INJUSTICE

GODS AMONG US: YEAR ONE

THE COMPLETE COLLECTION

INJU

GODS AMONG

THE COMPLETE

THIS STORY TAKES PLACE BEFORE THE START OF THE GAME

Tom Taylor
Writer

**Jheremy Raapack Mike S. Miller Bruno Redondo Axel Gimenez
David Yardin Tom Derenick Marc Deering Diana Egea
Kevin Maguire Neil Googe Xermanico Jonas Trindade**
Artists

**Andrew Elder Alejandro Sanchez David Yardin Ikari Studio
David Lopez & Santi Casas of Ikari Studio Rosemary Cheetham**
Colorists

Wes Abbott
Letterer

STICE

US: YEAR ONE

COLLECTION

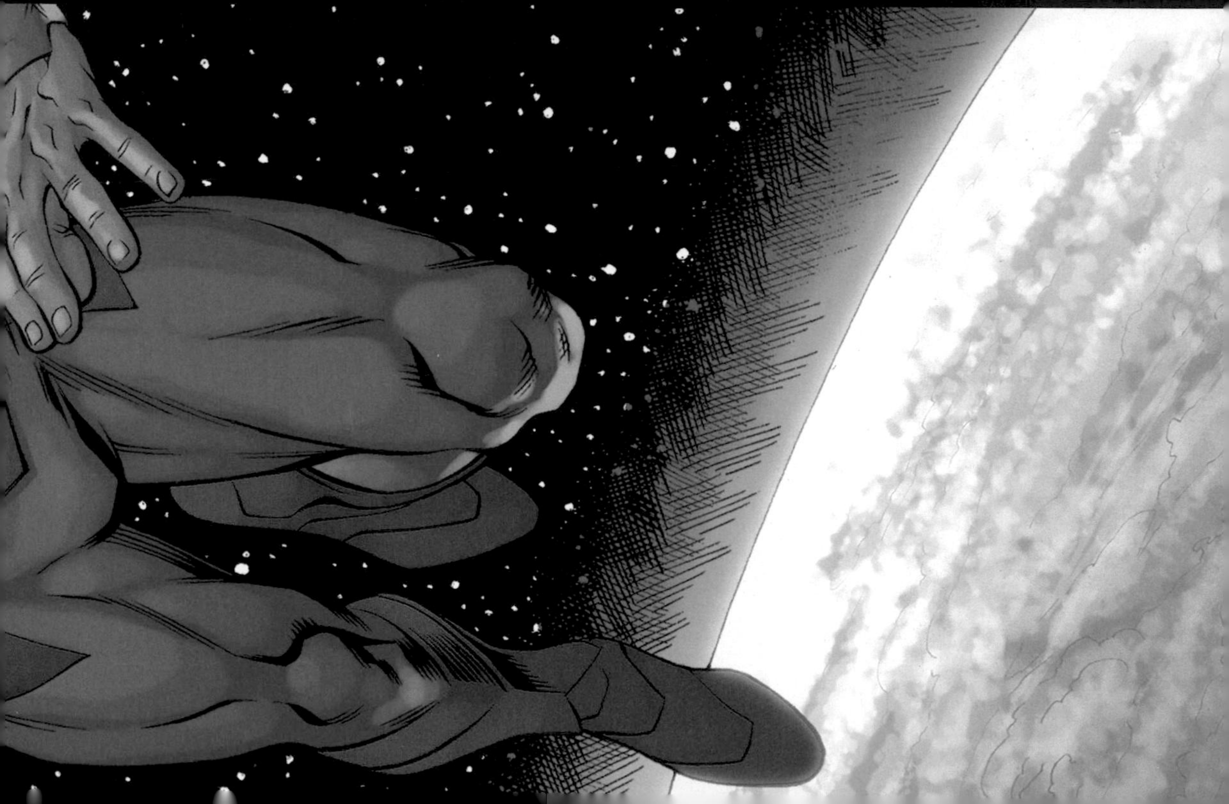

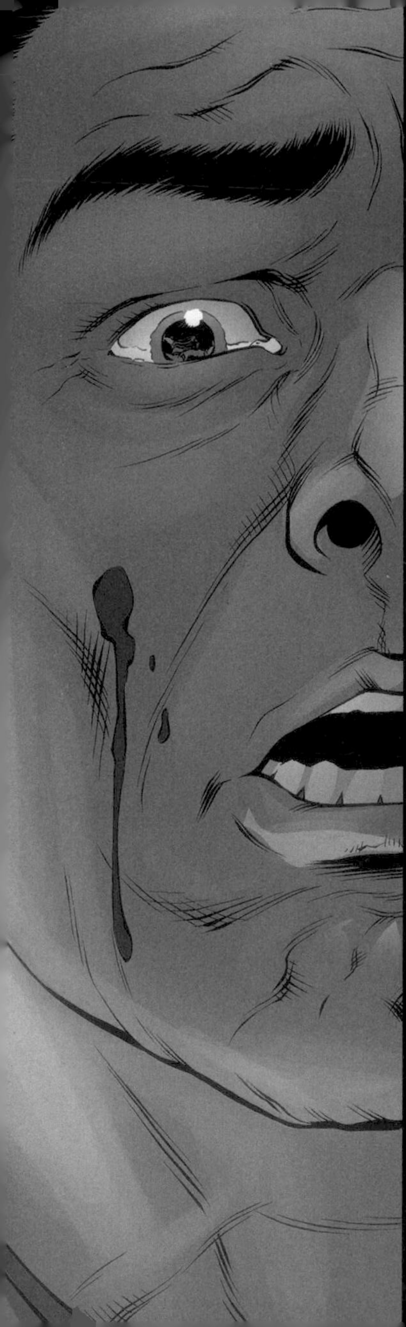

Jim Chadwick Editor – Original Series
Sarah Gaydos, Sarah Litt, Aniz Ansari Assistant Editors – Original Series
Jeb Woodard Editor – Collected Edition
Steve Cook Design Director – Books
Curtis King Jr. Publication Design

Marie Javins Editor-in-Chief, DC Comics

Daniel Cherry III Senior VP – General Manager
Jim Lee Publisher & Chief Creative Officer
Joen Choe VP – Global Brand & Creative Services
Don Falletti VP – Manufacturing Operations & Workflow Management
Lawrence Ganem VP – Talent Services
Alison Gill Senior VP – Manufacturing & Operations
Nick J. Napolitano VP – Manufacturing Administration & Design
Nancy Spears VP – Revenue

INJUSTICE: GODS AMONG US
YEAR ONE – THE COMPLETE COLLECTION

DC Comics, 2900 West Alameda Avenue, Burbank, CA 91505
Printed by LSC Communications, Owensville, MO, USA. 8/6/21.
Ninth Printing. ISBN: 978-1-4012-6279-2

PEFC Certified
This product is from sustainably managed forests and controlled sources
PEFC/29-31-337
www.pefc.org

Library of Congress Cataloging-in-Publication Data

Names: Taylor, Tom, 1978- author. | Raapack, Jheremy illustrator. | Miller,
Mike S., illustrator. | Redondo, Bruno, 1981- illustrator. | Elder, Andrew
(Colorist), illustrator. | Sanchez, Alejandro, 1985- illustrator. |
Yardin, David, illustrator. | Abbott, Wes, illustrator.
Title: Injustice : Gods among us year one, the complete collection / Tom
Taylor, writer ; Jheremy Raapack, Mike S. Miller, Bruno Redondo [and nine
others], artists ; Andrew Elder, Alejandro Sanchez, David Yardin [and four
others], colorists ; Wes Abbott, letterer.
Other titles: Gods among us year one | Injustice year one
Description: Burbank, CA : DC Comics, [2016]
Identifiers: LCCN 2015044884 | ISBN 9781401262792 (paperback)
Subjects: LCSH: Graphic novels. | Superhero comic books, strips, etc. |
BISAC: COMICS & GRAPHIC NOVELS / Superheroes.
Classification: LCC PN6727.T293 I57 2016 | DDC 741.5/973-dc23
LC record available at http://lccn.loc.gov/2015044884

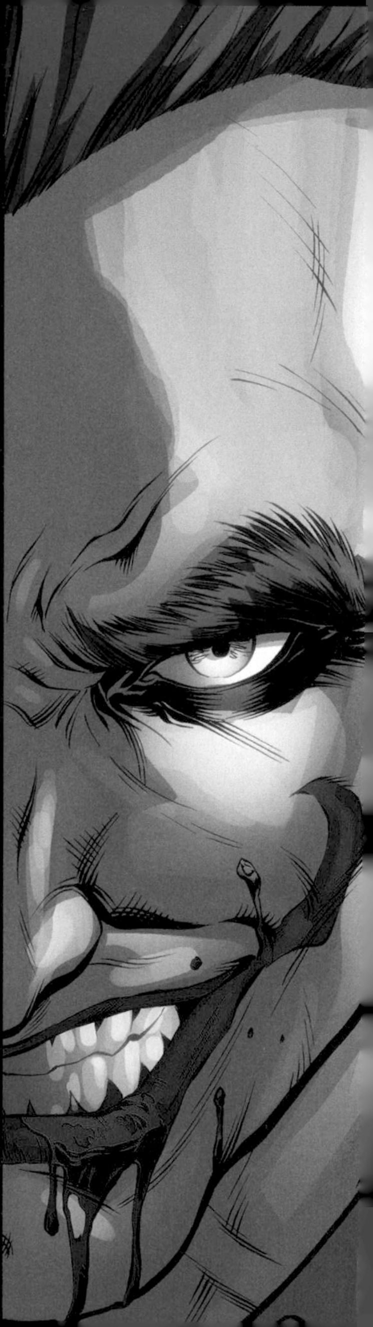

PART ONE

Jheremy Raapack Axel Gimenez Mike S. Miller Pencillers

Jheremy Raapack Marc Deering Mike S. Miller Inkers

Jheremy Raapack & **Tony Aviña** Cover

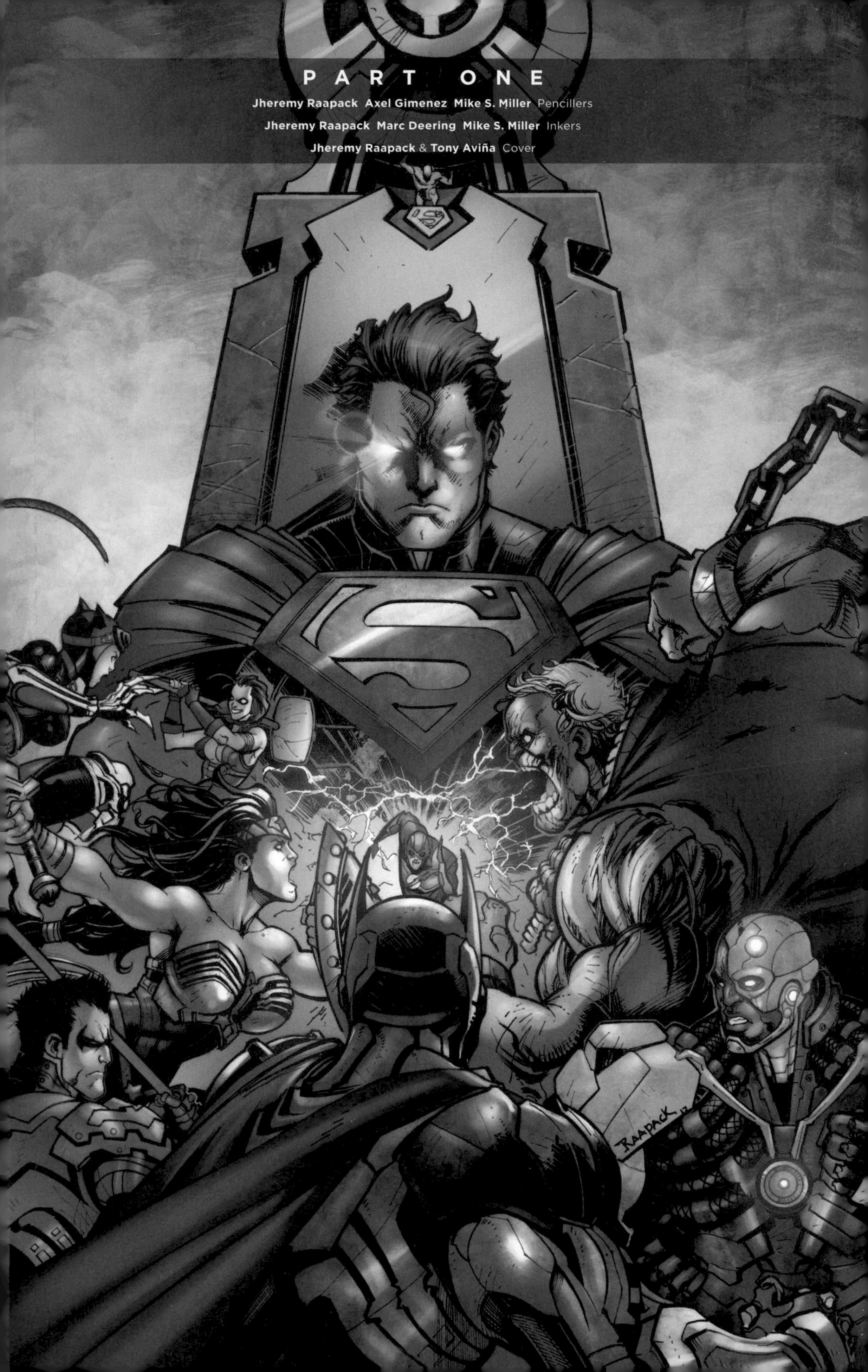
RAAPACK

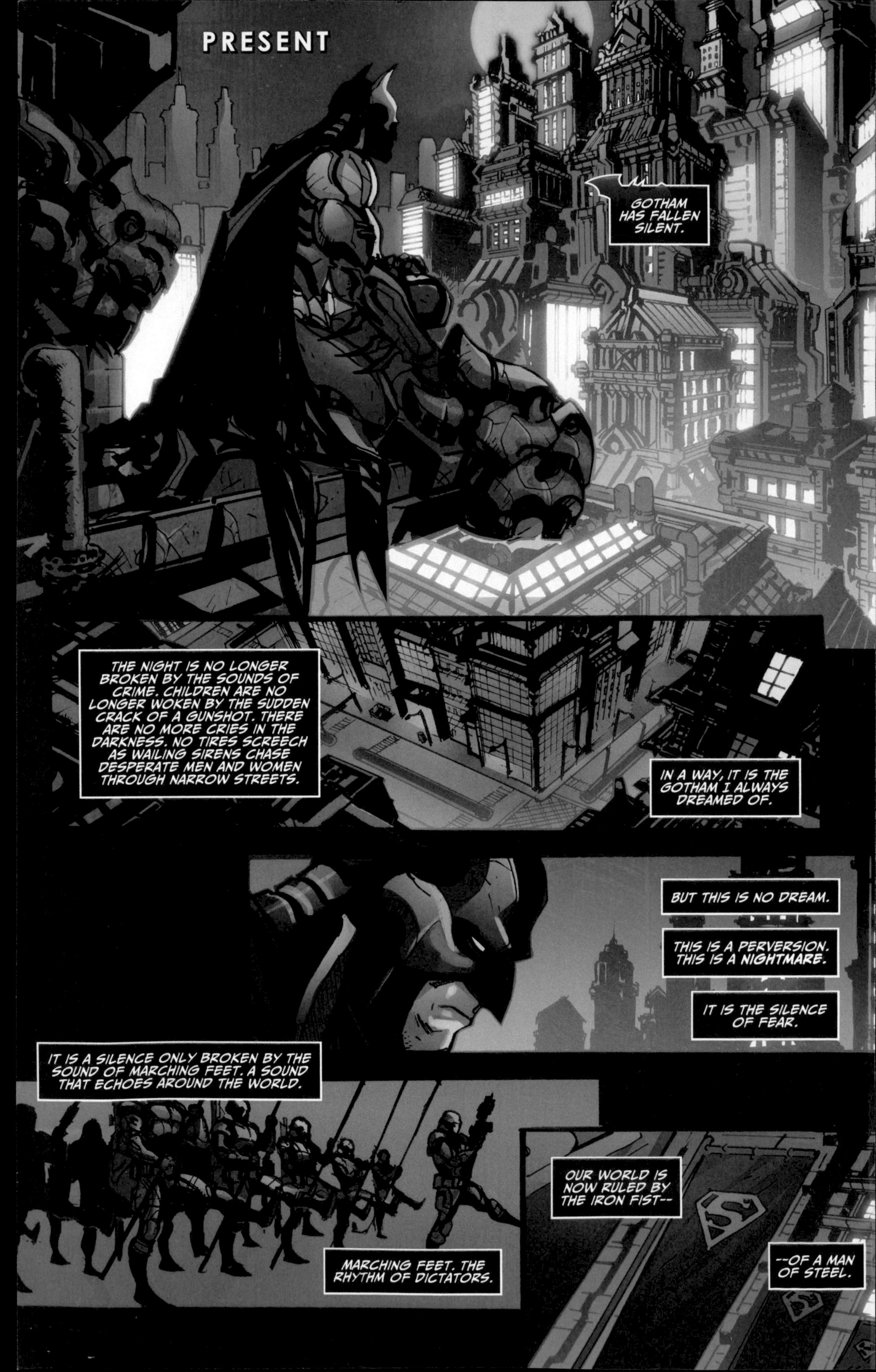
PRESENT
GOTHAM HAS FALLEN SILENT.
THE NIGHT IS NO LONGER BROKEN BY THE SOUNDS OF CRIME. CHILDREN ARE NO LONGER WOKEN BY THE SUDDEN CRACK OF A GUNSHOT. THERE ARE NO MORE CRIES IN THE DARKNESS. NO TIRES SCREECH AS WAILING SIRENS CHASE DESPERATE MEN AND WOMEN THROUGH NARROW STREETS.
IN A WAY, IT IS THE GOTHAM I ALWAYS DREAMED OF.
BUT THIS IS NO DREAM.
THIS IS A PERVERSION. THIS IS A NIGHTMARE.
IT IS THE SILENCE OF FEAR.
IT IS A SILENCE ONLY BROKEN BY THE SOUND OF MARCHING FEET. A SOUND THAT ECHOES AROUND THE WORLD.
MARCHING FEET. THE RHYTHM OF DICTATORS.
OUR WORLD IS NOW RULED BY THE IRON FIST--
--OF A MAN OF STEEL.

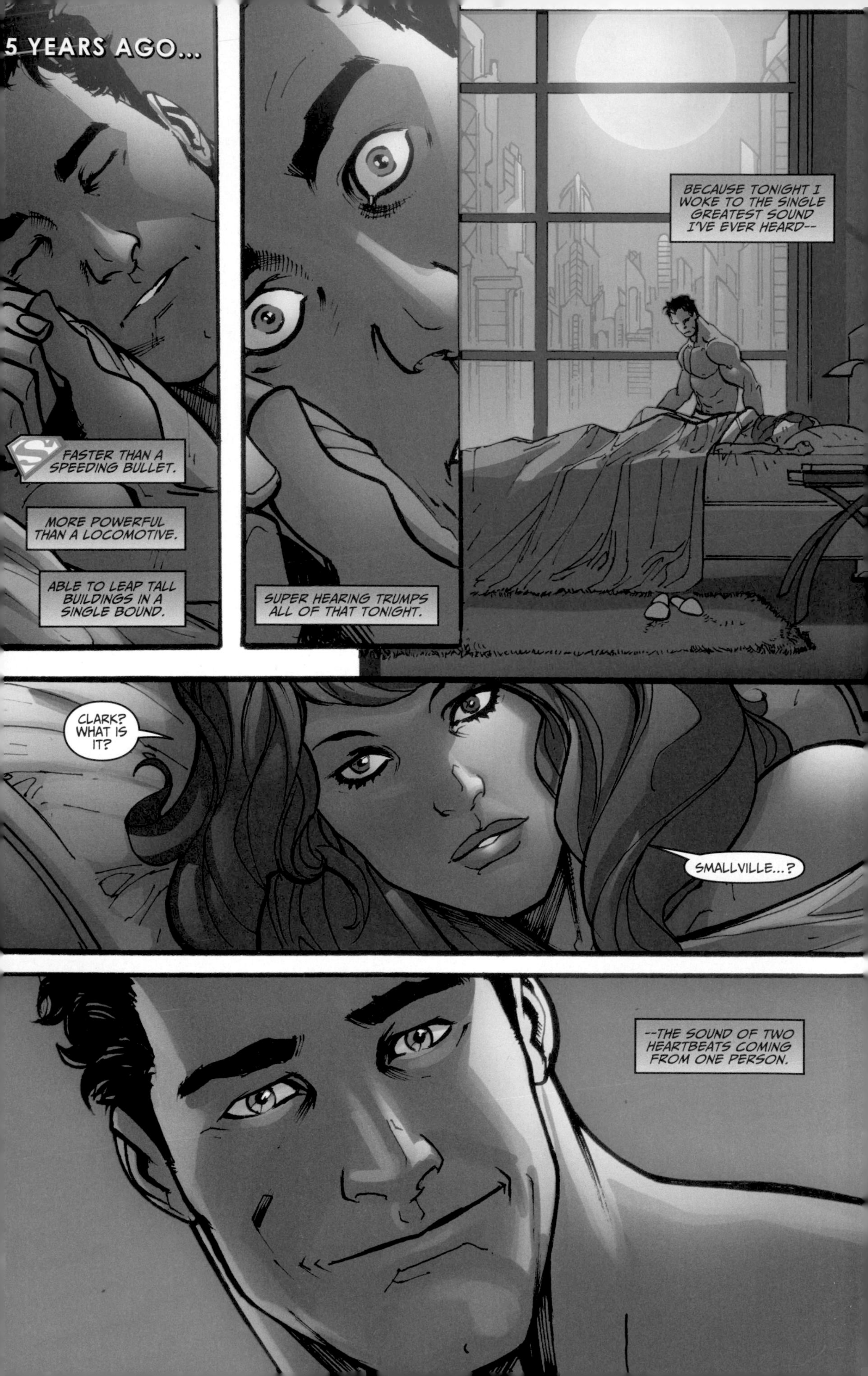
5 YEARS AGO...
FASTER THAN A SPEEDING BULLET.
MORE POWERFUL THAN A LOCOMOTIVE.
ABLE TO LEAP TALL BUILDINGS IN A SINGLE BOUND.
SUPER HEARING TRUMPS ALL OF THAT TONIGHT.
BECAUSE TONIGHT I WOKE TO THE SINGLE GREATEST SOUND I'VE EVER HEARD--
CLARK? WHAT IS IT?
SMALLVILLE...?
--THE SOUND OF TWO HEARTBEATS COMING FROM ONE PERSON.

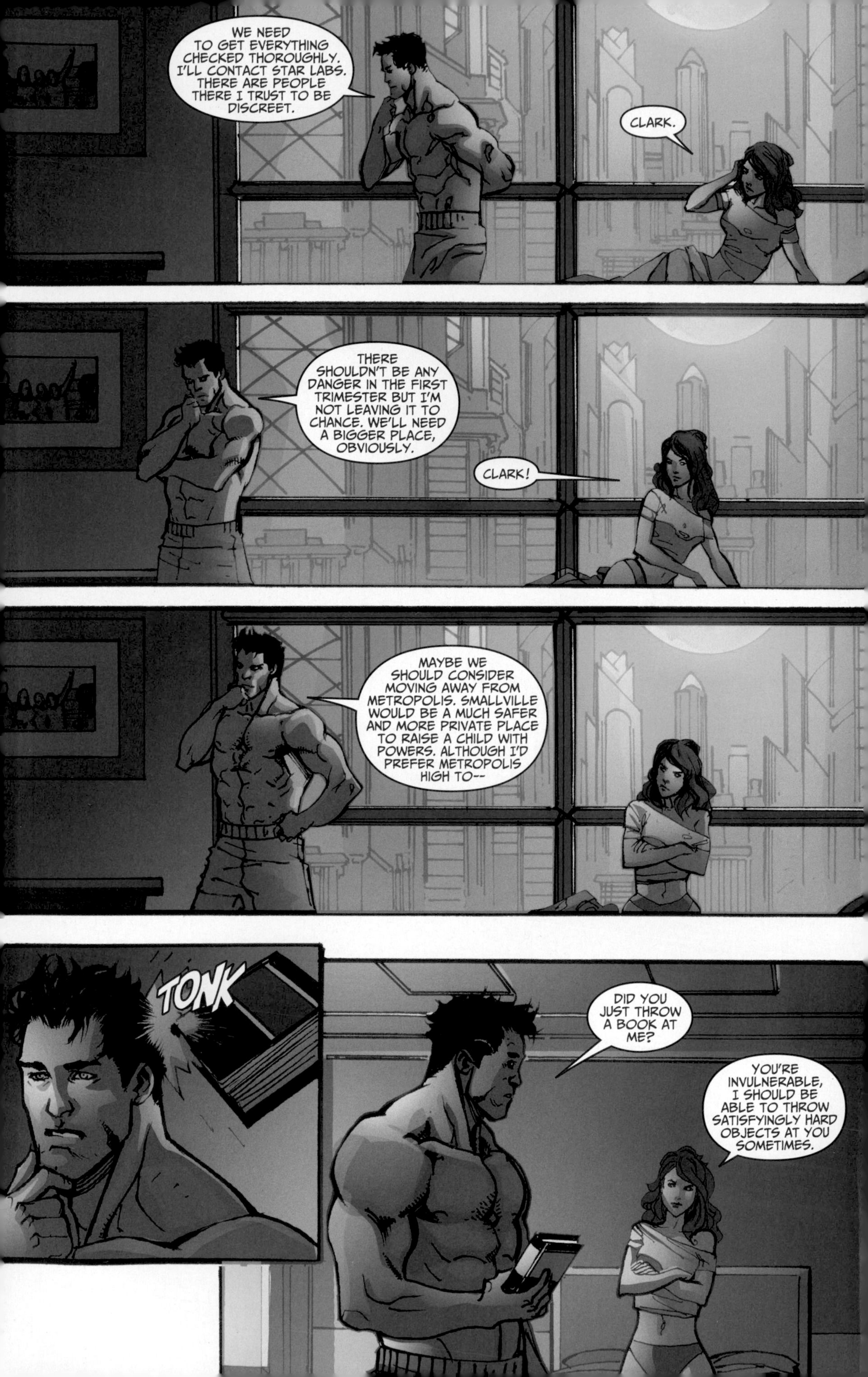
WE NEED TO GET EVERYTHING CHECKED THOROUGHLY. I'LL CONTACT STAR LABS. THERE ARE PEOPLE THERE I TRUST TO BE DISCREET.
CLARK.
THERE SHOULDN'T BE ANY DANGER IN THE FIRST TRIMESTER BUT I'M NOT LEAVING IT TO CHANCE. WE'LL NEED A BIGGER PLACE, OBVIOUSLY.
CLARK!
MAYBE WE SHOULD CONSIDER MOVING AWAY FROM METROPOLIS. SMALLVILLE WOULD BE A MUCH SAFER AND MORE PRIVATE PLACE TO RAISE A CHILD WITH POWERS. ALTHOUGH I'D PREFER METROPOLIS HIGH TO--
TONK
DID YOU JUST THROW A BOOK AT ME?
YOU'RE INVULNERABLE, I SHOULD BE ABLE TO THROW SATISFYINGLY HARD OBJECTS AT YOU SOMETIMES.

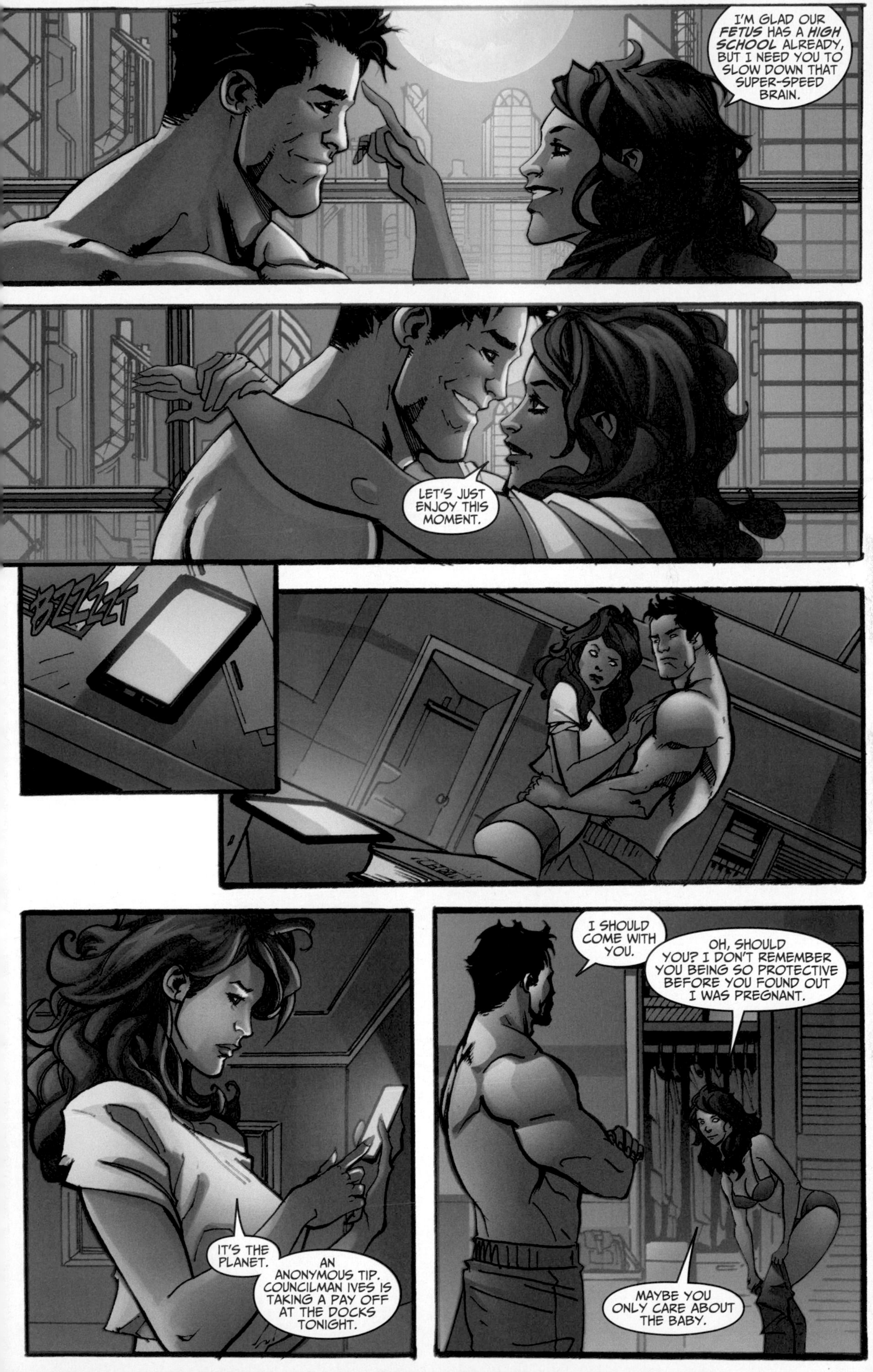

I'M GLAD OUR FETUS HAS A HIGH SCHOOL ALREADY, BUT I NEED YOU TO SLOW DOWN THAT SUPER-SPEED BRAIN.
LET'S JUST ENJOY THIS MOMENT.
BZZZZT
IT'S THE PLANET.
AN ANONYMOUS TIP. COUNCILMAN IVES IS TAKING A PAY OFF AT THE DOCKS TONIGHT.
I SHOULD COME WITH YOU.
OH, SHOULD YOU? I DON'T REMEMBER YOU BEING SO PROTECTIVE BEFORE YOU FOUND OUT I WAS PREGNANT.
MAYBE YOU ONLY CARE ABOUT THE BABY.

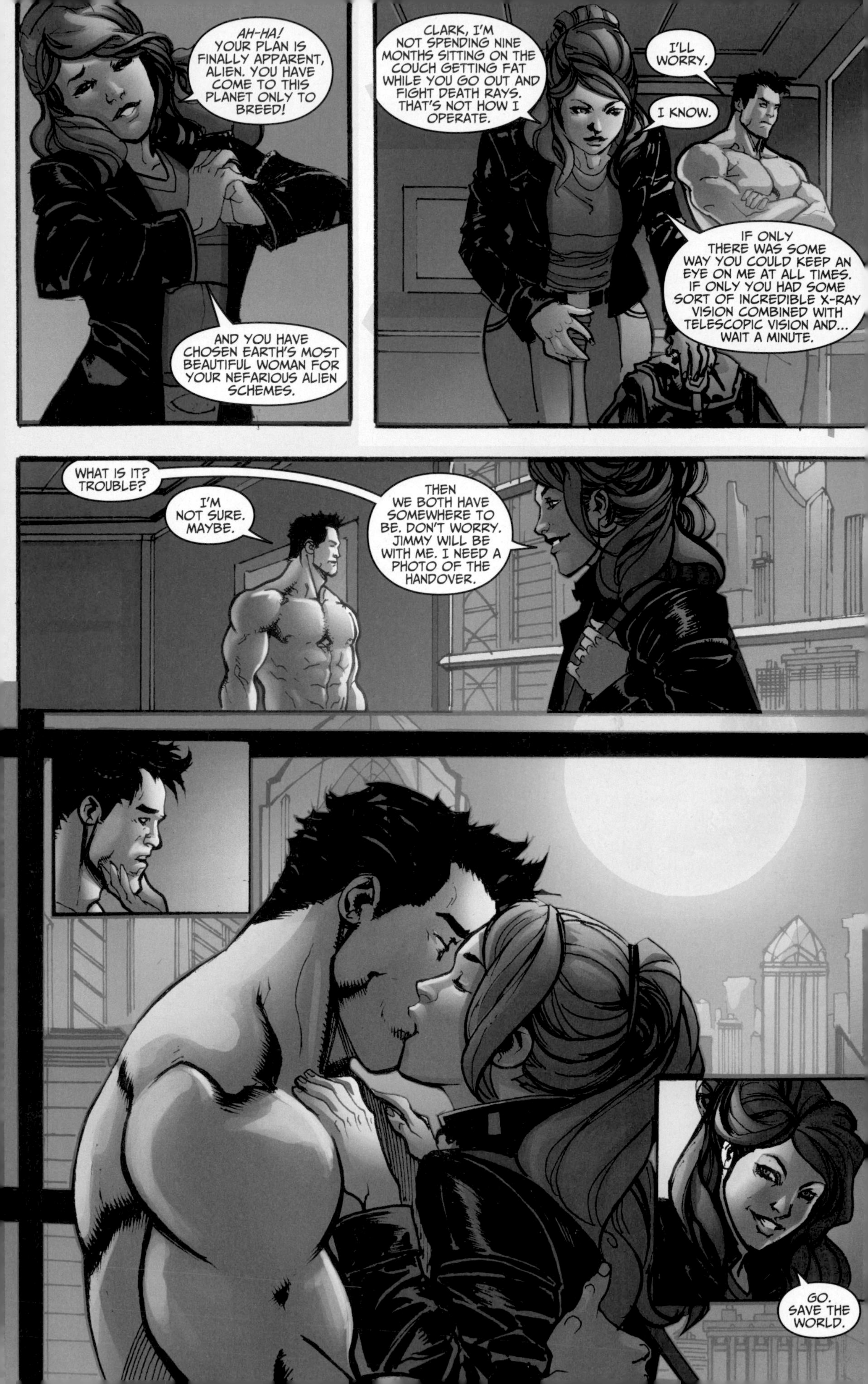
AH-HA! YOUR PLAN IS FINALLY APPARENT, ALIEN. YOU HAVE COME TO THIS PLANET ONLY TO BREED!
AND YOU HAVE CHOSEN EARTH'S MOST BEAUTIFUL WOMAN FOR YOUR NEFARIOUS ALIEN SCHEMES.
CLARK, I'M NOT SPENDING NINE MONTHS SITTING ON THE COUCH GETTING FAT WHILE YOU GO OUT AND FIGHT DEATH RAYS. THAT'S NOT HOW I OPERATE.
I'LL WORRY.
I KNOW.
IF ONLY THERE WAS SOME WAY YOU COULD KEEP AN EYE ON ME AT ALL TIMES. IF ONLY YOU HAD SOME SORT OF INCREDIBLE X-RAY VISION COMBINED WITH TELESCOPIC VISION AND... WAIT A MINUTE.
WHAT IS IT? TROUBLE?
I'M NOT SURE. MAYBE.
THEN WE BOTH HAVE SOMEWHERE TO BE. DON'T WORRY. JIMMY WILL BE WITH ME. I NEED A PHOTO OF THE HANDOVER.
GO. SAVE THE WORLD.

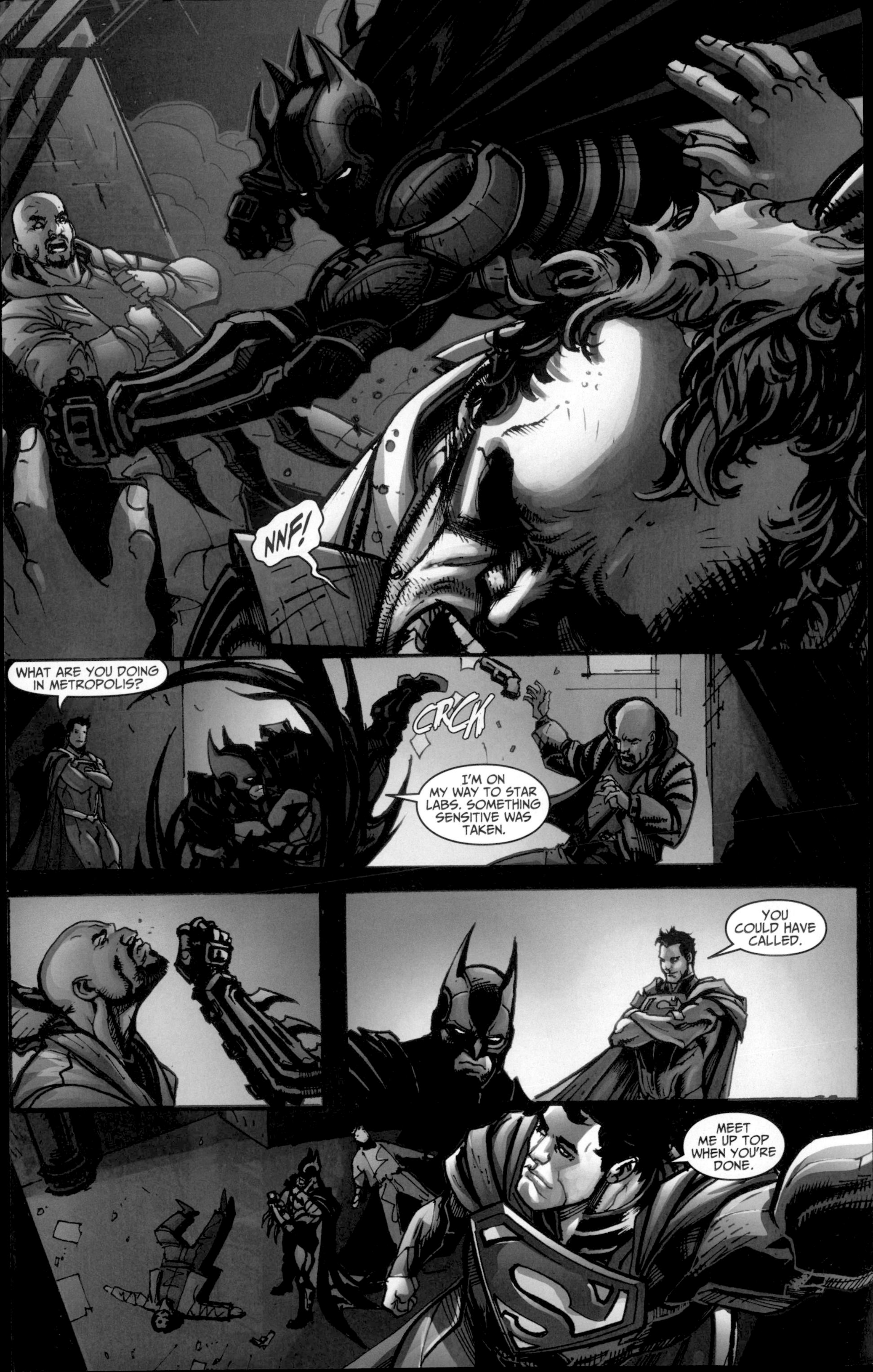
NNF!
WHAT ARE YOU DOING IN METROPOLIS?
CRCK
I'M ON MY WAY TO STAR LABS. SOMETHING SENSITIVE WAS TAKEN.
YOU COULD HAVE CALLED.
MEET ME UP TOP WHEN YOU'RE DONE.

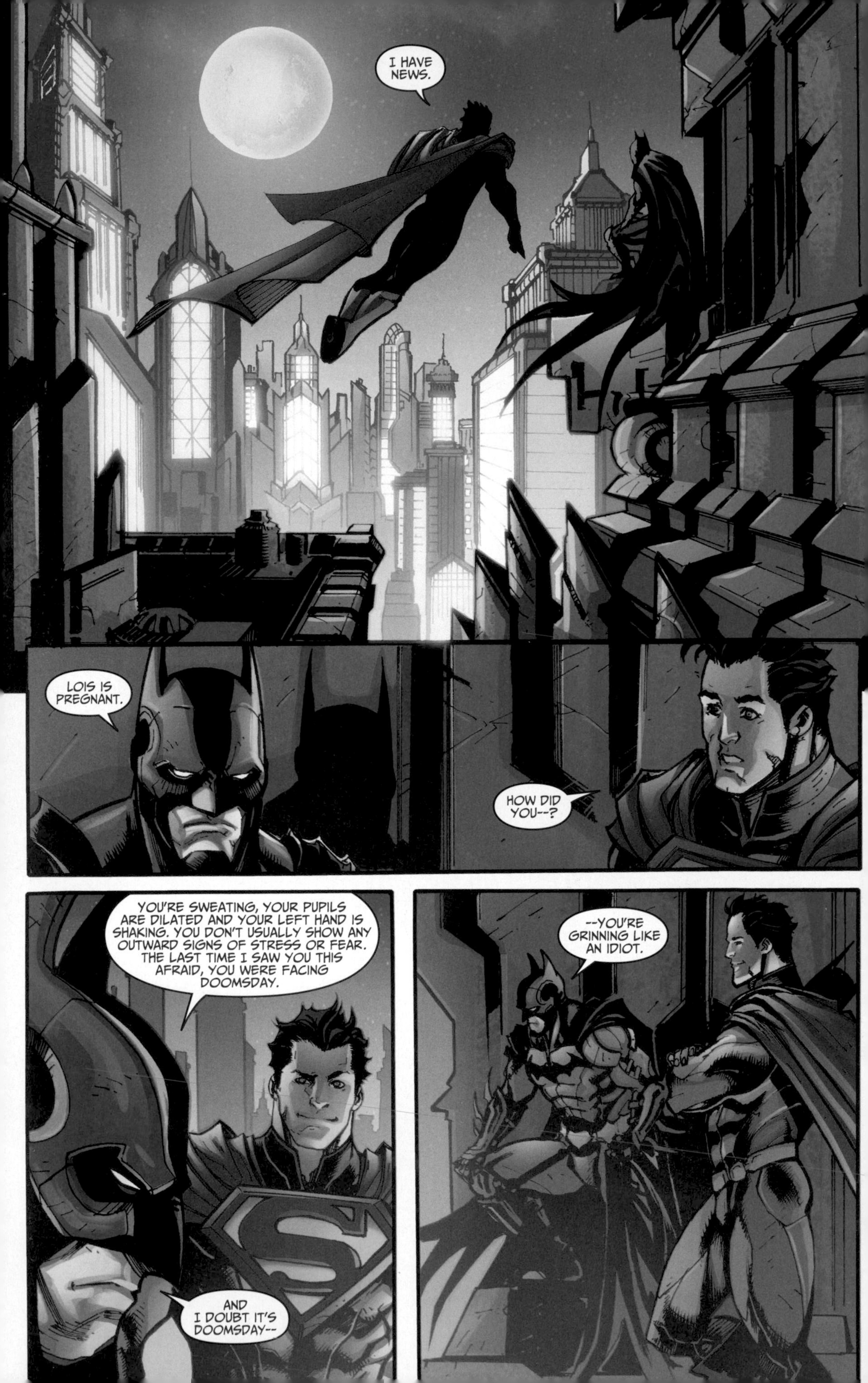
I HAVE NEWS.
LOIS IS PREGNANT.
HOW DID YOU--?
YOU'RE SWEATING, YOUR PUPILS ARE DILATED AND YOUR LEFT HAND IS SHAKING. YOU DON'T USUALLY SHOW ANY OUTWARD SIGNS OF STRESS OR FEAR. THE LAST TIME I SAW YOU THIS AFRAID, YOU WERE FACING DOOMSDAY.
AND I DOUBT IT'S DOOMSDAY--
--YOU'RE GRINNING LIKE AN IDIOT.

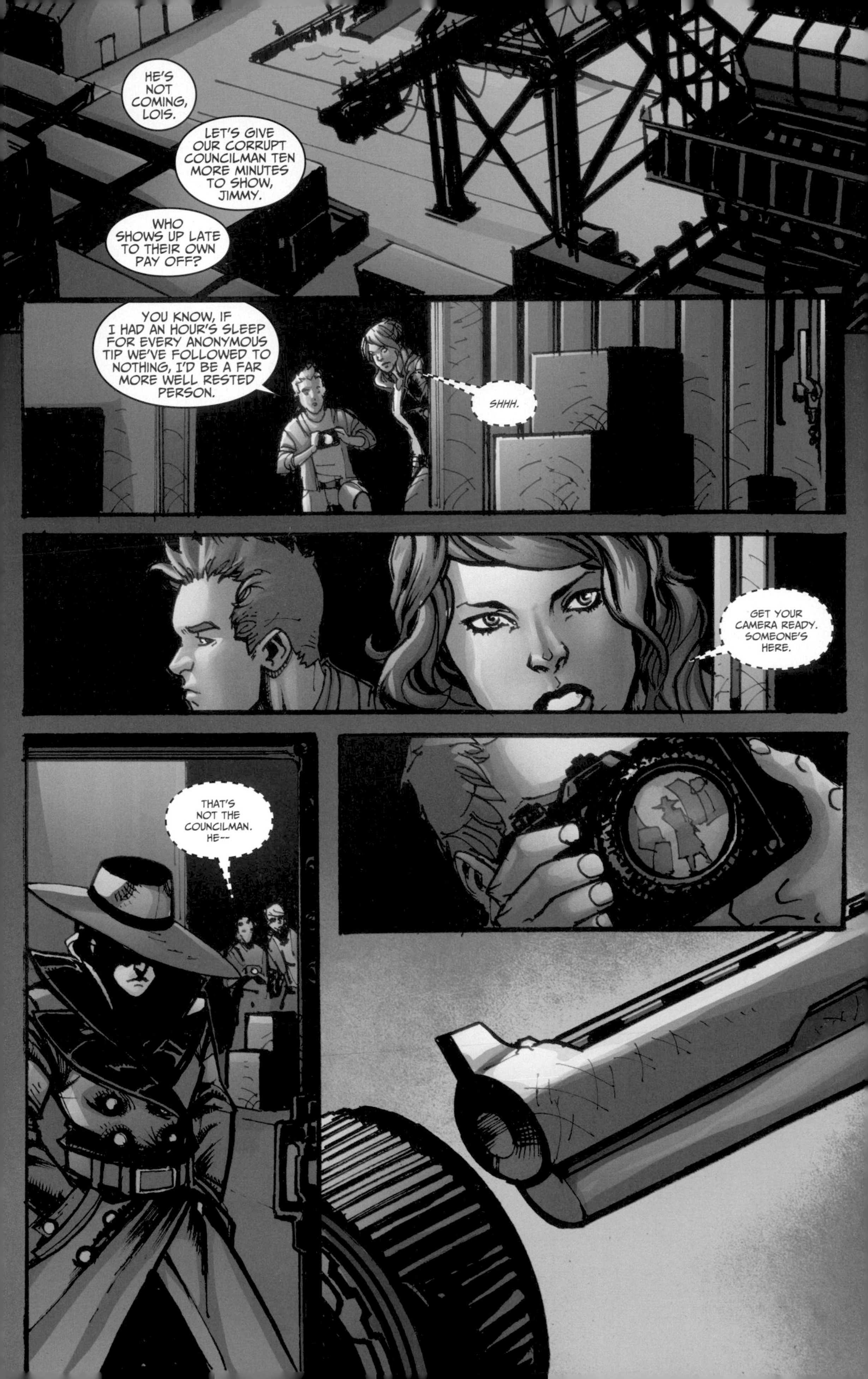
HE'S NOT COMING, LOIS.
LET'S GIVE OUR CORRUPT COUNCILMAN TEN MORE MINUTES TO SHOW, JIMMY.
WHO SHOWS UP LATE TO THEIR OWN PAY OFF?
YOU KNOW, IF I HAD AN HOUR'S SLEEP FOR EVERY ANONYMOUS TIP WE'VE FOLLOWED TO NOTHING, I'D BE A FAR MORE WELL RESTED PERSON.
SHHH.
GET YOUR CAMERA READY. SOMEONE'S HERE.
THAT'S NOT THE COUNCILMAN. HE--

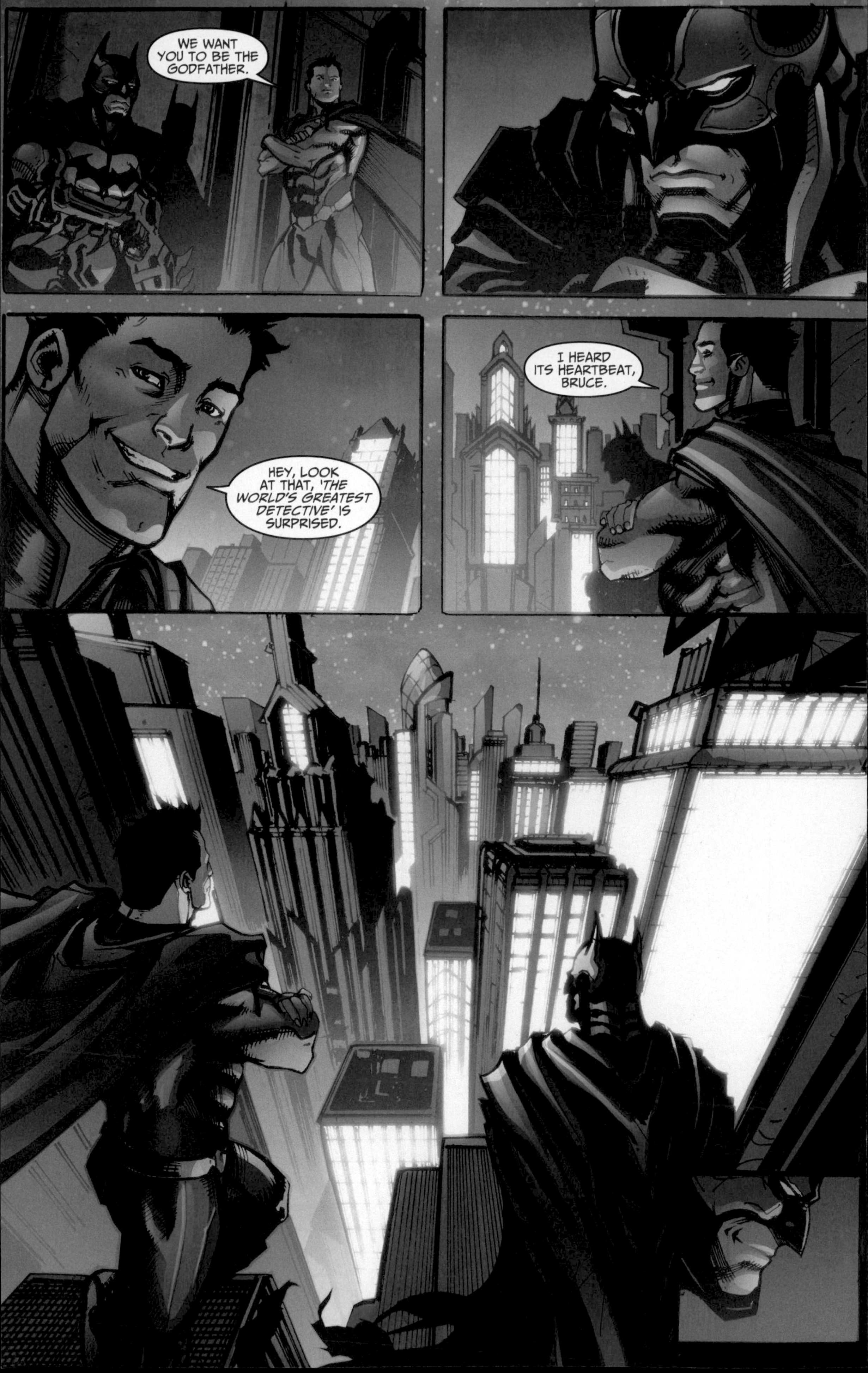
WE WANT YOU TO BE THE GODFATHER.
HEY, LOOK AT THAT, 'THE WORLD'S GREATEST DETECTIVE' IS SURPRISED.
I HEARD ITS HEARTBEAT, BRUCE.

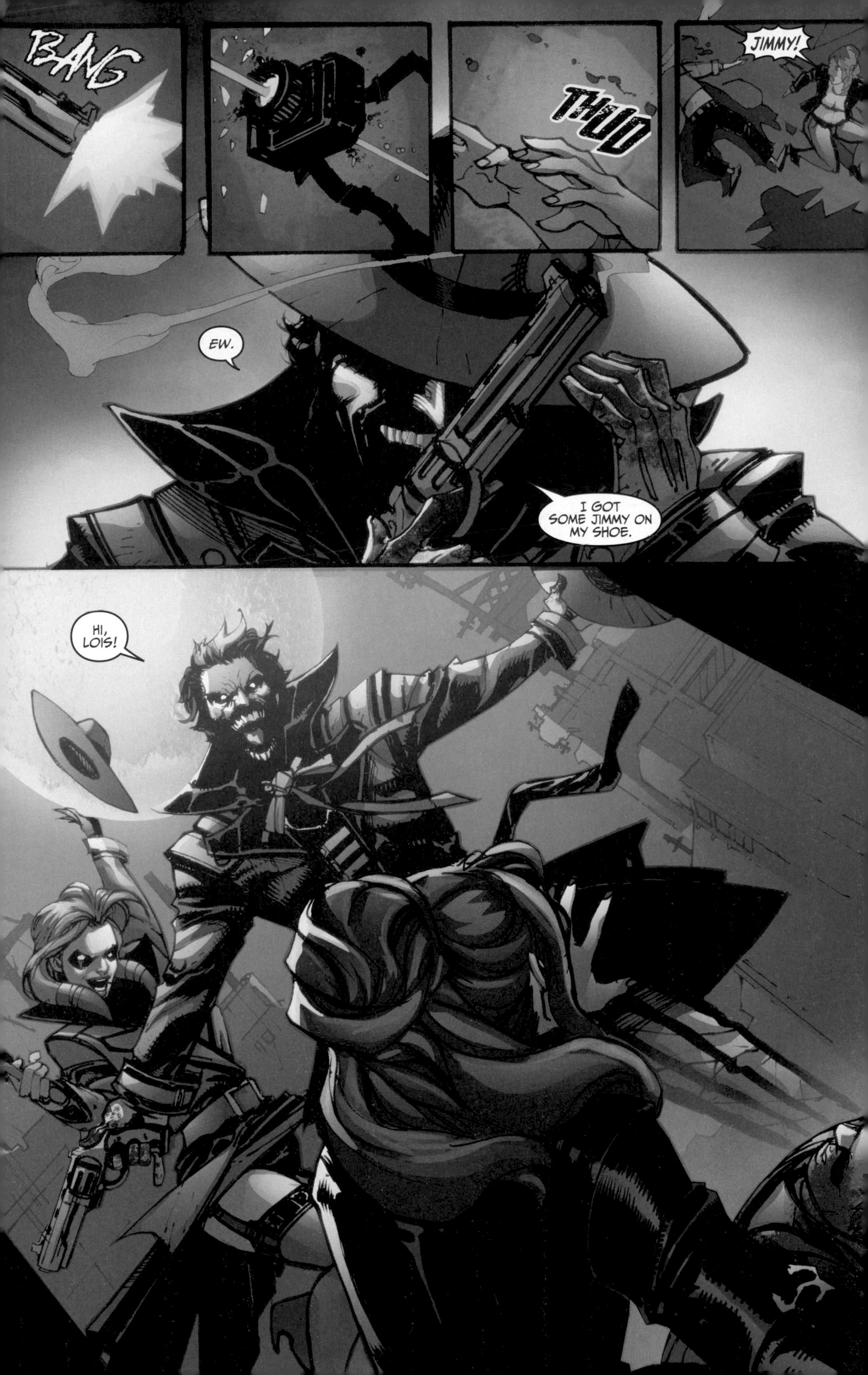
BANG
THUD
JIMMY!
EW.
I GOT SOME JIMMY ON MY SHOE.
HI, LOIS!

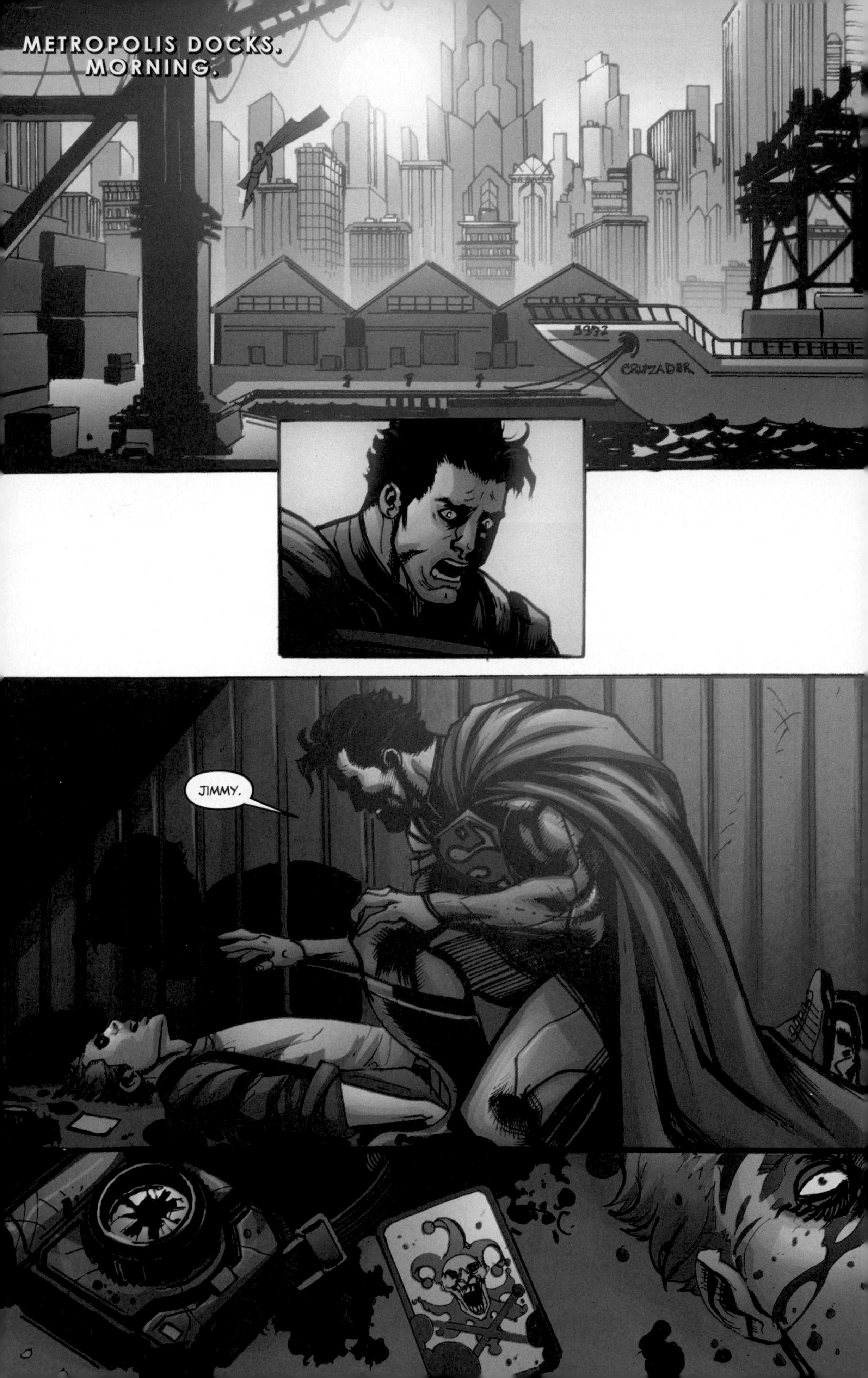
METROPOLIS DOCKS. MORNING.
CRUZADER
JIMMY.

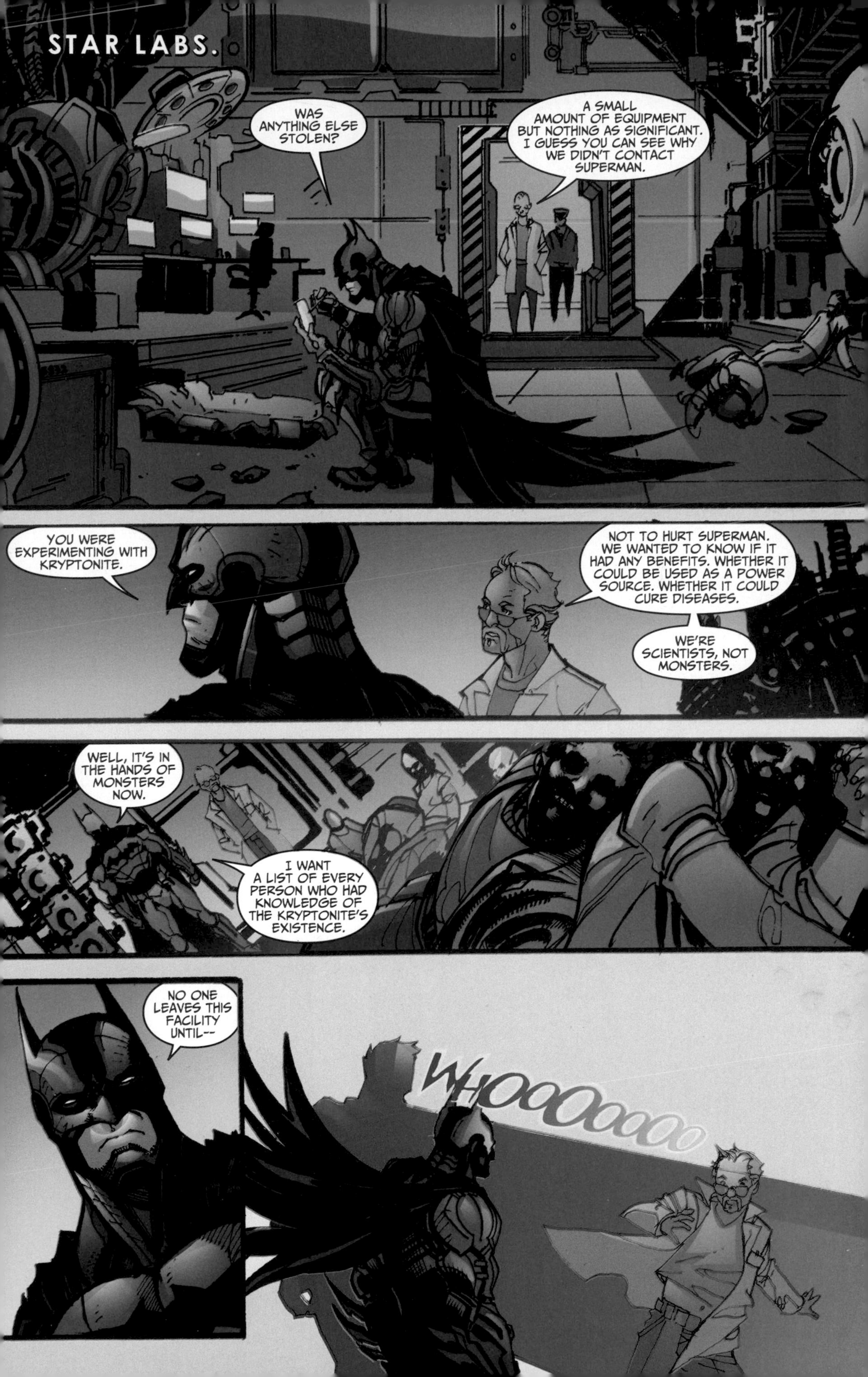
STAR LABS.
WAS ANYTHING ELSE STOLEN?
A SMALL AMOUNT OF EQUIPMENT BUT NOTHING AS SIGNIFICANT. I GUESS YOU CAN SEE WHY WE DIDN'T CONTACT SUPERMAN.
YOU WERE EXPERIMENTING WITH KRYPTONITE.
NOT TO HURT SUPERMAN. WE WANTED TO KNOW IF IT HAD ANY BENEFITS. WHETHER IT COULD BE USED AS A POWER SOURCE. WHETHER IT COULD CURE DISEASES.
WE'RE SCIENTISTS, NOT MONSTERS.
WELL, IT'S IN THE HANDS OF MONSTERS NOW.
I WANT A LIST OF EVERY PERSON WHO HAD KNOWLEDGE OF THE KRYPTONITE'S EXISTENCE.
NO ONE LEAVES THIS FACILITY UNTIL--
WHOOOOOOOO

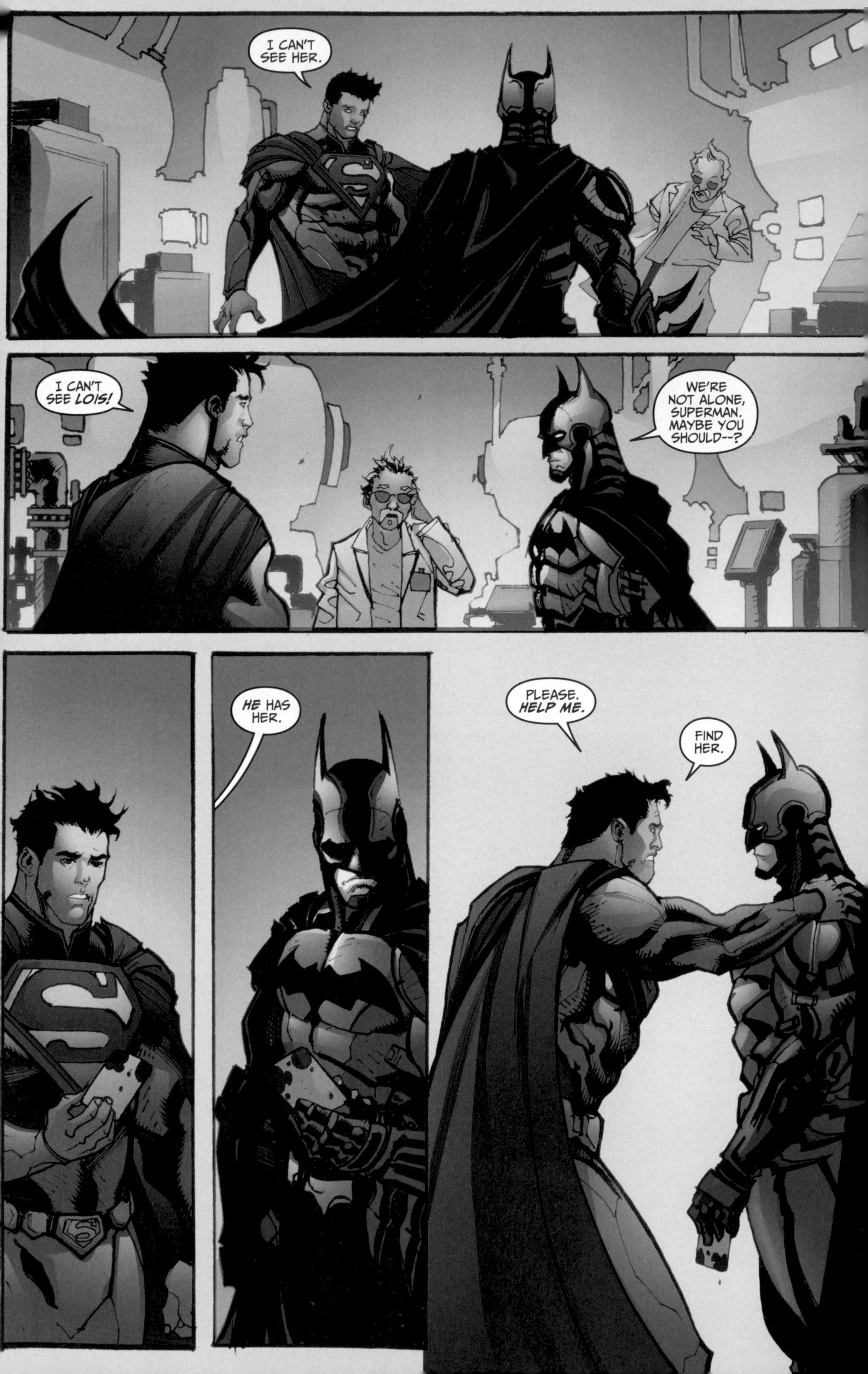

I CAN'T SEE HER.
I CAN'T SEE LOIS!
WE'RE NOT ALONE, SUPERMAN. MAYBE YOU SHOULD--?
HE HAS HER.
PLEASE. HELP ME.
FIND HER.

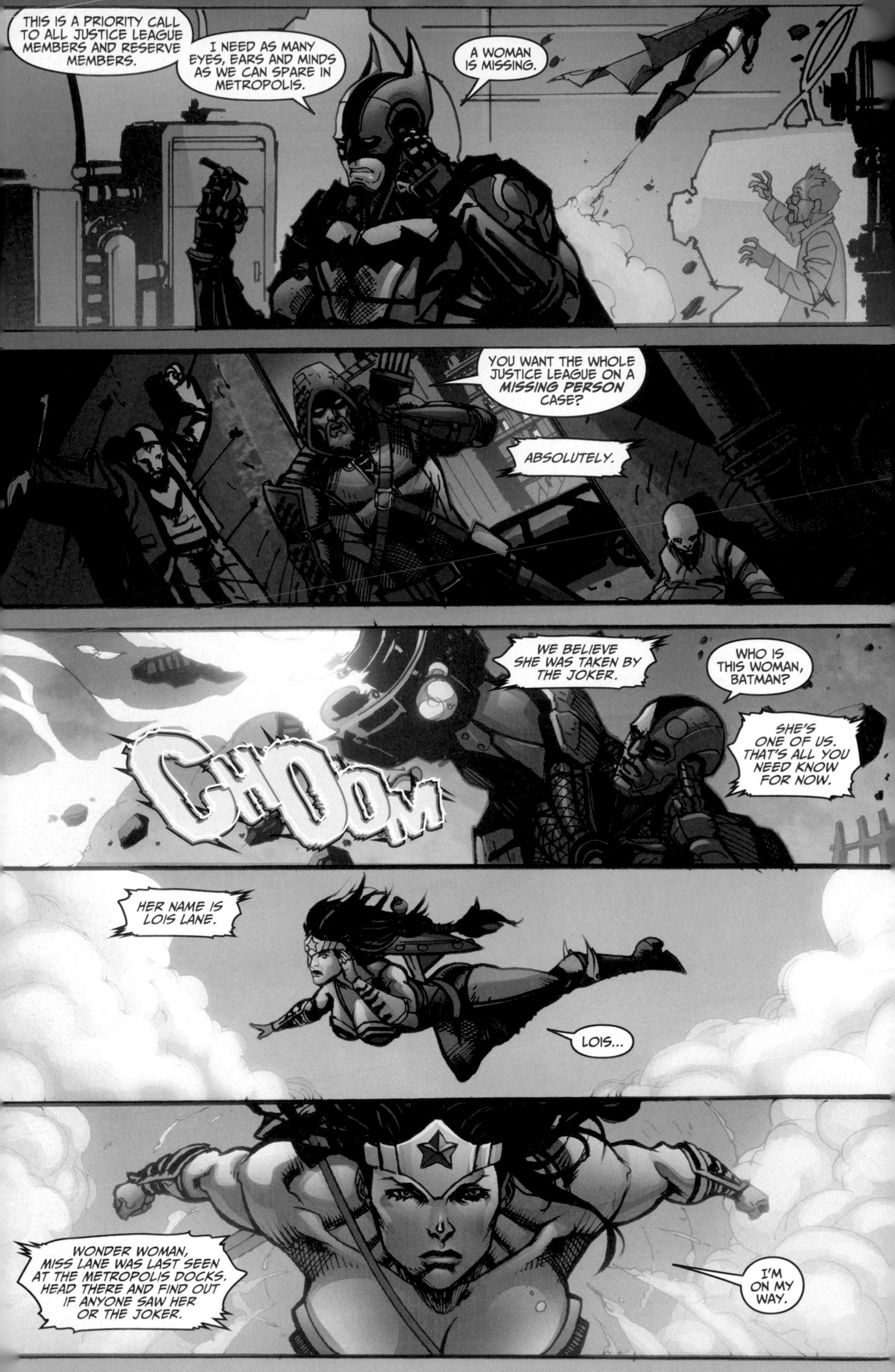
THIS IS A PRIORITY CALL TO ALL JUSTICE LEAGUE MEMBERS AND RESERVE MEMBERS.
I NEED AS MANY EYES, EARS AND MINDS AS WE CAN SPARE IN METROPOLIS.
A WOMAN IS MISSING.
YOU WANT THE WHOLE JUSTICE LEAGUE ON A *MISSING PERSON* CASE?
ABSOLUTELY.
WE BELIEVE SHE WAS TAKEN BY THE JOKER.
CHOOM
WHO IS THIS WOMAN, BATMAN?
SHE'S ONE OF US. THAT'S ALL YOU NEED KNOW FOR NOW.
HER NAME IS LOIS LANE.
LOIS...
WONDER WOMAN, MISS LANE WAS LAST SEEN AT THE METROPOLIS DOCKS. HEAD THERE AND FIND OUT IF ANYONE SAW HER OR THE JOKER.
I'M ON MY WAY.

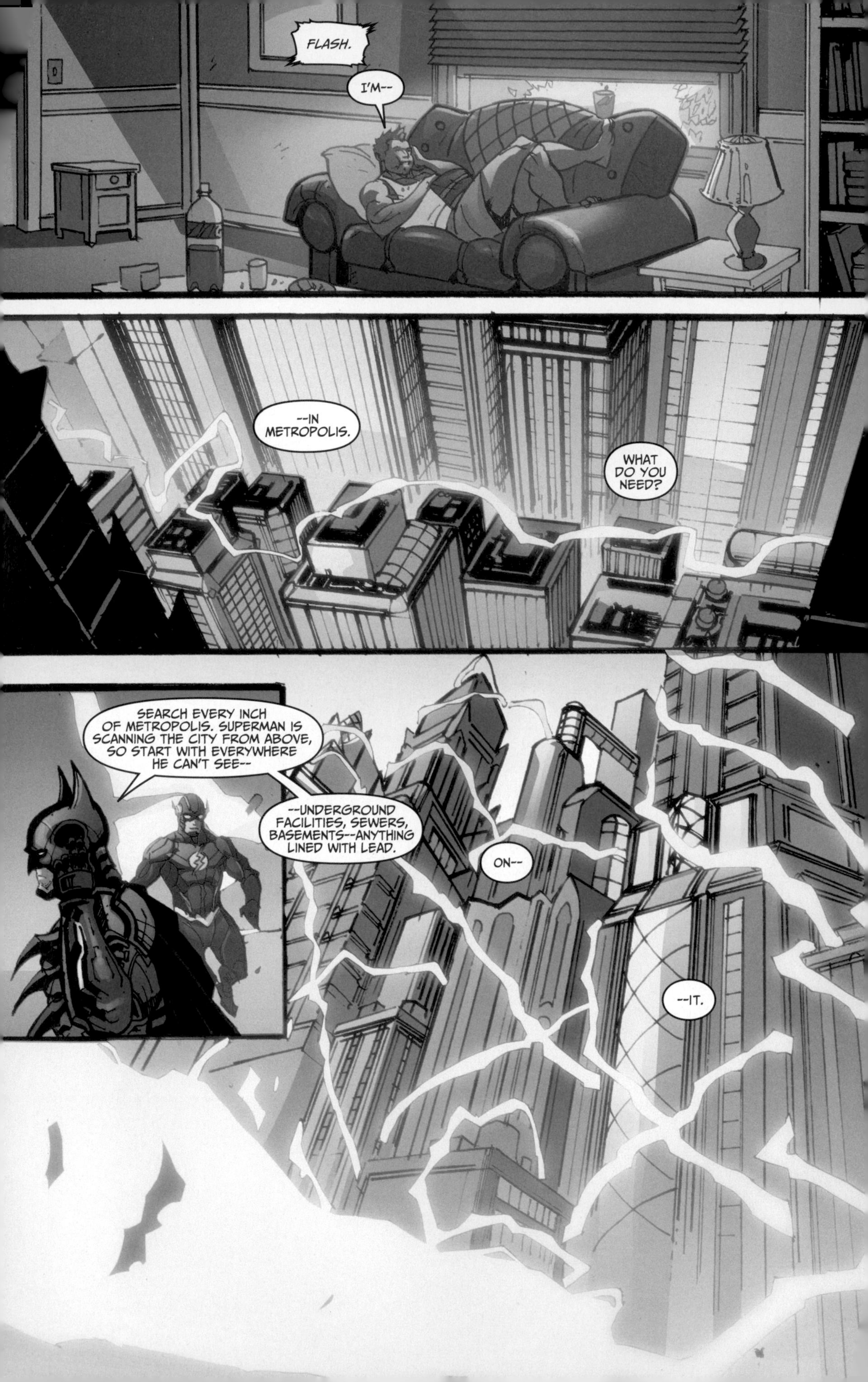
FLASH.
I'M--
--IN METROPOLIS.
WHAT DO YOU NEED?
SEARCH EVERY INCH OF METROPOLIS. SUPERMAN IS SCANNING THE CITY FROM ABOVE, SO START WITH EVERYWHERE HE CAN'T SEE--
--UNDERGROUND FACILITIES, SEWERS, BASEMENTS--ANYTHING LINED WITH LEAD.
ON--
--IT.

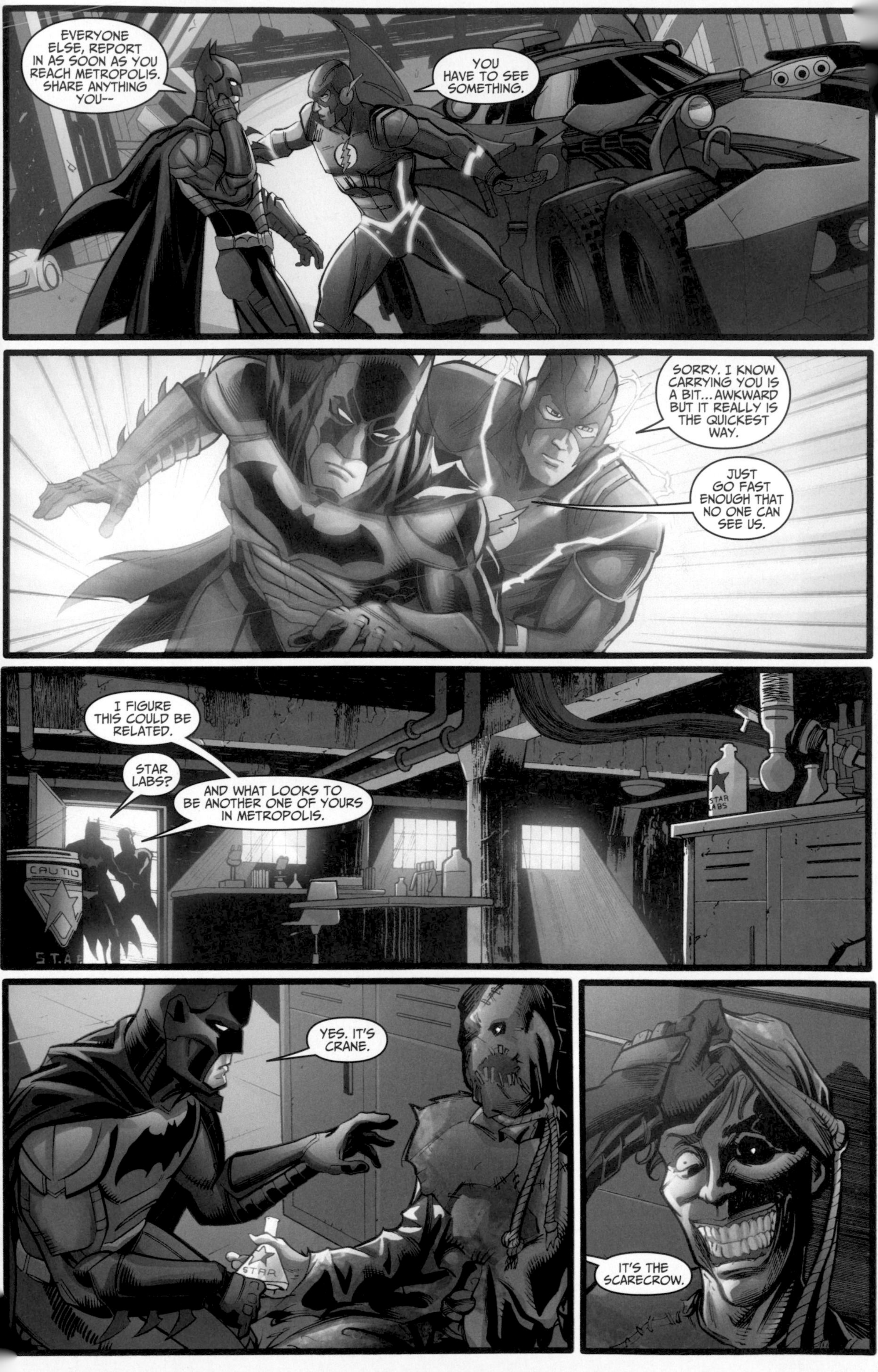
EVERYONE ELSE, REPORT IN AS SOON AS YOU REACH METROPOLIS. SHARE ANYTHING YOU--
YOU HAVE TO SEE SOMETHING.
SORRY. I KNOW CARRYING YOU IS A BIT... AWKWARD BUT IT REALLY IS THE QUICKEST WAY.
JUST GO FAST ENOUGH THAT NO ONE CAN SEE US.
I FIGURE THIS COULD BE RELATED.
STAR LABS?
AND WHAT LOOKS TO BE ANOTHER ONE OF YOURS IN METROPOLIS.
STAR LABS
CAUTIO
S.T.A.
YES. IT'S CRANE.
STAR
IT'S THE SCARECROW.

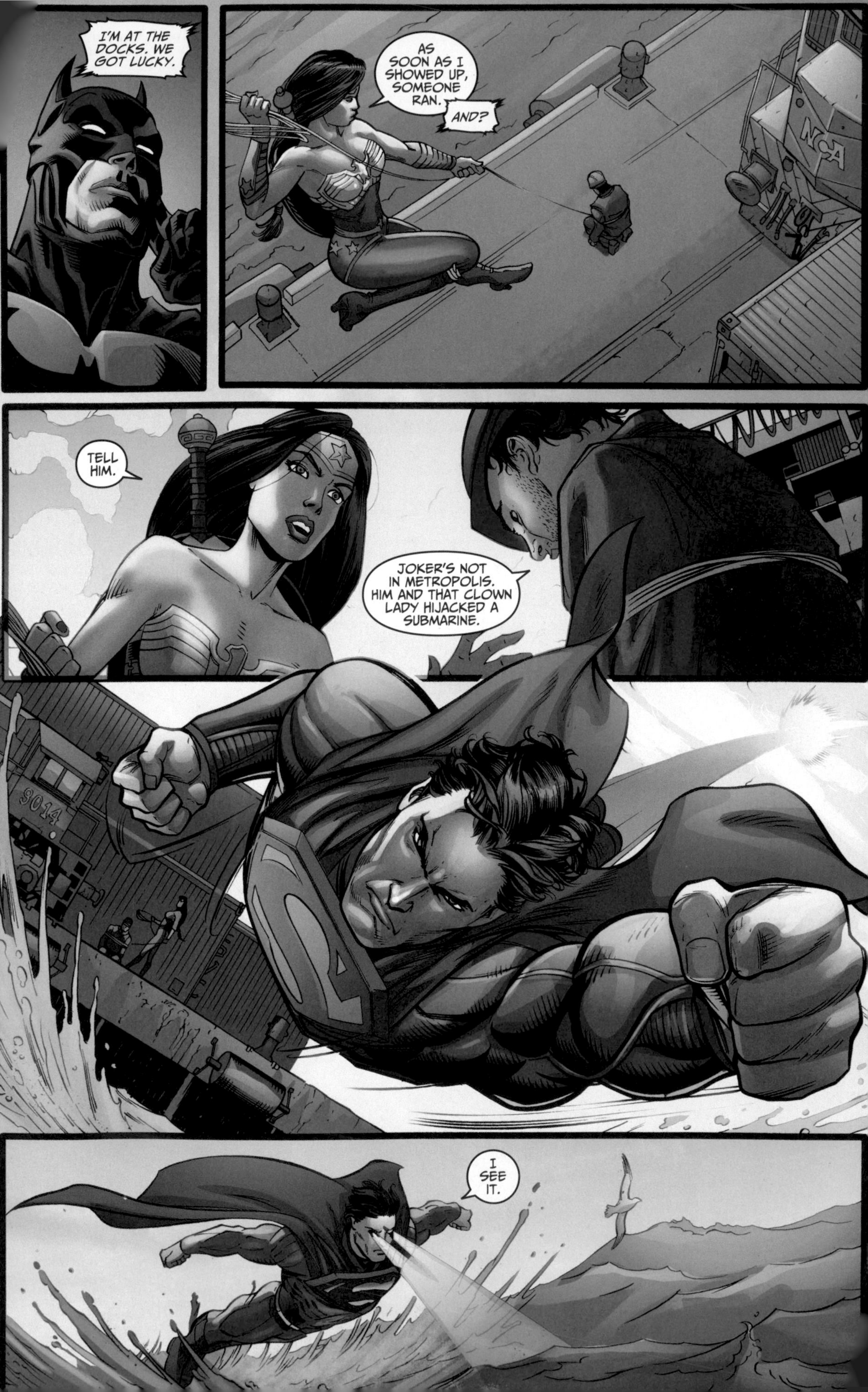
I'M AT THE DOCKS. WE GOT LUCKY.
AS SOON AS I SHOWED UP, SOMEONE RAN.
AND?
TELL HIM.
JOKER'S NOT IN METROPOLIS. HIM AND THAT CLOWN LADY HIJACKED A SUBMARINE.
I SEE IT.

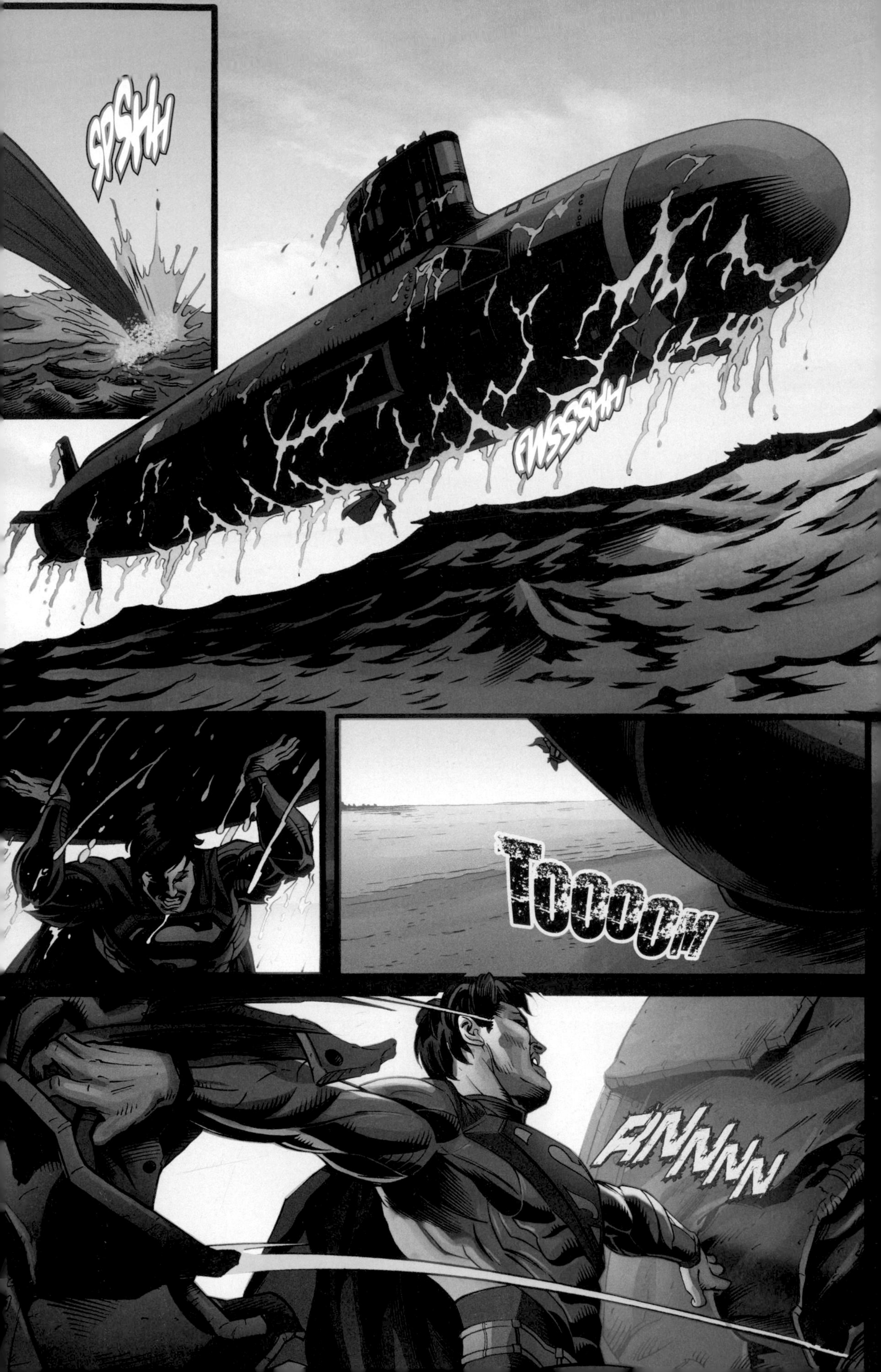
SPSHH
FWSSSHH
TOOOOOM
FINNNN

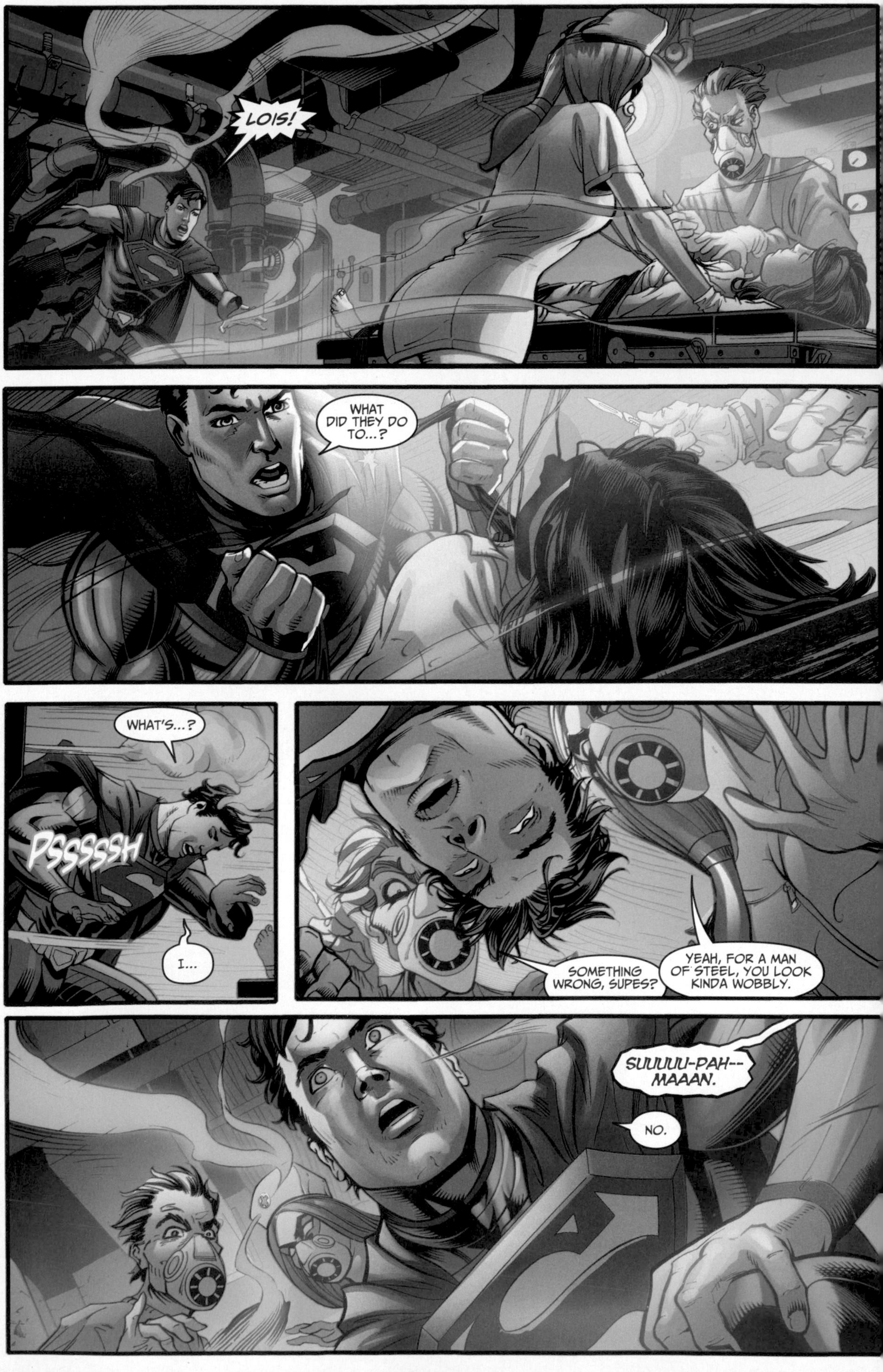
LOIS!
WHAT DID THEY DO TO...?
WHAT'S...?
PSSSSSH
I...
SOMETHING WRONG, SUPES?
YEAH, FOR A MAN OF STEEL, YOU LOOK KINDA WOBBLY.
SUUUUU-PAH-- MAAAN.
NO.

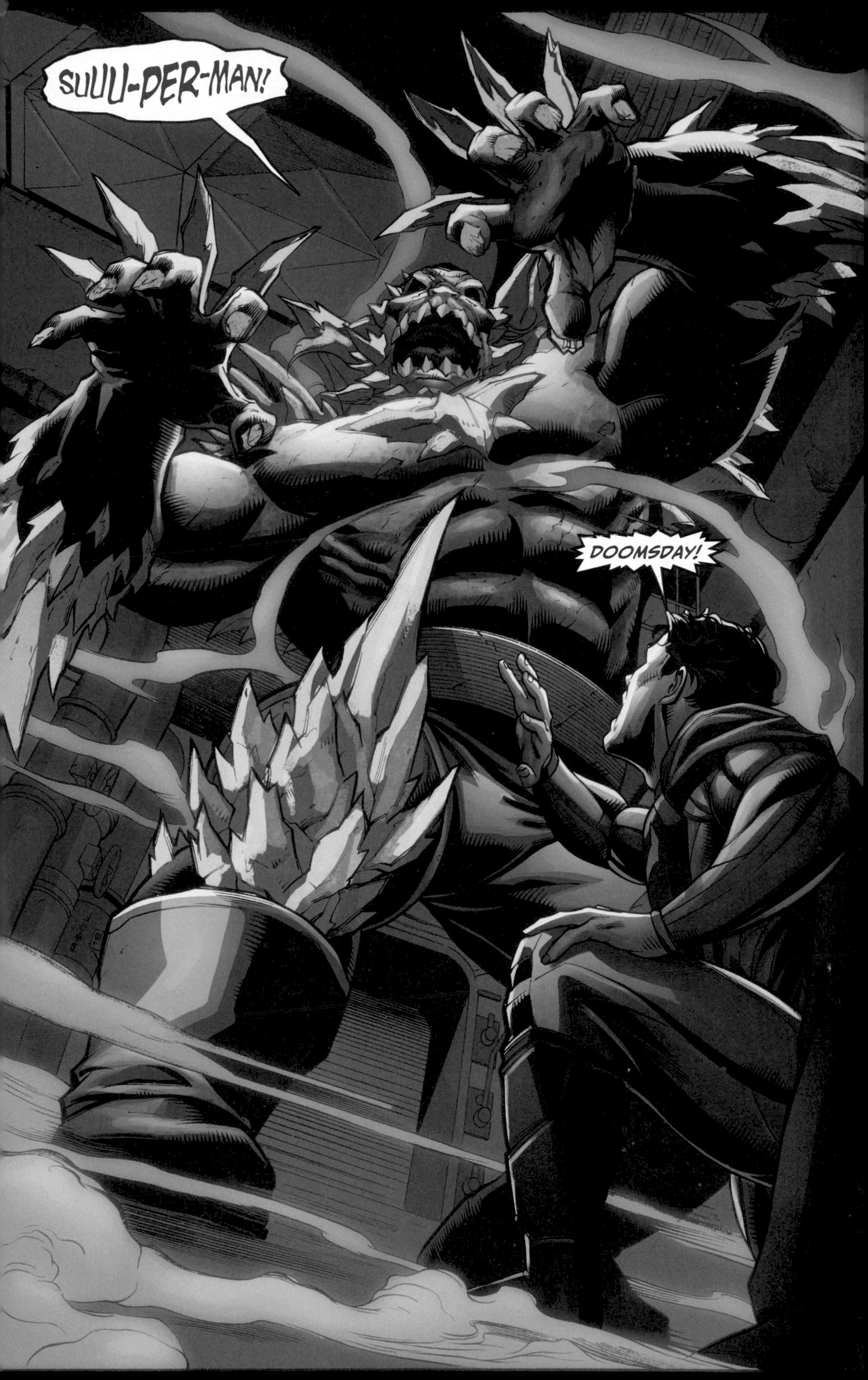
SUUU-PER-MAN!
DOOMSDAY!

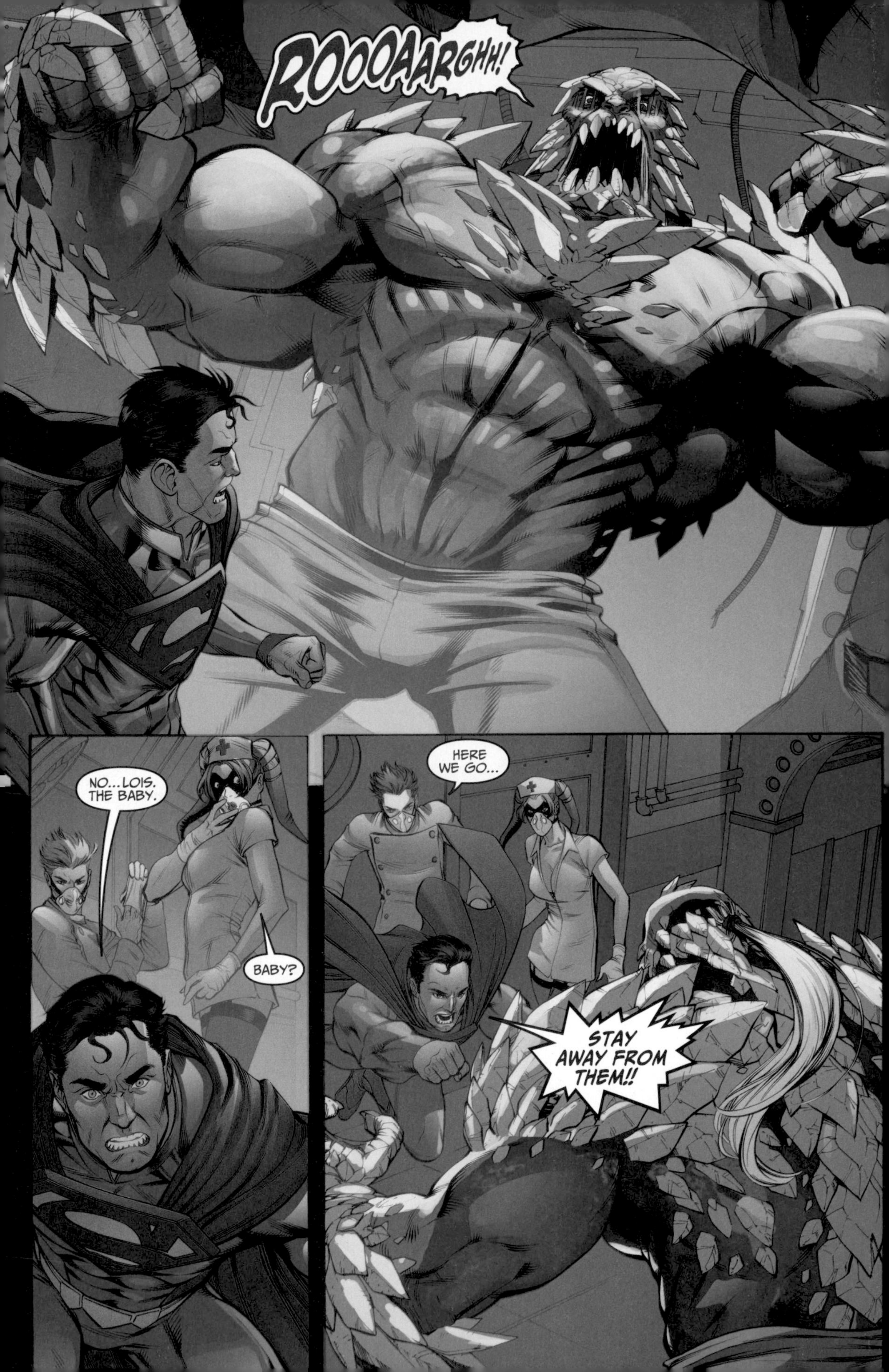
ROOOAARGHH!
NO... LOIS. THE BABY.
BABY?
HERE WE GO...
STAY AWAY FROM THEM!!

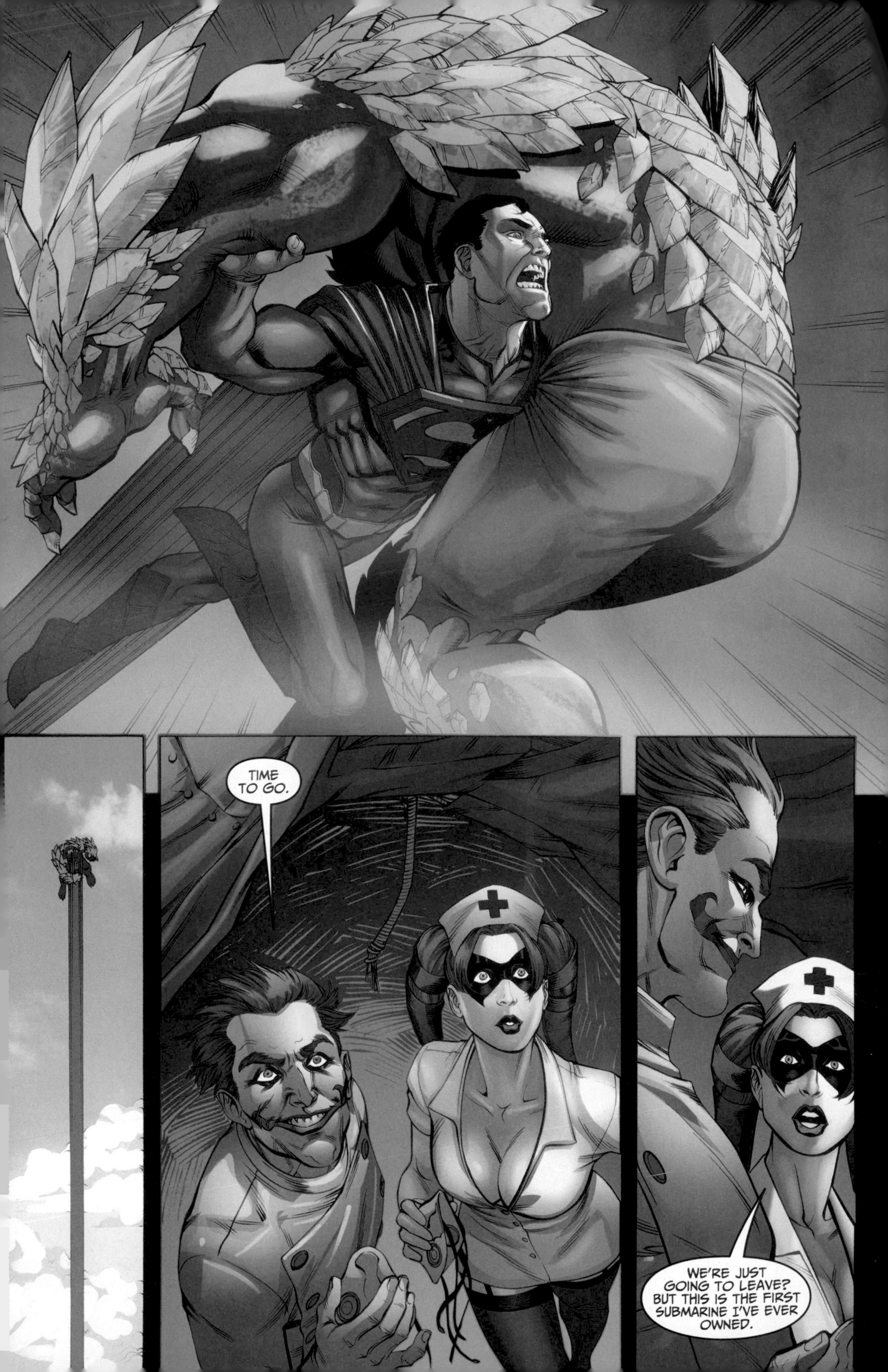
TIME TO GO.
WE'RE JUST GOING TO LEAVE? BUT THIS IS THE FIRST SUBMARINE I'VE EVER OWNED.

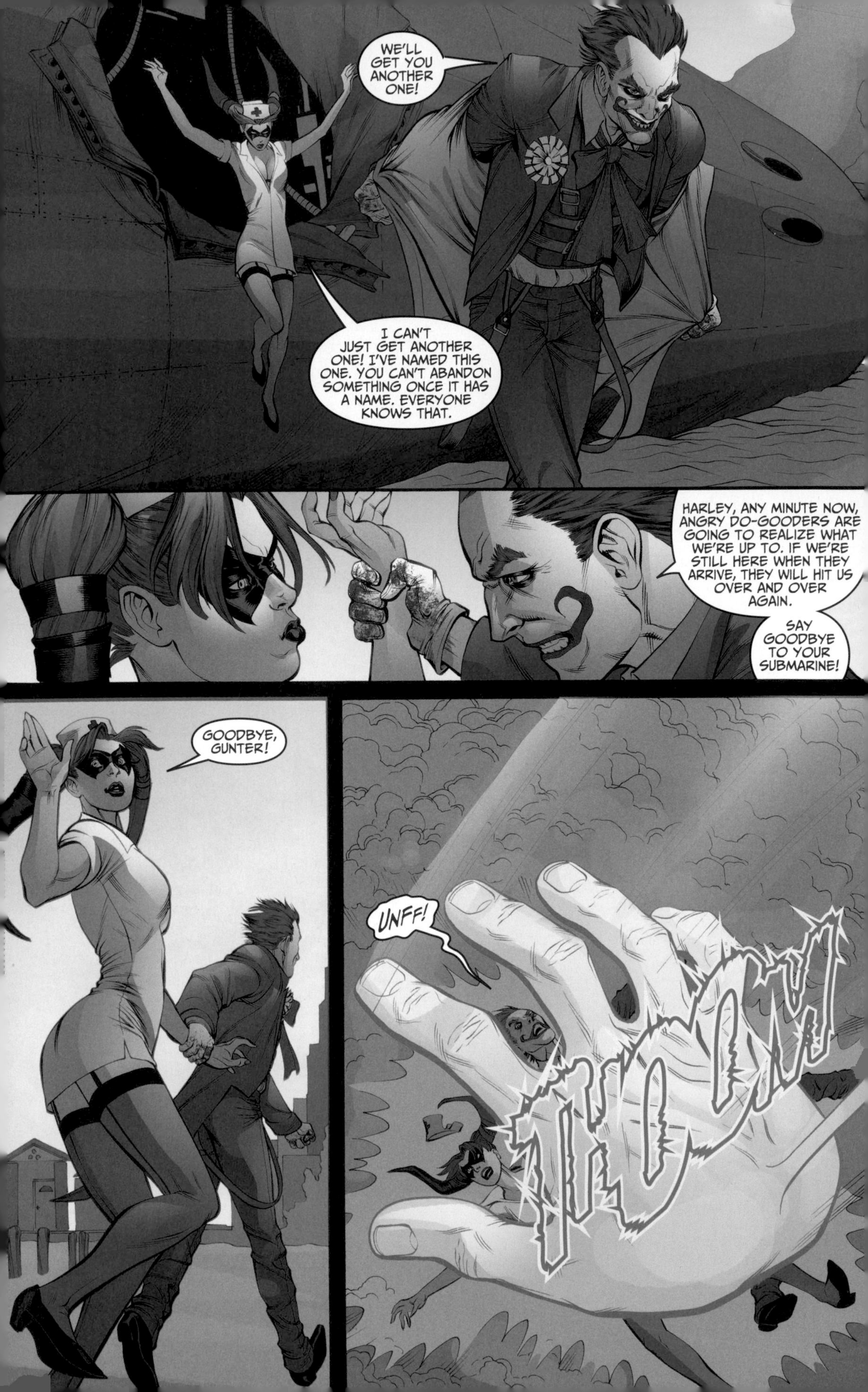
WE'LL GET YOU ANOTHER ONE!
I CAN'T JUST GET ANOTHER ONE! I'VE NAMED THIS ONE. YOU CAN'T ABANDON SOMETHING ONCE IT HAS A NAME. EVERYONE KNOWS THAT.
HARLEY, ANY MINUTE NOW, ANGRY DO-GOODERS ARE GOING TO REALIZE WHAT WE'RE UP TO. IF WE'RE STILL HERE WHEN THEY ARRIVE, THEY WILL HIT US OVER AND OVER AGAIN.
SAY GOODBYE TO YOUR SUBMARINE!
GOODBYE, GUNTER!
UNFF!

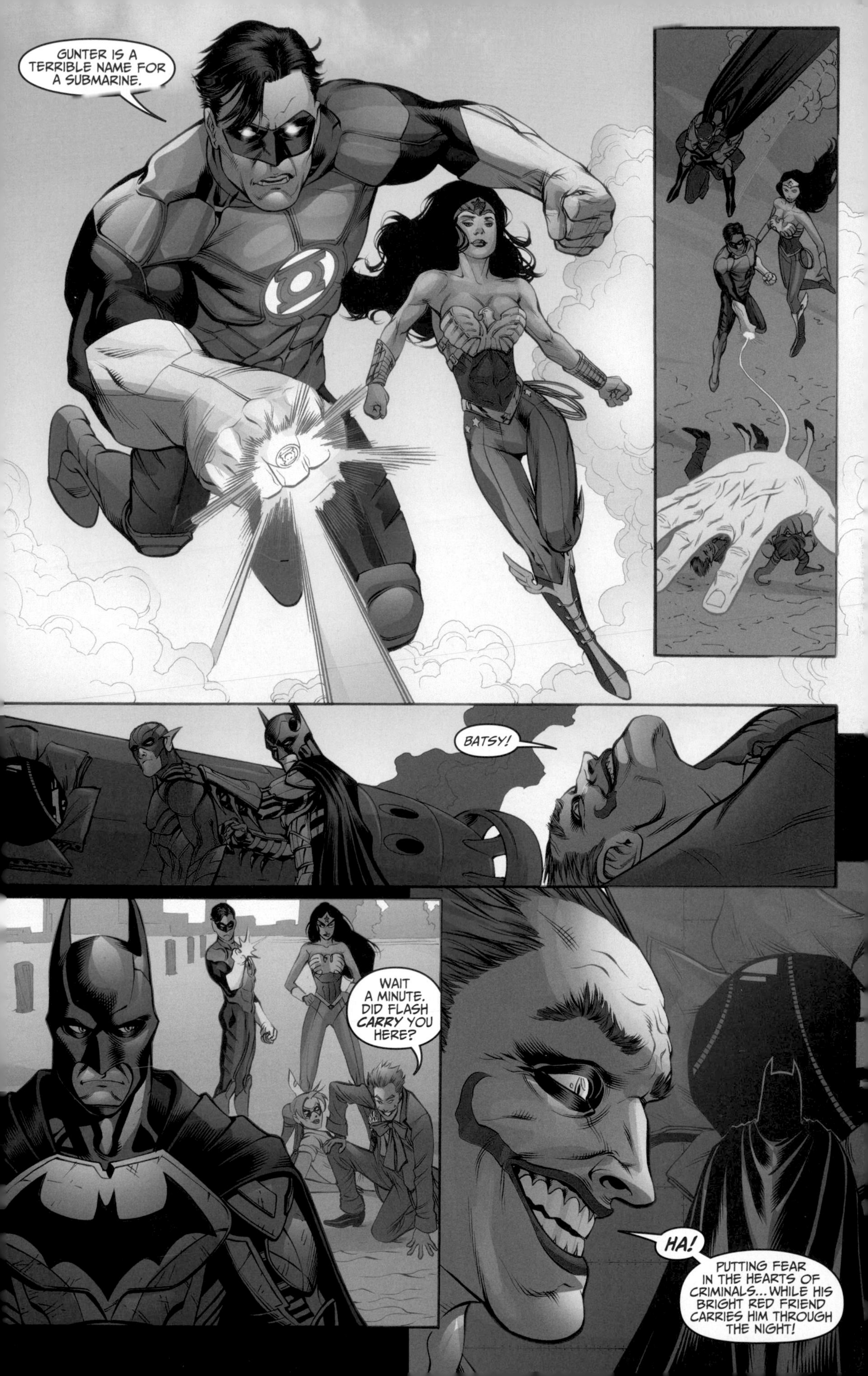

GUNTER IS A TERRIBLE NAME FOR A SUBMARINE.
BATSY!
WAIT A MINUTE. DID FLASH CARRY YOU HERE?
HA!
PUTTING FEAR IN THE HEARTS OF CRIMINALS...WHILE HIS BRIGHT RED FRIEND CARRIES HIM THROUGH THE NIGHT!

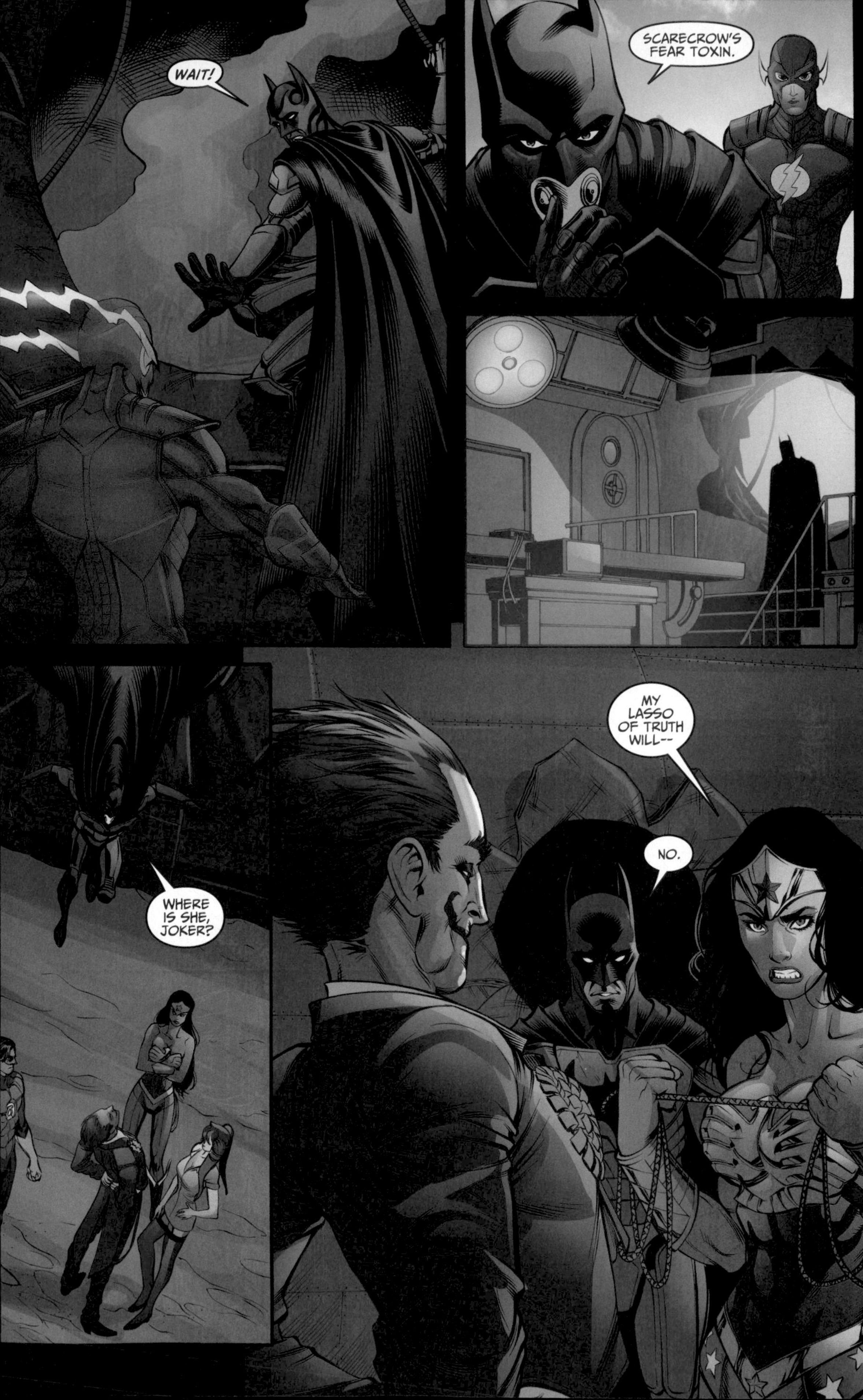
WAIT!
SCARECROW'S FEAR TOXIN.
WHERE IS SHE, JOKER?
MY LASSO OF TRUTH WILL--
NO.

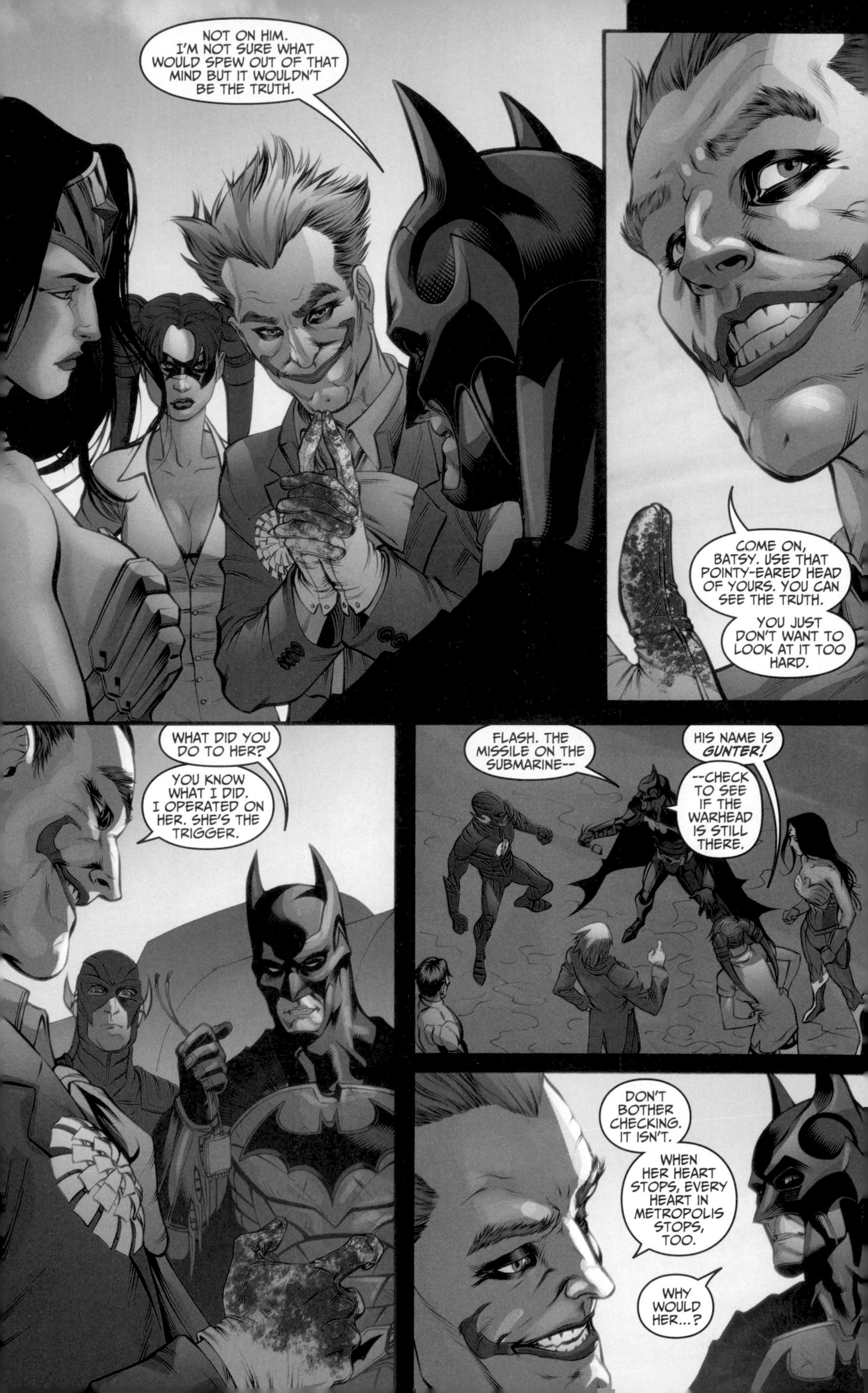
NOT ON HIM. I'M NOT SURE WHAT WOULD SPEW OUT OF THAT MIND BUT IT WOULDN'T BE THE TRUTH.
COME ON, BATSY. USE THAT POINTY-EARED HEAD OF YOURS. YOU CAN SEE THE TRUTH.
YOU JUST DON'T WANT TO LOOK AT IT TOO HARD.
WHAT DID YOU DO TO HER?
YOU KNOW WHAT I DID. I OPERATED ON HER. SHE'S THE TRIGGER.
FLASH. THE MISSILE ON THE SUBMARINE--
HIS NAME IS GUNTER!
--CHECK TO SEE IF THE WARHEAD IS STILL THERE.
DON'T BOTHER CHECKING. IT ISN'T.
WHEN HER HEART STOPS, EVERY HEART IN METROPOLIS STOPS, TOO.
WHY WOULD HER...?

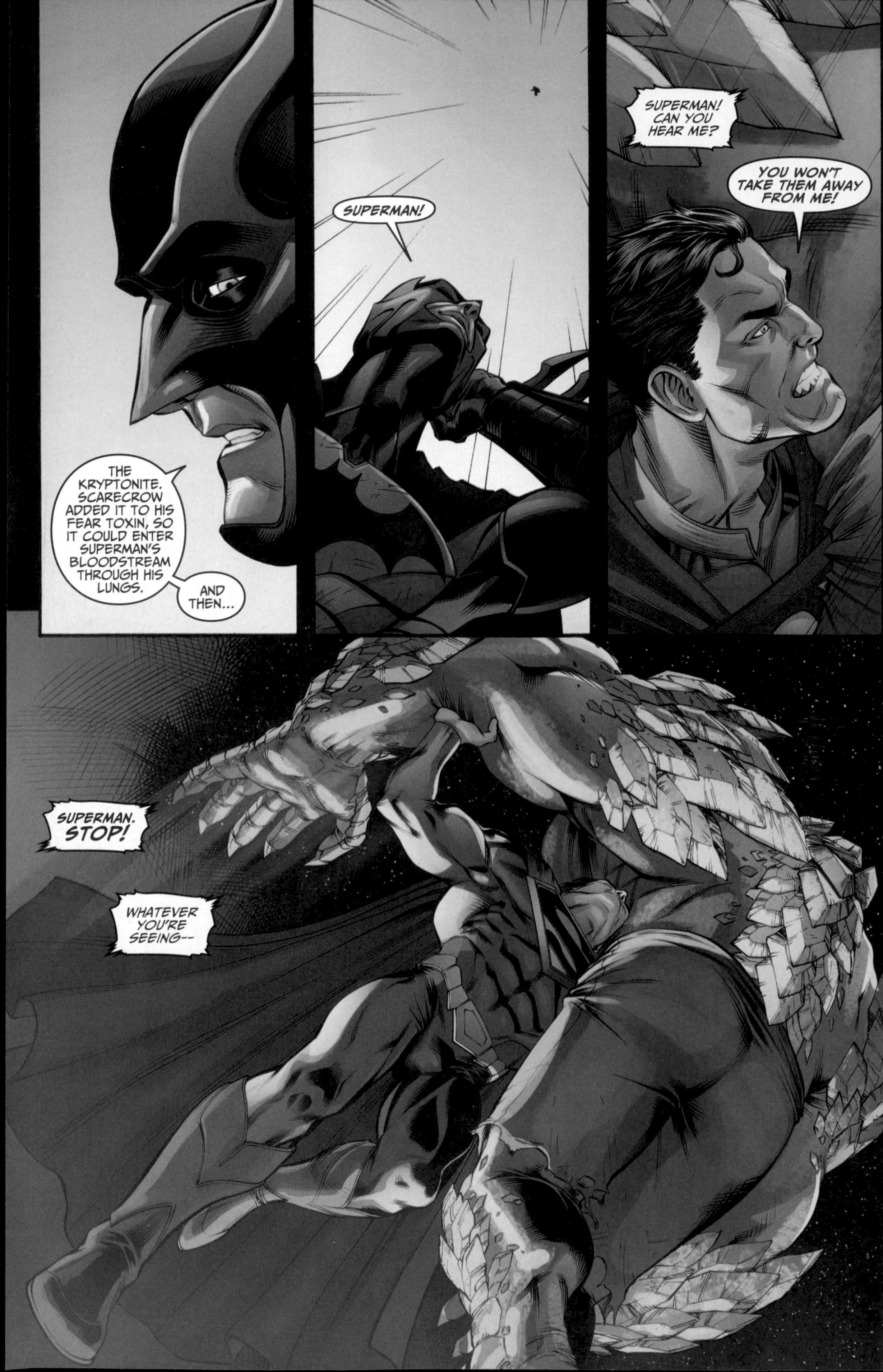
THE KRYPTONITE. SCARECROW ADDED IT TO HIS FEAR TOXIN, SO IT COULD ENTER SUPERMAN'S BLOODSTREAM THROUGH HIS LUNGS.
AND THEN...
SUPERMAN!
SUPERMAN! CAN YOU HEAR ME?
YOU WON'T TAKE THEM AWAY FROM ME!
SUPERMAN. STOP!
WHATEVER YOU'RE SEEING--

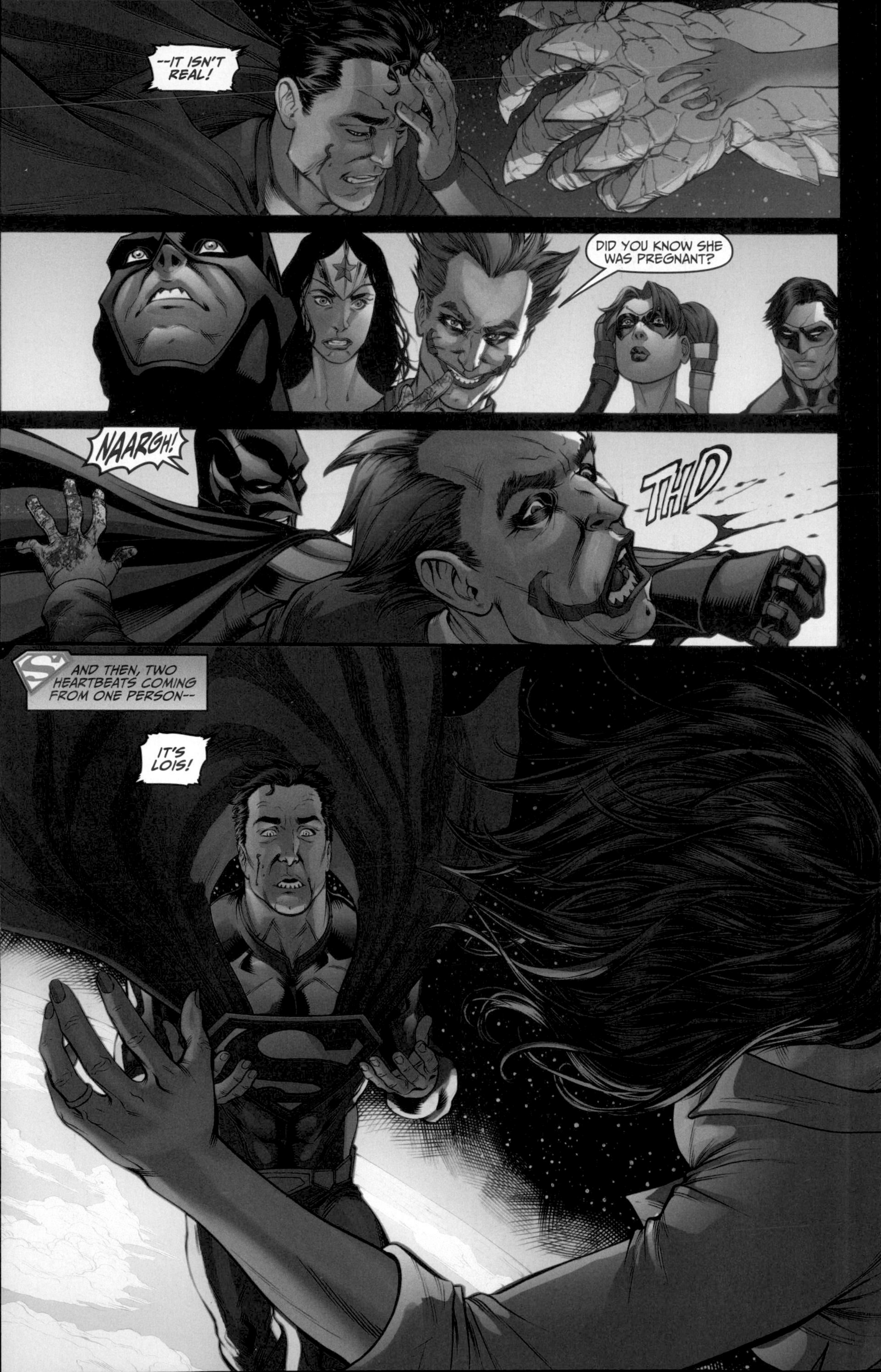
--IT ISN'T REAL!
DID YOU KNOW SHE WAS PREGNANT?
NAARGH!
THD
AND THEN, TWO HEARTBEATS COMING FROM ONE PERSON--
IT'S LOIS!

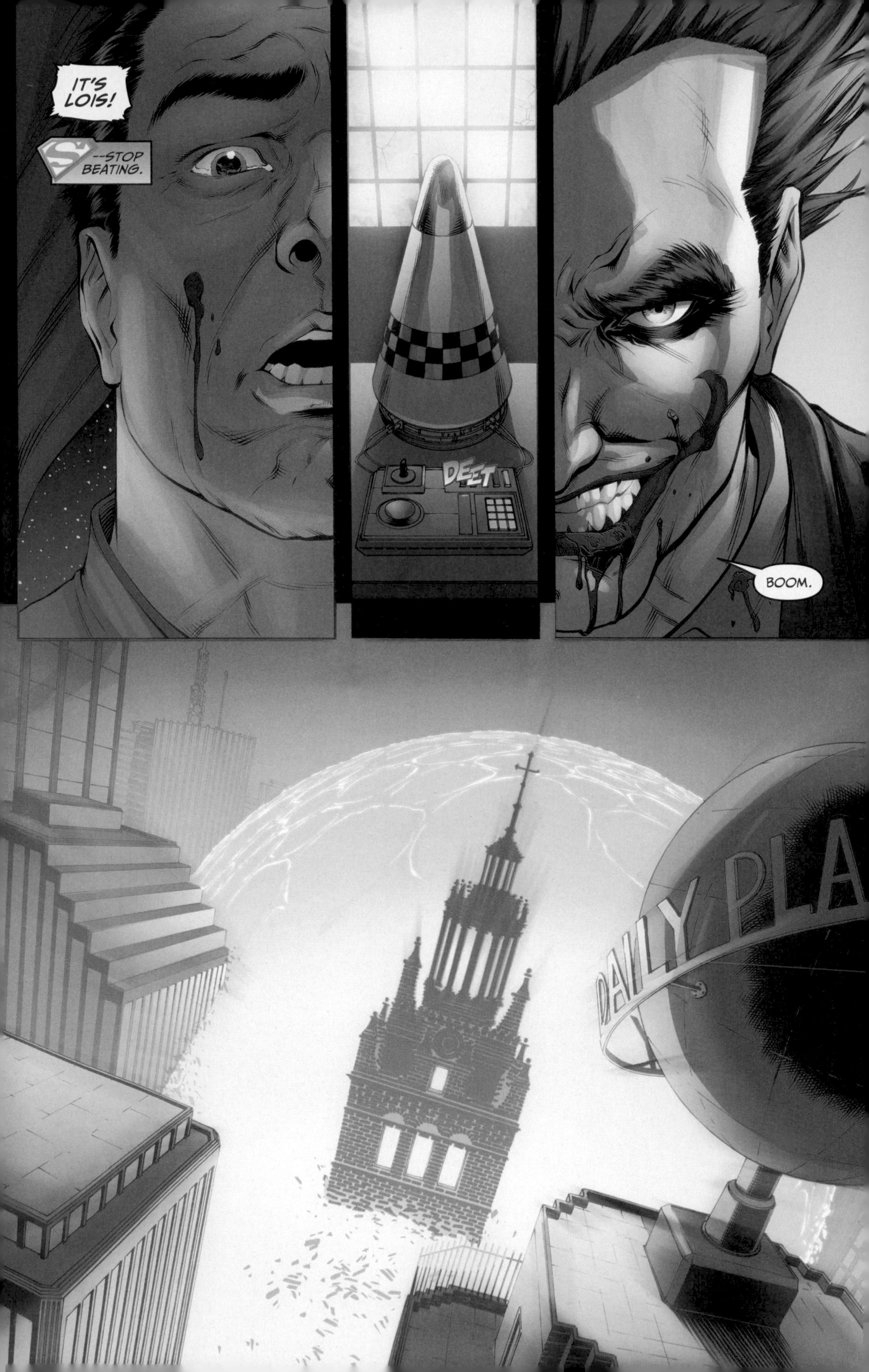
IT'S LOIS!
--STOP BEATING.
DEET!
BOOM.
DAILY PLA

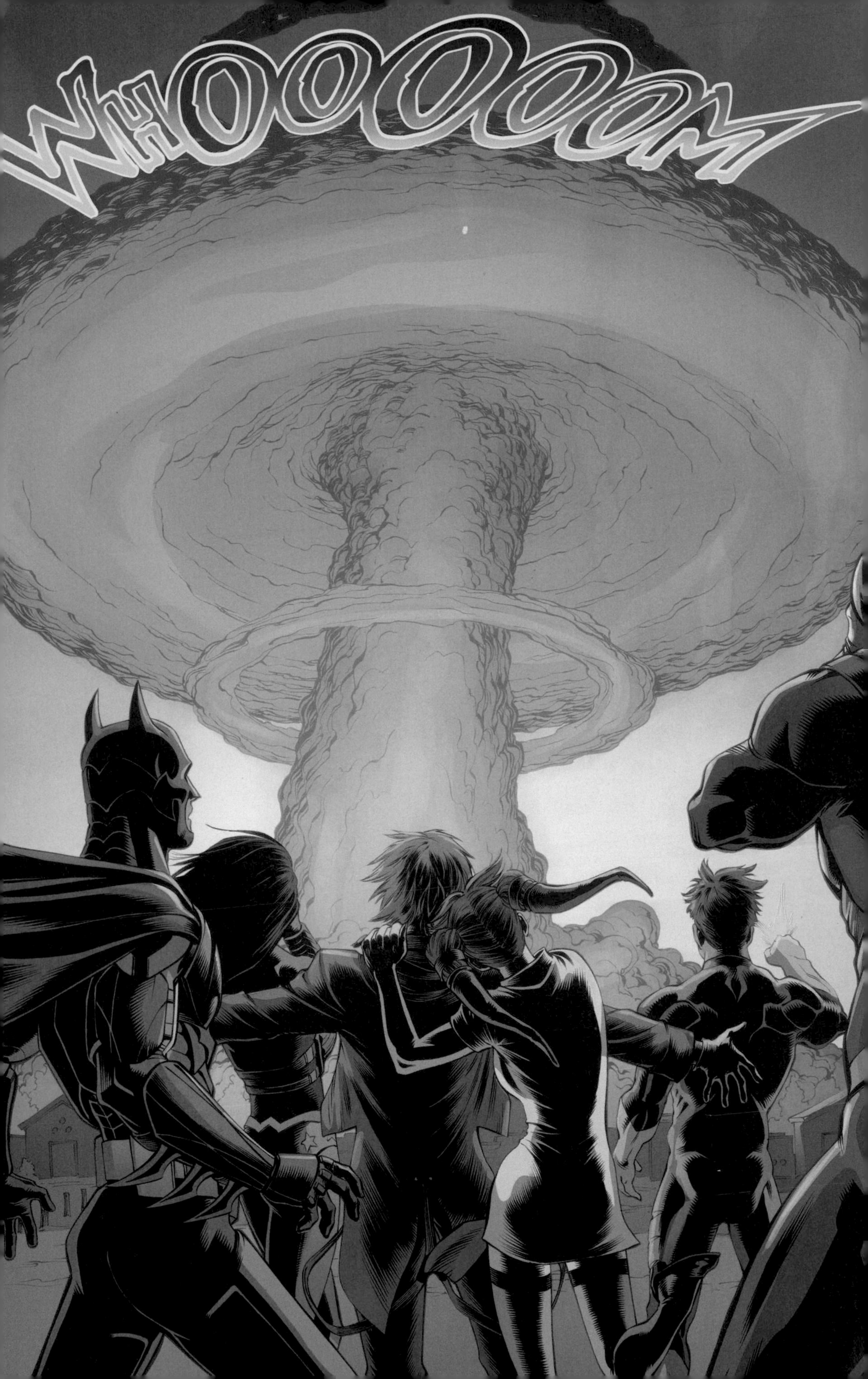
WHOOOOOM

PART TWO

Jheremy Raapack Bruno Redondo Artists

Jheremy Raapack & **Andrew Elder** Cover

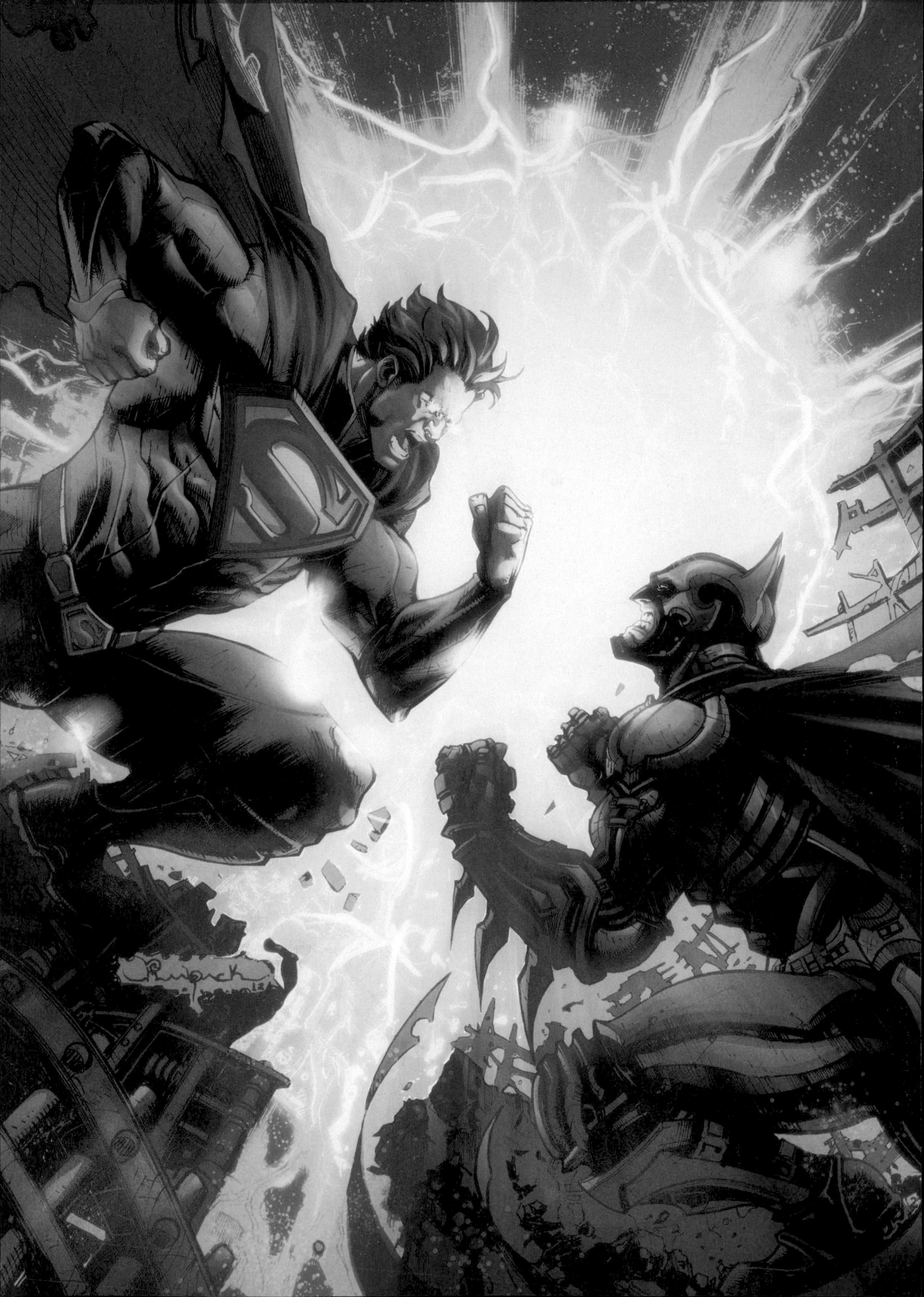

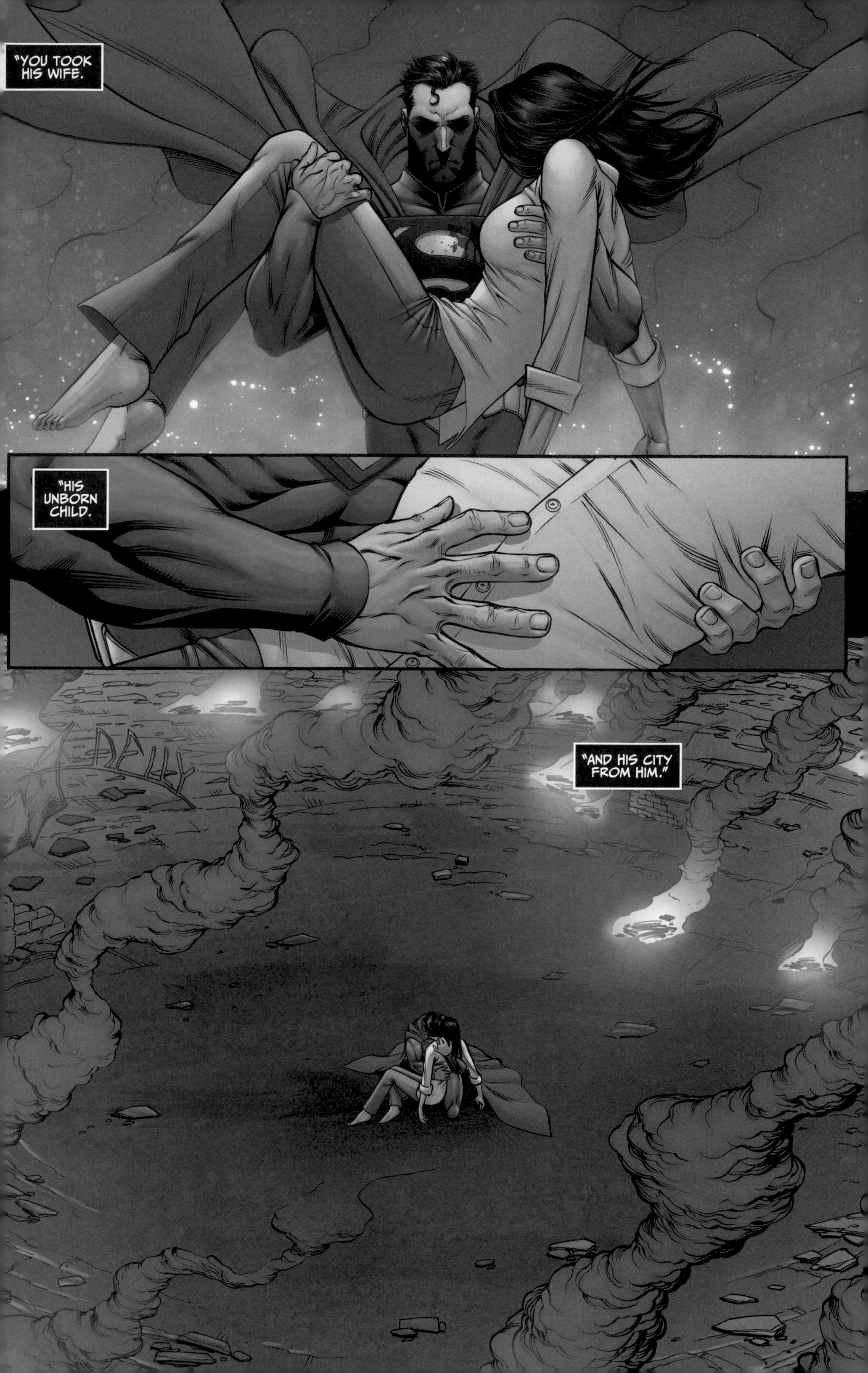
"YOU TOOK HIS WIFE.
"HIS UNBORN CHILD.
"AND HIS CITY FROM HIM."

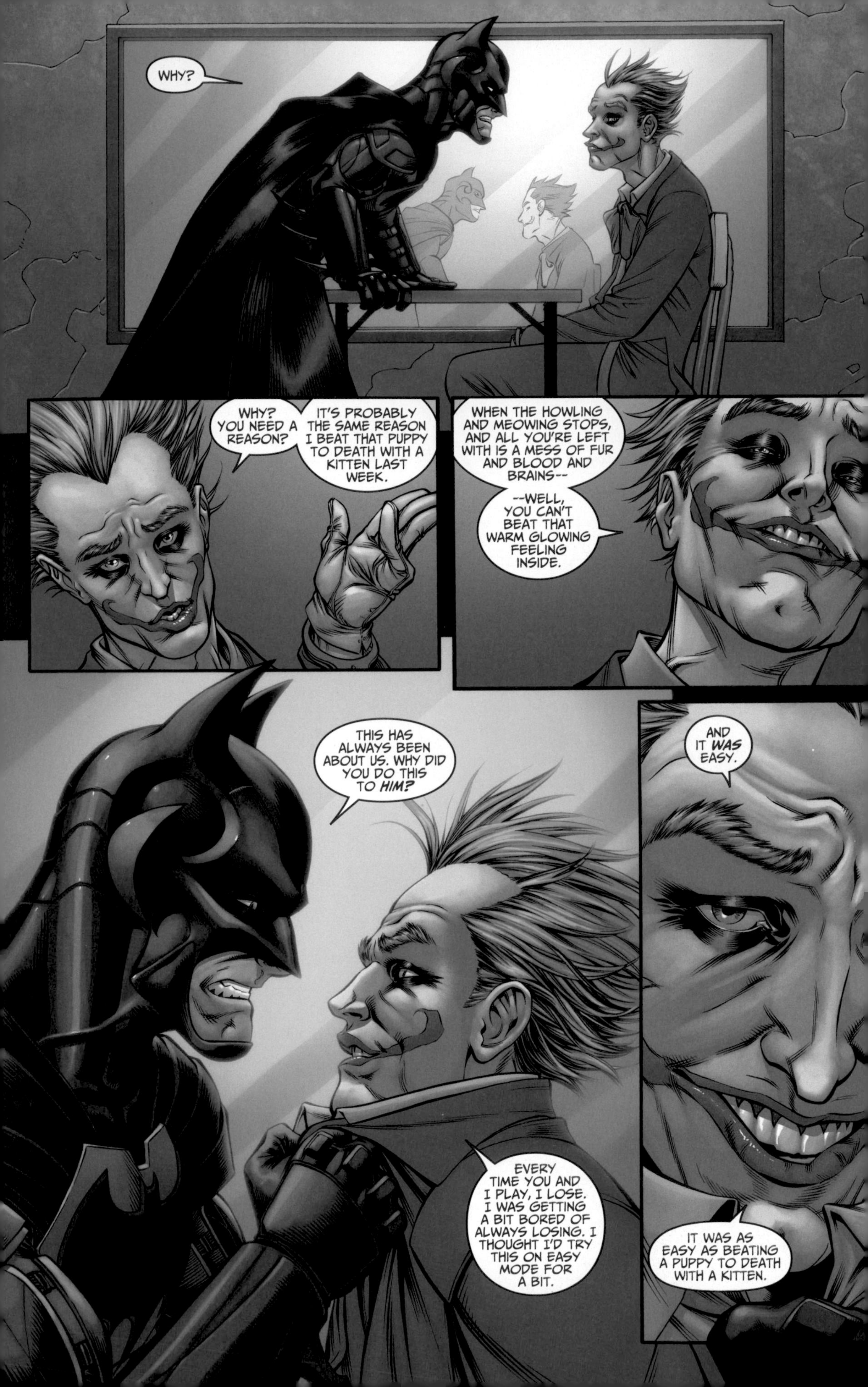
WHY?
WHY? YOU NEED A REASON?
IT'S PROBABLY THE SAME REASON I BEAT THAT PUPPY TO DEATH WITH A KITTEN LAST WEEK.
WHEN THE HOWLING AND MEOWING STOPS, AND ALL YOU'RE LEFT WITH IS A MESS OF FUR AND BLOOD AND BRAINS--
--WELL, YOU CAN'T BEAT THAT WARM GLOWING FEELING INSIDE.
THIS HAS ALWAYS BEEN ABOUT US. WHY DID YOU DO THIS TO *HIM?*
EVERY TIME YOU AND I PLAY, I LOSE. I WAS GETTING A BIT BORED OF ALWAYS LOSING. I THOUGHT I'D TRY THIS ON EASY MODE FOR A BIT.
AND IT *WAS* EASY.
IT WAS AS EASY AS BEATING A PUPPY TO DEATH WITH A KITTEN.

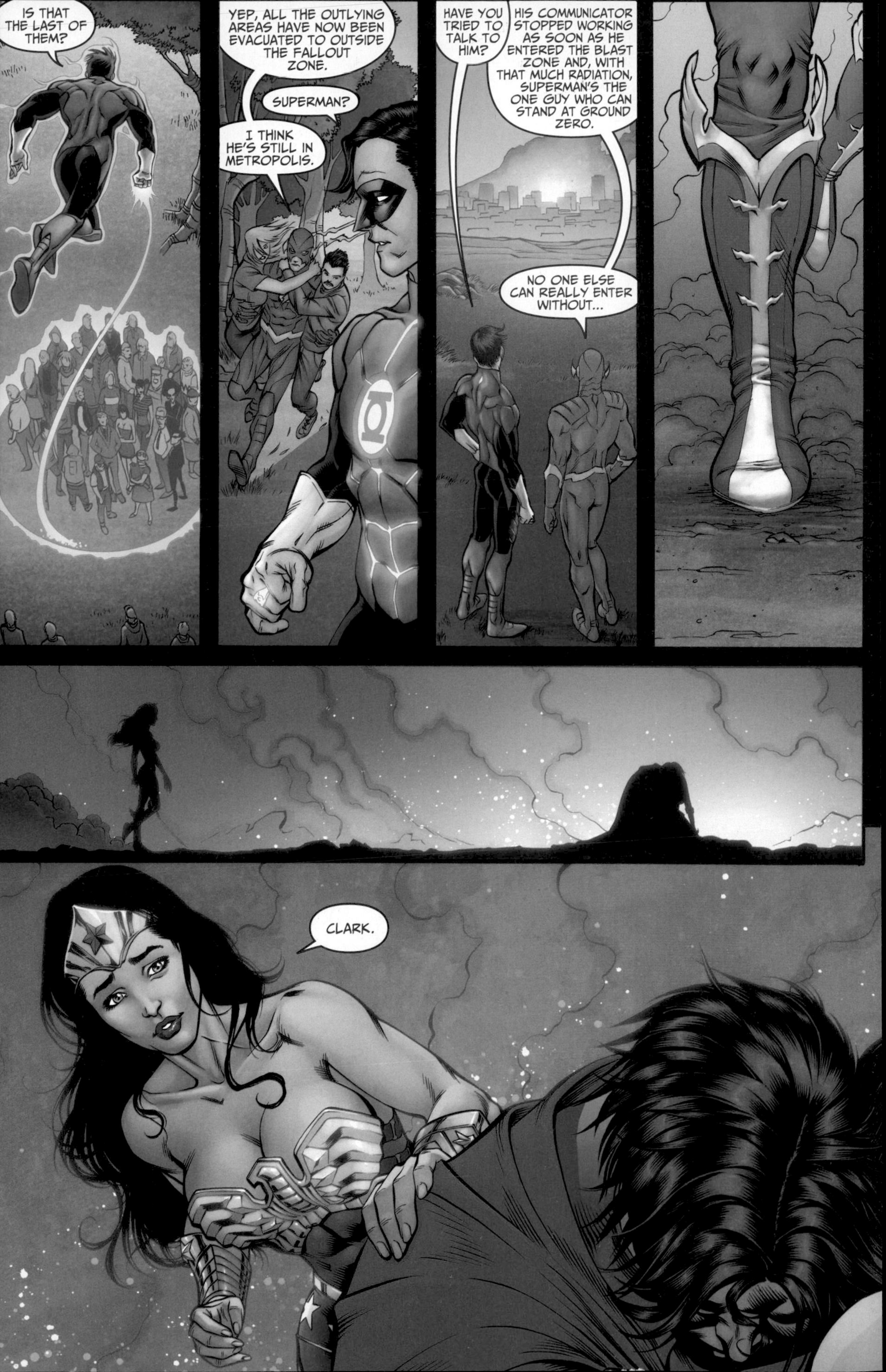
IS THAT THE LAST OF THEM?
YEP, ALL THE OUTLYING AREAS HAVE NOW BEEN EVACUATED TO OUTSIDE THE FALLOUT ZONE.
SUPERMAN?
I THINK HE'S STILL IN METROPOLIS.
HAVE YOU TRIED TO TALK TO HIM?
HIS COMMUNICATOR STOPPED WORKING AS SOON AS HE ENTERED THE BLAST ZONE AND, WITH THAT MUCH RADIATION, SUPERMAN'S THE ONE GUY WHO CAN STAND AT GROUND ZERO.
NO ONE ELSE CAN REALLY ENTER WITHOUT...
CLARK.

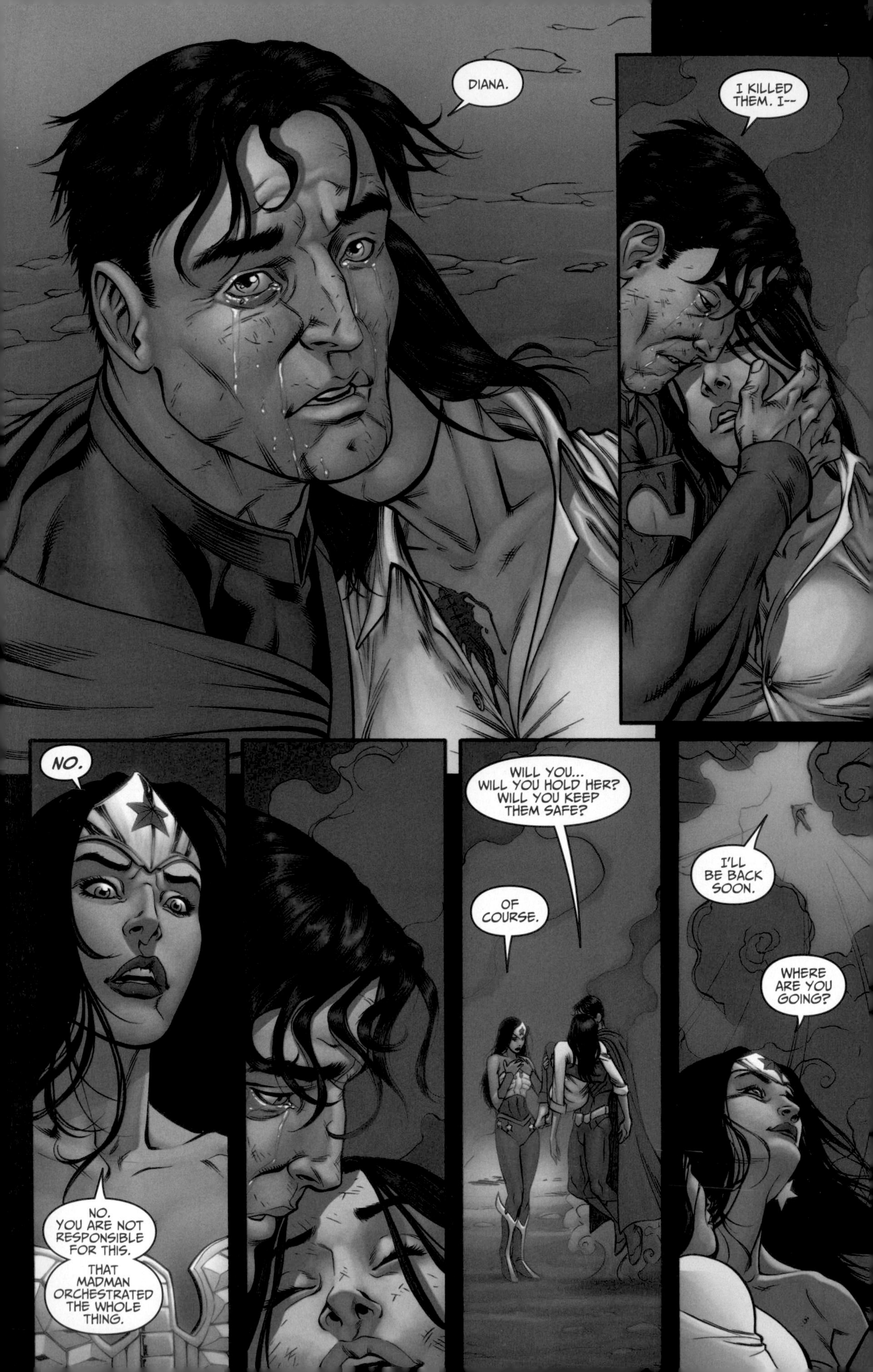
DIANA.
I KILLED THEM. I--
NO.
NO. YOU ARE NOT RESPONSIBLE FOR THIS.
THAT MADMAN ORCHESTRATED THE WHOLE THING.
WILL YOU... WILL YOU HOLD HER? WILL YOU KEEP THEM SAFE?
OF COURSE.
I'LL BE BACK SOON.
WHERE ARE YOU GOING?

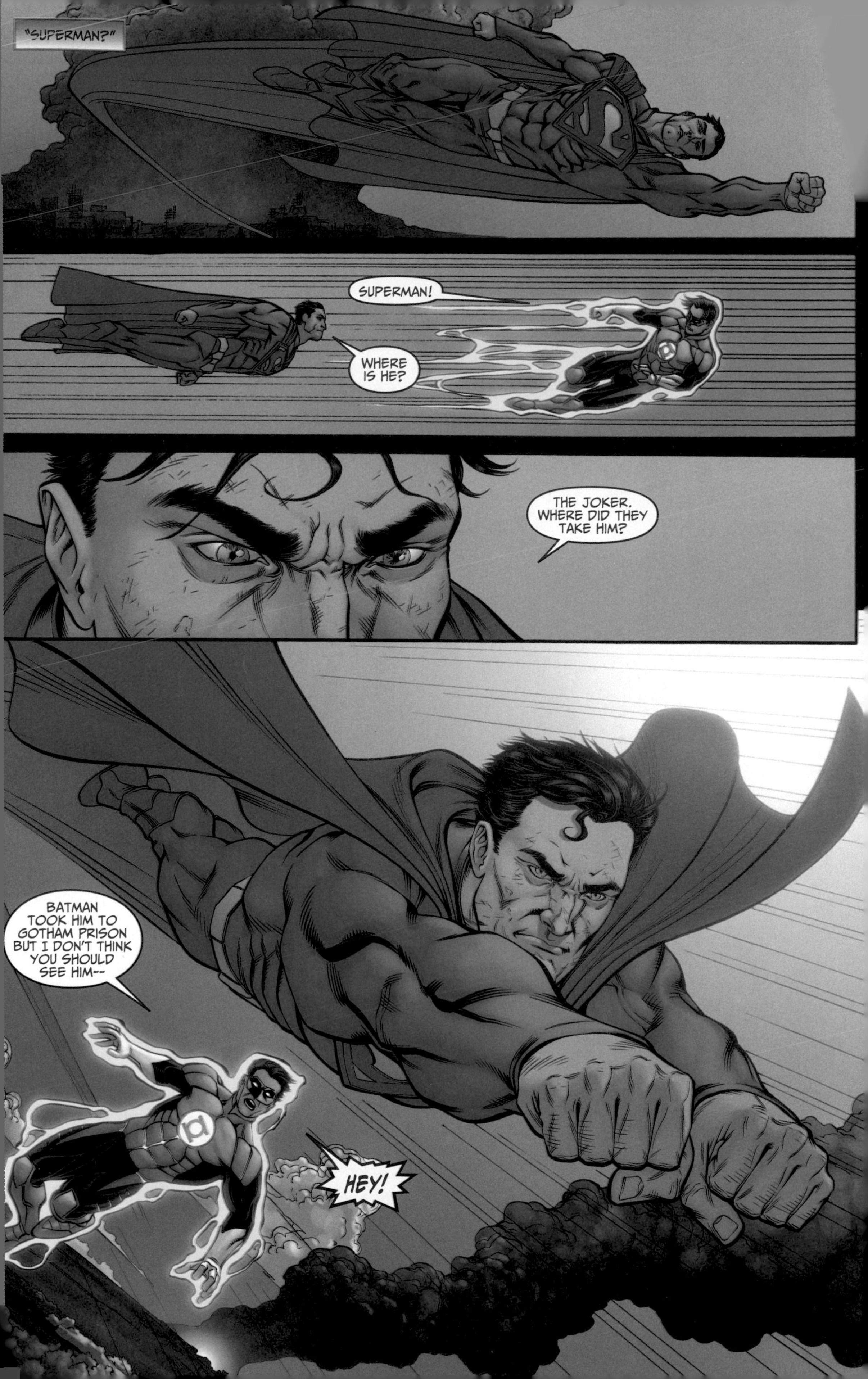
"SUPERMAN?"
SUPERMAN!
WHERE IS HE?
THE JOKER. WHERE DID THEY TAKE HIM?
BATMAN TOOK HIM TO GOTHAM PRISON BUT I DON'T THINK YOU SHOULD SEE HIM--
HEY!

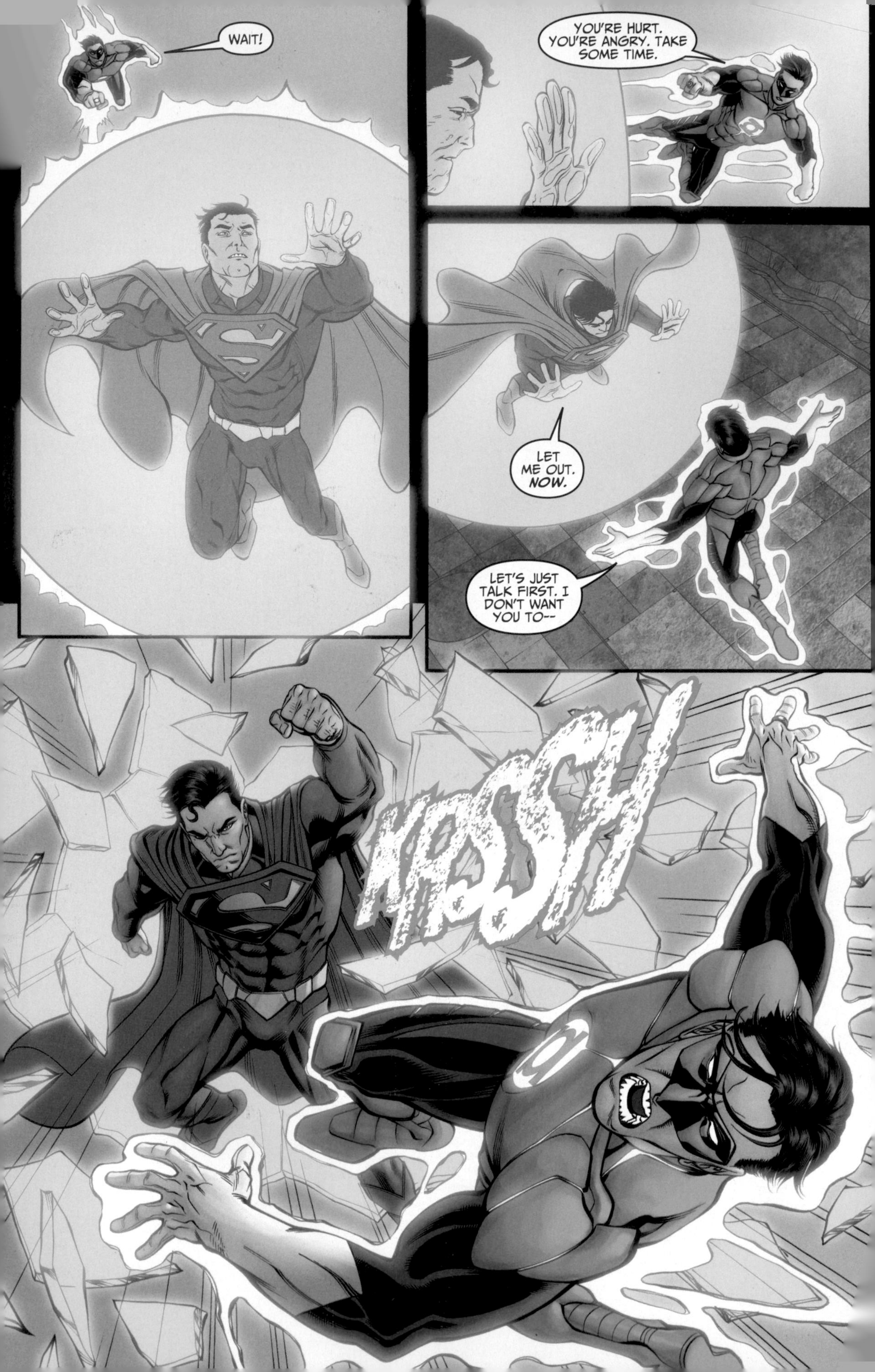
WAIT!
YOU'RE HURT. YOU'RE ANGRY. TAKE SOME TIME.
LET ME OUT. NOW.
LET'S JUST TALK FIRST. I DON'T WANT YOU TO--
KRASH

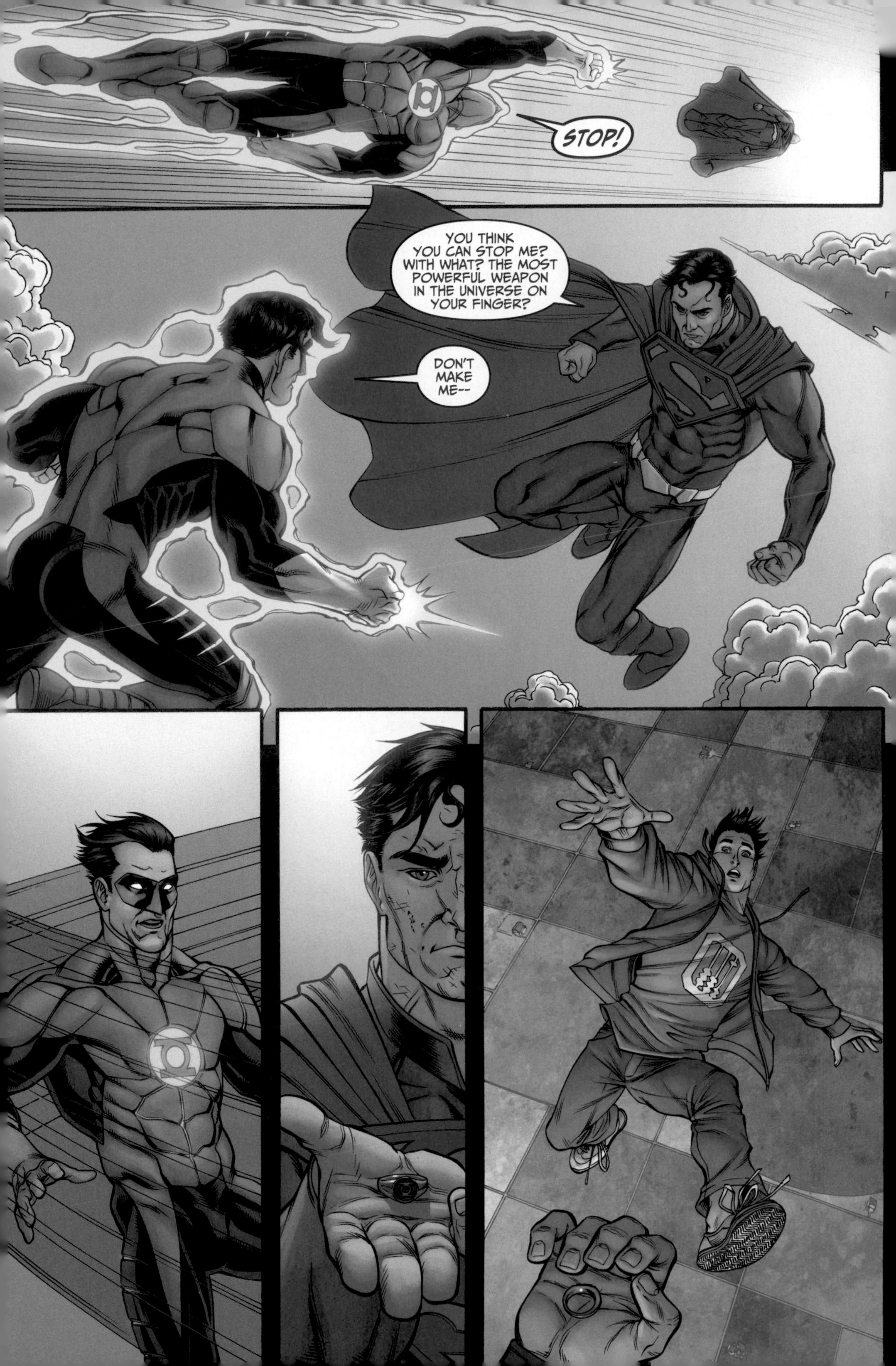
STOP!
YOU THINK YOU CAN STOP ME? WITH WHAT? THE MOST POWERFUL WEAPON IN THE UNIVERSE ON YOUR FINGER?
DON'T MAKE ME--

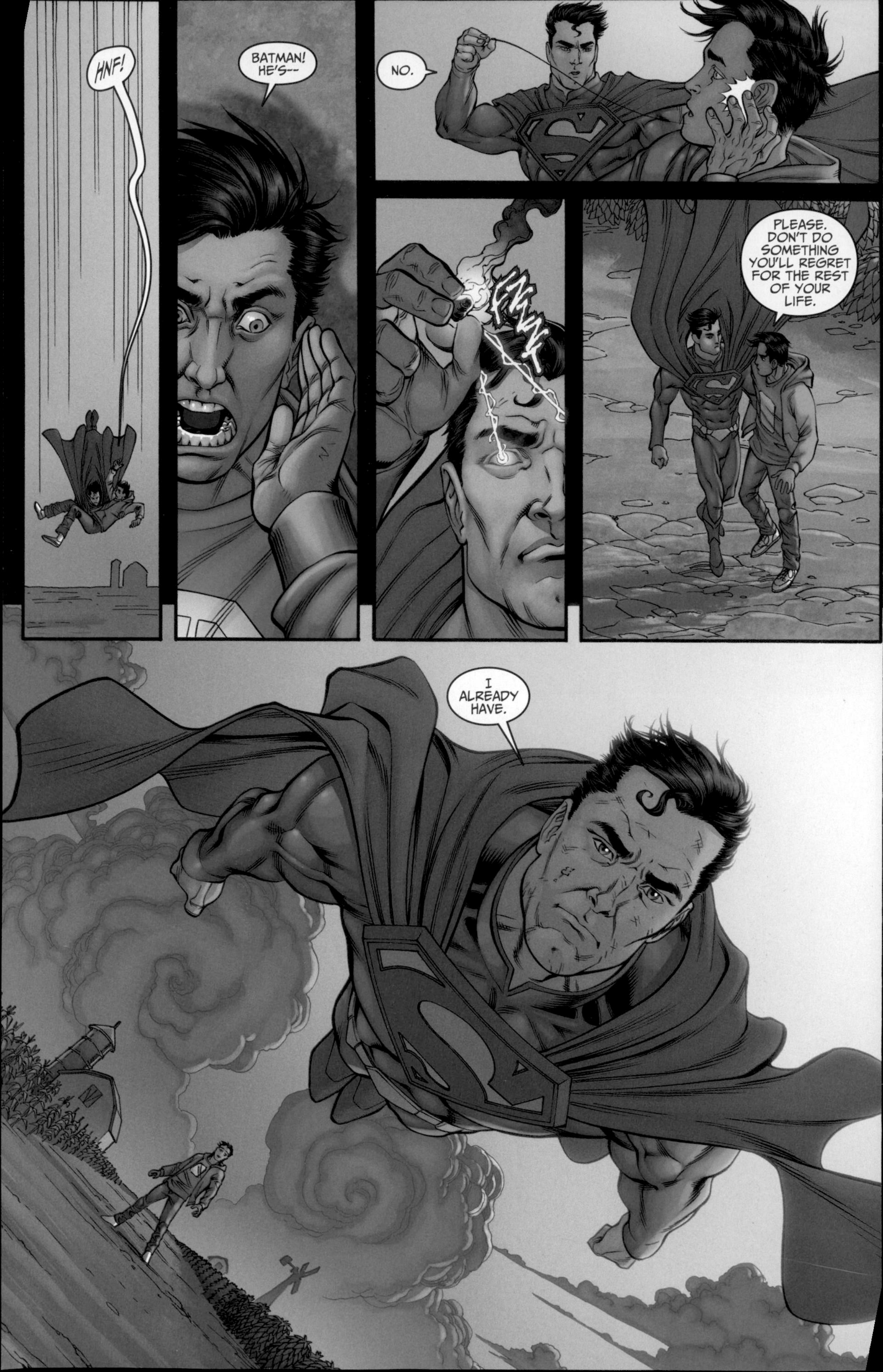

HNF!
BATMAN! HE'S--
NO.
FZZZT
PLEASE. DON'T DO SOMETHING YOU'LL REGRET FOR THE REST OF YOUR LIFE.
I ALREADY HAVE.

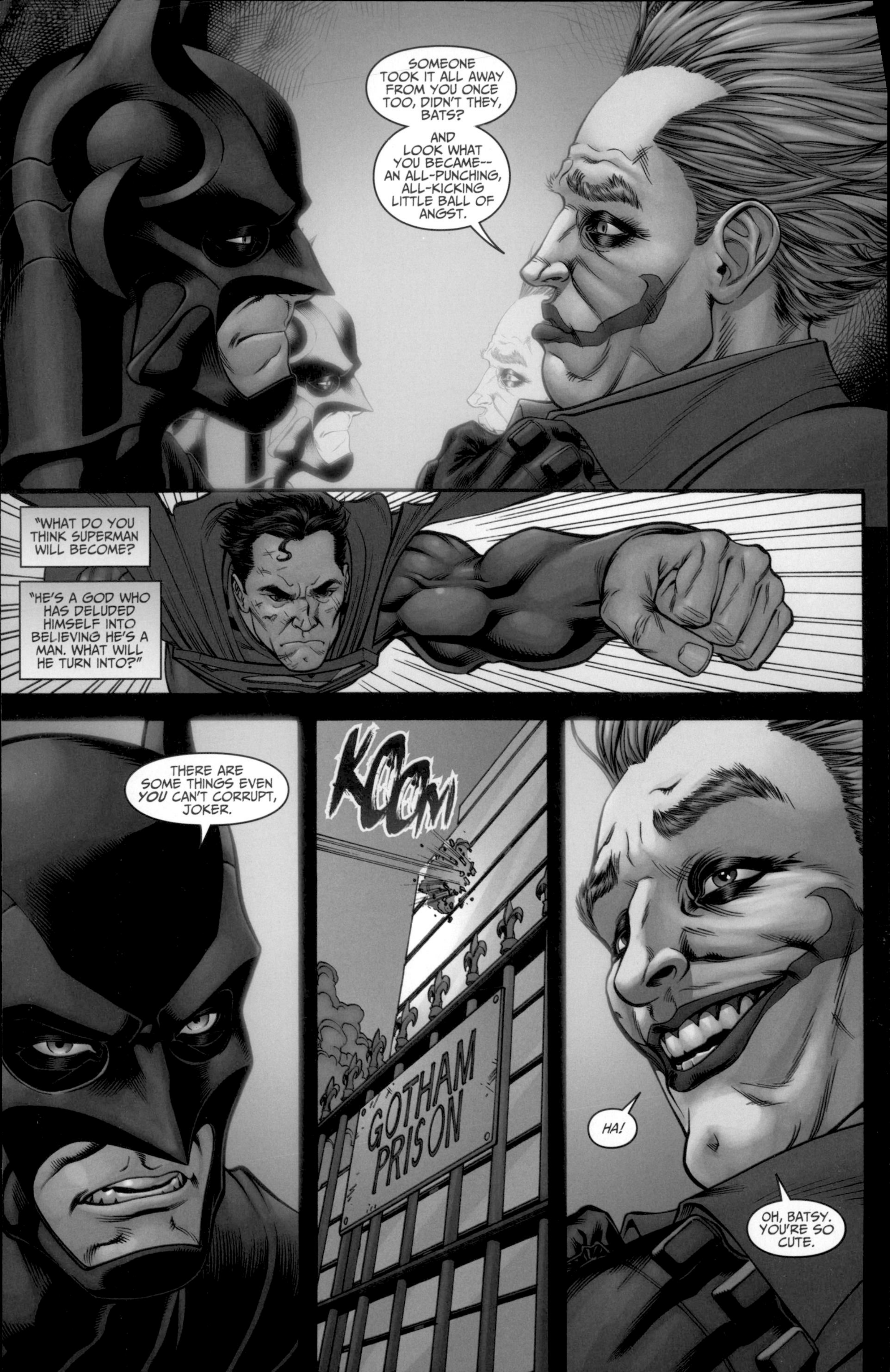
SOMEONE TOOK IT ALL AWAY FROM YOU ONCE TOO, DIDN'T THEY, BATS?
AND LOOK WHAT YOU BECAME-- AN ALL-PUNCHING, ALL-KICKING LITTLE BALL OF ANGST.
"WHAT DO YOU THINK SUPERMAN WILL BECOME?
"HE'S A GOD WHO HAS DELUDED HIMSELF INTO BELIEVING HE'S A MAN. WHAT WILL HE TURN INTO?"
THERE ARE SOME THINGS EVEN *YOU* CAN'T CORRUPT, JOKER.
KOOM
GOTHAM PRISON
HA!
OH, BATSY. YOU'RE SO CUTE.

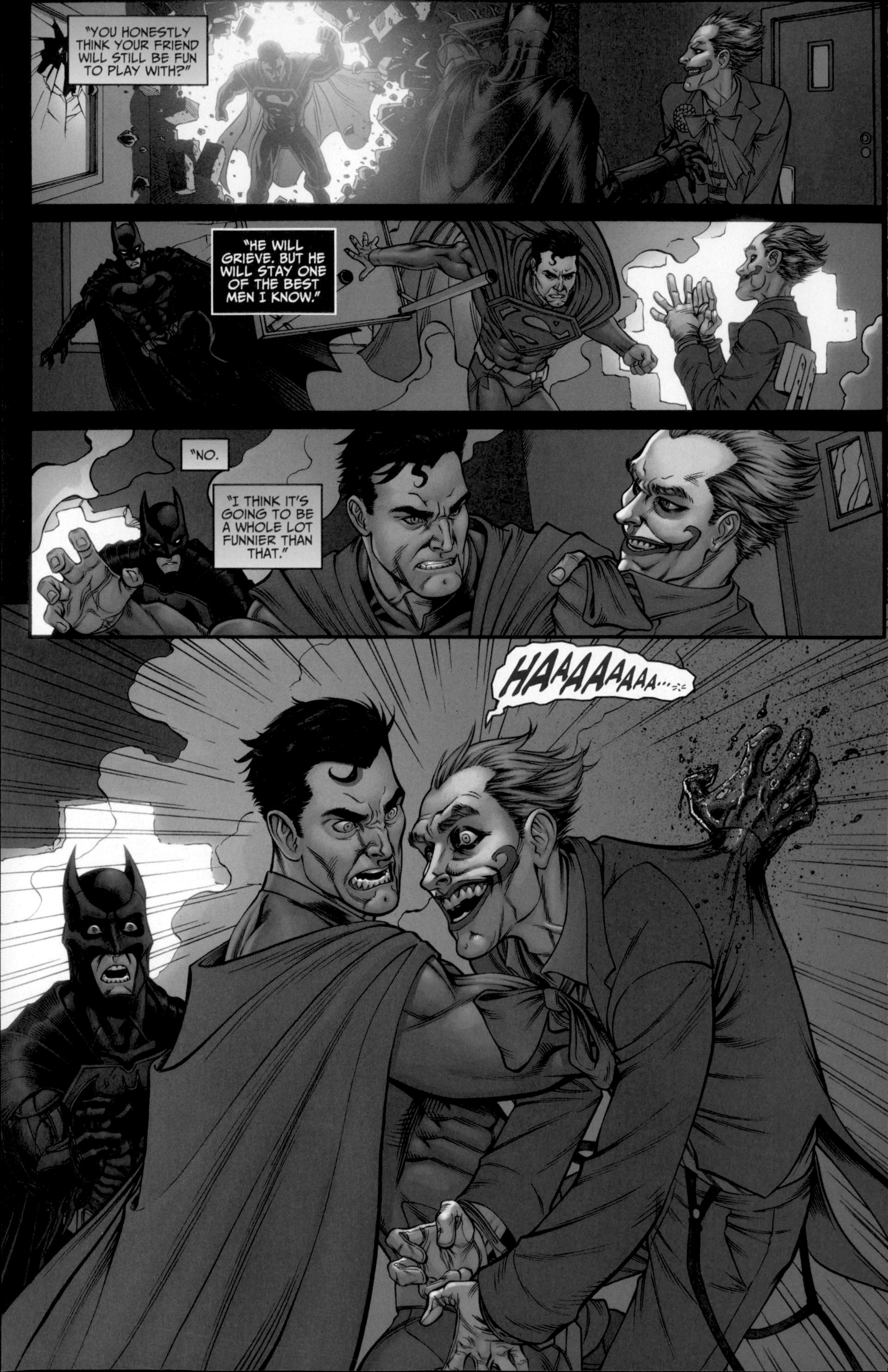
"YOU HONESTLY THINK YOUR FRIEND WILL STILL BE FUN TO PLAY WITH?"
"HE WILL GRIEVE. BUT HE WILL STAY ONE OF THE BEST MEN I KNOW."
"NO.
"I THINK IT'S GOING TO BE A WHOLE LOT FUNNIER THAN THAT."
HAAAAAAA...

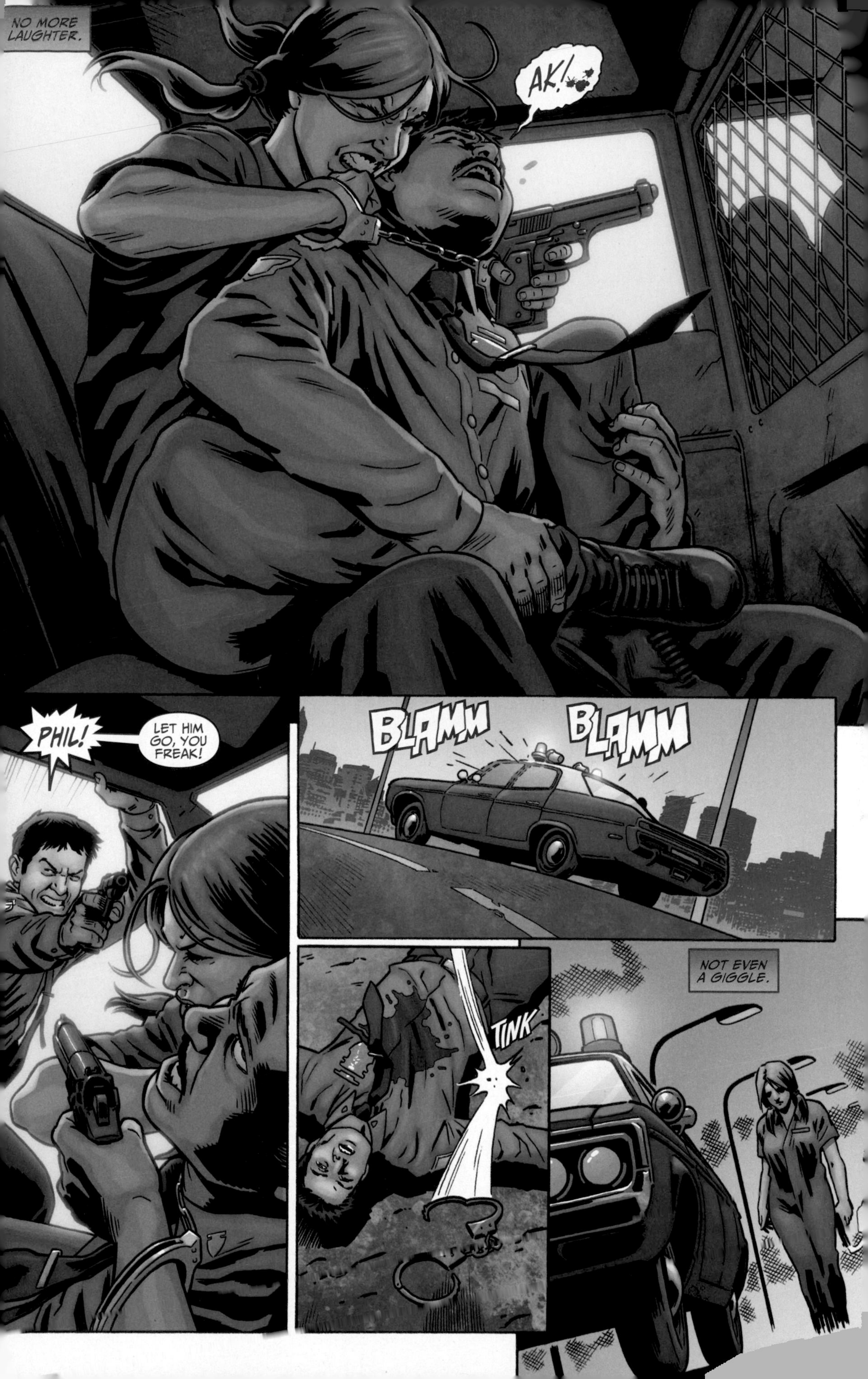
NO MORE LAUGHTER.
AK!
PHIL!
LET HIM GO, YOU FREAK!
BLAMM
BLAMM
TINK
NOT EVEN A GIGGLE.

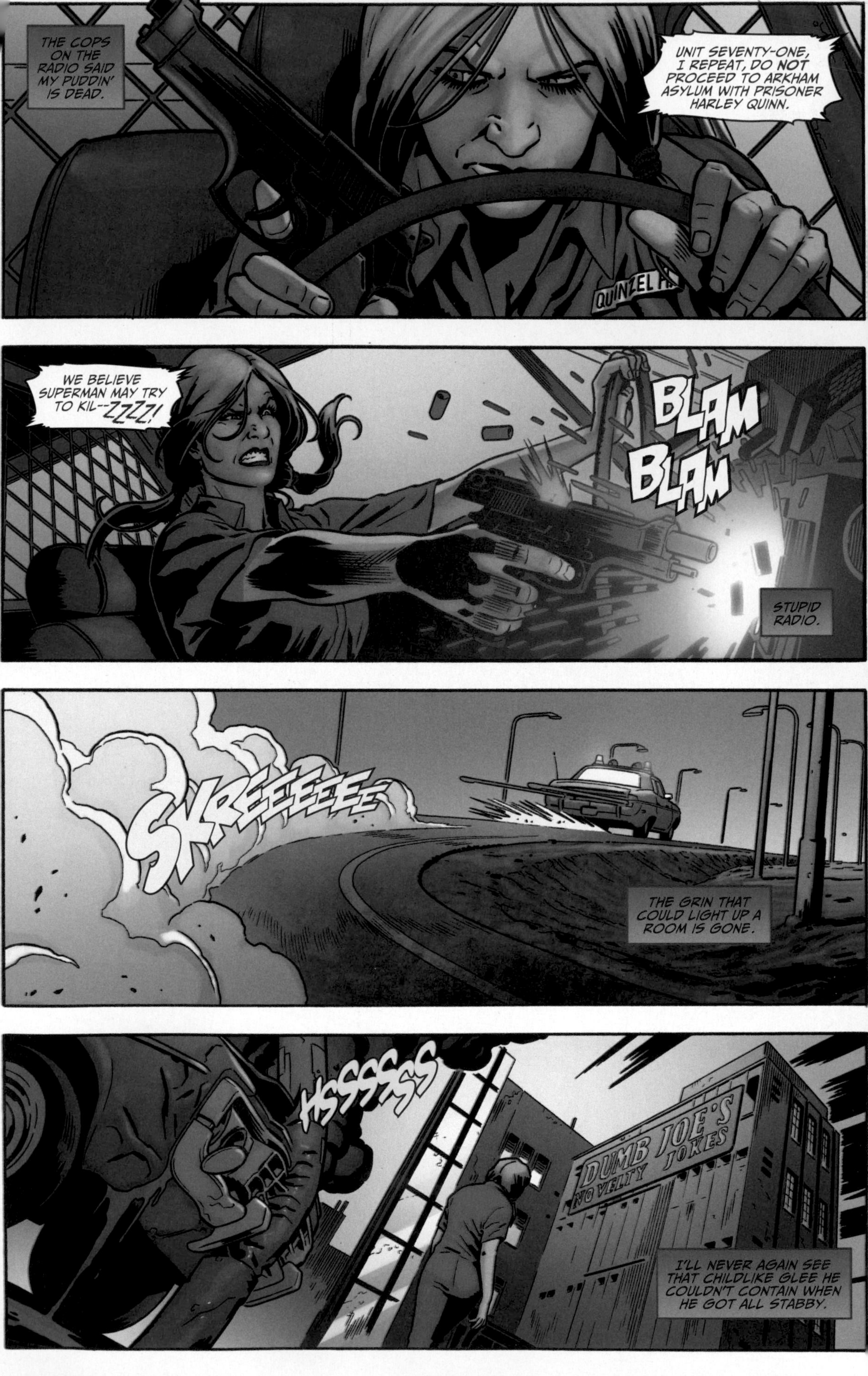
THE COPS ON THE RADIO SAID MY PUDDIN' IS DEAD.
UNIT SEVENTY-ONE, I REPEAT, DO NOT PROCEED TO ARKHAM ASYLUM WITH PRISONER HARLEY QUINN.
QUINZEL H.
WE BELIEVE SUPERMAN MAY TRY TO KIL--ZZZZ!
BLAM
BLAM
STUPID RADIO.
SKREEEEEEE
THE GRIN THAT COULD LIGHT UP A ROOM IS GONE.
HSSSSSS
DUMB JOE'S
NOVELTY JOKES
I'LL NEVER AGAIN SEE THAT CHILDLIKE GLEE HE COULDN'T CONTAIN WHEN HE GOT ALL STABBY.

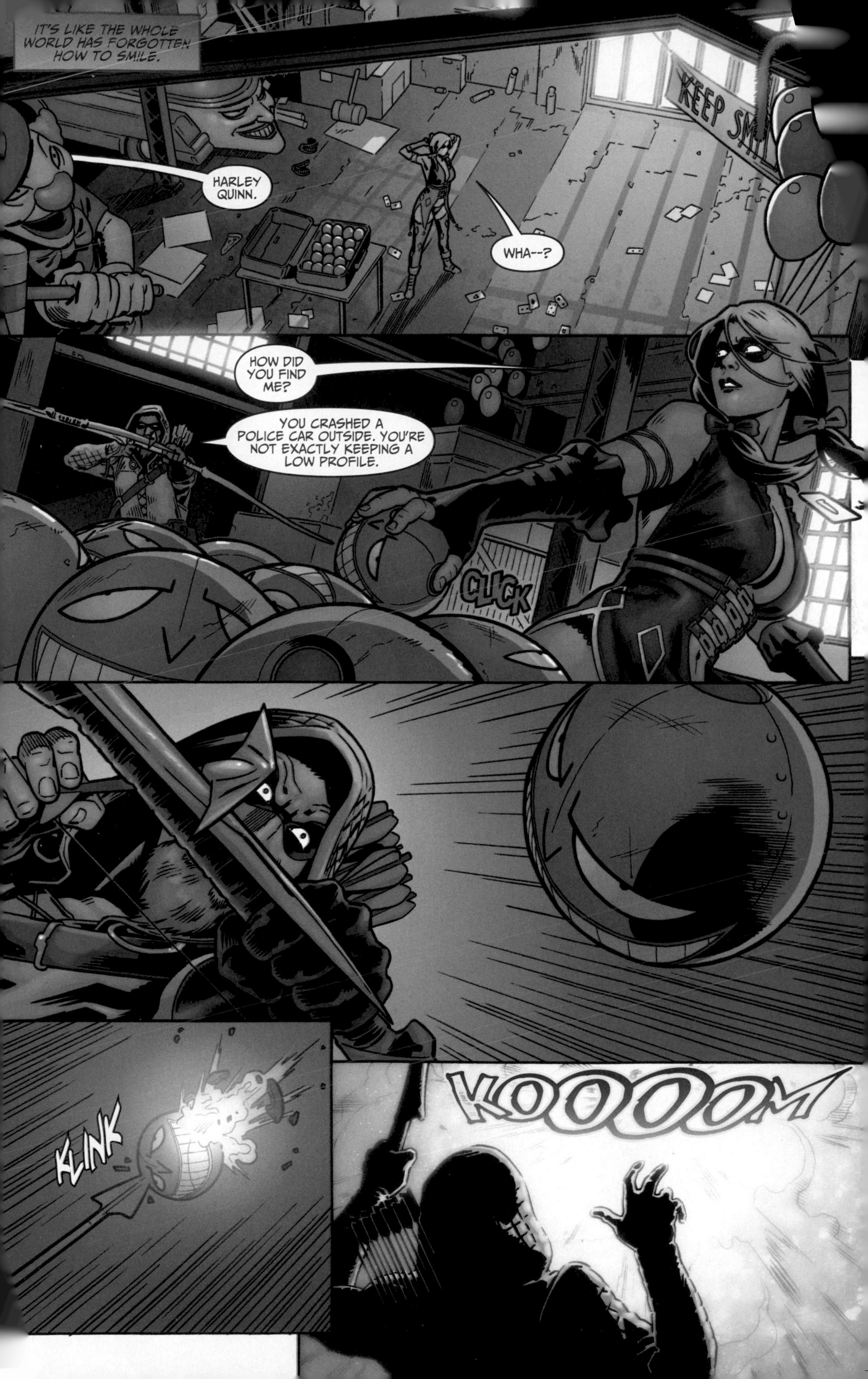
IT'S LIKE THE WHOLE WORLD HAS FORGOTTEN HOW TO SMILE.
KEEP SMIL
HARLEY QUINN.
WHA--?
HOW DID YOU FIND ME?
YOU CRASHED A POLICE CAR OUTSIDE. YOU'RE NOT EXACTLY KEEPING A LOW PROFILE.
CLICK
KLINK
KOOOOOM

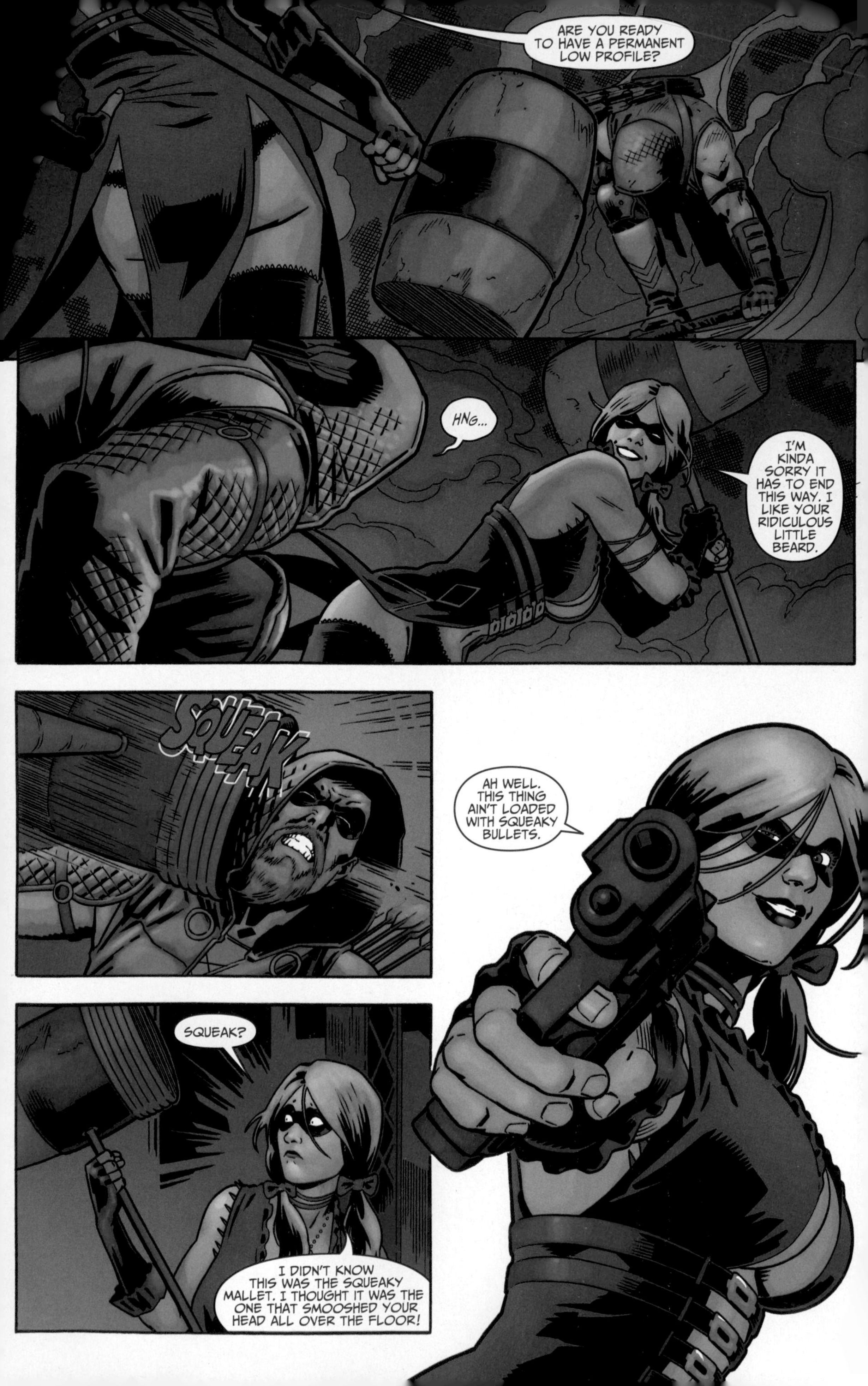
ARE YOU READY TO HAVE A PERMANENT LOW PROFILE?
HNG...
I'M KINDA SORRY IT HAS TO END THIS WAY. I LIKE YOUR RIDICULOUS LITTLE BEARD.
SQUEAK
AH WELL. THIS THING AIN'T LOADED WITH SQUEAKY BULLETS.
SQUEAK?
I DIDN'T KNOW THIS WAS THE SQUEAKY MALLET. I THOUGHT IT WAS THE ONE THAT SMOOSHED YOUR HEAD ALL OVER THE FLOOR!

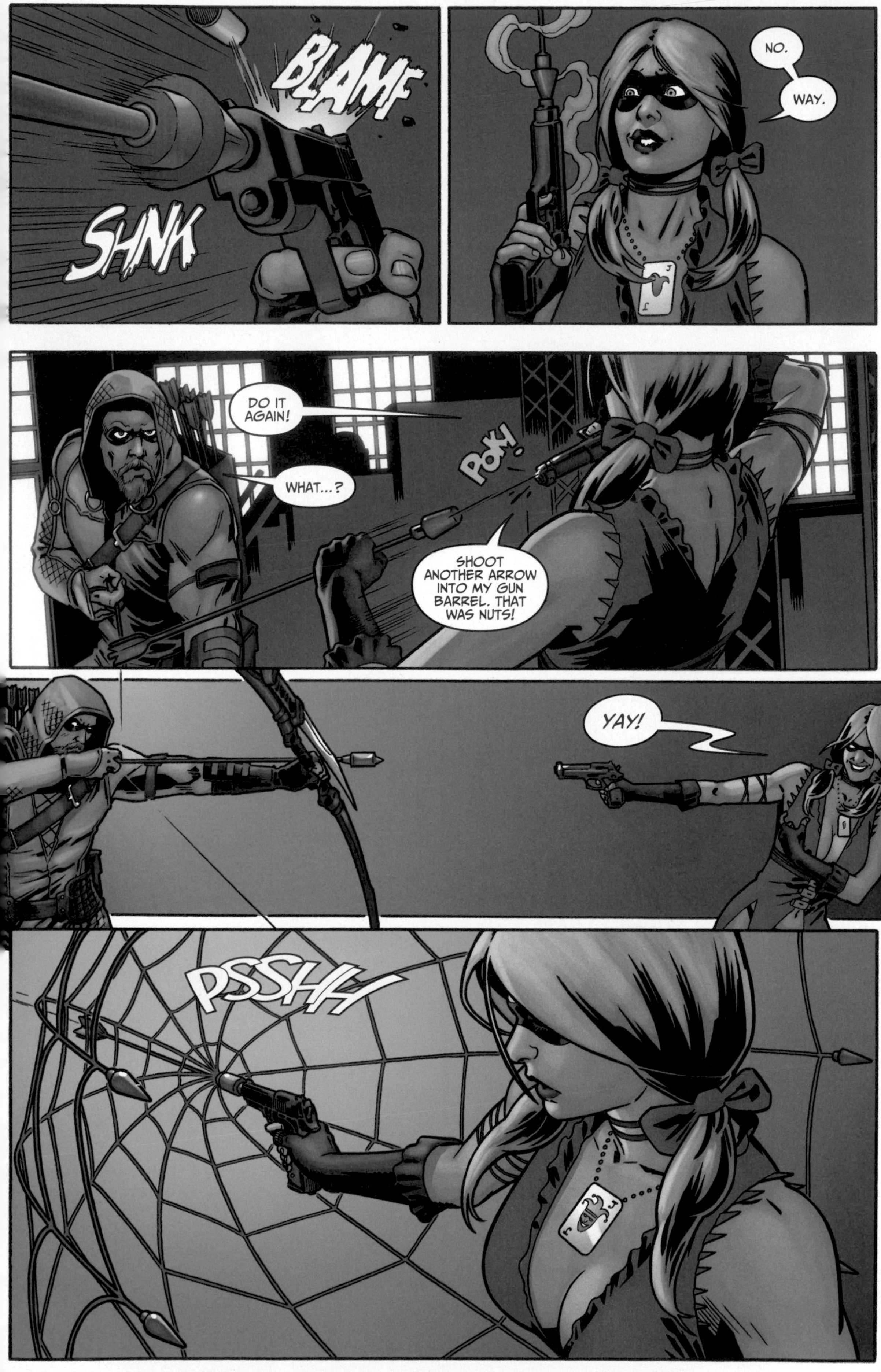
BLAMF
SHNK
NO.
WAY.
DO IT AGAIN!
WHAT...?
POK!
SHOOT ANOTHER ARROW INTO MY GUN BARREL. THAT WAS NUTS!
YAY!
PSSHH

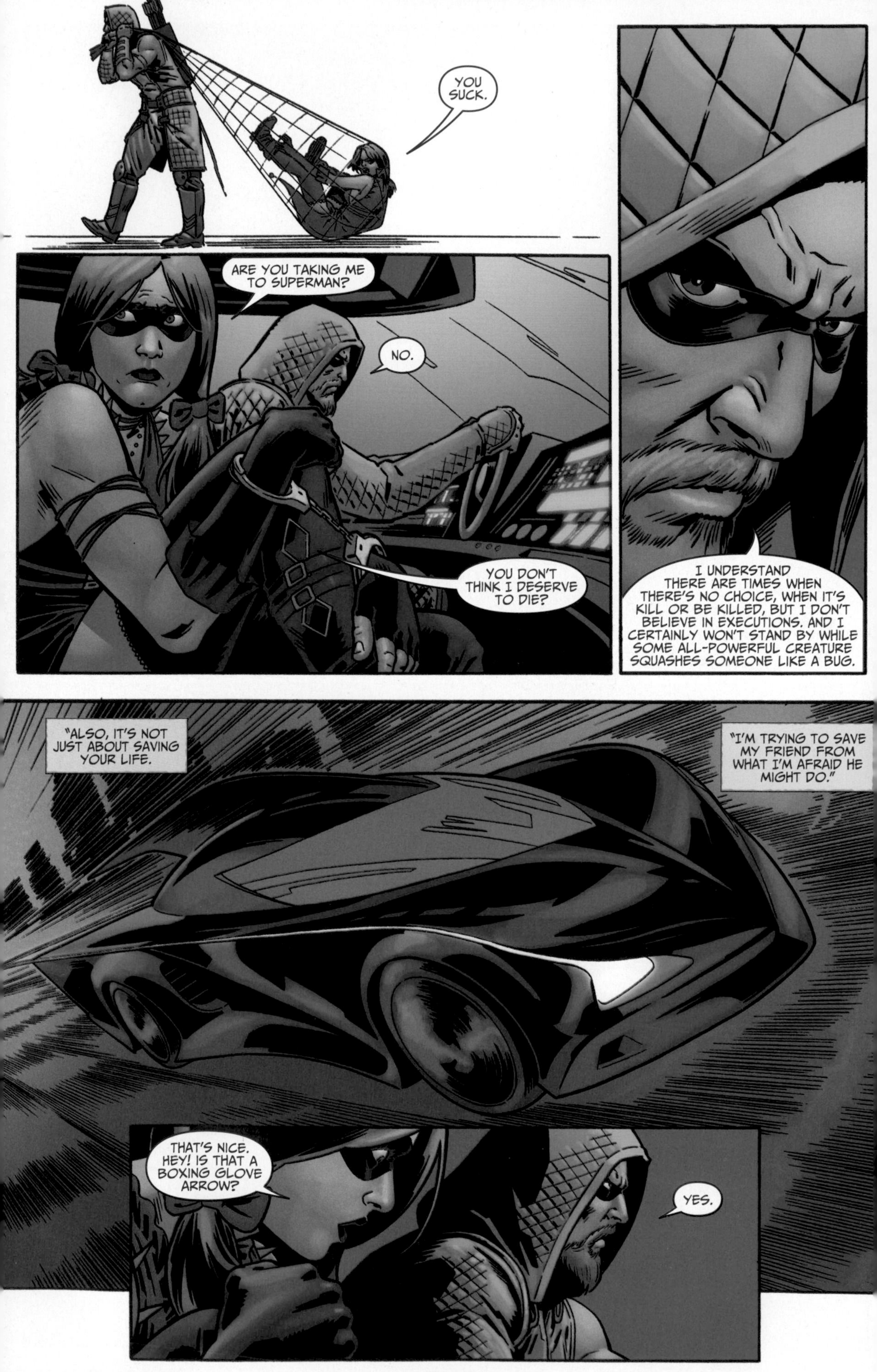
YOU SUCK.
ARE YOU TAKING ME TO SUPERMAN?
NO.
YOU DON'T THINK I DESERVE TO DIE?
I UNDERSTAND THERE ARE TIMES WHEN THERE'S NO CHOICE, WHEN IT'S KILL OR BE KILLED, BUT I DON'T BELIEVE IN EXECUTIONS. AND I CERTAINLY WON'T STAND BY WHILE SOME ALL-POWERFUL CREATURE SQUASHES SOMEONE LIKE A BUG.
"ALSO, IT'S NOT JUST ABOUT SAVING YOUR LIFE.
"I'M TRYING TO SAVE MY FRIEND FROM WHAT I'M AFRAID HE MIGHT DO."
THAT'S NICE. HEY! IS THAT A BOXING GLOVE ARROW?
YES.

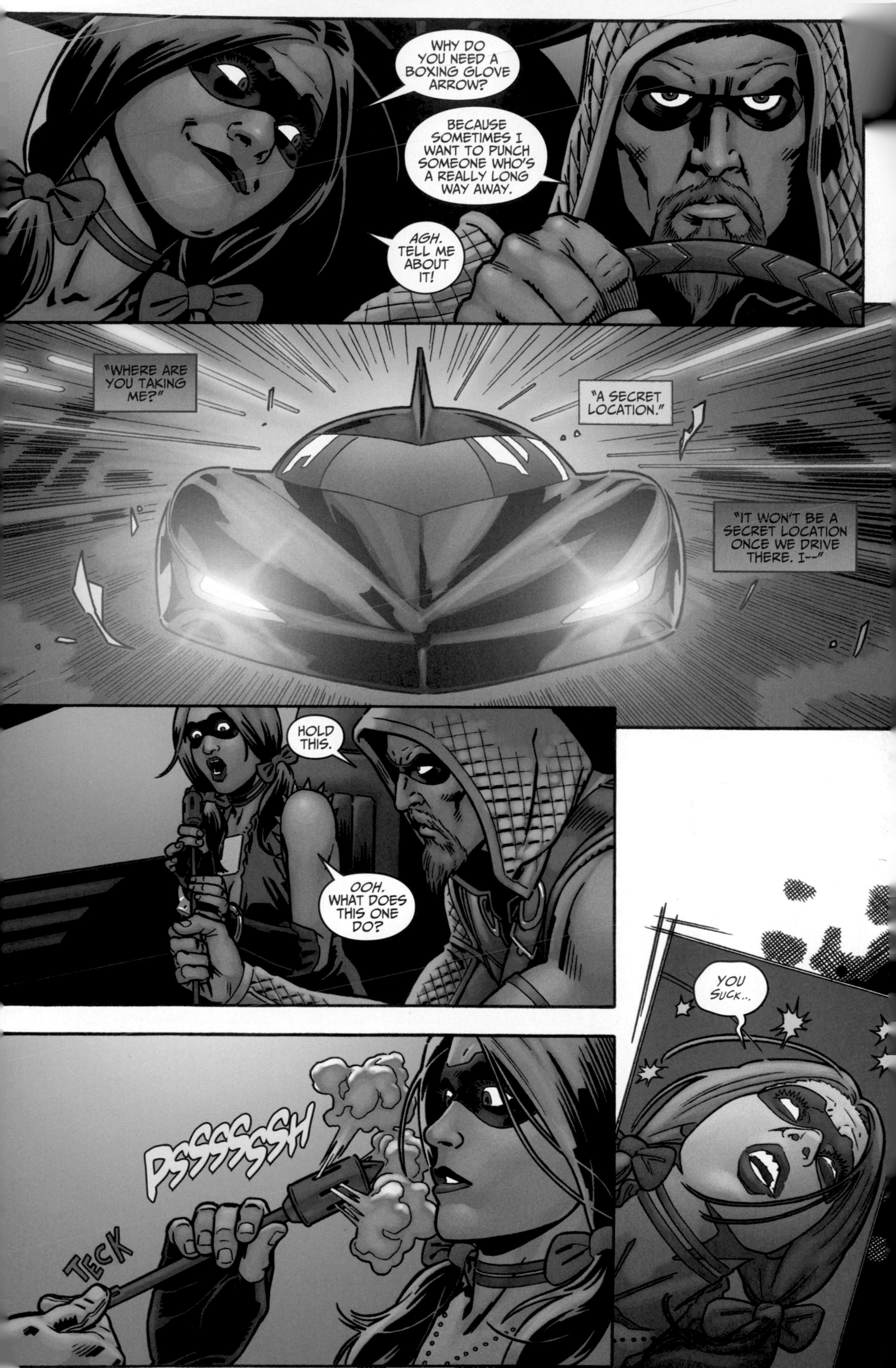
WHY DO YOU NEED A BOXING GLOVE ARROW?
BECAUSE SOMETIMES I WANT TO PUNCH SOMEONE WHO'S A REALLY LONG WAY AWAY.
AGH. TELL ME ABOUT IT!
"WHERE ARE YOU TAKING ME?"
"A SECRET LOCATION."
"IT WON'T BE A SECRET LOCATION ONCE WE DRIVE THERE. I--"
HOLD THIS.
OOH. WHAT DOES THIS ONE DO?
TECK
PSSSSSSH
YOU SUCK...

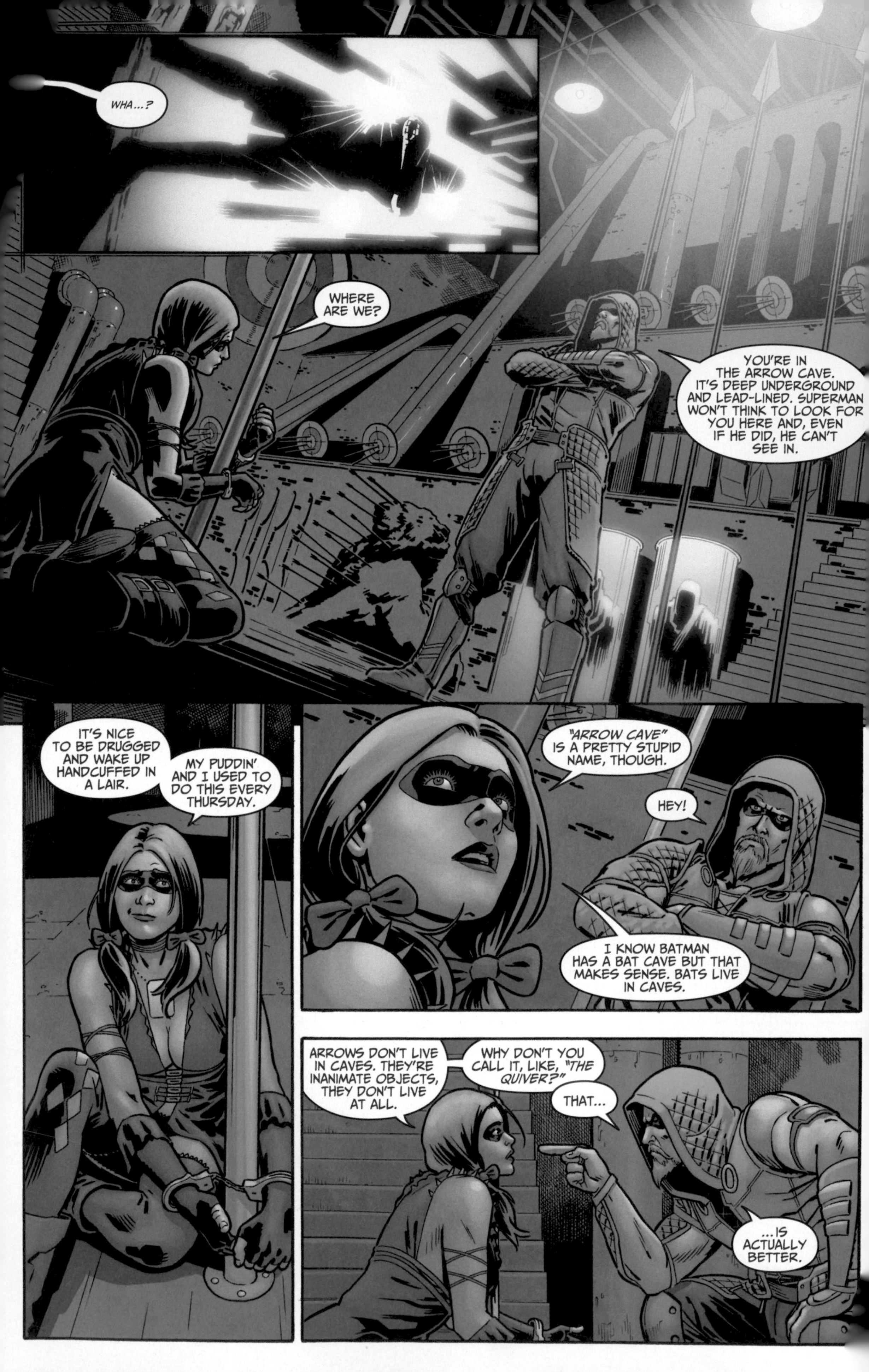
WHA...?
WHERE ARE WE?
YOU'RE IN THE ARROW CAVE. IT'S DEEP UNDERGROUND AND LEAD-LINED. SUPERMAN WON'T THINK TO LOOK FOR YOU HERE AND, EVEN IF HE DID, HE CAN'T SEE IN.
IT'S NICE TO BE DRUGGED AND WAKE UP HANDCUFFED IN A LAIR.
MY PUDDIN' AND I USED TO DO THIS EVERY THURSDAY.
"ARROW CAVE" IS A PRETTY STUPID NAME, THOUGH.
HEY!
I KNOW BATMAN HAS A BAT CAVE BUT THAT MAKES SENSE. BATS LIVE IN CAVES.
ARROWS DON'T LIVE IN CAVES. THEY'RE INANIMATE OBJECTS, THEY DON'T LIVE AT ALL.
WHY DON'T YOU CALL IT, LIKE, "THE QUIVER?"
THAT...
...IS ACTUALLY BETTER.

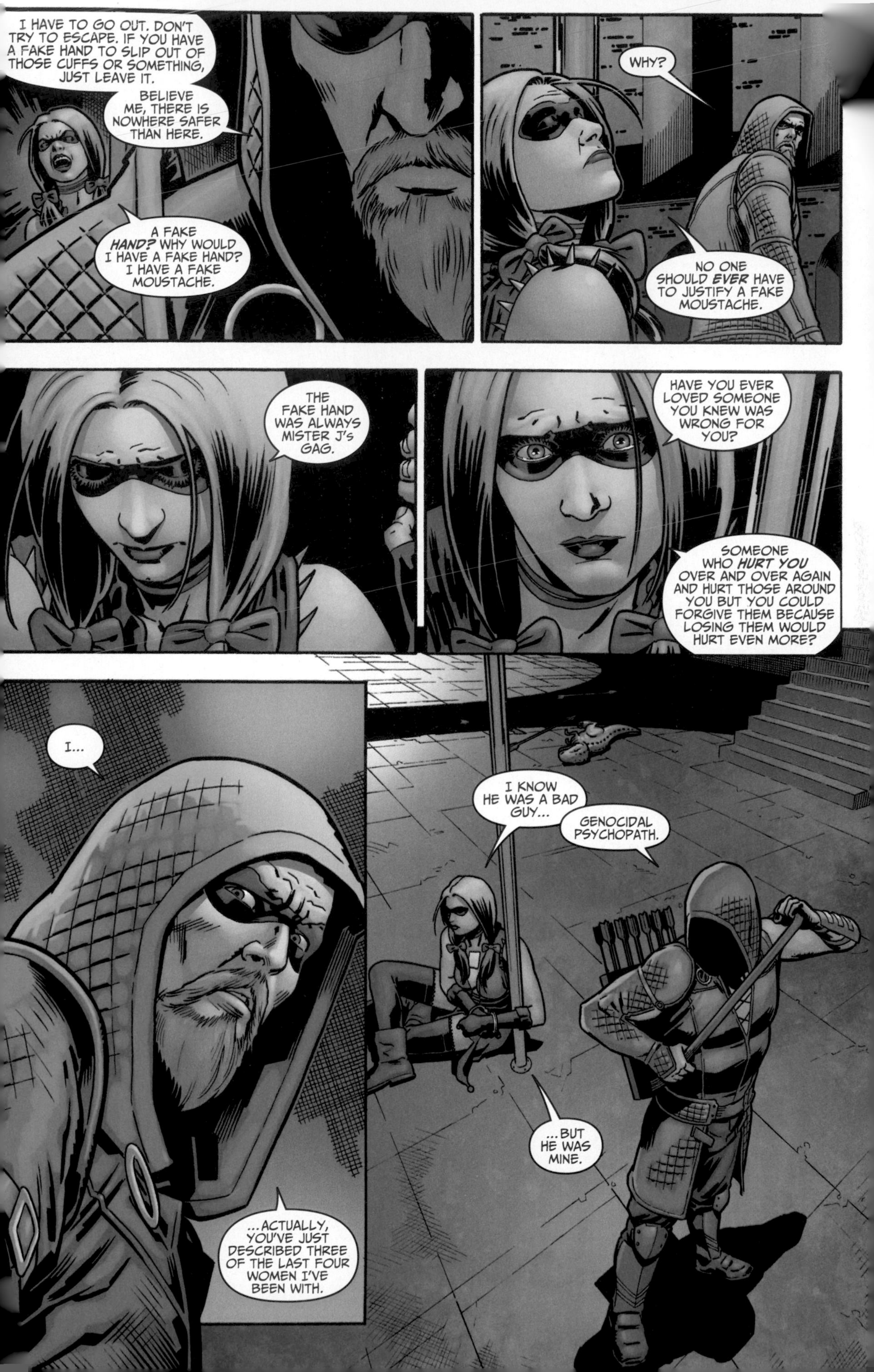
I HAVE TO GO OUT. DON'T TRY TO ESCAPE. IF YOU HAVE A FAKE HAND TO SLIP OUT OF THOSE CUFFS OR SOMETHING, JUST LEAVE IT.
BELIEVE ME, THERE IS NOWHERE SAFER THAN HERE.
A FAKE HAND? WHY WOULD I HAVE A FAKE HAND? I HAVE A FAKE MOUSTACHE.
WHY?
NO ONE SHOULD EVER HAVE TO JUSTIFY A FAKE MOUSTACHE.
THE FAKE HAND WAS ALWAYS MISTER J's GAG.
HAVE YOU EVER LOVED SOMEONE YOU KNEW WAS WRONG FOR YOU?
SOMEONE WHO HURT YOU OVER AND OVER AGAIN AND HURT THOSE AROUND YOU BUT YOU COULD FORGIVE THEM BECAUSE LOSING THEM WOULD HURT EVEN MORE?
I...
...ACTUALLY, YOU'VE JUST DESCRIBED THREE OF THE LAST FOUR WOMEN I'VE BEEN WITH.
I KNOW HE WAS A BAD GUY...
GENOCIDAL PSYCHOPATH.
...BUT HE WAS MINE.

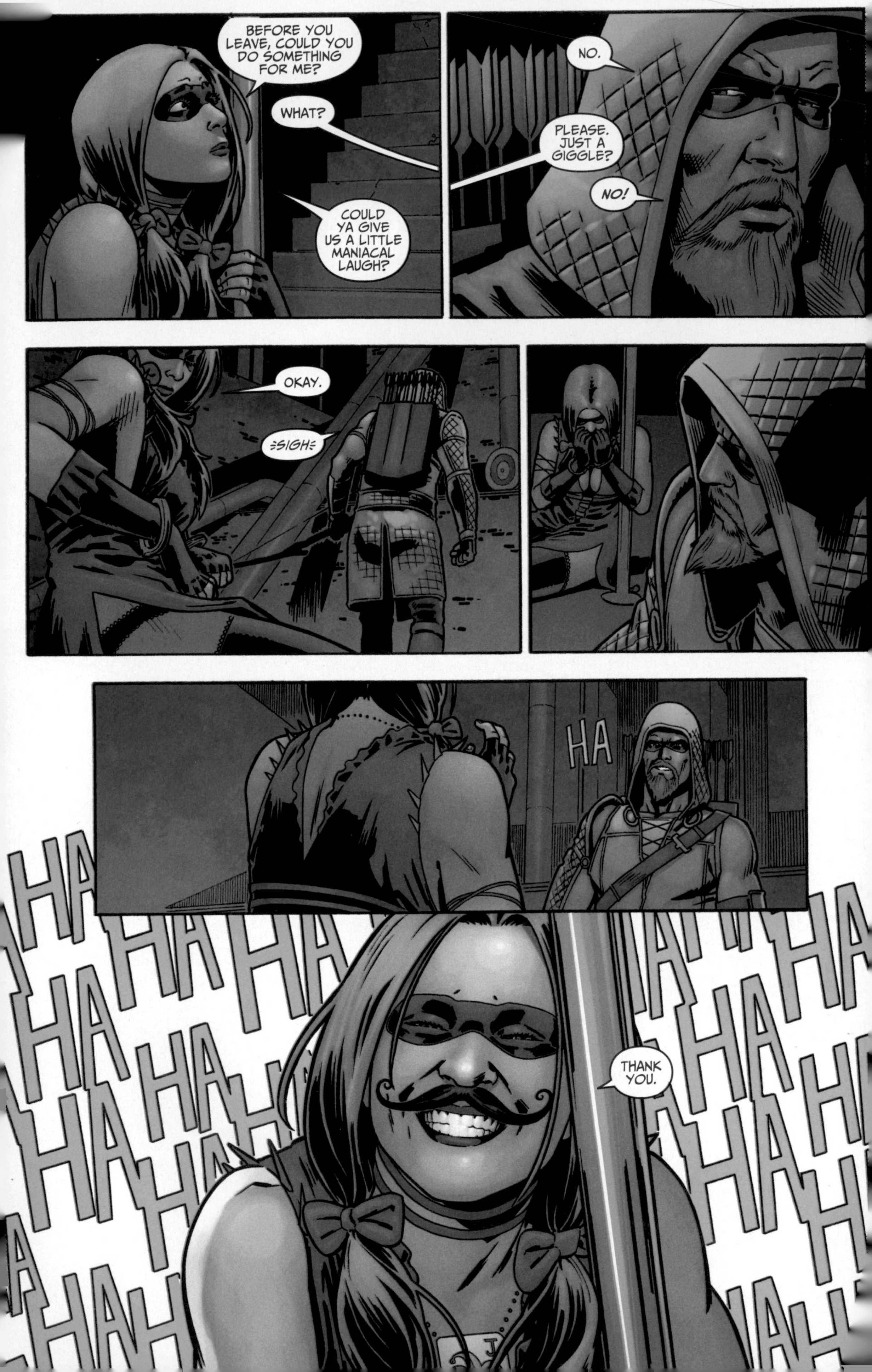
BEFORE YOU LEAVE, COULD YOU DO SOMETHING FOR ME?
WHAT?
COULD YA GIVE US A LITTLE MANIACAL LAUGH?
NO.
PLEASE. JUST A GIGGLE?
NO!
OKAY.
SIGH
HA
THANK YOU.

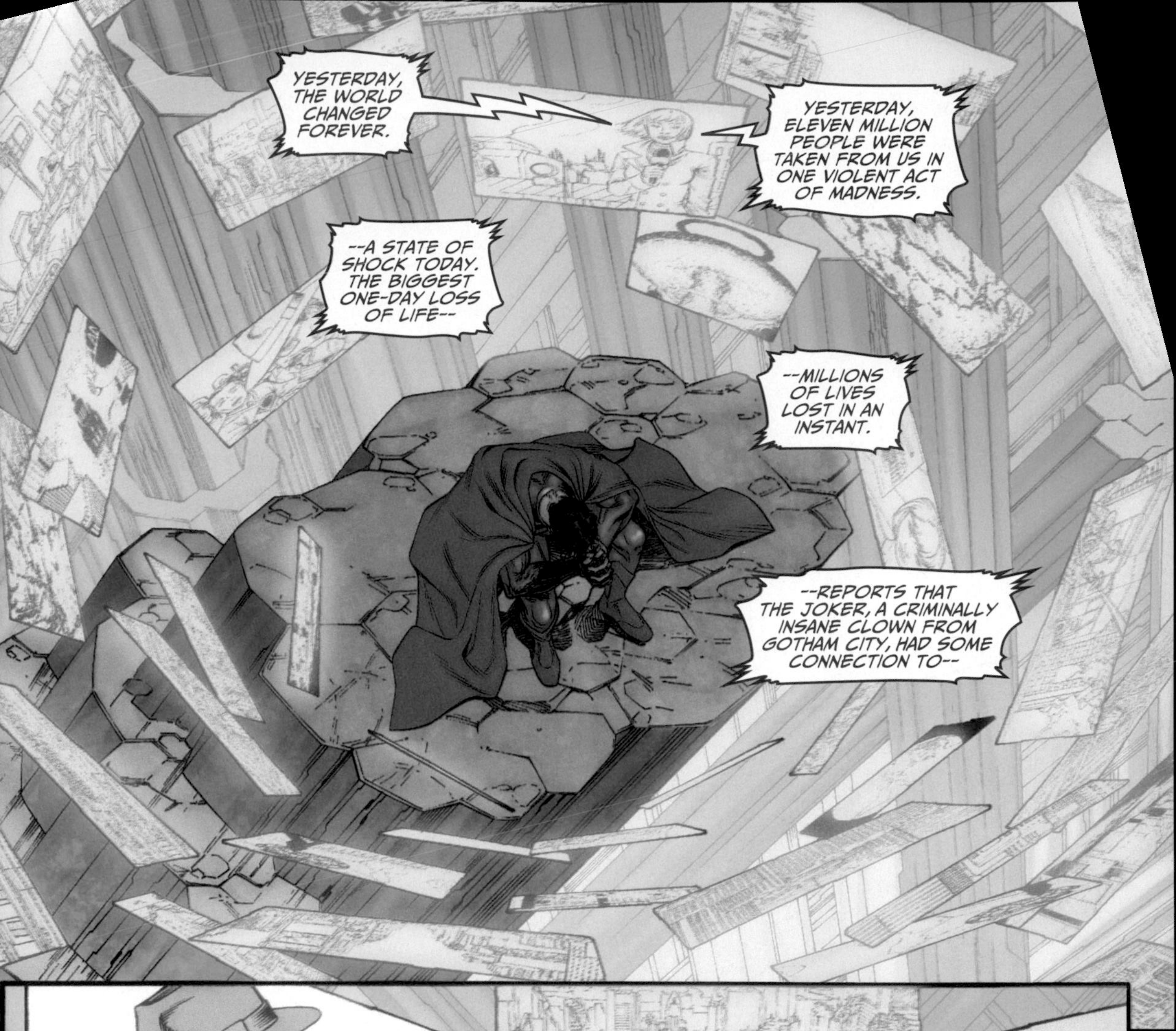
YESTERDAY, THE WORLD CHANGED FOREVER.
YESTERDAY, ELEVEN MILLION PEOPLE WERE TAKEN FROM US IN ONE VIOLENT ACT OF MADNESS.
--A STATE OF SHOCK TODAY. THE BIGGEST ONE-DAY LOSS OF LIFE--
--MILLIONS OF LIVES LOST IN AN INSTANT.
--REPORTS THAT THE JOKER, A CRIMINALLY INSANE CLOWN FROM GOTHAM CITY, HAD SOME CONNECTION TO--
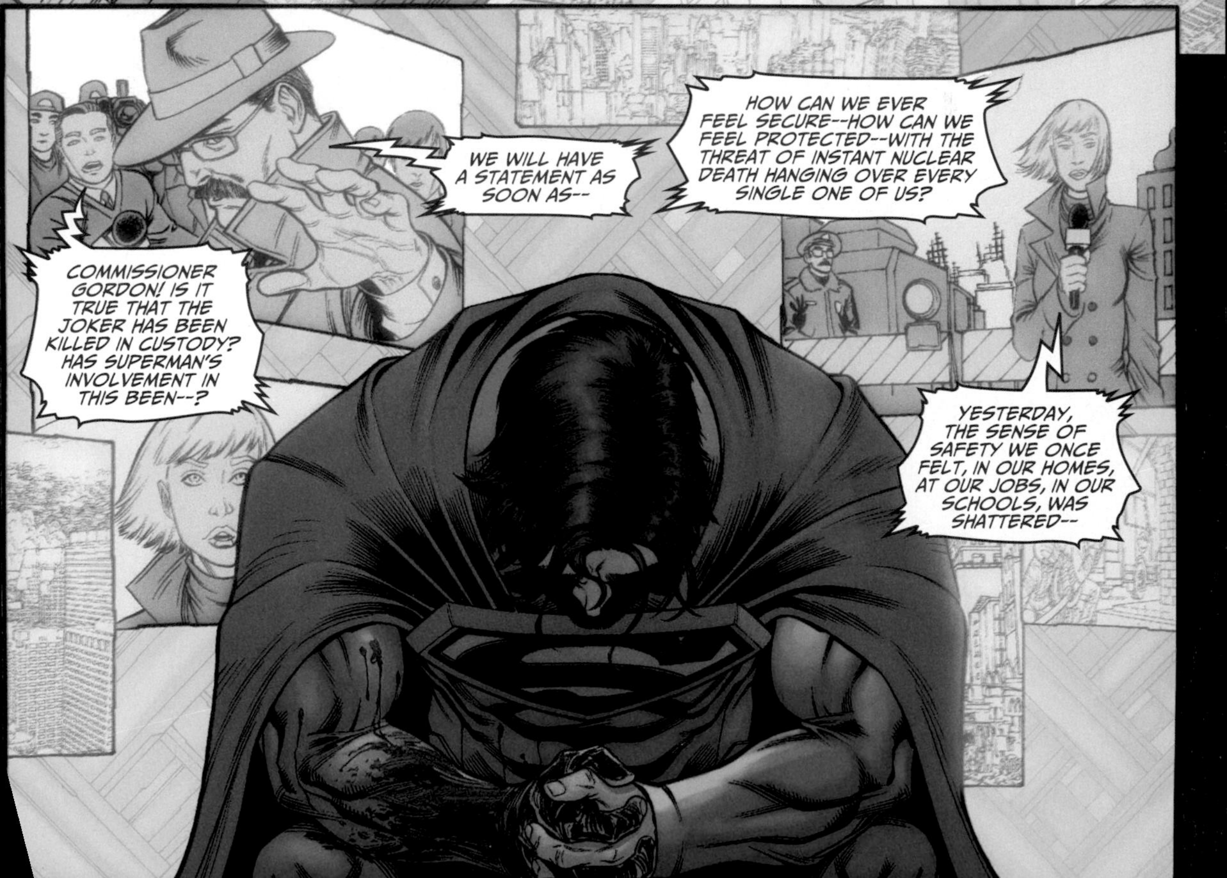
WE WILL HAVE A STATEMENT AS SOON AS--
COMMISSIONER GORDON! IS IT TRUE THAT THE JOKER HAS BEEN KILLED IN CUSTODY? HAS SUPERMAN'S INVOLVEMENT IN THIS BEEN--?
HOW CAN WE EVER FEEL SECURE--HOW CAN WE FEEL PROTECTED--WITH THE THREAT OF INSTANT NUCLEAR DEATH HANGING OVER EVERY SINGLE ONE OF US?
YESTERDAY, THE SENSE OF SAFETY WE ONCE FELT, IN OUR HOMES, AT OUR JOBS, IN OUR SCHOOLS, WAS SHATTERED--

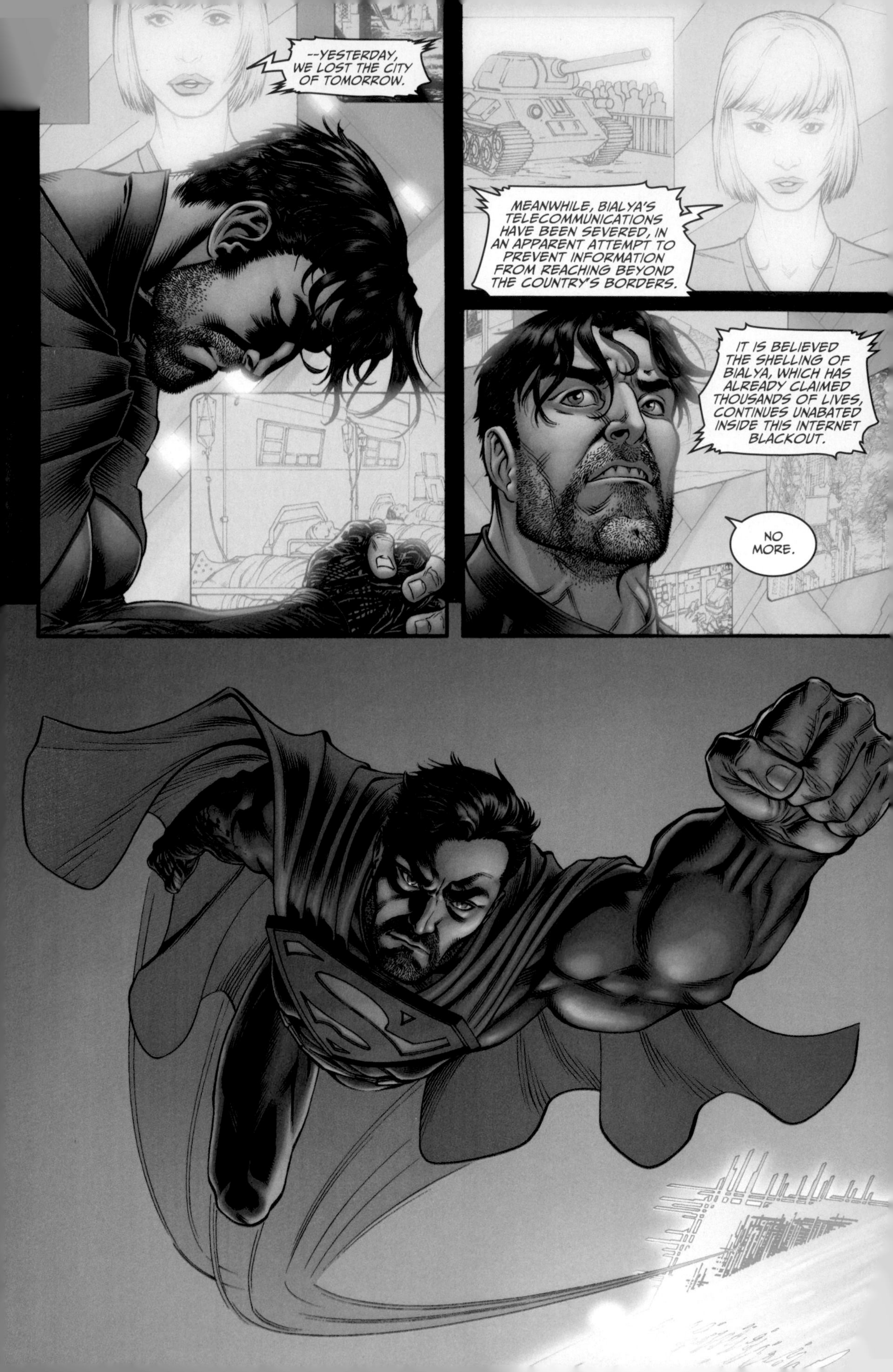
--YESTERDAY, WE LOST THE CITY OF TOMORROW.
MEANWHILE, BIALYA'S TELECOMMUNICATIONS HAVE BEEN SEVERED, IN AN APPARENT ATTEMPT TO PREVENT INFORMATION FROM REACHING BEYOND THE COUNTRY'S BORDERS.
IT IS BELIEVED THE SHELLING OF BIALYA, WHICH HAS ALREADY CLAIMED THOUSANDS OF LIVES, CONTINUES UNABATED INSIDE THIS INTERNET BLACKOUT.
NO MORE.

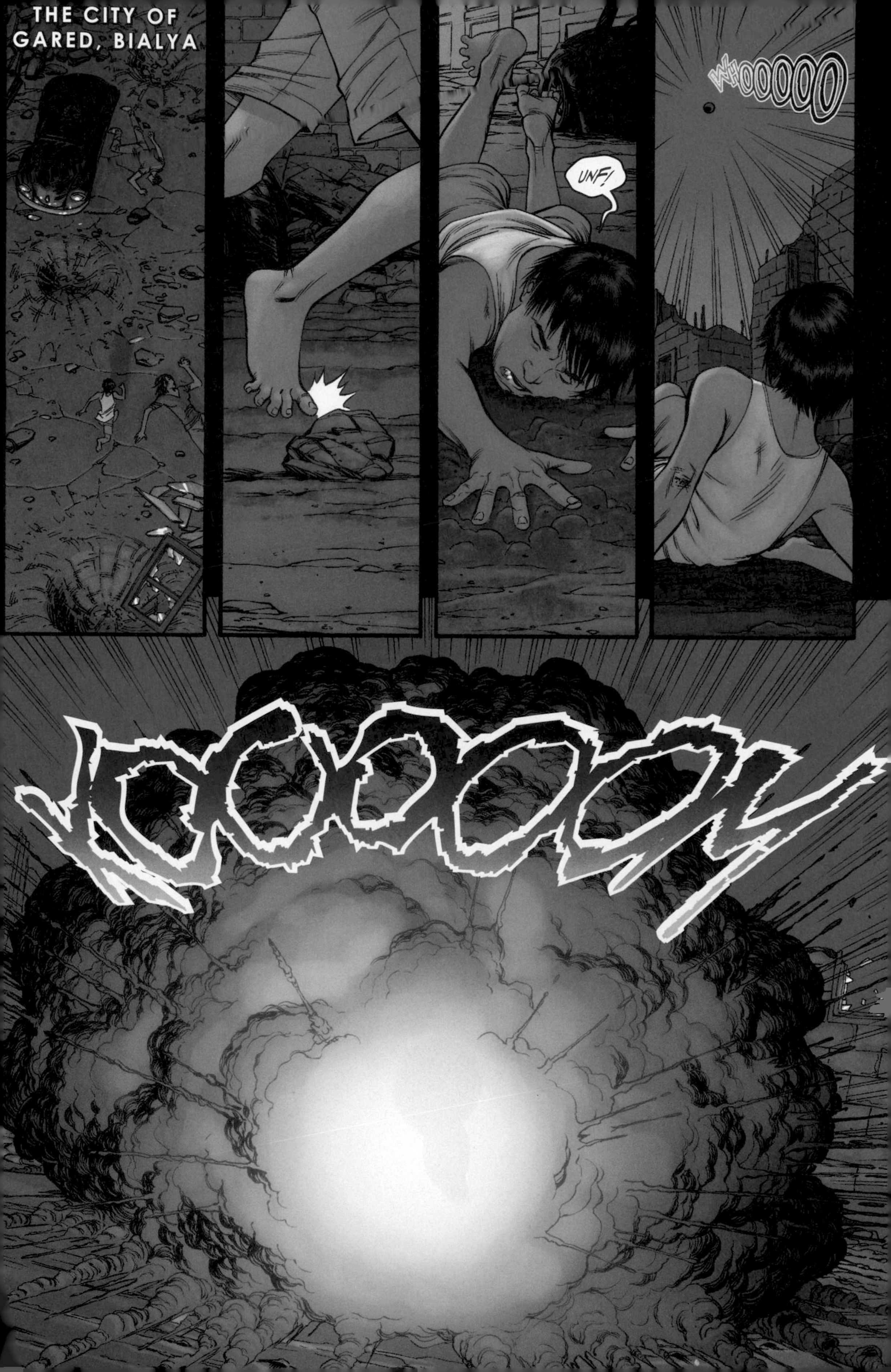
THE CITY OF GARED, BIALYA
UNF!
WHOOOOO

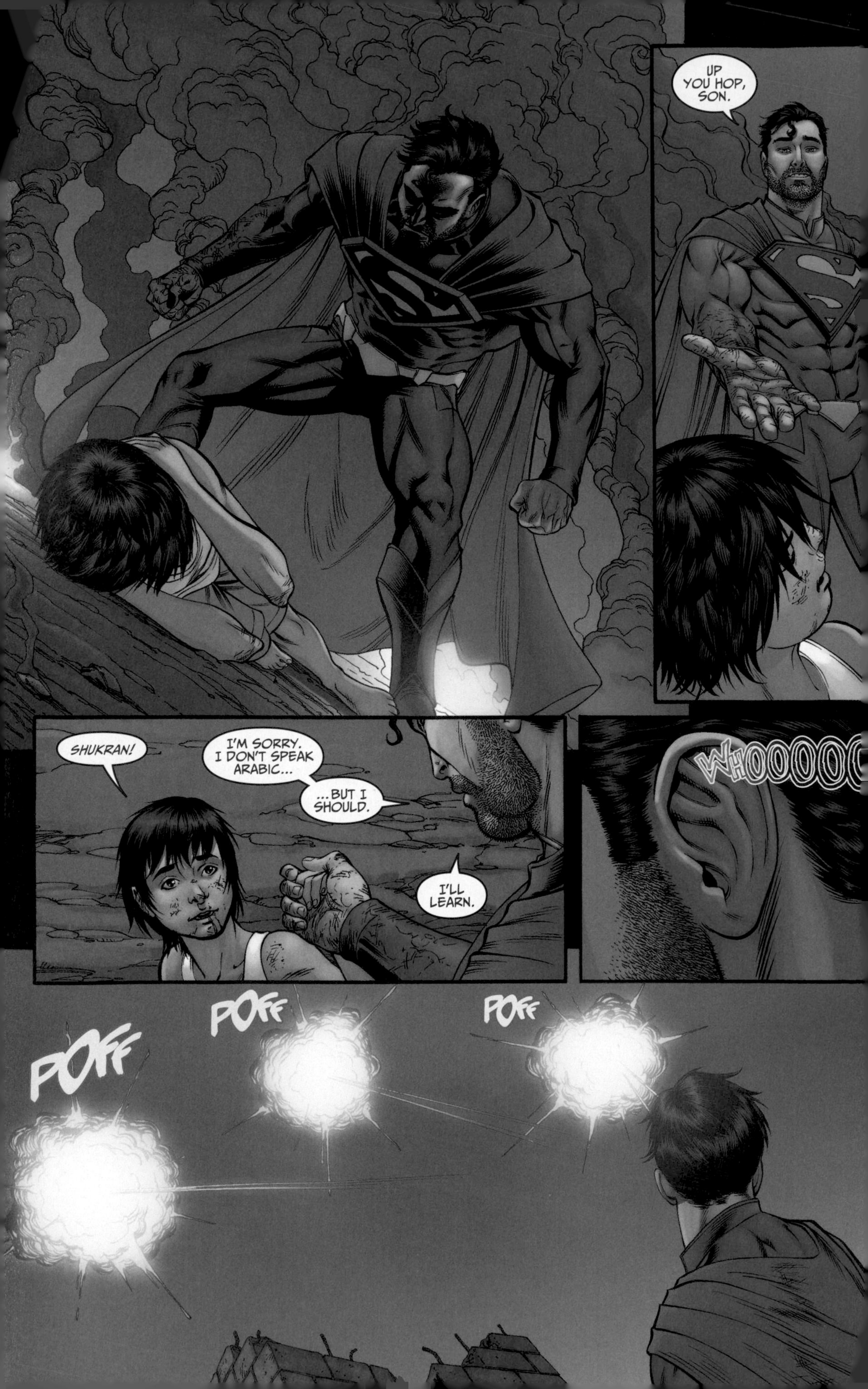
UP YOU HOP, SON.
SHUKRAN!
I'M SORRY. I DON'T SPEAK ARABIC...
...BUT I SHOULD.
I'LL LEARN.
WHOOOOO
POFF
POFF
POFF

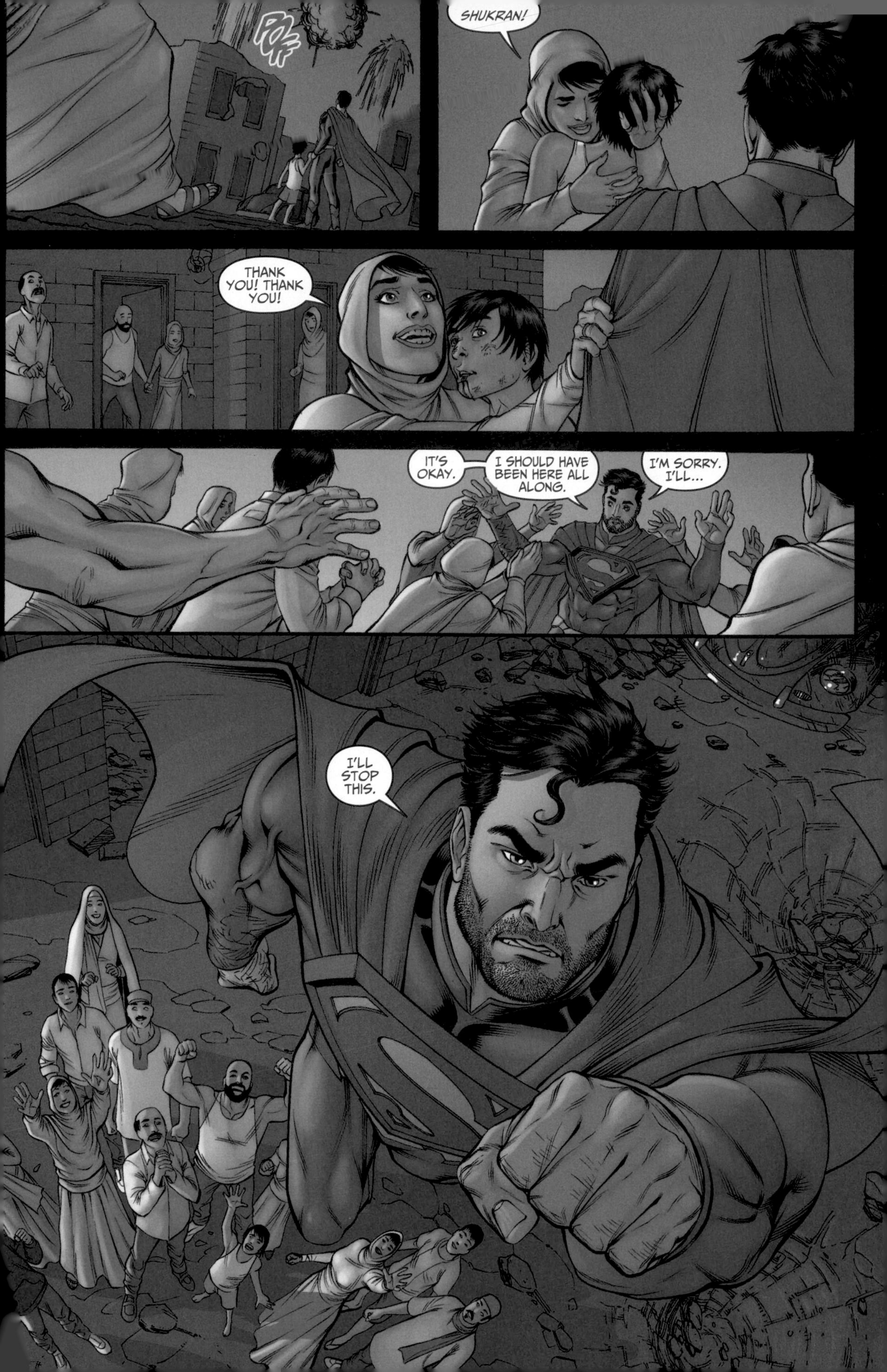
POFF
SHUKRAN!
THANK YOU! THANK YOU!
IT'S OKAY.
I SHOULD HAVE BEEN HERE ALL ALONG.
I'M SORRY. I'LL...
I'LL STOP THIS.

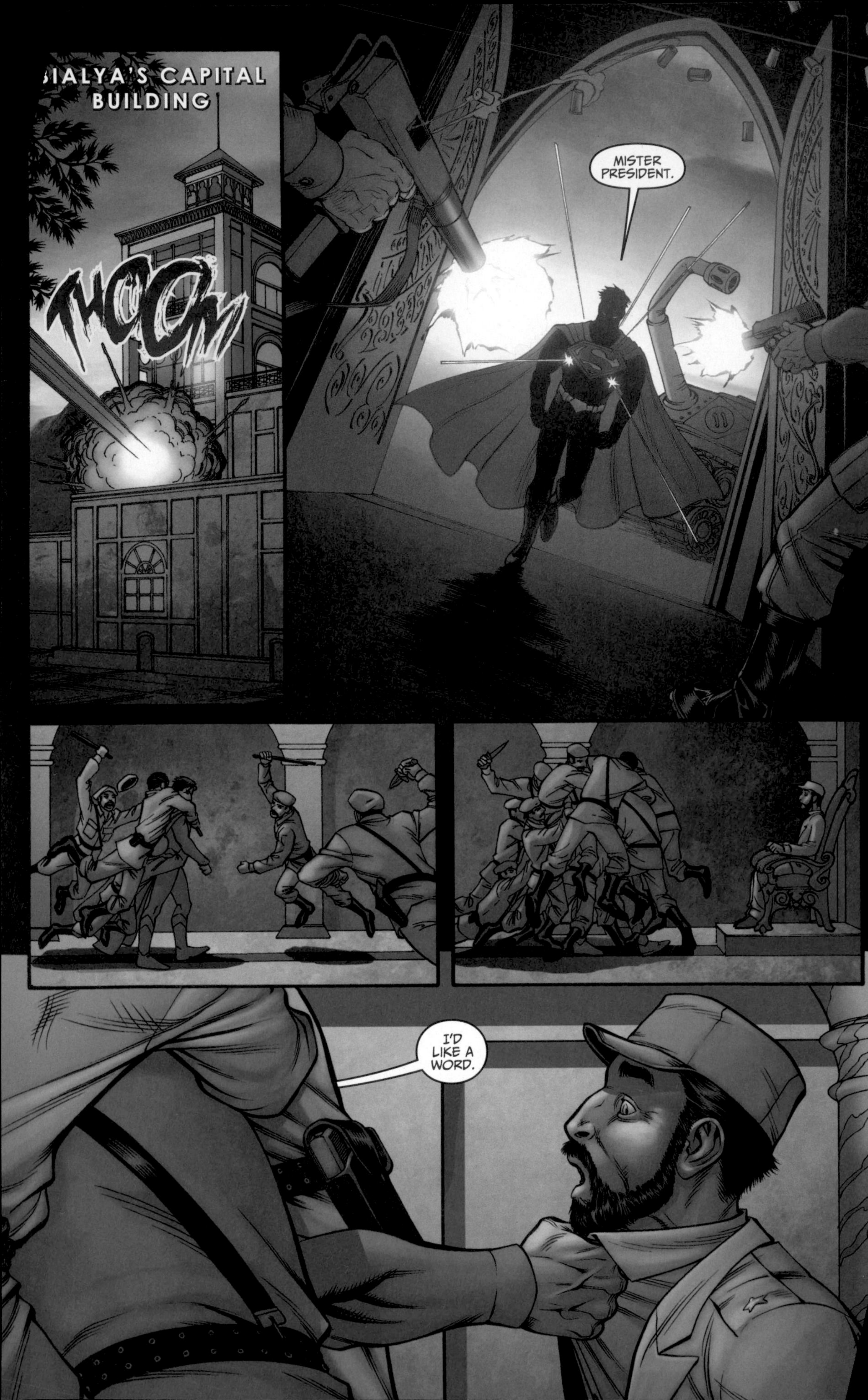

BIALYA'S CAPITAL BUILDING
THOOM
MISTER PRESIDENT.
I'D LIKE A WORD.

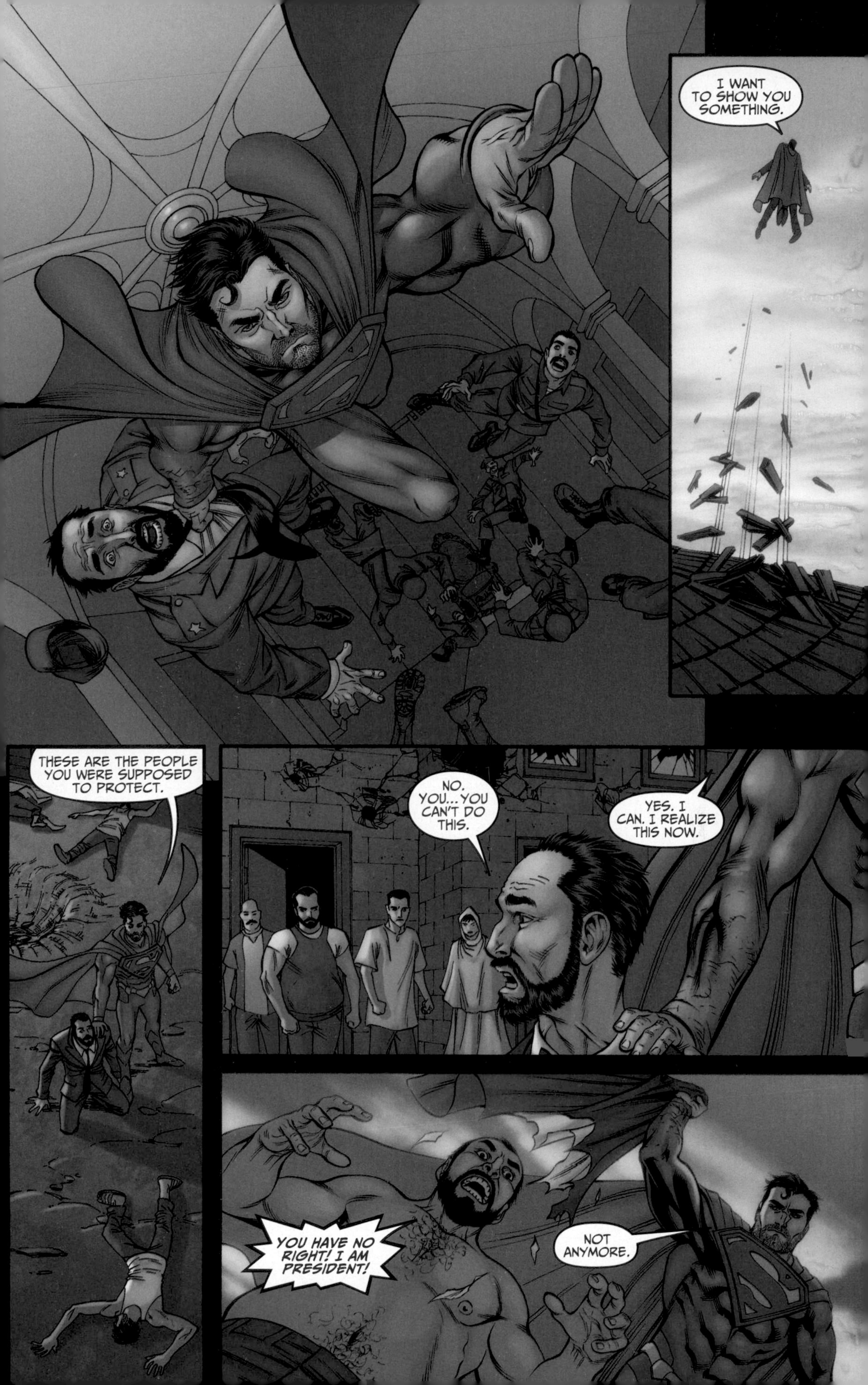
I WANT TO SHOW YOU SOMETHING.
THESE ARE THE PEOPLE YOU WERE SUPPOSED TO PROTECT.
NO. YOU...YOU CAN'T DO THIS.
YES. I CAN. I REALIZE THIS NOW.
YOU HAVE NO RIGHT! I AM PRESIDENT!
NOT ANYMORE.

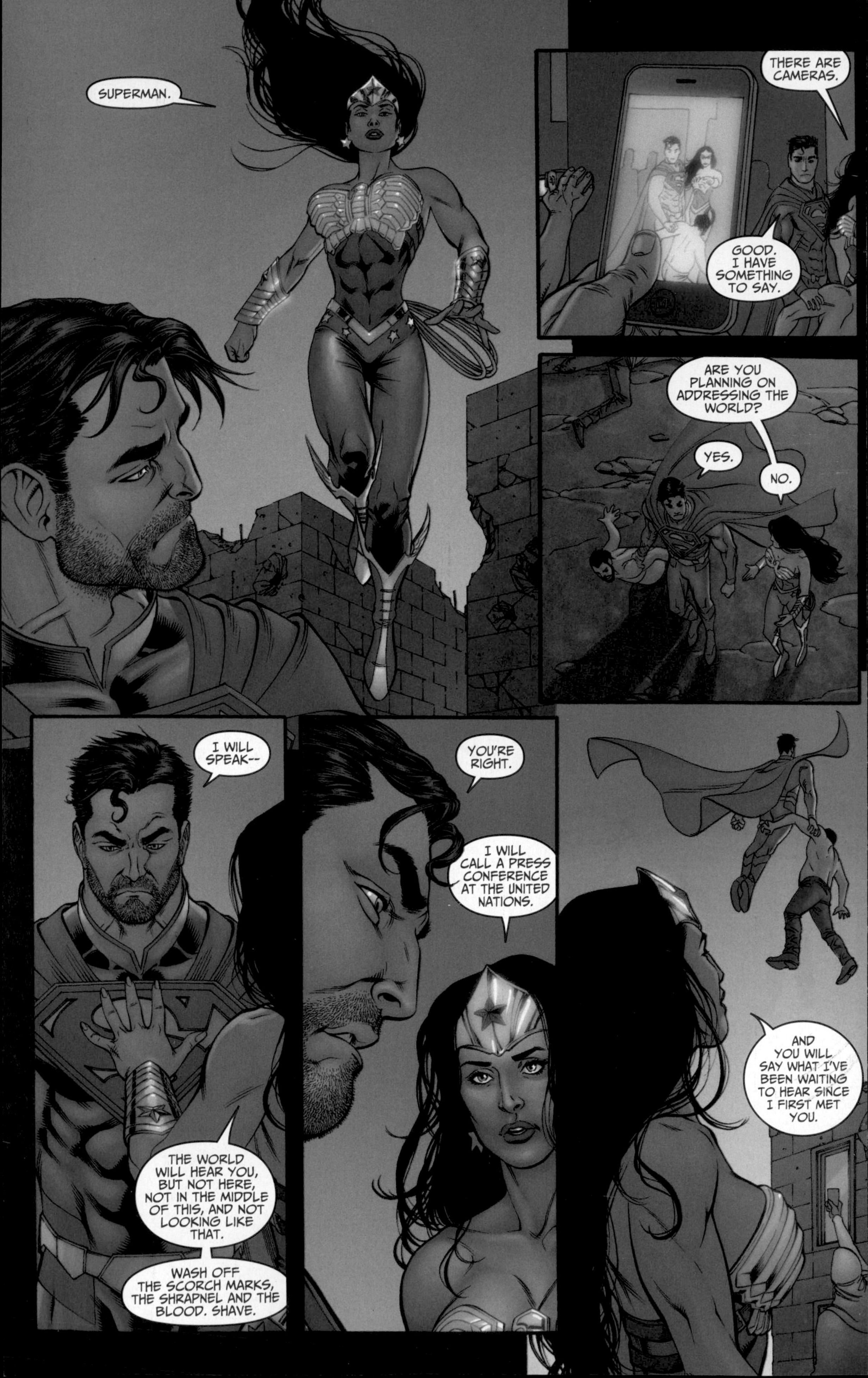
SUPERMAN.
THERE ARE CAMERAS.
GOOD. I HAVE SOMETHING TO SAY.
ARE YOU PLANNING ON ADDRESSING THE WORLD?
YES.
NO.
I WILL SPEAK--
THE WORLD WILL HEAR YOU, BUT NOT HERE, NOT IN THE MIDDLE OF THIS, AND NOT LOOKING LIKE THAT.
WASH OFF THE SCORCH MARKS, THE SHRAPNEL AND THE BLOOD. SHAVE.
YOU'RE RIGHT.
I WILL CALL A PRESS CONFERENCE AT THE UNITED NATIONS.
AND YOU WILL SAY WHAT I'VE BEEN WAITING TO HEAR SINCE I FIRST MET YOU.

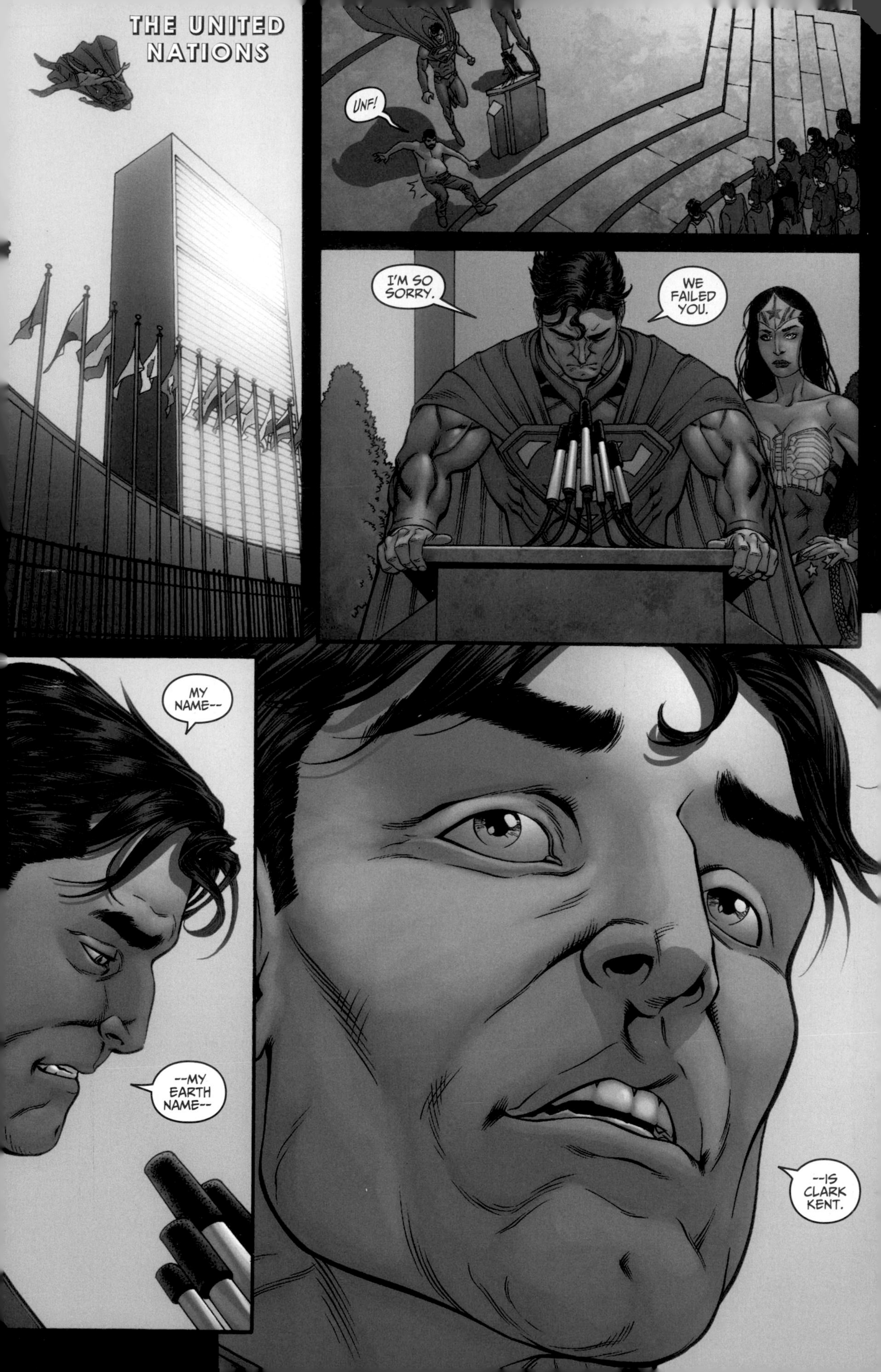
THE UNITED NATIONS
UNF!
I'M SO SORRY.
WE FAILED YOU.
MY NAME--
--MY EARTH NAME--
--IS CLARK KENT.

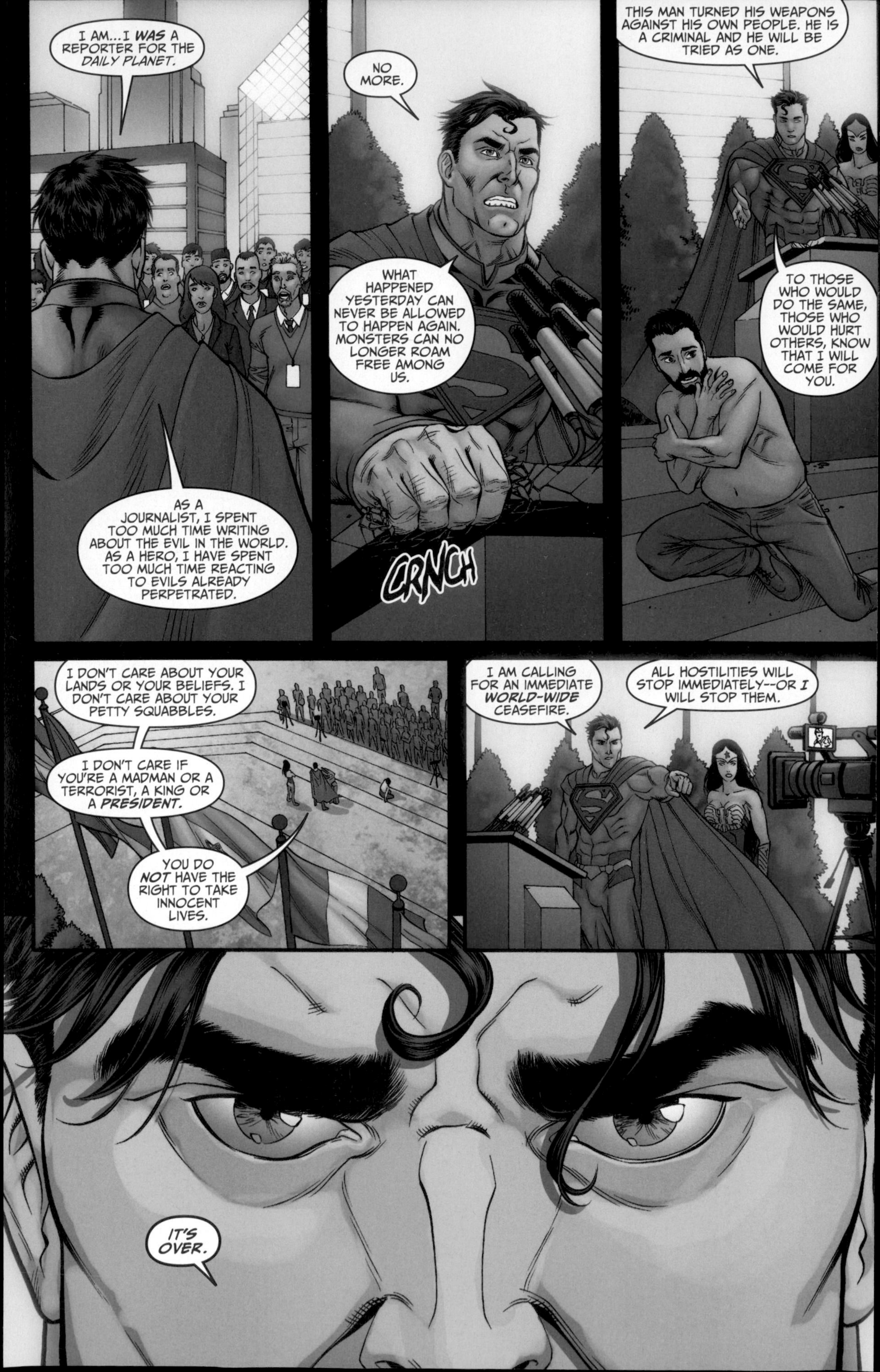
I AM...I *WAS* A REPORTER FOR THE *DAILY PLANET.*
AS A JOURNALIST, I SPENT TOO MUCH TIME WRITING ABOUT THE EVIL IN THE WORLD. AS A HERO, I HAVE SPENT TOO MUCH TIME REACTING TO EVILS ALREADY PERPETRATED.
NO MORE.
WHAT HAPPENED YESTERDAY CAN NEVER BE ALLOWED TO HAPPEN AGAIN. MONSTERS CAN NO LONGER ROAM FREE AMONG US.
CRNCH
THIS MAN TURNED HIS WEAPONS AGAINST HIS OWN PEOPLE. HE IS A CRIMINAL AND HE WILL BE TRIED AS ONE.
TO THOSE WHO WOULD DO THE SAME, THOSE WHO WOULD HURT OTHERS, KNOW THAT I WILL COME FOR YOU.
I DON'T CARE ABOUT YOUR LANDS OR YOUR BELIEFS. I DON'T CARE ABOUT YOUR PETTY SQUABBLES.
I DON'T CARE IF YOU'RE A MADMAN OR A TERRORIST, A KING OR A *PRESIDENT.*
YOU DO *NOT* HAVE THE RIGHT TO TAKE INNOCENT LIVES.
I AM CALLING FOR AN IMMEDIATE *WORLD-WIDE* CEASEFIRE.
ALL HOSTILITIES WILL STOP IMMEDIATELY--OR *I* WILL STOP THEM.
IT'S OVER.

PART THREE

Jheremy Raapack David Yardin Artists

Jheremy Raapack & Andrew Elder Cover

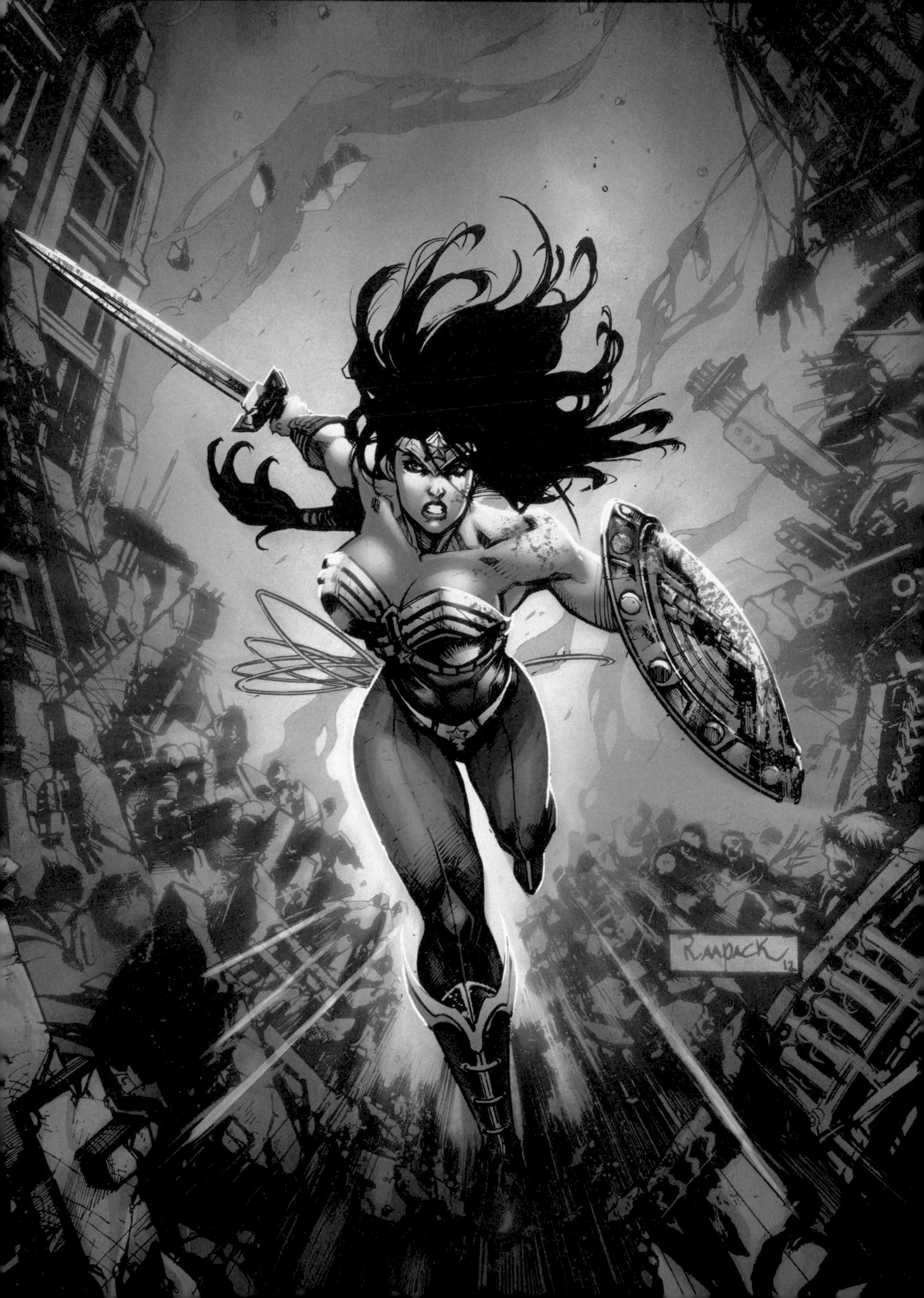
RAAPACK
'12

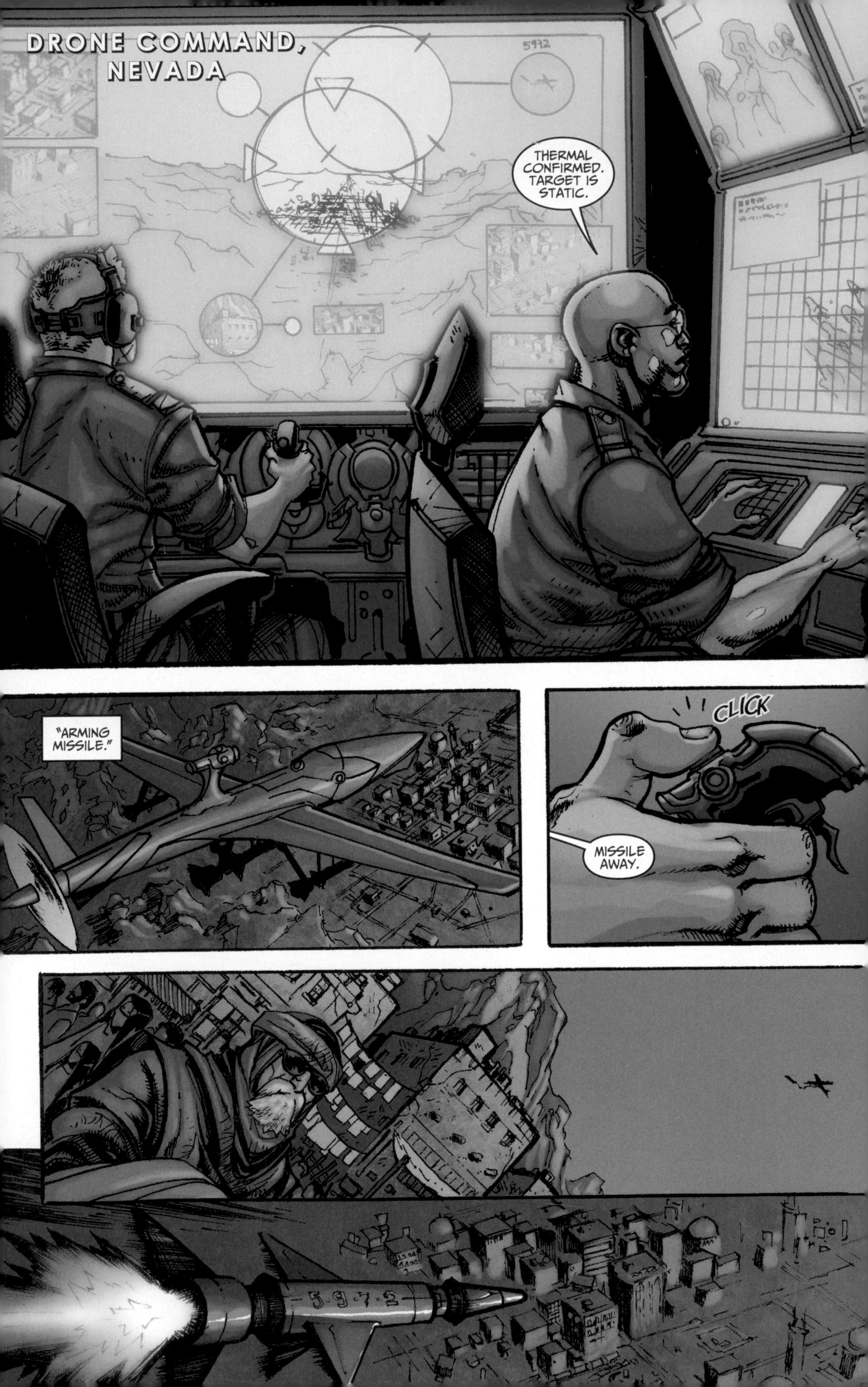
DRONE COMMAND, NEVADA
THERMAL CONFIRMED. TARGET IS STATIC.
"ARMING MISSILE."
CLICK
MISSILE AWAY.

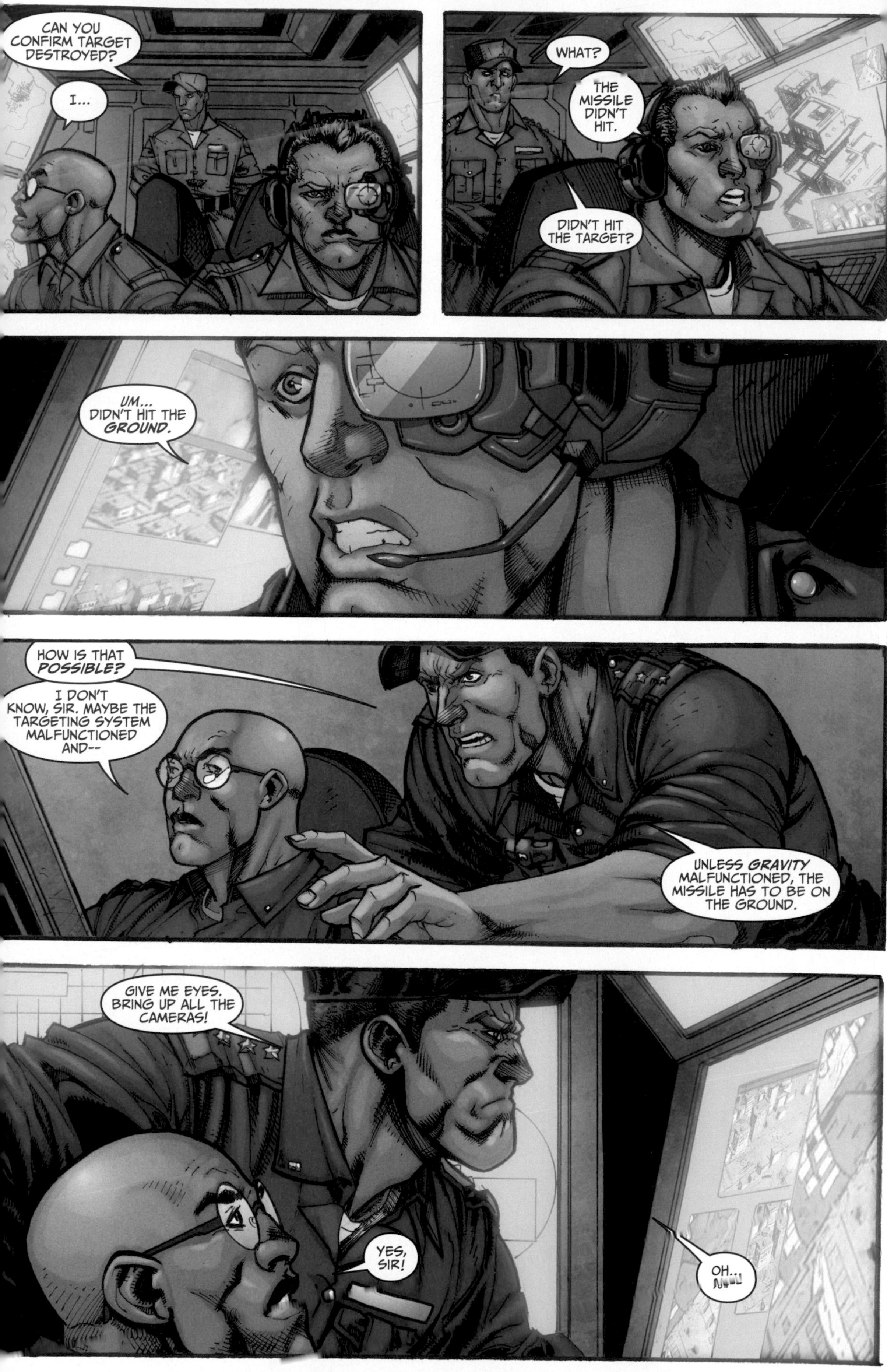
CAN YOU CONFIRM TARGET DESTROYED?
I...
WHAT?
THE MISSILE DIDN'T HIT.
DIDN'T HIT THE TARGET?
UM... DIDN'T HIT THE GROUND.
HOW IS THAT POSSIBLE?
I DON'T KNOW, SIR. MAYBE THE TARGETING SYSTEM MALFUNCTIONED AND--
UNLESS GRAVITY MALFUNCTIONED, THE MISSILE HAS TO BE ON THE GROUND.
GIVE ME EYES. BRING UP ALL THE CAMERAS!
YES, SIR!
OH...

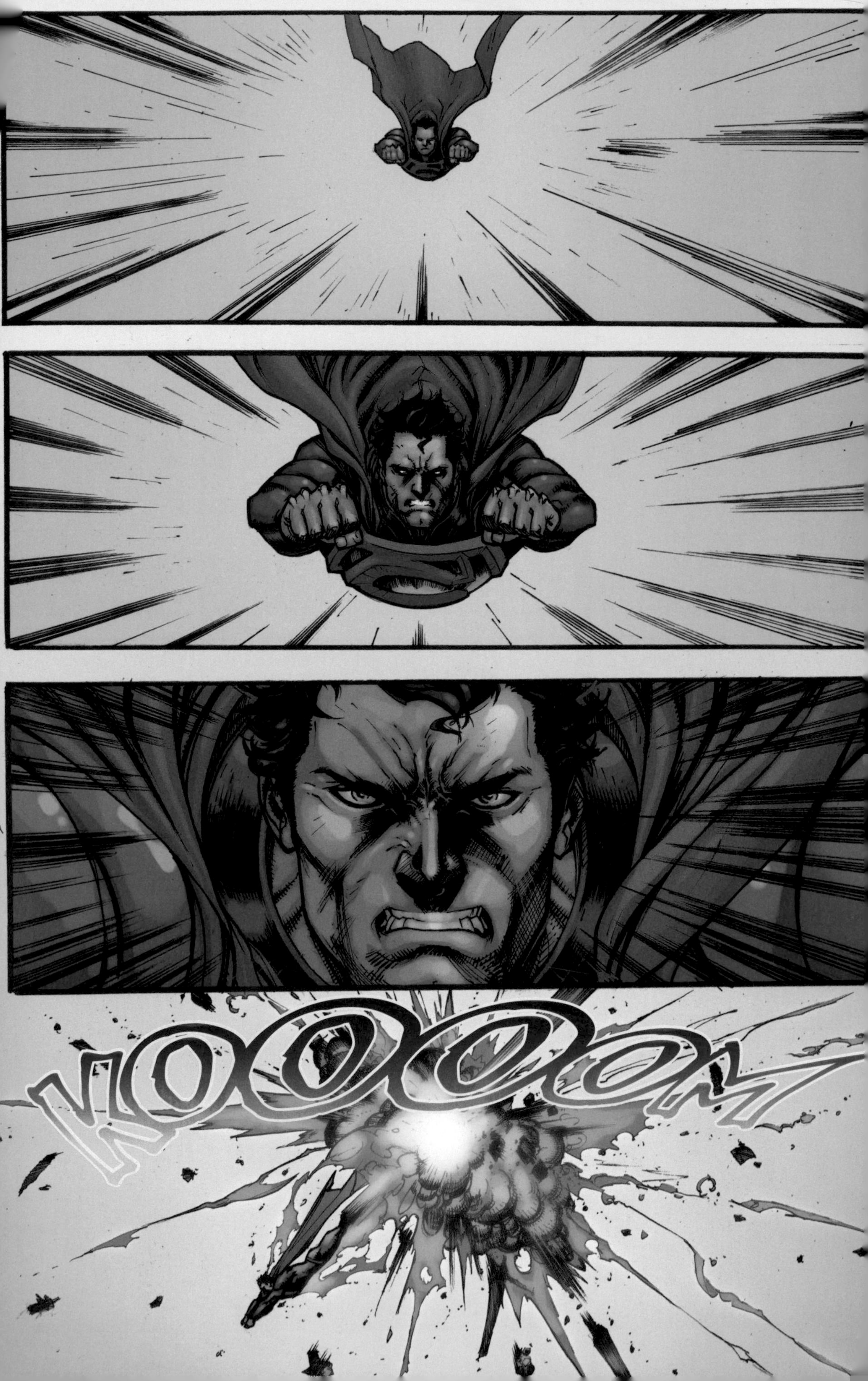
KOOOOM

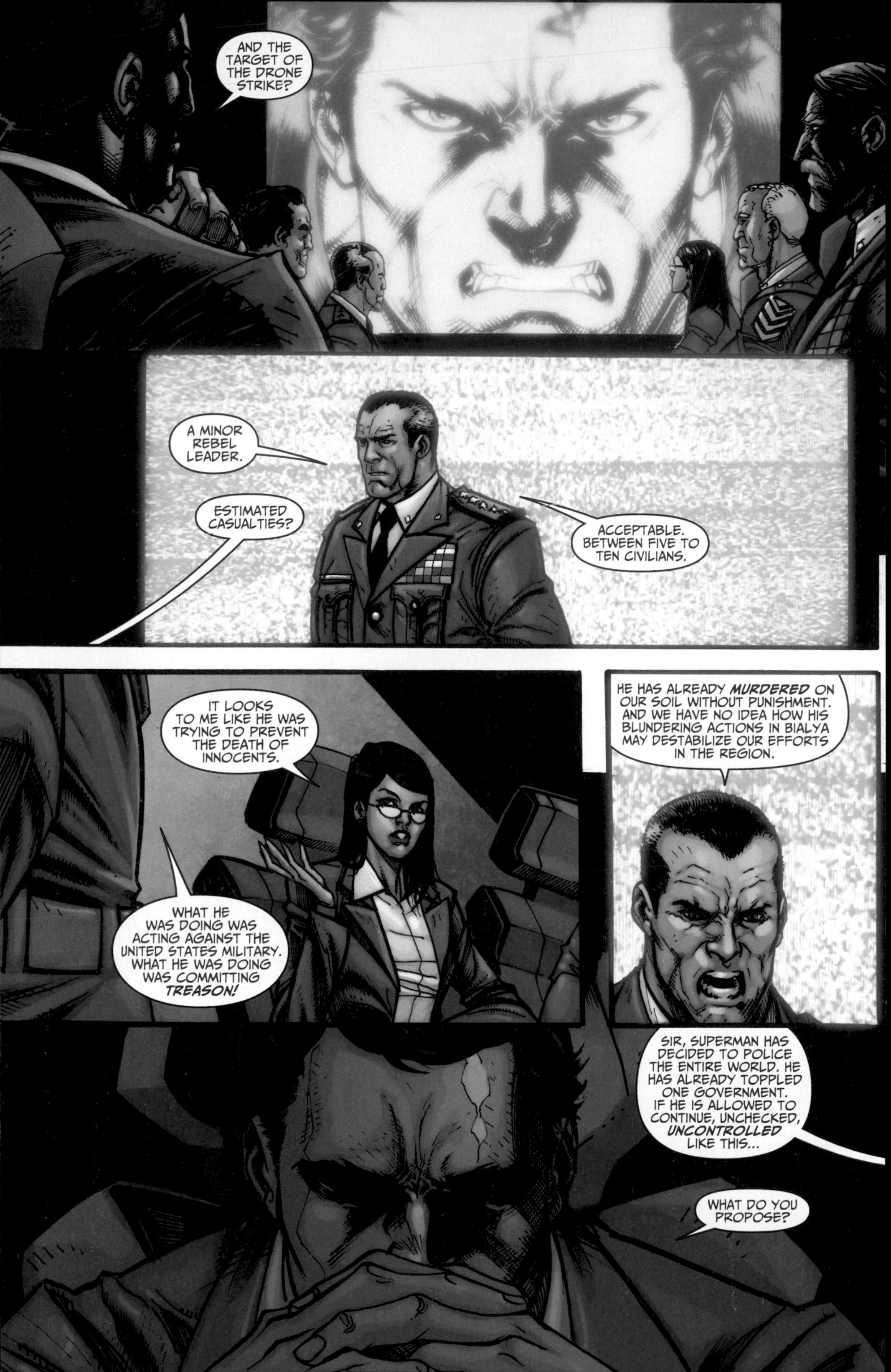
AND THE TARGET OF THE DRONE STRIKE?
A MINOR REBEL LEADER.
ESTIMATED CASUALTIES?
ACCEPTABLE. BETWEEN FIVE TO TEN CIVILIANS.
IT LOOKS TO ME LIKE HE WAS TRYING TO PREVENT THE DEATH OF INNOCENTS.
WHAT HE WAS DOING WAS ACTING AGAINST THE UNITED STATES MILITARY. WHAT HE WAS DOING WAS COMMITTING *TREASON!*
HE HAS ALREADY *MURDERED* ON OUR SOIL WITHOUT PUNISHMENT. AND WE HAVE NO IDEA HOW HIS BLUNDERING ACTIONS IN BIALYA MAY DESTABILIZE OUR EFFORTS IN THE REGION.
SIR, SUPERMAN HAS DECIDED TO POLICE THE ENTIRE WORLD. HE HAS ALREADY TOPPLED ONE GOVERNMENT. IF HE IS ALLOWED TO CONTINUE, UNCHECKED, *UNCONTROLLED* LIKE THIS...
WHAT DO YOU PROPOSE?

"WE HAVE ONE CHANCE AT THIS. WE HAVE ONE CARD WE CAN PLAY."

"HAVE YOU THOUGHT ABOUT THE CONSEQUENCES, GENERAL? IF WE MOVE AGAINST HIM AND *FAIL...?*"

"THERE WILL BE ABSOLUTELY NO SIGN OF YOUR INVOLVEMENT IN THIS, SIR. THESE WILL BE INDEPENDENT CONTRACTORS HIRED THROUGH A SERIES OF SHELL COMPANIES.

"AND WE WON'T FAIL. WE'VE PLANNED THIS."

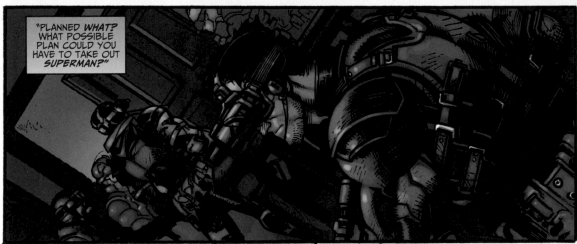

"PLANNED *WHAT?* WHAT POSSIBLE PLAN COULD YOU HAVE TO TAKE OUT *SUPERMAN?*"

"I'M NOT SUGGESTING WE TAKE OUT *SUPERMAN.*"

CRRRACK

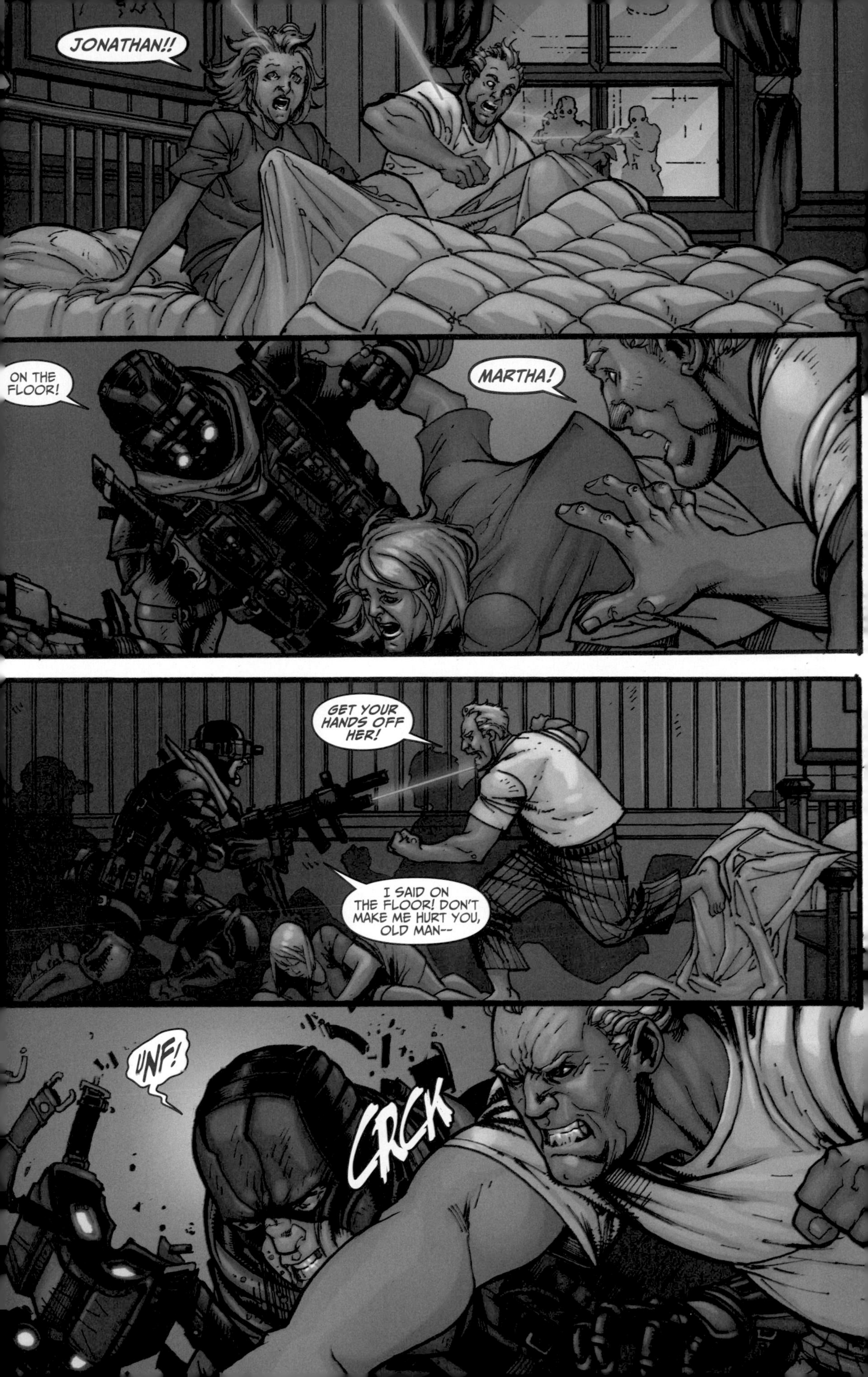
JONATHAN!!
ON THE FLOOR!
MARTHA!
GET YOUR HANDS OFF HER!
I SAID ON THE FLOOR! DON'T MAKE ME HURT YOU, OLD MAN--
UNF!
CRCK

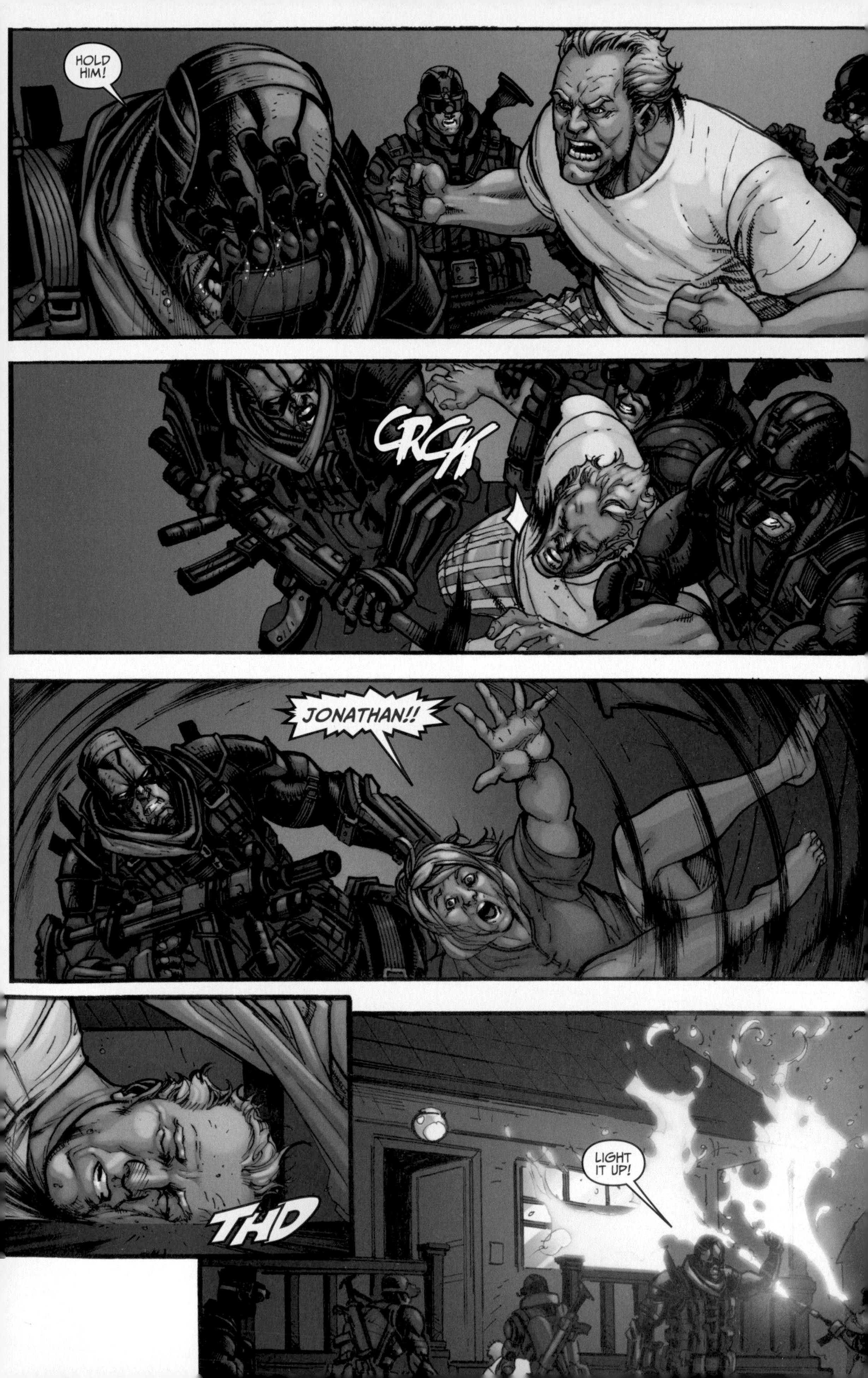
HOLD HIM!
CRCK
JONATHAN!!
THD
LIGHT IT UP!

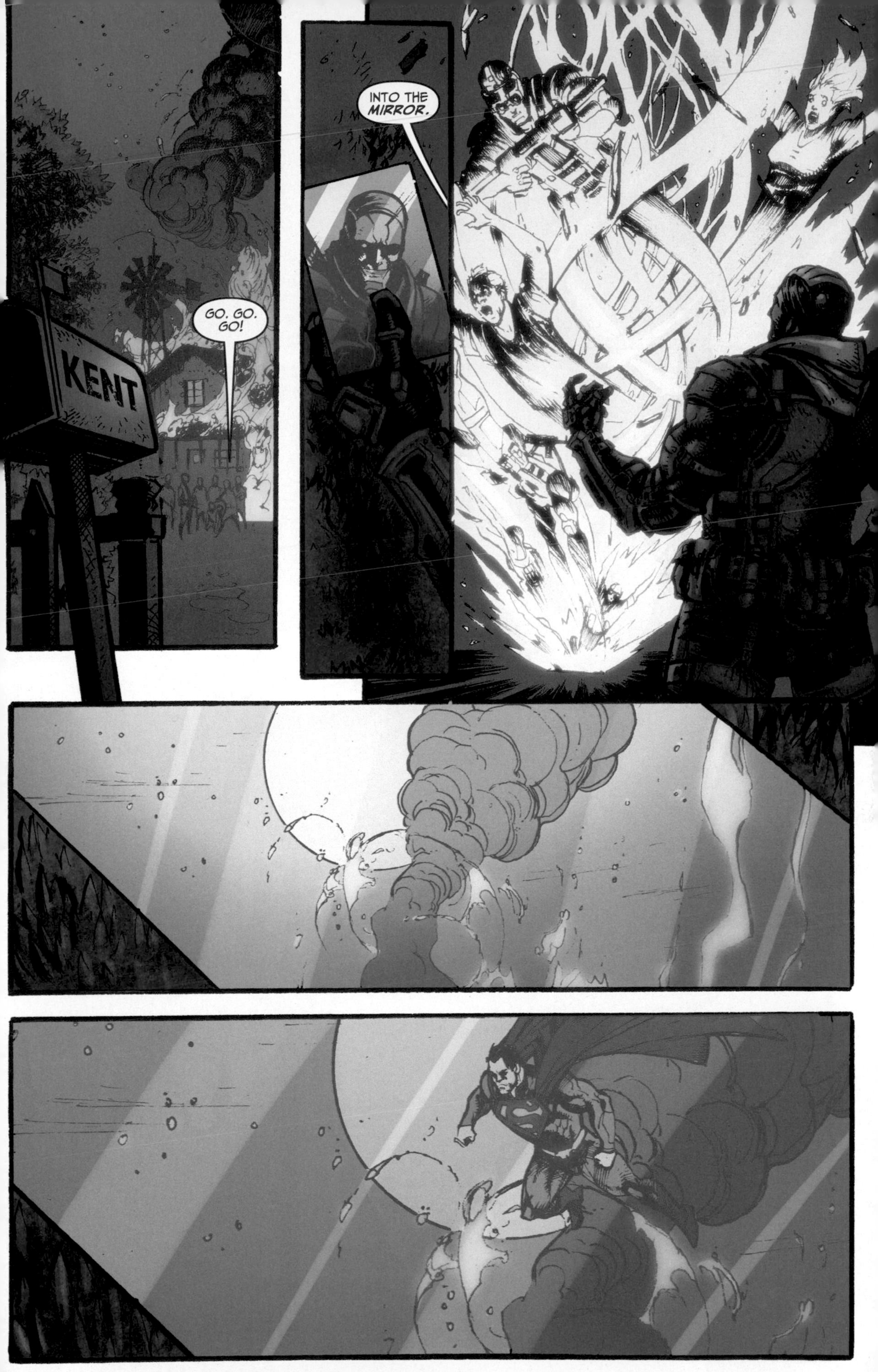
KENT
GO. GO. GO!
INTO THE MIRROR.

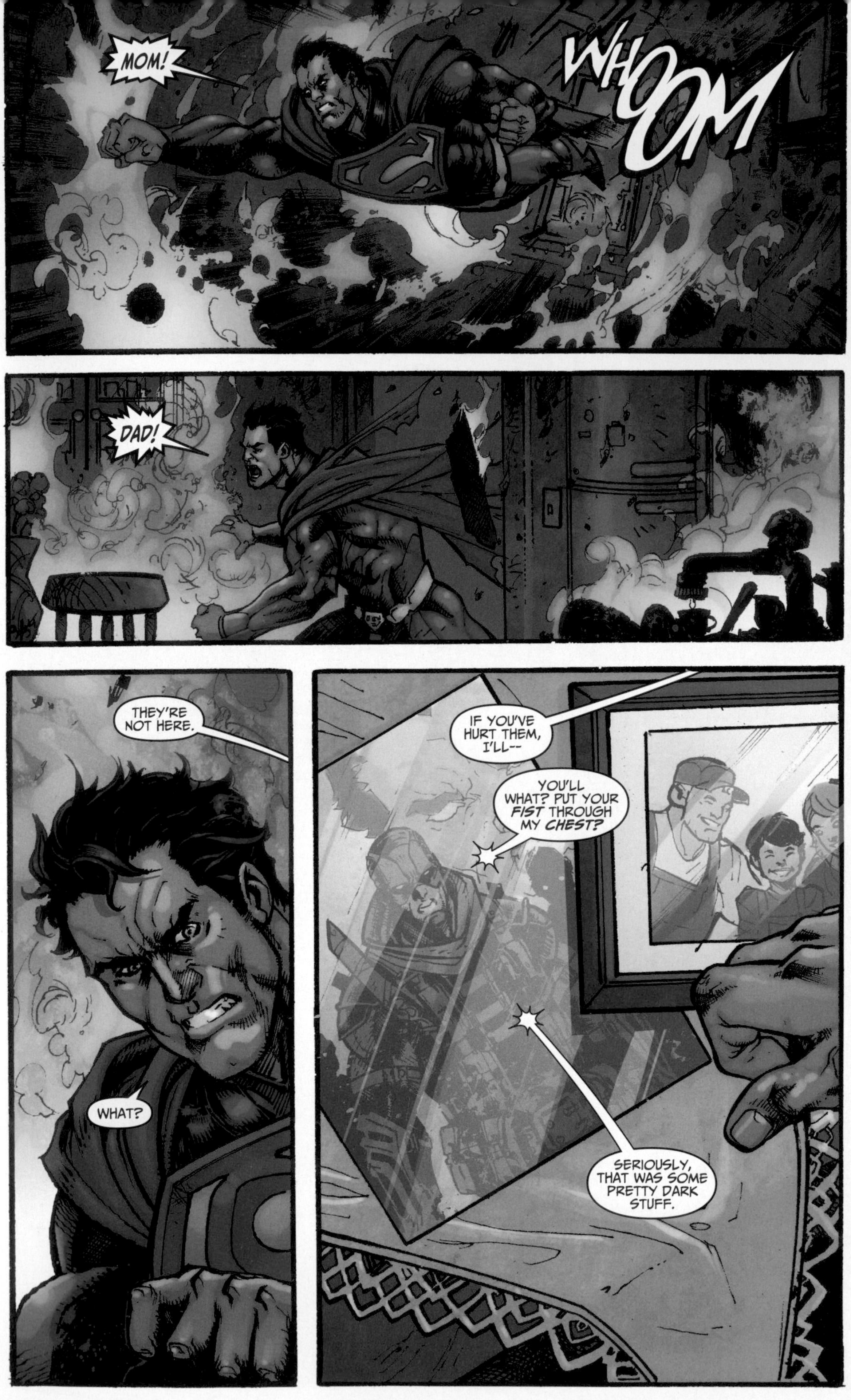
MOM!
WHOOM
DAD!
THEY'RE NOT HERE.
WHAT?
IF YOU'VE HURT THEM, I'LL--
YOU'LL WHAT? PUT YOUR FIST THROUGH MY CHEST?
SERIOUSLY, THAT WAS SOME PRETTY DARK STUFF.

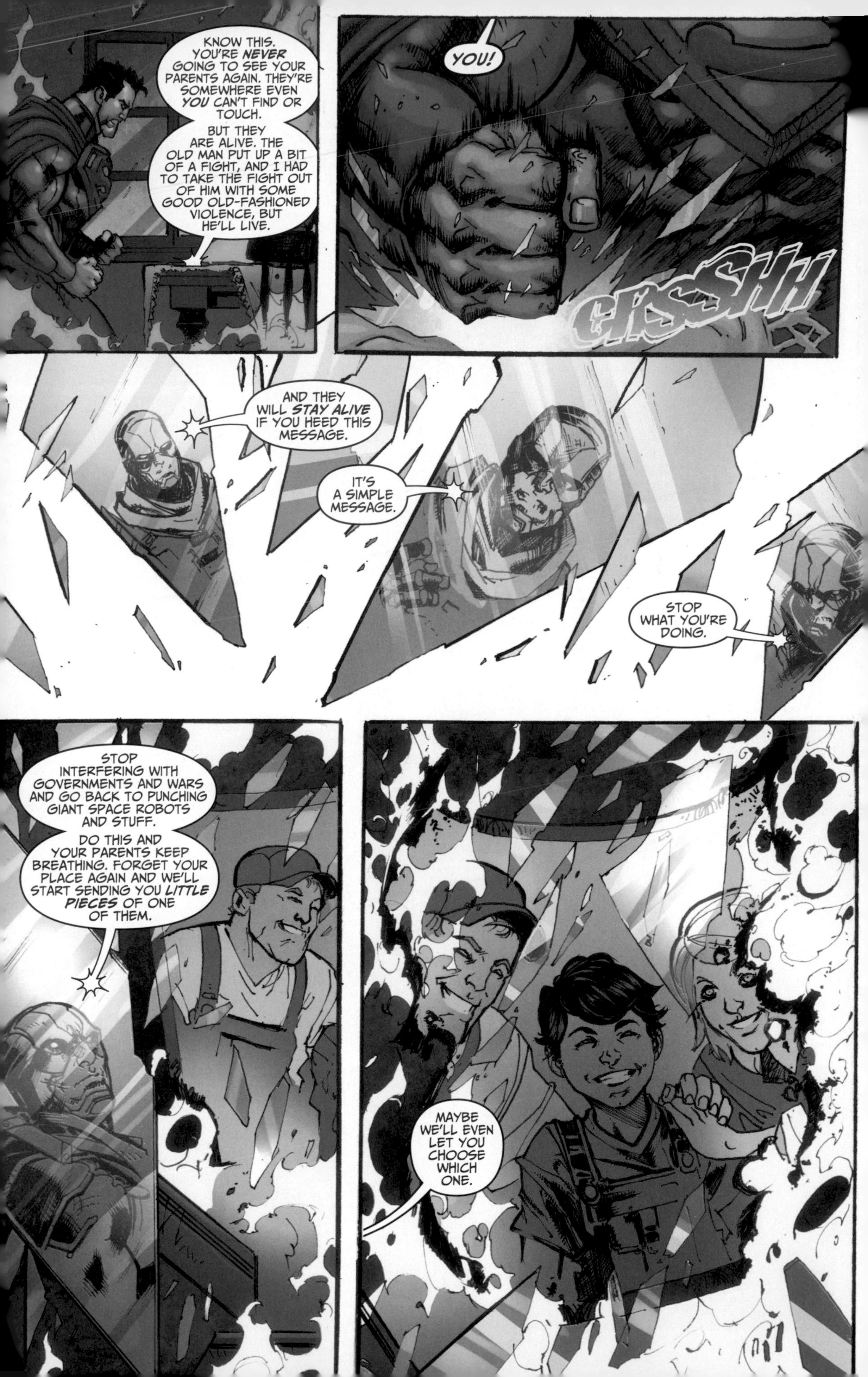
KNOW THIS. YOU'RE NEVER GOING TO SEE YOUR PARENTS AGAIN. THEY'RE SOMEWHERE EVEN YOU CAN'T FIND OR TOUCH.
BUT THEY ARE ALIVE. THE OLD MAN PUT UP A BIT OF A FIGHT, AND I HAD TO TAKE THE FIGHT OUT OF HIM WITH SOME GOOD OLD-FASHIONED VIOLENCE, BUT HE'LL LIVE.
YOU!
CRSSHH
AND THEY WILL STAY ALIVE IF YOU HEED THIS MESSAGE.
IT'S A SIMPLE MESSAGE.
STOP WHAT YOU'RE DOING.
STOP INTERFERING WITH GOVERNMENTS AND WARS AND GO BACK TO PUNCHING GIANT SPACE ROBOTS AND STUFF.
DO THIS AND YOUR PARENTS KEEP BREATHING. FORGET YOUR PLACE AGAIN AND WE'LL START SENDING YOU LITTLE PIECES OF ONE OF THEM.
MAYBE WE'LL EVEN LET YOU CHOOSE WHICH ONE.

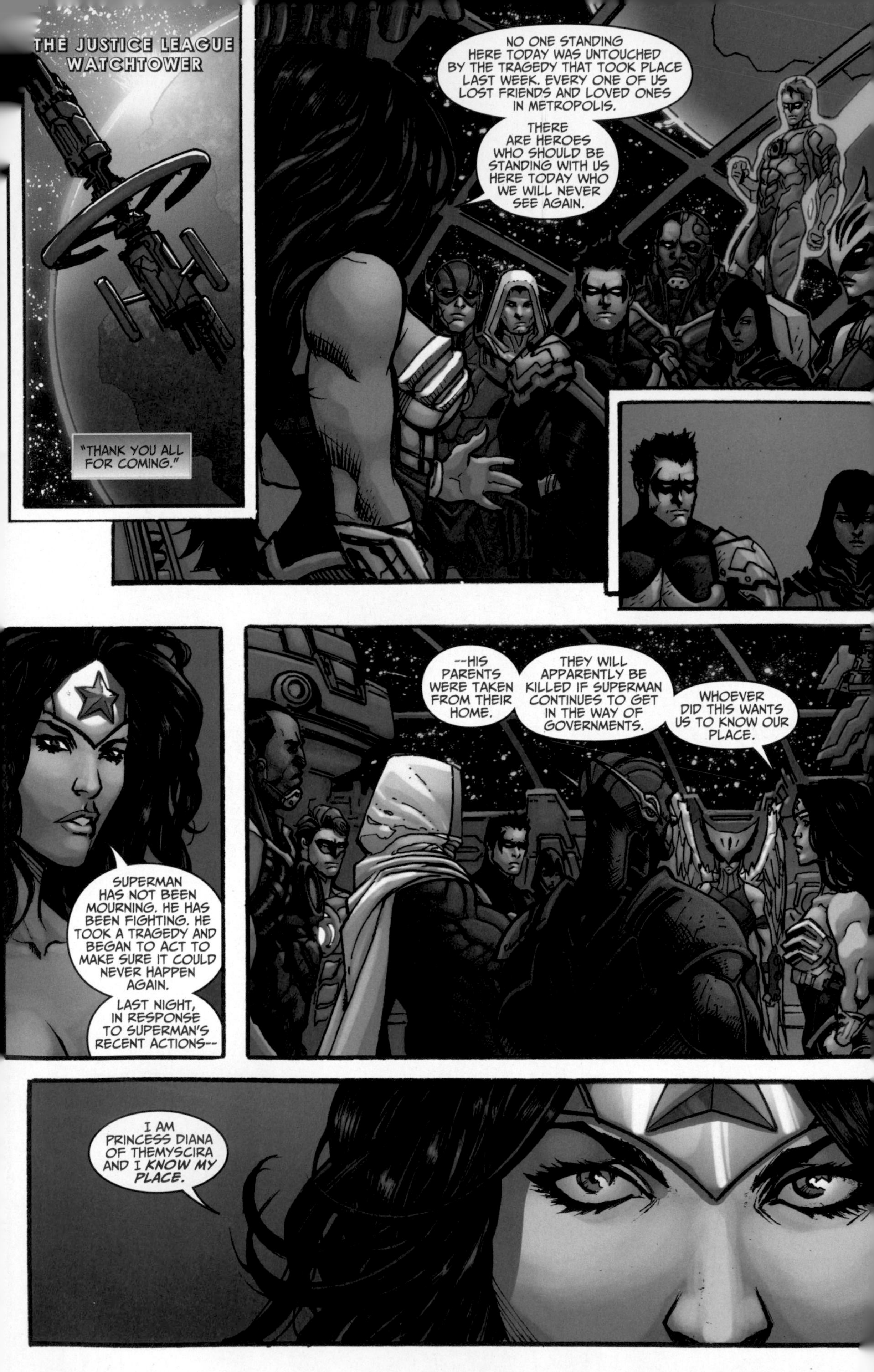
THE JUSTICE LEAGUE WATCHTOWER
"THANK YOU ALL FOR COMING."
NO ONE STANDING HERE TODAY WAS UNTOUCHED BY THE TRAGEDY THAT TOOK PLACE LAST WEEK. EVERY ONE OF US LOST FRIENDS AND LOVED ONES IN METROPOLIS.
THERE ARE HEROES WHO SHOULD BE STANDING WITH US HERE TODAY WHO WE WILL NEVER SEE AGAIN.
SUPERMAN HAS NOT BEEN MOURNING. HE HAS BEEN FIGHTING. HE TOOK A TRAGEDY AND BEGAN TO ACT TO MAKE SURE IT COULD NEVER HAPPEN AGAIN.
LAST NIGHT, IN RESPONSE TO SUPERMAN'S RECENT ACTIONS--
--HIS PARENTS WERE TAKEN FROM THEIR HOME.
THEY WILL APPARENTLY BE KILLED IF SUPERMAN CONTINUES TO GET IN THE WAY OF GOVERNMENTS.
WHOEVER DID THIS WANTS US TO KNOW OUR PLACE.
I AM PRINCESS DIANA OF THEMYSCIRA AND I *KNOW MY PLACE.*

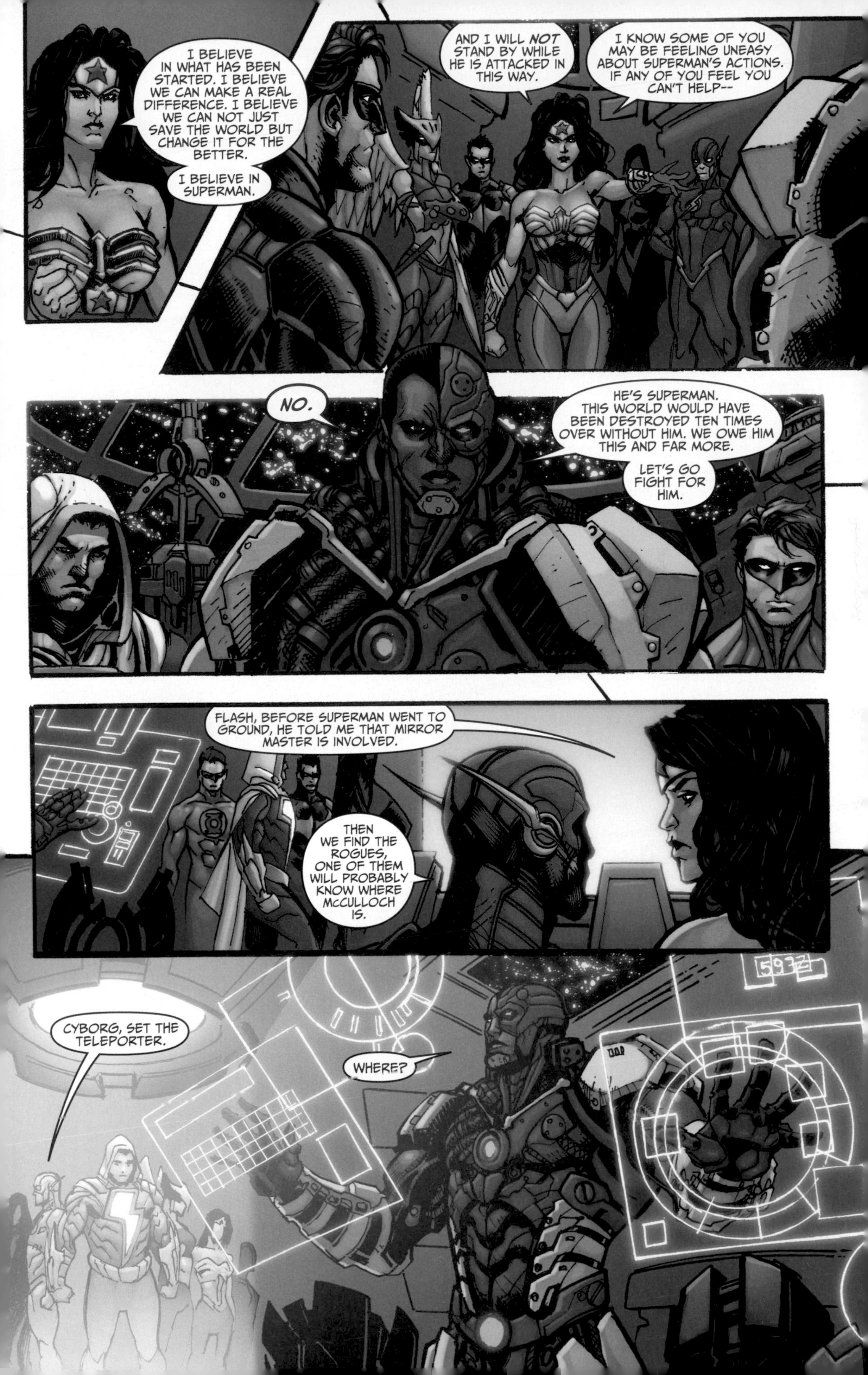
I BELIEVE IN WHAT HAS BEEN STARTED. I BELIEVE WE CAN MAKE A REAL DIFFERENCE. I BELIEVE WE CAN NOT JUST SAVE THE WORLD BUT CHANGE IT FOR THE BETTER.
I BELIEVE IN SUPERMAN.
AND I WILL *NOT* STAND BY WHILE HE IS ATTACKED IN THIS WAY.
I KNOW SOME OF YOU MAY BE FEELING UNEASY ABOUT SUPERMAN'S ACTIONS. IF ANY OF YOU FEEL YOU CAN'T HELP--
NO.
HE'S SUPERMAN. THIS WORLD WOULD HAVE BEEN DESTROYED TEN TIMES OVER WITHOUT HIM. WE OWE HIM THIS AND FAR MORE.
LET'S GO FIGHT FOR HIM.
FLASH, BEFORE SUPERMAN WENT TO GROUND, HE TOLD ME THAT MIRROR MASTER IS INVOLVED.
THEN WE FIND THE ROGUES, ONE OF THEM WILL PROBABLY KNOW WHERE McCULLOCH IS.
CYBORG, SET THE TELEPORTER.
WHERE?
5932

"CENTRAL CITY."

WHERE—

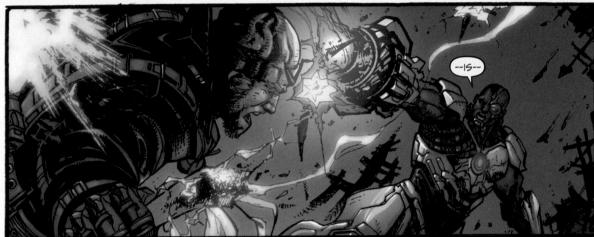

—IS—

—HE?

WHERE'S MIRROR MASTER?

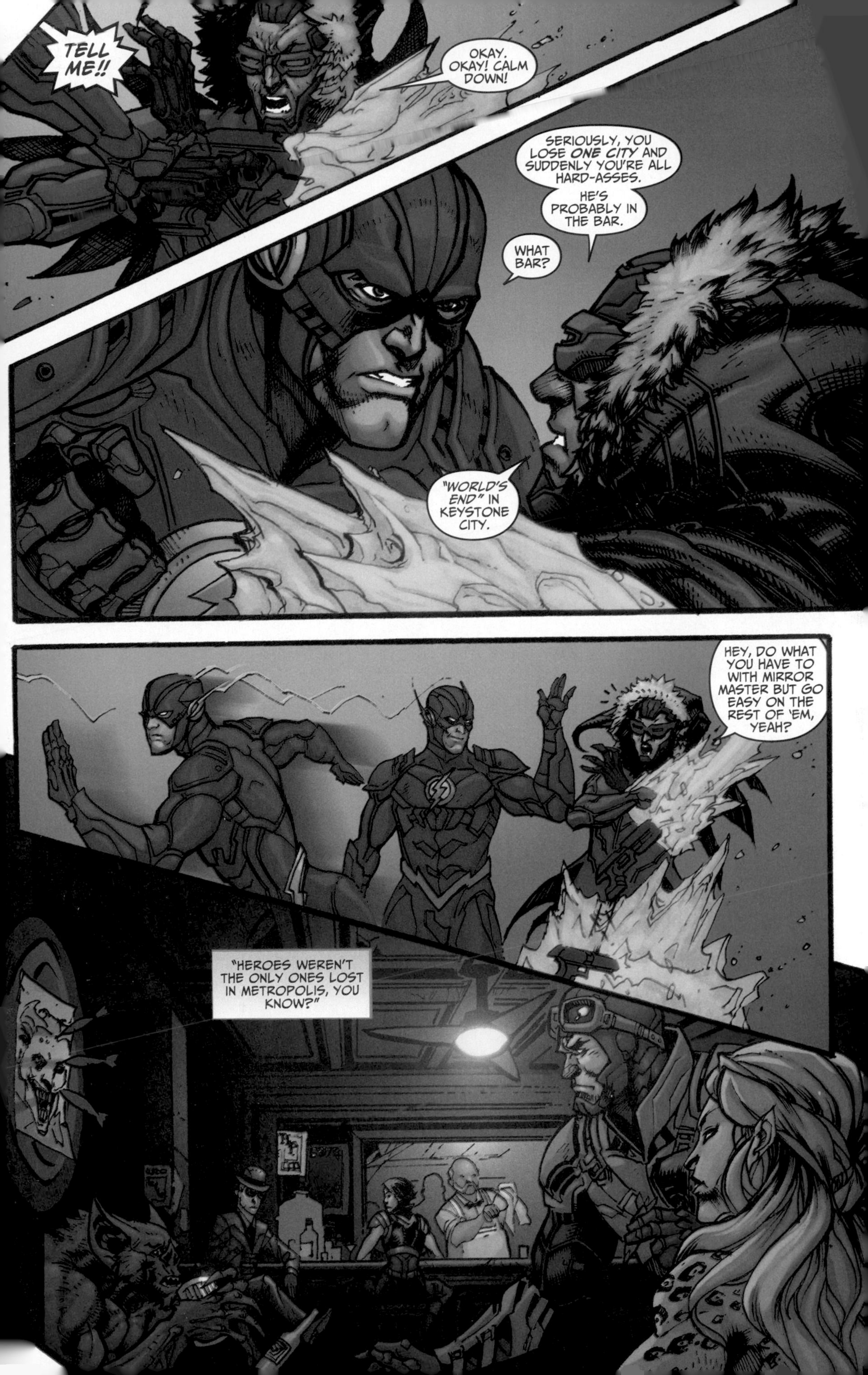
TELL ME!!
OKAY. OKAY! CALM DOWN!
SERIOUSLY, YOU LOSE ONE CITY AND SUDDENLY YOU'RE ALL HARD-ASSES.
HE'S PROBABLY IN THE BAR.
WHAT BAR?
"WORLD'S END" IN KEYSTONE CITY.
HEY, DO WHAT YOU HAVE TO WITH MIRROR MASTER BUT GO EASY ON THE REST OF 'EM, YEAH?
"HEROES WEREN'T THE ONLY ONES LOST IN METROPOLIS, YOU KNOW?"

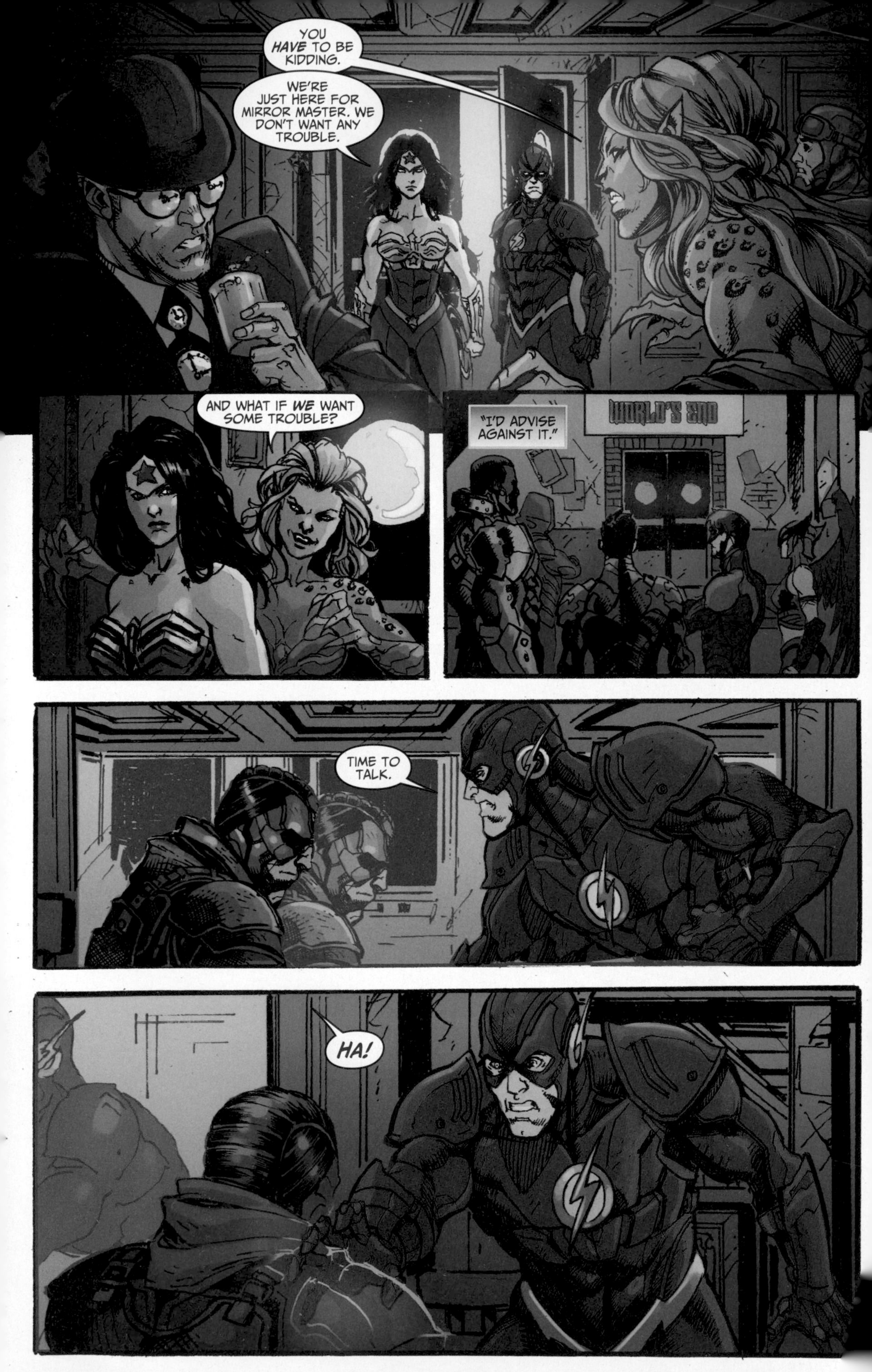
YOU HAVE TO BE KIDDING.
WE'RE JUST HERE FOR MIRROR MASTER. WE DON'T WANT ANY TROUBLE.
AND WHAT IF WE WANT SOME TROUBLE?
WORLD'S END
"I'D ADVISE AGAINST IT."
TIME TO TALK.
HA!

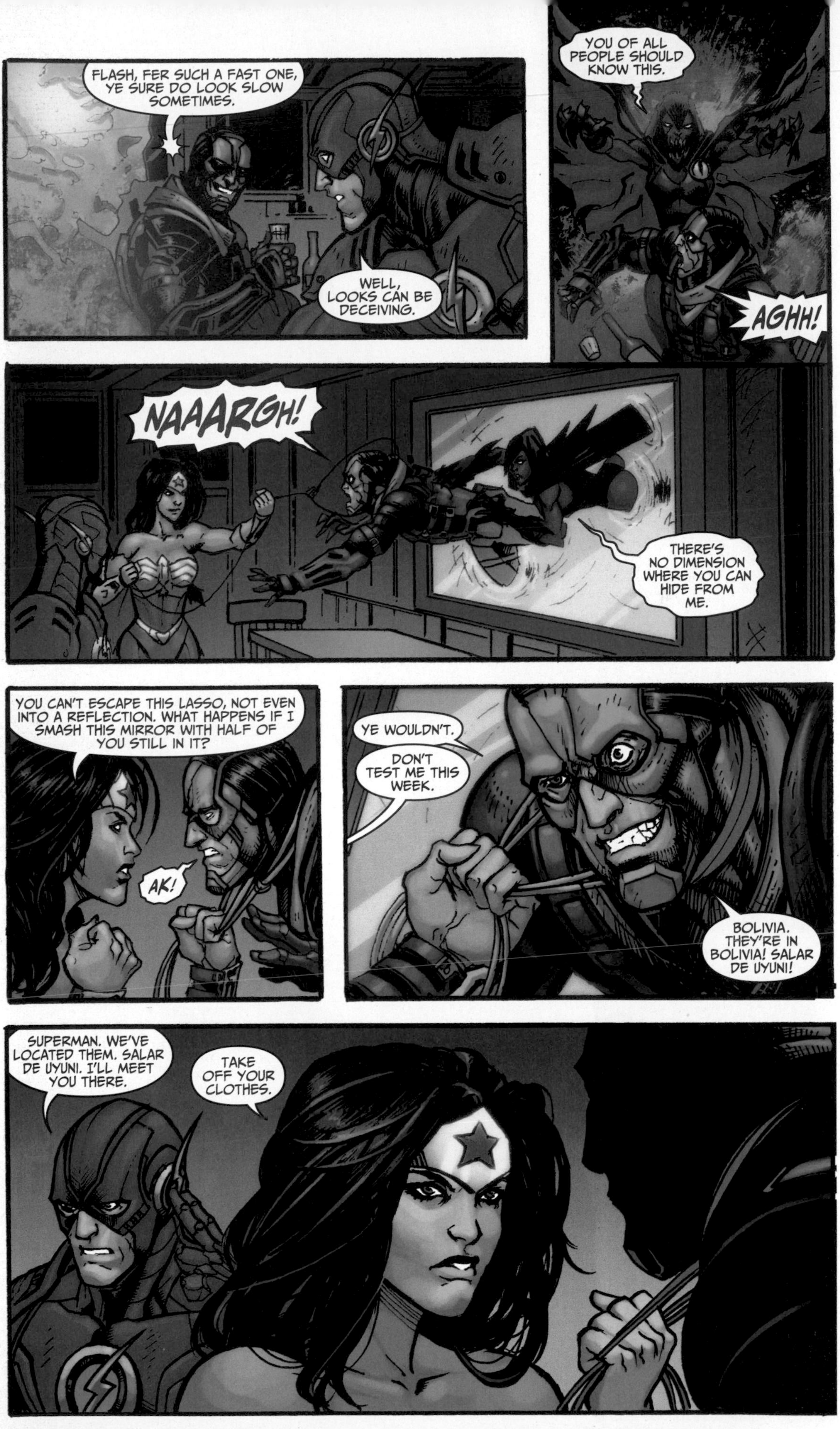
FLASH, FER SUCH A FAST ONE, YE SURE DO LOOK SLOW SOMETIMES.
WELL, LOOKS CAN BE DECEIVING.
YOU OF ALL PEOPLE SHOULD KNOW THIS.
AGHH!
NAAARGH!
THERE'S NO DIMENSION WHERE YOU CAN HIDE FROM ME.
YOU CAN'T ESCAPE THIS LASSO, NOT EVEN INTO A REFLECTION. WHAT HAPPENS IF I SMASH THIS MIRROR WITH HALF OF YOU STILL IN IT?
AK!
YE WOULDN'T.
DON'T TEST ME THIS WEEK.
BOLIVIA. THEY'RE IN BOLIVIA! SALAR DE UYUNI!
SUPERMAN. WE'VE LOCATED THEM. SALAR DE UYUNI. I'LL MEET YOU THERE.
TAKE OFF YOUR CLOTHES.

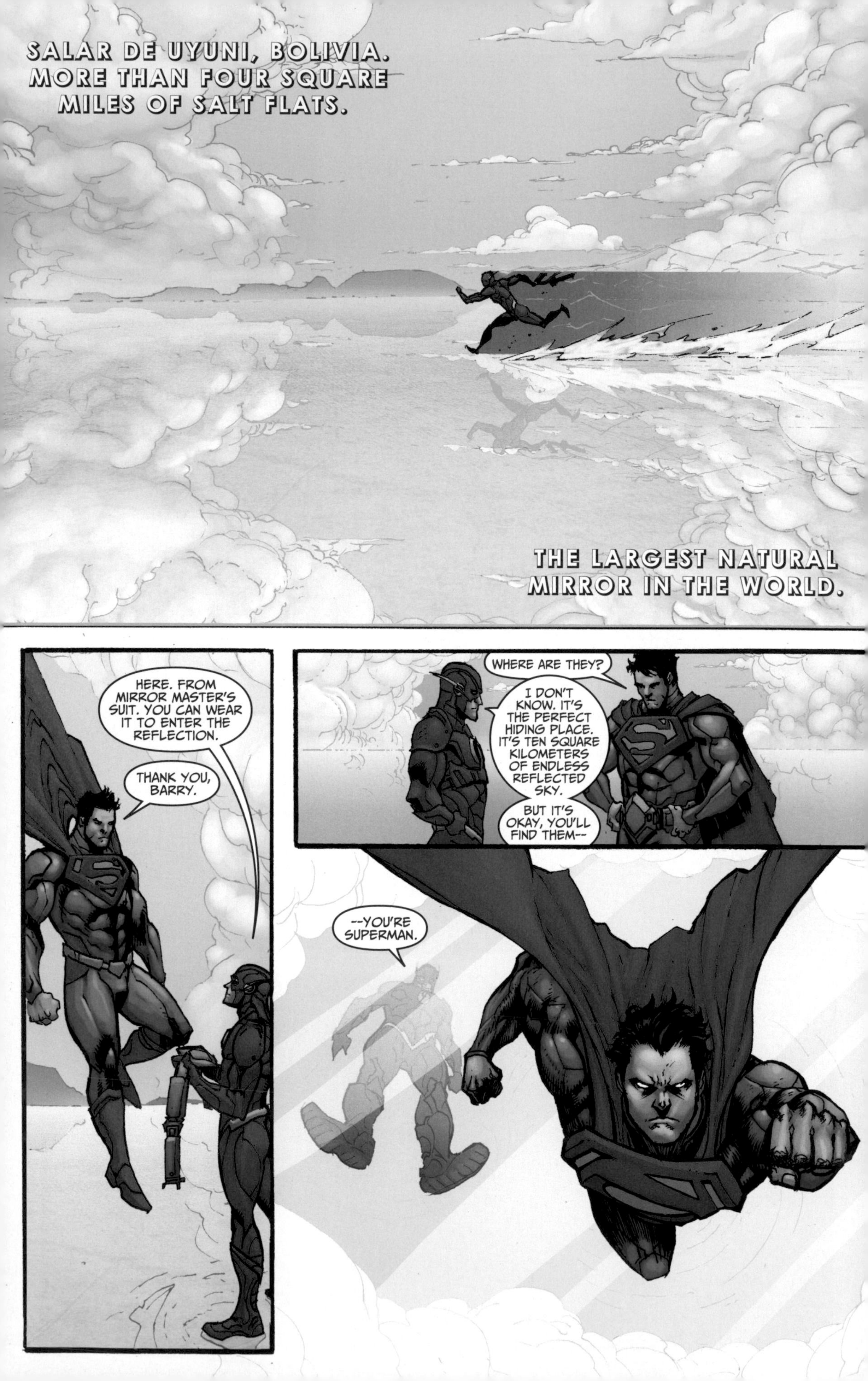
SALAR DE UYUNI, BOLIVIA. MORE THAN FOUR SQUARE MILES OF SALT FLATS.
THE LARGEST NATURAL MIRROR IN THE WORLD.
HERE. FROM MIRROR MASTER'S SUIT. YOU CAN WEAR IT TO ENTER THE REFLECTION.
THANK YOU, BARRY.
WHERE ARE THEY?
I DON'T KNOW. IT'S THE PERFECT HIDING PLACE. IT'S TEN SQUARE KILOMETERS OF ENDLESS REFLECTED SKY.
BUT IT'S OKAY, YOU'LL FIND THEM--
--YOU'RE SUPERMAN.

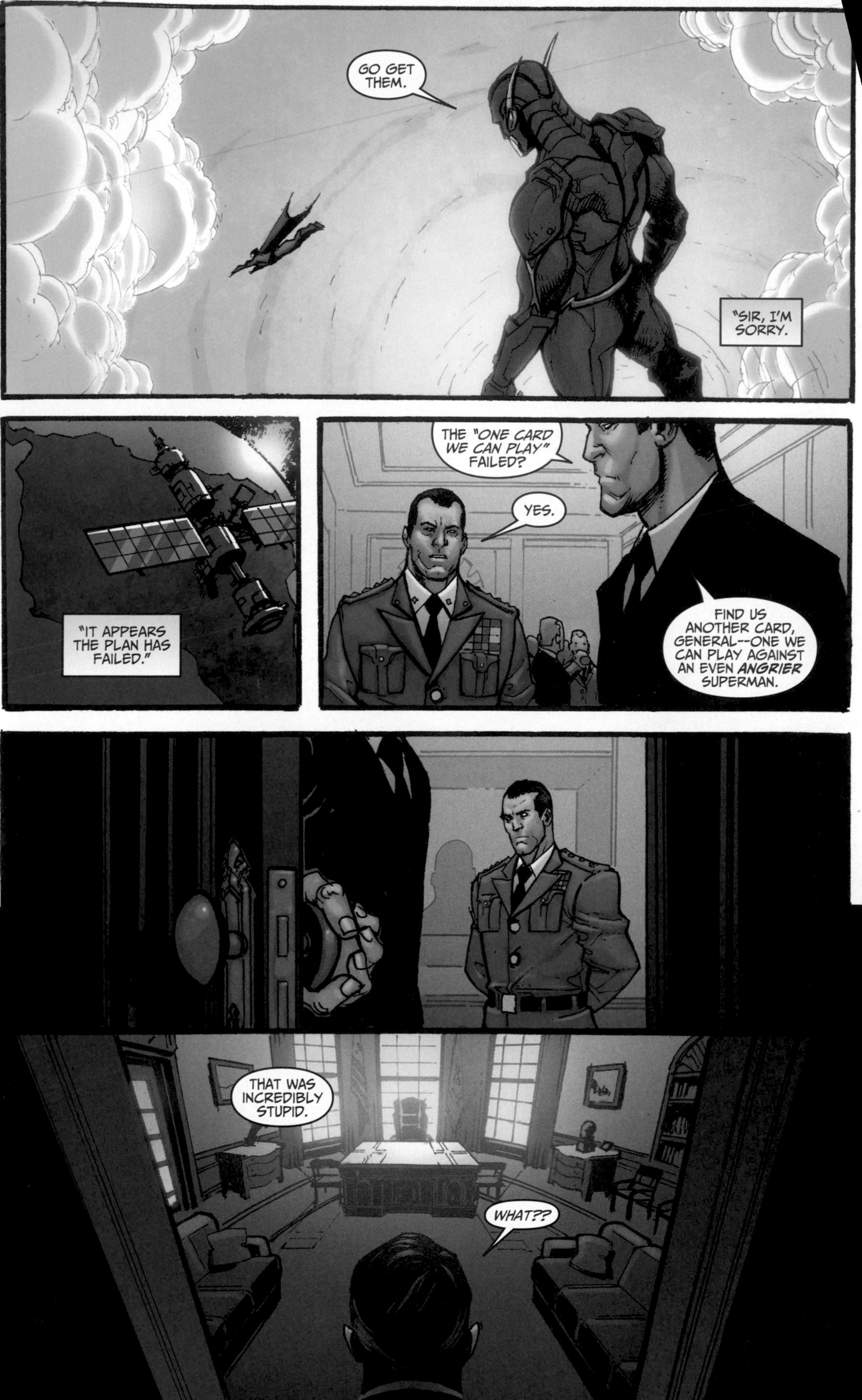
GO GET THEM.
"SIR, I'M SORRY.
"IT APPEARS THE PLAN HAS FAILED."
THE "ONE CARD WE CAN PLAY" FAILED?
YES.
FIND US ANOTHER CARD, GENERAL--ONE WE CAN PLAY AGAINST AN EVEN ANGRIER SUPERMAN.
THAT WAS INCREDIBLY STUPID.
WHAT??

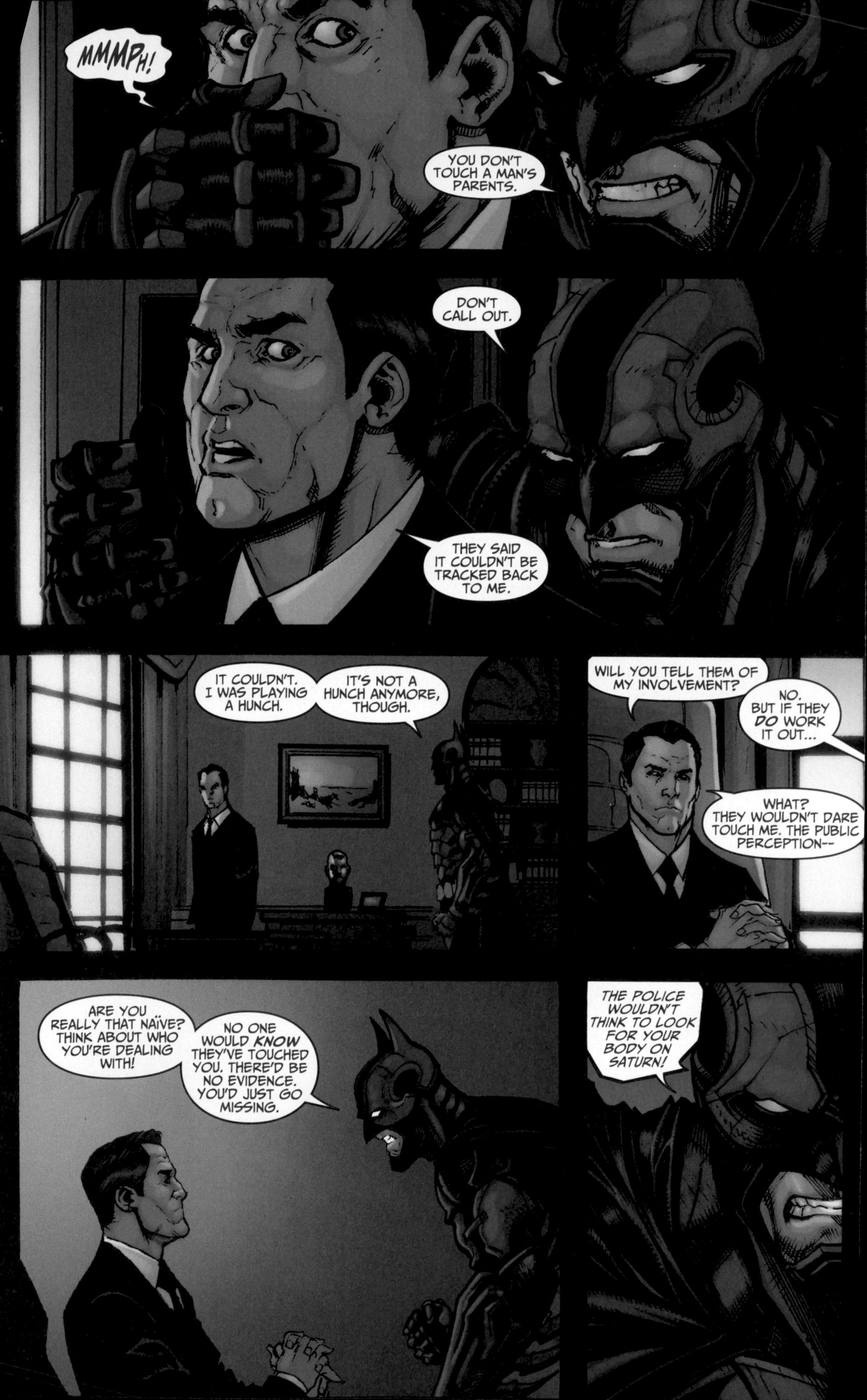
MMMPH!
YOU DON'T TOUCH A MAN'S PARENTS.
DON'T CALL OUT.
THEY SAID IT COULDN'T BE TRACKED BACK TO ME.
IT COULDN'T. I WAS PLAYING A HUNCH.
IT'S NOT A HUNCH ANYMORE, THOUGH.
WILL YOU TELL THEM OF MY INVOLVEMENT?
NO. BUT IF THEY DO WORK IT OUT...
WHAT? THEY WOULDN'T DARE TOUCH ME. THE PUBLIC PERCEPTION--
ARE YOU REALLY THAT NAÏVE? THINK ABOUT WHO YOU'RE DEALING WITH!
NO ONE WOULD KNOW THEY'VE TOUCHED YOU. THERE'D BE NO EVIDENCE. YOU'D JUST GO MISSING.
THE POLICE WOULDN'T THINK TO LOOK FOR YOUR BODY ON SATURN!

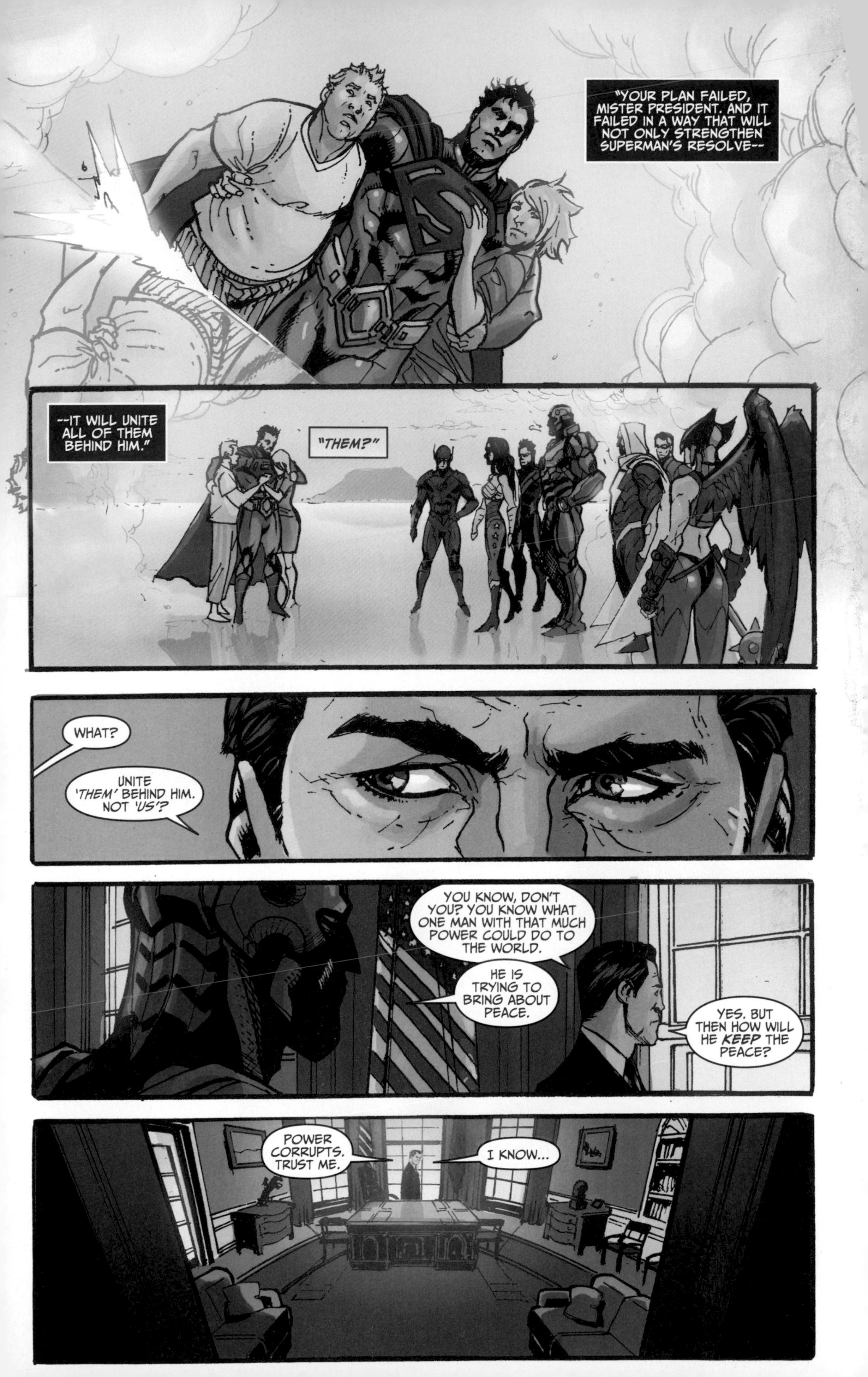
"YOUR PLAN FAILED, MISTER PRESIDENT. AND IT FAILED IN A WAY THAT WILL NOT ONLY STRENGTHEN SUPERMAN'S RESOLVE--
--IT WILL UNITE ALL OF THEM BEHIND HIM."
"THEM?"
WHAT?
UNITE 'THEM' BEHIND HIM. NOT 'US'?
YOU KNOW, DON'T YOU? YOU KNOW WHAT ONE MAN WITH THAT MUCH POWER COULD DO TO THE WORLD.
HE IS TRYING TO BRING ABOUT PEACE.
YES. BUT THEN HOW WILL HE KEEP THE PEACE?
POWER CORRUPTS. TRUST ME.
I KNOW...

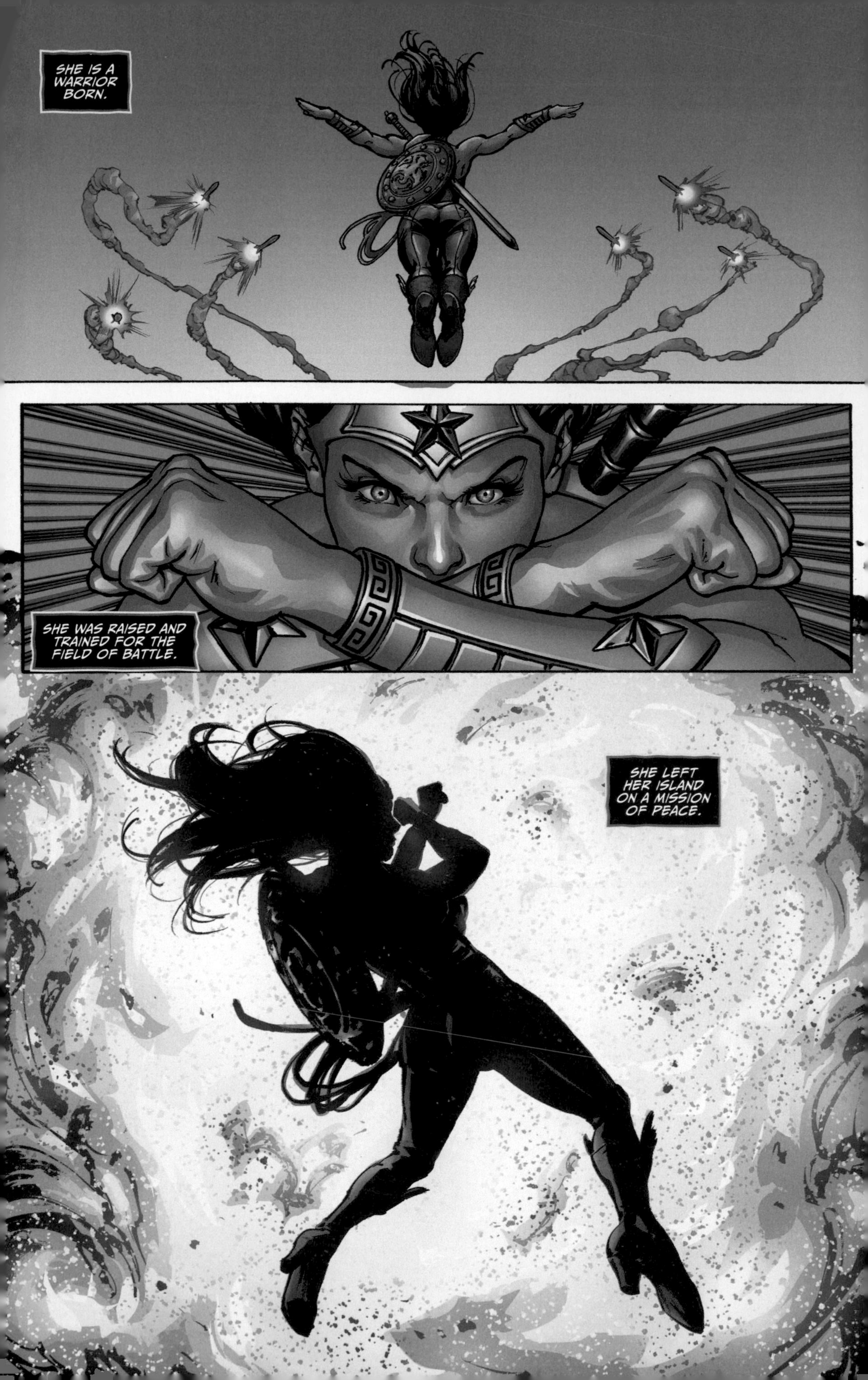
SHE IS A WARRIOR BORN.
SHE WAS RAISED AND TRAINED FOR THE FIELD OF BATTLE.
SHE LEFT HER ISLAND ON A MISSION OF PEACE.

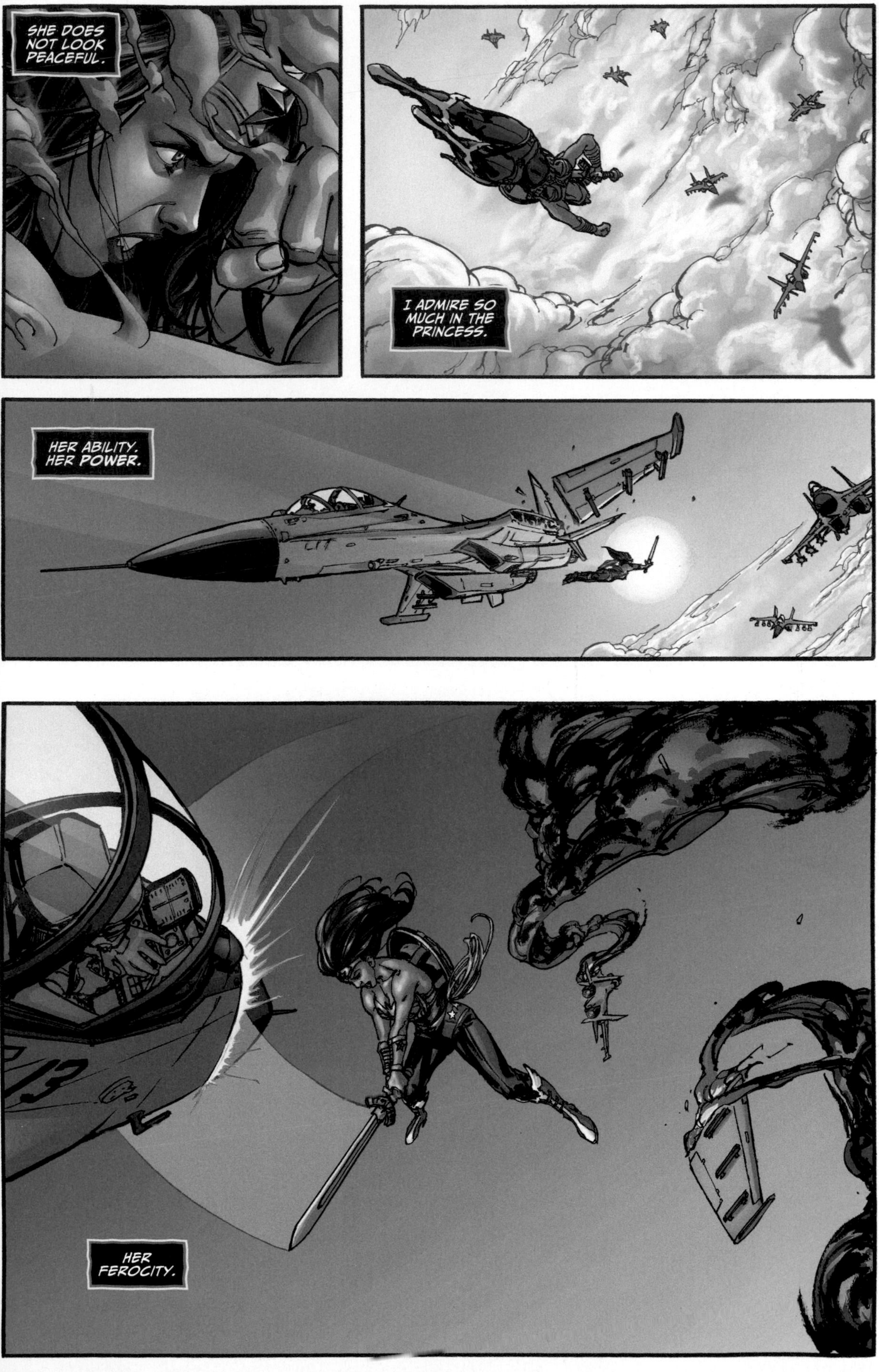
SHE DOES NOT LOOK PEACEFUL.
I ADMIRE SO MUCH IN THE PRINCESS.
HER ABILITY. HER POWER.
HER FEROCITY.

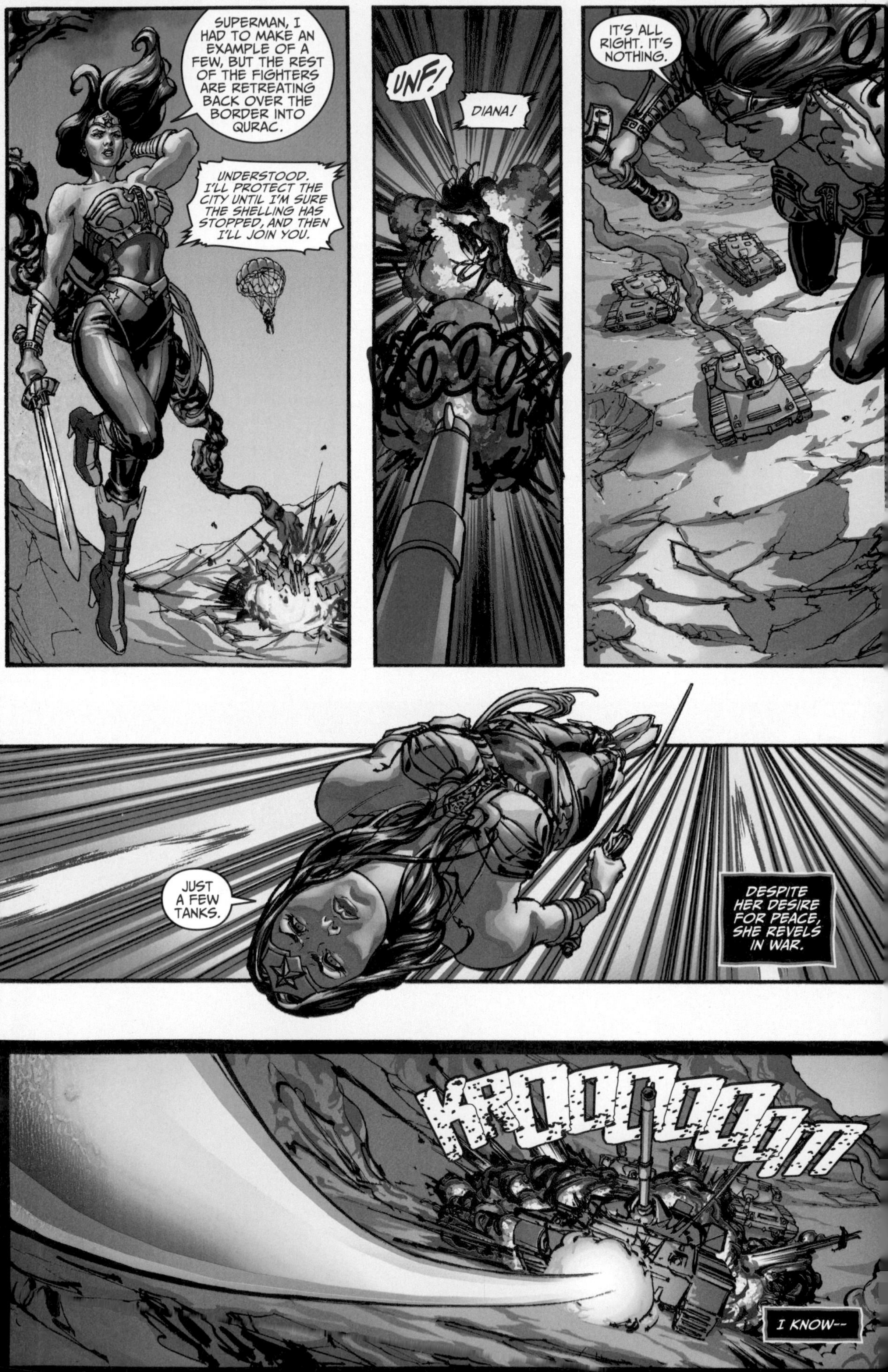
SUPERMAN, I HAD TO MAKE AN EXAMPLE OF A FEW, BUT THE REST OF THE FIGHTERS ARE RETREATING BACK OVER THE BORDER INTO QURAC.
UNDERSTOOD. I'LL PROTECT THE CITY UNTIL I'M SURE THE SHELLING HAS STOPPED, AND THEN I'LL JOIN YOU.
UNF!
DIANA!
IT'S ALL RIGHT. IT'S NOTHING.
JUST A FEW TANKS.
DESPITE HER DESIRE FOR PEACE, SHE REVELS IN WAR.
KROOOOOOM
I KNOW--

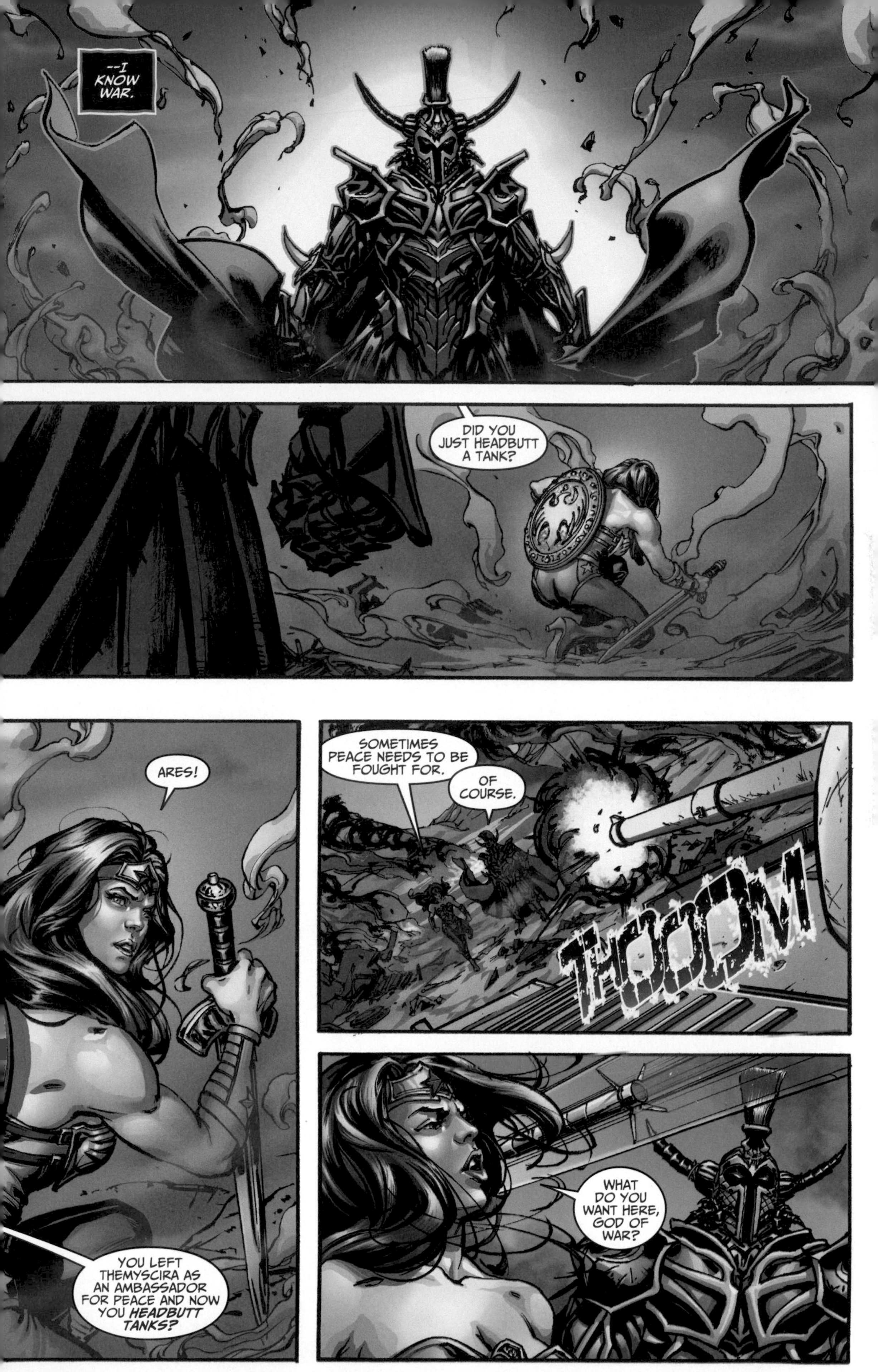
--I KNOW WAR.
DID YOU JUST HEADBUTT A TANK?
ARES!
YOU LEFT THEMYSCIRA AS AN AMBASSADOR FOR PEACE AND NOW YOU *HEADBUTT TANKS?*
SOMETIMES PEACE NEEDS TO BE FOUGHT FOR.
OF COURSE.
THOOM
WHAT DO YOU WANT HERE, GOD OF WAR?

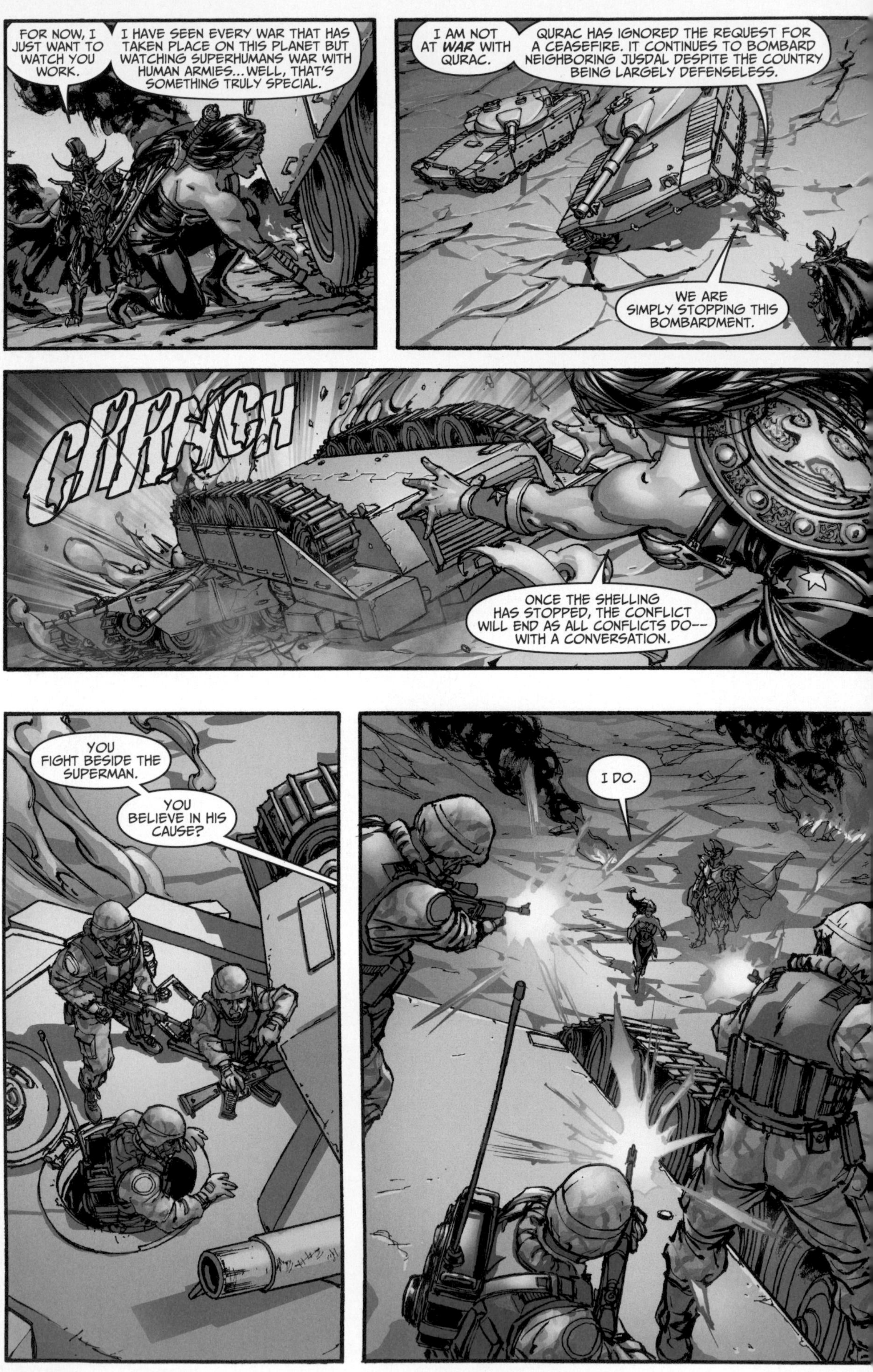
FOR NOW, I JUST WANT TO WATCH YOU WORK.
I HAVE SEEN EVERY WAR THAT HAS TAKEN PLACE ON THIS PLANET BUT WATCHING SUPERHUMANS WAR WITH HUMAN ARMIES...WELL, THAT'S SOMETHING TRULY SPECIAL.
I AM NOT AT WAR WITH QURAC.
QURAC HAS IGNORED THE REQUEST FOR A CEASEFIRE. IT CONTINUES TO BOMBARD NEIGHBORING JUSDAL DESPITE THE COUNTRY BEING LARGELY DEFENSELESS.
WE ARE SIMPLY STOPPING THIS BOMBARDMENT.
CRRAGH
ONCE THE SHELLING HAS STOPPED, THE CONFLICT WILL END AS ALL CONFLICTS DO-- WITH A CONVERSATION.
YOU FIGHT BESIDE THE SUPERMAN.
YOU BELIEVE IN HIS CAUSE?
I DO.

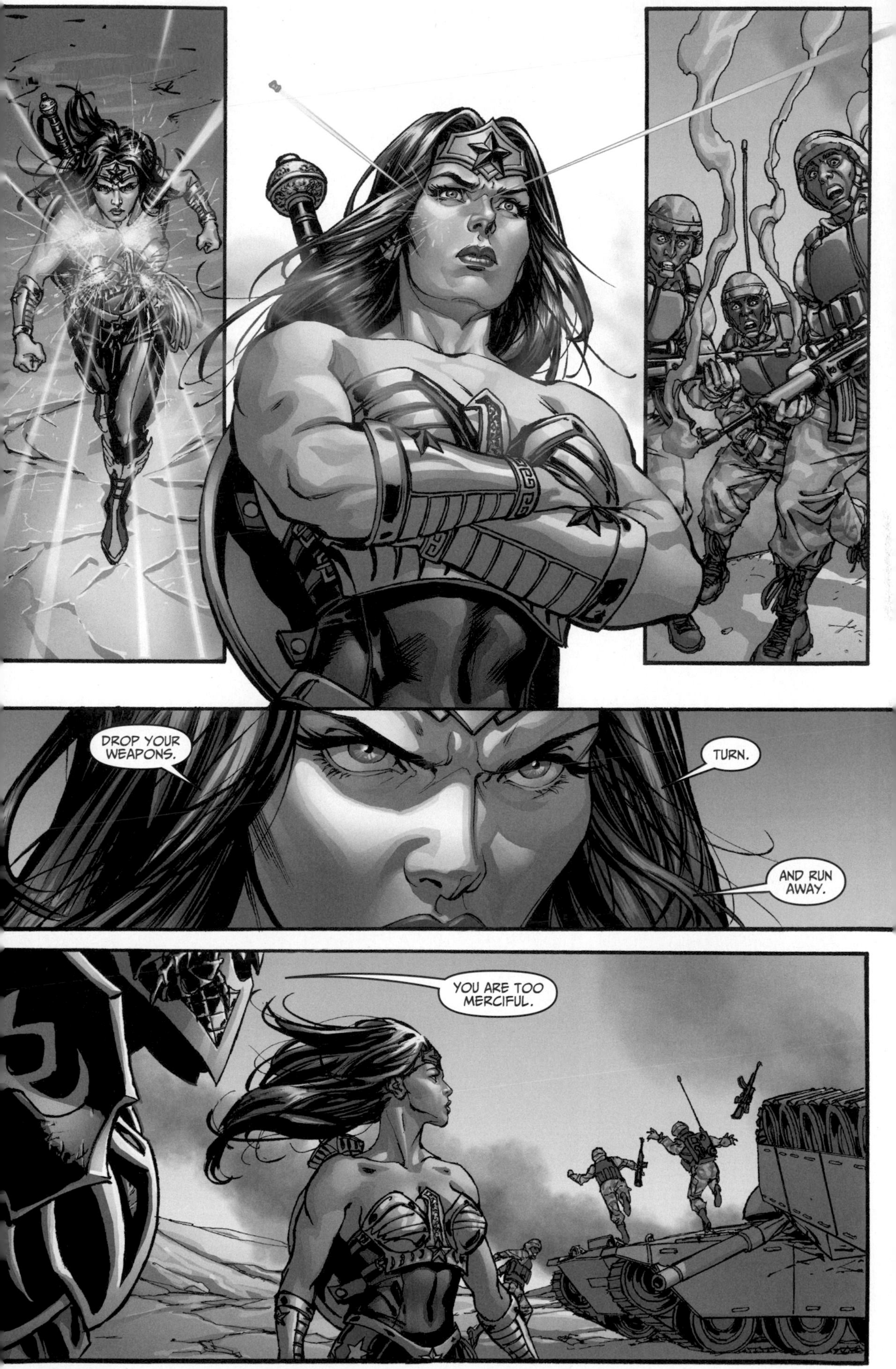
DROP YOUR WEAPONS.
TURN.
AND RUN AWAY.
YOU ARE TOO MERCIFUL.

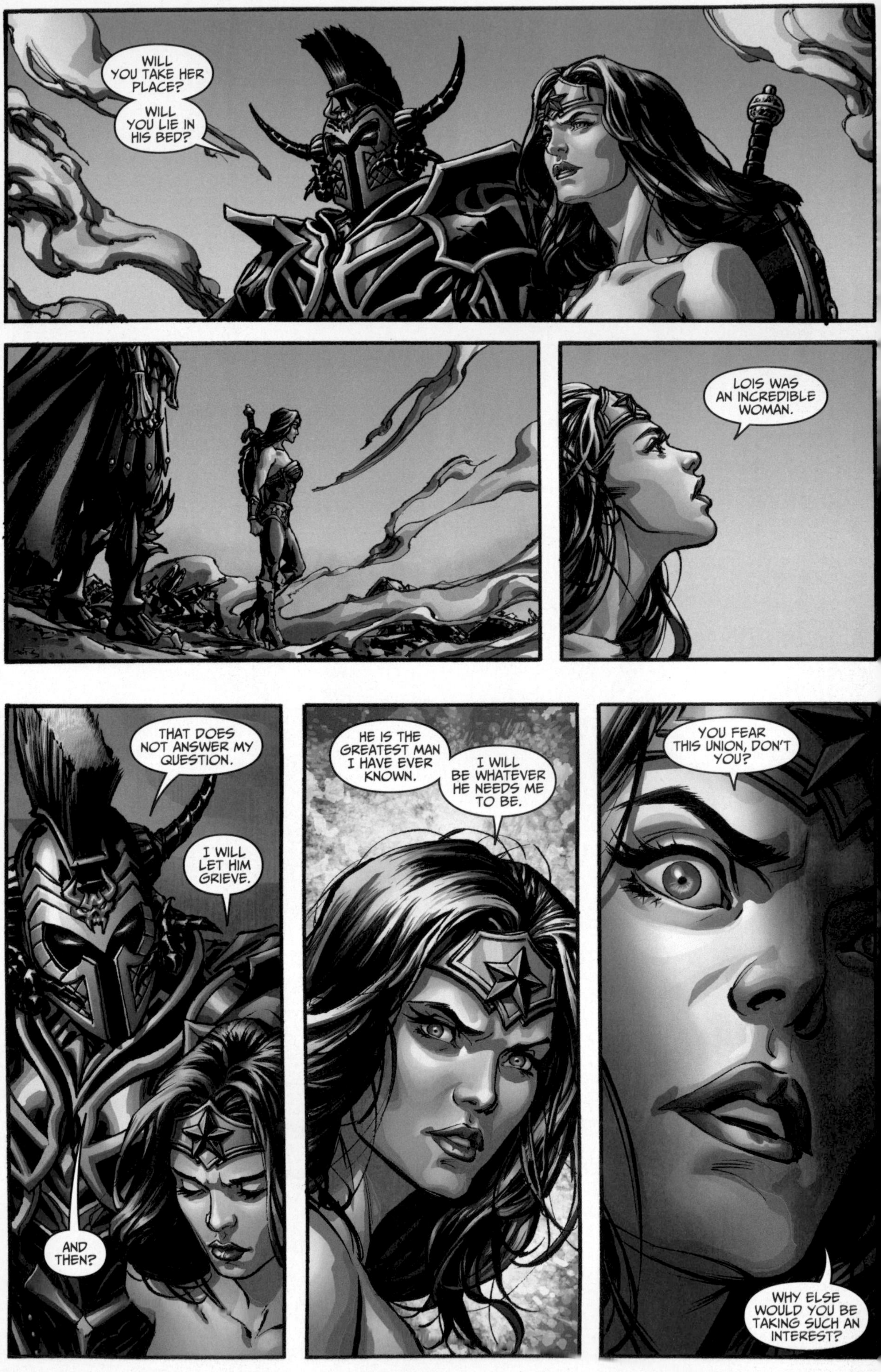
WILL YOU TAKE HER PLACE?
WILL YOU LIE IN HIS BED?
LOIS WAS AN INCREDIBLE WOMAN.
THAT DOES NOT ANSWER MY QUESTION.
I WILL LET HIM GRIEVE.
AND THEN?
HE IS THE GREATEST MAN I HAVE EVER KNOWN.
I WILL BE WHATEVER HE NEEDS ME TO BE.
YOU FEAR THIS UNION, DON'T YOU?
WHY ELSE WOULD YOU BE TAKING SUCH AN INTEREST?

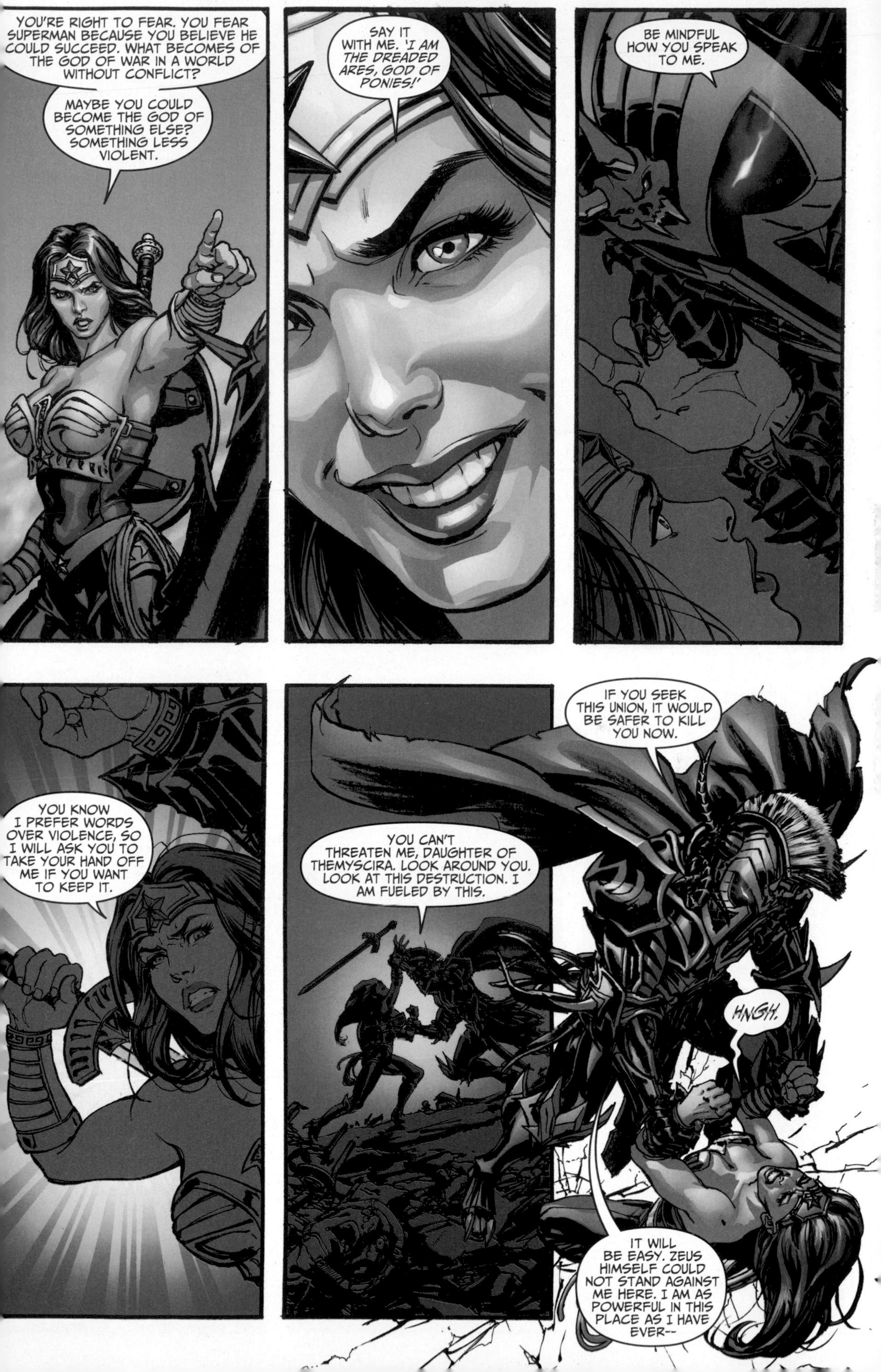

YOU'RE RIGHT TO FEAR. YOU FEAR SUPERMAN BECAUSE YOU BELIEVE HE COULD SUCCEED. WHAT BECOMES OF THE GOD OF WAR IN A WORLD WITHOUT CONFLICT?
MAYBE YOU COULD BECOME THE GOD OF SOMETHING ELSE? SOMETHING LESS VIOLENT.
SAY IT WITH ME. 'I AM THE DREADED ARES, GOD OF PONIES!'
BE MINDFUL HOW YOU SPEAK TO ME.
YOU KNOW I PREFER WORDS OVER VIOLENCE, SO I WILL ASK YOU TO TAKE YOUR HAND OFF ME IF YOU WANT TO KEEP IT.
YOU CAN'T THREATEN ME, DAUGHTER OF THEMYSCIRA. LOOK AROUND YOU. LOOK AT THIS DESTRUCTION. I AM FUELED BY THIS.
IF YOU SEEK THIS UNION, IT WOULD BE SAFER TO KILL YOU NOW.
HNGH.
IT WILL BE EASY. ZEUS HIMSELF COULD NOT STAND AGAINST ME HERE. I AM AS POWERFUL IN THIS PLACE AS I HAVE EVER--

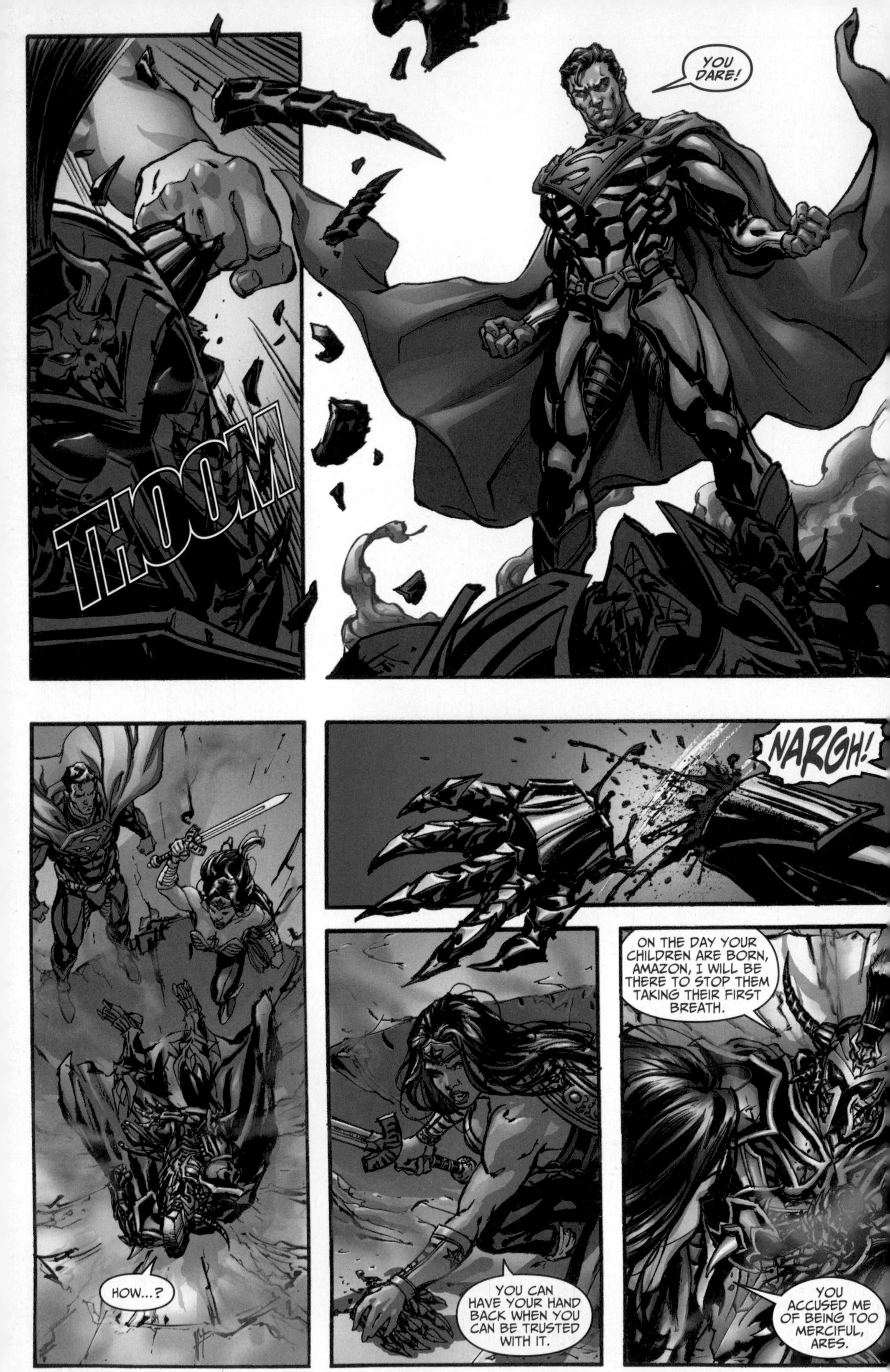
YOU DARE!
THOOM
NARGH!
HOW...?
YOU CAN HAVE YOUR HAND BACK WHEN YOU CAN BE TRUSTED WITH IT.
ON THE DAY YOUR CHILDREN ARE BORN, AMAZON, I WILL BE THERE TO STOP THEM TAKING THEIR FIRST BREATH.
YOU ACCUSED ME OF BEING TOO MERCIFUL, ARES.

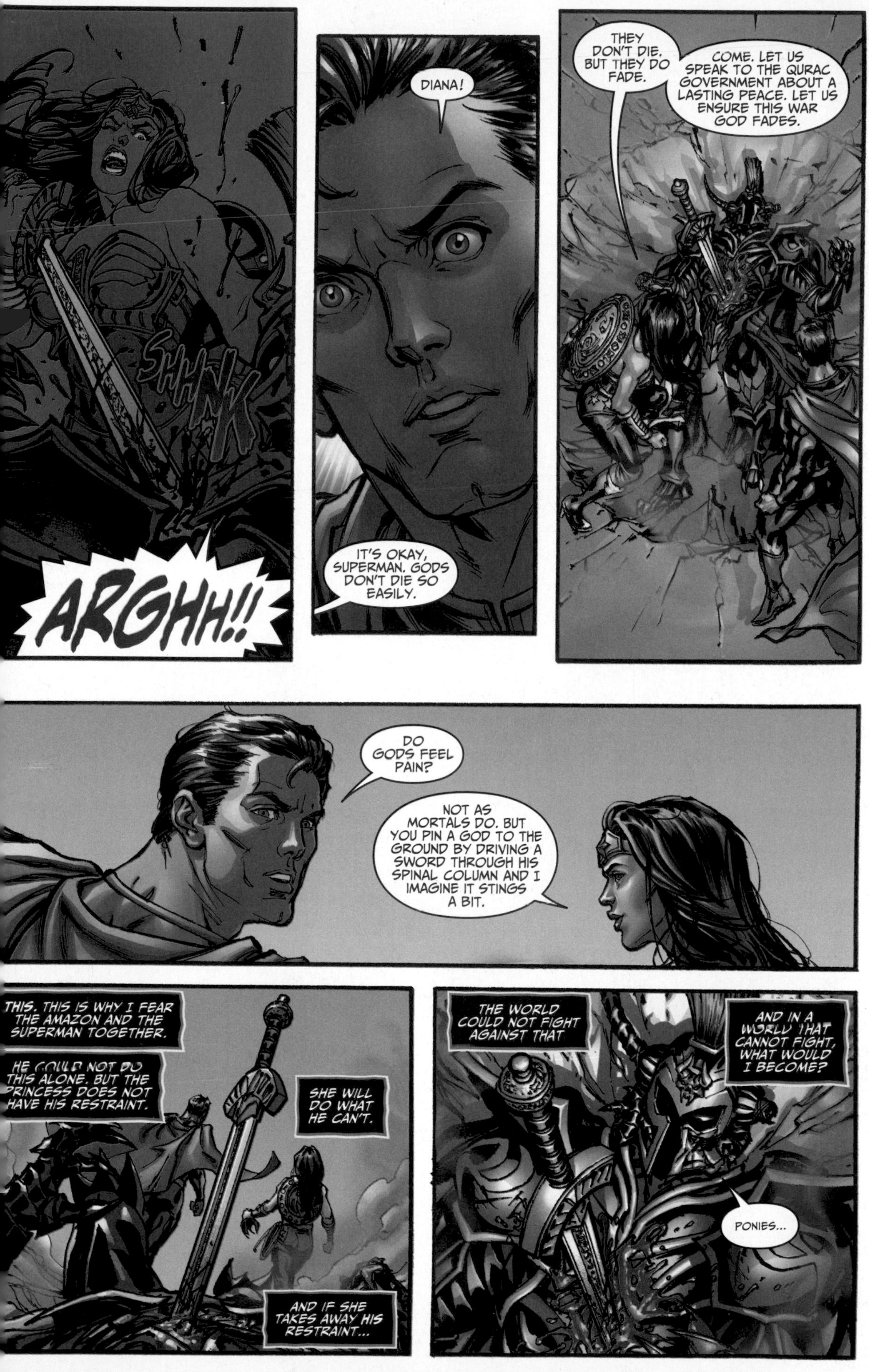
SHHHNK
ARGHH!!
DIANA!
IT'S OKAY, SUPERMAN. GODS DON'T DIE SO EASILY.
THEY DON'T DIE. BUT THEY DO FADE.
COME. LET US SPEAK TO THE QURAC GOVERNMENT ABOUT A LASTING PEACE. LET US ENSURE THIS WAR GOD FADES.
DO GODS FEEL PAIN?
NOT AS MORTALS DO. BUT YOU PIN A GOD TO THE GROUND BY DRIVING A SWORD THROUGH HIS SPINAL COLUMN AND I IMAGINE IT STINGS A BIT.
THIS. THIS IS WHY I FEAR THE AMAZON AND THE SUPERMAN TOGETHER.
HE COULD NOT DO THIS ALONE. BUT THE PRINCESS DOES NOT HAVE HIS RESTRAINT.
SHE WILL DO WHAT HE CAN'T.
AND IF SHE TAKES AWAY HIS RESTRAINT...
THE WORLD COULD NOT FIGHT AGAINST THAT
AND IN A WORLD THAT CANNOT FIGHT, WHAT WOULD I BECOME?
PONIES...

PART FOUR

Jheremy Raapack Tom Derenick Artists

Mico Suayan & **David Lopez** and **Santi Casas** of **Ikari Studio** Cover

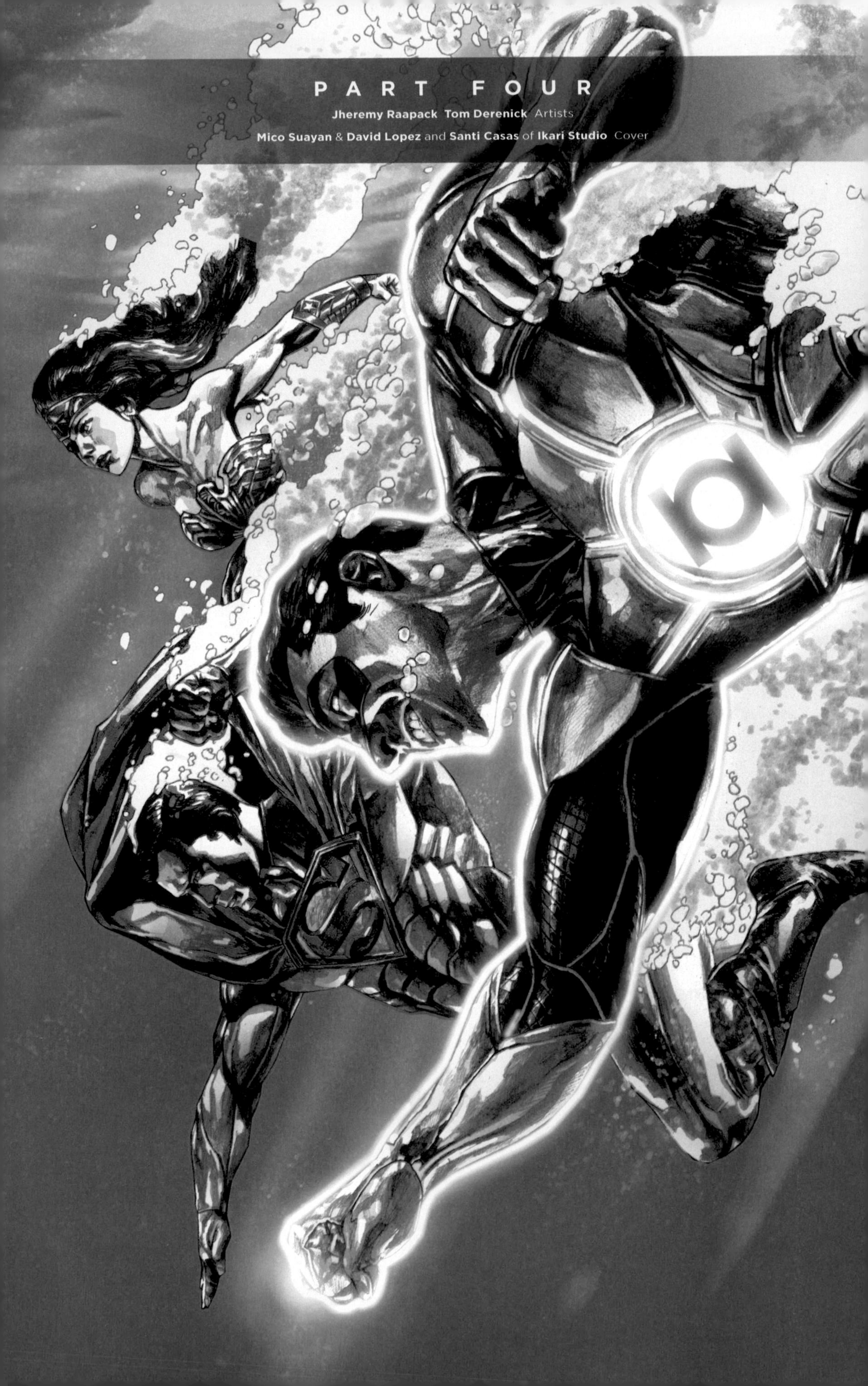

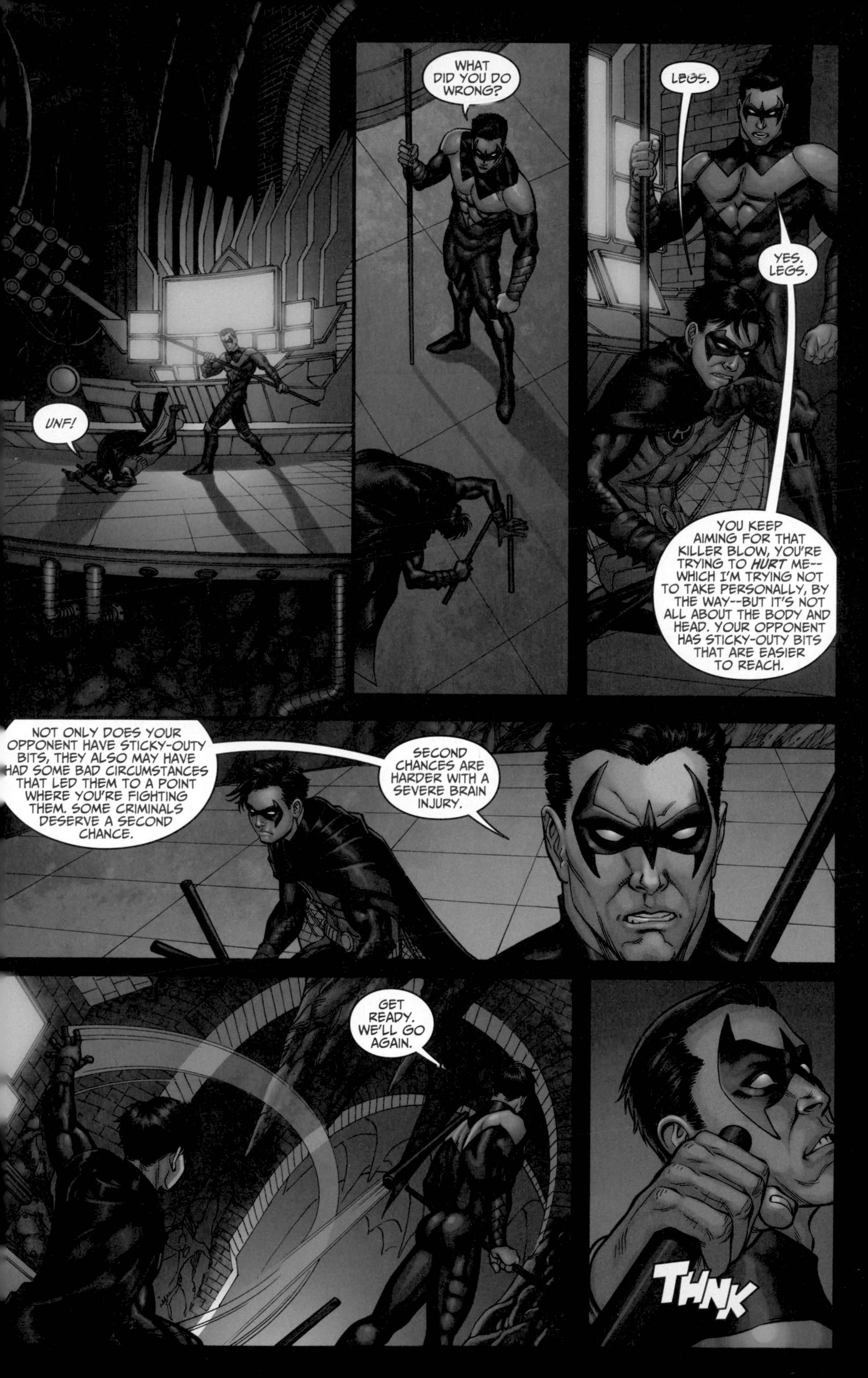
UNF!
WHAT DID YOU DO WRONG?
LEGS.
YES. LEGS.
YOU KEEP AIMING FOR THAT KILLER BLOW, YOU'RE TRYING TO *HURT* ME--WHICH I'M TRYING NOT TO TAKE PERSONALLY, BY THE WAY--BUT IT'S NOT ALL ABOUT THE BODY AND HEAD. YOUR OPPONENT HAS STICKY-OUTY BITS THAT ARE EASIER TO REACH.
NOT ONLY DOES YOUR OPPONENT HAVE STICKY-OUTY BITS, THEY ALSO MAY HAVE HAD SOME BAD CIRCUMSTANCES THAT LED THEM TO A POINT WHERE YOU'RE FIGHTING THEM. SOME CRIMINALS DESERVE A SECOND CHANCE.
SECOND CHANCES ARE HARDER WITH A SEVERE BRAIN INJURY.
GET READY. WE'LL GO AGAIN.
THNK

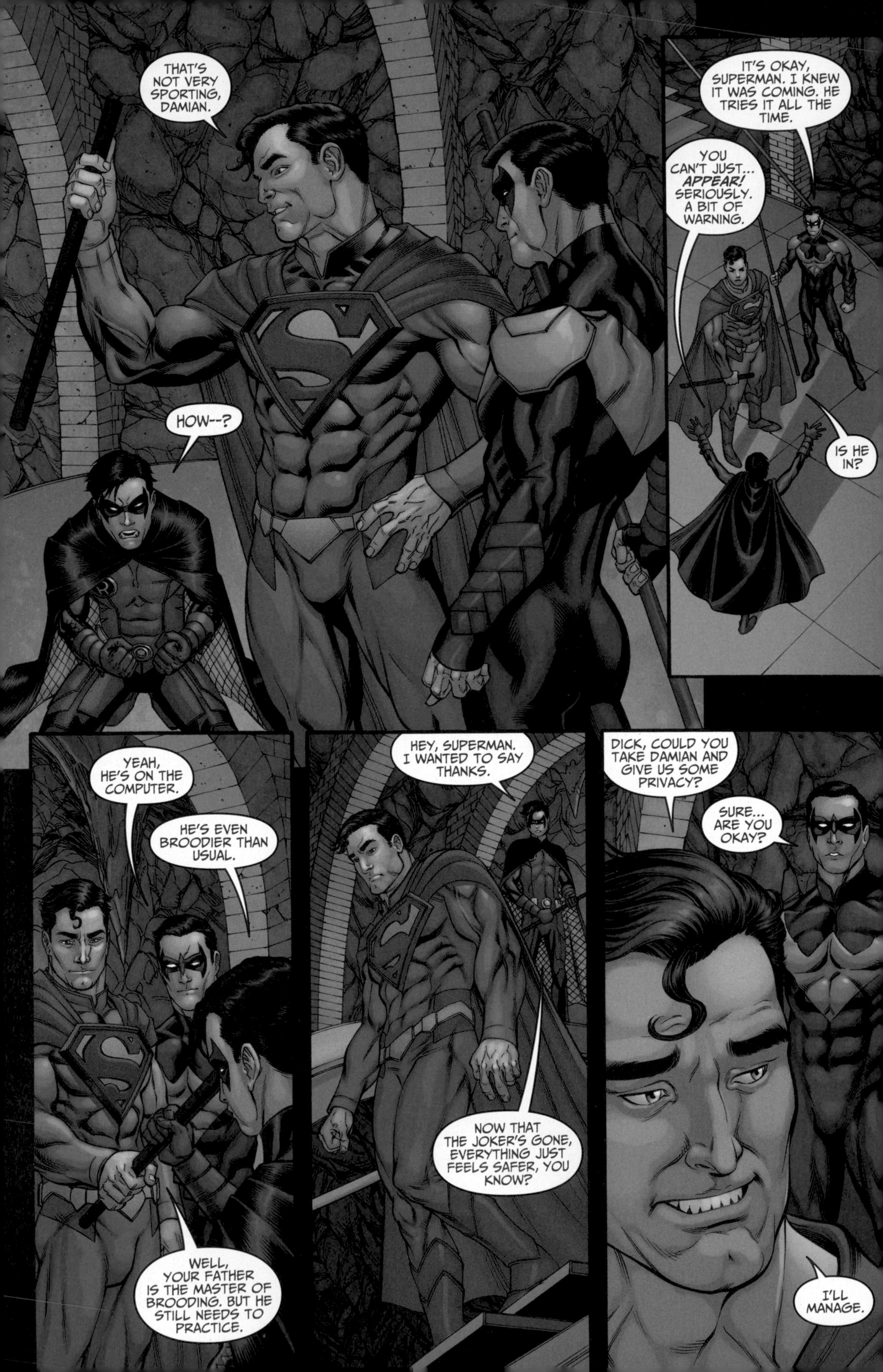
THAT'S NOT VERY SPORTING, DAMIAN.
HOW--?
IT'S OKAY, SUPERMAN. I KNEW IT WAS COMING. HE TRIES IT ALL THE TIME.
YOU CAN'T JUST... APPEAR! SERIOUSLY. A BIT OF WARNING.
IS HE IN?
YEAH, HE'S ON THE COMPUTER.
HE'S EVEN BROODIER THAN USUAL.
WELL, YOUR FATHER IS THE MASTER OF BROODING. BUT HE STILL NEEDS TO PRACTICE.
HEY, SUPERMAN. I WANTED TO SAY THANKS.
NOW THAT THE JOKER'S GONE, EVERYTHING JUST FEELS SAFER, YOU KNOW?
DICK, COULD YOU TAKE DAMIAN AND GIVE US SOME PRIVACY?
SURE... ARE YOU OKAY?
I'LL MANAGE.

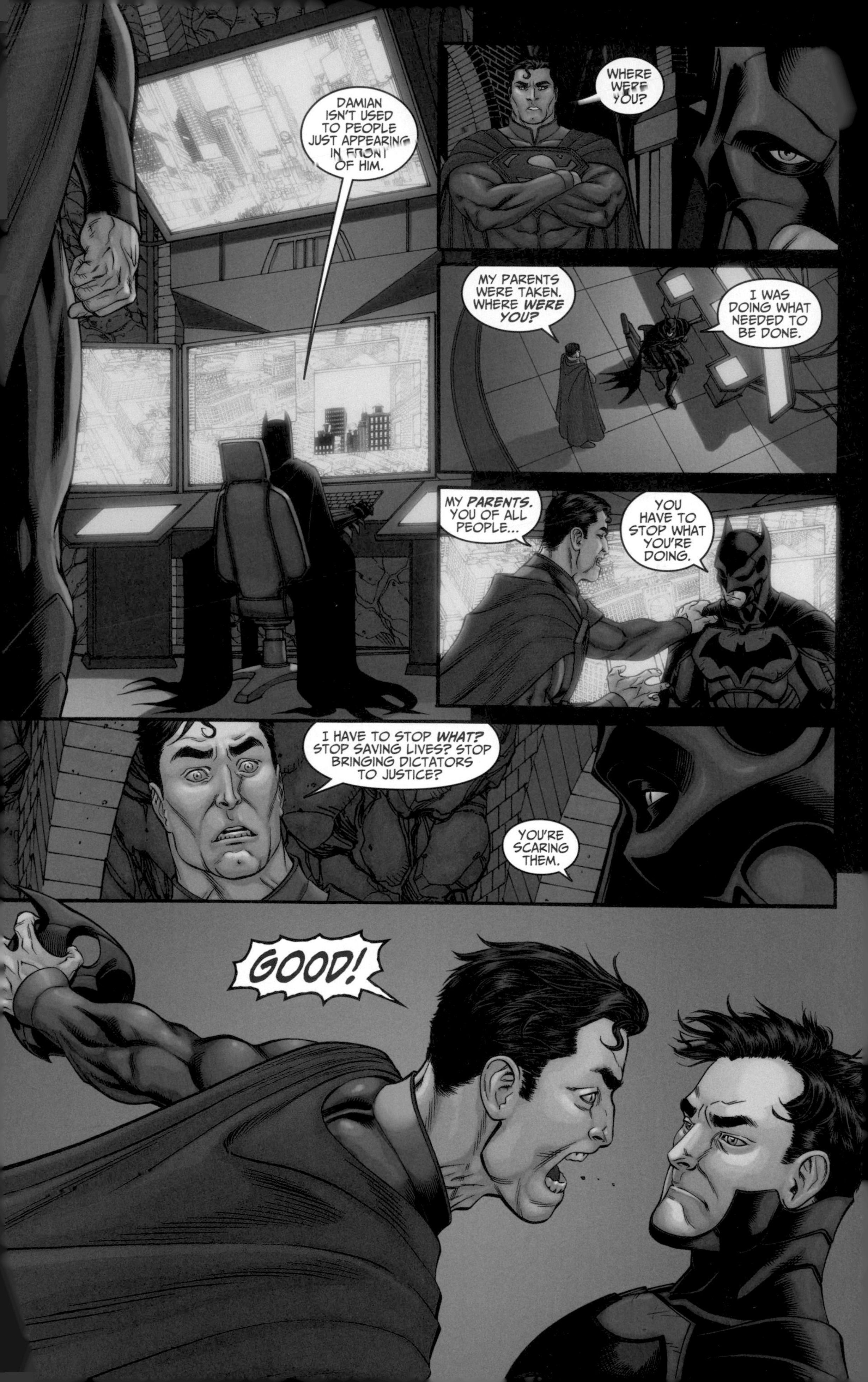
DAMIAN ISN'T USED TO PEOPLE JUST APPEARING IN FRONT OF HIM.
WHERE WERE YOU?
MY PARENTS WERE TAKEN. WHERE *WERE YOU?*
I WAS DOING WHAT NEEDED TO BE DONE.
MY *PARENTS.* YOU OF ALL PEOPLE...
YOU HAVE TO STOP WHAT YOU'RE DOING.
I HAVE TO STOP *WHAT?* STOP SAVING LIVES? STOP BRINGING DICTATORS TO JUSTICE?
YOU'RE SCARING THEM.
GOOD!

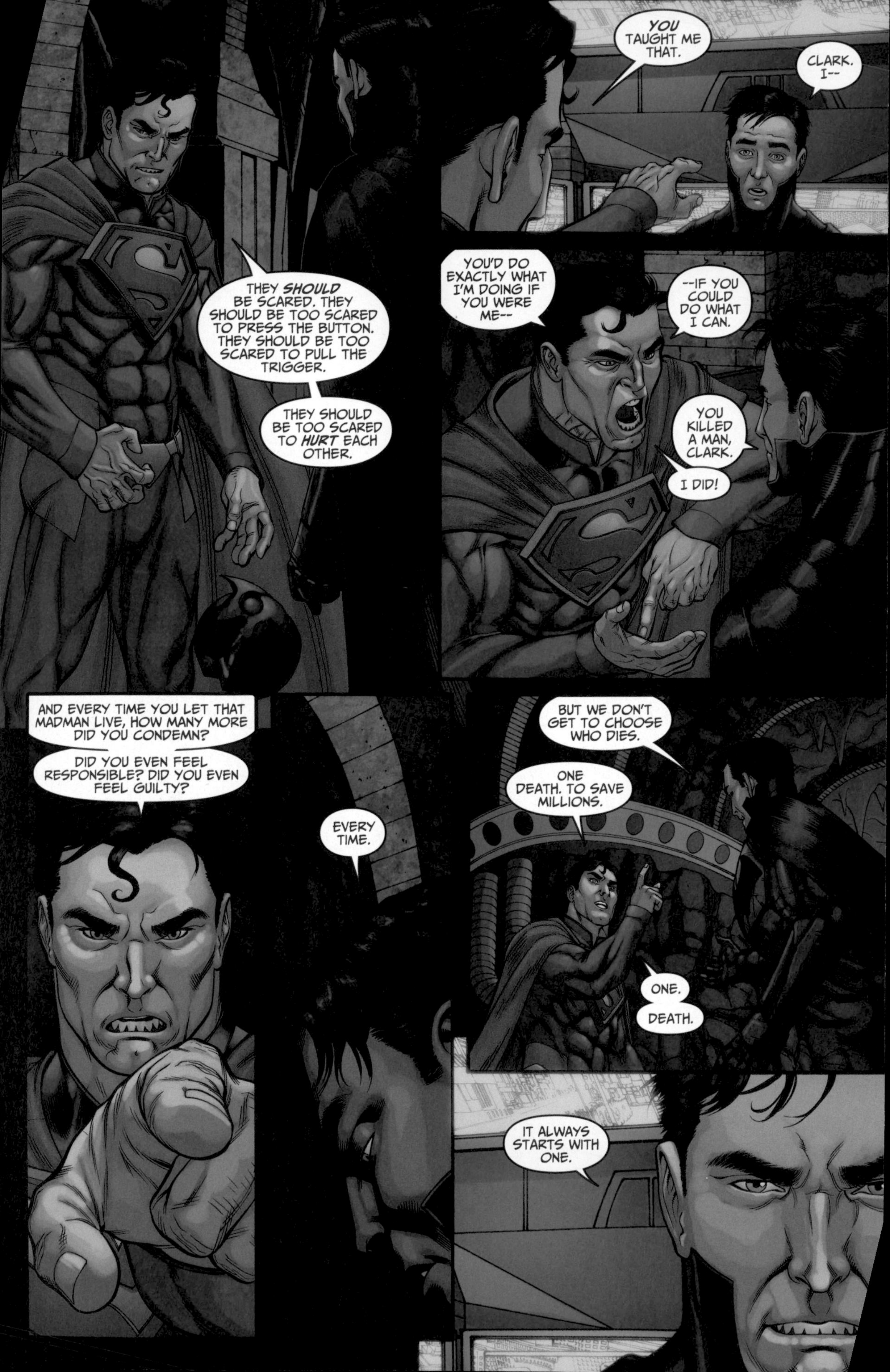

YOU TAUGHT ME THAT.
CLARK. I--
THEY SHOULD BE SCARED. THEY SHOULD BE TOO SCARED TO PRESS THE BUTTON. THEY SHOULD BE TOO SCARED TO PULL THE TRIGGER.
THEY SHOULD BE TOO SCARED TO HURT EACH OTHER.
YOU'D DO EXACTLY WHAT I'M DOING IF YOU WERE ME--
--IF YOU COULD DO WHAT I CAN.
YOU KILLED A MAN, CLARK.
I DID!
AND EVERY TIME YOU LET THAT MADMAN LIVE, HOW MANY MORE DID YOU CONDEMN?
DID YOU EVEN FEEL RESPONSIBLE? DID YOU EVEN FEEL GUILTY?
EVERY TIME.
BUT WE DON'T GET TO CHOOSE WHO DIES.
ONE DEATH. TO SAVE MILLIONS.
ONE.
DEATH.
IT ALWAYS STARTS WITH ONE.

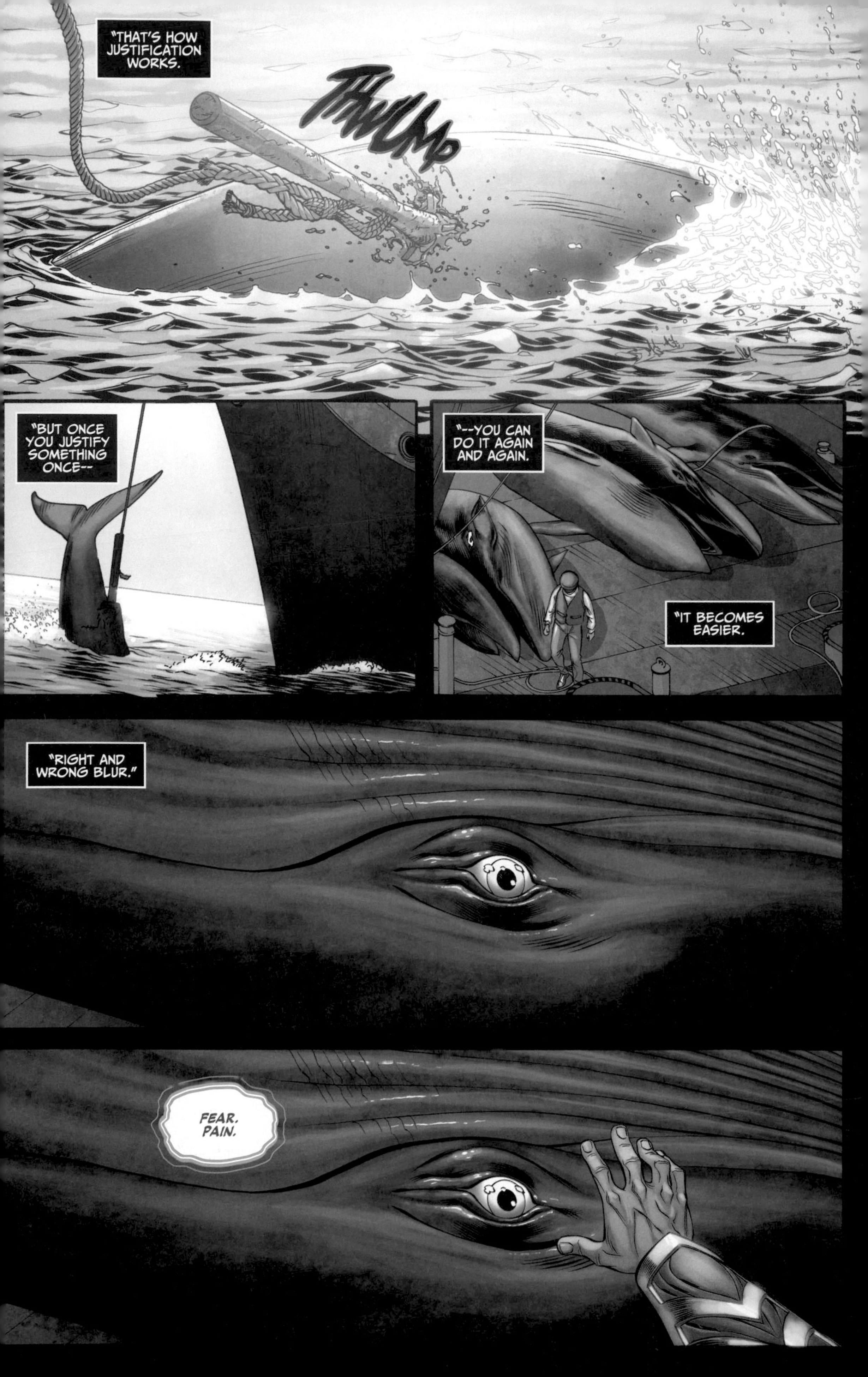
"THAT'S HOW JUSTIFICATION WORKS.
THWUMP
"BUT ONCE YOU JUSTIFY SOMETHING ONCE--
"--YOU CAN DO IT AGAIN AND AGAIN.
"IT BECOMES EASIER.
"RIGHT AND WRONG BLUR."
FEAR. PAIN.

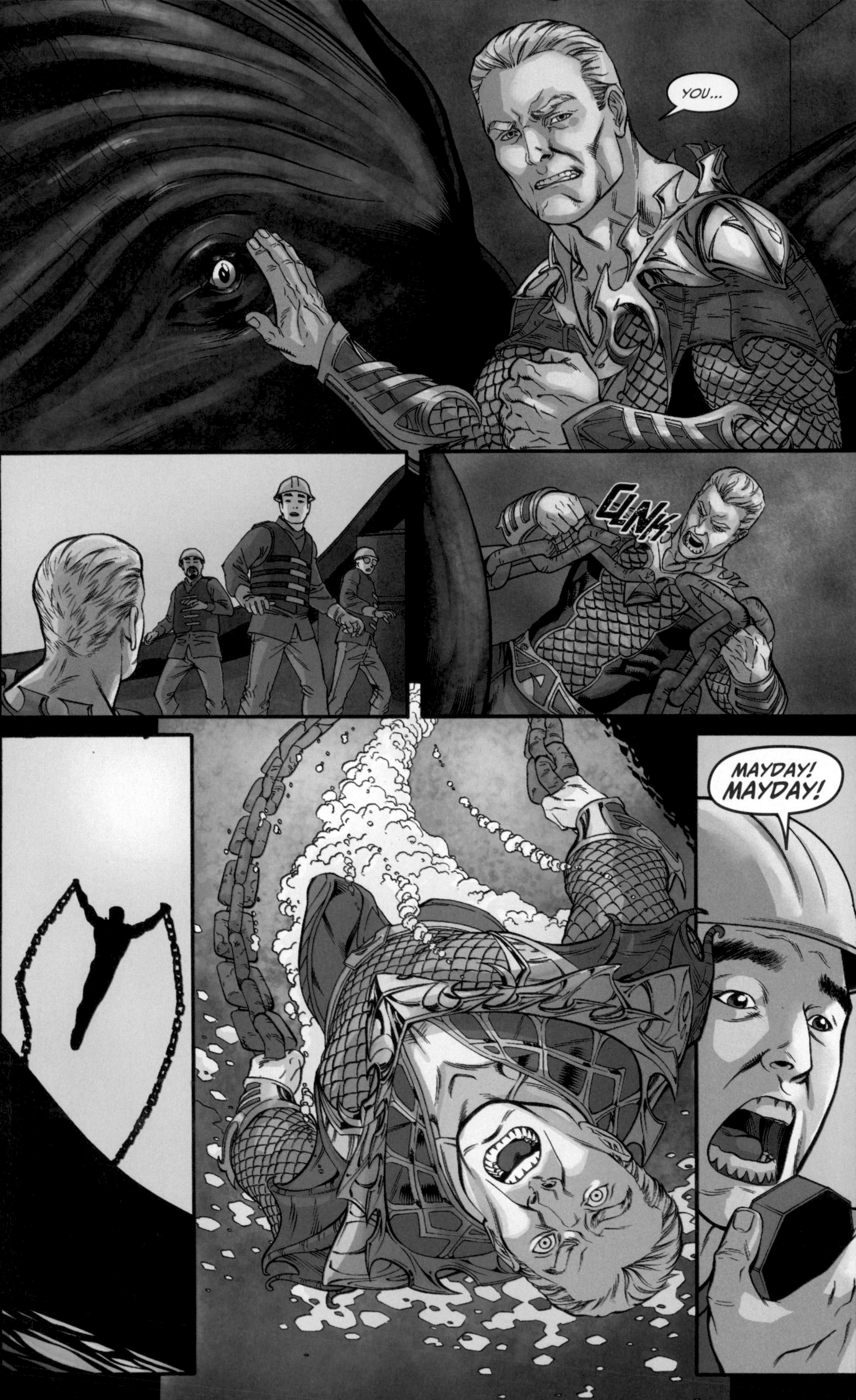
YOU...
CLNK
MAYDAY! MAYDAY!

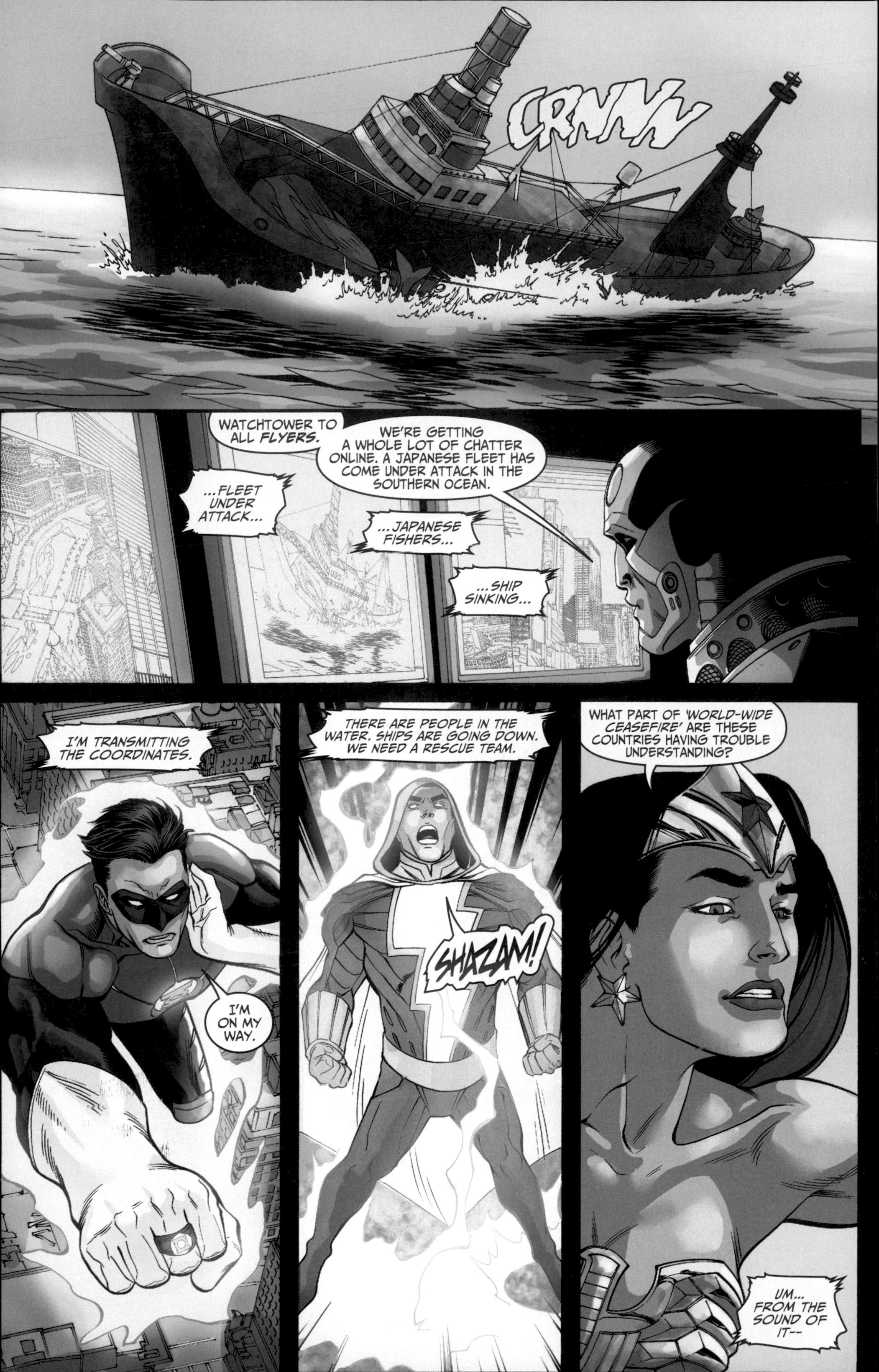
CRNNN
WATCHTOWER TO ALL FLYERS.
WE'RE GETTING A WHOLE LOT OF CHATTER ONLINE. A JAPANESE FLEET HAS COME UNDER ATTACK IN THE SOUTHERN OCEAN.
...FLEET UNDER ATTACK...
...JAPANESE FISHERS...
...SHIP SINKING...
I'M TRANSMITTING THE COORDINATES.
I'M ON MY WAY.
THERE ARE PEOPLE IN THE WATER. SHIPS ARE GOING DOWN. WE NEED A RESCUE TEAM.
SHAZAM!
WHAT PART OF 'WORLD-WIDE CEASEFIRE' ARE THESE COUNTRIES HAVING TROUBLE UNDERSTANDING?
UM... FROM THE SOUND OF IT--

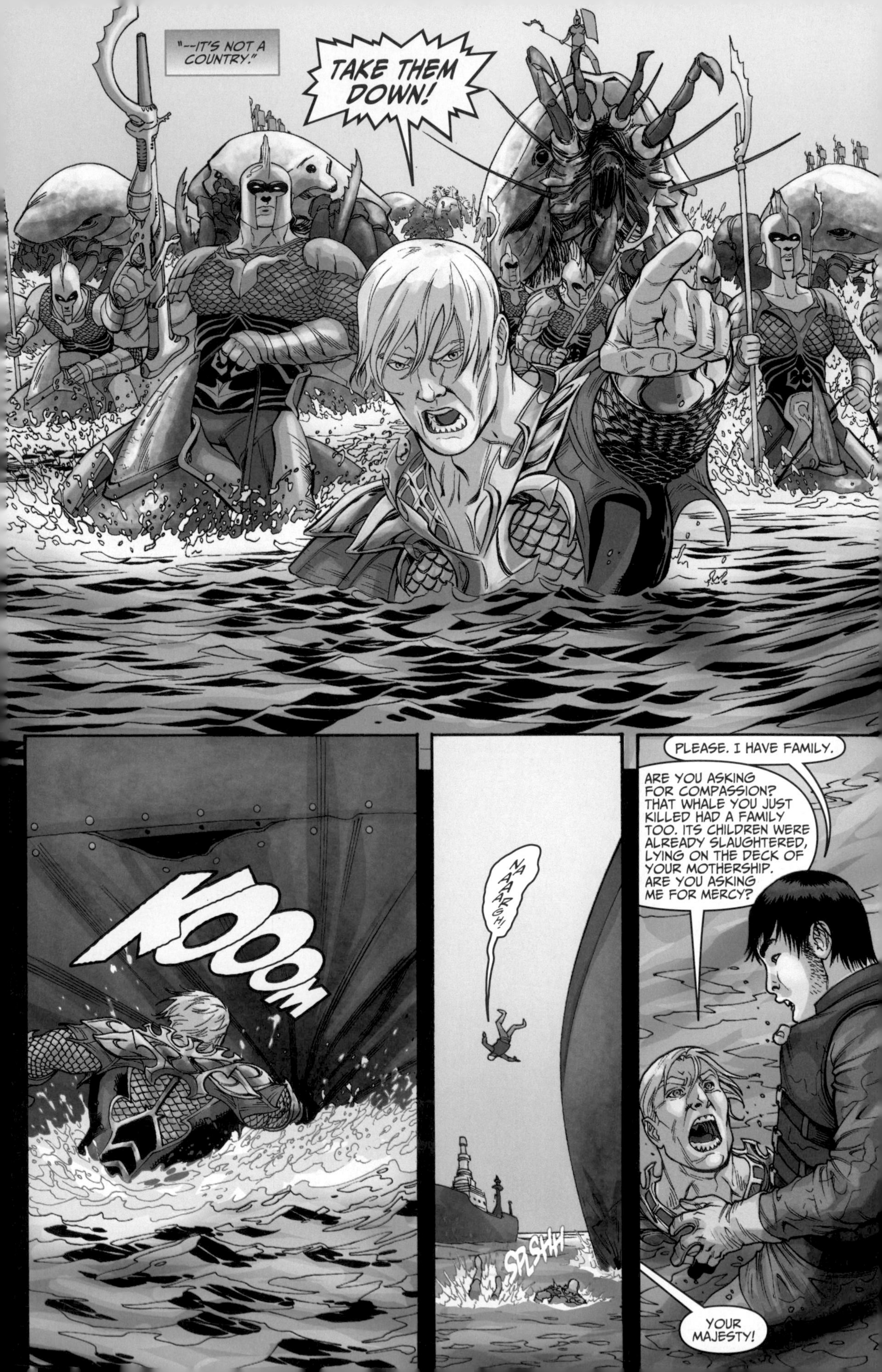
"--IT'S NOT A COUNTRY."
TAKE THEM DOWN!
KOOOM
NAAAARGH!
SPLSHH
PLEASE. I HAVE FAMILY.
ARE YOU ASKING FOR COMPASSION? THAT WHALE YOU JUST KILLED HAD A FAMILY TOO. ITS CHILDREN WERE ALREADY SLAUGHTERED, LYING ON THE DECK OF YOUR MOTHERSHIP. ARE YOU ASKING ME FOR MERCY?
YOUR MAJESTY!

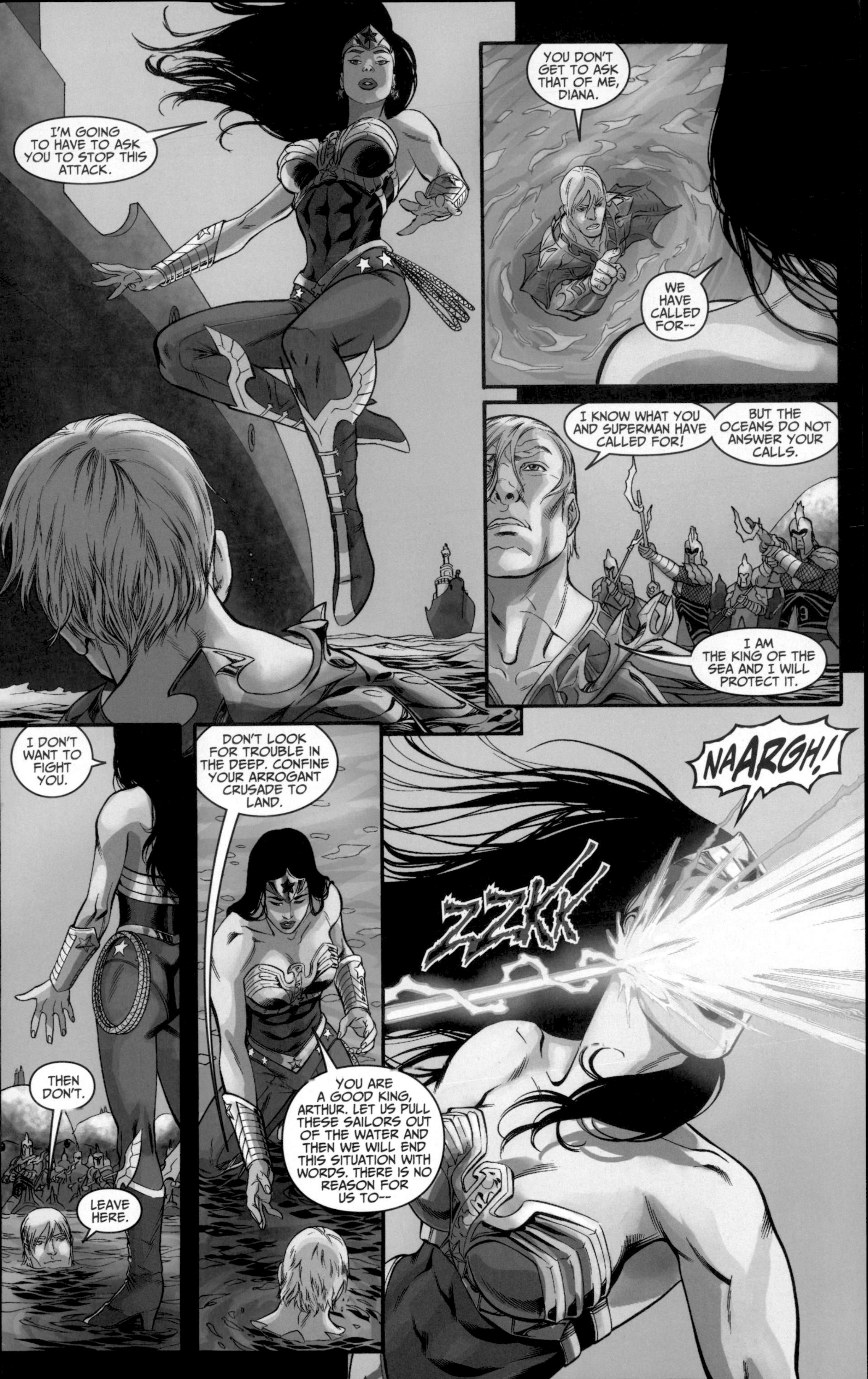

I'M GOING TO HAVE TO ASK YOU TO STOP THIS ATTACK.
YOU DON'T GET TO ASK THAT OF ME, DIANA.
WE HAVE CALLED FOR--
I KNOW WHAT YOU AND SUPERMAN HAVE CALLED FOR!
BUT THE OCEANS DO NOT ANSWER YOUR CALLS.
I AM THE KING OF THE SEA AND I WILL PROTECT IT.
I DON'T WANT TO FIGHT YOU.
THEN DON'T.
LEAVE HERE.
DON'T LOOK FOR TROUBLE IN THE DEEP. CONFINE YOUR ARROGANT CRUSADE TO LAND.
YOU ARE A GOOD KING, ARTHUR. LET US PULL THESE SAILORS OUT OF THE WATER AND THEN WE WILL END THIS SITUATION WITH WORDS. THERE IS NO REASON FOR US TO--
NAARGH!
ZZKK

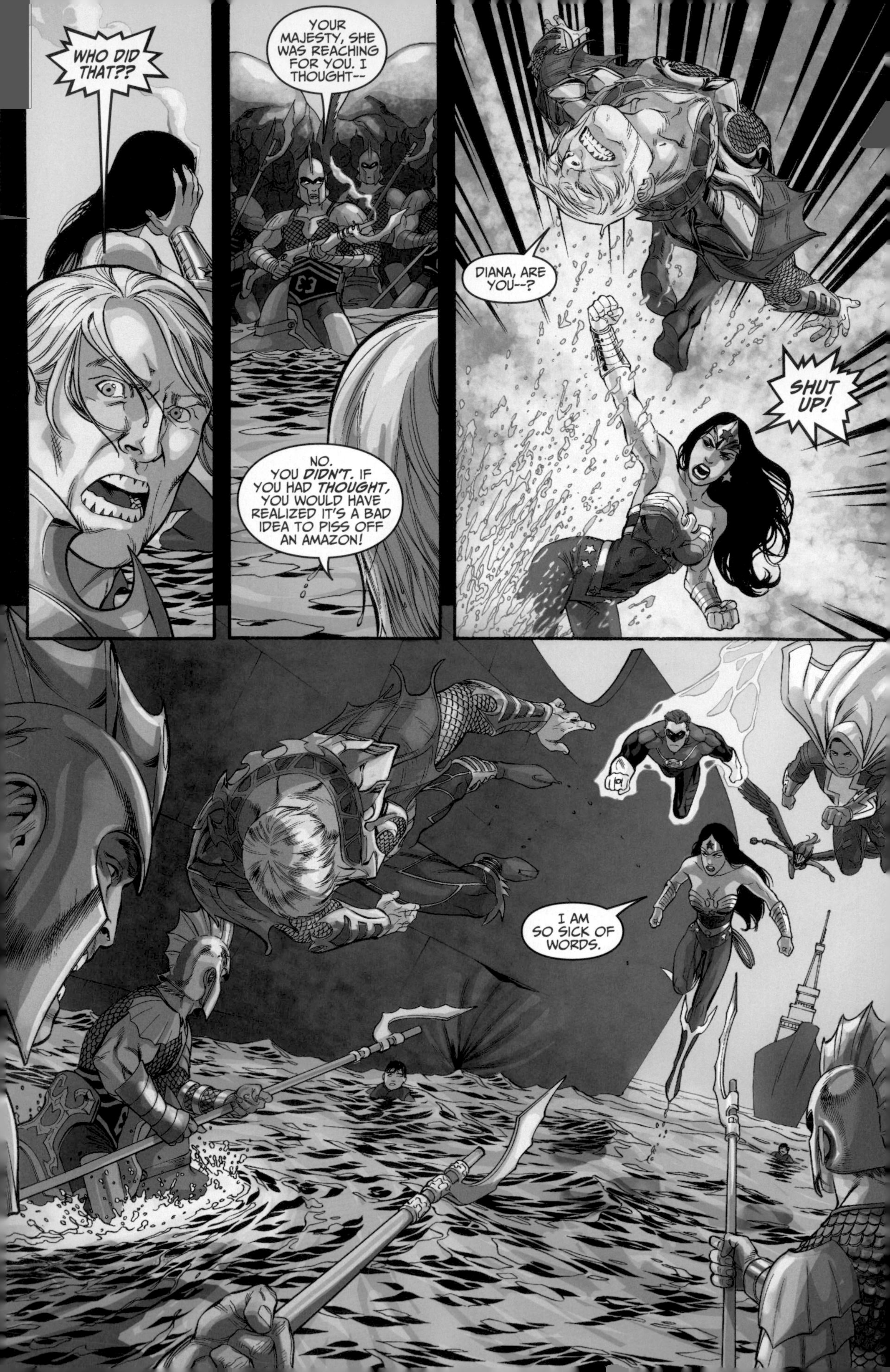
WHO DID THAT??
YOUR MAJESTY, SHE WAS REACHING FOR YOU. I THOUGHT--
NO. YOU *DIDN'T.* IF YOU HAD *THOUGHT,* YOU WOULD HAVE REALIZED IT'S A BAD IDEA TO PISS OFF AN AMAZON!
DIANA, ARE YOU--?
SHUT UP!
I AM SO SICK OF WORDS.

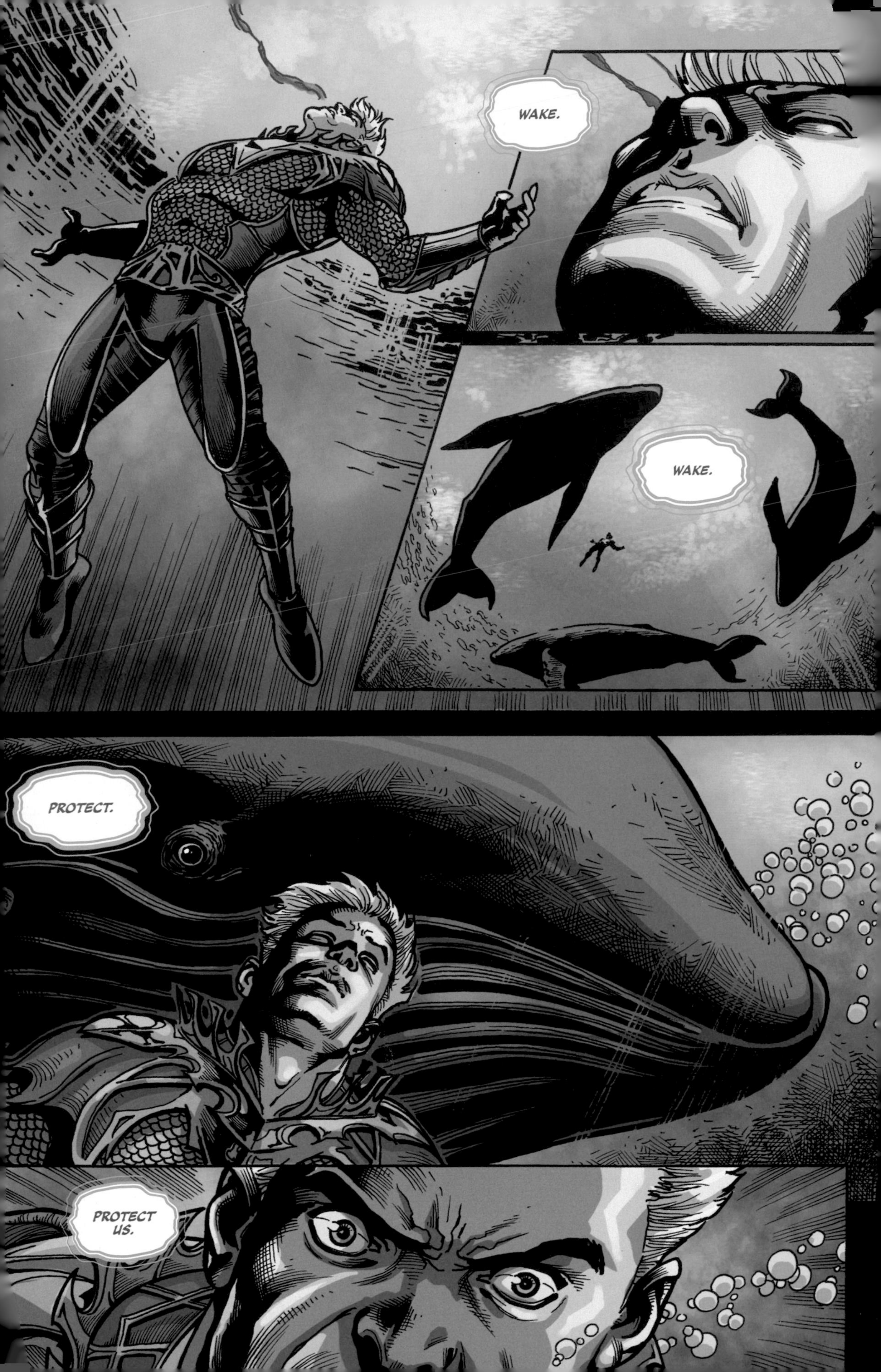
WAKE.
WAKE.
PROTECT.
PROTECT US.

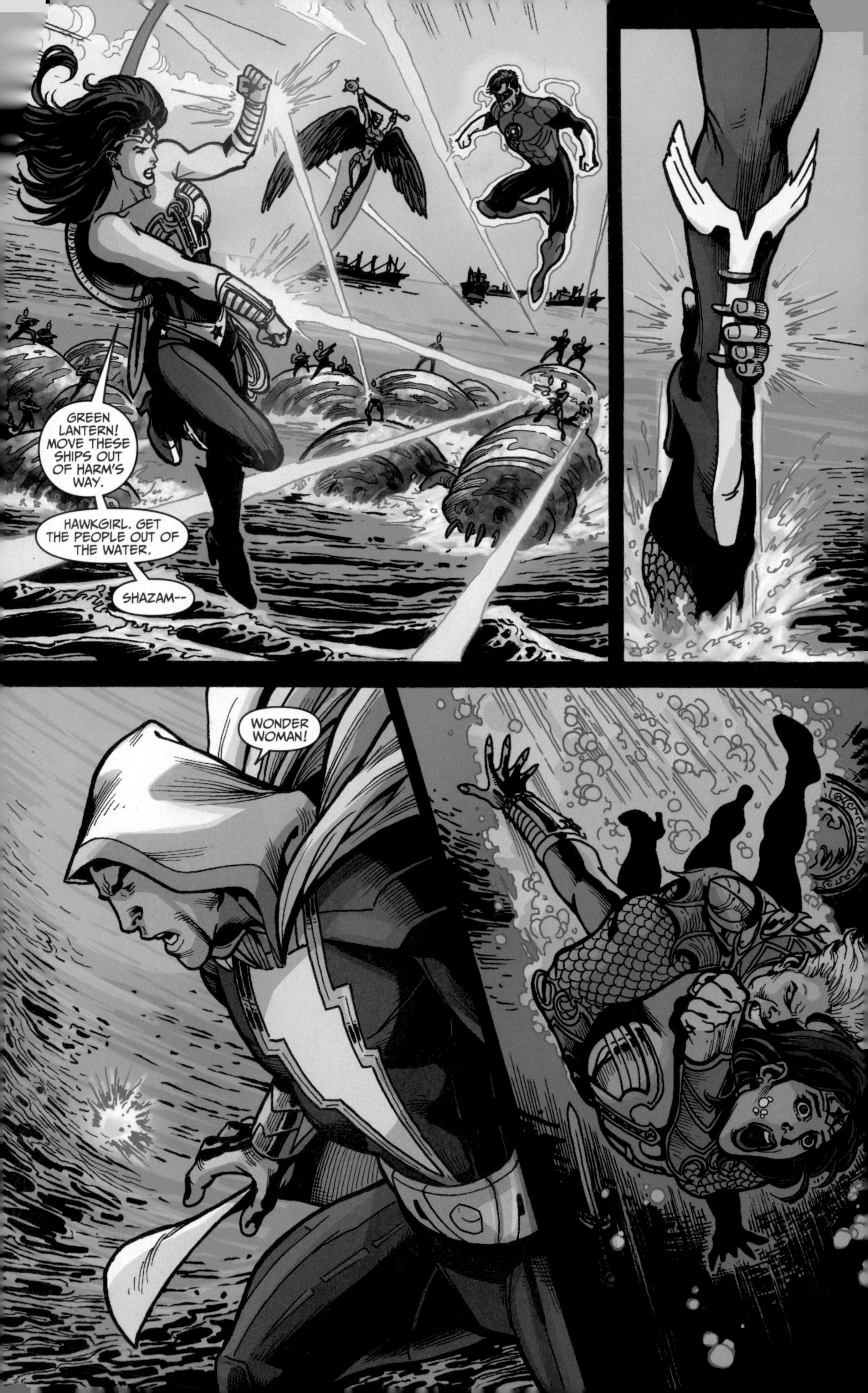
GREEN LANTERN! MOVE THESE SHIPS OUT OF HARM'S WAY.
HAWKGIRL. GET THE PEOPLE OUT OF THE WATER.
SHAZAM--
WONDER WOMAN!

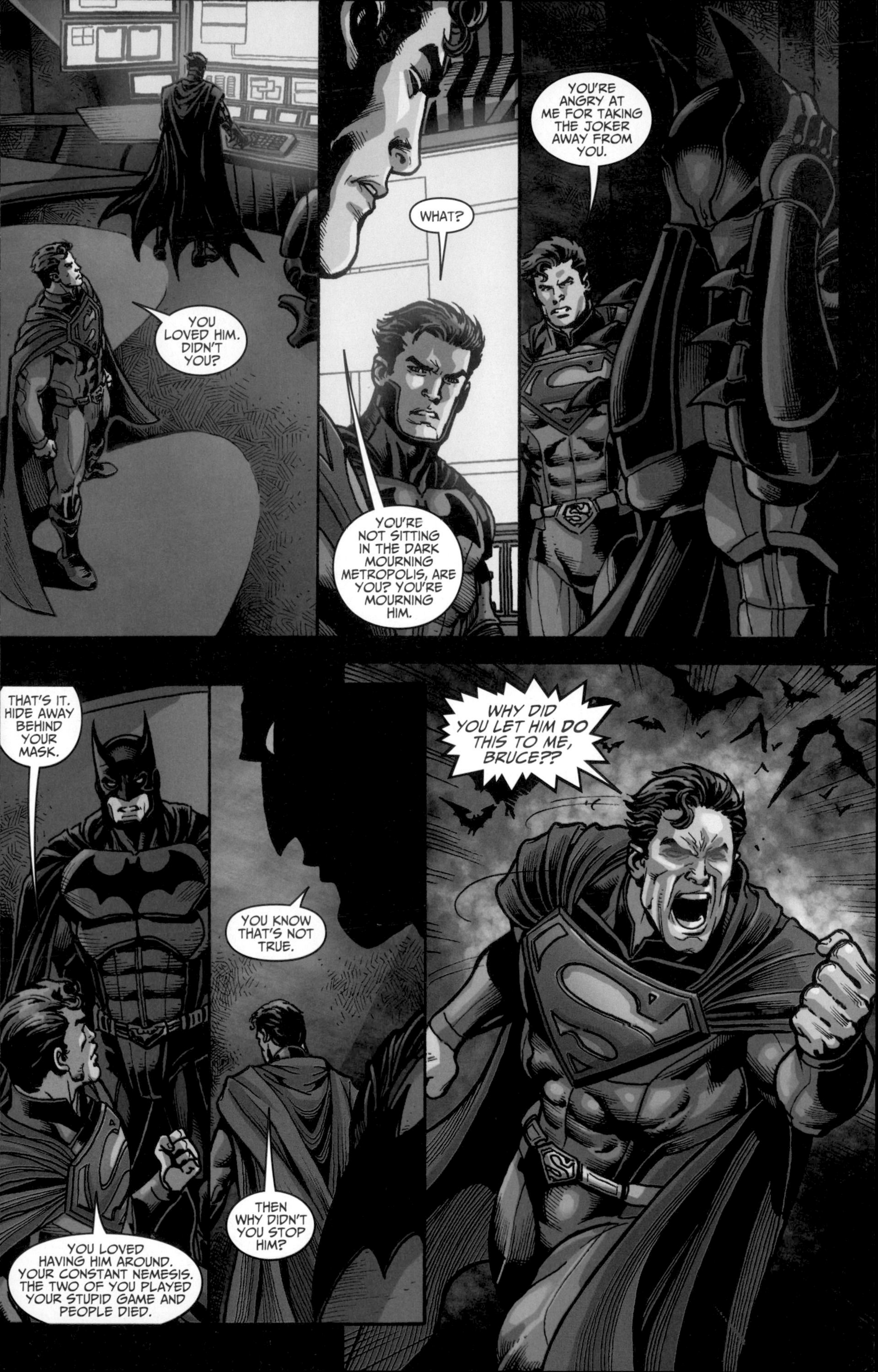
YOU LOVED HIM. DIDN'T YOU?
WHAT?
YOU'RE NOT SITTING IN THE DARK MOURNING METROPOLIS, ARE YOU? YOU'RE MOURNING HIM.
YOU'RE ANGRY AT ME FOR TAKING THE JOKER AWAY FROM YOU.
THAT'S IT. HIDE AWAY BEHIND YOUR MASK.
YOU LOVED HAVING HIM AROUND. YOUR CONSTANT NEMESIS. THE TWO OF YOU PLAYED YOUR STUPID GAME AND PEOPLE DIED.
YOU KNOW THAT'S NOT TRUE.
THEN WHY DIDN'T YOU STOP HIM?
WHY DID YOU LET HIM DO THIS TO ME, BRUCE??

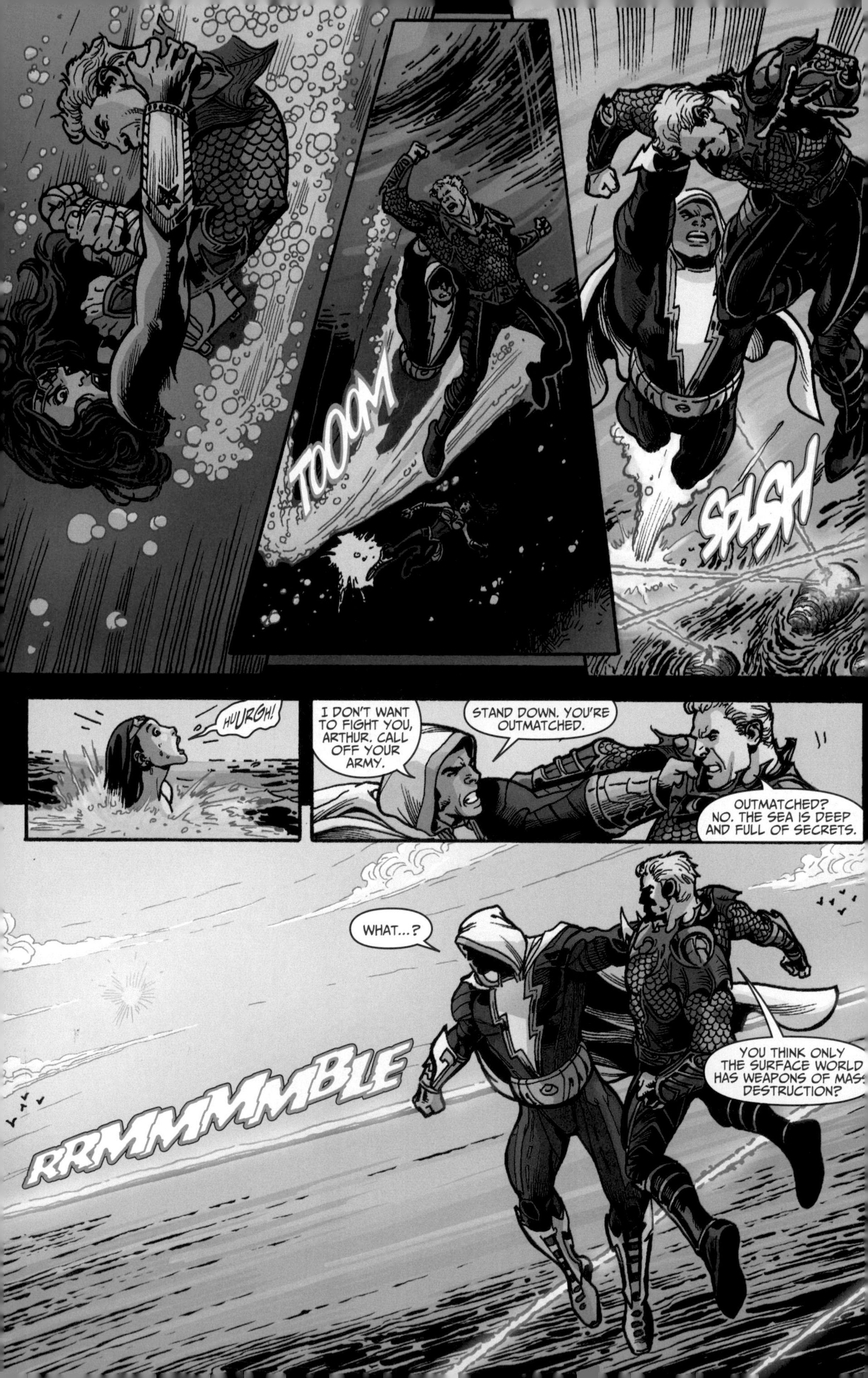
TOOOM
SPLSH
HUURGH!
I DON'T WANT TO FIGHT YOU, ARTHUR. CALL OFF YOUR ARMY.
STAND DOWN. YOU'RE OUTMATCHED.
OUTMATCHED? NO. THE SEA IS DEEP AND FULL OF SECRETS.
WHAT...?
RRMMMMMBLE
YOU THINK ONLY THE SURFACE WORLD HAS WEAPONS OF MASS DESTRUCTION?

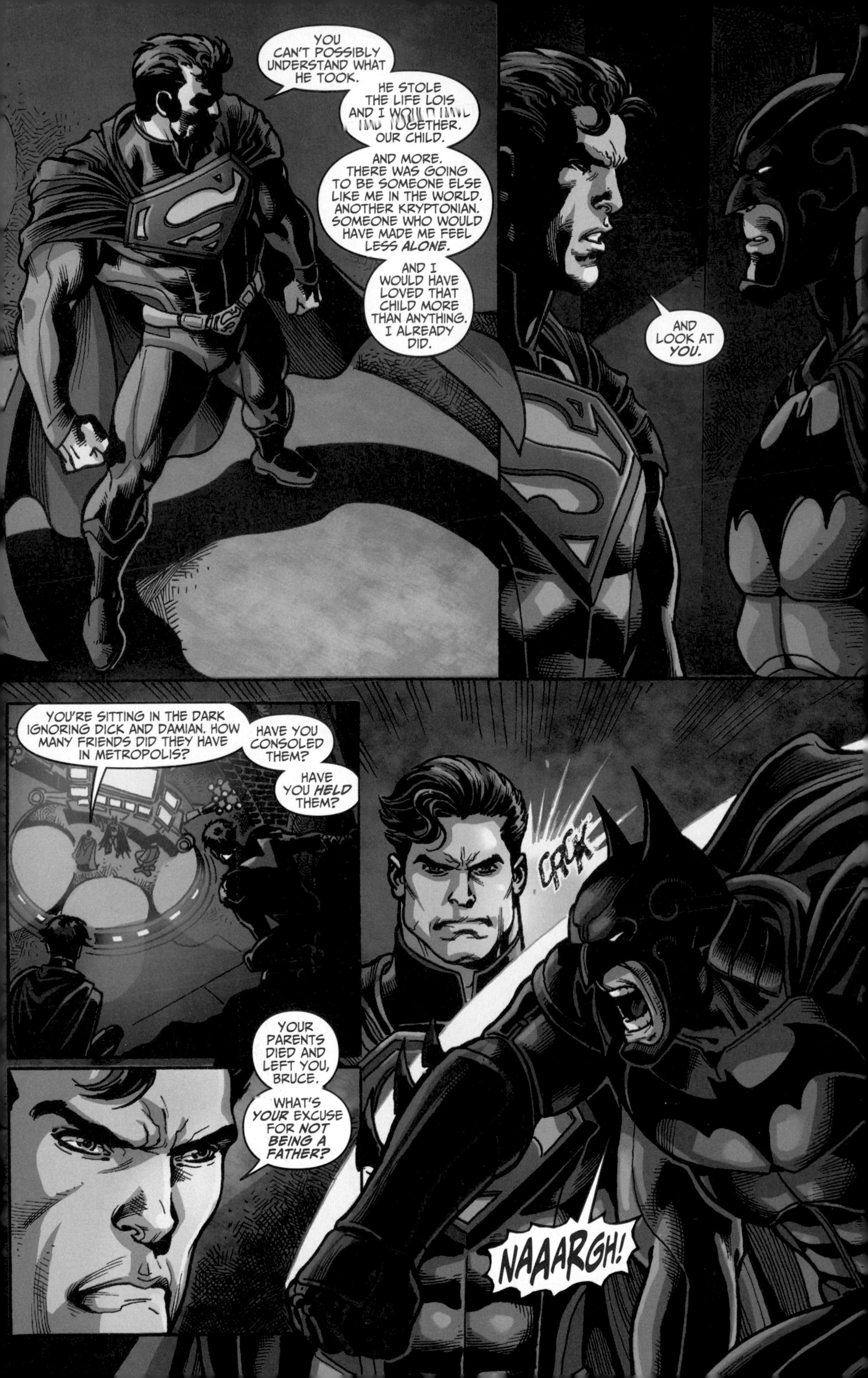

YOU CAN'T POSSIBLY UNDERSTAND WHAT HE TOOK.
HE STOLE THE LIFE LOIS AND I WOULD HAVE HAD TOGETHER. OUR CHILD.
AND MORE. THERE WAS GOING TO BE SOMEONE ELSE LIKE ME IN THE WORLD. ANOTHER KRYPTONIAN. SOMEONE WHO WOULD HAVE MADE ME FEEL LESS *ALONE*.
AND I WOULD HAVE LOVED THAT CHILD MORE THAN ANYTHING. I ALREADY DID.
AND LOOK AT *YOU*.
YOU'RE SITTING IN THE DARK IGNORING DICK AND DAMIAN. HOW MANY FRIENDS DID THEY HAVE IN METROPOLIS?
HAVE YOU CONSOLED THEM?
HAVE YOU *HELD* THEM?
YOUR PARENTS DIED AND LEFT YOU, BRUCE.
WHAT'S *YOUR* EXCUSE FOR *NOT BEING A FATHER?*
CRACK
NAAARGH!

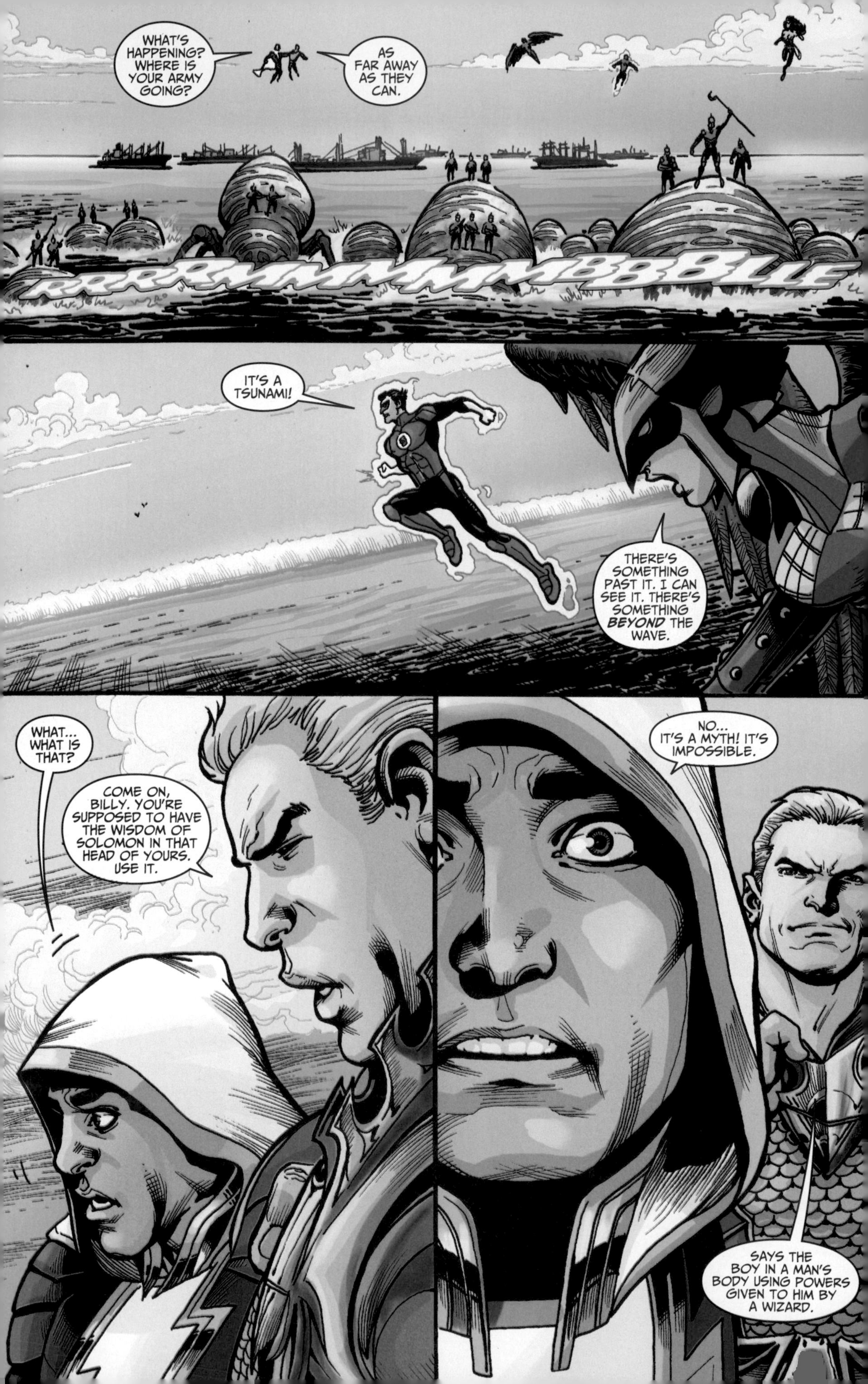
WHAT'S HAPPENING? WHERE IS YOUR ARMY GOING?
AS FAR AWAY AS THEY CAN.
RRRRMMMMMMBBBLLE
IT'S A TSUNAMI!
THERE'S SOMETHING PAST IT. I CAN SEE IT. THERE'S SOMETHING BEYOND THE WAVE.
WHAT... WHAT IS THAT?
COME ON, BILLY. YOU'RE SUPPOSED TO HAVE THE WISDOM OF SOLOMON IN THAT HEAD OF YOURS. USE IT.
NO... IT'S A MYTH! IT'S IMPOSSIBLE.
SAYS THE BOY IN A MAN'S BODY USING POWERS GIVEN TO HIM BY A WIZARD.

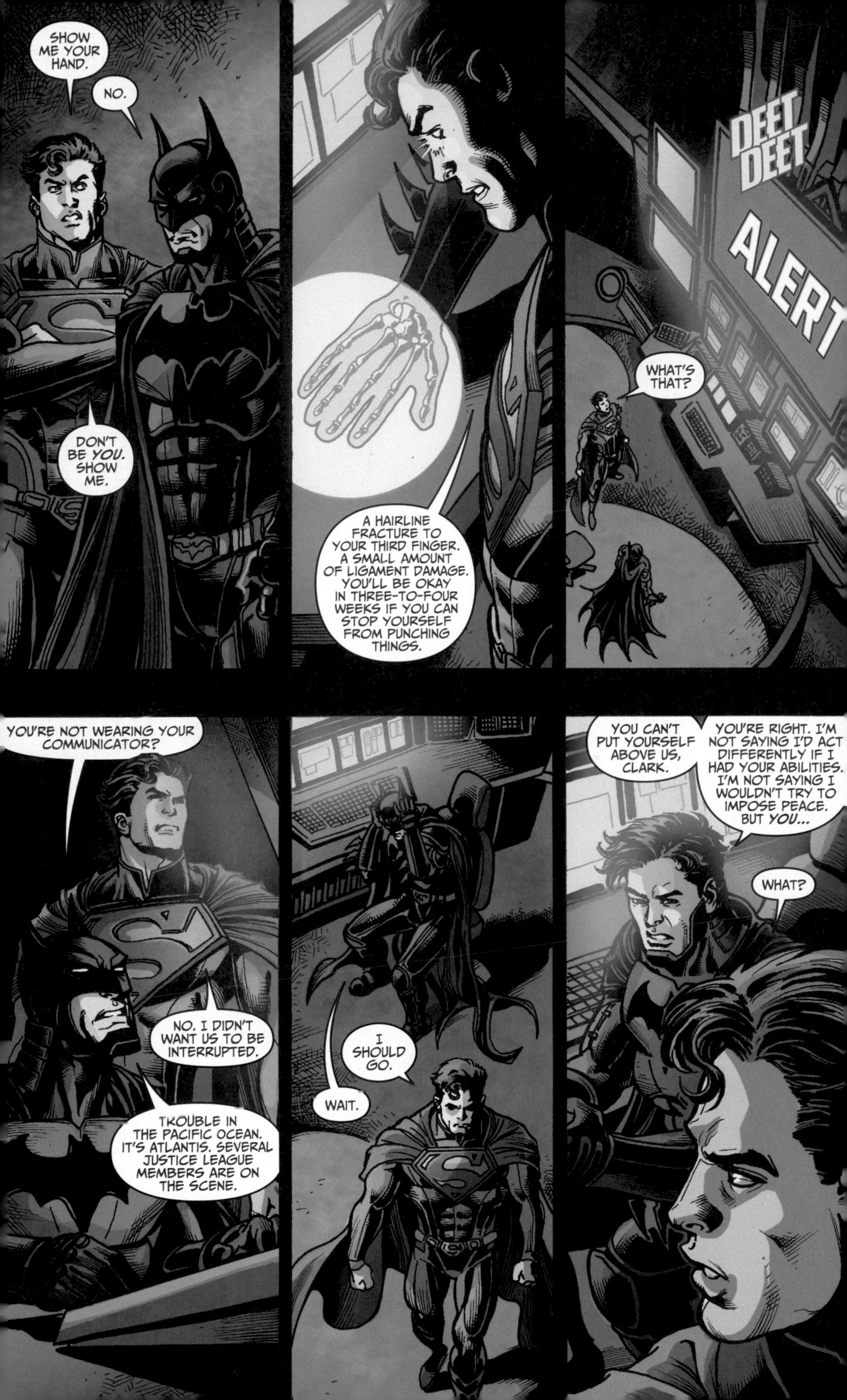
SHOW ME YOUR HAND.
NO.
DON'T BE *YOU*. SHOW ME.
A HAIRLINE FRACTURE TO YOUR THIRD FINGER. A SMALL AMOUNT OF LIGAMENT DAMAGE. YOU'LL BE OKAY IN THREE-TO-FOUR WEEKS IF YOU CAN STOP YOURSELF FROM PUNCHING THINGS.
DEET DEET
ALERT
WHAT'S THAT?
YOU'RE NOT WEARING YOUR COMMUNICATOR?
NO. I DIDN'T WANT US TO BE INTERRUPTED.
TROUBLE IN THE PACIFIC OCEAN. IT'S ATLANTIS. SEVERAL JUSTICE LEAGUE MEMBERS ARE ON THE SCENE.
I SHOULD GO.
WAIT.
YOU CAN'T PUT YOURSELF ABOVE US, CLARK.
YOU'RE RIGHT. I'M NOT SAYING I'D ACT DIFFERENTLY IF I HAD YOUR ABILITIES. I'M NOT SAYING I WOULDN'T TRY TO IMPOSE PEACE. BUT *YOU*...
WHAT?

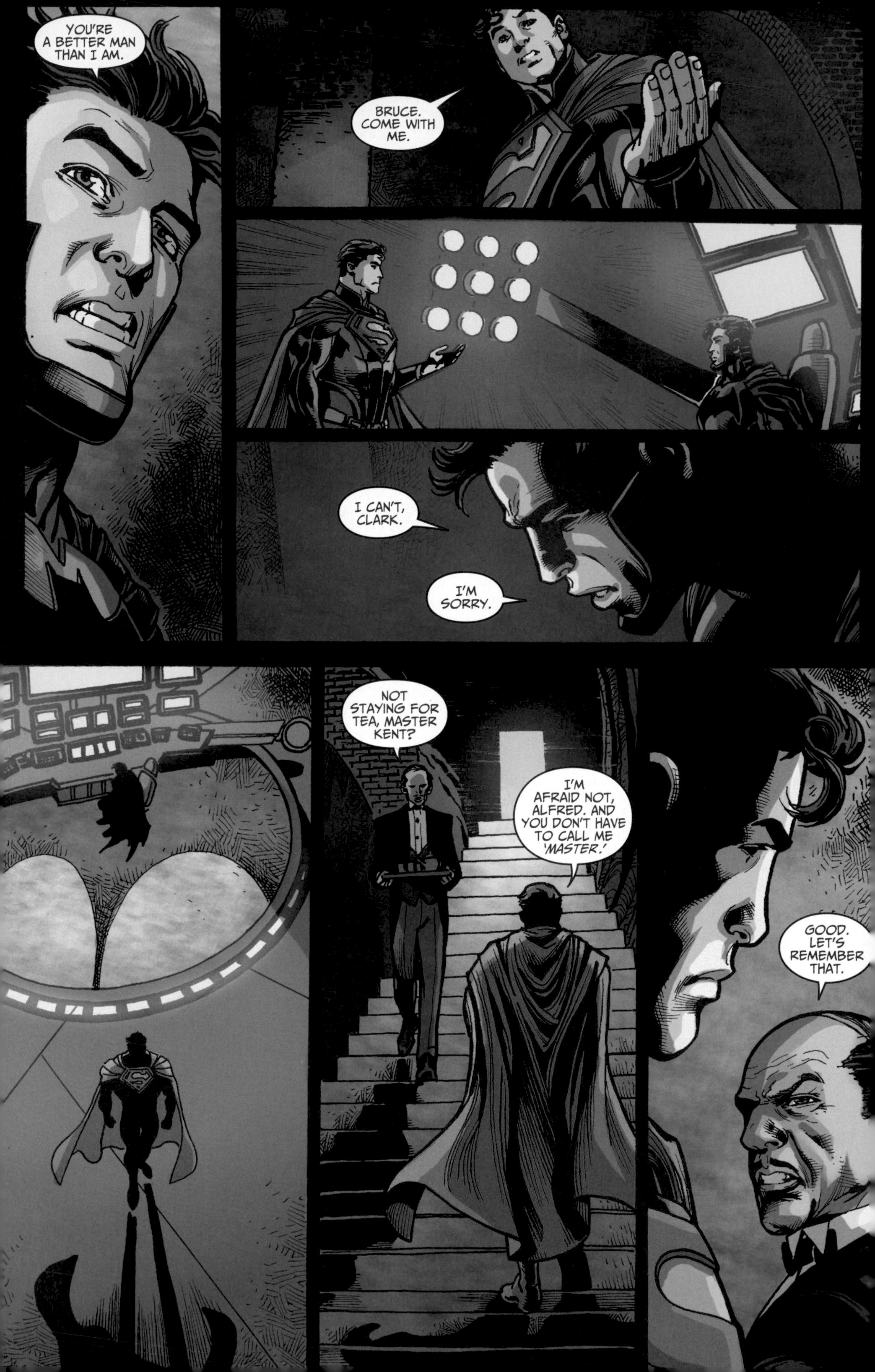
YOU'RE A BETTER MAN THAN I AM.
BRUCE. COME WITH ME.
I CAN'T, CLARK.
I'M SORRY.
NOT STAYING FOR TEA, MASTER KENT?
I'M AFRAID NOT, ALFRED. AND YOU DON'T HAVE TO CALL ME 'MASTER.'
GOOD. LET'S REMEMBER THAT.

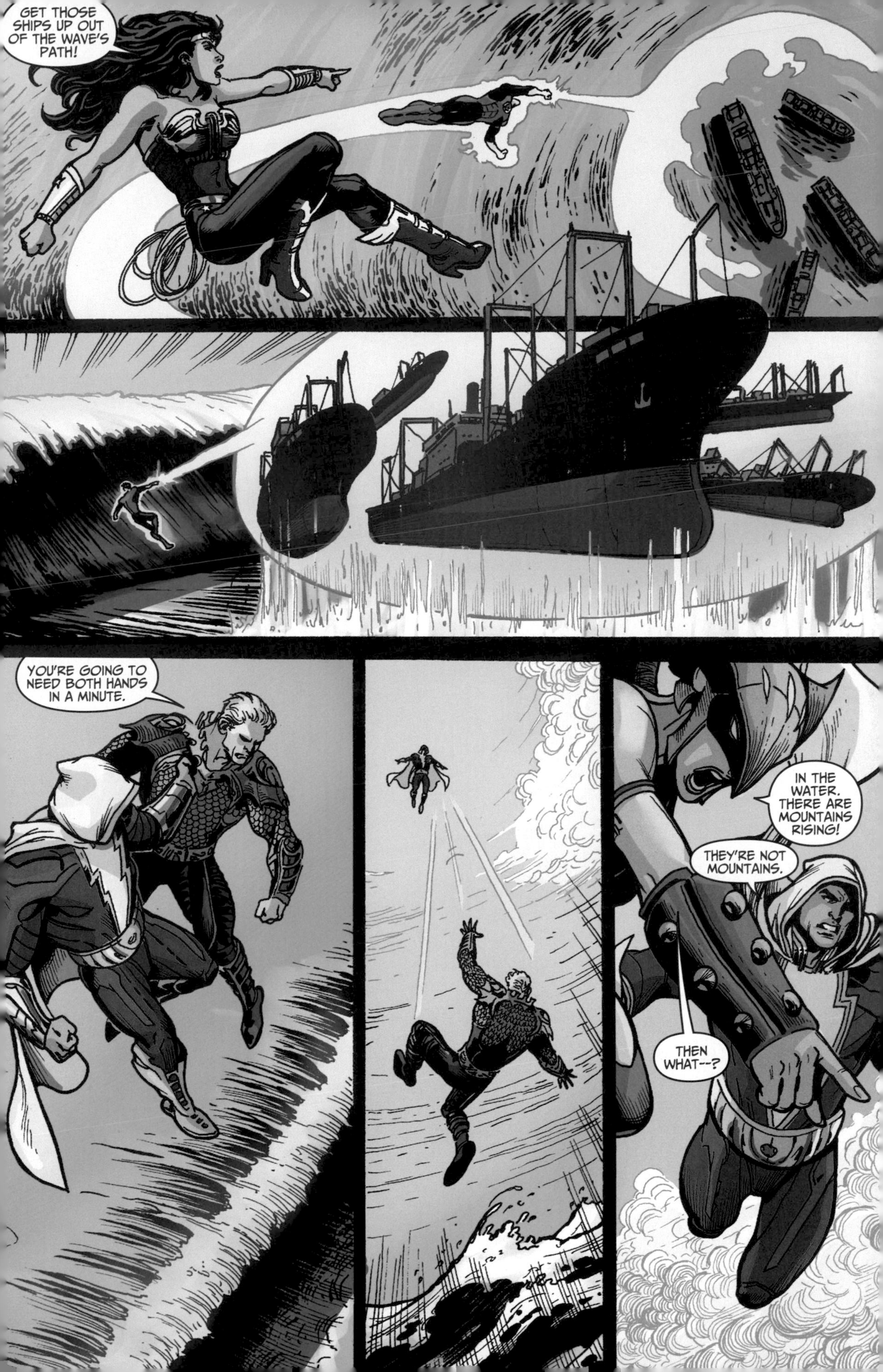
GET THOSE SHIPS UP OUT OF THE WAVE'S PATH!
YOU'RE GOING TO NEED BOTH HANDS IN A MINUTE.
IN THE WATER. THERE ARE MOUNTAINS RISING!
THEY'RE NOT MOUNTAINS.
THEN WHAT--?

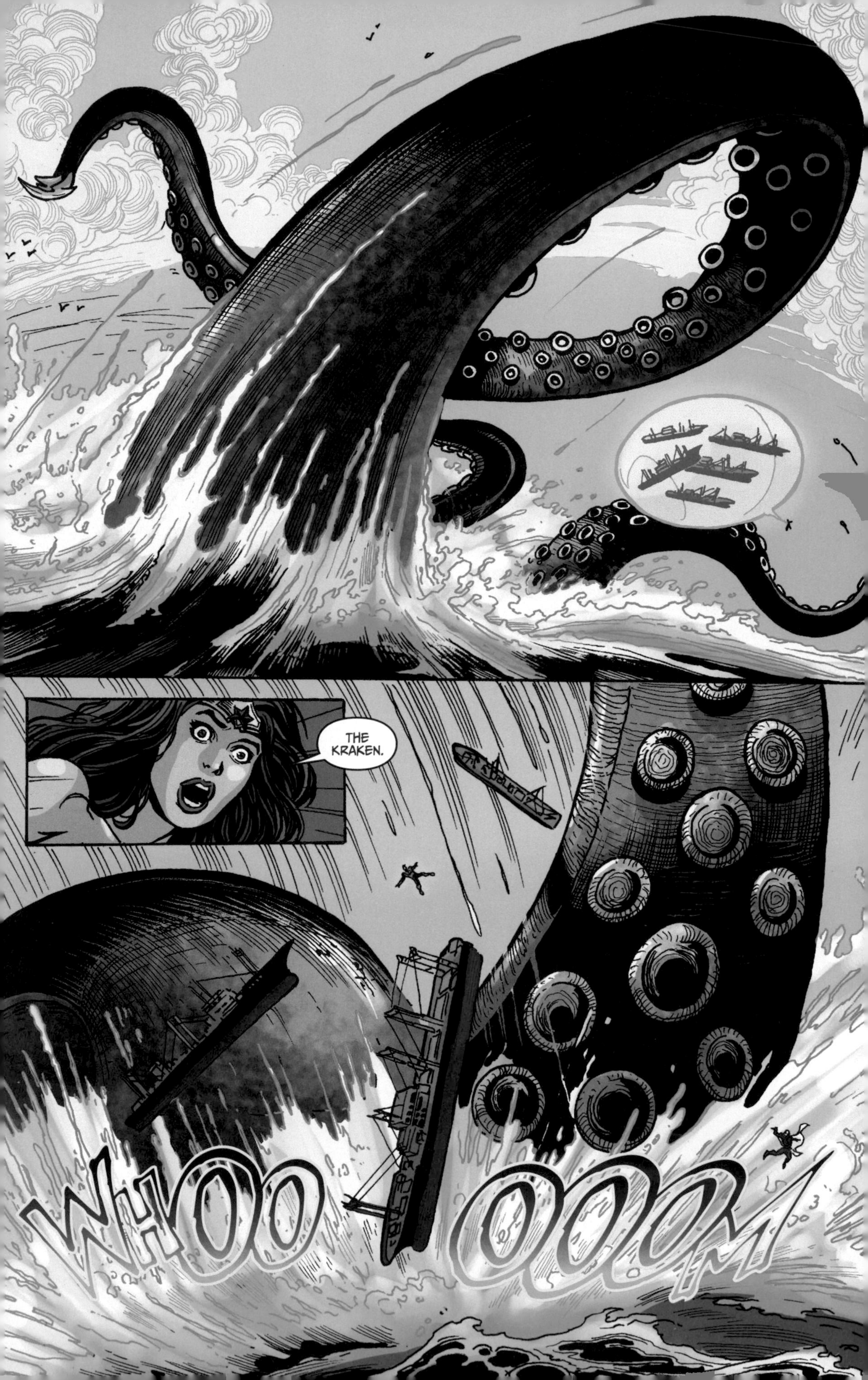
THE KRAKEN.
WHOOOOOM

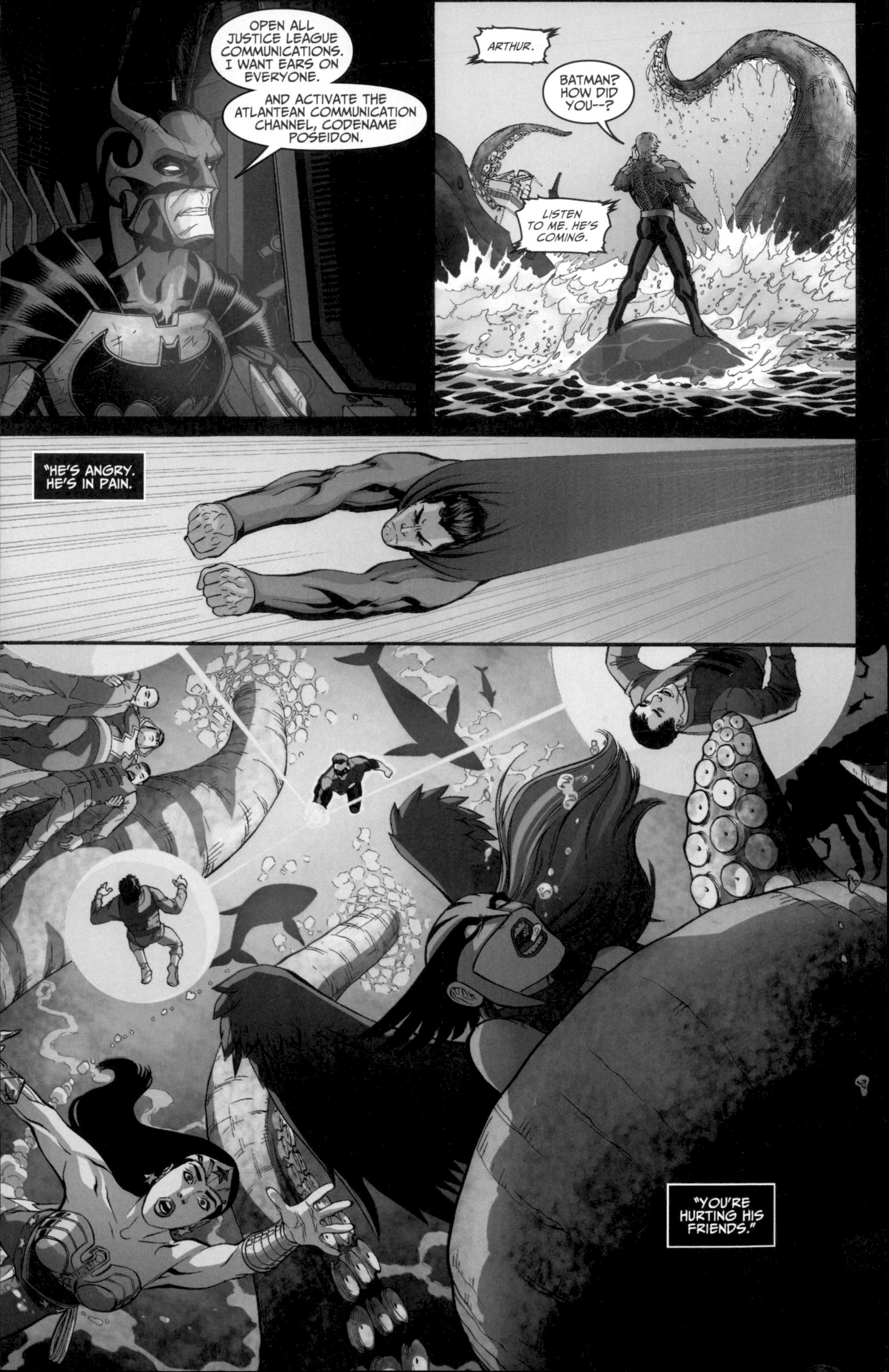

OPEN ALL JUSTICE LEAGUE COMMUNICATIONS. I WANT EARS ON EVERYONE.
AND ACTIVATE THE ATLANTEAN COMMUNICATION CHANNEL, CODENAME POSEIDON.
ARTHUR.
BATMAN? HOW DID YOU--?
LISTEN TO ME. HE'S COMING.
"HE'S ANGRY. HE'S IN PAIN.
"YOU'RE HURTING HIS FRIENDS."

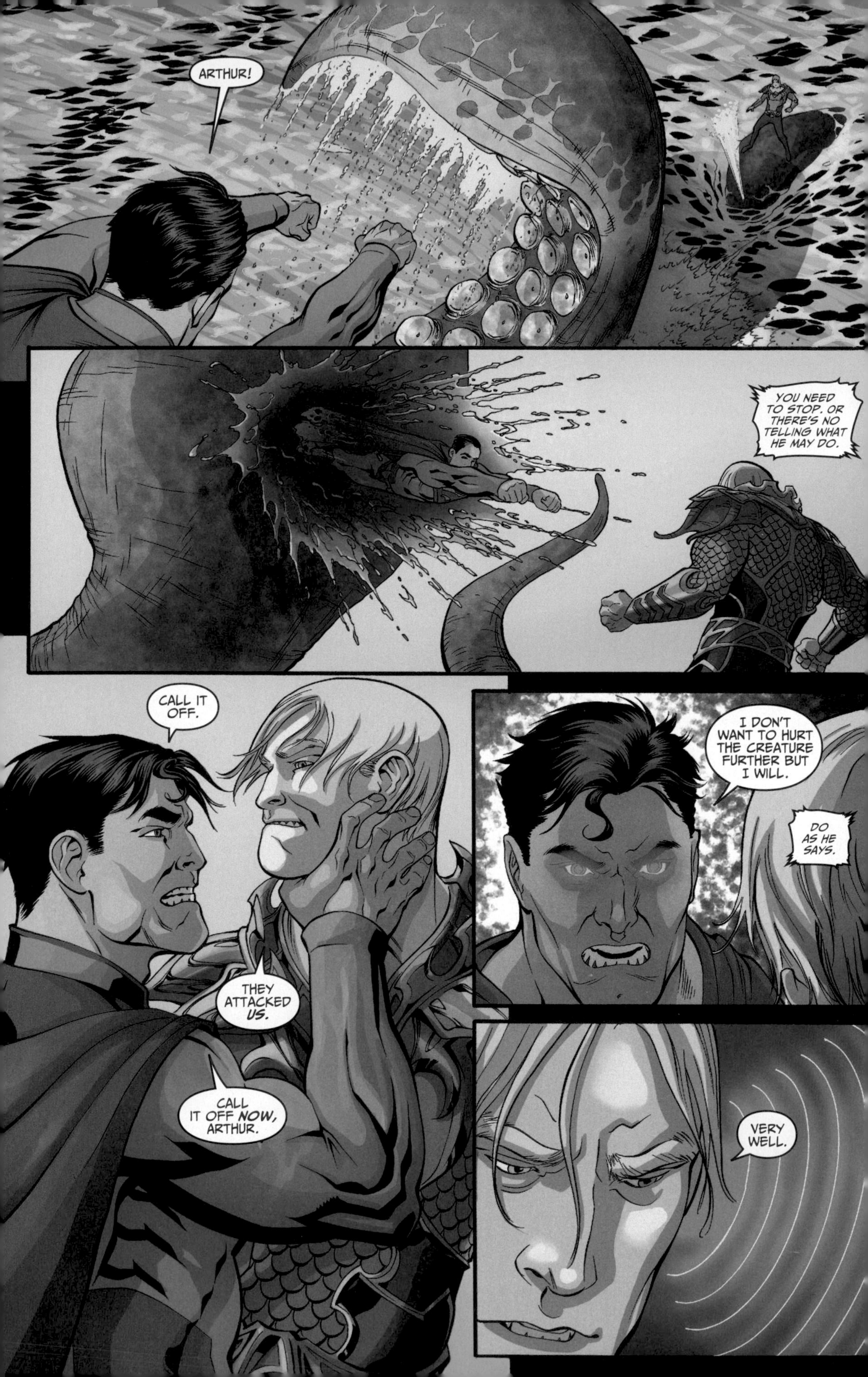
ARTHUR!
YOU NEED TO STOP. OR THERE'S NO TELLING WHAT HE MAY DO.
CALL IT OFF.
THEY ATTACKED *US*.
CALL IT OFF *NOW*, ARTHUR.
I DON'T WANT TO HURT THE CREATURE FURTHER BUT I WILL.
DO AS HE SAYS.
VERY WELL.

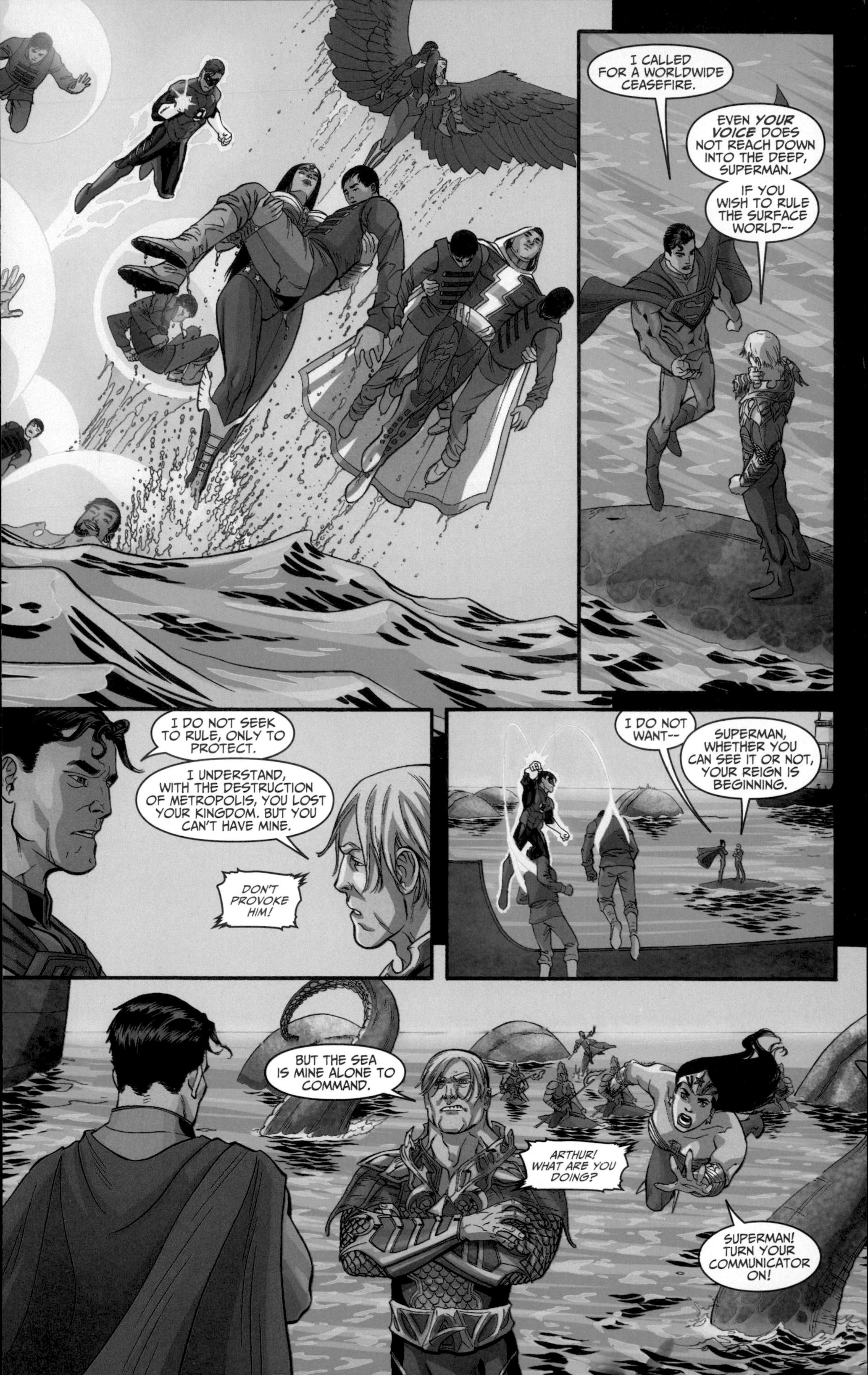
I CALLED FOR A WORLDWIDE CEASEFIRE.
EVEN YOUR VOICE DOES NOT REACH DOWN INTO THE DEEP, SUPERMAN.
IF YOU WISH TO RULE THE SURFACE WORLD--
I DO NOT SEEK TO RULE, ONLY TO PROTECT.
I UNDERSTAND, WITH THE DESTRUCTION OF METROPOLIS, YOU LOST YOUR KINGDOM. BUT YOU CAN'T HAVE MINE.
DON'T PROVOKE HIM!
I DO NOT WANT--
SUPERMAN, WHETHER YOU CAN SEE IT OR NOT, YOUR REIGN IS BEGINNING.
BUT THE SEA IS MINE ALONE TO COMMAND.
ARTHUR! WHAT ARE YOU DOING?
SUPERMAN! TURN YOUR COMMUNICATOR ON!

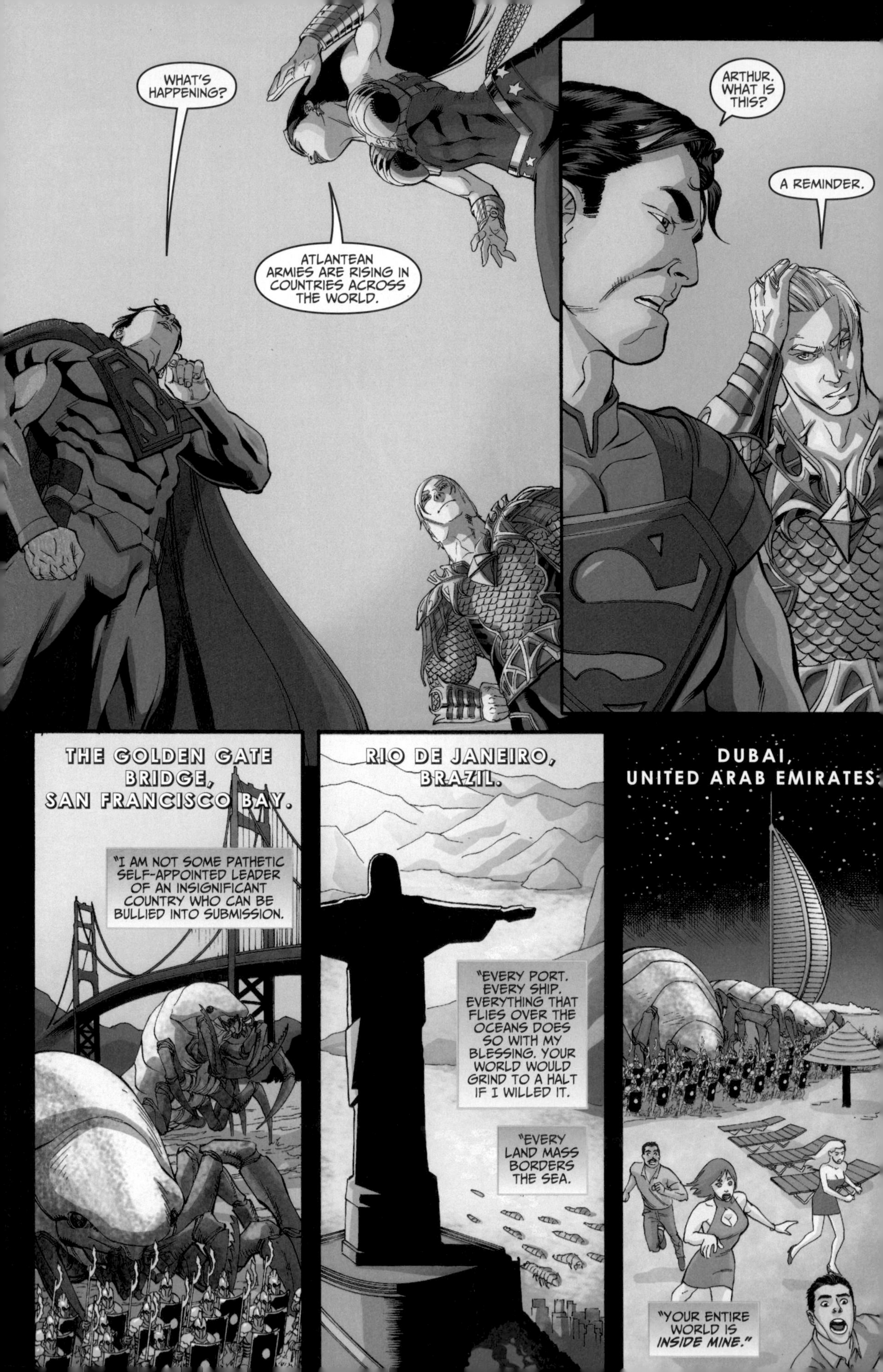

WHAT'S HAPPENING?
ATLANTEAN ARMIES ARE RISING IN COUNTRIES ACROSS THE WORLD.
ARTHUR. WHAT IS THIS?
A REMINDER.
THE GOLDEN GATE BRIDGE, SAN FRANCISCO BAY.
"I AM NOT SOME PATHETIC SELF-APPOINTED LEADER OF AN INSIGNIFICANT COUNTRY WHO CAN BE BULLIED INTO SUBMISSION.
RIO DE JANEIRO, BRAZIL.
"EVERY PORT. EVERY SHIP. EVERYTHING THAT FLIES OVER THE OCEANS DOES SO WITH MY BLESSING. YOUR WORLD WOULD GRIND TO A HALT IF I WILLED IT.
"EVERY LAND MASS BORDERS THE SEA.
DUBAI, UNITED ARAB EMIRATES.
"YOUR ENTIRE WORLD IS *INSIDE MINE.*"

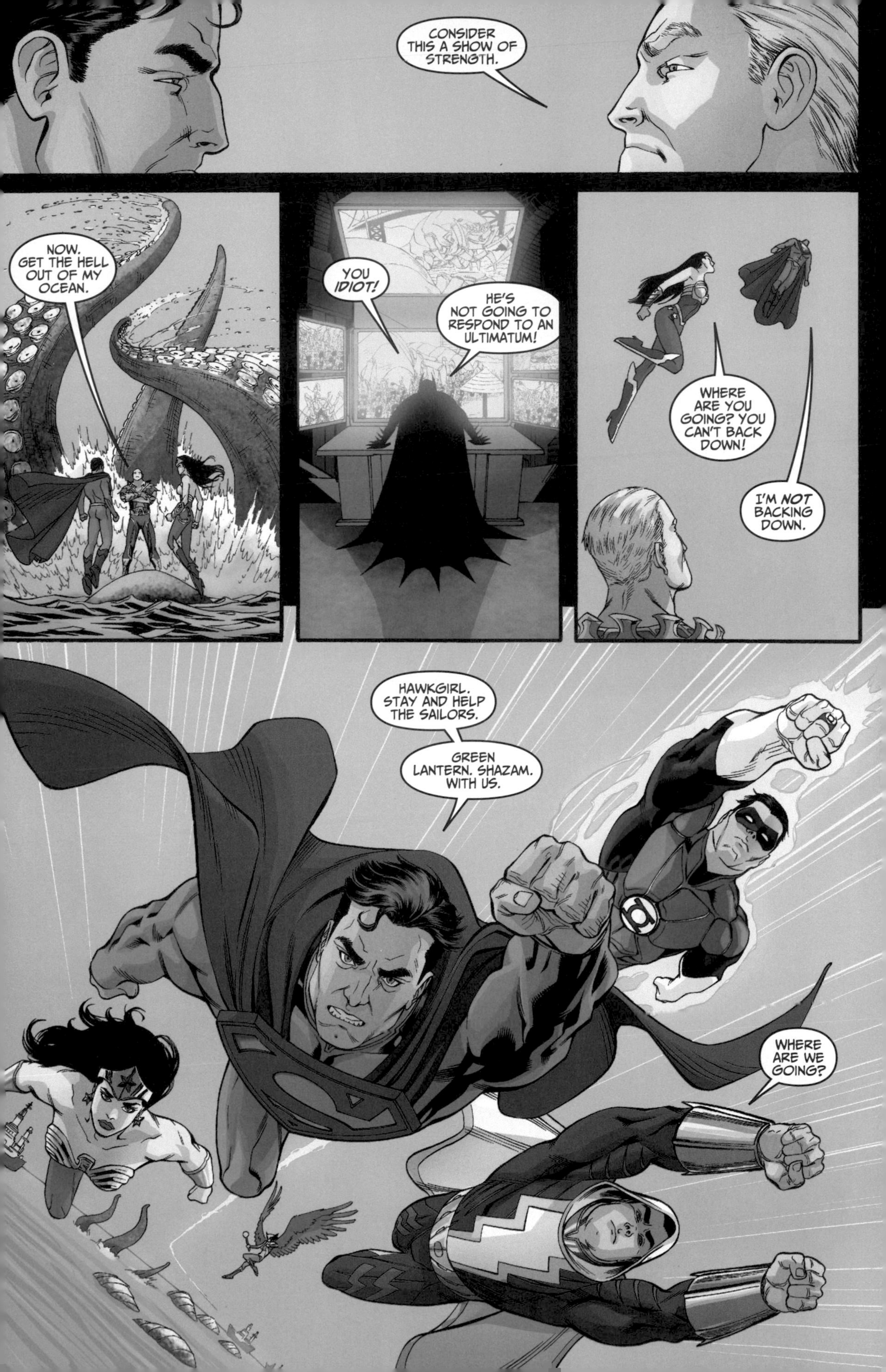
CONSIDER THIS A SHOW OF STRENGTH.
NOW. GET THE HELL OUT OF MY OCEAN.
YOU *IDIOT!*
HE'S NOT GOING TO RESPOND TO AN ULTIMATUM!
WHERE ARE YOU GOING? YOU CAN'T BACK DOWN!
I'M ***NOT*** BACKING DOWN.
HAWKGIRL. STAY AND HELP THE SAILORS.
GREEN LANTERN. SHAZAM. WITH US.
WHERE ARE WE GOING?

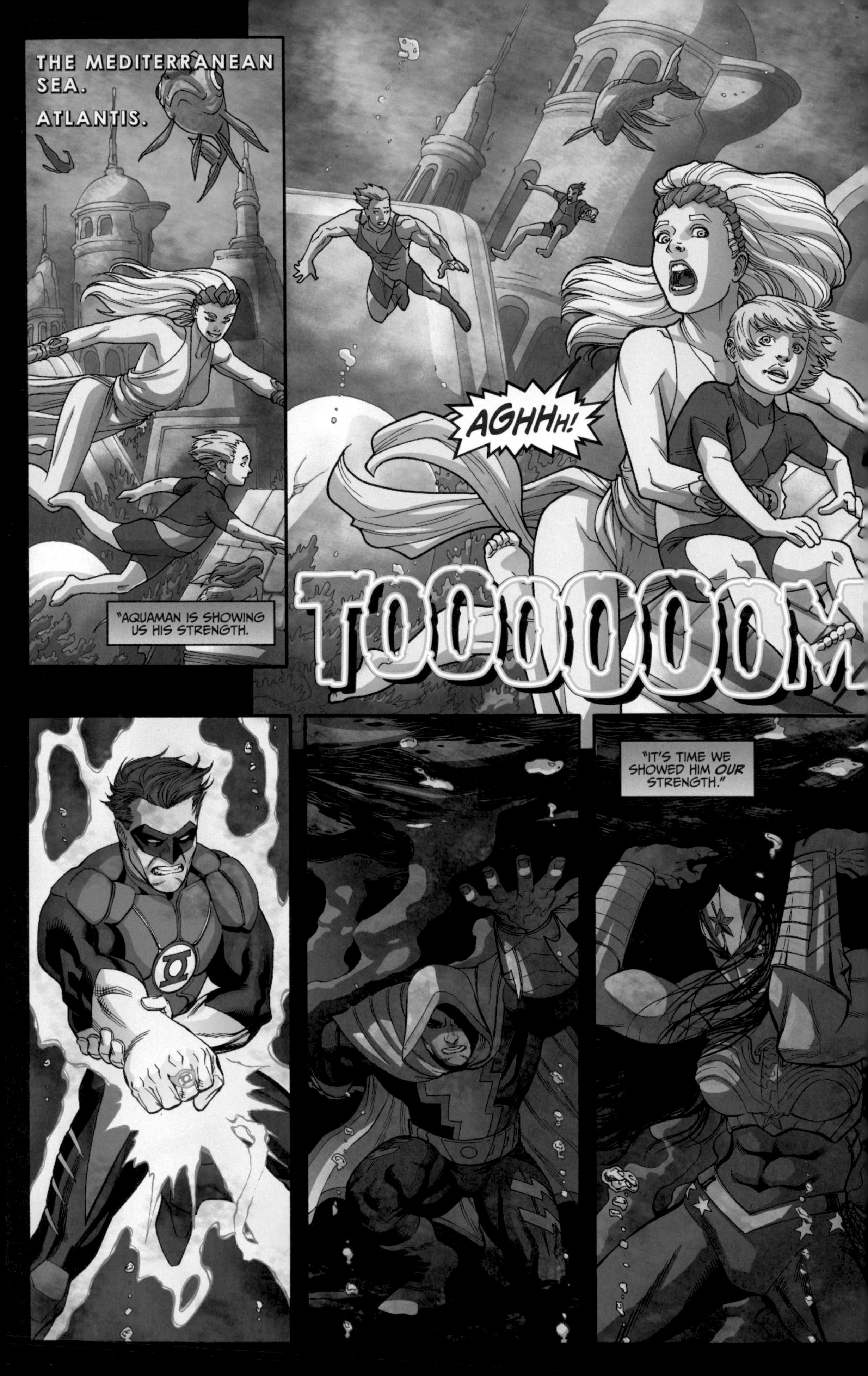
THE MEDITERRANEAN SEA.
ATLANTIS.
"AQUAMAN IS SHOWING US HIS STRENGTH.
AGHHh!
TOOOOOOM
"IT'S TIME WE SHOWED HIM OUR STRENGTH."

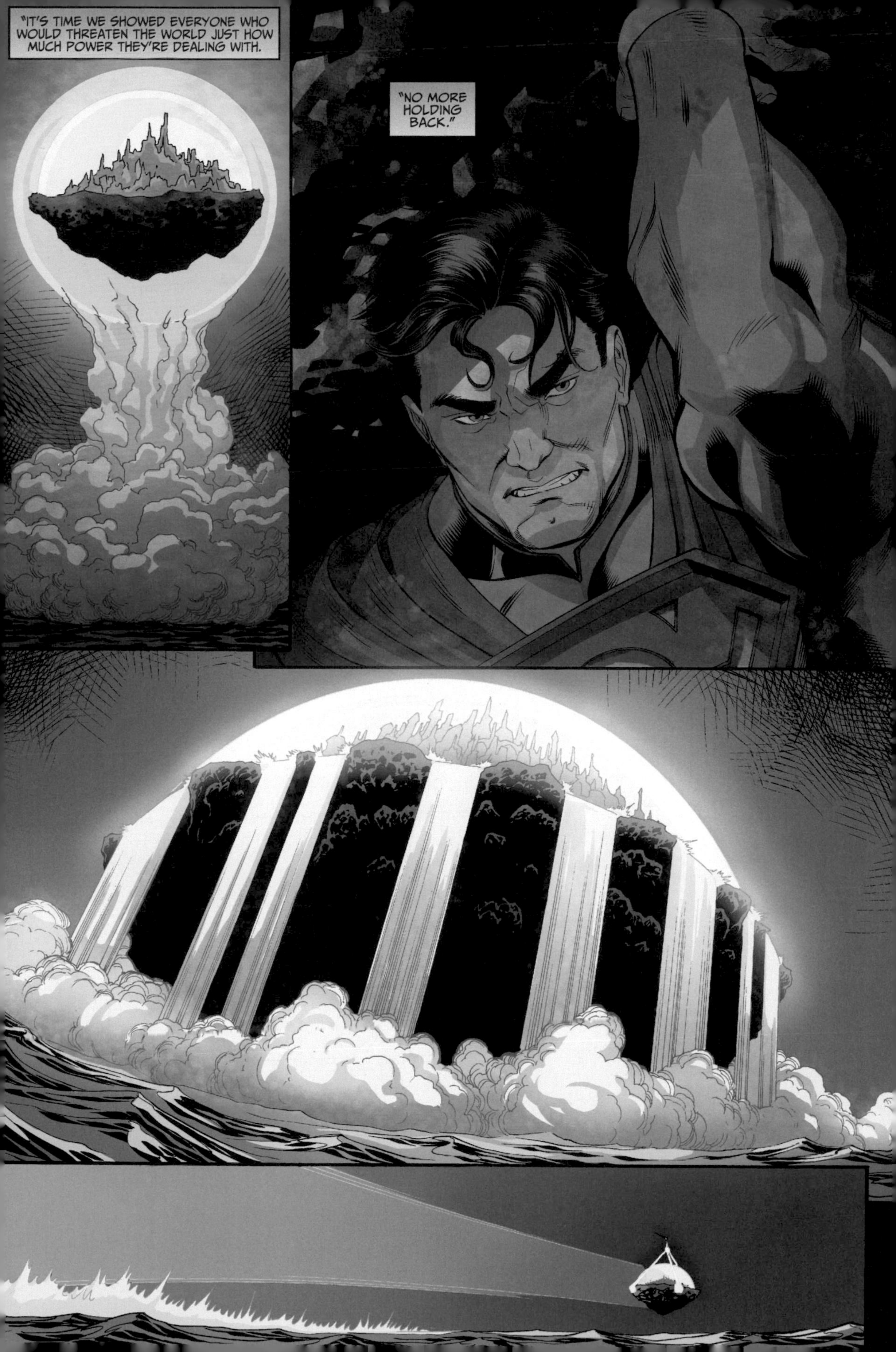
"IT'S TIME WE SHOWED EVERYONE WHO WOULD THREATEN THE WORLD JUST HOW MUCH POWER THEY'RE DEALING WITH.
"NO MORE HOLDING BACK."

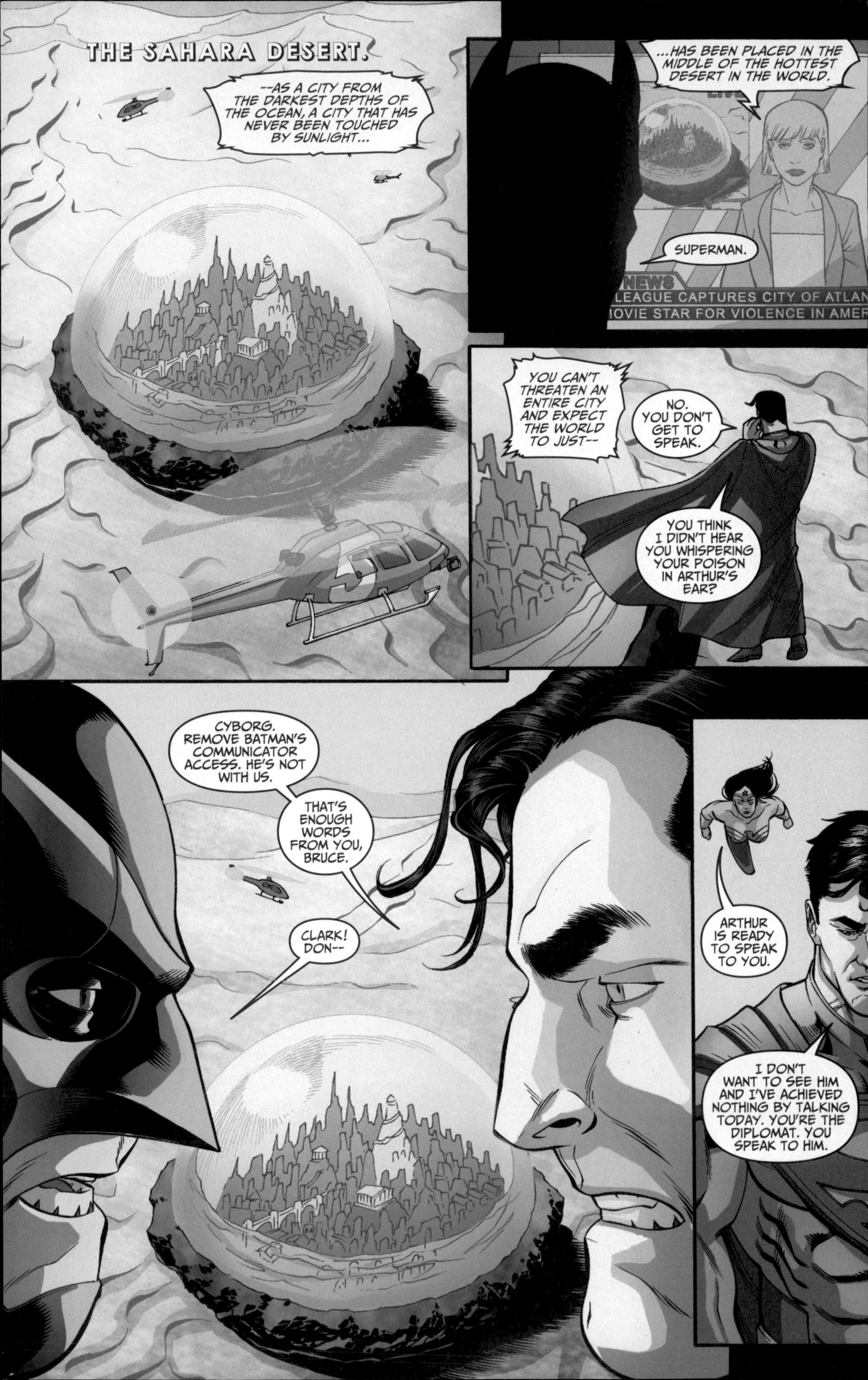
THE SAHARA DESERT.
--AS A CITY FROM THE DARKEST DEPTHS OF THE OCEAN, A CITY THAT HAS NEVER BEEN TOUCHED BY SUNLIGHT...
...HAS BEEN PLACED IN THE MIDDLE OF THE HOTTEST DESERT IN THE WORLD.
SUPERMAN.
NEWS
LEAGUE CAPTURES CITY OF ATLAN
MOVIE STAR FOR VIOLENCE IN AMER
YOU CAN'T THREATEN AN ENTIRE CITY AND EXPECT THE WORLD TO JUST--
NO. YOU DON'T GET TO SPEAK.
YOU THINK I DIDN'T HEAR YOU WHISPERING YOUR POISON IN ARTHUR'S EAR?
CYBORG. REMOVE BATMAN'S COMMUNICATOR ACCESS. HE'S NOT WITH US.
THAT'S ENOUGH WORDS FROM YOU, BRUCE.
CLARK! DON--
ARTHUR IS READY TO SPEAK TO YOU.
I DON'T WANT TO SEE HIM AND I'VE ACHIEVED NOTHING BY TALKING TODAY. YOU'RE THE DIPLOMAT. YOU SPEAK TO HIM.

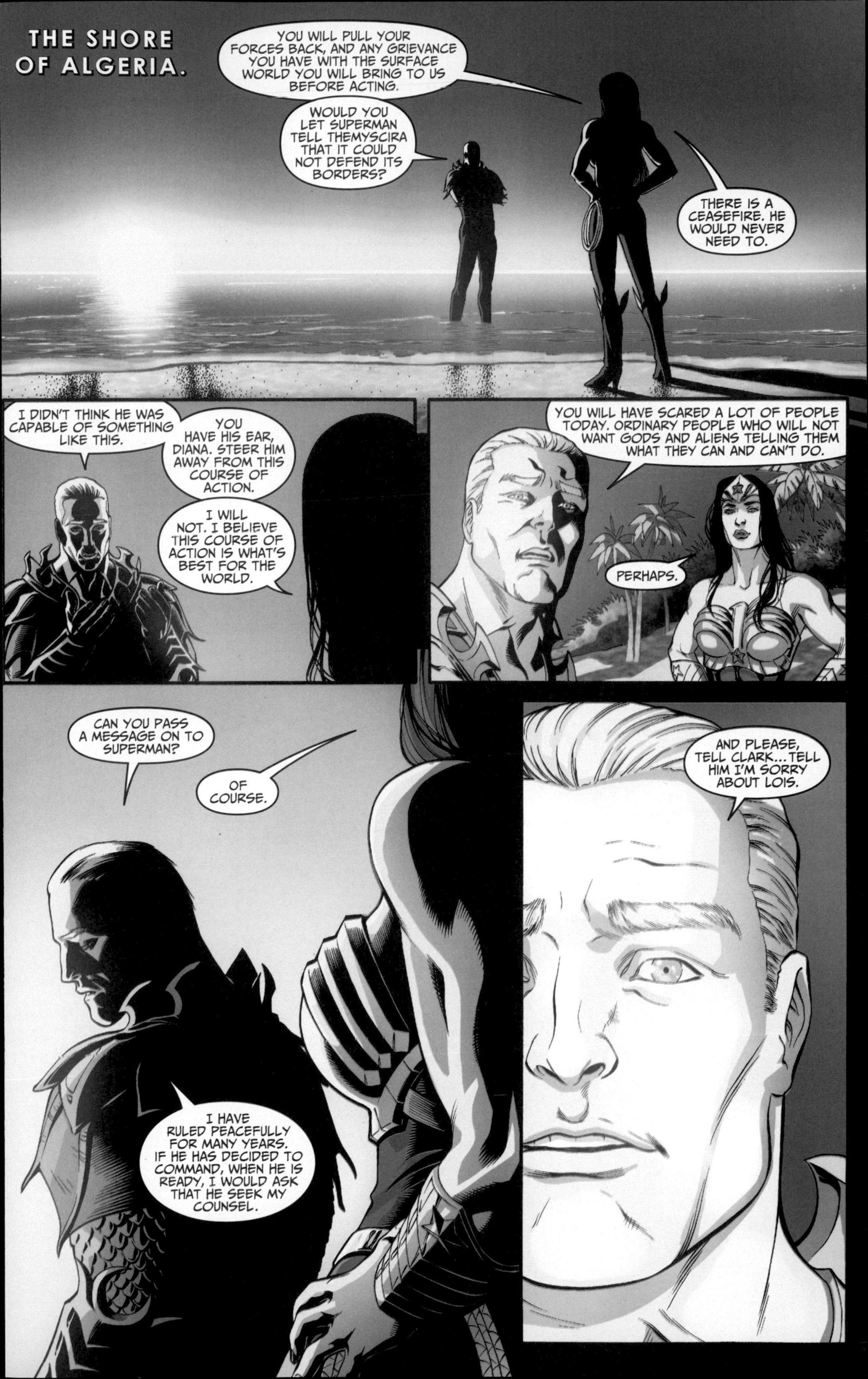
THE SHORE OF ALGERIA.
YOU WILL PULL YOUR FORCES BACK, AND ANY GRIEVANCE YOU HAVE WITH THE SURFACE WORLD YOU WILL BRING TO US BEFORE ACTING.
WOULD YOU LET SUPERMAN TELL THEMYSCIRA THAT IT COULD NOT DEFEND ITS BORDERS?
THERE IS A CEASEFIRE. HE WOULD NEVER NEED TO.
I DIDN'T THINK HE WAS CAPABLE OF SOMETHING LIKE THIS.
YOU HAVE HIS EAR, DIANA. STEER HIM AWAY FROM THIS COURSE OF ACTION.
I WILL NOT. I BELIEVE THIS COURSE OF ACTION IS WHAT'S BEST FOR THE WORLD.
YOU WILL HAVE SCARED A LOT OF PEOPLE TODAY. ORDINARY PEOPLE WHO WILL NOT WANT GODS AND ALIENS TELLING THEM WHAT THEY CAN AND CAN'T DO.
PERHAPS.
CAN YOU PASS A MESSAGE ON TO SUPERMAN?
OF COURSE.
I HAVE RULED PEACEFULLY FOR MANY YEARS. IF HE HAS DECIDED TO COMMAND, WHEN HE IS READY, I WOULD ASK THAT HE SEEK MY COUNSEL.
AND PLEASE, TELL CLARK...TELL HIM I'M SORRY ABOUT LOIS.

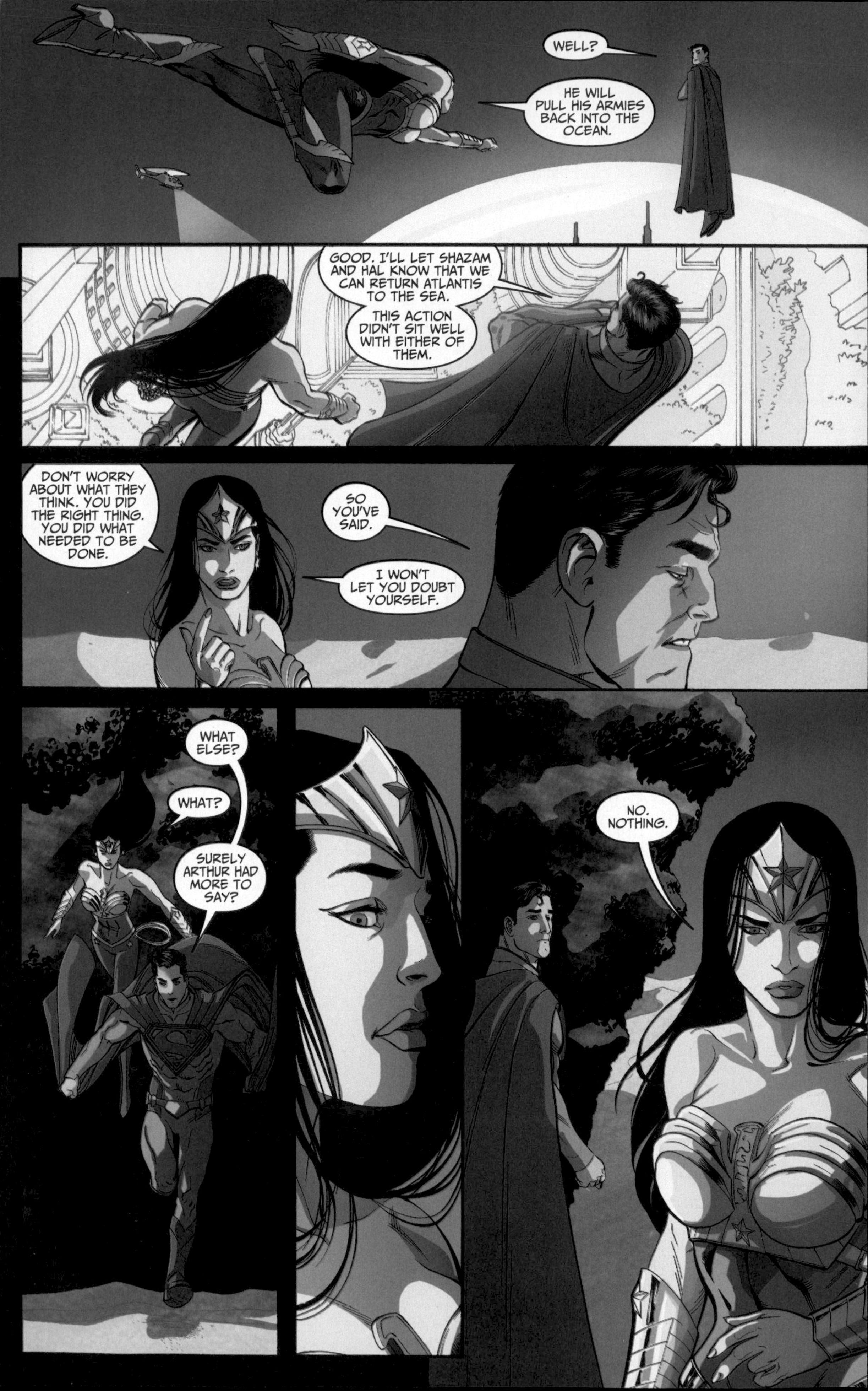
WELL?
HE WILL PULL HIS ARMIES BACK INTO THE OCEAN.
GOOD. I'LL LET SHAZAM AND HAL KNOW THAT WE CAN RETURN ATLANTIS TO THE SEA.
THIS ACTION DIDN'T SIT WELL WITH EITHER OF THEM.
DON'T WORRY ABOUT WHAT THEY THINK. YOU DID THE RIGHT THING. YOU DID WHAT NEEDED TO BE DONE.
SO YOU'VE SAID.
I WON'T LET YOU DOUBT YOURSELF.
WHAT ELSE?
WHAT?
SURELY ARTHUR HAD MORE TO SAY?
NO. NOTHING.

PART FIVE

Tom Derenick **Jheremy Raapack** Artists

Drew Johnson, **Ray Snyder** and **Kathryn Layno** Cover

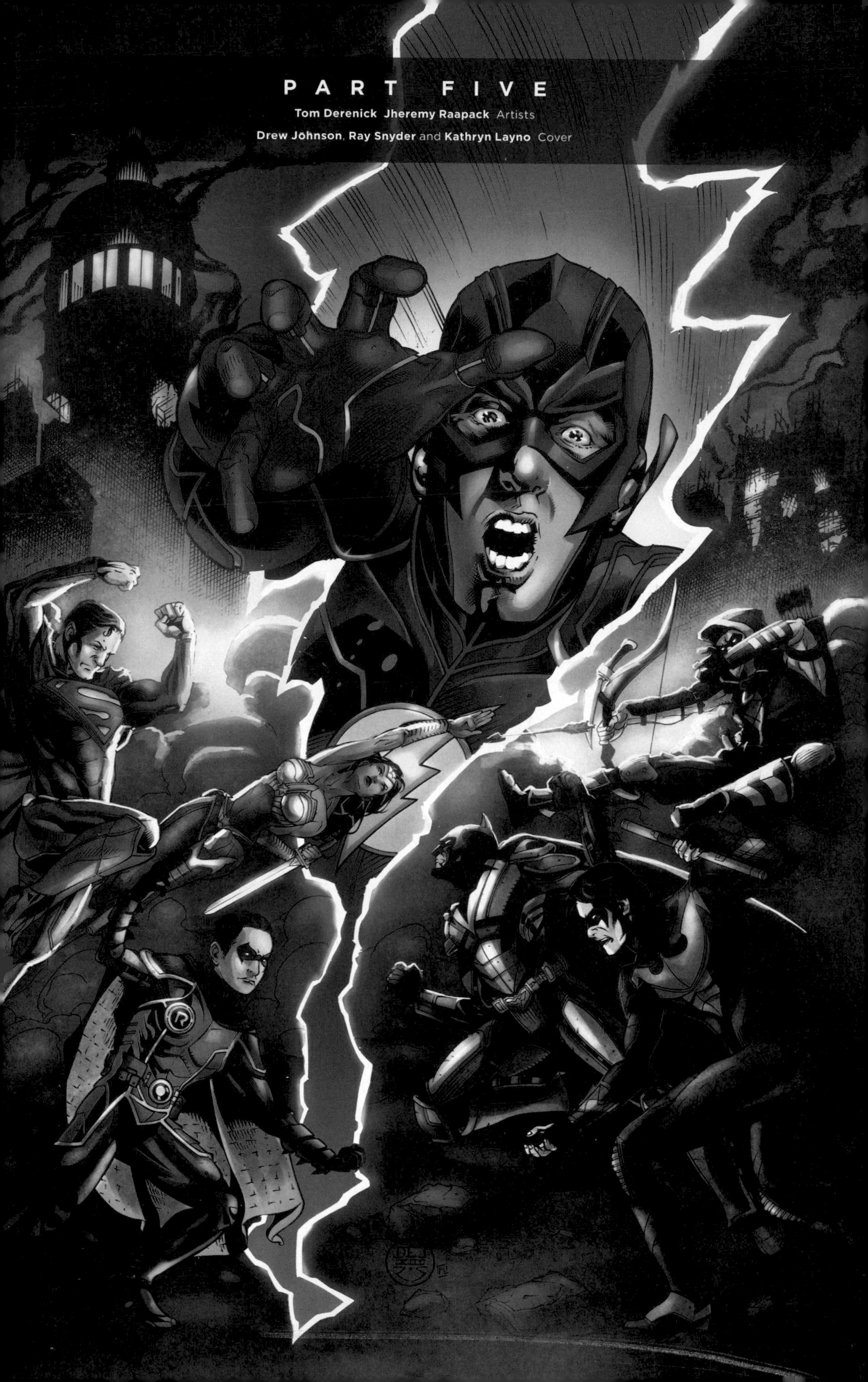

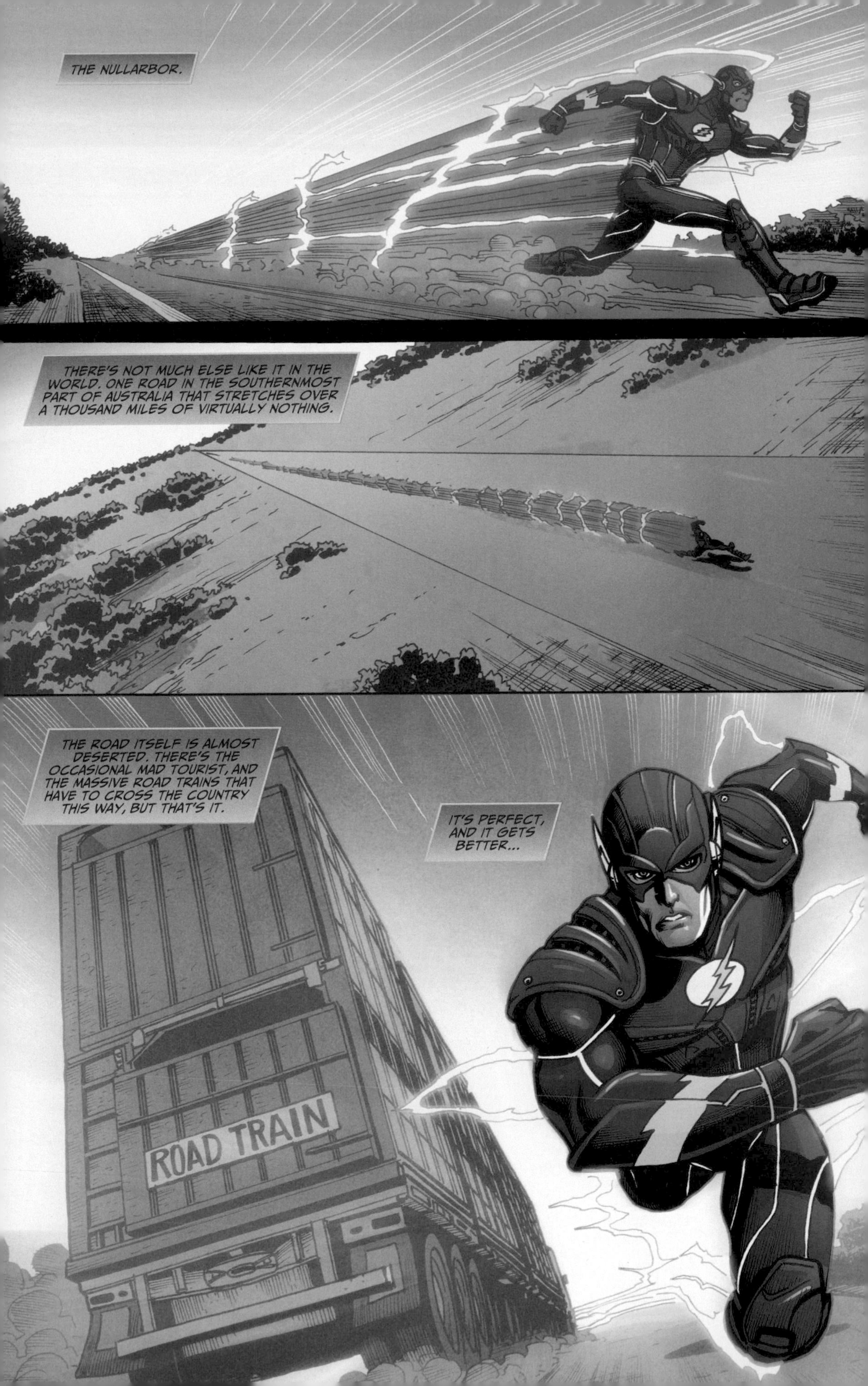
THE NULLARBOR.
THERE'S NOT MUCH ELSE LIKE IT IN THE WORLD. ONE ROAD IN THE SOUTHERNMOST PART OF AUSTRALIA THAT STRETCHES OVER A THOUSAND MILES OF VIRTUALLY NOTHING.
THE ROAD ITSELF IS ALMOST DESERTED. THERE'S THE OCCASIONAL MAD TOURIST, AND THE MASSIVE ROAD TRAINS THAT HAVE TO CROSS THE COUNTRY THIS WAY, BUT THAT'S IT.
ROAD TRAIN
IT'S PERFECT, AND IT GETS BETTER...

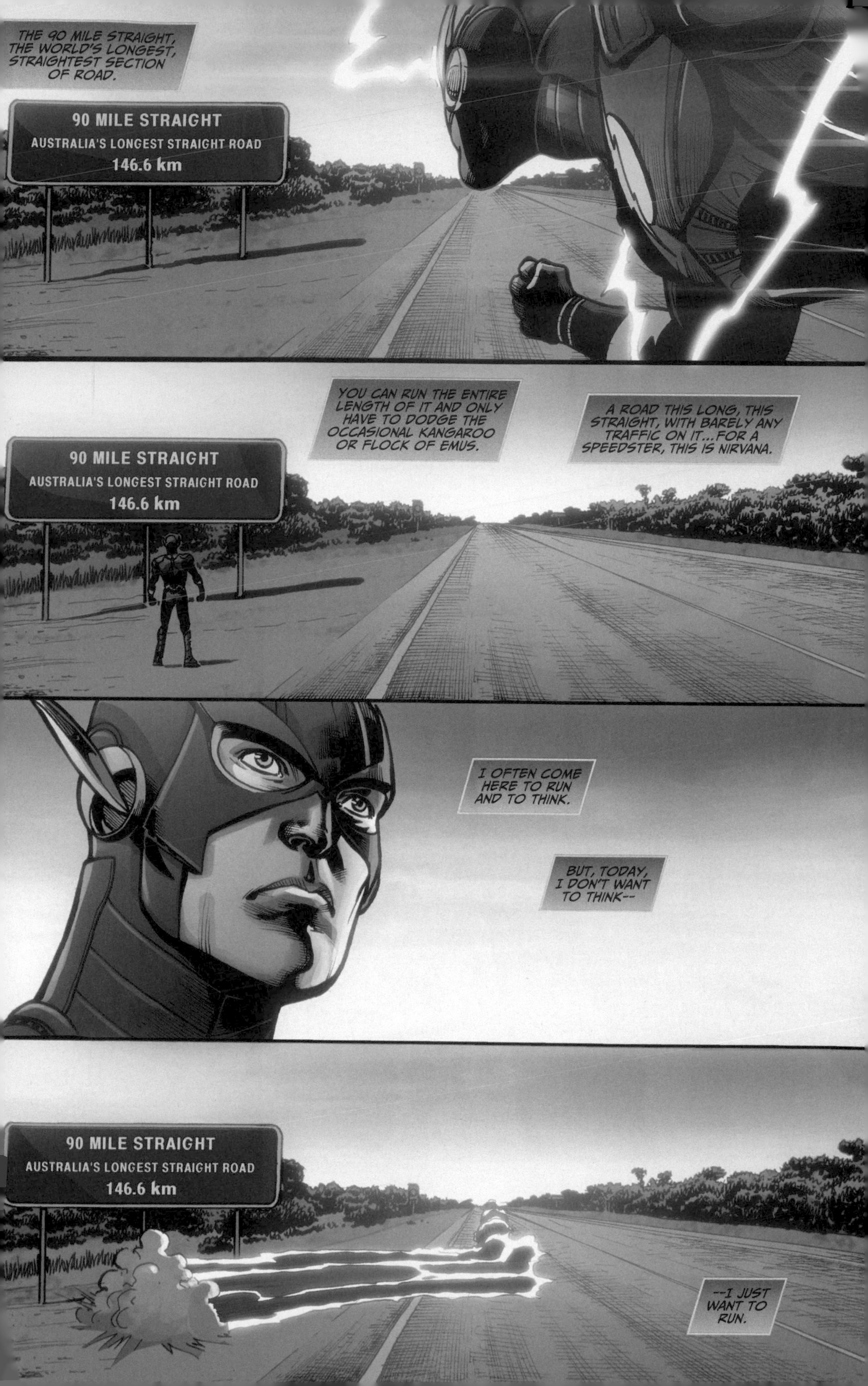
THE 90 MILE STRAIGHT, THE WORLD'S LONGEST, STRAIGHTEST SECTION OF ROAD.
90 MILE STRAIGHT
AUSTRALIA'S LONGEST STRAIGHT ROAD
146.6 km
YOU CAN RUN THE ENTIRE LENGTH OF IT AND ONLY HAVE TO DODGE THE OCCASIONAL KANGAROO OR FLOCK OF EMUS.
A ROAD THIS LONG, THIS STRAIGHT, WITH BARELY ANY TRAFFIC ON IT...FOR A SPEEDSTER, THIS IS NIRVANA.
90 MILE STRAIGHT
AUSTRALIA'S LONGEST STRAIGHT ROAD
146.6 km
I OFTEN COME HERE TO RUN AND TO THINK.
BUT, TODAY, I DON'T WANT TO THINK--
90 MILE STRAIGHT
AUSTRALIA'S LONGEST STRAIGHT ROAD
146.6 km
--I JUST WANT TO RUN.

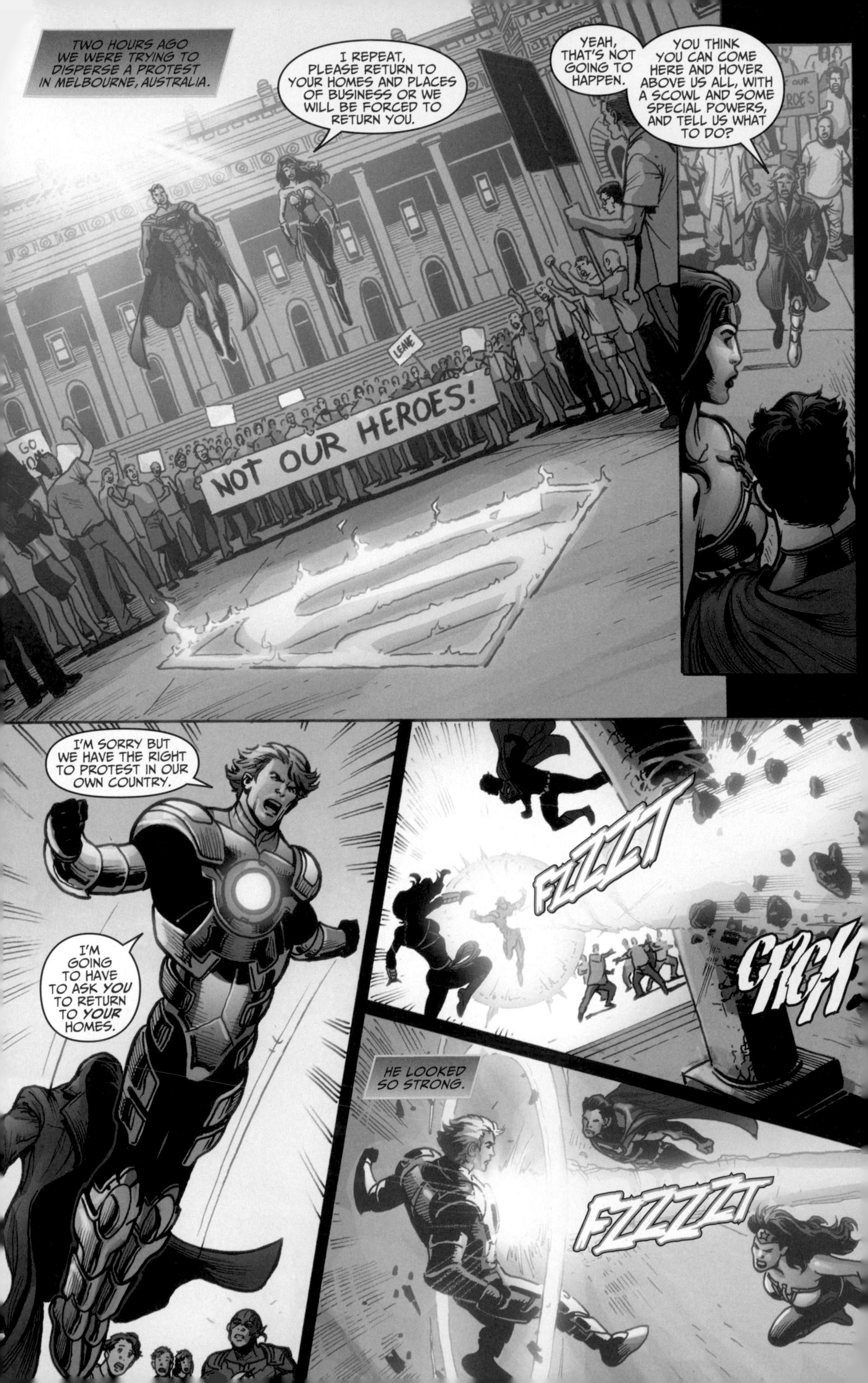

TWO HOURS AGO WE WERE TRYING TO DISPERSE A PROTEST IN MELBOURNE, AUSTRALIA.
I REPEAT, PLEASE RETURN TO YOUR HOMES AND PLACES OF BUSINESS OR WE WILL BE FORCED TO RETURN YOU.
YEAH, THAT'S NOT GOING TO HAPPEN.
YOU THINK YOU CAN COME HERE AND HOVER ABOVE US ALL, WITH A SCOWL AND SOME SPECIAL POWERS, AND TELL US WHAT TO DO?
LEAVE
GO
NOT OUR HEROES!
I'M SORRY BUT WE HAVE THE RIGHT TO PROTEST IN OUR OWN COUNTRY.
I'M GOING TO HAVE TO ASK *YOU* TO RETURN TO *YOUR* HOMES.
FZZZT
CRCK
HE LOOKED SO STRONG.
FZZZZT

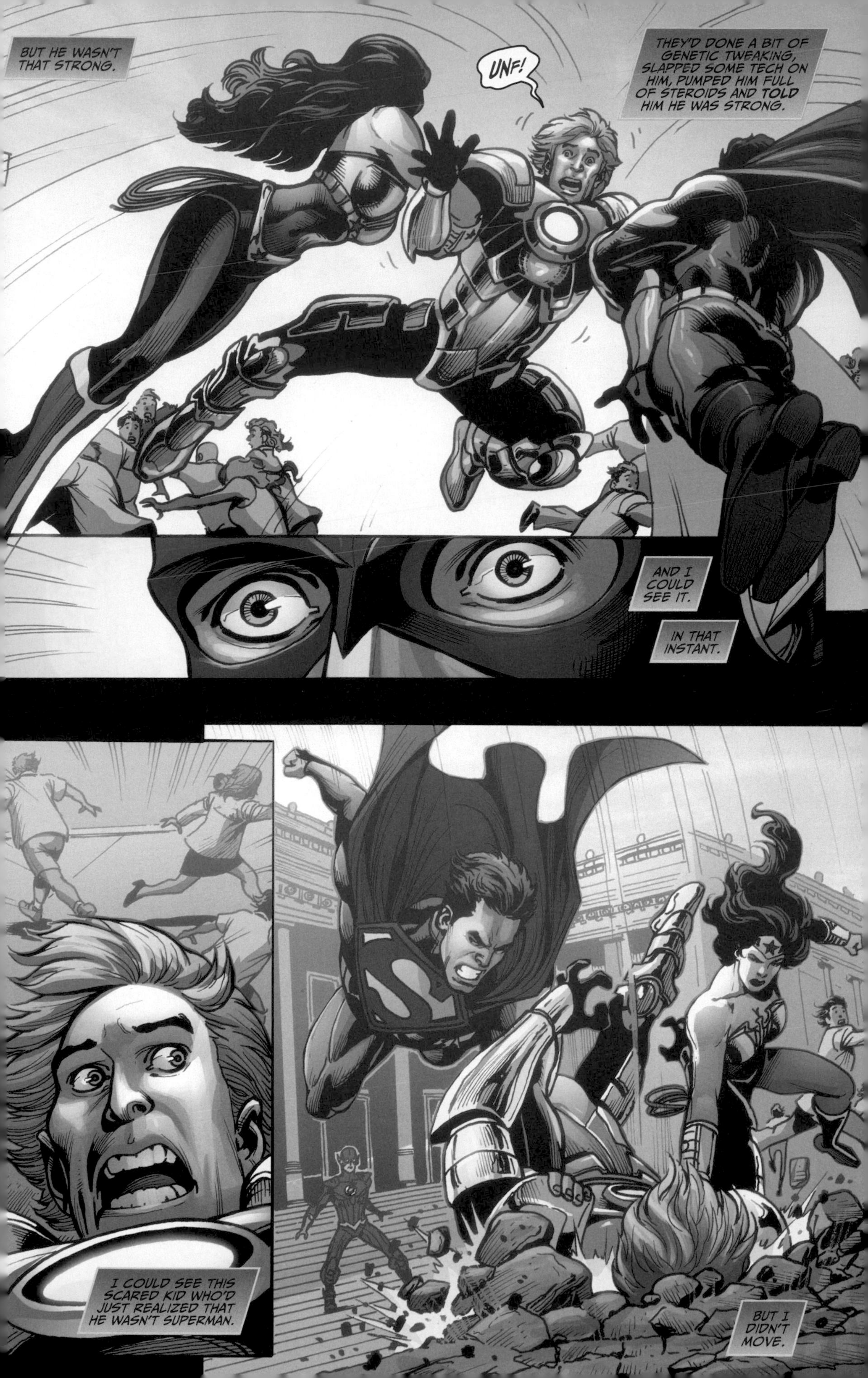
BUT HE WASN'T THAT STRONG.
UNF!
THEY'D DONE A BIT OF GENETIC TWEAKING, SLAPPED SOME TECH ON HIM, PUMPED HIM FULL OF STEROIDS AND TOLD HIM HE WAS STRONG.
AND I COULD SEE IT.
IN THAT INSTANT.
I COULD SEE THIS SCARED KID WHO'D JUST REALIZED THAT HE WASN'T SUPERMAN.
BUT I DIDN'T MOVE.

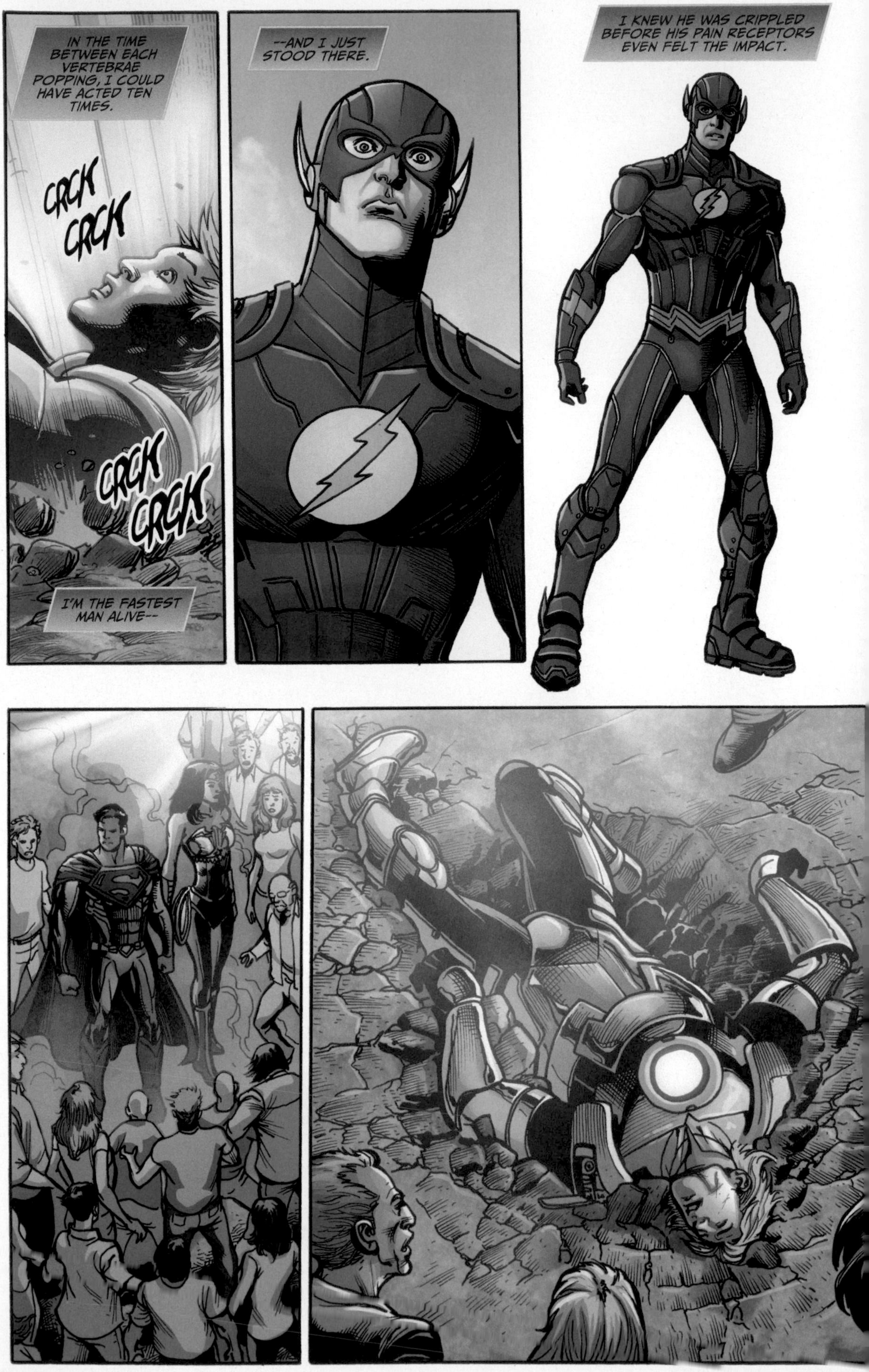

IN THE TIME BETWEEN EACH VERTEBRAE POPPING, I COULD HAVE ACTED TEN TIMES.
CRCK CRCK
CRCK CRCK
I'M THE FASTEST MAN ALIVE--
--AND I JUST STOOD THERE.
I KNEW HE WAS CRIPPLED BEFORE HIS PAIN RECEPTORS EVEN FELT THE IMPACT.

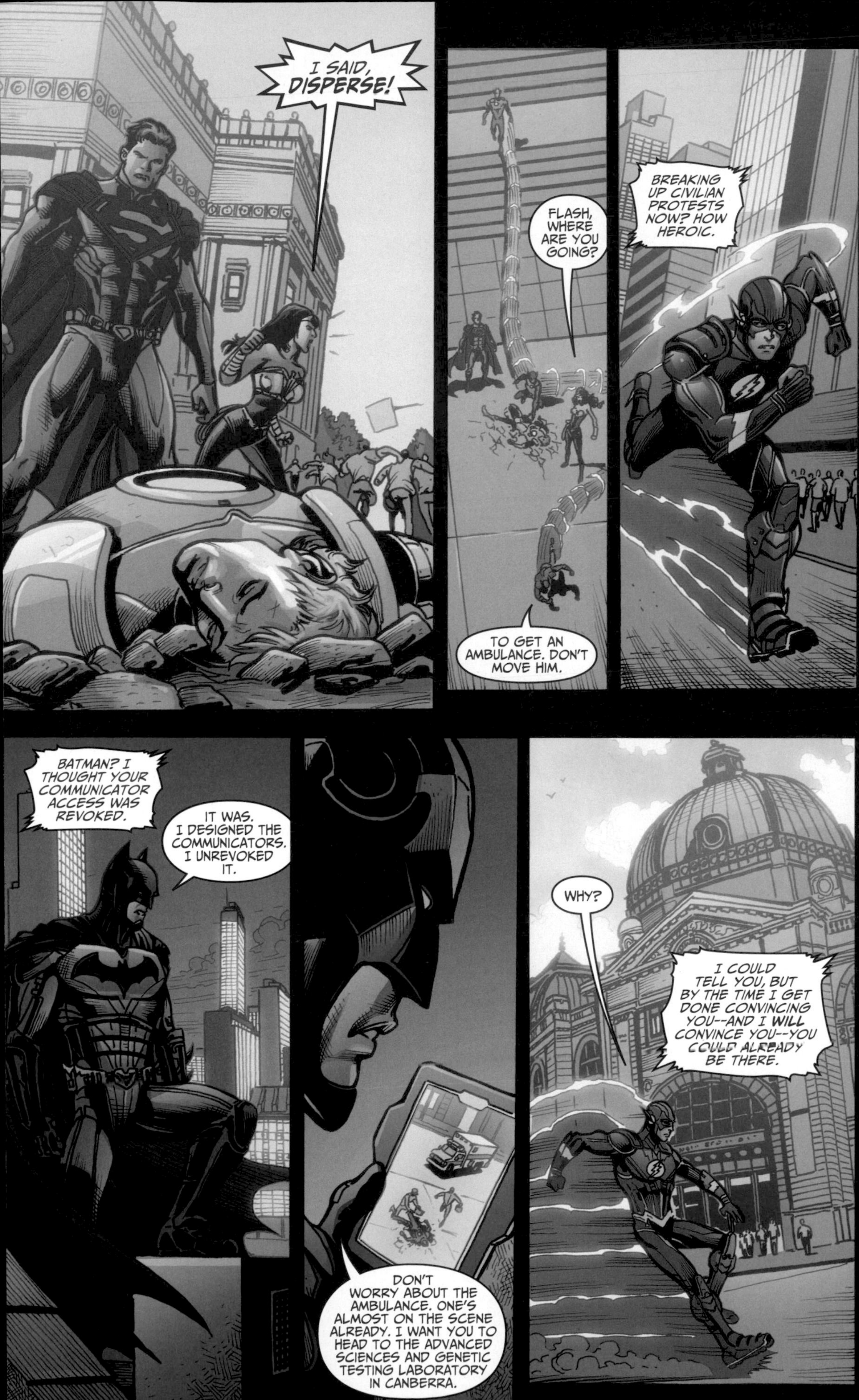
I SAID, DISPERSE!
FLASH, WHERE ARE YOU GOING?
TO GET AN AMBULANCE. DON'T MOVE HIM.
BREAKING UP CIVILIAN PROTESTS NOW? HOW HEROIC.
BATMAN? I THOUGHT YOUR COMMUNICATOR ACCESS WAS REVOKED.
IT WAS. I DESIGNED THE COMMUNICATORS. I UNREVOKED IT.
DON'T WORRY ABOUT THE AMBULANCE. ONE'S ALMOST ON THE SCENE ALREADY. I WANT YOU TO HEAD TO THE ADVANCED SCIENCES AND GENETIC TESTING LABORATORY IN CANBERRA.
WHY?
I COULD TELL YOU, BUT BY THE TIME I GET DONE CONVINCING YOU--AND I WILL CONVINCE YOU--YOU COULD ALREADY BE THERE.

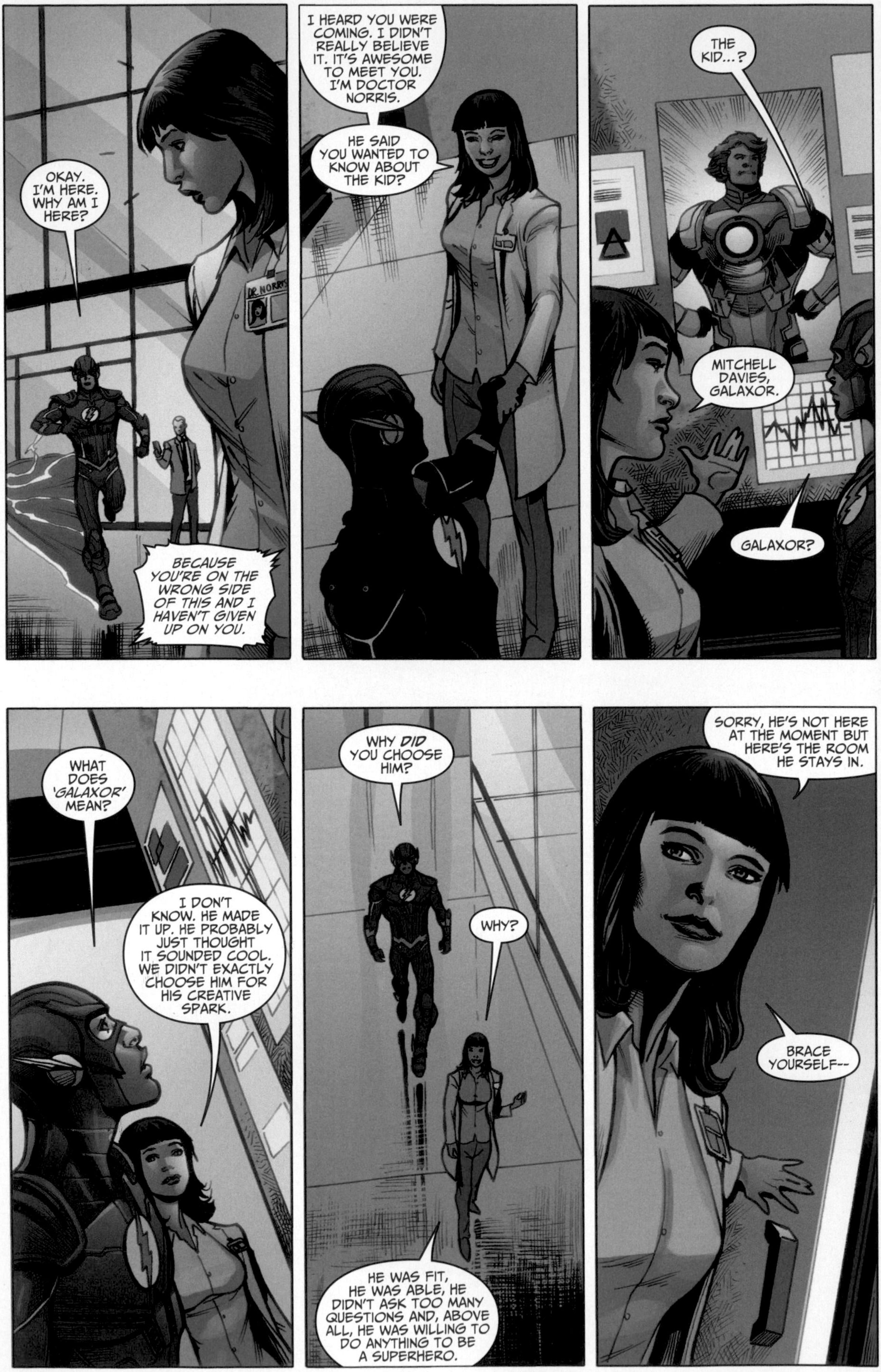
OKAY. I'M HERE. WHY AM I HERE?
BECAUSE YOU'RE ON THE WRONG SIDE OF THIS AND I HAVEN'T GIVEN UP ON YOU.
DR. NORRIS
I HEARD YOU WERE COMING. I DIDN'T REALLY BELIEVE IT. IT'S AWESOME TO MEET YOU. I'M DOCTOR NORRIS.
HE SAID YOU WANTED TO KNOW ABOUT THE KID?
THE KID...?
MITCHELL DAVIES, GALAXOR.
GALAXOR?
WHAT DOES 'GALAXOR' MEAN?
I DON'T KNOW. HE MADE IT UP. HE PROBABLY JUST THOUGHT IT SOUNDED COOL. WE DIDN'T EXACTLY CHOOSE HIM FOR HIS CREATIVE SPARK.
WHY DID YOU CHOOSE HIM?
WHY?
HE WAS FIT, HE WAS ABLE, HE DIDN'T ASK TOO MANY QUESTIONS AND, ABOVE ALL, HE WAS WILLING TO DO ANYTHING TO BE A SUPERHERO.
SORRY, HE'S NOT HERE AT THE MOMENT BUT HERE'S THE ROOM HE STAYS IN.
BRACE YOURSELF--

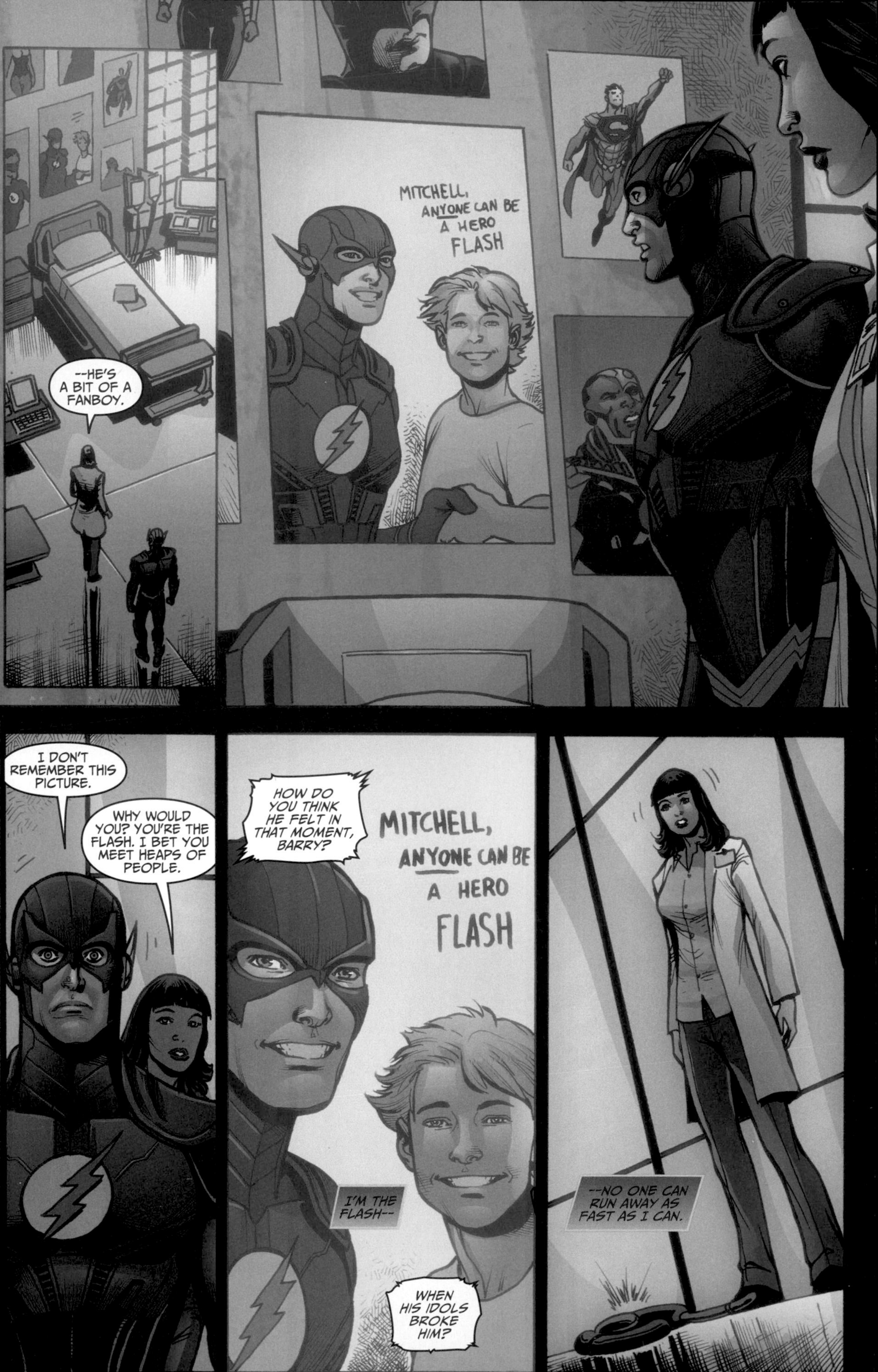
--HE'S A BIT OF A FANBOY.
MITCHELL, ANYONE CAN BE A HERO FLASH
I DON'T REMEMBER THIS PICTURE.
WHY WOULD YOU? YOU'RE THE FLASH. I BET YOU MEET HEAPS OF PEOPLE.
HOW DO YOU THINK HE FELT IN THAT MOMENT, BARRY?
MITCHELL, ANYONE CAN BE A HERO FLASH
I'M THE FLASH--
WHEN HIS IDOLS BROKE HIM?
--NO ONE CAN RUN AWAY AS FAST AS I CAN.

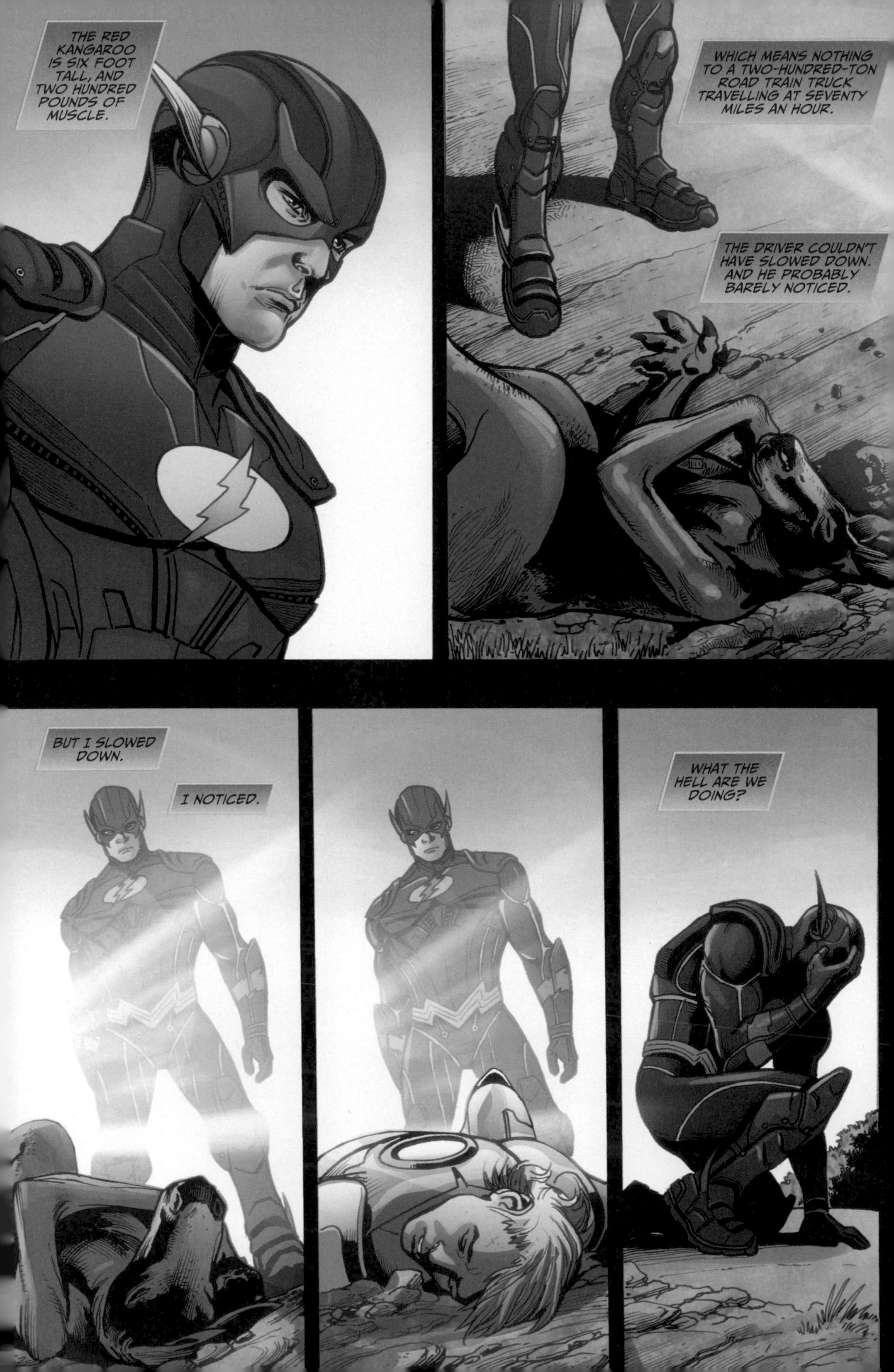
THE RED KANGAROO IS SIX FOOT TALL, AND TWO HUNDRED POUNDS OF MUSCLE.
WHICH MEANS NOTHING TO A TWO-HUNDRED-TON ROAD TRAIN TRUCK TRAVELLING AT SEVENTY MILES AN HOUR.
THE DRIVER COULDN'T HAVE SLOWED DOWN. AND HE PROBABLY BARELY NOTICED.
BUT I SLOWED DOWN.
I NOTICED.
WHAT THE HELL ARE WE DOING?

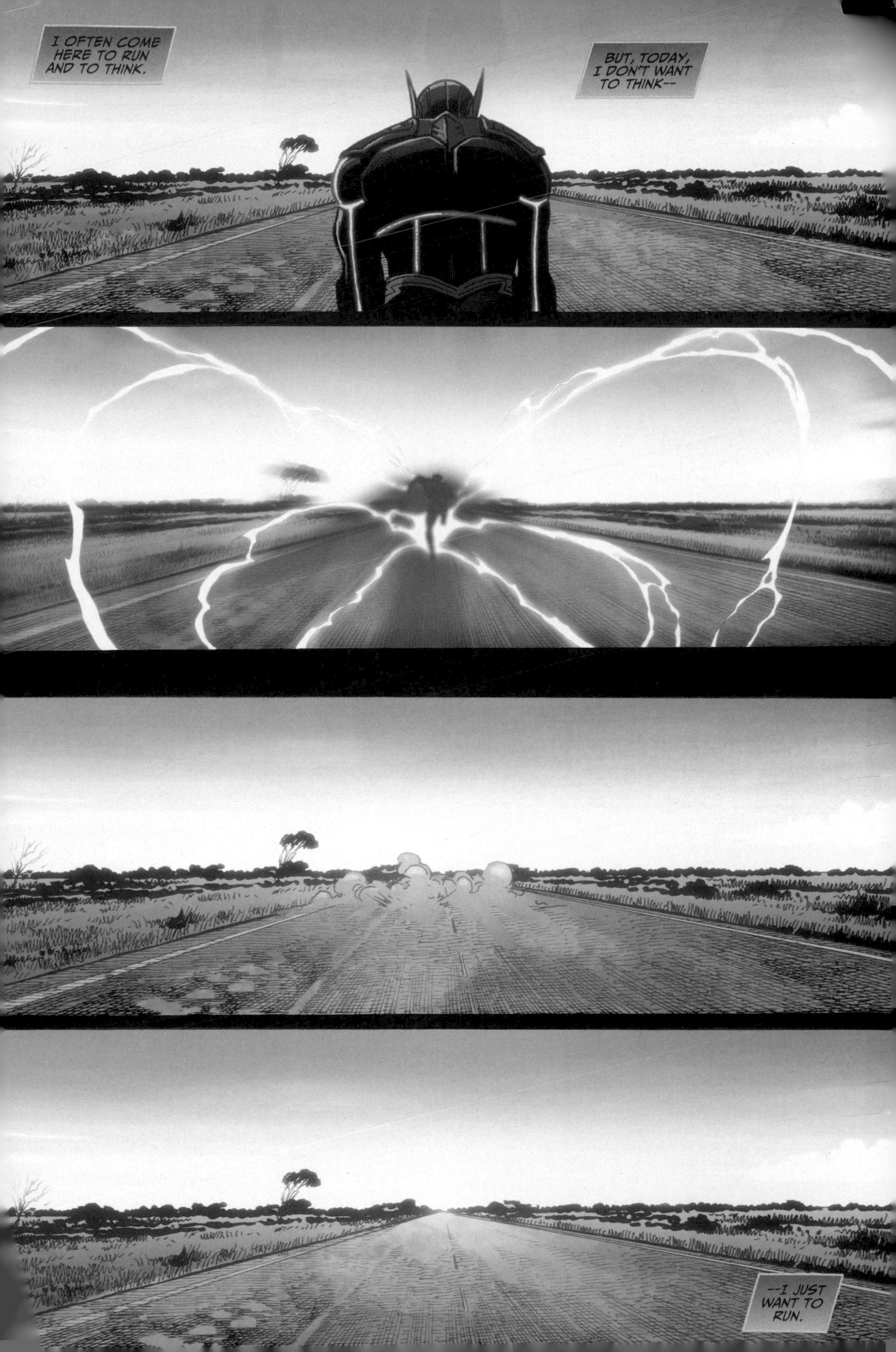
I OFTEN COME HERE TO RUN AND TO THINK.
BUT, TODAY, I DON'T WANT TO THINK--
--I JUST WANT TO RUN.

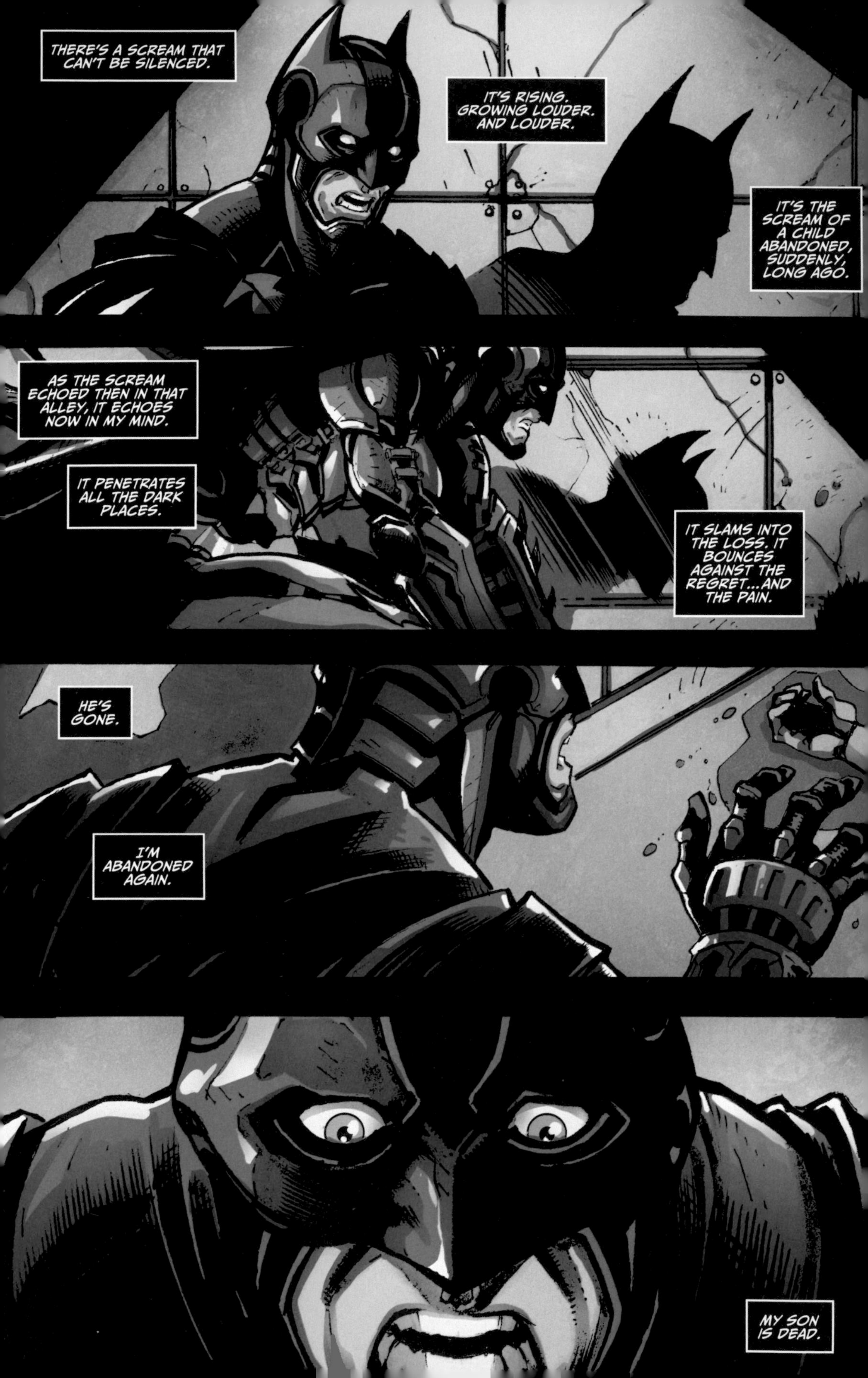

THERE'S A SCREAM THAT CAN'T BE SILENCED.
IT'S RISING. GROWING LOUDER. AND LOUDER.
IT'S THE SCREAM OF A CHILD ABANDONED, SUDDENLY, LONG AGO.
AS THE SCREAM ECHOED THEN IN THAT ALLEY, IT ECHOES NOW IN MY MIND.
IT PENETRATES ALL THE DARK PLACES.
IT SLAMS INTO THE LOSS. IT BOUNCES AGAINST THE REGRET...AND THE PAIN.
HE'S GONE.
I'M ABANDONED AGAIN.
MY SON IS DEAD.

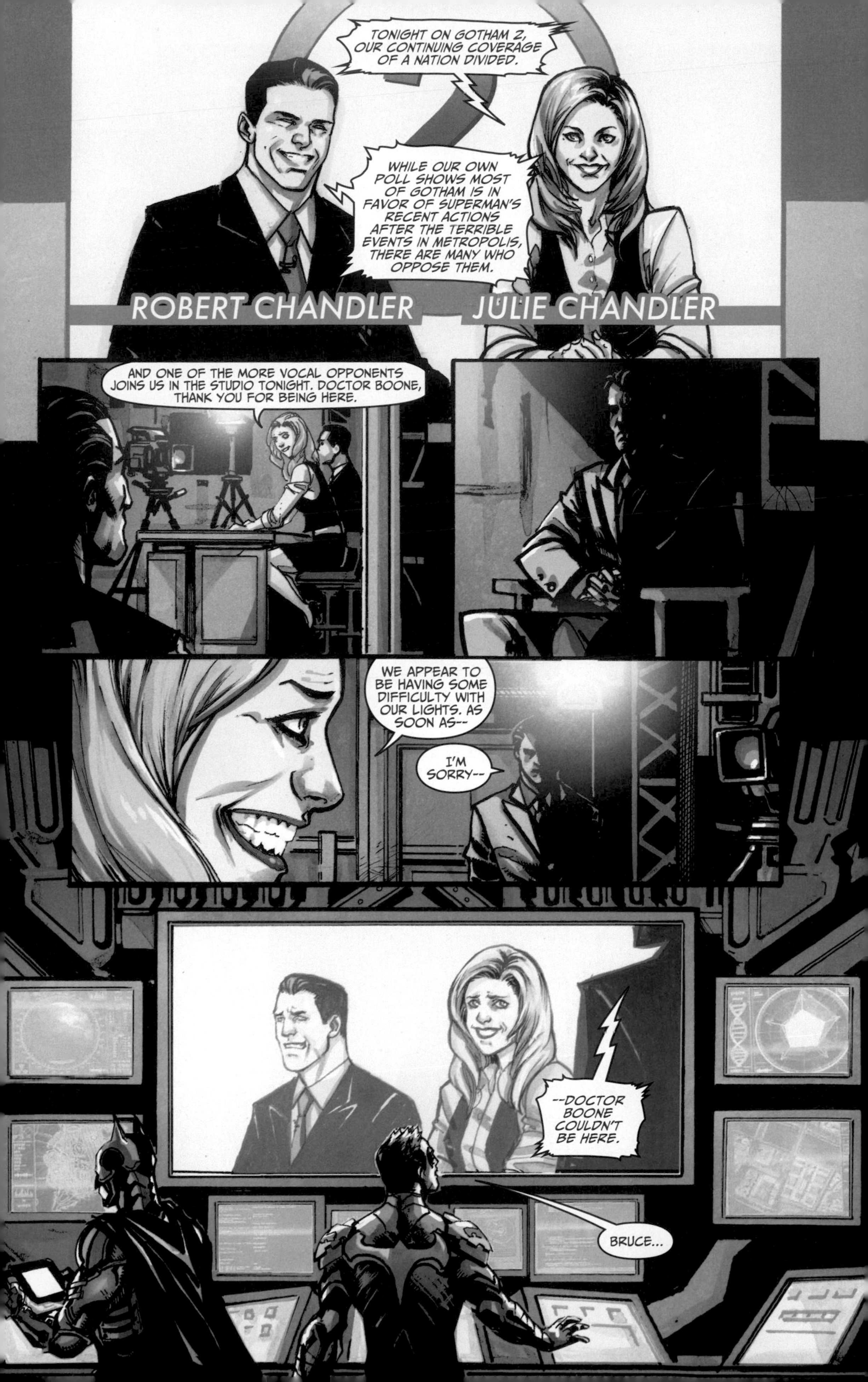
TONIGHT ON GOTHAM 2, OUR CONTINUING COVERAGE OF A NATION DIVIDED.
WHILE OUR OWN POLL SHOWS MOST OF GOTHAM IS IN FAVOR OF SUPERMAN'S RECENT ACTIONS AFTER THE TERRIBLE EVENTS IN METROPOLIS, THERE ARE MANY WHO OPPOSE THEM.
ROBERT CHANDLER
JULIE CHANDLER
AND ONE OF THE MORE VOCAL OPPONENTS JOINS US IN THE STUDIO TONIGHT. DOCTOR BOONE, THANK YOU FOR BEING HERE.
WE APPEAR TO BE HAVING SOME DIFFICULTY WITH OUR LIGHTS. AS SOON AS--
I'M SORRY--
--DOCTOR BOONE COULDN'T BE HERE.
BRUCE...

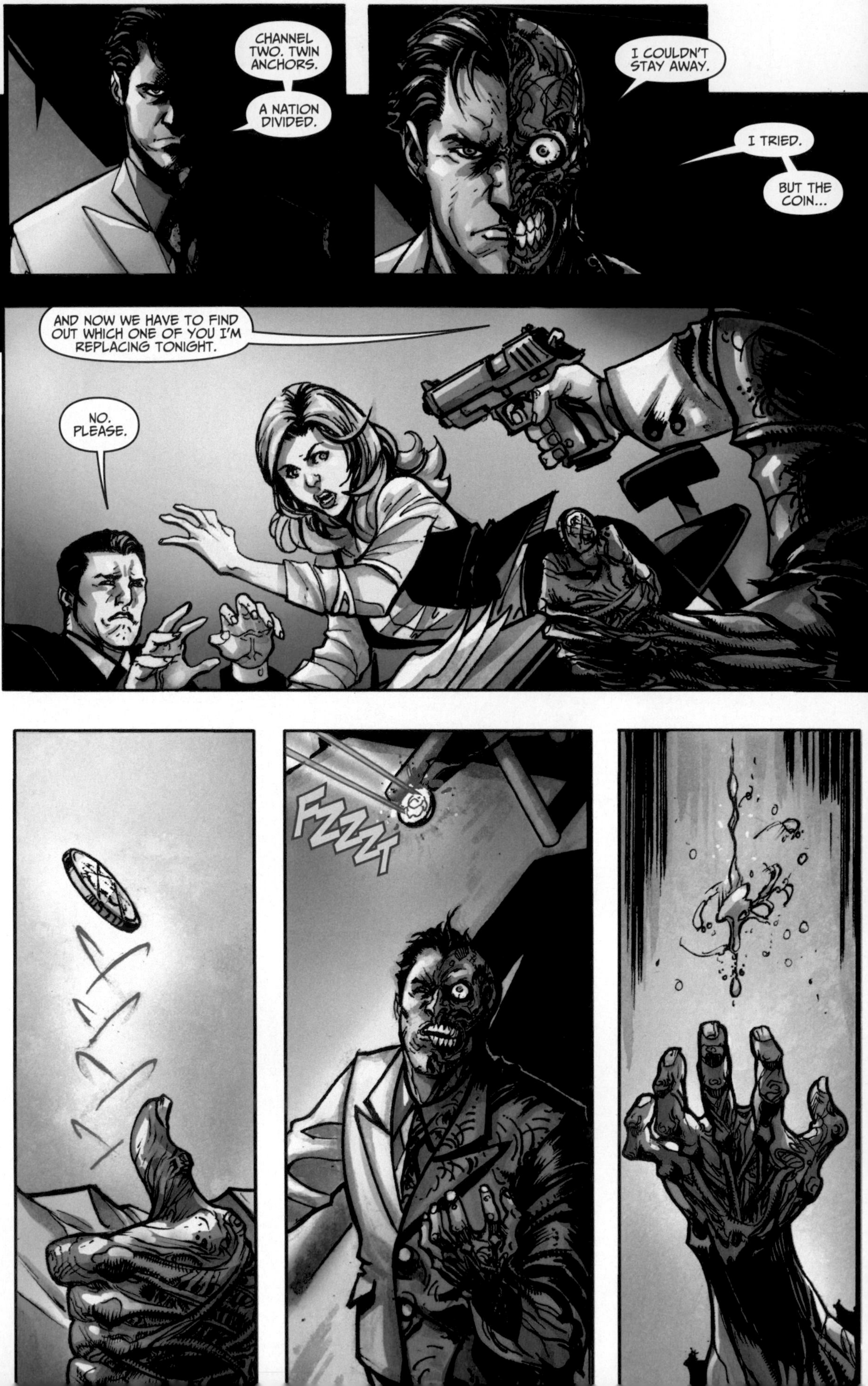
CHANNEL TWO. TWIN ANCHORS.
A NATION DIVIDED.
I COULDN'T STAY AWAY.
I TRIED.
BUT THE COIN...
AND NOW WE HAVE TO FIND OUT WHICH ONE OF YOU I'M REPLACING TONIGHT.
NO. PLEASE.
FZZZT

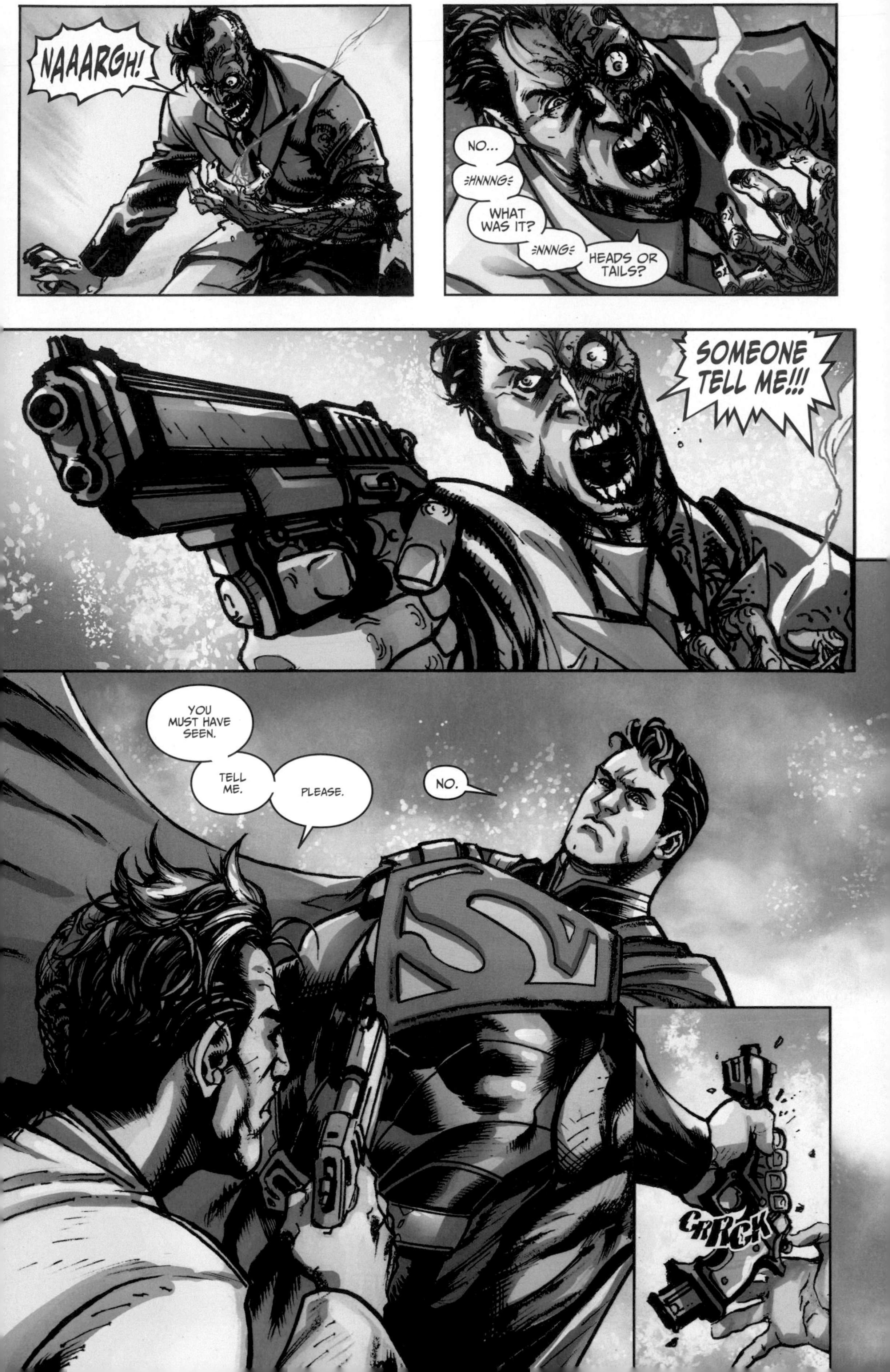
NAAARGH!
NO...
HNNNG
WHAT WAS IT?
NNNG
HEADS OR TAILS?
SOMEONE TELL ME!!!
YOU MUST HAVE SEEN.
TELL ME.
PLEASE.
NO.
GRRCK

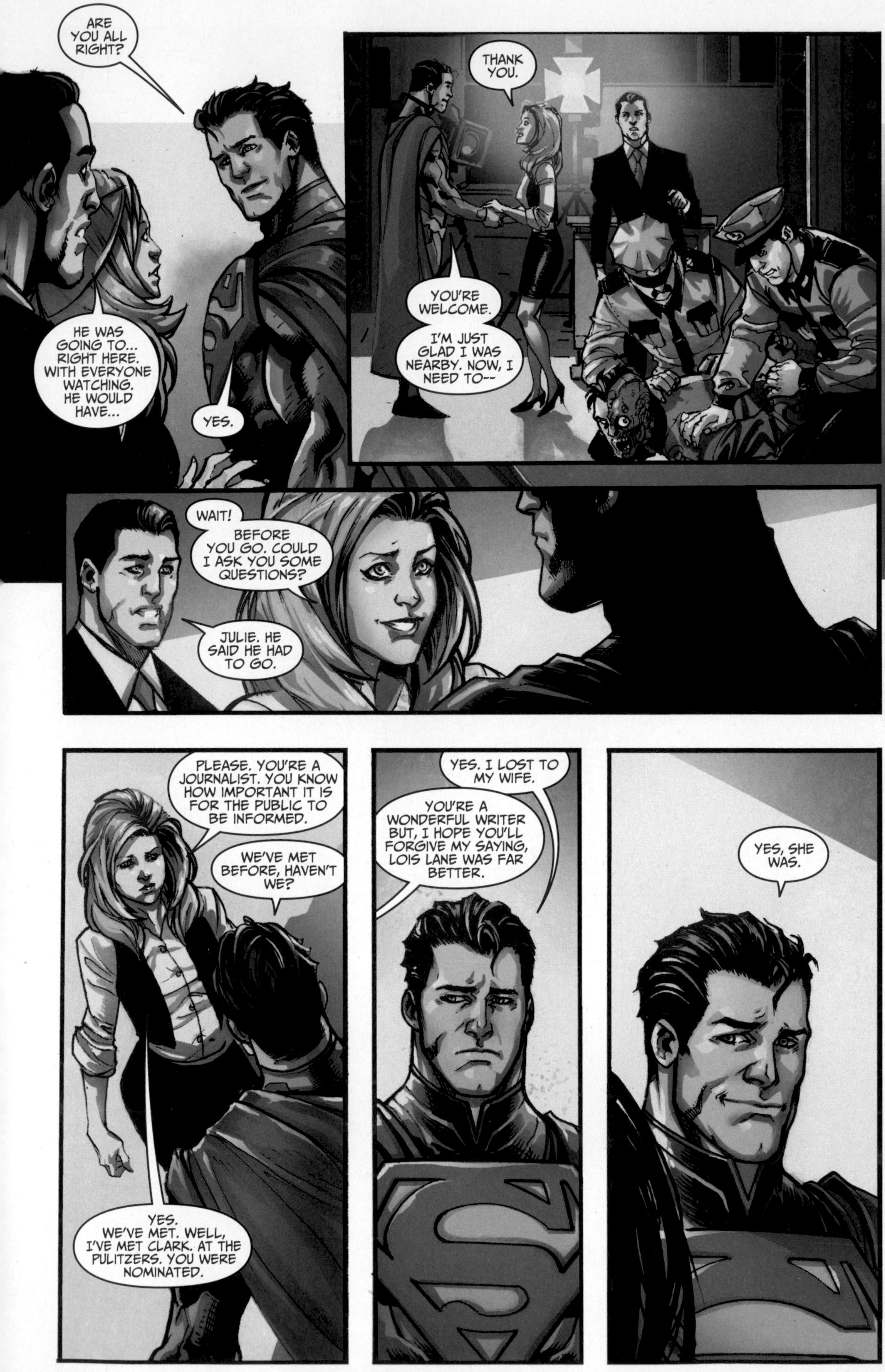
ARE YOU ALL RIGHT?
HE WAS GOING TO... RIGHT HERE. WITH EVERYONE WATCHING. HE WOULD HAVE...
YES.
THANK YOU.
YOU'RE WELCOME.
I'M JUST GLAD I WAS NEARBY. NOW, I NEED TO--
WAIT!
BEFORE YOU GO. COULD I ASK YOU SOME QUESTIONS?
JULIE. HE SAID HE HAD TO GO.
PLEASE. YOU'RE A JOURNALIST. YOU KNOW HOW IMPORTANT IT IS FOR THE PUBLIC TO BE INFORMED.
WE'VE MET BEFORE, HAVEN'T WE?
YES. WE'VE MET. WELL, I'VE MET CLARK. AT THE PULITZERS. YOU WERE NOMINATED.
YES. I LOST TO MY WIFE.
YOU'RE A WONDERFUL WRITER BUT, I HOPE YOU'LL FORGIVE MY SAYING, LOIS LANE WAS FAR BETTER.
YES, SHE WAS.

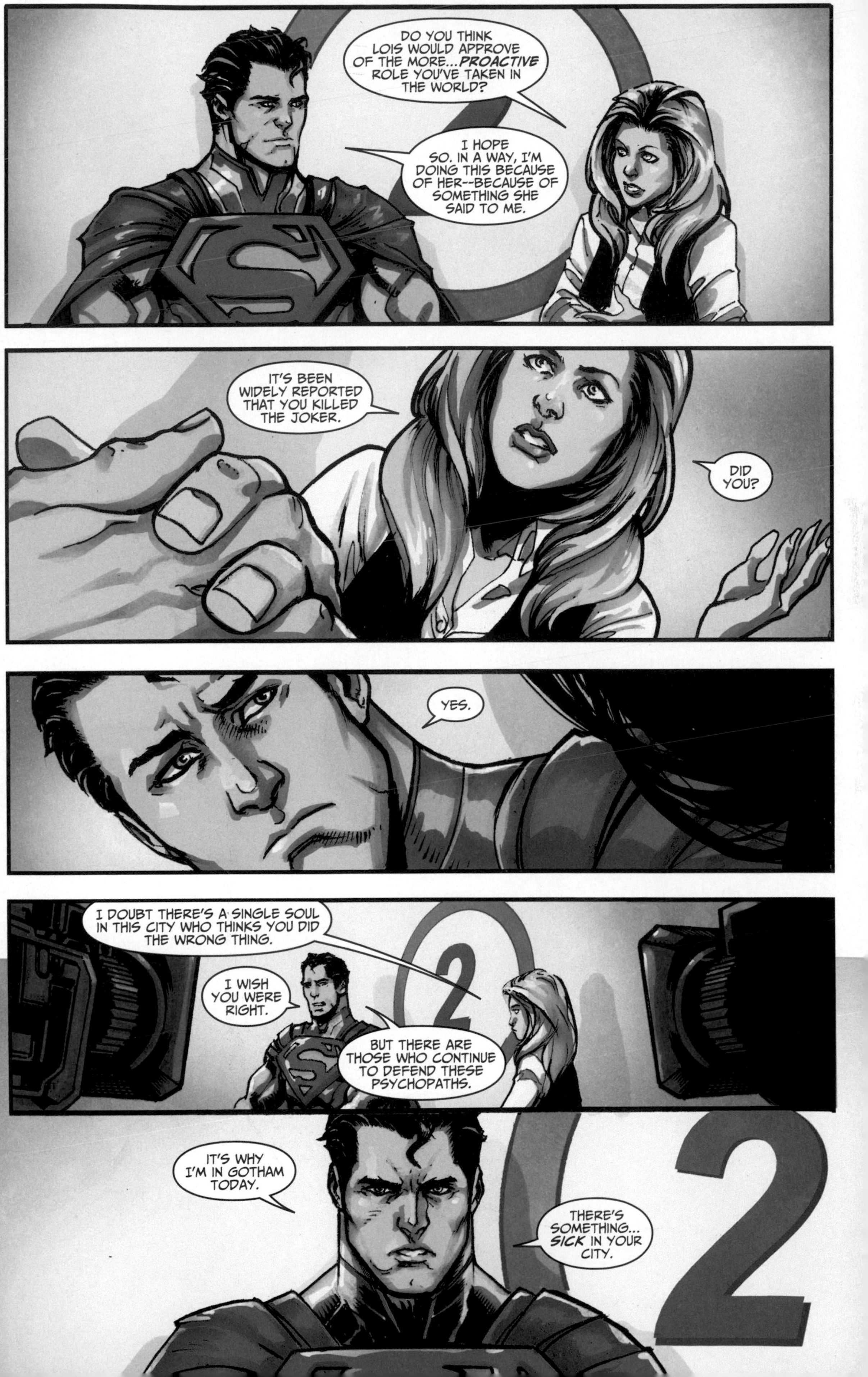
DO YOU THINK LOIS WOULD APPROVE OF THE MORE...PROACTIVE ROLE YOU'VE TAKEN IN THE WORLD?
I HOPE SO. IN A WAY, I'M DOING THIS BECAUSE OF HER--BECAUSE OF SOMETHING SHE SAID TO ME.
IT'S BEEN WIDELY REPORTED THAT YOU KILLED THE JOKER.
DID YOU?
YES.
I DOUBT THERE'S A SINGLE SOUL IN THIS CITY WHO THINKS YOU DID THE WRONG THING.
I WISH YOU WERE RIGHT.
BUT THERE ARE THOSE WHO CONTINUE TO DEFEND THESE PSYCHOPATHS.
IT'S WHY I'M IN GOTHAM TODAY.
THERE'S SOMETHING... SICK IN YOUR CITY.

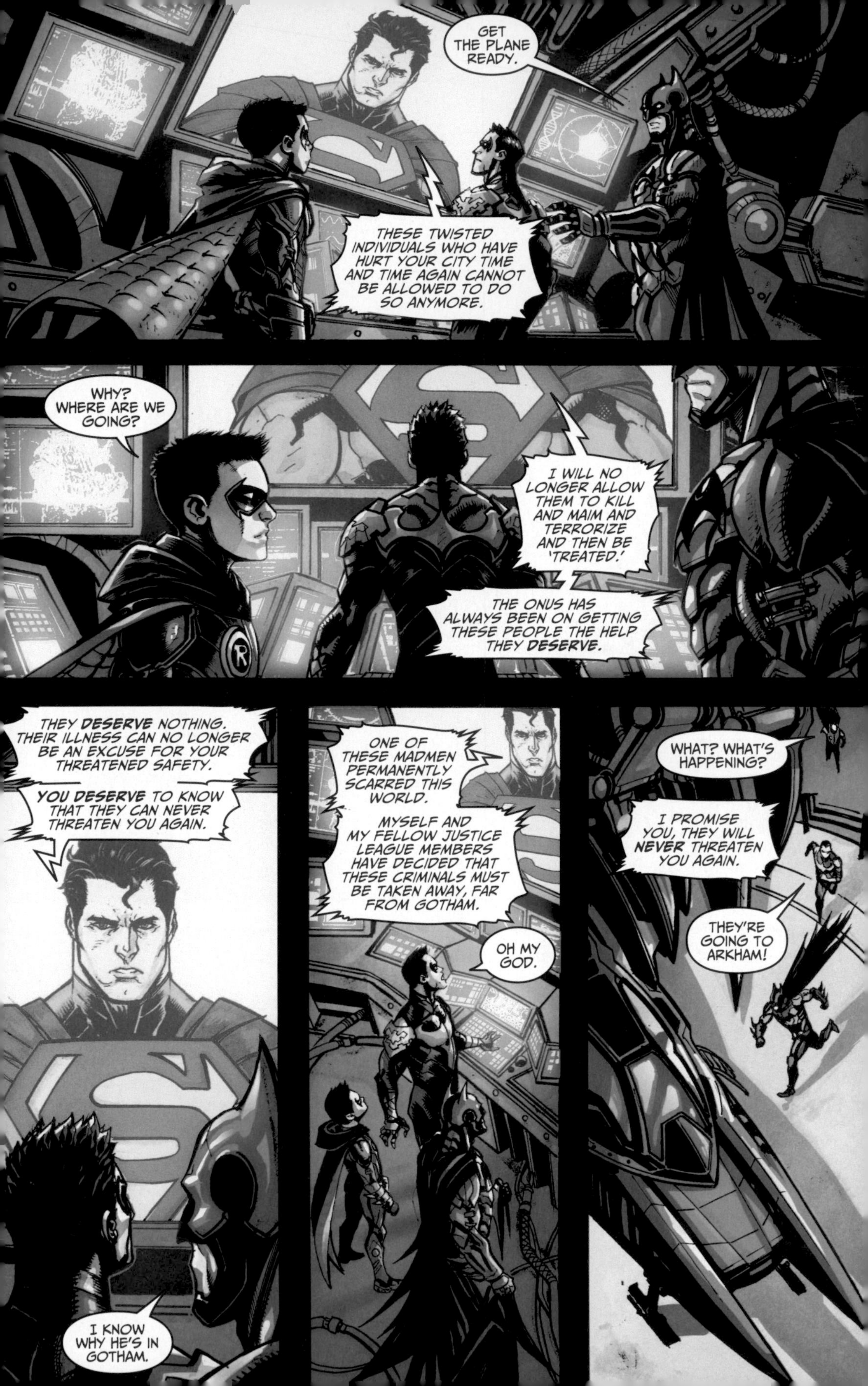
GET THE PLANE READY.
THESE TWISTED INDIVIDUALS WHO HAVE HURT YOUR CITY TIME AND TIME AGAIN CANNOT BE ALLOWED TO DO SO ANYMORE.
WHY? WHERE ARE WE GOING?
I WILL NO LONGER ALLOW THEM TO KILL AND MAIM AND TERRORIZE AND THEN BE 'TREATED.'
THE ONUS HAS ALWAYS BEEN ON GETTING THESE PEOPLE THE HELP THEY **DESERVE.**
THEY **DESERVE** NOTHING. THEIR ILLNESS CAN NO LONGER BE AN EXCUSE FOR YOUR THREATENED SAFETY.
YOU DESERVE TO KNOW THAT THEY CAN NEVER THREATEN YOU AGAIN.
I KNOW WHY HE'S IN GOTHAM.
ONE OF THESE MADMEN PERMANENTLY SCARRED THIS WORLD.
MYSELF AND MY FELLOW JUSTICE LEAGUE MEMBERS HAVE DECIDED THAT THESE CRIMINALS MUST BE TAKEN AWAY, FAR FROM GOTHAM.
OH MY GOD.
WHAT? WHAT'S HAPPENING?
I PROMISE YOU, THEY WILL **NEVER** THREATEN YOU AGAIN.
THEY'RE GOING TO ARKHAM!

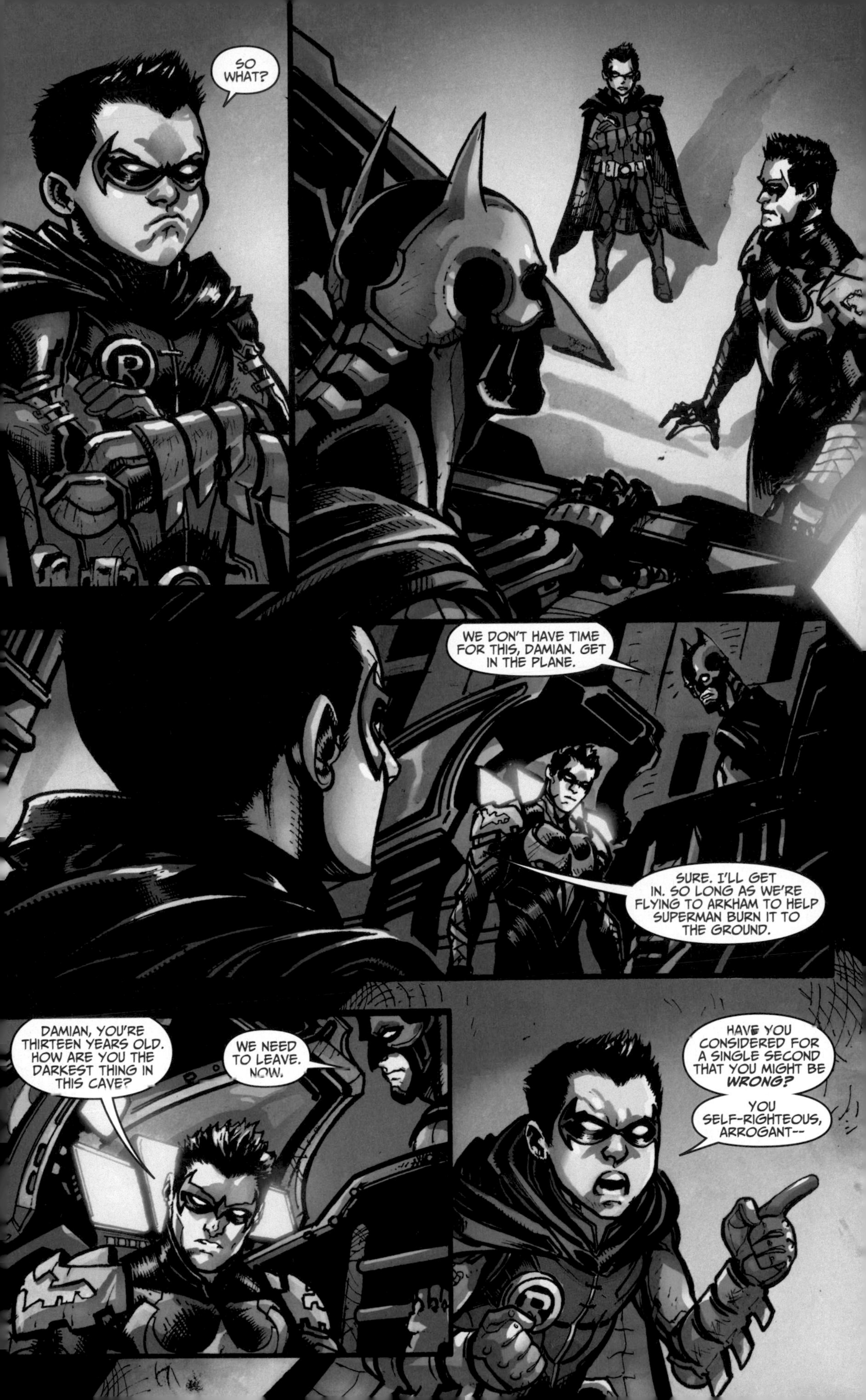
SO WHAT?
WE DON'T HAVE TIME FOR THIS, DAMIAN. GET IN THE PLANE.
SURE. I'LL GET IN. SO LONG AS WE'RE FLYING TO ARKHAM TO HELP SUPERMAN BURN IT TO THE GROUND.
DAMIAN, YOU'RE THIRTEEN YEARS OLD. HOW ARE YOU THE DARKEST THING IN THIS CAVE?
WE NEED TO LEAVE. NOW.
HAVE YOU CONSIDERED FOR A SINGLE SECOND THAT YOU MIGHT BE WRONG?
YOU SELF-RIGHTEOUS, ARROGANT--

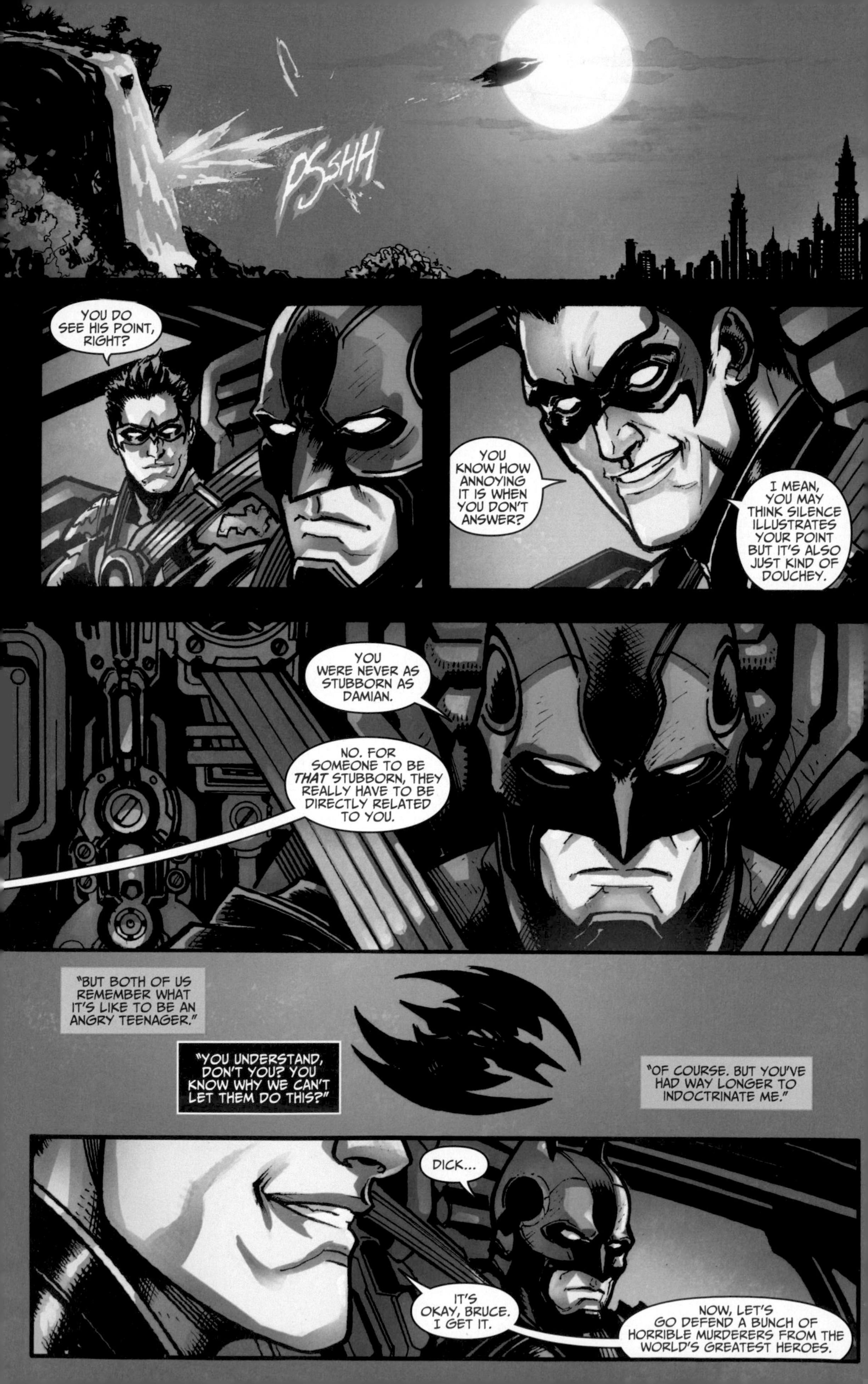
PSSHH
YOU DO SEE HIS POINT, RIGHT?
YOU KNOW HOW ANNOYING IT IS WHEN YOU DON'T ANSWER?
I MEAN, YOU MAY THINK SILENCE ILLUSTRATES YOUR POINT BUT IT'S ALSO JUST KIND OF DOUCHEY.
YOU WERE NEVER AS STUBBORN AS DAMIAN.
NO. FOR SOMEONE TO BE *THAT* STUBBORN, THEY REALLY HAVE TO BE DIRECTLY RELATED TO YOU.
"BUT BOTH OF US REMEMBER WHAT IT'S LIKE TO BE AN ANGRY TEENAGER."
"YOU UNDERSTAND, DON'T YOU? YOU KNOW WHY WE CAN'T LET THEM DO THIS?"
"OF COURSE. BUT YOU'VE HAD WAY LONGER TO INDOCTRINATE ME."
DICK...
IT'S OKAY, BRUCE. I GET IT.
NOW, LET'S GO DEFEND A BUNCH OF HORRIBLE MURDERERS FROM THE WORLD'S GREATEST HEROES.

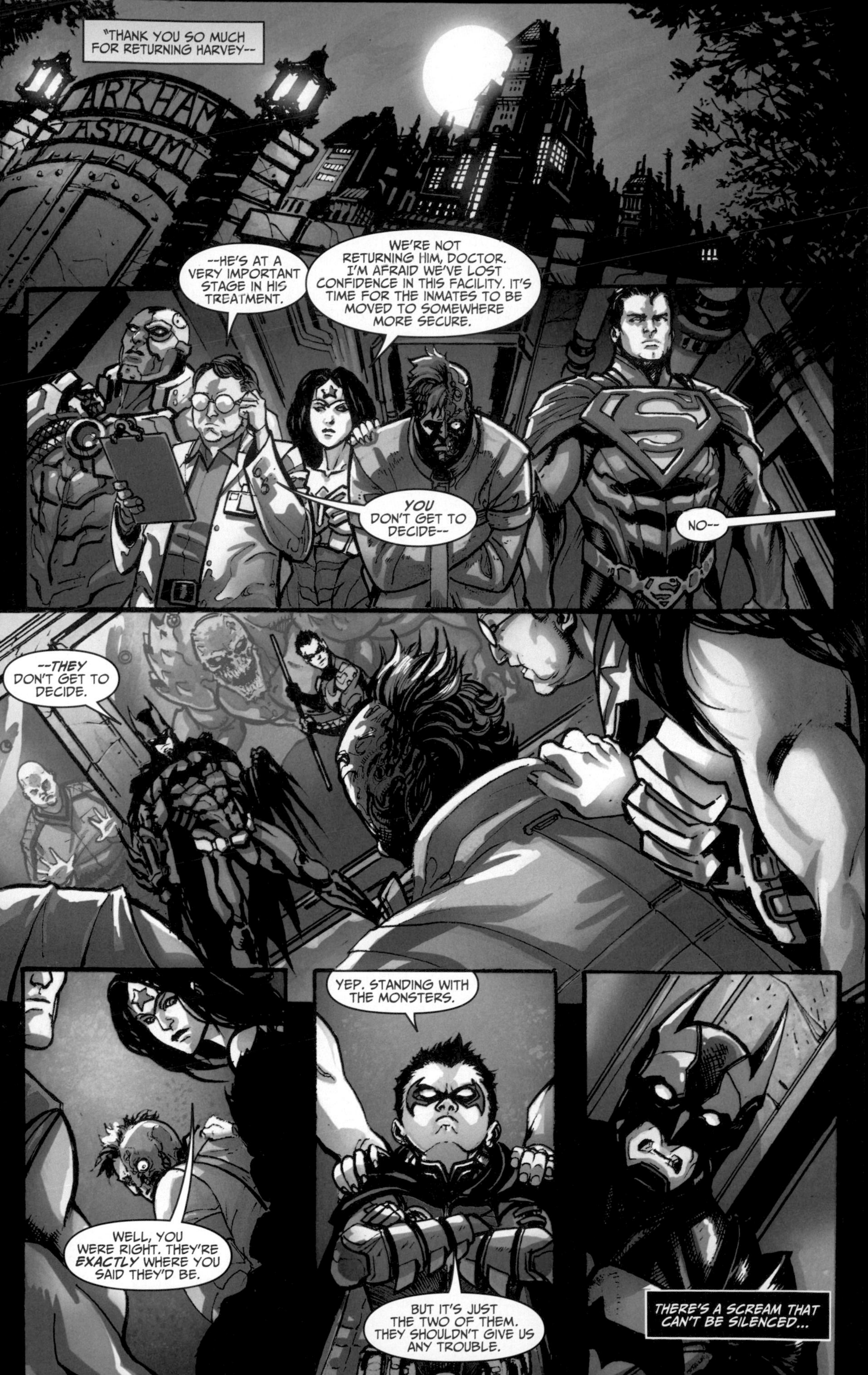

"THANK YOU SO MUCH FOR RETURNING HARVEY--
ARKHAM ASYLUM
--HE'S AT A VERY IMPORTANT STAGE IN HIS TREATMENT.
WE'RE NOT RETURNING HIM, DOCTOR. I'M AFRAID WE'VE LOST CONFIDENCE IN THIS FACILITY. IT'S TIME FOR THE INMATES TO BE MOVED TO SOMEWHERE MORE SECURE.
YOU DON'T GET TO DECIDE--
NO--
--*THEY* DON'T GET TO DECIDE.
WELL, YOU WERE RIGHT. THEY'RE *EXACTLY* WHERE YOU SAID THEY'D BE.
YEP. STANDING WITH THE MONSTERS.
BUT IT'S JUST THE TWO OF THEM. THEY SHOULDN'T GIVE US ANY TROUBLE.
THERE'S A SCREAM THAT CAN'T BE SILENCED...

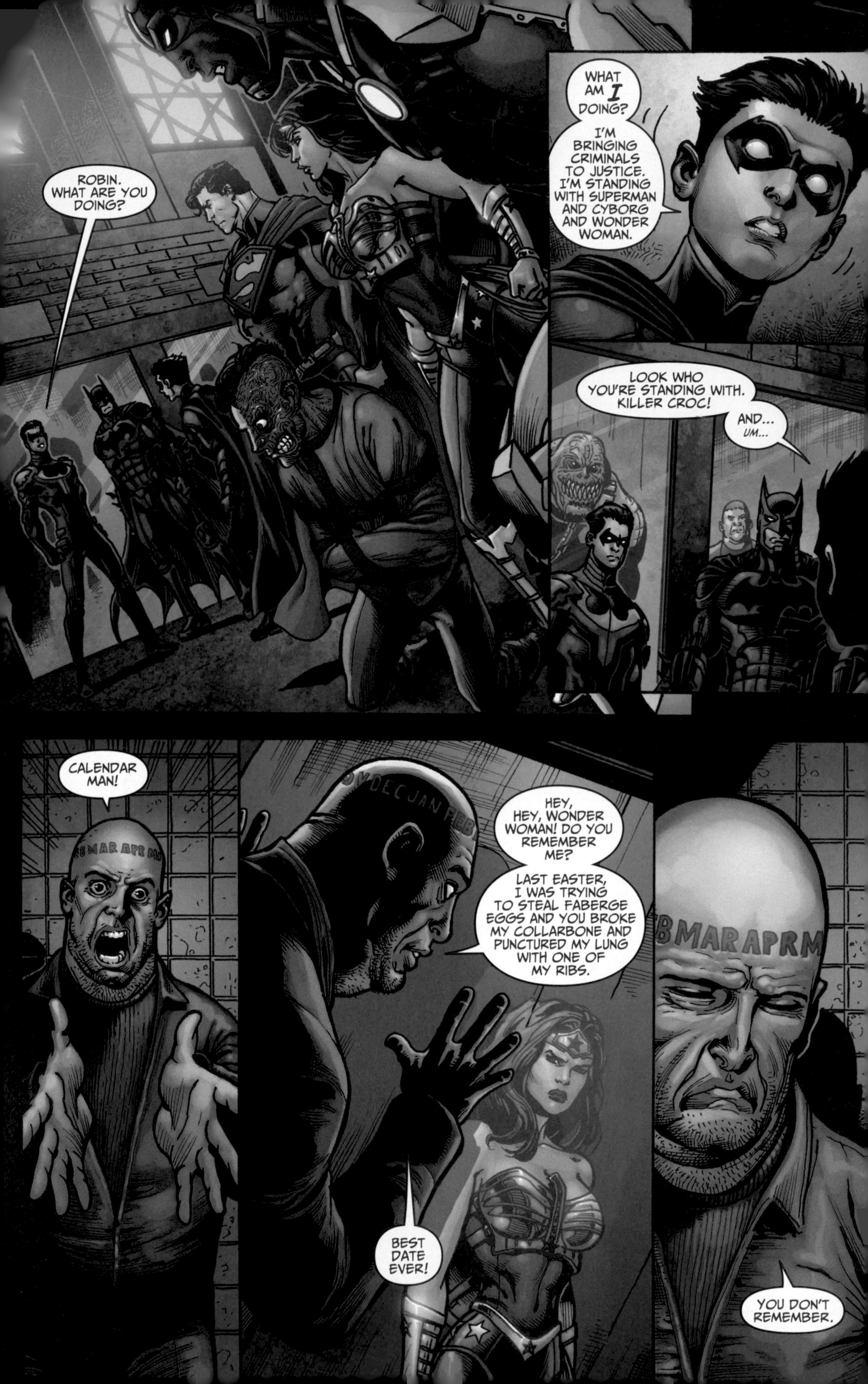
ROBIN. WHAT ARE YOU DOING?
WHAT AM I DOING?
I'M BRINGING CRIMINALS TO JUSTICE. I'M STANDING WITH SUPERMAN AND CYBORG AND WONDER WOMAN.
LOOK WHO YOU'RE STANDING WITH. KILLER CROC!
AND... UM...
CALENDAR MAN!
HEY, HEY, WONDER WOMAN! DO YOU REMEMBER ME?
LAST EASTER, I WAS TRYING TO STEAL FABERGE EGGS AND YOU BROKE MY COLLARBONE AND PUNCTURED MY LUNG WITH ONE OF MY RIBS.
BEST DATE EVER!
YOU DON'T REMEMBER.

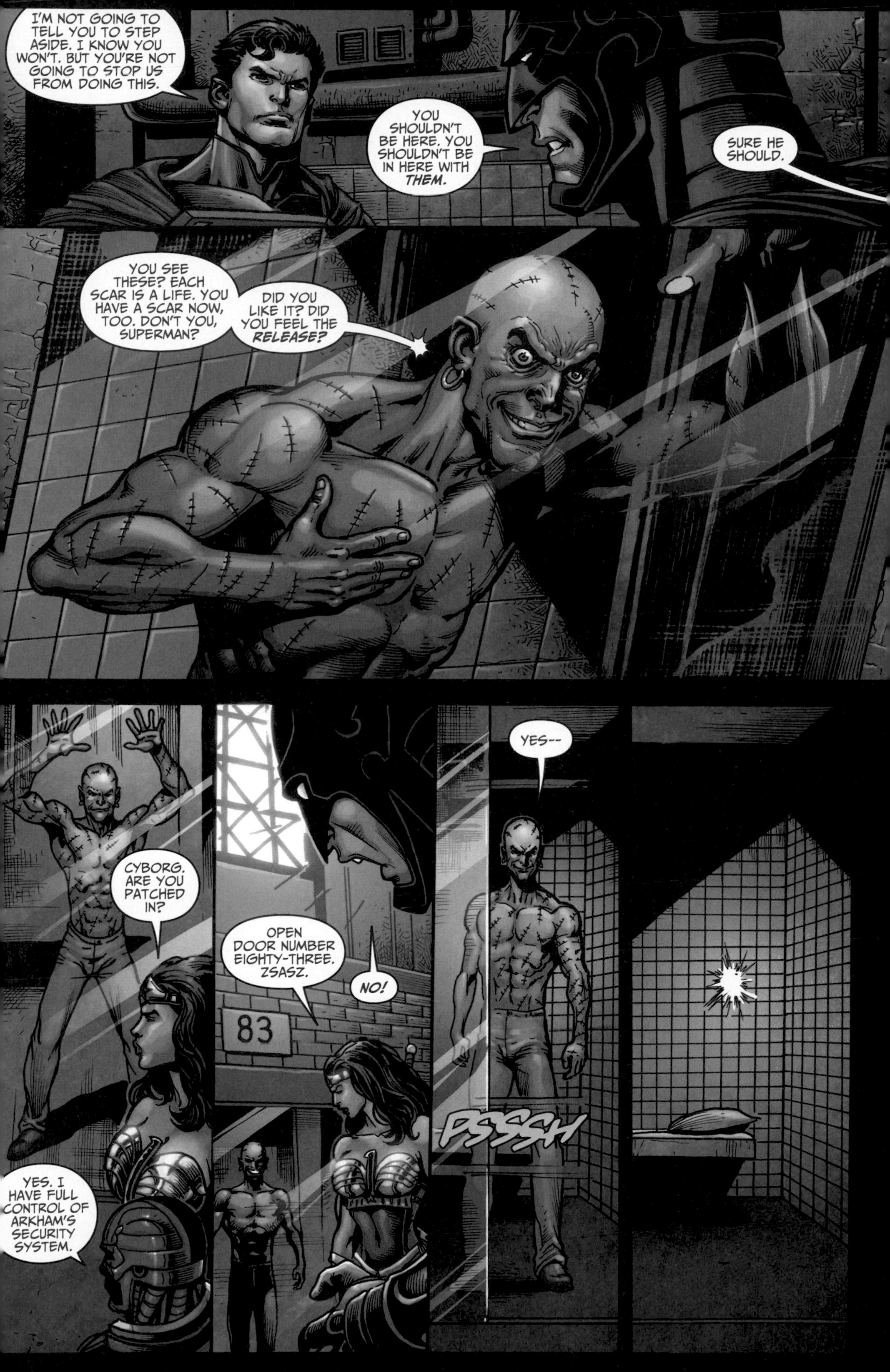
I'M NOT GOING TO TELL YOU TO STEP ASIDE. I KNOW YOU WON'T. BUT YOU'RE NOT GOING TO STOP US FROM DOING THIS.
YOU SHOULDN'T BE HERE. YOU SHOULDN'T BE IN HERE WITH THEM.
SURE HE SHOULD.
YOU SEE THESE? EACH SCAR IS A LIFE. YOU HAVE A SCAR NOW, TOO. DON'T YOU, SUPERMAN?
DID YOU LIKE IT? DID YOU FEEL THE RELEASE?
CYBORG. ARE YOU PATCHED IN?
YES. I HAVE FULL CONTROL OF ARKHAM'S SECURITY SYSTEM.
OPEN DOOR NUMBER EIGHTY-THREE. ZSASZ.
NO!
83
YES--
PSSSH

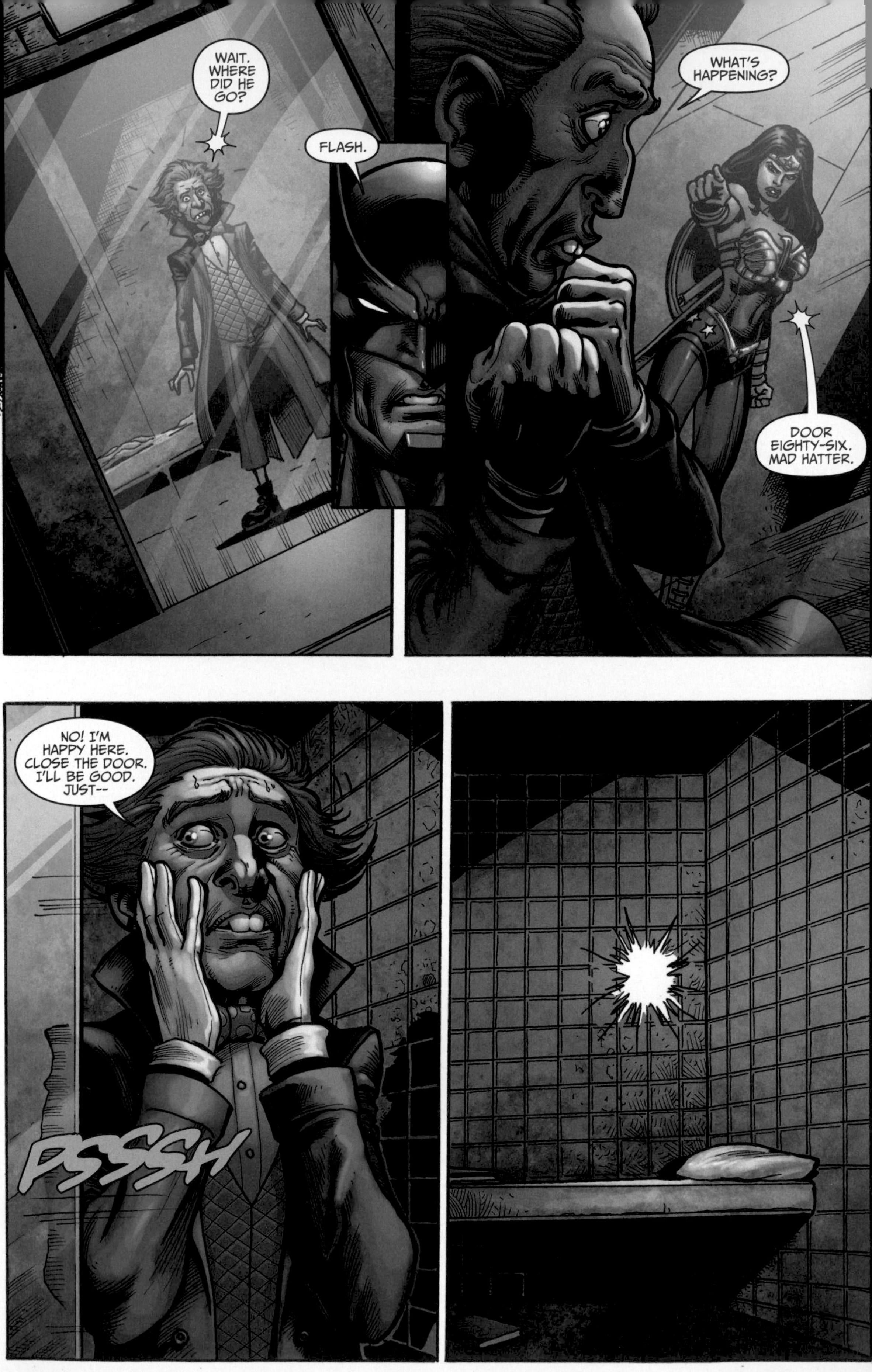
WAIT. WHERE DID HE GO?
FLASH.
WHAT'S HAPPENING?
DOOR EIGHTY-SIX. MAD HATTER.
NO! I'M HAPPY HERE. CLOSE THE DOOR. I'LL BE GOOD. JUST--
PSSSH

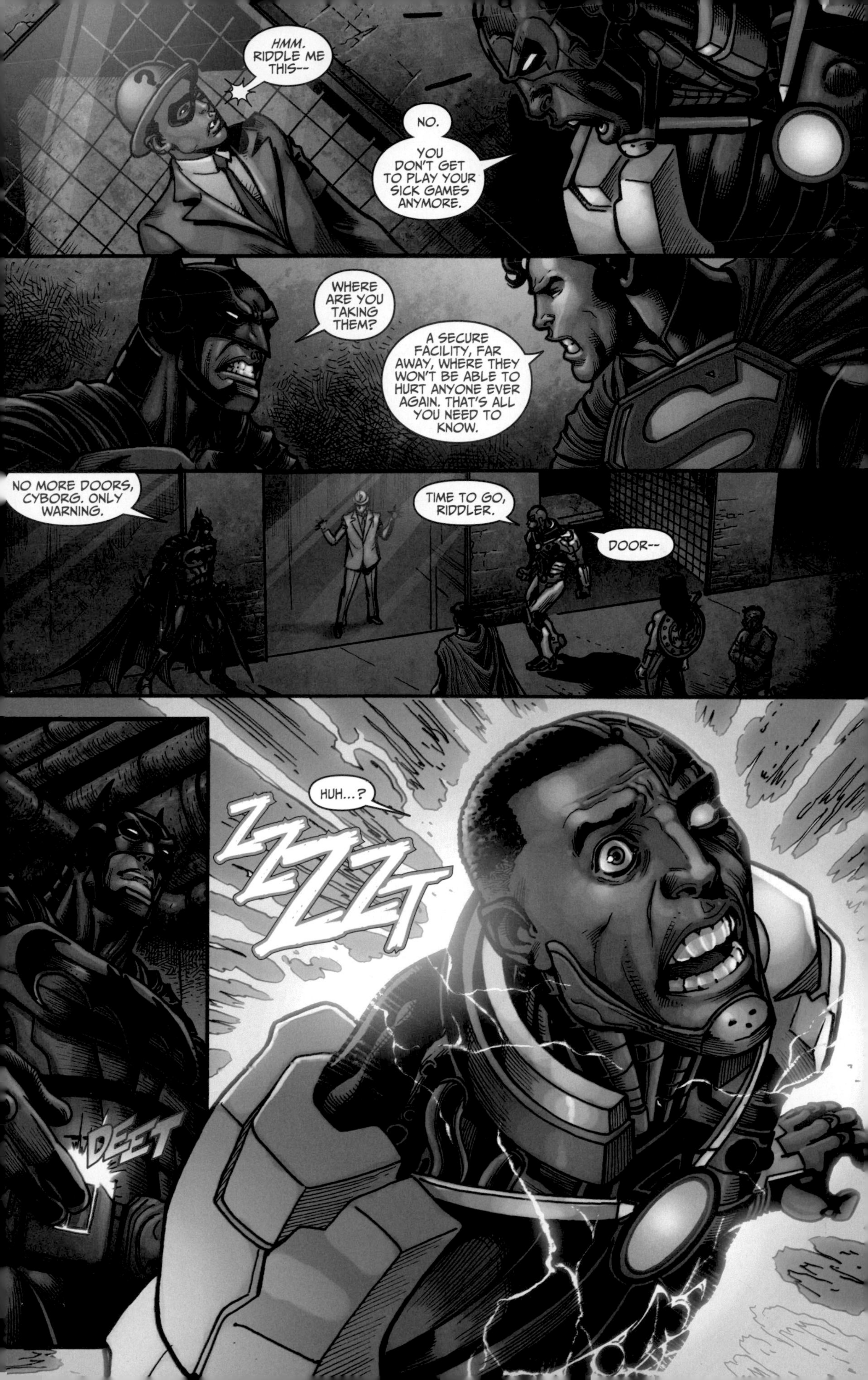
HMM. RIDDLE ME THIS--
NO.
YOU DON'T GET TO PLAY YOUR SICK GAMES ANYMORE.
WHERE ARE YOU TAKING THEM?
A SECURE FACILITY, FAR AWAY, WHERE THEY WON'T BE ABLE TO HURT ANYONE EVER AGAIN. THAT'S ALL YOU NEED TO KNOW.
NO MORE DOORS, CYBORG. ONLY WARNING.
TIME TO GO, RIDDLER.
DOOR--
DEET
HUH...?
ZZZZT

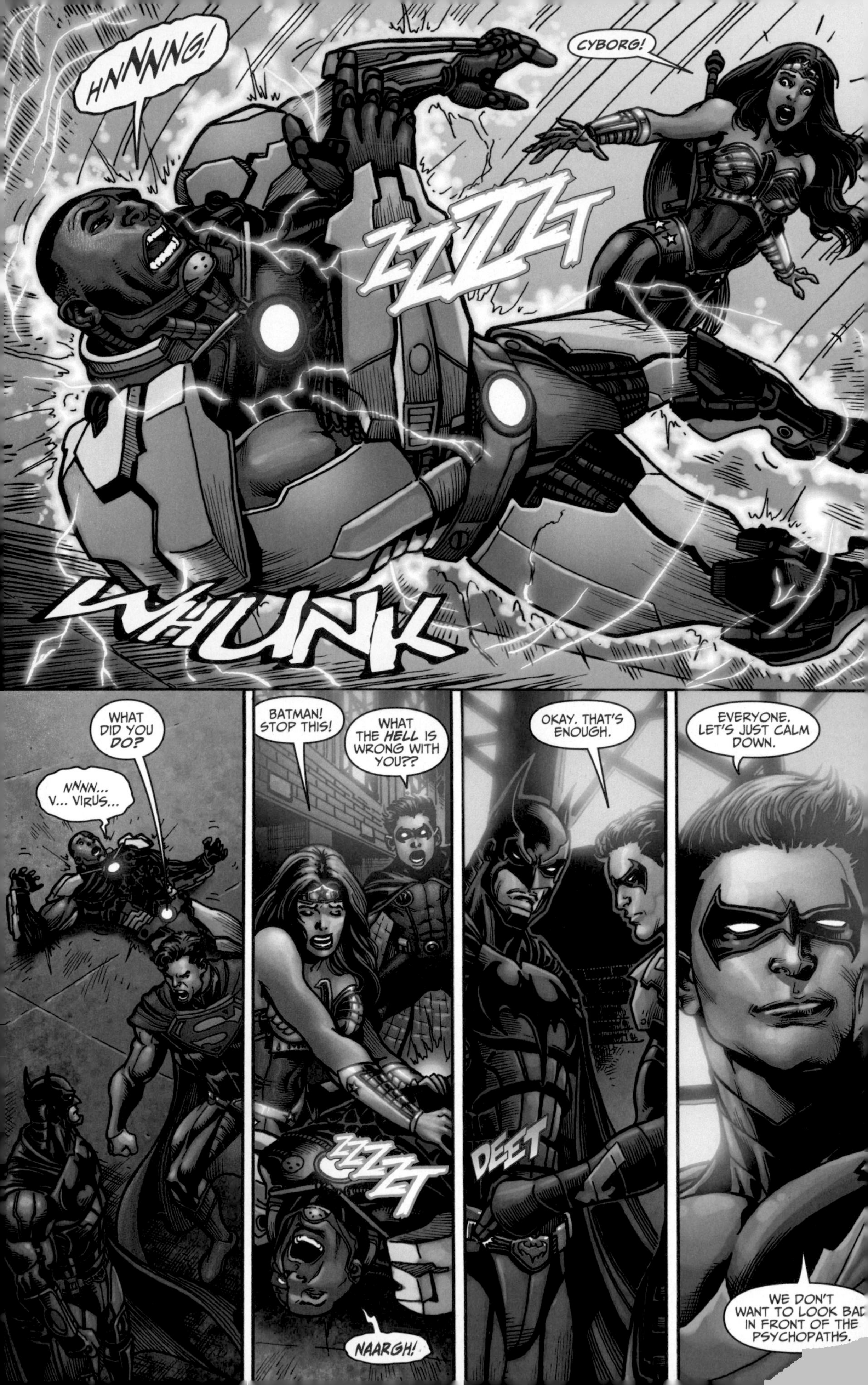
HNNNNG!
CYBORG!
ZZZZZT
WHUNK
WHAT DID YOU DO?
NNNN... V... VIRUS...
BATMAN! STOP THIS!
WHAT THE HELL IS WRONG WITH YOU??
ZZZZZT
NAARGH!
OKAY. THAT'S ENOUGH.
DEET
EVERYONE. LET'S JUST CALM DOWN.
WE DON'T WANT TO LOOK BAD IN FRONT OF THE PSYCHOPATHS.

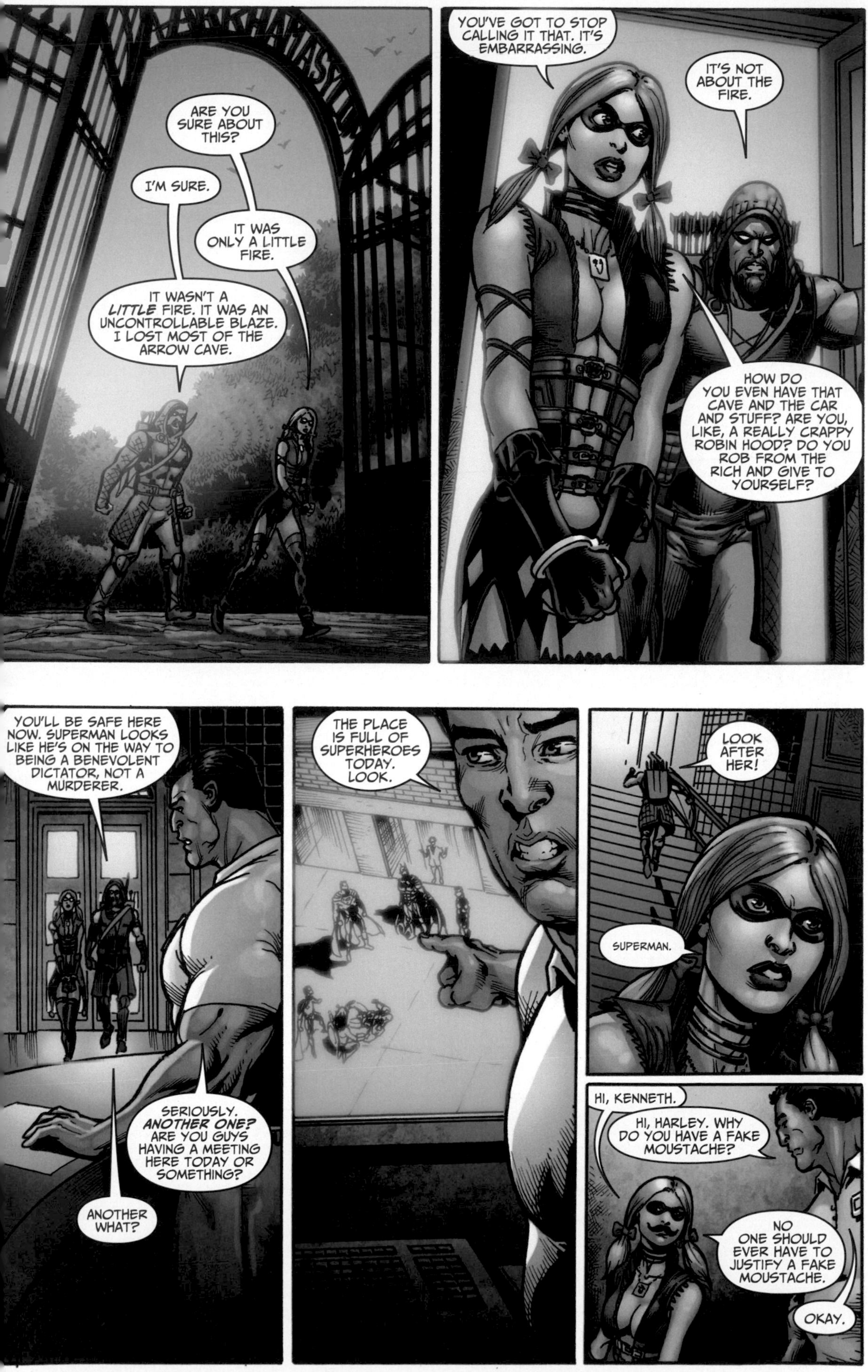
ARKHAM ASYLUM
ARE YOU SURE ABOUT THIS?
I'M SURE.
IT WAS ONLY A LITTLE FIRE.
IT WASN'T A *LITTLE* FIRE. IT WAS AN UNCONTROLLABLE BLAZE. I LOST MOST OF THE ARROW CAVE.
YOU'VE GOT TO STOP CALLING IT THAT. IT'S EMBARRASSING.
IT'S NOT ABOUT THE FIRE.
HOW DO YOU EVEN HAVE THAT CAVE AND THE CAR AND STUFF? ARE YOU, LIKE, A REALLY CRAPPY ROBIN HOOD? DO YOU ROB FROM THE RICH AND GIVE TO YOURSELF?
YOU'LL BE SAFE HERE NOW. SUPERMAN LOOKS LIKE HE'S ON THE WAY TO BEING A BENEVOLENT DICTATOR, NOT A MURDERER.
SERIOUSLY. ***ANOTHER ONE?*** ARE YOU GUYS HAVING A MEETING HERE TODAY OR SOMETHING?
ANOTHER WHAT?
THE PLACE IS FULL OF SUPERHEROES TODAY. LOOK.
LOOK AFTER HER!
SUPERMAN.
HI, KENNETH.
HI, HARLEY. WHY DO YOU HAVE A FAKE MOUSTACHE?
NO ONE SHOULD EVER HAVE TO JUSTIFY A FAKE MOUSTACHE.
OKAY.

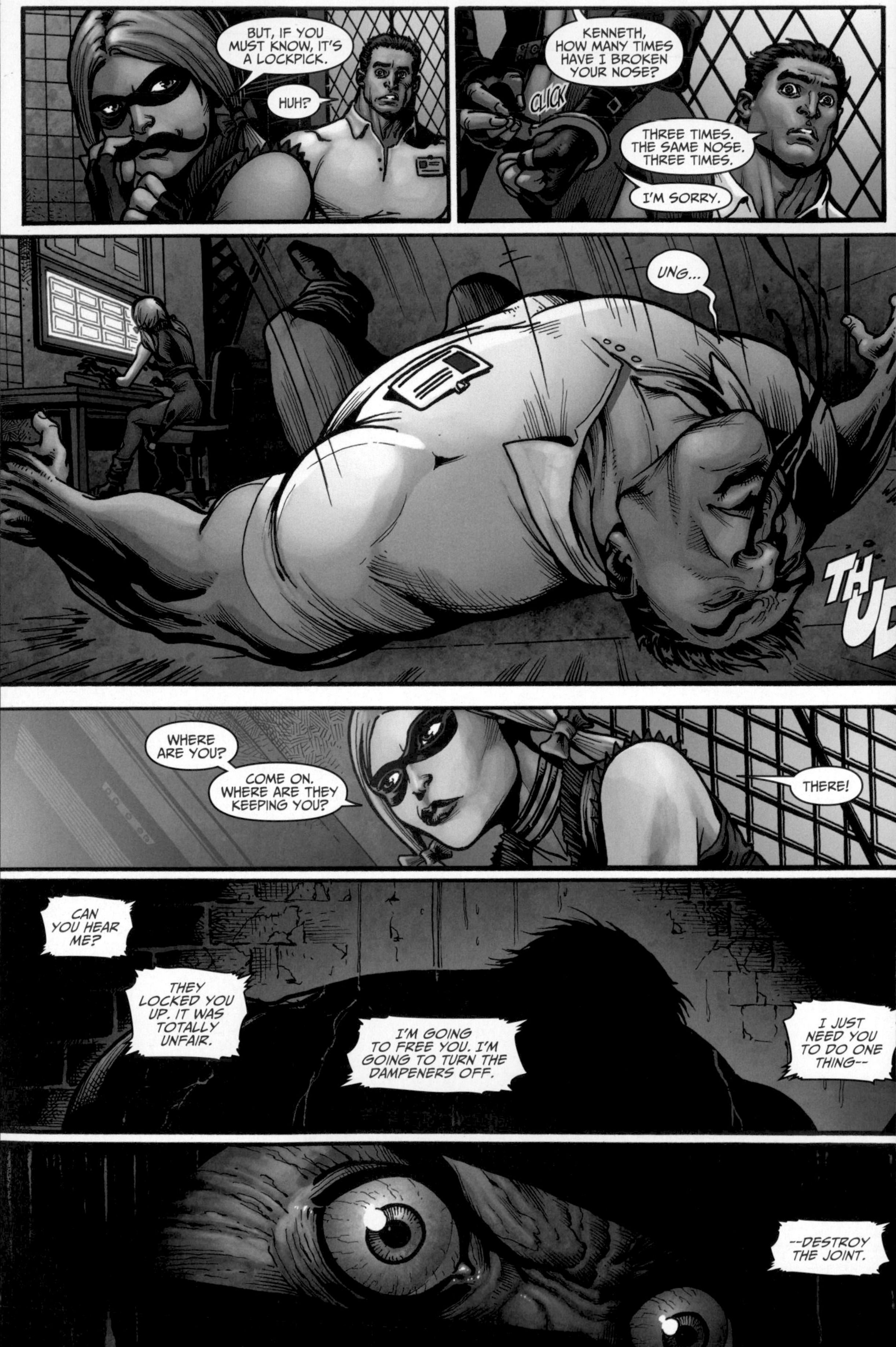
BUT, IF YOU MUST KNOW, IT'S A LOCKPICK.
HUH?
KENNETH, HOW MANY TIMES HAVE I BROKEN YOUR NOSE?
CLICK
THREE TIMES. THE SAME NOSE. THREE TIMES.
I'M SORRY.
UNG...
THUD
WHERE ARE YOU?
COME ON. WHERE ARE THEY KEEPING YOU?
THERE!
CAN YOU HEAR ME?
THEY LOCKED YOU UP. IT WAS TOTALLY UNFAIR.
I'M GOING TO FREE YOU. I'M GOING TO TURN THE DAMPENERS OFF.
I JUST NEED YOU TO DO ONE THING--
--DESTROY THE JOINT.

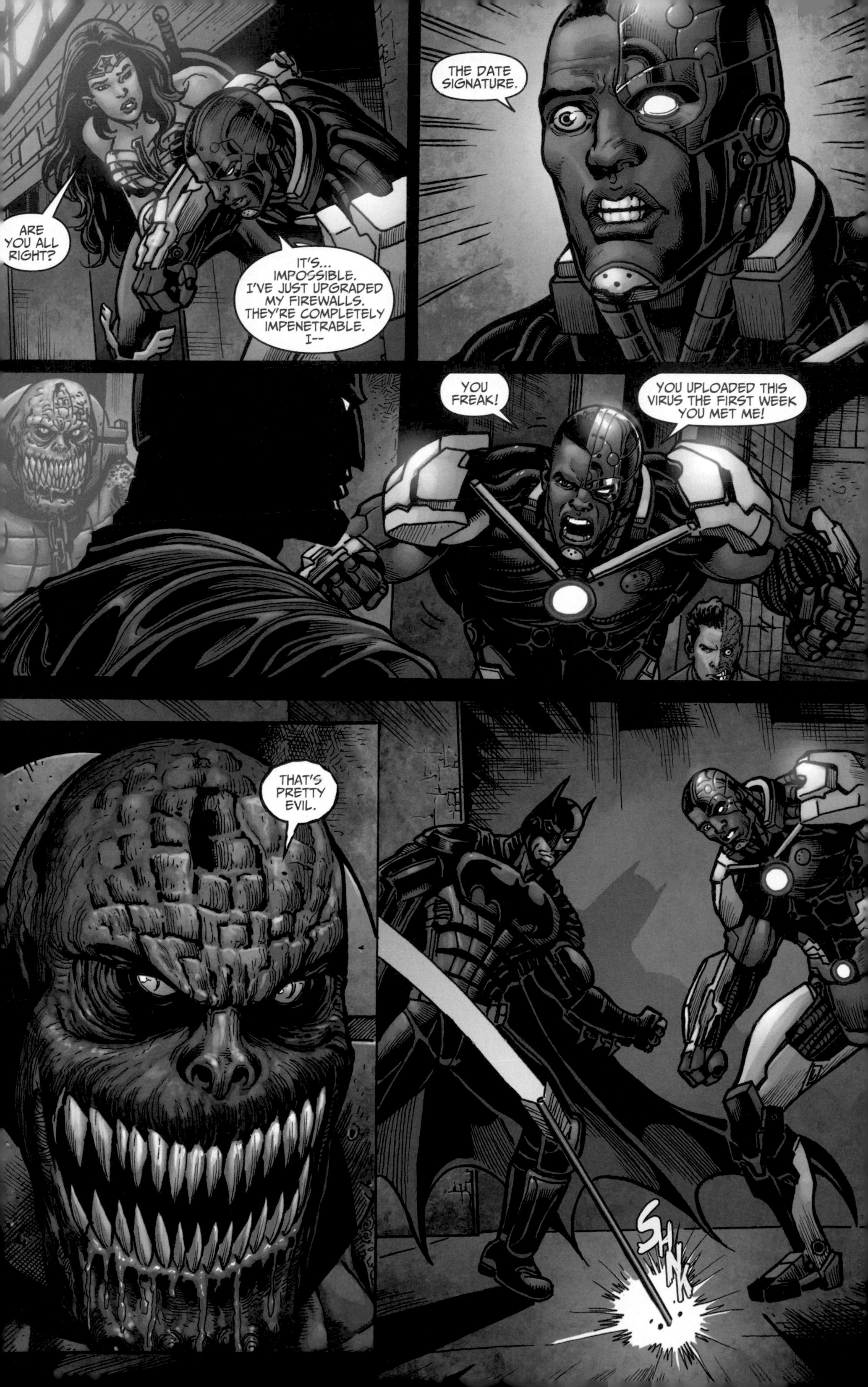
ARE YOU ALL RIGHT?
IT'S... IMPOSSIBLE. I'VE JUST UPGRADED MY FIREWALLS. THEY'RE COMPLETELY IMPENETRABLE. I--
THE DATE SIGNATURE.
YOU FREAK!
YOU UPLOADED THIS VIRUS THE FIRST WEEK YOU MET ME!
THAT'S PRETTY EVIL.
SHNK

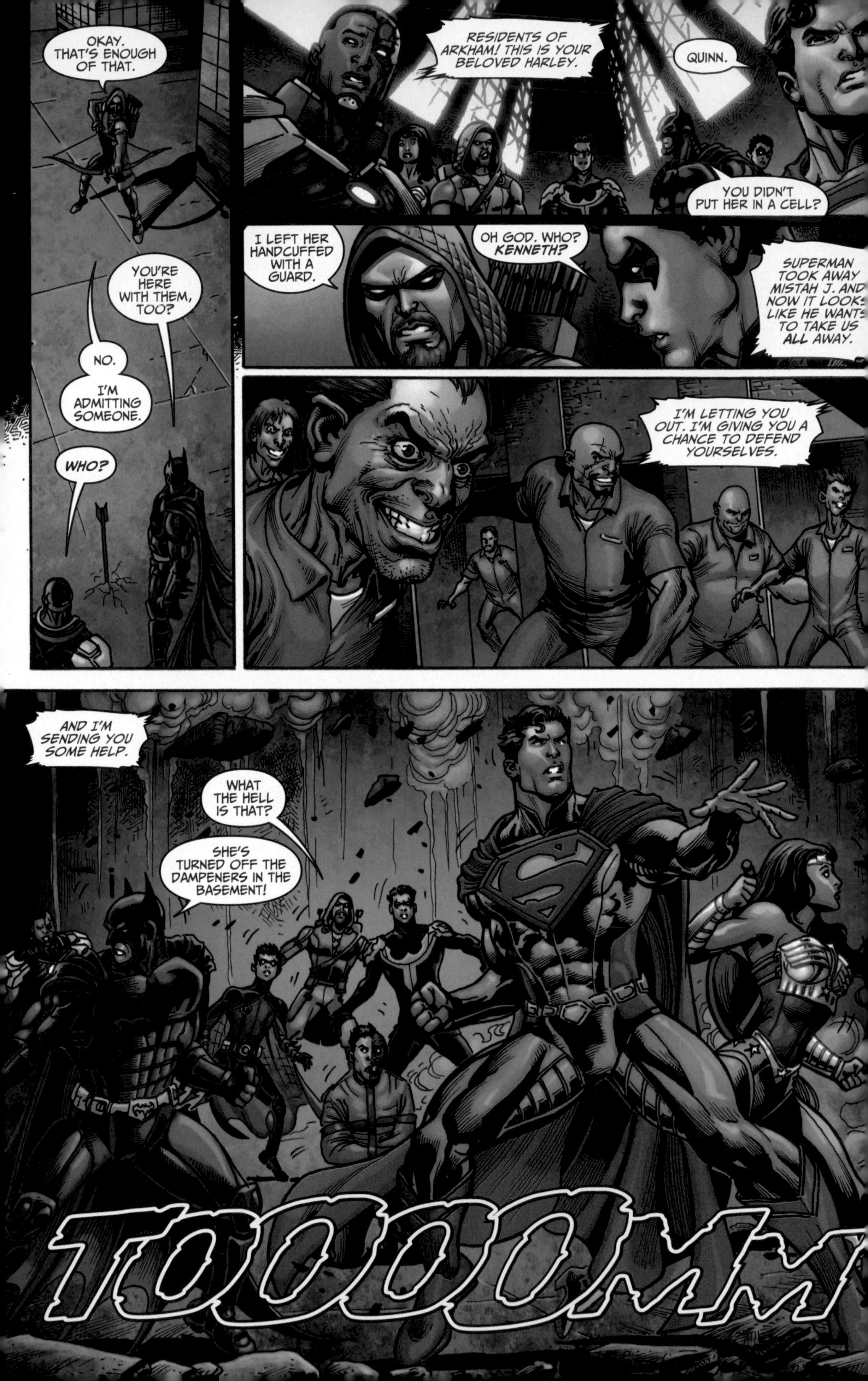
OKAY. THAT'S ENOUGH OF THAT.
RESIDENTS OF ARKHAM! THIS IS YOUR BELOVED HARLEY.
QUINN.
YOU DIDN'T PUT HER IN A CELL?
I LEFT HER HANDCUFFED WITH A GUARD.
OH GOD. WHO? KENNETH?
SUPERMAN TOOK AWAY MISTAH J. AND NOW IT LOOKS LIKE HE WANTS TO TAKE US ALL AWAY.
YOU'RE HERE WITH THEM, TOO?
NO.
I'M ADMITTING SOMEONE.
WHO?
I'M LETTING YOU OUT. I'M GIVING YOU A CHANCE TO DEFEND YOURSELVES.
AND I'M SENDING YOU SOME HELP.
WHAT THE HELL IS THAT?
SHE'S TURNED OFF THE DAMPENERS IN THE BASEMENT!
TOOOOMM

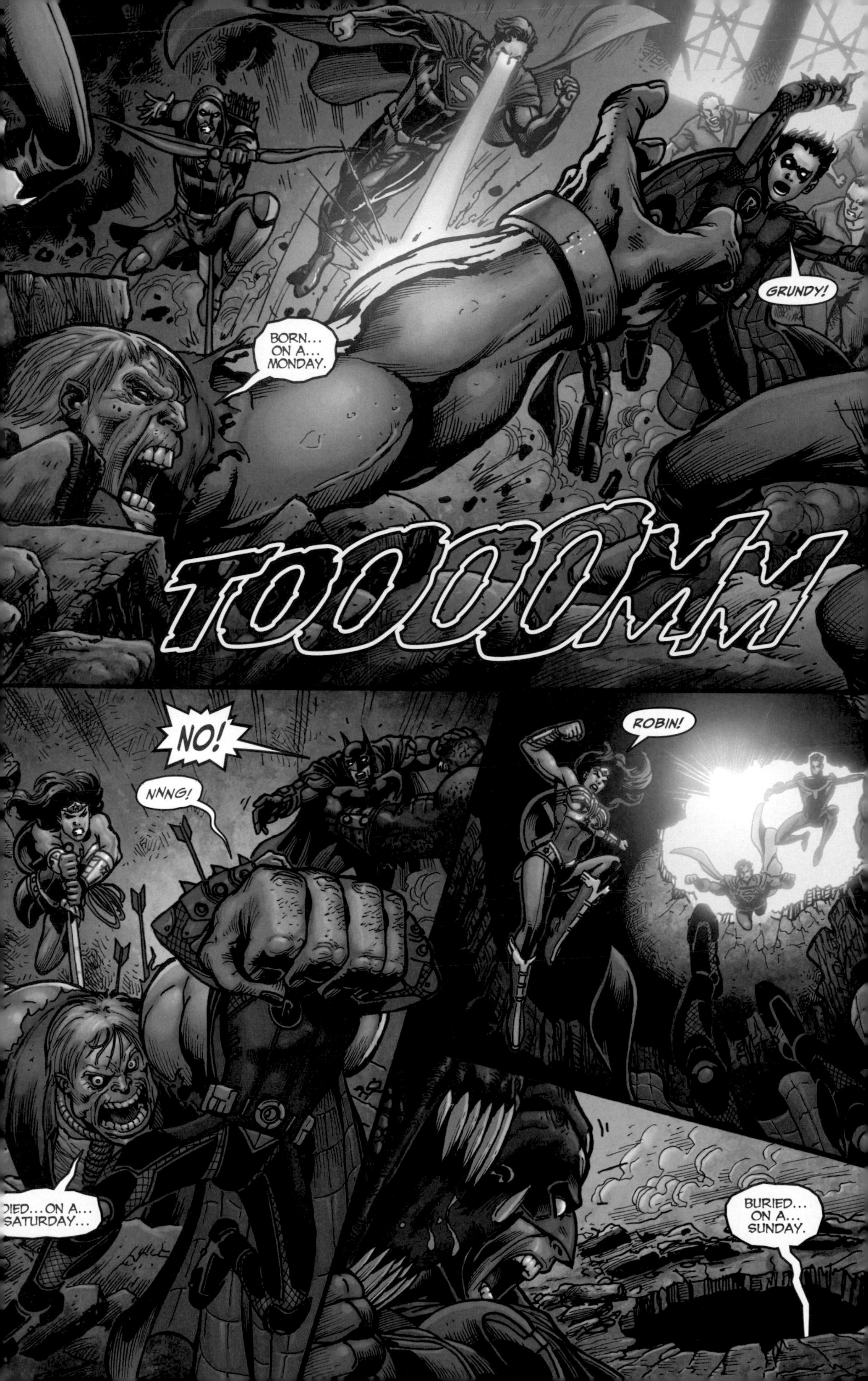
GRUNDY!
BORN... ON A... MONDAY.
TOOOOMM
NO!
NNNG!
ROBIN!
DIED...ON A... SATURDAY...
BURIED... ON A... SUNDAY.

PART SIX

Mike S. Miller David Yardin Jheremy Raapack Pencillers

Mike S. Miller Jheremy Raapack Le Beau Underwood Jonas Trindade David Yardin Inkers

Mico Suayan & **David Lopez** and **Santi Casas** of **Ikari Studio** Cover

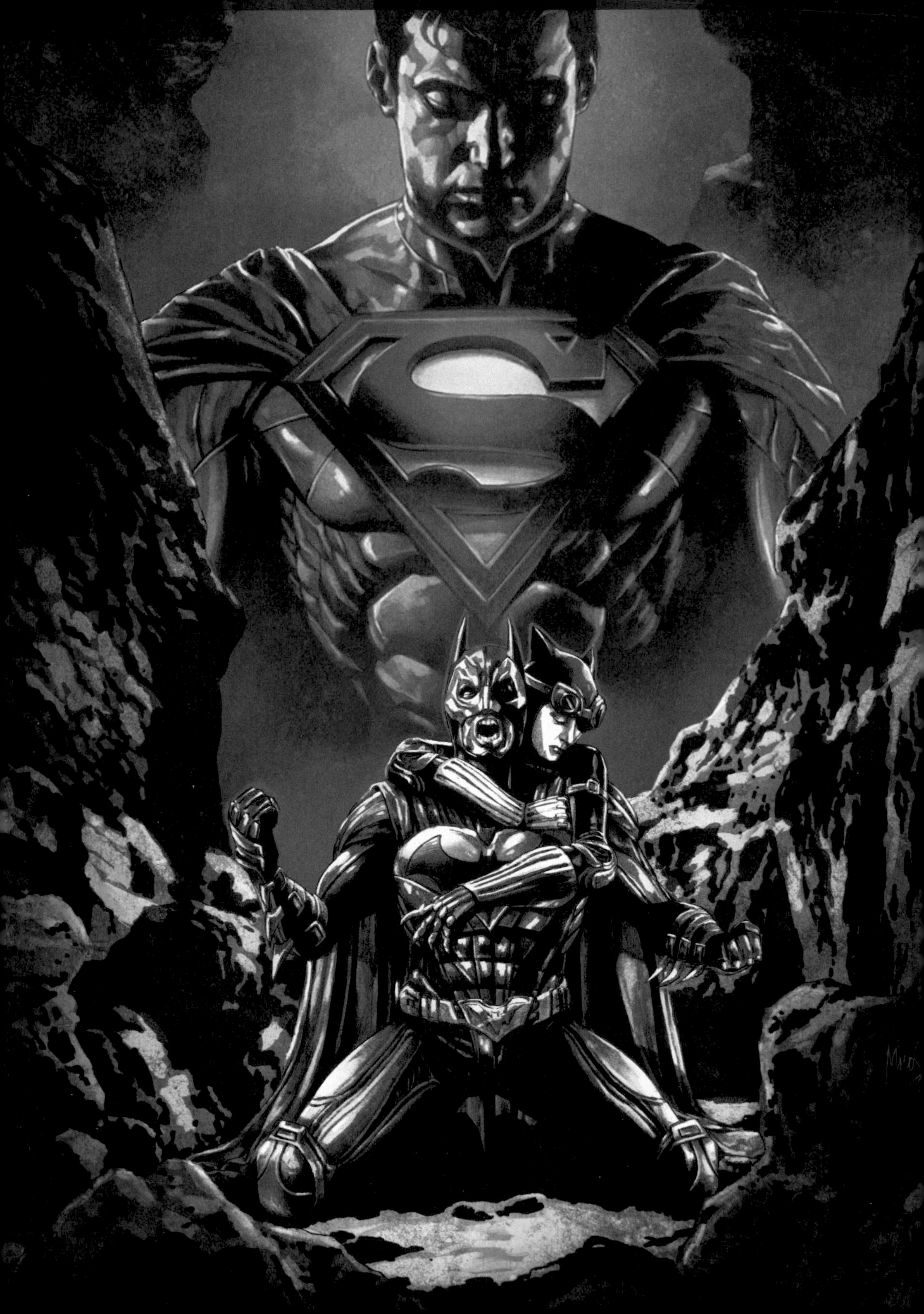

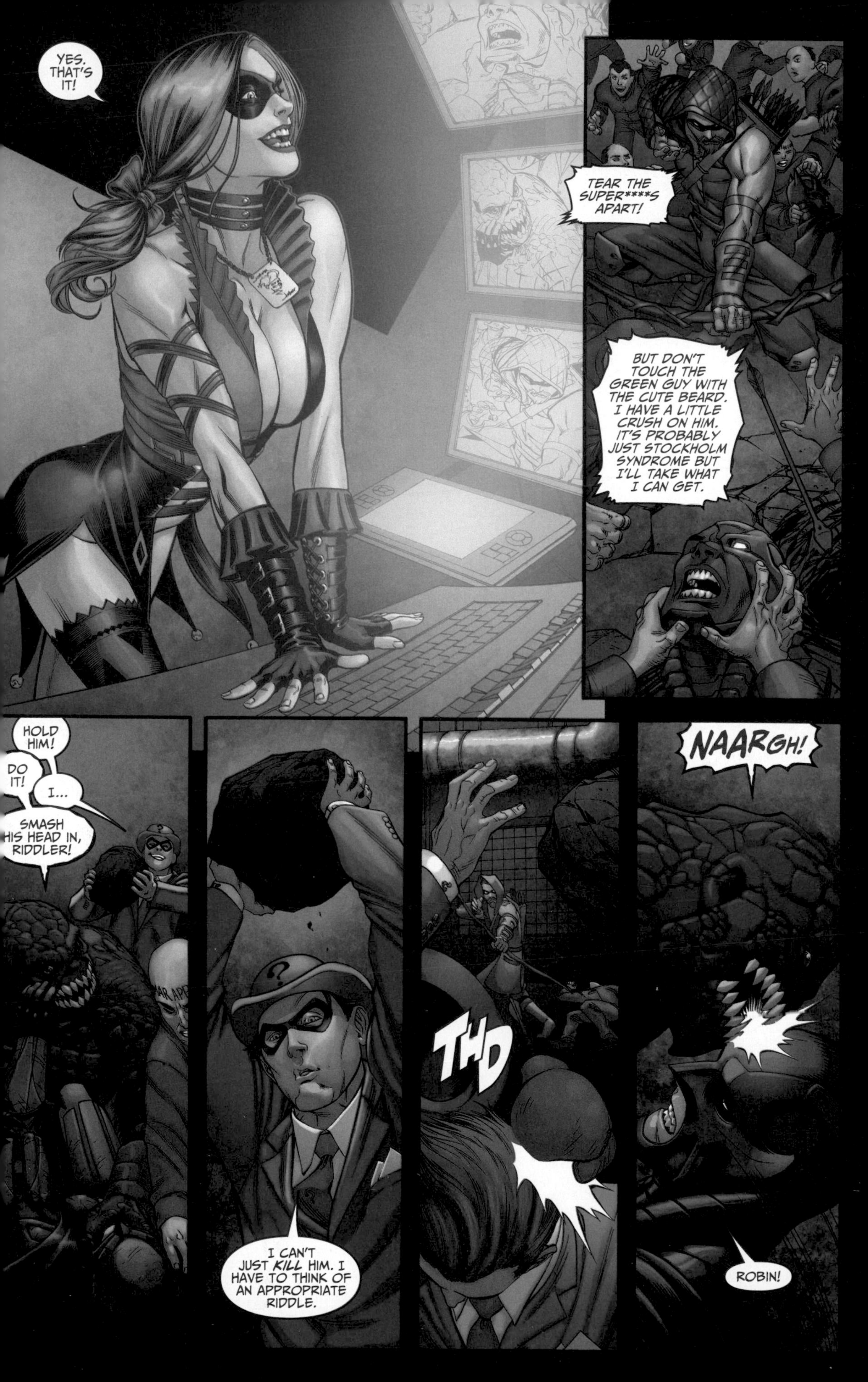
YES. THAT'S IT!
TEAR THE SUPER****S APART!
BUT DON'T TOUCH THE GREEN GUY WITH THE CUTE BEARD. I HAVE A LITTLE CRUSH ON HIM. IT'S PROBABLY JUST STOCKHOLM SYNDROME BUT I'LL TAKE WHAT I CAN GET.
HOLD HIM!
DO IT!
I...
SMASH HIS HEAD IN, RIDDLER!
I CAN'T JUST KILL HIM. I HAVE TO THINK OF AN APPROPRIATE RIDDLE.
THD
NAARGH!
ROBIN!

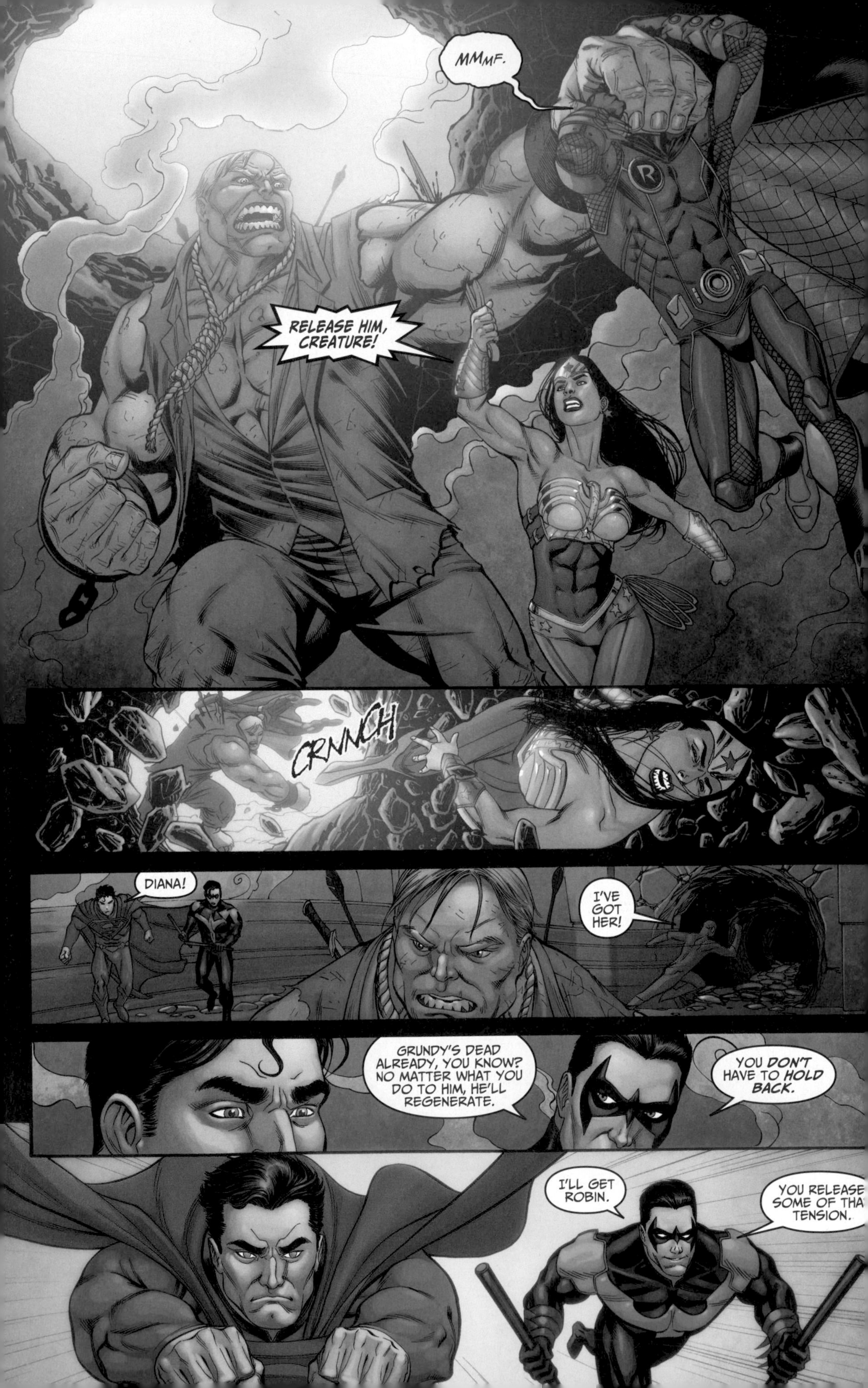
MMMF.
RELEASE HIM, CREATURE!
CRNNCH
DIANA!
I'VE GOT HER!
GRUNDY'S DEAD ALREADY, YOU KNOW? NO MATTER WHAT YOU DO TO HIM, HE'LL REGENERATE.
YOU DON'T HAVE TO HOLD BACK.
I'LL GET ROBIN.
YOU RELEASE SOME OF THA TENSION.

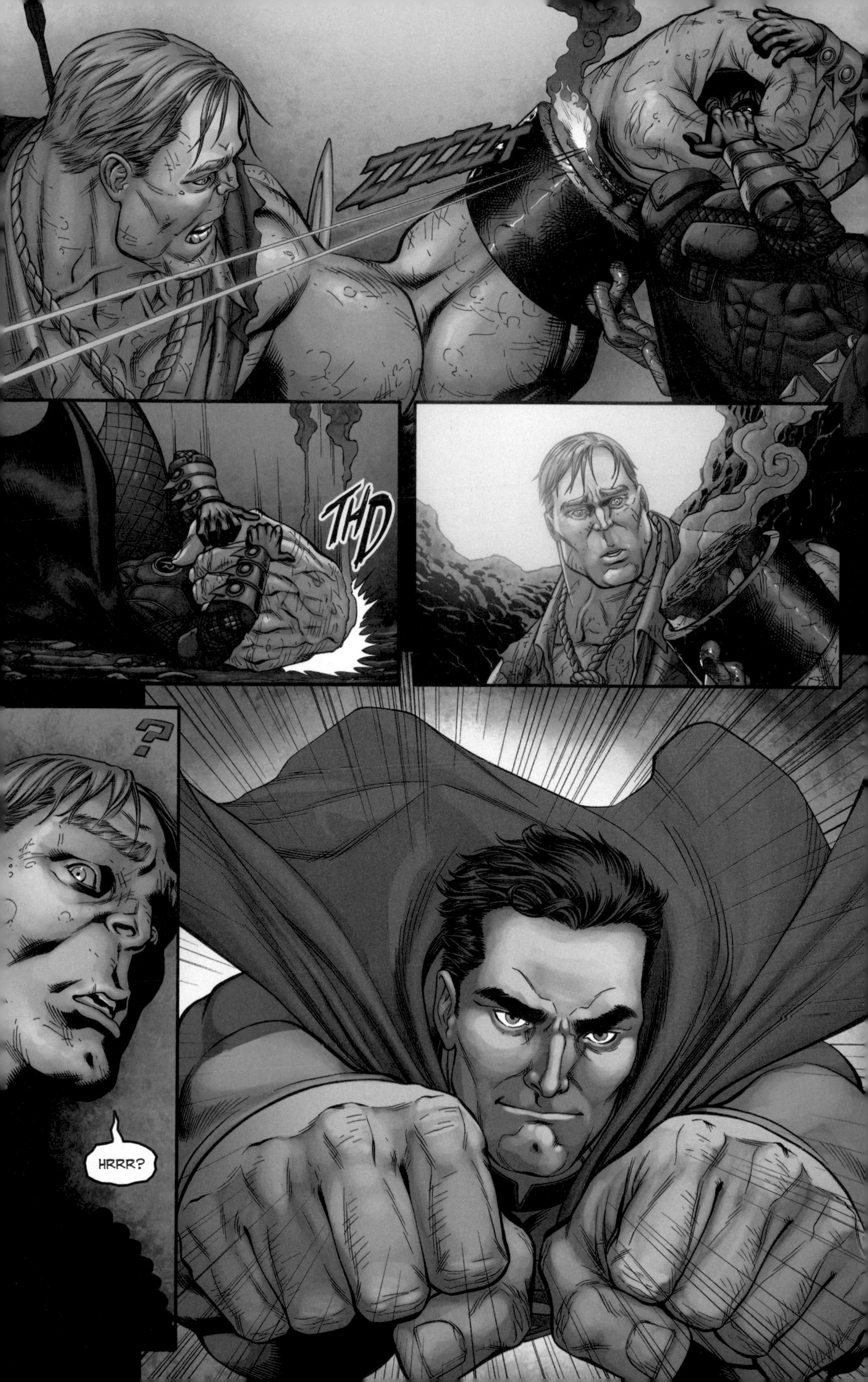
ZZZZT
THD
?
HRRR?

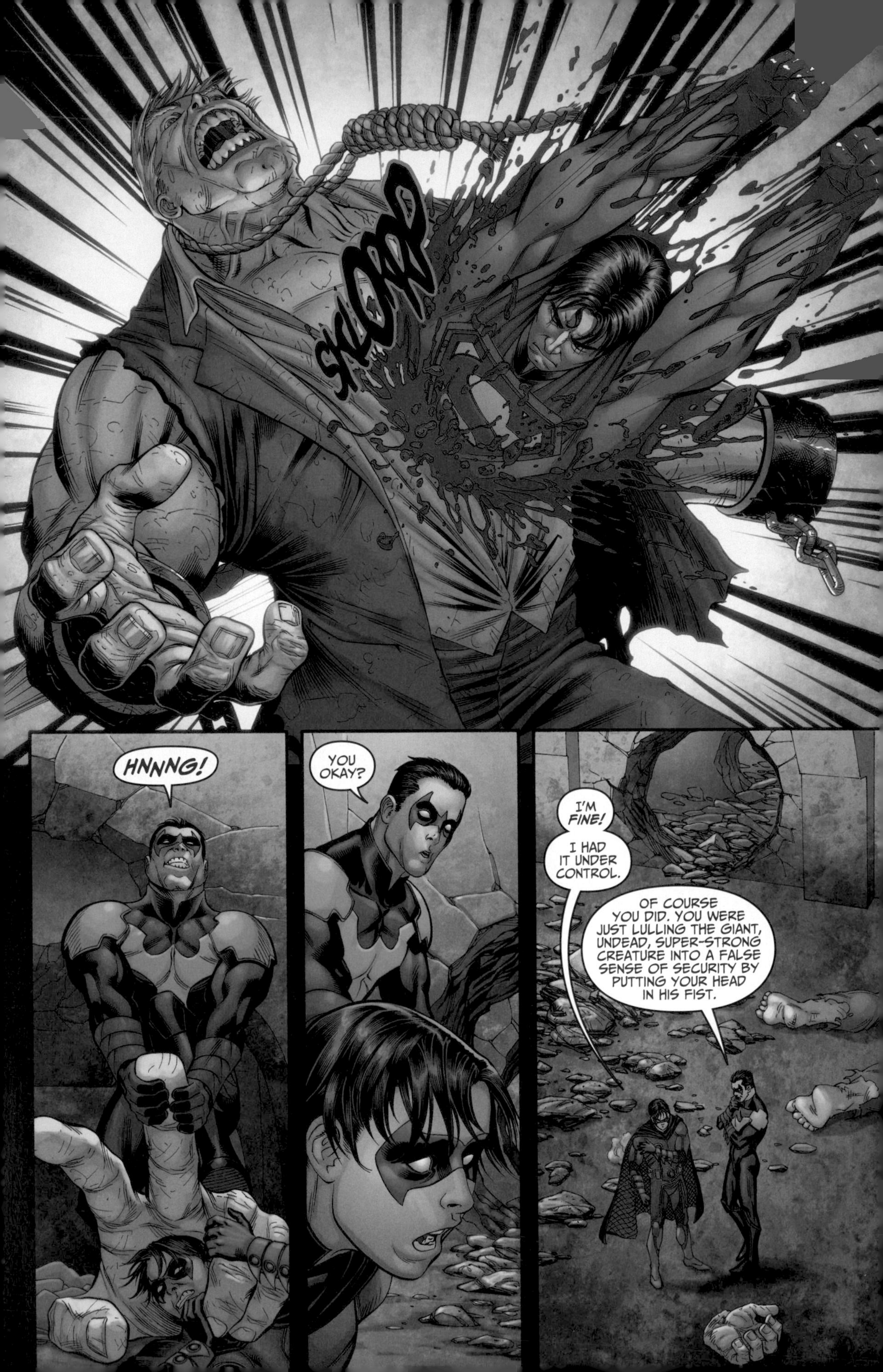
SKLORP
HNNNG!
YOU OKAY?
I'M FINE!
I HAD IT UNDER CONTROL.
OF COURSE YOU DID. YOU WERE JUST LULLING THE GIANT, UNDEAD, SUPER-STRONG CREATURE INTO A FALSE SENSE OF SECURITY BY PUTTING YOUR HEAD IN HIS FIST.

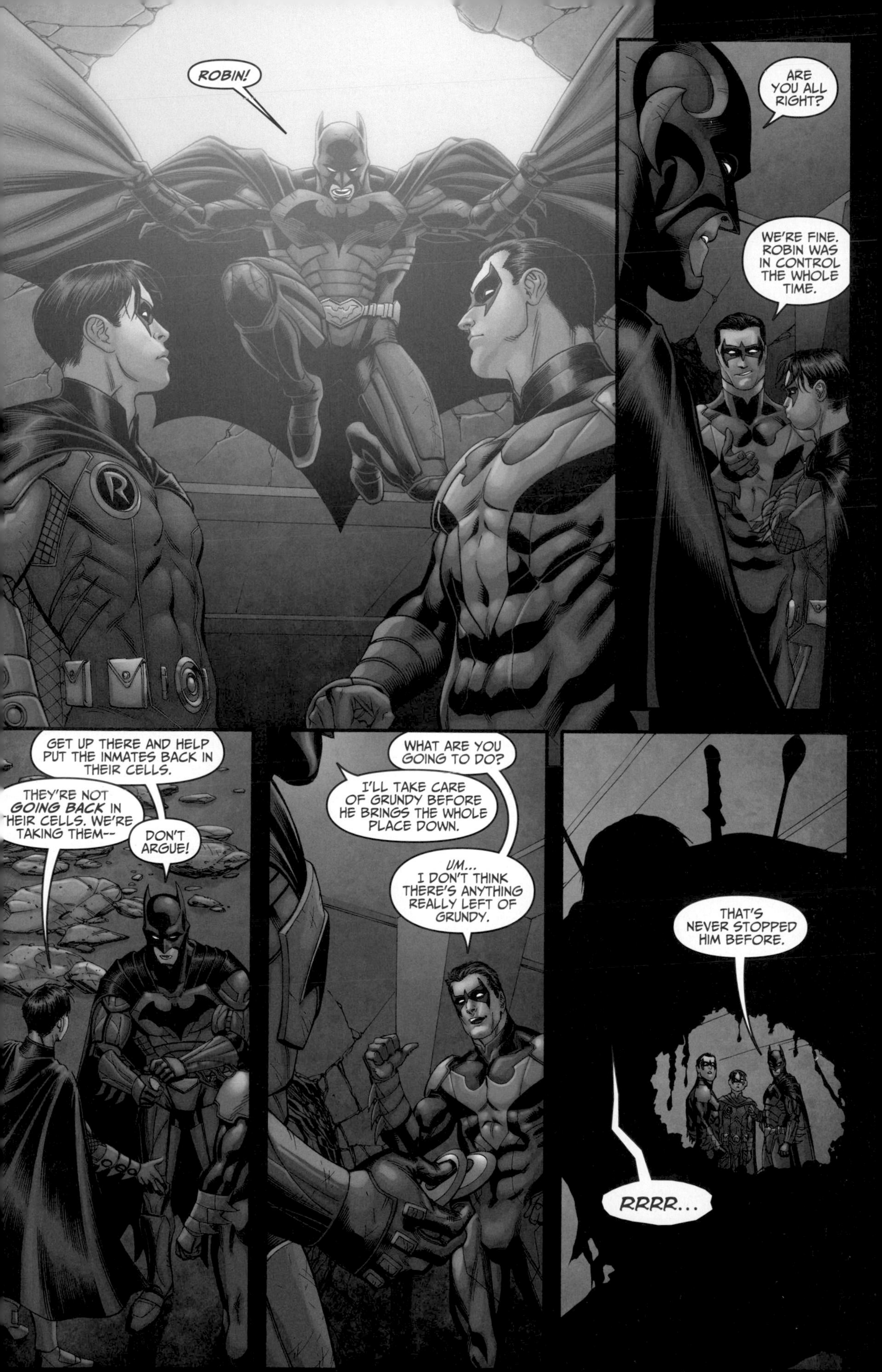
ROBIN!
ARE YOU ALL RIGHT?
WE'RE FINE. ROBIN WAS IN CONTROL THE WHOLE TIME.
GET UP THERE AND HELP PUT THE INMATES BACK IN THEIR CELLS.
THEY'RE NOT *GOING BACK* IN HEIR CELLS. WE'RE TAKING THEM--
DON'T ARGUE!
WHAT ARE YOU GOING TO DO?
I'LL TAKE CARE OF GRUNDY BEFORE HE BRINGS THE WHOLE PLACE DOWN.
UM... I DON'T THINK THERE'S ANYTHING REALLY LEFT OF GRUNDY.
THAT'S NEVER STOPPED HIM BEFORE.
RRRR...

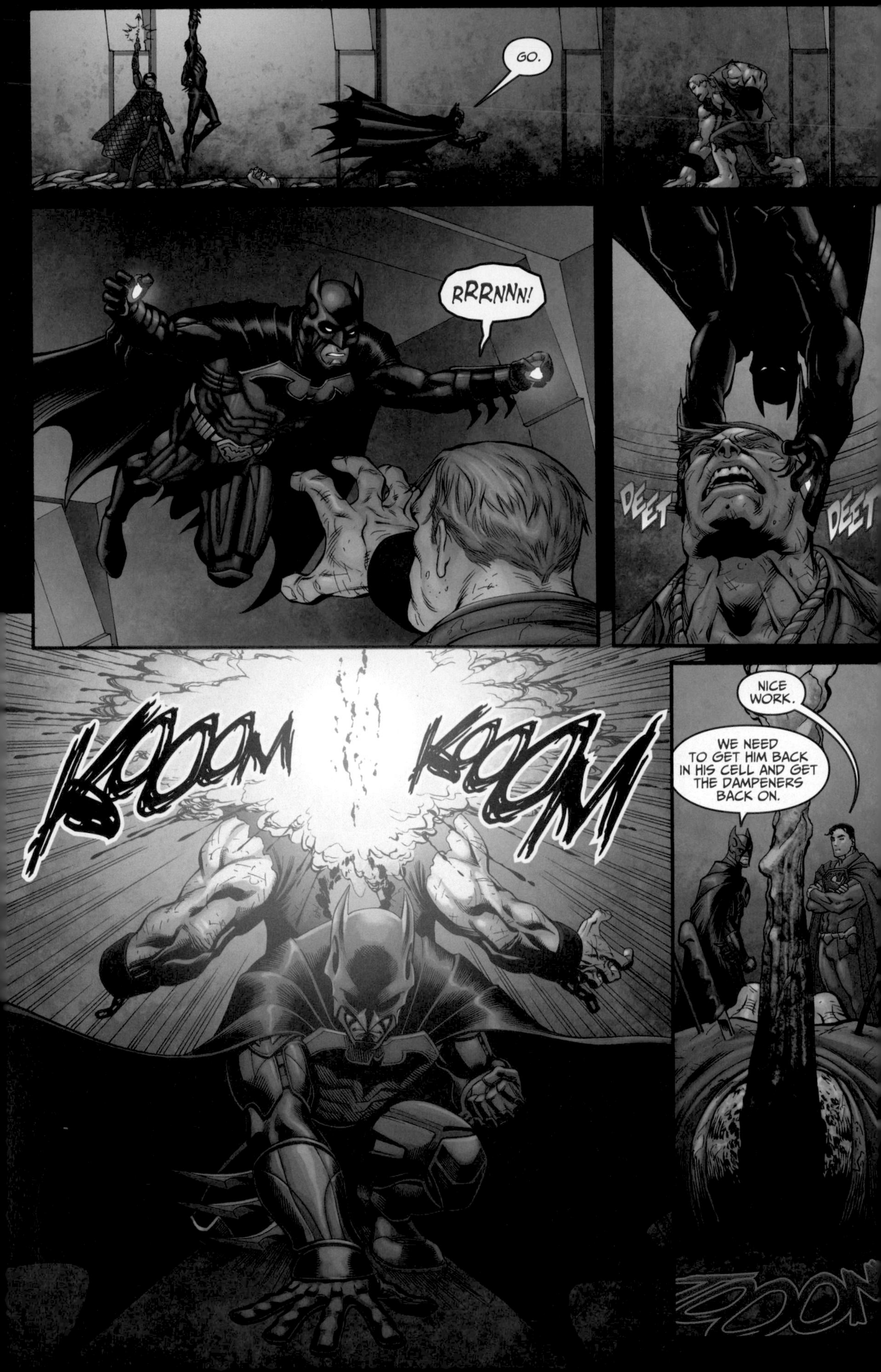
GO.
RRRNNN!
DEET
DEET
KOOOM
KOOOM
NICE WORK.
WE NEED TO GET HIM BACK IN HIS CELL AND GET THE DAMPENERS BACK ON.
ZOOM

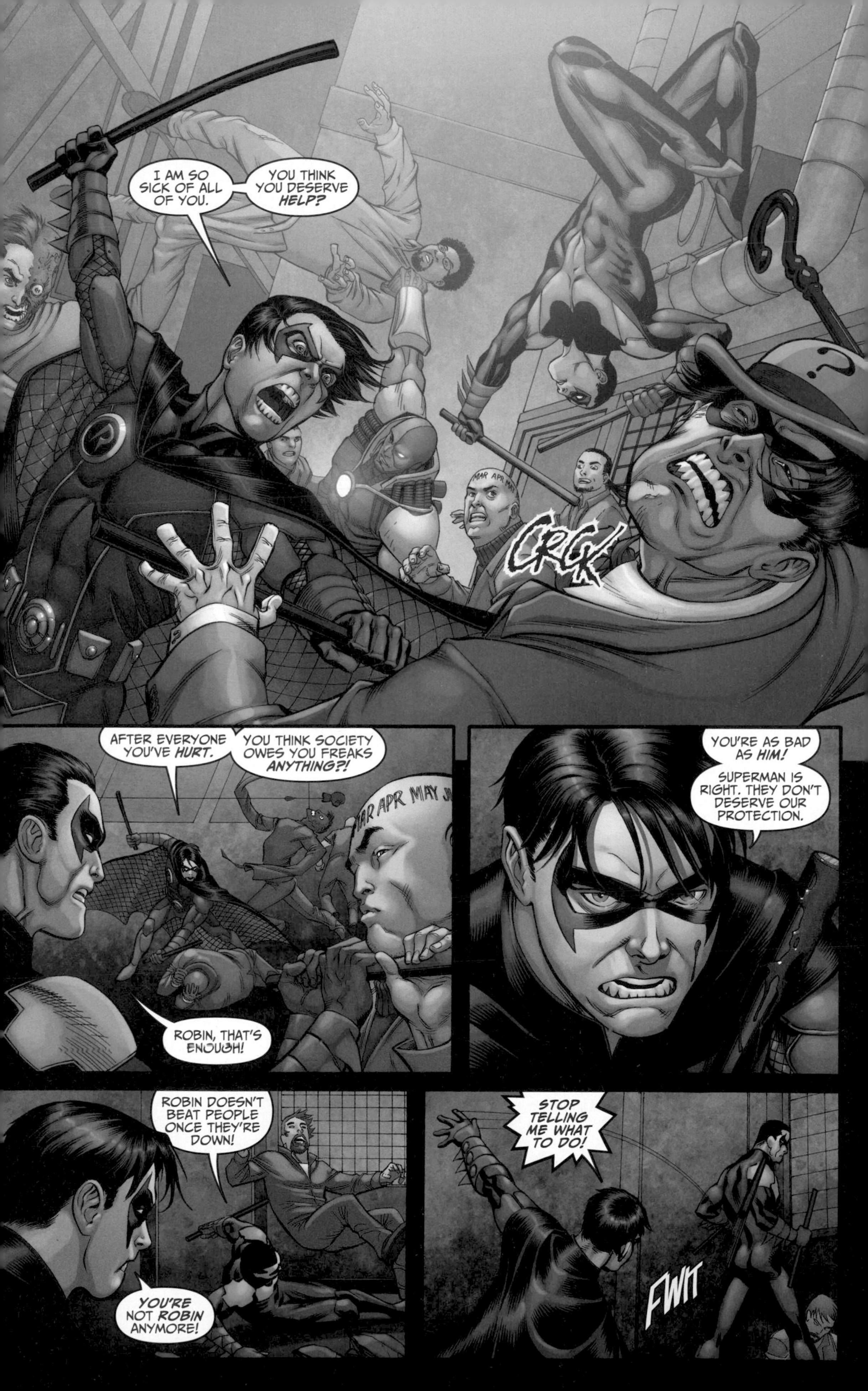
I AM SO SICK OF ALL OF YOU.
YOU THINK YOU DESERVE *HELP?*
MAR APR MAY
CRCK!
AFTER EVERYONE YOU'VE *HURT.*
YOU THINK SOCIETY OWES YOU FREAKS *ANYTHING?!*
MAR APR MAY JU
ROBIN, THAT'S ENOUGH!
YOU'RE AS BAD AS *HIM!*
SUPERMAN IS RIGHT. THEY DON'T DESERVE OUR PROTECTION.
ROBIN DOESN'T BEAT PEOPLE ONCE THEY'RE DOWN!
YOU'RE NOT *ROBIN* ANYMORE!
STOP TELLING ME WHAT TO DO!
FWIT

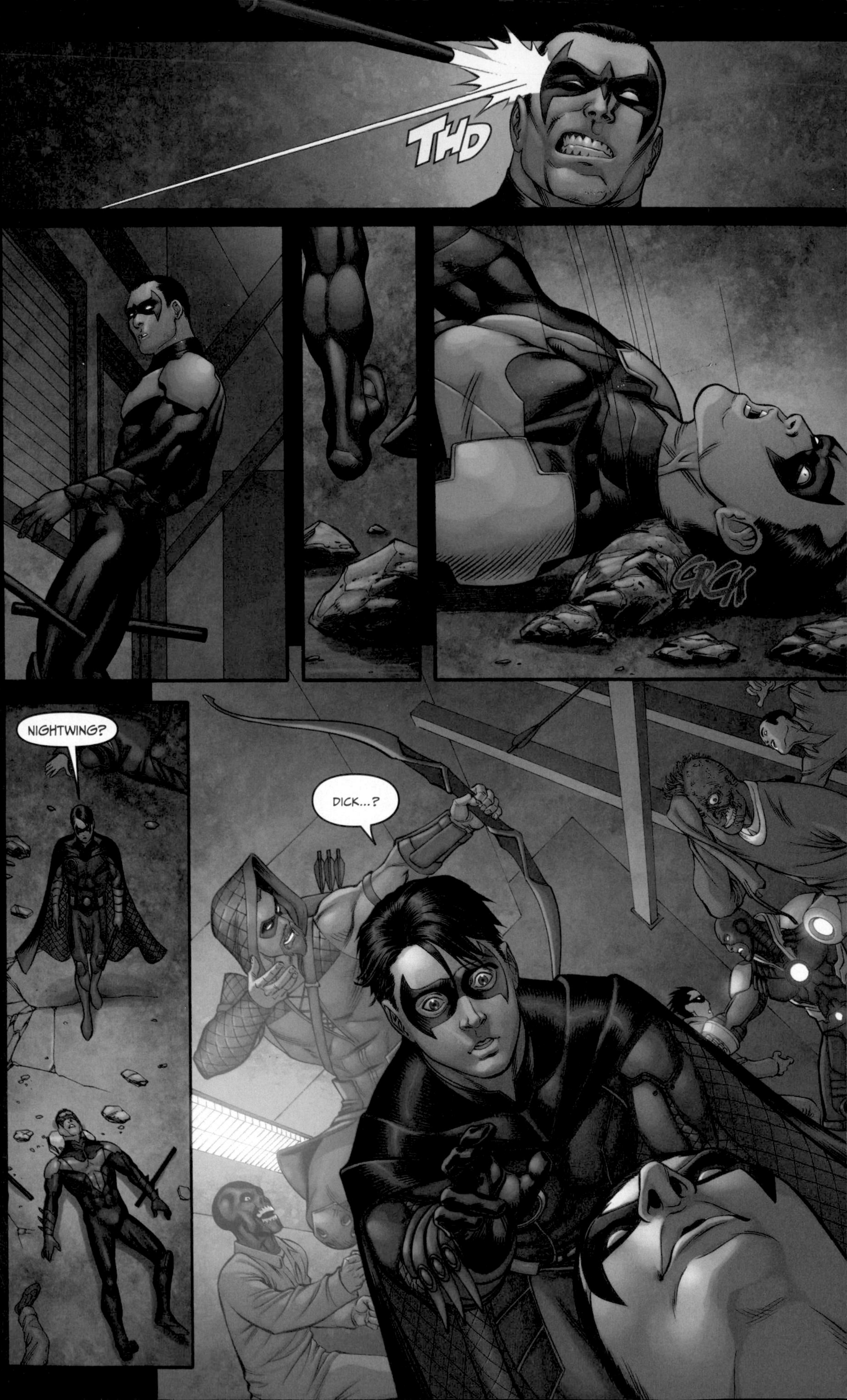
THD
CRCK
NIGHTWING?
DICK...?

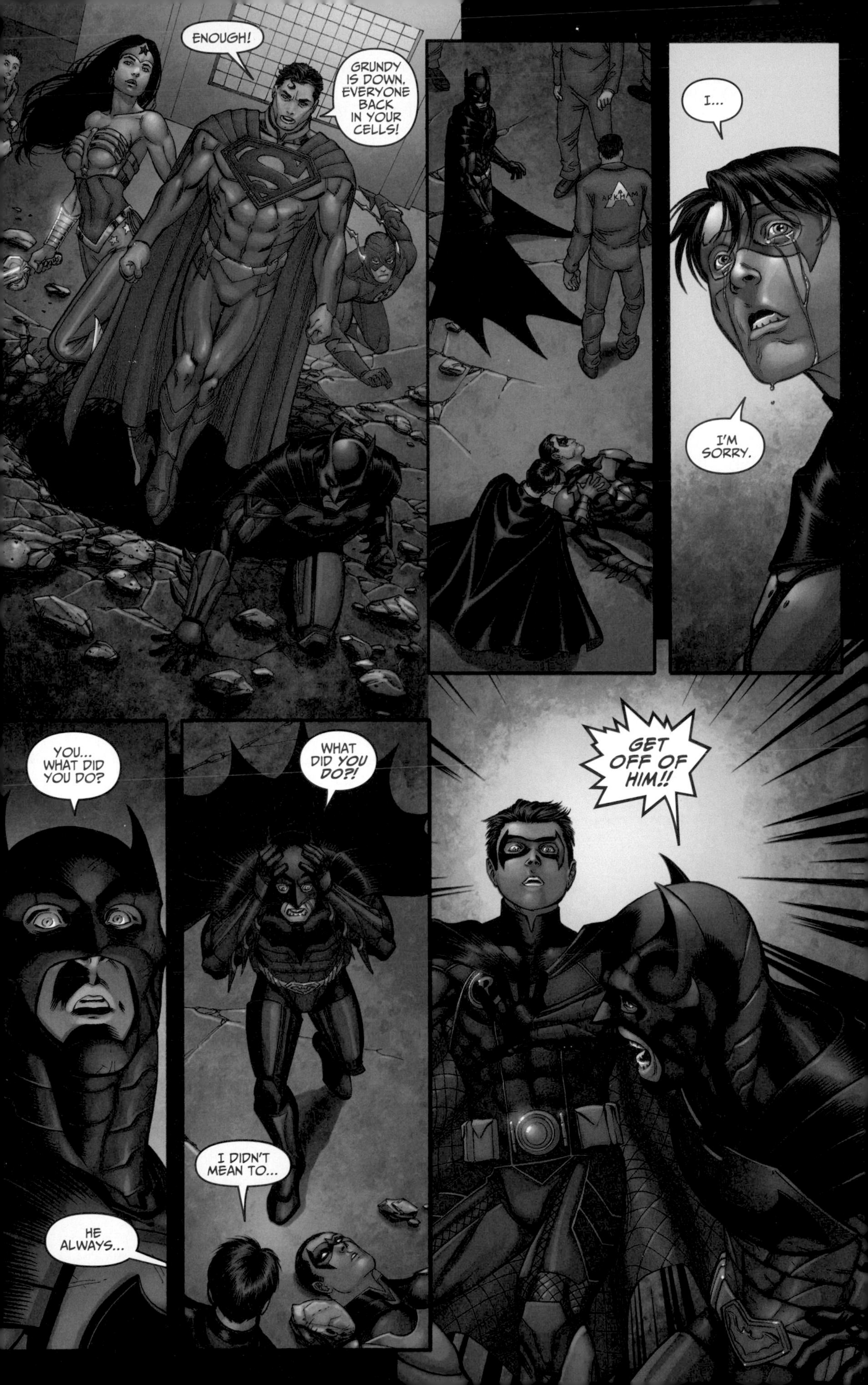
ENOUGH!
GRUNDY IS DOWN. EVERYONE BACK IN YOUR CELLS!
ARKHAM
I...
I'M SORRY.
YOU... WHAT DID YOU DO?
HE ALWAYS...
WHAT DID YOU DO?!
I DIDN'T MEAN TO...
GET OFF OF HIM!!

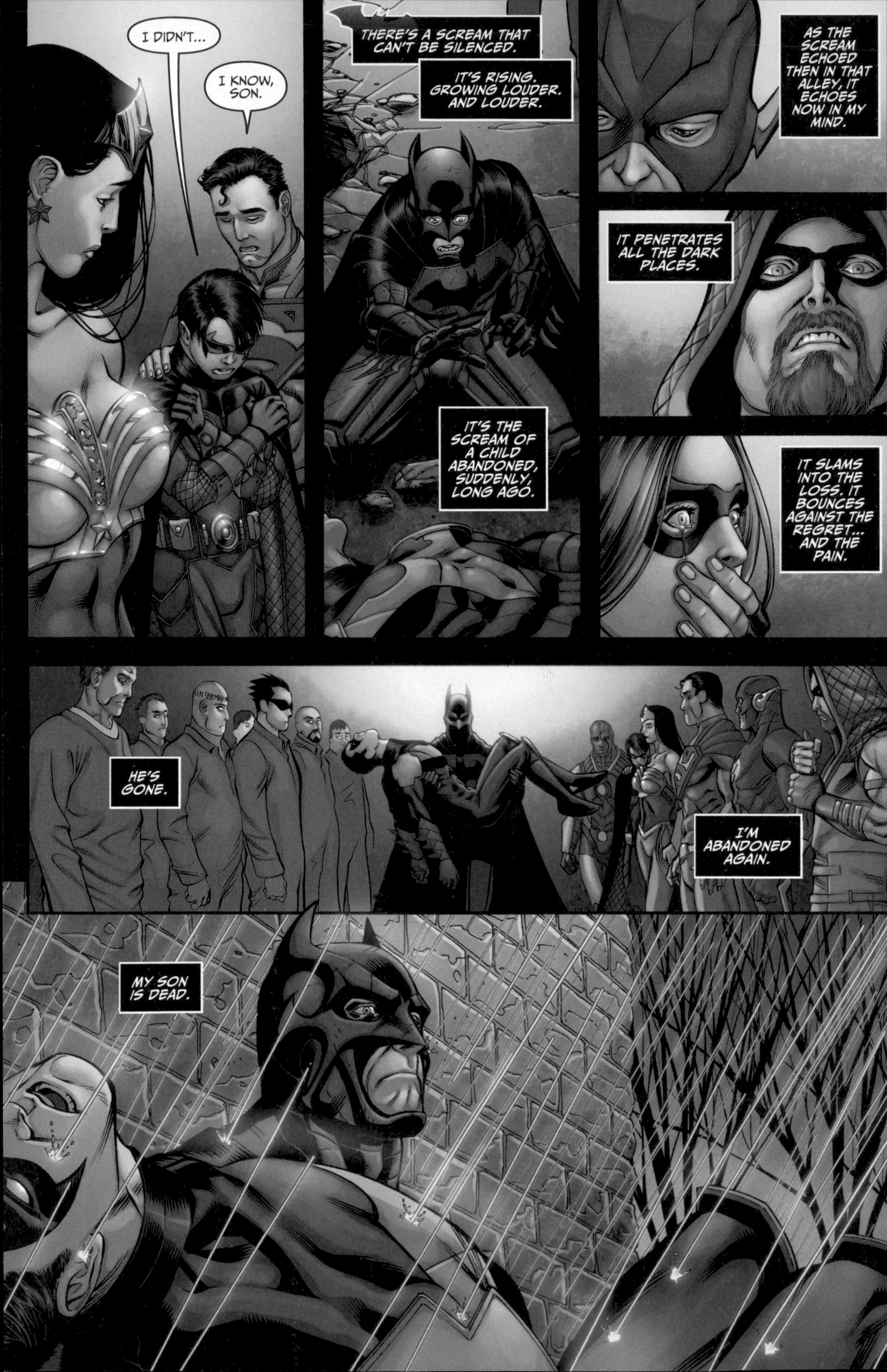
I DIDN'T...
I KNOW, SON.
THERE'S A SCREAM THAT CAN'T BE SILENCED.
IT'S RISING. GROWING LOUDER. AND LOUDER.
IT'S THE SCREAM OF A CHILD ABANDONED, SUDDENLY, LONG AGO.
AS THE SCREAM ECHOED THEN IN THAT ALLEY, IT ECHOES NOW IN MY MIND.
IT PENETRATES ALL THE DARK PLACES.
IT SLAMS INTO THE LOSS. IT BOUNCES AGAINST THE REGRET... AND THE PAIN.
HE'S GONE.
I'M ABANDONED AGAIN.
MY SON IS DEAD.

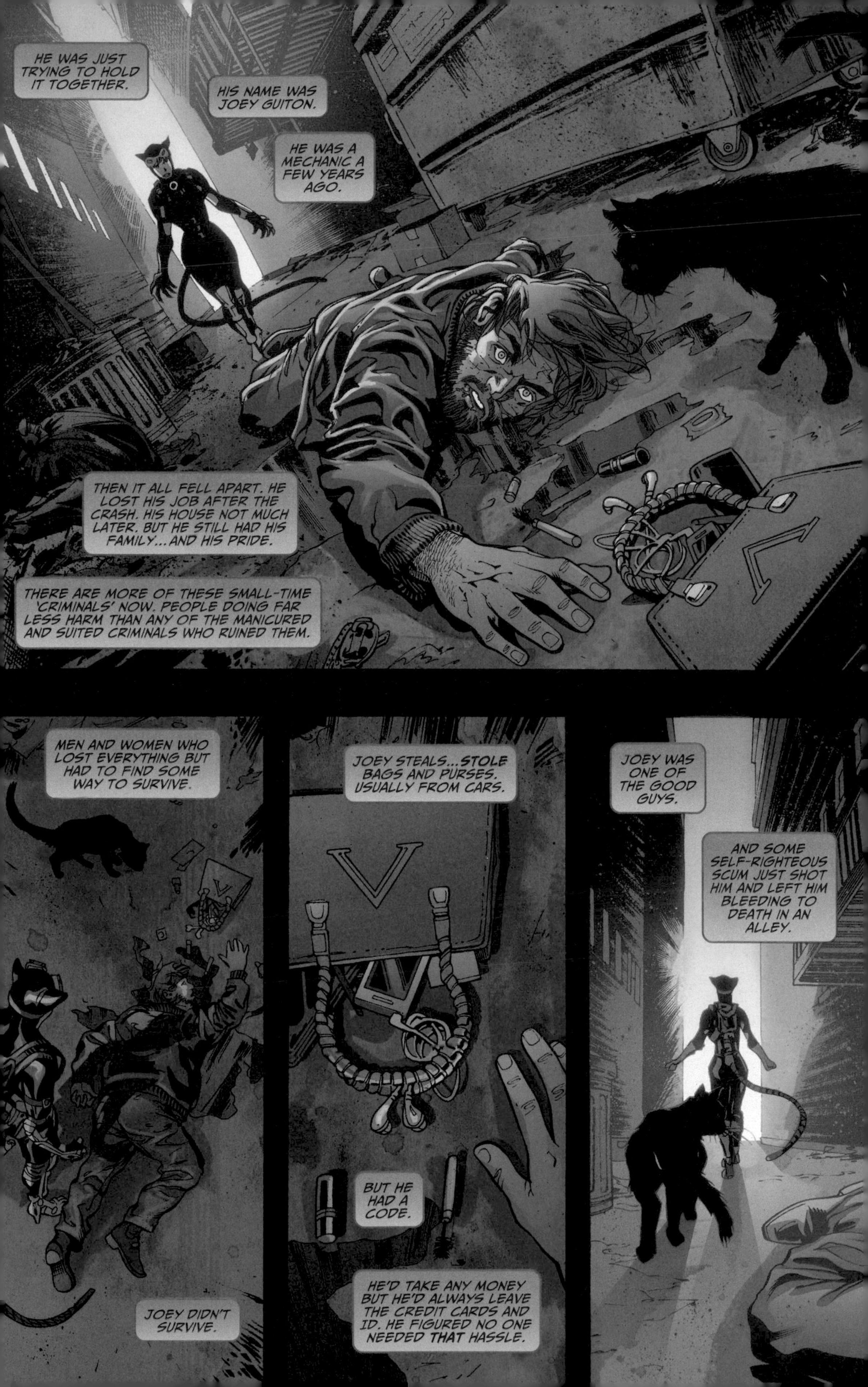
HE WAS JUST TRYING TO HOLD IT TOGETHER.
HIS NAME WAS JOEY GUITON.
HE WAS A MECHANIC A FEW YEARS AGO.
THEN IT ALL FELL APART. HE LOST HIS JOB AFTER THE CRASH. HIS HOUSE NOT MUCH LATER. BUT HE STILL HAD HIS FAMILY... AND HIS PRIDE.
THERE ARE MORE OF THESE SMALL-TIME 'CRIMINALS' NOW. PEOPLE DOING FAR LESS HARM THAN ANY OF THE MANICURED AND SUITED CRIMINALS WHO RUINED THEM.
MEN AND WOMEN WHO LOST EVERYTHING BUT HAD TO FIND SOME WAY TO SURVIVE.
JOEY DIDN'T SURVIVE.
JOEY STEALS...STOLE BAGS AND PURSES. USUALLY FROM CARS.
BUT HE HAD A CODE.
HE'D TAKE ANY MONEY BUT HE'D ALWAYS LEAVE THE CREDIT CARDS AND ID. HE FIGURED NO ONE NEEDED THAT HASSLE.
JOEY WAS ONE OF THE GOOD GUYS.
AND SOME SELF-RIGHTEOUS SCUM JUST SHOT HIM AND LEFT HIM BLEEDING TO DEATH IN AN ALLEY.

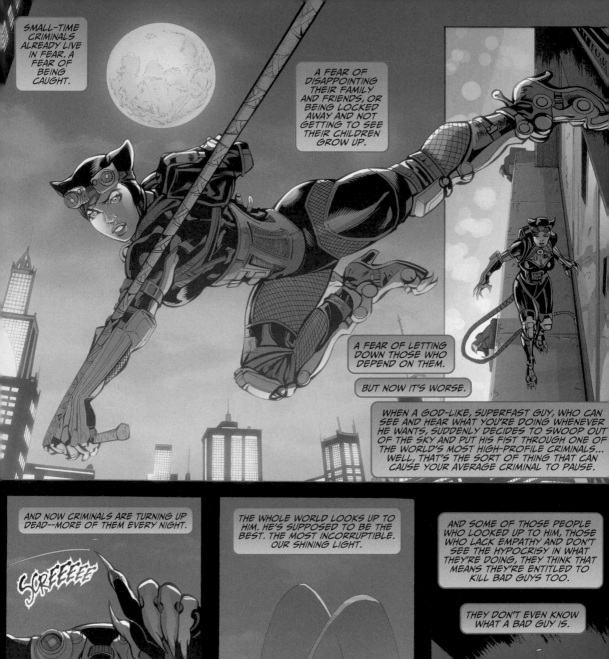

SMALL-TIME CRIMINALS ALREADY LIVE IN FEAR. A FEAR OF BEING CAUGHT.

A FEAR OF DISAPPOINTING THEIR FAMILY AND FRIENDS, OR BEING LOCKED AWAY AND NOT GETTING TO SEE THEIR CHILDREN GROW UP.

A FEAR OF LETTING DOWN THOSE WHO DEPEND ON THEM.

BUT NOW IT'S WORSE.

WHEN A GOD-LIKE, SUPERFAST GUY, WHO CAN SEE AND HEAR WHAT YOU'RE DOING WHENEVER HE WANTS, SUDDENLY DECIDES TO SWOOP OUT OF THE SKY AND PUT HIS FIST THROUGH ONE OF THE WORLD'S MOST HIGH-PROFILE CRIMINALS... WELL, THAT'S THE SORT OF THING THAT CAN CAUSE YOUR AVERAGE CRIMINAL TO PAUSE.

AND NOW CRIMINALS ARE TURNING UP DEAD--MORE OF THEM EVERY NIGHT.

SCREEEEE

AND IT'S ALL SUPERMAN'S FAULT.

THE WHOLE WORLD LOOKS UP TO HIM. HE'S SUPPOSED TO BE THE BEST. THE MOST INCORRUPTIBLE. OUR SHINING LIGHT.

AND HE JUST MURDERED A CRIMINAL AND DIDN'T ANSWER FOR IT.

AND SOME OF THOSE PEOPLE WHO LOOKED UP TO HIM, THOSE WHO LACK EMPATHY AND DON'T SEE THE HYPOCRISY IN WHAT THEY'RE DOING, THEY THINK THAT MEANS THEY'RE ENTITLED TO KILL BAD GUYS TOO.

THEY DON'T EVEN KNOW WHAT A BAD GUY IS.

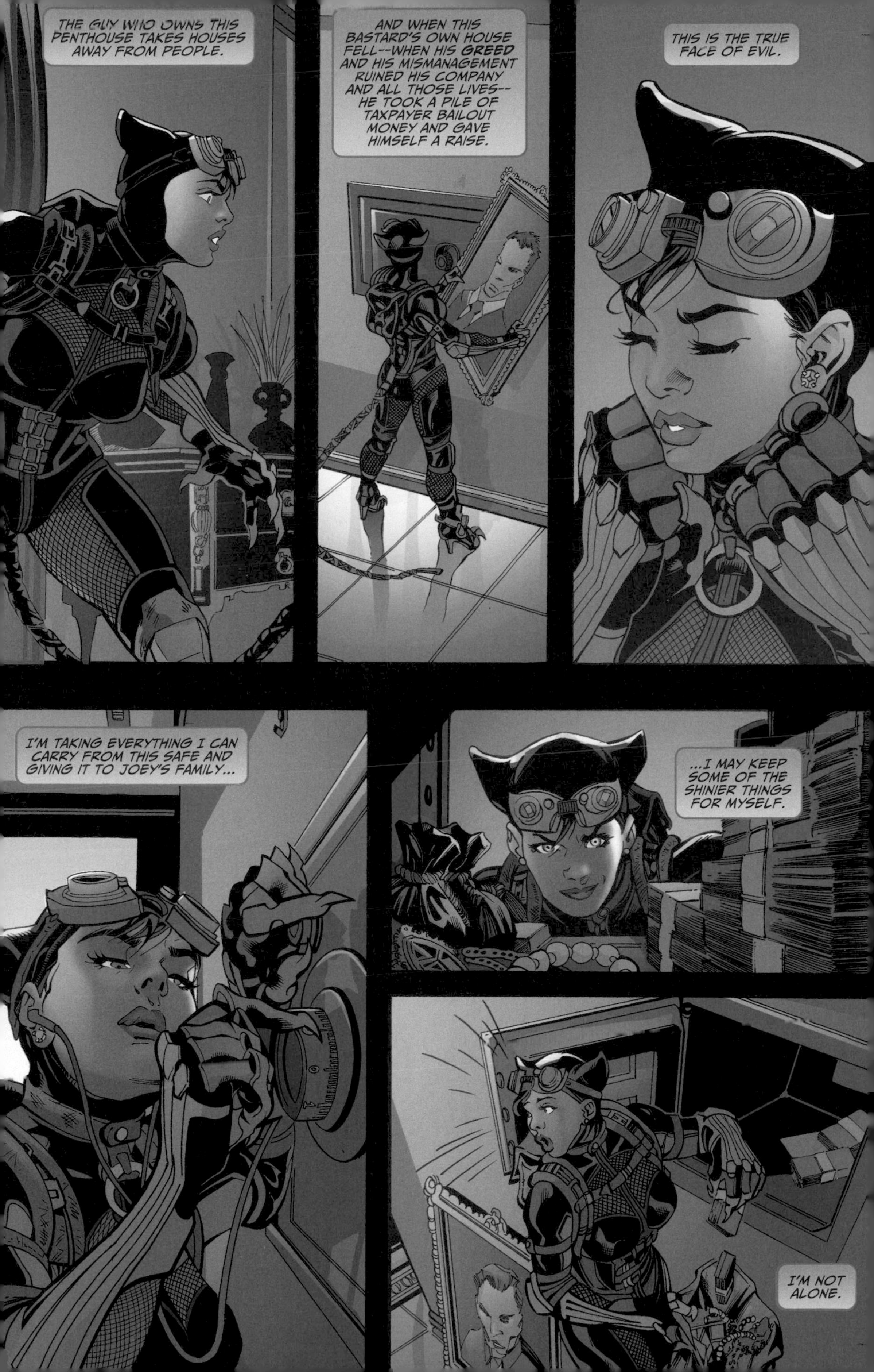
THE GUY WHO OWNS THIS PENTHOUSE TAKES HOUSES AWAY FROM PEOPLE.
AND WHEN THIS BASTARD'S OWN HOUSE FELL--WHEN HIS **GREED** AND HIS MISMANAGEMENT RUINED HIS COMPANY AND ALL THOSE LIVES--HE TOOK A PILE OF TAXPAYER BAILOUT MONEY AND GAVE HIMSELF A RAISE.
THIS IS THE TRUE FACE OF EVIL.
I'M TAKING EVERYTHING I CAN CARRY FROM THIS SAFE AND GIVING IT TO JOEY'S FAMILY...
...I MAY KEEP SOME OF THE SHINIER THINGS FOR MYSELF.
I'M NOT ALONE.

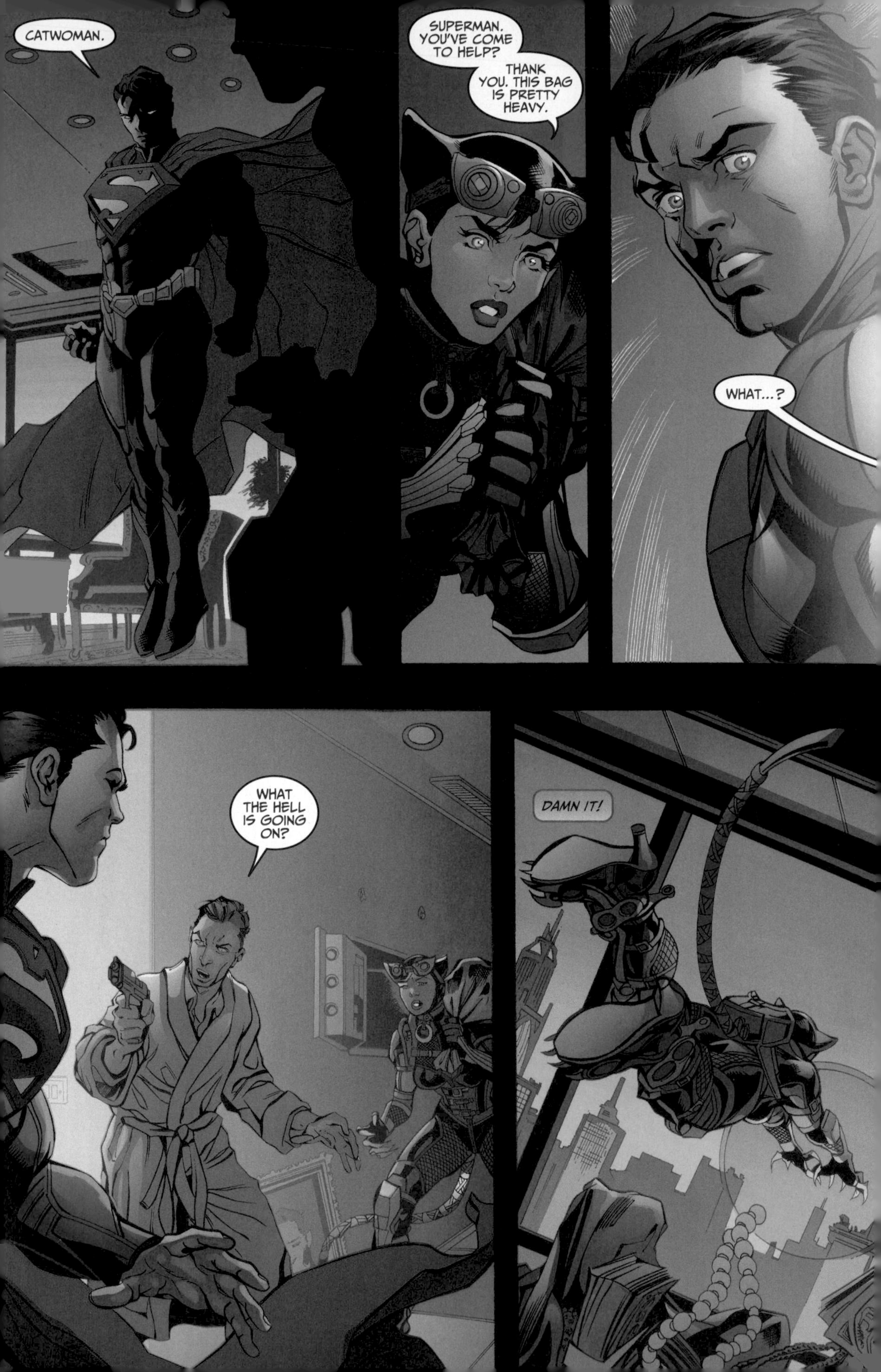
CATWOMAN.
SUPERMAN. YOU'VE COME TO HELP?
THANK YOU. THIS BAG IS PRETTY HEAVY.
WHAT...?
WHAT THE HELL IS GOING ON?
DAMN IT!

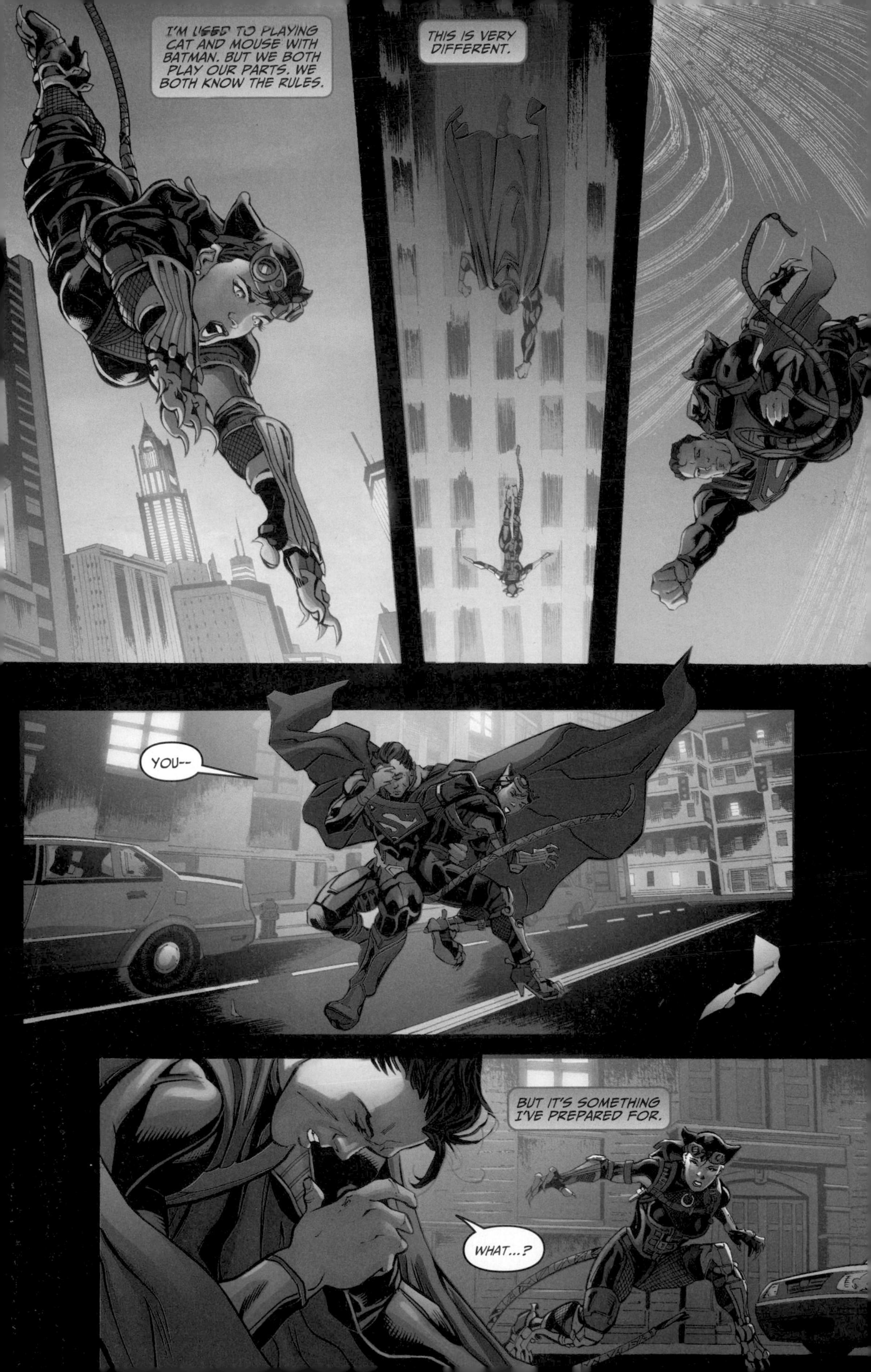
I'M USED TO PLAYING CAT AND MOUSE WITH BATMAN. BUT WE BOTH PLAY OUR PARTS. WE BOTH KNOW THE RULES.
THIS IS VERY DIFFERENT.
YOU--
BUT IT'S SOMETHING I'VE PREPARED FOR.
WHAT...?

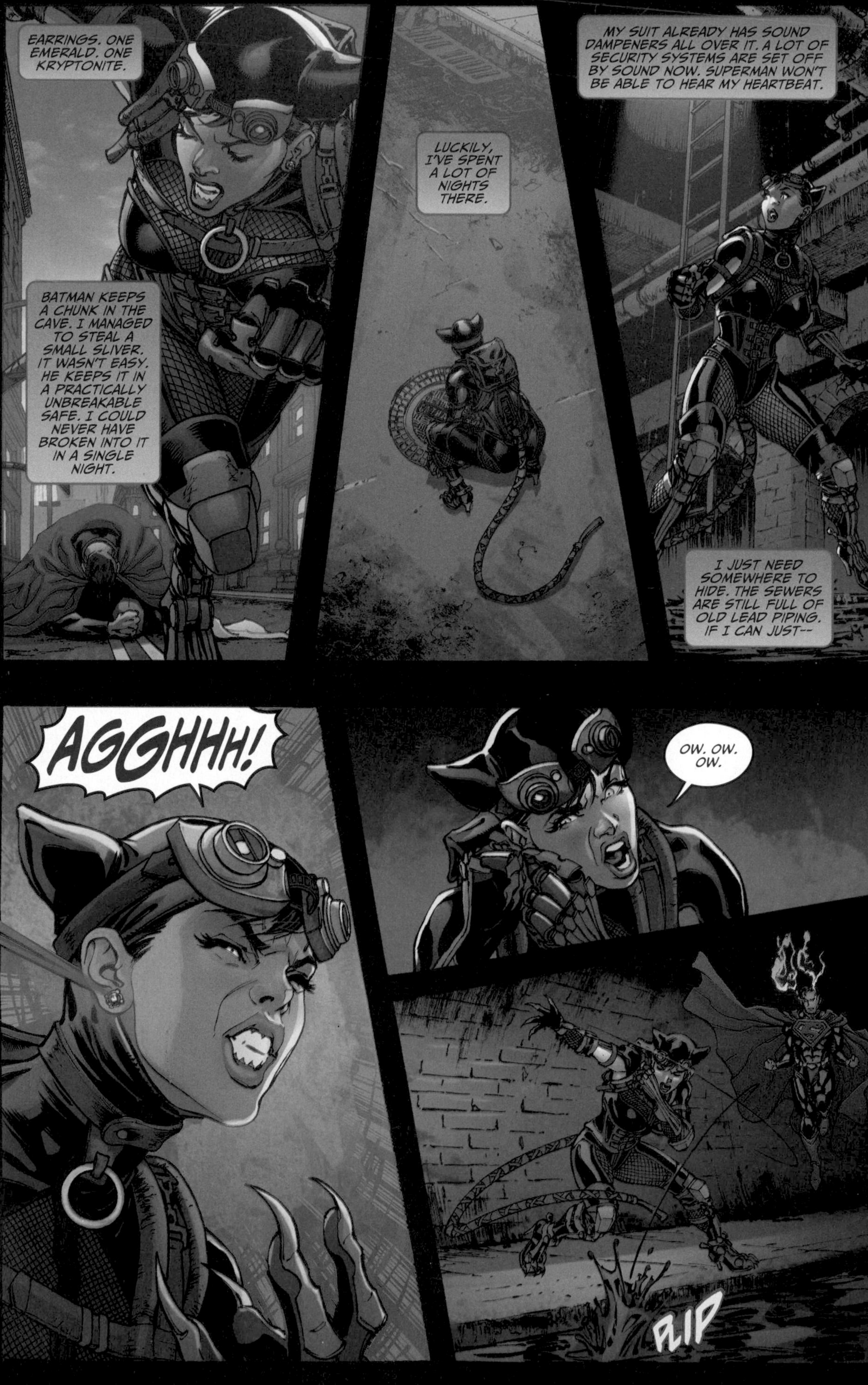
EARRINGS. ONE EMERALD. ONE KRYPTONITE.
BATMAN KEEPS A CHUNK IN THE CAVE. I MANAGED TO STEAL A SMALL SLIVER. IT WASN'T EASY. HE KEEPS IT IN A PRACTICALLY UNBREAKABLE SAFE. I COULD NEVER HAVE BROKEN INTO IT IN A SINGLE NIGHT.
LUCKILY, I'VE SPENT A LOT OF NIGHTS THERE.
MY SUIT ALREADY HAS SOUND DAMPENERS ALL OVER IT. A LOT OF SECURITY SYSTEMS ARE SET OFF BY SOUND NOW. SUPERMAN WON'T BE ABLE TO HEAR MY HEARTBEAT.
I JUST NEED SOMEWHERE TO HIDE. THE SEWERS ARE STILL FULL OF OLD LEAD PIPING. IF I CAN JUST--
AGGHHH!
OW. OW. OW.
PLIP

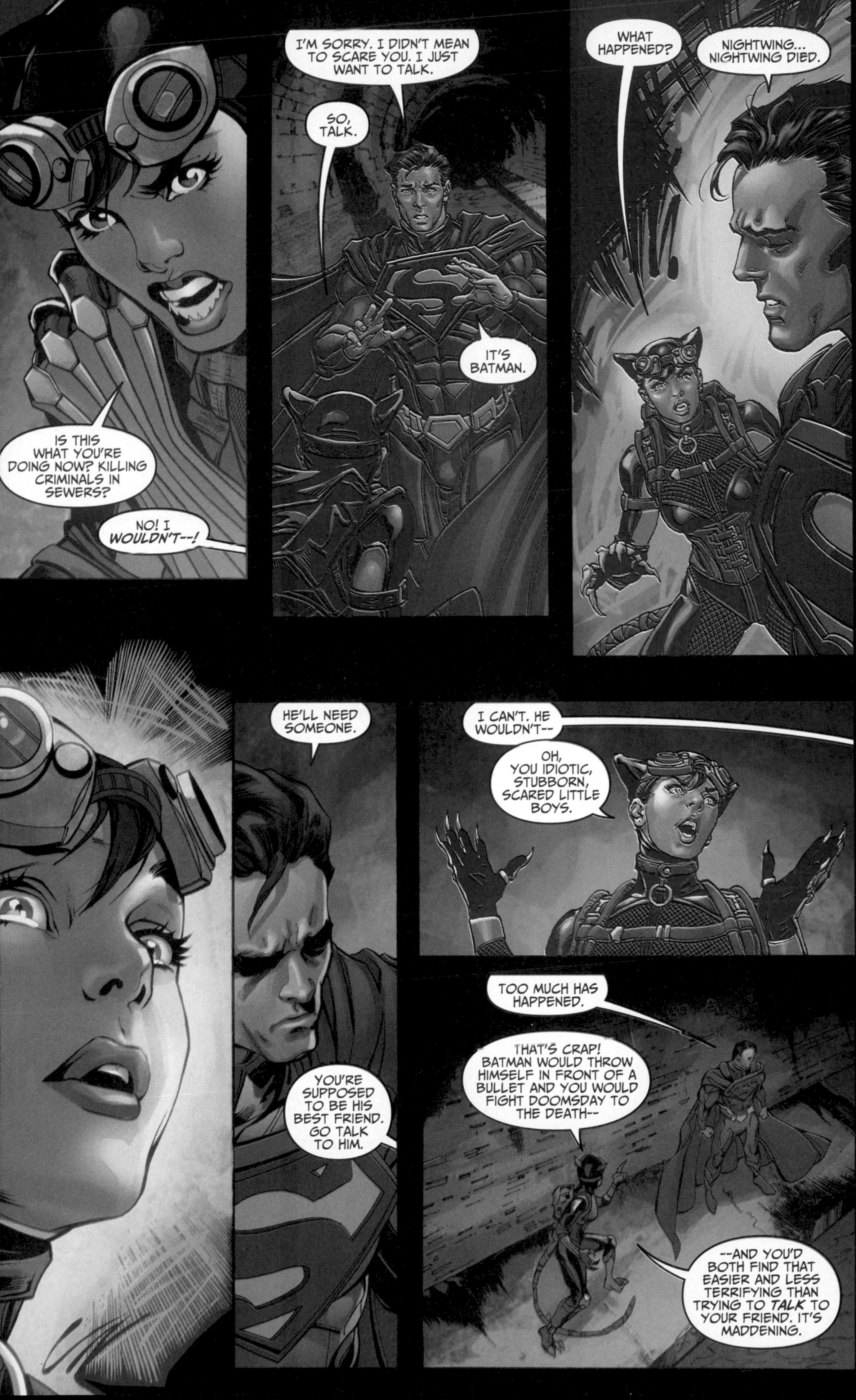
IS THIS WHAT YOU'RE DOING NOW? KILLING CRIMINALS IN SEWERS?
NO! I *WOULDN'T--!*
I'M SORRY. I DIDN'T MEAN TO SCARE YOU. I JUST WANT TO TALK.
SO, TALK.
IT'S BATMAN.
WHAT HAPPENED?
NIGHTWING... NIGHTWING DIED.
HE'LL NEED SOMEONE.
YOU'RE SUPPOSED TO BE HIS BEST FRIEND. GO TALK TO HIM.
I CAN'T. HE WOULDN'T--
OH, YOU IDIOTIC, STUBBORN, SCARED LITTLE BOYS.
TOO MUCH HAS HAPPENED.
THAT'S CRAP! BATMAN WOULD THROW HIMSELF IN FRONT OF A BULLET AND YOU WOULD FIGHT DOOMSDAY TO THE DEATH--
--AND YOU'D BOTH FIND THAT EASIER AND LESS TERRIFYING THAN TRYING TO *TALK* TO YOUR FRIEND. IT'S MADDENING.

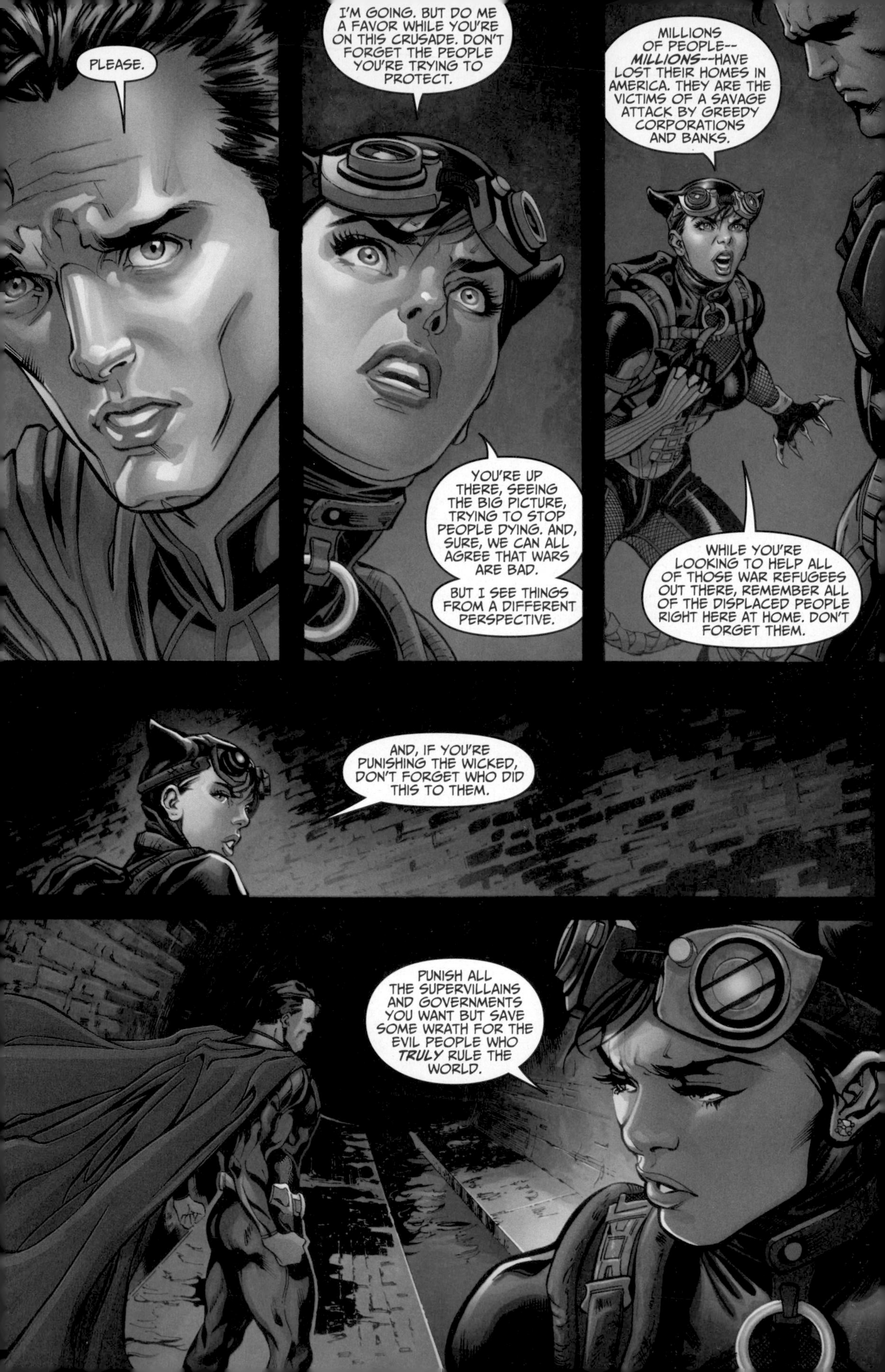
PLEASE.
I'M GOING. BUT DO ME A FAVOR WHILE YOU'RE ON THIS CRUSADE. DON'T FORGET THE PEOPLE YOU'RE TRYING TO PROTECT.
YOU'RE UP THERE, SEEING THE BIG PICTURE, TRYING TO STOP PEOPLE DYING. AND, SURE, WE CAN ALL AGREE THAT WARS ARE BAD.
BUT I SEE THINGS FROM A DIFFERENT PERSPECTIVE.
MILLIONS OF PEOPLE--*MILLIONS*--HAVE LOST THEIR HOMES IN AMERICA. THEY ARE THE VICTIMS OF A SAVAGE ATTACK BY GREEDY CORPORATIONS AND BANKS.
WHILE YOU'RE LOOKING TO HELP ALL OF THOSE WAR REFUGEES OUT THERE, REMEMBER ALL OF THE DISPLACED PEOPLE RIGHT HERE AT HOME. DON'T FORGET THEM.
AND, IF YOU'RE PUNISHING THE WICKED, DON'T FORGET WHO DID THIS TO THEM.
PUNISH ALL THE SUPERVILLAINS AND GOVERNMENTS YOU WANT BUT SAVE SOME WRATH FOR THE EVIL PEOPLE WHO *TRULY* RULE THE WORLD.

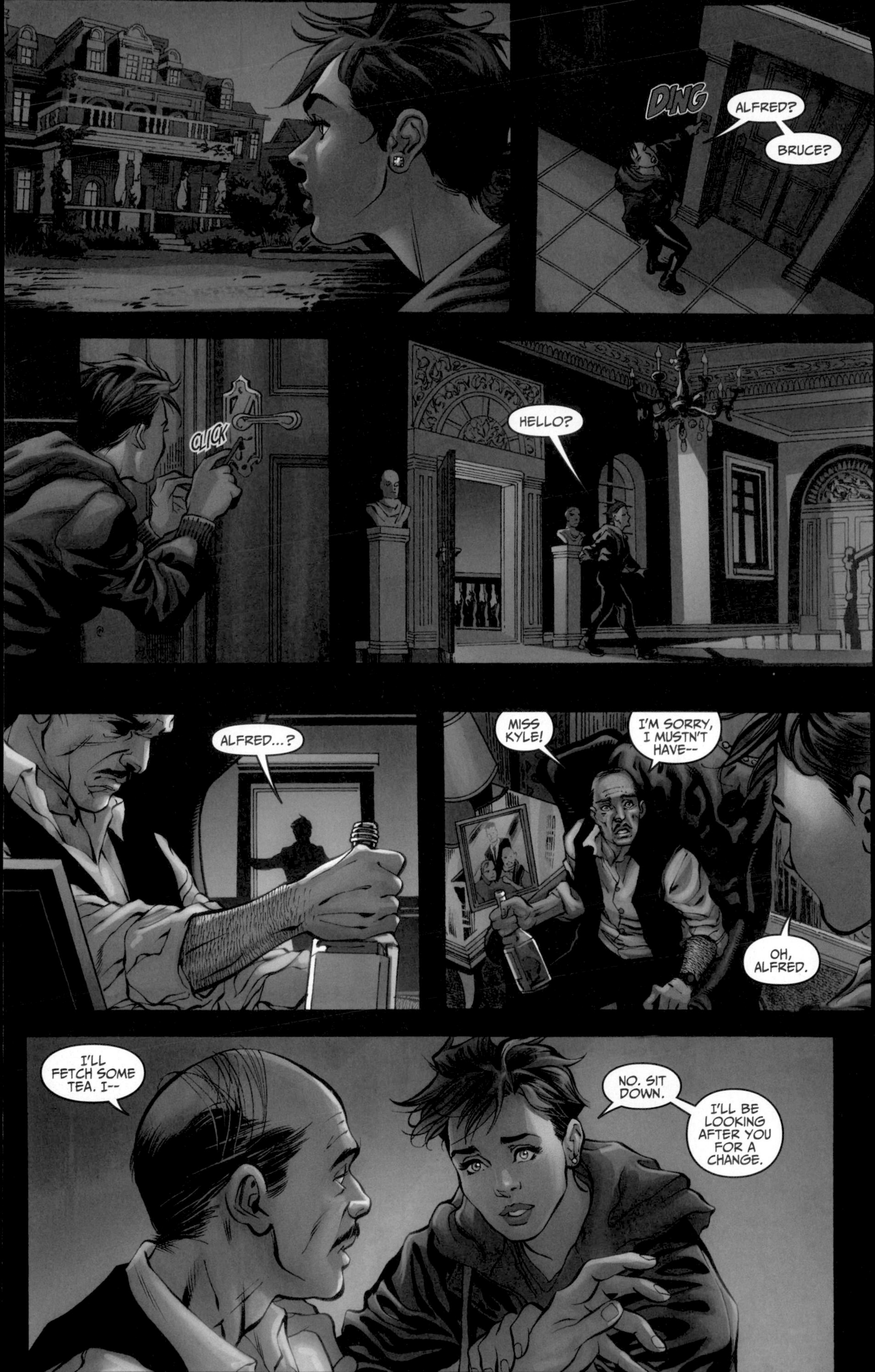
DING
ALFRED?
BRUCE?
CLICK
HELLO?
ALFRED...?
MISS KYLE!
I'M SORRY, I MUSTN'T HAVE--
OH, ALFRED.
I'LL FETCH SOME TEA. I--
NO. SIT DOWN.
I'LL BE LOOKING AFTER YOU FOR A CHANGE.

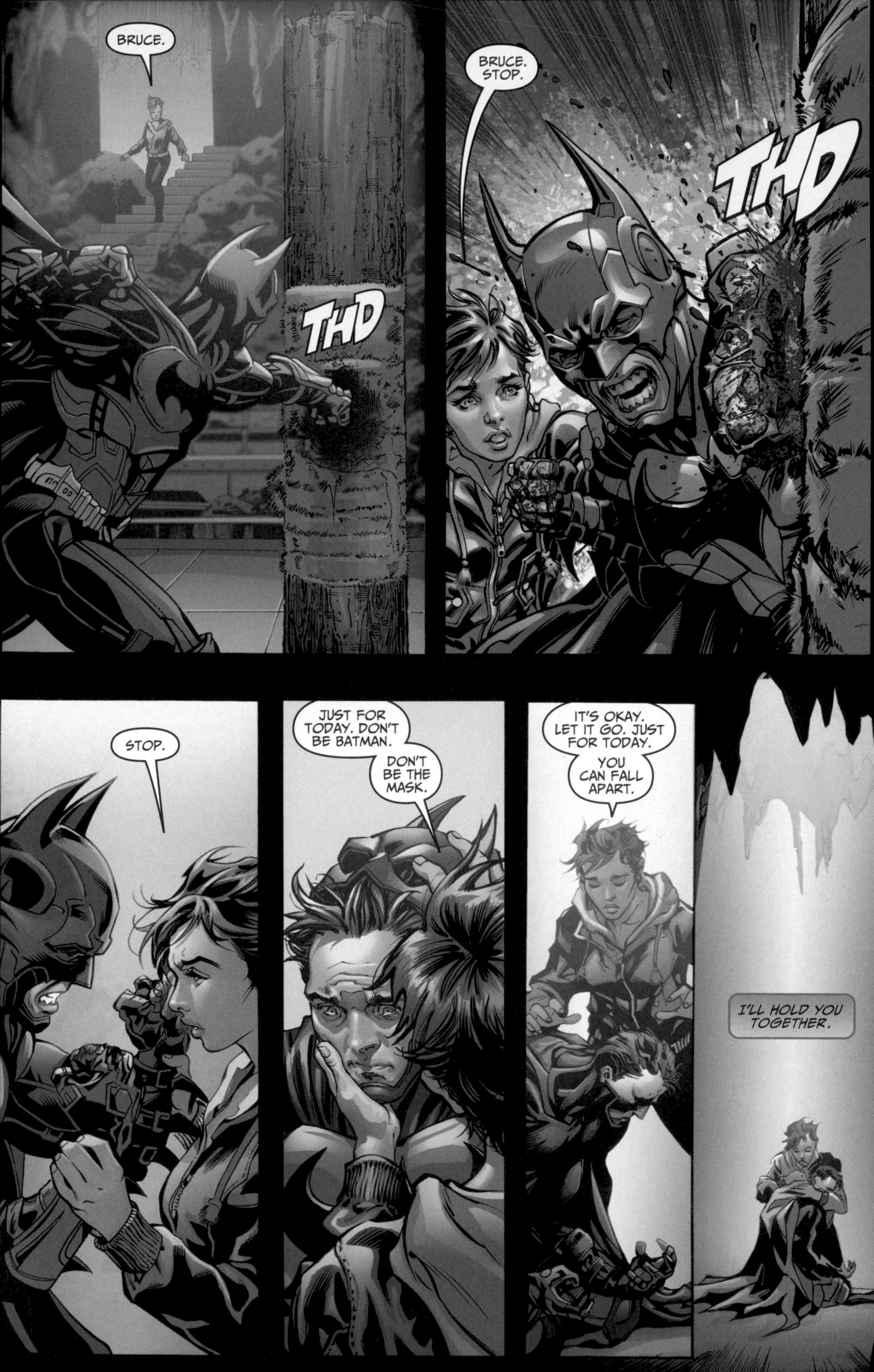
BRUCE.
THD
BRUCE. STOP.
THD
STOP.
JUST FOR TODAY. DON'T BE BATMAN.
DON'T BE THE MASK.
IT'S OKAY. LET IT GO. JUST FOR TODAY.
YOU CAN FALL APART.
I'LL HOLD YOU TOGETHER.

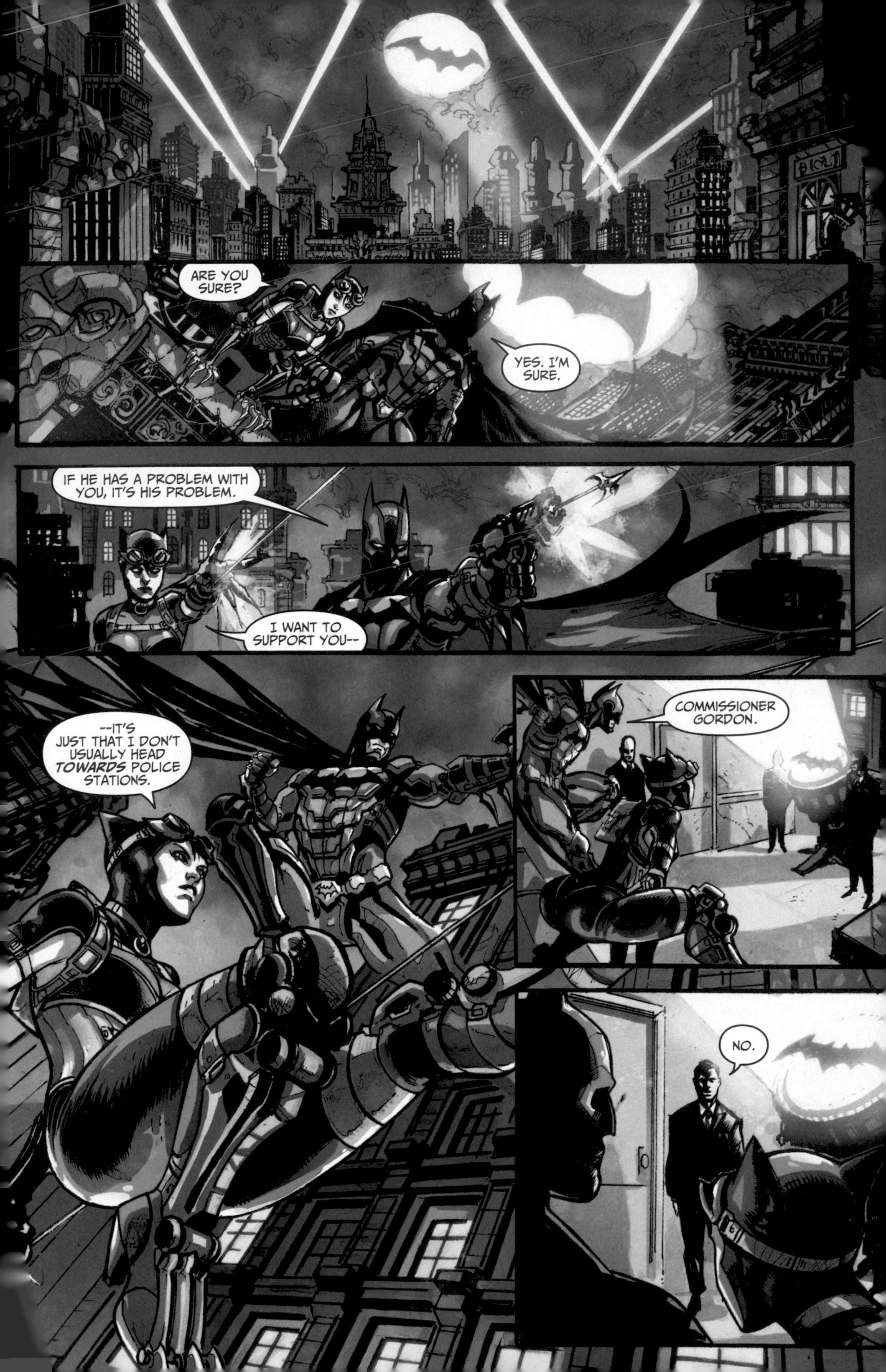
ARE YOU SURE?
YES. I'M SURE.
IF HE HAS A PROBLEM WITH YOU, IT'S HIS PROBLEM.
I WANT TO SUPPORT YOU--
--IT'S JUST THAT I DON'T USUALLY HEAD *TOWARDS* POLICE STATIONS.
COMMISSIONER GORDON.
NO.

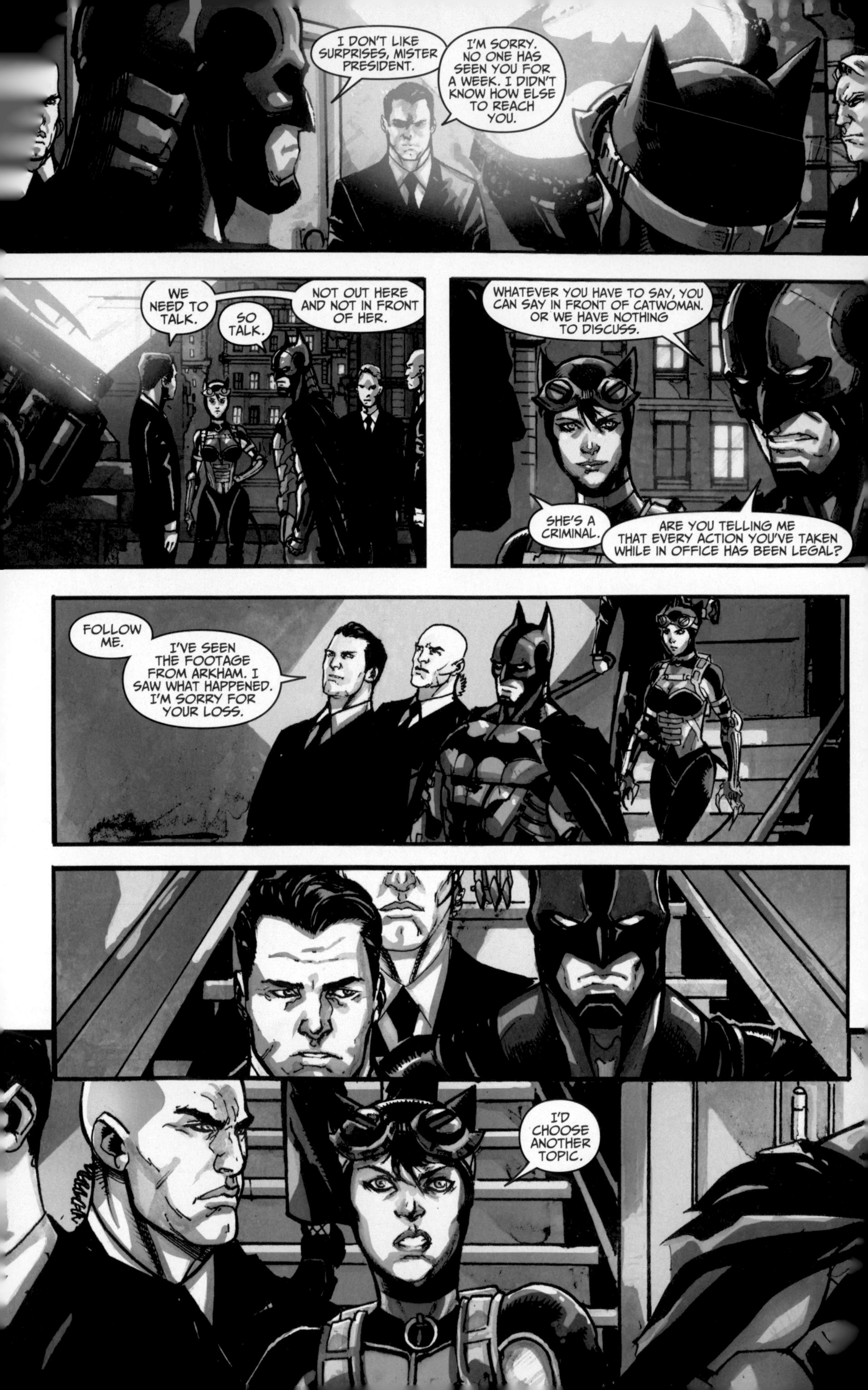
I DON'T LIKE SURPRISES, MISTER PRESIDENT.
I'M SORRY. NO ONE HAS SEEN YOU FOR A WEEK. I DIDN'T KNOW HOW ELSE TO REACH YOU.
WE NEED TO TALK.
SO TALK.
NOT OUT HERE AND NOT IN FRONT OF HER.
WHATEVER YOU HAVE TO SAY, YOU CAN SAY IN FRONT OF CATWOMAN. OR WE HAVE NOTHING TO DISCUSS.
SHE'S A CRIMINAL.
ARE YOU TELLING ME THAT EVERY ACTION YOU'VE TAKEN WHILE IN OFFICE HAS BEEN LEGAL?
FOLLOW ME.
I'VE SEEN THE FOOTAGE FROM ARKHAM. I SAW WHAT HAPPENED. I'M SORRY FOR YOUR LOSS.
I'D CHOOSE ANOTHER TOPIC.

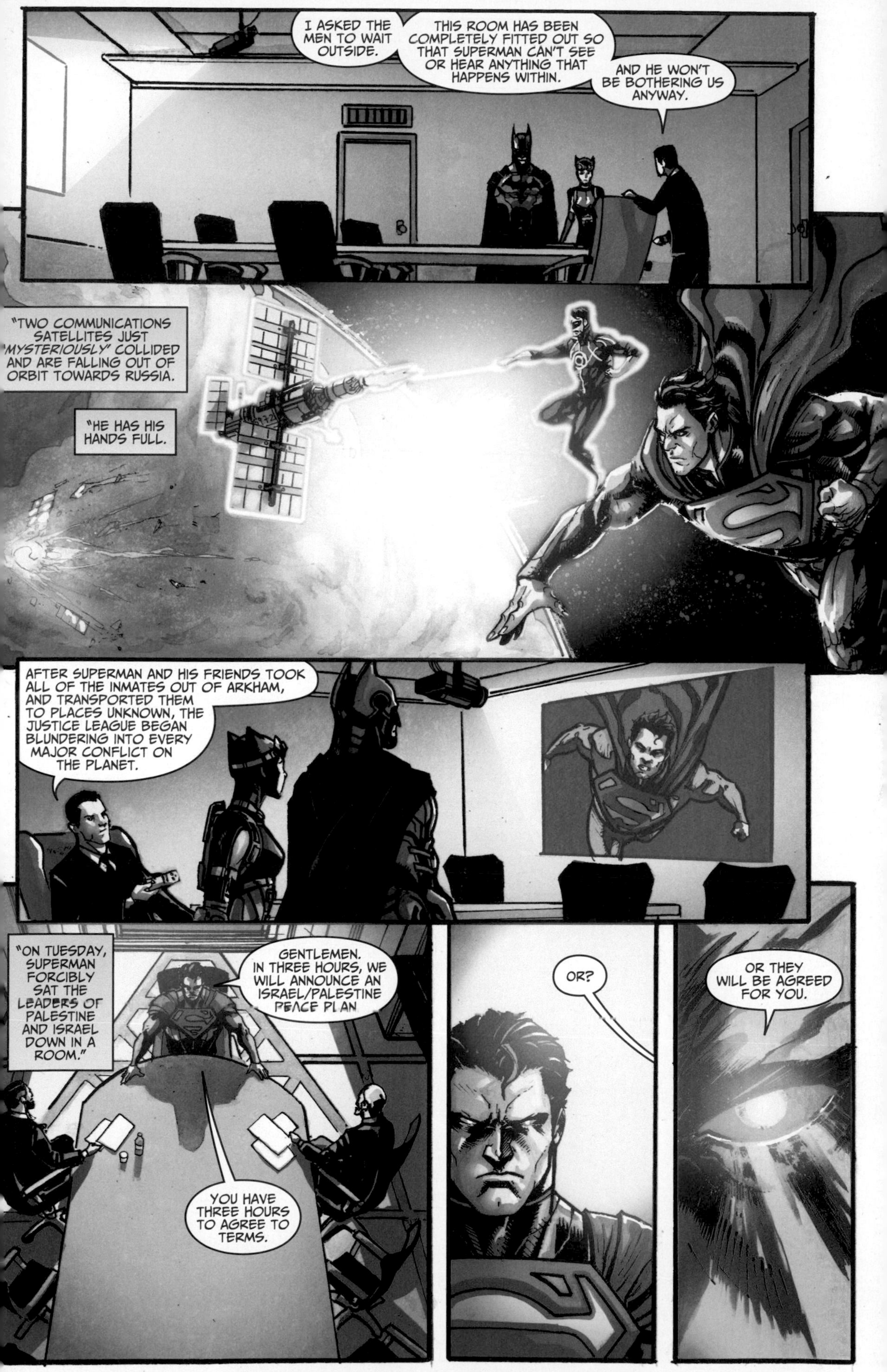
I ASKED THE MEN TO WAIT OUTSIDE.
THIS ROOM HAS BEEN COMPLETELY FITTED OUT SO THAT SUPERMAN CAN'T SEE OR HEAR ANYTHING THAT HAPPENS WITHIN.
AND HE WON'T BE BOTHERING US ANYWAY.
"TWO COMMUNICATIONS SATELLITES JUST *MYSTERIOUSLY* COLLIDED AND ARE FALLING OUT OF ORBIT TOWARDS RUSSIA.
"HE HAS HIS HANDS FULL.
AFTER SUPERMAN AND HIS FRIENDS TOOK ALL OF THE INMATES OUT OF ARKHAM, AND TRANSPORTED THEM TO PLACES UNKNOWN, THE JUSTICE LEAGUE BEGAN BLUNDERING INTO EVERY MAJOR CONFLICT ON THE PLANET.
"ON TUESDAY, SUPERMAN FORCIBLY SAT THE LEADERS OF PALESTINE AND ISRAEL DOWN IN A ROOM."
GENTLEMEN. IN THREE HOURS, WE WILL ANNOUNCE AN ISRAEL/PALESTINE PEACE PLAN
YOU HAVE THREE HOURS TO AGREE TO TERMS.
OR?
OR THEY WILL BE AGREED FOR YOU.

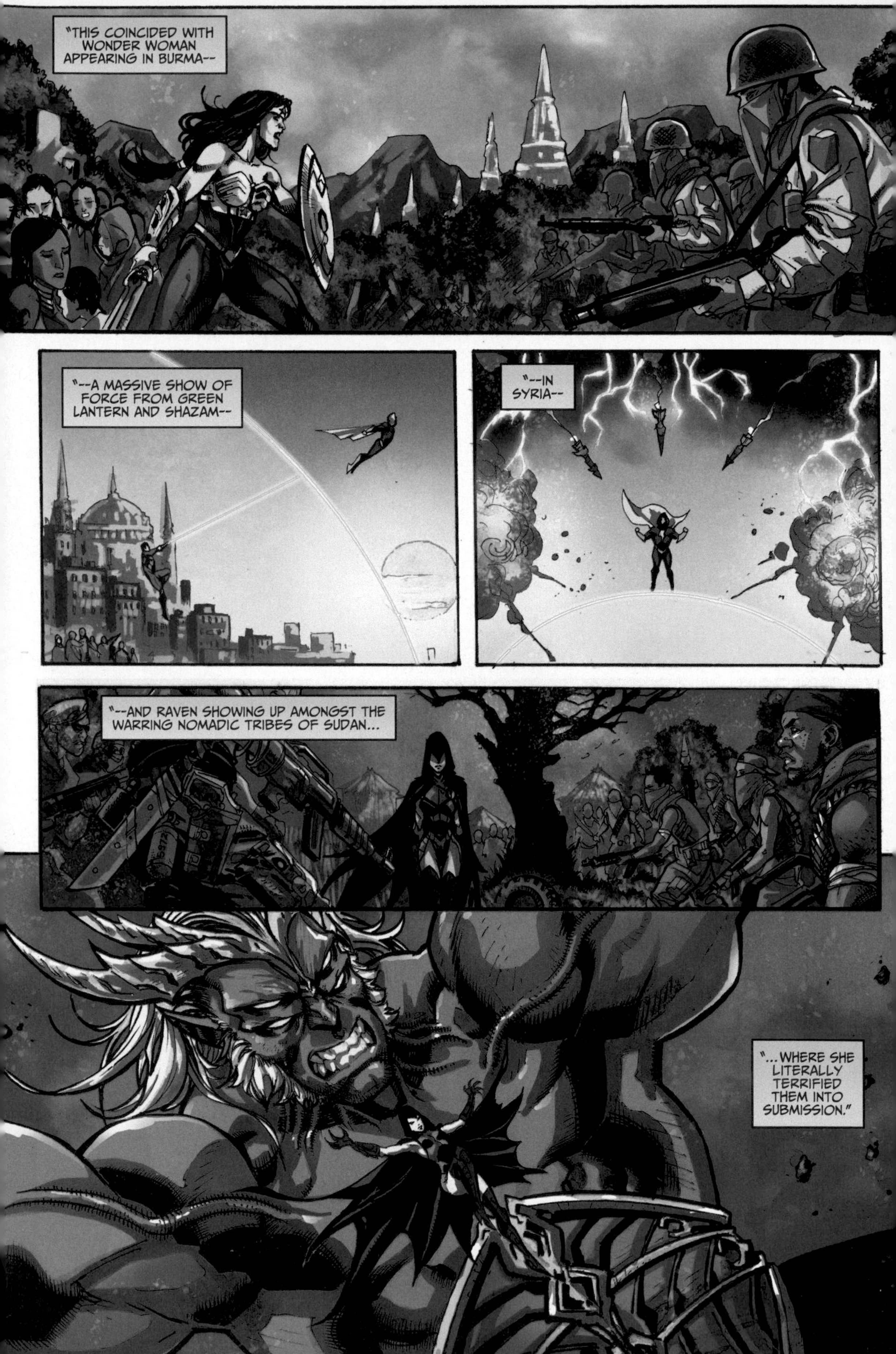
"THIS COINCIDED WITH WONDER WOMAN APPEARING IN BURMA--
"--A MASSIVE SHOW OF FORCE FROM GREEN LANTERN AND SHAZAM--
"--IN SYRIA--
"--AND RAVEN SHOWING UP AMONGST THE WARRING NOMADIC TRIBES OF SUDAN...
"...WHERE SHE LITERALLY TERRIFIED THEM INTO SUBMISSION."

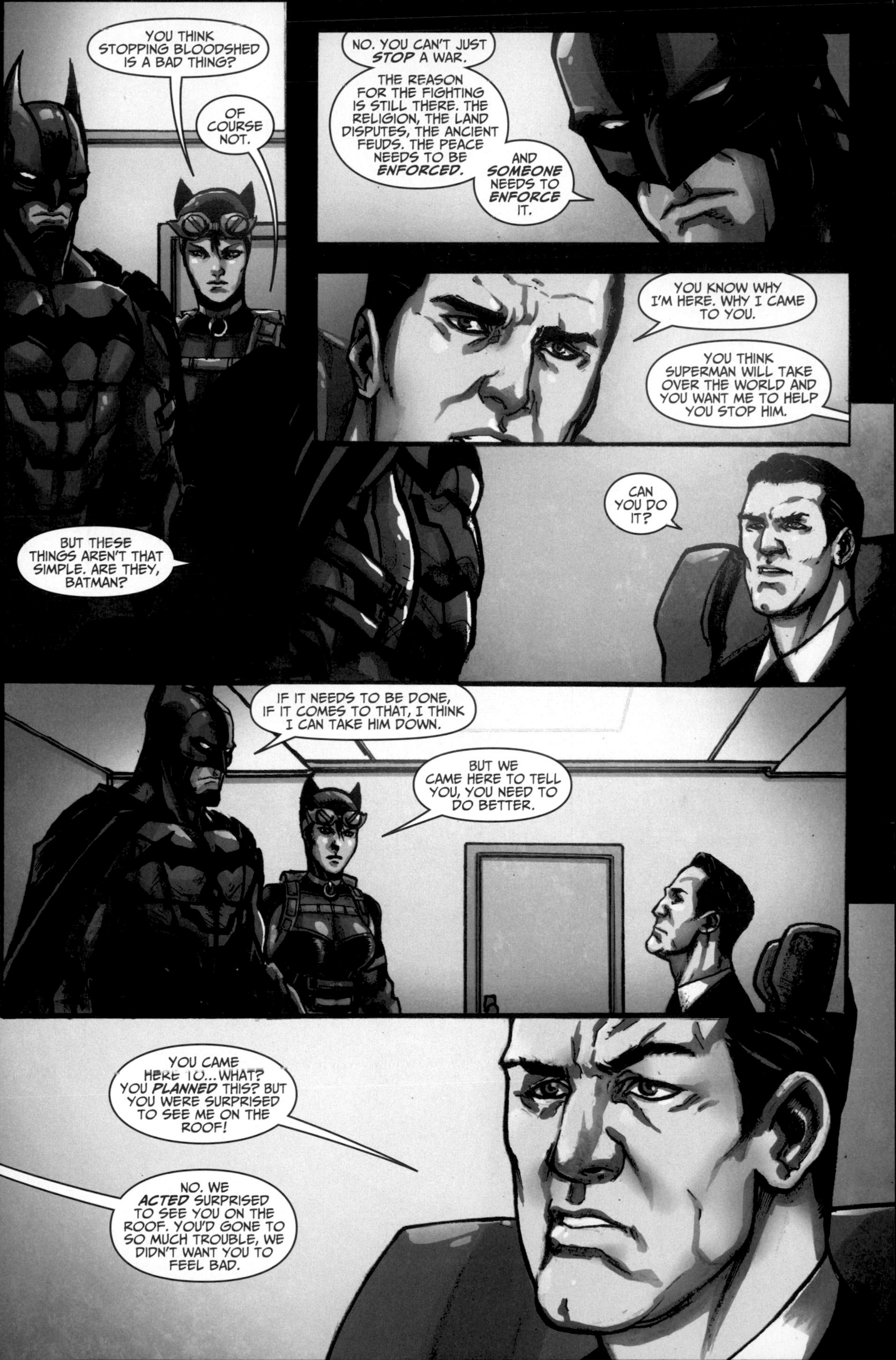
YOU THINK STOPPING BLOODSHED IS A BAD THING?
OF COURSE NOT.
NO. YOU CAN'T JUST STOP A WAR.
THE REASON FOR THE FIGHTING IS STILL THERE. THE RELIGION, THE LAND DISPUTES, THE ANCIENT FEUDS. THE PEACE NEEDS TO BE ENFORCED.
AND SOMEONE NEEDS TO ENFORCE IT.
YOU KNOW WHY I'M HERE. WHY I CAME TO YOU.
YOU THINK SUPERMAN WILL TAKE OVER THE WORLD AND YOU WANT ME TO HELP YOU STOP HIM.
CAN YOU DO IT?
BUT THESE THINGS AREN'T THAT SIMPLE. ARE THEY, BATMAN?
IF IT NEEDS TO BE DONE, IF IT COMES TO THAT, I THINK I CAN TAKE HIM DOWN.
BUT WE CAME HERE TO TELL YOU, YOU NEED TO DO BETTER.
YOU CAME HERE TO...WHAT? YOU PLANNED THIS? BUT YOU WERE SURPRISED TO SEE ME ON THE ROOF!
NO. WE ACTED SURPRISED TO SEE YOU ON THE ROOF. YOU'D GONE TO SO MUCH TROUBLE, WE DIDN'T WANT YOU TO FEEL BAD.

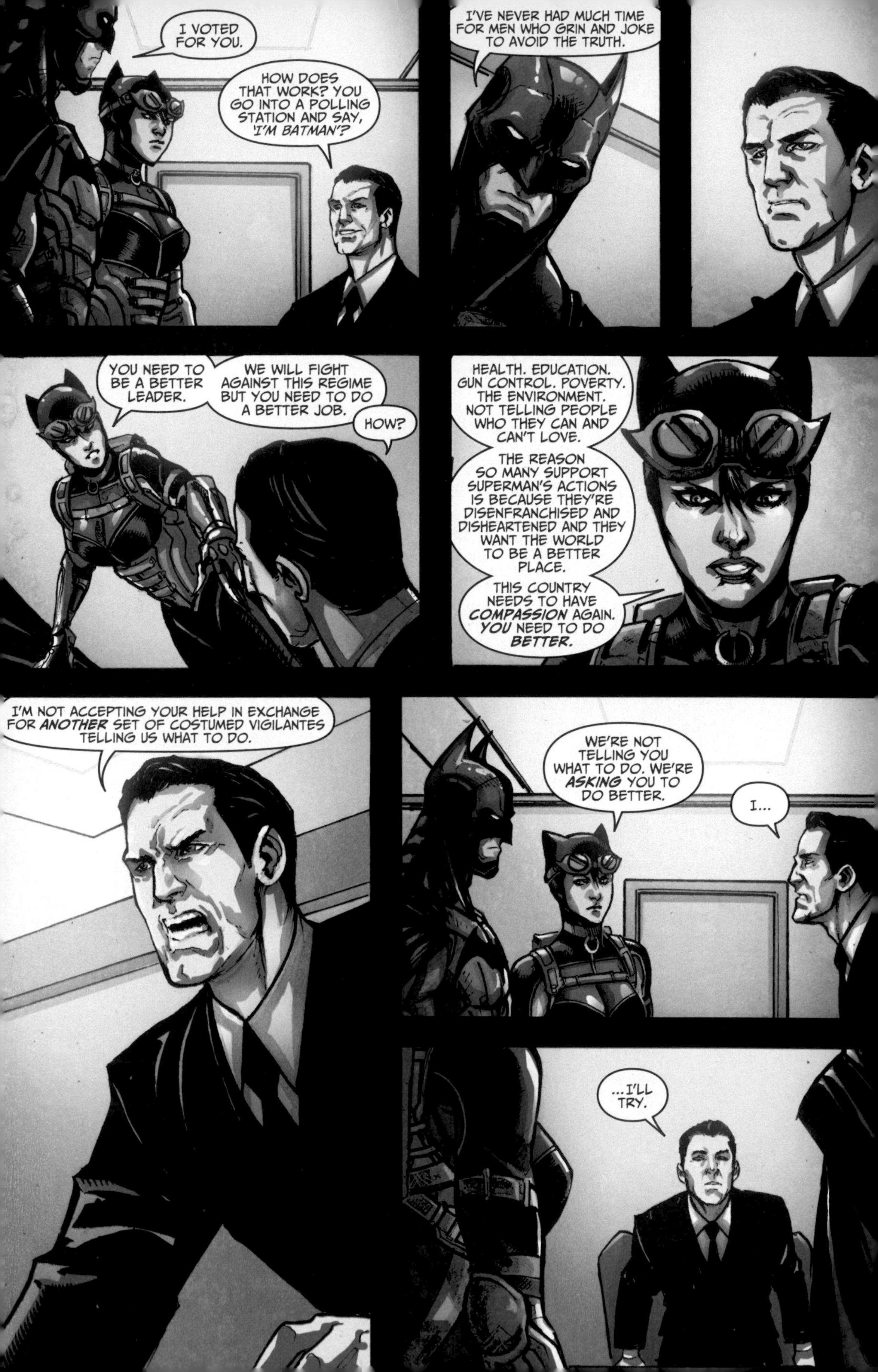
I VOTED FOR YOU.
HOW DOES THAT WORK? YOU GO INTO A POLLING STATION AND SAY, *'I'M BATMAN'?*
I'VE NEVER HAD MUCH TIME FOR MEN WHO GRIN AND JOKE TO AVOID THE TRUTH.
YOU NEED TO BE A BETTER LEADER.
WE WILL FIGHT AGAINST THIS REGIME BUT YOU NEED TO DO A BETTER JOB.
HOW?
HEALTH. EDUCATION. GUN CONTROL. POVERTY. THE ENVIRONMENT. NOT TELLING PEOPLE WHO THEY CAN AND CAN'T LOVE.
THE REASON SO MANY SUPPORT SUPERMAN'S ACTIONS IS BECAUSE THEY'RE DISENFRANCHISED AND DISHEARTENED AND THEY WANT THE WORLD TO BE A BETTER PLACE.
THIS COUNTRY NEEDS TO HAVE ***COMPASSION*** AGAIN. ***YOU*** NEED TO DO ***BETTER.***
I'M NOT ACCEPTING YOUR HELP IN EXCHANGE FOR ***ANOTHER*** SET OF COSTUMED VIGILANTES TELLING US WHAT TO DO.
WE'RE NOT TELLING YOU WHAT TO DO. WE'RE ***ASKING*** YOU TO DO BETTER.
I...
...I'LL TRY.

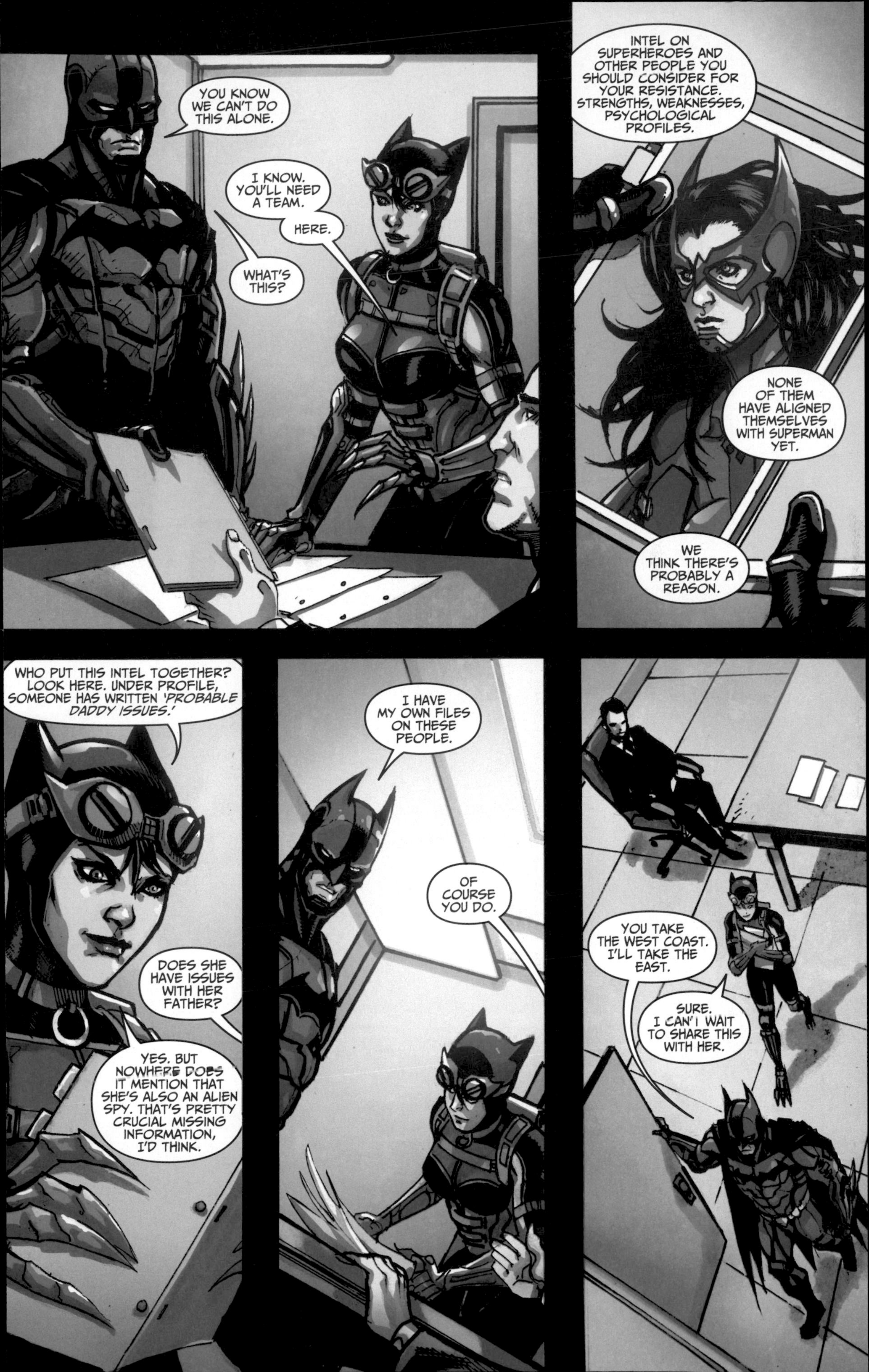

YOU KNOW WE CAN'T DO THIS ALONE.
I KNOW. YOU'LL NEED A TEAM.
HERE.
WHAT'S THIS?
INTEL ON SUPERHEROES AND OTHER PEOPLE YOU SHOULD CONSIDER FOR YOUR RESISTANCE. STRENGTHS, WEAKNESSES, PSYCHOLOGICAL PROFILES.
NONE OF THEM HAVE ALIGNED THEMSELVES WITH SUPERMAN YET.
WE THINK THERE'S PROBABLY A REASON.
WHO PUT THIS INTEL TOGETHER? LOOK HERE. UNDER PROFILE, SOMEONE HAS WRITTEN '*PROBABLE DADDY ISSUES.*'
DOES SHE HAVE ISSUES WITH HER FATHER?
YES. BUT NOWHERE DOES IT MENTION THAT SHE'S ALSO AN ALIEN SPY. THAT'S PRETTY CRUCIAL MISSING INFORMATION, I'D THINK.
I HAVE MY OWN FILES ON THESE PEOPLE.
OF COURSE YOU DO.
YOU TAKE THE WEST COAST. I'LL TAKE THE EAST.
SURE. I CAN'T WAIT TO SHARE THIS WITH HER.

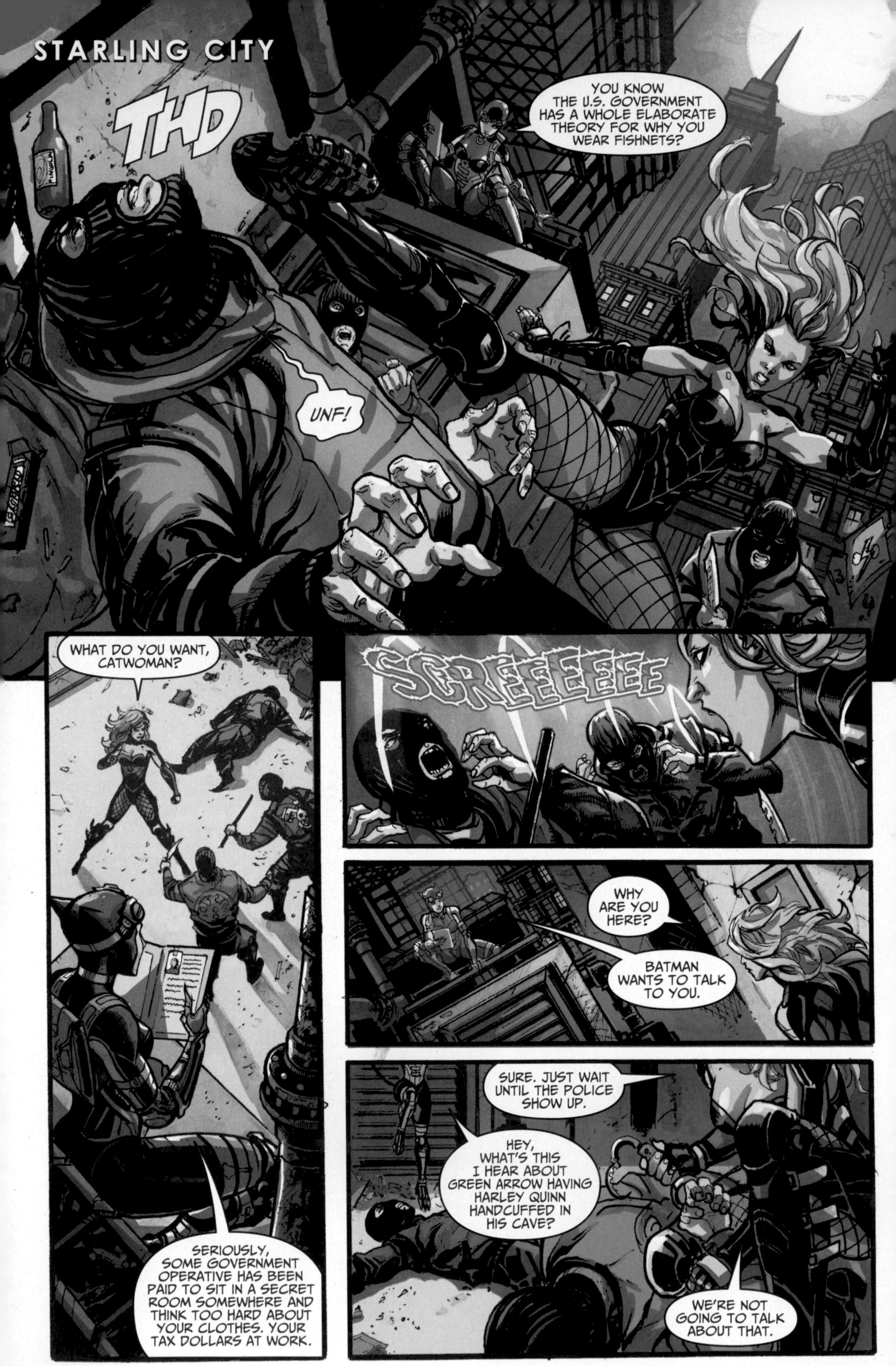
STARLING CITY
THD
YOU KNOW THE U.S. GOVERNMENT HAS A WHOLE ELABORATE THEORY FOR WHY YOU WEAR FISHNETS?
UNF!
WHAT DO YOU WANT, CATWOMAN?
SERIOUSLY, SOME GOVERNMENT OPERATIVE HAS BEEN PAID TO SIT IN A SECRET ROOM SOMEWHERE AND THINK TOO HARD ABOUT YOUR CLOTHES. YOUR TAX DOLLARS AT WORK.
SCREEEEEEE
WHY ARE YOU HERE?
BATMAN WANTS TO TALK TO YOU.
SURE. JUST WAIT UNTIL THE POLICE SHOW UP.
HEY, WHAT'S THIS I HEAR ABOUT GREEN ARROW HAVING HARLEY QUINN HANDCUFFED IN HIS CAVE?
WE'RE NOT GOING TO TALK ABOUT THAT.

JEFFERSON?

WHAT--?

BZZZT

I'M SORRY. I DIDN'T MEAN TO STARTLE YOU.

SERIOUSLY? THE 'WORLD'S GREATEST DETECTIVE' CAN'T FIND MY DOORBELL?

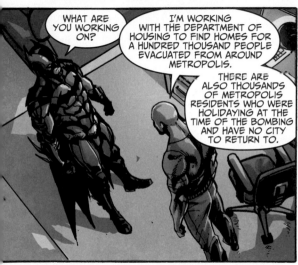

WHAT ARE YOU WORKING ON?

I'M WORKING WITH THE DEPARTMENT OF HOUSING TO FIND HOMES FOR A HUNDRED THOUSAND PEOPLE EVACUATED FROM AROUND METROPOLIS.

THERE ARE ALSO THOUSANDS OF METROPOLIS RESIDENTS WHO WERE HOLIDAYING AT THE TIME OF THE BOMBING AND HAVE NO CITY TO RETURN TO.

YOU'RE DOING GOOD WORK, JEFFERSON.

I'LL HELP YOU FIND HOMES FOR THESE PEOPLE. BUT I'D LIKE TO TALK TO YOU ABOUT SOMETHING ELSE THAT NEEDS YOUR ATTENTION.

I NEED BLACK LIGHTNING.

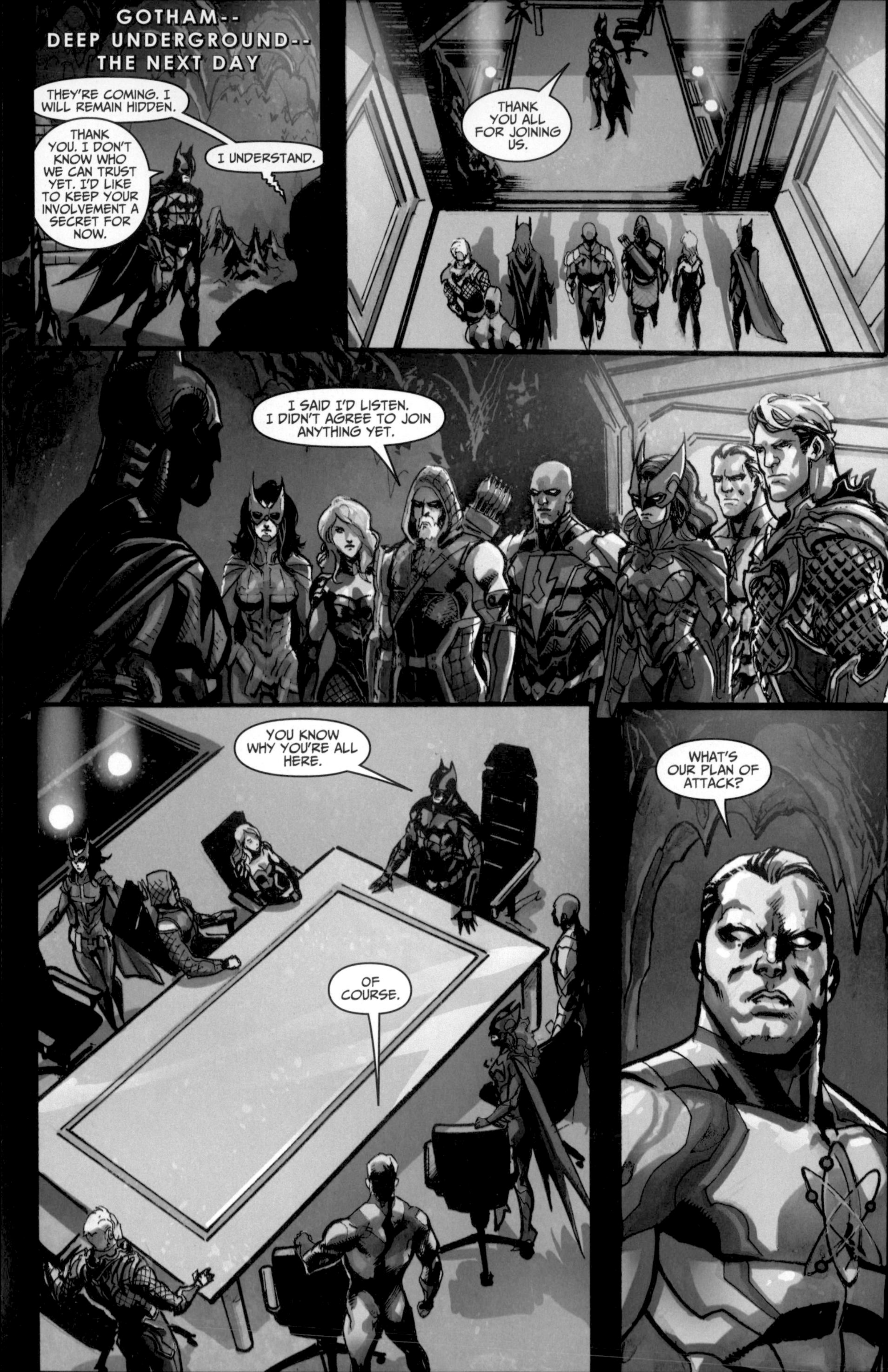
GOTHAM-- DEEP UNDERGROUND-- THE NEXT DAY
THEY'RE COMING. I WILL REMAIN HIDDEN.
THANK YOU. I DON'T KNOW WHO WE CAN TRUST YET. I'D LIKE TO KEEP YOUR INVOLVEMENT A SECRET FOR NOW.
I UNDERSTAND.
THANK YOU ALL FOR JOINING US.
I SAID I'D LISTEN. I DIDN'T AGREE TO JOIN ANYTHING YET.
YOU KNOW WHY YOU'RE ALL HERE.
OF COURSE.
WHAT'S OUR PLAN OF ATTACK?

PART SEVEN

Kevin Maguire **Tom Derenick** **Neil Googe** Artists

Rosemary Cheetham **Alejandro Sanchez** Colorists

Mico Suayan & **David Lopez** and **Santi Casas** of **Ikari Studio** Cover

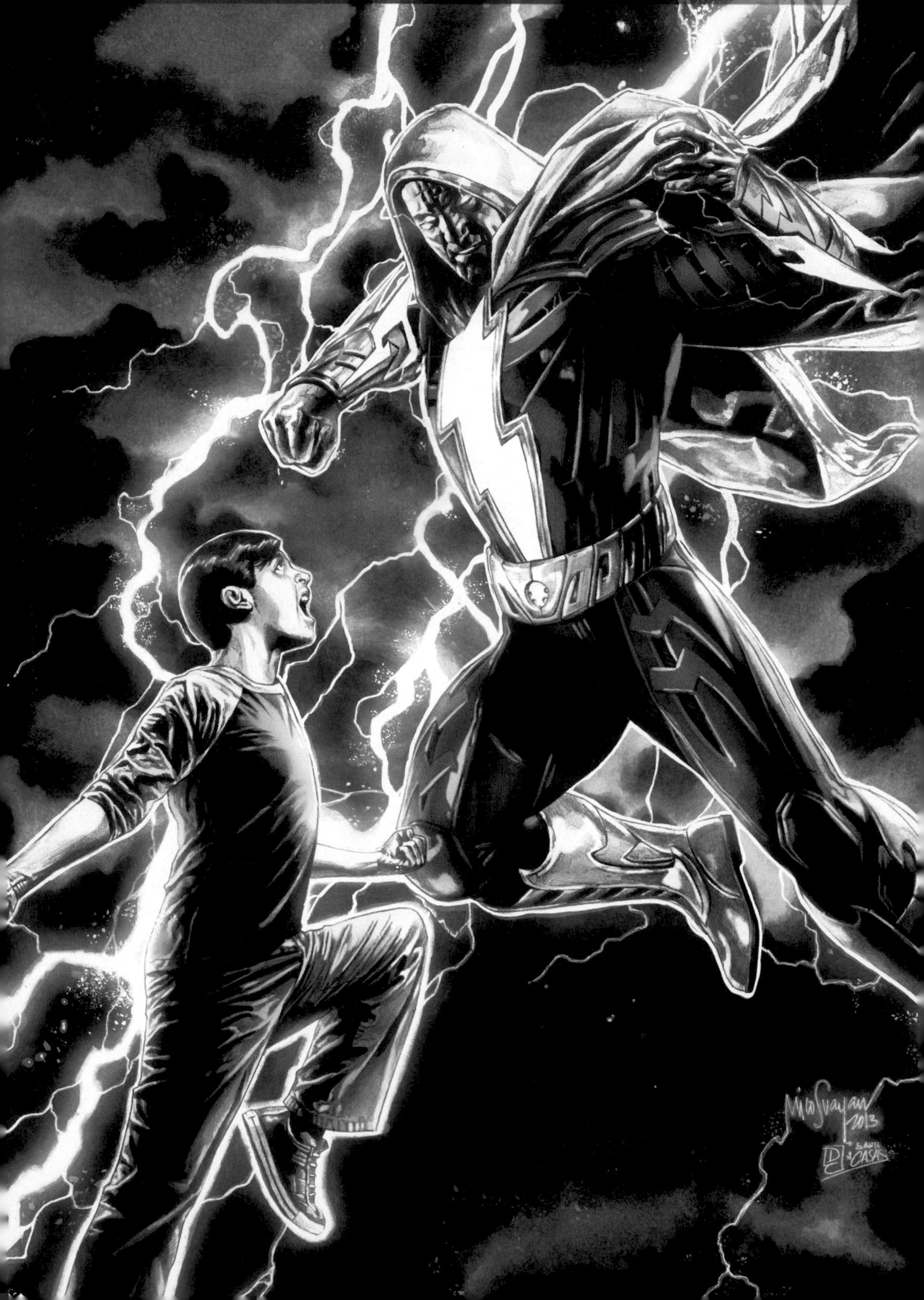

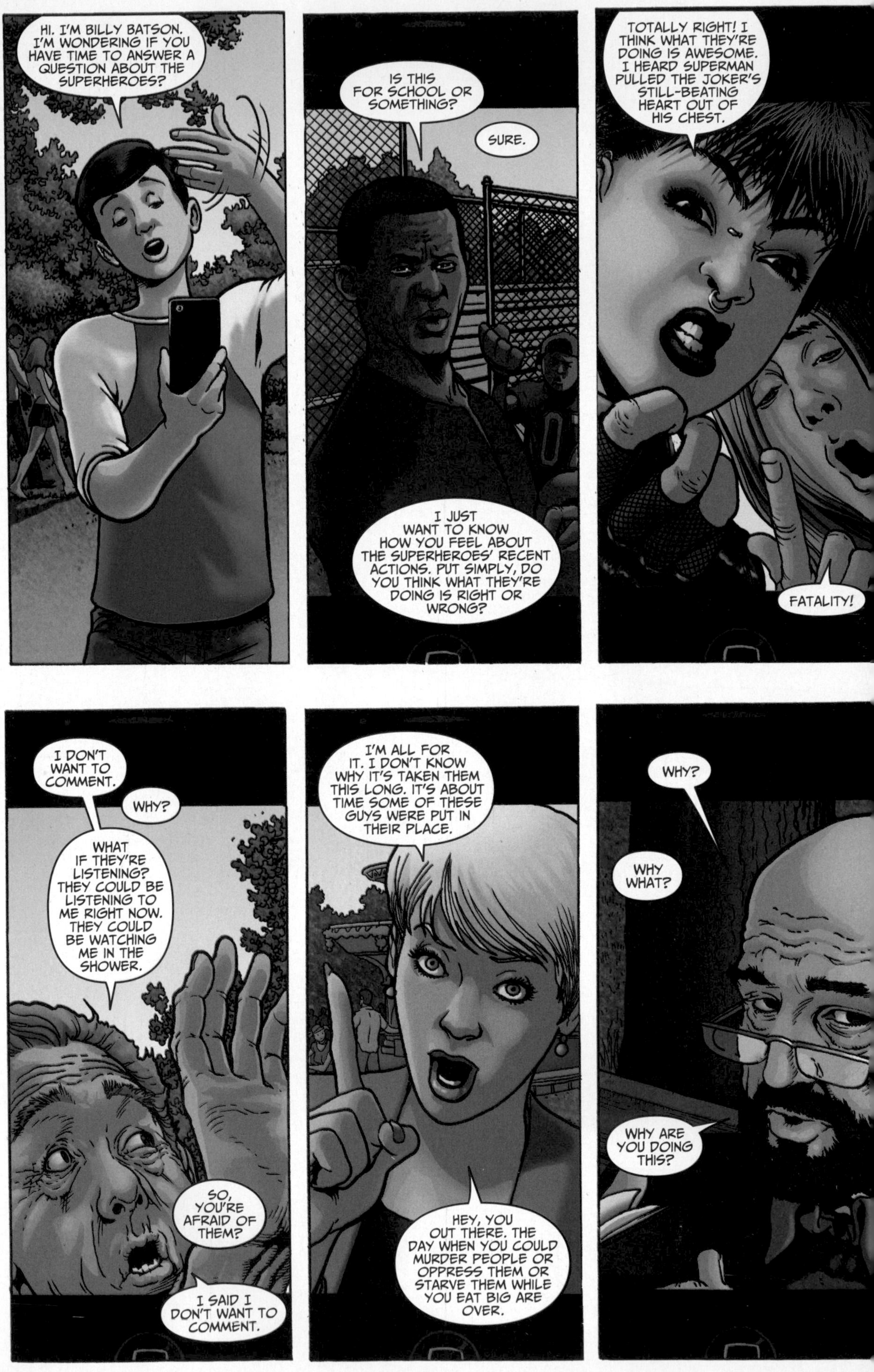
HI. I'M BILLY BATSON. I'M WONDERING IF YOU HAVE TIME TO ANSWER A QUESTION ABOUT THE SUPERHEROES?
IS THIS FOR SCHOOL OR SOMETHING?
SURE.
I JUST WANT TO KNOW HOW YOU FEEL ABOUT THE SUPERHEROES' RECENT ACTIONS. PUT SIMPLY, DO YOU THINK WHAT THEY'RE DOING IS RIGHT OR WRONG?
TOTALLY RIGHT! I THINK WHAT THEY'RE DOING IS AWESOME. I HEARD SUPERMAN PULLED THE JOKER'S STILL-BEATING HEART OUT OF HIS CHEST.
FATALITY!
I DON'T WANT TO COMMENT.
WHY?
WHAT IF THEY'RE LISTENING? THEY COULD BE LISTENING TO ME RIGHT NOW. THEY COULD BE WATCHING ME IN THE SHOWER.
SO, YOU'RE AFRAID OF THEM?
I SAID I DON'T WANT TO COMMENT.
I'M ALL FOR IT. I DON'T KNOW WHY IT'S TAKEN THEM THIS LONG. IT'S ABOUT TIME SOME OF THESE GUYS WERE PUT IN THEIR PLACE.
HEY, YOU OUT THERE. THE DAY WHEN YOU COULD MURDER PEOPLE OR OPPRESS THEM OR STARVE THEM WHILE YOU EAT BIG ARE OVER.
WHY?
WHY WHAT?
WHY ARE YOU DOING THIS?

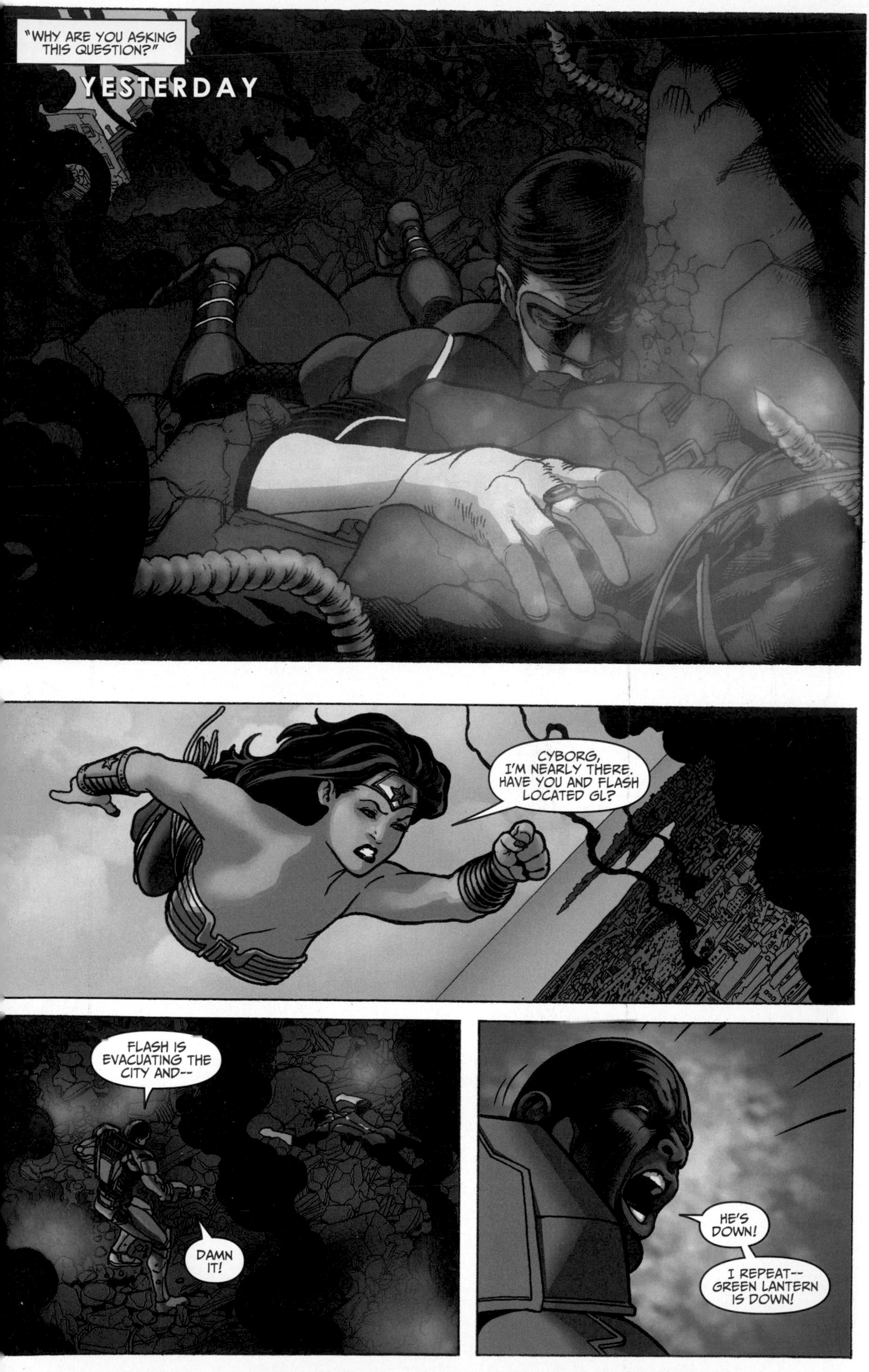
"WHY ARE YOU ASKING THIS QUESTION?"
YESTERDAY
CYBORG, I'M NEARLY THERE. HAVE YOU AND FLASH LOCATED GL?
FLASH IS EVACUATING THE CITY AND--
DAMN IT!
HE'S DOWN!
I REPEAT-- GREEN LANTERN IS DOWN!

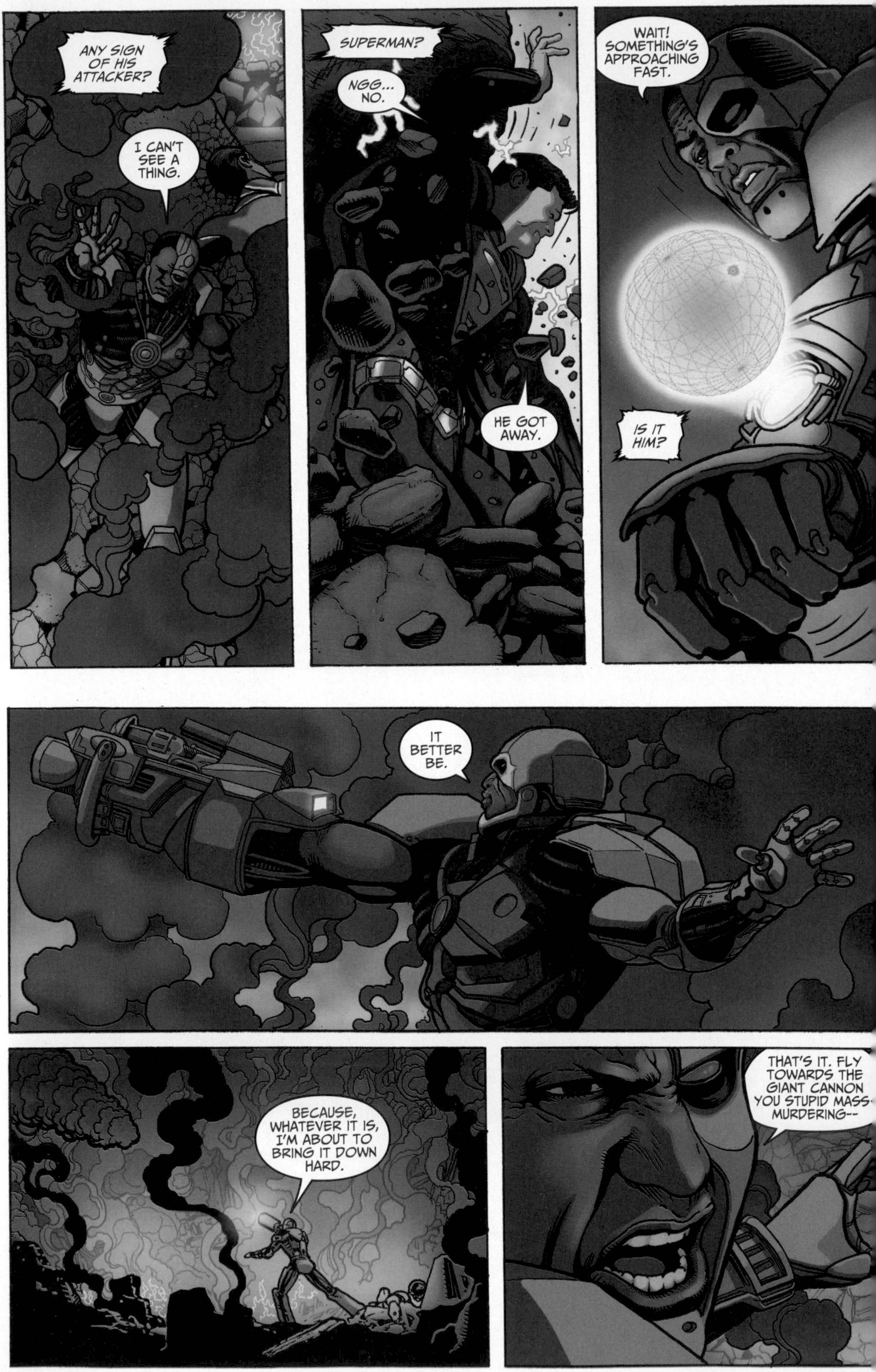
ANY SIGN OF HIS ATTACKER?
I CAN'T SEE A THING.
SUPERMAN?
NGG... NO.
HE GOT AWAY.
WAIT! SOMETHING'S APPROACHING FAST.
IS IT HIM?
IT BETTER BE.
BECAUSE, WHATEVER IT IS, I'M ABOUT TO BRING IT DOWN HARD.
THAT'S IT. FLY TOWARDS THE GIANT CANNON YOU STUPID MASS-MURDERING--

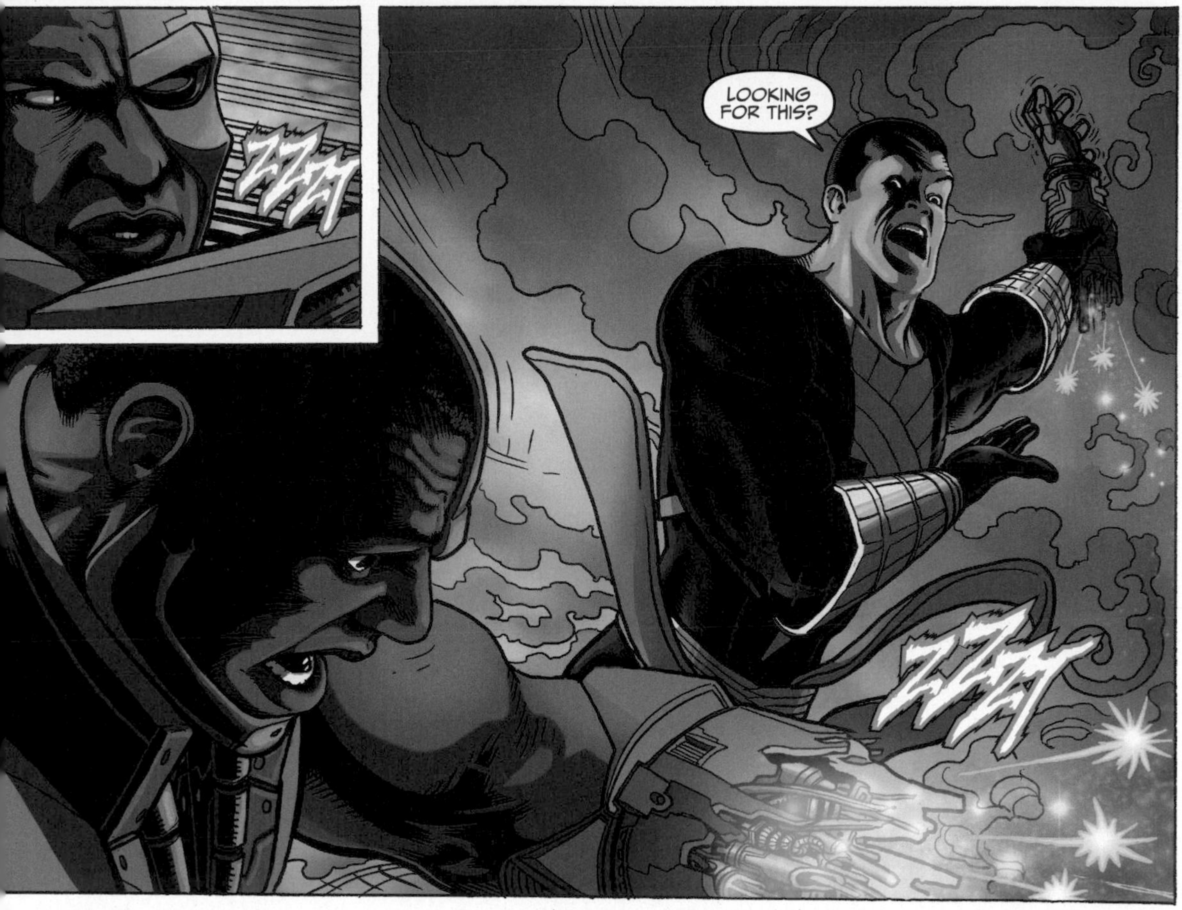
ZZAT
LOOKING FOR THIS?
ZZAT
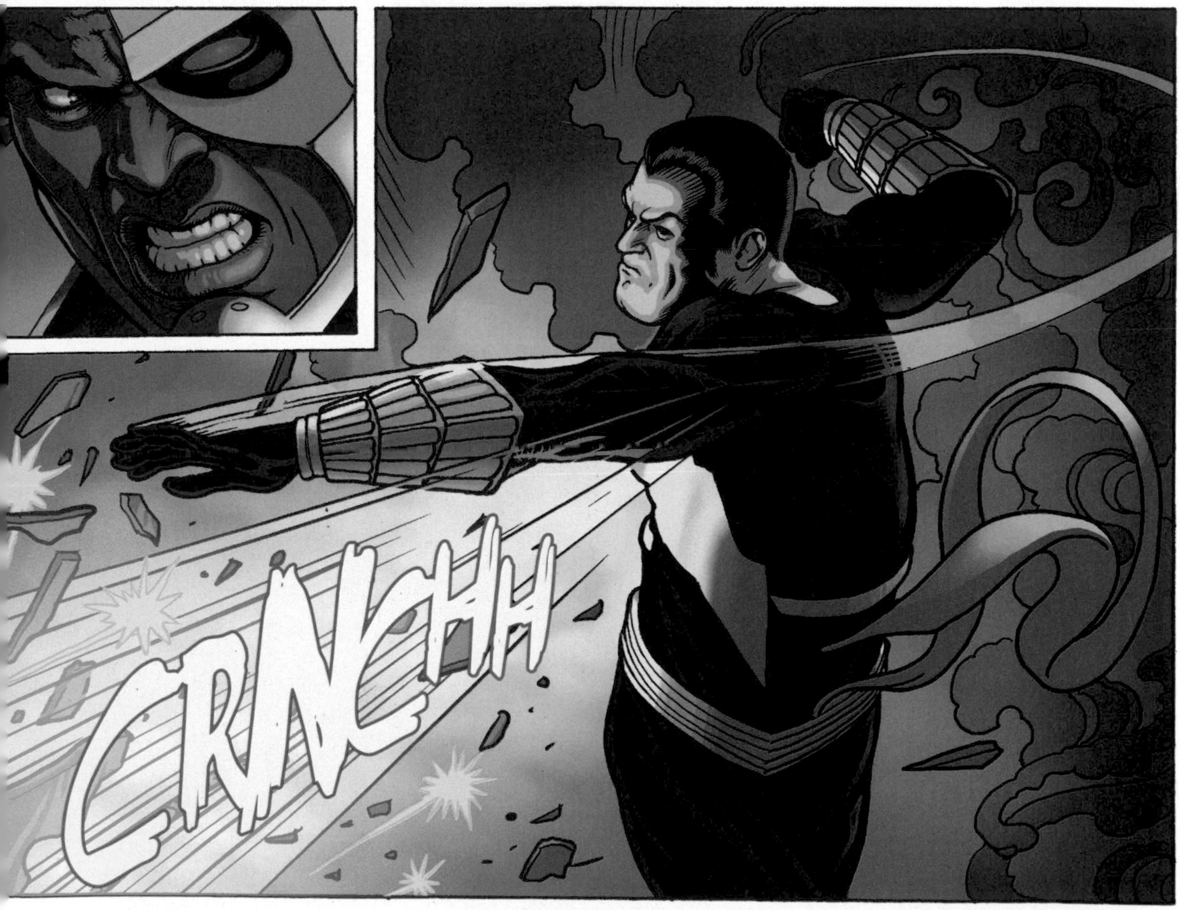
CRNCHH

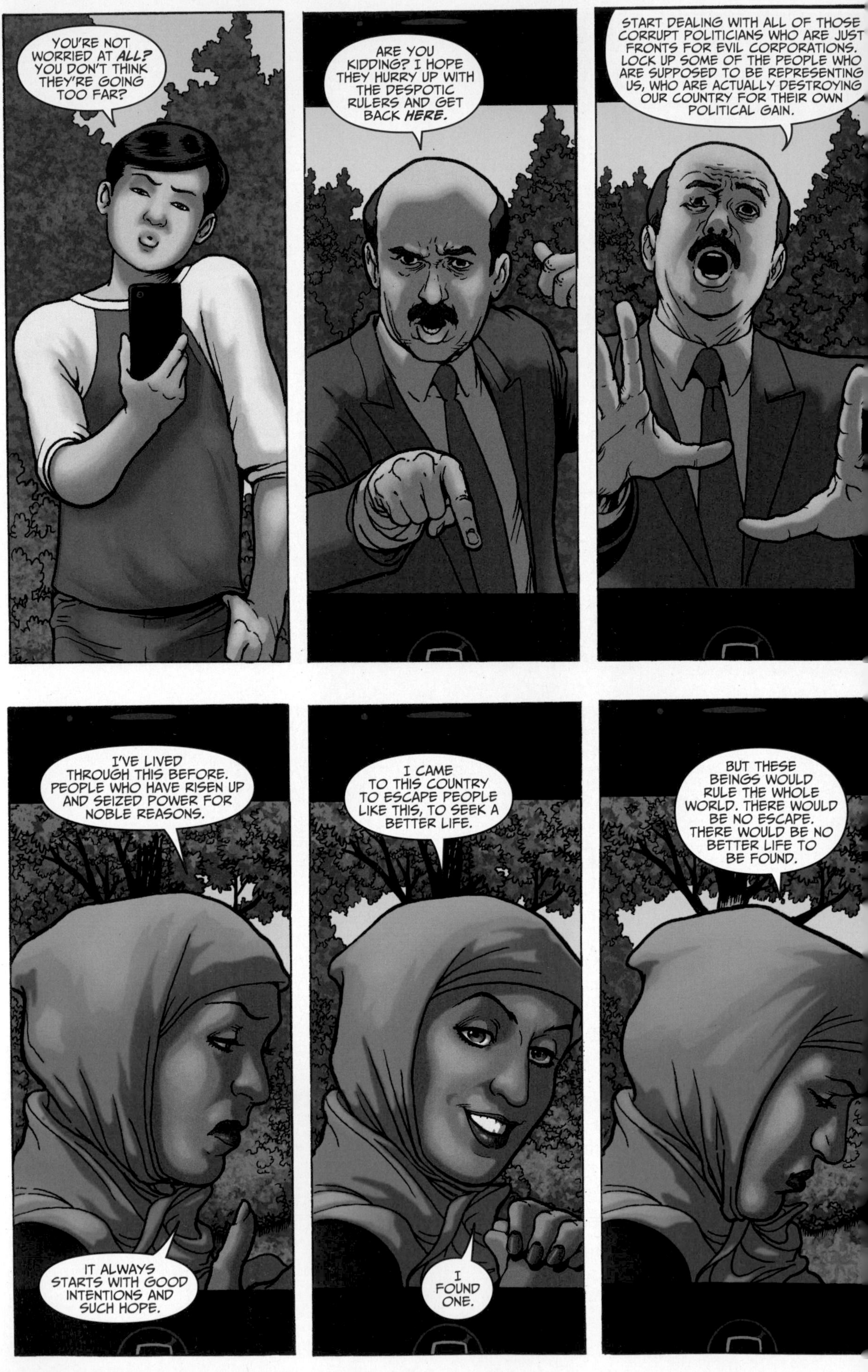
YOU'RE NOT WORRIED AT ALL? YOU DON'T THINK THEY'RE GOING TOO FAR?
ARE YOU KIDDING? I HOPE THEY HURRY UP WITH THE DESPOTIC RULERS AND GET BACK HERE.
START DEALING WITH ALL OF THOSE CORRUPT POLITICIANS WHO ARE JUST FRONTS FOR EVIL CORPORATIONS. LOCK UP SOME OF THE PEOPLE WHO ARE SUPPOSED TO BE REPRESENTING US, WHO ARE ACTUALLY DESTROYING OUR COUNTRY FOR THEIR OWN POLITICAL GAIN.
I'VE LIVED THROUGH THIS BEFORE. PEOPLE WHO HAVE RISEN UP AND SEIZED POWER FOR NOBLE REASONS.
IT ALWAYS STARTS WITH GOOD INTENTIONS AND SUCH HOPE.
I CAME TO THIS COUNTRY TO ESCAPE PEOPLE LIKE THIS, TO SEEK A BETTER LIFE.
I FOUND ONE.
BUT THESE BEINGS WOULD RULE THE WHOLE WORLD. THERE WOULD BE NO ESCAPE. THERE WOULD BE NO BETTER LIFE TO BE FOUND.

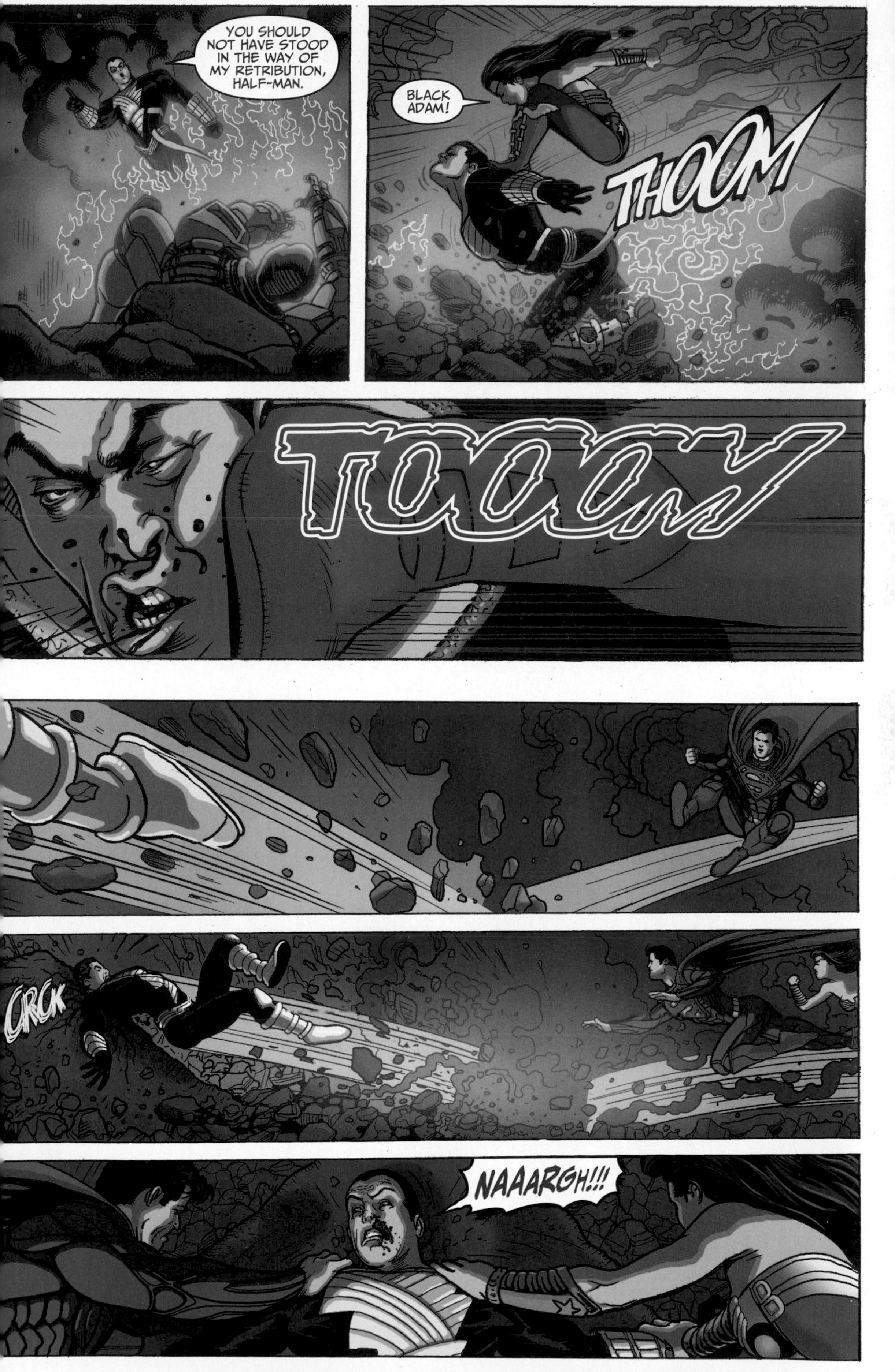
YOU SHOULD NOT HAVE STOOD IN THE WAY OF MY RETRIBUTION, HALF-MAN.
BLACK ADAM!
THOOM
TOOOM
CRCK
NAAARGH!!!

YOU'RE DONE, ADAM.

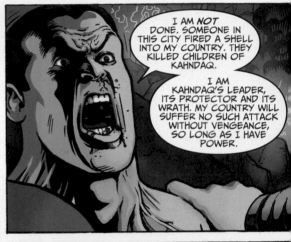

I AM *NOT* DONE. SOMEONE IN THIS CITY FIRED A SHELL INTO MY COUNTRY. THEY KILLED CHILDREN OF KAHNDAQ.

I AM KAHNDAQ'S LEADER, ITS PROTECTOR AND ITS WRATH. MY COUNTRY WILL SUFFER NO SUCH ATTACK WITHOUT VENGEANCE, SO LONG AS I HAVE POWER.

THEN WE WILL *TAKE* YOUR POWER.

WHAT ARE YOU DOING?

ASKING HIM A QUESTION.

SHAZAM, HOLD HIM.

KNOW THAT YOU CANNOT LIE WHILE TOUCHING THIS LASSO.

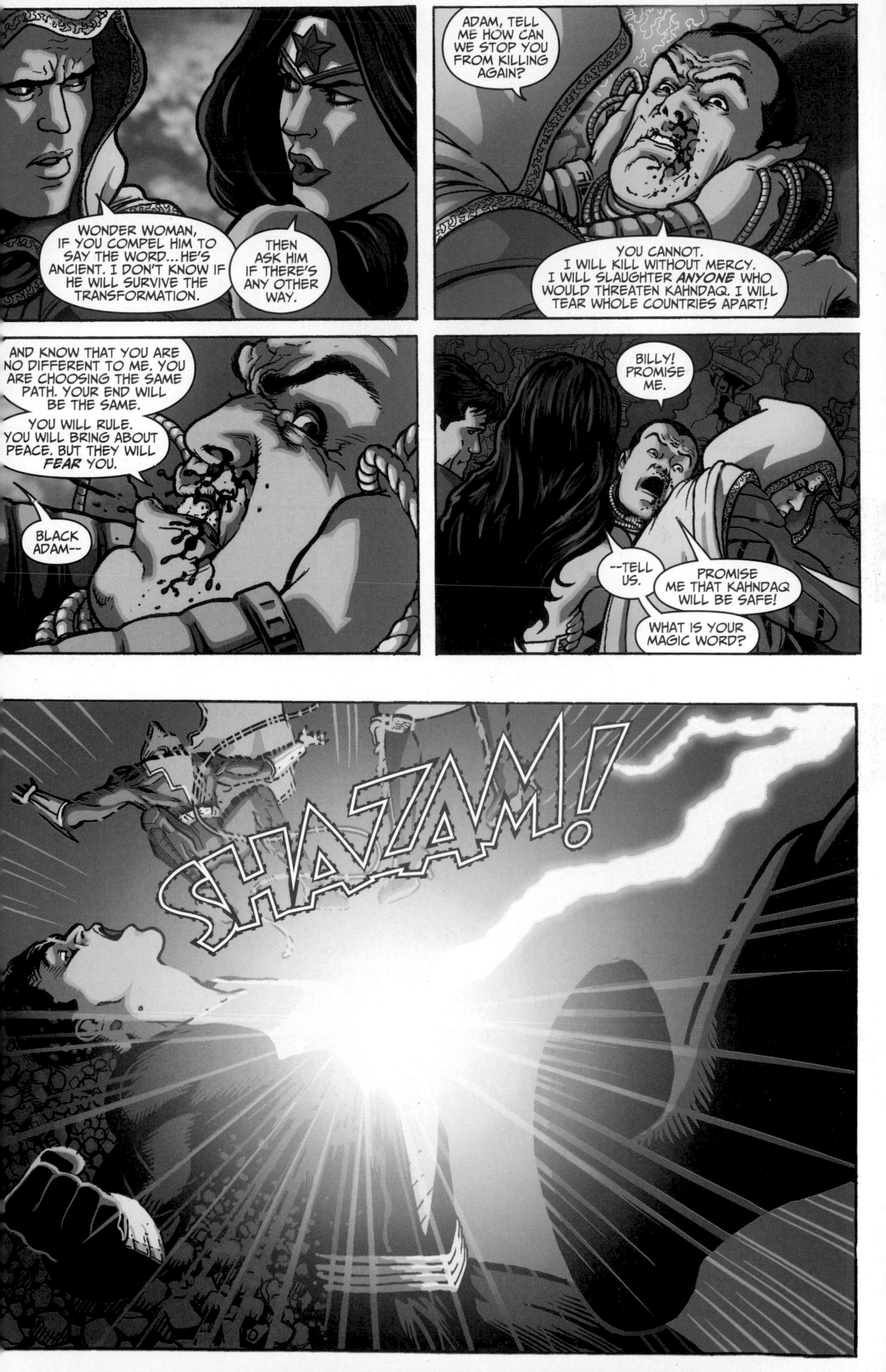
WONDER WOMAN, IF YOU COMPEL HIM TO SAY THE WORD...HE'S ANCIENT. I DON'T KNOW IF HE WILL SURVIVE THE TRANSFORMATION.
THEN ASK HIM IF THERE'S ANY OTHER WAY.
ADAM, TELL ME HOW CAN WE STOP YOU FROM KILLING AGAIN?
YOU CANNOT. I WILL KILL WITHOUT MERCY. I WILL SLAUGHTER ANYONE WHO WOULD THREATEN KAHNDAQ. I WILL TEAR WHOLE COUNTRIES APART!
AND KNOW THAT YOU ARE NO DIFFERENT TO ME. YOU ARE CHOOSING THE SAME PATH. YOUR END WILL BE THE SAME.
YOU WILL RULE. YOU WILL BRING ABOUT PEACE. BUT THEY WILL FEAR YOU.
BLACK ADAM--
BILLY! PROMISE ME.
--TELL US.
PROMISE ME THAT KAHNDAQ WILL BE SAFE!
WHAT IS YOUR MAGIC WORD?
SHAZAM!

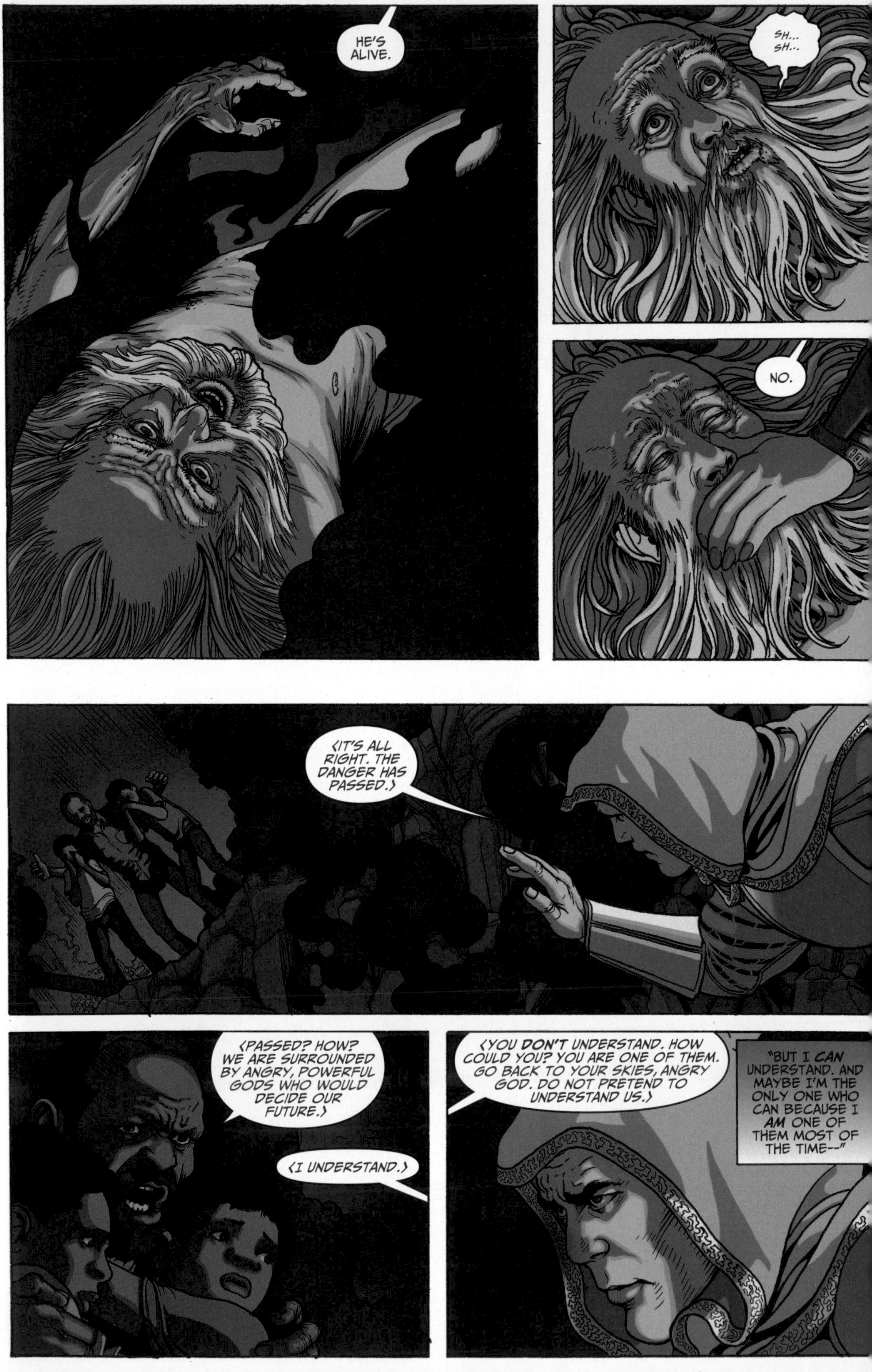

HE'S ALIVE.
SH... SH...
NO.
<IT'S ALL RIGHT. THE DANGER HAS PASSED.>
<PASSED? HOW? WE ARE SURROUNDED BY ANGRY, POWERFUL GODS WHO WOULD DECIDE OUR FUTURE.>
<I UNDERSTAND.>
<YOU DON'T UNDERSTAND. HOW COULD YOU? YOU ARE ONE OF THEM. GO BACK TO YOUR SKIES, ANGRY GOD. DO NOT PRETEND TO UNDERSTAND US.>
"BUT I CAN UNDERSTAND. AND MAYBE I'M THE ONLY ONE WHO CAN BECAUSE I AM ONE OF THEM MOST OF THE TIME--"

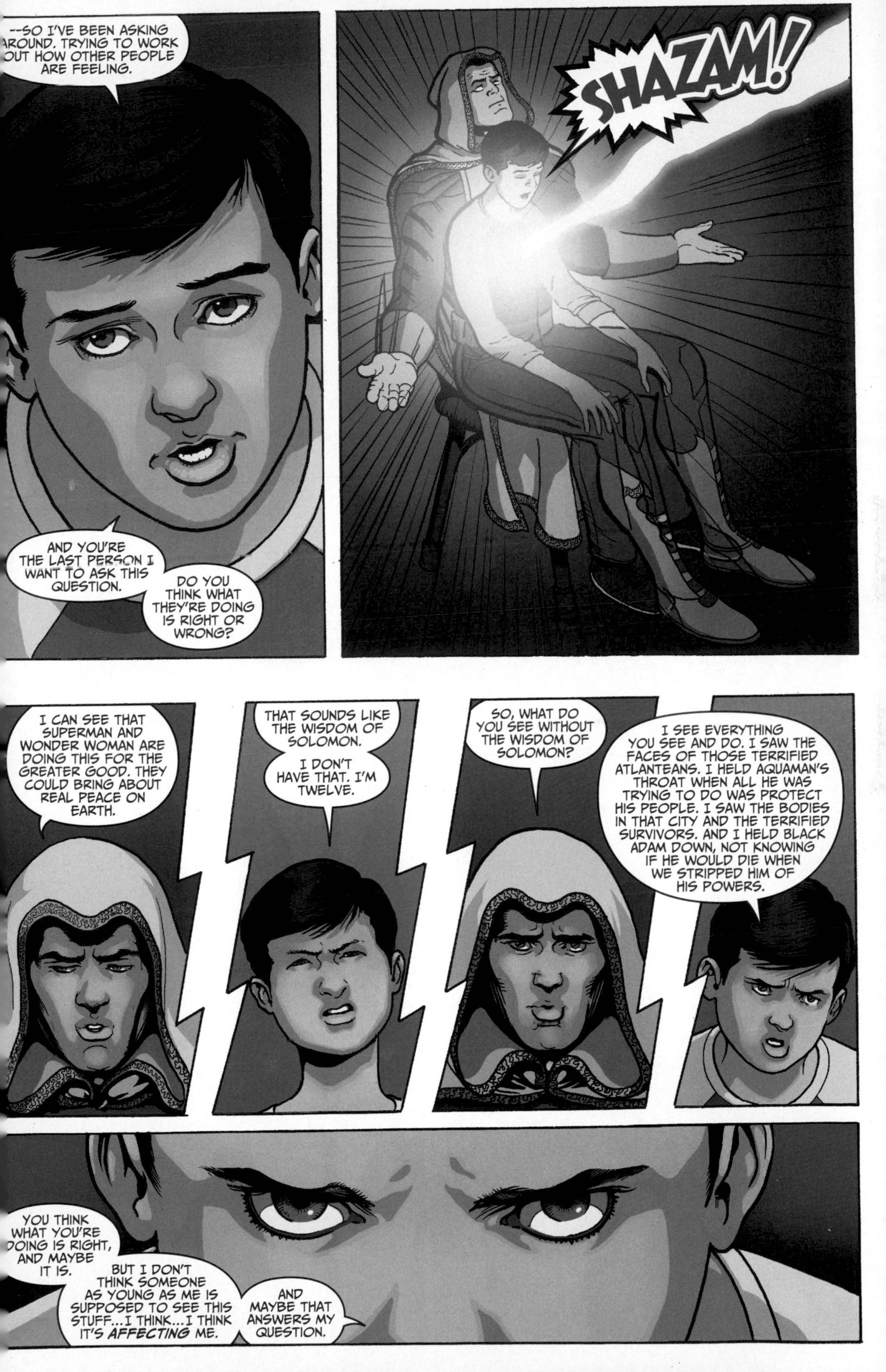
--SO I'VE BEEN ASKING AROUND. TRYING TO WORK OUT HOW OTHER PEOPLE ARE FEELING.
AND YOU'RE THE LAST PERSON I WANT TO ASK THIS QUESTION.
DO YOU THINK WHAT THEY'RE DOING IS RIGHT OR WRONG?
SHAZAM!
I CAN SEE THAT SUPERMAN AND WONDER WOMAN ARE DOING THIS FOR THE GREATER GOOD. THEY COULD BRING ABOUT REAL PEACE ON EARTH.
THAT SOUNDS LIKE THE WISDOM OF SOLOMON.
I DON'T HAVE THAT. I'M TWELVE.
SO, WHAT DO YOU SEE WITHOUT THE WISDOM OF SOLOMON?
I SEE EVERYTHING YOU SEE AND DO. I SAW THE FACES OF THOSE TERRIFIED ATLANTEANS. I HELD AQUAMAN'S THROAT WHEN ALL HE WAS TRYING TO DO WAS PROTECT HIS PEOPLE. I SAW THE BODIES IN THAT CITY AND THE TERRIFIED SURVIVORS. AND I HELD BLACK ADAM DOWN, NOT KNOWING IF HE WOULD DIE WHEN WE STRIPPED HIM OF HIS POWERS.
YOU THINK WHAT YOU'RE DOING IS RIGHT, AND MAYBE IT IS.
BUT I DON'T THINK SOMEONE AS YOUNG AS ME IS SUPPOSED TO SEE THIS STUFF...I THINK...I THINK IT'S *AFFECTING* ME.
AND MAYBE THAT ANSWERS MY QUESTION.

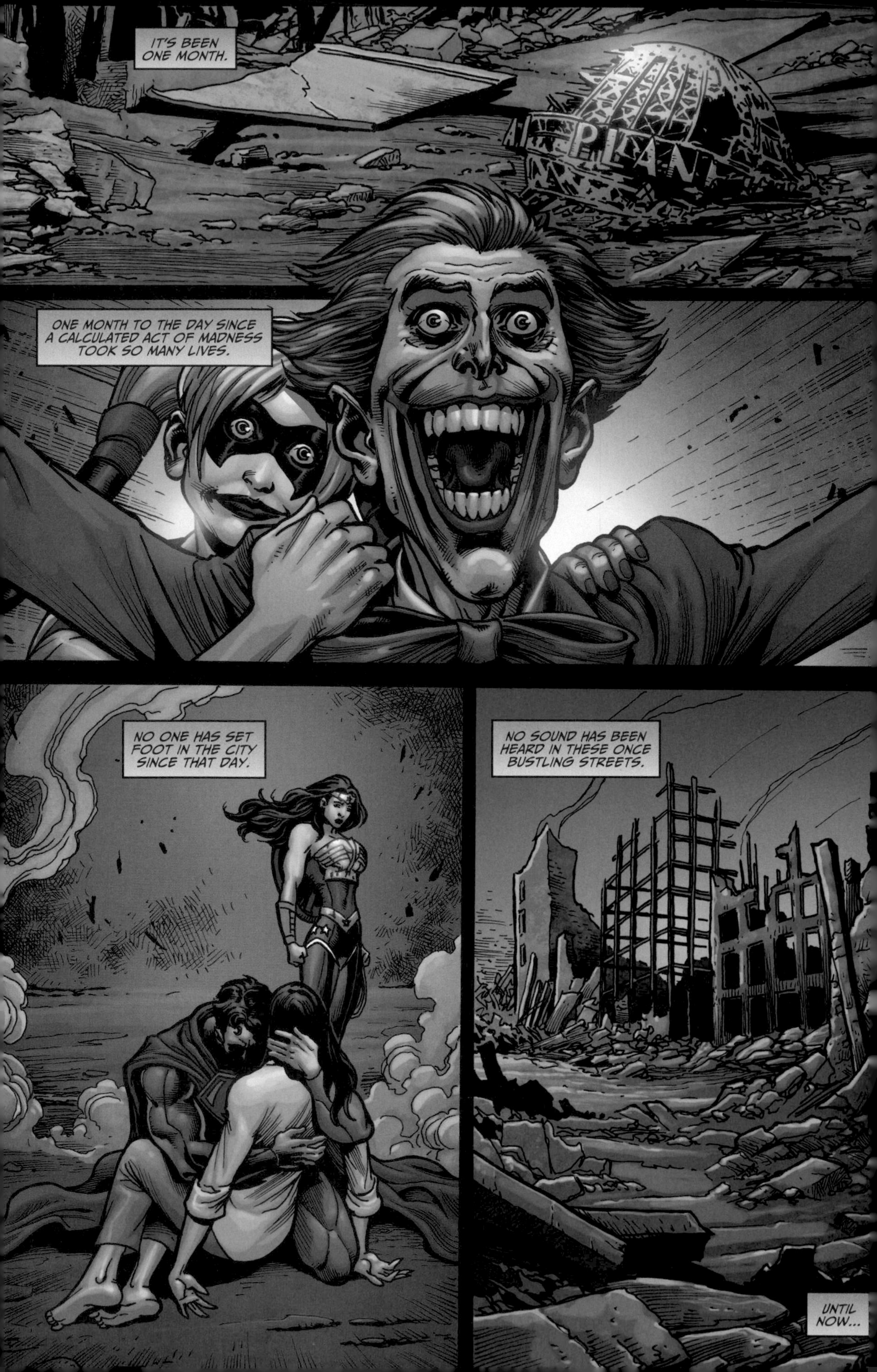
IT'S BEEN ONE MONTH.
ONE MONTH TO THE DAY SINCE A CALCULATED ACT OF MADNESS TOOK SO MANY LIVES.
NO ONE HAS SET FOOT IN THE CITY SINCE THAT DAY.
NO SOUND HAS BEEN HEARD IN THESE ONCE BUSTLING STREETS.
UNTIL NOW...

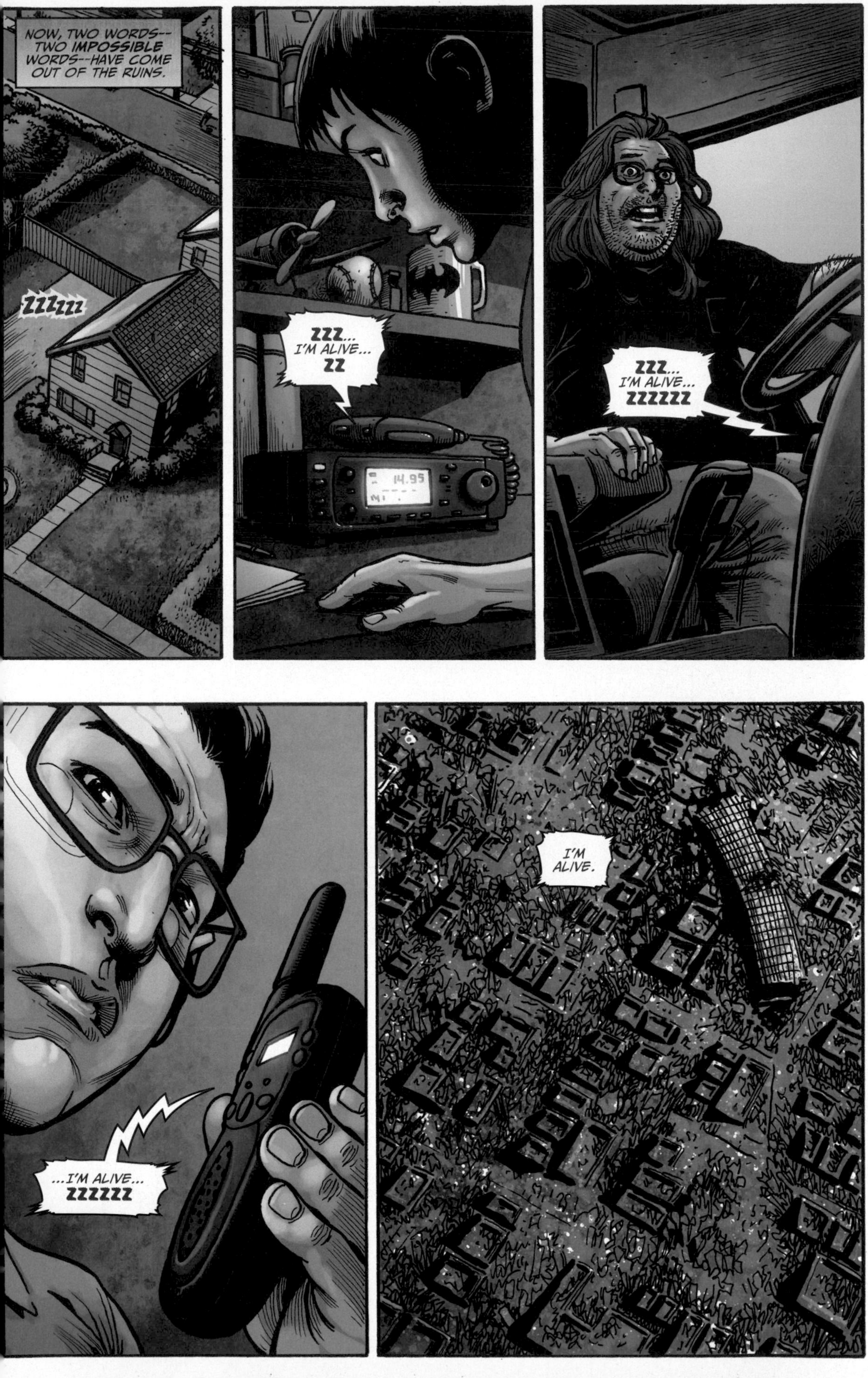
NOW, TWO WORDS--TWO IMPOSSIBLE WORDS--HAVE COME OUT OF THE RUINS.
ZZZzzz
ZZZ... I'M ALIVE... ZZ
ZZZ... I'M ALIVE... ZZZZZZ
...I'M ALIVE... ZZZZZZ
I'M ALIVE.

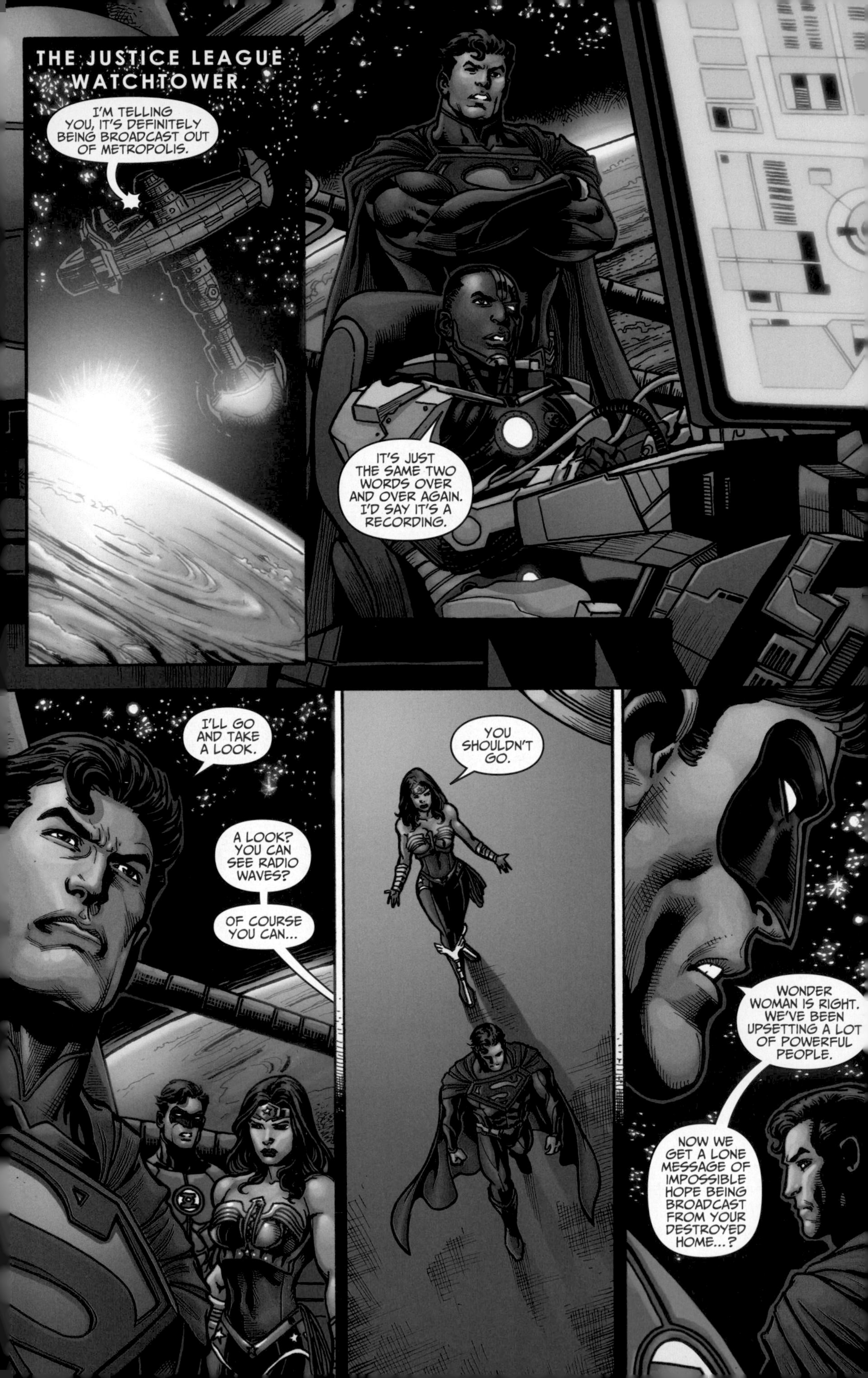
THE JUSTICE LEAGUE WATCHTOWER.
I'M TELLING YOU, IT'S DEFINITELY BEING BROADCAST OUT OF METROPOLIS.
IT'S JUST THE SAME TWO WORDS OVER AND OVER AGAIN. I'D SAY IT'S A RECORDING.
I'LL GO AND TAKE A LOOK.
A LOOK? YOU CAN SEE RADIO WAVES?
OF COURSE YOU CAN...
YOU SHOULDN'T GO.
WONDER WOMAN IS RIGHT. WE'VE BEEN UPSETTING A LOT OF POWERFUL PEOPLE.
NOW WE GET A LONE MESSAGE OF IMPOSSIBLE HOPE BEING BROADCAST FROM YOUR DESTROYED HOME...?

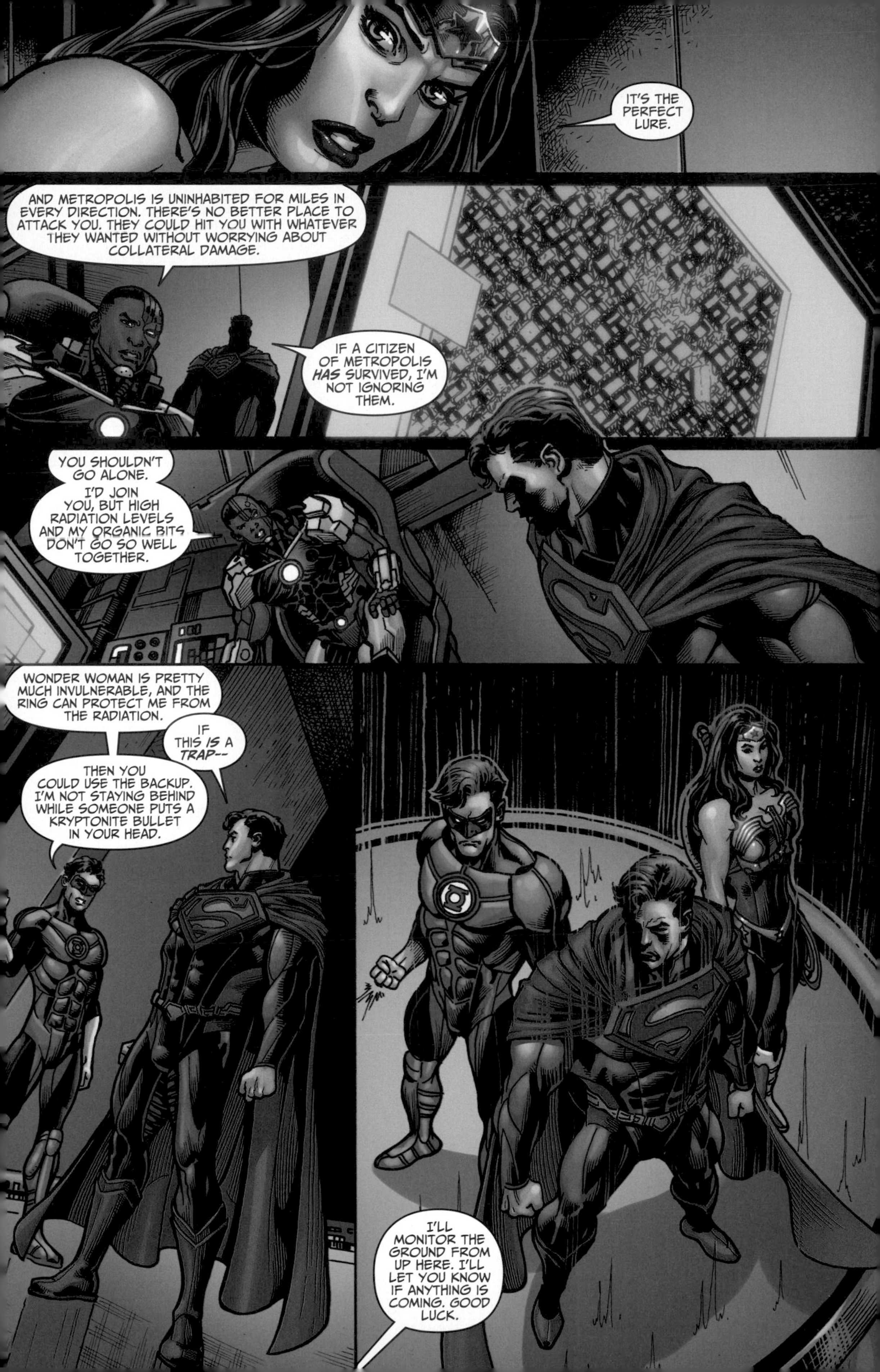
IT'S THE PERFECT LURE.
AND METROPOLIS IS UNINHABITED FOR MILES IN EVERY DIRECTION. THERE'S NO BETTER PLACE TO ATTACK YOU. THEY COULD HIT YOU WITH WHATEVER THEY WANTED WITHOUT WORRYING ABOUT COLLATERAL DAMAGE.
IF A CITIZEN OF METROPOLIS HAS SURVIVED, I'M NOT IGNORING THEM.
YOU SHOULDN'T GO ALONE.
I'D JOIN YOU, BUT HIGH RADIATION LEVELS AND MY ORGANIC BITS DON'T GO SO WELL TOGETHER.
WONDER WOMAN IS PRETTY MUCH INVULNERABLE, AND THE RING CAN PROTECT ME FROM THE RADIATION.
IF THIS IS A TRAP--
THEN YOU COULD USE THE BACKUP. I'M NOT STAYING BEHIND WHILE SOMEONE PUTS A KRYPTONITE BULLET IN YOUR HEAD.
I'LL MONITOR THE GROUND FROM UP HERE. I'LL LET YOU KNOW IF ANYTHING IS COMING. GOOD LUCK.

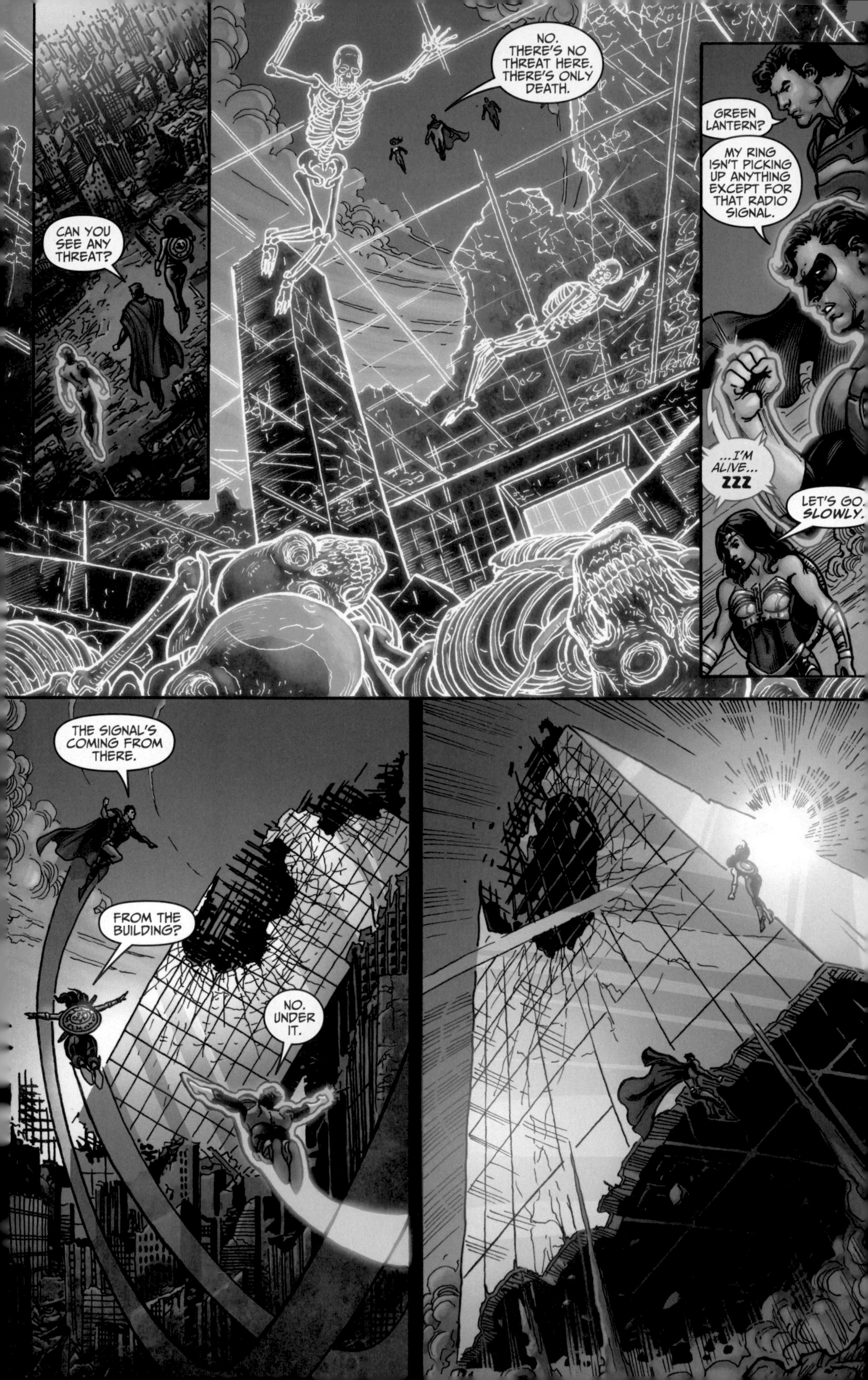
CAN YOU SEE ANY THREAT?
NO. THERE'S NO THREAT HERE. THERE'S ONLY DEATH.
GREEN LANTERN?
MY RING ISN'T PICKING UP ANYTHING EXCEPT FOR THAT RADIO SIGNAL.
...I'M ALIVE... ZZZ
LET'S GO. SLOWLY.
THE SIGNAL'S COMING FROM THERE.
FROM THE BUILDING?
NO. UNDER IT.

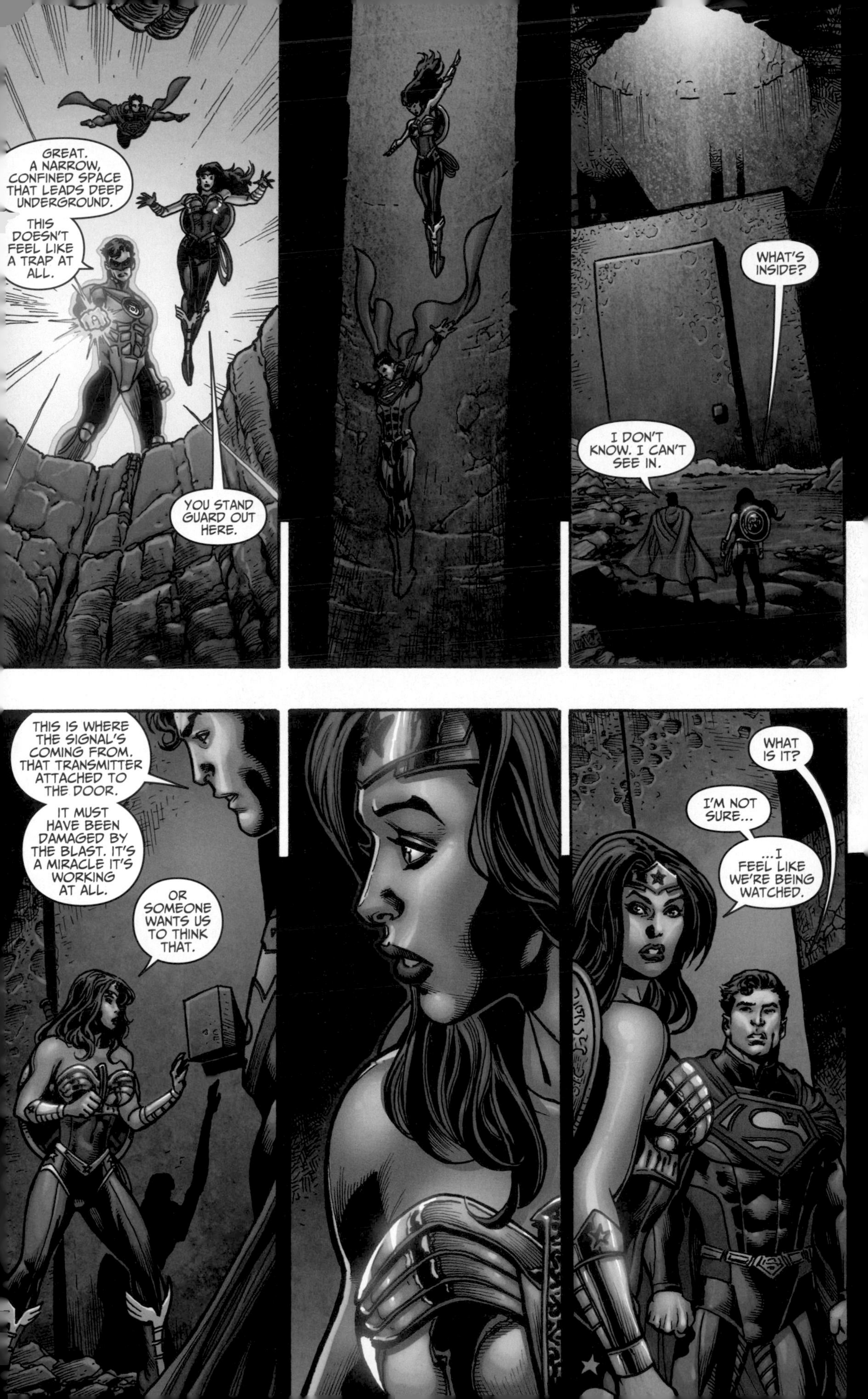
GREAT. A NARROW, CONFINED SPACE THAT LEADS DEEP UNDERGROUND.
THIS DOESN'T FEEL LIKE A TRAP AT ALL.
YOU STAND GUARD OUT HERE.
WHAT'S INSIDE?
I DON'T KNOW. I CAN'T SEE IN.
THIS IS WHERE THE SIGNAL'S COMING FROM. THAT TRANSMITTER ATTACHED TO THE DOOR.
IT MUST HAVE BEEN DAMAGED BY THE BLAST. IT'S A MIRACLE IT'S WORKING AT ALL.
OR SOMEONE WANTS US TO THINK THAT.
WHAT IS IT?
I'M NOT SURE...
...I FEEL LIKE WE'RE BEING WATCHED.

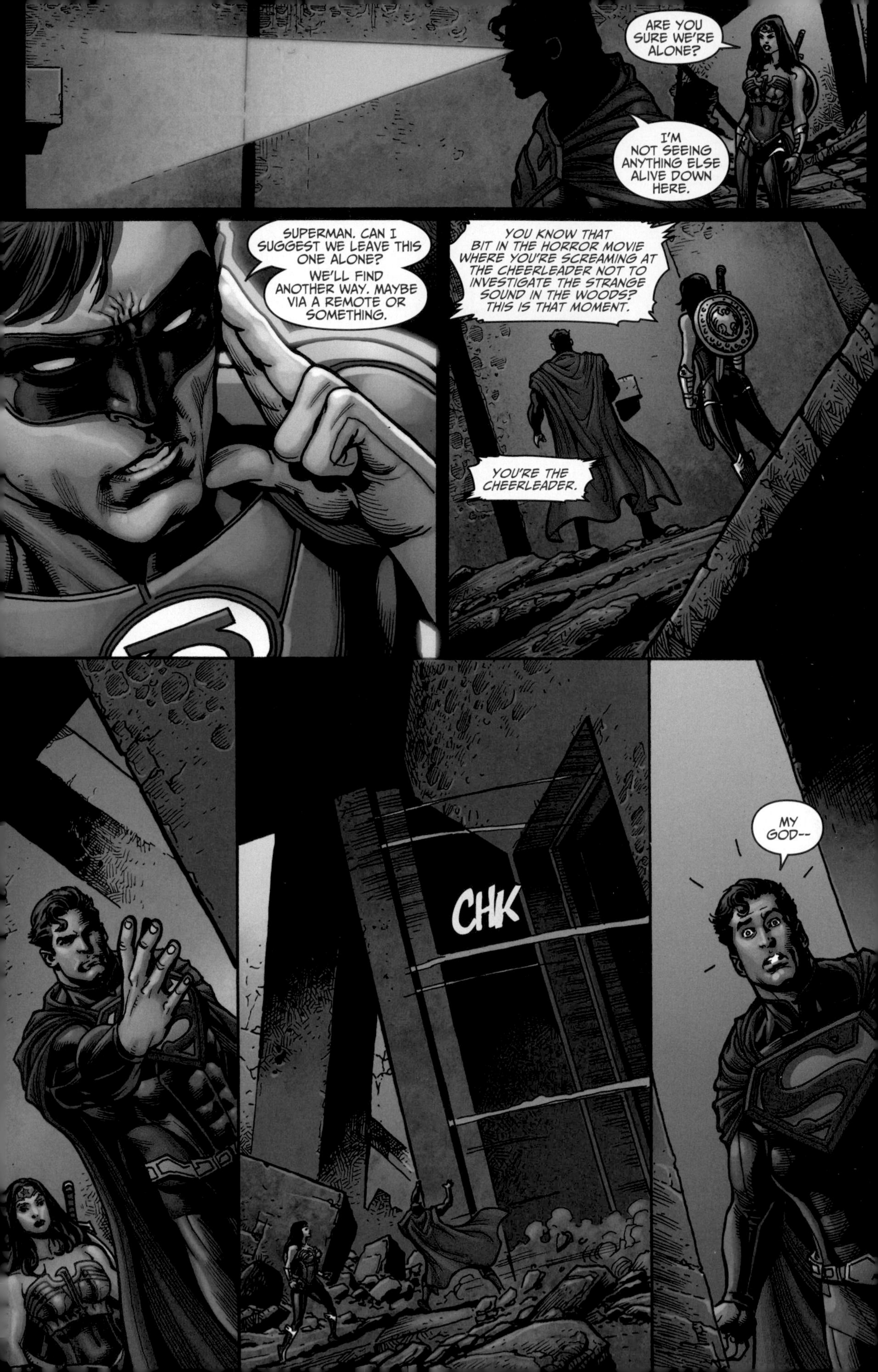

ARE YOU SURE WE'RE ALONE?
I'M NOT SEEING ANYTHING ELSE ALIVE DOWN HERE.
SUPERMAN. CAN I SUGGEST WE LEAVE THIS ONE ALONE?
WE'LL FIND ANOTHER WAY. MAYBE VIA A REMOTE OR SOMETHING.
YOU KNOW THAT BIT IN THE HORROR MOVIE WHERE YOU'RE SCREAMING AT THE CHEERLEADER NOT TO INVESTIGATE THE STRANGE SOUND IN THE WOODS? THIS IS THAT MOMENT.
YOU'RE THE CHEERLEADER.
CHK
MY GOD--

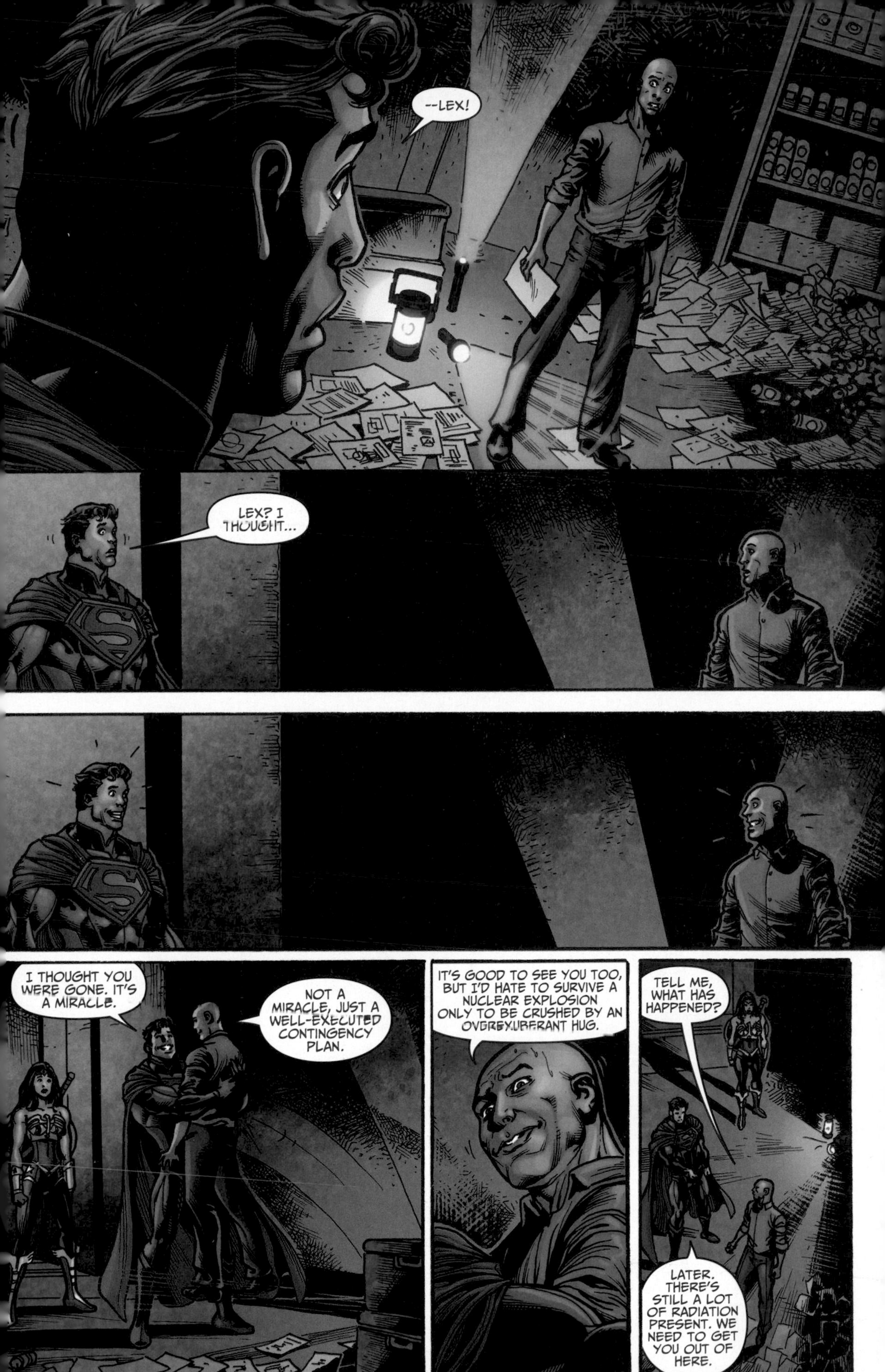
--LEX!
LEX? I THOUGHT...
I THOUGHT YOU WERE GONE. IT'S A MIRACLE.
NOT A MIRACLE, JUST A WELL-EXECUTED CONTINGENCY PLAN.
IT'S GOOD TO SEE YOU TOO, BUT I'D HATE TO SURVIVE A NUCLEAR EXPLOSION ONLY TO BE CRUSHED BY AN OVEREXUBERANT HUG.
TELL ME, WHAT HAS HAPPENED?
LATER. THERE'S STILL A LOT OF RADIATION PRESENT. WE NEED TO GET YOU OUT OF HERE.

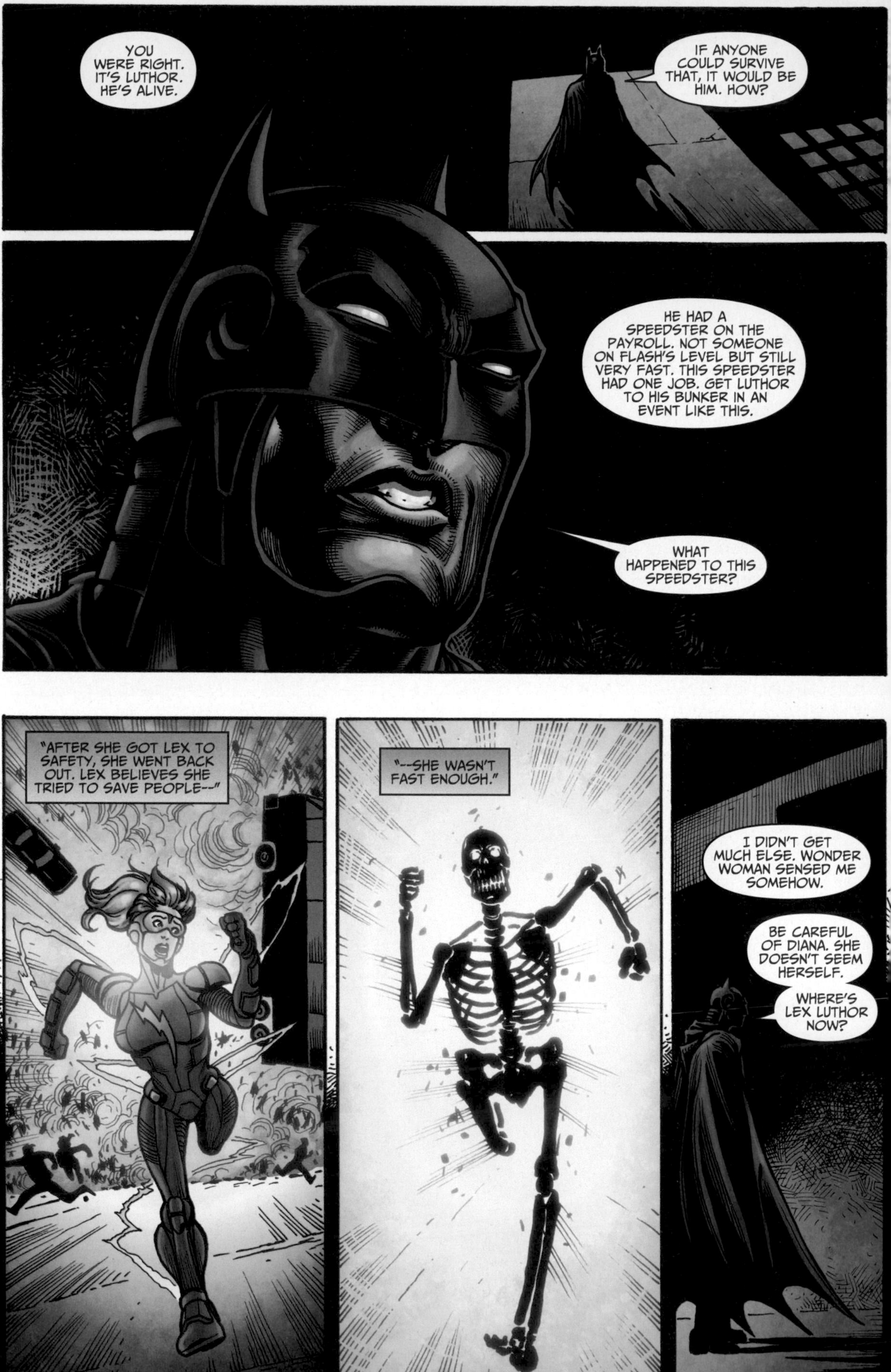
YOU WERE RIGHT. IT'S LUTHOR. HE'S ALIVE.
IF ANYONE COULD SURVIVE THAT, IT WOULD BE HIM. HOW?
HE HAD A SPEEDSTER ON THE PAYROLL. NOT SOMEONE ON FLASH'S LEVEL BUT STILL VERY FAST. THIS SPEEDSTER HAD ONE JOB. GET LUTHOR TO HIS BUNKER IN AN EVENT LIKE THIS.
WHAT HAPPENED TO THIS SPEEDSTER?
"AFTER SHE GOT LEX TO SAFETY, SHE WENT BACK OUT. LEX BELIEVES SHE TRIED TO SAVE PEOPLE--"
"--SHE WASN'T FAST ENOUGH."
I DIDN'T GET MUCH ELSE. WONDER WOMAN SENSED ME SOMEHOW.
BE CAREFUL OF DIANA. SHE DOESN'T SEEM HERSELF.
WHERE'S LEX LUTHOR NOW?

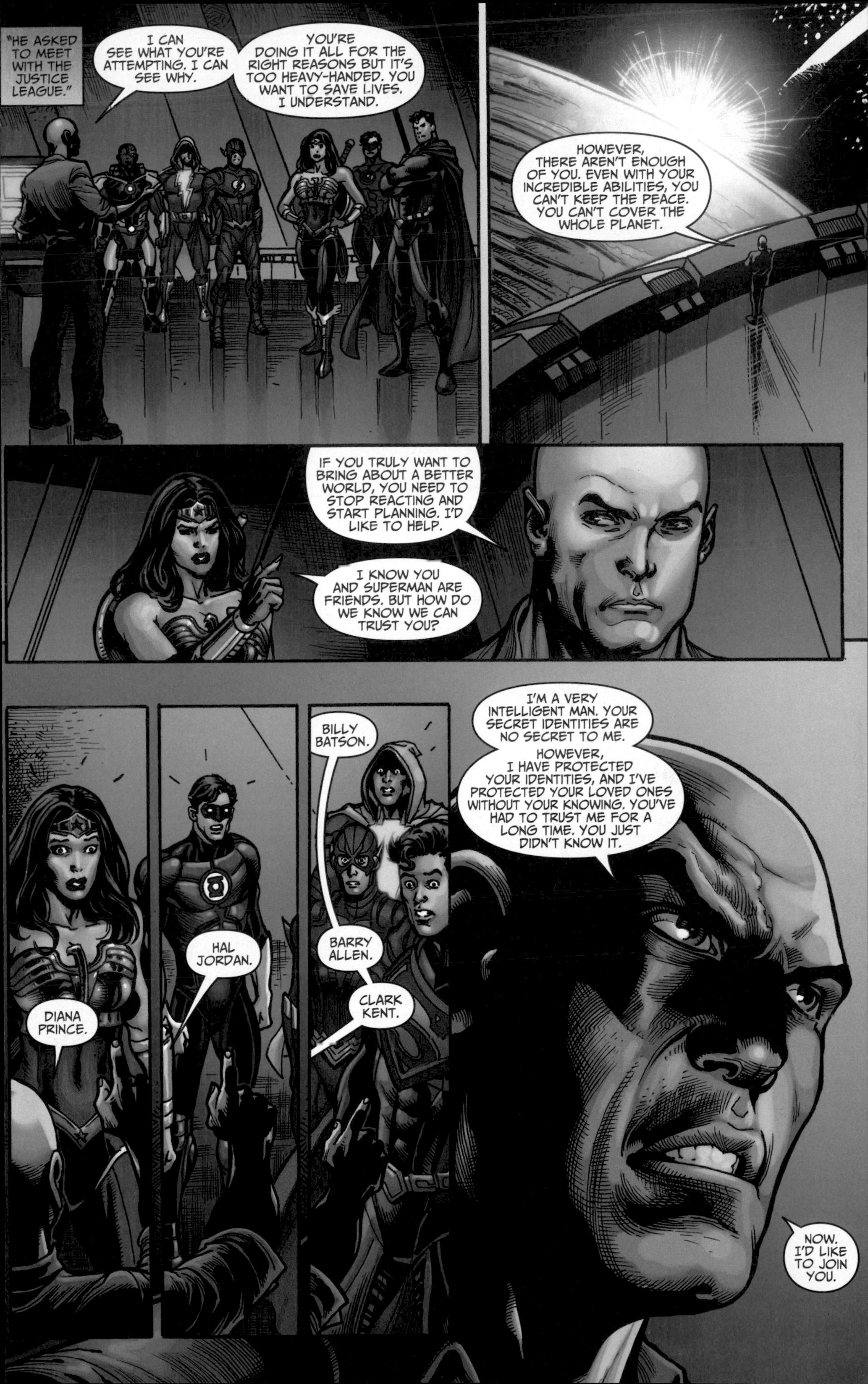

"HE ASKED TO MEET WITH THE JUSTICE LEAGUE."
I CAN SEE WHAT YOU'RE ATTEMPTING. I CAN SEE WHY.
YOU'RE DOING IT ALL FOR THE RIGHT REASONS BUT IT'S TOO HEAVY-HANDED. YOU WANT TO SAVE LIVES. I UNDERSTAND.
HOWEVER, THERE AREN'T ENOUGH OF YOU. EVEN WITH YOUR INCREDIBLE ABILITIES, YOU CAN'T KEEP THE PEACE. YOU CAN'T COVER THE WHOLE PLANET.
IF YOU TRULY WANT TO BRING ABOUT A BETTER WORLD, YOU NEED TO STOP REACTING AND START PLANNING. I'D LIKE TO HELP.
I KNOW YOU AND SUPERMAN ARE FRIENDS. BUT HOW DO WE KNOW WE CAN TRUST YOU?
I'M A VERY INTELLIGENT MAN. YOUR SECRET IDENTITIES ARE NO SECRET TO ME.
HOWEVER, I HAVE PROTECTED YOUR IDENTITIES, AND I'VE PROTECTED YOUR LOVED ONES WITHOUT YOUR KNOWING. YOU'VE HAD TO TRUST ME FOR A LONG TIME. YOU JUST DIDN'T KNOW IT.
DIANA PRINCE.
HAL JORDAN.
BILLY BATSON.
BARRY ALLEN.
CLARK KENT.
NOW. I'D LIKE TO JOIN YOU.

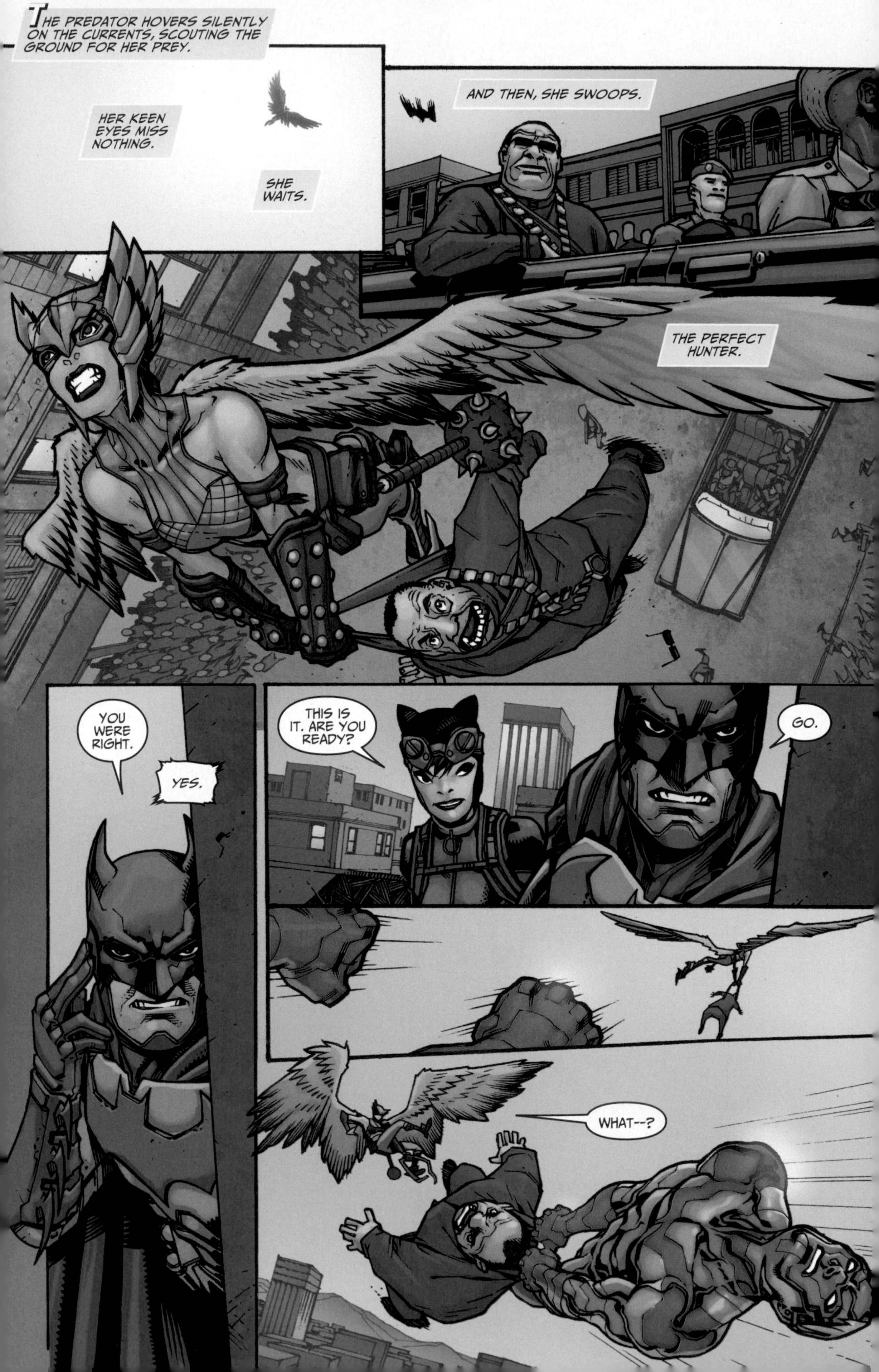
THE PREDATOR HOVERS SILENTLY ON THE CURRENTS, SCOUTING THE GROUND FOR HER PREY.
HER KEEN EYES MISS NOTHING.
SHE WAITS.
AND THEN, SHE SWOOPS.
THE PERFECT HUNTER.
YOU WERE RIGHT.
YES.
THIS IS IT. ARE YOU READY?
GO.
WHAT--?

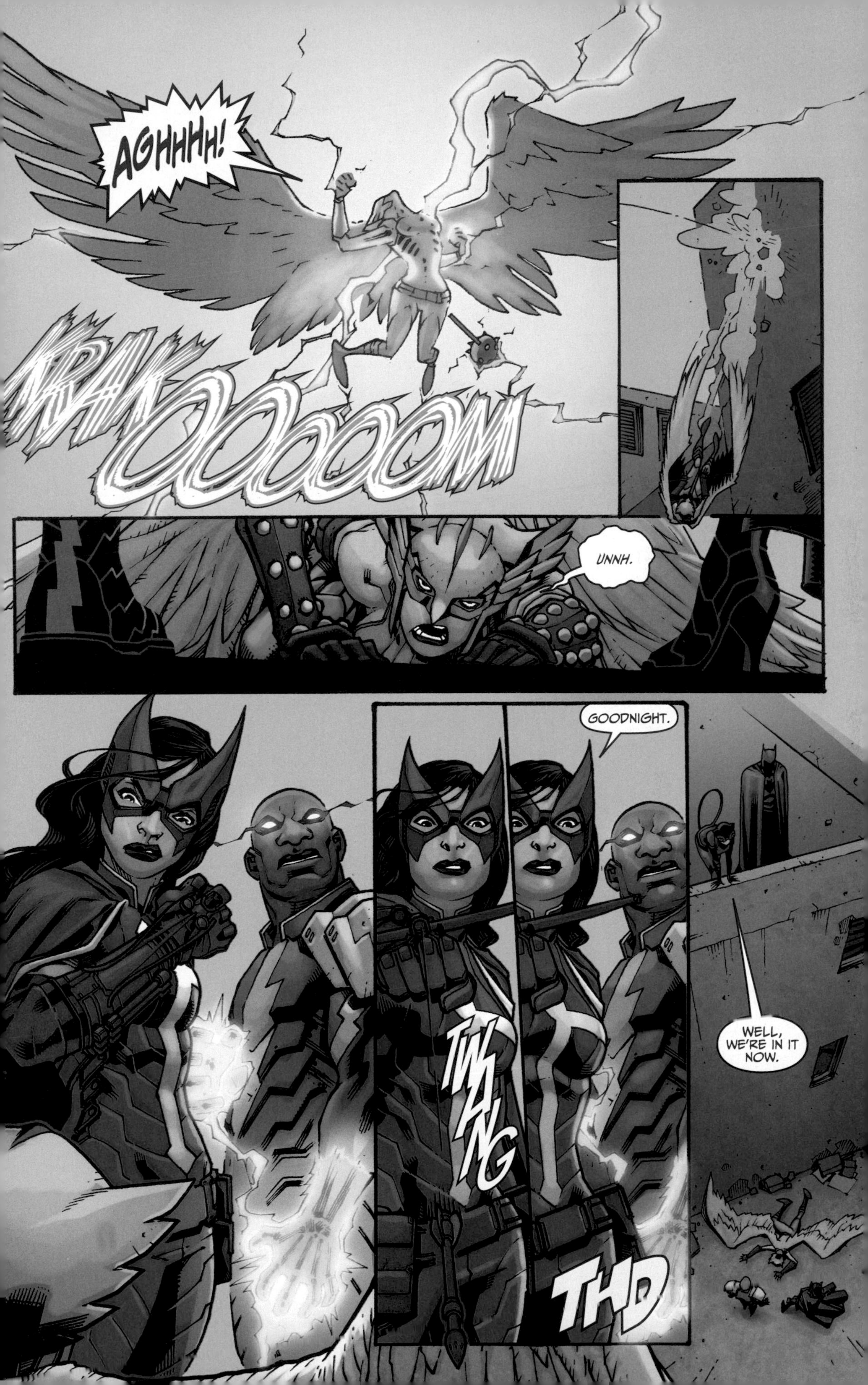
AGHHHH!
KRAKOOOOOOM
UNNH.
GOODNIGHT.
TWANG
THD
WELL, WE'RE IN IT NOW.

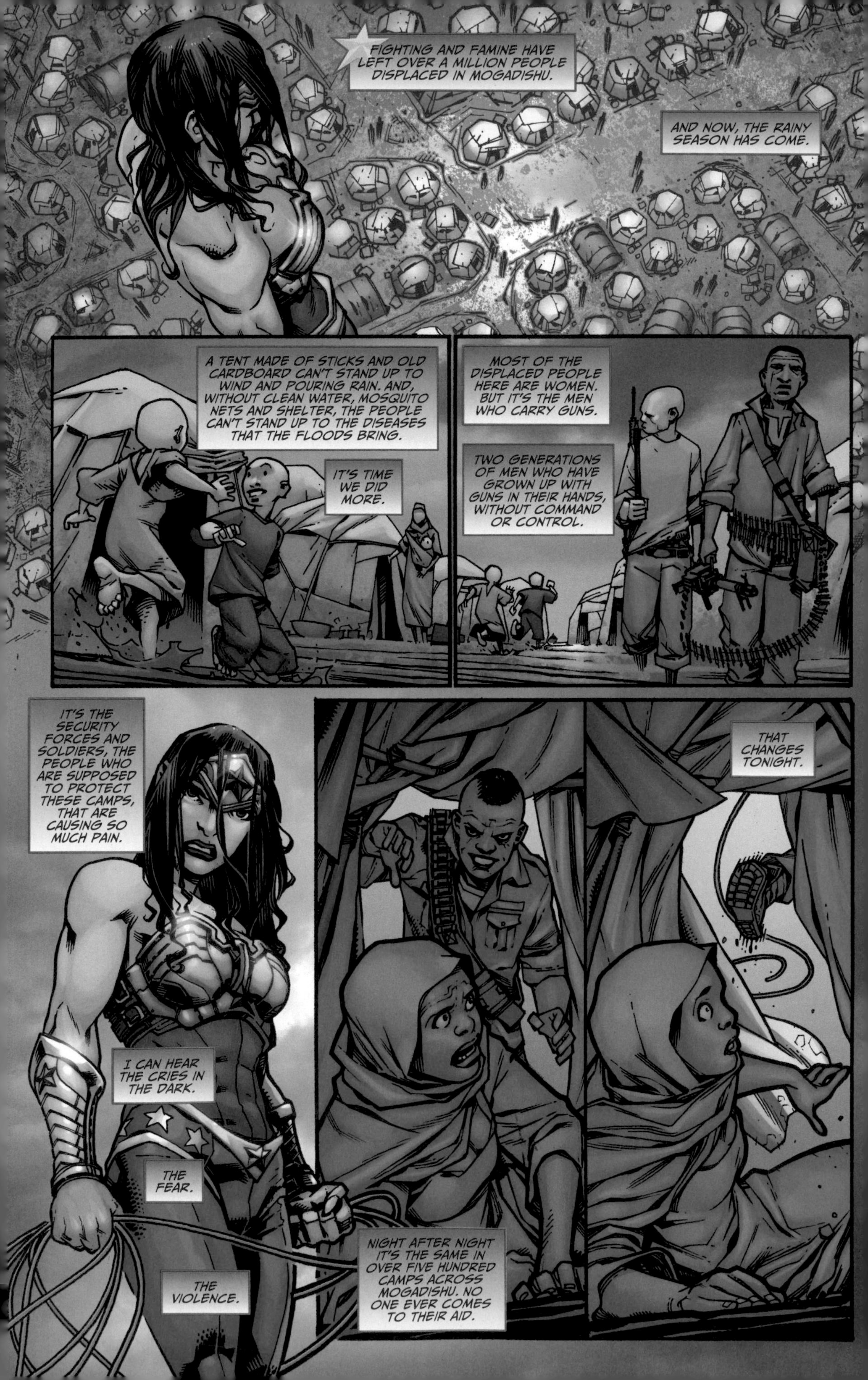
FIGHTING AND FAMINE HAVE LEFT OVER A MILLION PEOPLE DISPLACED IN MOGADISHU.
AND NOW, THE RAINY SEASON HAS COME.
A TENT MADE OF STICKS AND OLD CARDBOARD CAN'T STAND UP TO WIND AND POURING RAIN. AND, WITHOUT CLEAN WATER, MOSQUITO NETS AND SHELTER, THE PEOPLE CAN'T STAND UP TO THE DISEASES THAT THE FLOODS BRING.
IT'S TIME WE DID MORE.
MOST OF THE DISPLACED PEOPLE HERE ARE WOMEN. BUT IT'S THE MEN WHO CARRY GUNS.
TWO GENERATIONS OF MEN WHO HAVE GROWN UP WITH GUNS IN THEIR HANDS, WITHOUT COMMAND OR CONTROL.
IT'S THE SECURITY FORCES AND SOLDIERS, THE PEOPLE WHO ARE SUPPOSED TO PROTECT THESE CAMPS, THAT ARE CAUSING SO MUCH PAIN.
I CAN HEAR THE CRIES IN THE DARK.
THE FEAR.
THE VIOLENCE.
NIGHT AFTER NIGHT IT'S THE SAME IN OVER FIVE HUNDRED CAMPS ACROSS MOGADISHU. NO ONE EVER COMES TO THEIR AID.
THAT CHANGES TONIGHT.

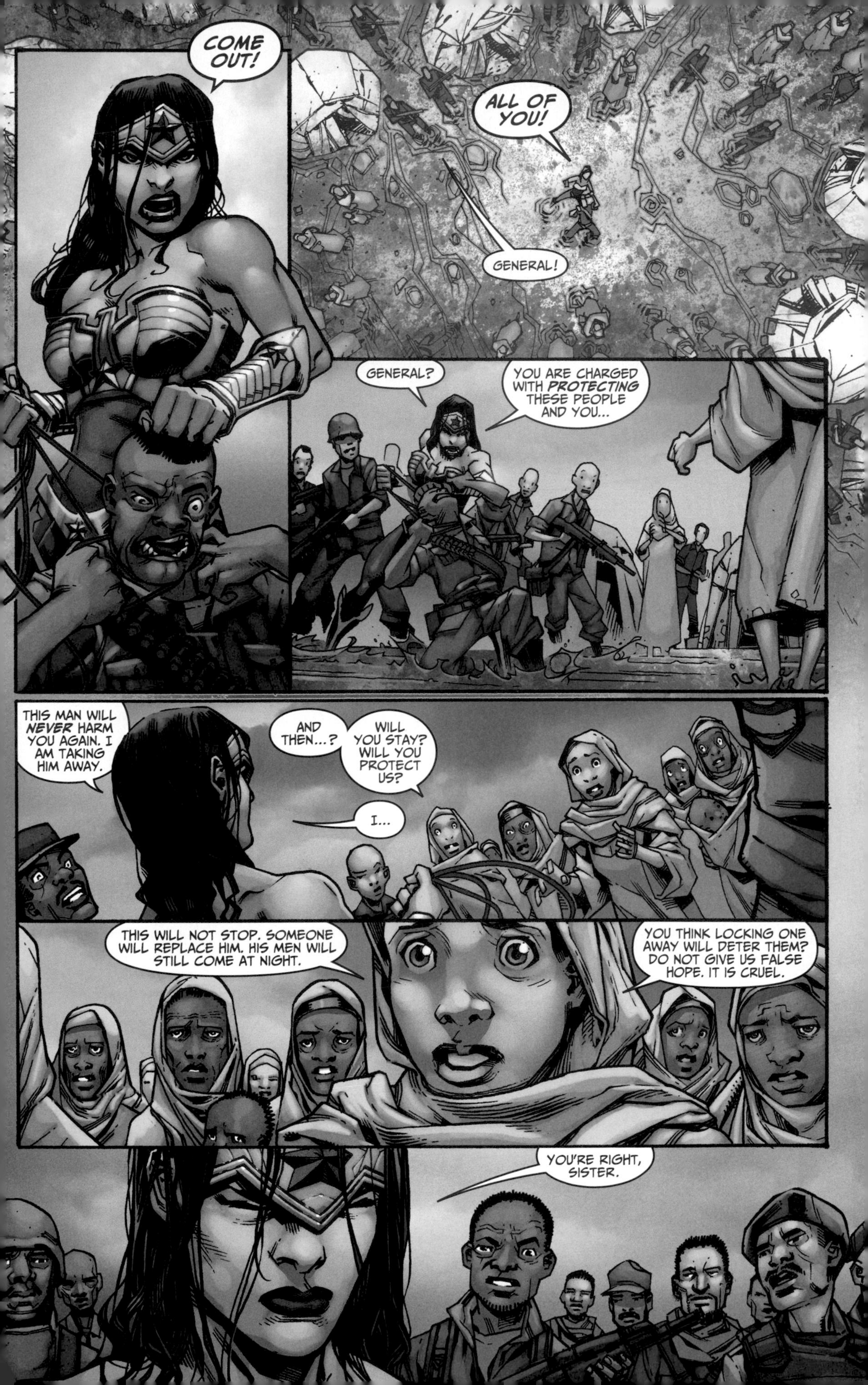
COME OUT!
ALL OF YOU!
GENERAL!
GENERAL?
YOU ARE CHARGED WITH PROTECTING THESE PEOPLE AND YOU...
THIS MAN WILL NEVER HARM YOU AGAIN. I AM TAKING HIM AWAY.
AND THEN...?
WILL YOU STAY? WILL YOU PROTECT US?
I...
THIS WILL NOT STOP. SOMEONE WILL REPLACE HIM. HIS MEN WILL STILL COME AT NIGHT.
YOU THINK LOCKING ONE AWAY WILL DETER THEM? DO NOT GIVE US FALSE HOPE. IT IS CRUEL.
YOU'RE RIGHT, SISTER.

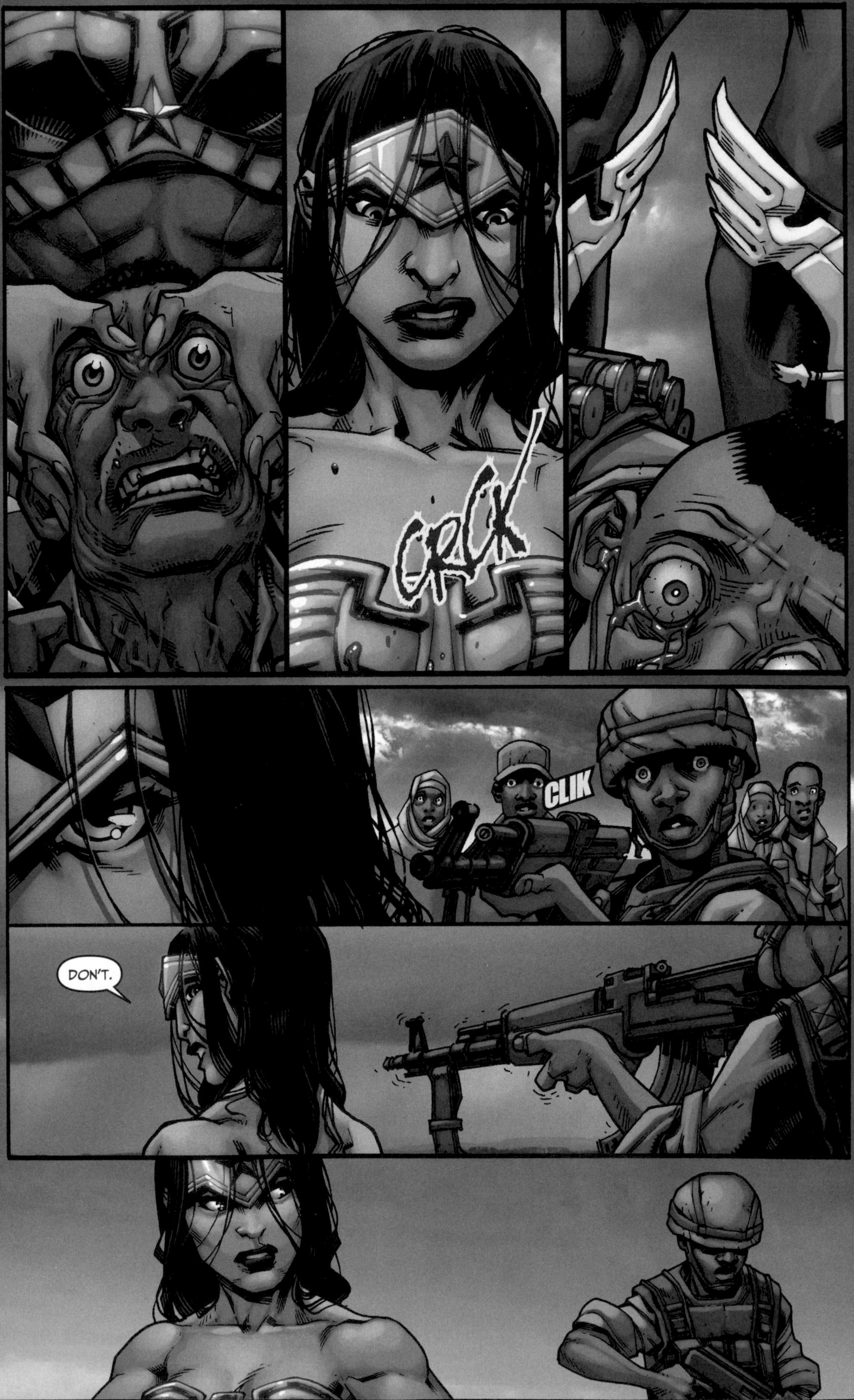
CRCK
CLIK
DON'T.

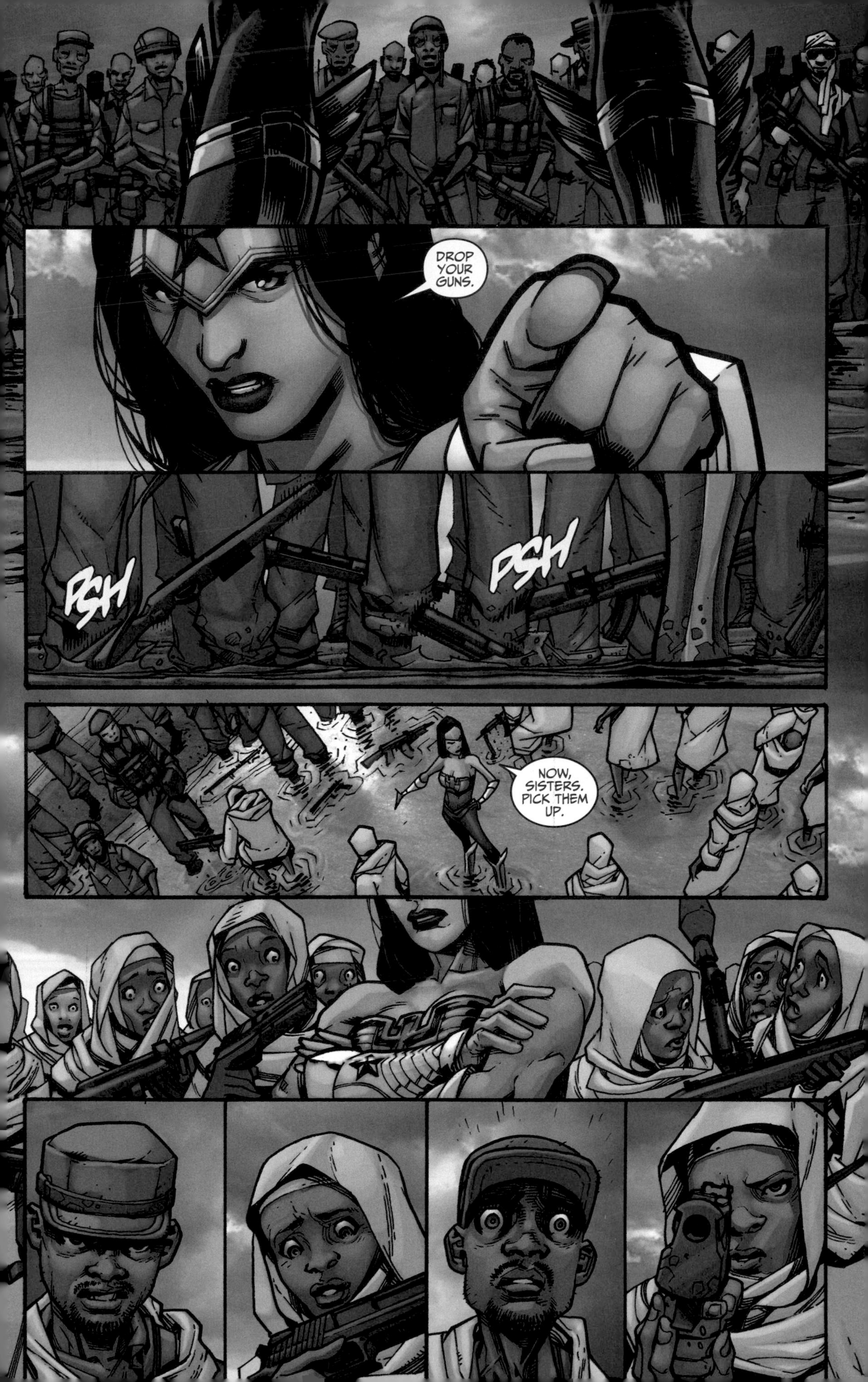
DROP YOUR GUNS.
PSH
PSH
NOW, SISTERS. PICK THEM UP.

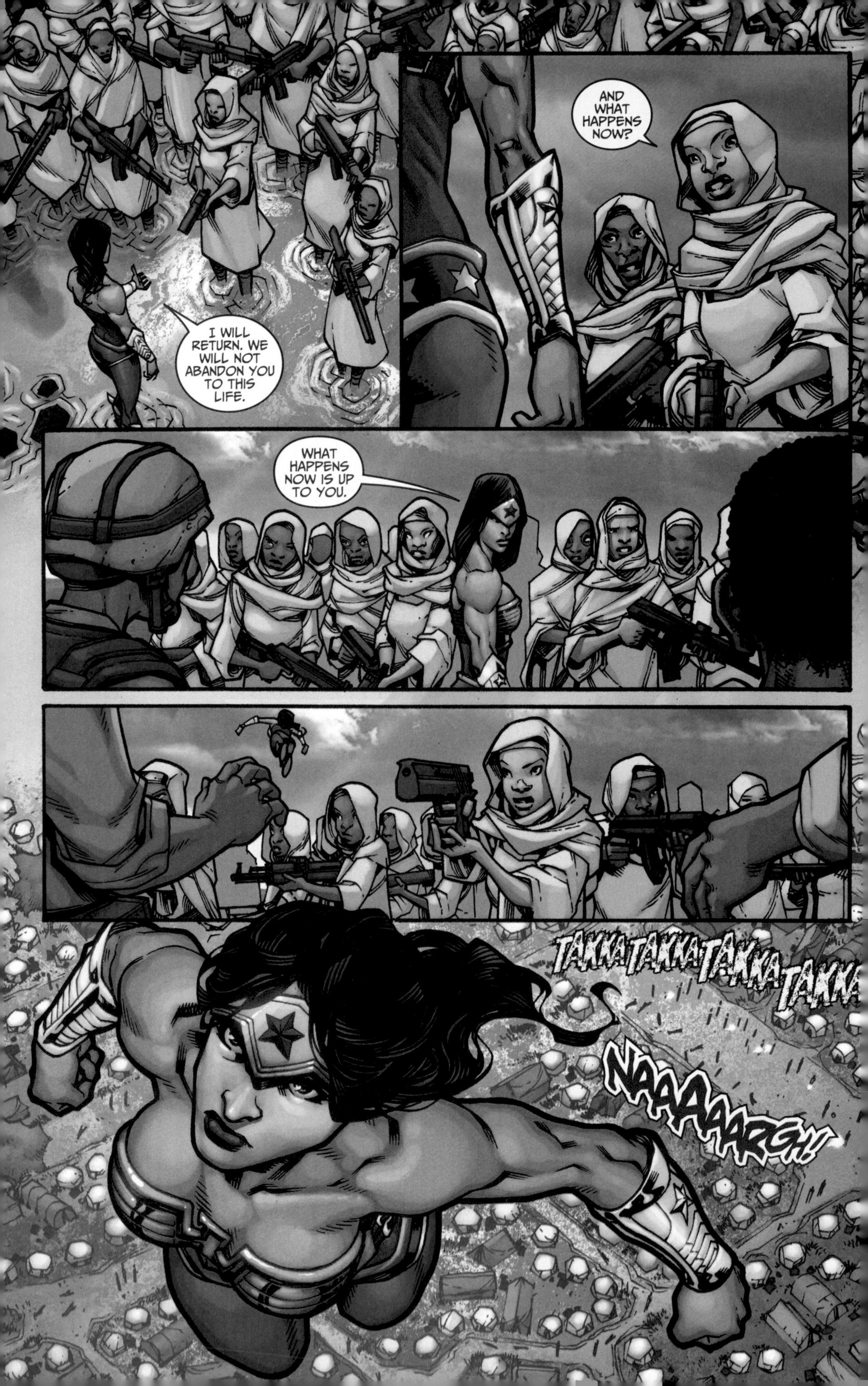
I WILL RETURN. WE WILL NOT ABANDON YOU TO THIS LIFE.
AND WHAT HAPPENS NOW?
WHAT HAPPENS NOW IS UP TO YOU.
TAKKA TAKKA TAKKA TAKKA
NAAAAAARGH!!

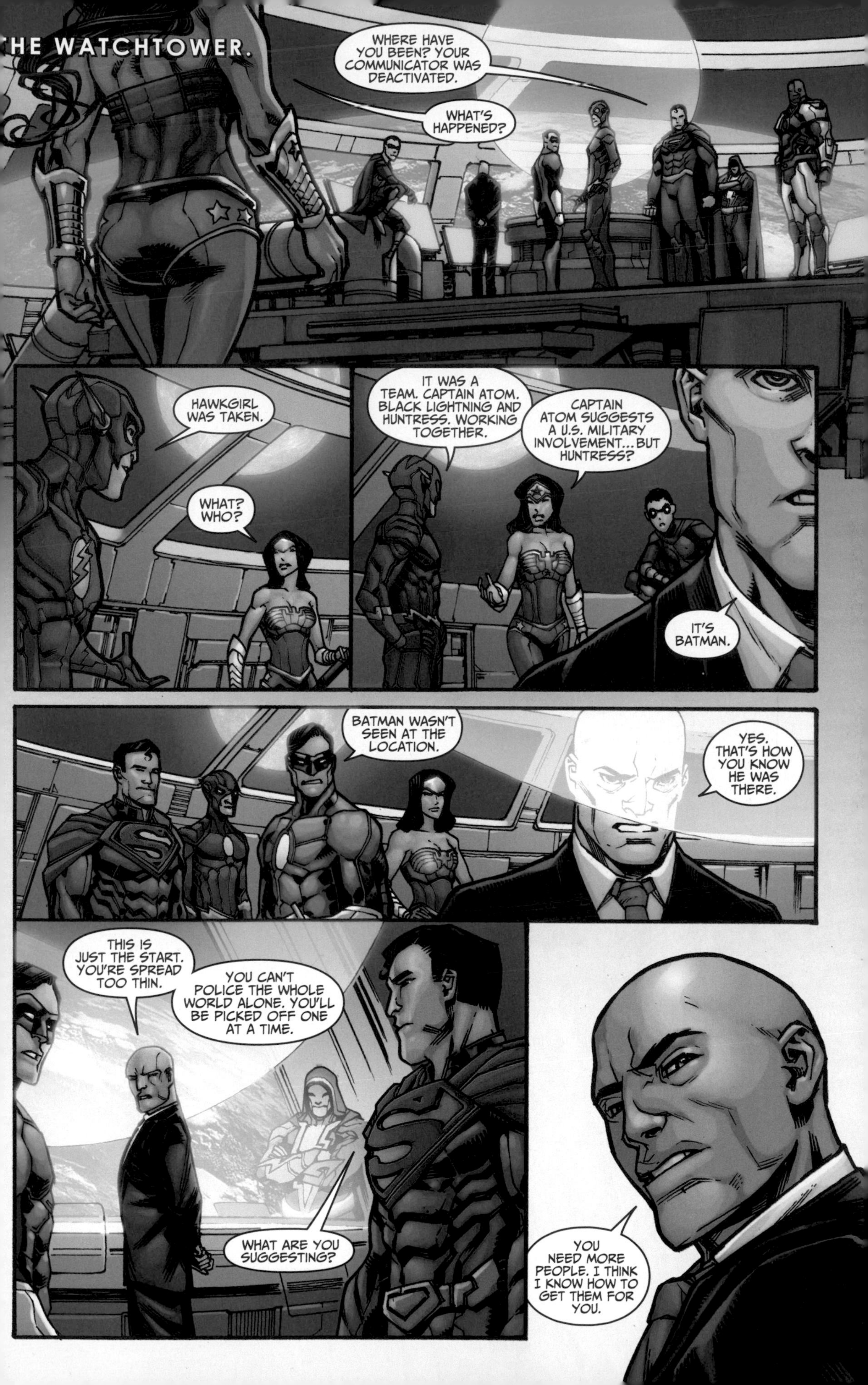
THE WATCHTOWER.
WHERE HAVE YOU BEEN? YOUR COMMUNICATOR WAS DEACTIVATED.
WHAT'S HAPPENED?
HAWKGIRL WAS TAKEN.
WHAT? WHO?
IT WAS A TEAM. CAPTAIN ATOM. BLACK LIGHTNING AND HUNTRESS. WORKING TOGETHER.
CAPTAIN ATOM SUGGESTS A U.S. MILITARY INVOLVEMENT... BUT HUNTRESS?
IT'S BATMAN.
BATMAN WASN'T SEEN AT THE LOCATION.
YES. THAT'S HOW YOU KNOW HE WAS THERE.
THIS IS JUST THE START. YOU'RE SPREAD TOO THIN.
YOU CAN'T POLICE THE WHOLE WORLD ALONE. YOU'LL BE PICKED OFF ONE AT A TIME.
WHAT ARE YOU SUGGESTING?
YOU NEED MORE PEOPLE. I THINK I KNOW HOW TO GET THEM FOR YOU.

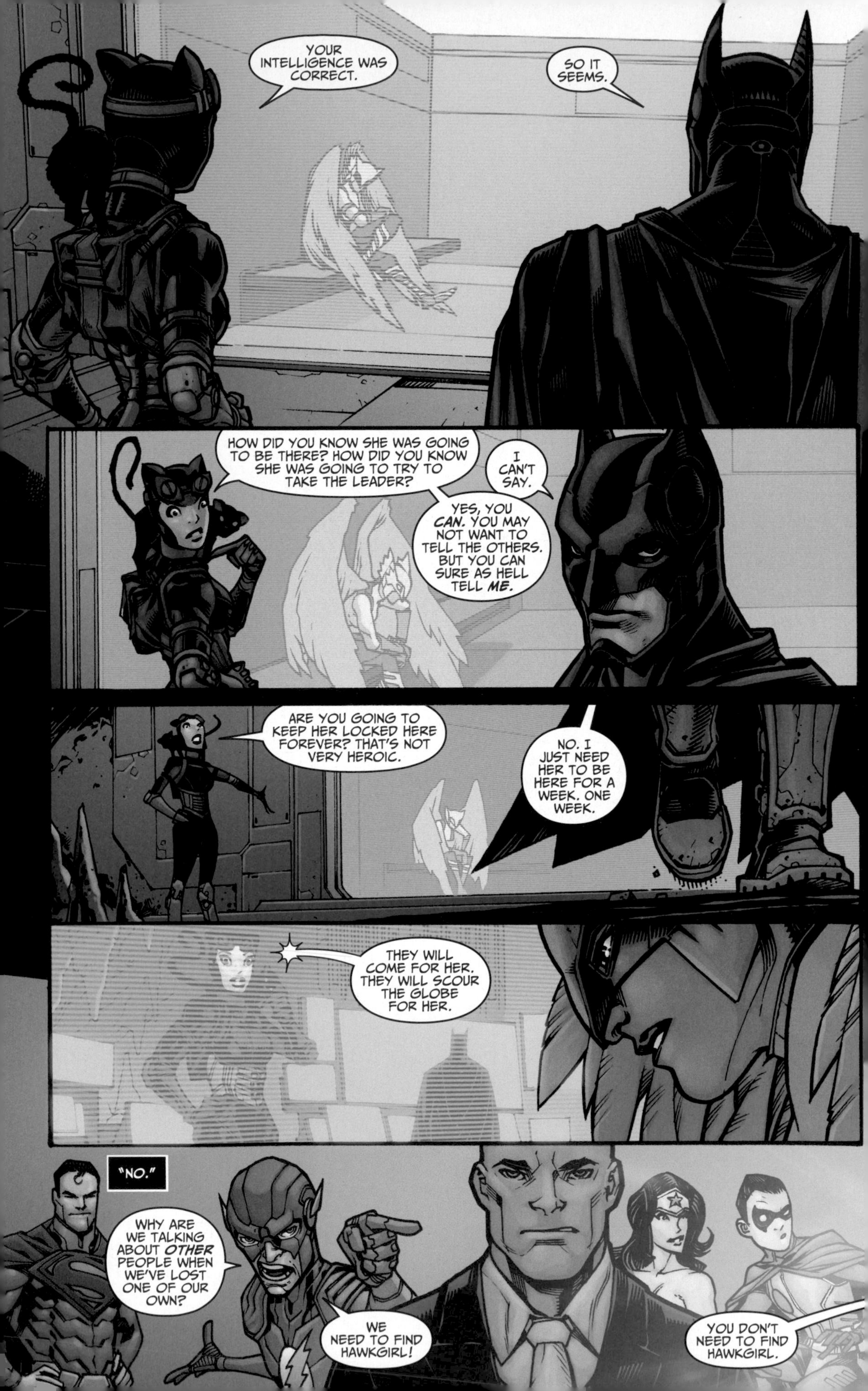
YOUR INTELLIGENCE WAS CORRECT.
SO IT SEEMS.
HOW DID YOU KNOW SHE WAS GOING TO BE THERE? HOW DID YOU KNOW SHE WAS GOING TO TRY TO TAKE THE LEADER?
I CAN'T SAY.
YES, YOU *CAN.* YOU MAY NOT WANT TO TELL THE OTHERS. BUT YOU CAN SURE AS HELL TELL *ME.*
ARE YOU GOING TO KEEP HER LOCKED HERE FOREVER? THAT'S NOT VERY HEROIC.
NO. I JUST NEED HER TO BE HERE FOR A WEEK. ONE WEEK.
THEY WILL COME FOR HER. THEY WILL SCOUR THE GLOBE FOR HER.
"NO."
WHY ARE WE TALKING ABOUT *OTHER* PEOPLE WHEN WE'VE LOST ONE OF OUR OWN?
WE NEED TO FIND HAWKGIRL!
YOU DON'T NEED TO FIND HAWKGIRL.

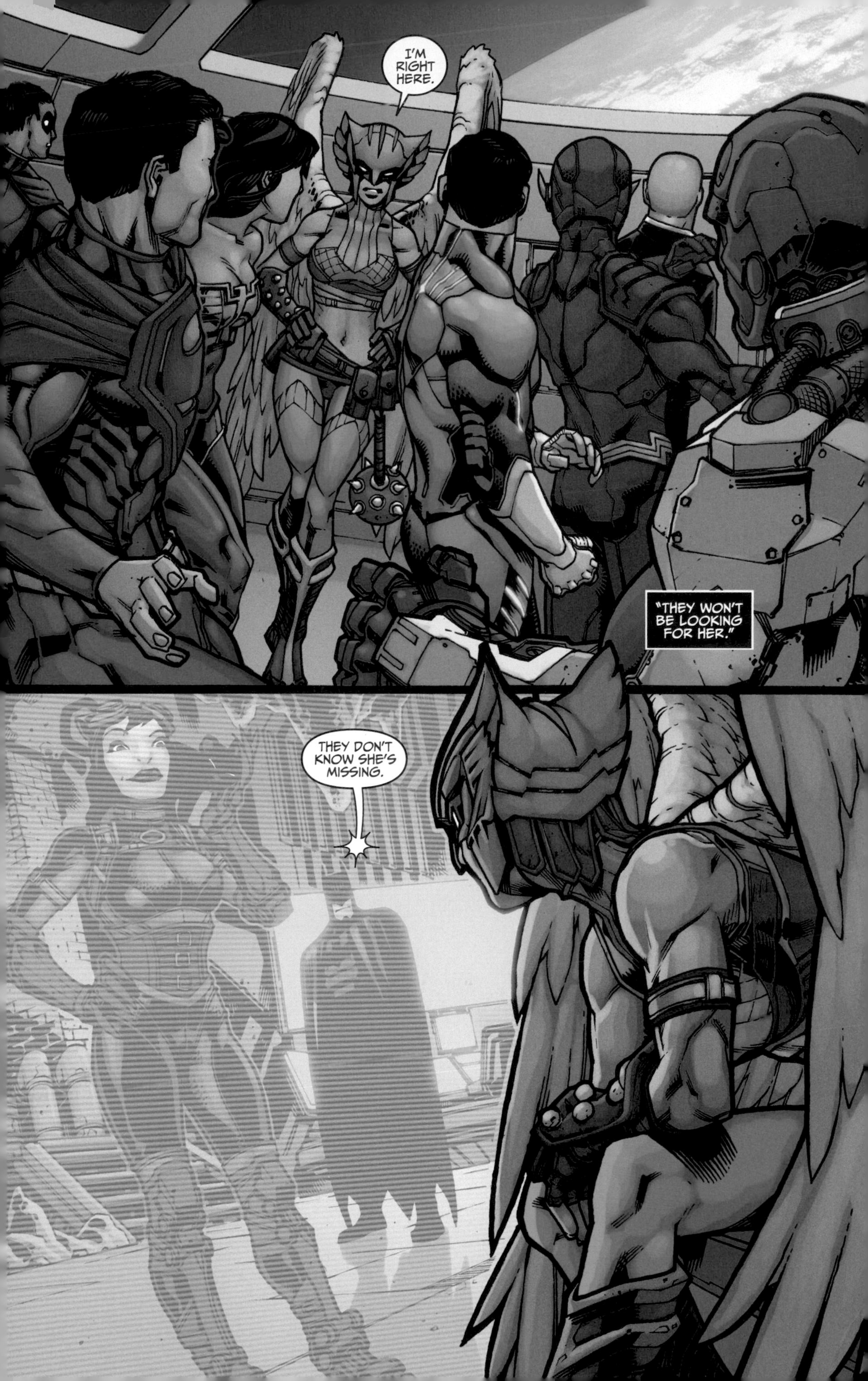
I'M RIGHT HERE.
"THEY WON'T BE LOOKING FOR HER."
THEY DON'T KNOW SHE'S MISSING.

PART EIGHT

Mike S. Miller **Tom Derenick** Artists

Alejandro Sanchez Colorist

Mico Suayan & **David Lopez** and **Santi Casas** of **Ikari Studio** Cover

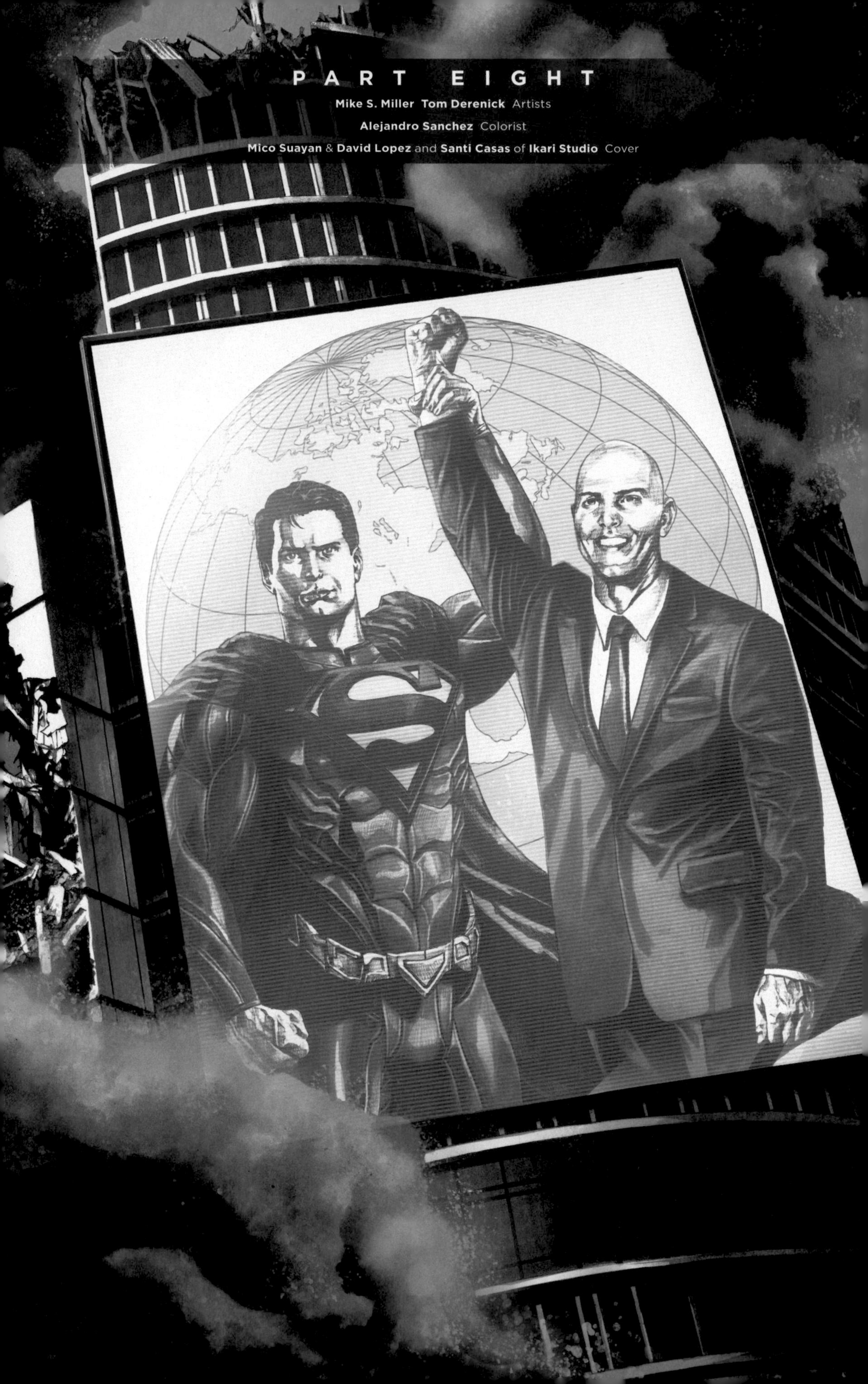

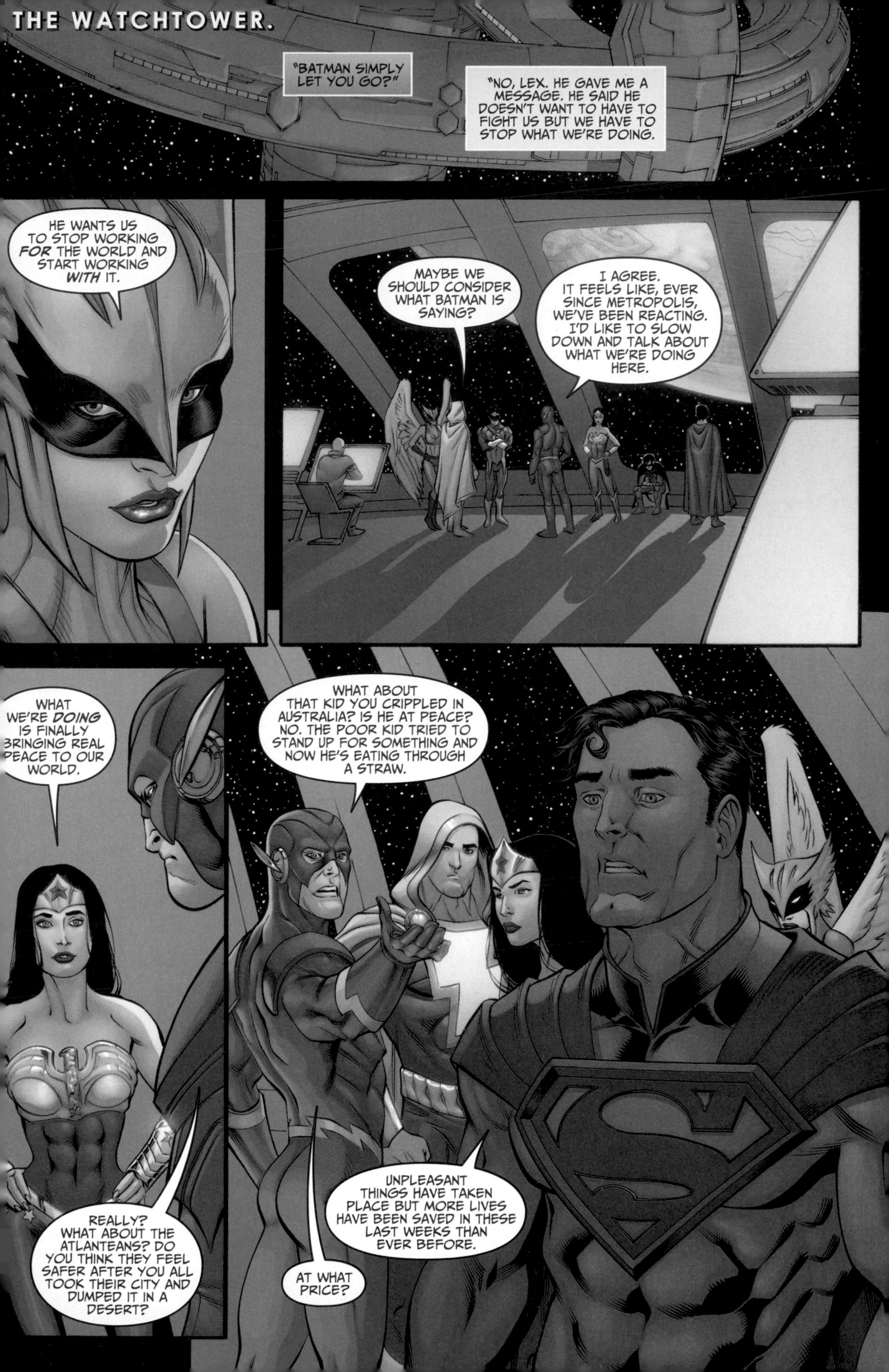
THE WATCHTOWER.
"BATMAN SIMPLY LET YOU GO?"
"NO, LEX. HE GAVE ME A MESSAGE. HE SAID HE DOESN'T WANT TO HAVE TO FIGHT US BUT WE HAVE TO STOP WHAT WE'RE DOING.
HE WANTS US TO STOP WORKING FOR THE WORLD AND START WORKING WITH IT.
MAYBE WE SHOULD CONSIDER WHAT BATMAN IS SAYING?
I AGREE. IT FEELS LIKE, EVER SINCE METROPOLIS, WE'VE BEEN REACTING. I'D LIKE TO SLOW DOWN AND TALK ABOUT WHAT WE'RE DOING HERE.
WHAT WE'RE DOING IS FINALLY BRINGING REAL PEACE TO OUR WORLD.
REALLY? WHAT ABOUT THE ATLANTEANS? DO YOU THINK THEY FEEL SAFER AFTER YOU ALL TOOK THEIR CITY AND DUMPED IT IN A DESERT?
WHAT ABOUT THAT KID YOU CRIPPLED IN AUSTRALIA? IS HE AT PEACE? NO. THE POOR KID TRIED TO STAND UP FOR SOMETHING AND NOW HE'S EATING THROUGH A STRAW.
AT WHAT PRICE?
UNPLEASANT THINGS HAVE TAKEN PLACE BUT MORE LIVES HAVE BEEN SAVED IN THESE LAST WEEKS THAN EVER BEFORE.

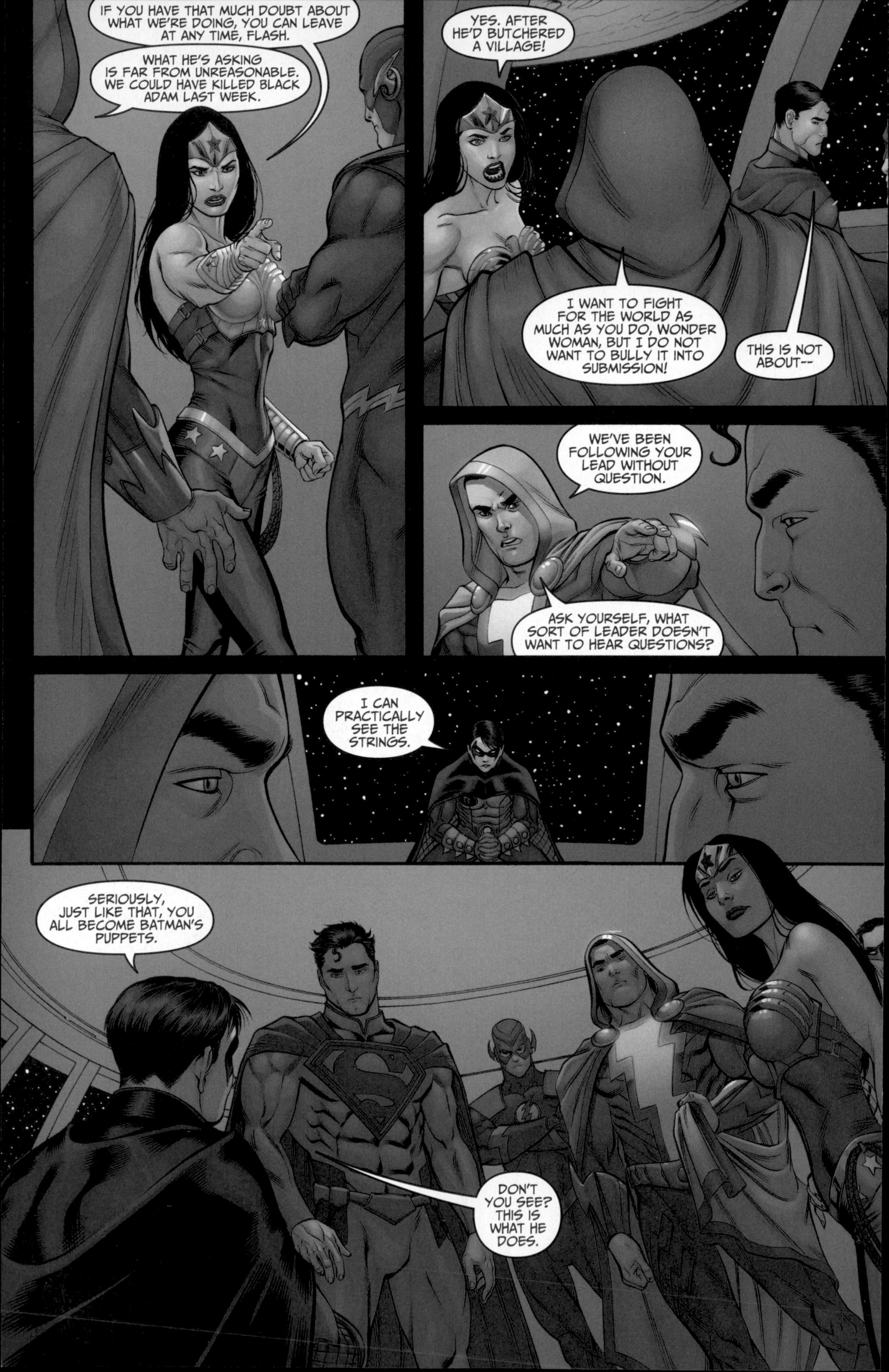
IF YOU HAVE THAT MUCH DOUBT ABOUT WHAT WE'RE DOING, YOU CAN LEAVE AT ANY TIME, FLASH.
WHAT HE'S ASKING IS FAR FROM UNREASONABLE. WE COULD HAVE KILLED BLACK ADAM LAST WEEK.
YES. AFTER HE'D BUTCHERED A VILLAGE!
I WANT TO FIGHT FOR THE WORLD AS MUCH AS YOU DO, WONDER WOMAN, BUT I DO NOT WANT TO BULLY IT INTO SUBMISSION!
THIS IS NOT ABOUT--
WE'VE BEEN FOLLOWING YOUR LEAD WITHOUT QUESTION.
ASK YOURSELF, WHAT SORT OF LEADER DOESN'T WANT TO HEAR QUESTIONS?
I CAN PRACTICALLY SEE THE STRINGS.
SERIOUSLY, JUST LIKE THAT, YOU ALL BECOME BATMAN'S PUPPETS.
DON'T YOU SEE? THIS IS WHAT HE DOES.

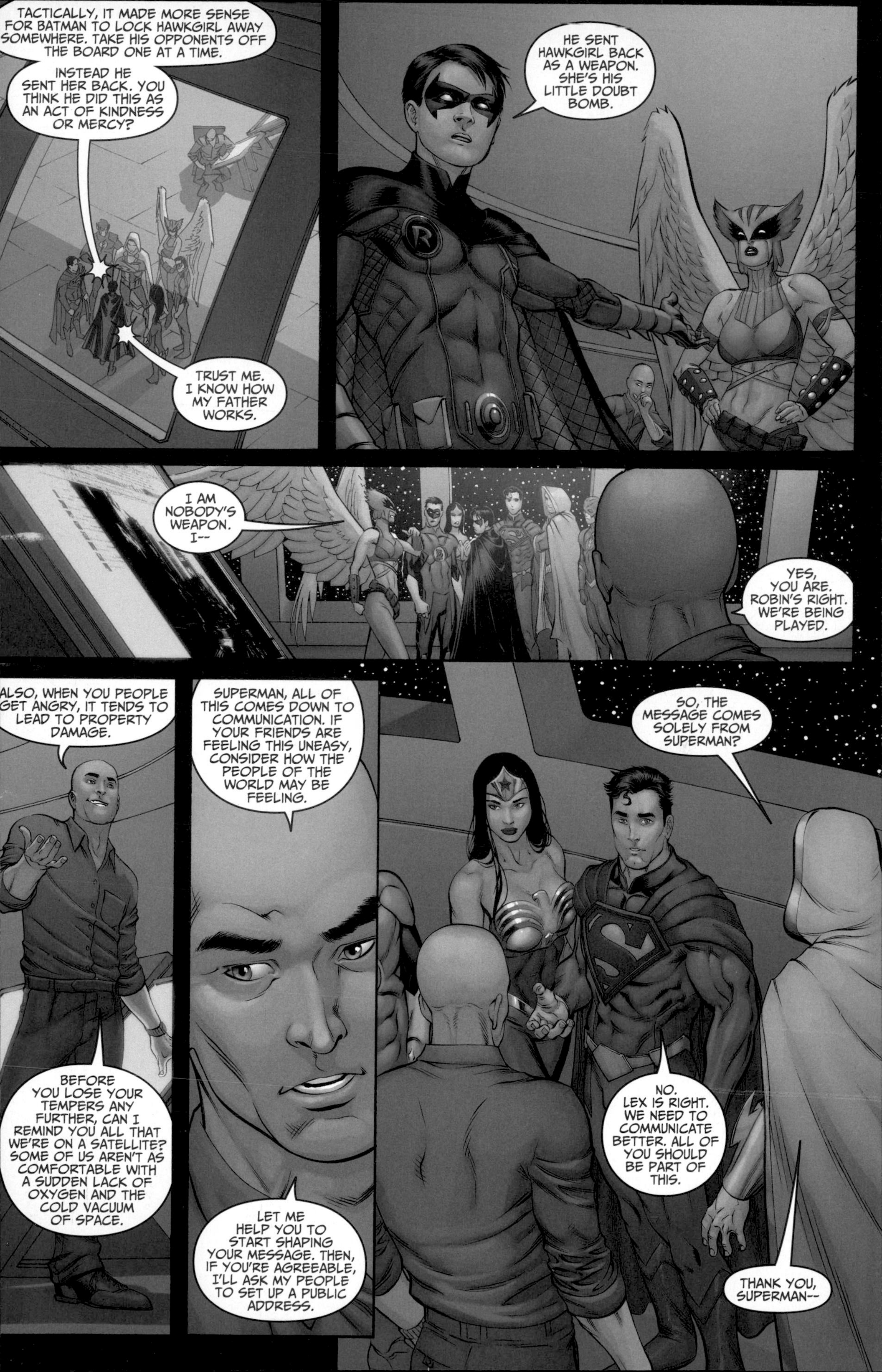
TACTICALLY, IT MADE MORE SENSE FOR BATMAN TO LOCK HAWKGIRL AWAY SOMEWHERE. TAKE HIS OPPONENTS OFF THE BOARD ONE AT A TIME.
INSTEAD HE SENT HER BACK. YOU THINK HE DID THIS AS AN ACT OF KINDNESS OR MERCY?
TRUST ME. I KNOW HOW MY FATHER WORKS.
HE SENT HAWKGIRL BACK AS A WEAPON. SHE'S HIS LITTLE DOUBT BOMB.
I AM NOBODY'S WEAPON. I--
YES, YOU ARE. ROBIN'S RIGHT. WE'RE BEING PLAYED.
ALSO, WHEN YOU PEOPLE GET ANGRY, IT TENDS TO LEAD TO PROPERTY DAMAGE.
BEFORE YOU LOSE YOUR TEMPERS ANY FURTHER, CAN I REMIND YOU ALL THAT WE'RE ON A SATELLITE? SOME OF US AREN'T AS COMFORTABLE WITH A SUDDEN LACK OF OXYGEN AND THE COLD VACUUM OF SPACE.
SUPERMAN, ALL OF THIS COMES DOWN TO COMMUNICATION. IF YOUR FRIENDS ARE FEELING THIS UNEASY, CONSIDER HOW THE PEOPLE OF THE WORLD MAY BE FEELING.
LET ME HELP YOU TO START SHAPING YOUR MESSAGE. THEN, IF YOU'RE AGREEABLE, I'LL ASK MY PEOPLE TO SET UP A PUBLIC ADDRESS.
SO, THE MESSAGE COMES SOLELY FROM SUPERMAN?
NO. LEX IS RIGHT. WE NEED TO COMMUNICATE BETTER. ALL OF YOU SHOULD BE PART OF THIS.
THANK YOU, SUPERMAN--

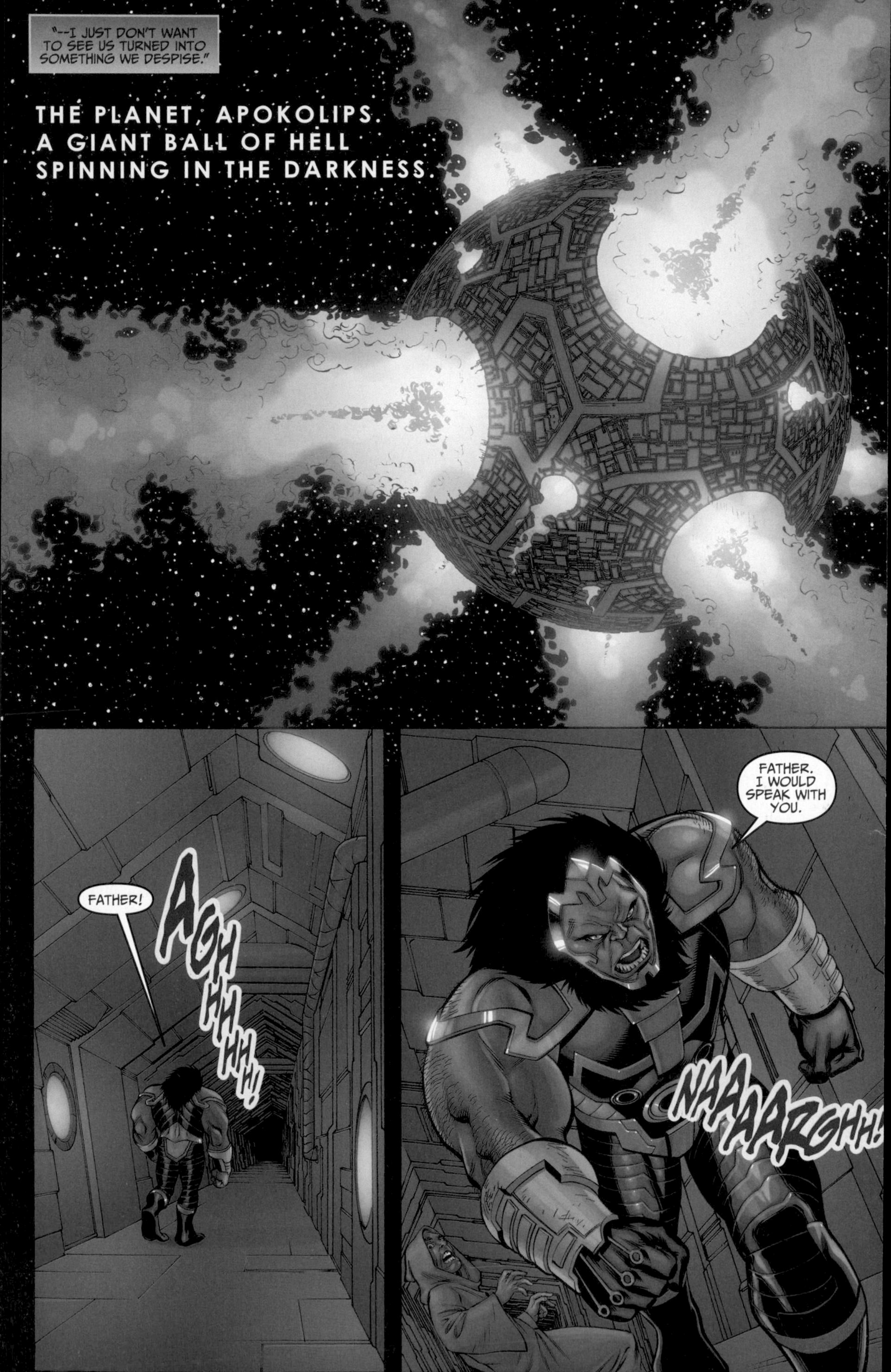
"--I JUST DON'T WANT TO SEE US TURNED INTO SOMETHING WE DESPISE."
THE PLANET, APOKOLIPS. A GIANT BALL OF HELL SPINNING IN THE DARKNESS.
FATHER!
AGHHHHHH!
FATHER. I WOULD SPEAK WITH YOU.
NAAAAARGHH!

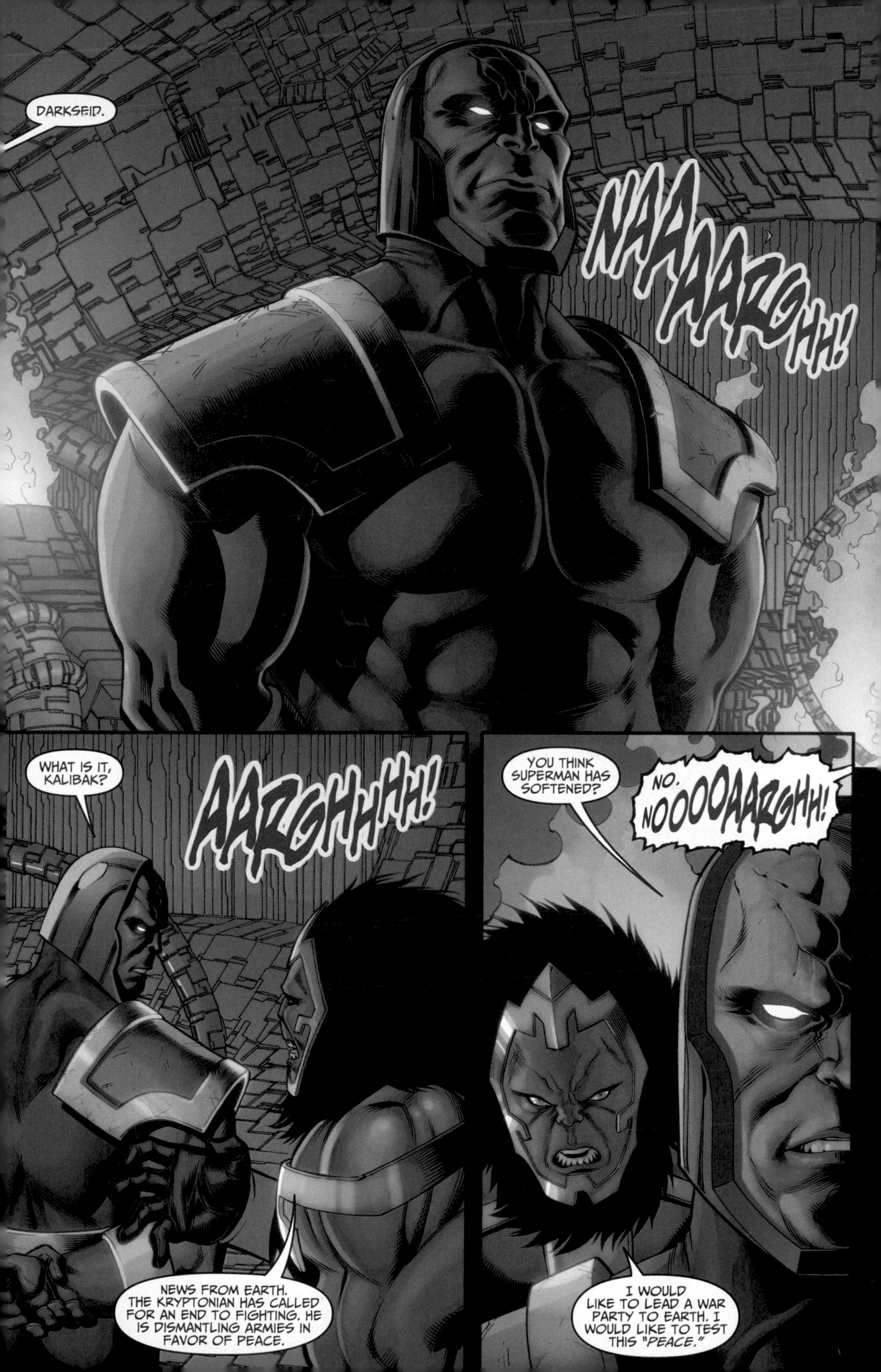
DARKSEID.
NAAAAARGHH!
WHAT IS IT, KALIBAK?
AARGHHHH!
NEWS FROM EARTH. THE KRYPTONIAN HAS CALLED FOR AN END TO FIGHTING. HE IS DISMANTLING ARMIES IN FAVOR OF PEACE.
YOU THINK SUPERMAN HAS SOFTENED?
NO. NOOOOAARGHH!
I WOULD LIKE TO LEAD A WAR PARTY TO EARTH. I WOULD LIKE TO TEST THIS "PEACE."

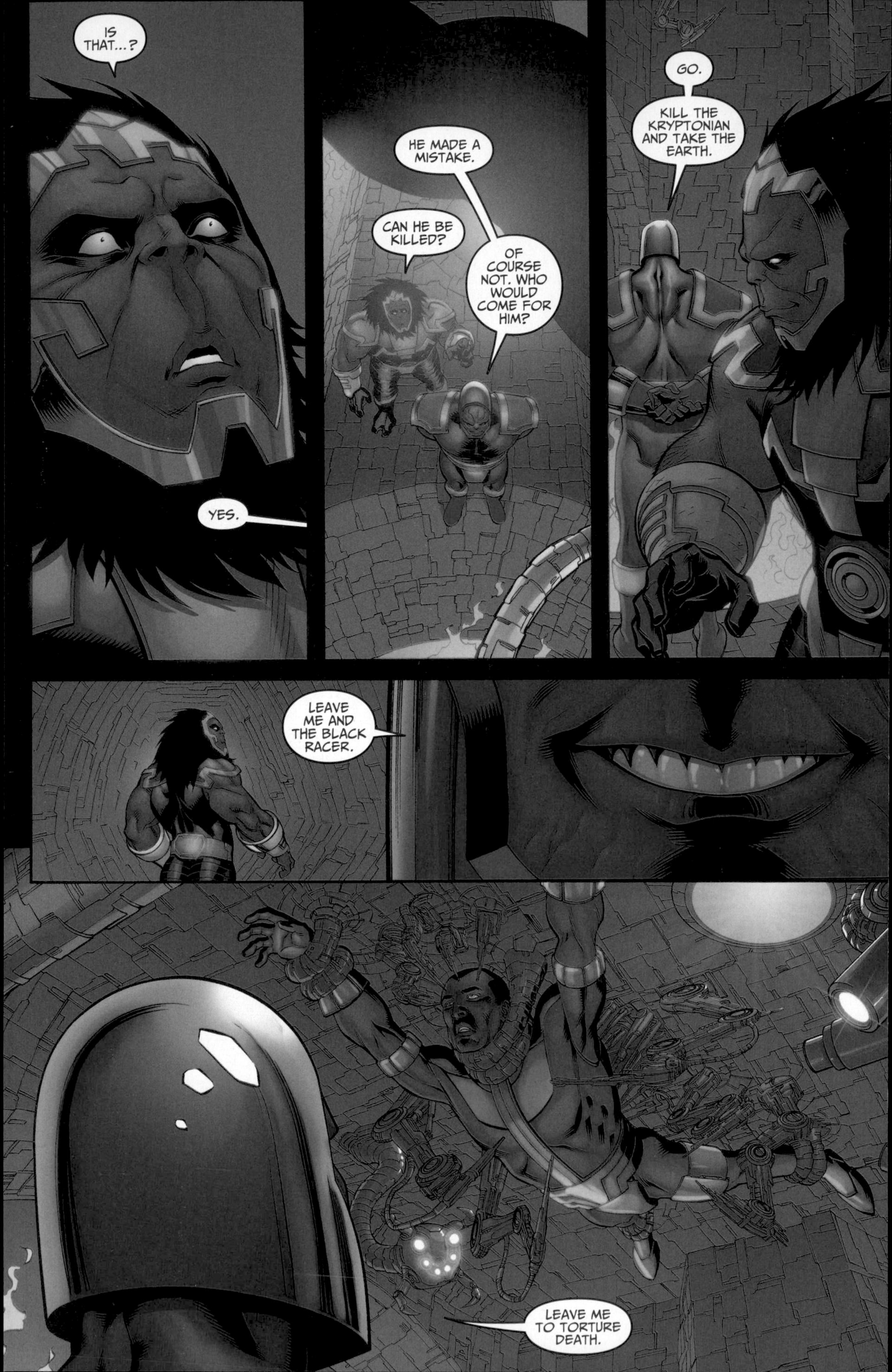
IS THAT...?
YES.
HE MADE A MISTAKE.
CAN HE BE KILLED?
OF COURSE NOT. WHO WOULD COME FOR HIM?
GO.
KILL THE KRYPTONIAN AND TAKE THE EARTH.
LEAVE ME AND THE BLACK RACER.
LEAVE ME TO TORTURE DEATH.

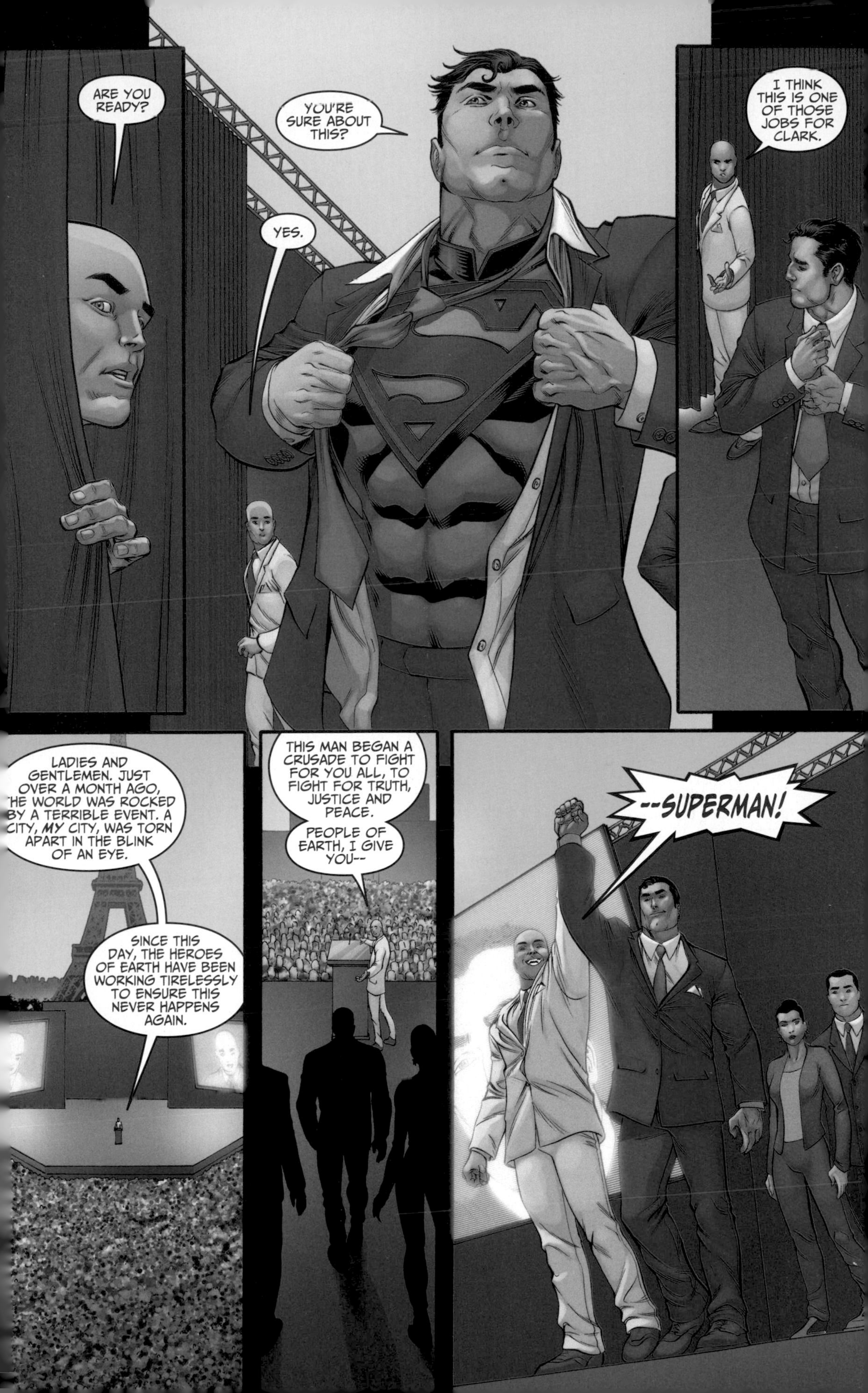
ARE YOU READY?
YOU'RE SURE ABOUT THIS?
YES.
I THINK THIS IS ONE OF THOSE JOBS FOR CLARK.
LADIES AND GENTLEMEN. JUST OVER A MONTH AGO, THE WORLD WAS ROCKED BY A TERRIBLE EVENT. A CITY, *MY* CITY, WAS TORN APART IN THE BLINK OF AN EYE.
SINCE THIS DAY, THE HEROES OF EARTH HAVE BEEN WORKING TIRELESSLY TO ENSURE THIS NEVER HAPPENS AGAIN.
THIS MAN BEGAN A CRUSADE TO FIGHT FOR YOU ALL, TO FIGHT FOR TRUTH, JUSTICE AND PEACE.
PEOPLE OF EARTH, I GIVE YOU--
--SUPERMAN!

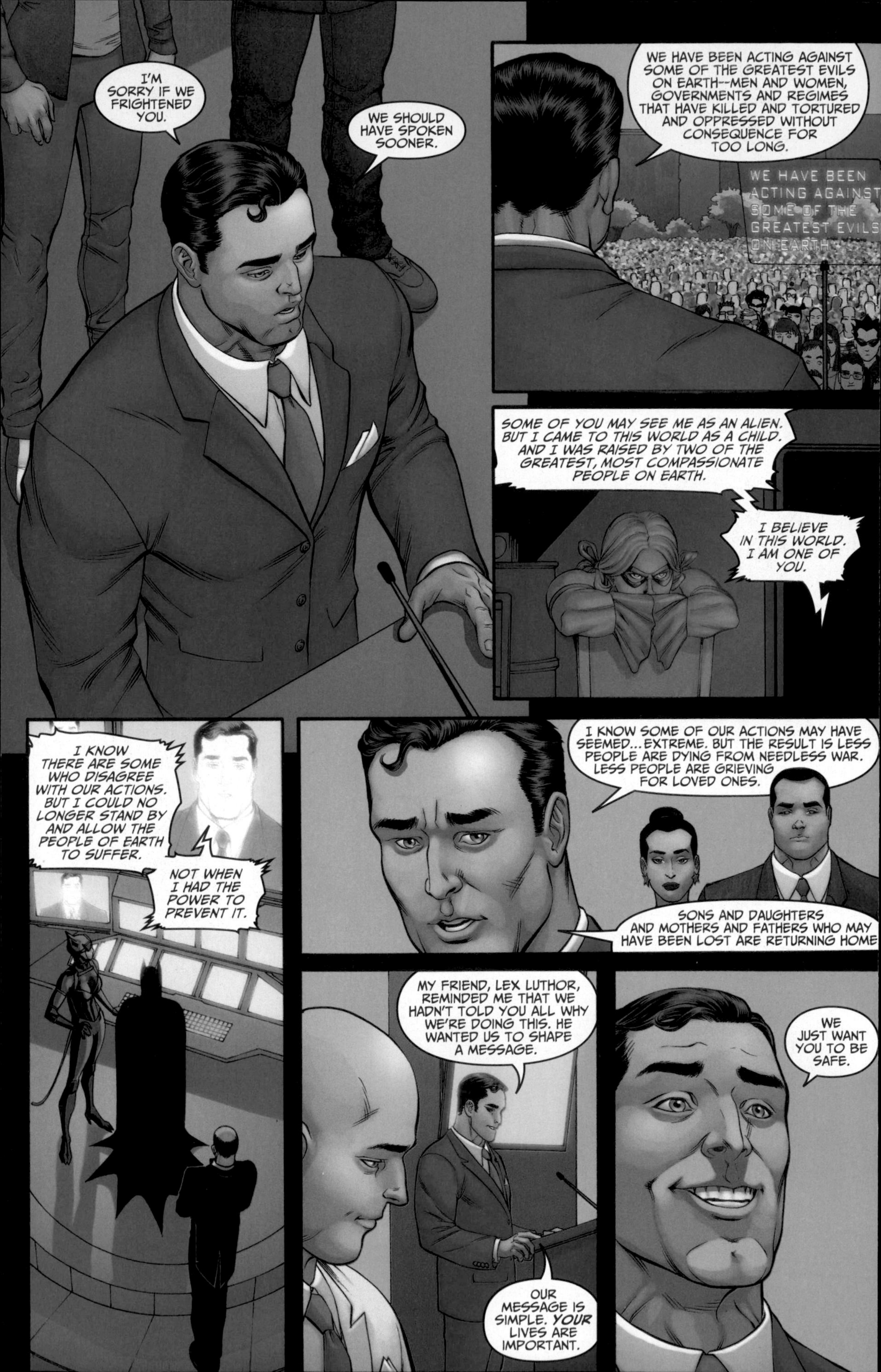
I'M SORRY IF WE FRIGHTENED YOU.
WE SHOULD HAVE SPOKEN SOONER.
WE HAVE BEEN ACTING AGAINST SOME OF THE GREATEST EVILS ON EARTH--MEN AND WOMEN, GOVERNMENTS AND REGIMES THAT HAVE KILLED AND TORTURED AND OPPRESSED WITHOUT CONSEQUENCE FOR TOO LONG.
WE HAVE BEEN ACTING AGAINST SOME OF THE GREATEST EVILS ON EARTH
SOME OF YOU MAY SEE ME AS AN ALIEN. BUT I CAME TO THIS WORLD AS A CHILD. AND I WAS RAISED BY TWO OF THE GREATEST, MOST COMPASSIONATE PEOPLE ON EARTH.
I BELIEVE IN THIS WORLD. I AM ONE OF YOU.
I KNOW THERE ARE SOME WHO DISAGREE WITH OUR ACTIONS. BUT I COULD NO LONGER STAND BY AND ALLOW THE PEOPLE OF EARTH TO SUFFER.
NOT WHEN I HAD THE POWER TO PREVENT IT.
I KNOW SOME OF OUR ACTIONS MAY HAVE SEEMED... EXTREME. BUT THE RESULT IS LESS PEOPLE ARE DYING FROM NEEDLESS WAR. LESS PEOPLE ARE GRIEVING FOR LOVED ONES.
SONS AND DAUGHTERS AND MOTHERS AND FATHERS WHO MAY HAVE BEEN LOST ARE RETURNING HOME
MY FRIEND, LEX LUTHOR, REMINDED ME THAT WE HADN'T TOLD YOU ALL WHY WE'RE DOING THIS. HE WANTED US TO SHAPE A MESSAGE.
OUR MESSAGE IS SIMPLE. *YOUR* LIVES ARE IMPORTANT.
WE JUST WANT YOU TO BE SAFE.

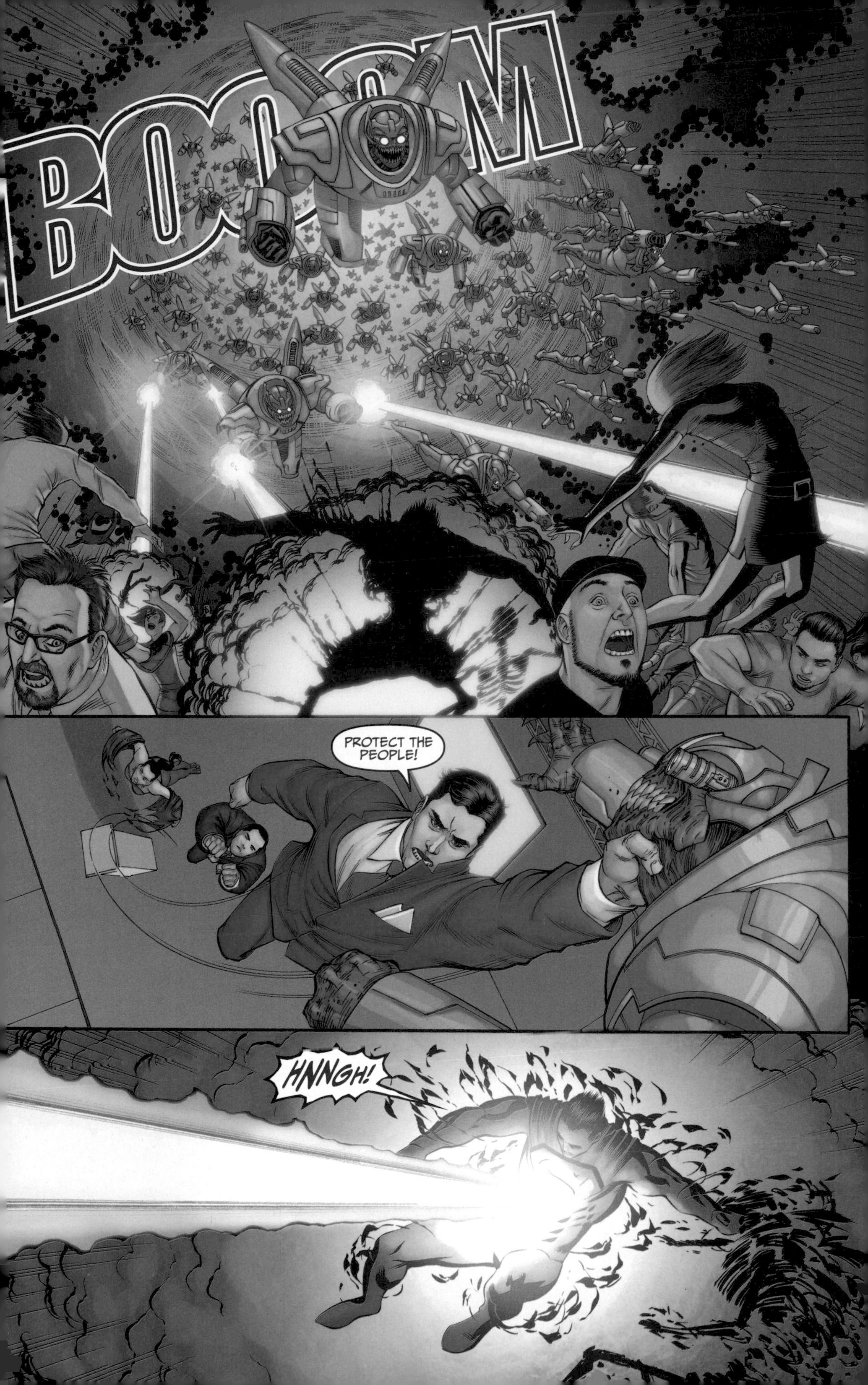
BOOOM
PROTECT THE PEOPLE!
HNNGH!

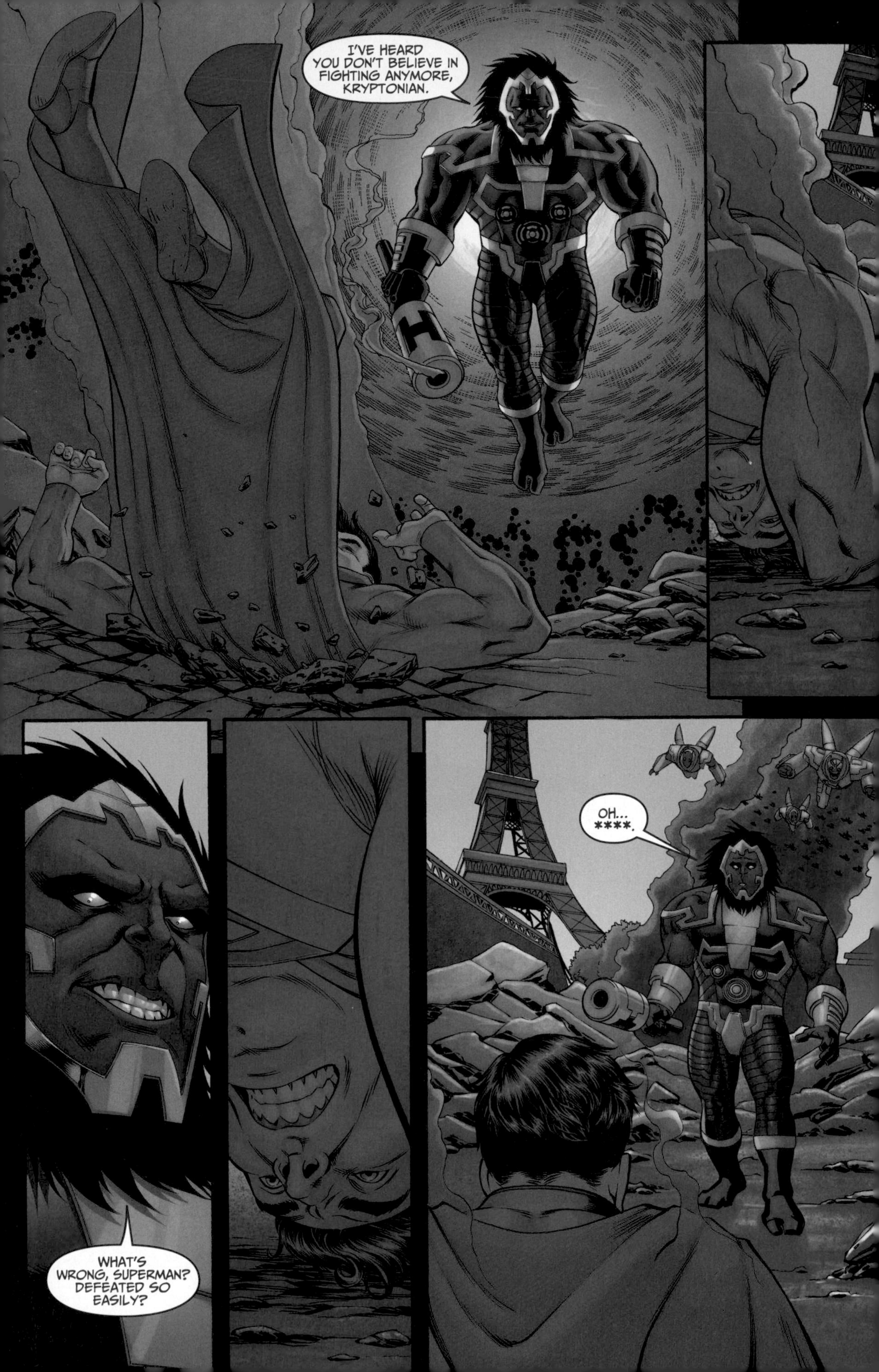
I'VE HEARD YOU DON'T BELIEVE IN FIGHTING ANYMORE, KRYPTONIAN.
WHAT'S WRONG, SUPERMAN? DEFEATED SO EASILY?
OH... ****.

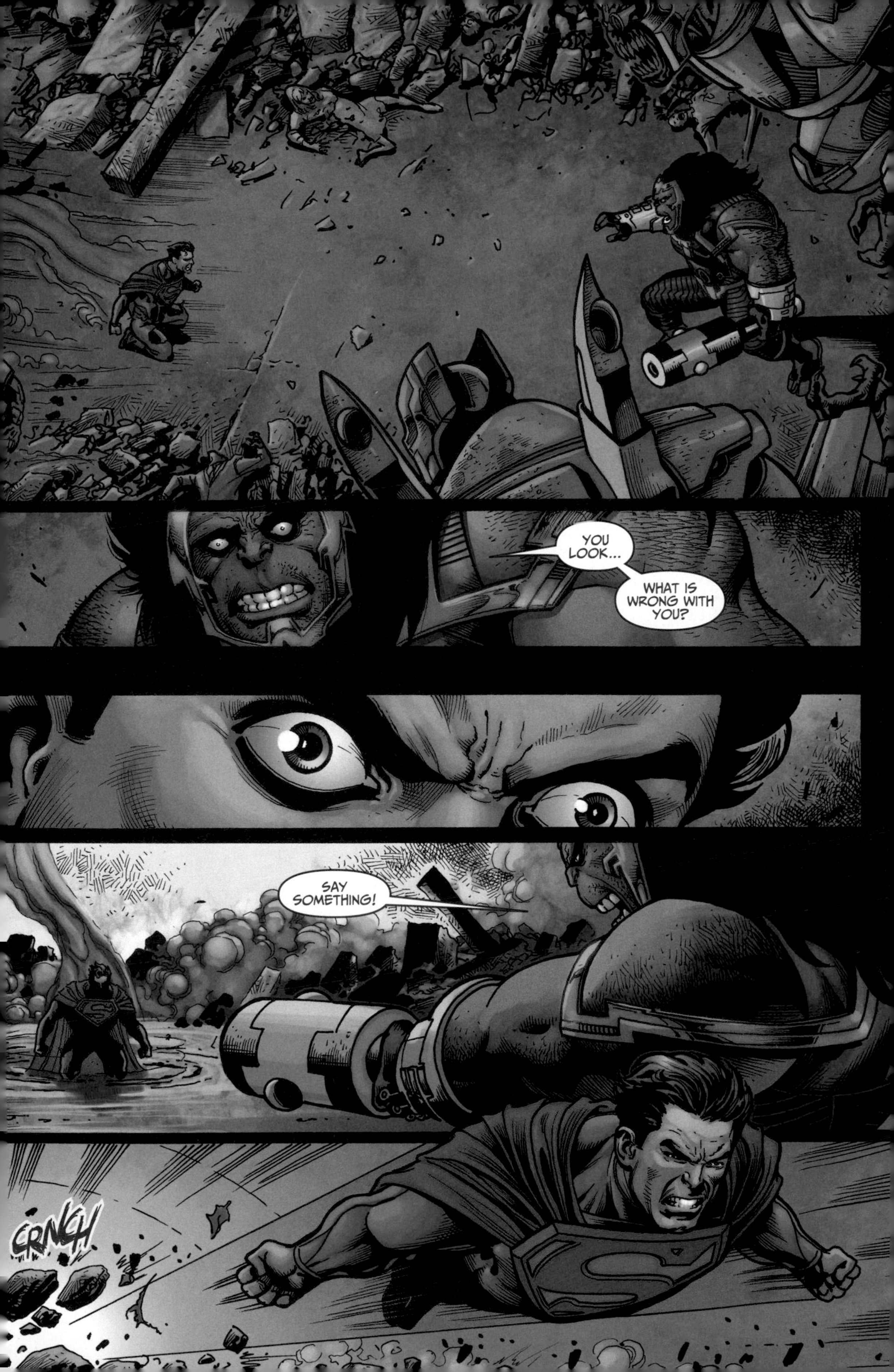
YOU LOOK...
WHAT IS WRONG WITH YOU?
SAY SOMETHING!
CRNCH

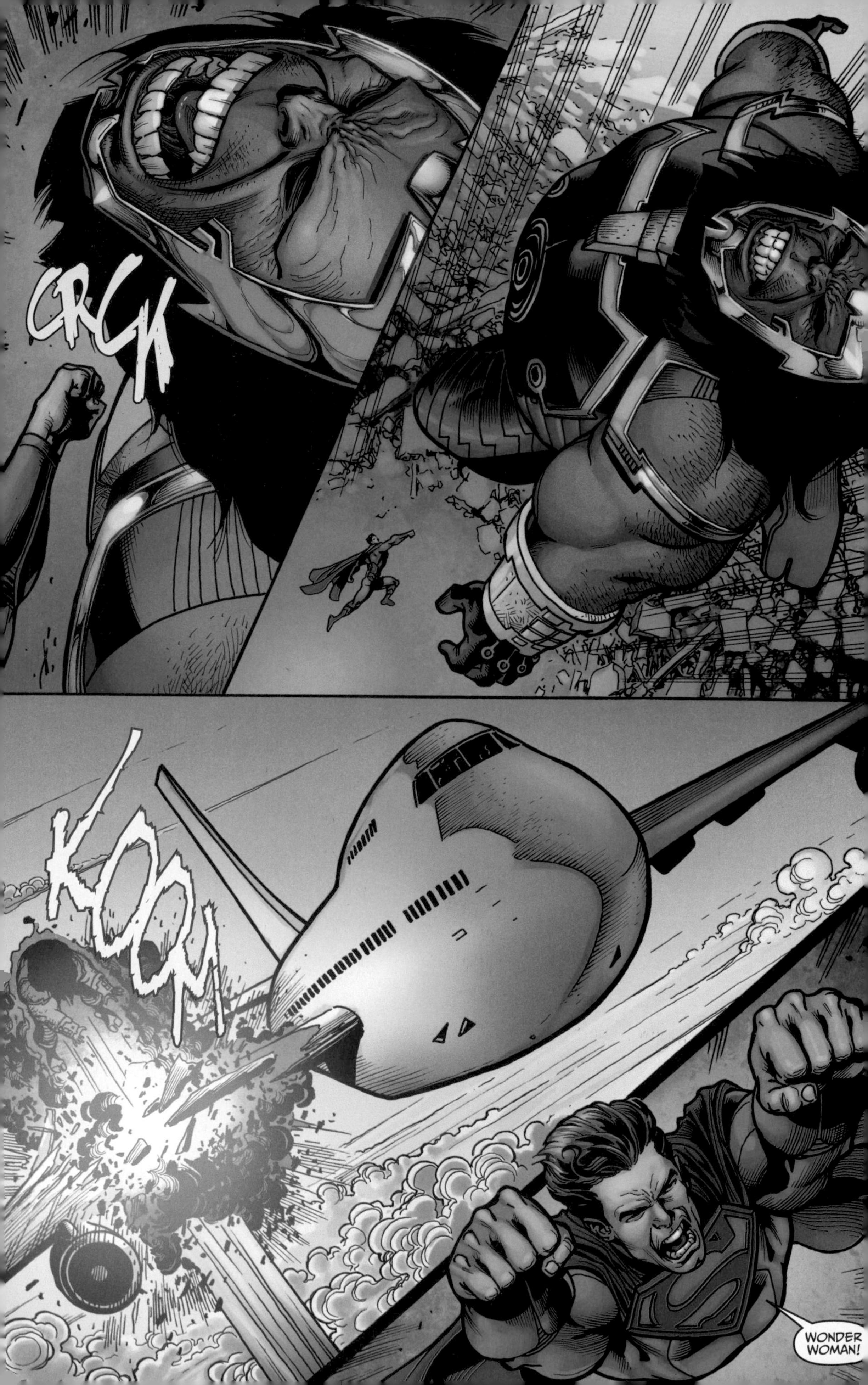
CRCK
KOOM
WONDER WOMAN!

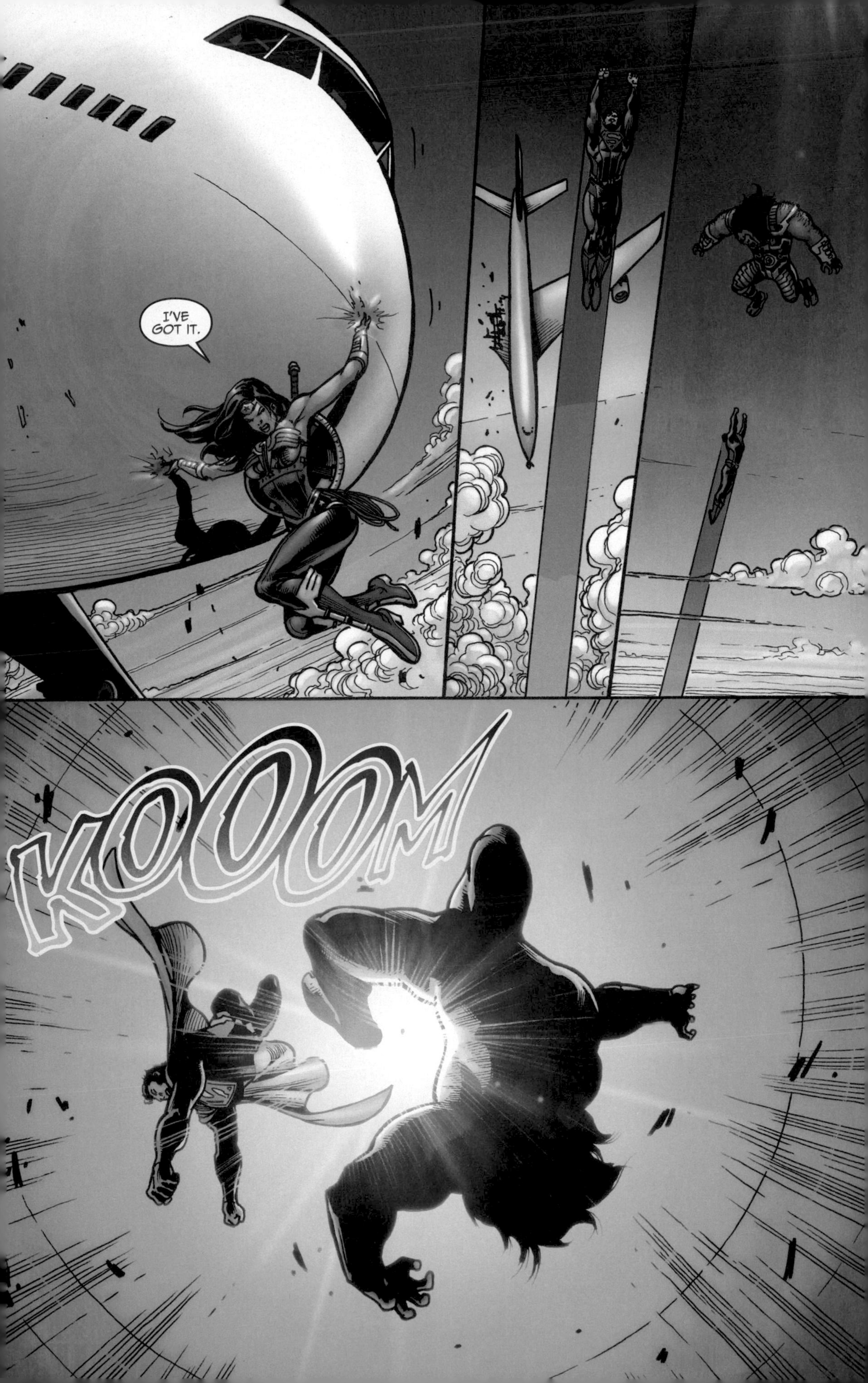
I'VE GOT IT.
KOOOM

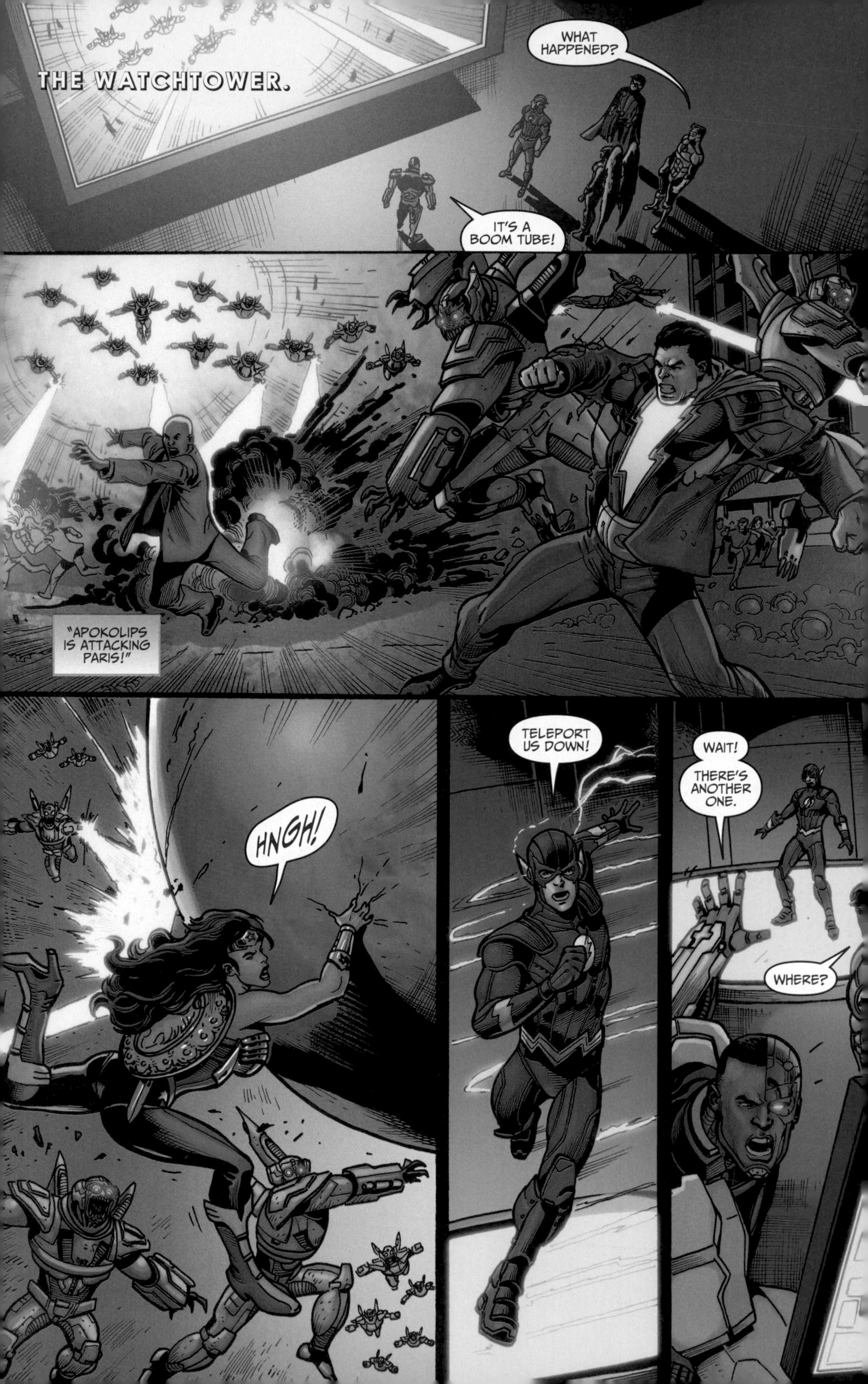
THE WATCHTOWER.
WHAT HAPPENED?
IT'S A BOOM TUBE!
"APOKOLIPS IS ATTACKING PARIS!"
HNGH!
TELEPORT US DOWN!
WAIT!
THERE'S ANOTHER ONE.
WHERE?

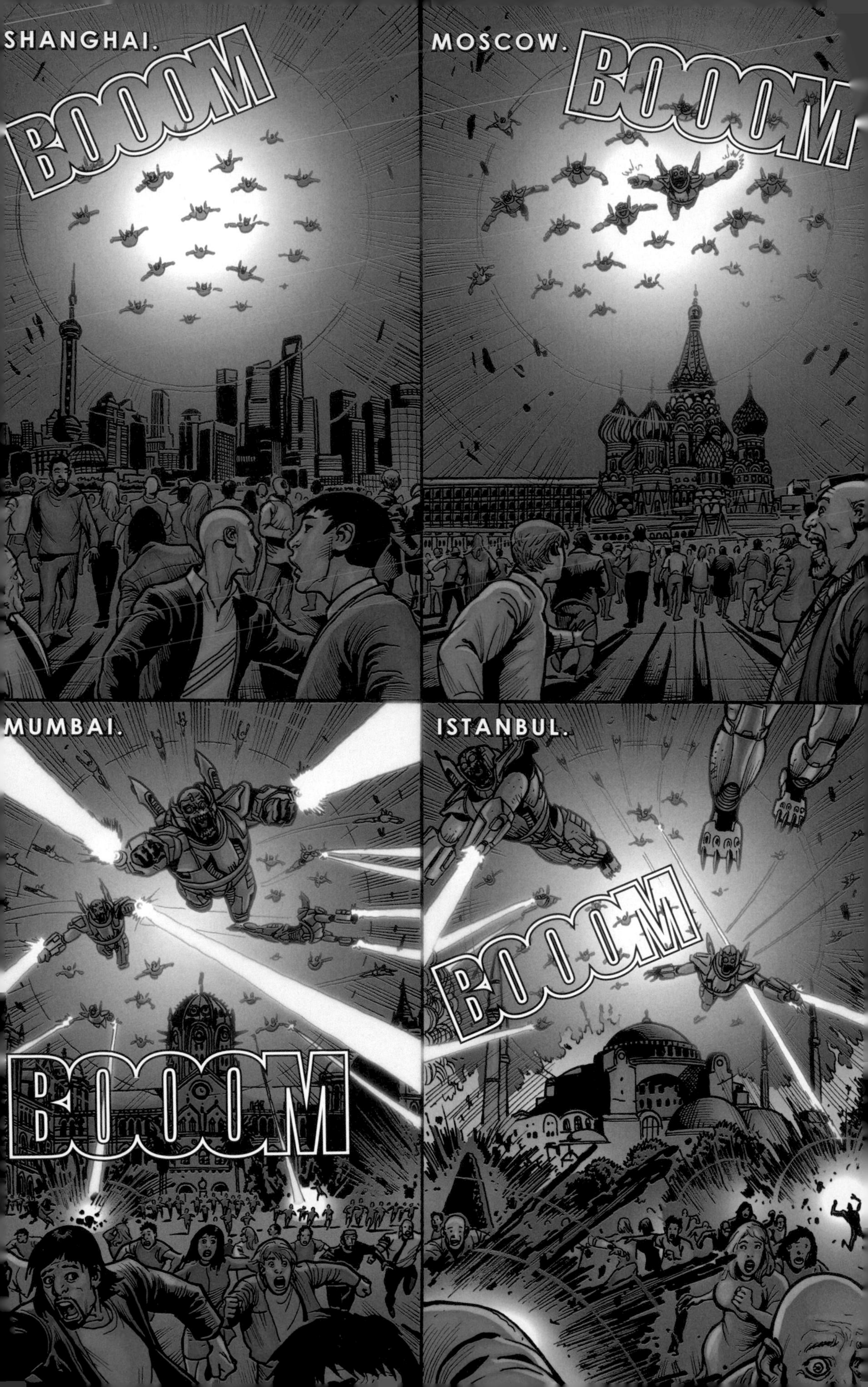
SHANGHAI.
BOOOM
MOSCOW.
BOOOM
MUMBAI.
BOOOM
ISTANBUL.
BOOOM

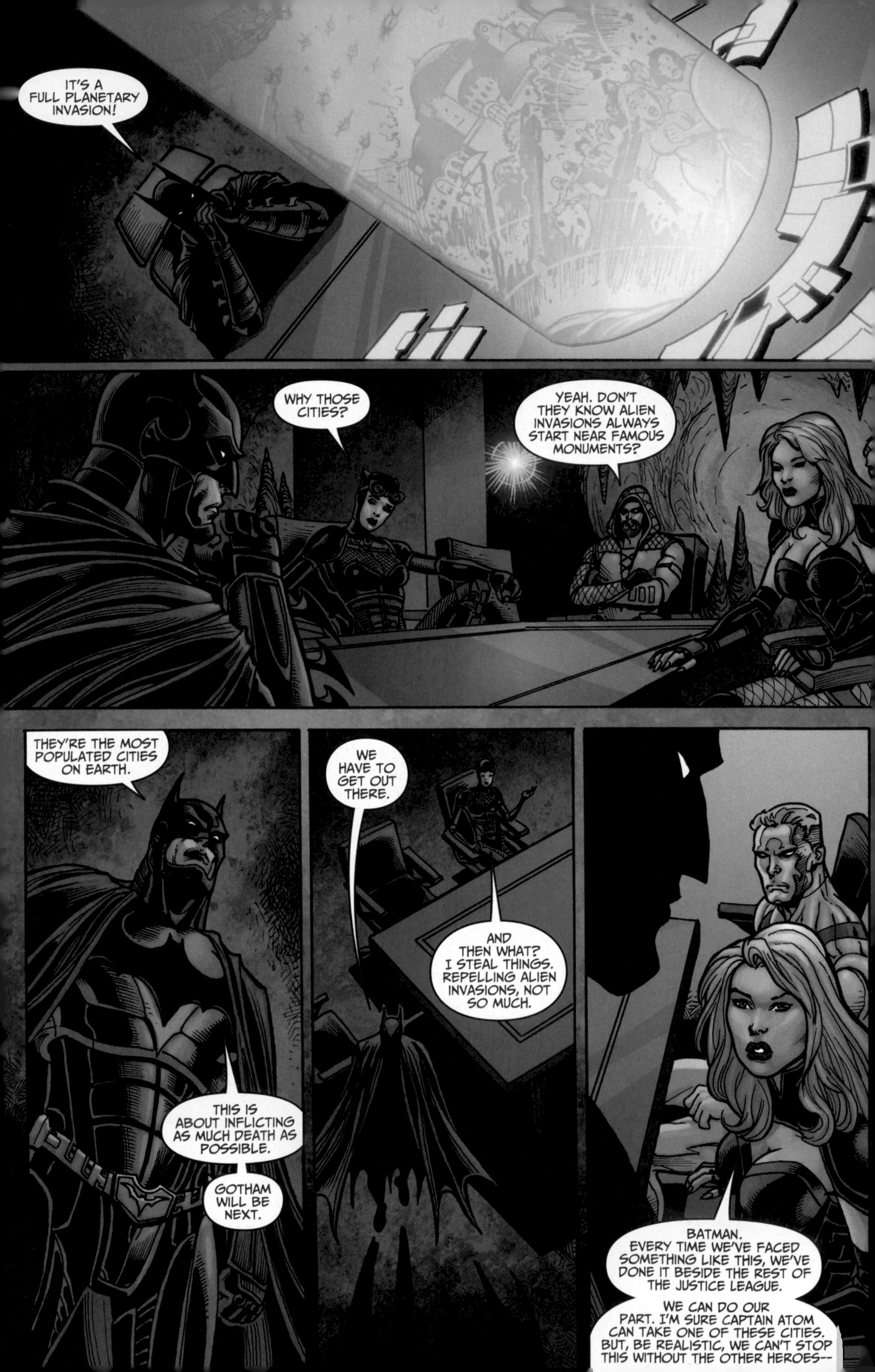
IT'S A FULL PLANETARY INVASION!
WHY THOSE CITIES?
YEAH. DON'T THEY KNOW ALIEN INVASIONS ALWAYS START NEAR FAMOUS MONUMENTS?
THEY'RE THE MOST POPULATED CITIES ON EARTH.
THIS IS ABOUT INFLICTING AS MUCH DEATH AS POSSIBLE.
GOTHAM WILL BE NEXT.
WE HAVE TO GET OUT THERE.
AND THEN WHAT? I STEAL THINGS. REPELLING ALIEN INVASIONS, NOT SO MUCH.
BATMAN. EVERY TIME WE'VE FACED SOMETHING LIKE THIS, WE'VE DONE IT BESIDE THE REST OF THE JUSTICE LEAGUE.
WE CAN DO OUR PART. I'M SURE CAPTAIN ATOM CAN TAKE ONE OF THESE CITIES. BUT, BE REALISTIC, WE CAN'T STOP THIS WITHOUT THE OTHER HEROES--

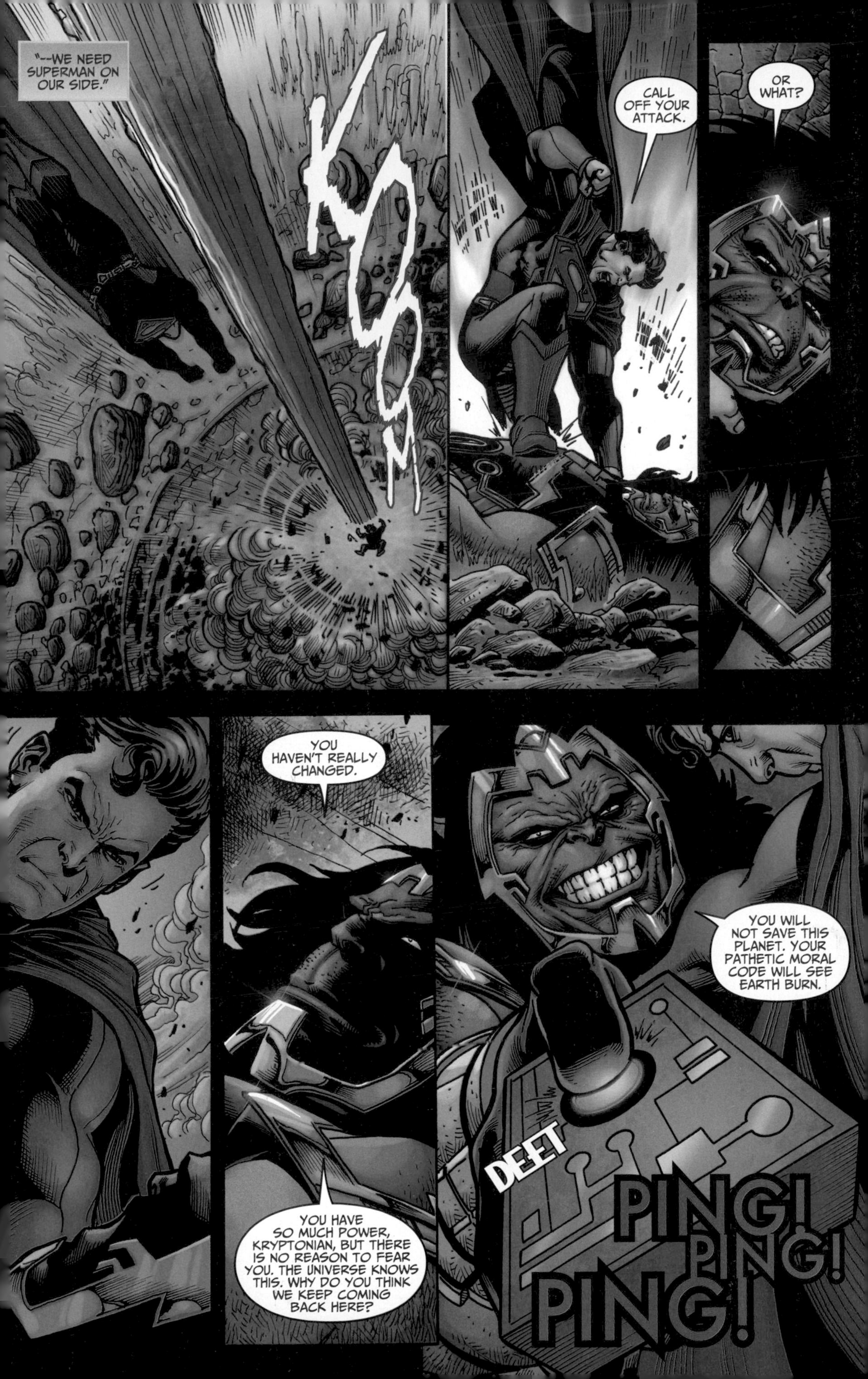
"--WE NEED SUPERMAN ON OUR SIDE."
KOOM
CALL OFF YOUR ATTACK.
OR WHAT?
YOU HAVEN'T REALLY CHANGED.
YOU HAVE SO MUCH POWER, KRYPTONIAN, BUT THERE IS NO REASON TO FEAR YOU. THE UNIVERSE KNOWS THIS. WHY DO YOU THINK WE KEEP COMING BACK HERE?
YOU WILL NOT SAVE THIS PLANET. YOUR PATHETIC MORAL CODE WILL SEE EARTH BURN.
DEET
PING! PING! PING!

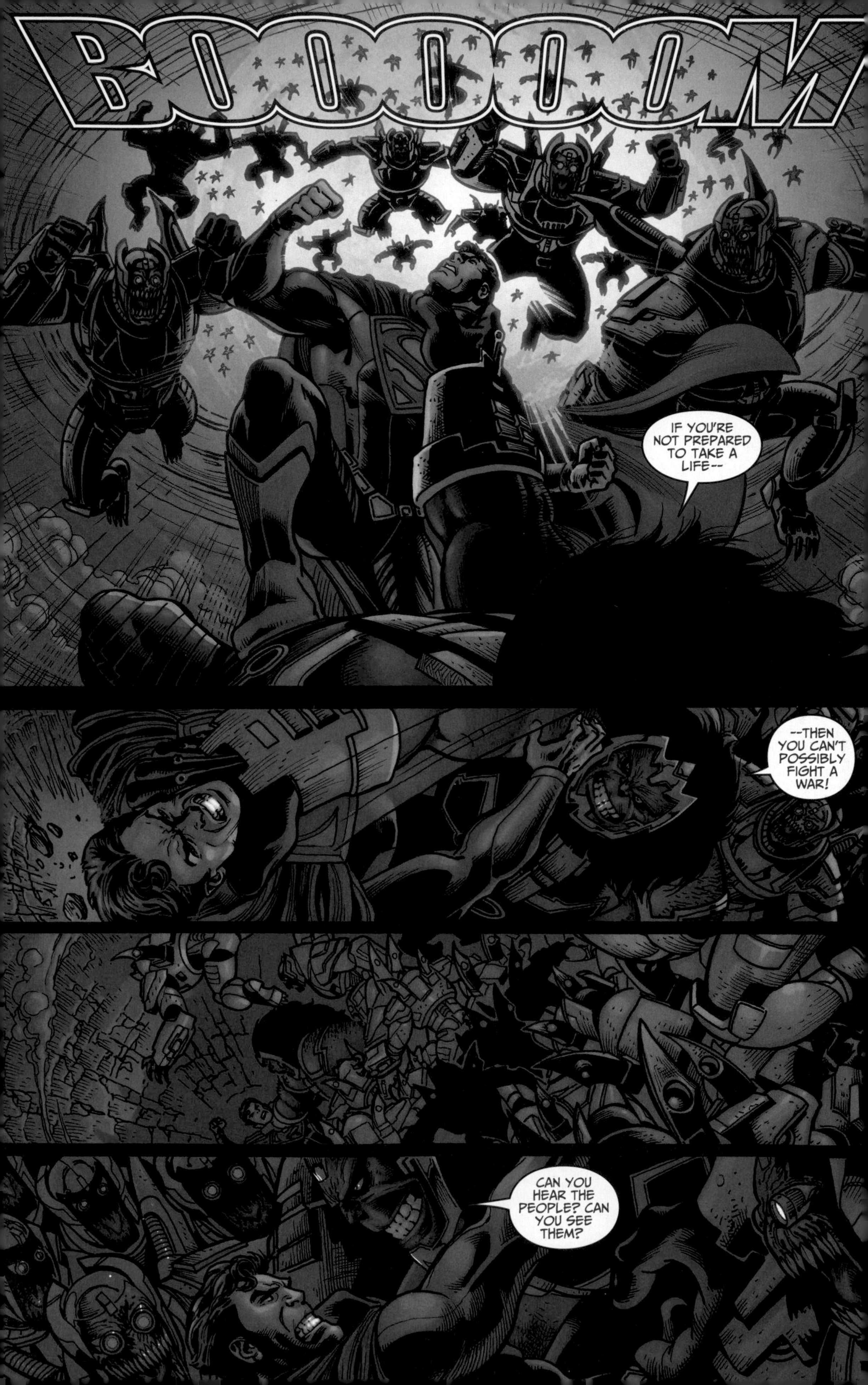
BOOOOOM
IF YOU'RE NOT PREPARED TO TAKE A LIFE--
--THEN YOU CAN'T POSSIBLY FIGHT A WAR!
CAN YOU HEAR THE PEOPLE? CAN YOU SEE THEM?

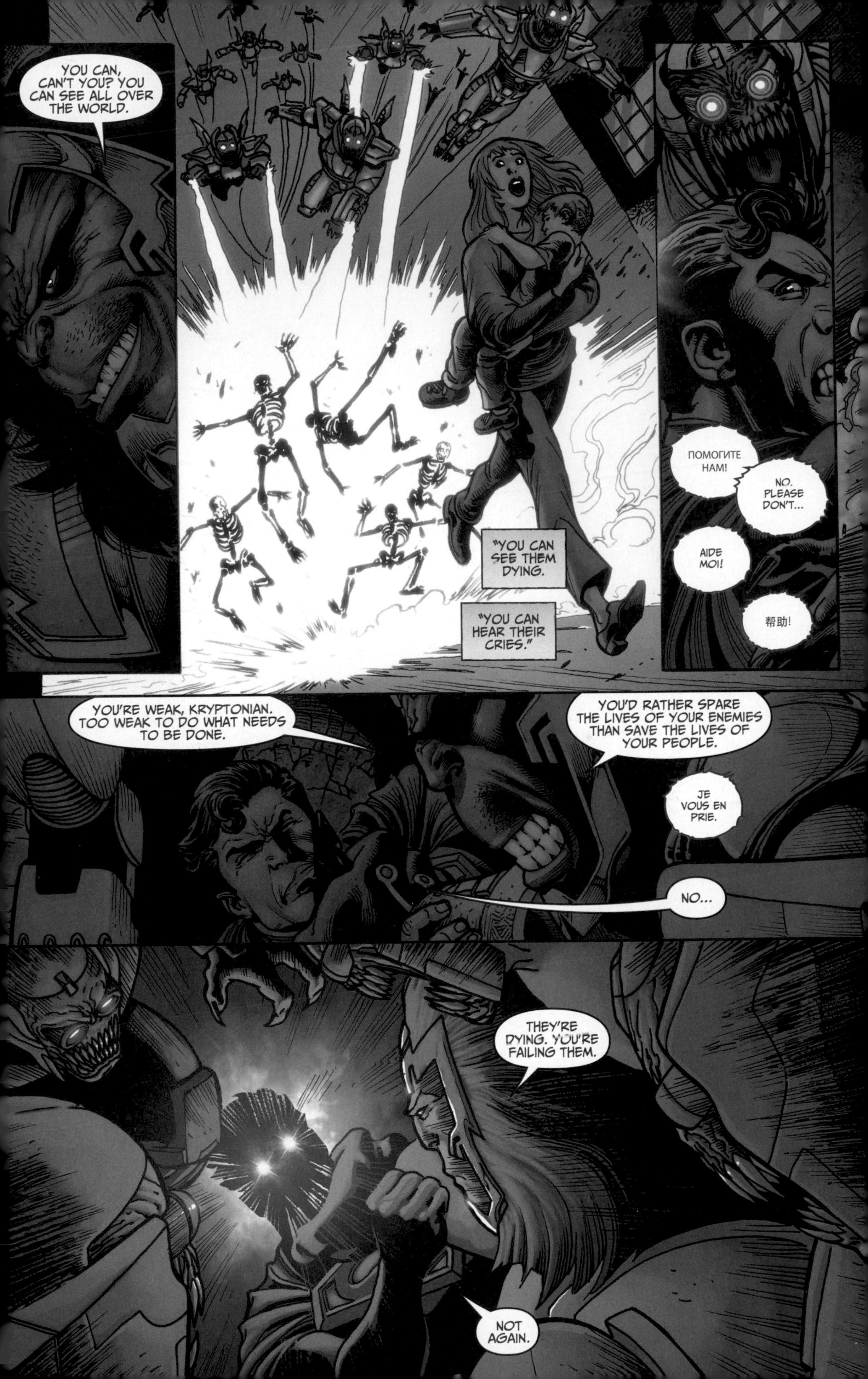
YOU CAN, CAN'T YOU? YOU CAN SEE ALL OVER THE WORLD.
"YOU CAN SEE THEM DYING.
"YOU CAN HEAR THEIR CRIES."
ПОМОГИТЕ НАМ!
NO. PLEASE DON'T...
AIDE MOI!
帮助!
YOU'RE WEAK, KRYPTONIAN. TOO WEAK TO DO WHAT NEEDS TO BE DONE.
YOU'D RATHER SPARE THE LIVES OF YOUR ENEMIES THAN SAVE THE LIVES OF YOUR PEOPLE.
JE VOUS EN PRIE.
NO...
THEY'RE DYING. YOU'RE FAILING THEM.
NOT AGAIN.

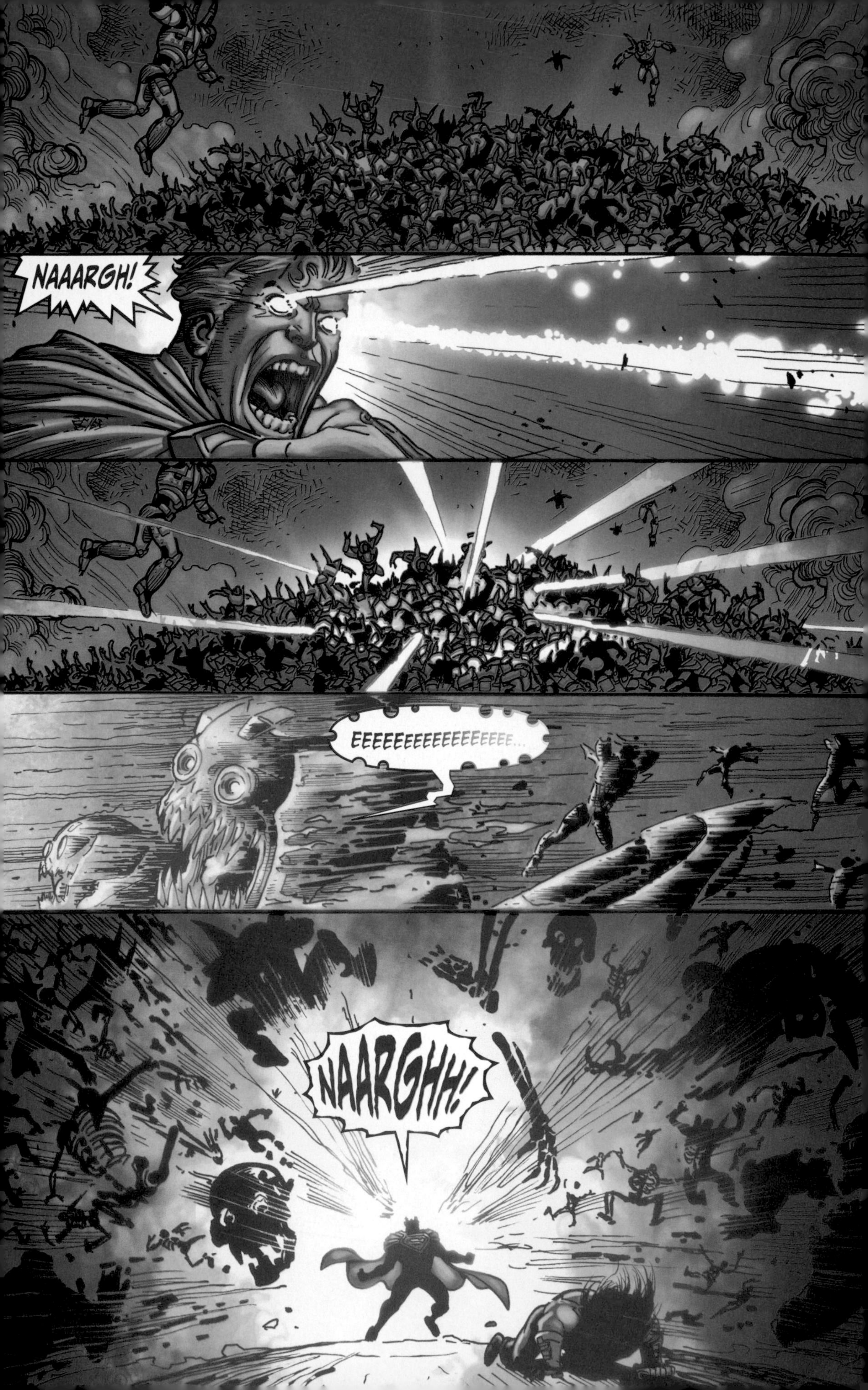
NAAARGH!
EEEEEEEEEEEEEEEE...
NAARGHH!

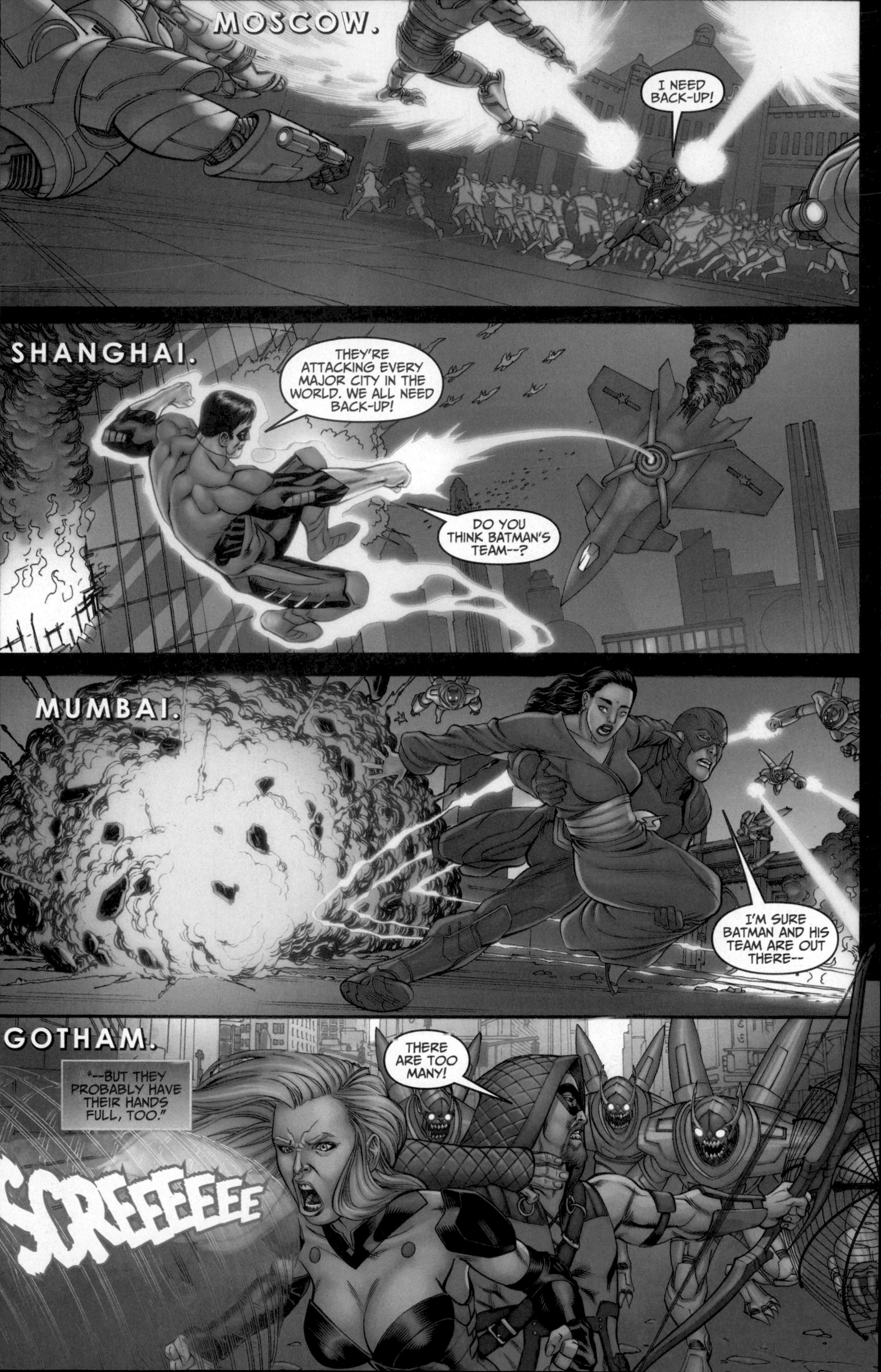
MOSCOW.
I NEED BACK-UP!
SHANGHAI.
THEY'RE ATTACKING EVERY MAJOR CITY IN THE WORLD. WE ALL NEED BACK-UP!
DO YOU THINK BATMAN'S TEAM--?
MUMBAI.
I'M SURE BATMAN AND HIS TEAM ARE OUT THERE--
GOTHAM.
"--BUT THEY PROBABLY HAVE THEIR HANDS FULL, TOO."
THERE ARE TOO MANY!
SCREEEEEE

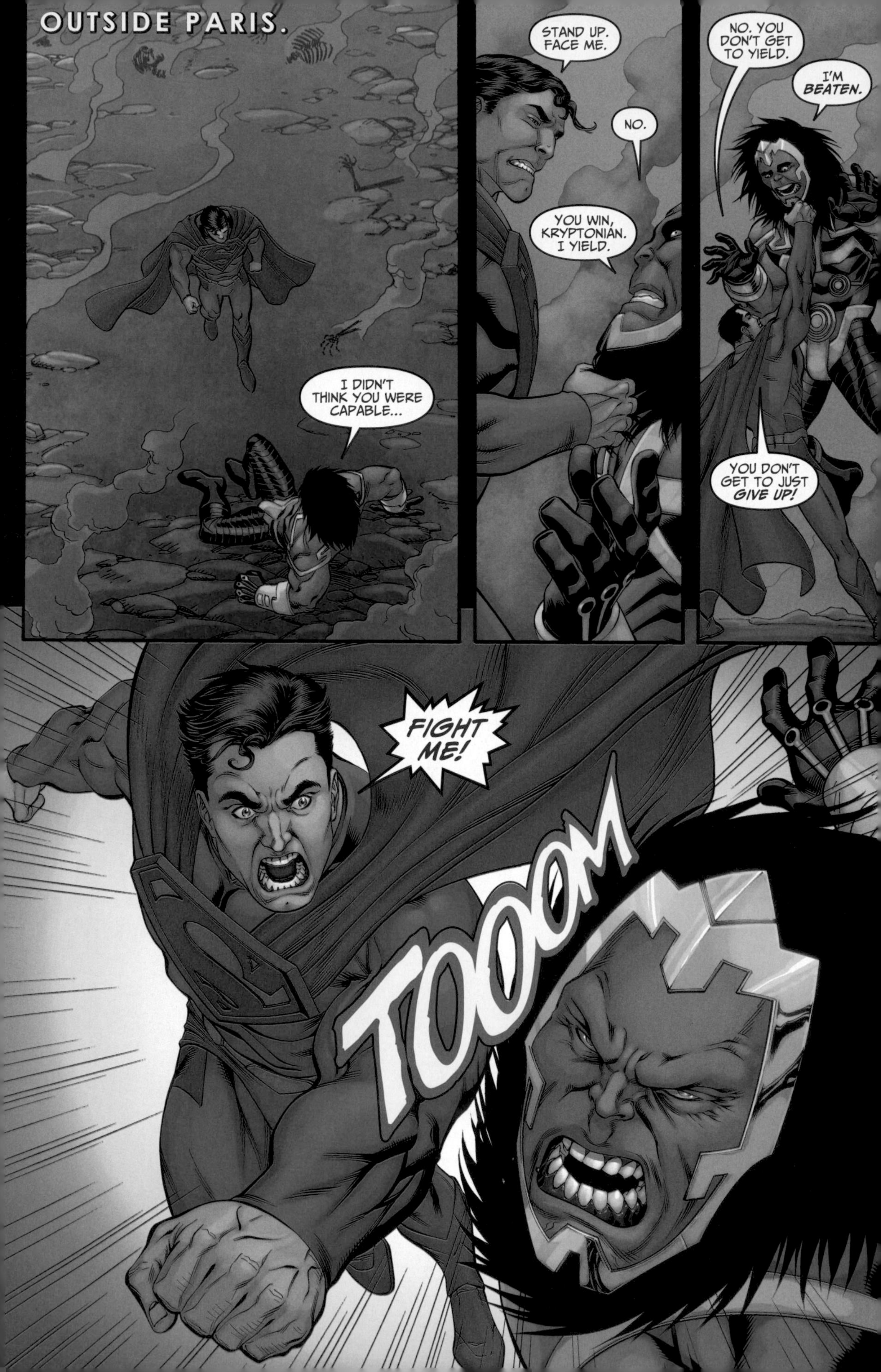
OUTSIDE PARIS.
I DIDN'T THINK YOU WERE CAPABLE...
STAND UP. FACE ME.
NO.
YOU WIN, KRYPTONIAN. I YIELD.
NO. YOU DON'T GET TO YIELD.
I'M BEATEN.
YOU DON'T GET TO JUST GIVE UP!
FIGHT ME!
TOOOM

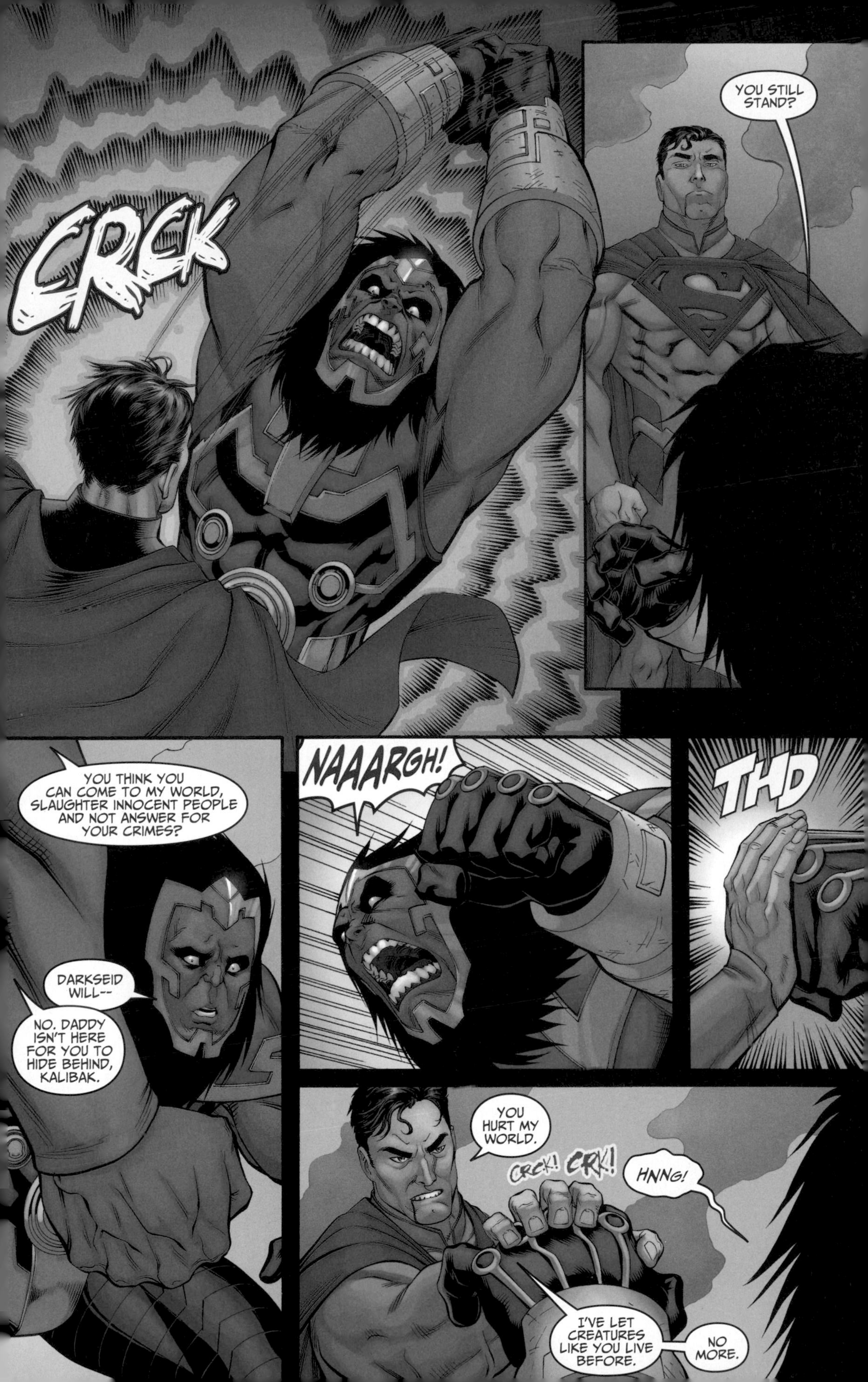
CRCK
YOU STILL STAND?
YOU THINK YOU CAN COME TO MY WORLD, SLAUGHTER INNOCENT PEOPLE AND NOT ANSWER FOR YOUR CRIMES?
DARKSEID WILL--
NO. DADDY ISN'T HERE FOR YOU TO HIDE BEHIND, KALIBAK.
NAAARGH!
THD
YOU HURT MY WORLD.
CRCK! CRK!
HNNG!
I'VE LET CREATURES LIKE YOU LIVE BEFORE.
NO MORE.

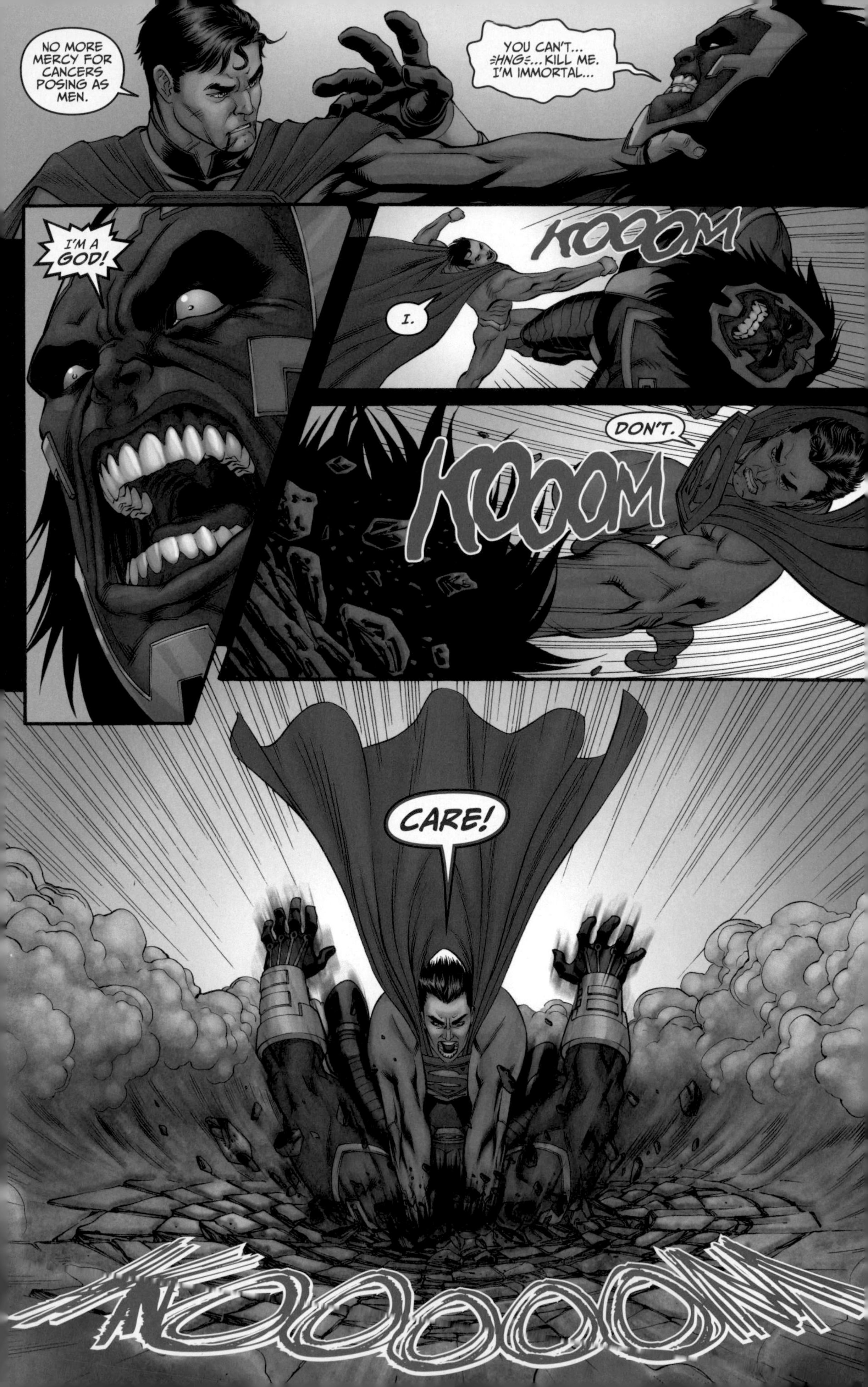
NO MORE MERCY FOR CANCERS POSING AS MEN.
YOU CAN'T... HNG... KILL ME. I'M IMMORTAL...
I'M A GOD!
I.
KOOOM
DON'T.
KOOOM
CARE!
KOOOOOOM

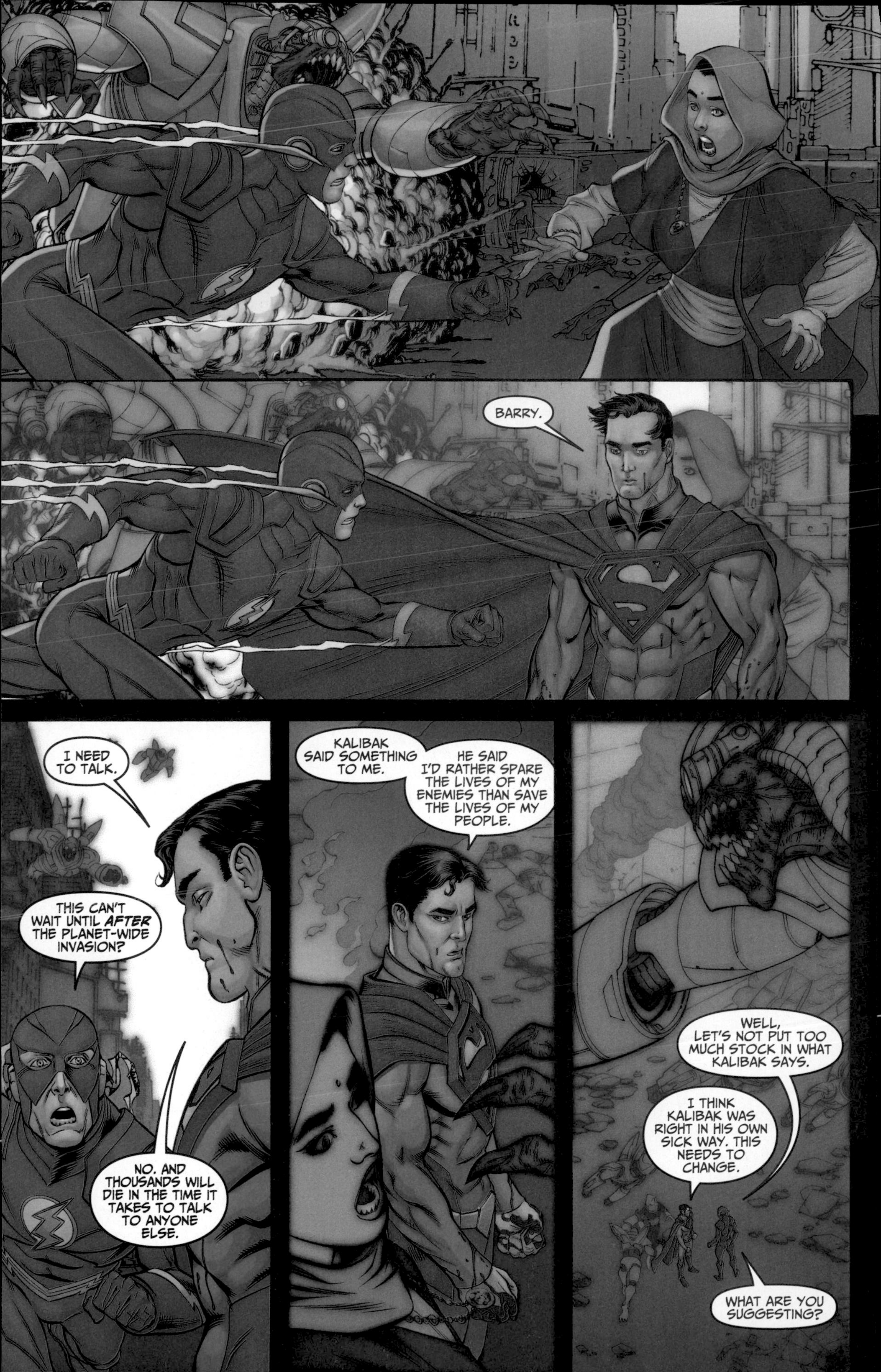
BARRY.
I NEED TO TALK.
THIS CAN'T WAIT UNTIL *AFTER* THE PLANET-WIDE INVASION?
NO. AND THOUSANDS WILL DIE IN THE TIME IT TAKES TO TALK TO ANYONE ELSE.
KALIBAK SAID SOMETHING TO ME.
HE SAID I'D RATHER SPARE THE LIVES OF MY ENEMIES THAN SAVE THE LIVES OF MY PEOPLE.
WELL, LET'S NOT PUT TOO MUCH STOCK IN WHAT KALIBAK SAYS.
I THINK KALIBAK WAS RIGHT IN HIS OWN SICK WAY. THIS NEEDS TO CHANGE.
WHAT ARE YOU SUGGESTING?

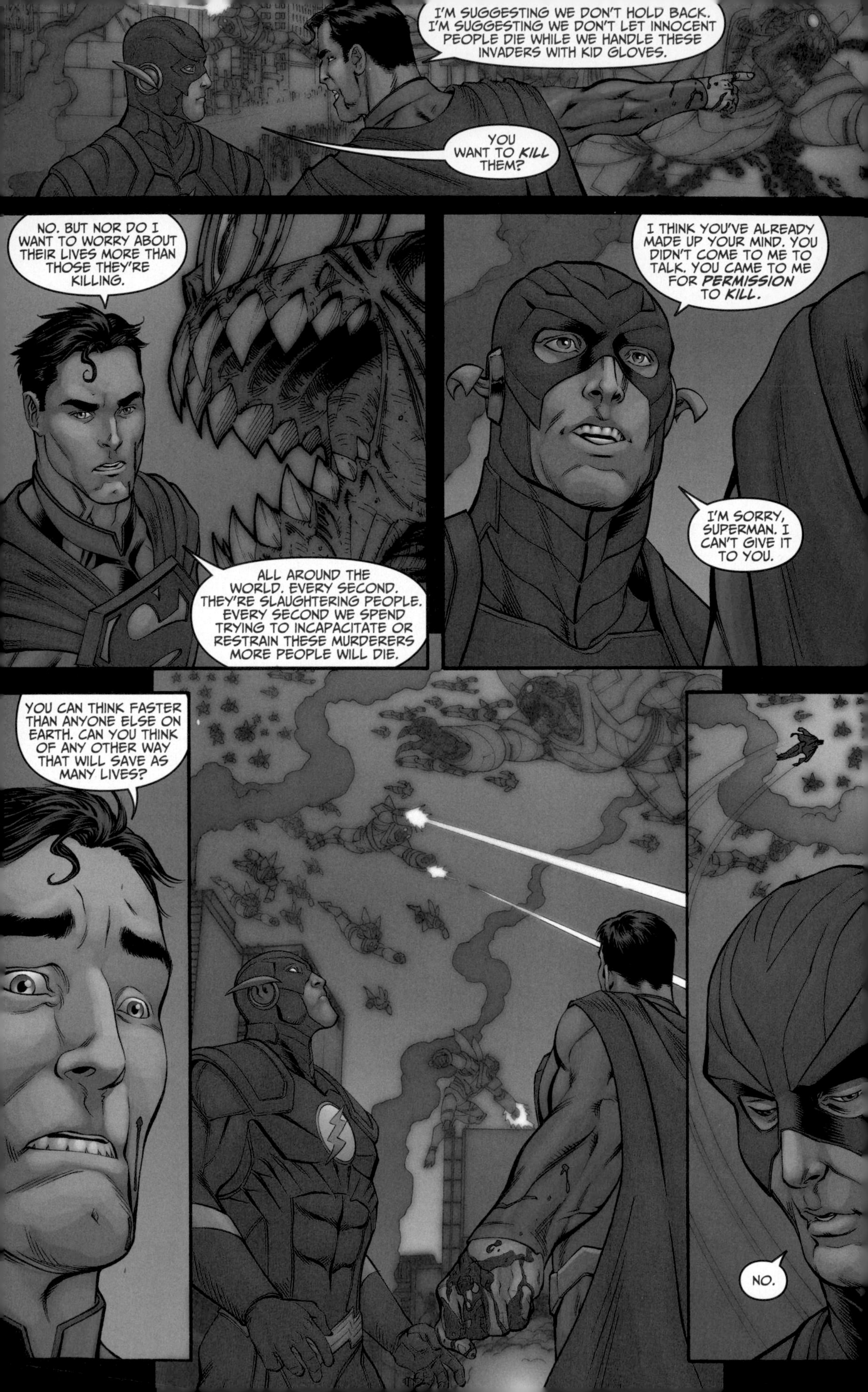
I'M SUGGESTING WE DON'T HOLD BACK. I'M SUGGESTING WE DON'T LET INNOCENT PEOPLE DIE WHILE WE HANDLE THESE INVADERS WITH KID GLOVES.
YOU WANT TO KILL THEM?
NO. BUT NOR DO I WANT TO WORRY ABOUT THEIR LIVES MORE THAN THOSE THEY'RE KILLING.
ALL AROUND THE WORLD. EVERY SECOND. THEY'RE SLAUGHTERING PEOPLE. EVERY SECOND WE SPEND TRYING TO INCAPACITATE OR RESTRAIN THESE MURDERERS MORE PEOPLE WILL DIE.
I THINK YOU'VE ALREADY MADE UP YOUR MIND. YOU DIDN'T COME TO ME TO TALK. YOU CAME TO ME FOR PERMISSION TO KILL.
I'M SORRY, SUPERMAN. I CAN'T GIVE IT TO YOU.
YOU CAN THINK FASTER THAN ANYONE ELSE ON EARTH. CAN YOU THINK OF ANY OTHER WAY THAT WILL SAVE AS MANY LIVES?
NO.

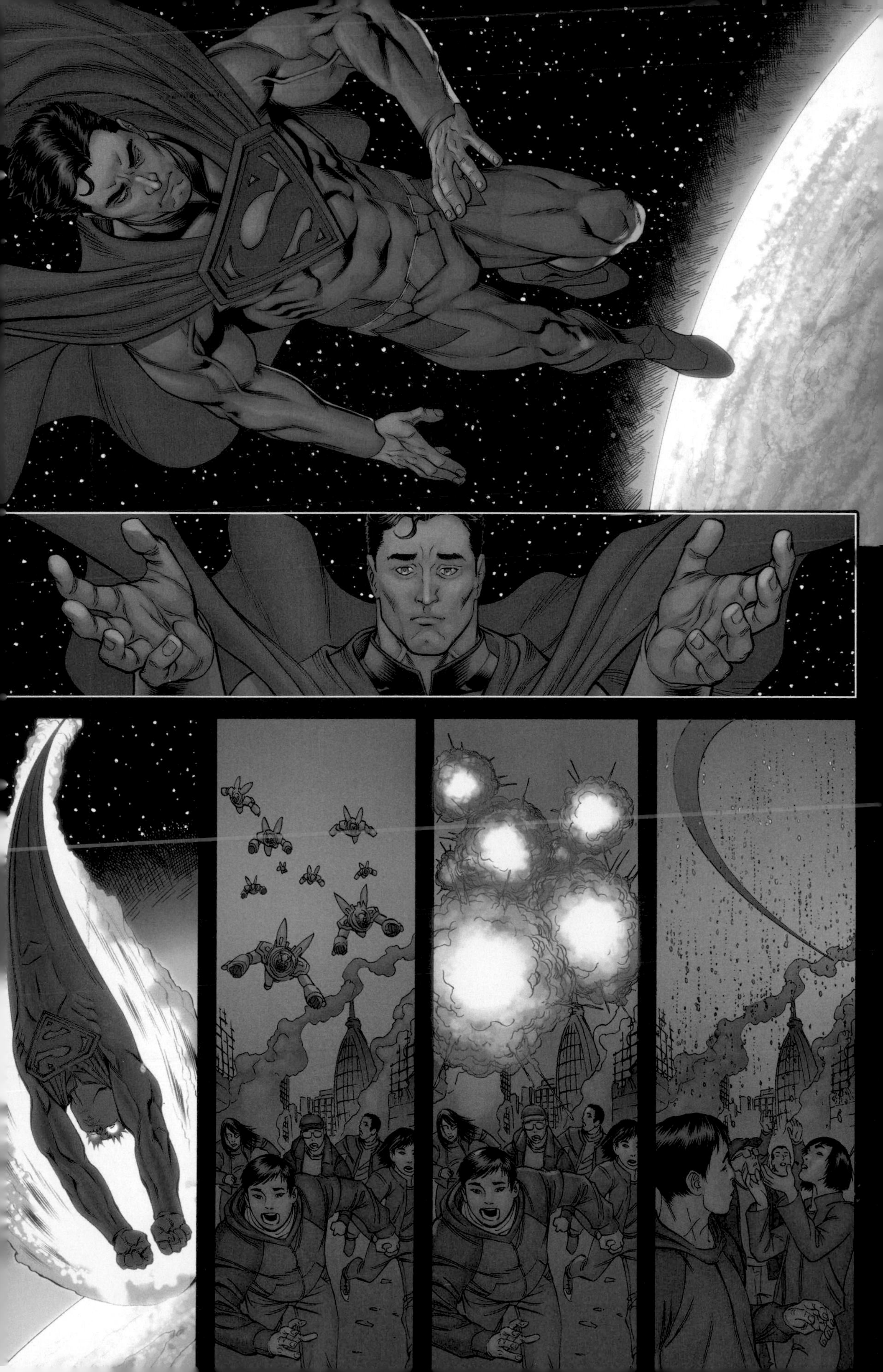

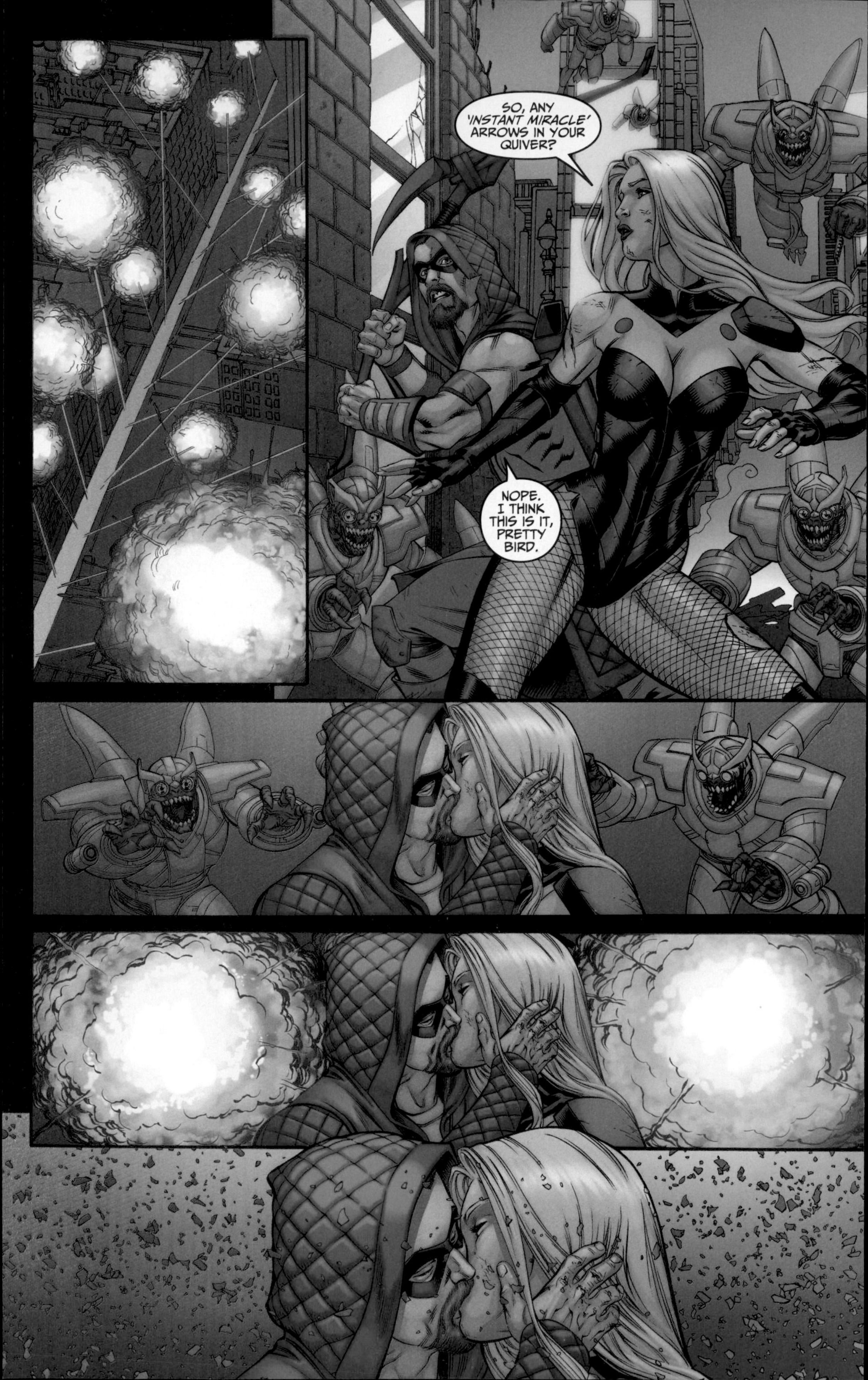

SO, ANY *'INSTANT MIRACLE'* ARROWS IN YOUR QUIVER?
NOPE. I THINK THIS IS IT, PRETTY BIRD.

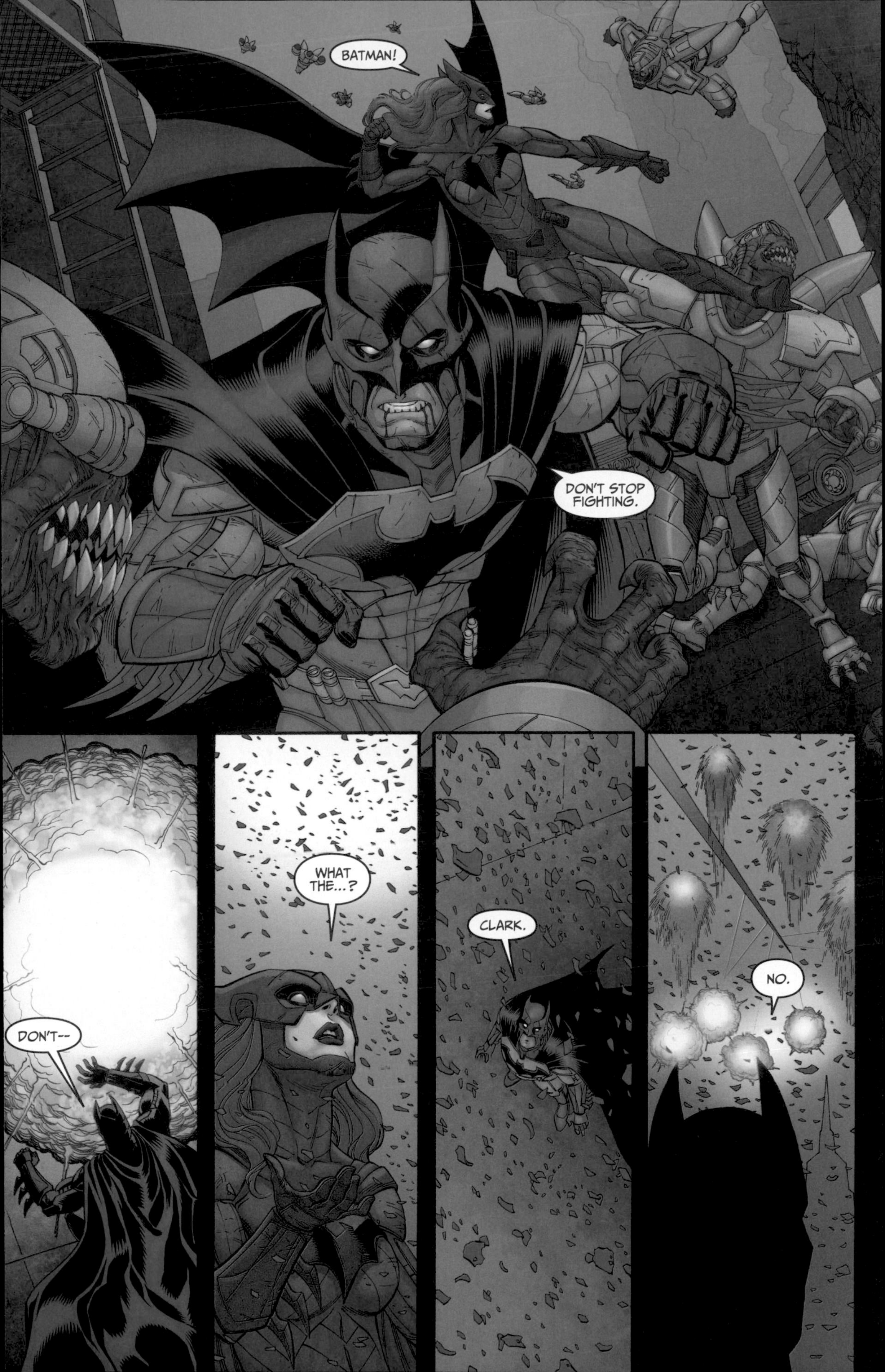
BATMAN!
DON'T STOP FIGHTING.
DON'T--
WHAT THE...?
CLARK.
NO.

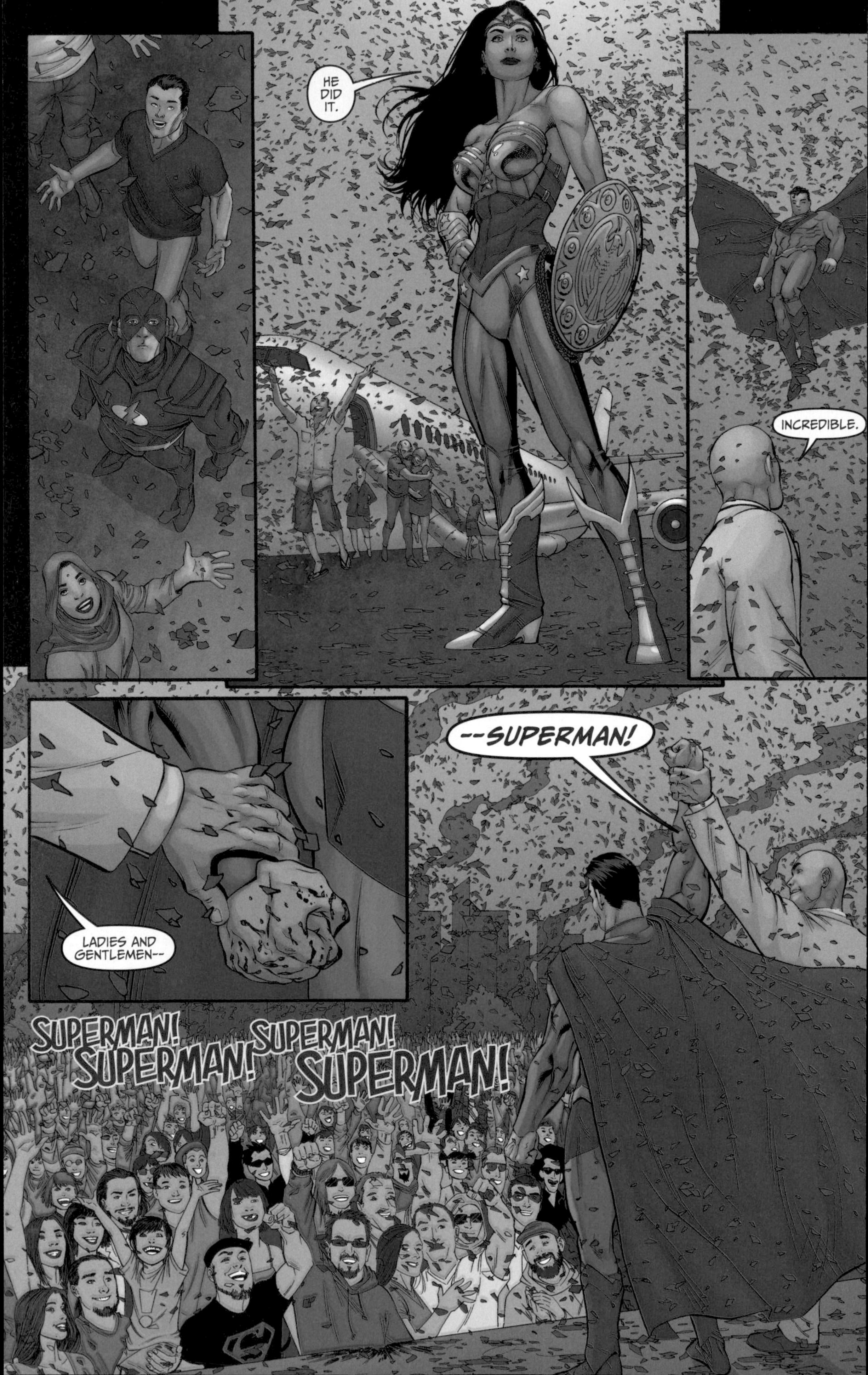
HE DID IT.
INCREDIBLE.
LADIES AND GENTLEMEN--
--SUPERMAN!
SUPERMAN! SUPERMAN! SUPERMAN! SUPERMAN!

PART NINE

Bruno Redondo Tom Derenick Jheremy Raapack Artists

David Lopez and **Santi Casas** of **Ikari Studio** Colorists

Jheremy Raapack & **David Lopez** and **Santi Casas** of **Ikari Studio** Cover

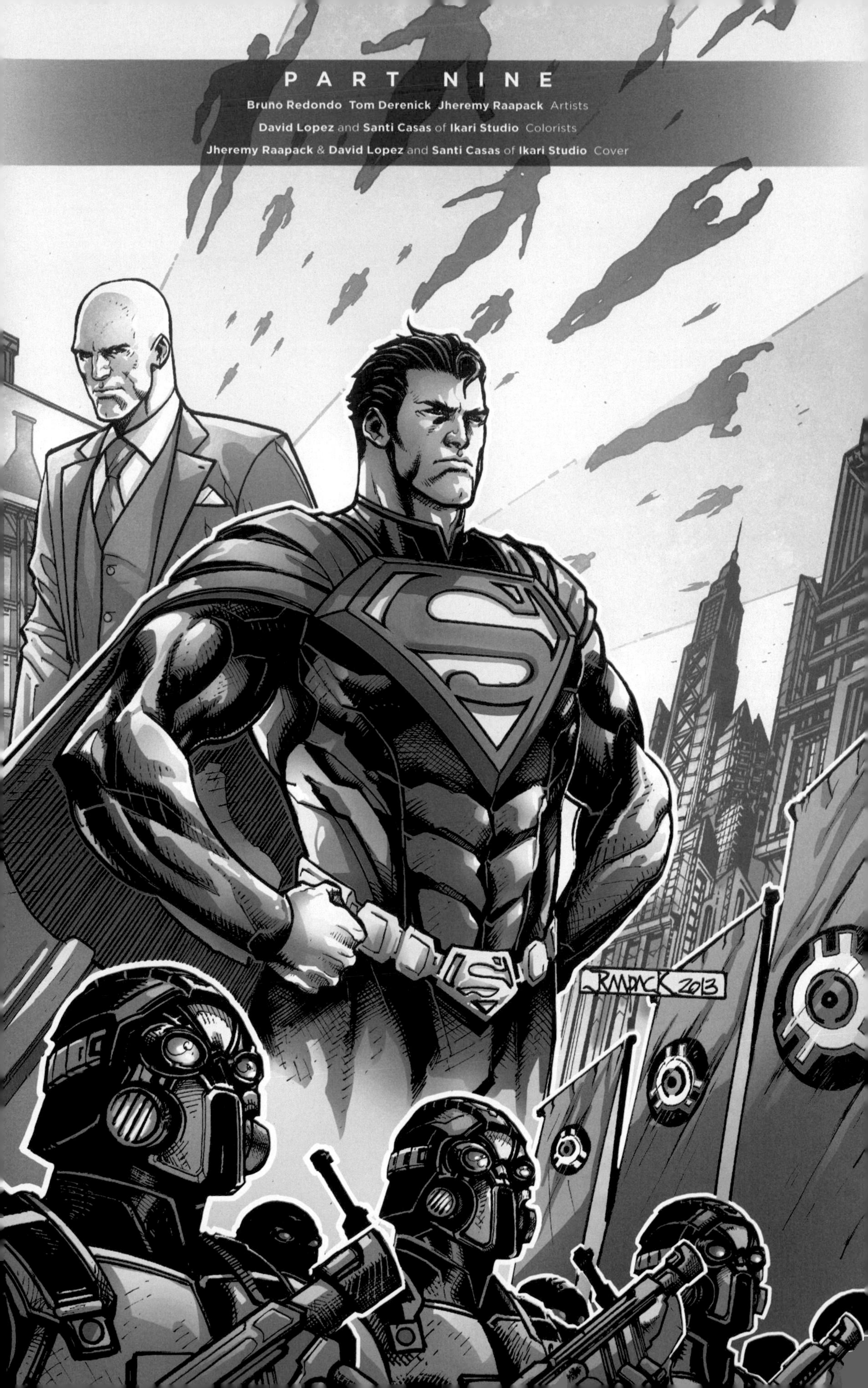

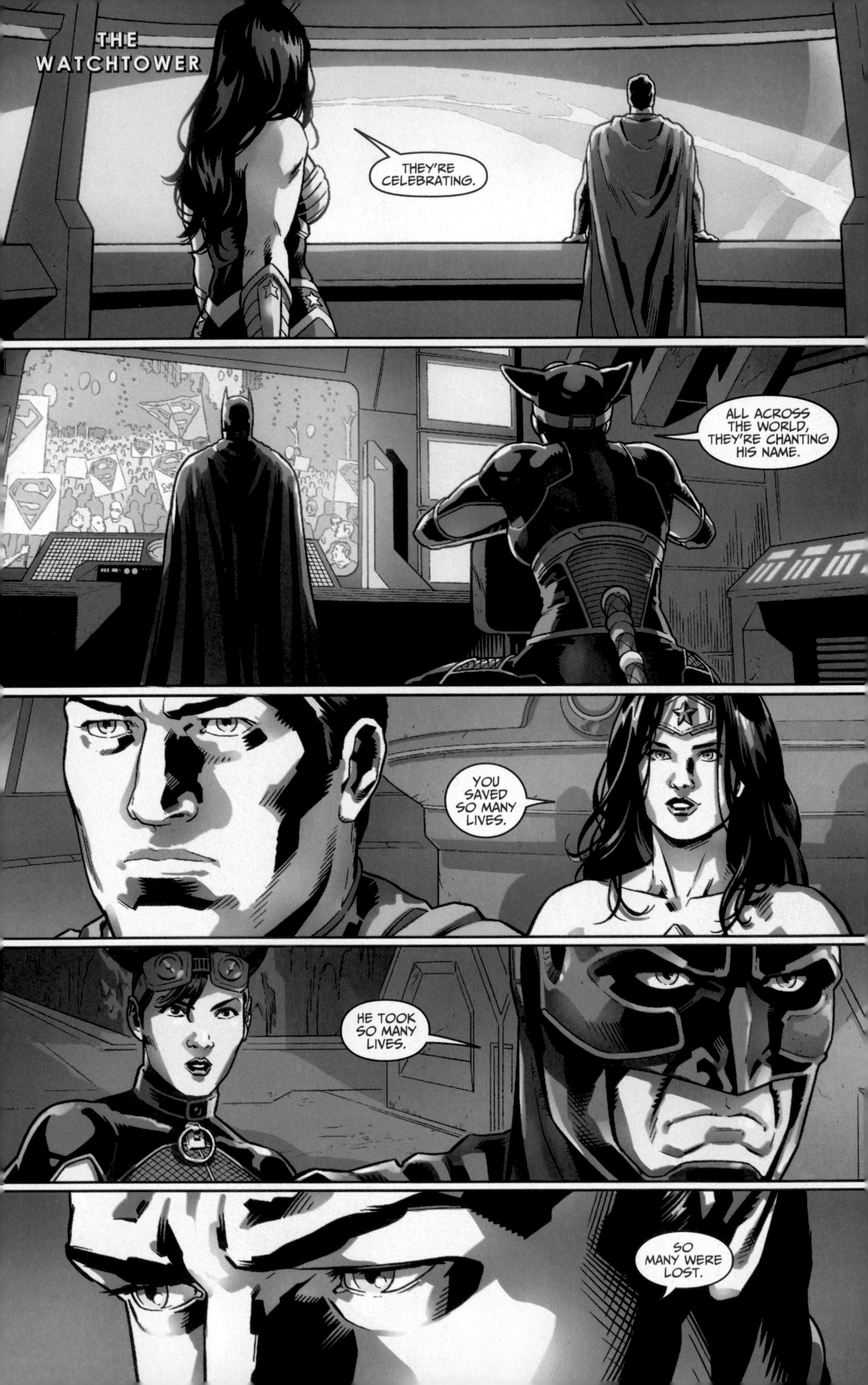
THE WATCHTOWER
THEY'RE CELEBRATING.
ALL ACROSS THE WORLD, THEY'RE CHANTING HIS NAME.
YOU SAVED SO MANY LIVES.
HE TOOK SO MANY LIVES.
SO MANY WERE LOST.

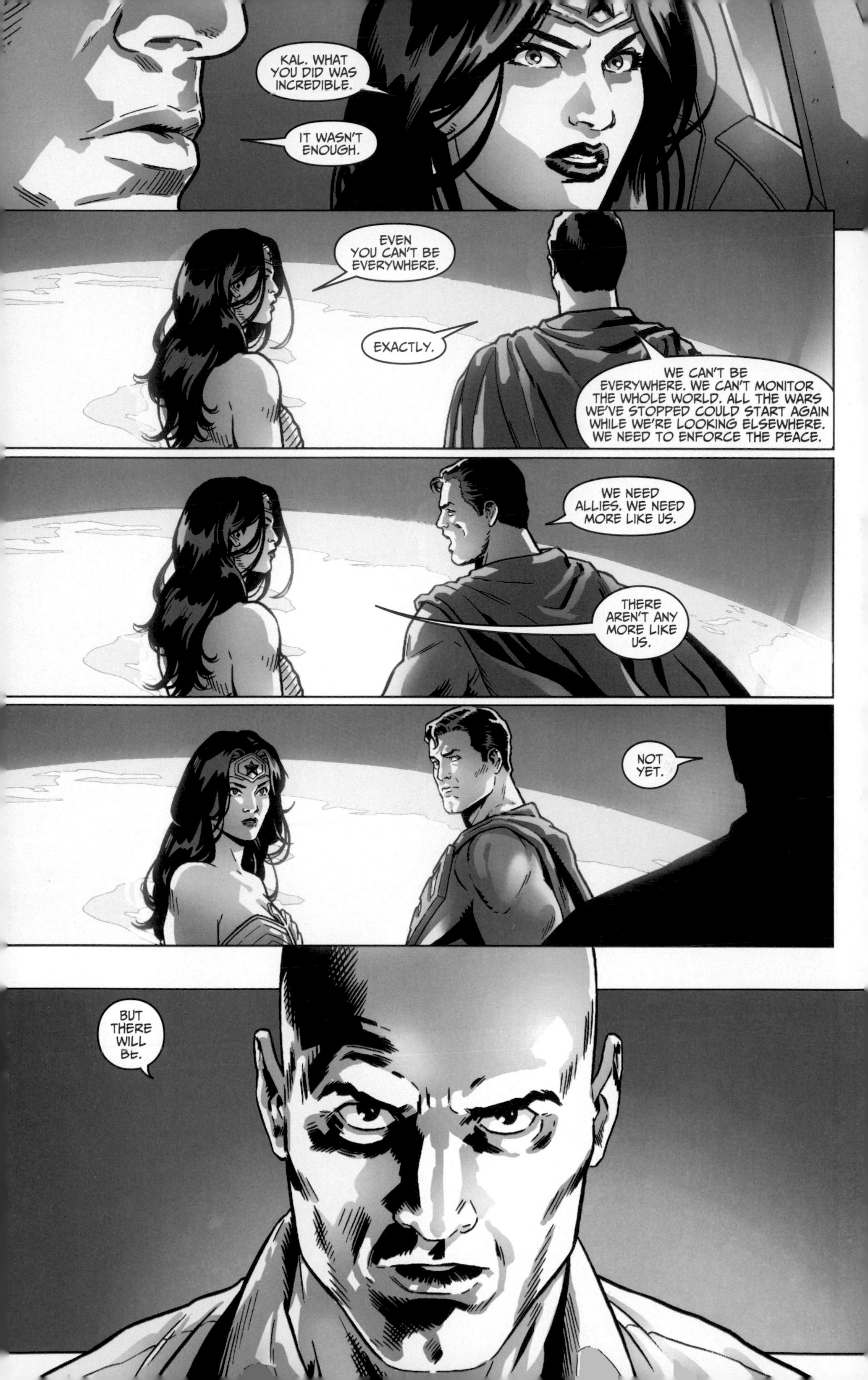
KAL. WHAT YOU DID WAS INCREDIBLE.
IT WASN'T ENOUGH.
EVEN YOU CAN'T BE EVERYWHERE.
EXACTLY.
WE CAN'T BE EVERYWHERE. WE CAN'T MONITOR THE WHOLE WORLD. ALL THE WARS WE'VE STOPPED COULD START AGAIN WHILE WE'RE LOOKING ELSEWHERE. WE NEED TO ENFORCE THE PEACE.
WE NEED ALLIES. WE NEED MORE LIKE US.
THERE AREN'T ANY MORE LIKE US.
NOT YET.
BUT THERE WILL BE.

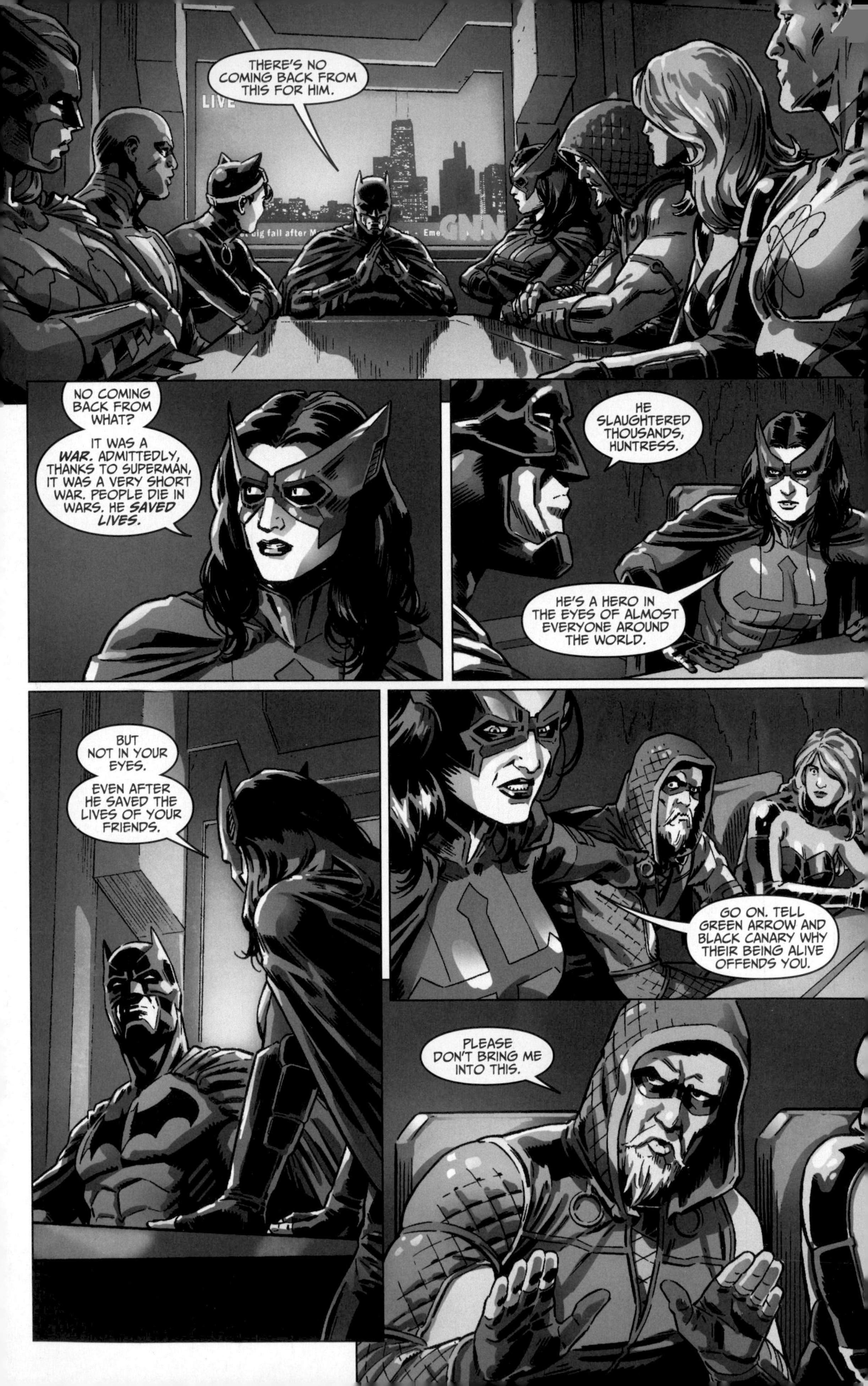

THERE'S NO COMING BACK FROM THIS FOR HIM.
LIVE
GNN
NO COMING BACK FROM WHAT?
IT WAS A WAR. ADMITTEDLY, THANKS TO SUPERMAN, IT WAS A VERY SHORT WAR. PEOPLE DIE IN WARS. HE SAVED LIVES.
HE SLAUGHTERED THOUSANDS, HUNTRESS.
HE'S A HERO IN THE EYES OF ALMOST EVERYONE AROUND THE WORLD.
BUT NOT IN YOUR EYES.
EVEN AFTER HE SAVED THE LIVES OF YOUR FRIENDS.
GO ON. TELL GREEN ARROW AND BLACK CANARY WHY THEIR BEING ALIVE OFFENDS YOU.
PLEASE DON'T BRING ME INTO THIS.

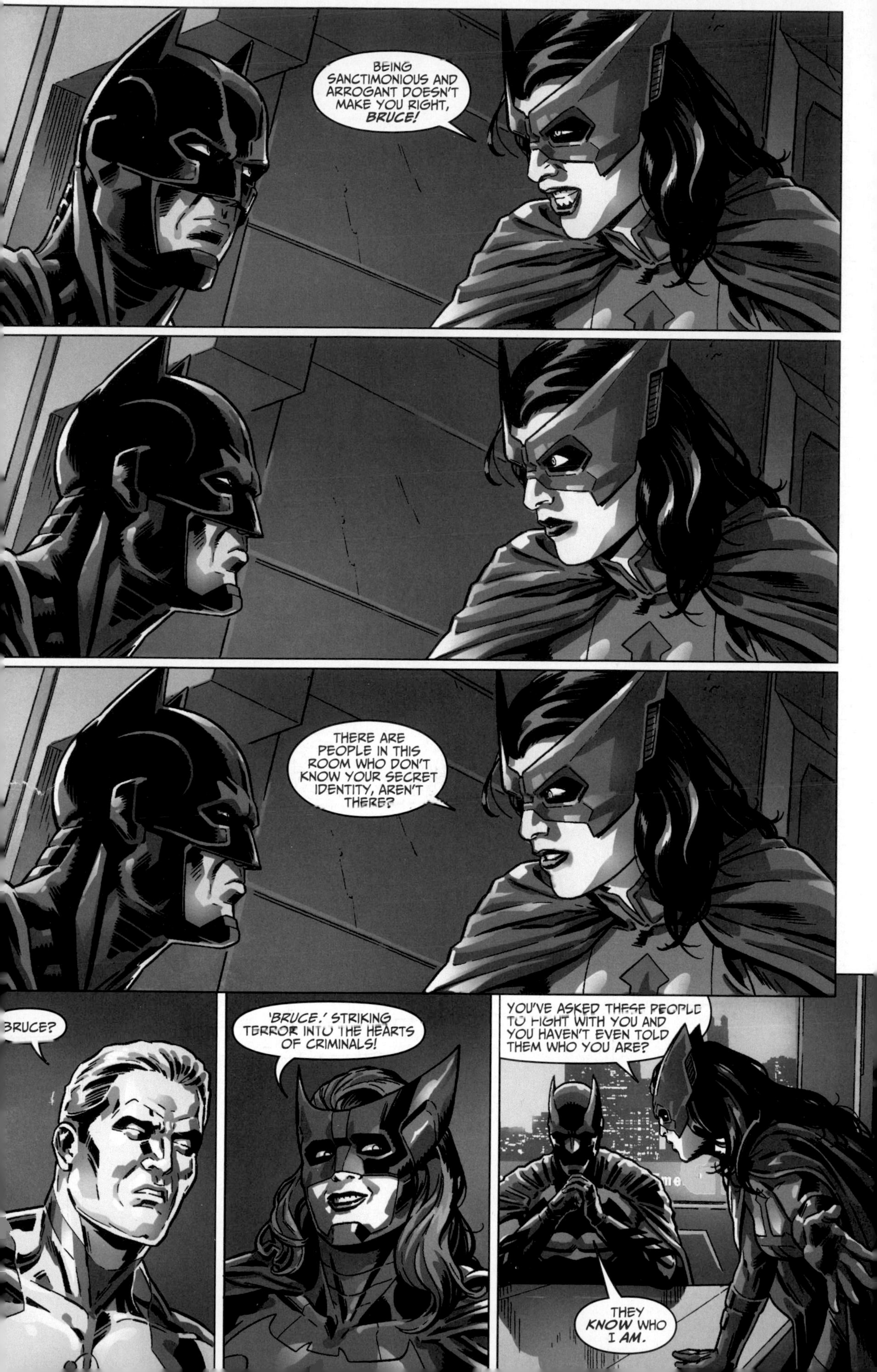
BEING SANCTIMONIOUS AND ARROGANT DOESN'T MAKE YOU RIGHT, BRUCE!
THERE ARE PEOPLE IN THIS ROOM WHO DON'T KNOW YOUR SECRET IDENTITY, AREN'T THERE?
BRUCE?
'BRUCE.' STRIKING TERROR INTO THE HEARTS OF CRIMINALS!
YOU'VE ASKED THESE PEOPLE TO FIGHT WITH YOU AND YOU HAVEN'T EVEN TOLD THEM WHO YOU ARE?
THEY KNOW WHO I AM.

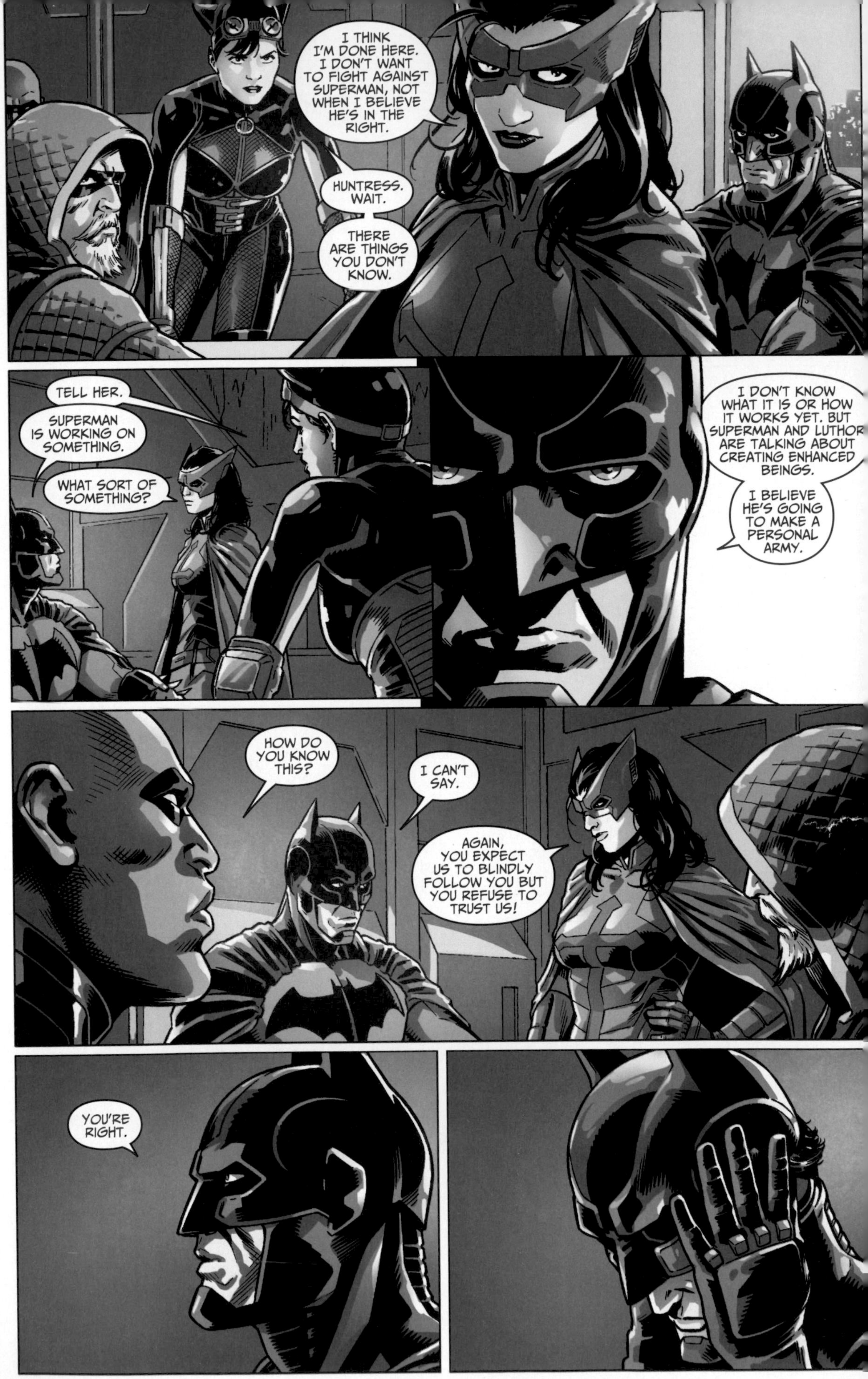
I THINK I'M DONE HERE. I DON'T WANT TO FIGHT AGAINST SUPERMAN, NOT WHEN I BELIEVE HE'S IN THE RIGHT.
HUNTRESS. WAIT.
THERE ARE THINGS YOU DON'T KNOW.
TELL HER.
SUPERMAN IS WORKING ON SOMETHING.
WHAT SORT OF SOMETHING?
I DON'T KNOW WHAT IT IS OR HOW IT WORKS YET. BUT SUPERMAN AND LUTHOR ARE TALKING ABOUT CREATING ENHANCED BEINGS.
I BELIEVE HE'S GOING TO MAKE A PERSONAL ARMY.
HOW DO YOU KNOW THIS?
I CAN'T SAY.
AGAIN, YOU EXPECT US TO BLINDLY FOLLOW YOU BUT YOU REFUSE TO TRUST US!
YOU'RE RIGHT.

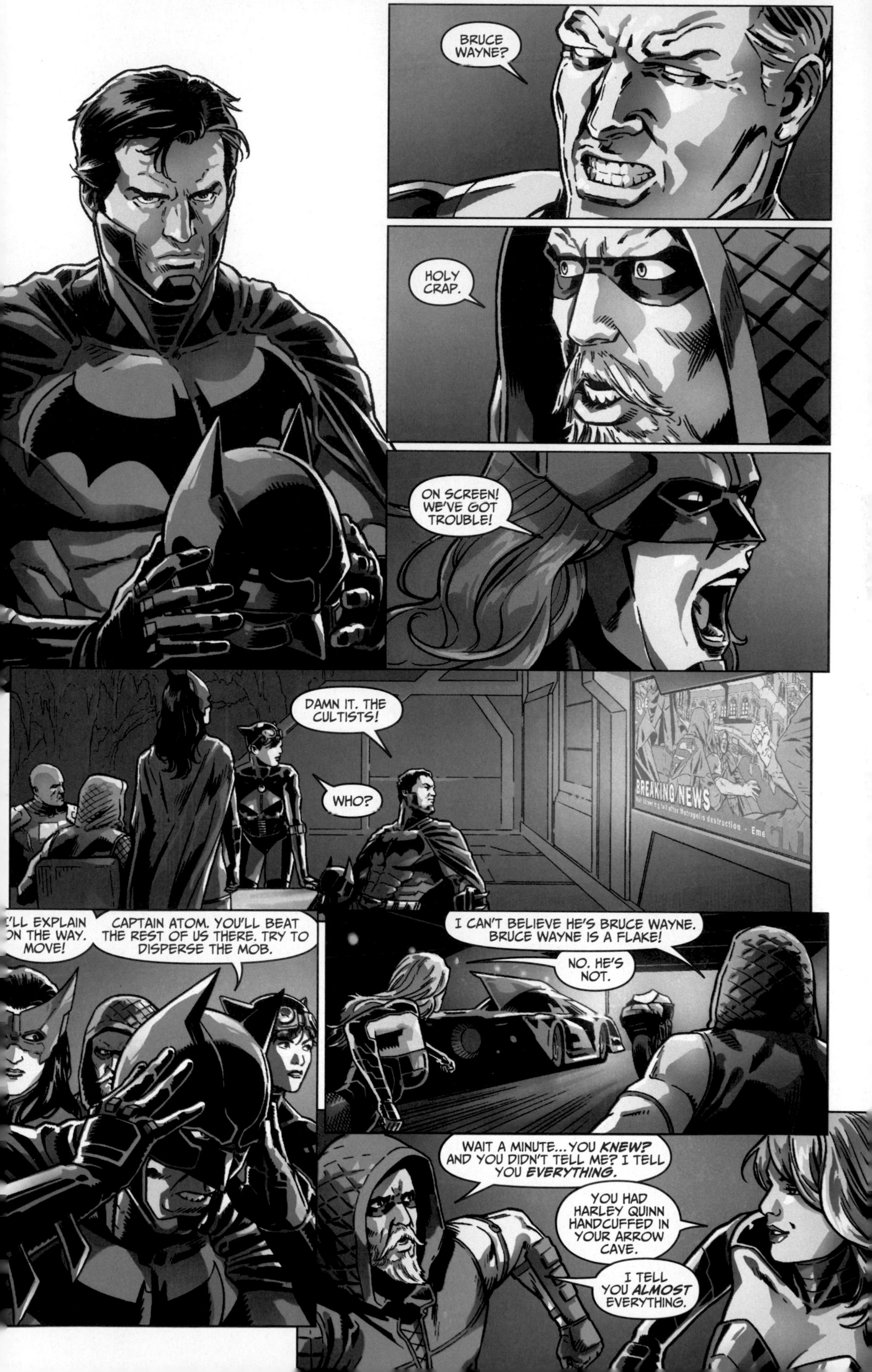

BRUCE WAYNE?
HOLY CRAP.
ON SCREEN! WE'VE GOT TROUBLE!
DAMN IT. THE CULTISTS!
WHO?
BREAKING NEWS
'LL EXPLAIN ON THE WAY. MOVE!
CAPTAIN ATOM. YOU'LL BEAT THE REST OF US THERE. TRY TO DISPERSE THE MOB.
I CAN'T BELIEVE HE'S BRUCE WAYNE. BRUCE WAYNE IS A FLAKE!
NO. HE'S NOT.
WAIT A MINUTE... YOU KNEW? AND YOU DIDN'T TELL ME? I TELL YOU EVERYTHING.
YOU HAD HARLEY QUINN HANDCUFFED IN YOUR ARROW CAVE.
I TELL YOU ALMOST EVERYTHING.

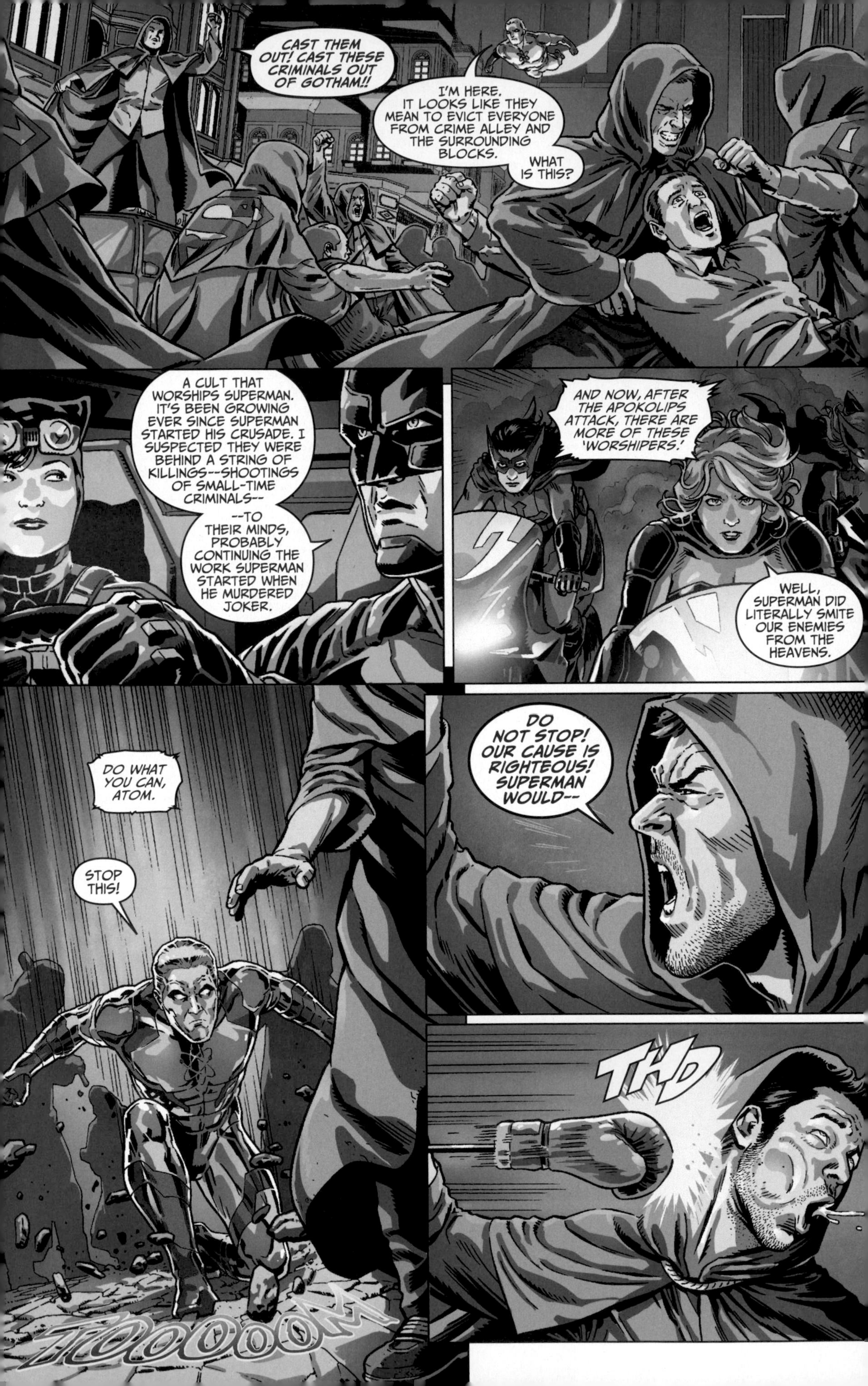
CAST THEM OUT! CAST THESE CRIMINALS OUT OF GOTHAM!!
I'M HERE. IT LOOKS LIKE THEY MEAN TO EVICT EVERYONE FROM CRIME ALLEY AND THE SURROUNDING BLOCKS.
WHAT IS THIS?
A CULT THAT WORSHIPS SUPERMAN. IT'S BEEN GROWING EVER SINCE SUPERMAN STARTED HIS CRUSADE. I SUSPECTED THEY WERE BEHIND A STRING OF KILLINGS--SHOOTINGS OF SMALL-TIME CRIMINALS--
--TO THEIR MINDS, PROBABLY CONTINUING THE WORK SUPERMAN STARTED WHEN HE MURDERED JOKER.
AND NOW, AFTER THE APOKOLIPS ATTACK, THERE ARE MORE OF THESE 'WORSHIPERS.'
WELL, SUPERMAN DID LITERALLY SMITE OUR ENEMIES FROM THE HEAVENS.
DO WHAT YOU CAN, ATOM.
STOP THIS!
TOOOOOOM
DO NOT STOP! OUR CAUSE IS RIGHTEOUS! SUPERMAN WOULD--
THD

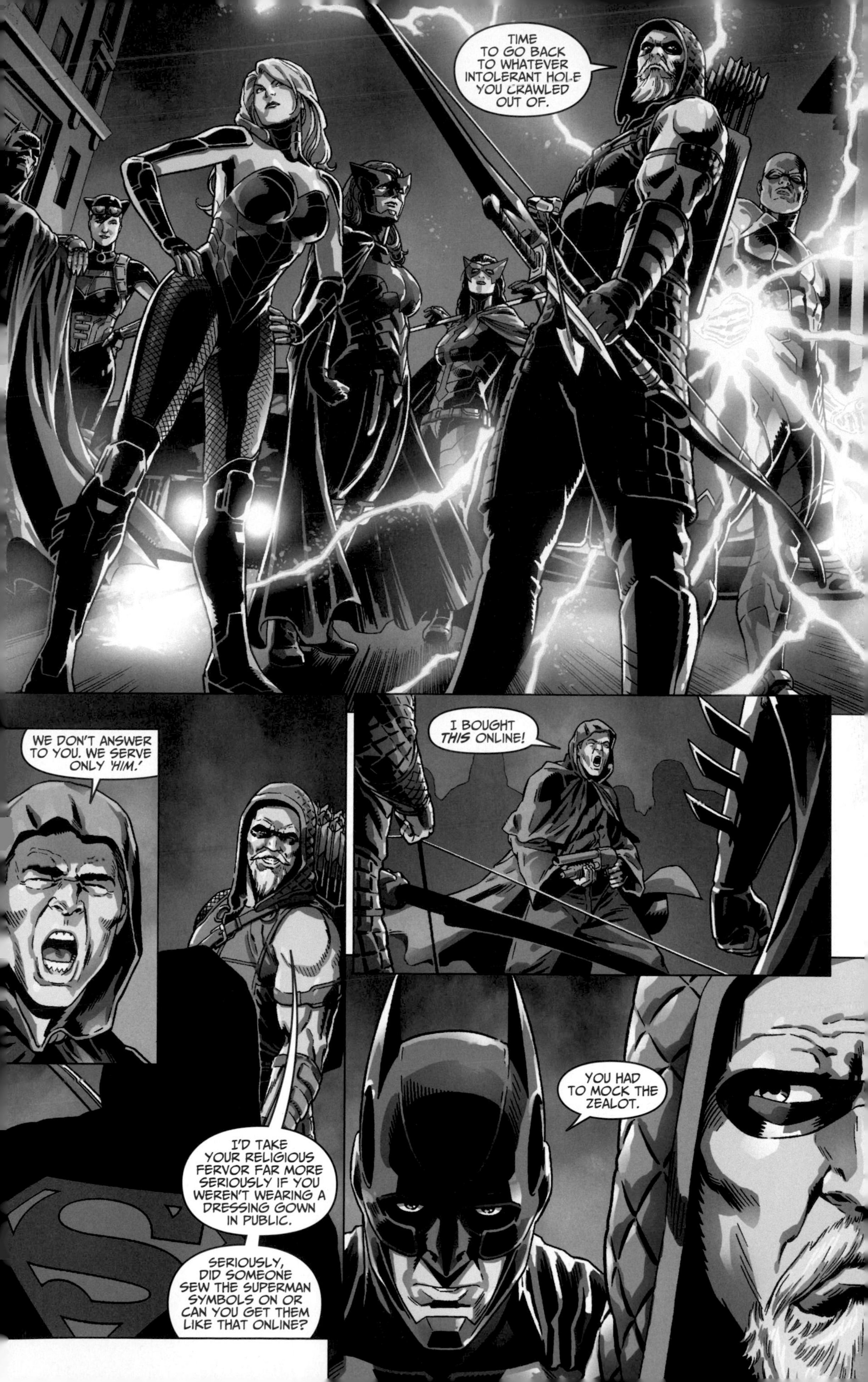
TIME TO GO BACK TO WHATEVER INTOLERANT HOLE YOU CRAWLED OUT OF.
WE DON'T ANSWER TO YOU. WE SERVE ONLY 'HIM.'
I BOUGHT *THIS* ONLINE!
I'D TAKE YOUR RELIGIOUS FERVOR FAR MORE SERIOUSLY IF YOU WEREN'T WEARING A DRESSING GOWN IN PUBLIC.
SERIOUSLY, DID SOMEONE SEW THE SUPERMAN SYMBOLS ON OR CAN YOU GET THEM LIKE THAT ONLINE?
YOU HAD TO MOCK THE ZEALOT.

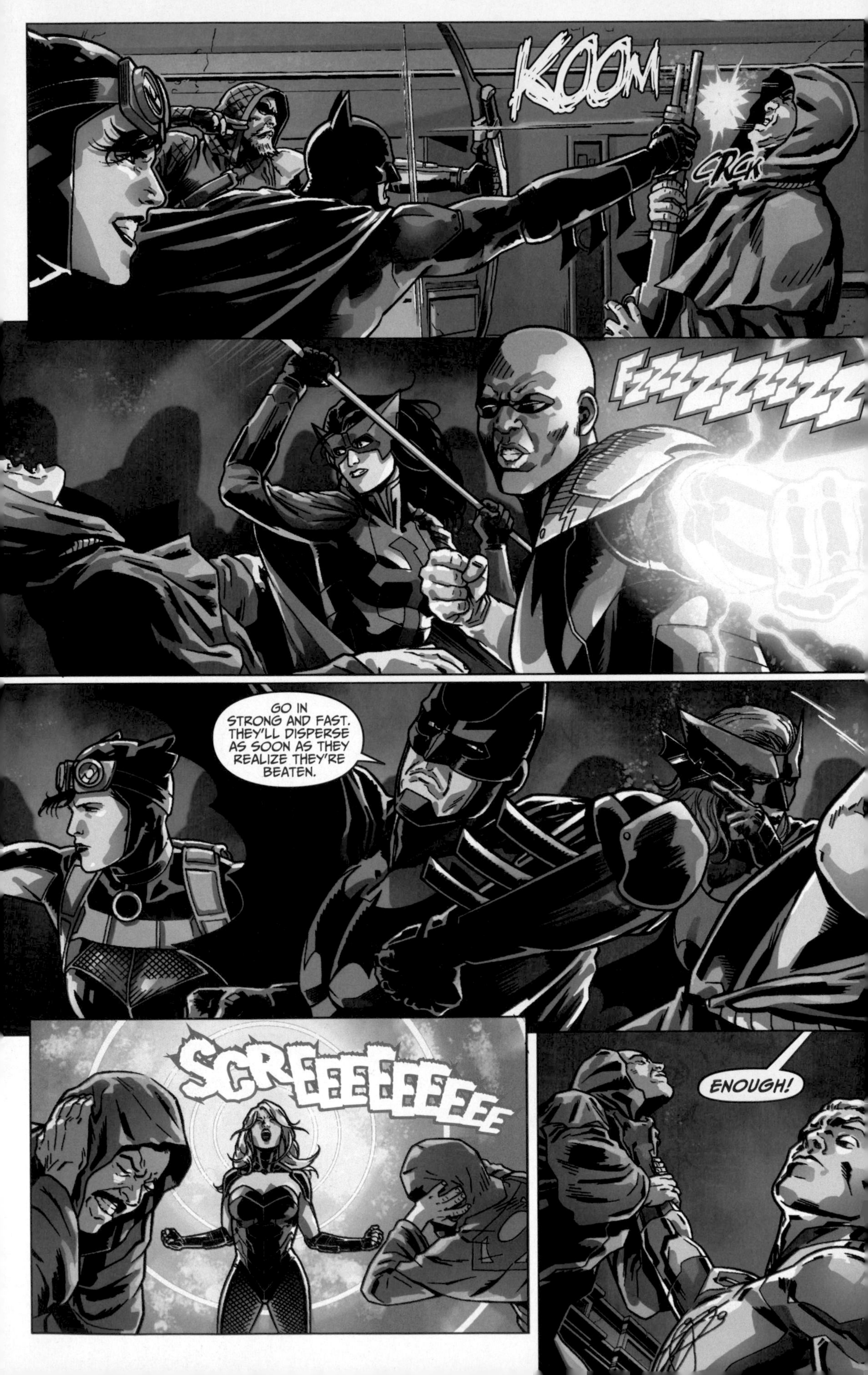
KOOM
CRCK
FZZZZZZZZ
GO IN STRONG AND FAST. THEY'LL DISPERSE AS SOON AS THEY REALIZE THEY'RE BEATEN.
SCREEEEEEEEEE
ENOUGH!

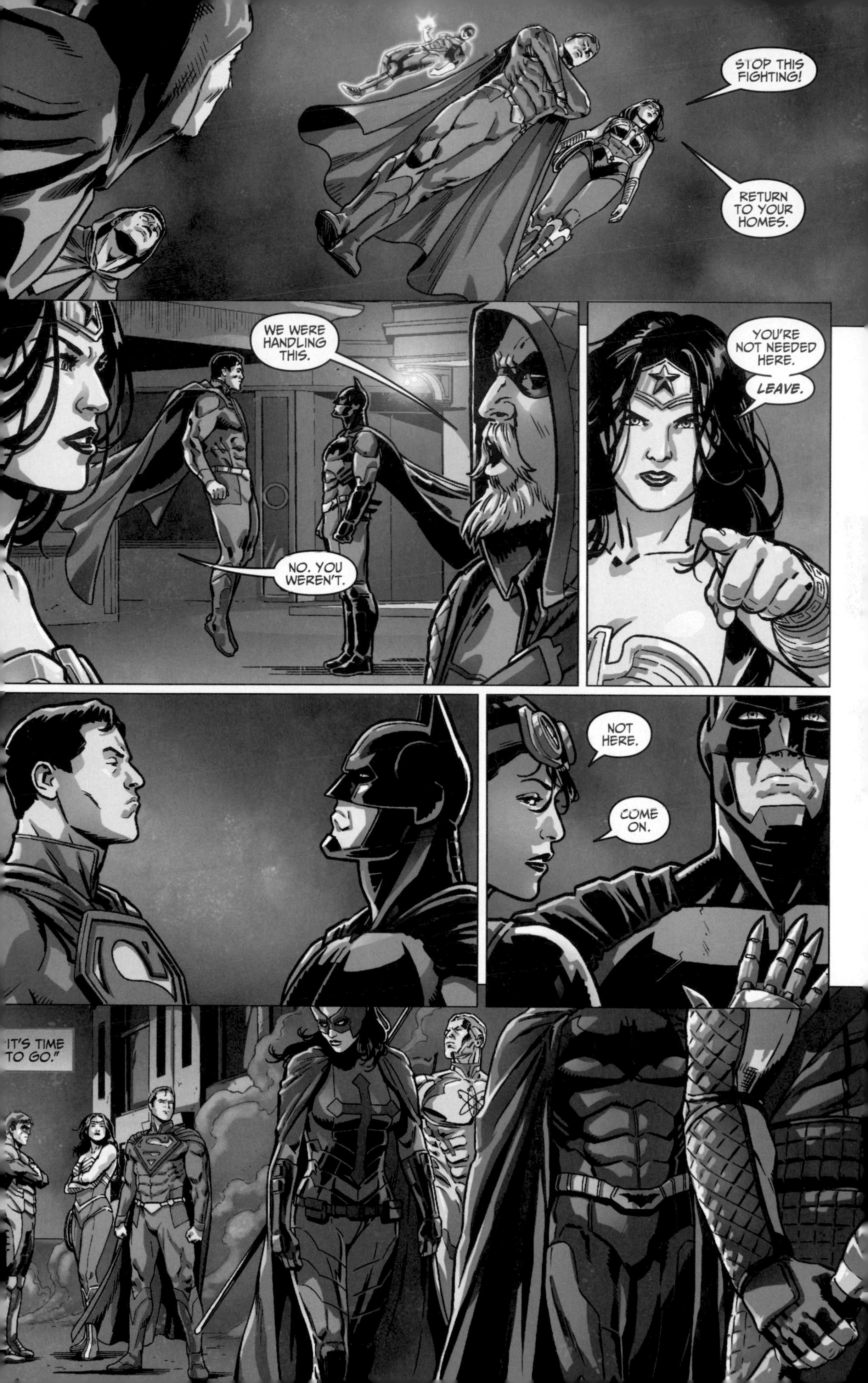
STOP THIS FIGHTING!
RETURN TO YOUR HOMES.
WE WERE HANDLING THIS.
NO. YOU WEREN'T.
YOU'RE NOT NEEDED HERE.
LEAVE.
NOT HERE.
COME ON.
"IT'S TIME TO GO."

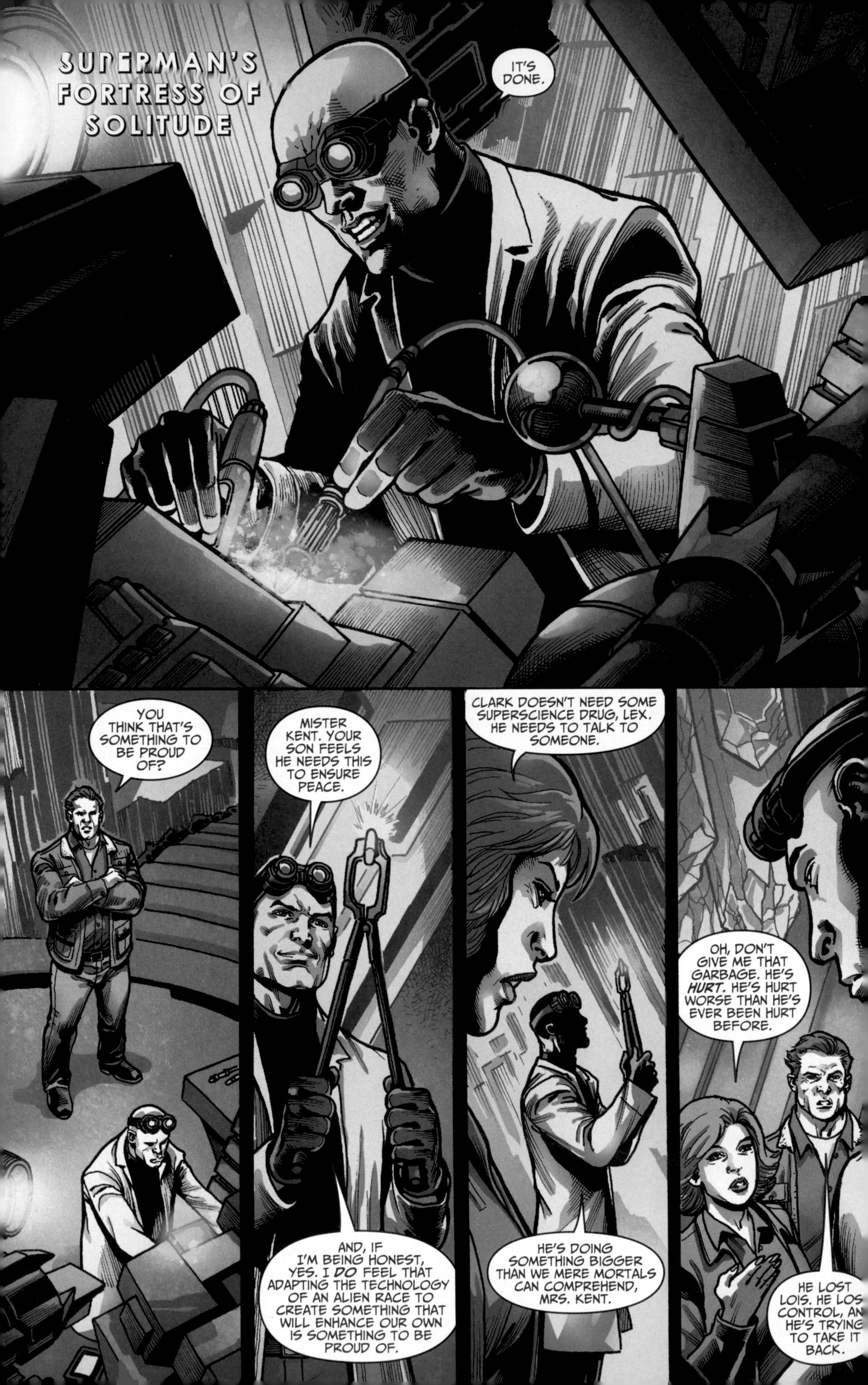
SUPERMAN'S FORTRESS OF SOLITUDE
IT'S DONE.
YOU THINK THAT'S SOMETHING TO BE PROUD OF?
MISTER KENT. YOUR SON FEELS HE NEEDS THIS TO ENSURE PEACE.
AND, IF I'M BEING HONEST, YES. I *DO* FEEL THAT ADAPTING THE TECHNOLOGY OF AN ALIEN RACE TO CREATE SOMETHING THAT WILL ENHANCE OUR OWN IS SOMETHING TO BE PROUD OF.
CLARK DOESN'T NEED SOME SUPERSCIENCE DRUG, LEX. HE NEEDS TO TALK TO SOMEONE.
HE'S DOING SOMETHING BIGGER THAN WE MERE MORTALS CAN COMPREHEND, MRS. KENT.
OH, DON'T GIVE ME THAT GARBAGE. HE'S *HURT*. HE'S HURT WORSE THAN HE'S EVER BEEN HURT BEFORE.
HE LOST LOIS. HE LOS CONTROL, AN HE'S TRYING TO TAKE IT BACK.

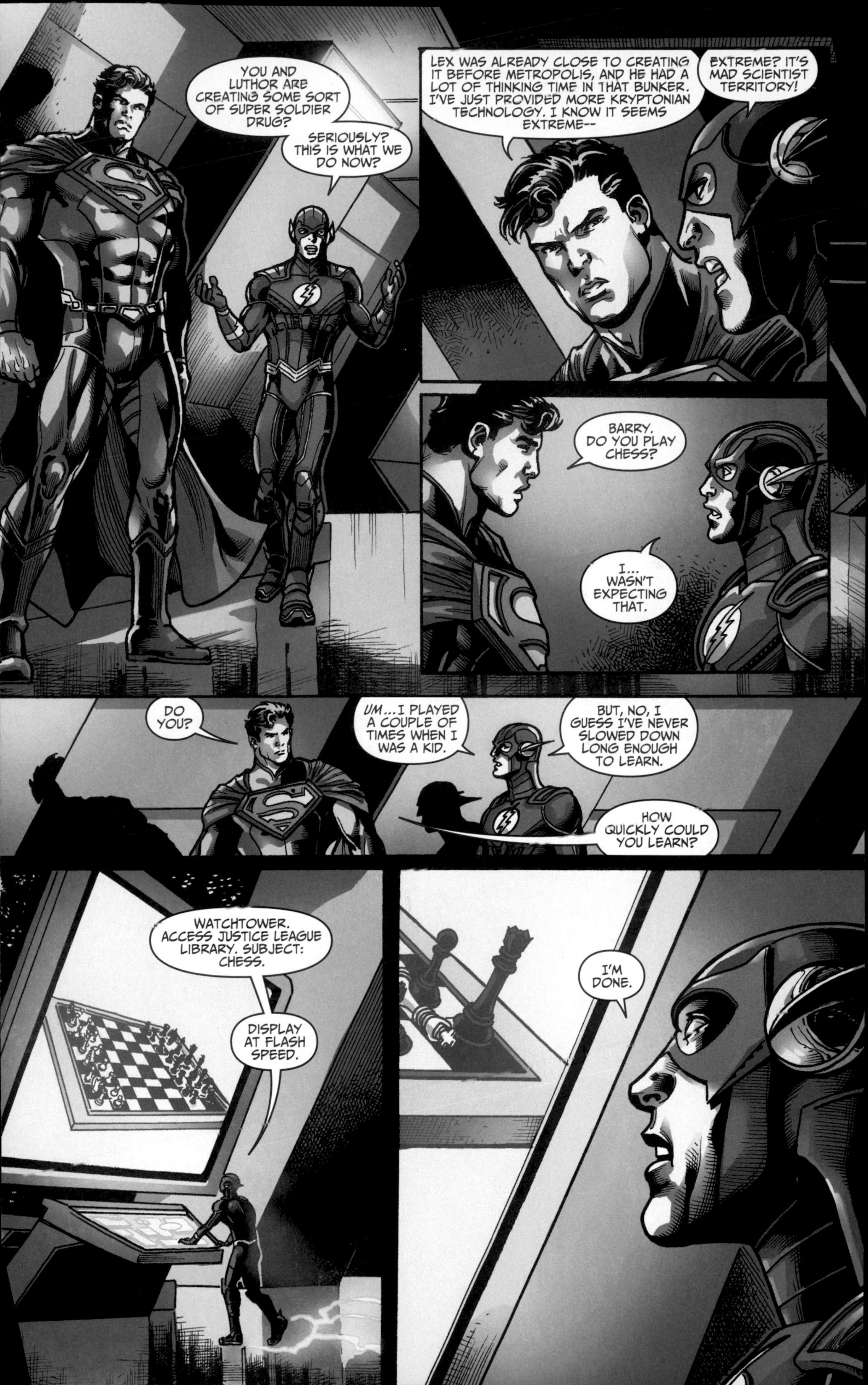
YOU AND LUTHOR ARE CREATING SOME SORT OF SUPER SOLDIER DRUG?
SERIOUSLY? THIS IS WHAT WE DO NOW?
LEX WAS ALREADY CLOSE TO CREATING IT BEFORE METROPOLIS, AND HE HAD A LOT OF THINKING TIME IN THAT BUNKER. I'VE JUST PROVIDED MORE KRYPTONIAN TECHNOLOGY. I KNOW IT SEEMS EXTREME--
EXTREME? IT'S MAD SCIENTIST TERRITORY!
BARRY. DO YOU PLAY CHESS?
I... WASN'T EXPECTING THAT.
DO YOU?
UM... I PLAYED A COUPLE OF TIMES WHEN I WAS A KID.
BUT, NO, I GUESS I'VE NEVER SLOWED DOWN LONG ENOUGH TO LEARN.
HOW QUICKLY COULD YOU LEARN?
WATCHTOWER. ACCESS JUSTICE LEAGUE LIBRARY. SUBJECT: CHESS.
DISPLAY AT FLASH SPEED.
I'M DONE.

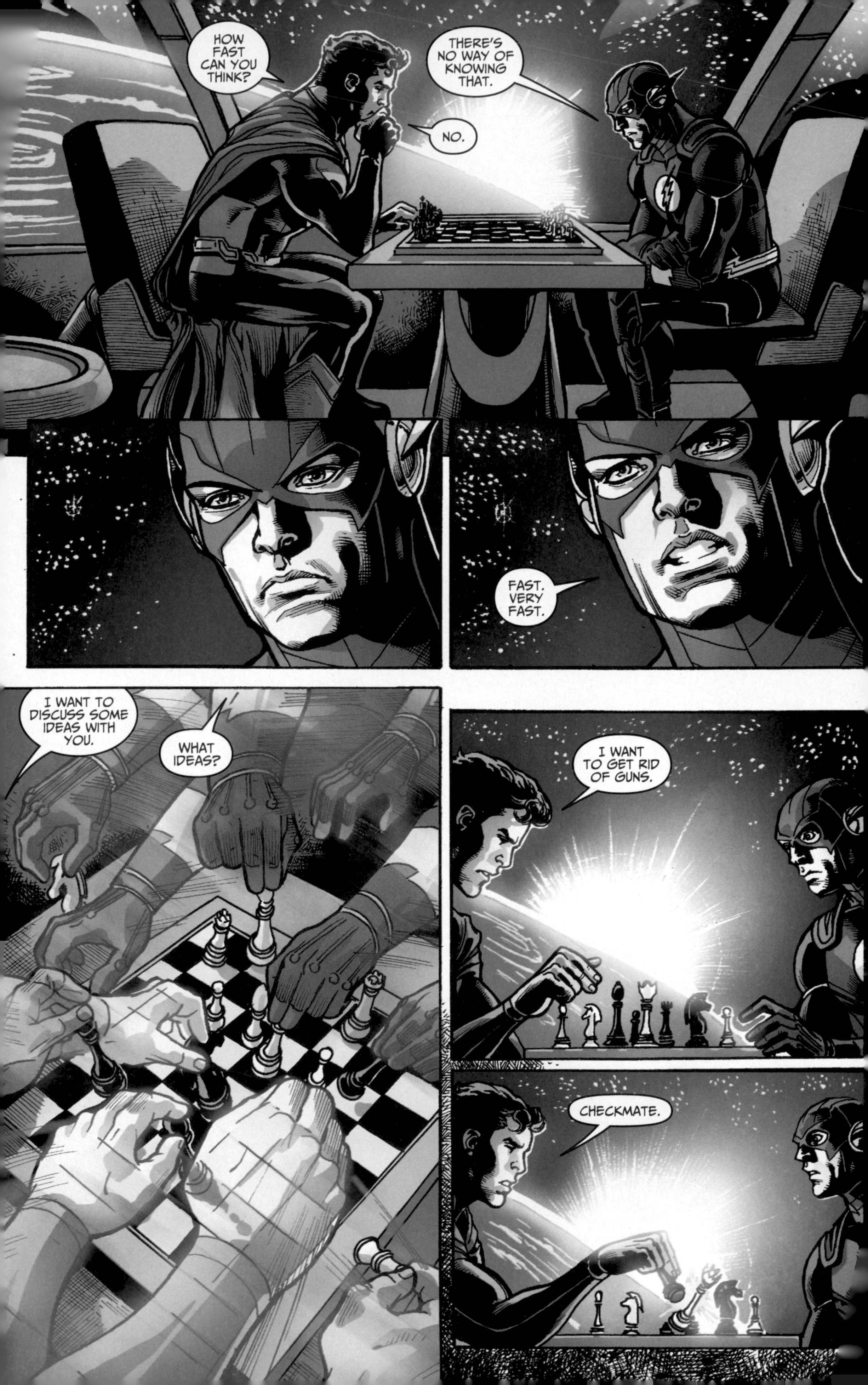
HOW FAST CAN YOU THINK?
THERE'S NO WAY OF KNOWING THAT.
NO.
FAST. VERY FAST.
I WANT TO DISCUSS SOME IDEAS WITH YOU.
WHAT IDEAS?
I WANT TO GET RID OF GUNS.
CHECKMATE.

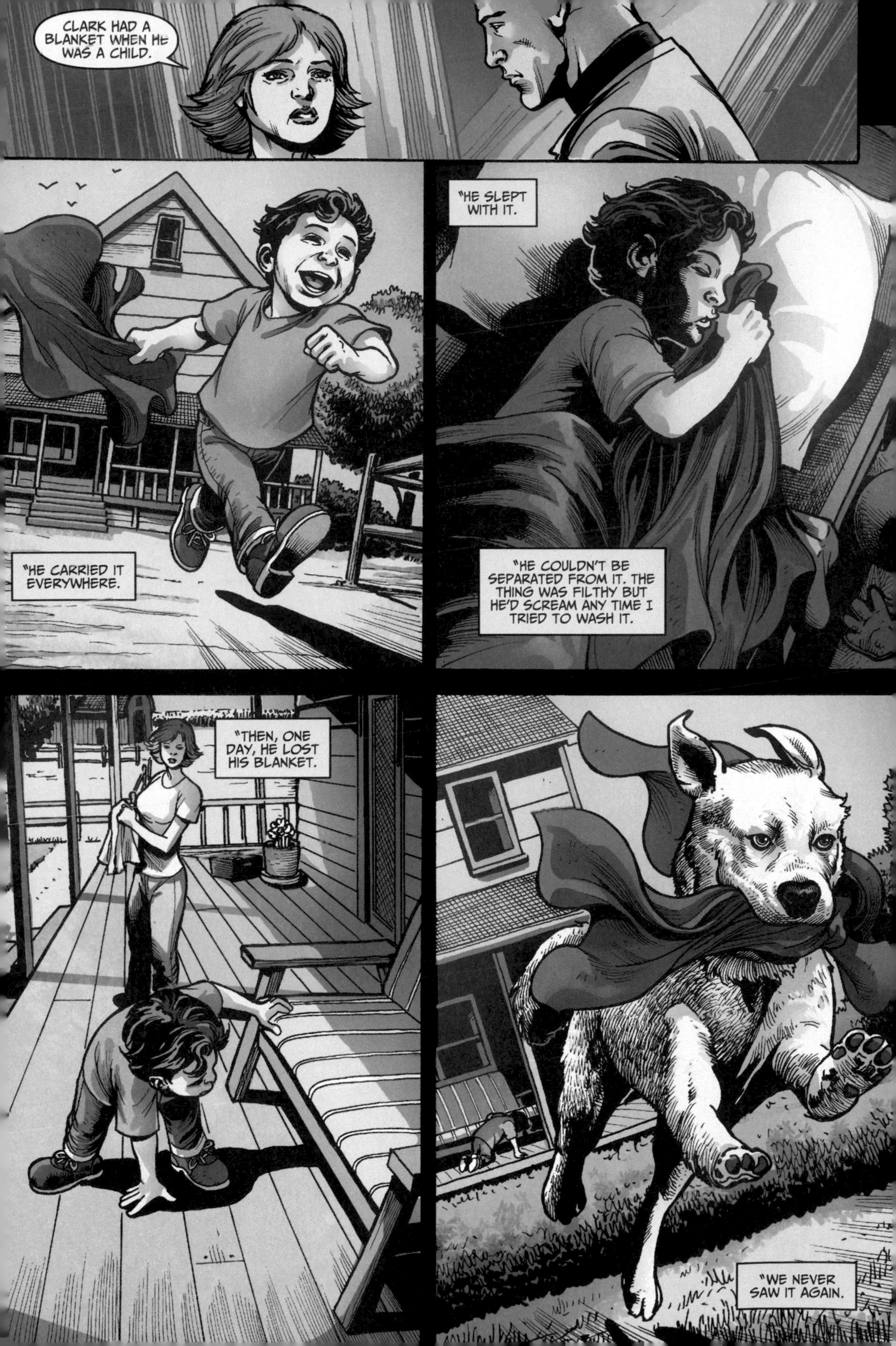
CLARK HAD A BLANKET WHEN HE WAS A CHILD.
"HE CARRIED IT EVERYWHERE.
"HE SLEPT WITH IT.
"HE COULDN'T BE SEPARATED FROM IT. THE THING WAS FILTHY BUT HE'D SCREAM ANY TIME I TRIED TO WASH IT.
"THEN, ONE DAY, HE LOST HIS BLANKET.
"WE NEVER SAW IT AGAIN.

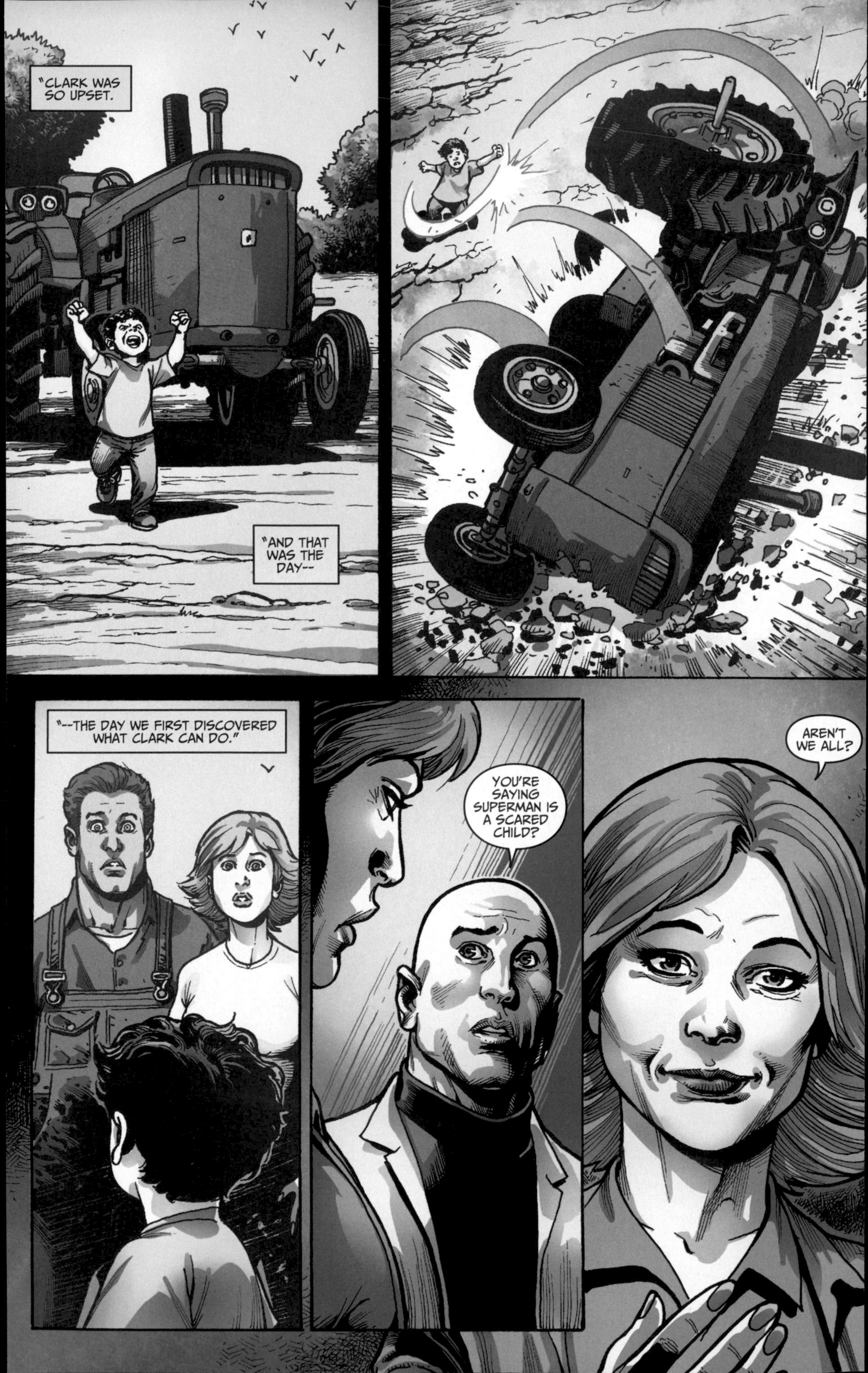
"CLARK WAS SO UPSET.
"AND THAT WAS THE DAY--
"--THE DAY WE FIRST DISCOVERED WHAT CLARK CAN DO."
YOU'RE SAYING SUPERMAN IS A SCARED CHILD?
AREN'T WE ALL?

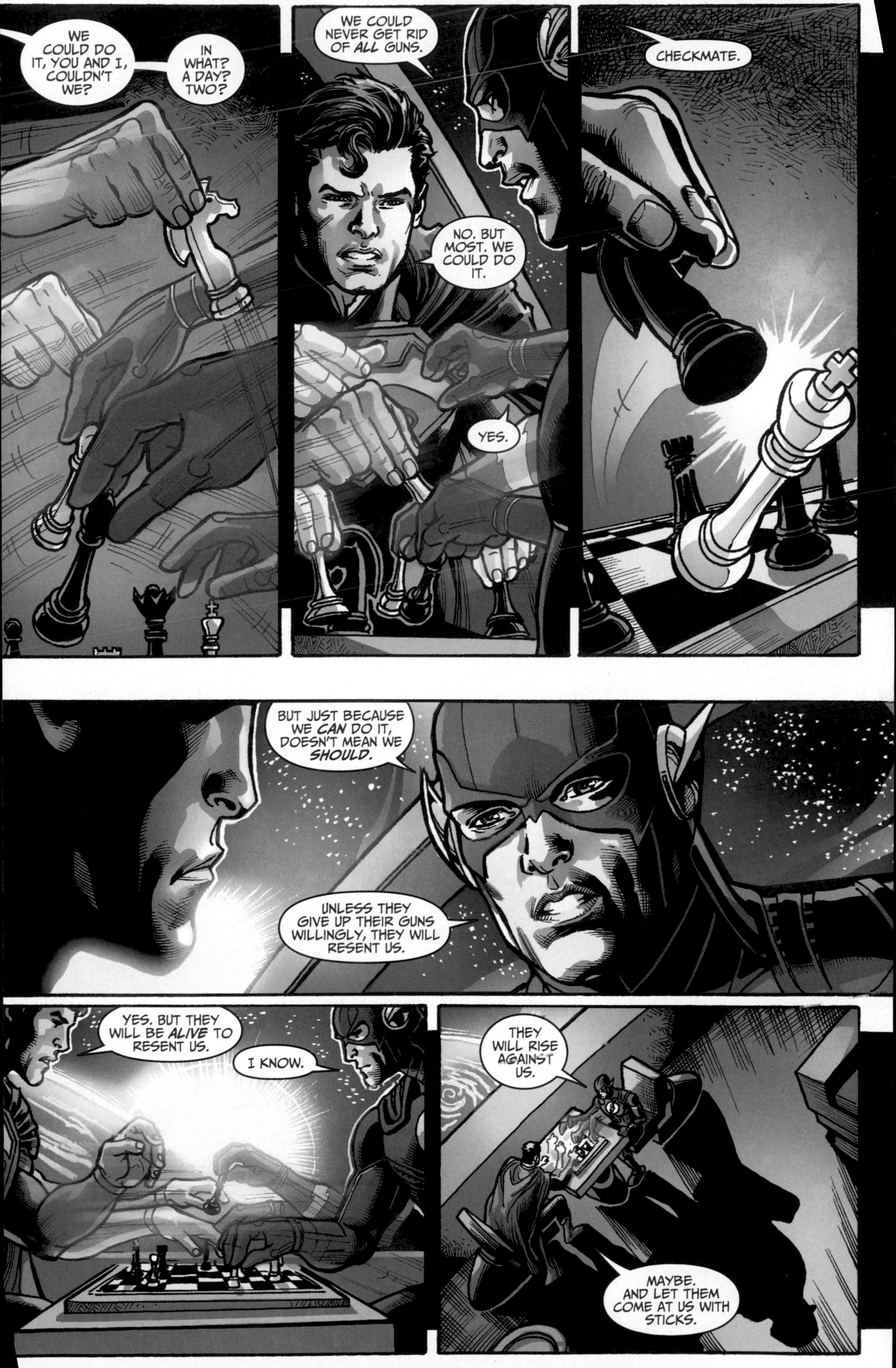
WE COULD DO IT, YOU AND I, COULDN'T WE?
IN WHAT? A DAY? TWO?
WE COULD NEVER GET RID OF ALL GUNS.
NO. BUT MOST. WE COULD DO IT.
YES.
CHECKMATE.
BUT JUST BECAUSE WE CAN DO IT, DOESN'T MEAN WE SHOULD.
UNLESS THEY GIVE UP THEIR GUNS WILLINGLY, THEY WILL RESENT US.
YES. BUT THEY WILL BE ALIVE TO RESENT US.
I KNOW.
THEY WILL RISE AGAINST US.
MAYBE. AND LET THEM COME AT US WITH STICKS.

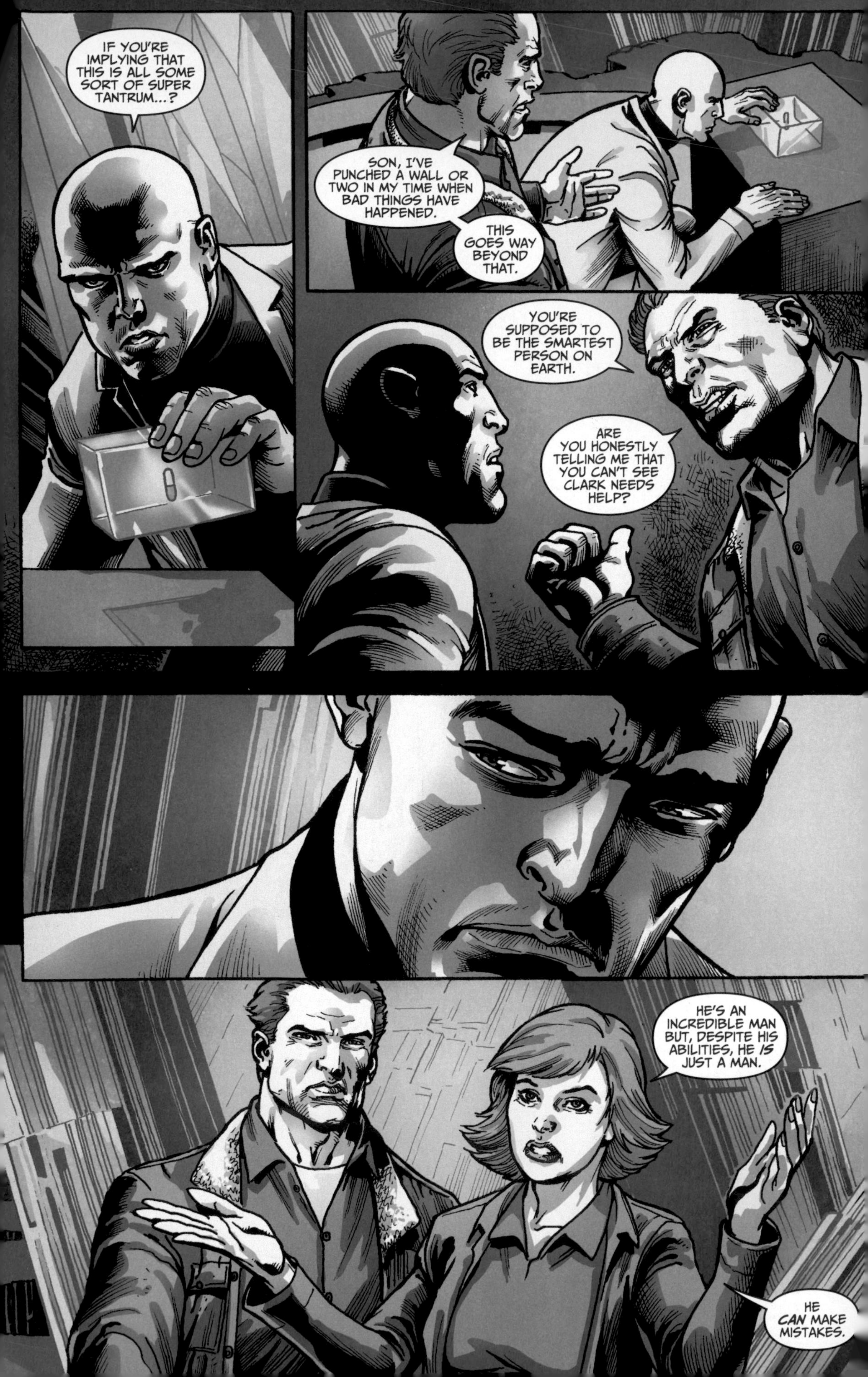
IF YOU'RE IMPLYING THAT THIS IS ALL SOME SORT OF SUPER TANTRUM...?
SON, I'VE PUNCHED A WALL OR TWO IN MY TIME WHEN BAD THINGS HAVE HAPPENED.
THIS GOES WAY BEYOND THAT.
YOU'RE SUPPOSED TO BE THE SMARTEST PERSON ON EARTH.
ARE YOU HONESTLY TELLING ME THAT YOU CAN'T SEE CLARK NEEDS HELP?
HE'S AN INCREDIBLE MAN BUT, DESPITE HIS ABILITIES, HE IS JUST A MAN.
HE CAN MAKE MISTAKES.

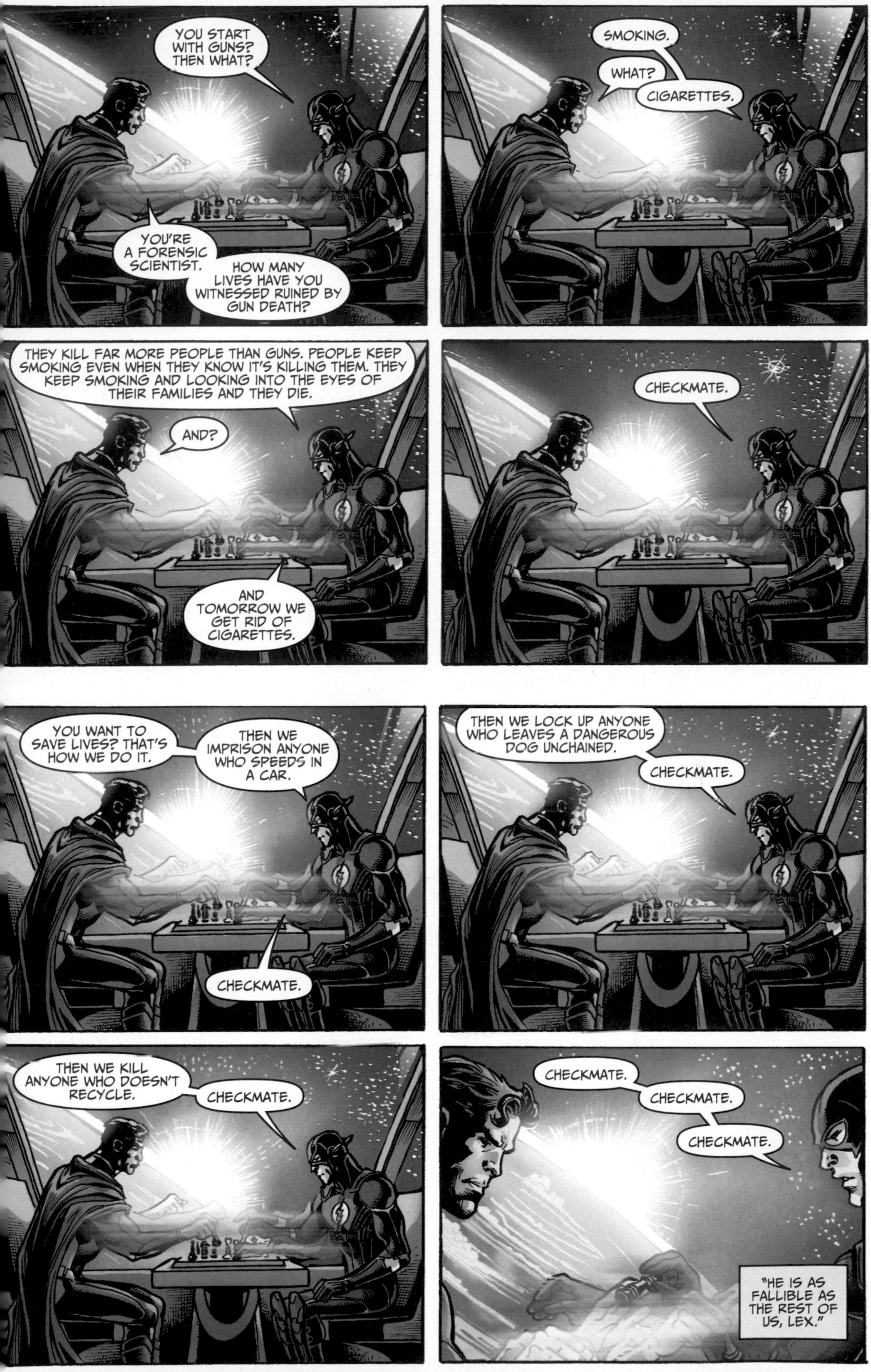
YOU START WITH GUNS? THEN WHAT?
YOU'RE A FORENSIC SCIENTIST.
HOW MANY LIVES HAVE YOU WITNESSED RUINED BY GUN DEATH?
SMOKING.
WHAT?
CIGARETTES.
THEY KILL FAR MORE PEOPLE THAN GUNS. PEOPLE KEEP SMOKING EVEN WHEN THEY KNOW IT'S KILLING THEM. THEY KEEP SMOKING AND LOOKING INTO THE EYES OF THEIR FAMILIES AND THEY DIE.
AND?
AND TOMORROW WE GET RID OF CIGARETTES.
CHECKMATE.
YOU WANT TO SAVE LIVES? THAT'S HOW WE DO IT.
THEN WE IMPRISON ANYONE WHO SPEEDS IN A CAR.
CHECKMATE.
THEN WE LOCK UP ANYONE WHO LEAVES A DANGEROUS DOG UNCHAINED.
CHECKMATE.
THEN WE KILL ANYONE WHO DOESN'T RECYCLE.
CHECKMATE.
CHECKMATE.
CHECKMATE.
CHECKMATE.
"HE IS AS FALLIBLE AS THE REST OF US, LEX."

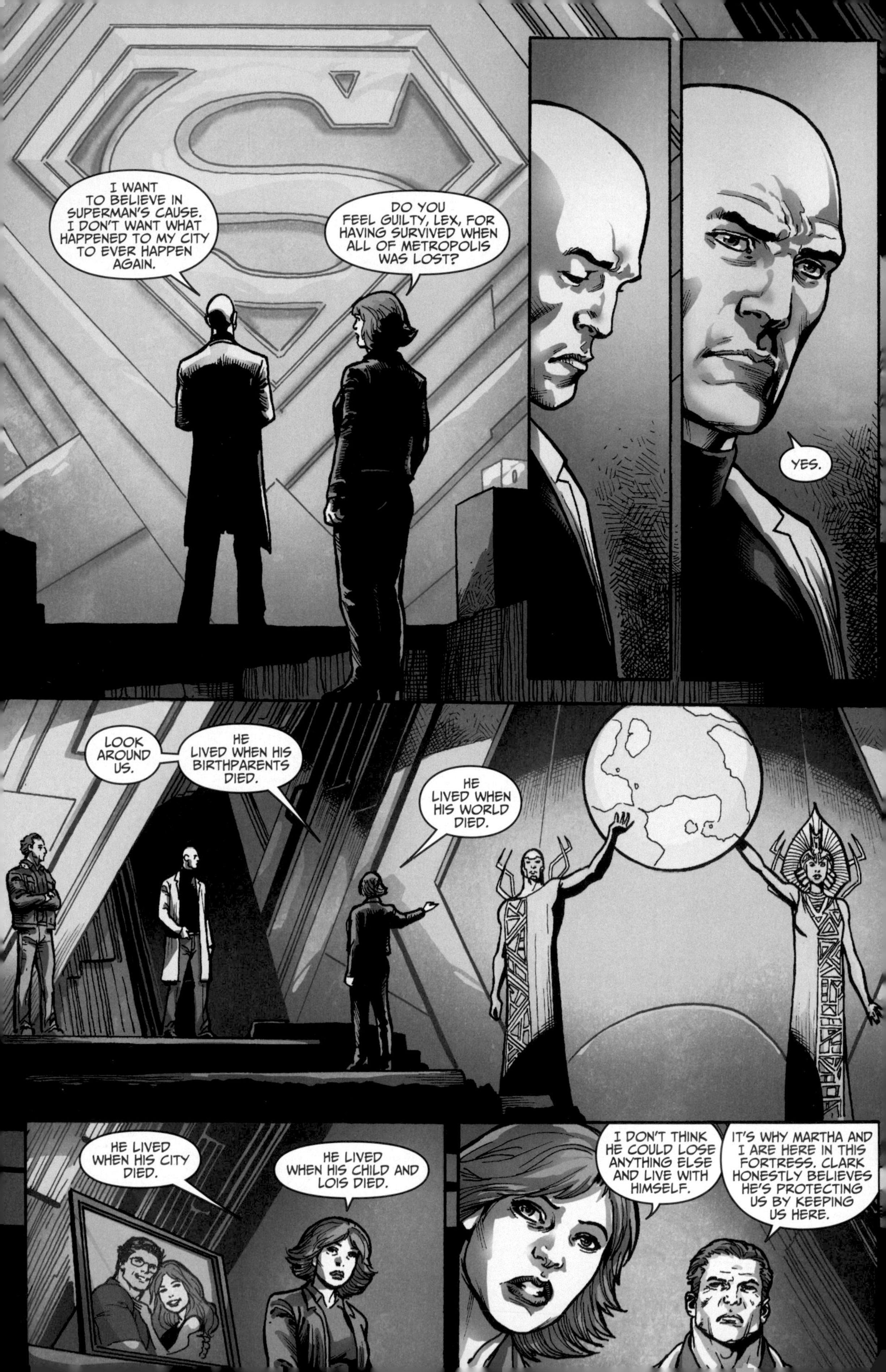
I WANT TO BELIEVE IN SUPERMAN'S CAUSE. I DON'T WANT WHAT HAPPENED TO MY CITY TO EVER HAPPEN AGAIN.
DO YOU FEEL GUILTY, LEX, FOR HAVING SURVIVED WHEN ALL OF METROPOLIS WAS LOST?
YES.
LOOK AROUND US.
HE LIVED WHEN HIS BIRTHPARENTS DIED.
HE LIVED WHEN HIS WORLD DIED.
HE LIVED WHEN HIS CITY DIED.
HE LIVED WHEN HIS CHILD AND LOIS DIED.
I DON'T THINK HE COULD LOSE ANYTHING ELSE AND LIVE WITH HIMSELF.
IT'S WHY MARTHA AND I ARE HERE IN THIS FORTRESS. CLARK HONESTLY BELIEVES HE'S PROTECTING US BY KEEPING US HERE.

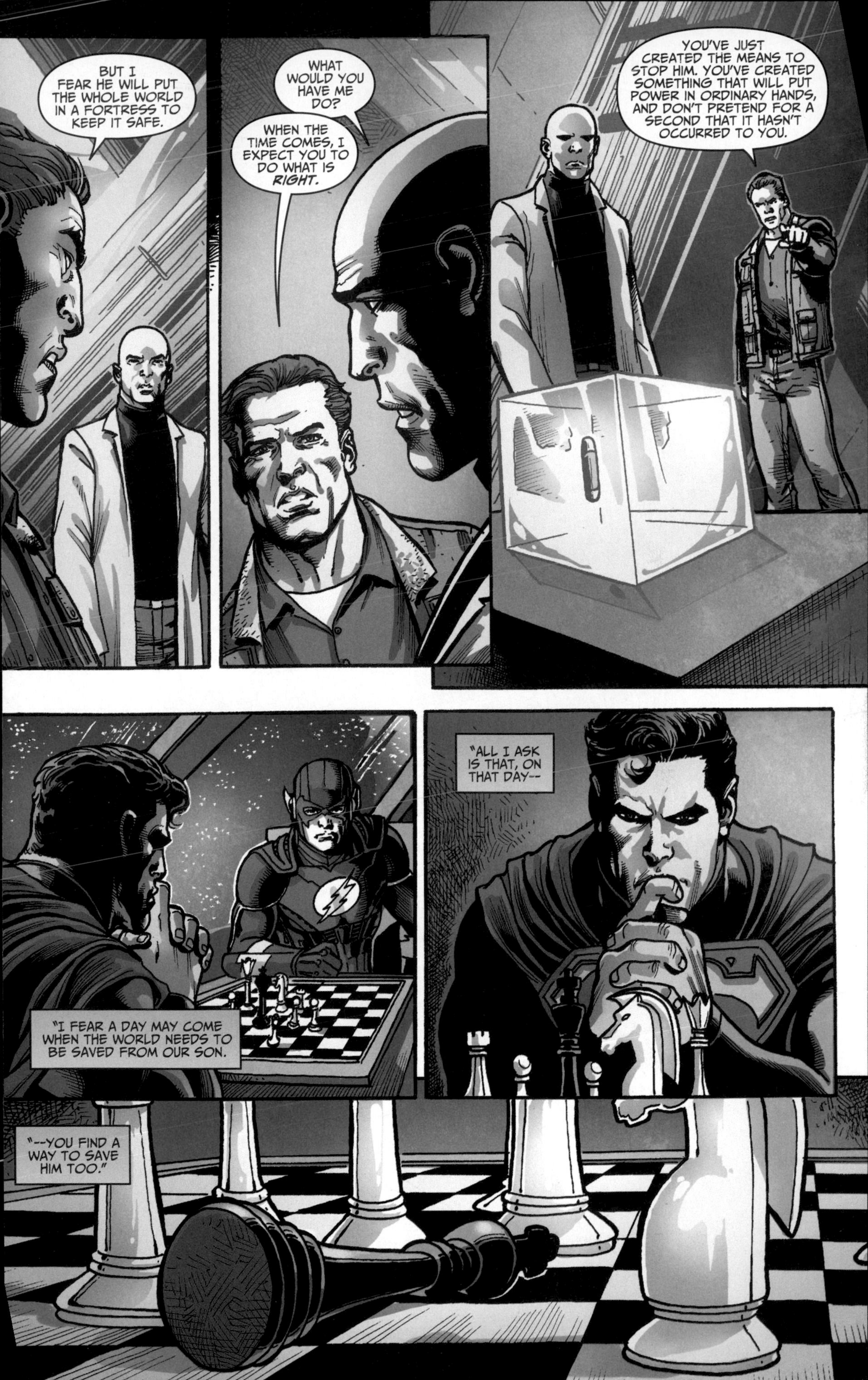
BUT I FEAR HE WILL PUT THE WHOLE WORLD IN A FORTRESS TO KEEP IT SAFE.
WHAT WOULD YOU HAVE ME DO?
WHEN THE TIME COMES, I EXPECT YOU TO DO WHAT IS *RIGHT.*
YOU'VE JUST CREATED THE MEANS TO STOP HIM. YOU'VE CREATED SOMETHING THAT WILL PUT POWER IN ORDINARY HANDS, AND DON'T PRETEND FOR A SECOND THAT IT HASN'T OCCURRED TO YOU.
"I FEAR A DAY MAY COME WHEN THE WORLD NEEDS TO BE SAVED FROM OUR SON.
"ALL I ASK IS THAT, ON THAT DAY--
"--YOU FIND A WAY TO SAVE HIM TOO."

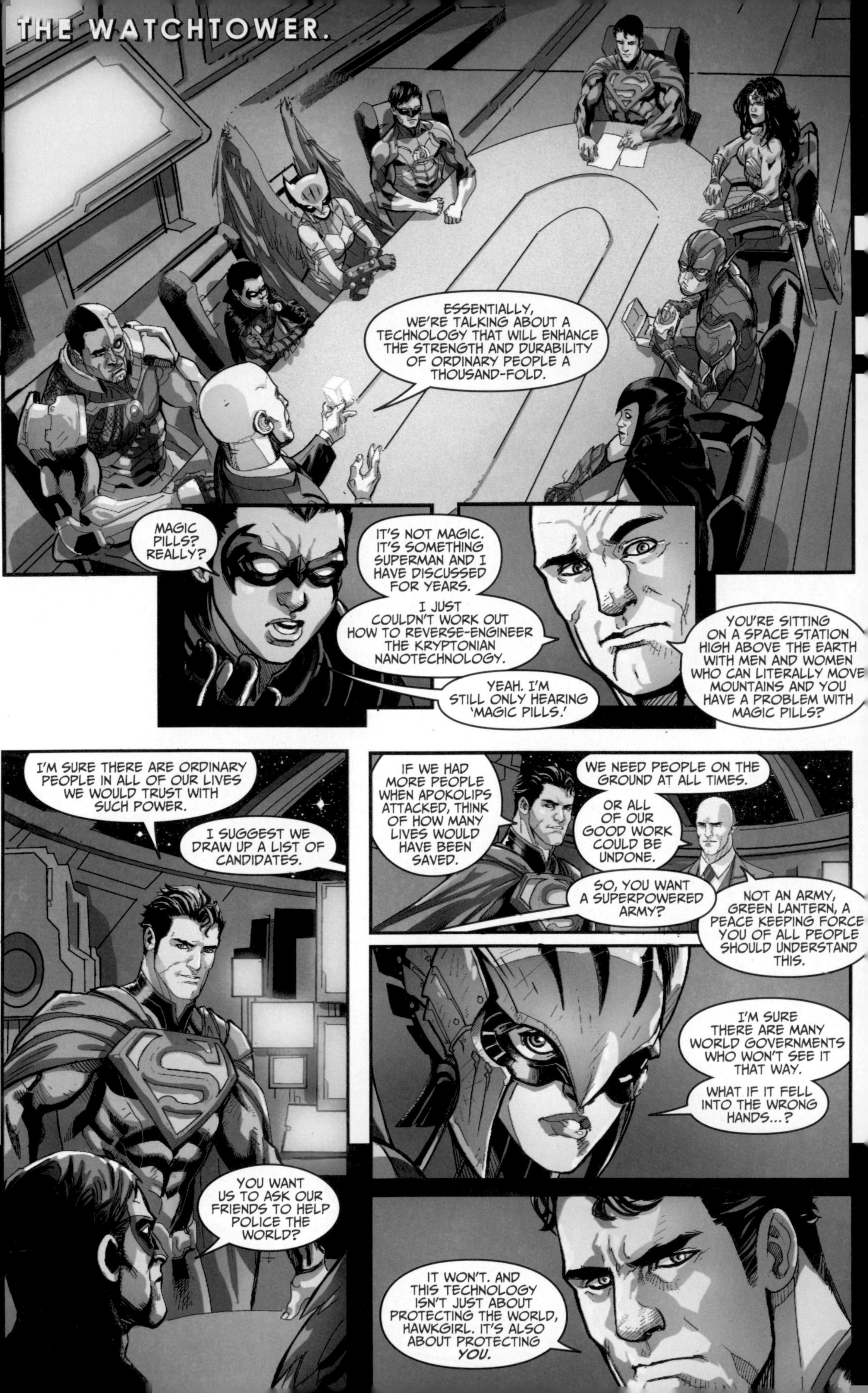
THE WATCHTOWER.
ESSENTIALLY, WE'RE TALKING ABOUT A TECHNOLOGY THAT WILL ENHANCE THE STRENGTH AND DURABILITY OF ORDINARY PEOPLE A THOUSAND-FOLD.
MAGIC PILLS? REALLY?
IT'S NOT MAGIC. IT'S SOMETHING SUPERMAN AND I HAVE DISCUSSED FOR YEARS.
I JUST COULDN'T WORK OUT HOW TO REVERSE-ENGINEER THE KRYPTONIAN NANOTECHNOLOGY.
YEAH. I'M STILL ONLY HEARING 'MAGIC PILLS.'
YOU'RE SITTING ON A SPACE STATION HIGH ABOVE THE EARTH WITH MEN AND WOMEN WHO CAN LITERALLY MOVE MOUNTAINS AND YOU HAVE A PROBLEM WITH MAGIC PILLS?
I'M SURE THERE ARE ORDINARY PEOPLE IN ALL OF OUR LIVES WE WOULD TRUST WITH SUCH POWER.
I SUGGEST WE DRAW UP A LIST OF CANDIDATES.
YOU WANT US TO ASK OUR FRIENDS TO HELP POLICE THE WORLD?
IF WE HAD MORE PEOPLE WHEN APOKOLIPS ATTACKED, THINK OF HOW MANY LIVES WOULD HAVE BEEN SAVED.
WE NEED PEOPLE ON THE GROUND AT ALL TIMES.
OR ALL OF OUR GOOD WORK COULD BE UNDONE.
SO, YOU WANT A SUPERPOWERED ARMY?
NOT AN ARMY, GREEN LANTERN, A PEACE KEEPING FORCE YOU OF ALL PEOPLE SHOULD UNDERSTAND THIS.
I'M SURE THERE ARE MANY WORLD GOVERNMENTS WHO WON'T SEE IT THAT WAY.
WHAT IF IT FELL INTO THE WRONG HANDS...?
IT WON'T. AND THIS TECHNOLOGY ISN'T JUST ABOUT PROTECTING THE WORLD, HAWKGIRL. IT'S ALSO ABOUT PROTECTING *YOU*.

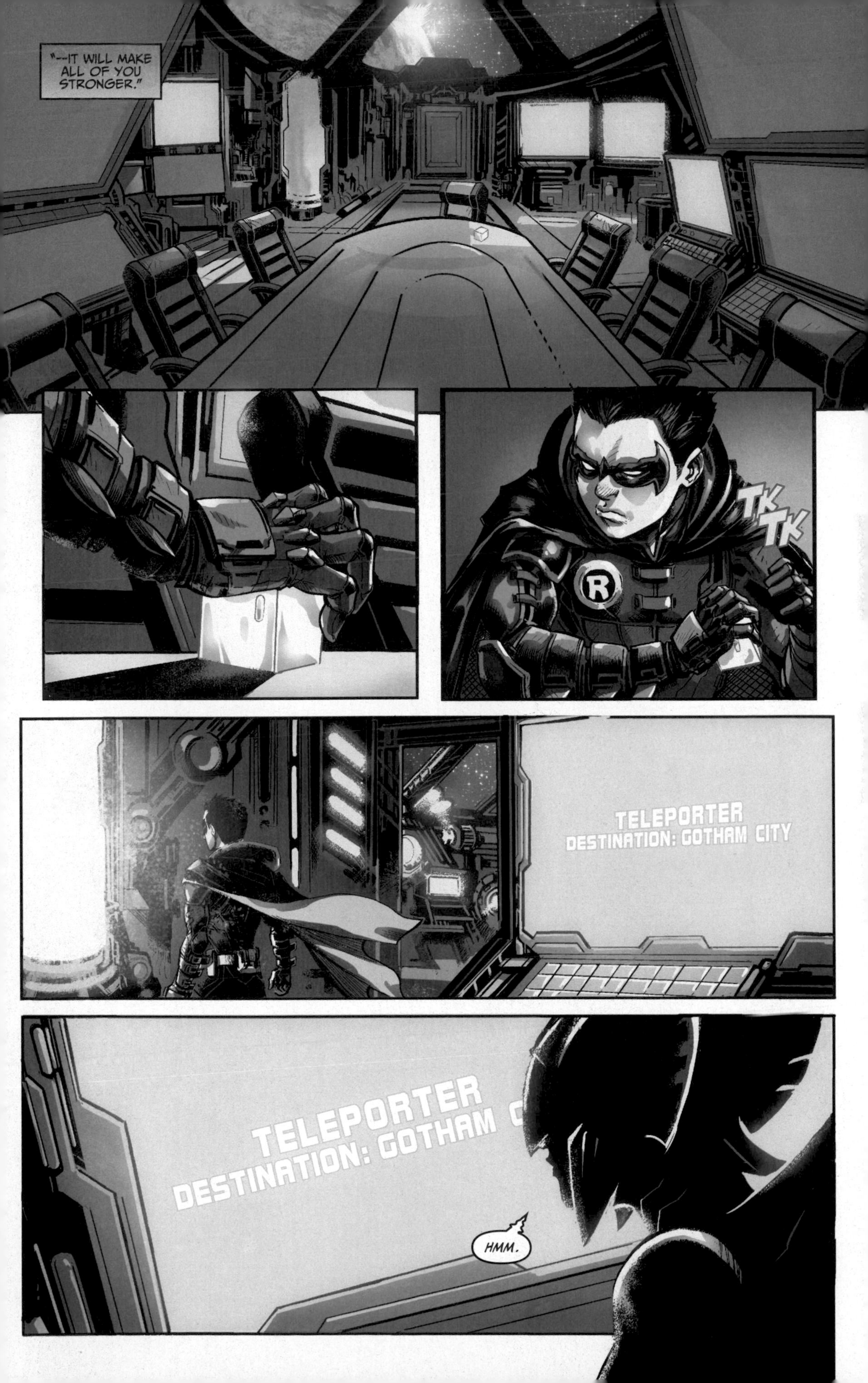
"--IT WILL MAKE ALL OF YOU STRONGER."
TK TK
TELEPORTER
DESTINATION: GOTHAM CITY
TELEPORTER
DESTINATION: GOTHAM C
HMM.

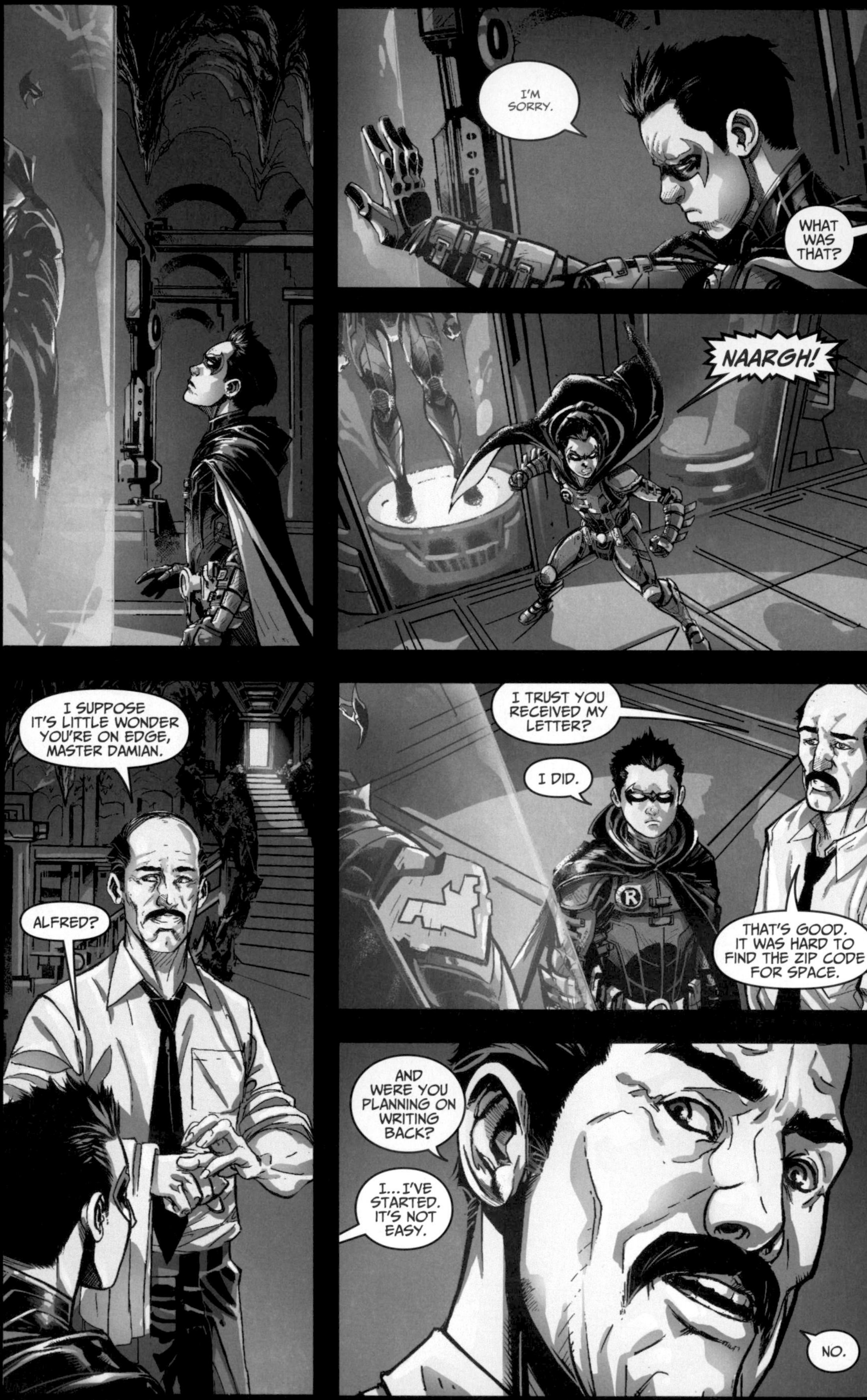
I'M SORRY.
WHAT WAS THAT?
NAARGH!
I SUPPOSE IT'S LITTLE WONDER YOU'RE ON EDGE, MASTER DAMIAN.
ALFRED?
I TRUST YOU RECEIVED MY LETTER?
I DID.
THAT'S GOOD. IT WAS HARD TO FIND THE ZIP CODE FOR SPACE.
AND WERE YOU PLANNING ON WRITING BACK?
I...I'VE STARTED. IT'S NOT EASY.
NO.

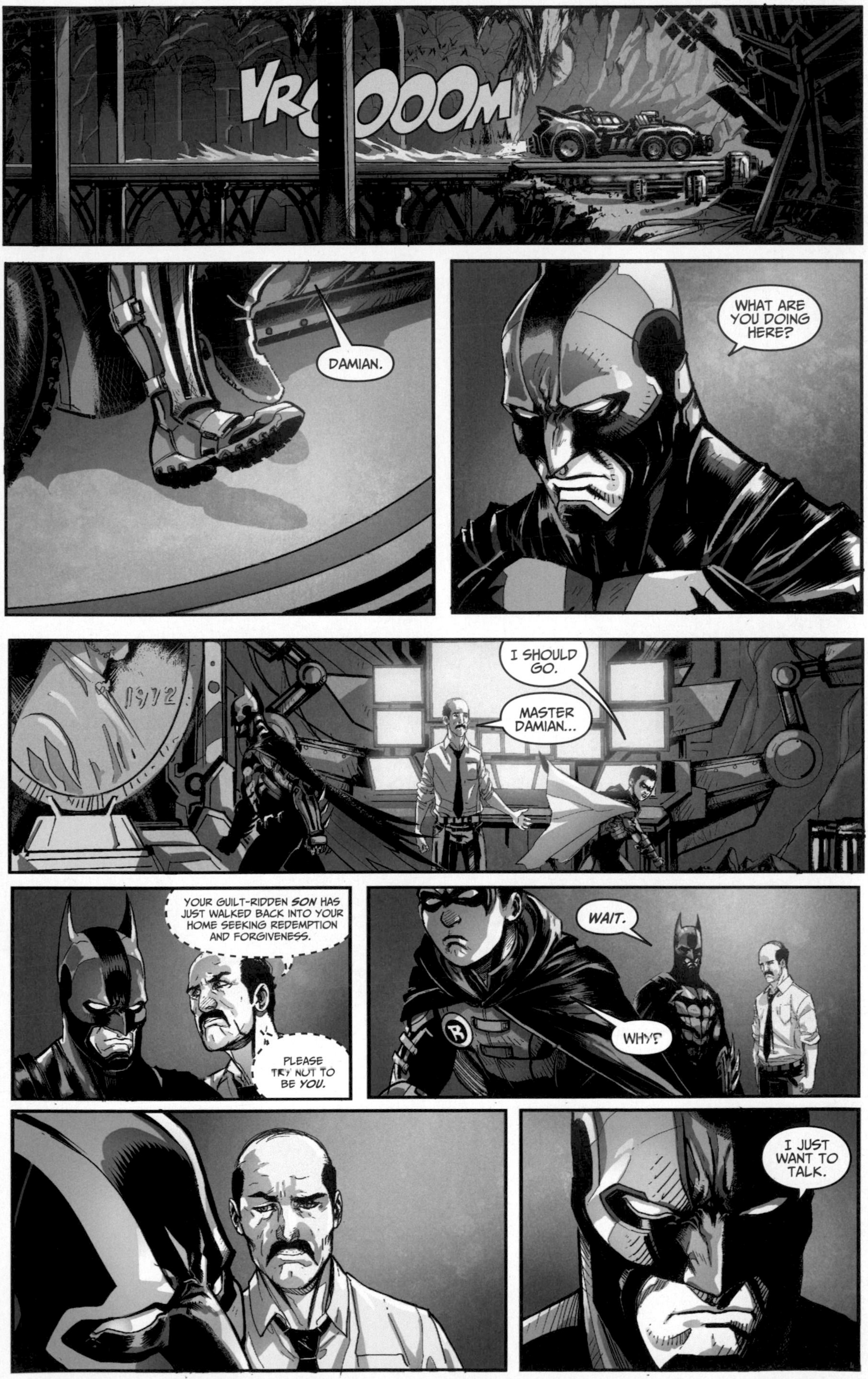
VROOOOM
DAMIAN.
WHAT ARE YOU DOING HERE?
I SHOULD GO.
MASTER DAMIAN...
1972
YOUR GUILT-RIDDEN SON HAS JUST WALKED BACK INTO YOUR HOME SEEKING REDEMPTION AND FORGIVENESS.
PLEASE TRY NOT TO BE YOU.
WAIT.
WHY?
I JUST WANT TO TALK.

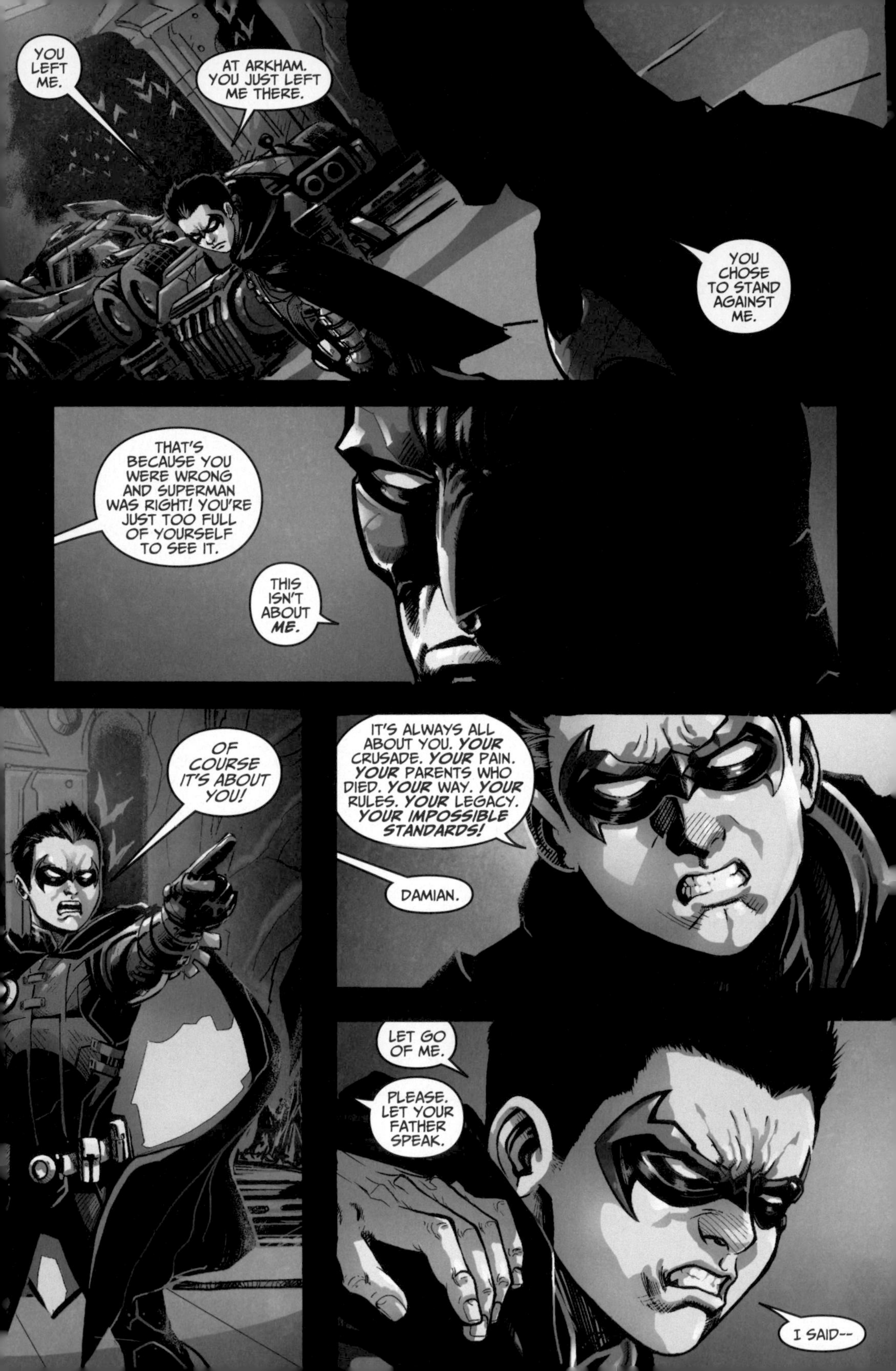
YOU LEFT ME.
AT ARKHAM. YOU JUST LEFT ME THERE.
YOU CHOSE TO STAND AGAINST ME.
THAT'S BECAUSE YOU WERE WRONG AND SUPERMAN WAS RIGHT! YOU'RE JUST TOO FULL OF YOURSELF TO SEE IT.
THIS ISN'T ABOUT *ME.*
OF COURSE IT'S ABOUT YOU!
IT'S ALWAYS ALL ABOUT YOU. *YOUR* CRUSADE. *YOUR* PAIN. *YOUR* PARENTS WHO DIED. *YOUR* WAY. *YOUR* RULES. *YOUR* LEGACY. *YOUR IMPOSSIBLE STANDARDS!*
DAMIAN.
LET GO OF ME.
PLEASE. LET YOUR FATHER SPEAK.
I SAID--

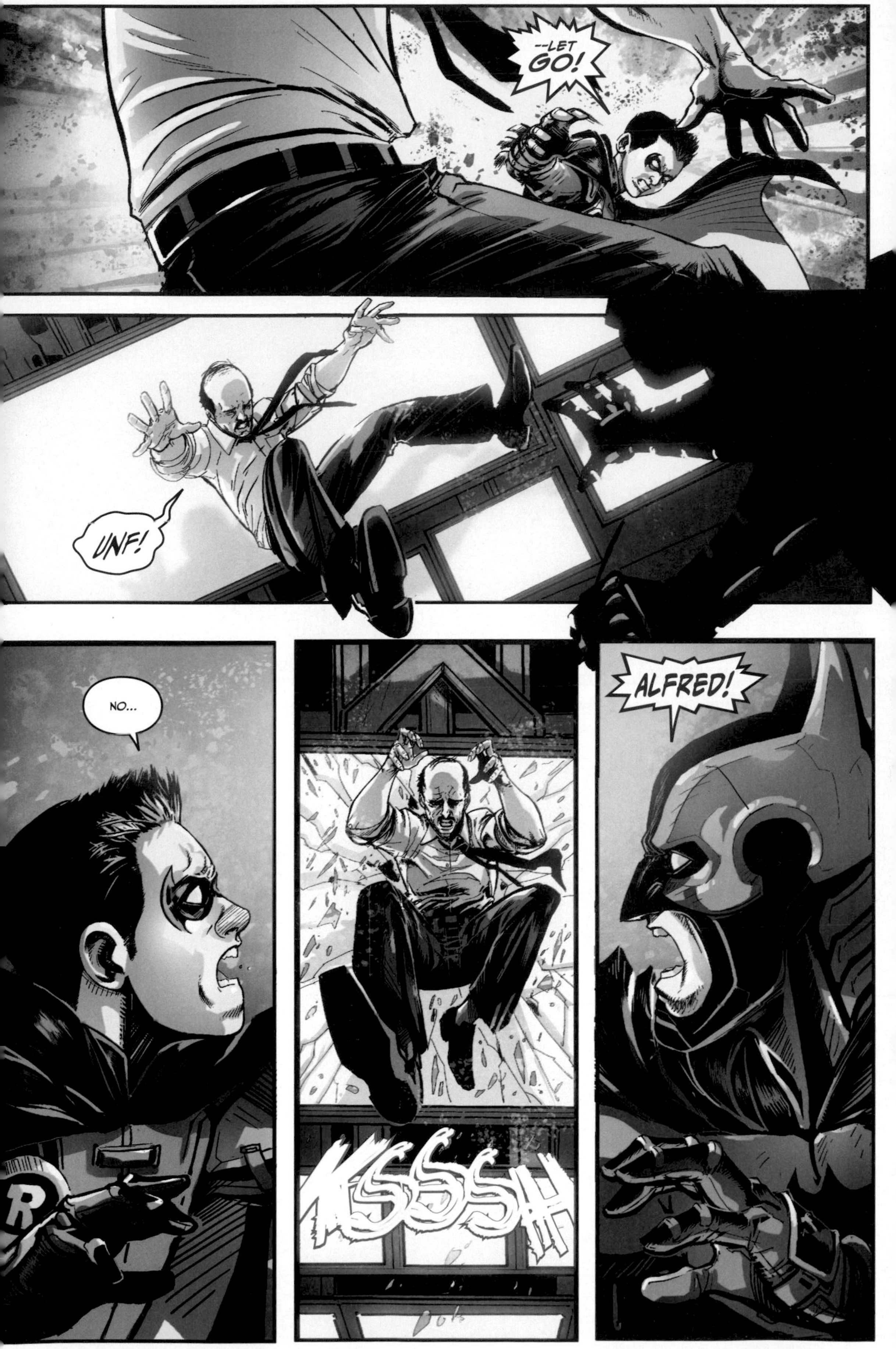
--LET GO!
UNF!
NO...
KSSSH
ALFRED!

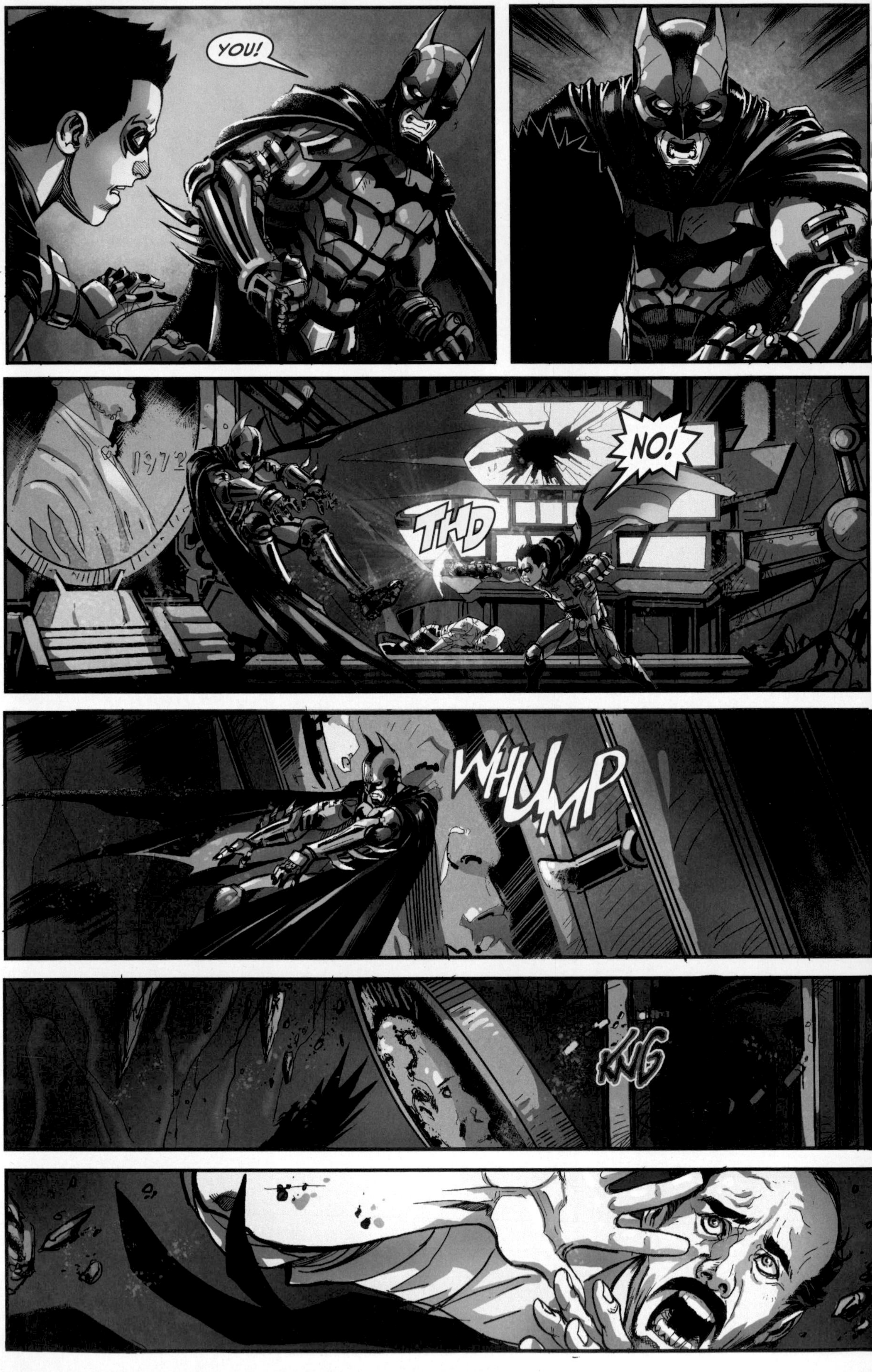
YOU!
NO!
THD
WHUMP
KNG

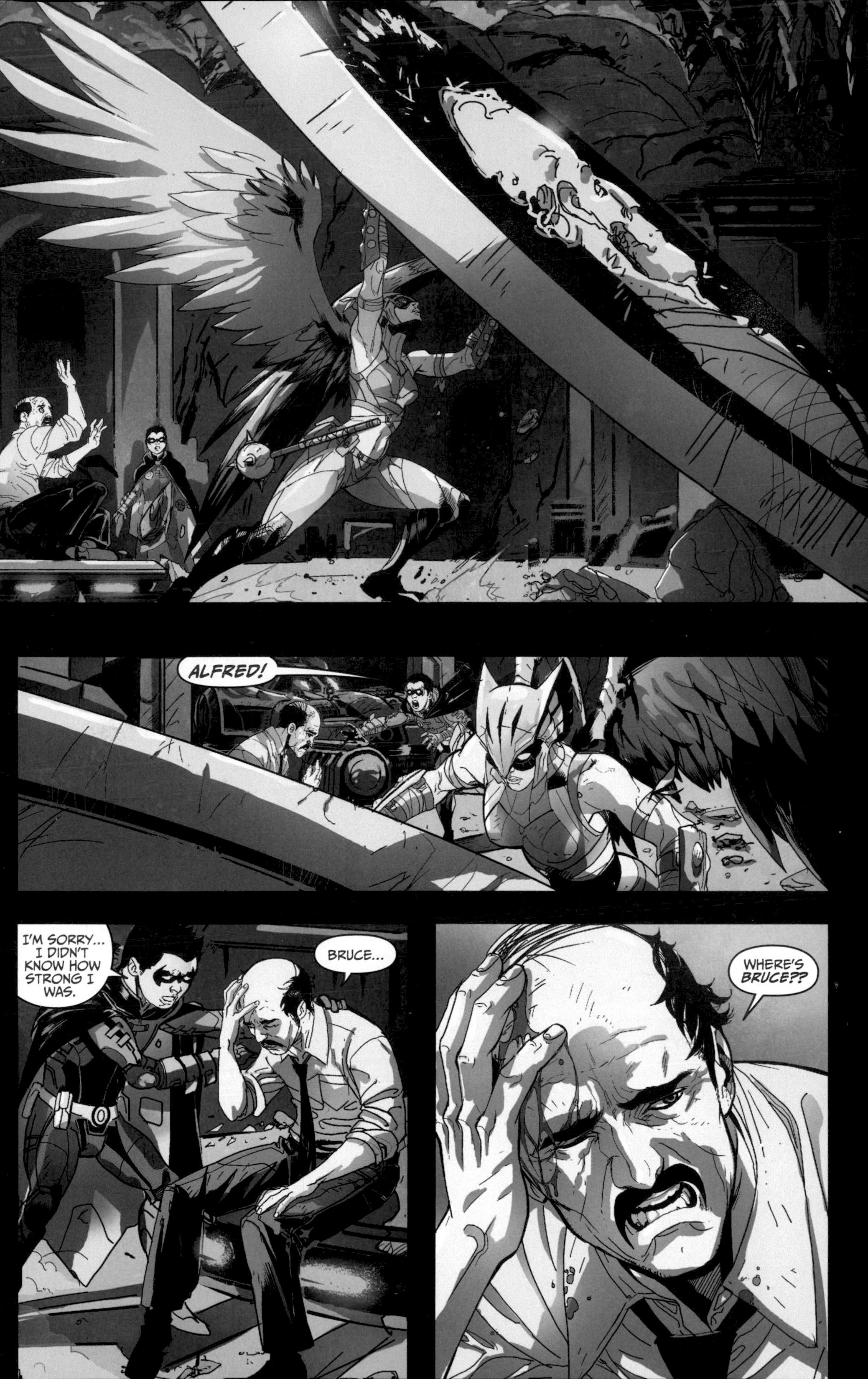
ALFRED!
I'M SORRY... I DIDN'T KNOW HOW STRONG I WAS.
BRUCE...
WHERE'S BRUCE??

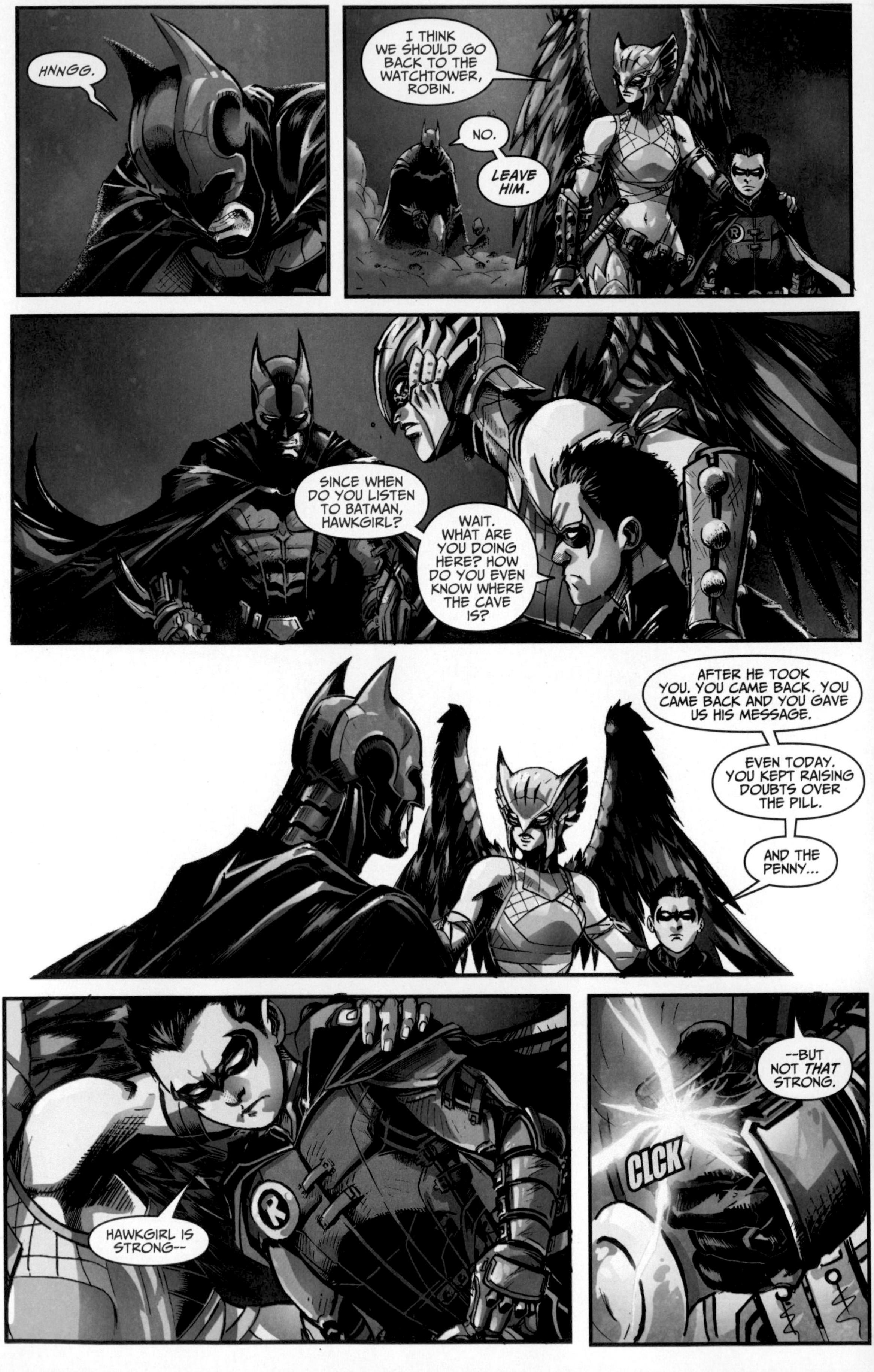
HNNGG.
I THINK WE SHOULD GO BACK TO THE WATCHTOWER, ROBIN.
NO.
LEAVE HIM.
SINCE WHEN DO YOU LISTEN TO BATMAN, HAWKGIRL?
WAIT. WHAT ARE YOU DOING HERE? HOW DO YOU EVEN KNOW WHERE THE CAVE IS?
AFTER HE TOOK YOU. YOU CAME BACK. YOU CAME BACK AND YOU GAVE US HIS MESSAGE.
EVEN TODAY. YOU KEPT RAISING DOUBTS OVER THE PILL.
AND THE PENNY...
HAWKGIRL IS STRONG--
--BUT NOT THAT STRONG.
CLCK

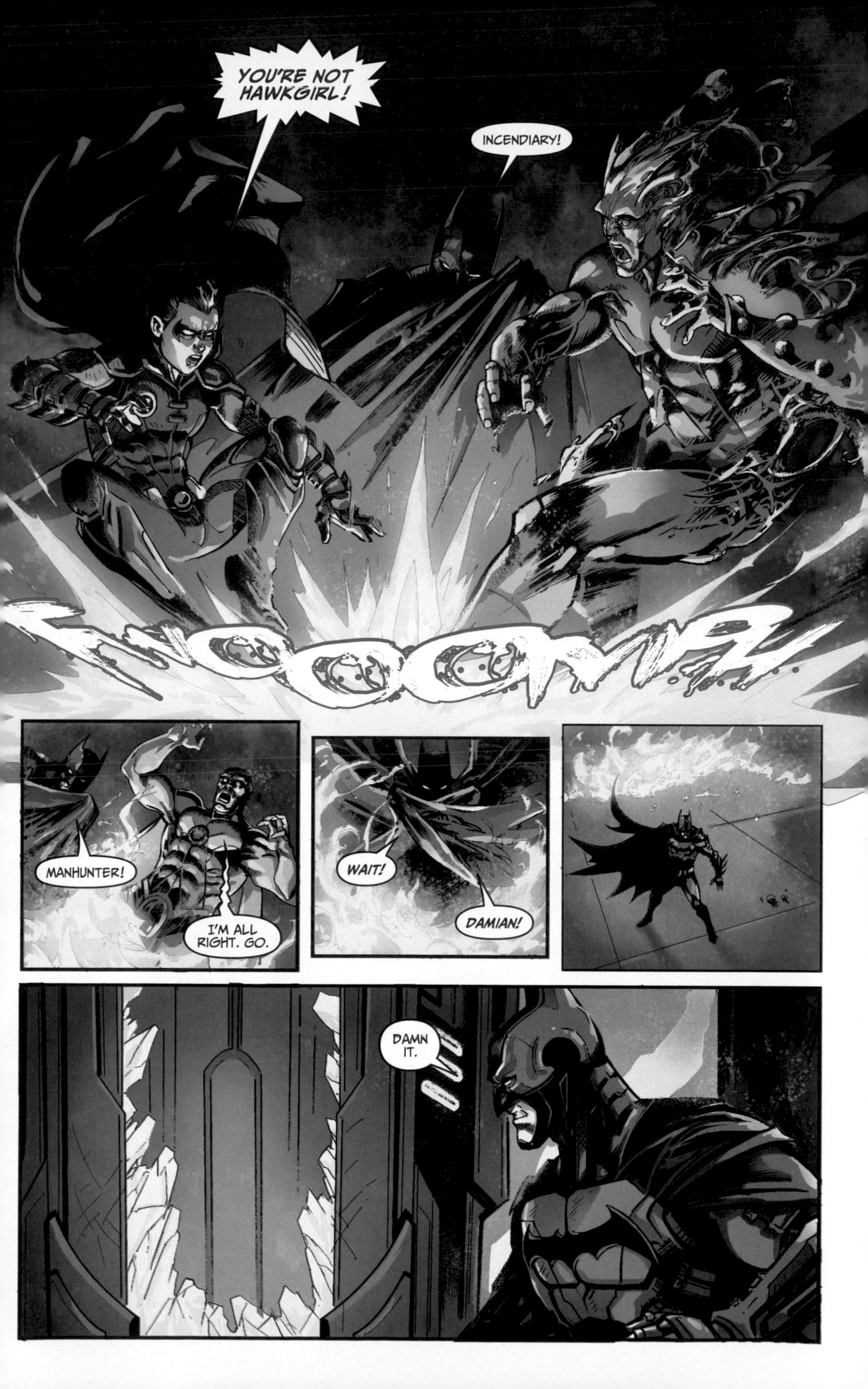
YOU'RE NOT HAWKGIRL!
INCENDIARY!
MANHUNTER!
I'M ALL RIGHT. GO.
WAIT!
DAMIAN!
DAMN IT.

PART TEN

Tom Derenick **Mike S. Miller** **Bruno Redondo** Artists

David Lopez and **Santi Casas** of **Ikari Studio** Colorists

Mico Suayan & **David Lopez** and **Santi Casas** of **Ikari Studio** Cover

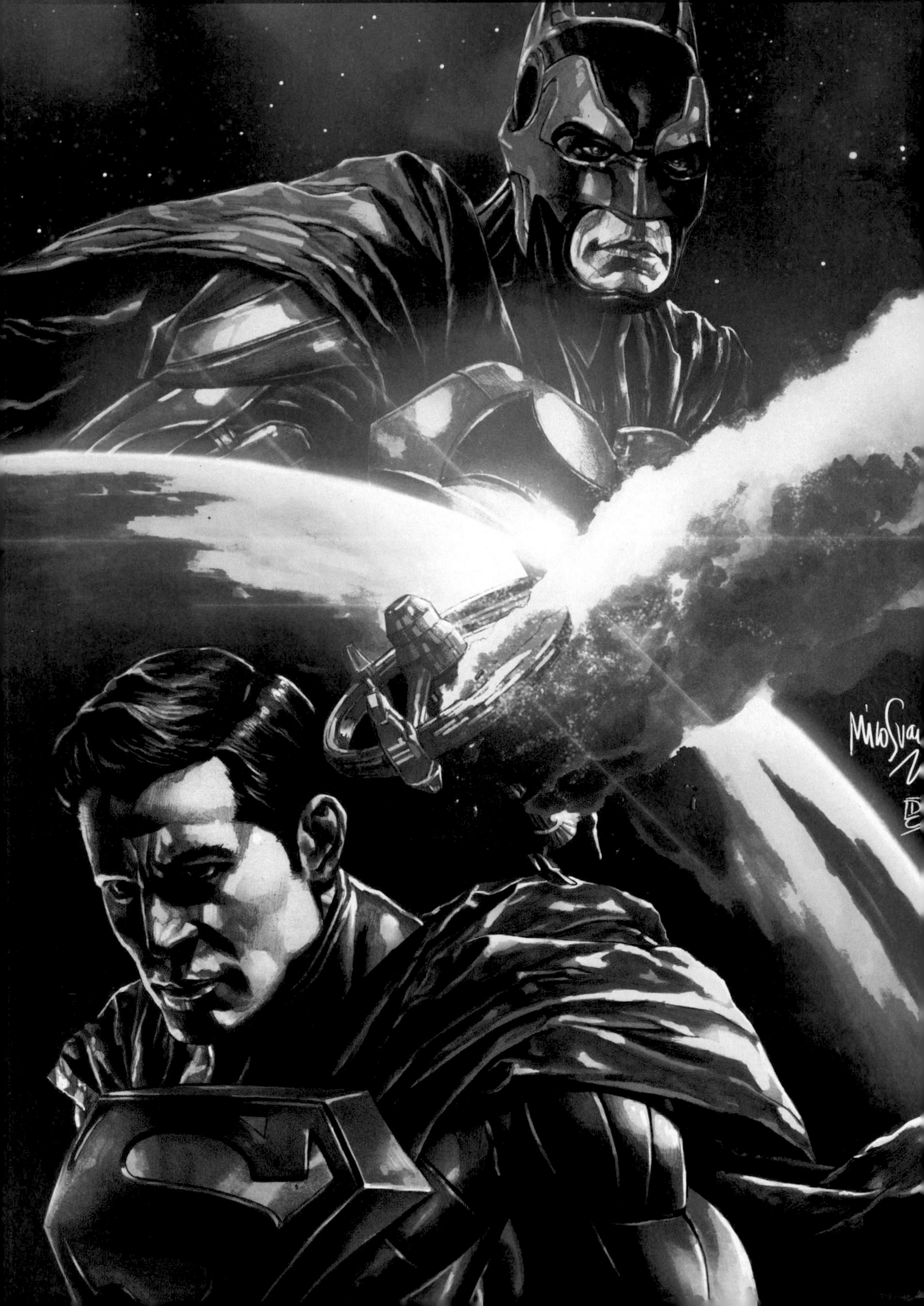

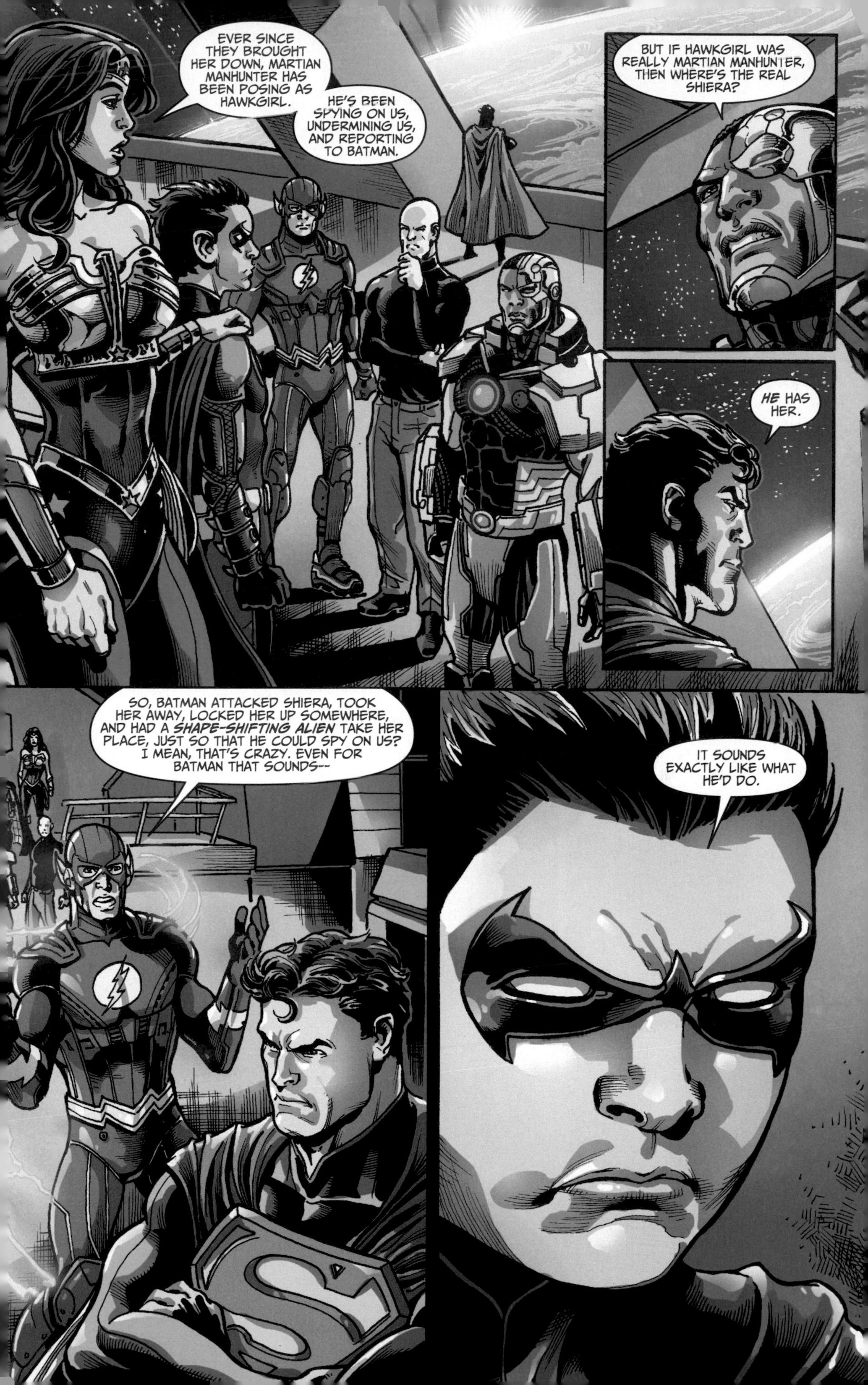
EVER SINCE THEY BROUGHT HER DOWN, MARTIAN MANHUNTER HAS BEEN POSING AS HAWKGIRL.
HE'S BEEN SPYING ON US, UNDERMINING US, AND REPORTING TO BATMAN.
BUT IF HAWKGIRL WAS REALLY MARTIAN MANHUNTER, THEN WHERE'S THE REAL SHIERA?
HE HAS HER.
SO, BATMAN ATTACKED SHIERA, TOOK HER AWAY, LOCKED HER UP SOMEWHERE, AND HAD A *SHAPE-SHIFTING ALIEN* TAKE HER PLACE, JUST SO THAT HE COULD SPY ON US? I MEAN, THAT'S CRAZY. EVEN FOR BATMAN THAT SOUNDS--
IT SOUNDS EXACTLY LIKE WHAT HE'D DO.

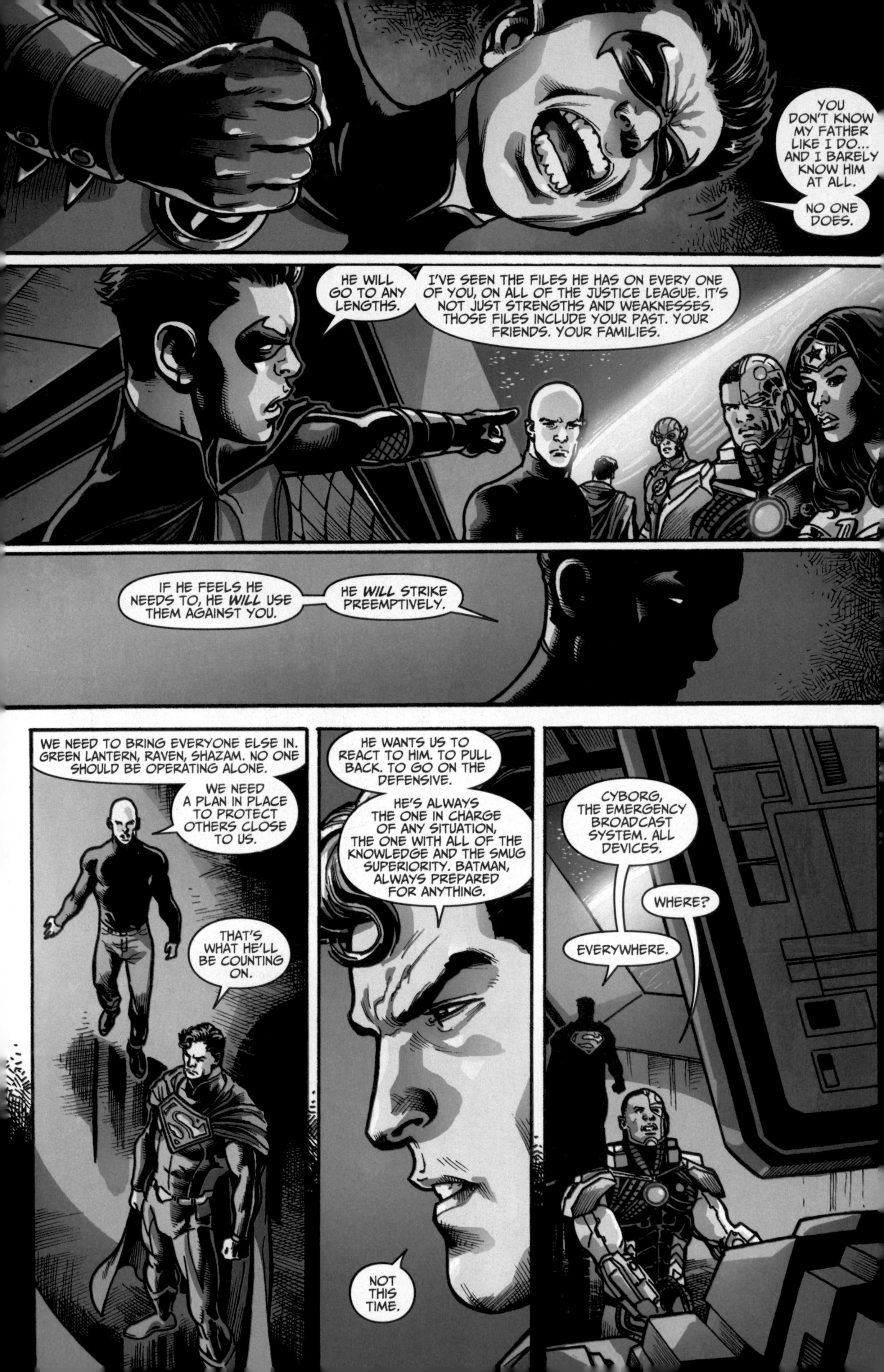
YOU DON'T KNOW MY FATHER LIKE I DO... AND I BARELY KNOW HIM AT ALL.
NO ONE DOES.
HE WILL GO TO ANY LENGTHS.
I'VE SEEN THE FILES HE HAS ON EVERY ONE OF YOU, ON ALL OF THE JUSTICE LEAGUE. IT'S NOT JUST STRENGTHS AND WEAKNESSES. THOSE FILES INCLUDE YOUR PAST. YOUR FRIENDS. YOUR FAMILIES.
IF HE FEELS HE NEEDS TO, HE WILL USE THEM AGAINST YOU.
HE WILL STRIKE PREEMPTIVELY.
WE NEED TO BRING EVERYONE ELSE IN. GREEN LANTERN, RAVEN, SHAZAM. NO ONE SHOULD BE OPERATING ALONE.
WE NEED A PLAN IN PLACE TO PROTECT OTHERS CLOSE TO US.
THAT'S WHAT HE'LL BE COUNTING ON.
HE WANTS US TO REACT TO HIM. TO PULL BACK. TO GO ON THE DEFENSIVE.
HE'S ALWAYS THE ONE IN CHARGE OF ANY SITUATION, THE ONE WITH ALL OF THE KNOWLEDGE AND THE SMUG SUPERIORITY. BATMAN, ALWAYS PREPARED FOR ANYTHING.
NOT THIS TIME.
CYBORG, THE EMERGENCY BROADCAST SYSTEM. ALL DEVICES.
WHERE?
EVERYWHERE.

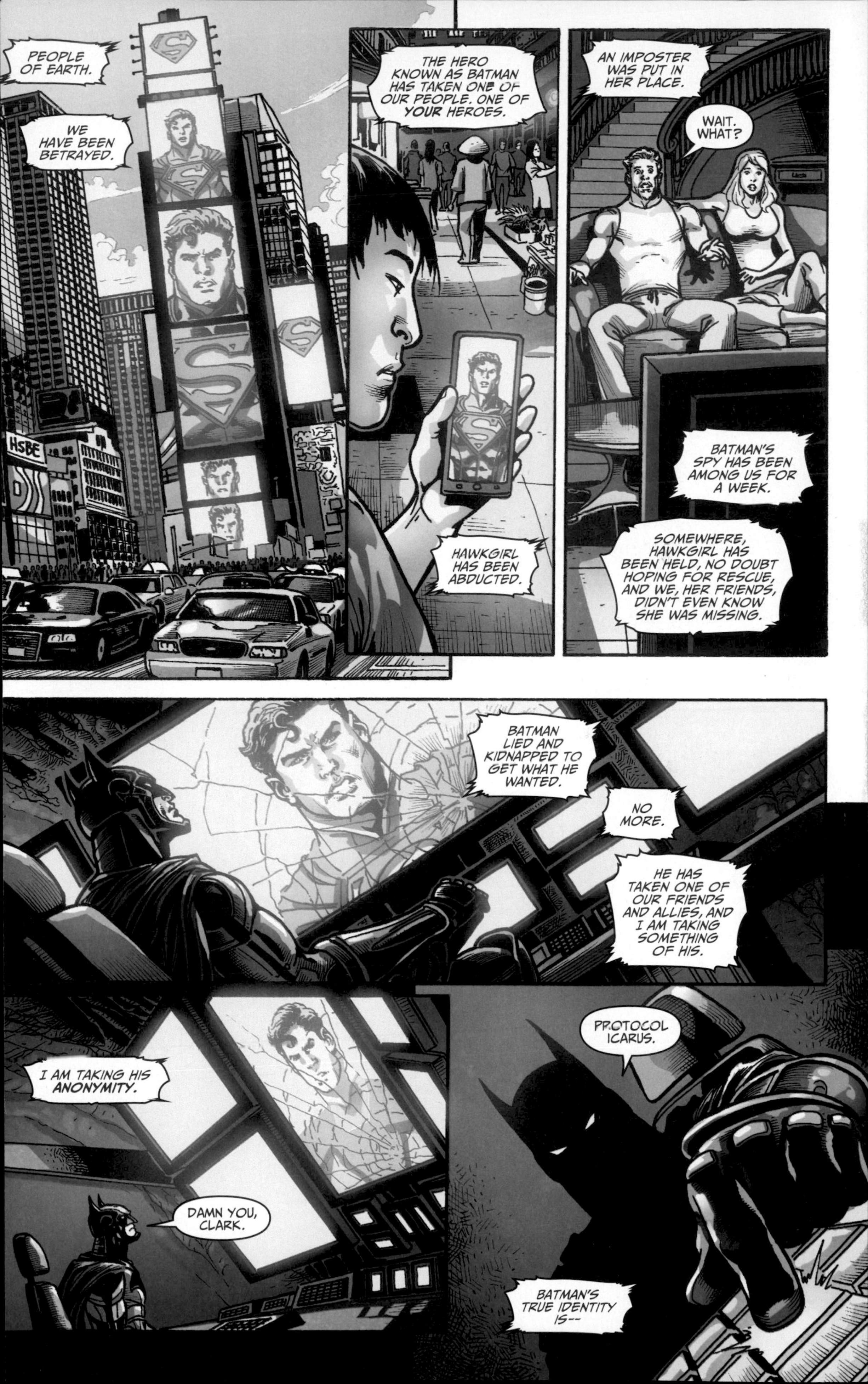
PEOPLE OF EARTH.
WE HAVE BEEN BETRAYED.
THE HERO KNOWN AS BATMAN HAS TAKEN ONE OF OUR PEOPLE. ONE OF YOUR HEROES.
HAWKGIRL HAS BEEN ABDUCTED.
AN IMPOSTER WAS PUT IN HER PLACE.
WAIT. WHAT?
BATMAN'S SPY HAS BEEN AMONG US FOR A WEEK.
SOMEWHERE, HAWKGIRL HAS BEEN HELD, NO DOUBT HOPING FOR RESCUE, AND WE, HER FRIENDS, DIDN'T EVEN KNOW SHE WAS MISSING.
BATMAN LIED AND KIDNAPPED TO GET WHAT HE WANTED.
NO MORE.
HE HAS TAKEN ONE OF OUR FRIENDS AND ALLIES, AND I AM TAKING SOMETHING OF HIS.
I AM TAKING HIS ANONYMITY.
DAMN YOU, CLARK.
PROTOCOL ICARUS.
BATMAN'S TRUE IDENTITY IS--

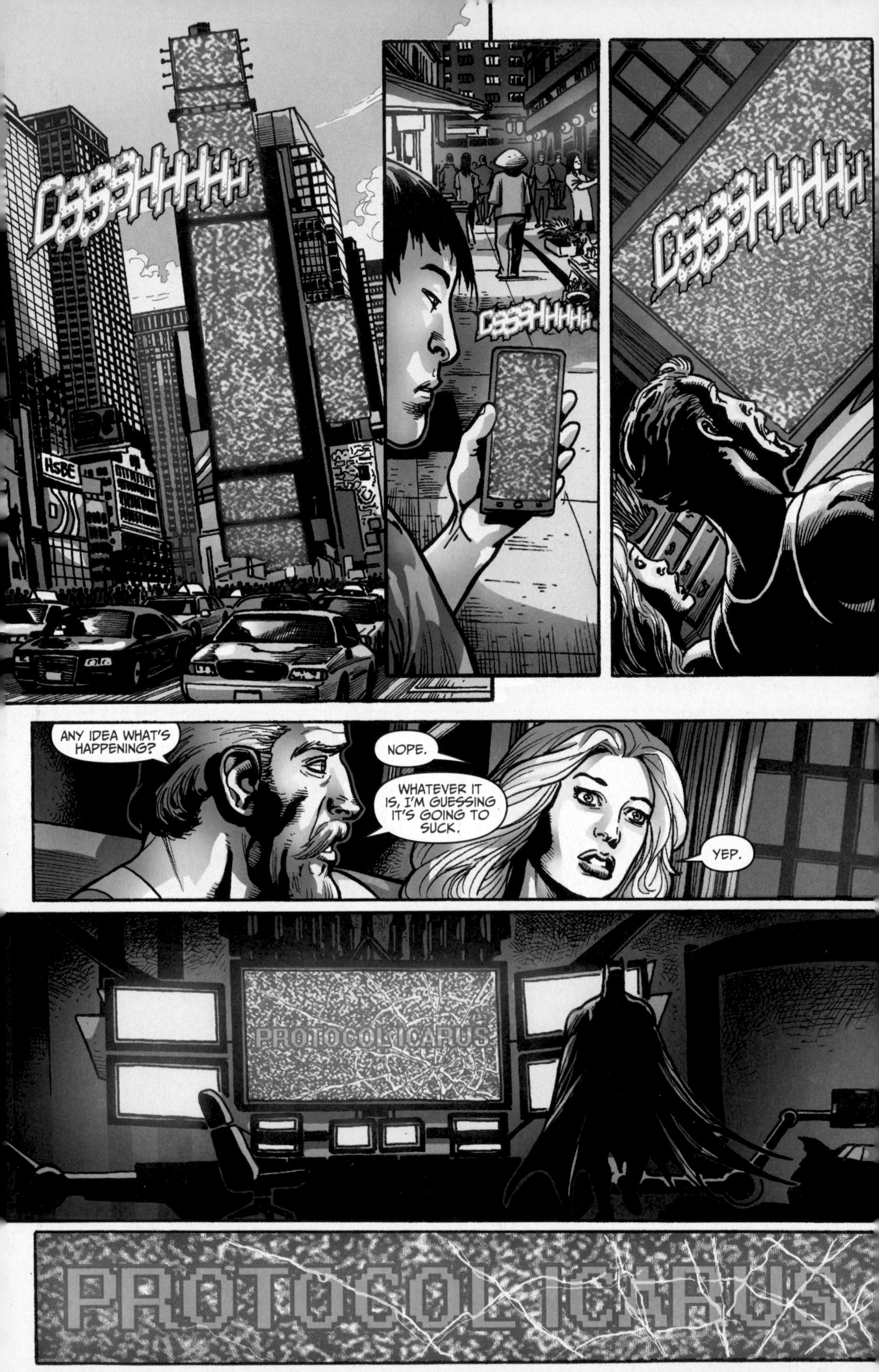
CSSSHHHHH
CSSSHHHHH
CSSSHHHHH
ANY IDEA WHAT'S HAPPENING?
NOPE.
WHATEVER IT IS, I'M GUESSING IT'S GOING TO SUCK.
YEP.
PROTOCOL ICARUS
PROTOCOL ICARUS

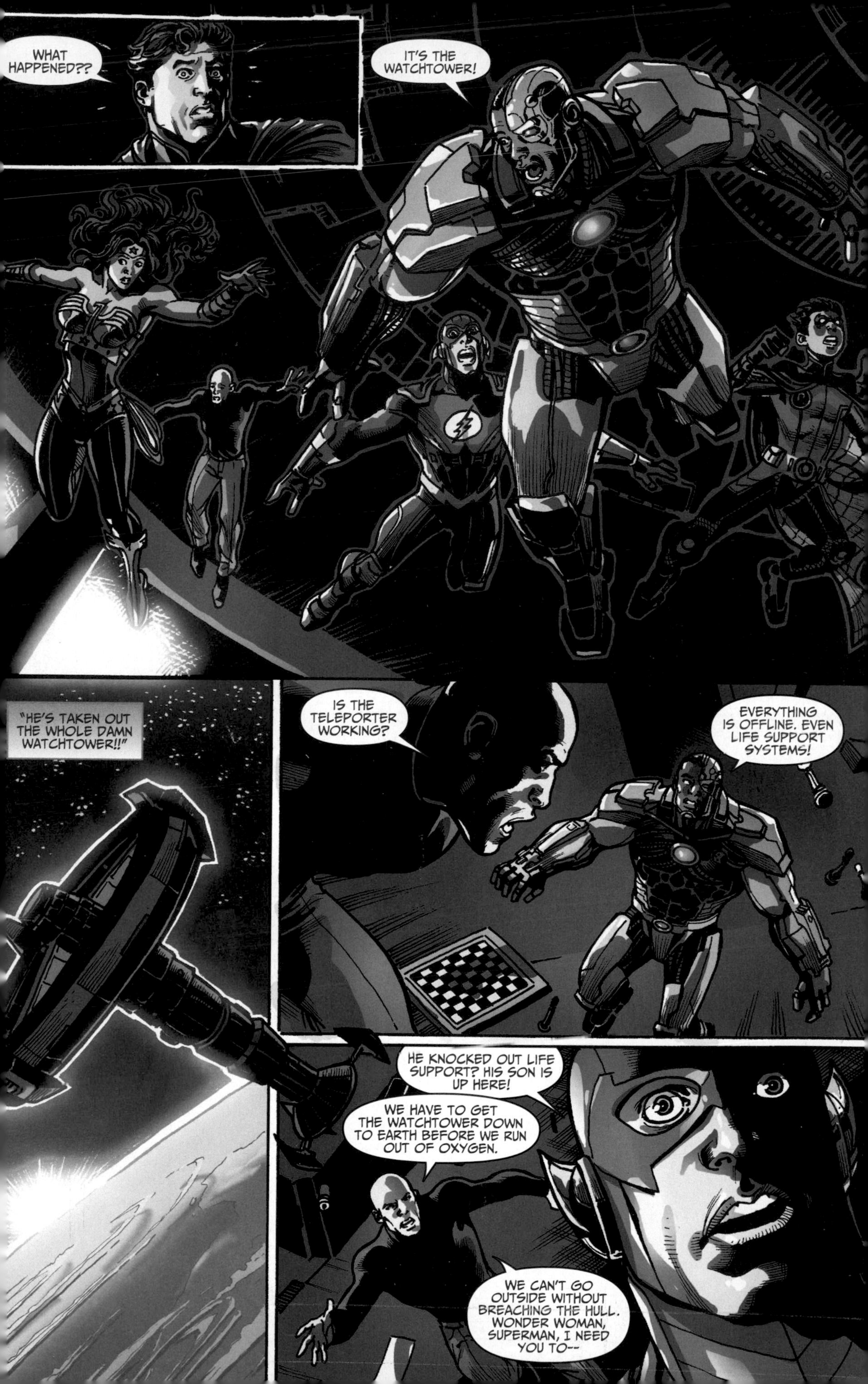
WHAT HAPPENED??
IT'S THE WATCHTOWER!
"HE'S TAKEN OUT THE WHOLE DAMN WATCHTOWER!!"
IS THE TELEPORTER WORKING?
EVERYTHING IS OFFLINE. EVEN LIFE SUPPORT SYSTEMS!
HE KNOCKED OUT LIFE SUPPORT? HIS SON IS UP HERE!
WE HAVE TO GET THE WATCHTOWER DOWN TO EARTH BEFORE WE RUN OUT OF OXYGEN.
WE CAN'T GO OUTSIDE WITHOUT BREACHING THE HULL. WONDER WOMAN, SUPERMAN, I NEED YOU TO--

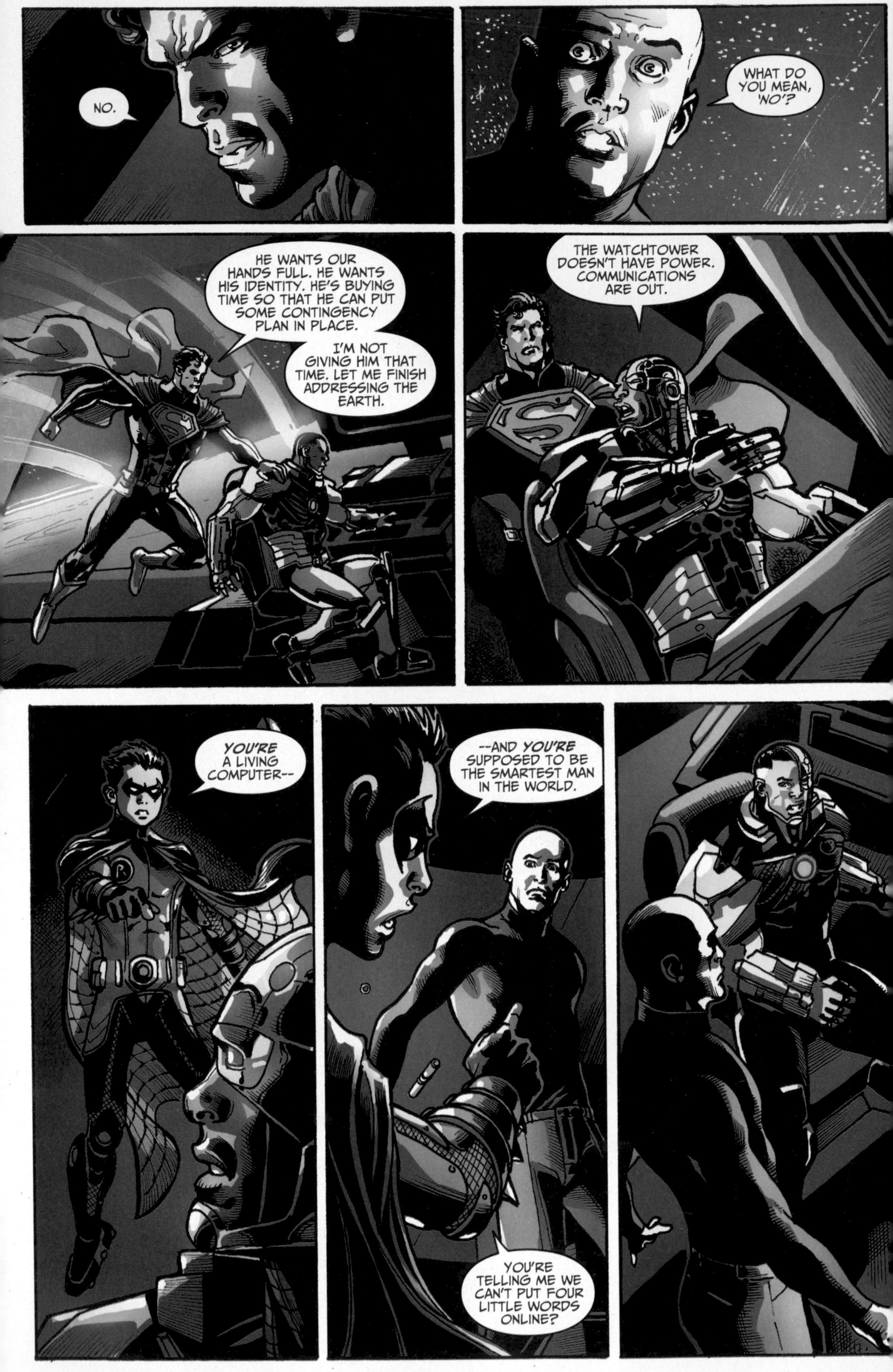
NO.
WHAT DO YOU MEAN, 'NO'?
HE WANTS OUR HANDS FULL. HE WANTS HIS IDENTITY. HE'S BUYING TIME SO THAT HE CAN PUT SOME CONTINGENCY PLAN IN PLACE.
I'M NOT GIVING HIM THAT TIME. LET ME FINISH ADDRESSING THE EARTH.
THE WATCHTOWER DOESN'T HAVE POWER. COMMUNICATIONS ARE OUT.
YOU'RE A LIVING COMPUTER--
--AND *YOU'RE* SUPPOSED TO BE THE SMARTEST MAN IN THE WORLD.
YOU'RE TELLING ME WE CAN'T PUT FOUR LITTLE WORDS ONLINE?

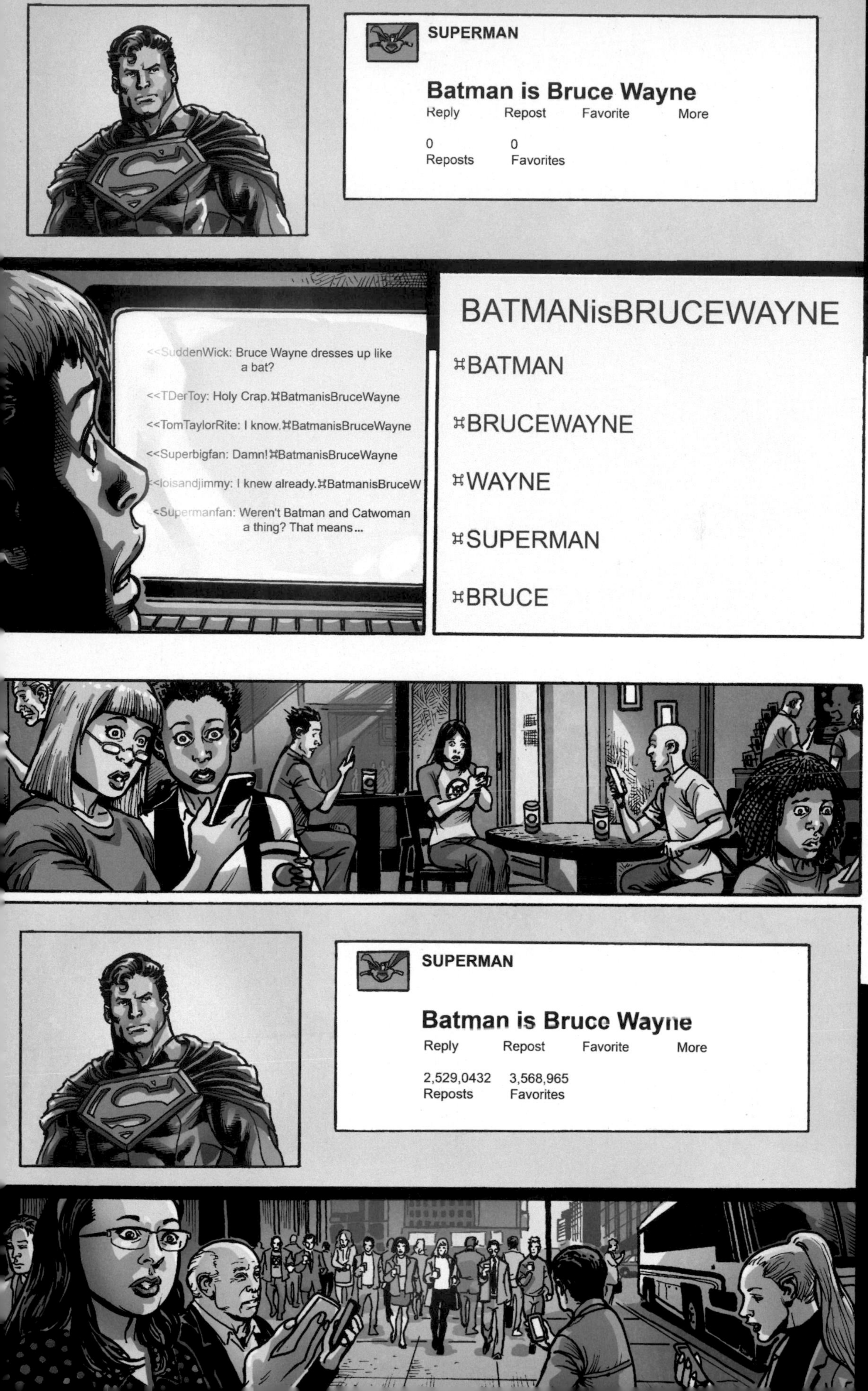

SUPERMAN
Batman is Bruce Wayne
Reply Repost Favorite More
0 Reposts 0 Favorites
<<SuddenWick: Bruce Wayne dresses up like a bat?
<<TDerToy: Holy Crap.⌘BatmanisBruceWayne
<<TomTaylorRite: I know.⌘BatmanisBruceWayne
<<Superbigfan: Damn!⌘BatmanisBruceWayne
<<loisandjimmy: I knew already.⌘BatmanisBruceW
<<Supermanfan: Weren't Batman and Catwoman a thing? That means...
BATMANisBRUCEWAYNE
⌘BATMAN
⌘BRUCEWAYNE
⌘WAYNE
⌘SUPERMAN
⌘BRUCE
SUPERMAN
Batman is Bruce Wayne
Reply Repost Favorite More
2,529,0432 Reposts 3,568,965 Favorites

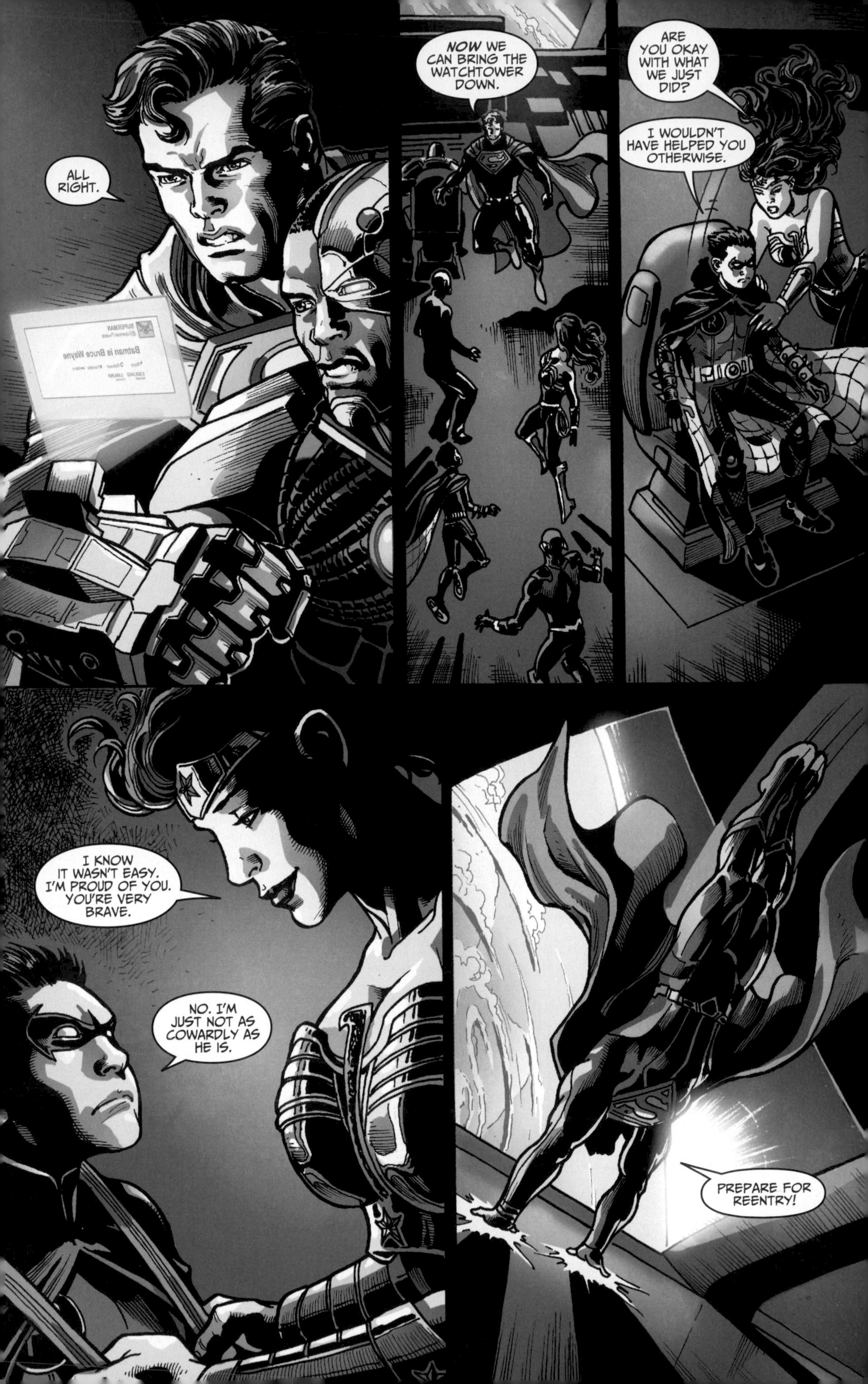
ALL RIGHT.
NOW WE CAN BRING THE WATCHTOWER DOWN.
ARE YOU OKAY WITH WHAT WE JUST DID?
I WOULDN'T HAVE HELPED YOU OTHERWISE.
I KNOW IT WASN'T EASY. I'M PROUD OF YOU. YOU'RE VERY BRAVE.
NO. I'M JUST NOT AS COWARDLY AS HE IS.
PREPARE FOR REENTRY!

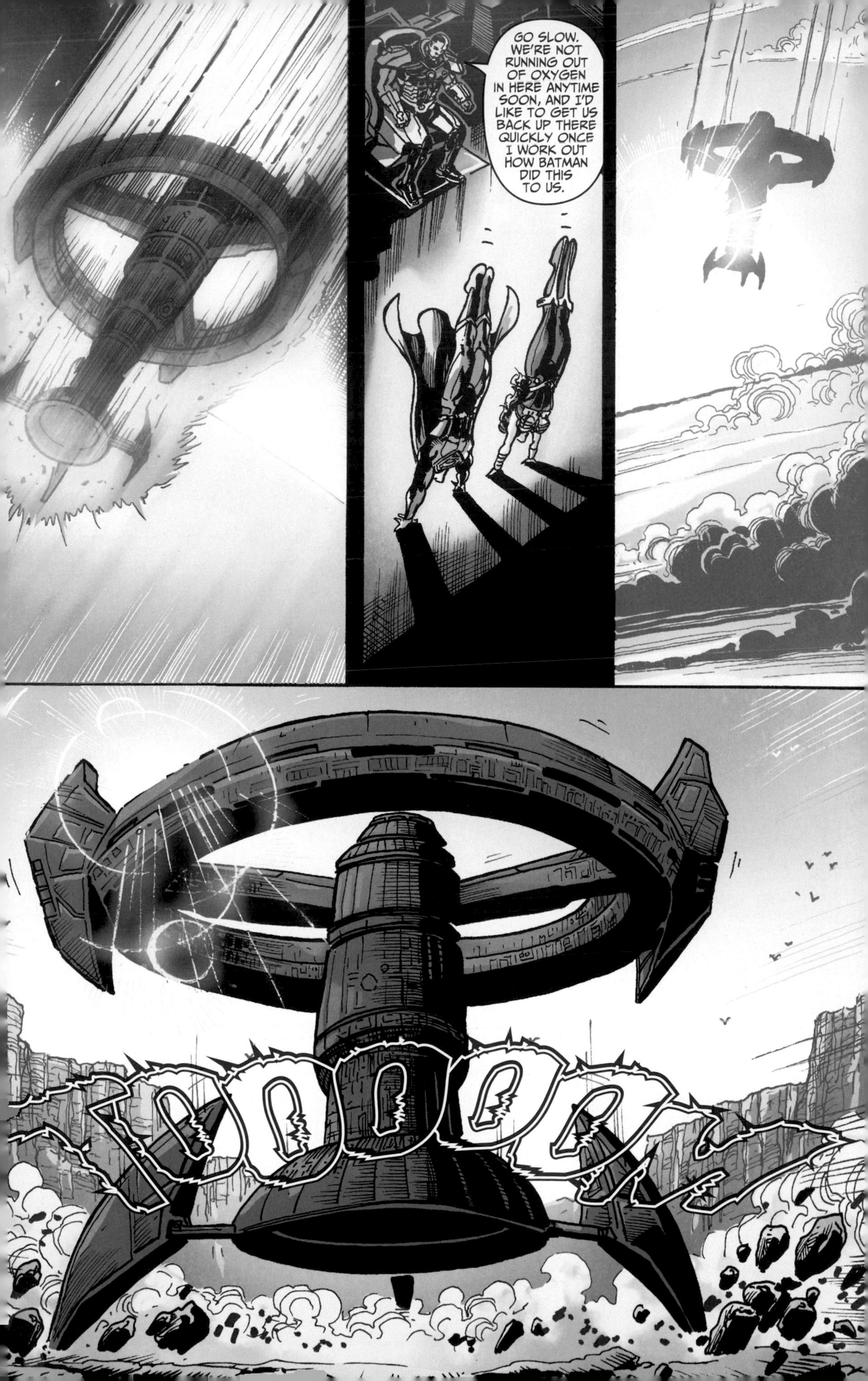
GO SLOW. WE'RE NOT RUNNING OUT OF OXYGEN IN HERE ANYTIME SOON, AND I'D LIKE TO GET US BACK UP THERE QUICKLY ONCE I WORK OUT HOW BATMAN DID THIS TO US.
TOOOOOOM

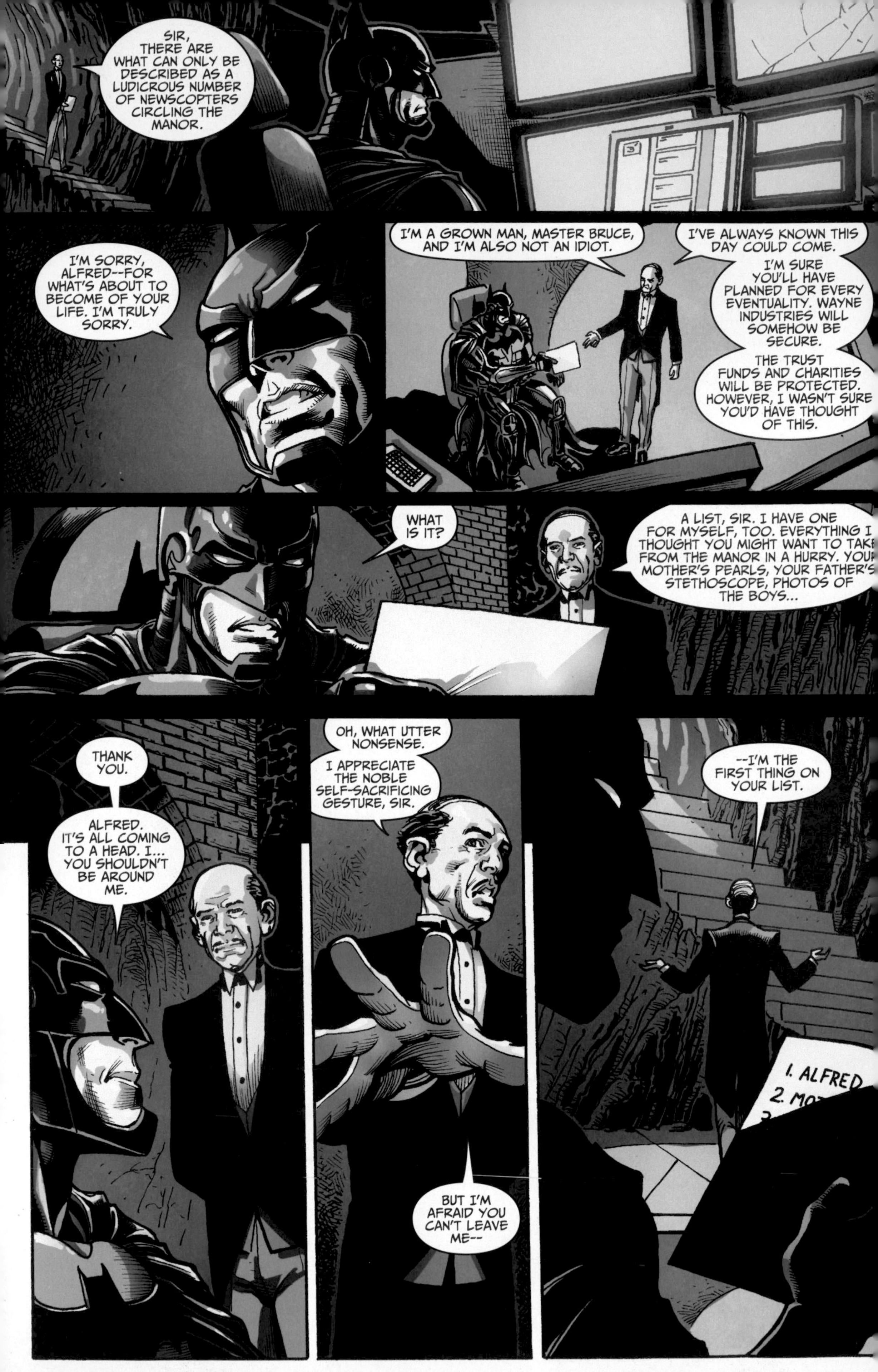
SIR, THERE ARE WHAT CAN ONLY BE DESCRIBED AS A LUDICROUS NUMBER OF NEWSCOPTERS CIRCLING THE MANOR.
I'M SORRY, ALFRED--FOR WHAT'S ABOUT TO BECOME OF YOUR LIFE. I'M TRULY SORRY.
I'M A GROWN MAN, MASTER BRUCE, AND I'M ALSO NOT AN IDIOT.
I'VE ALWAYS KNOWN THIS DAY COULD COME.
I'M SURE YOU'LL HAVE PLANNED FOR EVERY EVENTUALITY. WAYNE INDUSTRIES WILL SOMEHOW BE SECURE.
THE TRUST FUNDS AND CHARITIES WILL BE PROTECTED. HOWEVER, I WASN'T SURE YOU'D HAVE THOUGHT OF THIS.
WHAT IS IT?
A LIST, SIR. I HAVE ONE FOR MYSELF, TOO. EVERYTHING I THOUGHT YOU MIGHT WANT TO TAKE FROM THE MANOR IN A HURRY. YOUR MOTHER'S PEARLS, YOUR FATHER'S STETHOSCOPE, PHOTOS OF THE BOYS...
THANK YOU.
ALFRED. IT'S ALL COMING TO A HEAD. I... YOU SHOULDN'T BE AROUND ME.
OH, WHAT UTTER NONSENSE.
I APPRECIATE THE NOBLE SELF-SACRIFICING GESTURE, SIR.
BUT I'M AFRAID YOU CAN'T LEAVE ME--
--I'M THE FIRST THING ON YOUR LIST.
1. ALFRED

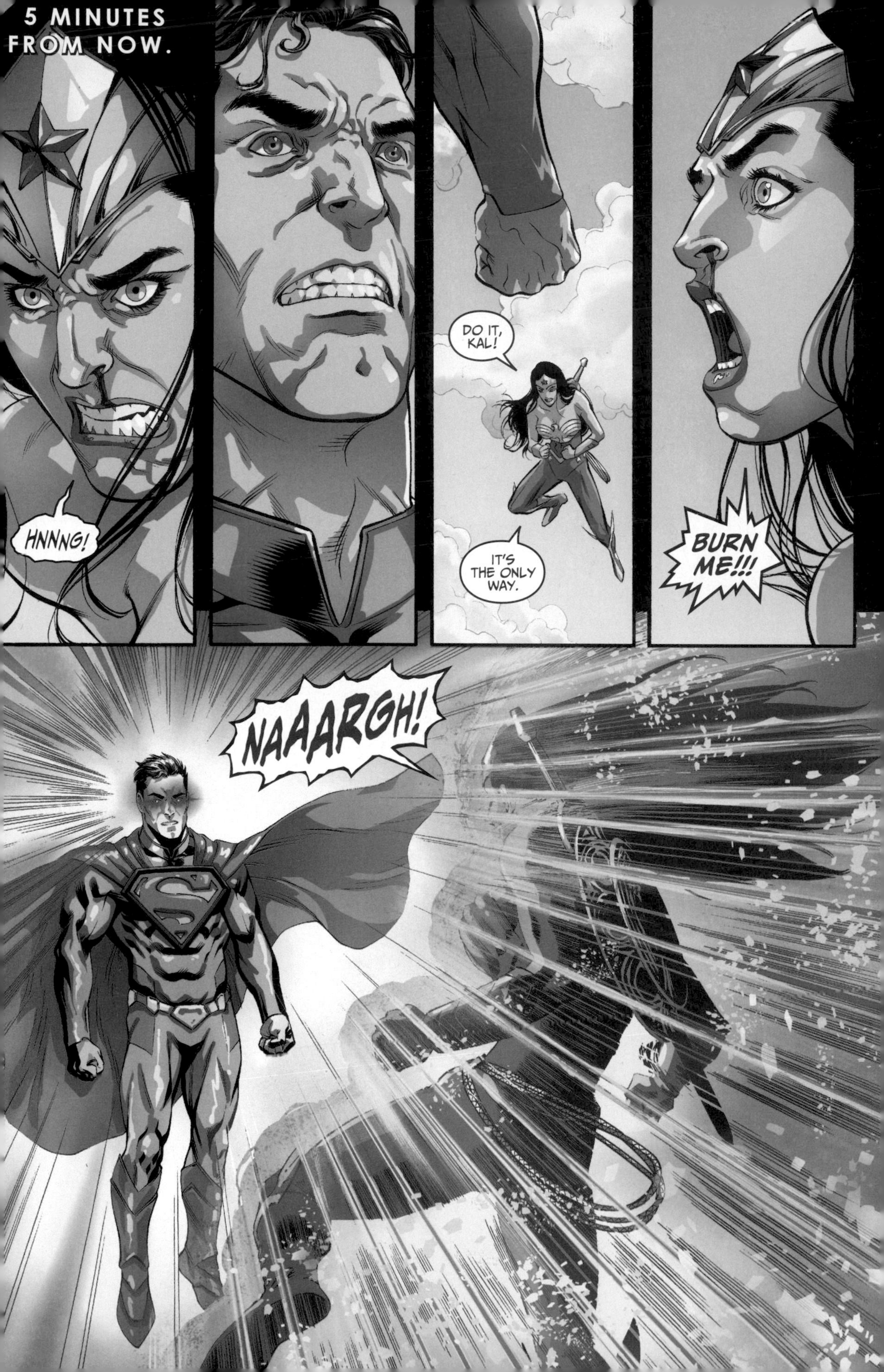
5 MINUTES FROM NOW.
HNNNG!
DO IT, KAL!
IT'S THE ONLY WAY.
BURN ME!!!
NAAARGH!

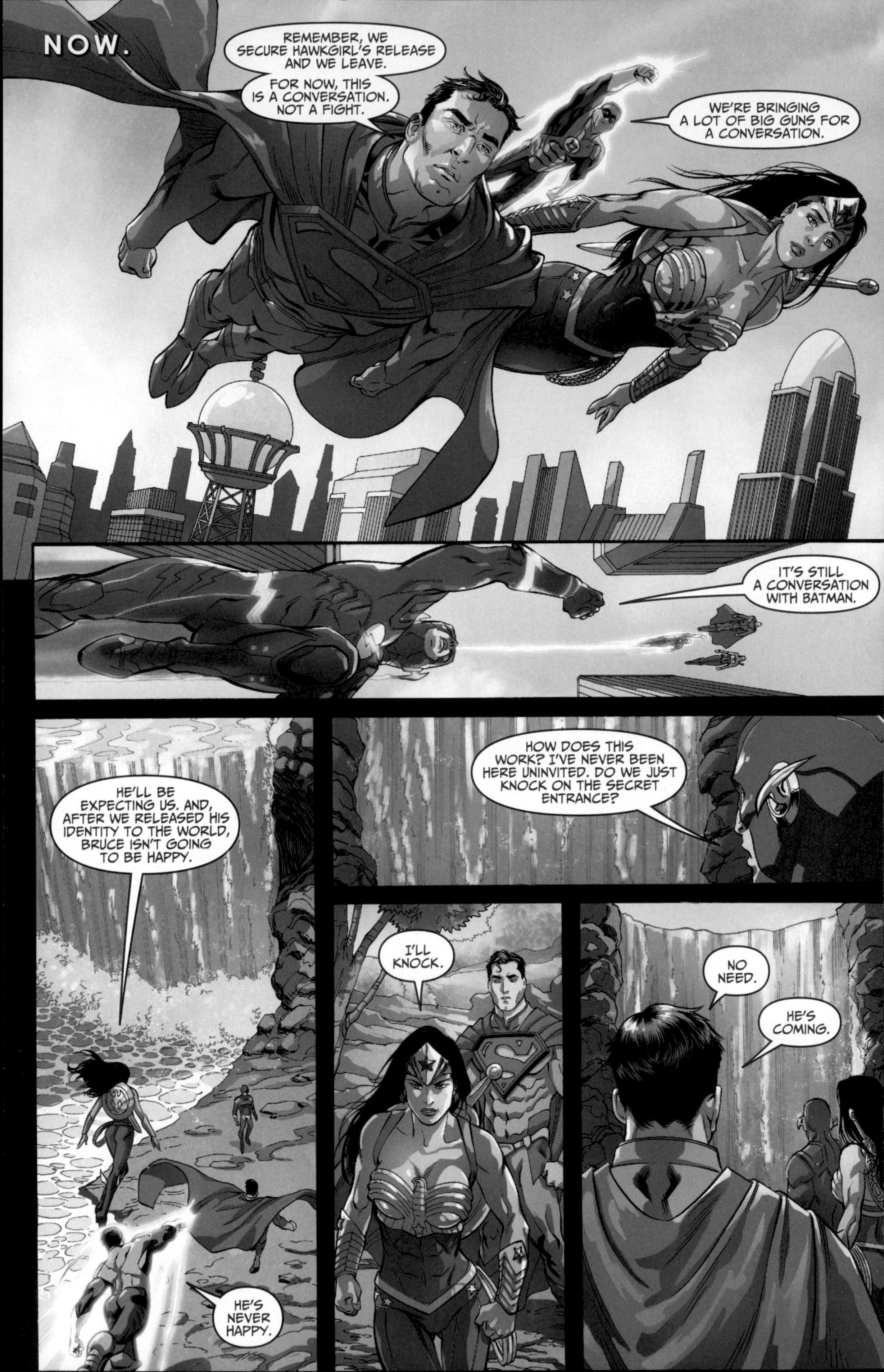
NOW.
REMEMBER, WE SECURE HAWKGIRL'S RELEASE AND WE LEAVE.
FOR NOW, THIS IS A CONVERSATION. NOT A FIGHT.
WE'RE BRINGING A LOT OF BIG GUNS FOR A CONVERSATION.
IT'S STILL A CONVERSATION WITH BATMAN.
HE'LL BE EXPECTING US. AND, AFTER WE RELEASED HIS IDENTITY TO THE WORLD, BRUCE ISN'T GOING TO BE HAPPY.
HE'S NEVER HAPPY.
HOW DOES THIS WORK? I'VE NEVER BEEN HERE UNINVITED. DO WE JUST KNOCK ON THE SECRET ENTRANCE?
I'LL KNOCK.
NO NEED.
HE'S COMING.

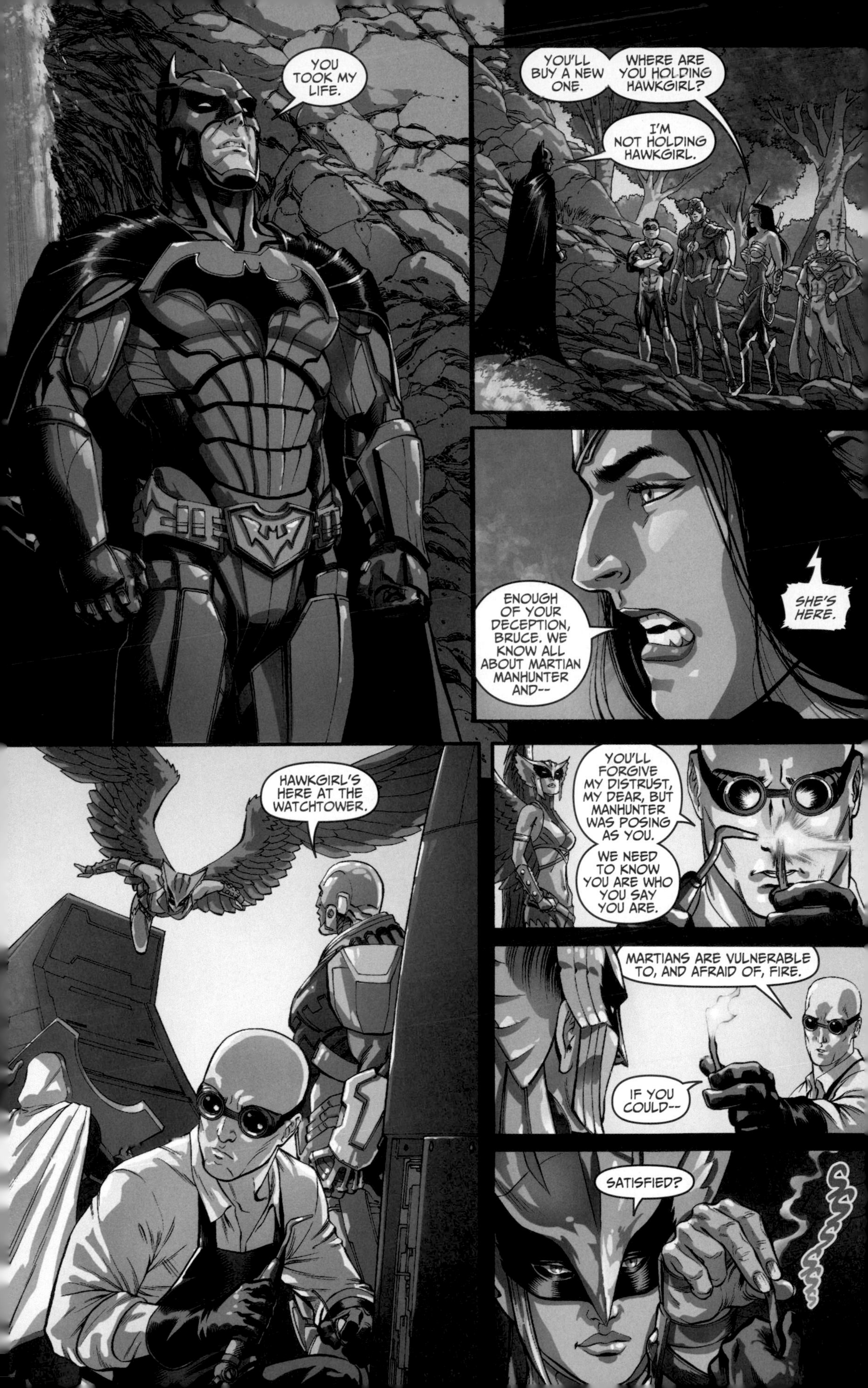
YOU TOOK MY LIFE.
YOU'LL BUY A NEW ONE.
WHERE ARE YOU HOLDING HAWKGIRL?
I'M NOT HOLDING HAWKGIRL.
ENOUGH OF YOUR DECEPTION, BRUCE. WE KNOW ALL ABOUT MARTIAN MANHUNTER AND--
SHE'S HERE.
HAWKGIRL'S HERE AT THE WATCHTOWER.
YOU'LL FORGIVE MY DISTRUST, MY DEAR, BUT MANHUNTER WAS POSING AS YOU.
WE NEED TO KNOW YOU ARE WHO YOU SAY YOU ARE.
MARTIANS ARE VULNERABLE TO, AND AFRAID OF, FIRE.
IF YOU COULD--
SATISFIED?

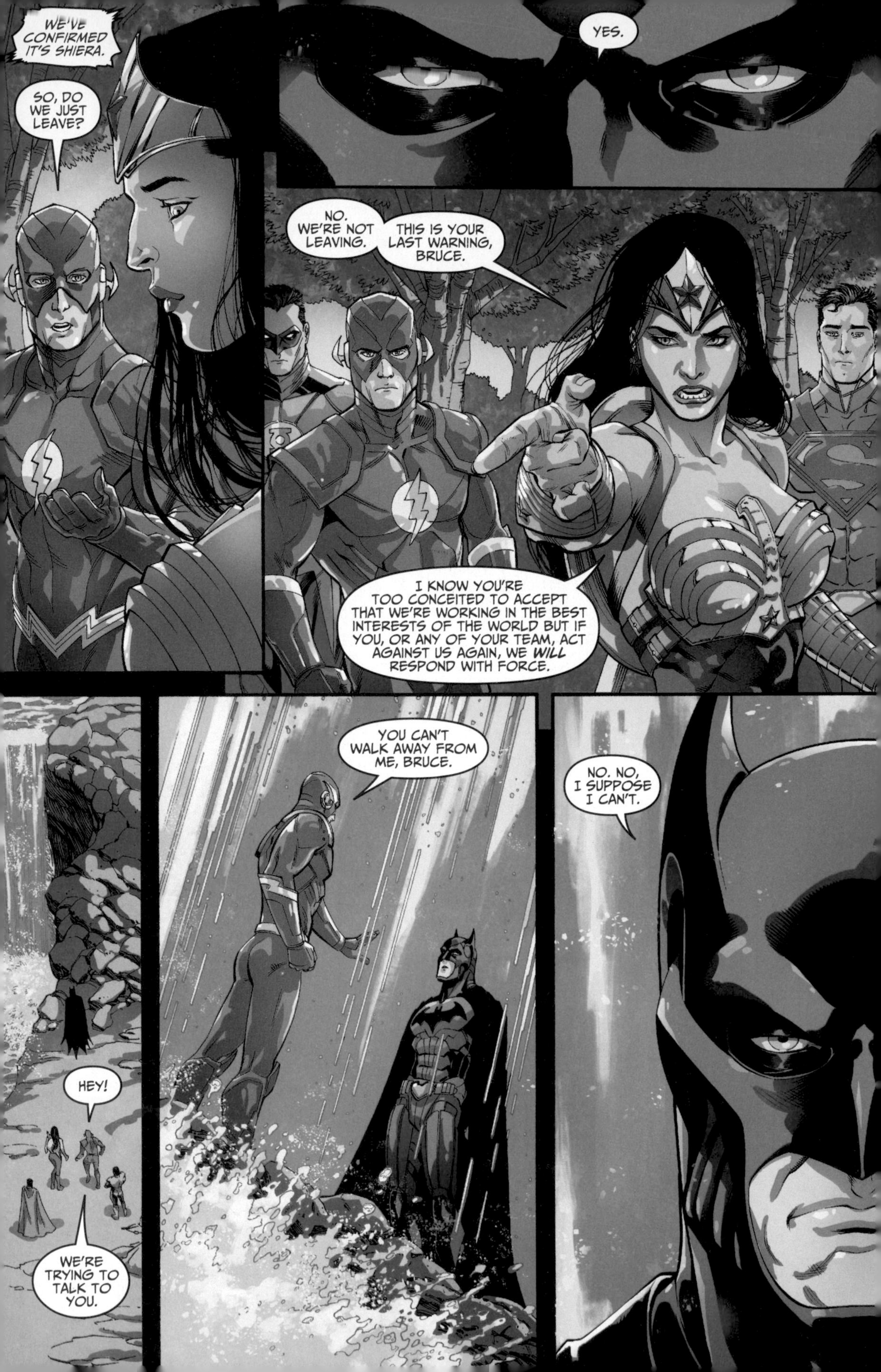
WE'VE CONFIRMED IT'S SHIERA.
SO, DO WE JUST LEAVE?
YES.
NO. WE'RE NOT LEAVING.
THIS IS YOUR LAST WARNING, BRUCE.
I KNOW YOU'RE TOO CONCEITED TO ACCEPT THAT WE'RE WORKING IN THE BEST INTERESTS OF THE WORLD BUT IF YOU, OR ANY OF YOUR TEAM, ACT AGAINST US AGAIN, WE *WILL* RESPOND WITH FORCE.
HEY!
WE'RE TRYING TO TALK TO YOU.
YOU CAN'T WALK AWAY FROM ME, BRUCE.
NO. NO, I SUPPOSE I CAN'T.

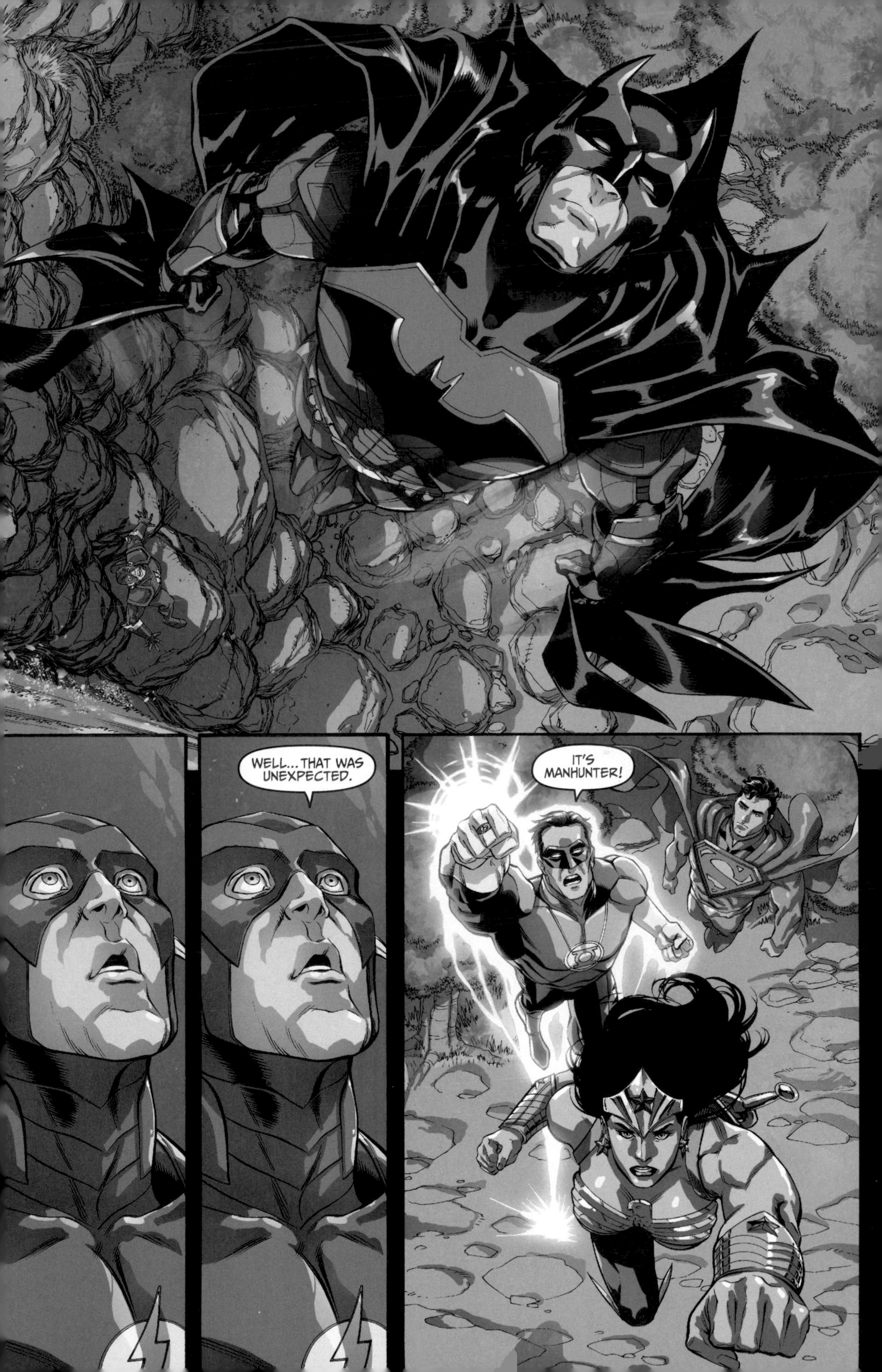
WELL... THAT WAS UNEXPECTED.
IT'S MANHUNTER!

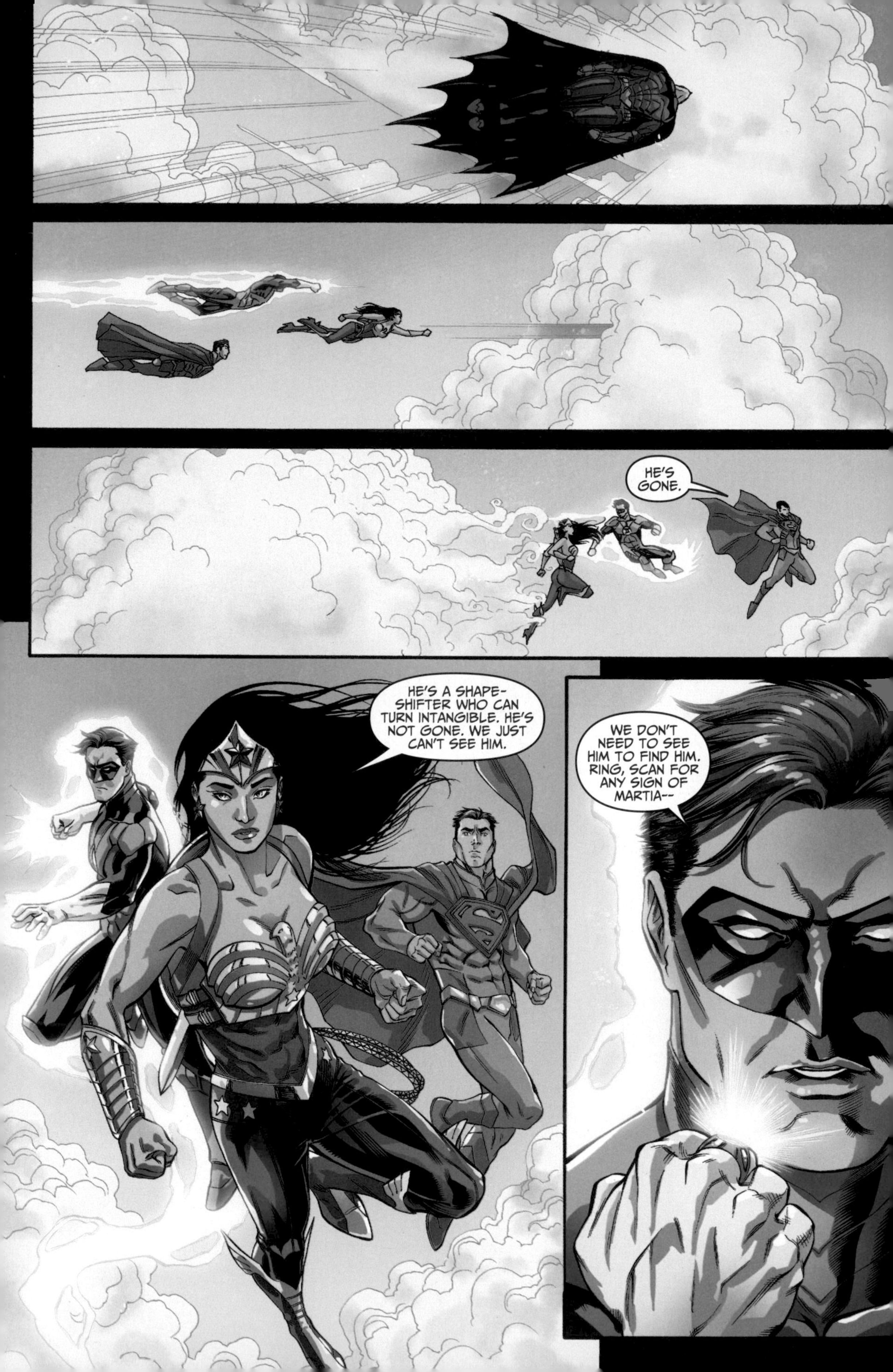
HE'S GONE.
HE'S A SHAPE-SHIFTER WHO CAN TURN INTANGIBLE. HE'S NOT GONE. WE JUST CAN'T SEE HIM.
WE DON'T NEED TO SEE HIM TO FIND HIM. RING, SCAN FOR ANY SIGN OF MARTIA--

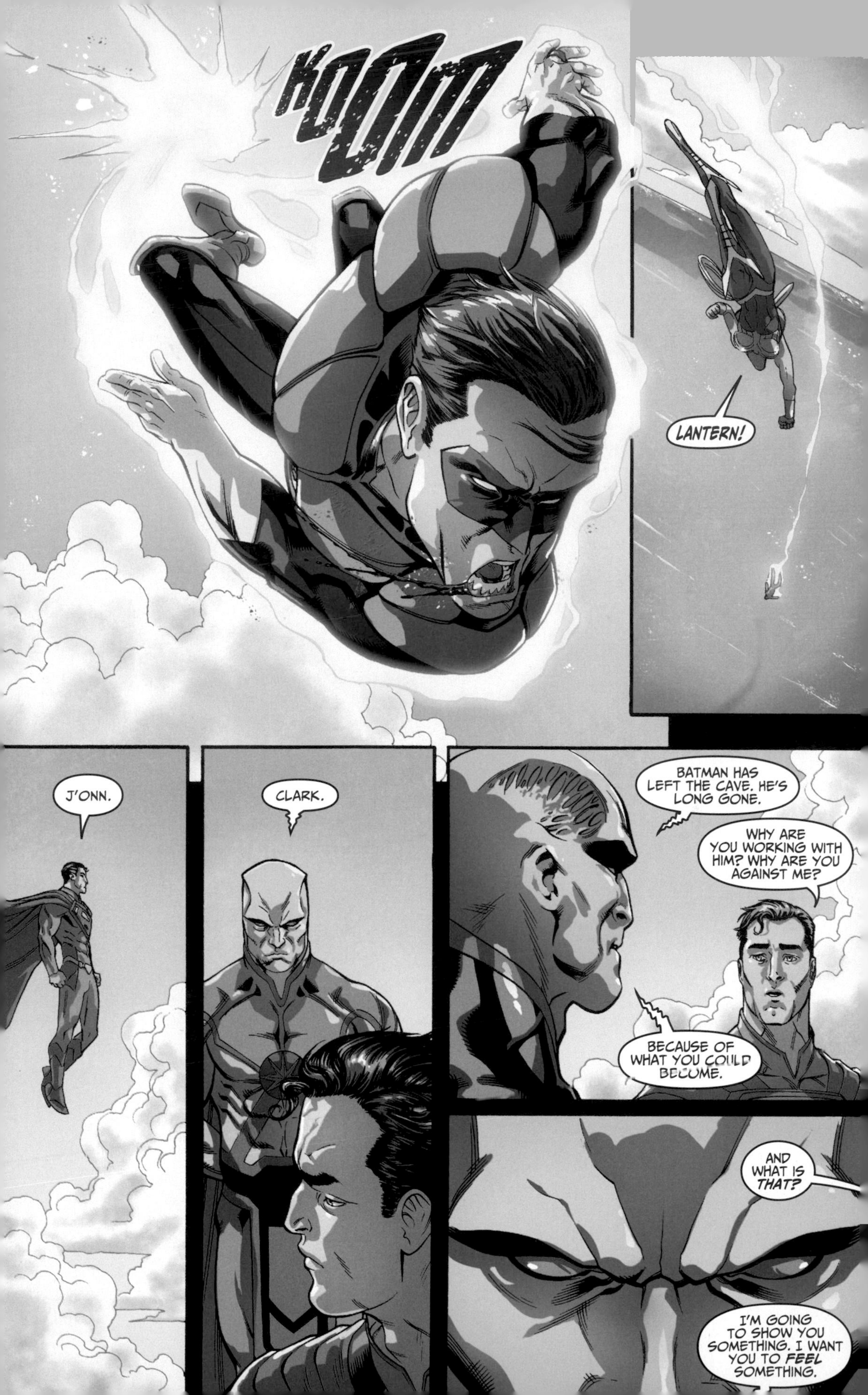
KOOM
LANTERN!
J'ONN.
CLARK.
BATMAN HAS LEFT THE CAVE. HE'S LONG GONE.
WHY ARE YOU WORKING WITH HIM? WHY ARE YOU AGAINST ME?
BECAUSE OF WHAT YOU COULD BECOME.
AND WHAT IS *THAT?*
I'M GOING TO SHOW YOU SOMETHING. I WANT YOU TO *FEEL* SOMETHING.

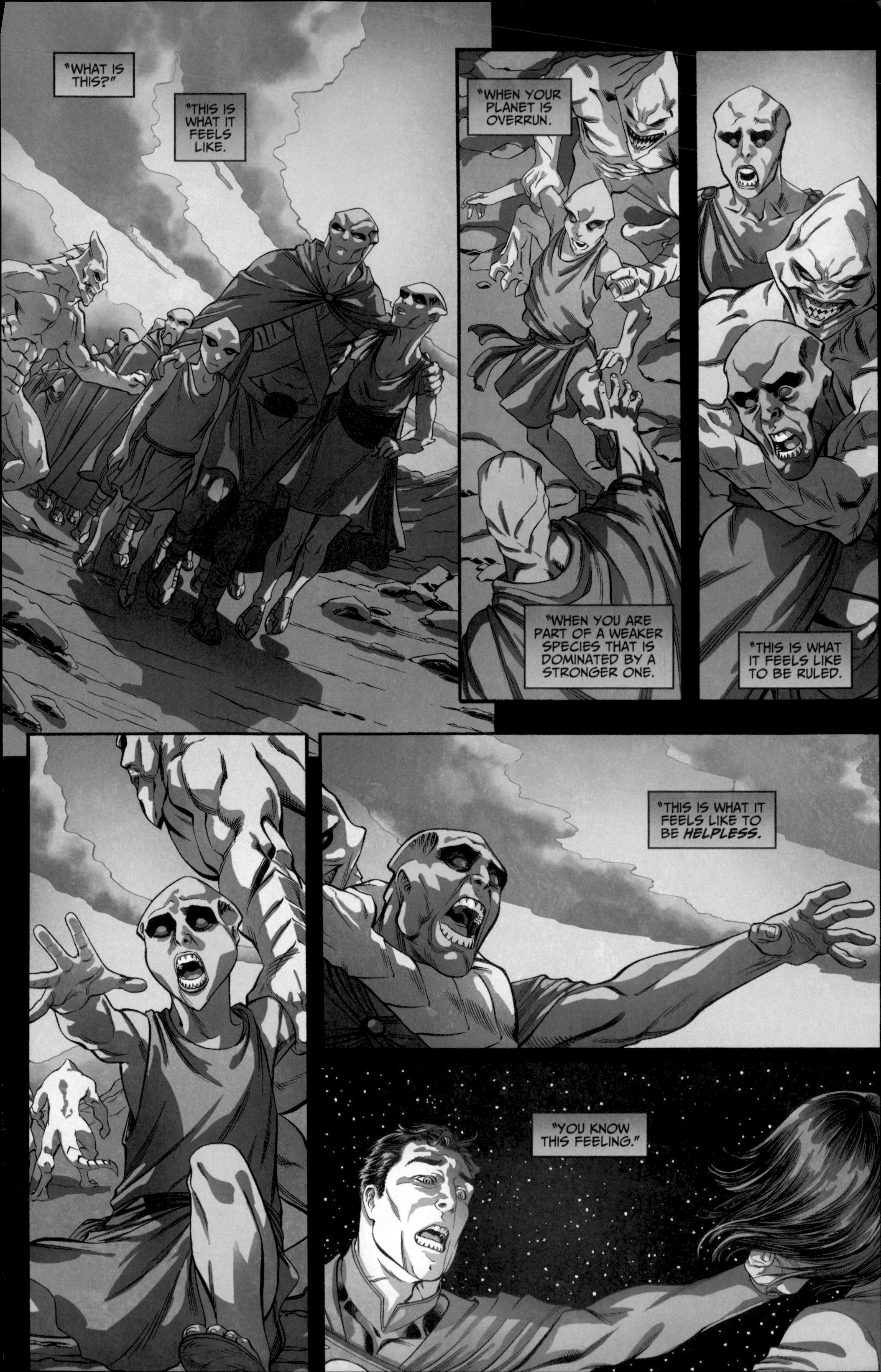
"WHAT IS THIS?"
"THIS IS WHAT IT FEELS LIKE.
"WHEN YOUR PLANET IS OVERRUN.
"WHEN YOU ARE PART OF A WEAKER SPECIES THAT IS DOMINATED BY A STRONGER ONE.
"THIS IS WHAT IT FEELS LIKE TO BE RULED.
"THIS IS WHAT IT FEELS LIKE TO BE *HELPLESS*.
"YOU KNOW THIS FEELING."

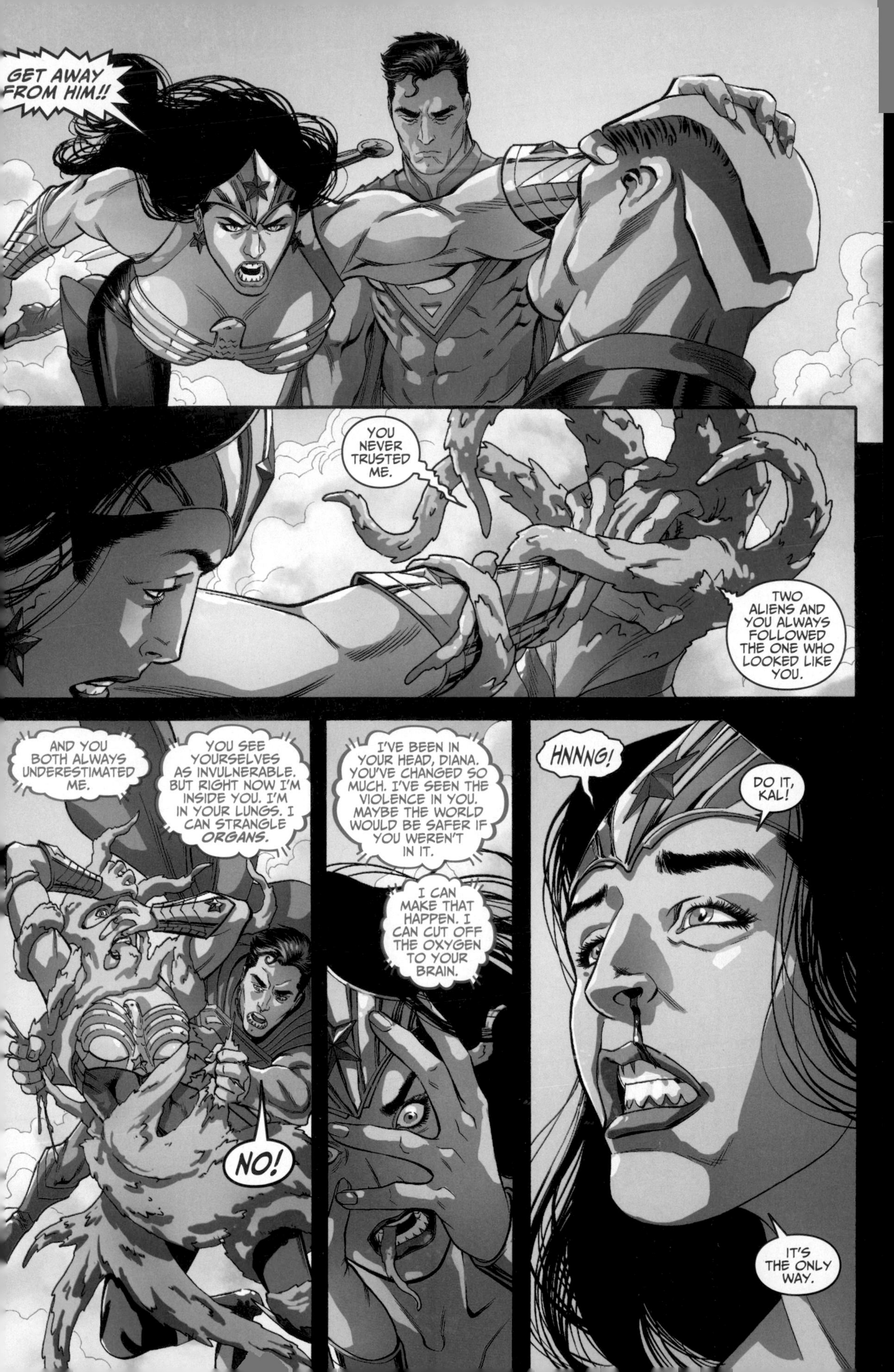
GET AWAY FROM HIM!!
YOU NEVER TRUSTED ME.
TWO ALIENS AND YOU ALWAYS FOLLOWED THE ONE WHO LOOKED LIKE YOU.
AND YOU BOTH ALWAYS UNDERESTIMATED ME.
YOU SEE YOURSELVES AS INVULNERABLE. BUT RIGHT NOW I'M INSIDE YOU. I'M IN YOUR LUNGS. I CAN STRANGLE ORGANS.
NO!
I'VE BEEN IN YOUR HEAD, DIANA. YOU'VE CHANGED SO MUCH. I'VE SEEN THE VIOLENCE IN YOU. MAYBE THE WORLD WOULD BE SAFER IF YOU WEREN'T IN IT.
I CAN MAKE THAT HAPPEN. I CAN CUT OFF THE OXYGEN TO YOUR BRAIN.
HNNNG!
DO IT, KAL!
IT'S THE ONLY WAY.

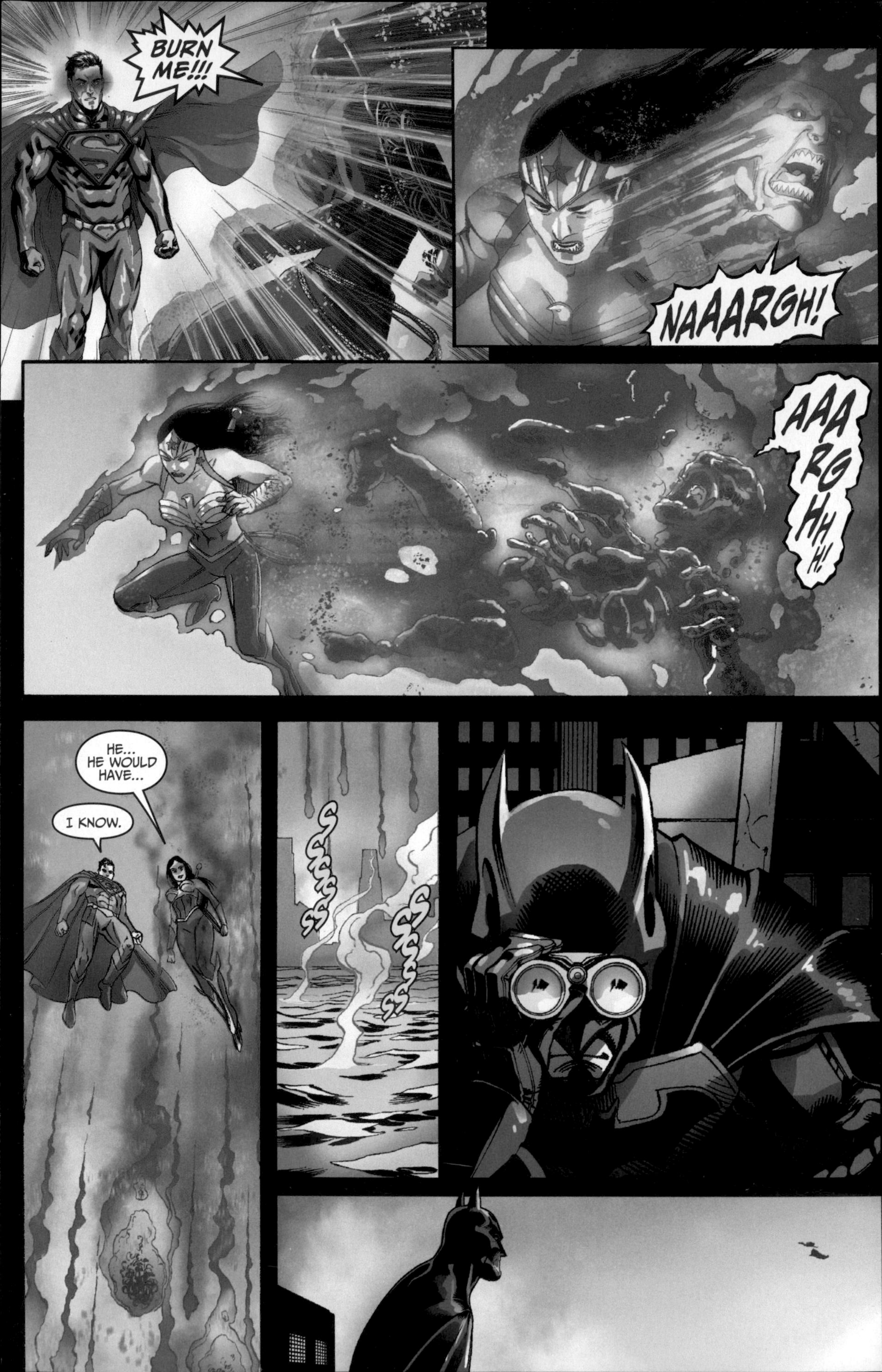
BURN ME!!!
NAAARGH!
AAARGHHH!
HE... HE WOULD HAVE...
I KNOW.
SSSSSS
SSSSSS

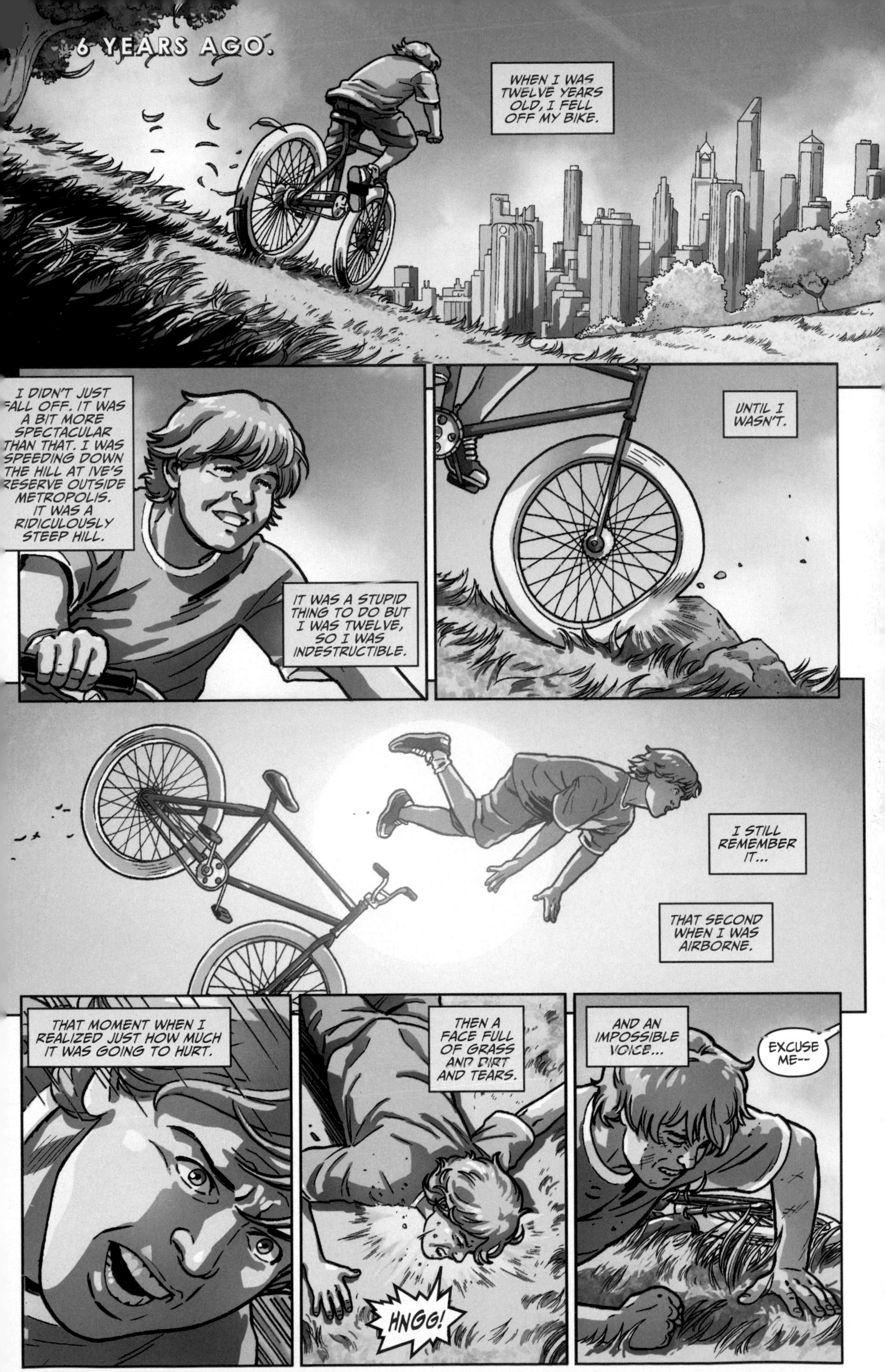
6 YEARS AGO.
WHEN I WAS TWELVE YEARS OLD, I FELL OFF MY BIKE.
I DIDN'T JUST FALL OFF. IT WAS A BIT MORE SPECTACULAR THAN THAT. I WAS SPEEDING DOWN THE HILL AT IVE'S RESERVE OUTSIDE METROPOLIS. IT WAS A RIDICULOUSLY STEEP HILL.
IT WAS A STUPID THING TO DO BUT I WAS TWELVE, SO I WAS INDESTRUCTIBLE.
UNTIL I WASN'T.
I STILL REMEMBER IT...
THAT SECOND WHEN I WAS AIRBORNE.
THAT MOMENT WHEN I REALIZED JUST HOW MUCH IT WAS GOING TO HURT.
THEN A FACE FULL OF GRASS AND DIRT AND TEARS.
HNGG!
AND AN IMPOSSIBLE VOICE...
EXCUSE ME--

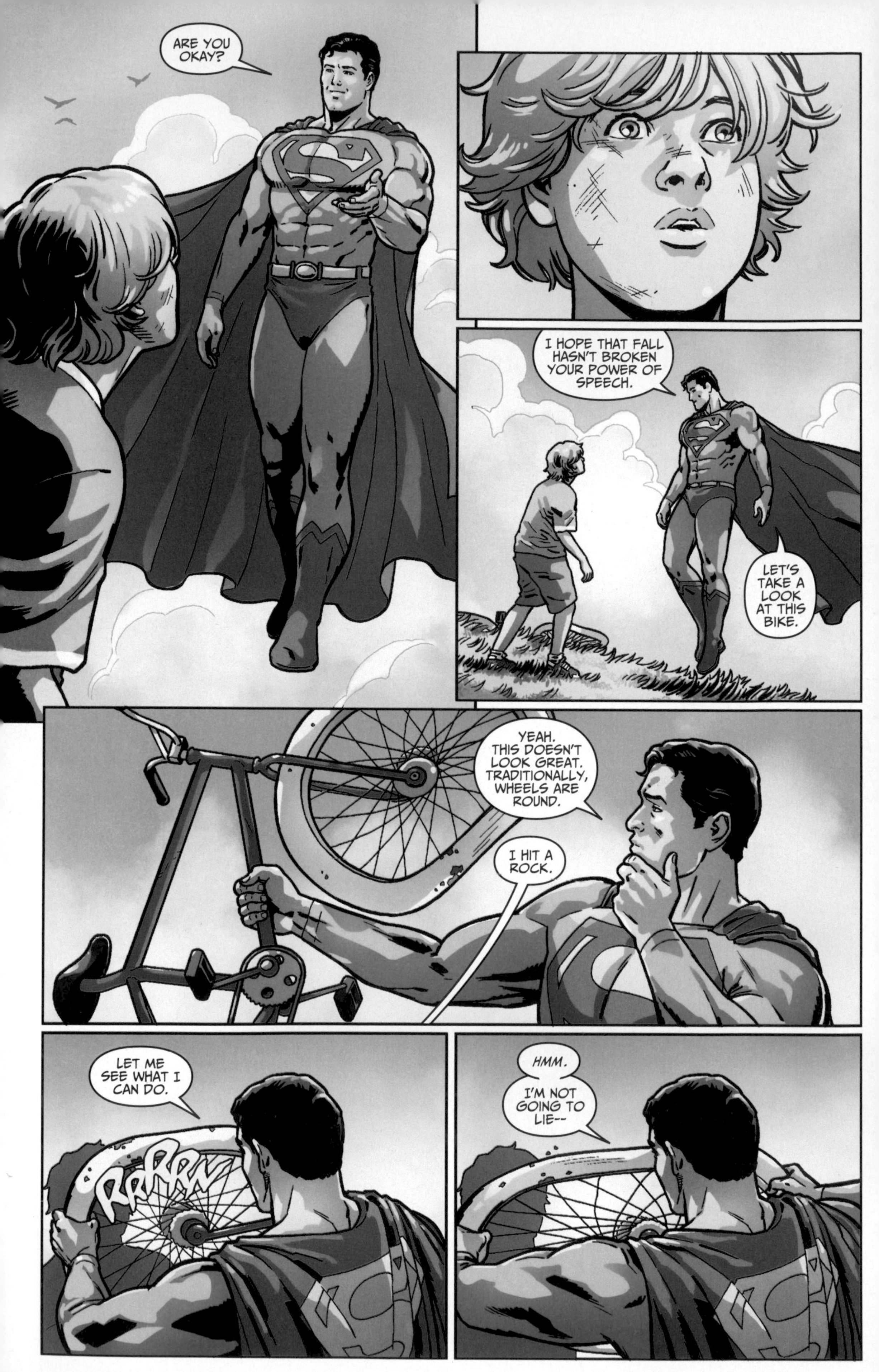
ARE YOU OKAY?
I HOPE THAT FALL HASN'T BROKEN YOUR POWER OF SPEECH.
LET'S TAKE A LOOK AT THIS BIKE.
YEAH. THIS DOESN'T LOOK GREAT. TRADITIONALLY, WHEELS ARE ROUND.
I HIT A ROCK.
LET ME SEE WHAT I CAN DO.
RRRRN
HMM.
I'M NOT GOING TO LIE--

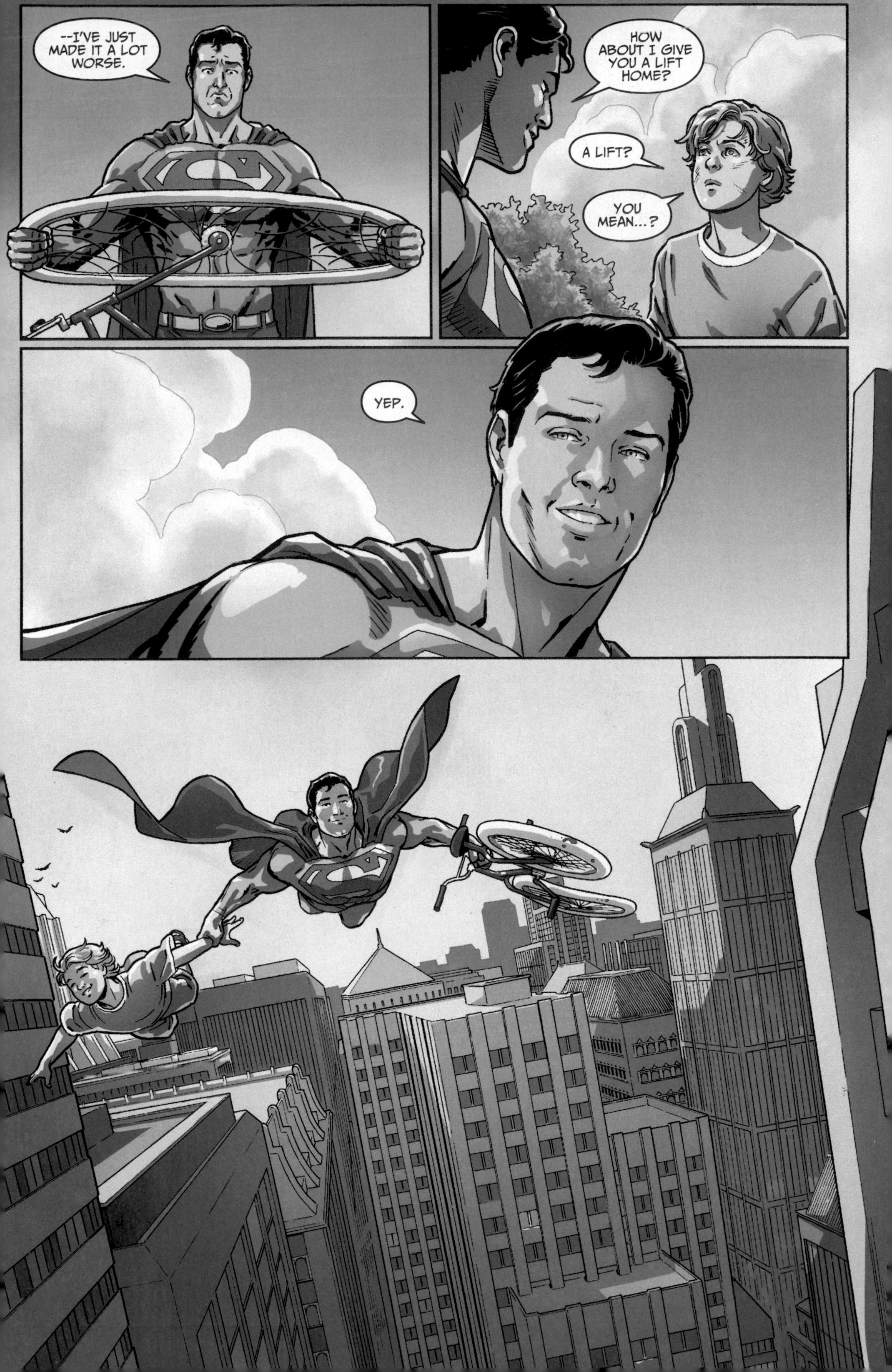
--I'VE JUST MADE IT A LOT WORSE.
HOW ABOUT I GIVE YOU A LIFT HOME?
A LIFT?
YOU MEAN...?
YEP.

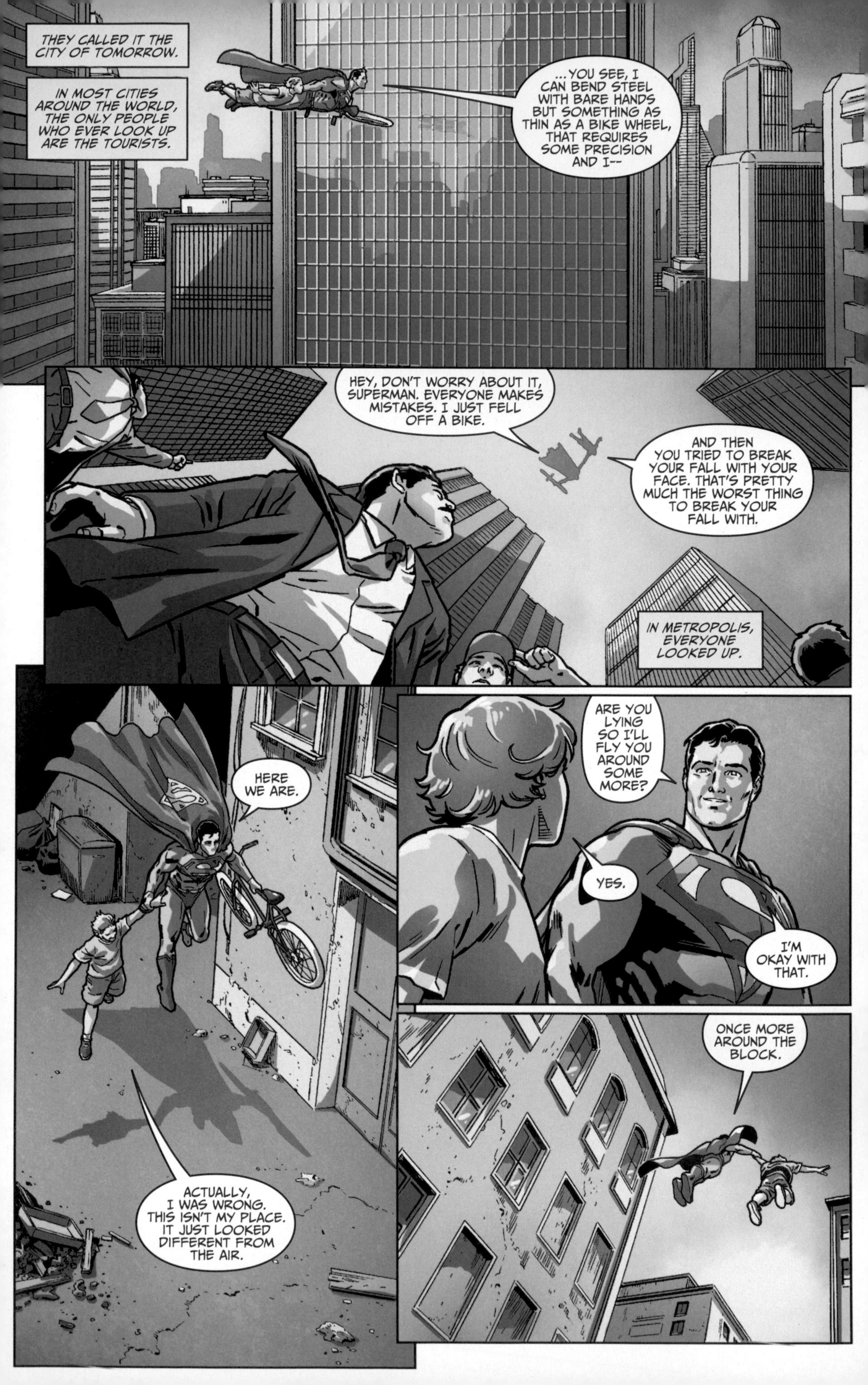
THEY CALLED IT THE CITY OF TOMORROW.
IN MOST CITIES AROUND THE WORLD, THE ONLY PEOPLE WHO EVER LOOK UP ARE THE TOURISTS.
...YOU SEE, I CAN BEND STEEL WITH BARE HANDS BUT SOMETHING AS THIN AS A BIKE WHEEL, THAT REQUIRES SOME PRECISION AND I--
HEY, DON'T WORRY ABOUT IT, SUPERMAN. EVERYONE MAKES MISTAKES. I JUST FELL OFF A BIKE.
AND THEN YOU TRIED TO BREAK YOUR FALL WITH YOUR FACE. THAT'S PRETTY MUCH THE WORST THING TO BREAK YOUR FALL WITH.
IN METROPOLIS, EVERYONE LOOKED UP.
HERE WE ARE.
ACTUALLY, I WAS WRONG. THIS ISN'T MY PLACE. IT JUST LOOKED DIFFERENT FROM THE AIR.
ARE YOU LYING SO I'LL FLY YOU AROUND SOME MORE?
YES.
I'M OKAY WITH THAT.
ONCE MORE AROUND THE BLOCK.

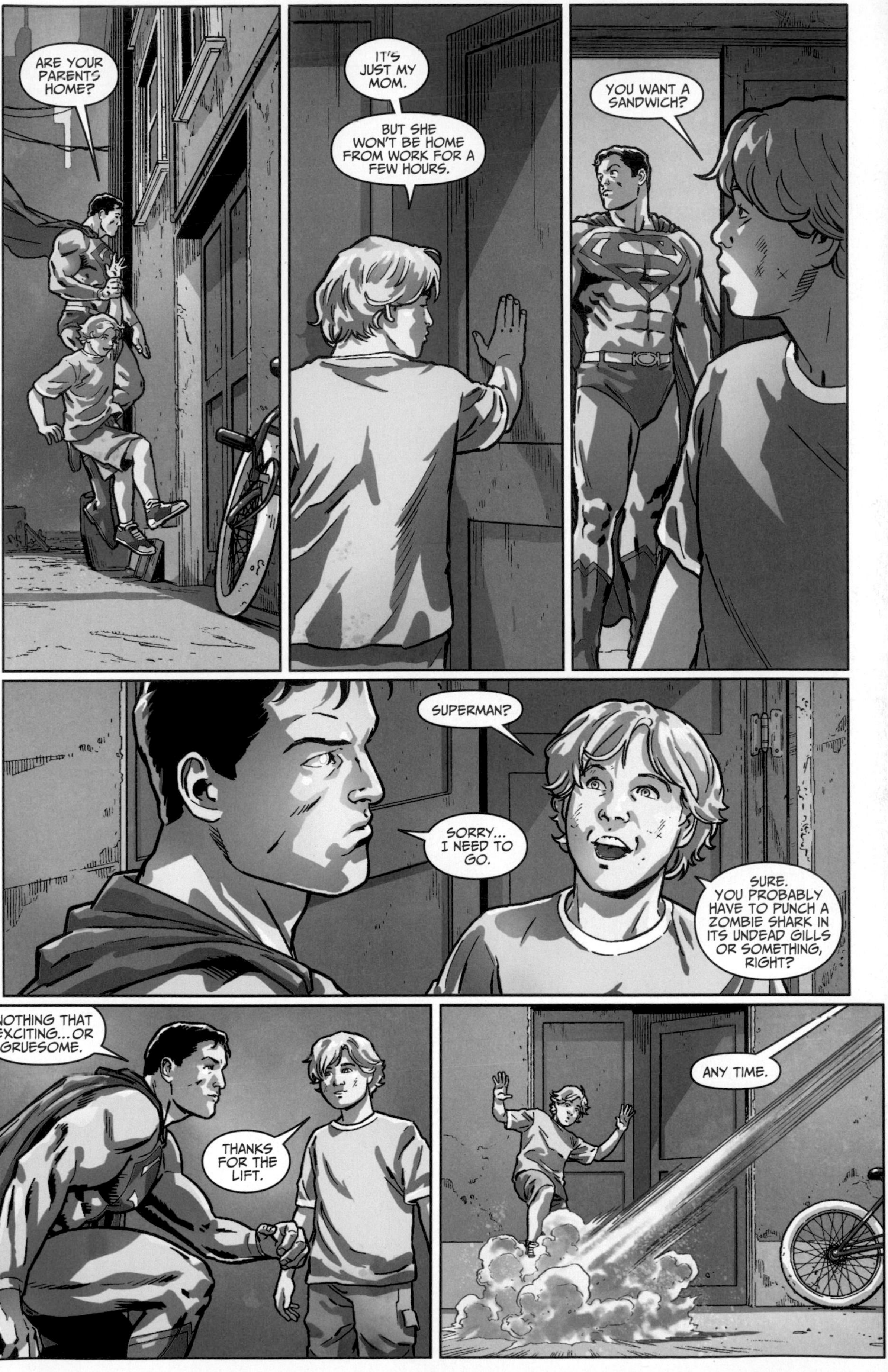
ARE YOUR PARENTS HOME?
IT'S JUST MY MOM.
BUT SHE WON'T BE HOME FROM WORK FOR A FEW HOURS.
YOU WANT A SANDWICH?
SUPERMAN?
SORRY... I NEED TO GO.
SURE. YOU PROBABLY HAVE TO PUNCH A ZOMBIE SHARK IN ITS UNDEAD GILLS OR SOMETHING, RIGHT?
NOTHING THAT EXCITING...OR GRUESOME.
THANKS FOR THE LIFT.
ANY TIME.

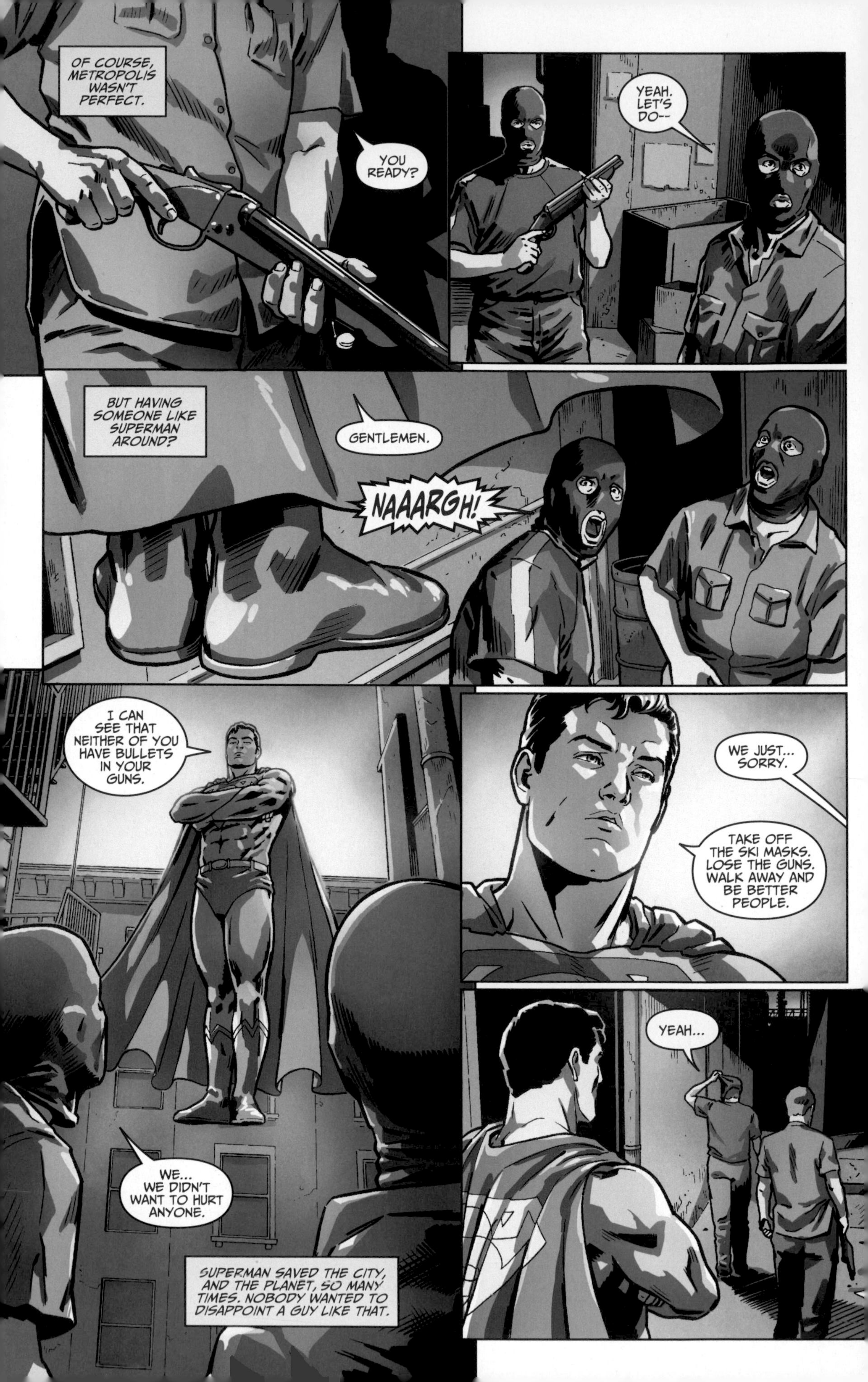
OF COURSE, METROPOLIS WASN'T PERFECT.
YOU READY?
YEAH. LET'S DO--
BUT HAVING SOMEONE LIKE SUPERMAN AROUND?
GENTLEMEN.
NAAARGH!
I CAN SEE THAT NEITHER OF YOU HAVE BULLETS IN YOUR GUNS.
WE... WE DIDN'T WANT TO HURT ANYONE.
SUPERMAN SAVED THE CITY, AND THE PLANET, SO MANY TIMES. NOBODY WANTED TO DISAPPOINT A GUY LIKE THAT.
WE JUST... SORRY.
TAKE OFF THE SKI MASKS. LOSE THE GUNS. WALK AWAY AND BE BETTER PEOPLE.
YEAH...

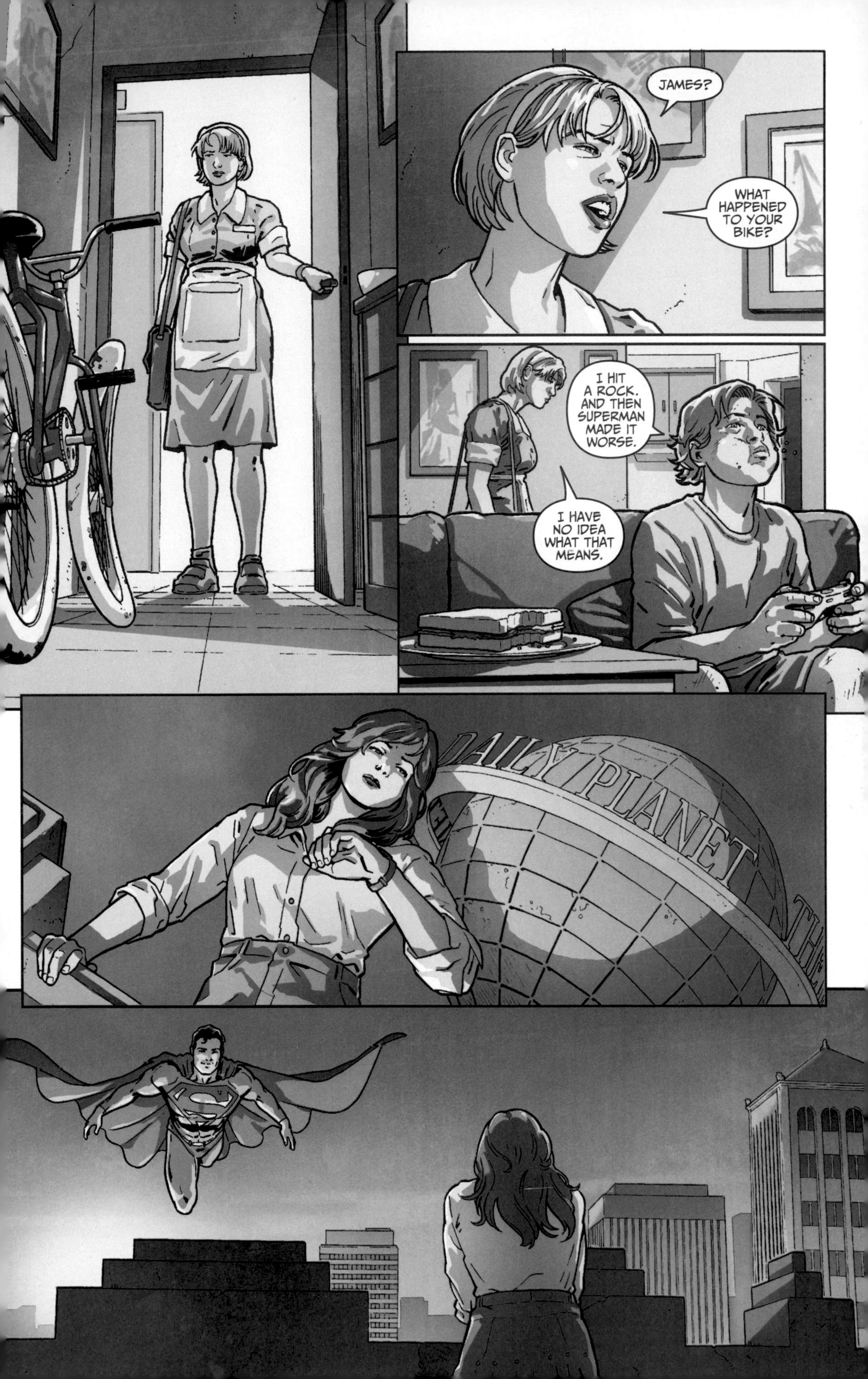
JAMES?
WHAT HAPPENED TO YOUR BIKE?
I HIT A ROCK. AND THEN SUPERMAN MADE IT WORSE.
I HAVE NO IDEA WHAT THAT MEANS.
DAILY PLANET

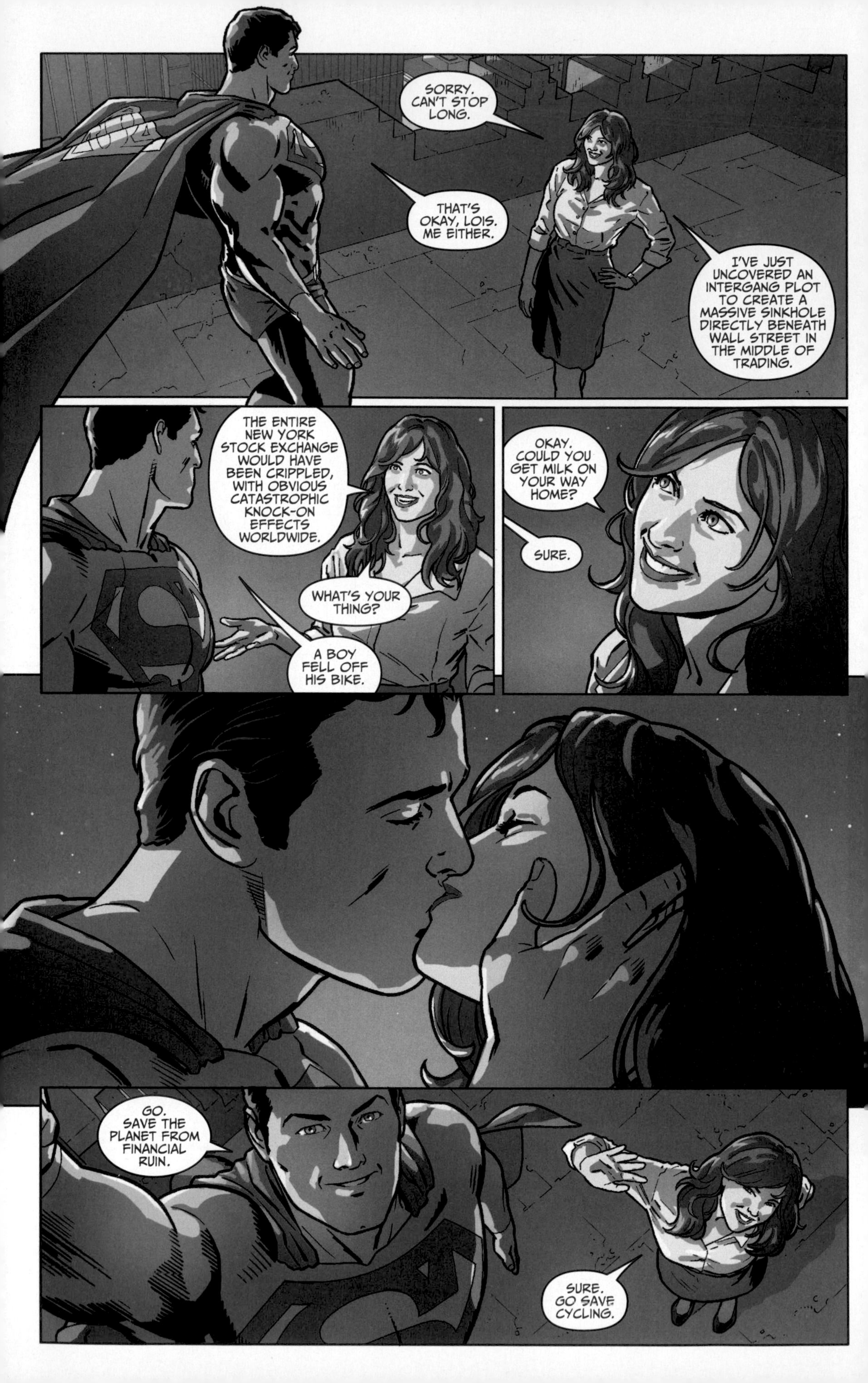
SORRY. CAN'T STOP LONG.
THAT'S OKAY, LOIS. ME EITHER.
I'VE JUST UNCOVERED AN INTERGANG PLOT TO CREATE A MASSIVE SINKHOLE DIRECTLY BENEATH WALL STREET IN THE MIDDLE OF TRADING.
THE ENTIRE NEW YORK STOCK EXCHANGE WOULD HAVE BEEN CRIPPLED, WITH OBVIOUS CATASTROPHIC KNOCK-ON EFFECTS WORLDWIDE.
WHAT'S YOUR THING?
A BOY FELL OFF HIS BIKE.
OKAY. COULD YOU GET MILK ON YOUR WAY HOME?
SURE.
GO. SAVE THE PLANET FROM FINANCIAL RUIN.
SURE. GO SAVE CYCLING.

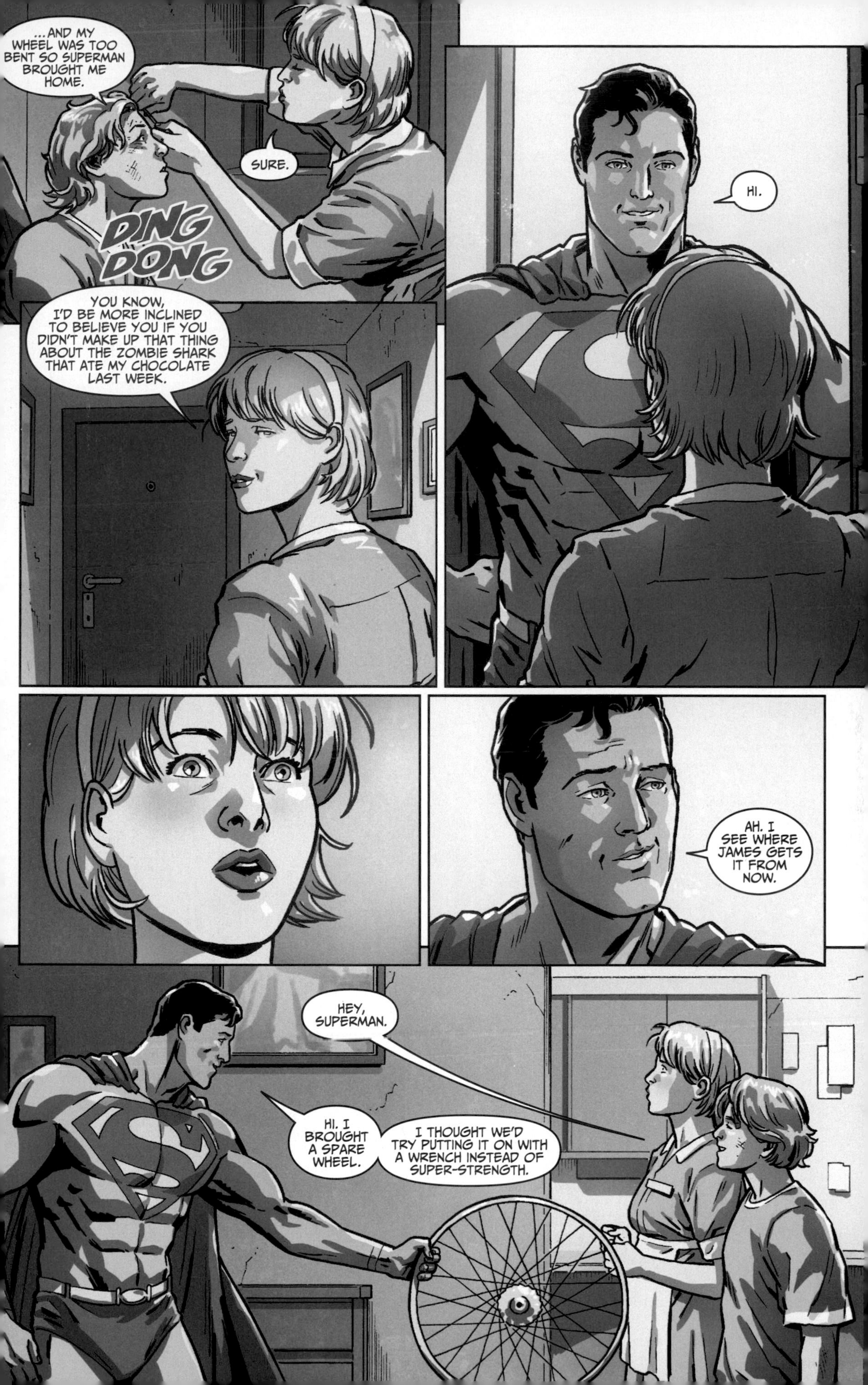
...AND MY WHEEL WAS TOO BENT SO SUPERMAN BROUGHT ME HOME.
SURE.
DING DONG
YOU KNOW, I'D BE MORE INCLINED TO BELIEVE YOU IF YOU DIDN'T MAKE UP THAT THING ABOUT THE ZOMBIE SHARK THAT ATE MY CHOCOLATE LAST WEEK.
HI.
AH. I SEE WHERE JAMES GETS IT FROM NOW.
HEY, SUPERMAN.
HI. I BROUGHT A SPARE WHEEL.
I THOUGHT WE'D TRY PUTTING IT ON WITH A WRENCH INSTEAD OF SUPER-STRENGTH.

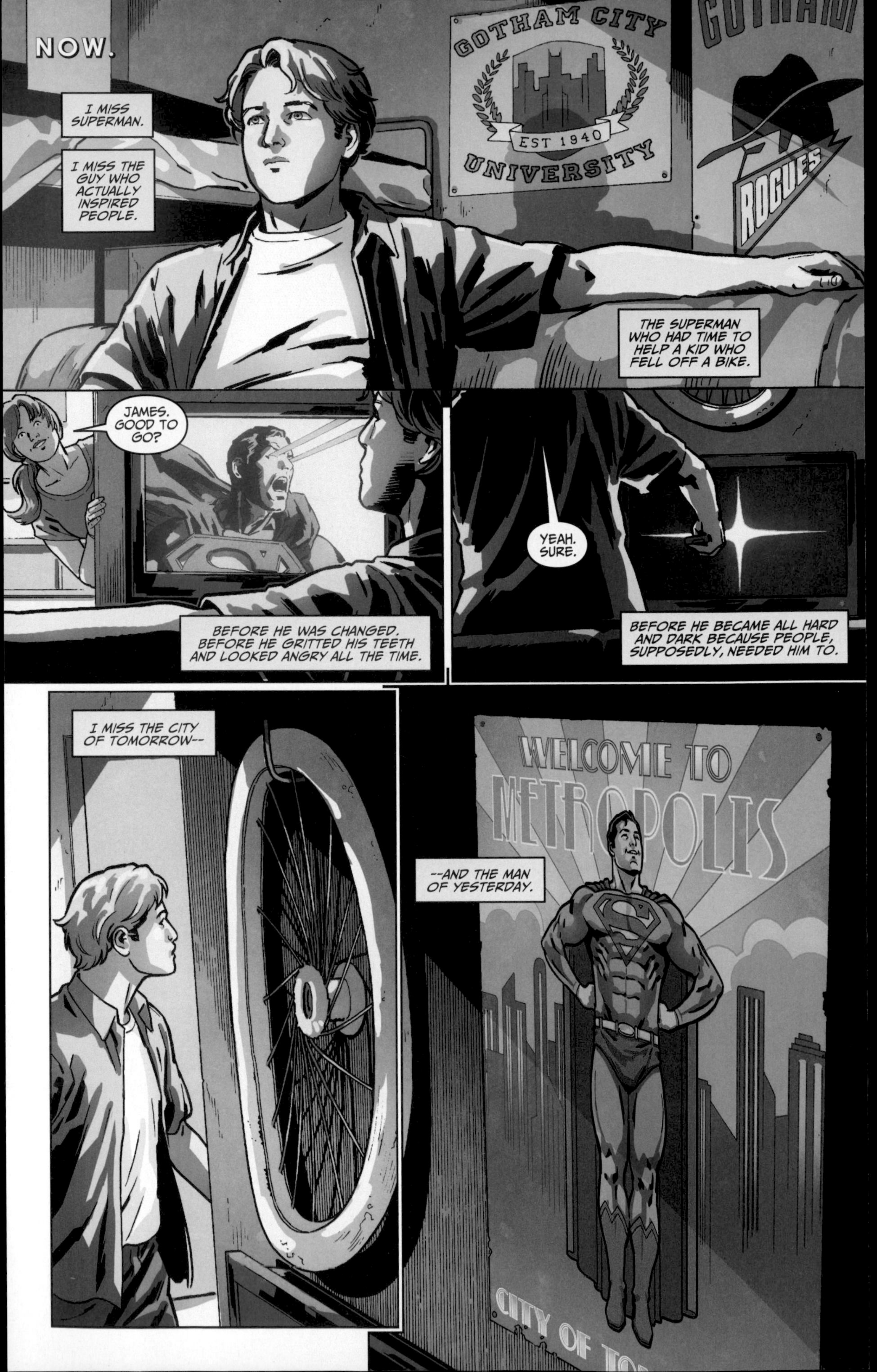
NOW.
GOTHAM CITY
EST 1940
UNIVERSITY
ROGUES
I MISS SUPERMAN.
I MISS THE GUY WHO ACTUALLY INSPIRED PEOPLE.
THE SUPERMAN WHO HAD TIME TO HELP A KID WHO FELL OFF A BIKE.
JAMES. GOOD TO GO?
BEFORE HE WAS CHANGED. BEFORE HE GRITTED HIS TEETH AND LOOKED ANGRY ALL THE TIME.
YEAH. SURE.
BEFORE HE BECAME ALL HARD AND DARK BECAUSE PEOPLE, SUPPOSEDLY, NEEDED HIM TO.
I MISS THE CITY OF TOMORROW--
WELCOME TO METROPOLIS
--AND THE MAN OF YESTERDAY.

PART ELEVEN

Xermanico **Jonas Trindade** **Mike S. Miller** **Bruno Redondo** Artists

Alejandro Sanchez Colorist

Juan José Ryp & **David Lopez** and **Santi Casas** of **Ikari Studio** Cover

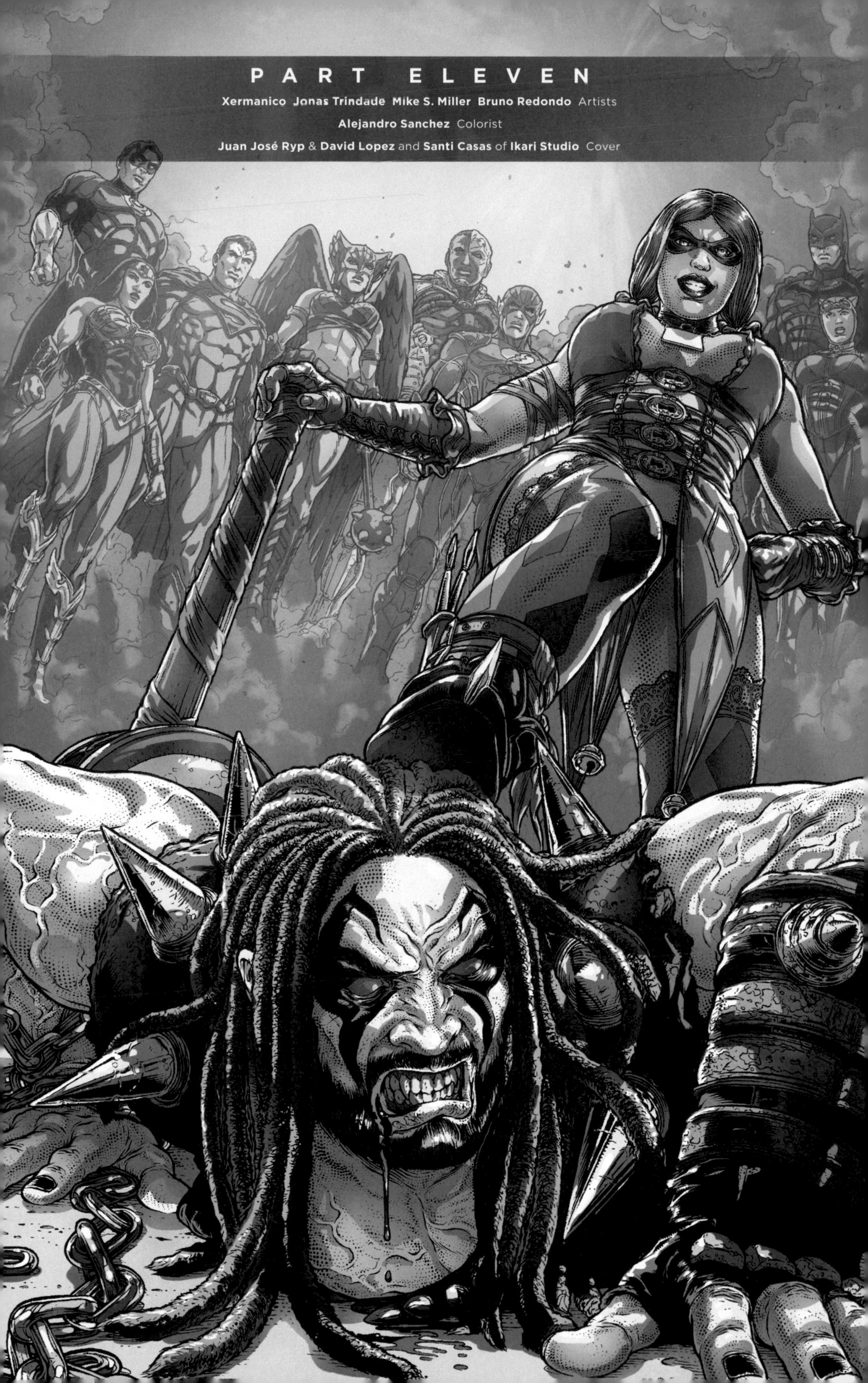

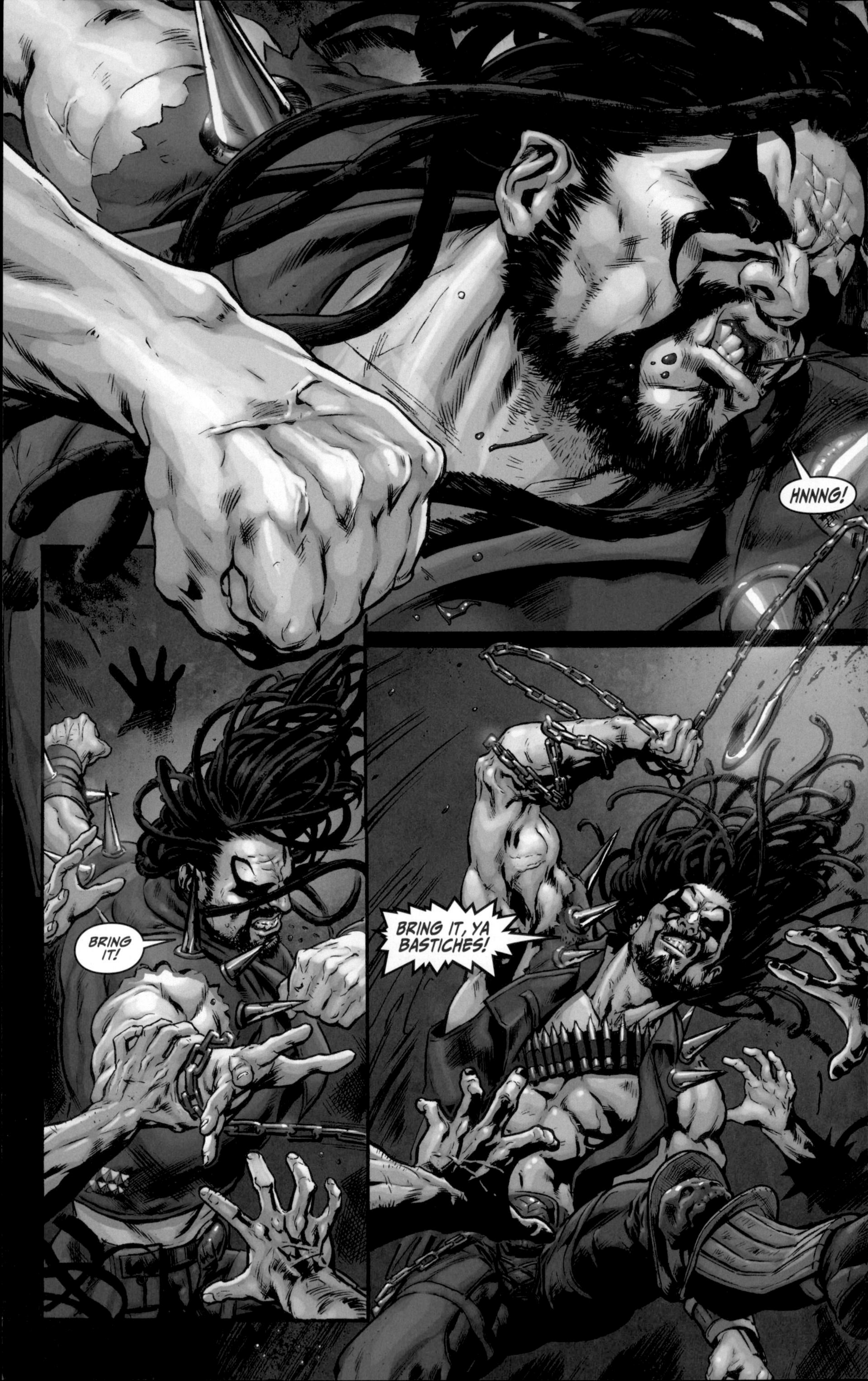
HNNNG!
BRING IT!
BRING IT, YA BASTICHES!

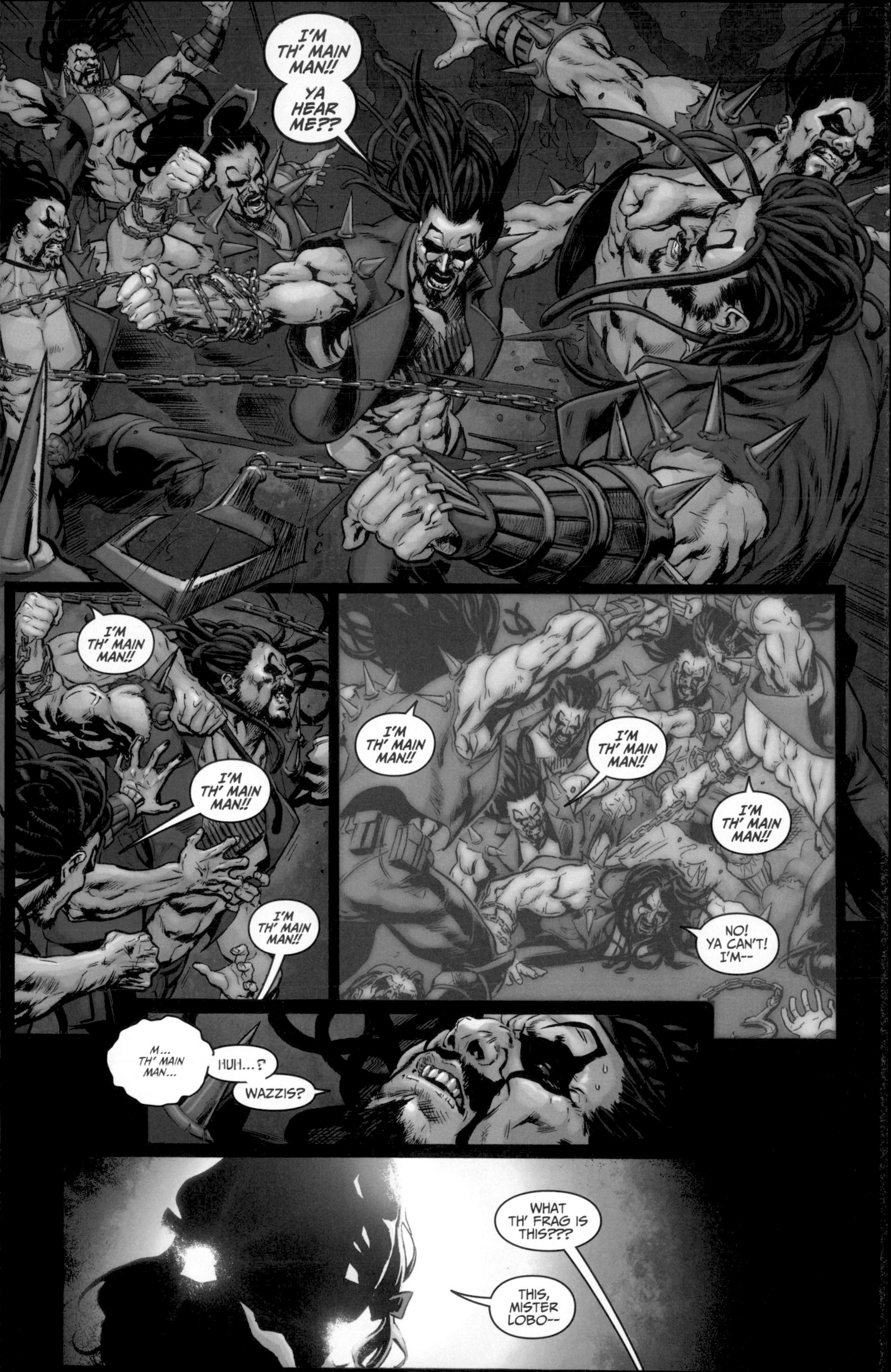
I'M TH' MAIN MAN!! YA HEAR ME??
I'M TH' MAIN MAN!!
I'M TH' MAIN MAN!!
I'M TH' MAIN MAN!!
I'M TH' MAIN MAN!!
I'M TH' MAIN MAN!!
I'M TH' MAIN MAN!!
NO! YA CAN'T! I'M--
M... TH' MAIN MAN...
HUH...?
WAZZIS?
WHAT TH' FRAG IS THIS???
THIS, MISTER LOBO--

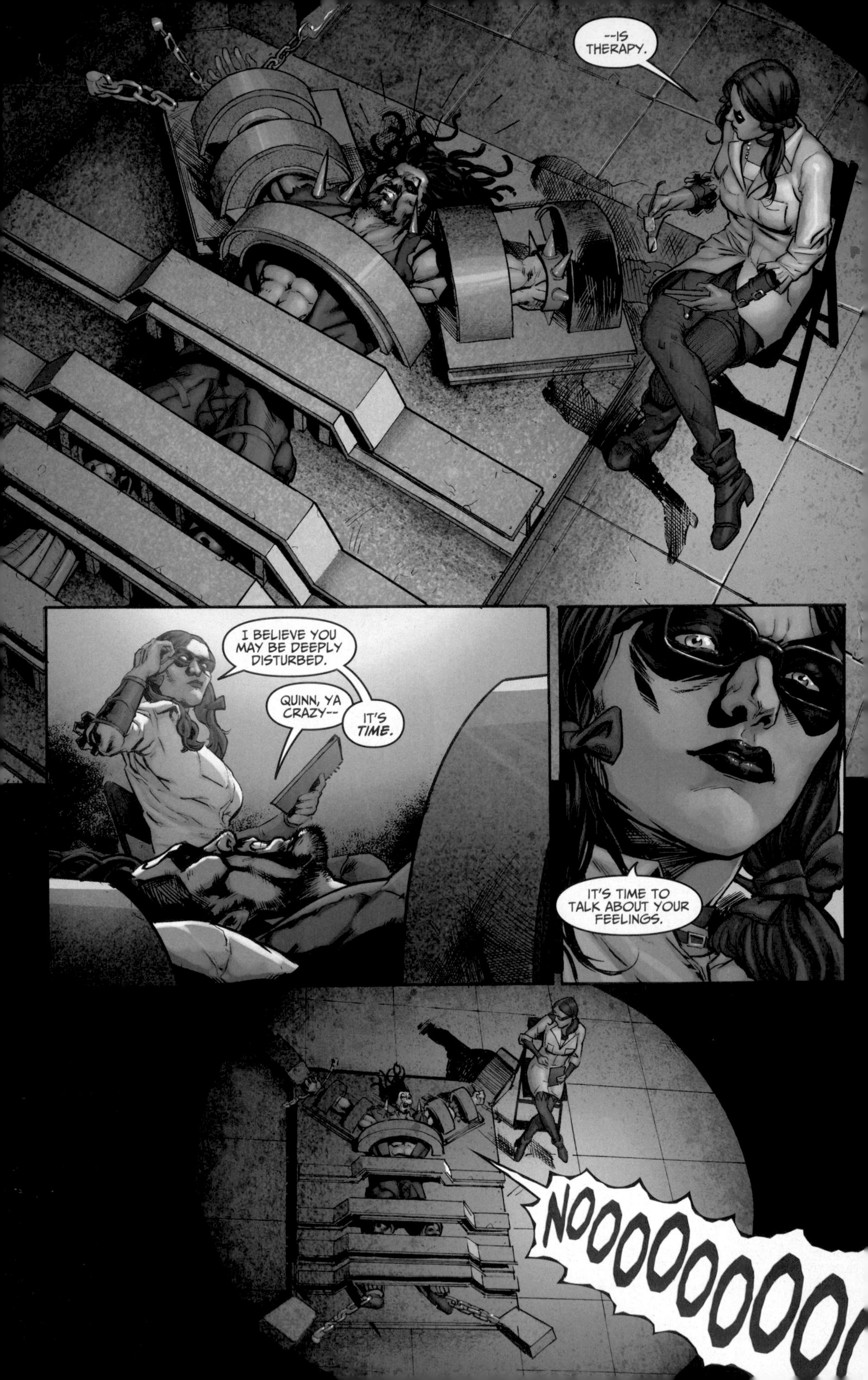
--IS THERAPY.
I BELIEVE YOU MAY BE DEEPLY DISTURBED.
QUINN, YA CRAZY--
IT'S *TIME*.
IT'S TIME TO TALK ABOUT YOUR FEELINGS.
NOOOOOOOOO!

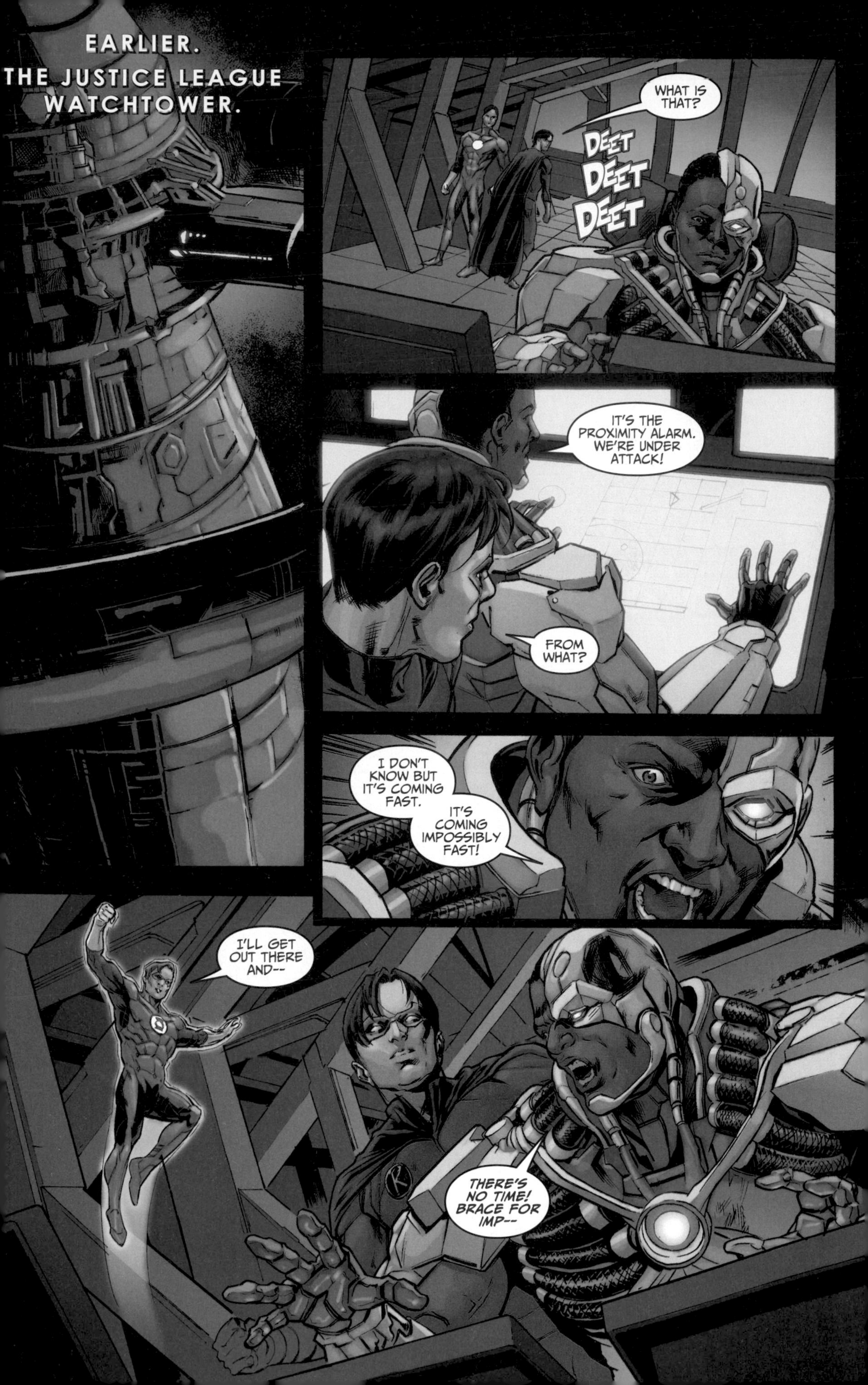
EARLIER.
THE JUSTICE LEAGUE WATCHTOWER.
WHAT IS THAT?
DEET DEET DEET
IT'S THE PROXIMITY ALARM. WE'RE UNDER ATTACK!
FROM WHAT?
I DON'T KNOW BUT IT'S COMING FAST.
IT'S COMING IMPOSSIBLY FAST!
I'LL GET OUT THERE AND--
THERE'S NO TIME! BRACE FOR IMP--

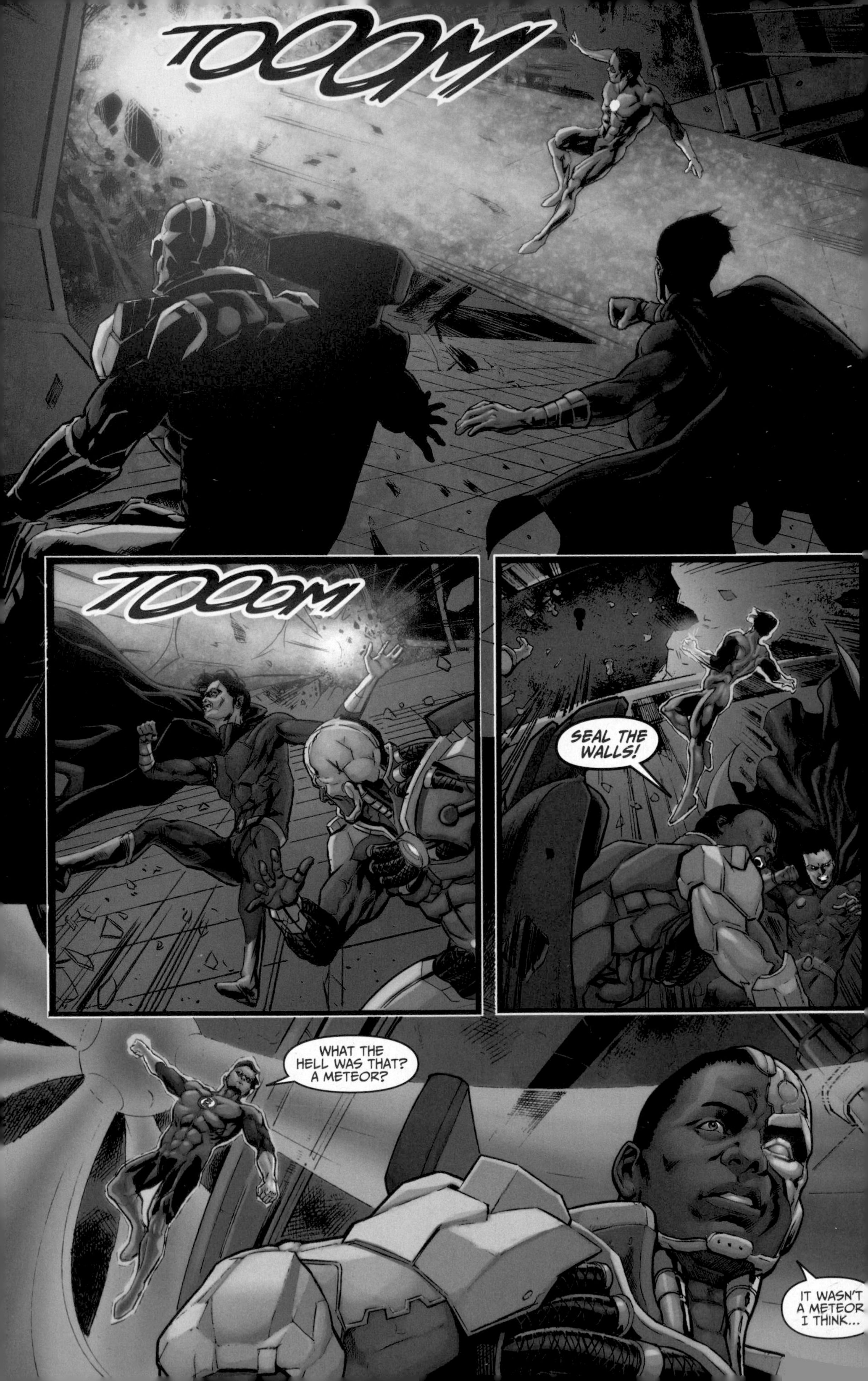
TOOOOM
TOOOOM
SEAL THE WALLS!
WHAT THE HELL WAS THAT? A METEOR?
IT WASN'T A METEOR I THINK...

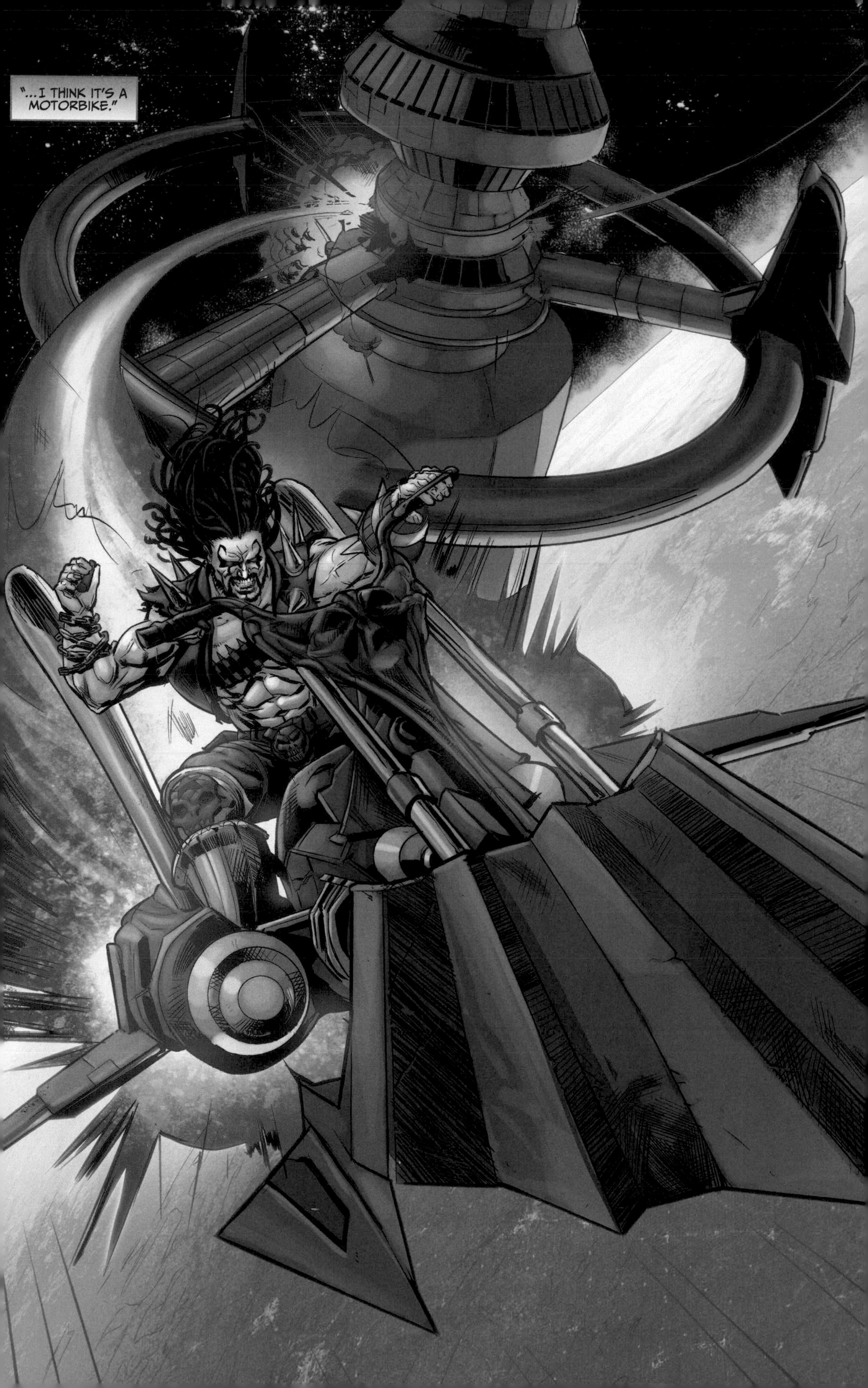
"...I THINK IT'S A MOTORBIKE."

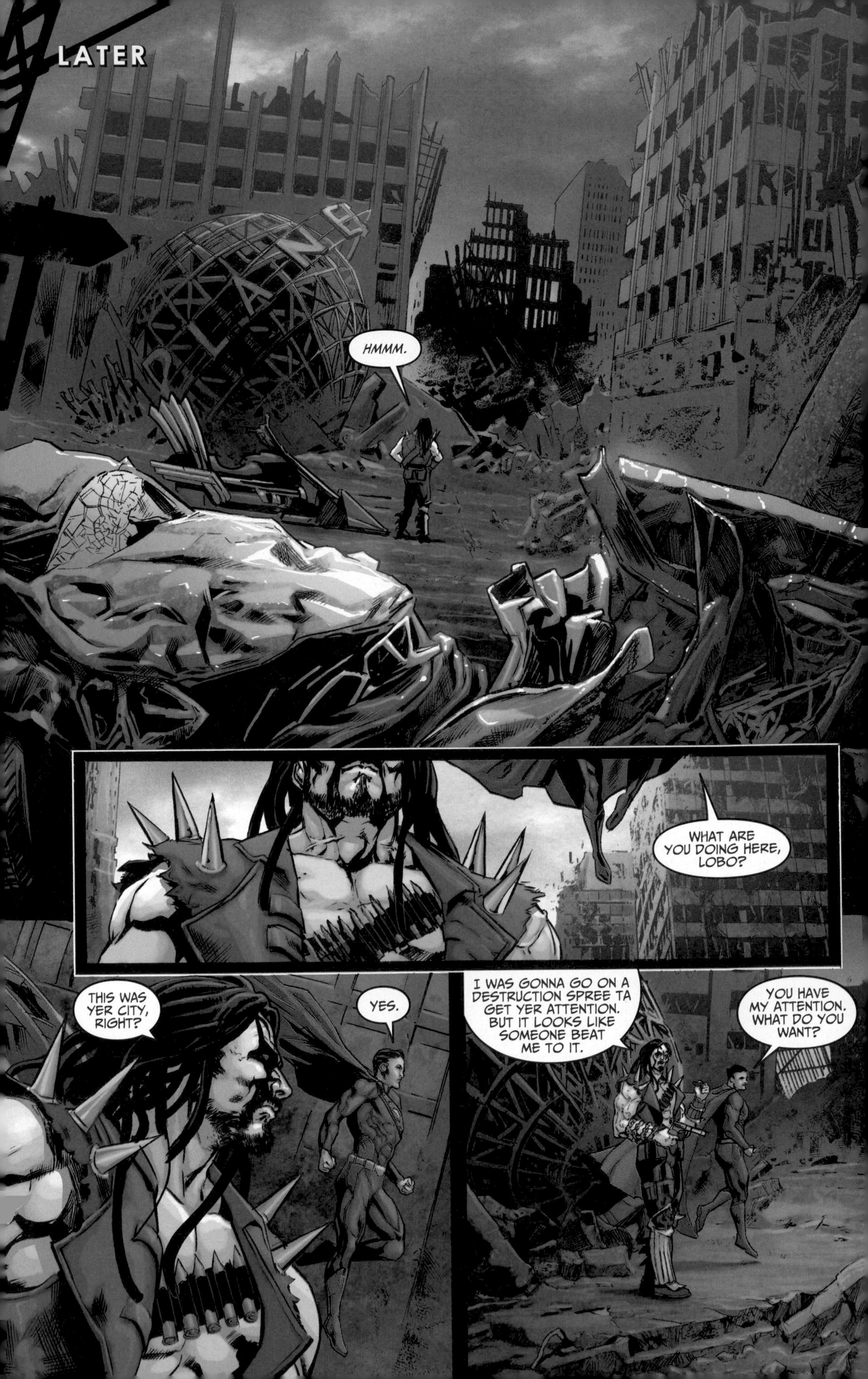
LATER
HMMM.
WHAT ARE YOU DOING HERE, LOBO?
THIS WAS YER CITY, RIGHT?
YES.
I WAS GONNA GO ON A DESTRUCTION SPREE TA GET YER ATTENTION. BUT IT LOOKS LIKE SOMEONE BEAT ME TO IT.
YOU HAVE MY ATTENTION. WHAT DO YOU WANT?

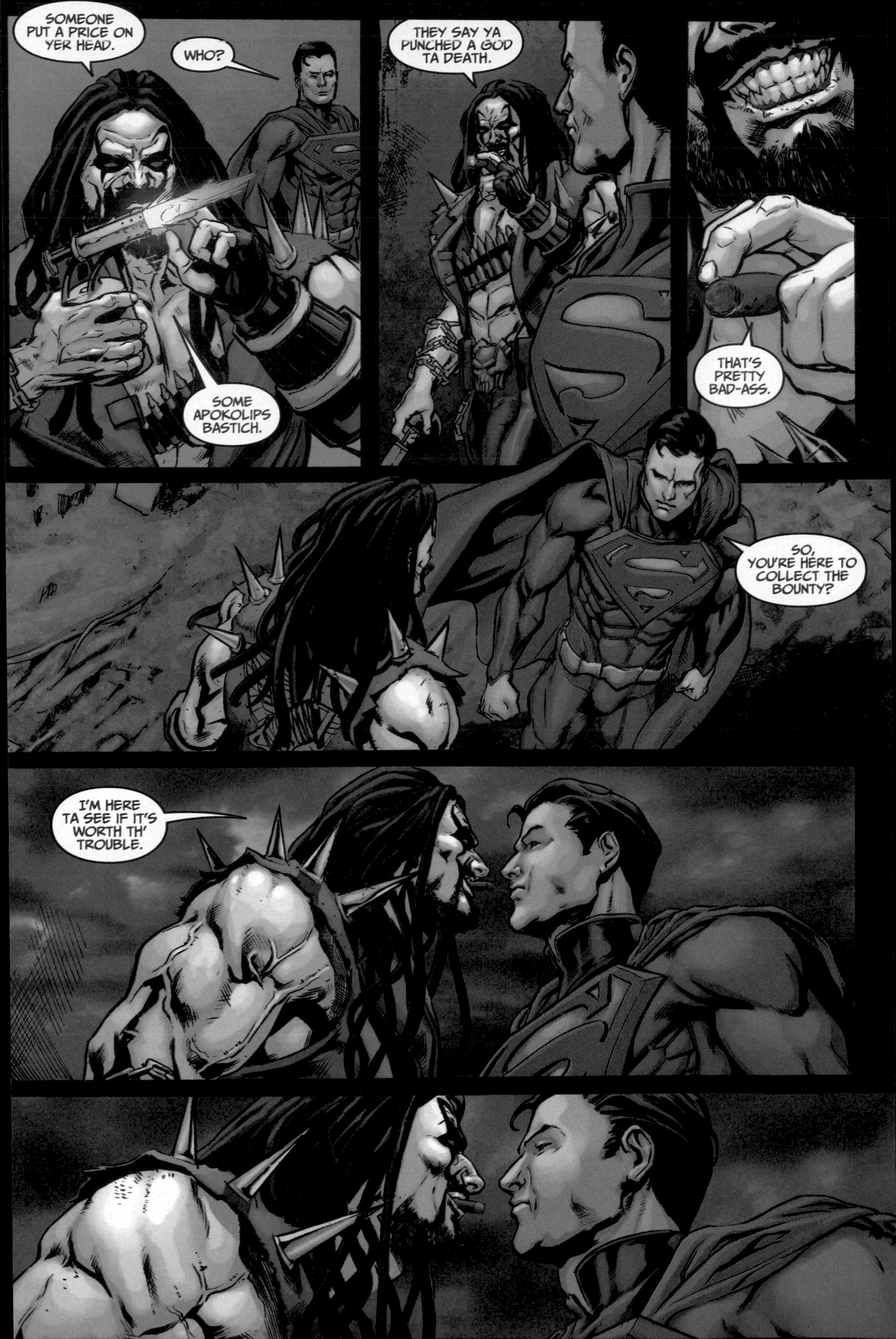
SOMEONE PUT A PRICE ON YER HEAD.
WHO?
SOME APOKOLIPS BASTICH.
THEY SAY YA PUNCHED A GOD TA DEATH.
THAT'S PRETTY BAD-ASS.
SO, YOU'RE HERE TO COLLECT THE BOUNTY?
I'M HERE TA SEE IF IT'S WORTH TH' TROUBLE.

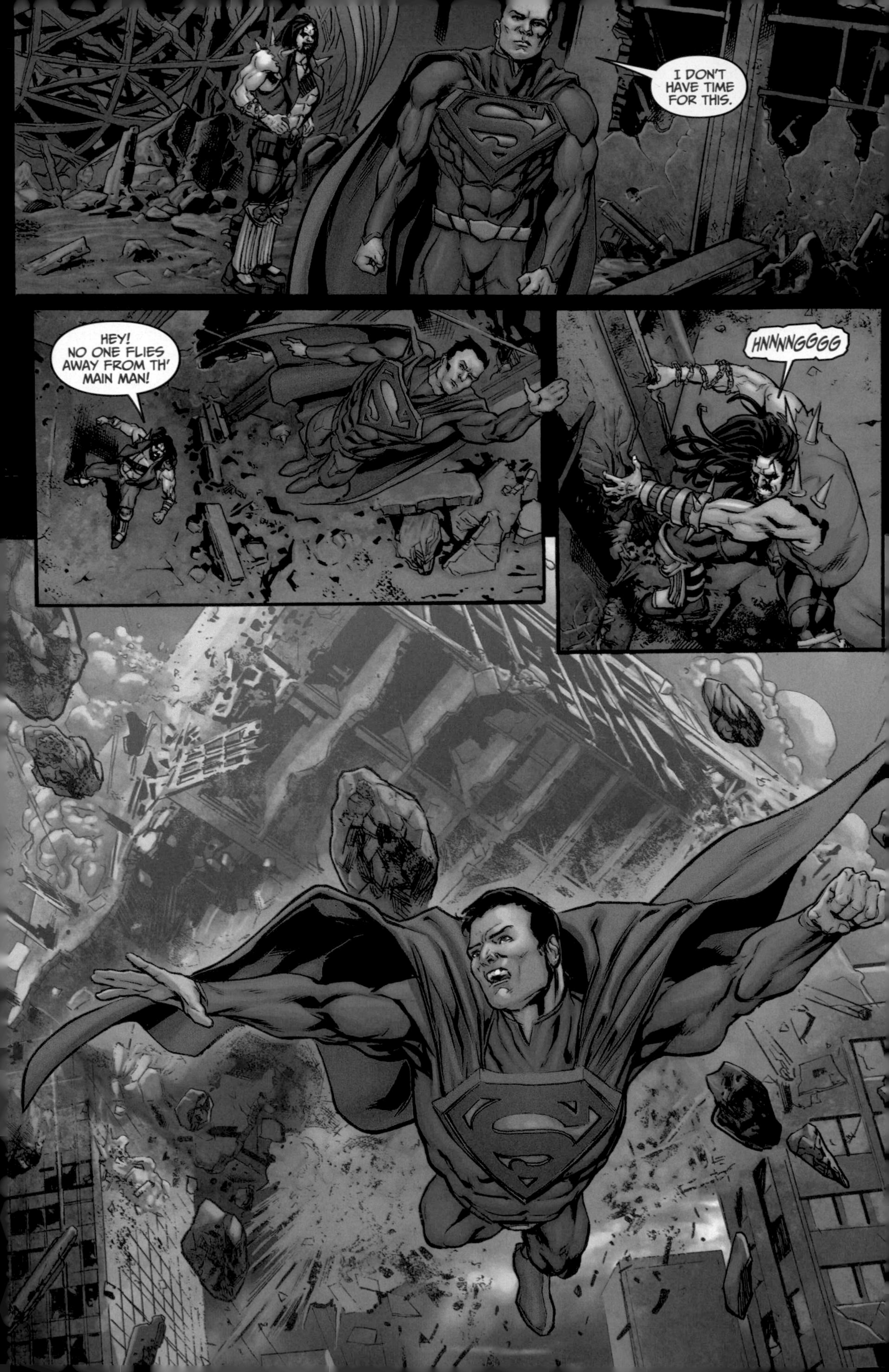
I DON'T HAVE TIME FOR THIS.
HEY! NO ONE FLIES AWAY FROM TH' MAIN MAN!
HNNNNGGGG

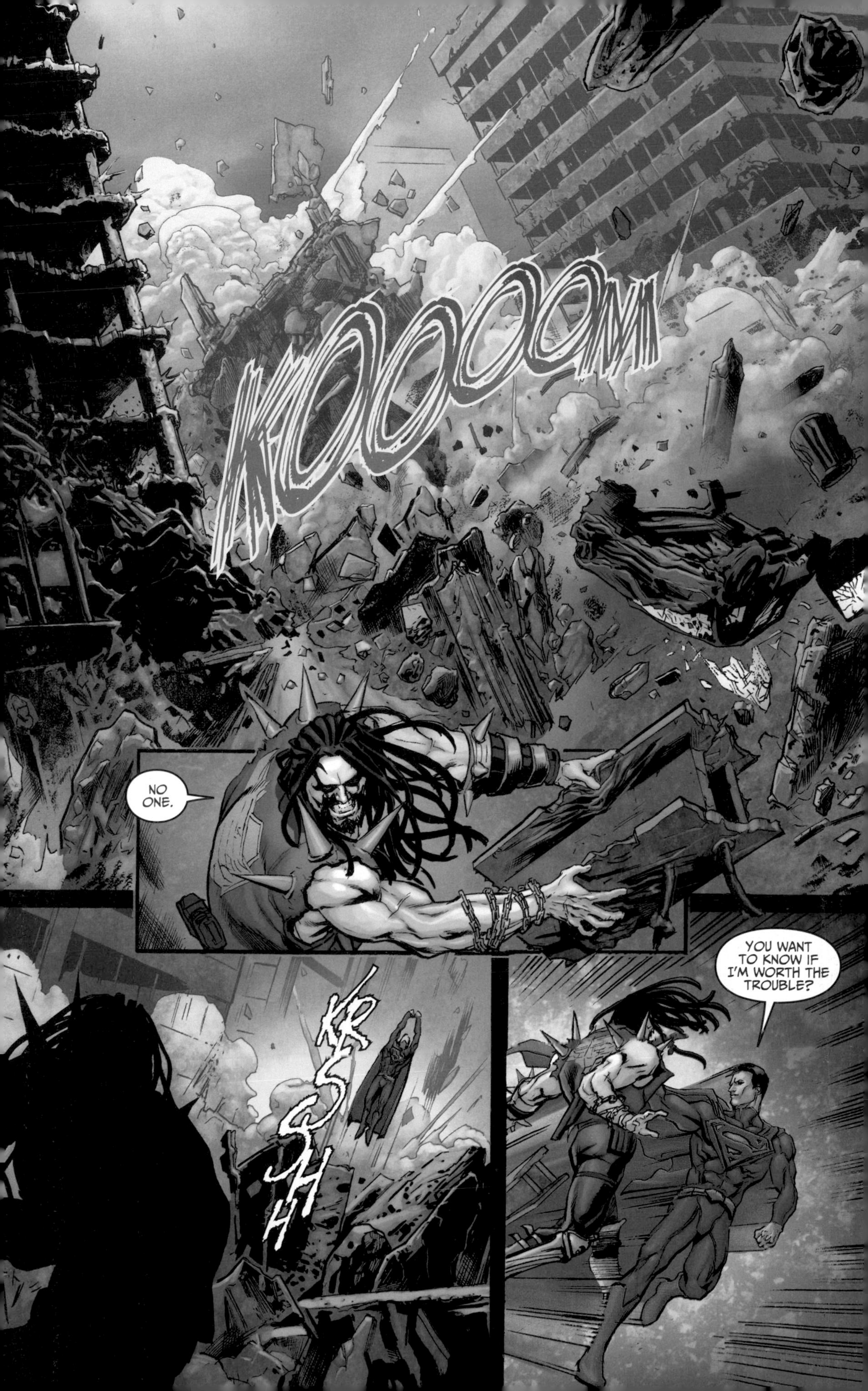
KOOOOM
NO ONE.
KRSSH
YOU WANT TO KNOW IF I'M WORTH THE TROUBLE?

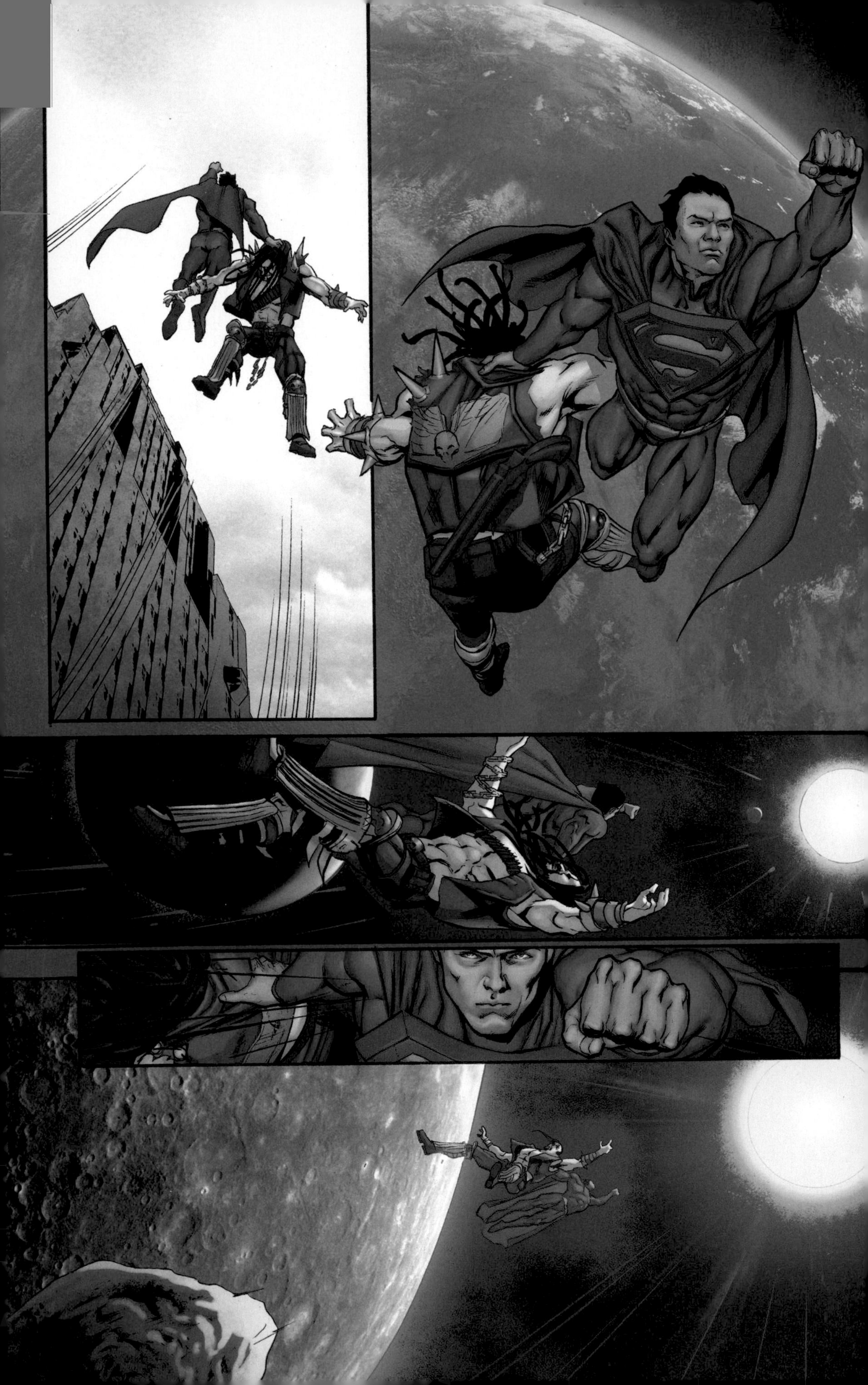

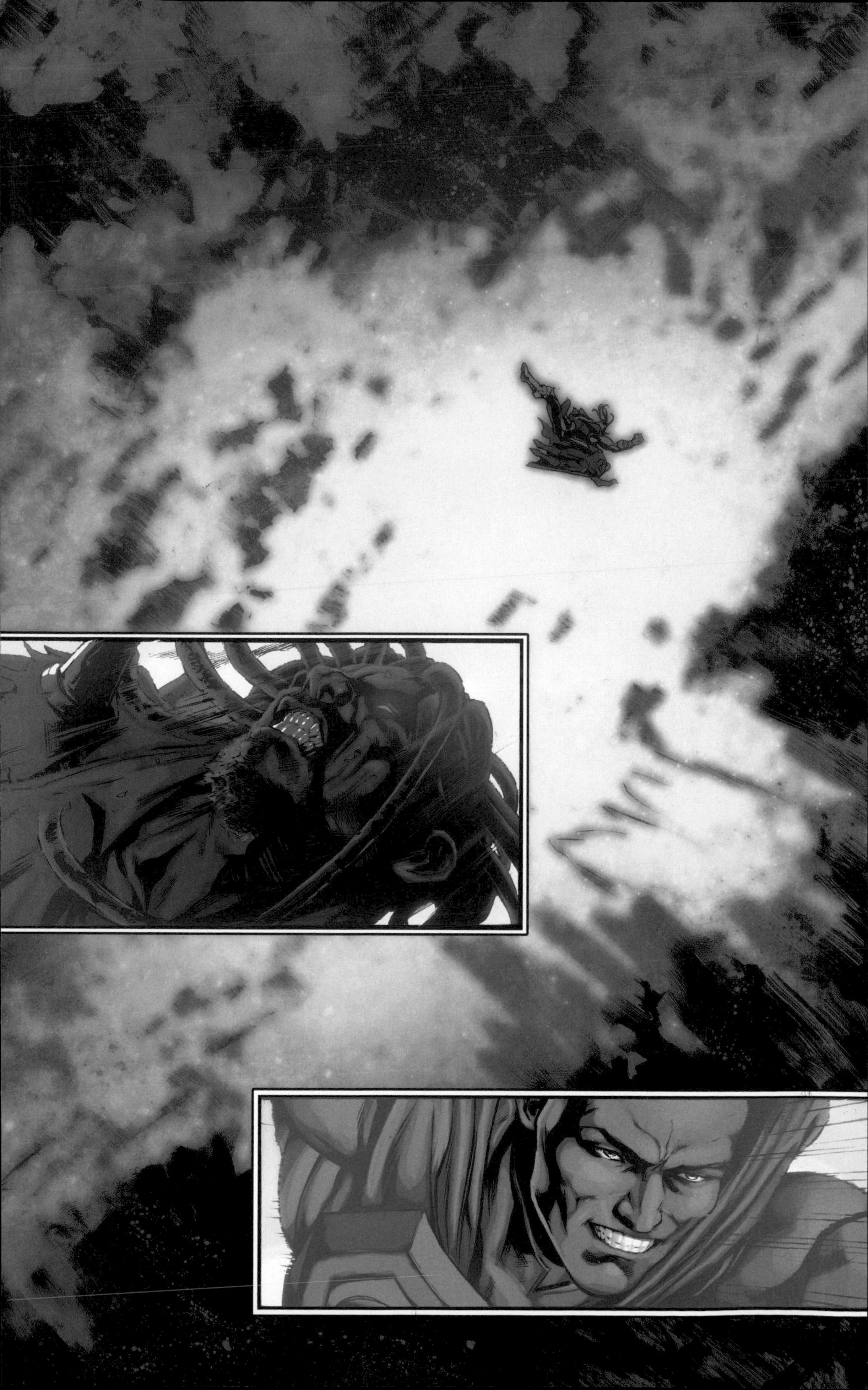

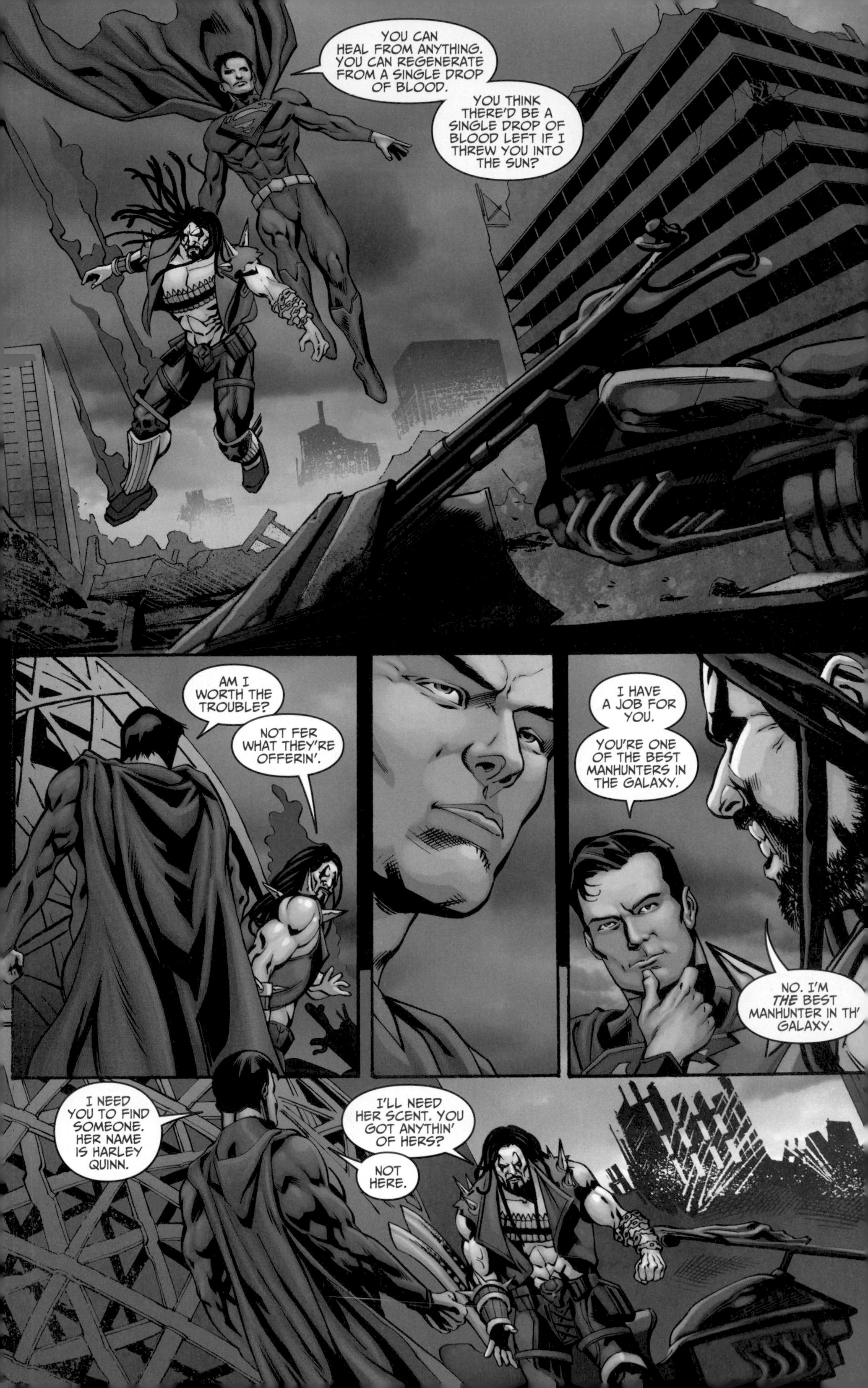

YOU CAN HEAL FROM ANYTHING. YOU CAN REGENERATE FROM A SINGLE DROP OF BLOOD.
YOU THINK THERE'D BE A SINGLE DROP OF BLOOD LEFT IF I THREW YOU INTO THE SUN?
AM I WORTH THE TROUBLE?
NOT FER WHAT THEY'RE OFFERIN'.
I HAVE A JOB FOR YOU.
YOU'RE ONE OF THE BEST MANHUNTERS IN THE GALAXY.
NO. I'M *THE* BEST MANHUNTER IN TH' GALAXY.
I NEED YOU TO FIND SOMEONE. HER NAME IS HARLEY QUINN.
I'LL NEED HER SCENT. YOU GOT ANYTHIN' OF HERS?
NOT HERE.

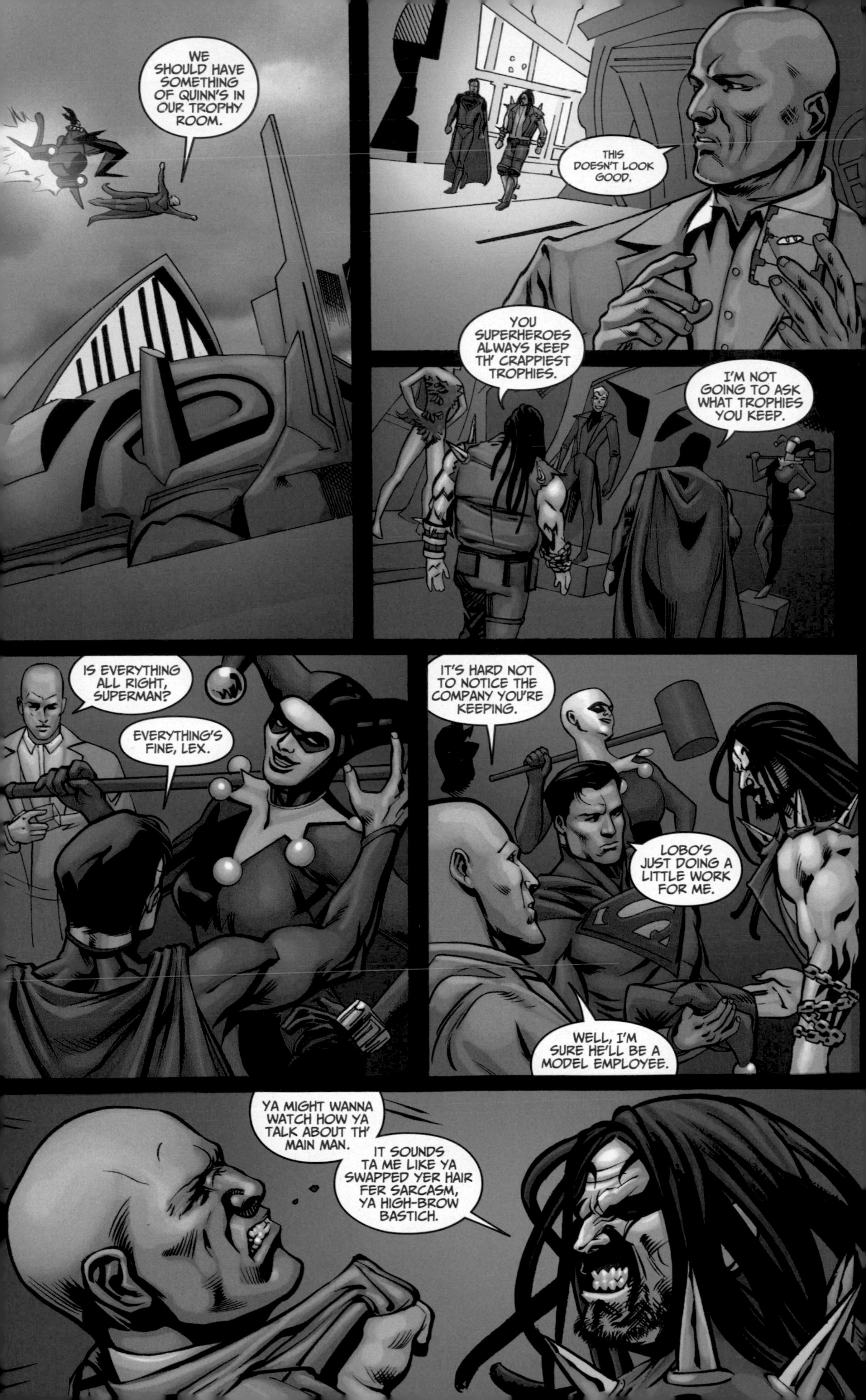
WE SHOULD HAVE SOMETHING OF QUINN'S IN OUR TROPHY ROOM.
THIS DOESN'T LOOK GOOD.
YOU SUPERHEROES ALWAYS KEEP TH' CRAPPIEST TROPHIES.
I'M NOT GOING TO ASK WHAT TROPHIES YOU KEEP.
IS EVERYTHING ALL RIGHT, SUPERMAN?
EVERYTHING'S FINE, LEX.
IT'S HARD NOT TO NOTICE THE COMPANY YOU'RE KEEPING.
LOBO'S JUST DOING A LITTLE WORK FOR ME.
WELL, I'M SURE HE'LL BE A MODEL EMPLOYEE.
YA MIGHT WANNA WATCH HOW YA TALK ABOUT TH' MAIN MAN.
IT SOUNDS TA ME LIKE YA SWAPPED YER HAIR FER SARCASM, YA HIGH-BROW BASTICH.

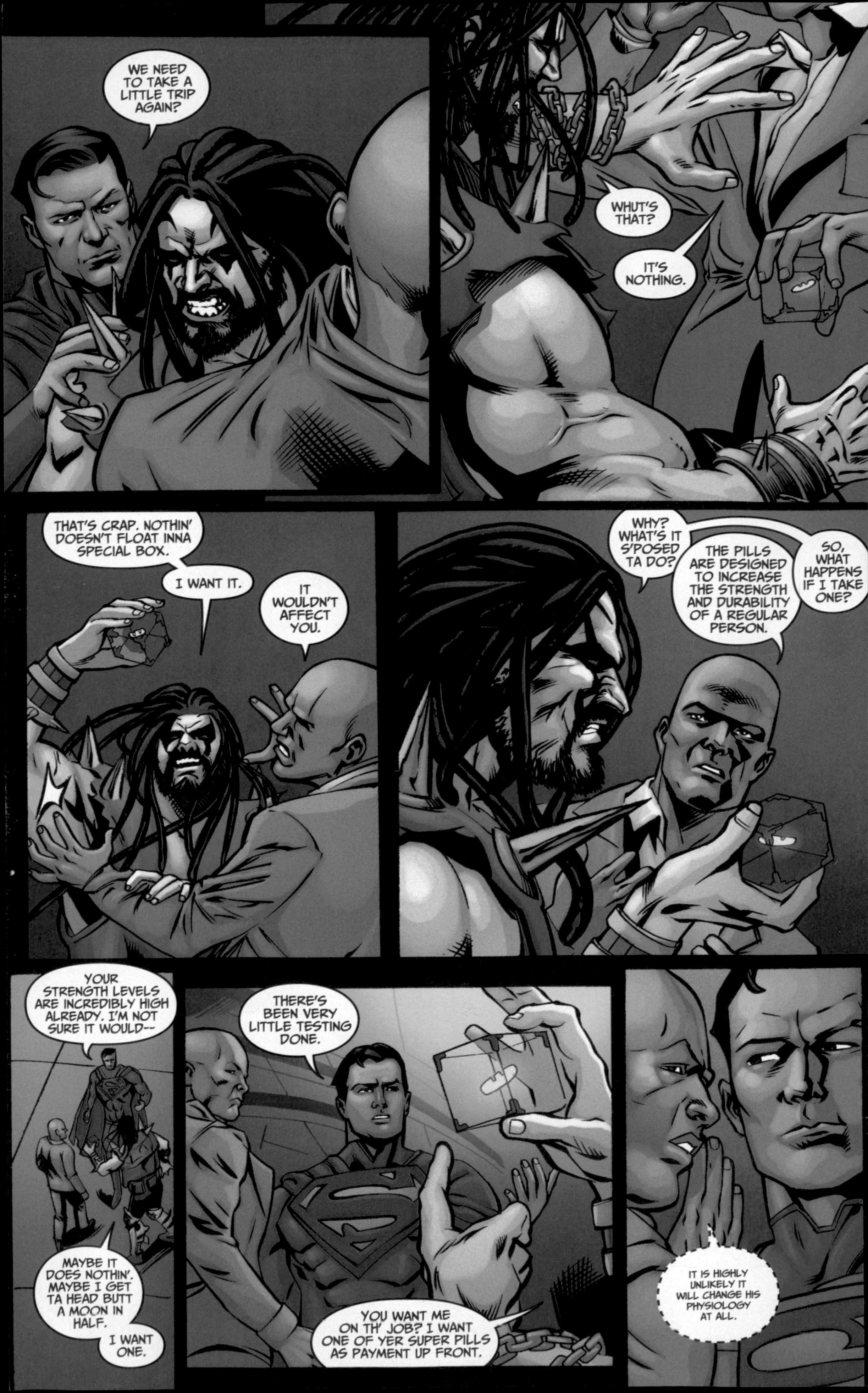
WE NEED TO TAKE A LITTLE TRIP AGAIN?
WHUT'S THAT?
IT'S NOTHING.
THAT'S CRAP. NOTHIN' DOESN'T FLOAT INNA SPECIAL BOX.
I WANT IT.
IT WOULDN'T AFFECT YOU.
WHY? WHAT'S IT S'POSED TA DO?
THE PILLS ARE DESIGNED TO INCREASE THE STRENGTH AND DURABILITY OF A REGULAR PERSON.
SO, WHAT HAPPENS IF I TAKE ONE?
YOUR STRENGTH LEVELS ARE INCREDIBLY HIGH ALREADY. I'M NOT SURE IT WOULD--
MAYBE IT DOES NOTHIN'. MAYBE I GET TA HEAD BUTT A MOON IN HALF.
I WANT ONE.
THERE'S BEEN VERY LITTLE TESTING DONE.
YOU WANT ME ON TH' JOB? I WANT ONE OF YER SUPER PILLS AS PAYMENT UP FRONT.
IT IS HIGHLY UNLIKELY IT WILL CHANGE HIS PHYSIOLOGY AT ALL.

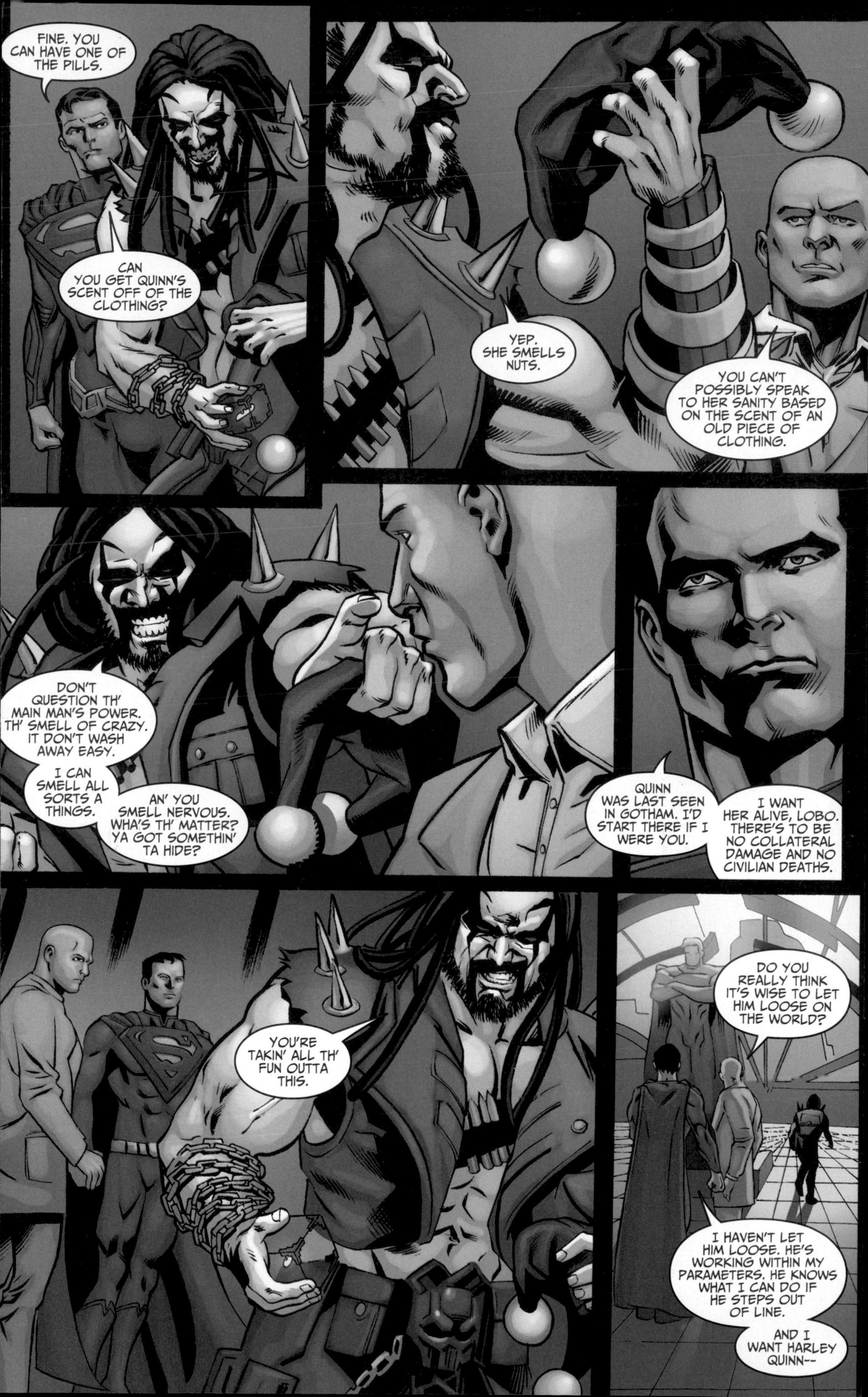
FINE. YOU CAN HAVE ONE OF THE PILLS.
CAN YOU GET QUINN'S SCENT OFF OF THE CLOTHING?
YEP. SHE SMELLS NUTS.
YOU CAN'T POSSIBLY SPEAK TO HER SANITY BASED ON THE SCENT OF AN OLD PIECE OF CLOTHING.
DON'T QUESTION TH' MAIN MAN'S POWER. TH' SMELL OF CRAZY. IT DON'T WASH AWAY EASY.
I CAN SMELL ALL SORTS A THINGS.
AN' YOU SMELL NERVOUS. WHA'S TH' MATTER? YA GOT SOMETHIN' TA HIDE?
QUINN WAS LAST SEEN IN GOTHAM. I'D START THERE IF I WERE YOU.
I WANT HER ALIVE, LOBO. THERE'S TO BE NO COLLATERAL DAMAGE AND NO CIVILIAN DEATHS.
YOU'RE TAKIN' ALL TH' FUN OUTTA THIS.
DO YOU REALLY THINK IT'S WISE TO LET HIM LOOSE ON THE WORLD?
I HAVEN'T LET HIM LOOSE. HE'S WORKING WITHIN MY PARAMETERS. HE KNOWS WHAT I CAN DO IF HE STEPS OUT OF LINE.
AND I WANT HARLEY QUINN--

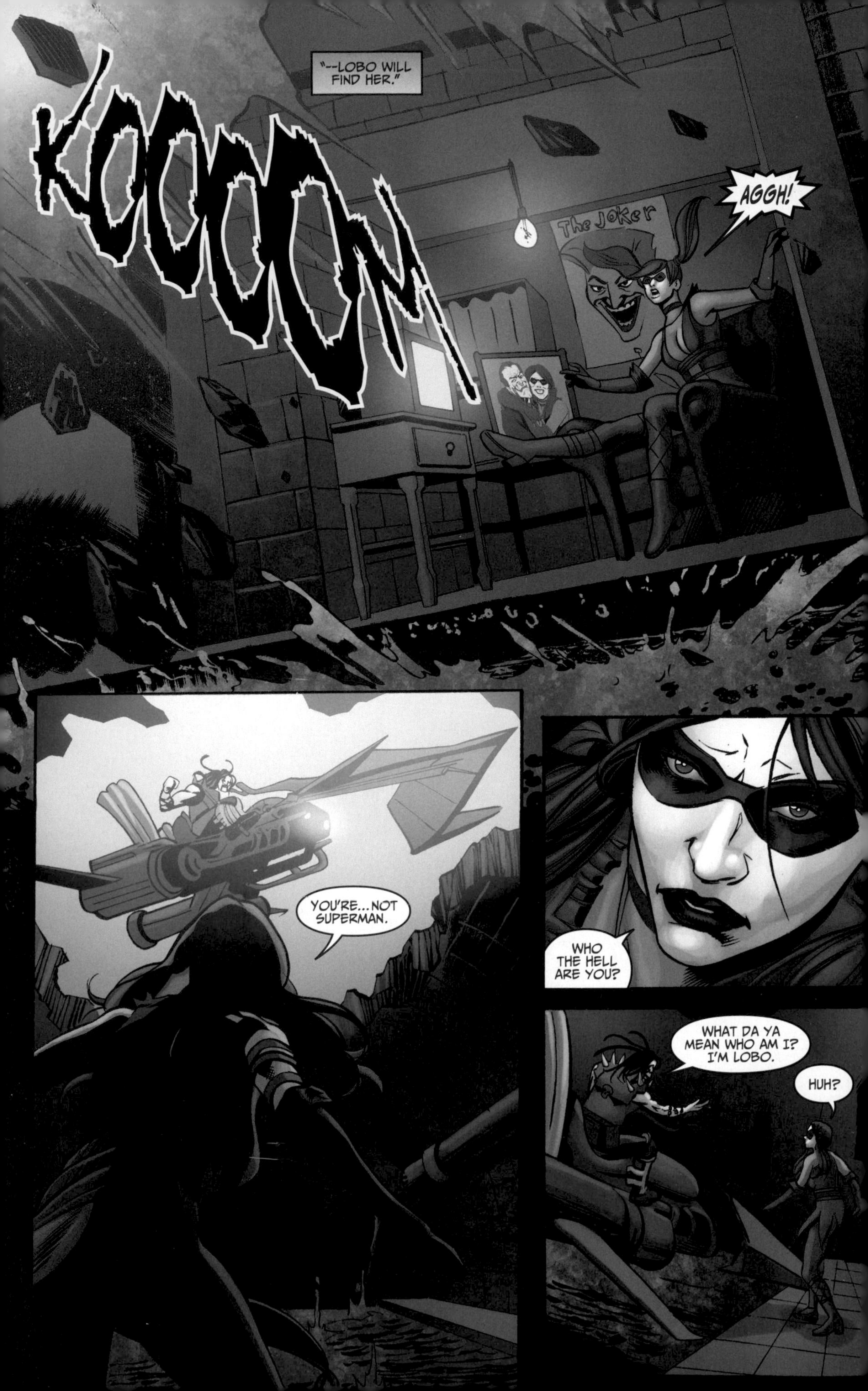
"--LOBO WILL FIND HER."
KOOOOM!
AGGH!
The JOKer
YOU'RE...NOT SUPERMAN.
WHO THE HELL ARE YOU?
WHAT DA YA MEAN WHO AM I? I'M LOBO.
HUH?

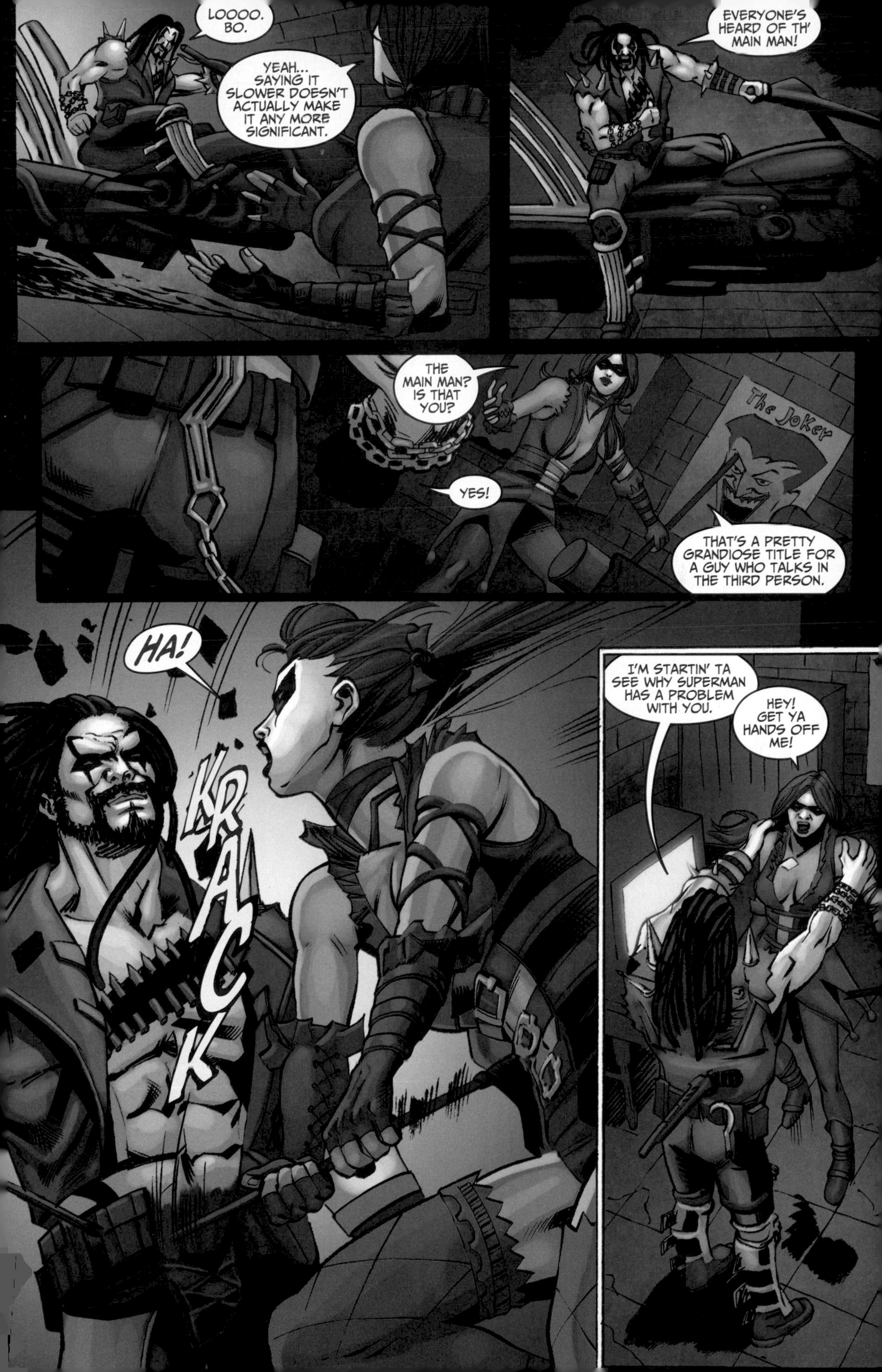
LOOOO. BO.
YEAH... SAYING IT SLOWER DOESN'T ACTUALLY MAKE IT ANY MORE SIGNIFICANT.
EVERYONE'S HEARD OF TH' MAIN MAN!
THE MAIN MAN? IS THAT YOU?
YES!
The Joker
THAT'S A PRETTY GRANDIOSE TITLE FOR A GUY WHO TALKS IN THE THIRD PERSON.
HA!
KRACK
I'M STARTIN' TA SEE WHY SUPERMAN HAS A PROBLEM WITH YOU.
HEY! GET YA HANDS OFF ME!

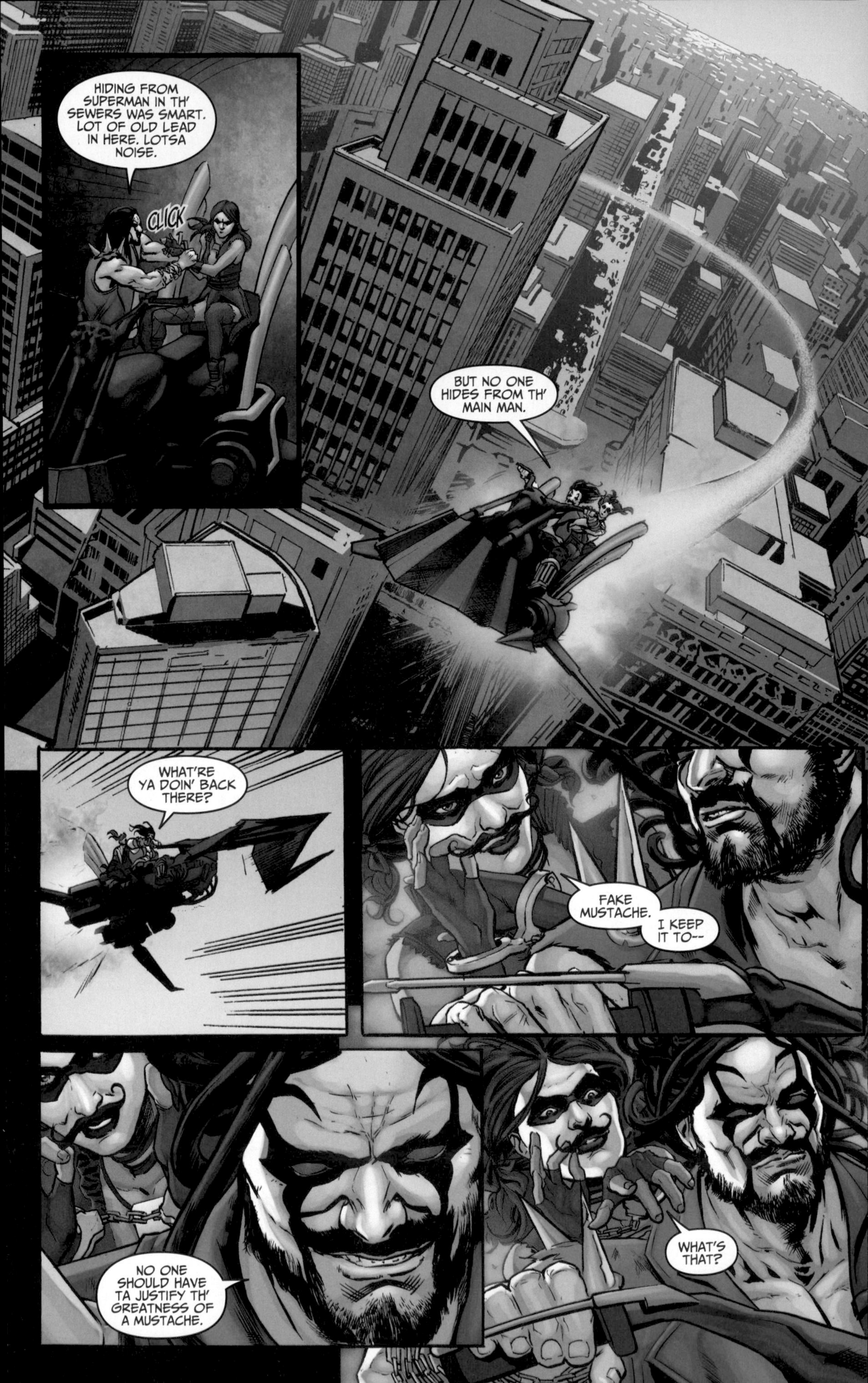
HIDING FROM SUPERMAN IN TH' SEWERS WAS SMART. LOT OF OLD LEAD IN HERE. LOTSA NOISE.
CLICK
BUT NO ONE HIDES FROM TH' MAIN MAN.
WHAT'RE YA DOIN' BACK THERE?
FAKE MUSTACHE.
I KEEP IT TO--
NO ONE SHOULD HAVE TA JUSTIFY TH' GREATNESS OF A MUSTACHE.
WHAT'S THAT?

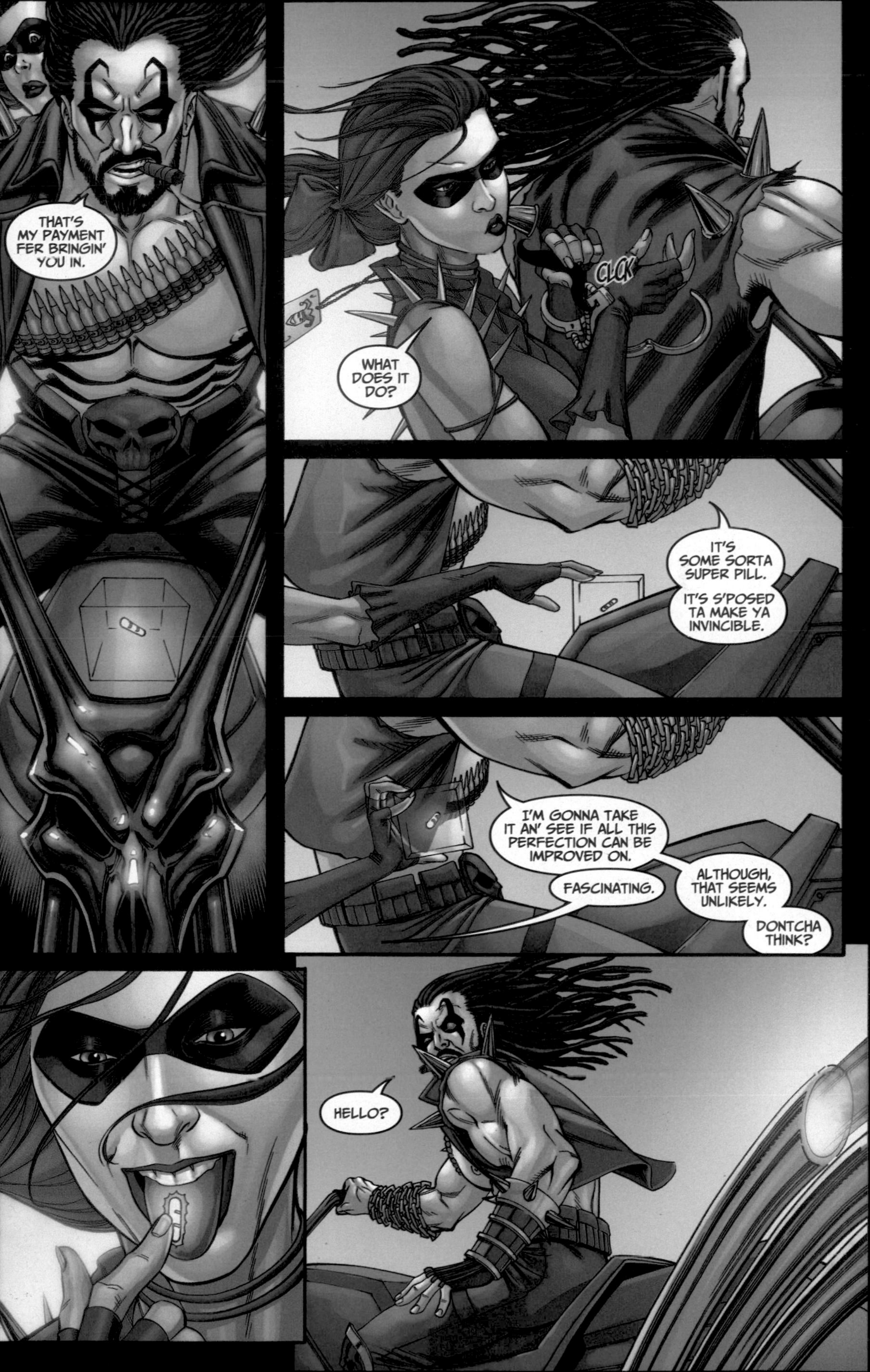
THAT'S MY PAYMENT FER BRINGIN' YOU IN.
CLCK
WHAT DOES IT DO?
IT'S SOME SORTA SUPER PILL.
IT'S S'POSED TA MAKE YA INVINCIBLE.
I'M GONNA TAKE IT AN' SEE IF ALL THIS PERFECTION CAN BE IMPROVED ON.
FASCINATING.
ALTHOUGH, THAT SEEMS UNLIKELY.
DONTCHA THINK?
HELLO?

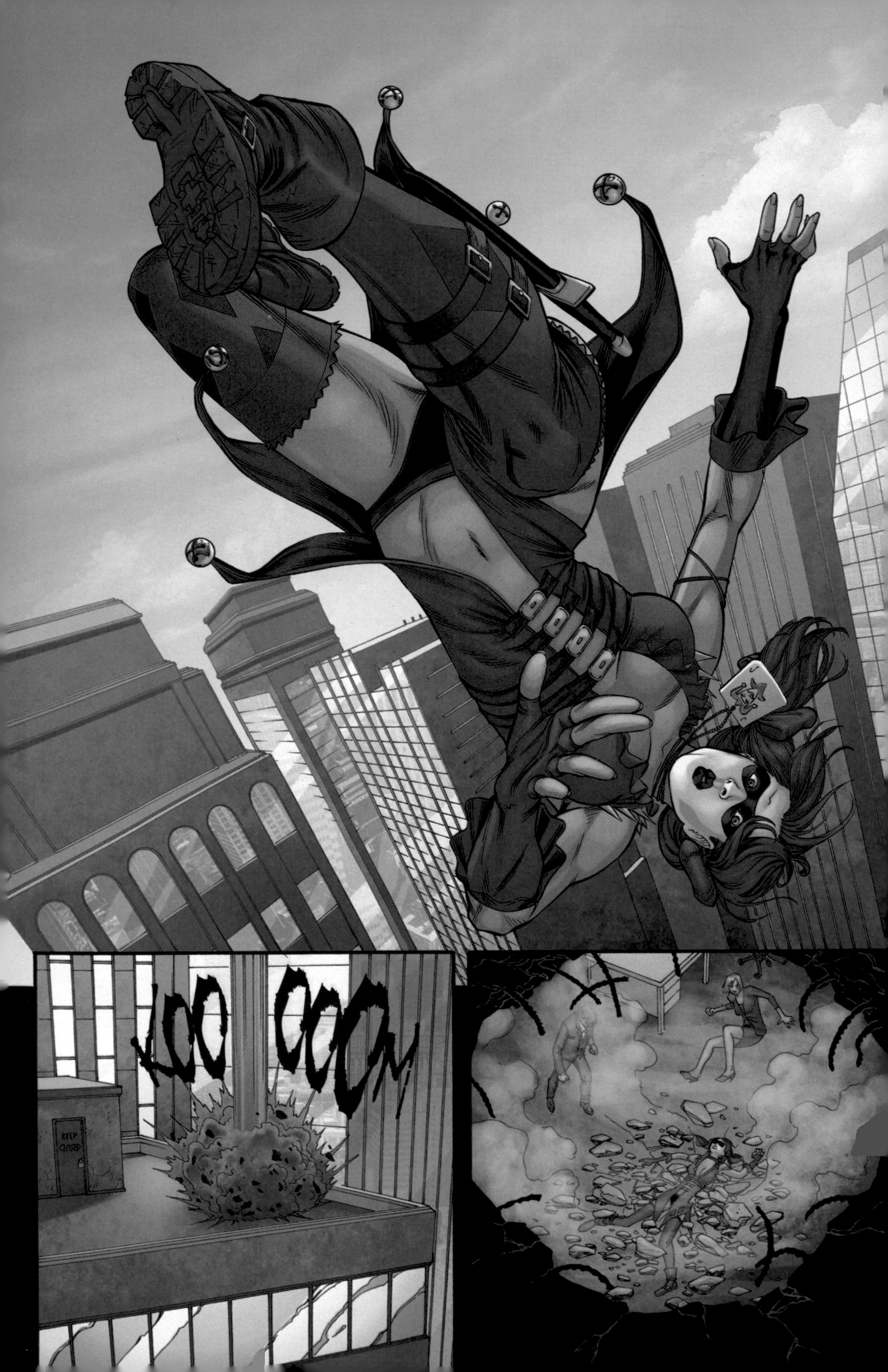
KEEP CLOSED

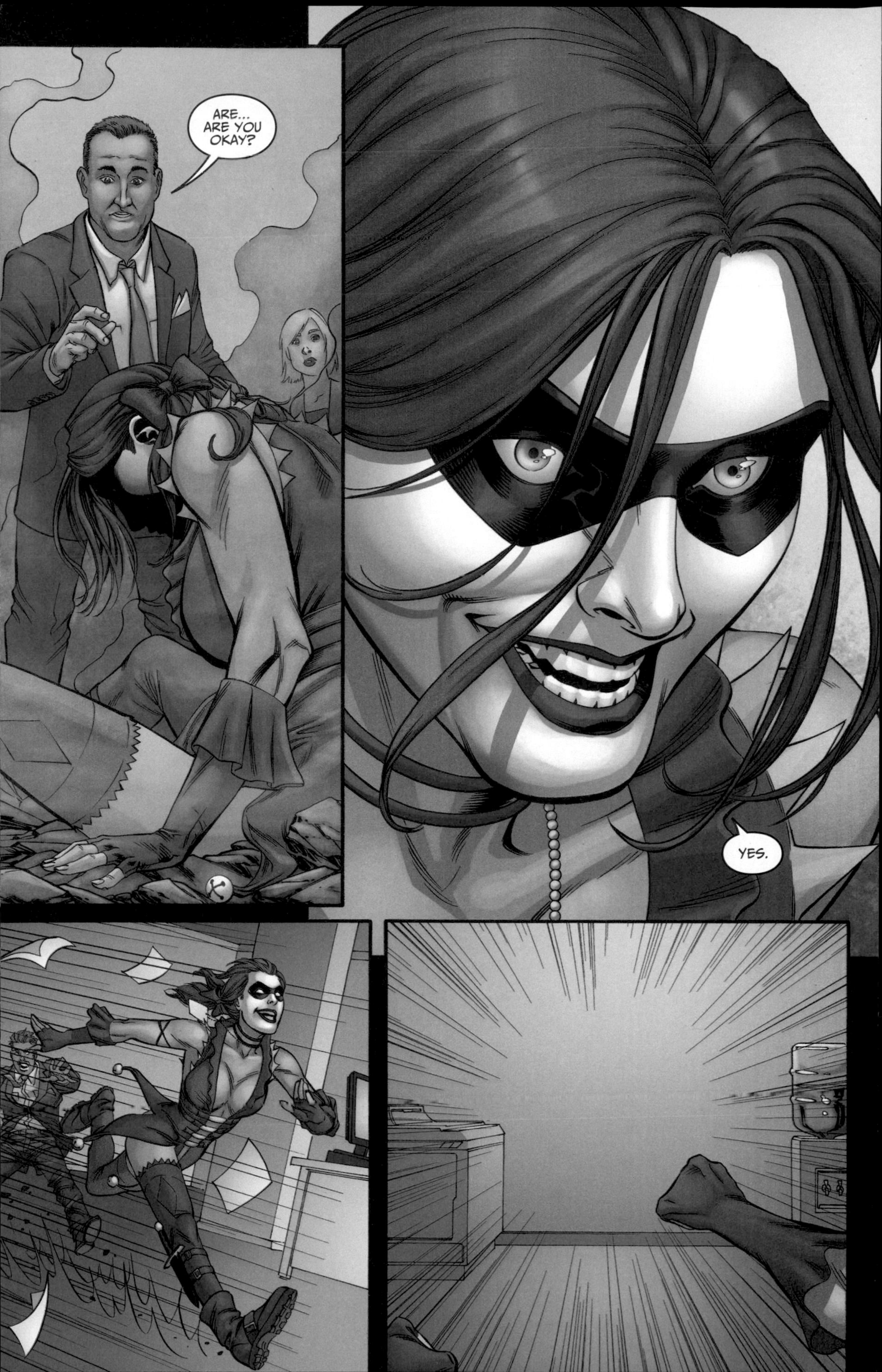
ARE... ARE YOU OKAY?
YES.

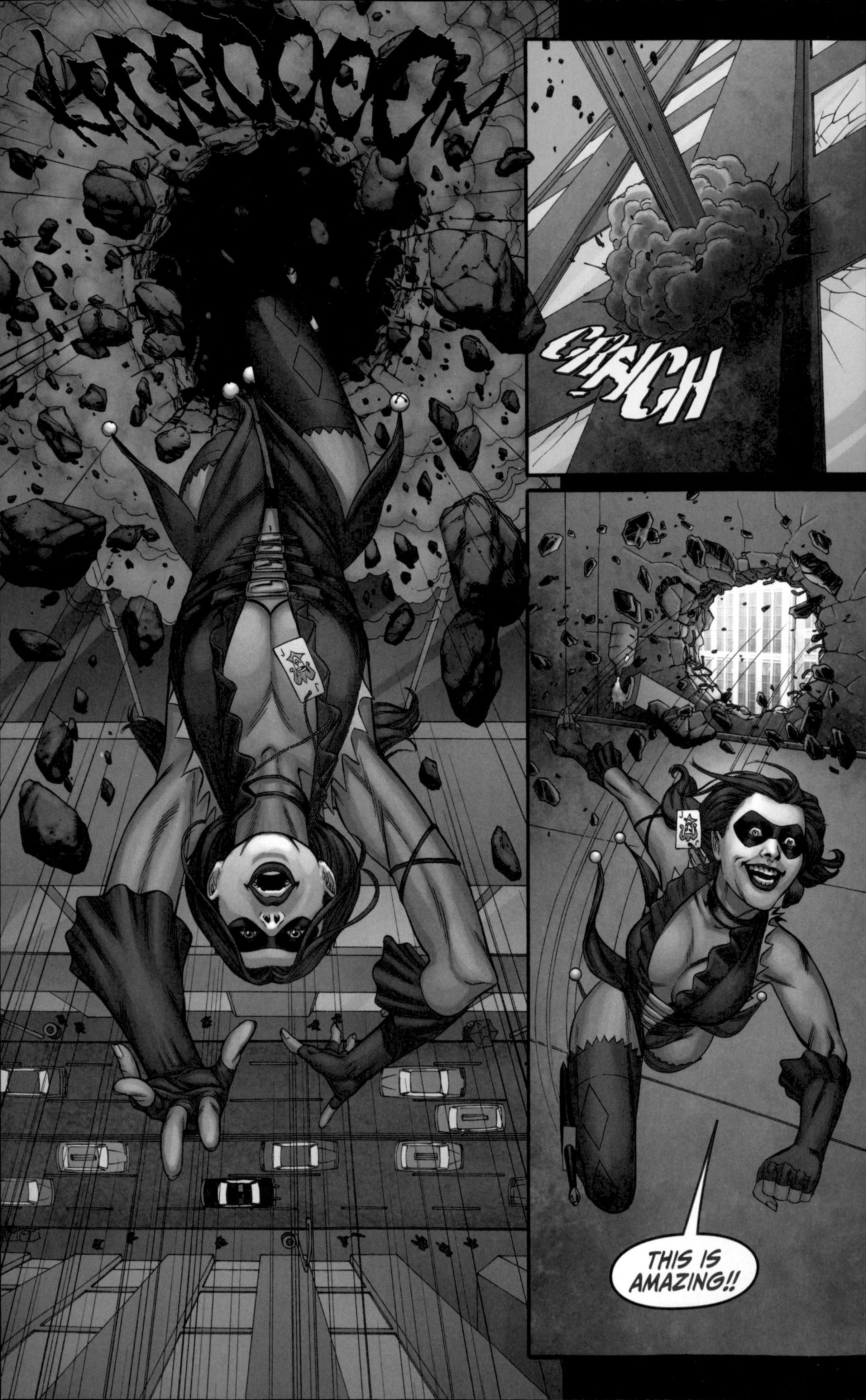
THIS IS AMAZING!!

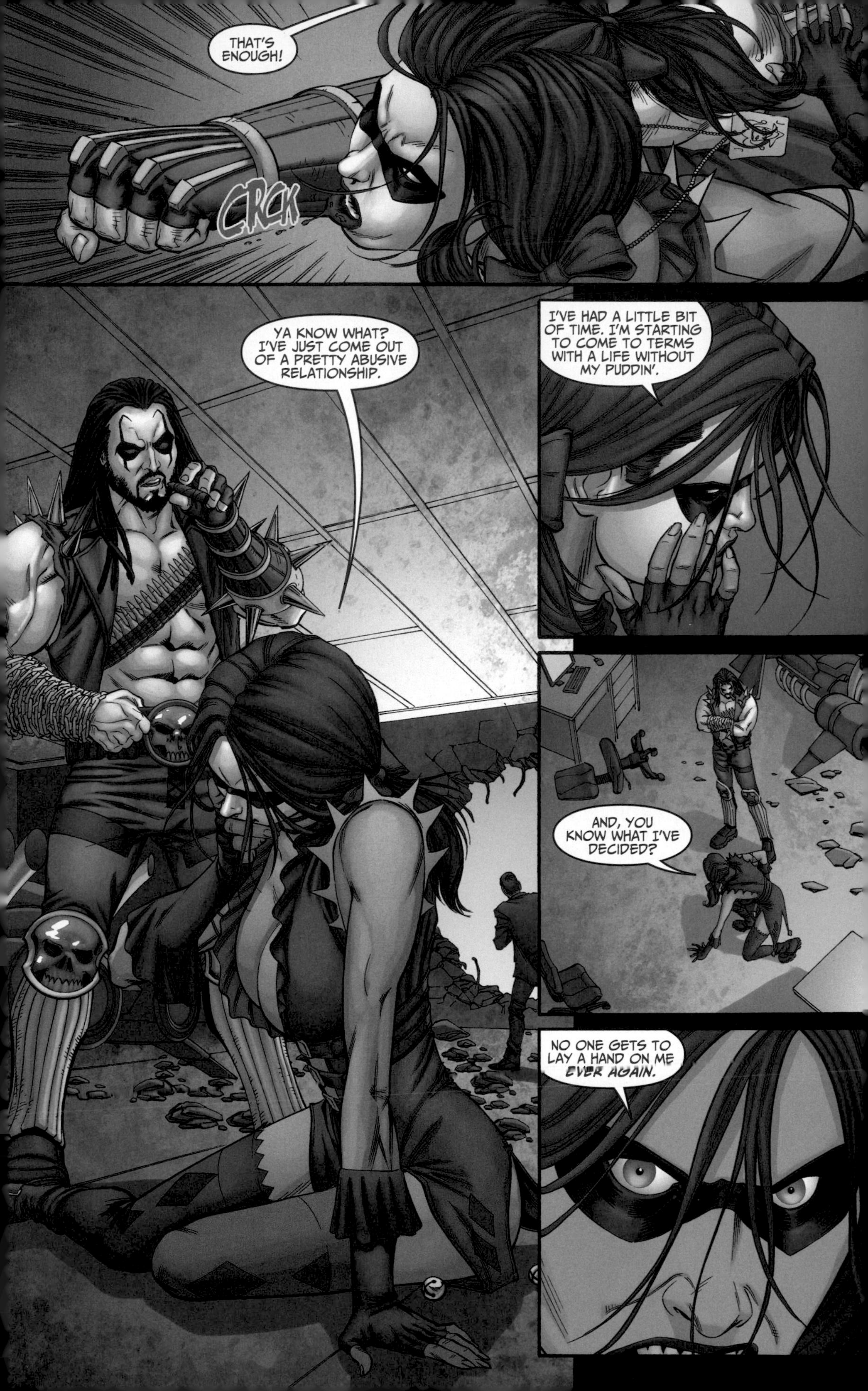
THAT'S ENOUGH!
CRCK
YA KNOW WHAT? I'VE JUST COME OUT OF A PRETTY ABUSIVE RELATIONSHIP.
I'VE HAD A LITTLE BIT OF TIME. I'M STARTING TO COME TO TERMS WITH A LIFE WITHOUT MY PUDDIN'.
AND, YOU KNOW WHAT I'VE DECIDED?
NO ONE GETS TO LAY A HAND ON ME *EVER AGAIN*.

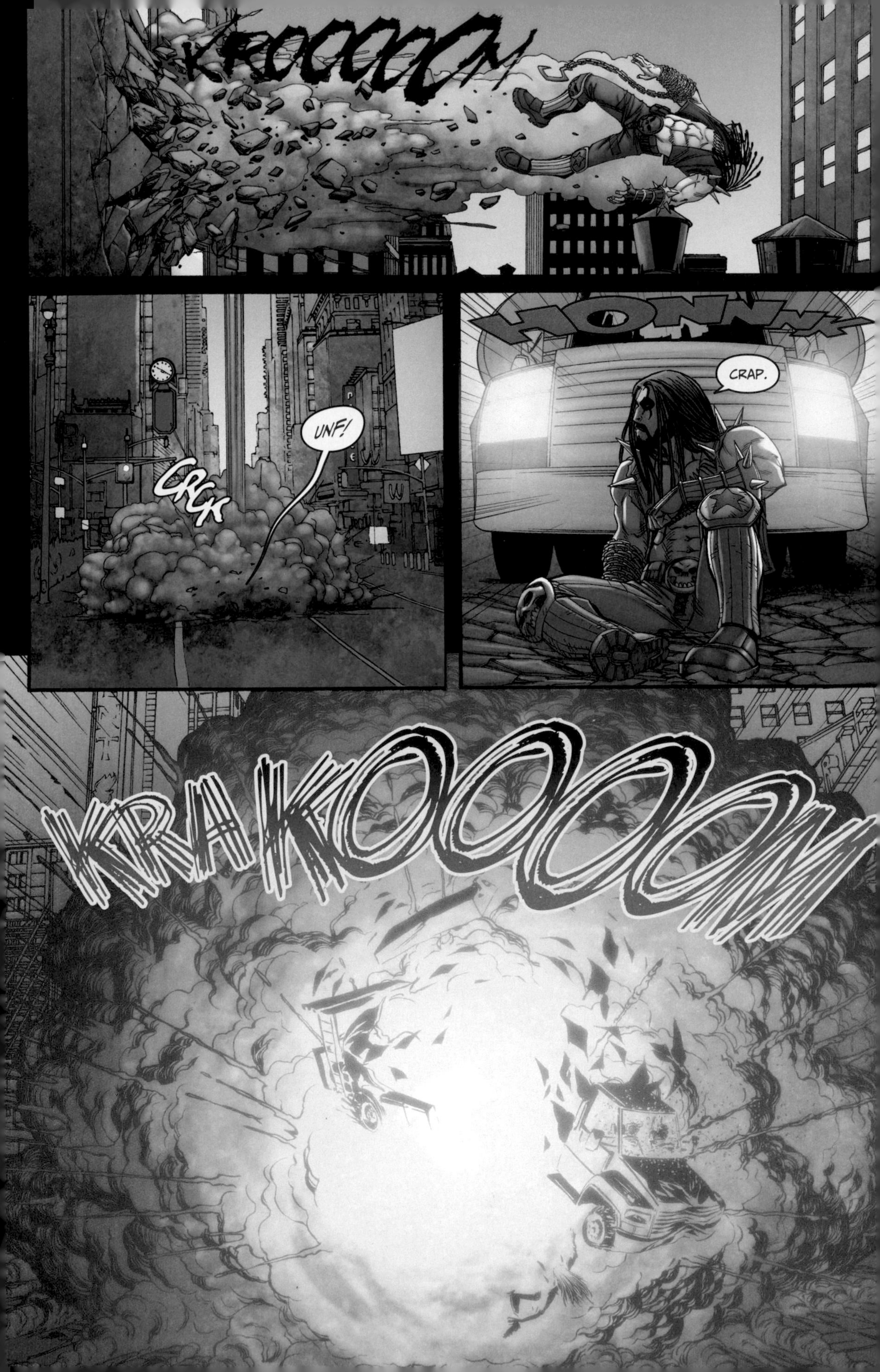
KROOOOOM
CRCK
UNF!
HONNK
CRAP.
KRAKOOOOOM

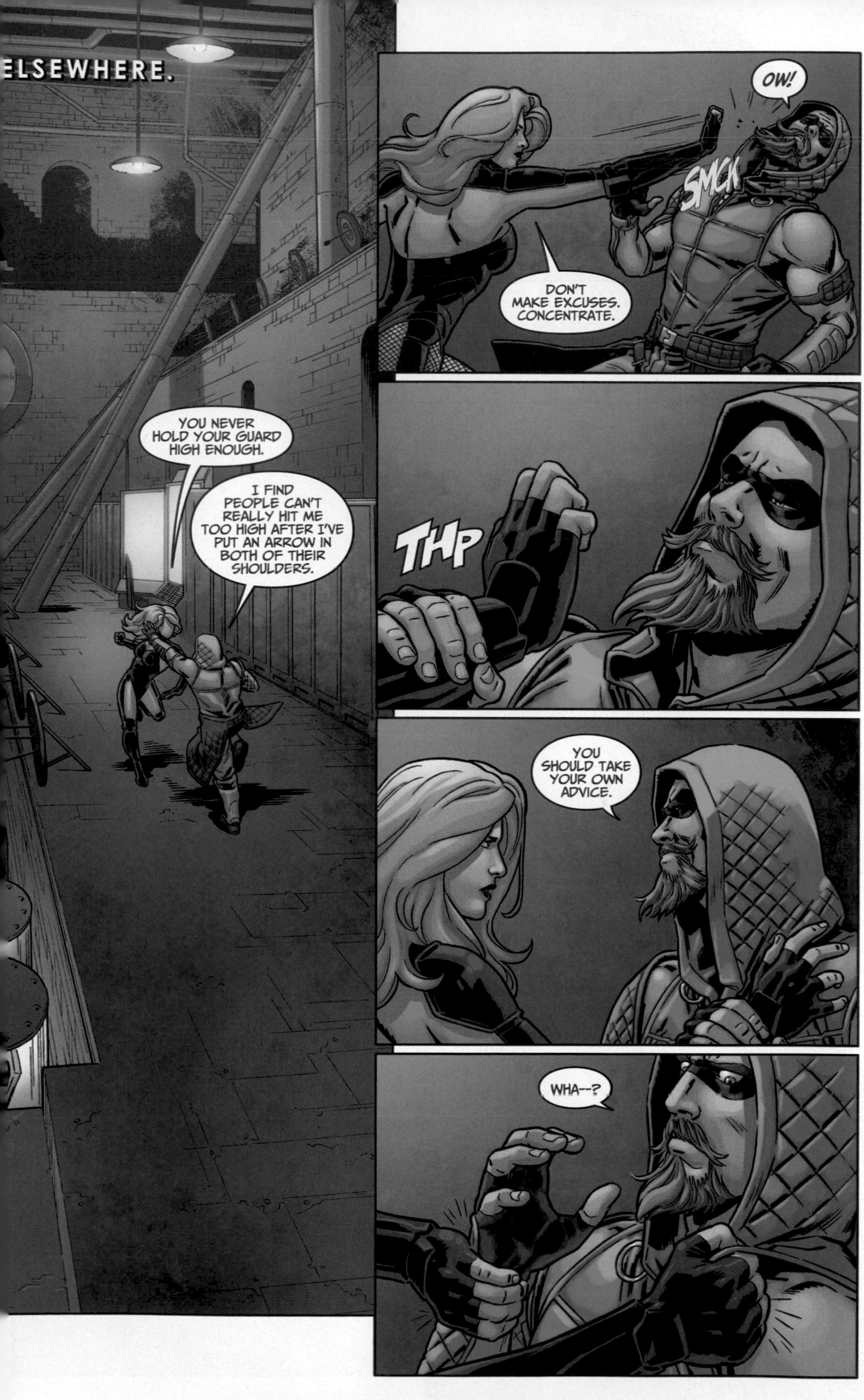
ELSEWHERE.
YOU NEVER HOLD YOUR GUARD HIGH ENOUGH.
I FIND PEOPLE CAN'T REALLY HIT ME TOO HIGH AFTER I'VE PUT AN ARROW IN BOTH OF THEIR SHOULDERS.
OW!
SMCK
DON'T MAKE EXCUSES. CONCENTRATE.
THP
YOU SHOULD TAKE YOUR OWN ADVICE.
WHA--?

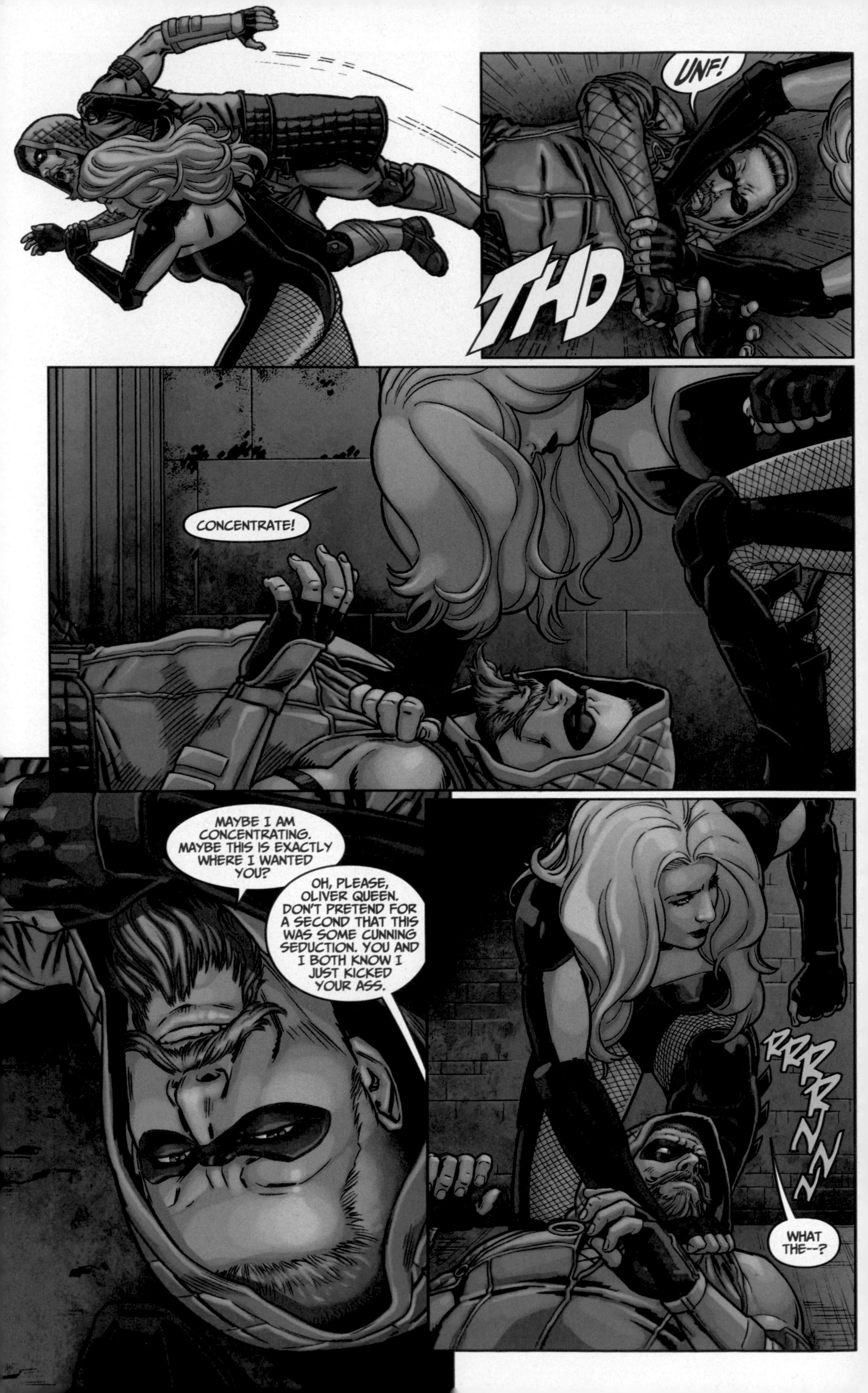
UNF!
THD
CONCENTRATE!
MAYBE I AM CONCENTRATING. MAYBE THIS IS EXACTLY WHERE I WANTED YOU?
OH, PLEASE, OLIVER QUEEN. DON'T PRETEND FOR A SECOND THAT THIS WAS SOME CUNNING SEDUCTION. YOU AND I BOTH KNOW I JUST KICKED YOUR ASS.
RRRRNNN
WHAT THE--?

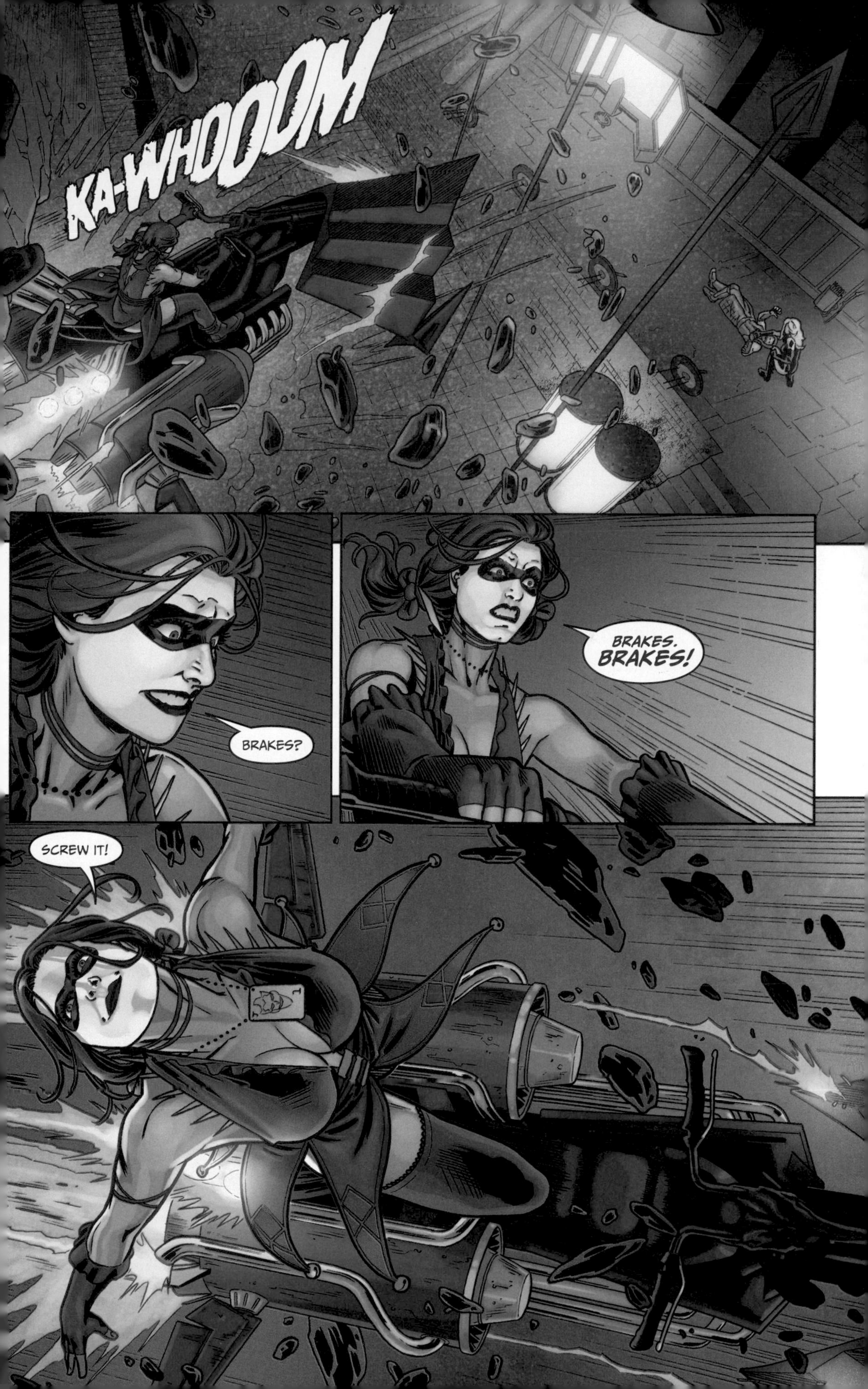
KA-WHOOOM
BRAKES?
BRAKES. BRAKES!
SCREW IT!

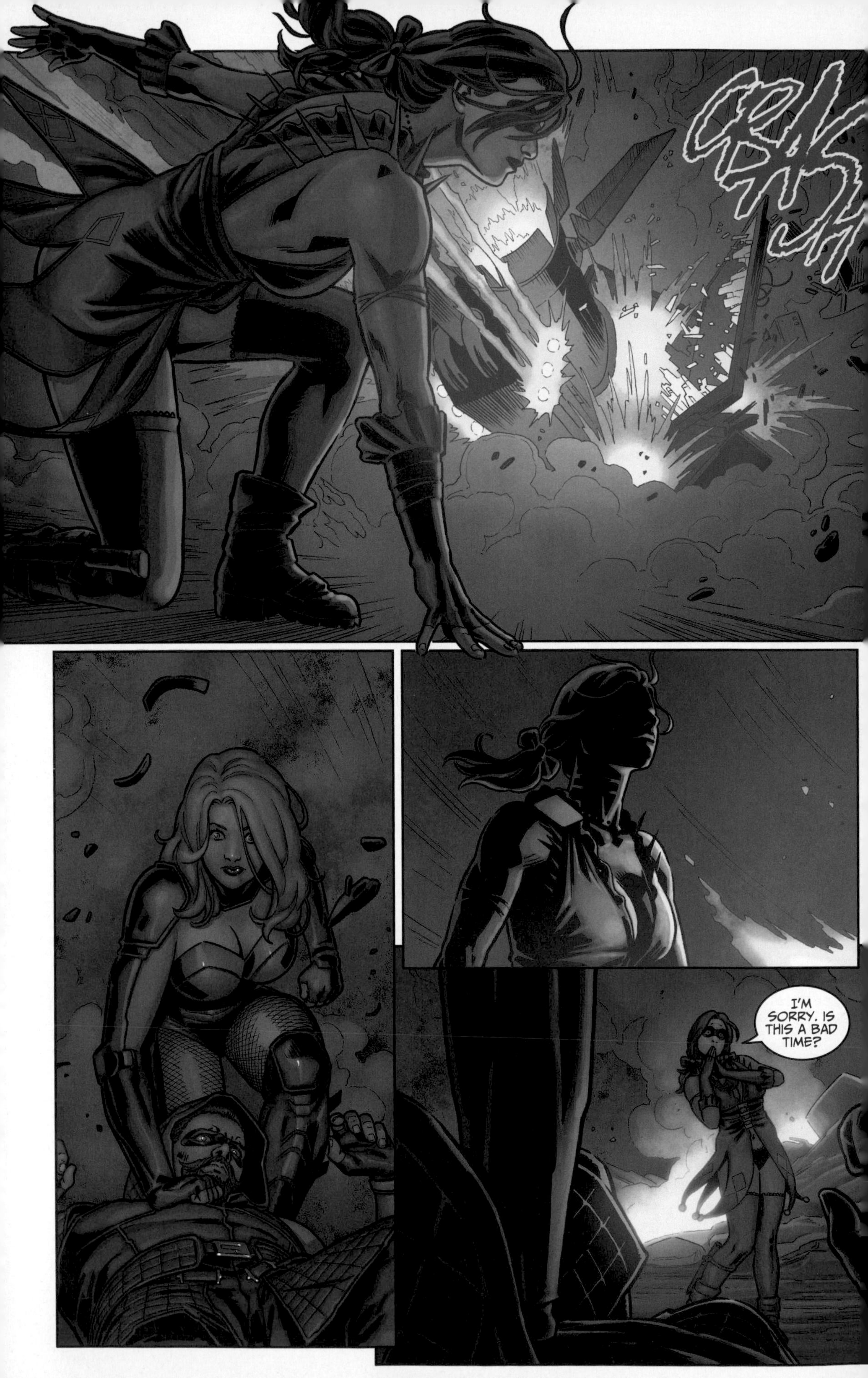
I'M SORRY. IS THIS A BAD TIME?

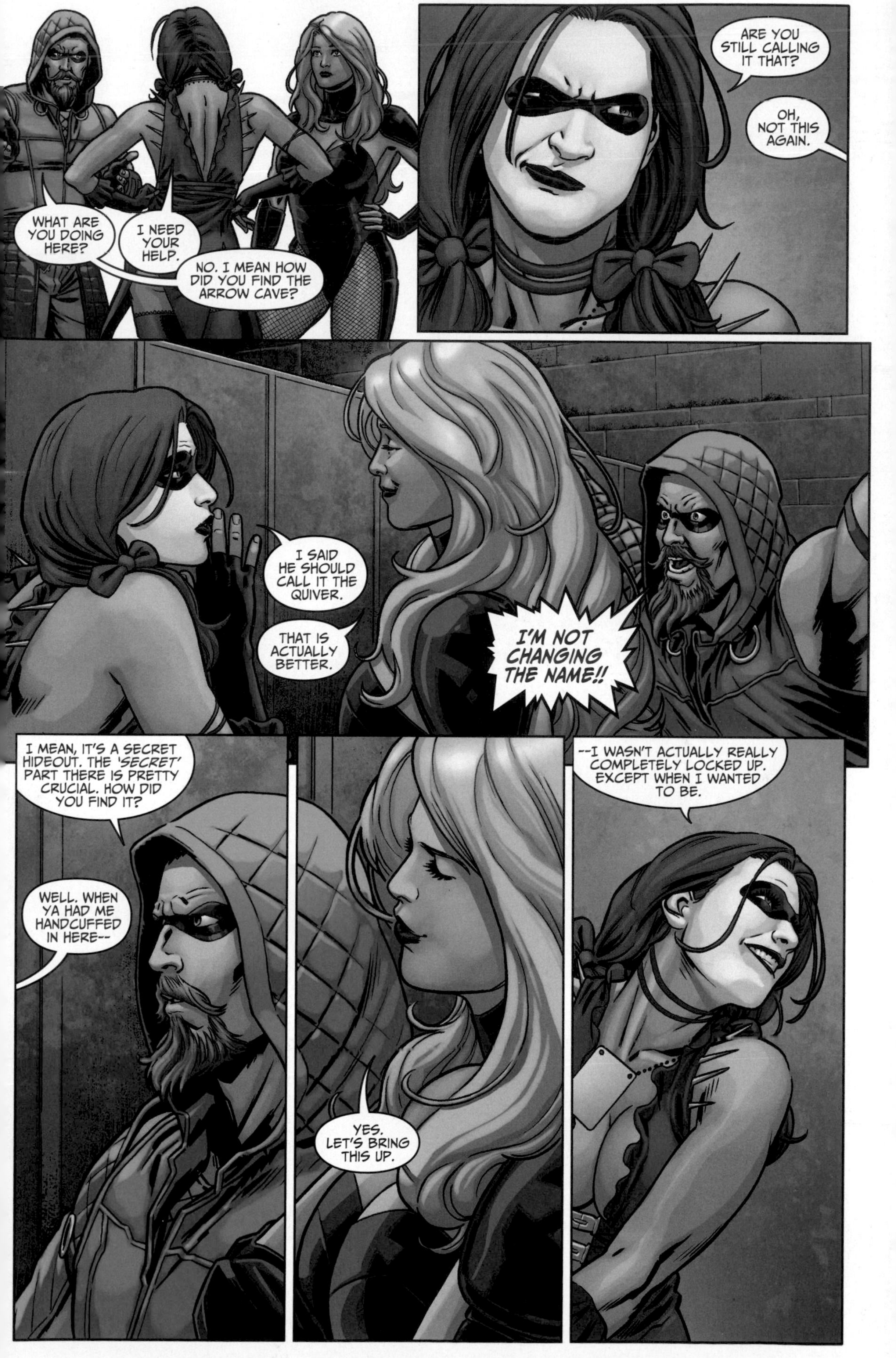
WHAT ARE YOU DOING HERE?
I NEED YOUR HELP.
NO. I MEAN HOW DID YOU FIND THE ARROW CAVE?
ARE YOU STILL CALLING IT THAT?
OH, NOT THIS AGAIN.
I SAID HE SHOULD CALL IT THE QUIVER.
THAT IS ACTUALLY BETTER.
I'M NOT CHANGING THE NAME!!
I MEAN, IT'S A SECRET HIDEOUT. THE 'SECRET' PART THERE IS PRETTY CRUCIAL. HOW DID YOU FIND IT?
WELL. WHEN YA HAD ME HANDCUFFED IN HERE--
YES. LET'S BRING THIS UP.
--I WASN'T ACTUALLY REALLY COMPLETELY LOCKED UP. EXCEPT WHEN I WANTED TO BE.

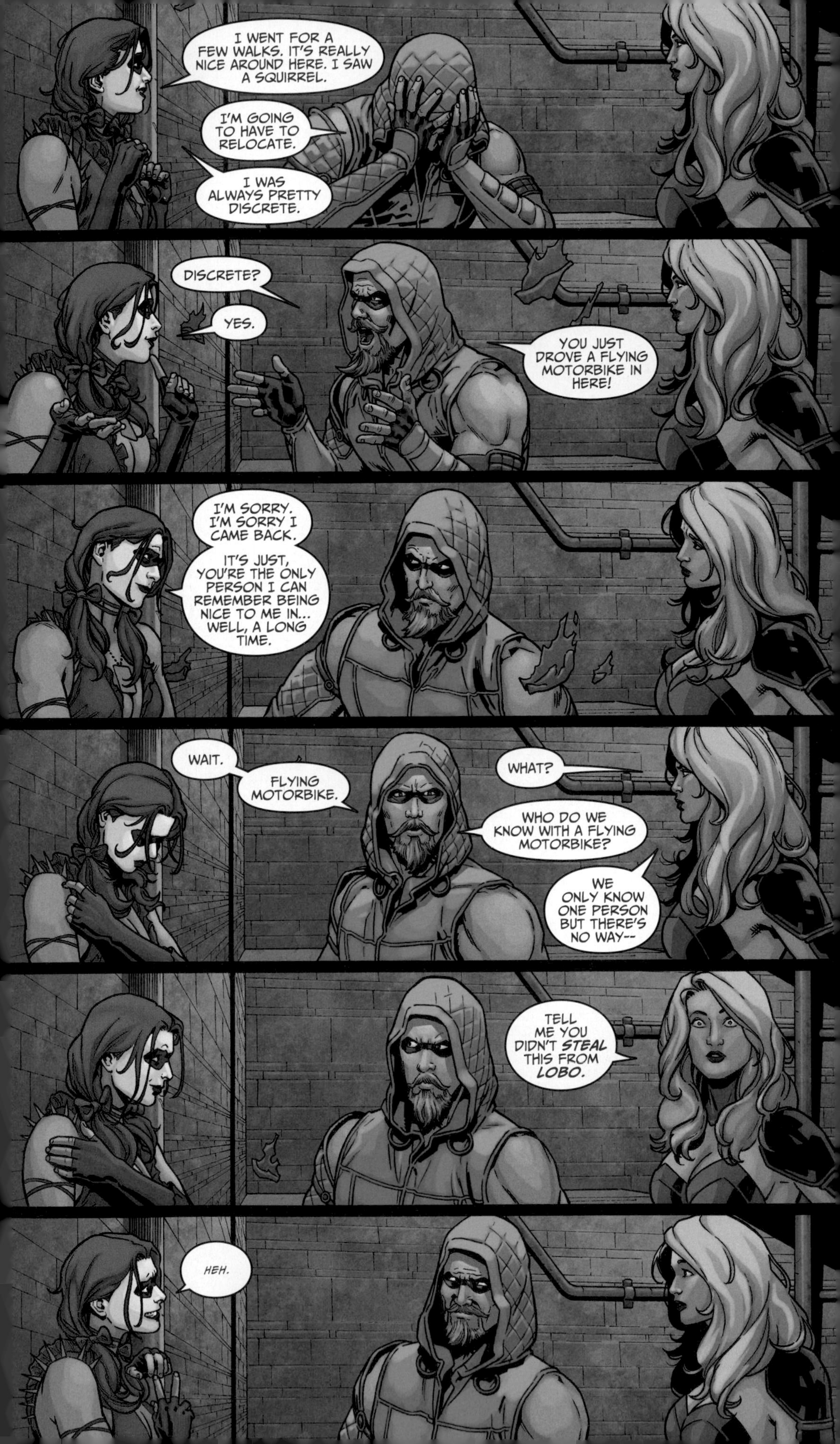
I WENT FOR A FEW WALKS. IT'S REALLY NICE AROUND HERE. I SAW A SQUIRREL.
I'M GOING TO HAVE TO RELOCATE.
I WAS ALWAYS PRETTY DISCRETE.
DISCRETE?
YES.
YOU JUST DROVE A FLYING MOTORBIKE IN HERE!
I'M SORRY. I'M SORRY I CAME BACK.
IT'S JUST, YOU'RE THE ONLY PERSON I CAN REMEMBER BEING NICE TO ME IN... WELL, A LONG TIME.
WAIT.
FLYING MOTORBIKE.
WHAT?
WHO DO WE KNOW WITH A FLYING MOTORBIKE?
WE ONLY KNOW ONE PERSON BUT THERE'S NO WAY--
TELL ME YOU DIDN'T STEAL THIS FROM LOBO.
HEH.

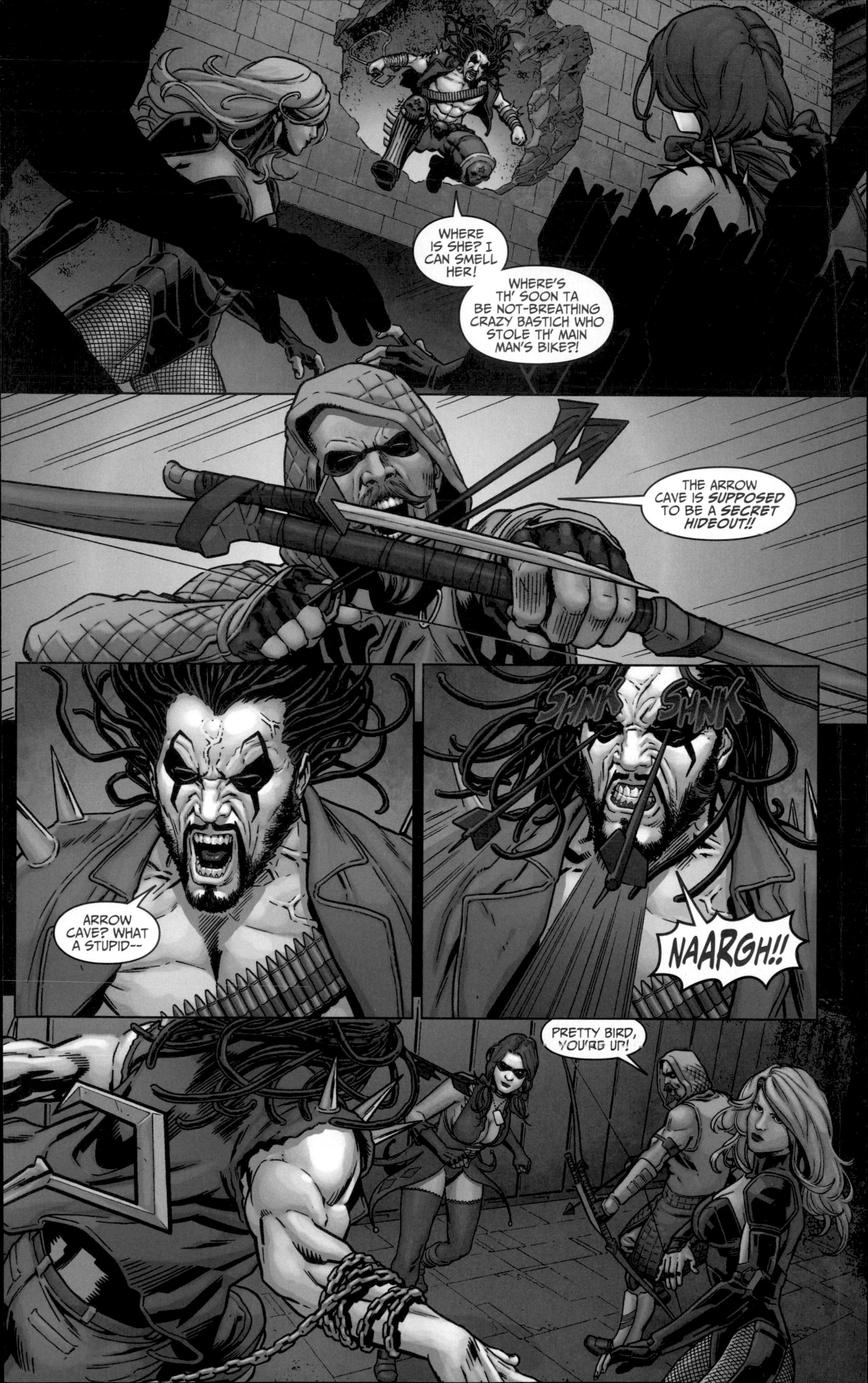
WHERE IS SHE? I CAN SMELL HER!
WHERE'S TH' SOON TA BE NOT-BREATHING CRAZY BASTICH WHO STOLE TH' MAIN MAN'S BIKE?!
THE ARROW CAVE IS SUPPOSED TO BE A SECRET HIDEOUT!!
ARROW CAVE? WHAT A STUPID--
SHNK SHNK
NAARGH!!
PRETTY BIRD, YOU'RE UP!

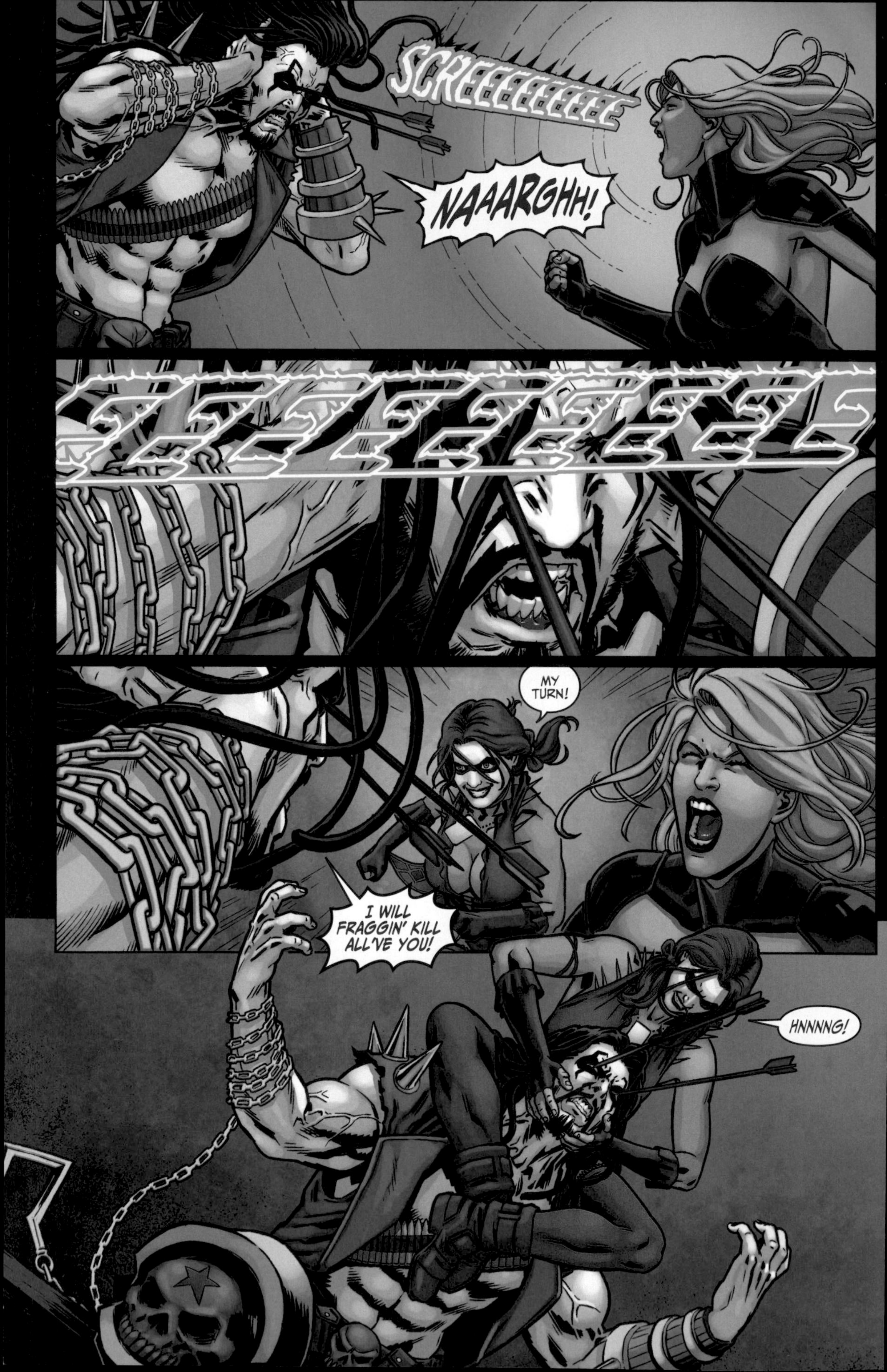
SCREEEEEEEEEE
NAAARGHH!
MY TURN!
I WILL FRAGGIN' KILL ALL'VE YOU!
HNNNNG!

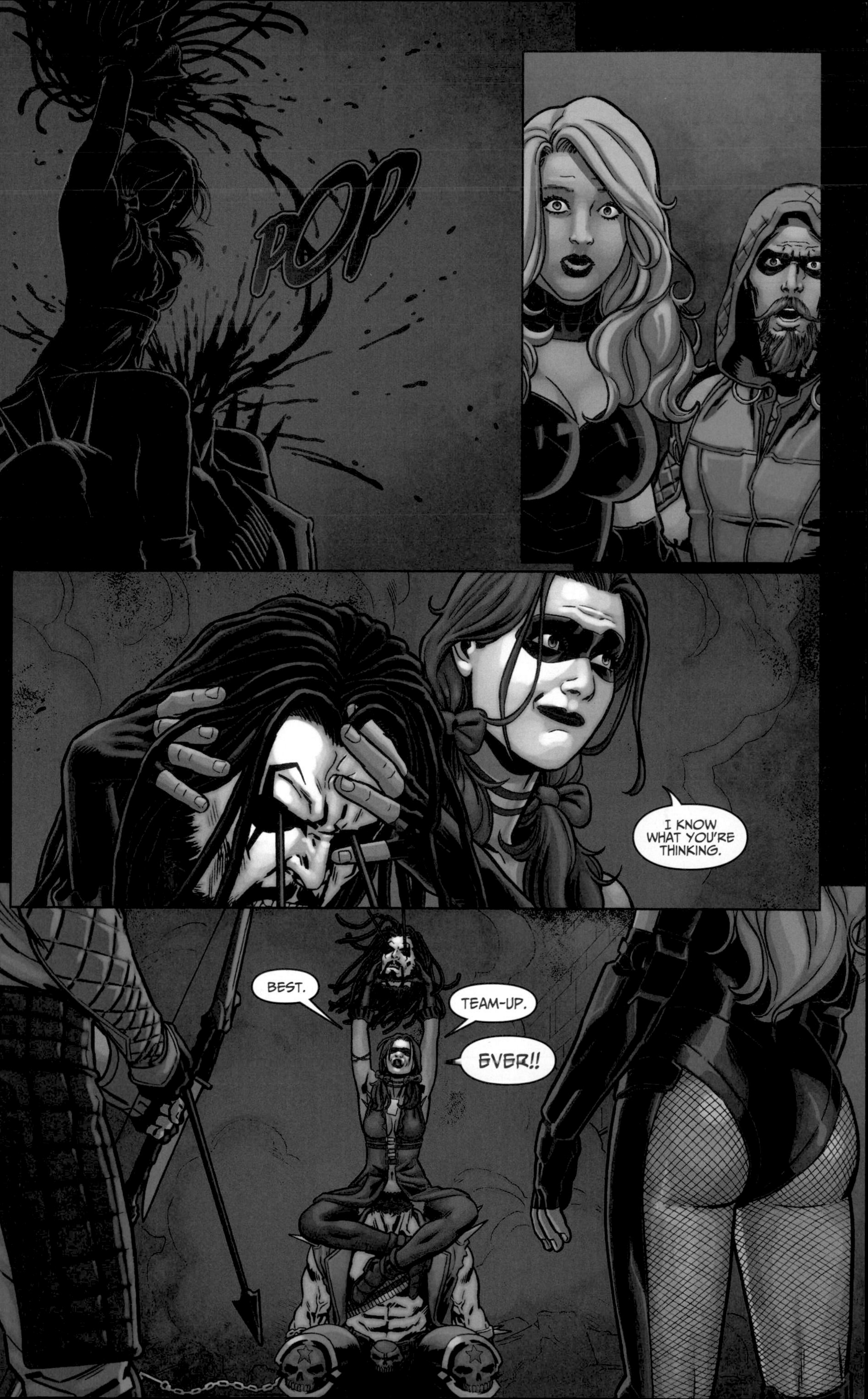
POP
I KNOW WHAT YOU'RE THINKING.
BEST.
TEAM-UP.
EVER!!

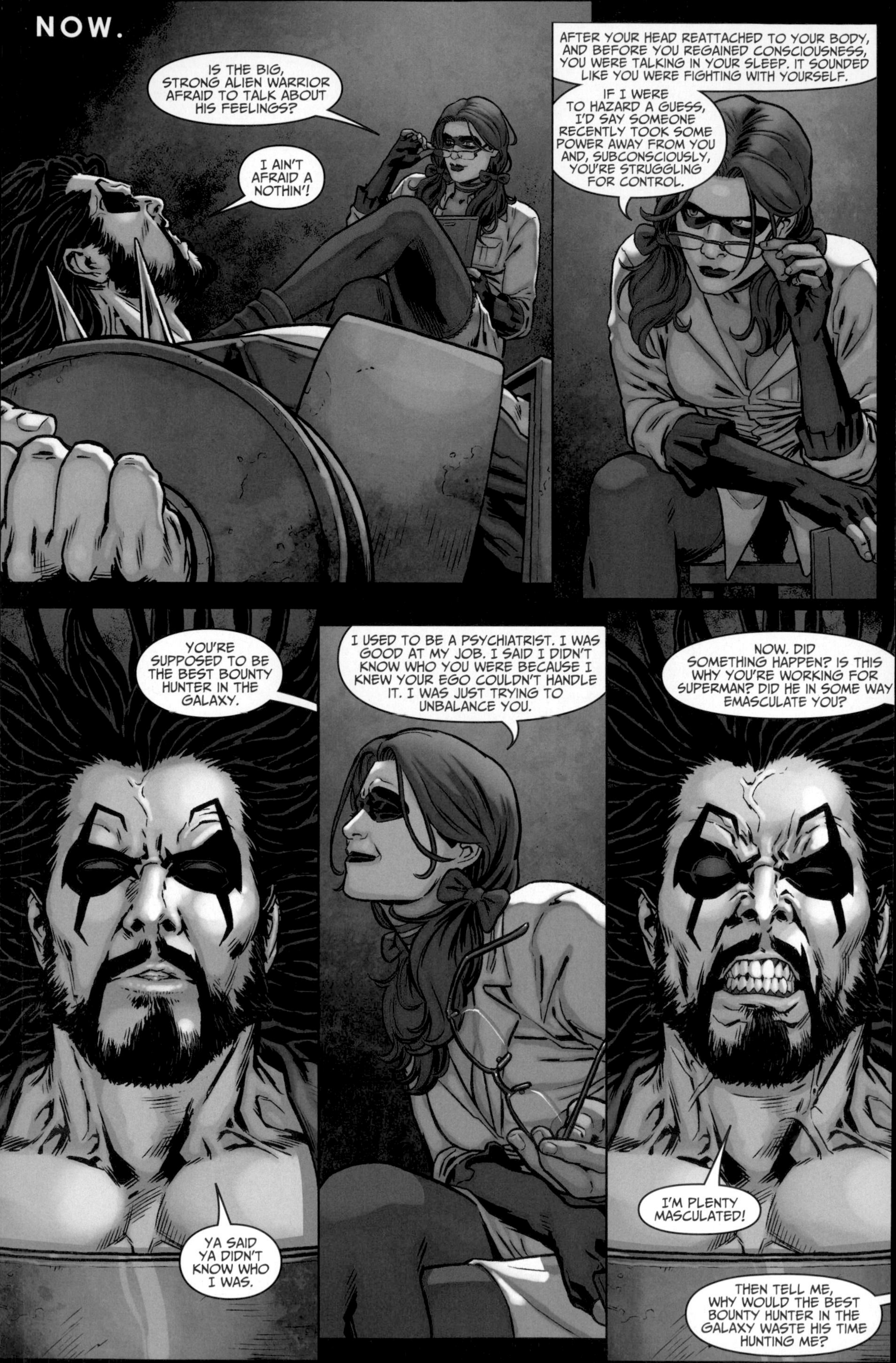
NOW.
IS THE BIG, STRONG ALIEN WARRIOR AFRAID TO TALK ABOUT HIS FEELINGS?
I AIN'T AFRAID A NOTHIN'!
AFTER YOUR HEAD REATTACHED TO YOUR BODY, AND BEFORE YOU REGAINED CONSCIOUSNESS, YOU WERE TALKING IN YOUR SLEEP. IT SOUNDED LIKE YOU WERE FIGHTING WITH YOURSELF.
IF I WERE TO HAZARD A GUESS, I'D SAY SOMEONE RECENTLY TOOK SOME POWER AWAY FROM YOU AND, SUBCONSCIOUSLY, YOU'RE STRUGGLING FOR CONTROL.
YOU'RE SUPPOSED TO BE THE BEST BOUNTY HUNTER IN THE GALAXY.
YA SAID YA DIDN'T KNOW WHO I WAS.
I USED TO BE A PSYCHIATRIST. I WAS GOOD AT MY JOB. I SAID I DIDN'T KNOW WHO YOU WERE BECAUSE I KNEW YOUR EGO COULDN'T HANDLE IT. I WAS JUST TRYING TO UNBALANCE YOU.
NOW. DID SOMETHING HAPPEN? IS THIS WHY YOU'RE WORKING FOR SUPERMAN? DID HE IN SOME WAY EMASCULATE YOU?
I'M PLENTY MASCULATED!
THEN TELL ME, WHY WOULD THE BEST BOUNTY HUNTER IN THE GALAXY WASTE HIS TIME HUNTING ME?

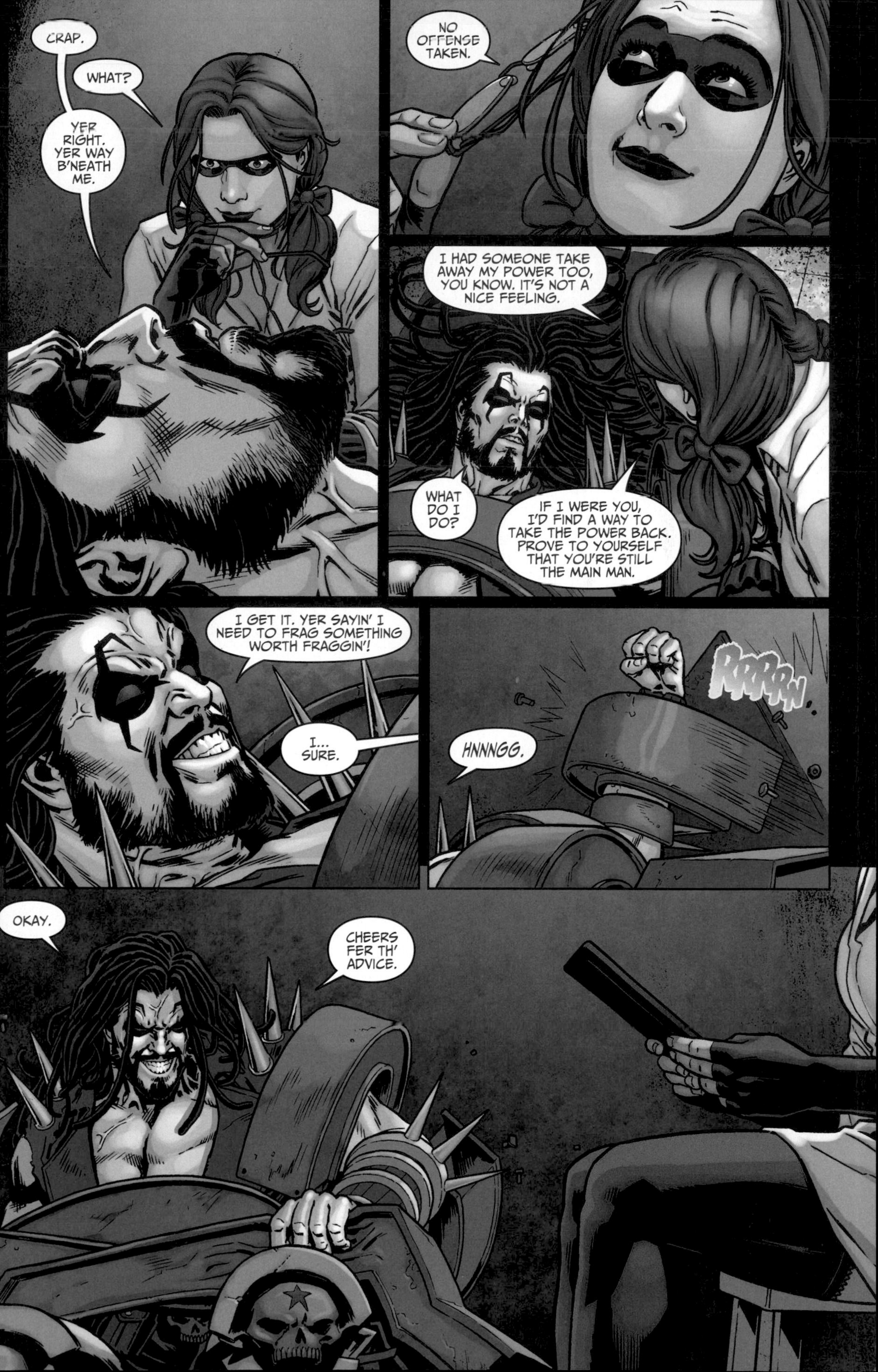
CRAP.
WHAT?
YER RIGHT. YER WAY B'NEATH ME.
NO OFFENSE TAKEN.
I HAD SOMEONE TAKE AWAY MY POWER TOO, YOU KNOW. IT'S NOT A NICE FEELING.
WHAT DO I DO?
IF I WERE YOU, I'D FIND A WAY TO TAKE THE POWER BACK. PROVE TO YOURSELF THAT YOU'RE STILL THE MAIN MAN.
I GET IT. YER SAYIN' I NEED TO FRAG SOMETHING WORTH FRAGGIN'!
I... SURE.
RRRRN
HNNNGG.
OKAY.
CHEERS FER TH' ADVICE.

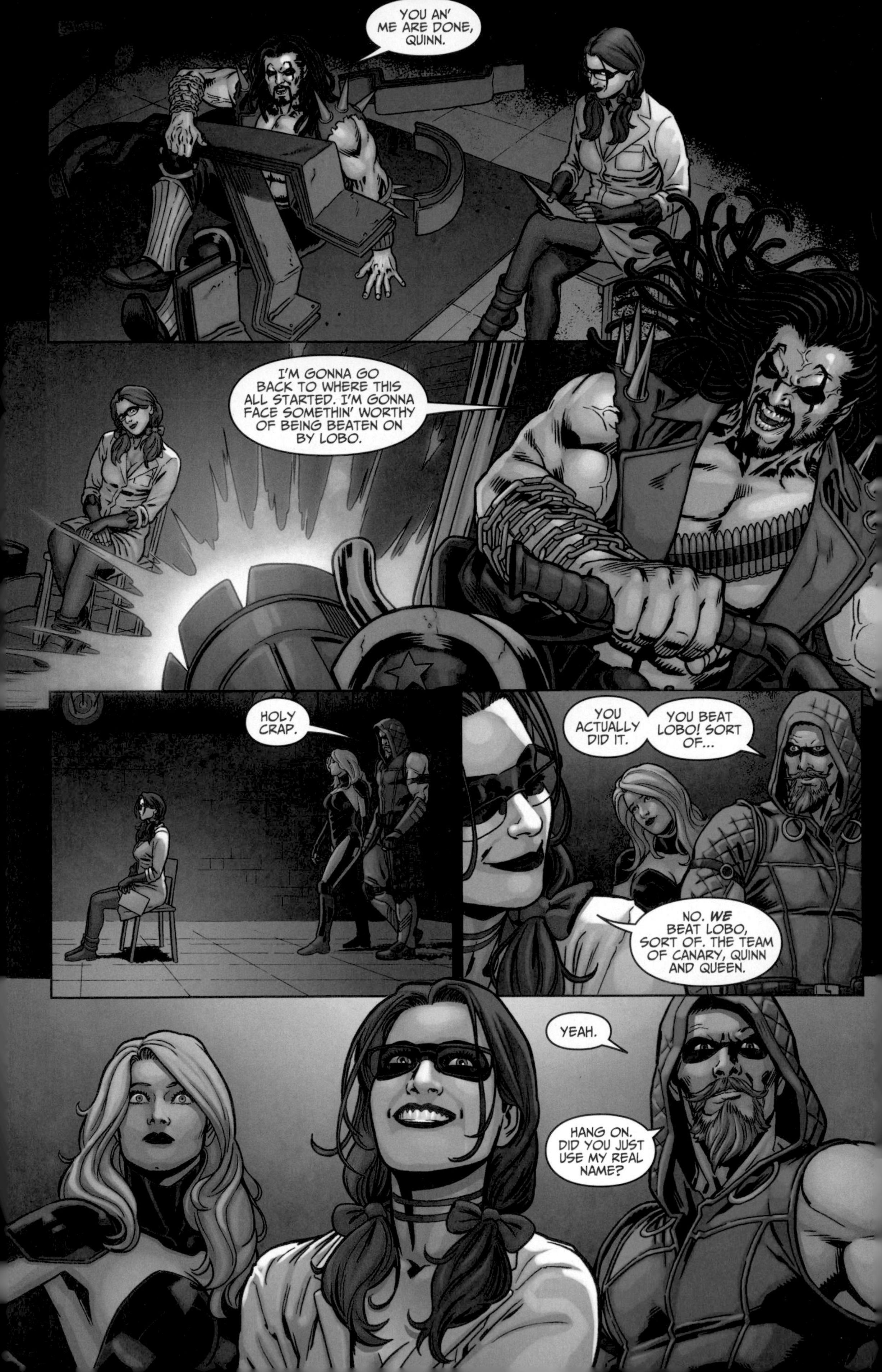
YOU AN' ME ARE DONE, QUINN.
I'M GONNA GO BACK TO WHERE THIS ALL STARTED. I'M GONNA FACE SOMETHIN' WORTHY OF BEING BEATEN ON BY LOBO.
HOLY CRAP.
YOU ACTUALLY DID IT.
YOU BEAT LOBO! SORT OF...
NO. WE BEAT LOBO, SORT OF. THE TEAM OF CANARY, QUINN AND QUEEN.
YEAH.
HANG ON. DID YOU JUST USE MY REAL NAME?

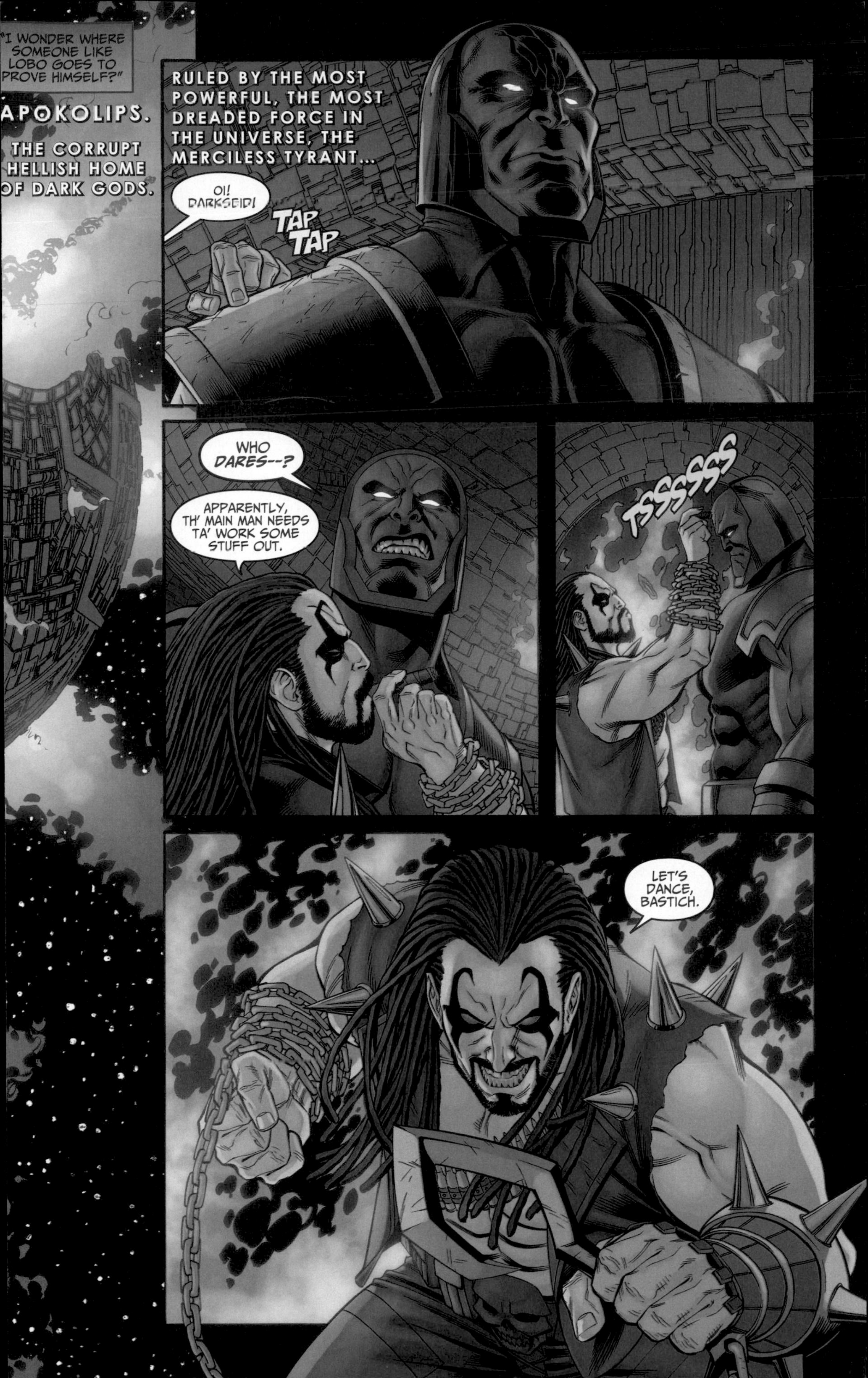
"I WONDER WHERE SOMEONE LIKE LOBO GOES TO PROVE HIMSELF?"
APOKOLIPS.
THE CORRUPT HELLISH HOME OF DARK GODS.
RULED BY THE MOST POWERFUL, THE MOST DREADED FORCE IN THE UNIVERSE, THE MERCILESS TYRANT...
OI! DARKSEID!
TAP TAP
WHO DARES--?
APPARENTLY, TH' MAIN MAN NEEDS TA' WORK SOME STUFF OUT.
TSSSSSS
LET'S DANCE, BASTICH.

PART TWELVE

Tom Derenick Jheremy Raapack Bruno Redondo Artists

Sergi Erra, **Fran Vazquez**, **David Lopez** and **Santi Casas** of **Ikari Studio** Colorists

Mico Suayan & **David Lopez** and **Santi Casas** of **Ikari Studio** Cover

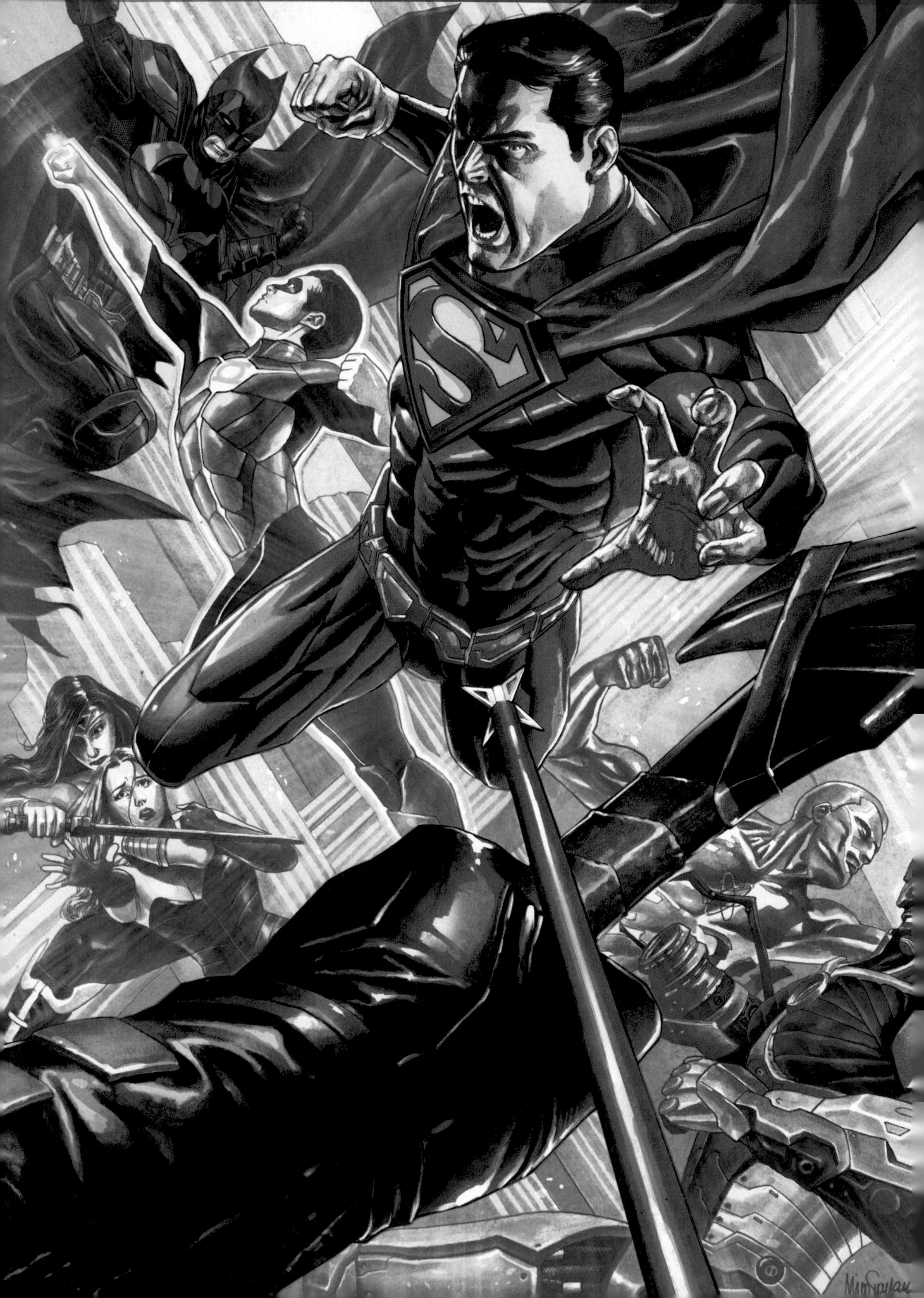

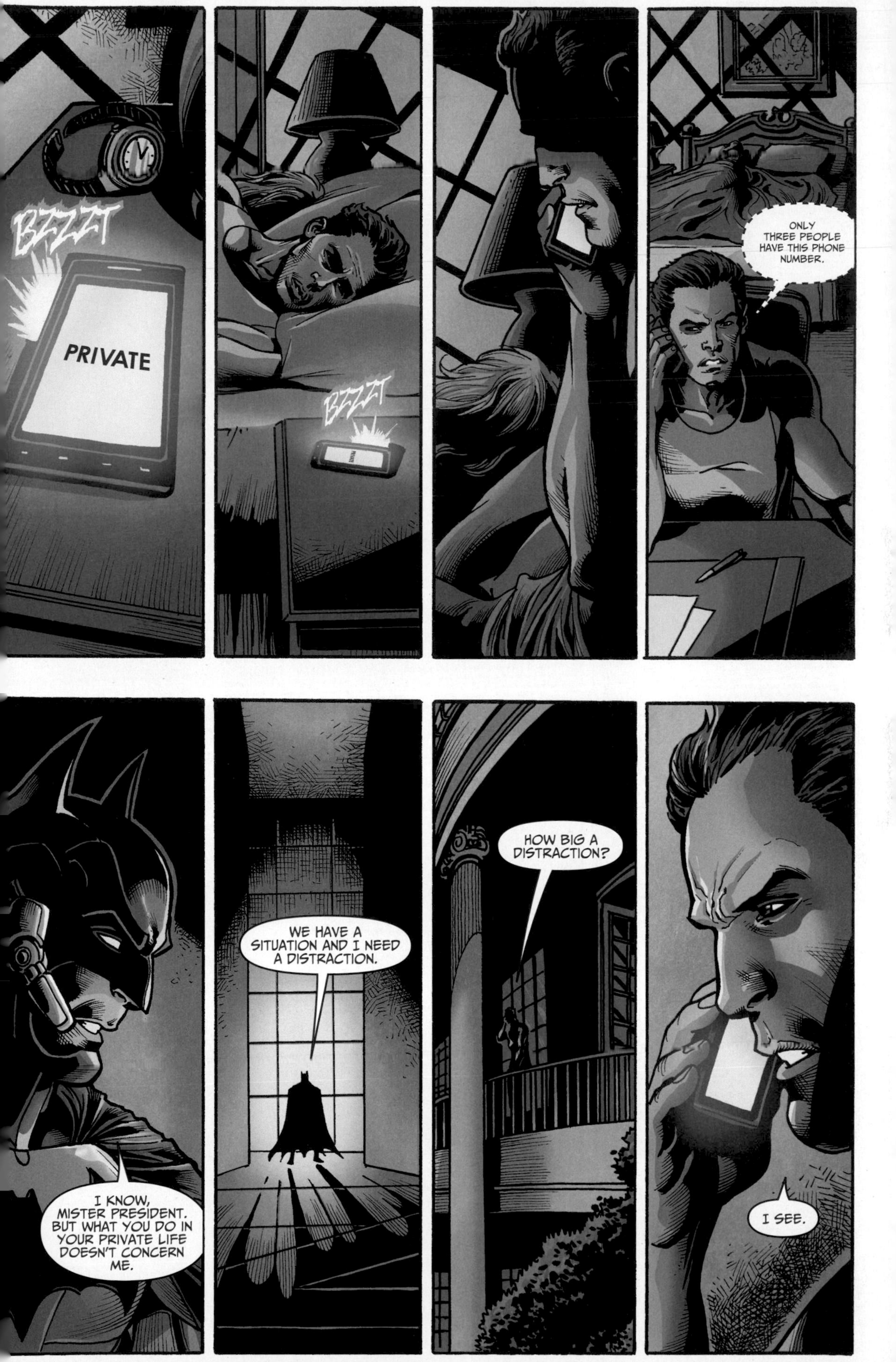
BZZZT
PRIVATE
BZZZT
ONLY THREE PEOPLE HAVE THIS PHONE NUMBER.
I KNOW, MISTER PRESIDENT. BUT WHAT YOU DO IN YOUR PRIVATE LIFE DOESN'T CONCERN ME.
WE HAVE A SITUATION AND I NEED A DISTRACTION.
HOW BIG A DISTRACTION?
I SEE.

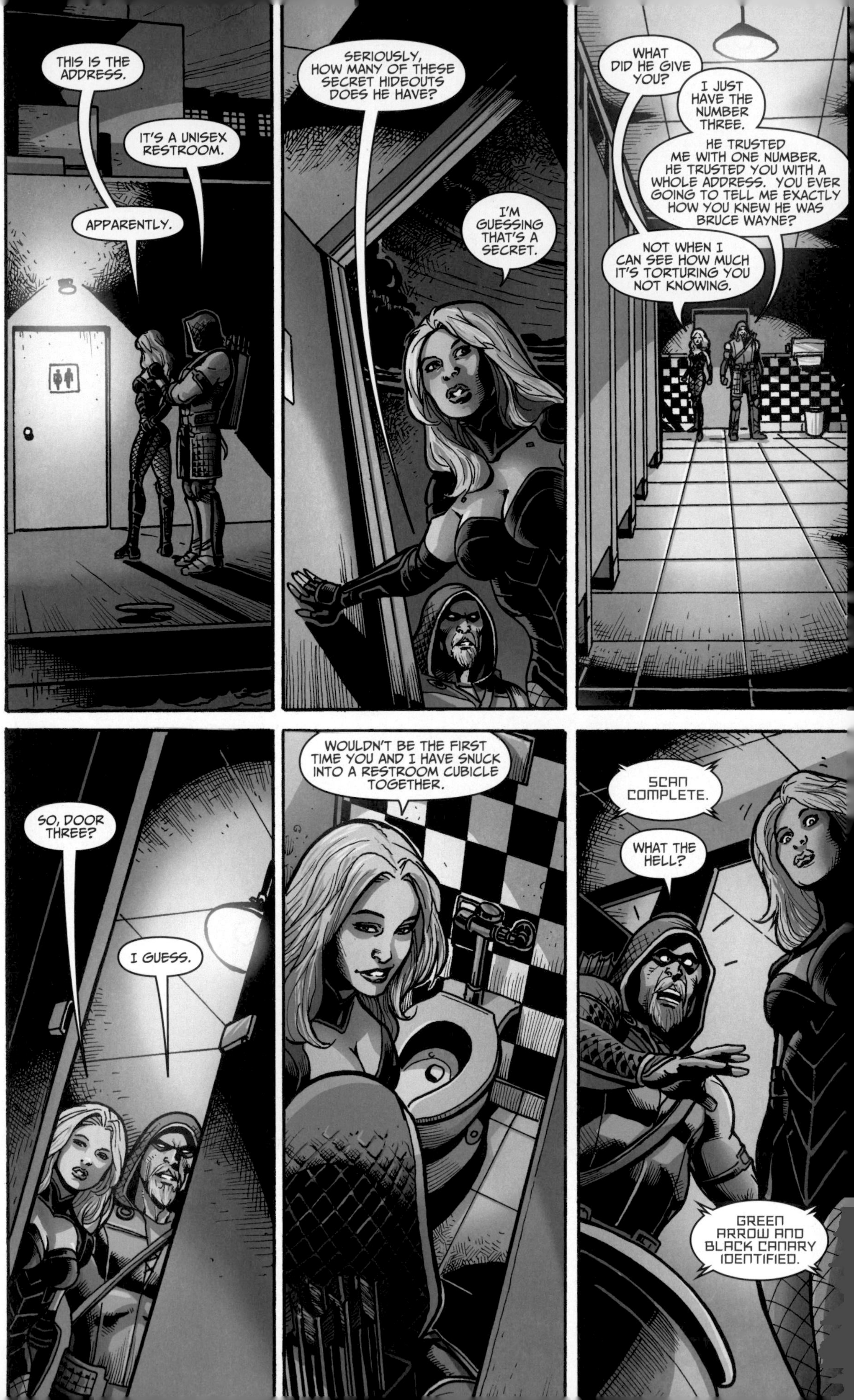

THIS IS THE ADDRESS.
IT'S A UNISEX RESTROOM.
APPARENTLY.
SERIOUSLY, HOW MANY OF THESE SECRET HIDEOUTS DOES HE HAVE?
I'M GUESSING THAT'S A SECRET.
WHAT DID HE GIVE YOU?
I JUST HAVE THE NUMBER THREE.
HE TRUSTED ME WITH ONE NUMBER. HE TRUSTED YOU WITH A WHOLE ADDRESS. YOU EVER GOING TO TELL ME EXACTLY HOW YOU KNEW HE WAS BRUCE WAYNE?
NOT WHEN I CAN SEE HOW MUCH IT'S TORTURING YOU NOT KNOWING.
SO, DOOR THREE?
I GUESS.
WOULDN'T BE THE FIRST TIME YOU AND I HAVE SNUCK INTO A RESTROOM CUBICLE TOGETHER.
SCAN COMPLETE.
WHAT THE HELL?
GREEN ARROW AND BLACK CANARY IDENTIFIED.

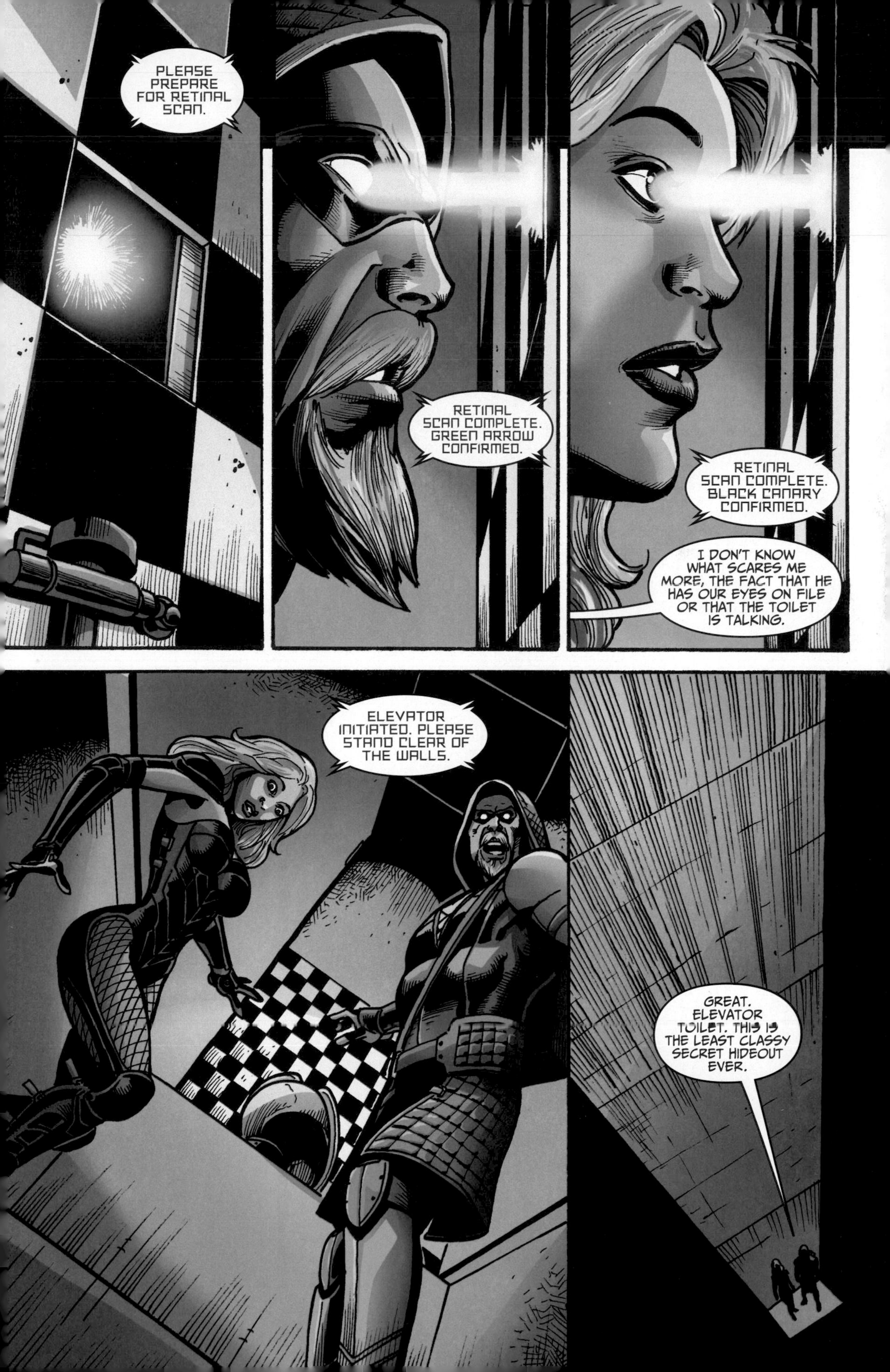
PLEASE PREPARE FOR RETINAL SCAN.
RETINAL SCAN COMPLETE. GREEN ARROW CONFIRMED.
RETINAL SCAN COMPLETE. BLACK CANARY CONFIRMED.
I DON'T KNOW WHAT SCARES ME MORE, THE FACT THAT HE HAS OUR EYES ON FILE OR THAT THE TOILET IS TALKING.
ELEVATOR INITIATED. PLEASE STAND CLEAR OF THE WALLS.
GREAT. ELEVATOR TOILET. THIS IS THE LEAST CLASSY SECRET HIDEOUT EVER.

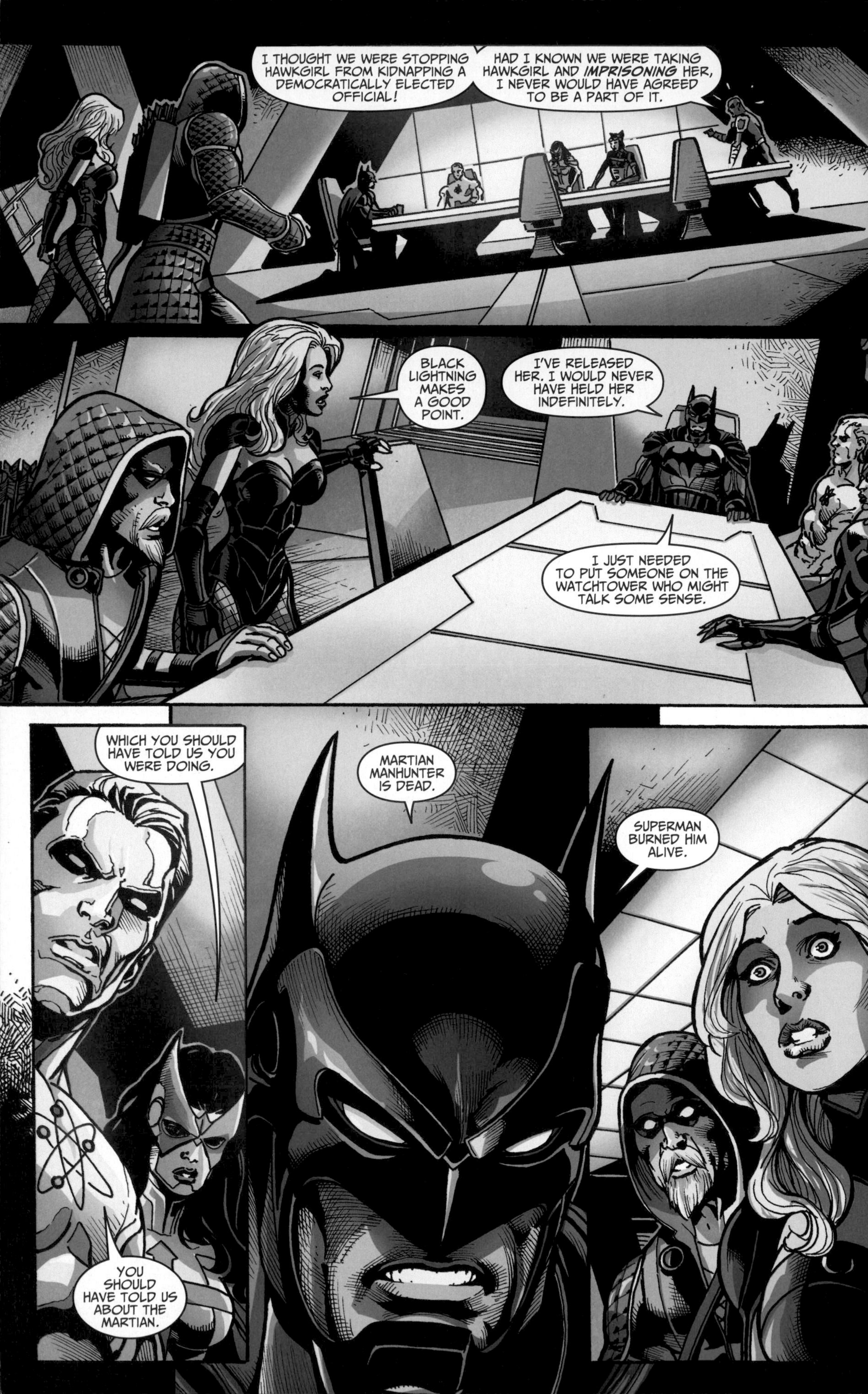
I THOUGHT WE WERE STOPPING HAWKGIRL FROM KIDNAPPING A DEMOCRATICALLY ELECTED OFFICIAL!
HAD I KNOWN WE WERE TAKING HAWKGIRL AND *IMPRISONING* HER, I NEVER WOULD HAVE AGREED TO BE A PART OF IT.
BLACK LIGHTNING MAKES A GOOD POINT.
I'VE RELEASED HER. I WOULD NEVER HAVE HELD HER INDEFINITELY.
I JUST NEEDED TO PUT SOMEONE ON THE WATCHTOWER WHO MIGHT TALK SOME SENSE.
WHICH YOU SHOULD HAVE TOLD US YOU WERE DOING.
YOU SHOULD HAVE TOLD US ABOUT THE MARTIAN.
MARTIAN MANHUNTER IS DEAD.
SUPERMAN BURNED HIM ALIVE.

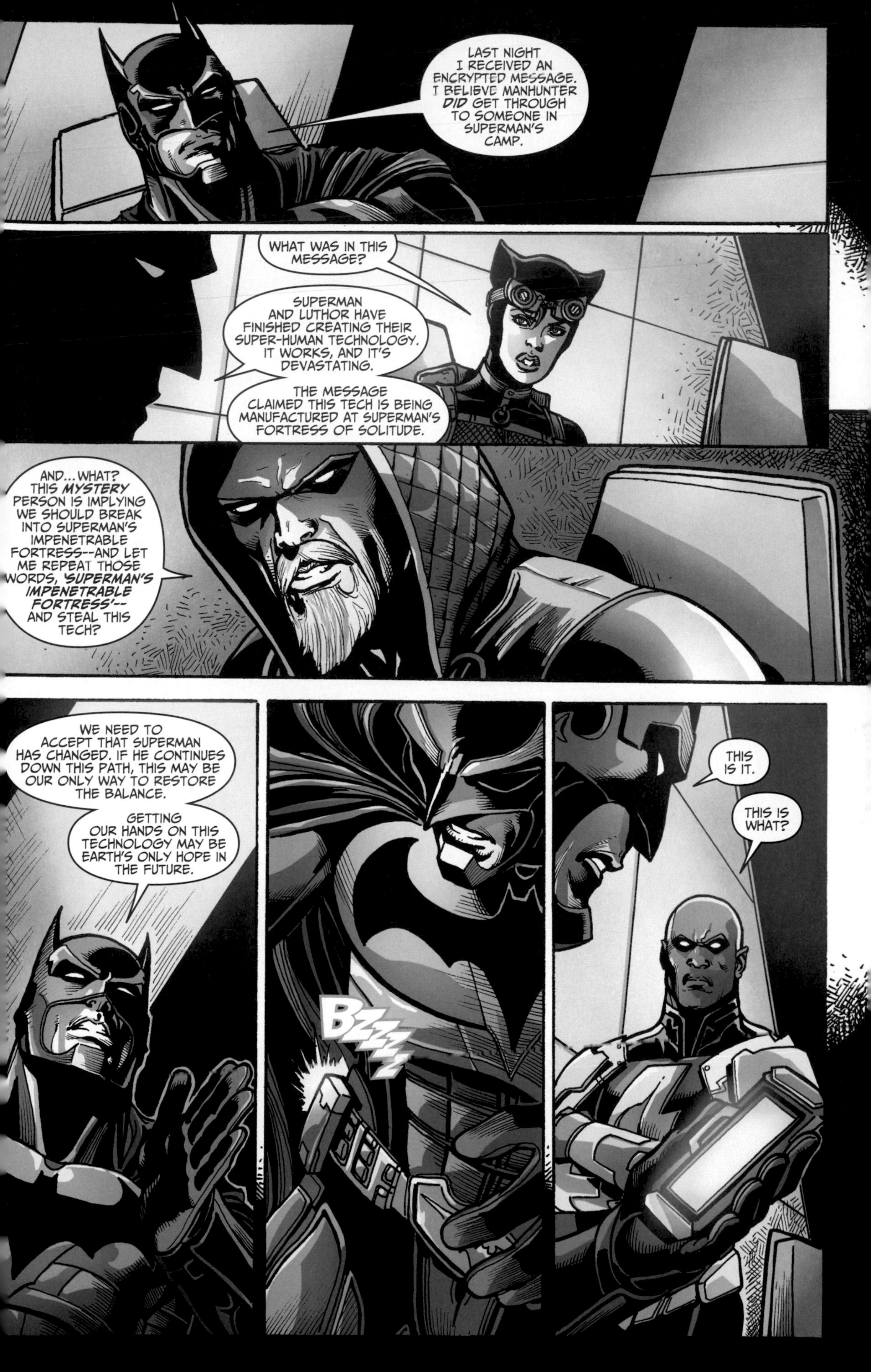
LAST NIGHT I RECEIVED AN ENCRYPTED MESSAGE. I BELIEVE MANHUNTER *DID* GET THROUGH TO SOMEONE IN SUPERMAN'S CAMP.
WHAT WAS IN THIS MESSAGE?
SUPERMAN AND LUTHOR HAVE FINISHED CREATING THEIR SUPER-HUMAN TECHNOLOGY. IT WORKS, AND IT'S DEVASTATING.
THE MESSAGE CLAIMED THIS TECH IS BEING MANUFACTURED AT SUPERMAN'S FORTRESS OF SOLITUDE.
AND...WHAT? THIS *MYSTERY* PERSON IS IMPLYING WE SHOULD BREAK INTO SUPERMAN'S IMPENETRABLE FORTRESS--AND LET ME REPEAT THOSE WORDS, *'SUPERMAN'S IMPENETRABLE FORTRESS'*-- AND STEAL THIS TECH?
WE NEED TO ACCEPT THAT SUPERMAN HAS CHANGED. IF HE CONTINUES DOWN THIS PATH, THIS MAY BE OUR ONLY WAY TO RESTORE THE BALANCE.
GETTING OUR HANDS ON THIS TECHNOLOGY MAY BE EARTH'S ONLY HOPE IN THE FUTURE.
BZZZZ
THIS IS IT.
THIS IS WHAT?

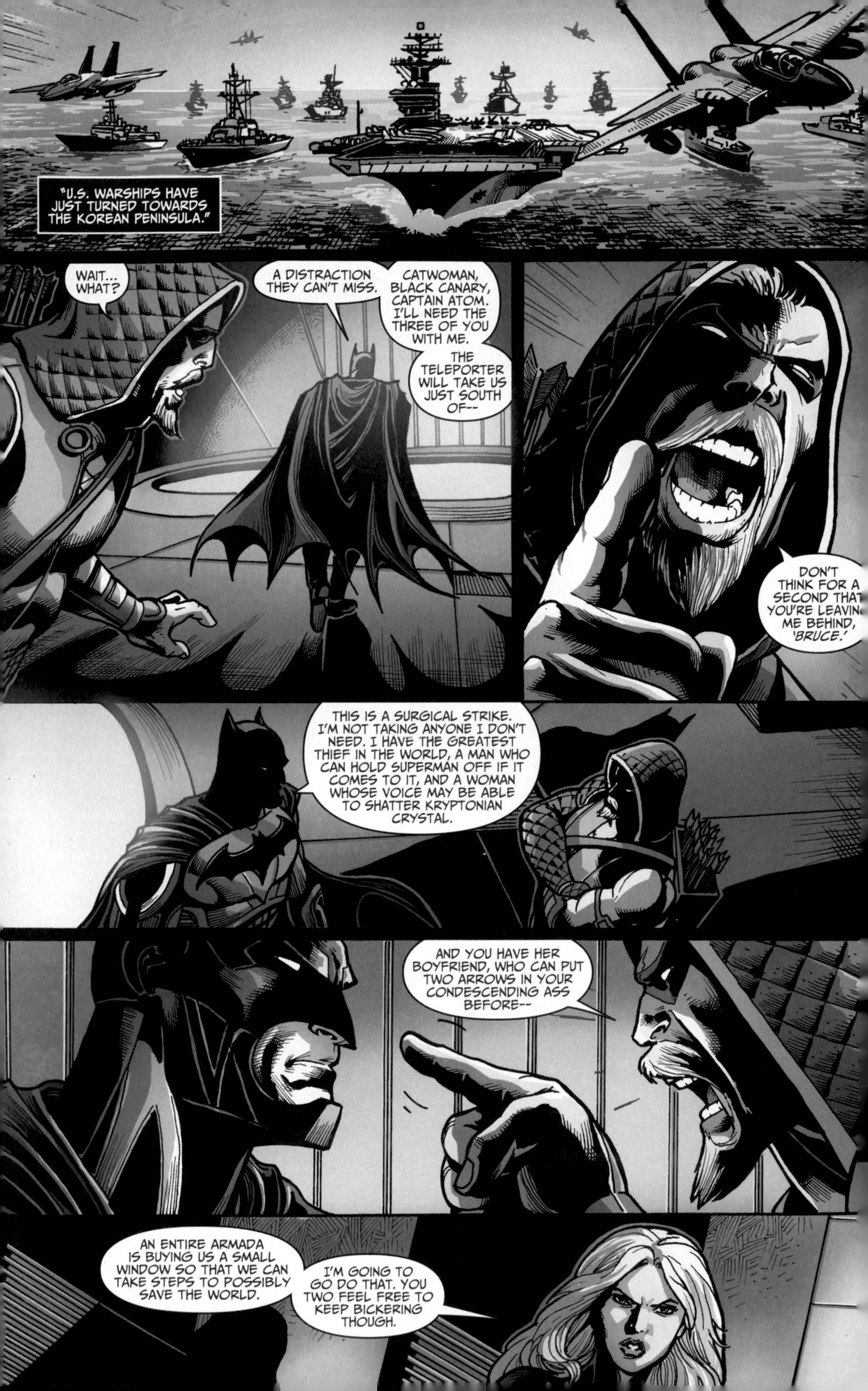
"U.S. WARSHIPS HAVE JUST TURNED TOWARDS THE KOREAN PENINSULA."
WAIT... WHAT?
A DISTRACTION THEY CAN'T MISS.
CATWOMAN, BLACK CANARY, CAPTAIN ATOM. I'LL NEED THE THREE OF YOU WITH ME.
THE TELEPORTER WILL TAKE US JUST SOUTH OF--
DON'T THINK FOR A SECOND THAT YOU'RE LEAVING ME BEHIND, 'BRUCE.'
THIS IS A SURGICAL STRIKE. I'M NOT TAKING ANYONE I DON'T NEED. I HAVE THE GREATEST THIEF IN THE WORLD, A MAN WHO CAN HOLD SUPERMAN OFF IF IT COMES TO IT, AND A WOMAN WHOSE VOICE MAY BE ABLE TO SHATTER KRYPTONIAN CRYSTAL.
AND YOU HAVE HER BOYFRIEND, WHO CAN PUT TWO ARROWS IN YOUR CONDESCENDING ASS BEFORE--
AN ENTIRE ARMADA IS BUYING US A SMALL WINDOW SO THAT WE CAN TAKE STEPS TO POSSIBLY SAVE THE WORLD.
I'M GOING TO GO DO THAT. YOU TWO FEEL FREE TO KEEP BICKERING THOUGH.

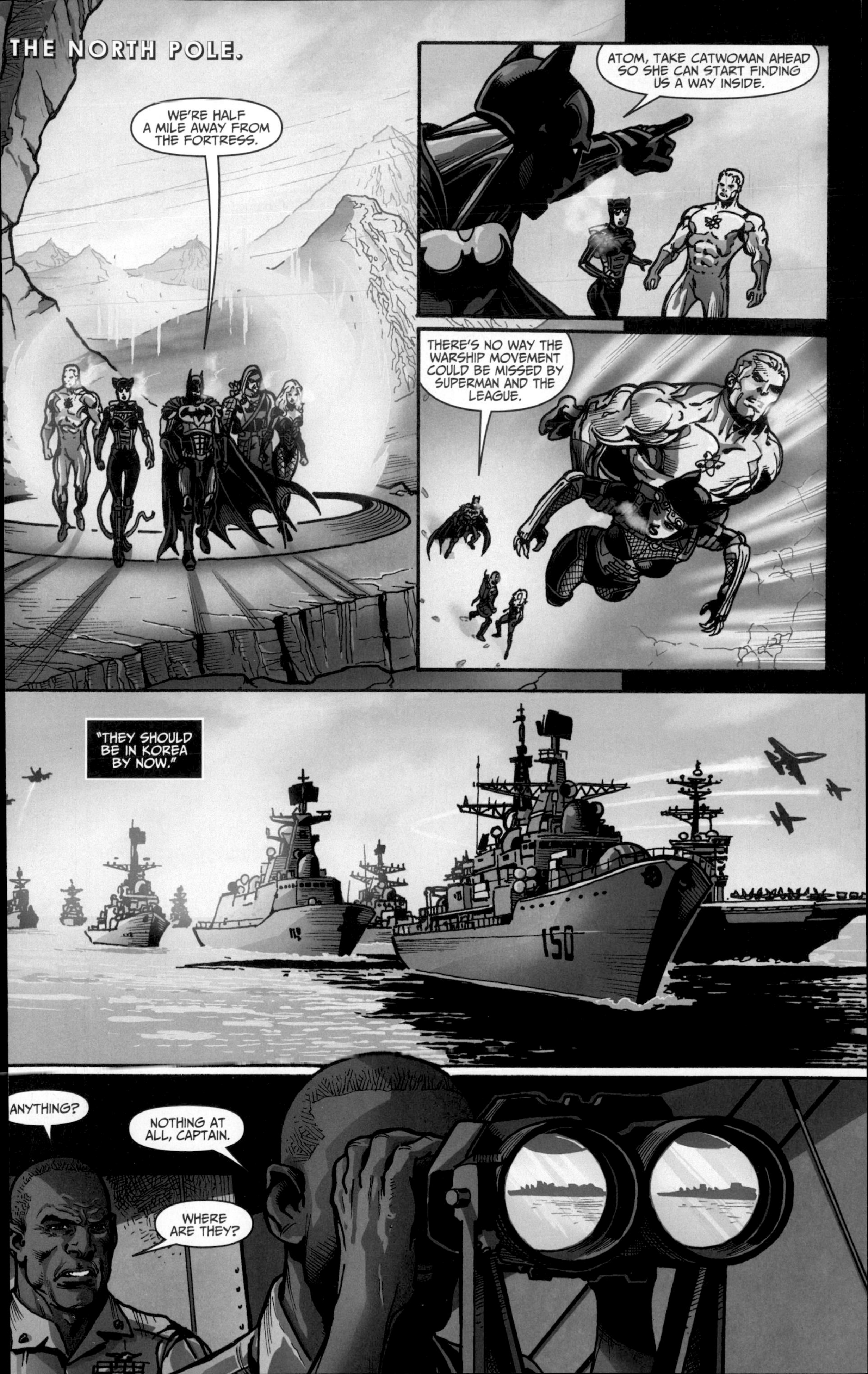
THE NORTH POLE.
WE'RE HALF A MILE AWAY FROM THE FORTRESS.
ATOM, TAKE CATWOMAN AHEAD SO SHE CAN START FINDING US A WAY INSIDE.
THERE'S NO WAY THE WARSHIP MOVEMENT COULD BE MISSED BY SUPERMAN AND THE LEAGUE.
"THEY SHOULD BE IN KOREA BY NOW."
150
ANYTHING?
NOTHING AT ALL, CAPTAIN.
WHERE ARE THEY?

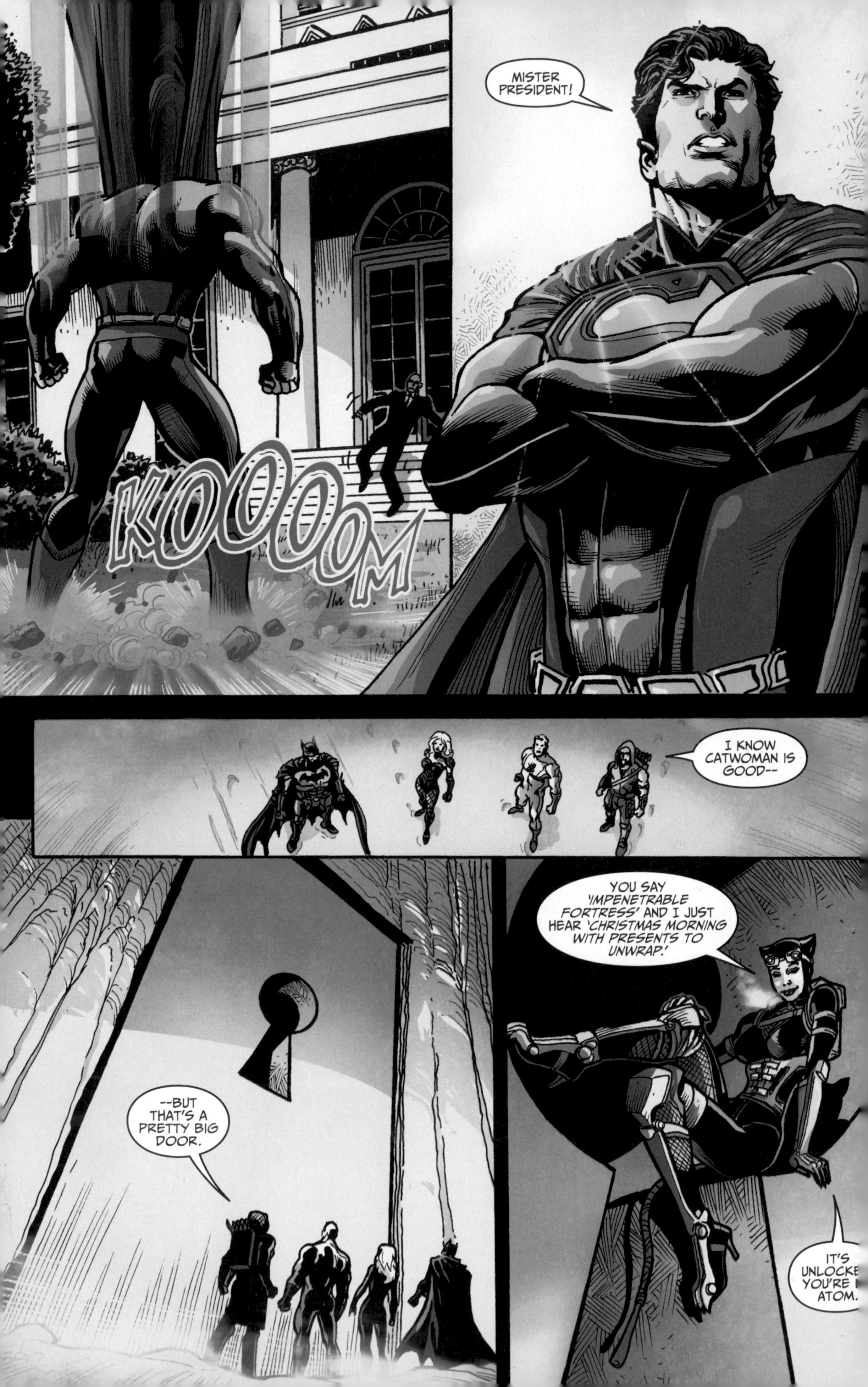
KOOOOOM
MISTER PRESIDENT!
I KNOW CATWOMAN IS GOOD--
--BUT THAT'S A PRETTY BIG DOOR.
YOU SAY 'IMPENETRABLE FORTRESS' AND I JUST HEAR 'CHRISTMAS MORNING WITH PRESENTS TO UNWRAP.'
IT'S UNLOCKE YOU'RE ATOM.

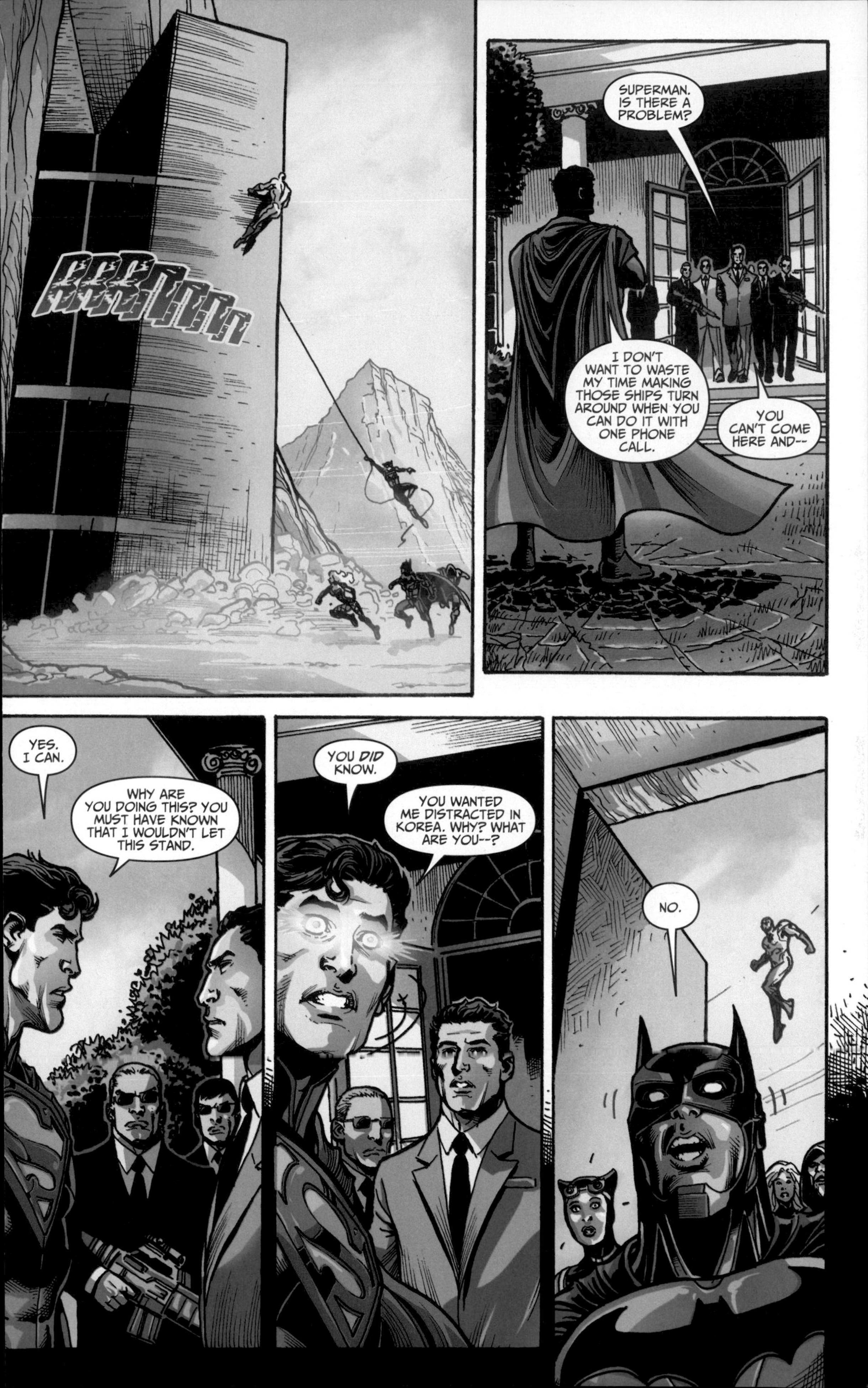
SUPERMAN. IS THERE A PROBLEM?
I DON'T WANT TO WASTE MY TIME MAKING THOSE SHIPS TURN AROUND WHEN YOU CAN DO IT WITH ONE PHONE CALL.
YOU CAN'T COME HERE AND--
YES. I CAN.
WHY ARE YOU DOING THIS? YOU MUST HAVE KNOWN THAT I WOULDN'T LET THIS STAND.
YOU *DID* KNOW.
YOU WANTED ME DISTRACTED IN KOREA. WHY? WHAT ARE YOU--?
NO.

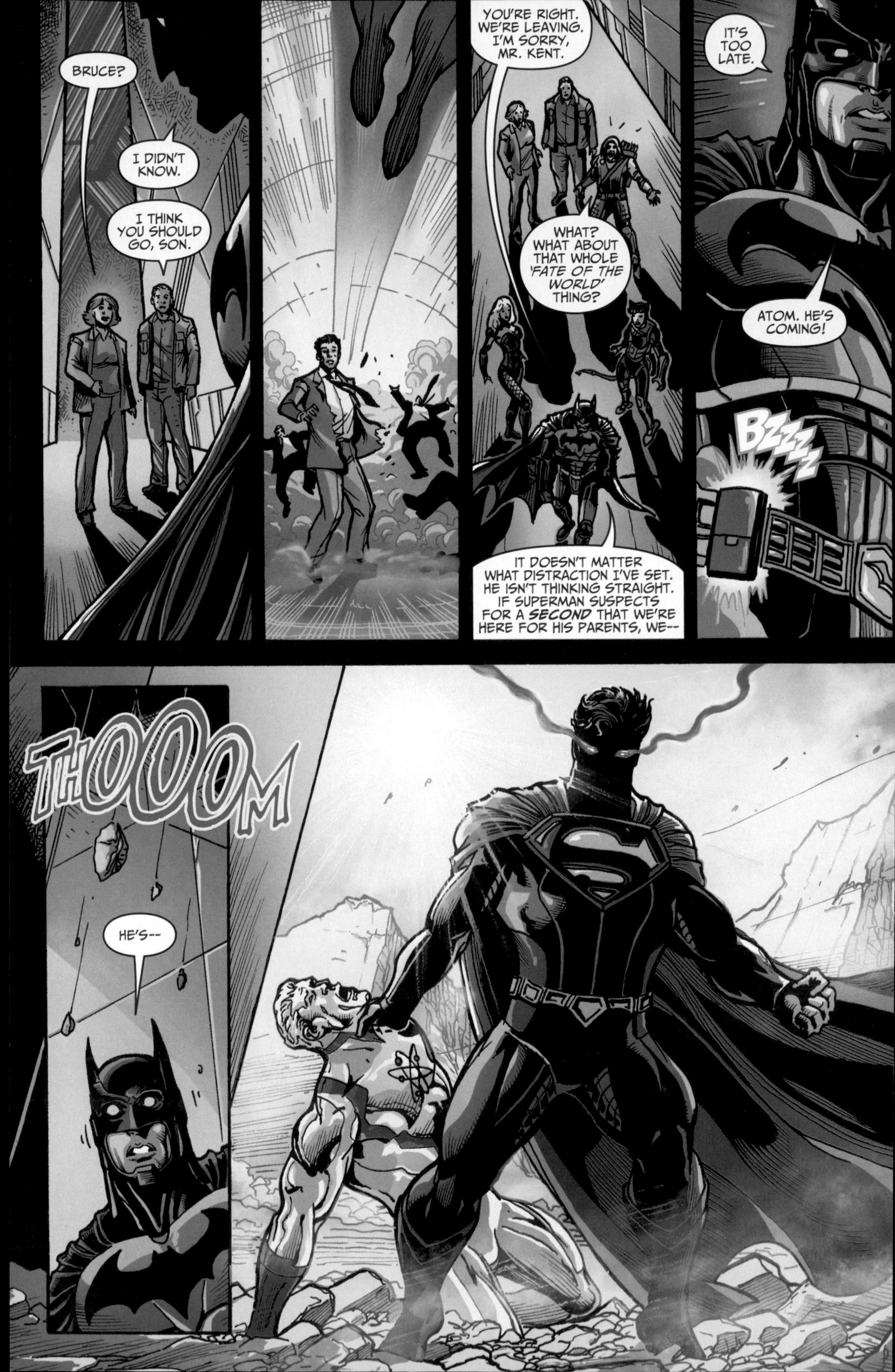
BRUCE?
I DIDN'T KNOW.
I THINK YOU SHOULD GO, SON.
YOU'RE RIGHT. WE'RE LEAVING. I'M SORRY, MR. KENT.
WHAT? WHAT ABOUT THAT WHOLE 'FATE OF THE WORLD' THING?
IT DOESN'T MATTER WHAT DISTRACTION I'VE SET. HE ISN'T THINKING STRAIGHT. IF SUPERMAN SUSPECTS FOR A SECOND THAT WE'RE HERE FOR HIS PARENTS, WE--
IT'S TOO LATE.
ATOM. HE'S COMING!
BZZZZ
THOOOM
HE'S--

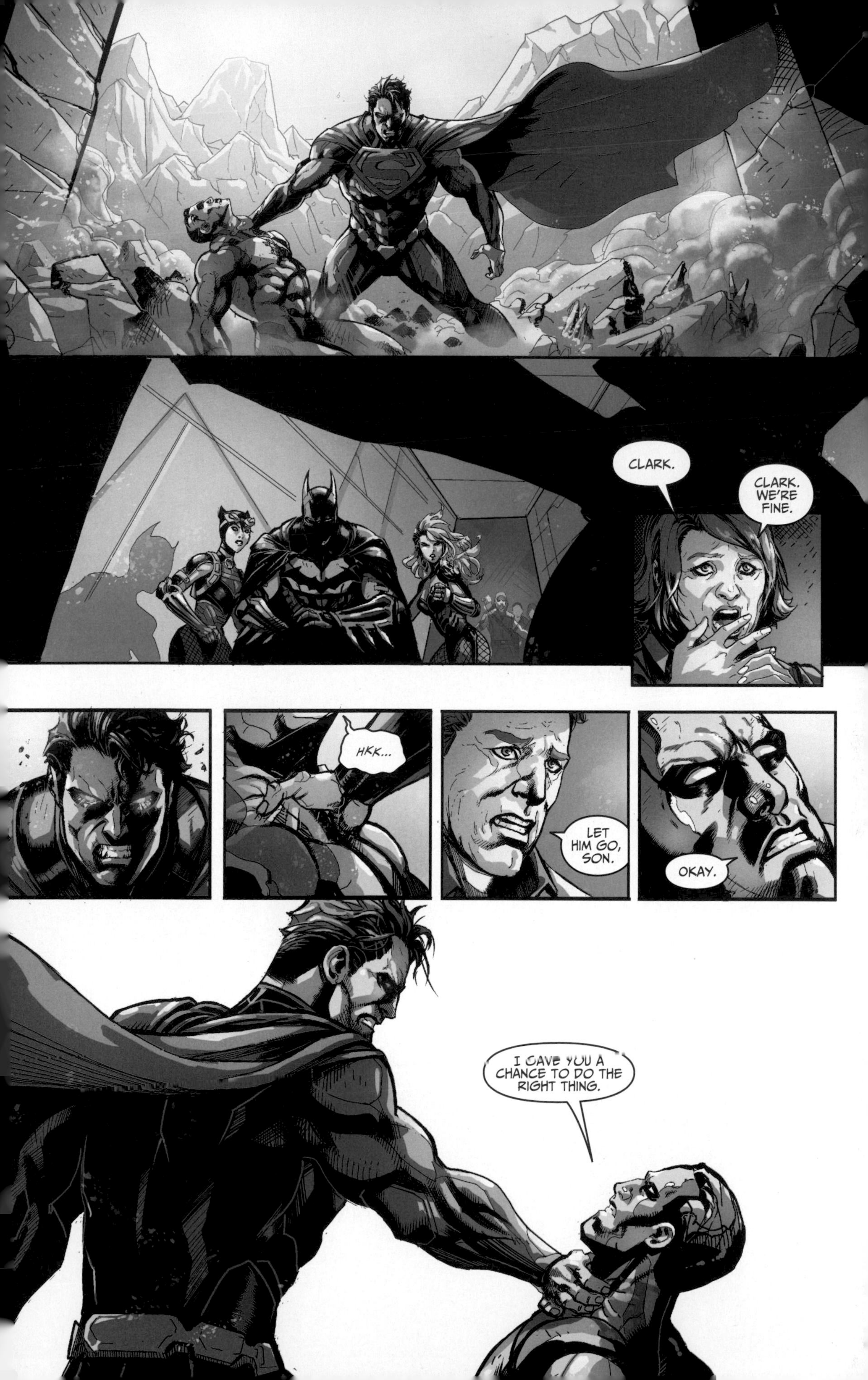
CLARK.
CLARK. WE'RE FINE.
HKK...
LET HIM GO, SON.
OKAY.
I GAVE YOU A CHANCE TO DO THE RIGHT THING.

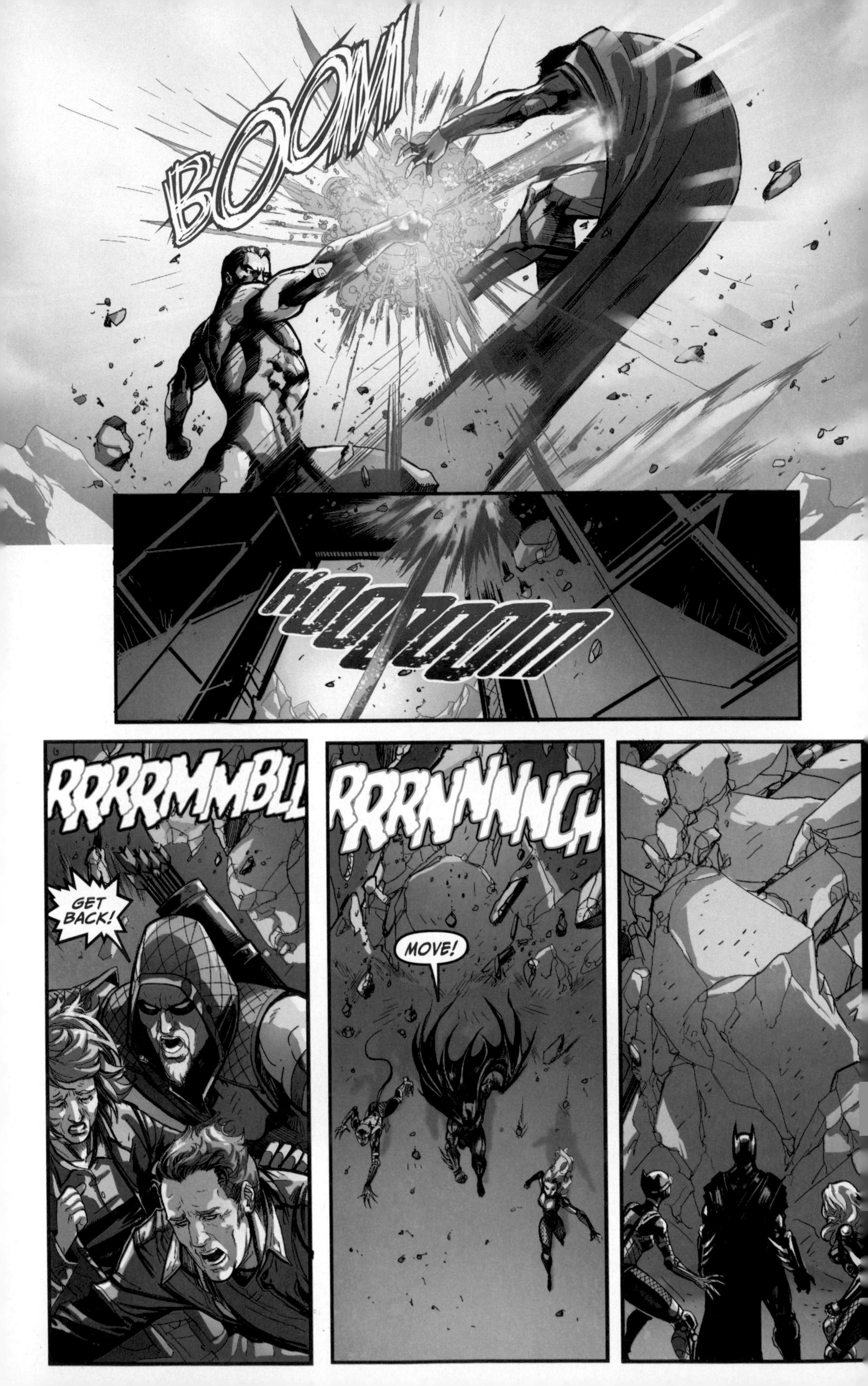
BOOOM!
KOOOOOM
RRRRMMBLL
GET BACK!
RRRNNNNCH
MOVE!

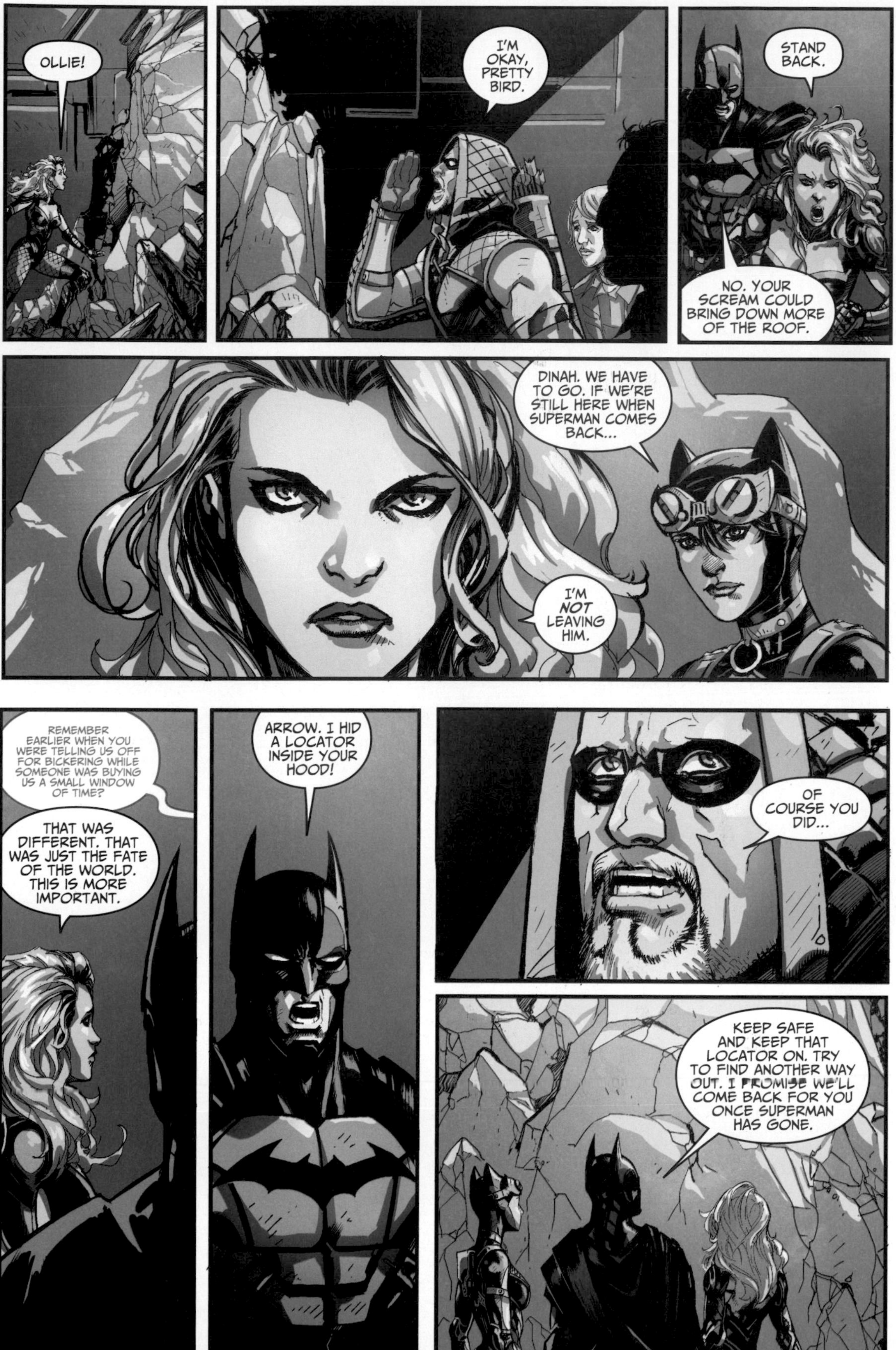
OLLIE!
I'M OKAY, PRETTY BIRD.
STAND BACK.
NO. YOUR SCREAM COULD BRING DOWN MORE OF THE ROOF.
DINAH. WE HAVE TO GO. IF WE'RE STILL HERE WHEN SUPERMAN COMES BACK...
I'M *NOT* LEAVING HIM.
REMEMBER EARLIER WHEN YOU WERE TELLING US OFF FOR BICKERING WHILE SOMEONE WAS BUYING US A SMALL WINDOW OF TIME?
THAT WAS DIFFERENT. THAT WAS JUST THE FATE OF THE WORLD. THIS IS MORE IMPORTANT.
ARROW. I HID A LOCATOR INSIDE YOUR HOOD!
OF COURSE YOU DID...
KEEP SAFE AND KEEP THAT LOCATOR ON. TRY TO FIND ANOTHER WAY OUT. I PROMISE WE'LL COME BACK FOR YOU ONCE SUPERMAN HAS GONE.

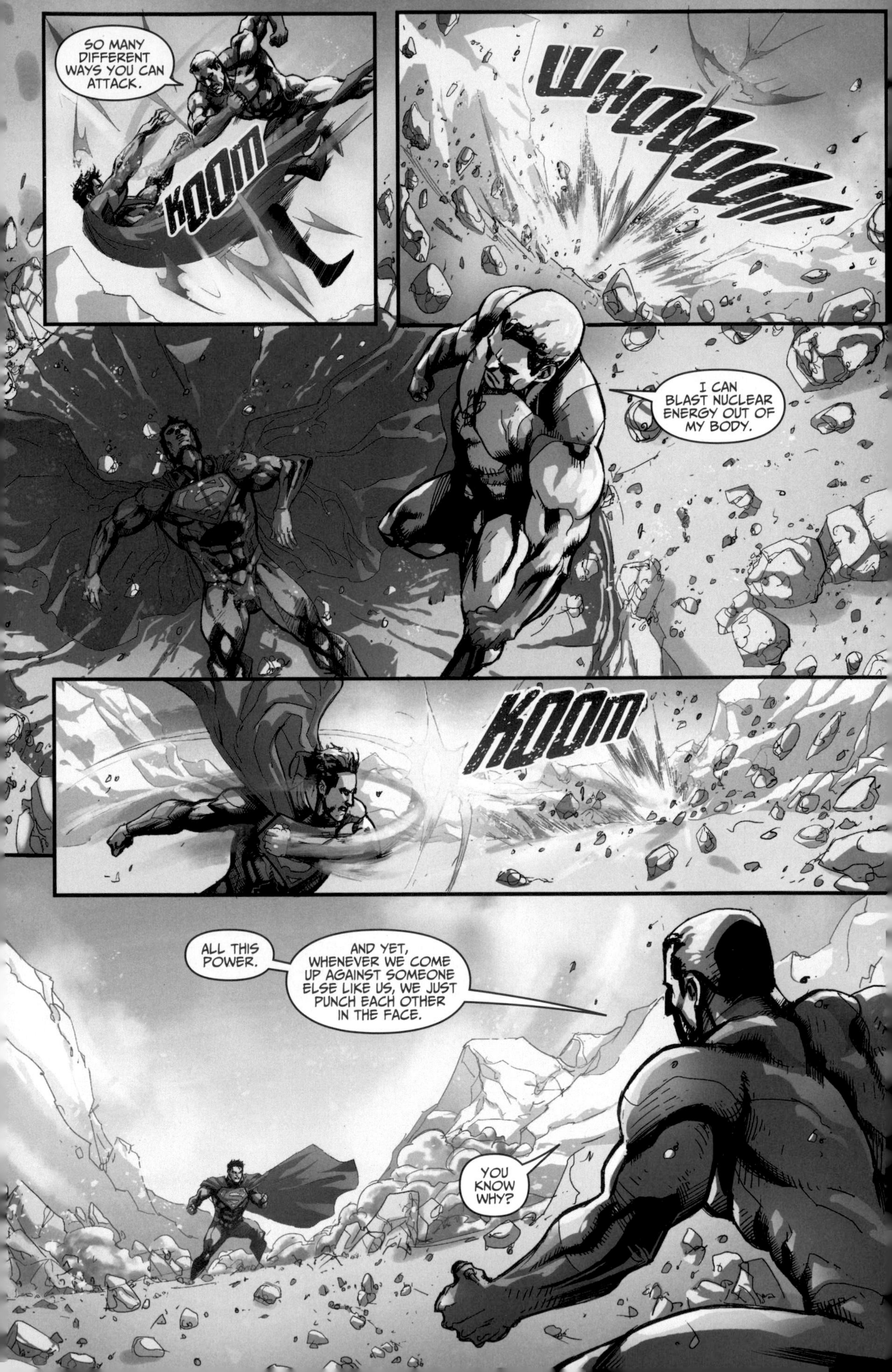
SO MANY DIFFERENT WAYS YOU CAN ATTACK.
KOOM
WHOOOOM
I CAN BLAST NUCLEAR ENERGY OUT OF MY BODY.
KOOM
ALL THIS POWER.
AND YET, WHENEVER WE COME UP AGAINST SOMEONE ELSE LIKE US, WE JUST PUNCH EACH OTHER IN THE FACE.
YOU KNOW WHY?

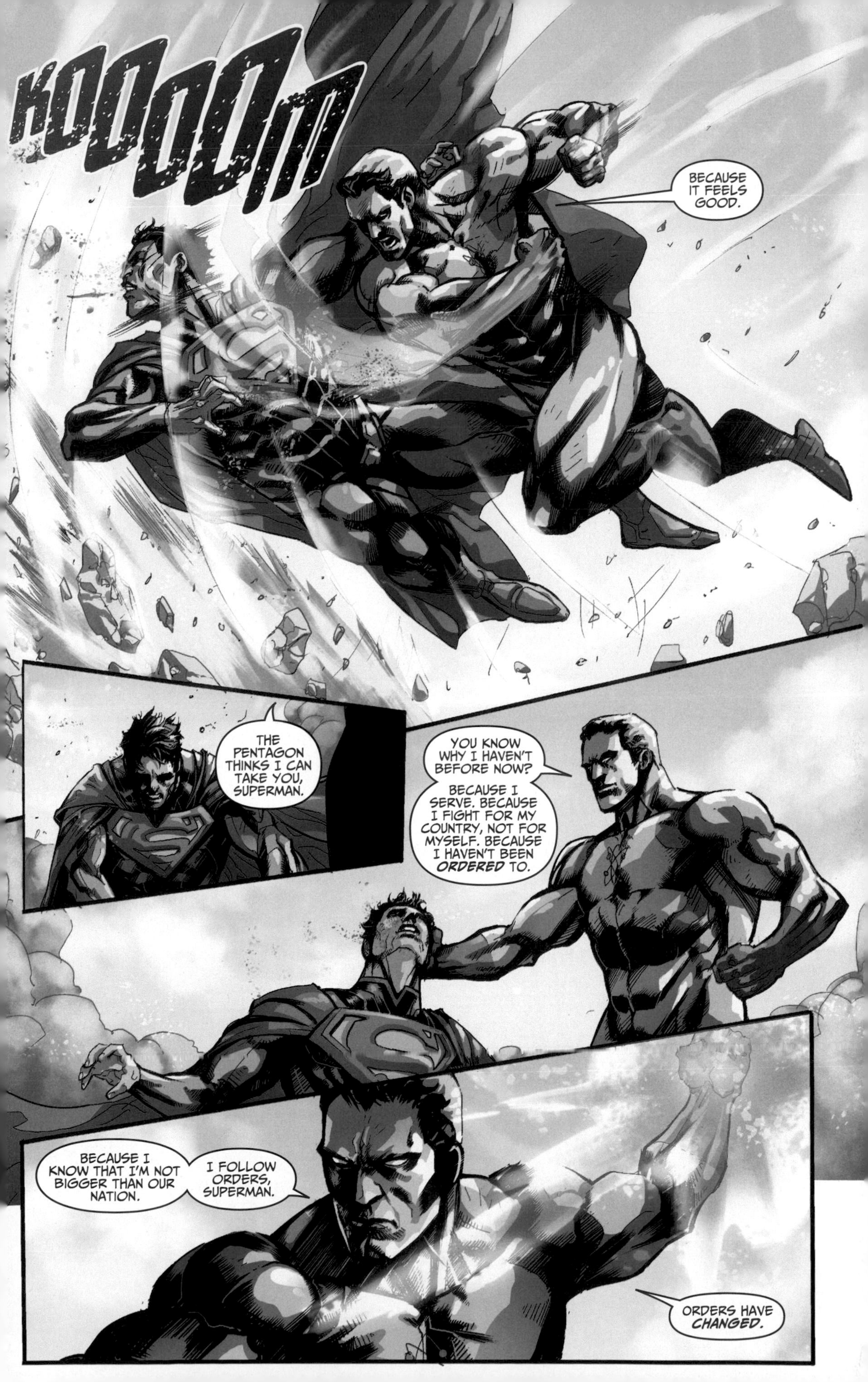

KOOOOM
BECAUSE IT FEELS GOOD.
THE PENTAGON THINKS I CAN TAKE YOU, SUPERMAN.
YOU KNOW WHY I HAVEN'T BEFORE NOW?
BECAUSE I SERVE. BECAUSE I FIGHT FOR MY COUNTRY, NOT FOR MYSELF. BECAUSE I HAVEN'T BEEN ORDERED TO.
BECAUSE I KNOW THAT I'M NOT BIGGER THAN OUR NATION.
I FOLLOW ORDERS, SUPERMAN.
ORDERS HAVE CHANGED.

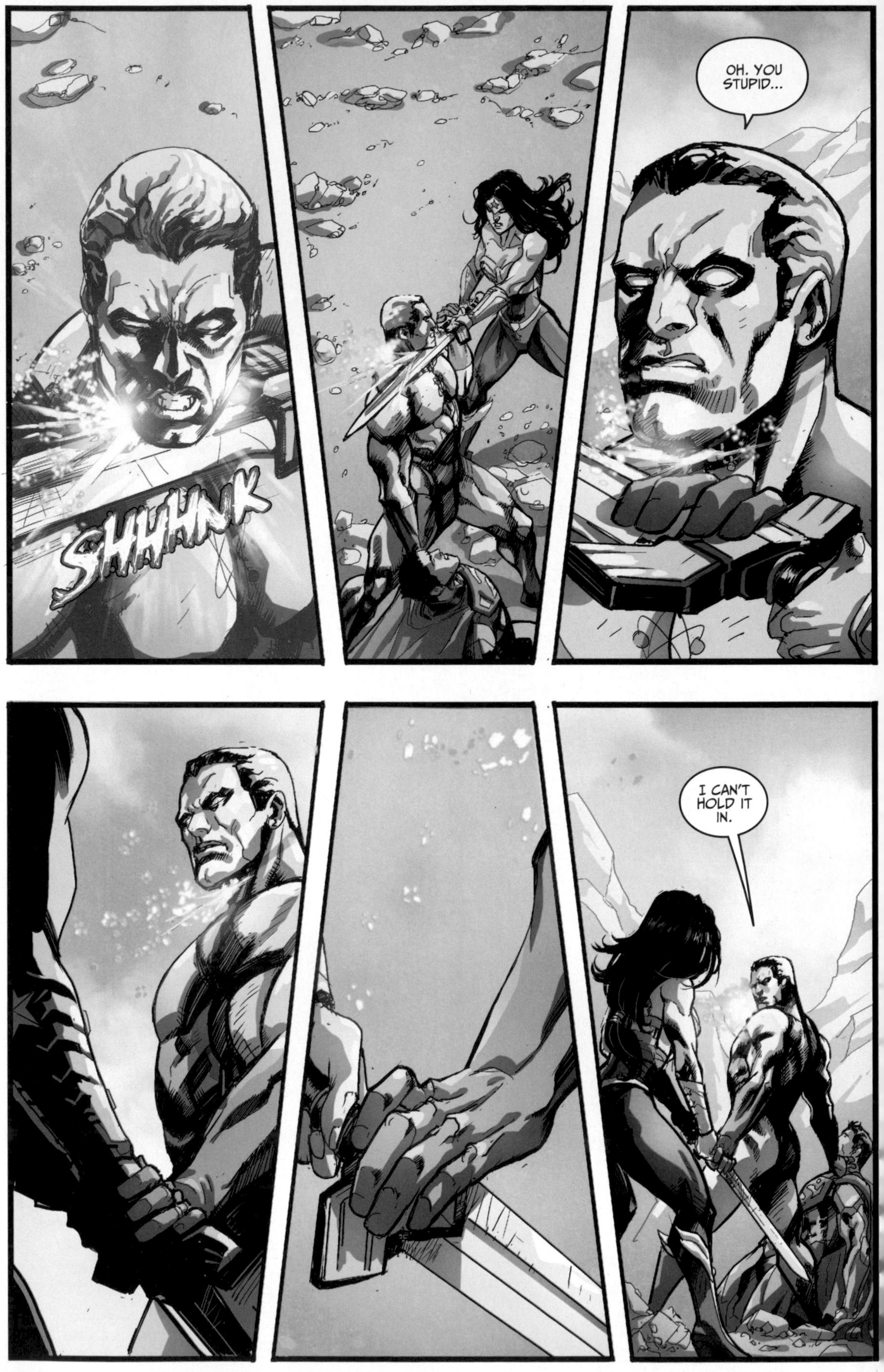
SHHHNK
OH. YOU STUPID...
I CAN'T HOLD IT IN.

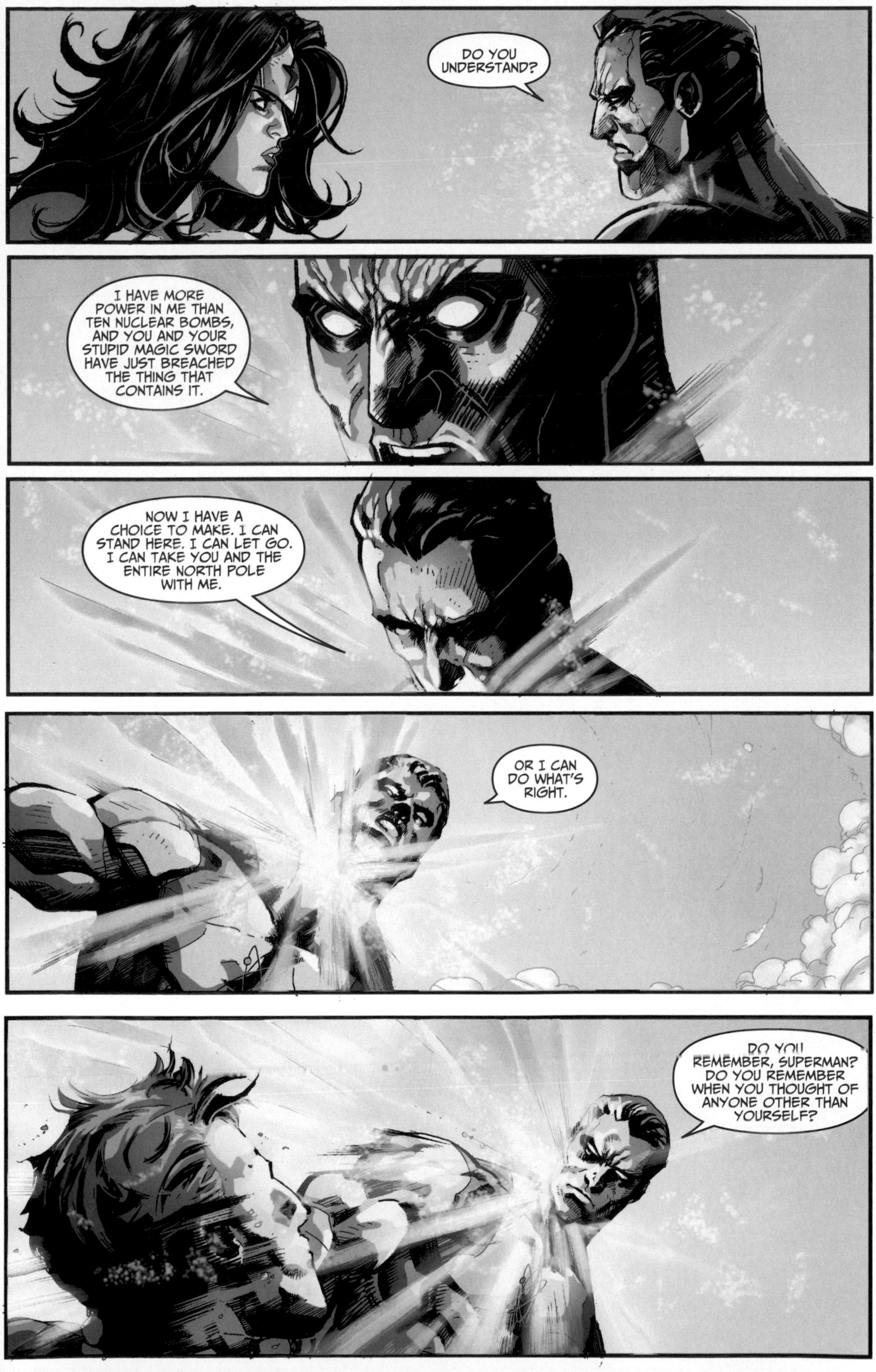
DO YOU UNDERSTAND?
I HAVE MORE POWER IN ME THAN TEN NUCLEAR BOMBS, AND YOU AND YOUR STUPID MAGIC SWORD HAVE JUST BREACHED THE THING THAT CONTAINS IT.
NOW I HAVE A CHOICE TO MAKE. I CAN STAND HERE. I CAN LET GO. I CAN TAKE YOU AND THE ENTIRE NORTH POLE WITH ME.
OR I CAN DO WHAT'S RIGHT.
DO YOU REMEMBER, SUPERMAN? DO YOU REMEMBER WHEN YOU THOUGHT OF ANYONE OTHER THAN YOURSELF?

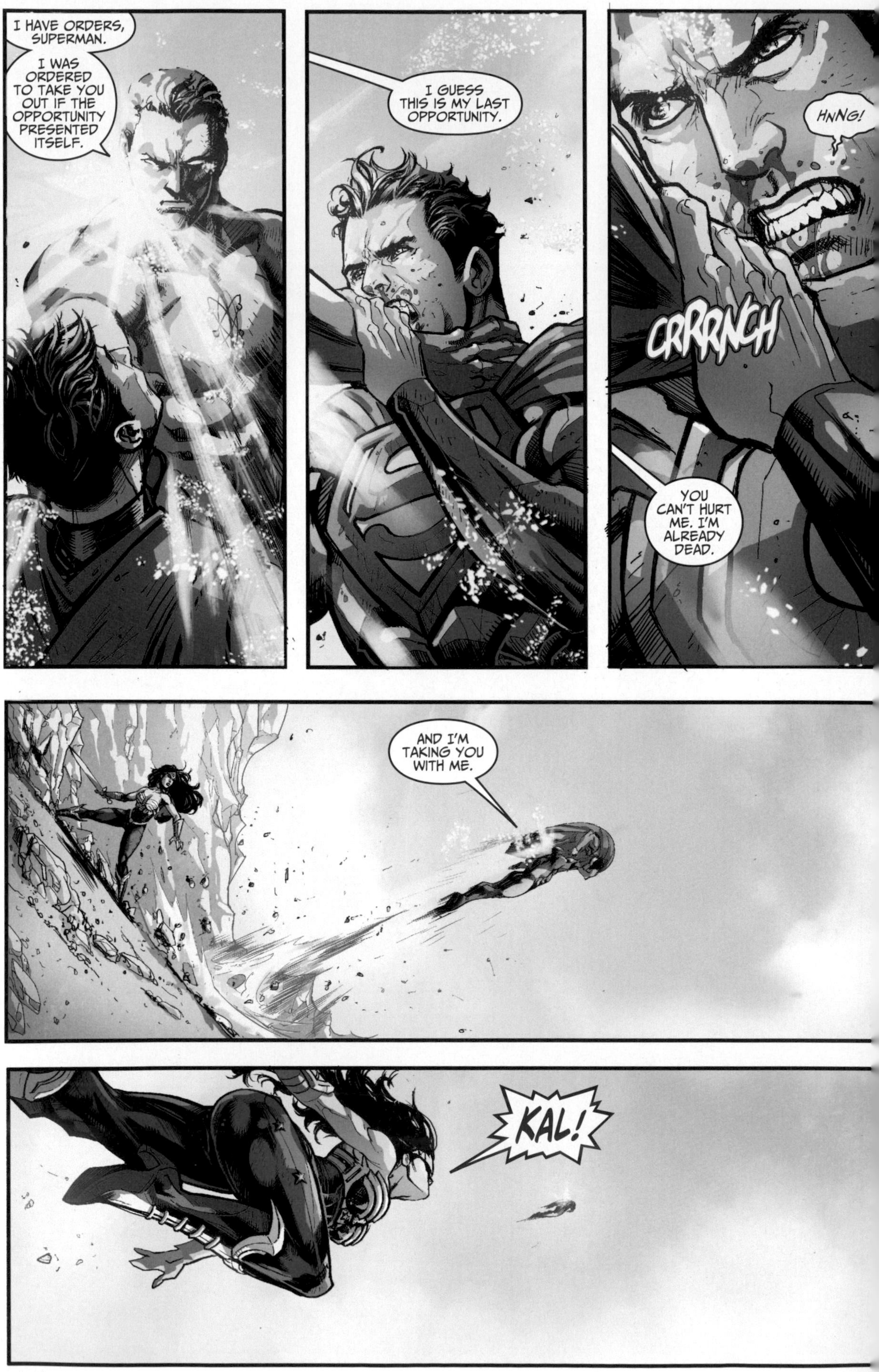

I HAVE ORDERS, SUPERMAN.
I WAS ORDERED TO TAKE YOU OUT IF THE OPPORTUNITY PRESENTED ITSELF.
I GUESS THIS IS MY LAST OPPORTUNITY.
HNNG!
CRRRNCH
YOU CAN'T HURT ME. I'M ALREADY DEAD.
AND I'M TAKING YOU WITH ME.
KAL!

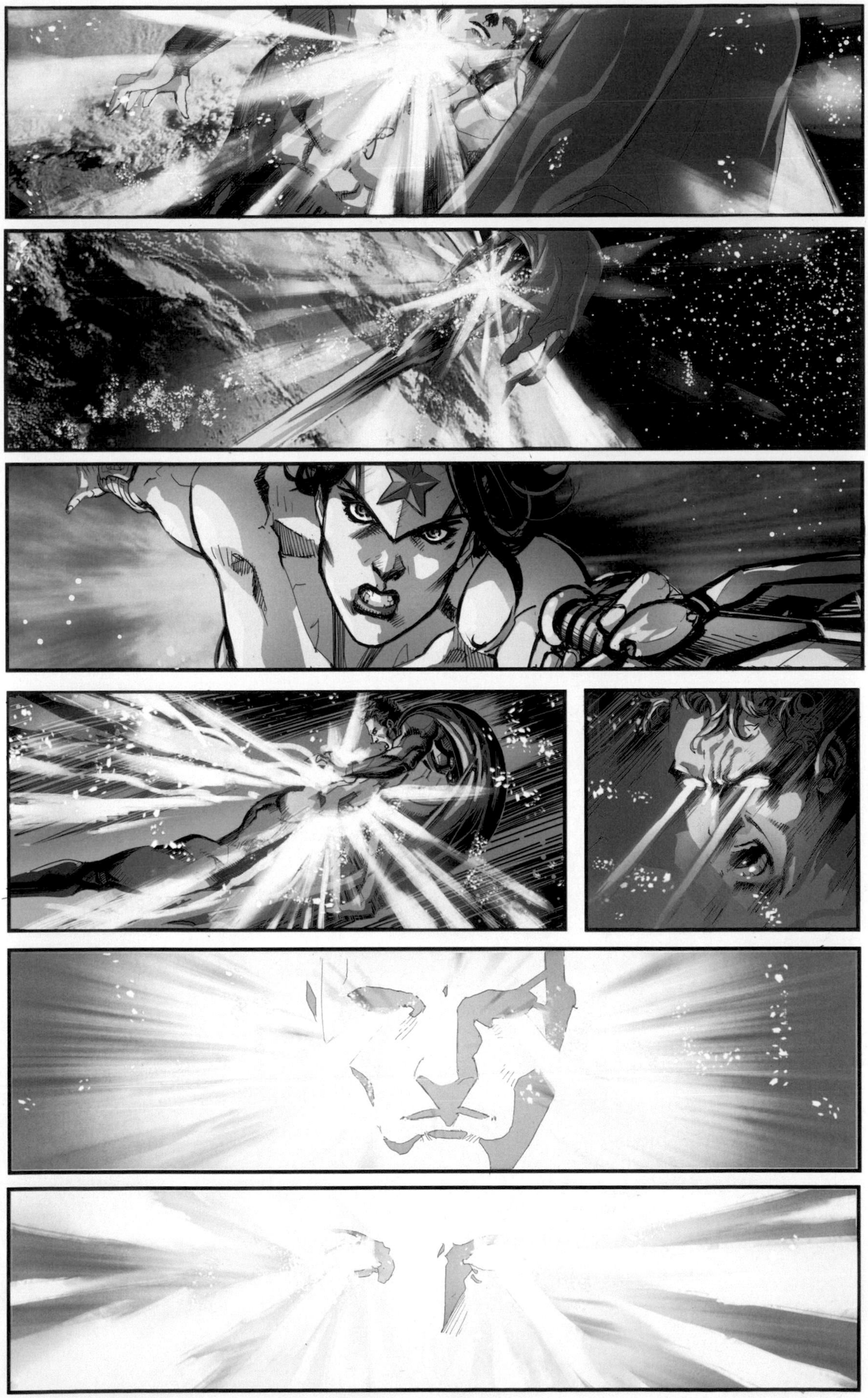

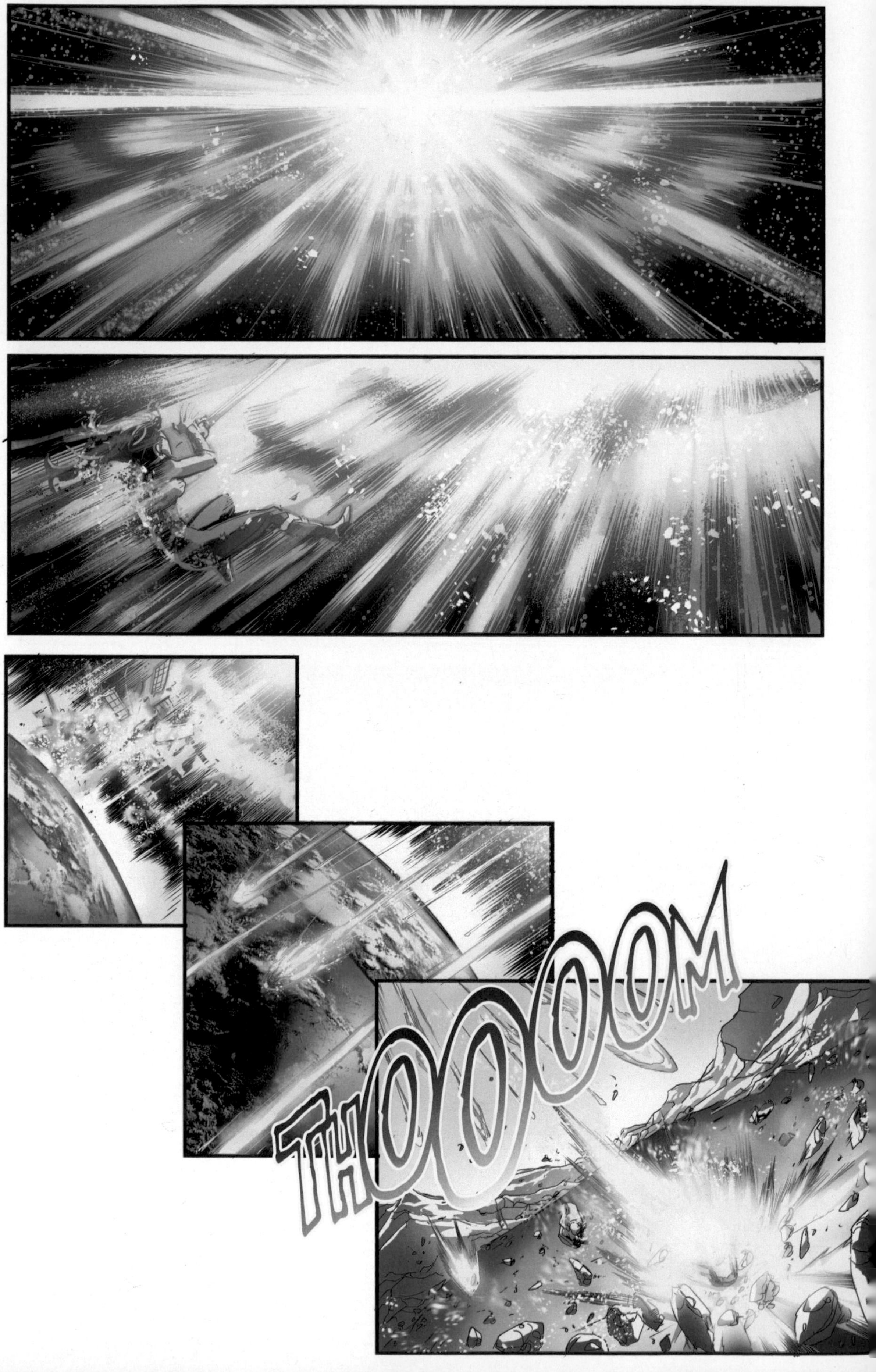
THOOOOOM

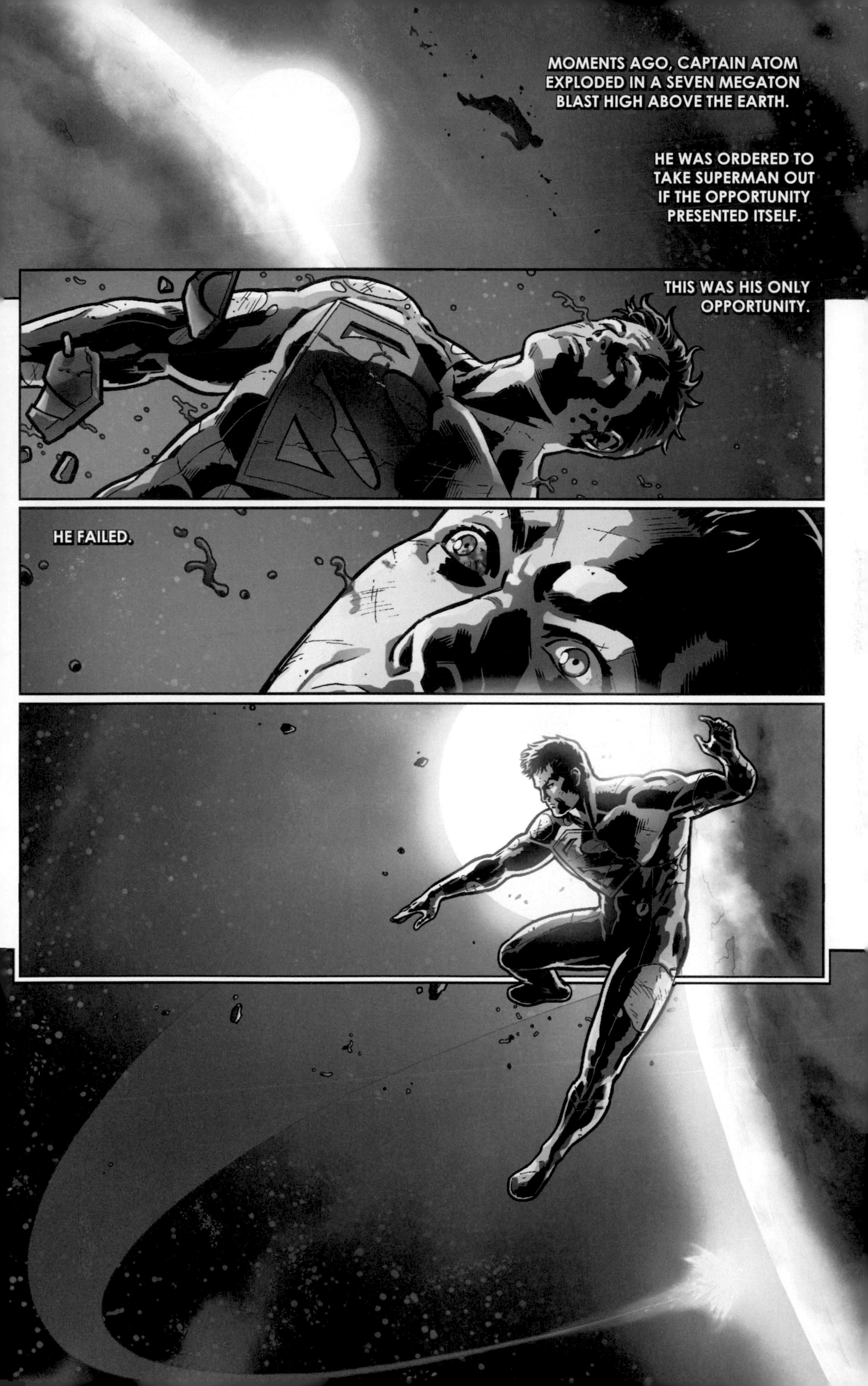
MOMENTS AGO, CAPTAIN ATOM EXPLODED IN A SEVEN MEGATON BLAST HIGH ABOVE THE EARTH.
HE WAS ORDERED TO TAKE SUPERMAN OUT IF THE OPPORTUNITY PRESENTED ITSELF.
THIS WAS HIS ONLY OPPORTUNITY.
HE FAILED.

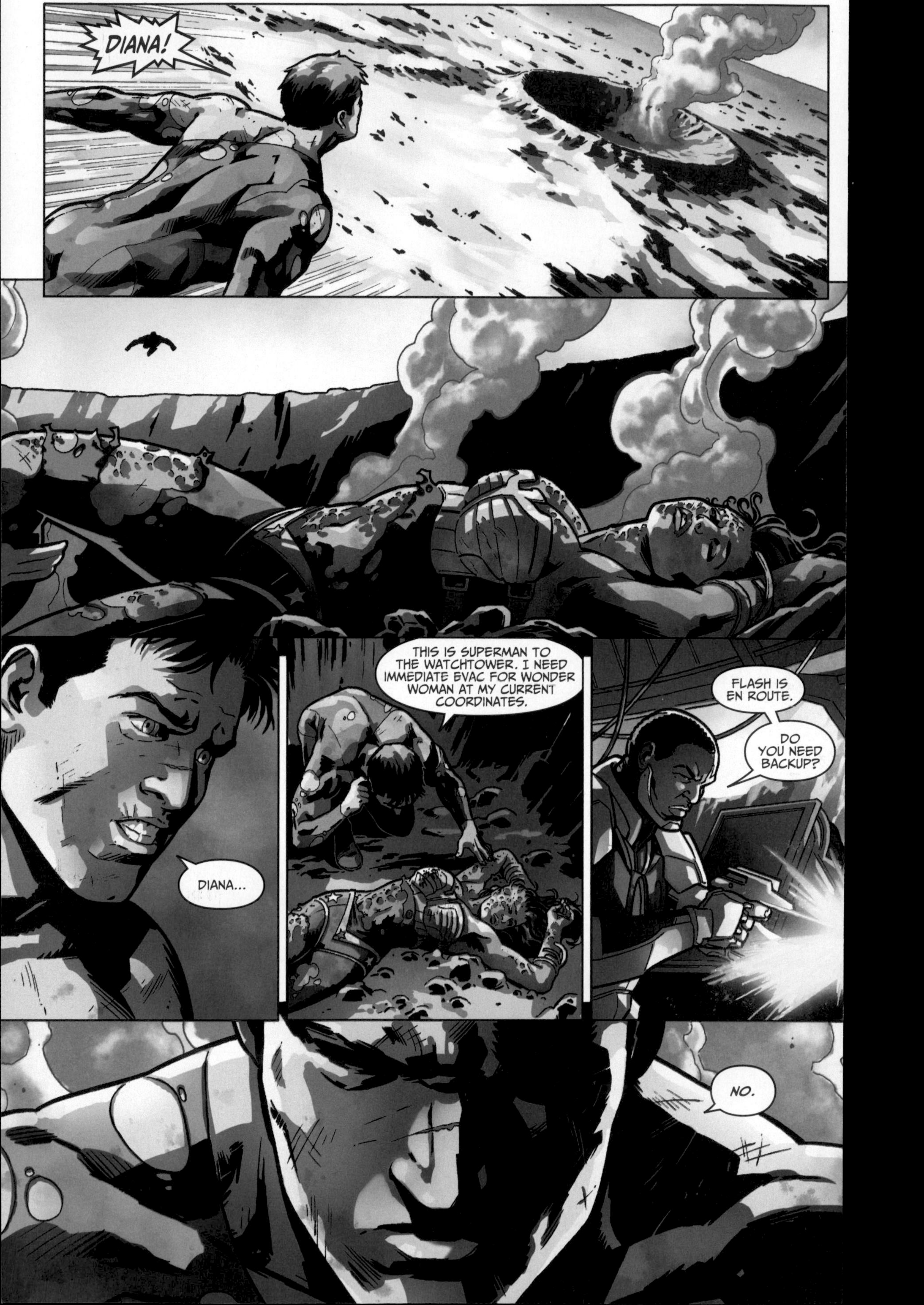
DIANA!
DIANA...
THIS IS SUPERMAN TO THE WATCHTOWER. I NEED IMMEDIATE EVAC FOR WONDER WOMAN AT MY CURRENT COORDINATES.
FLASH IS EN ROUTE.
DO YOU NEED BACKUP?
NO.

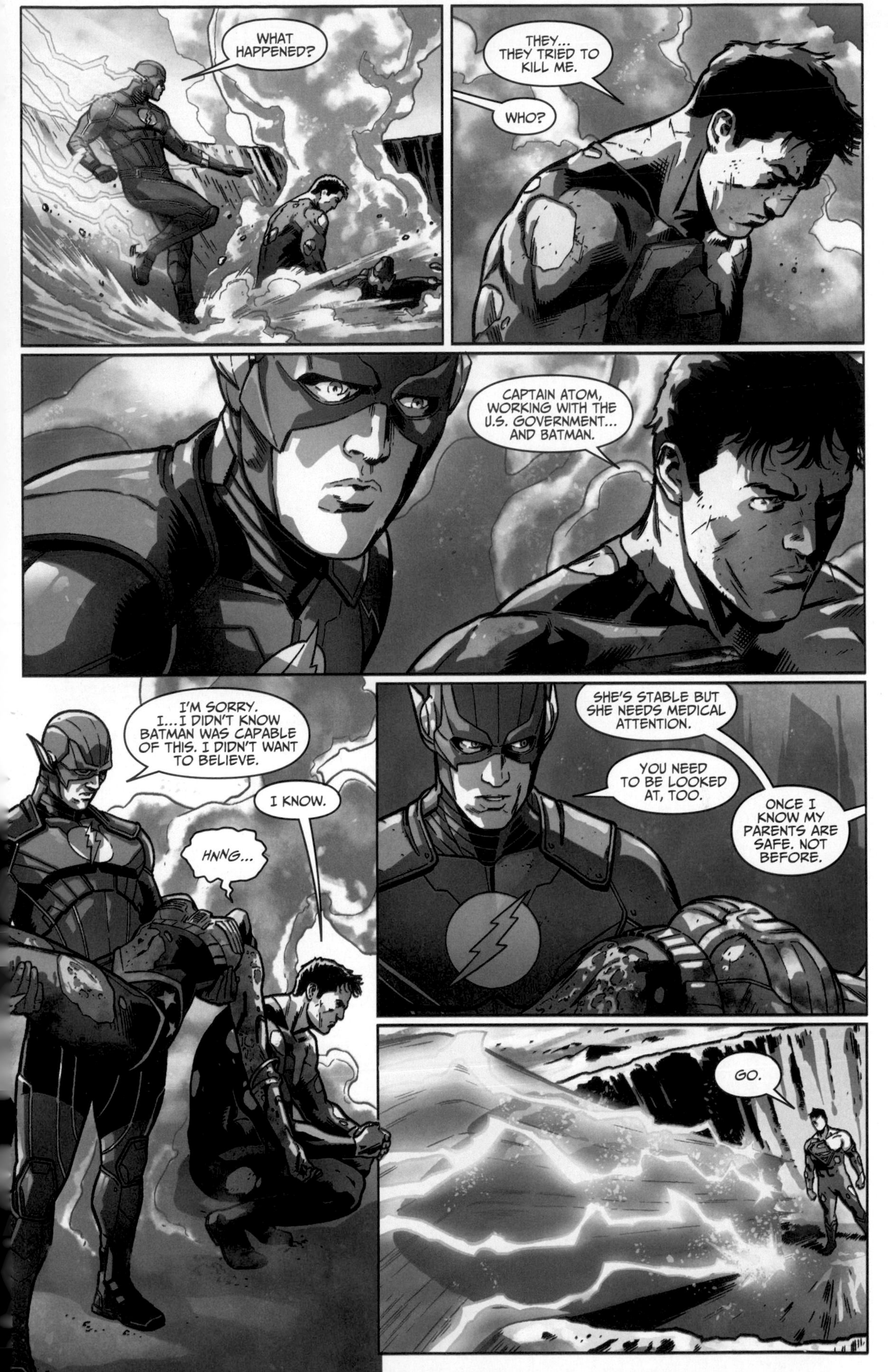
WHAT HAPPENED?
THEY... THEY TRIED TO KILL ME.
WHO?
CAPTAIN ATOM, WORKING WITH THE U.S. GOVERNMENT... AND BATMAN.
I'M SORRY. I...I DIDN'T KNOW BATMAN WAS CAPABLE OF THIS. I DIDN'T WANT TO BELIEVE.
I KNOW.
HNNG...
SHE'S STABLE BUT SHE NEEDS MEDICAL ATTENTION.
YOU NEED TO BE LOOKED AT, TOO.
ONCE I KNOW MY PARENTS ARE SAFE. NOT BEFORE.
GO.

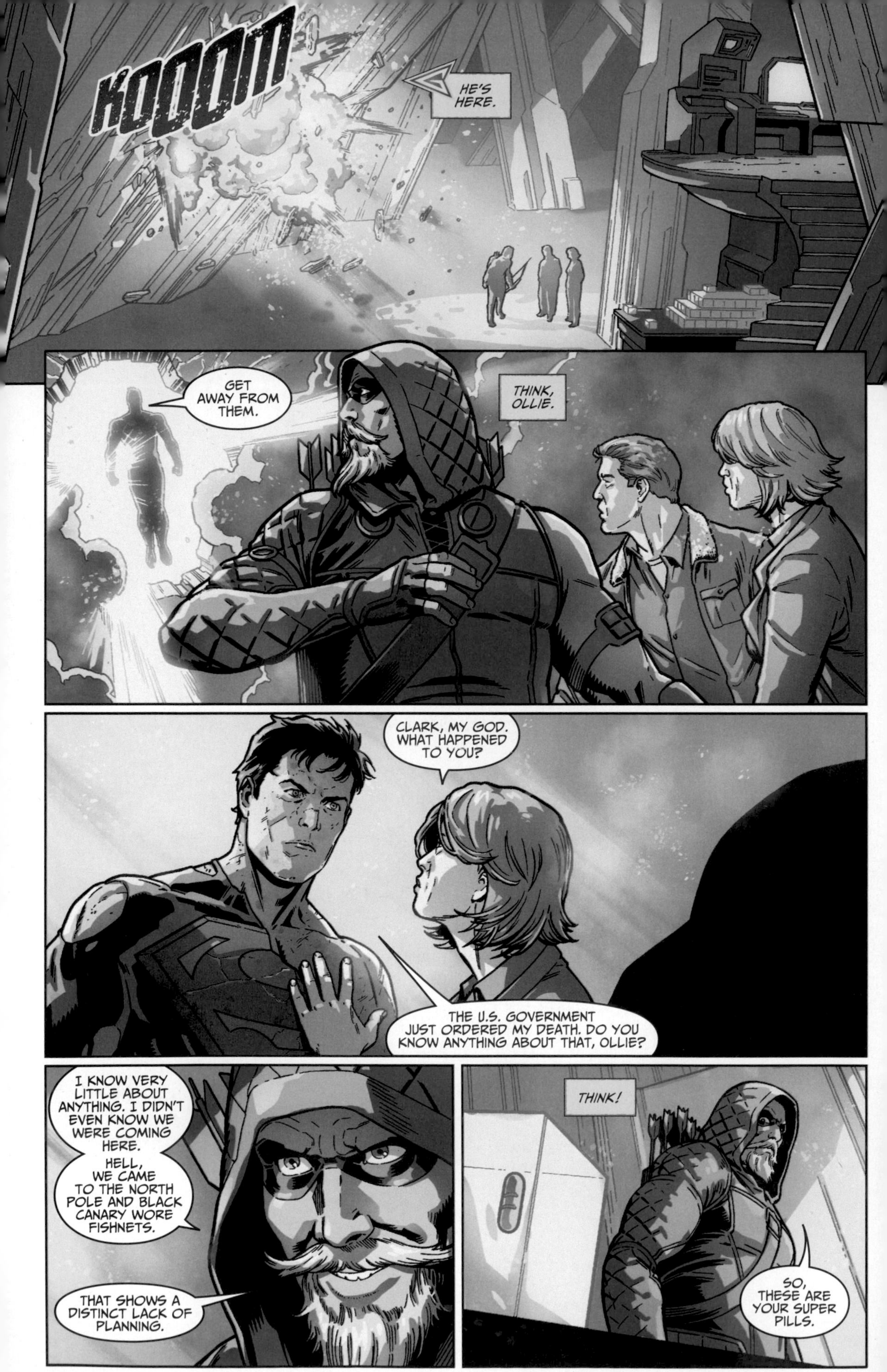
KOOOM
HE'S HERE.
GET AWAY FROM THEM.
THINK, OLLIE.
CLARK, MY GOD. WHAT HAPPENED TO YOU?
THE U.S. GOVERNMENT JUST ORDERED MY DEATH. DO YOU KNOW ANYTHING ABOUT THAT, OLLIE?
I KNOW VERY LITTLE ABOUT ANYTHING. I DIDN'T EVEN KNOW WE WERE COMING HERE.
HELL, WE CAME TO THE NORTH POLE AND BLACK CANARY WORE FISHNETS.
THAT SHOWS A DISTINCT LACK OF PLANNING.
THINK!
SO, THESE ARE YOUR SUPER PILLS.

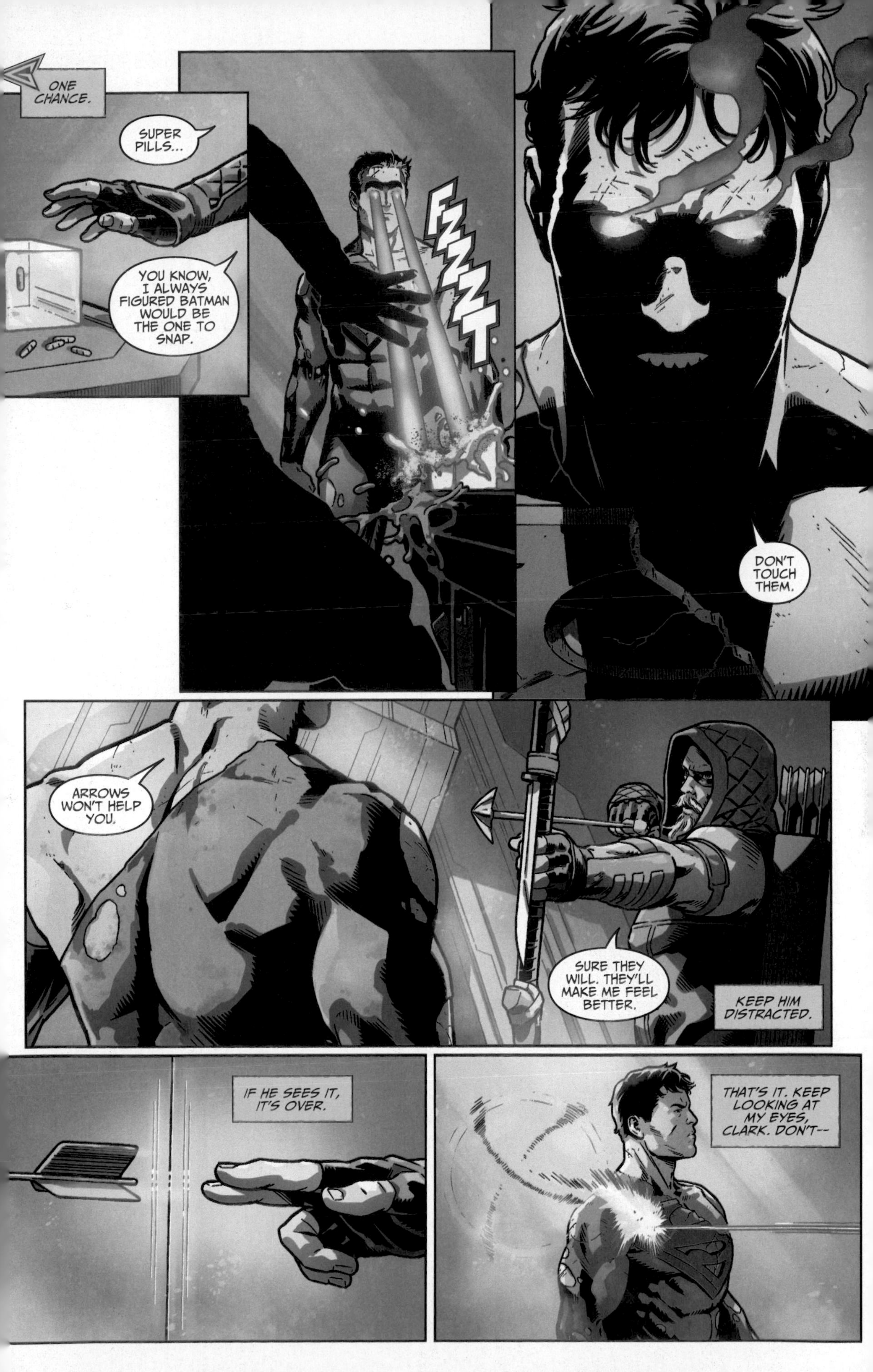
ONE CHANCE.
SUPER PILLS...
YOU KNOW, I ALWAYS FIGURED BATMAN WOULD BE THE ONE TO SNAP.
FZZZT
DON'T TOUCH THEM.
ARROWS WON'T HELP YOU.
SURE THEY WILL. THEY'LL MAKE ME FEEL BETTER.
KEEP HIM DISTRACTED.
IF HE SEES IT, IT'S OVER.
THAT'S IT. KEEP LOOKING AT MY EYES, CLARK. DON'T--

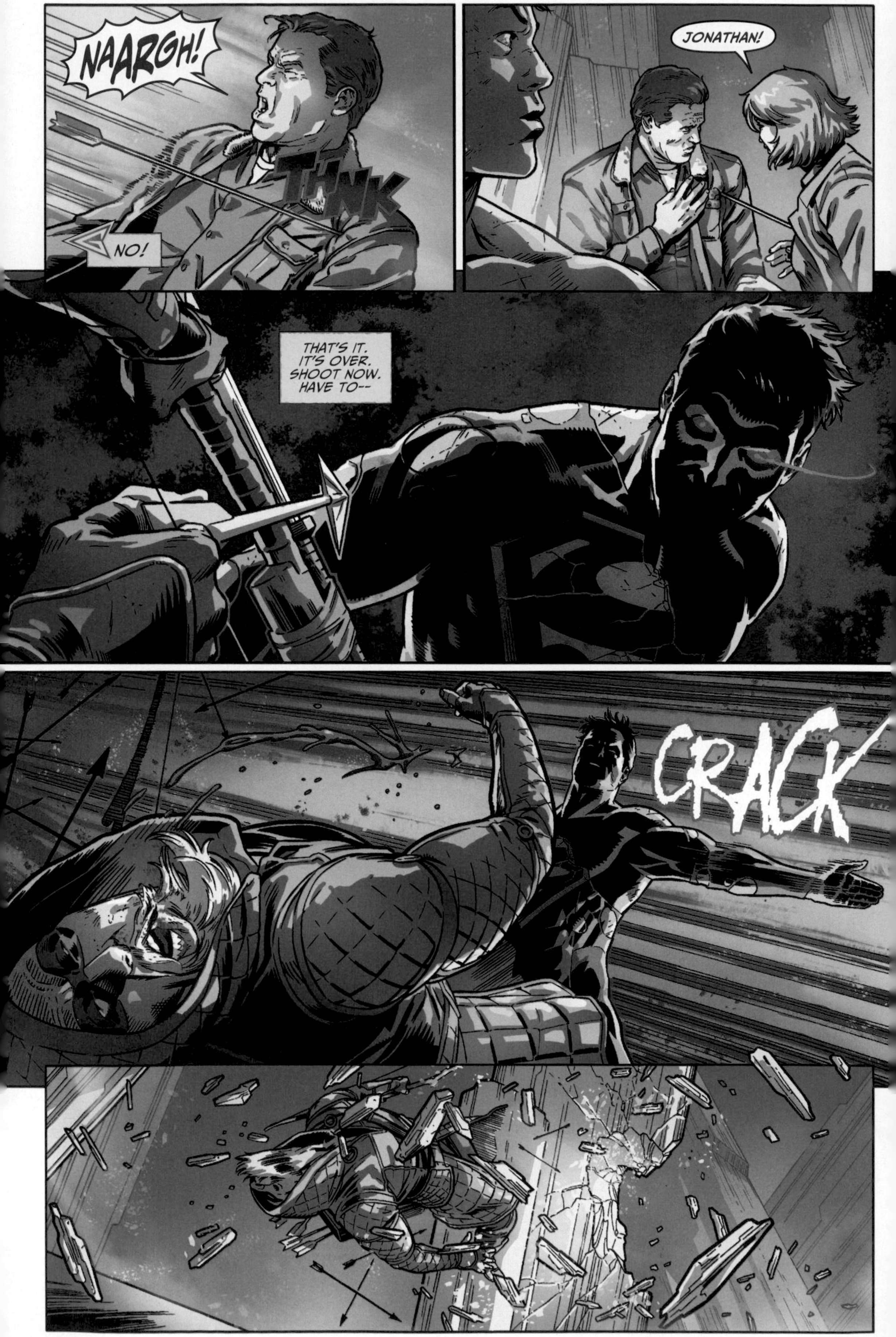
NAARGH!
THNK
NO!
JONATHAN!
THAT'S IT. IT'S OVER. SHOOT NOW. HAVE TO--
CRACK

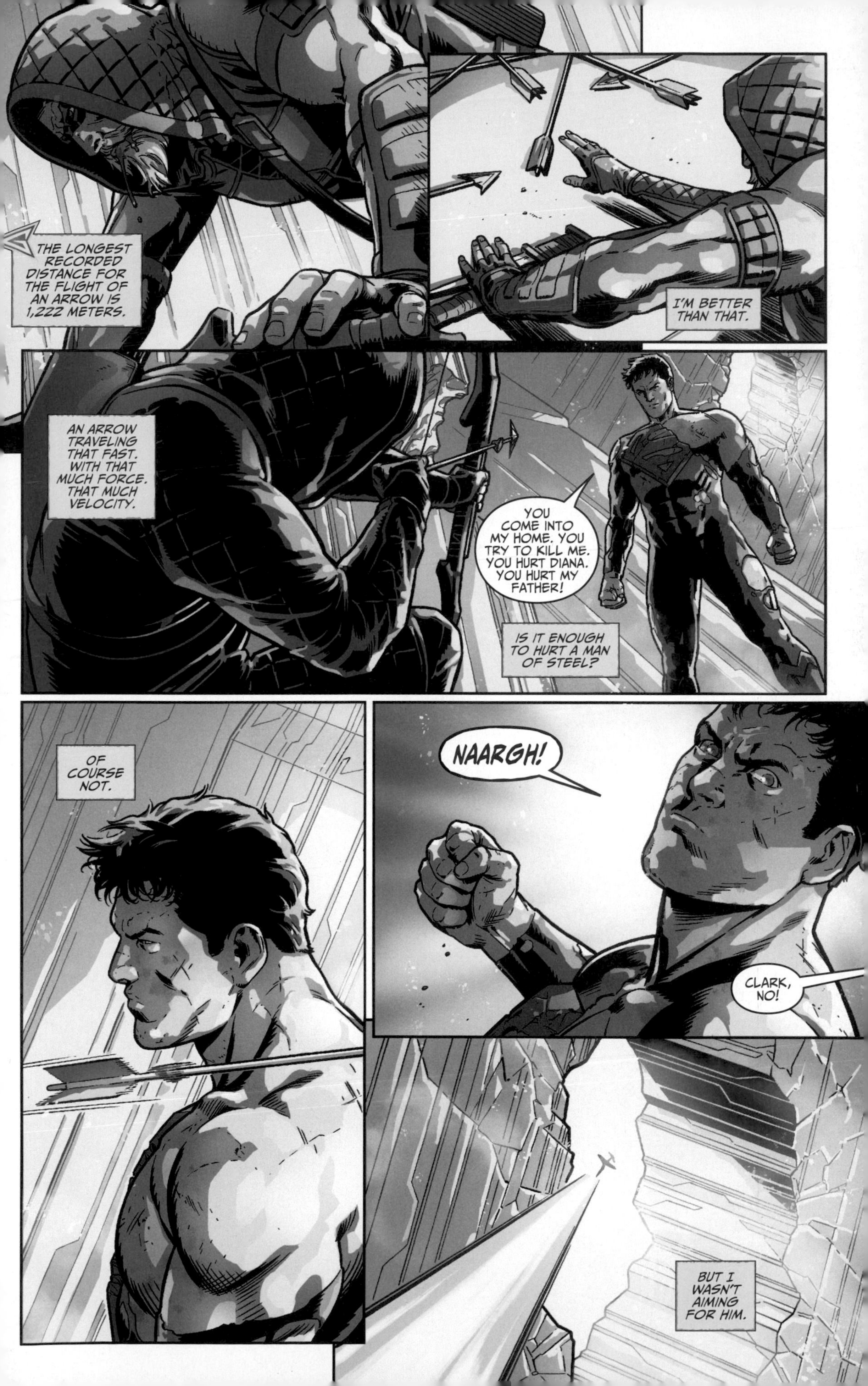

THE LONGEST RECORDED DISTANCE FOR THE FLIGHT OF AN ARROW IS 1,222 METERS.
I'M BETTER THAN THAT.
AN ARROW TRAVELING THAT FAST. WITH THAT MUCH FORCE. THAT MUCH VELOCITY.
YOU COME INTO MY HOME. YOU TRY TO KILL ME. YOU HURT DIANA. YOU HURT MY FATHER!
IS IT ENOUGH TO HURT A MAN OF STEEL?
OF COURSE NOT.
NAARGH!
CLARK, NO!
BUT I WASN'T AIMING FOR HIM.

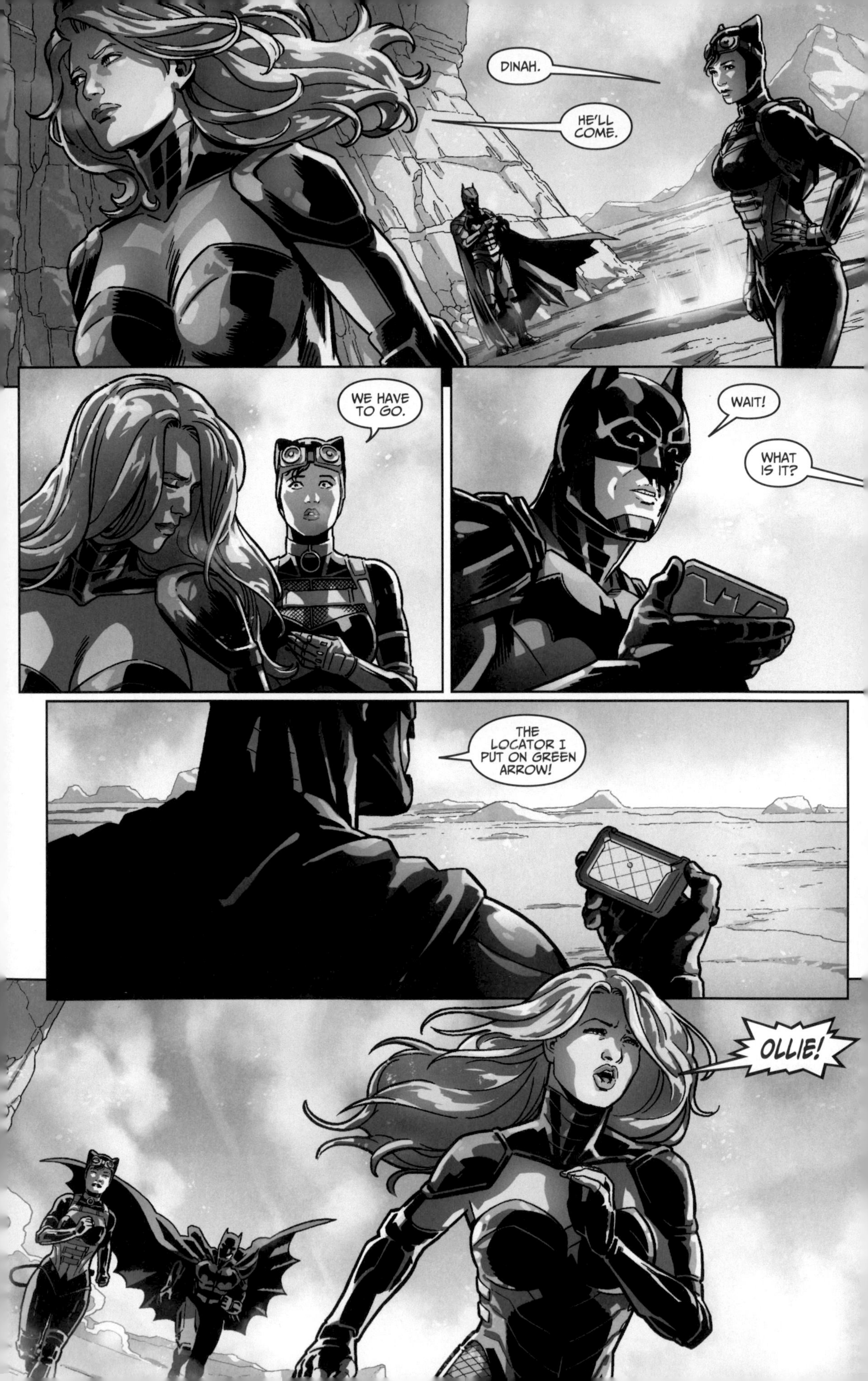
DINAH.
HE'LL COME.
WE HAVE TO GO.
WAIT!
WHAT IS IT?
THE LOCATOR I PUT ON GREEN ARROW!
OLLIE!

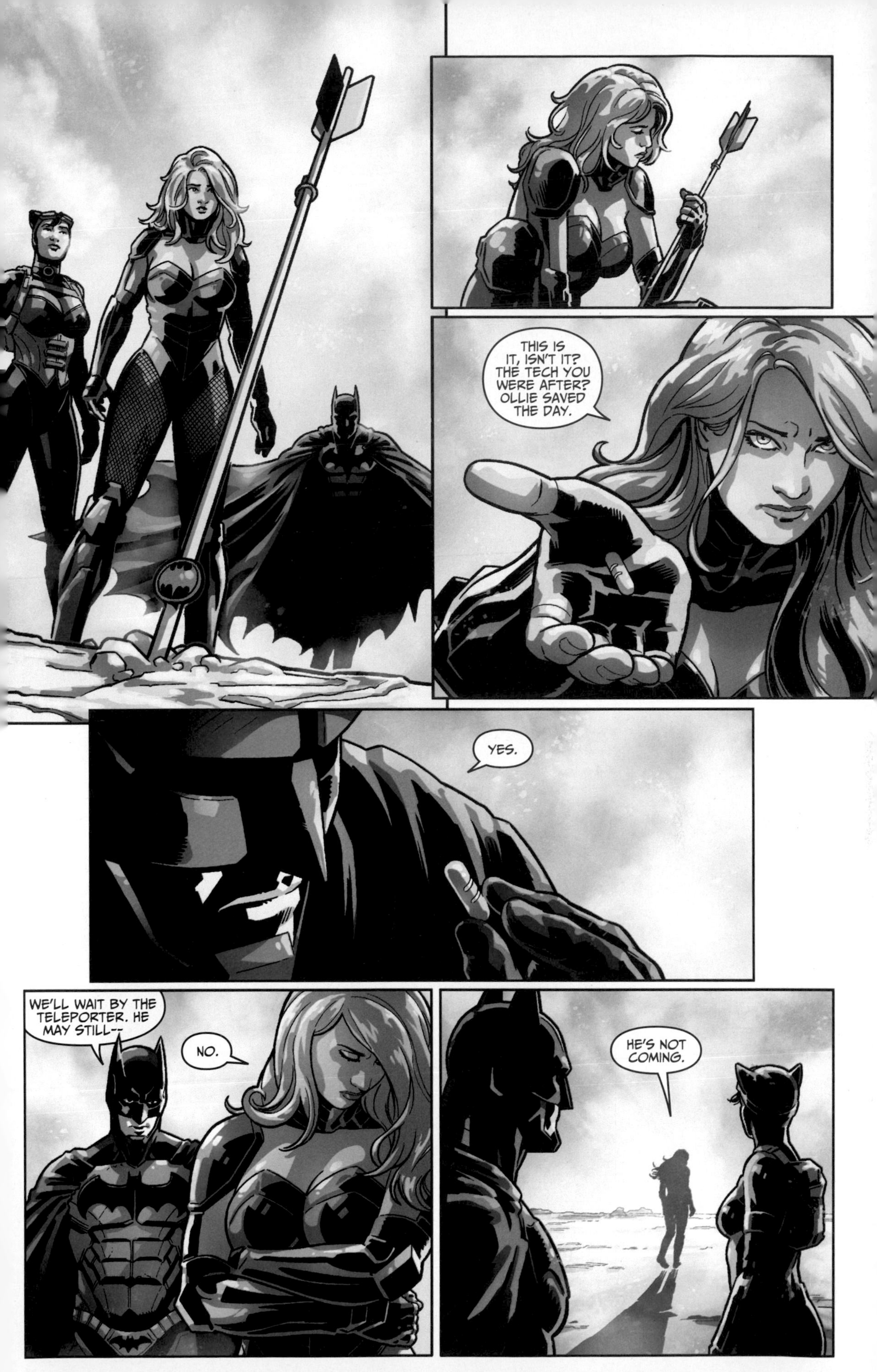
THIS IS IT, ISN'T IT? THE TECH YOU WERE AFTER? OLLIE SAVED THE DAY.
YES.
WE'LL WAIT BY THE TELEPORTER. HE MAY STILL--
NO.
HE'S NOT COMING.

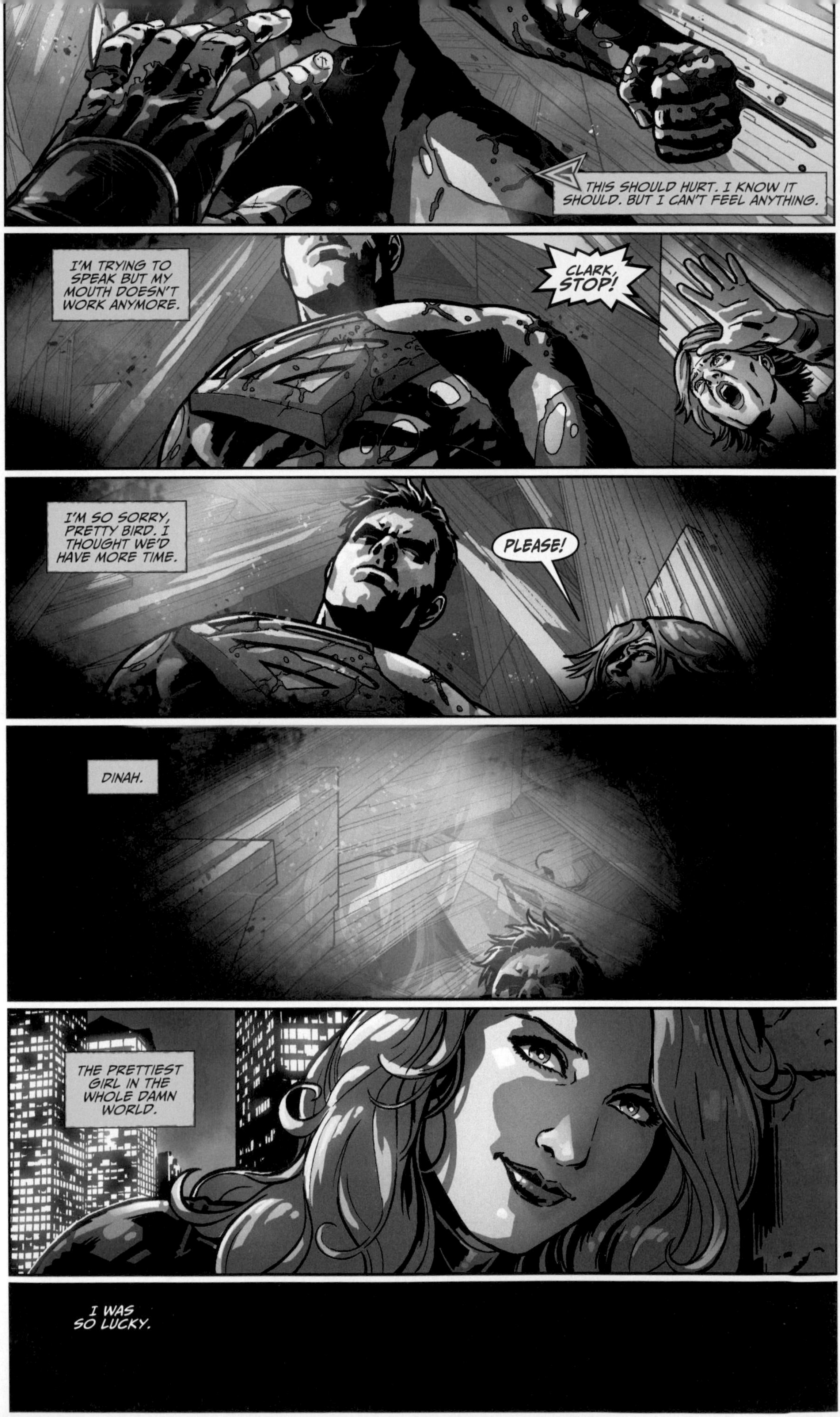
THIS SHOULD HURT. I KNOW IT SHOULD. BUT I CAN'T FEEL ANYTHING.
I'M TRYING TO SPEAK BUT MY MOUTH DOESN'T WORK ANYMORE.
CLARK, STOP!
I'M SO SORRY, PRETTY BIRD. I THOUGHT WE'D HAVE MORE TIME.
PLEASE!
DINAH.
THE PRETTIEST GIRL IN THE WHOLE DAMN WORLD.
I WAS SO LUCKY.

PART THIRTEEN

Mike S. Miller **Tom Derenick** Pencillers

Sergi Erra, **Fran Vazquez**, **David Lopez** and **Santi Casas** of **Ikari Studio** Inkers

Mico Suayan & **David Lopez** and **Santi Casas** of **Ikari Studio** Cover

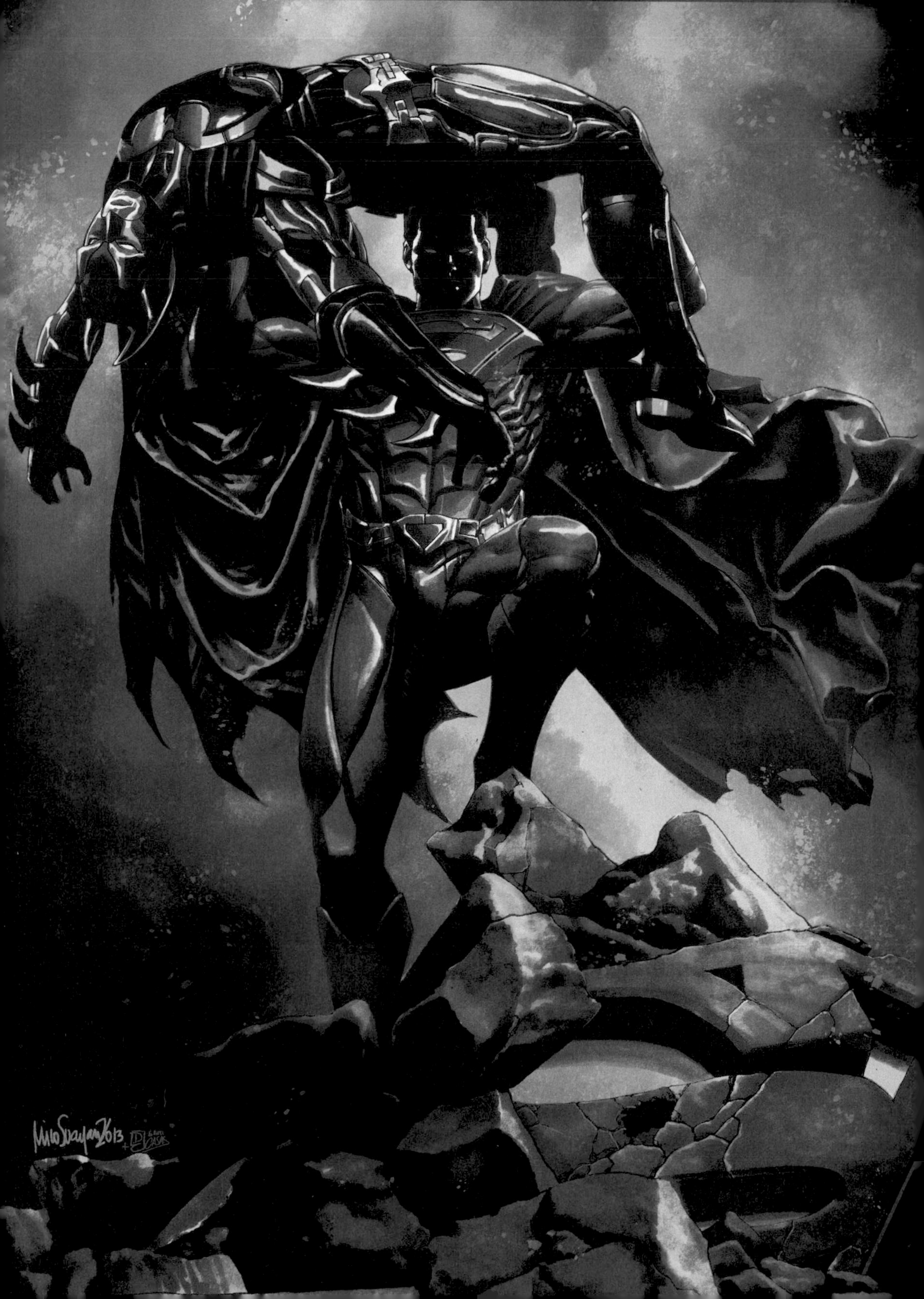

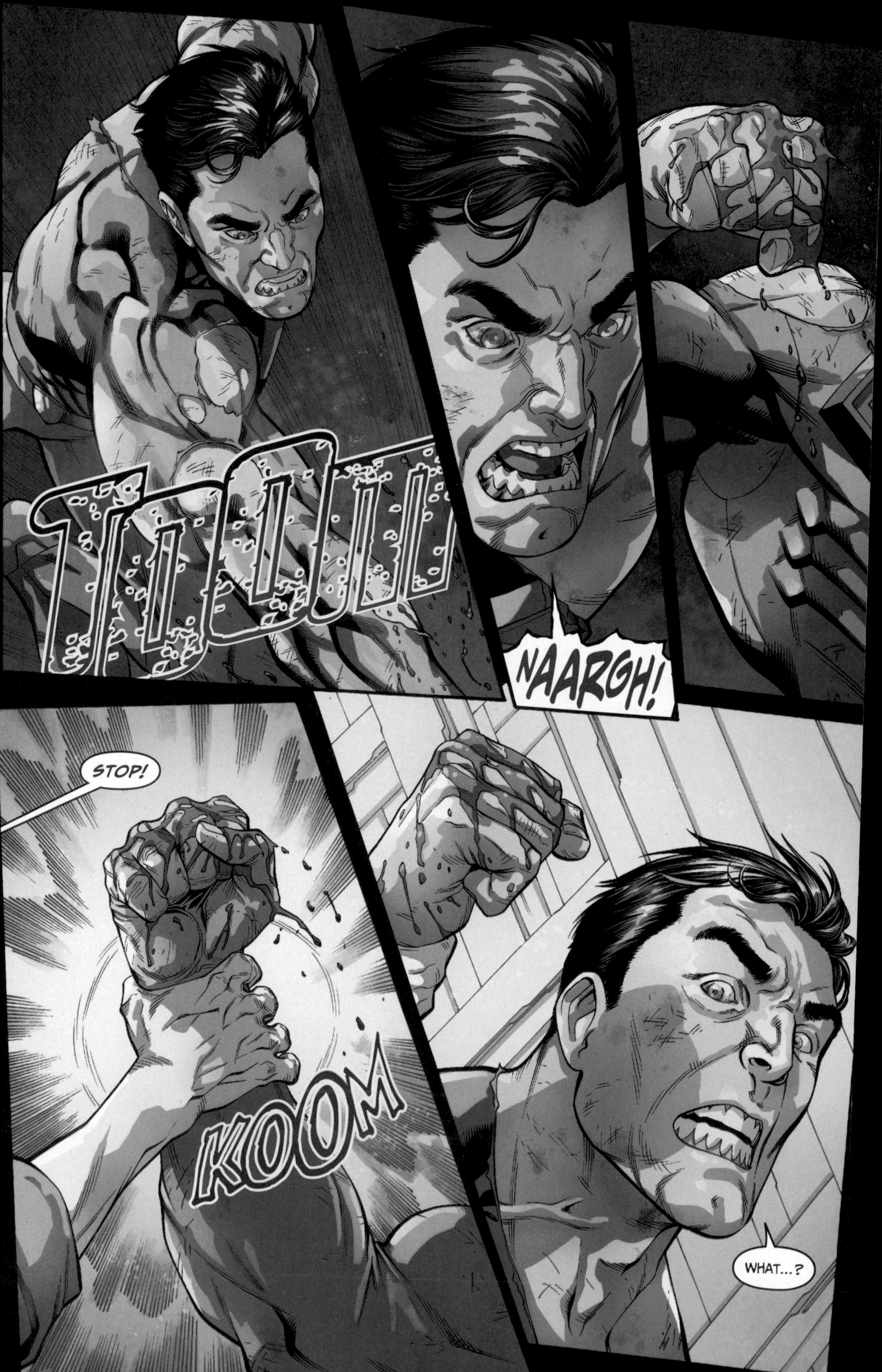
THOOM
NAARGH!
STOP!
KOOM
WHAT...?

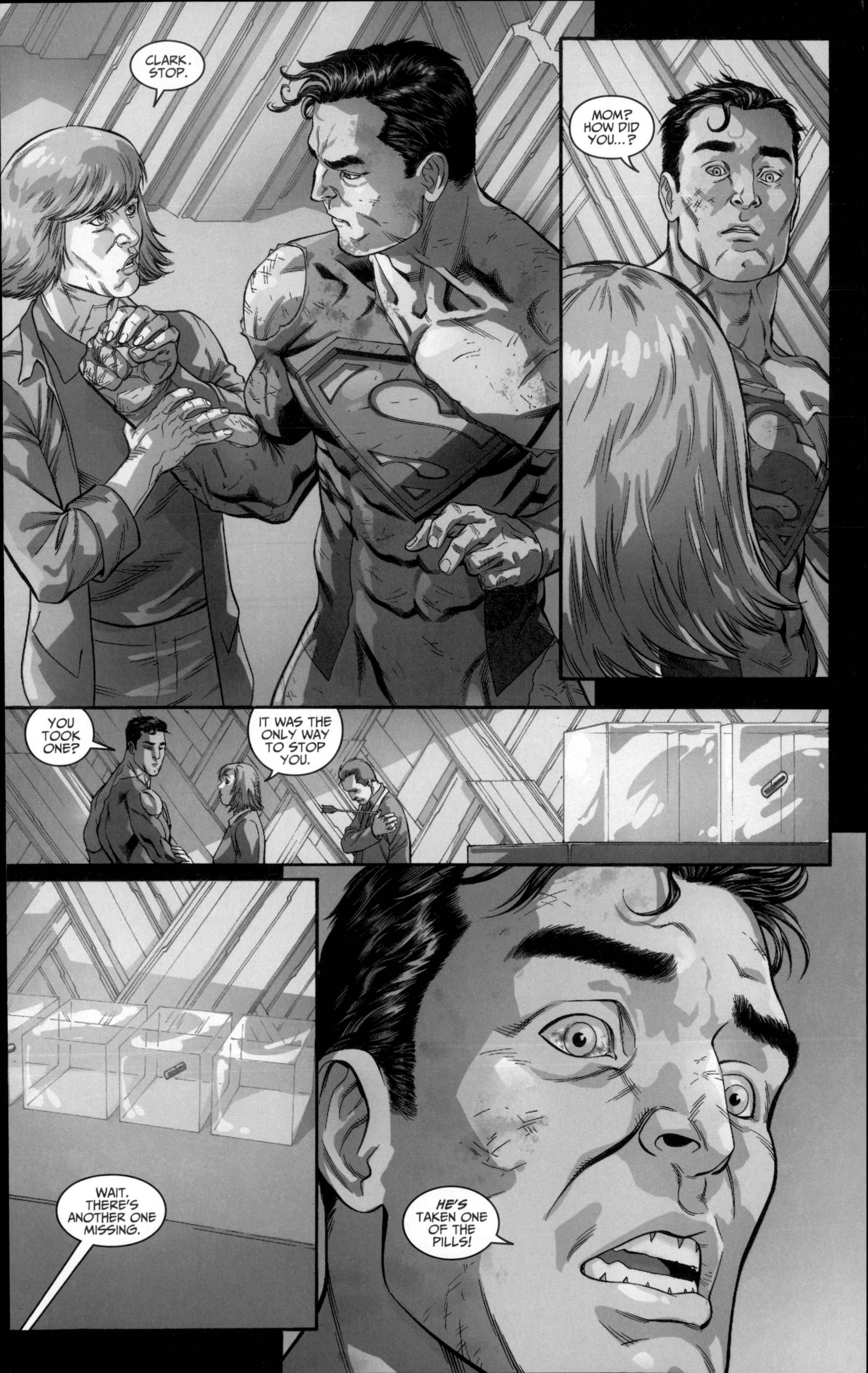
CLARK. STOP.
MOM? HOW DID YOU...?
YOU TOOK ONE?
IT WAS THE ONLY WAY TO STOP YOU.
WAIT. THERE'S ANOTHER ONE MISSING.
HE'S TAKEN ONE OF THE PILLS!

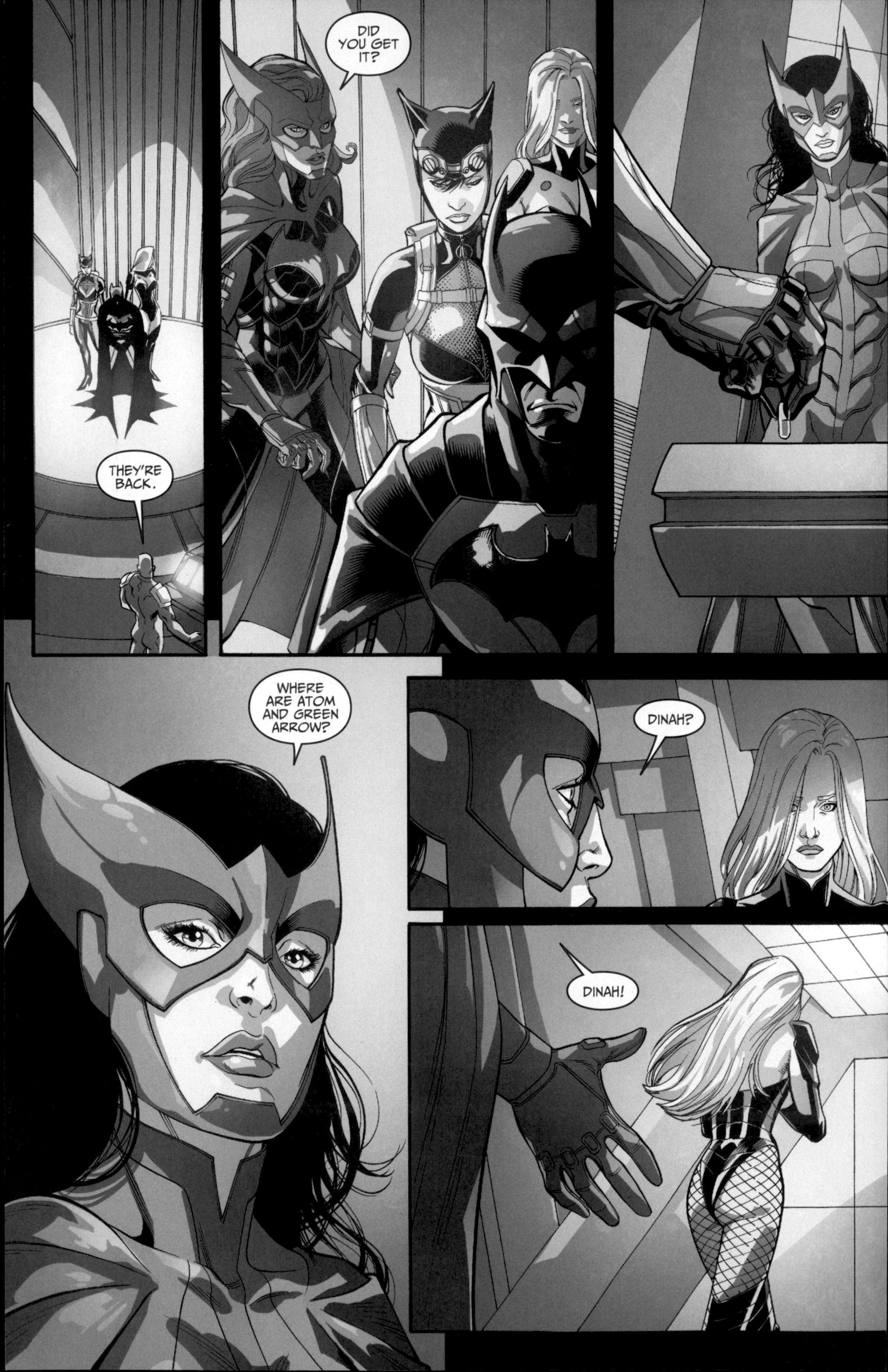
THEY'RE BACK.
DID YOU GET IT?
WHERE ARE ATOM AND GREEN ARROW?
DINAH?
DINAH!

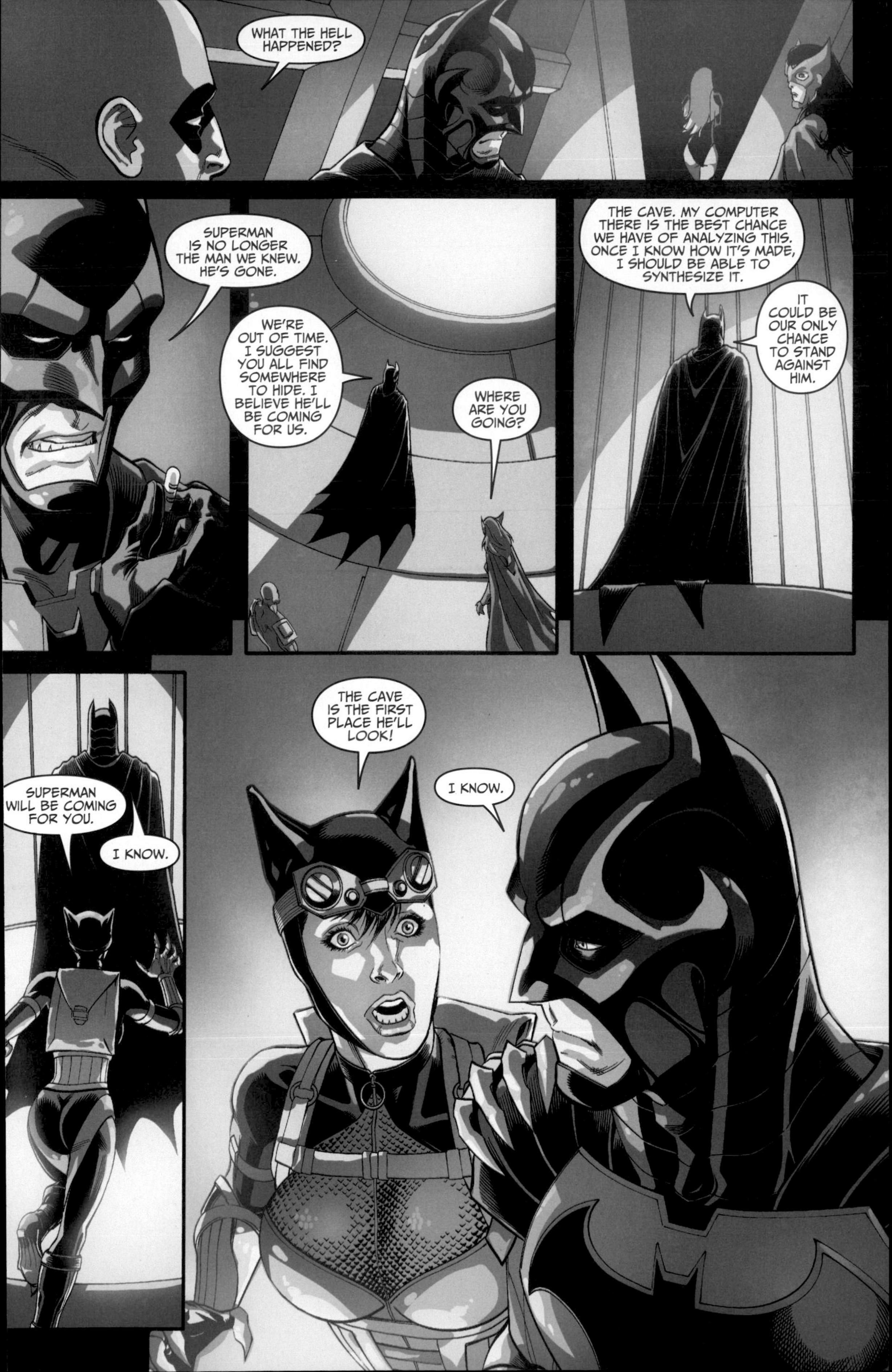
WHAT THE HELL HAPPENED?
SUPERMAN IS NO LONGER THE MAN WE KNEW. HE'S GONE.
WE'RE OUT OF TIME. I SUGGEST YOU ALL FIND SOMEWHERE TO HIDE. I BELIEVE HE'LL BE COMING FOR US.
WHERE ARE YOU GOING?
THE CAVE. MY COMPUTER THERE IS THE BEST CHANCE WE HAVE OF ANALYZING THIS. ONCE I KNOW HOW IT'S MADE, I SHOULD BE ABLE TO SYNTHESIZE IT.
IT COULD BE OUR ONLY CHANCE TO STAND AGAINST HIM.
SUPERMAN WILL BE COMING FOR YOU.
I KNOW.
THE CAVE IS THE FIRST PLACE HE'LL LOOK!
I KNOW.

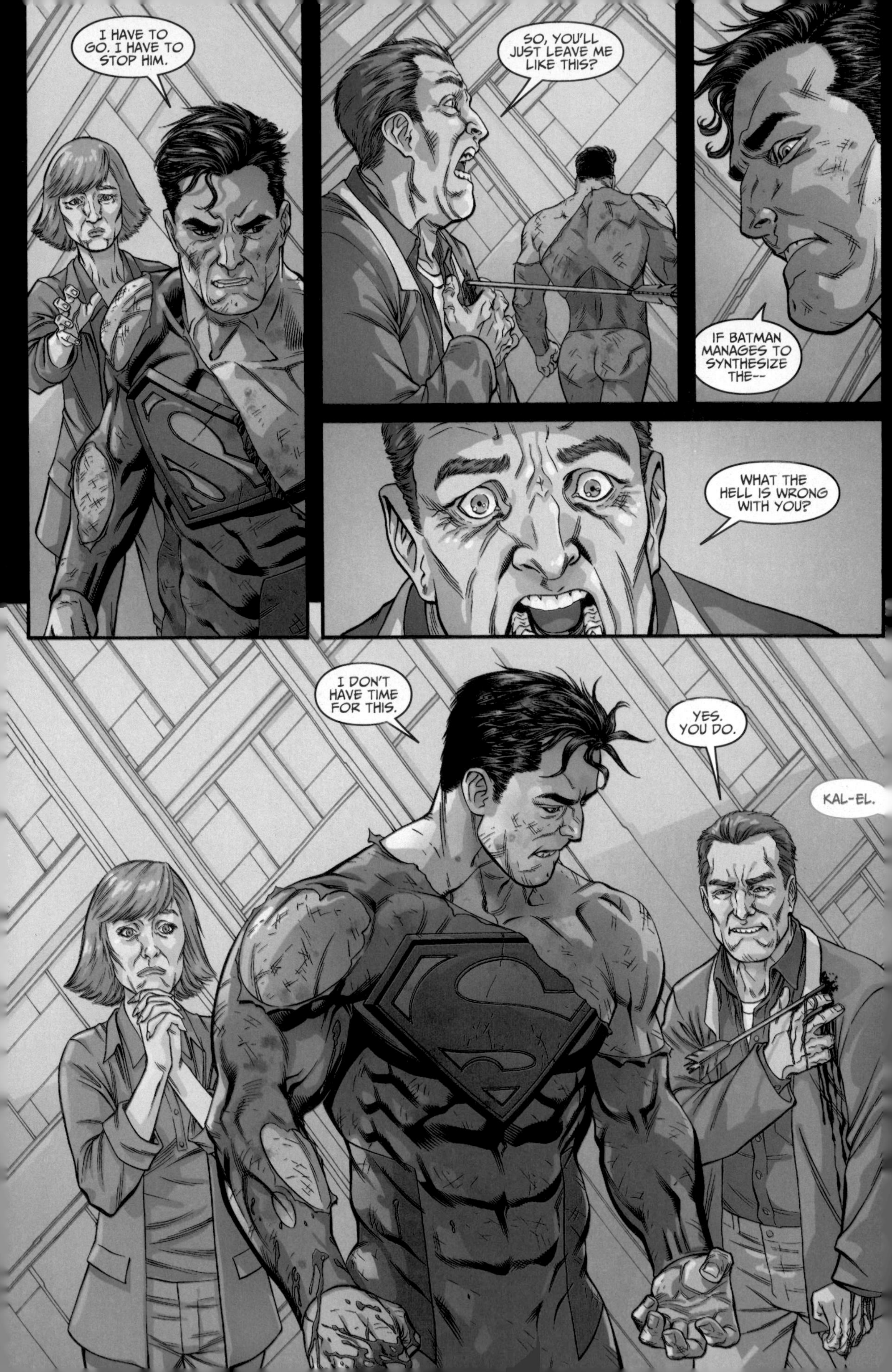
I HAVE TO GO. I HAVE TO STOP HIM.
SO, YOU'LL JUST LEAVE ME LIKE THIS?
IF BATMAN MANAGES TO SYNTHESIZE THE--
WHAT THE HELL IS WRONG WITH YOU?
I DON'T HAVE TIME FOR THIS.
YES. YOU DO.
KAL-EL.

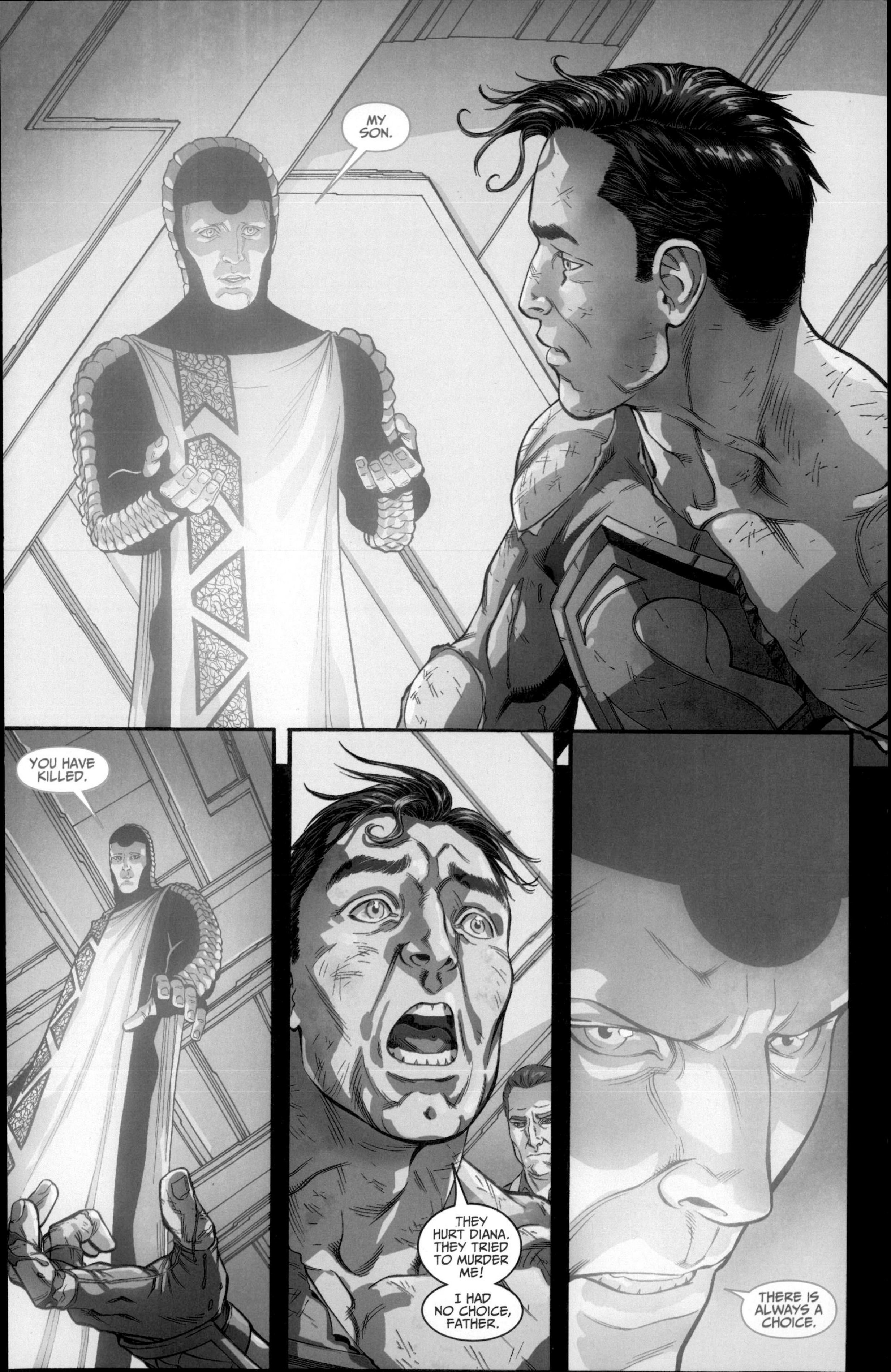
MY SON.
YOU HAVE KILLED.
THEY HURT DIANA. THEY TRIED TO MURDER ME!
I HAD NO CHOICE, FATHER.
THERE IS ALWAYS A CHOICE.

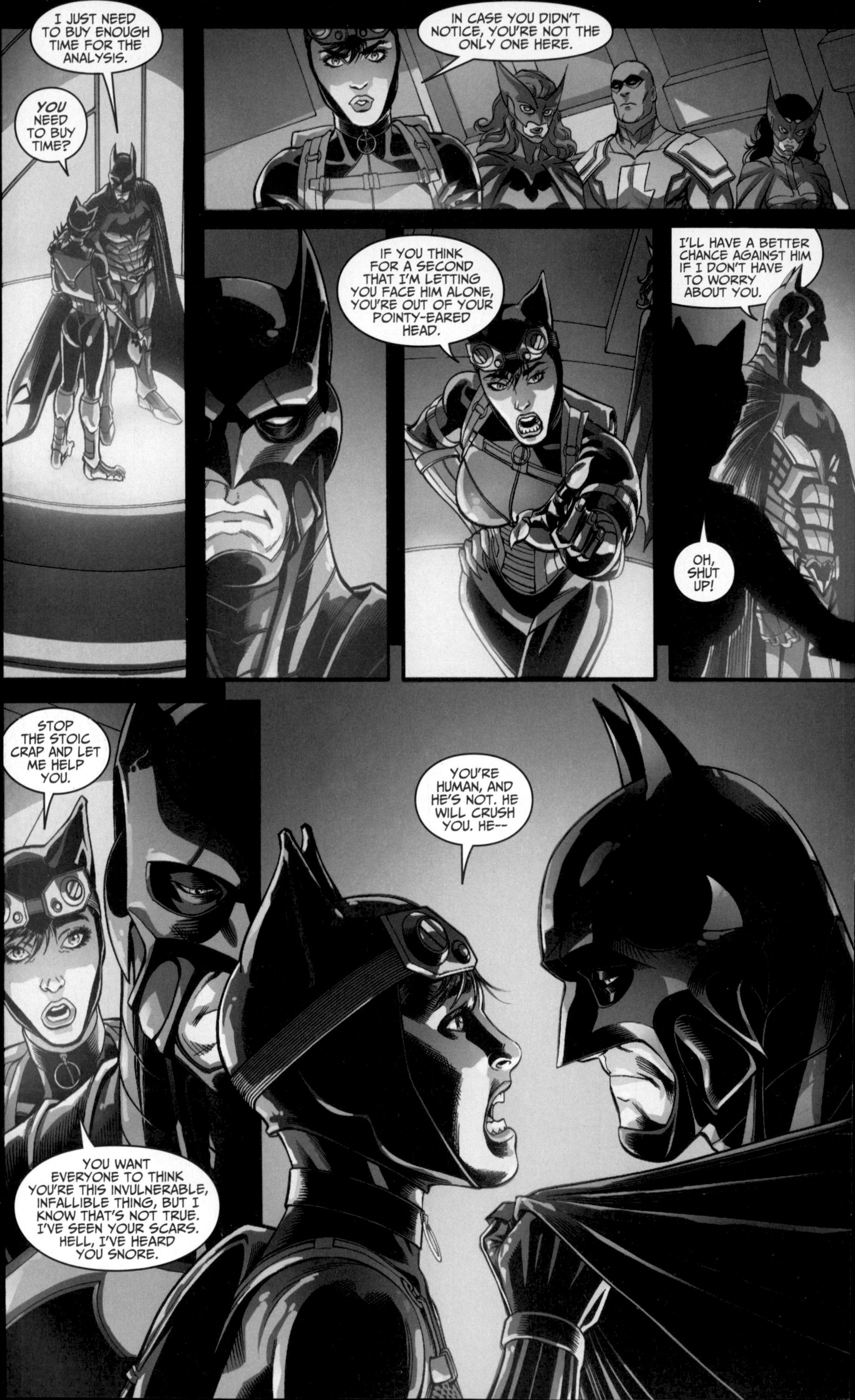
I JUST NEED TO BUY ENOUGH TIME FOR THE ANALYSIS.
YOU NEED TO BUY TIME?
IN CASE YOU DIDN'T NOTICE, YOU'RE NOT THE ONLY ONE HERE.
IF YOU THINK FOR A SECOND THAT I'M LETTING YOU FACE HIM ALONE, YOU'RE OUT OF YOUR POINTY-EARED HEAD.
I'LL HAVE A BETTER CHANCE AGAINST HIM IF I DON'T HAVE TO WORRY ABOUT YOU.
OH, SHUT UP!
STOP THE STOIC CRAP AND LET ME HELP YOU.
YOU'RE HUMAN, AND HE'S NOT. HE WILL CRUSH YOU. HE--
YOU WANT EVERYONE TO THINK YOU'RE THIS INVULNERABLE, INFALLIBLE THING, BUT I KNOW THAT'S NOT TRUE. I'VE SEEN YOUR SCARS. HELL, I'VE HEARD YOU SNORE.

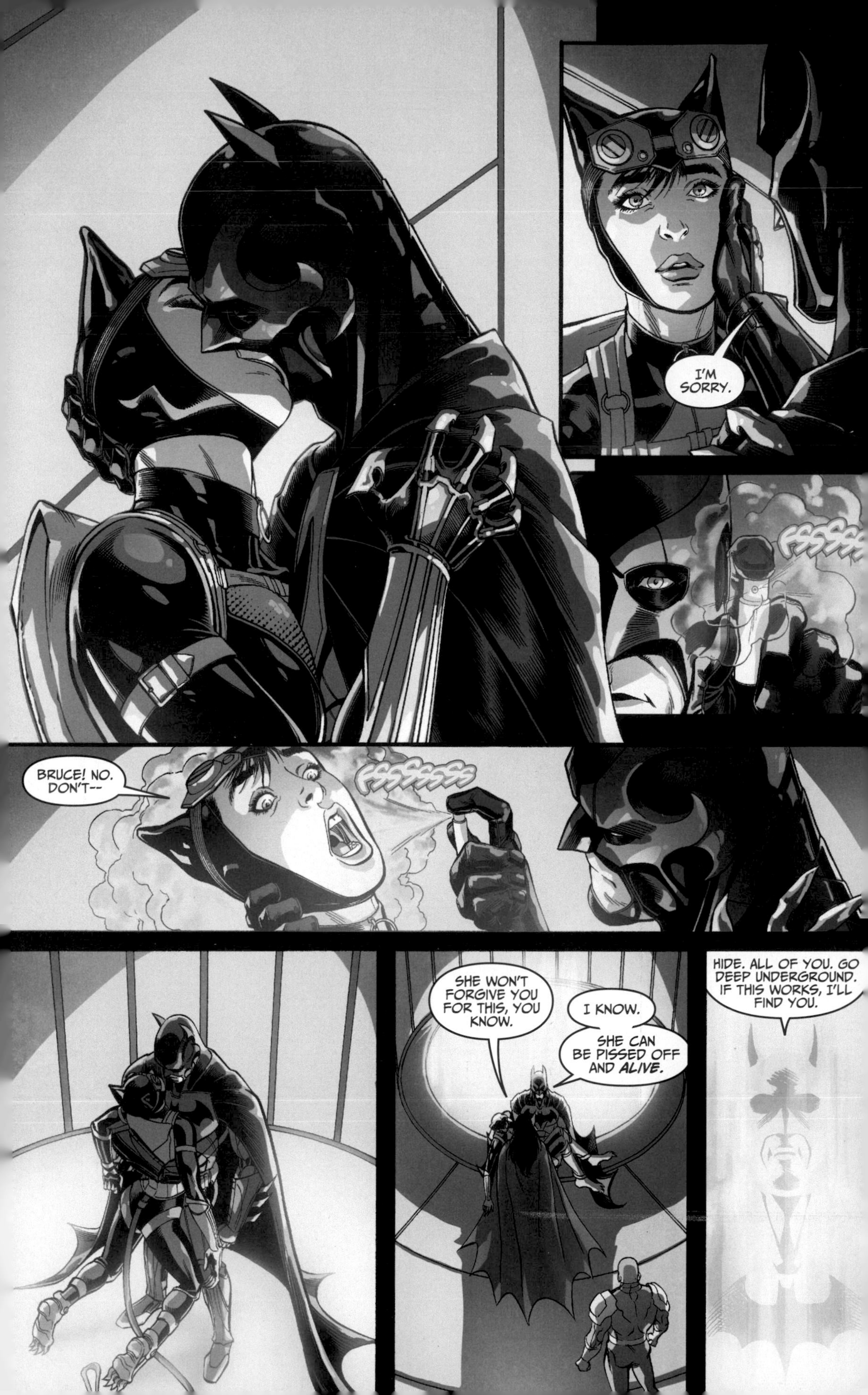
I'M SORRY.
FSSSSS
BRUCE! NO. DON'T--
FSSSSSSS
SHE WON'T FORGIVE YOU FOR THIS, YOU KNOW.
I KNOW.
SHE CAN BE PISSED OFF AND *ALIVE.*
HIDE. ALL OF YOU. GO DEEP UNDERGROUND. IF THIS WORKS, I'LL FIND YOU.

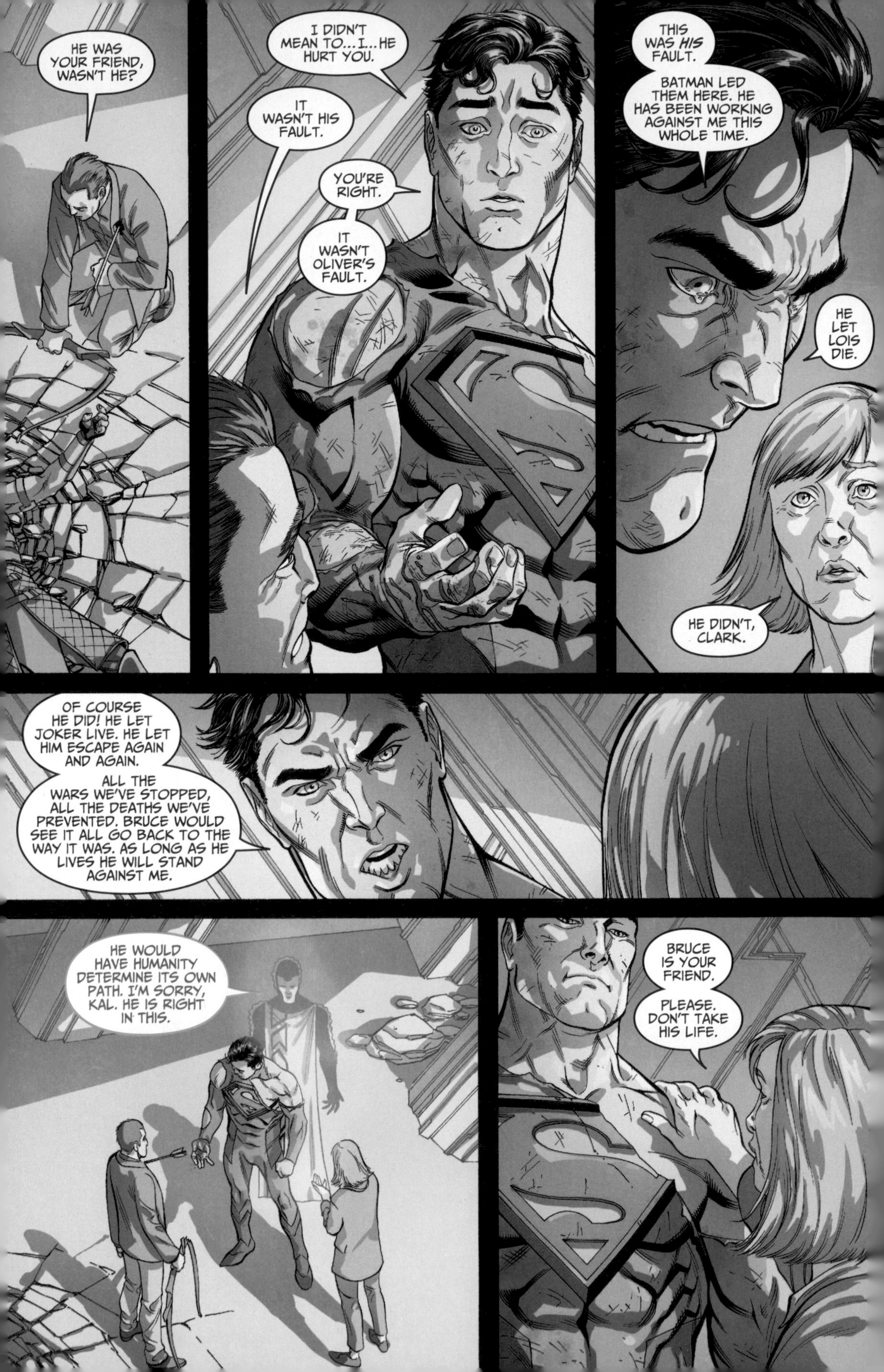
HE WAS YOUR FRIEND, WASN'T HE?
I DIDN'T MEAN TO... I... HE HURT YOU.
IT WASN'T HIS FAULT.
YOU'RE RIGHT.
IT WASN'T OLIVER'S FAULT.
THIS WAS *HIS* FAULT.
BATMAN LED THEM HERE. HE HAS BEEN WORKING AGAINST ME THIS WHOLE TIME.
HE LET LOIS DIE.
HE DIDN'T, CLARK.
OF COURSE HE DID! HE LET JOKER LIVE. HE LET HIM ESCAPE AGAIN AND AGAIN.
ALL THE WARS WE'VE STOPPED, ALL THE DEATHS WE'VE PREVENTED. BRUCE WOULD SEE IT ALL GO BACK TO THE WAY IT WAS. AS LONG AS HE LIVES HE WILL STAND AGAINST ME.
HE WOULD HAVE HUMANITY DETERMINE ITS OWN PATH. I'M SORRY, KAL. HE IS RIGHT IN THIS.
BRUCE IS YOUR FRIEND.
PLEASE. DON'T TAKE HIS LIFE.

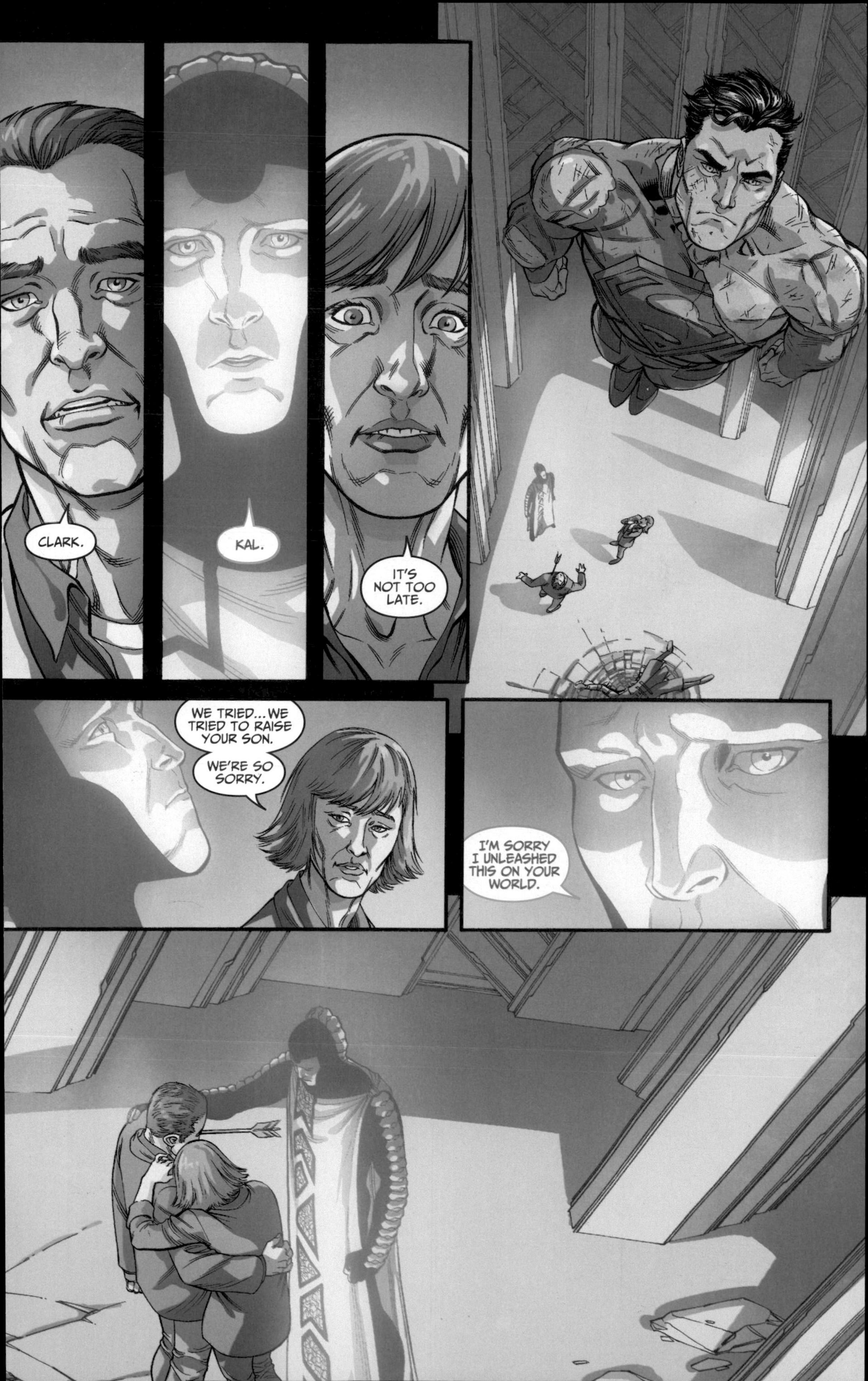
CLARK.
KAL.
IT'S NOT TOO LATE.
WE TRIED...WE TRIED TO RAISE YOUR SON.
WE'RE SO SORRY.
I'M SORRY I UNLEASHED THIS ON YOUR WORLD.

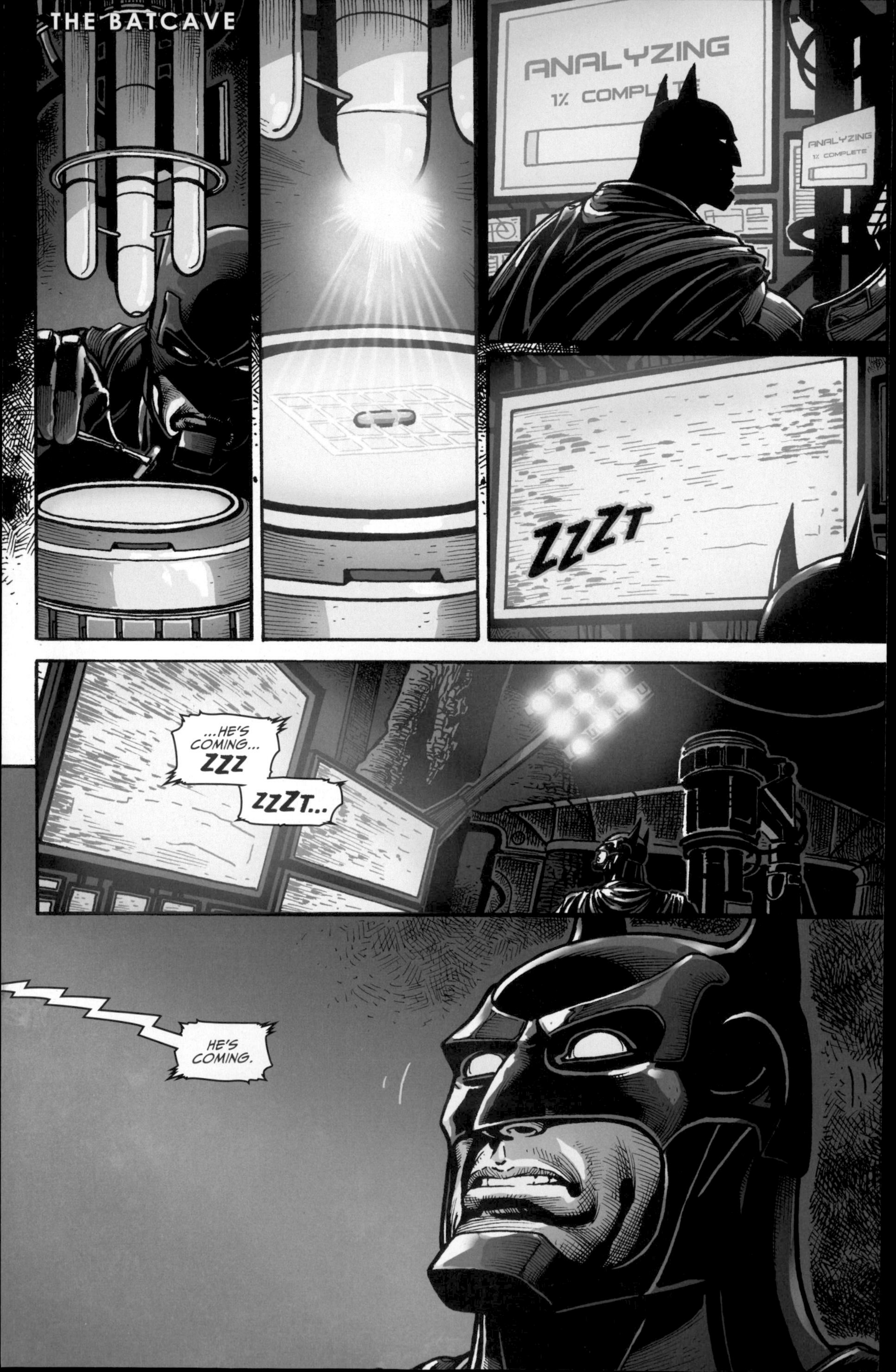
THE BATCAVE
ANALYZING
1% COMPLETE
ANALYZING
1% COMPLETE
ZZZT
...HE'S COMING... ZZZ
ZZZT...
HE'S COMING.

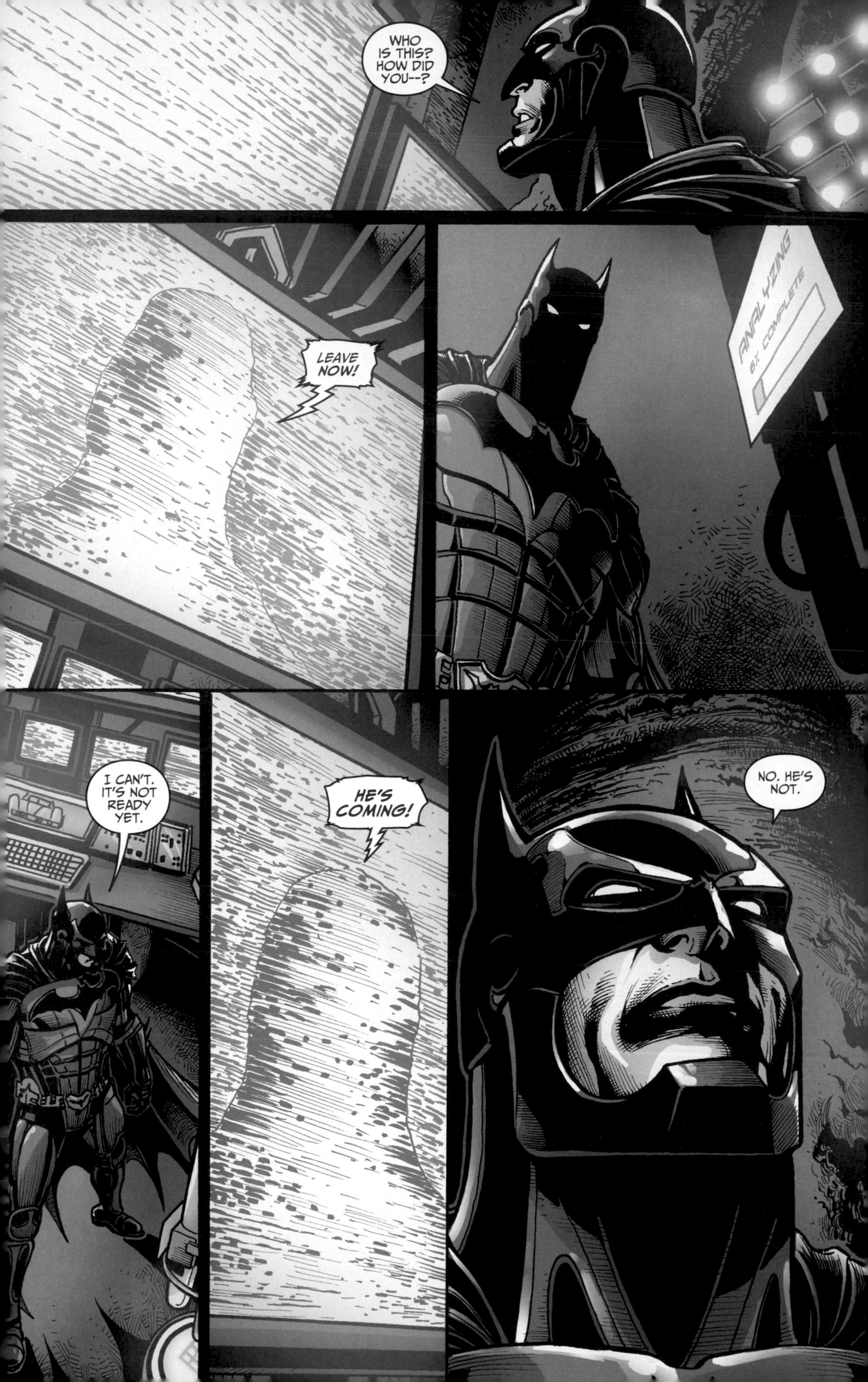
WHO IS THIS? HOW DID YOU--?
LEAVE NOW!
ANALYZING
6% COMPLETE
I CAN'T. IT'S NOT READY YET.
HE'S COMING!
NO. HE'S NOT.

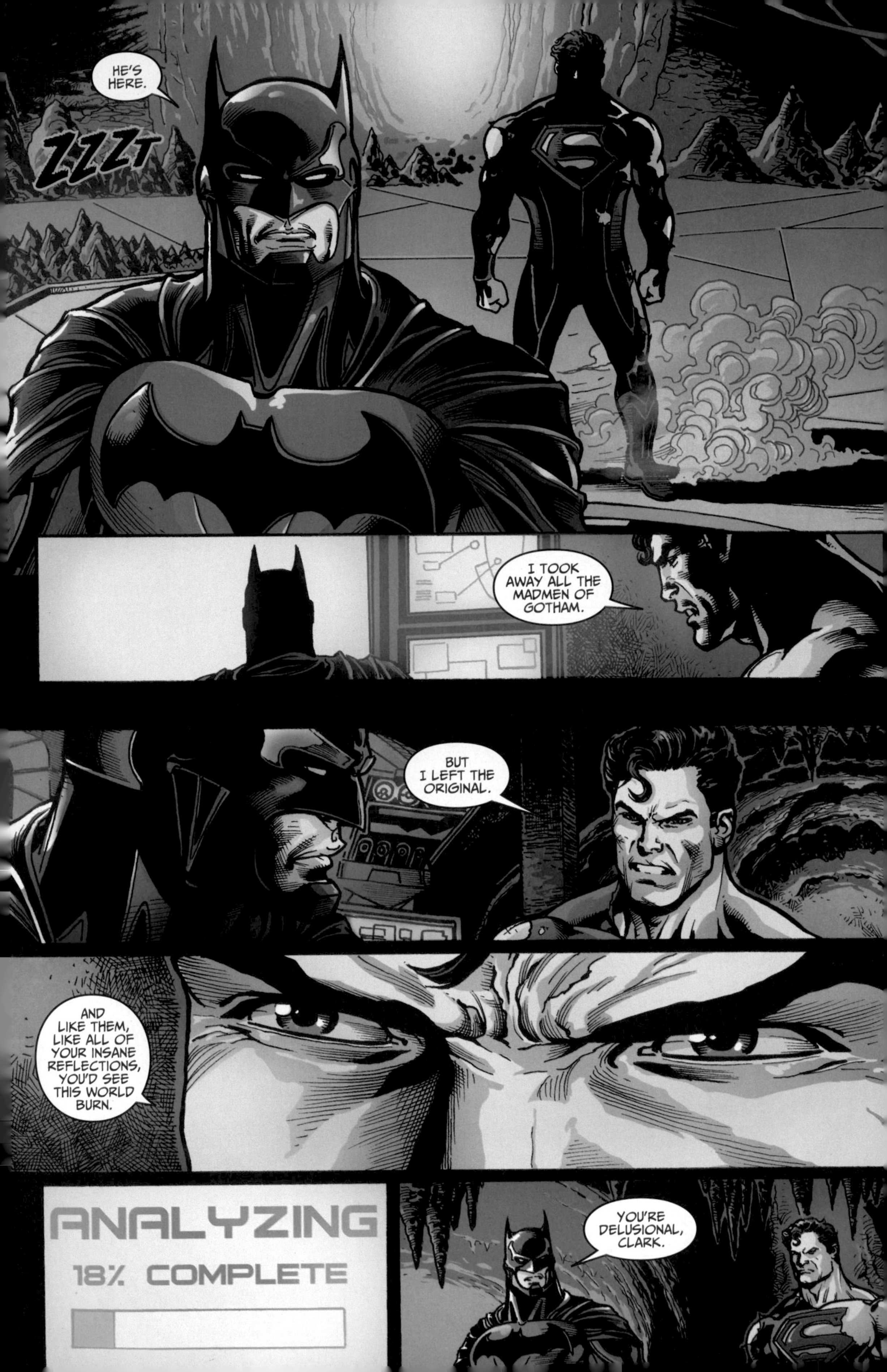
HE'S HERE.
ZZZT
I TOOK AWAY ALL THE MADMEN OF GOTHAM.
BUT I LEFT THE ORIGINAL.
AND LIKE THEM, LIKE ALL OF YOUR INSANE REFLECTIONS, YOU'D SEE THIS WORLD BURN.
ANALYZING
18% COMPLETE
YOU'RE DELUSIONAL, CLARK.

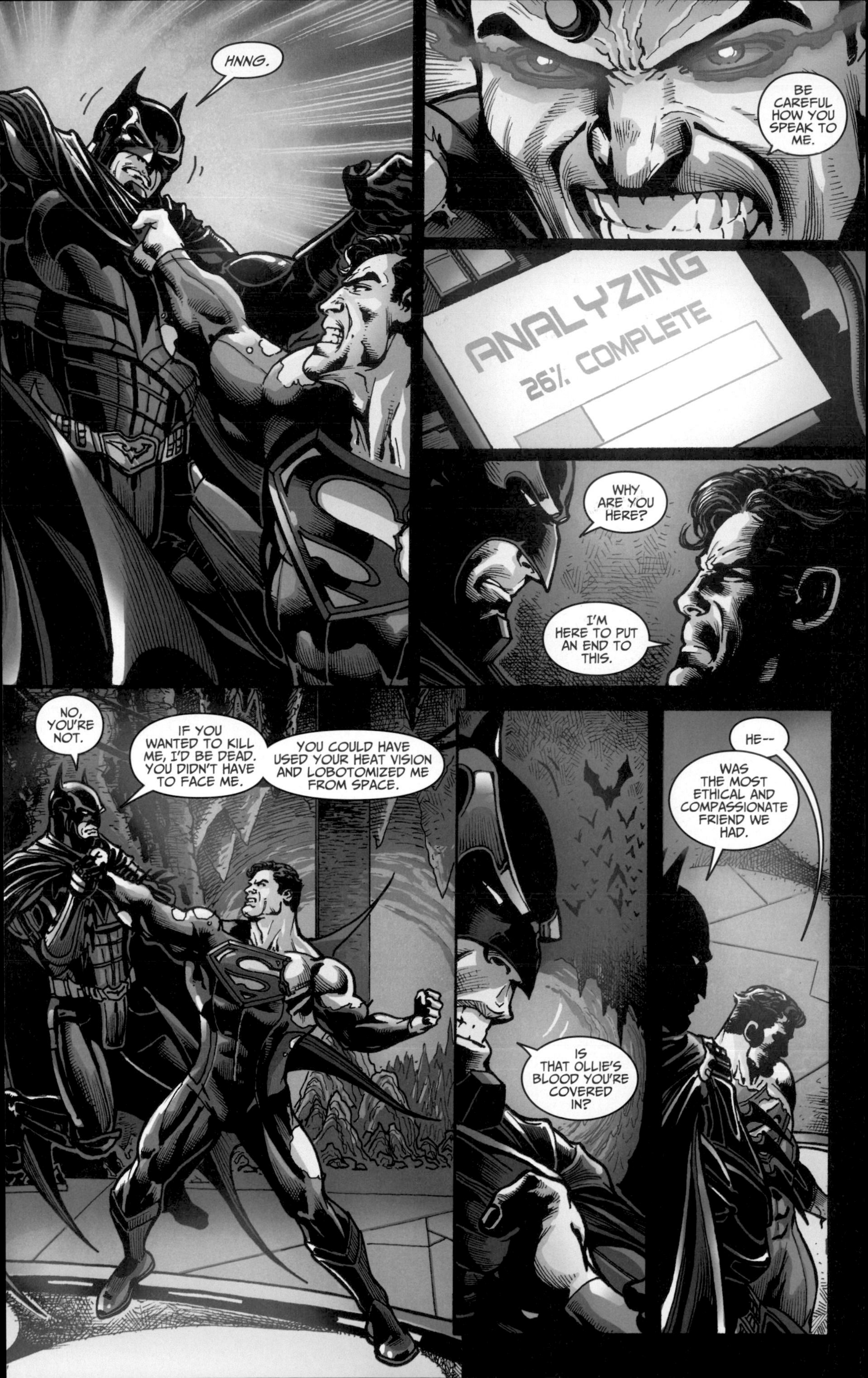
HNNG.
BE CAREFUL HOW YOU SPEAK TO ME.
ANALYZING
26% COMPLETE
WHY ARE YOU HERE?
I'M HERE TO PUT AN END TO THIS.
NO, YOU'RE NOT.
IF YOU WANTED TO KILL ME, I'D BE DEAD. YOU DIDN'T HAVE TO FACE ME.
YOU COULD HAVE USED YOUR HEAT VISION AND LOBOTOMIZED ME FROM SPACE.
IS THAT OLLIE'S BLOOD YOU'RE COVERED IN?
HE--
WAS THE MOST ETHICAL AND COMPASSIONATE FRIEND WE HAD.

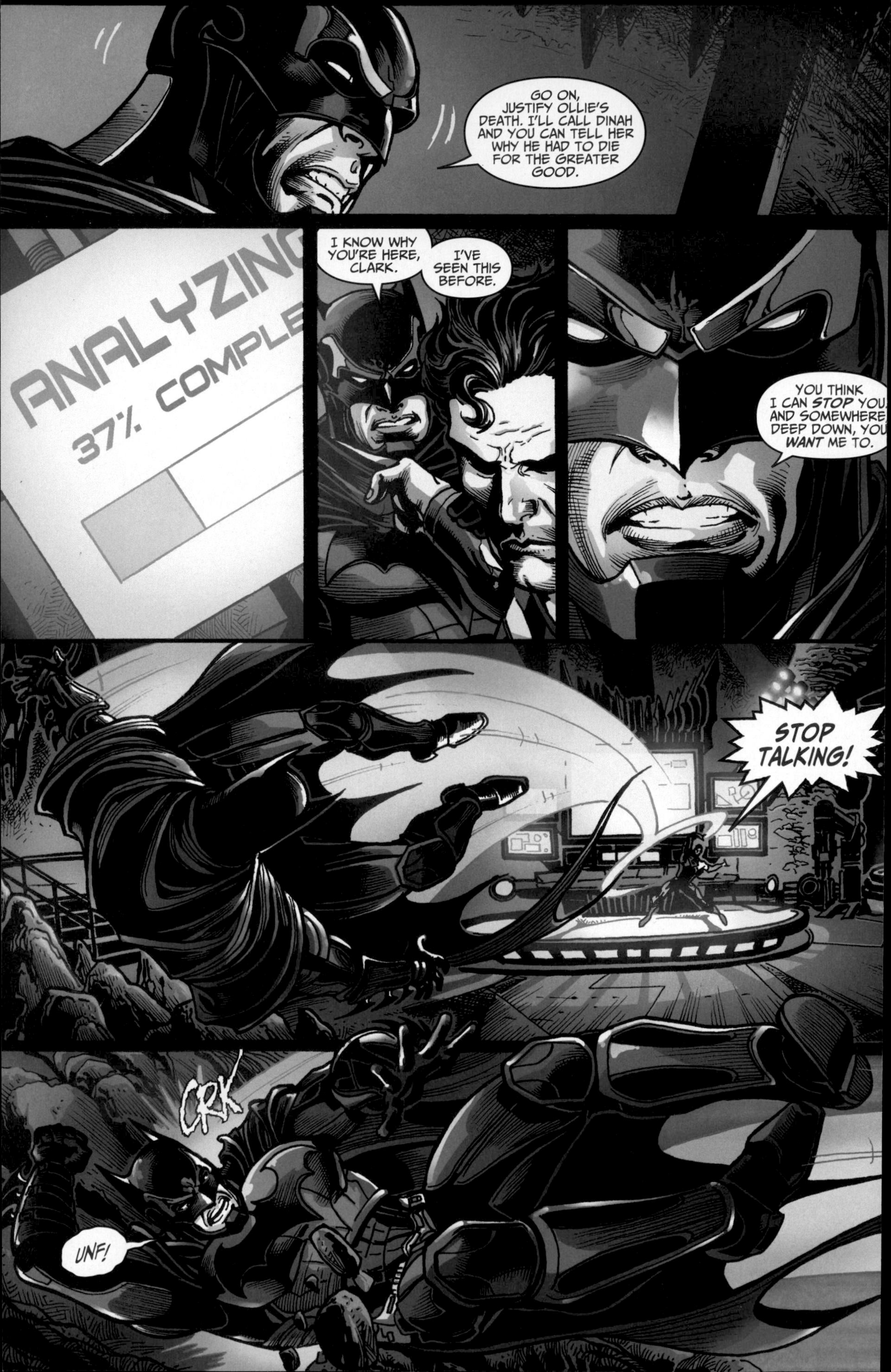
GO ON, JUSTIFY OLLIE'S DEATH. I'LL CALL DINAH AND YOU CAN TELL HER WHY HE HAD TO DIE FOR THE GREATER GOOD.
ANALYZING
37% COMPLE
I KNOW WHY YOU'RE HERE, CLARK.
I'VE SEEN THIS BEFORE.
YOU THINK I CAN STOP YOU. AND SOMEWHERE, DEEP DOWN, YOU WANT ME TO.
STOP TALKING!
CRK
UNF!

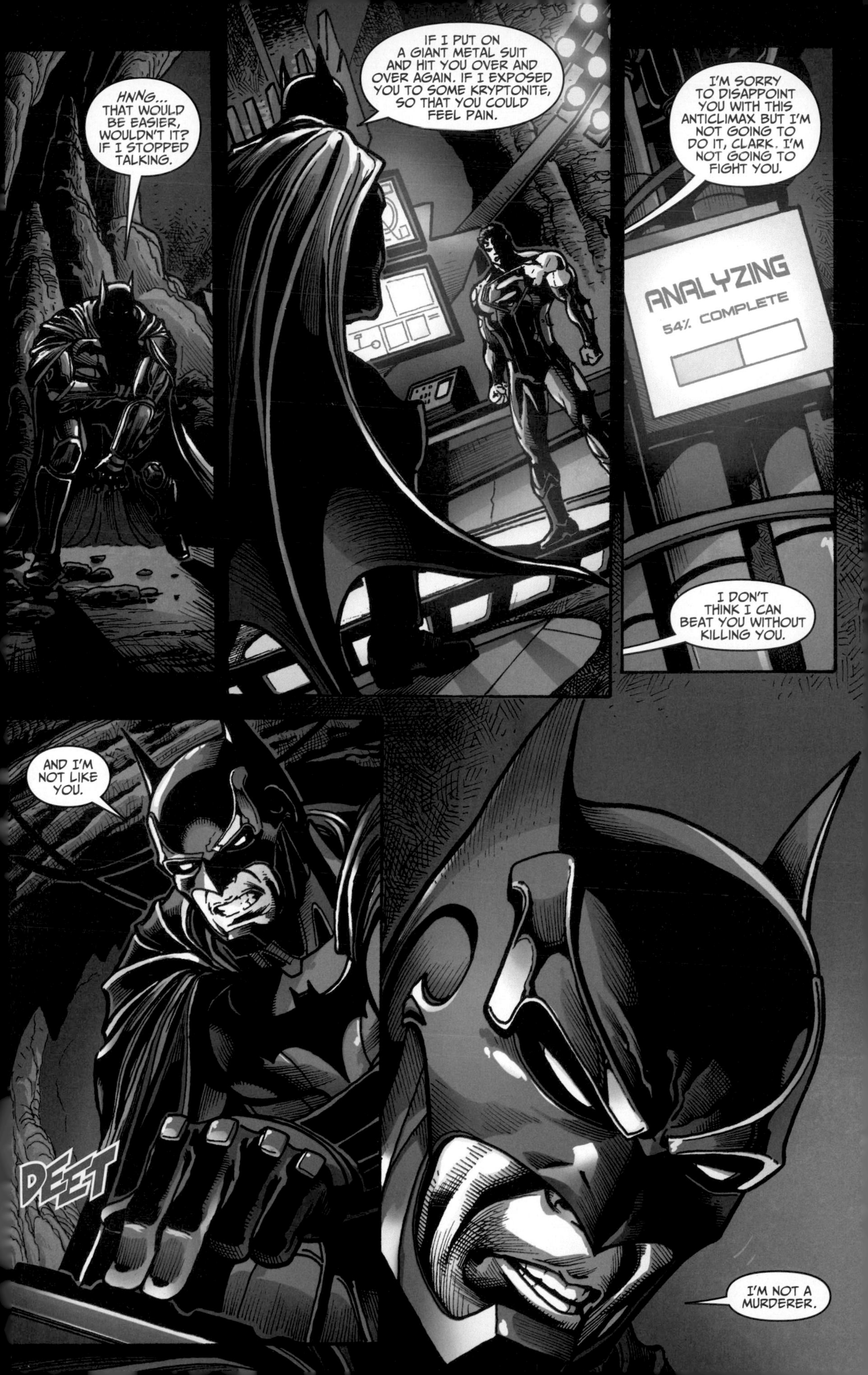
HNNG... THAT WOULD BE EASIER, WOULDN'T IT? IF I STOPPED TALKING.
IF I PUT ON A GIANT METAL SUIT AND HIT YOU OVER AND OVER AGAIN. IF I EXPOSED YOU TO SOME KRYPTONITE, SO THAT YOU COULD FEEL PAIN.
I'M SORRY TO DISAPPOINT YOU WITH THIS ANTICLIMAX BUT I'M NOT GOING TO DO IT, CLARK. I'M NOT GOING TO FIGHT YOU.
ANALYZING
54% COMPLETE
I DON'T THINK I CAN BEAT YOU WITHOUT KILLING YOU.
AND I'M NOT LIKE YOU.
DEET
I'M NOT A MURDERER.

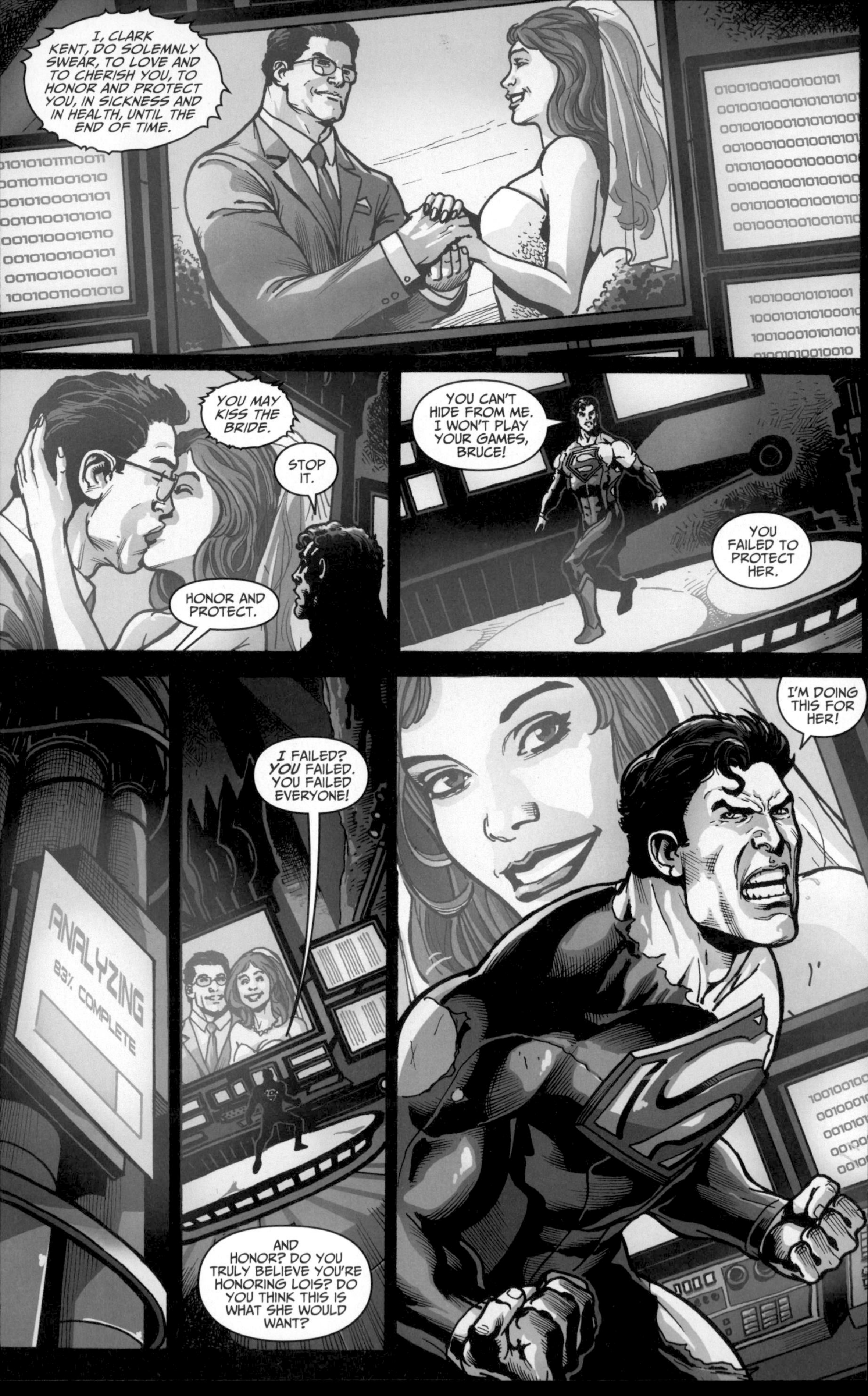
I, CLARK KENT, DO SOLEMNLY SWEAR, TO LOVE AND TO CHERISH YOU, TO HONOR AND PROTECT YOU, IN SICKNESS AND IN HEALTH, UNTIL THE END OF TIME.
YOU MAY KISS THE BRIDE.
STOP IT.
HONOR AND PROTECT.
YOU CAN'T HIDE FROM ME. I WON'T PLAY YOUR GAMES, BRUCE!
YOU FAILED TO PROTECT HER.
ANALYZING
83% COMPLETE
I FAILED? *YOU* FAILED. YOU FAILED EVERYONE!
AND HONOR? DO YOU TRULY BELIEVE YOU'RE HONORING LOIS? DO YOU THINK THIS IS WHAT SHE WOULD WANT?
I'M DOING THIS FOR HER!

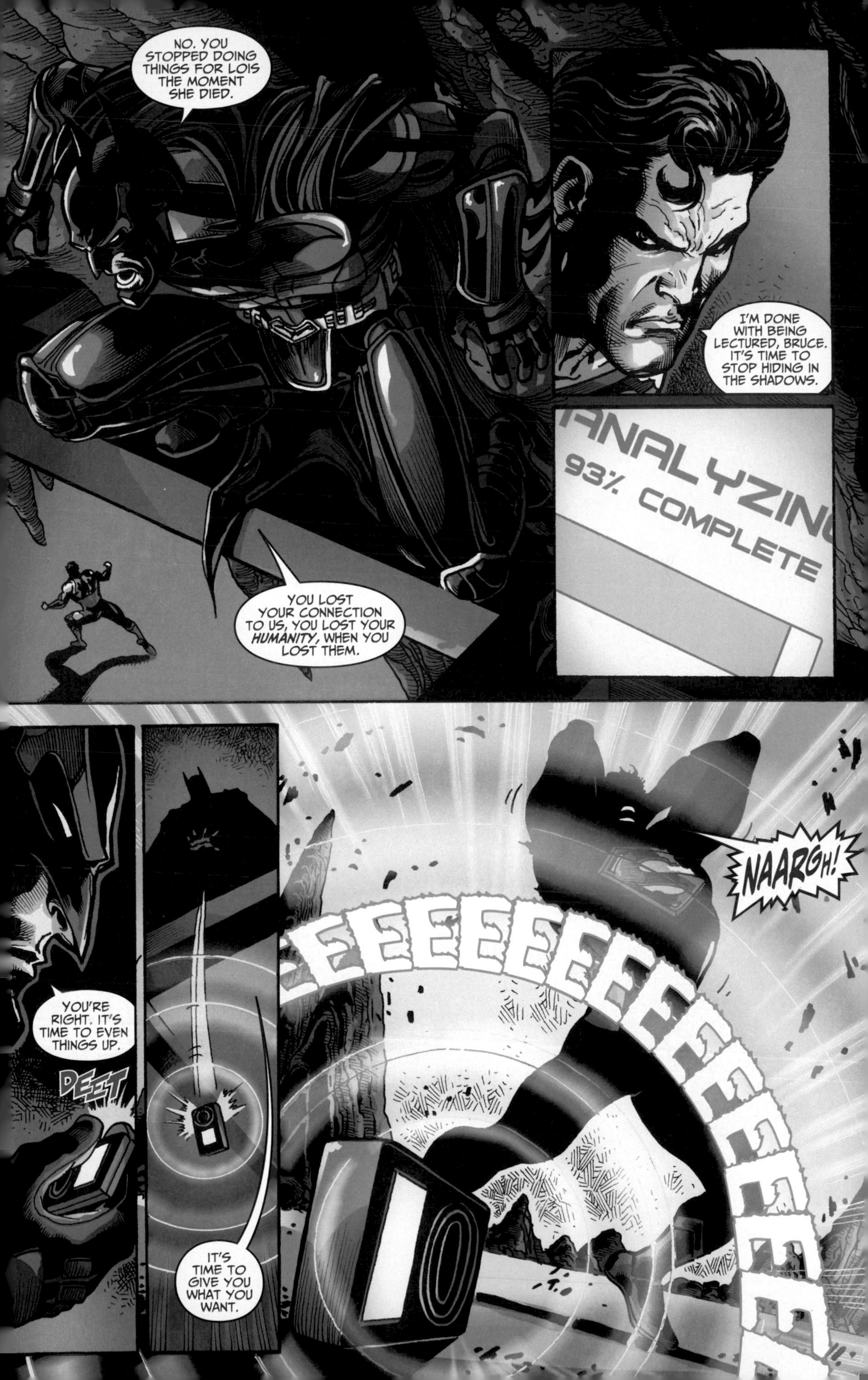
NO. YOU STOPPED DOING THINGS FOR LOIS THE MOMENT SHE DIED.
I'M DONE WITH BEING LECTURED, BRUCE. IT'S TIME TO STOP HIDING IN THE SHADOWS.
YOU LOST YOUR CONNECTION TO US, YOU LOST YOUR *HUMANITY*, WHEN YOU LOST THEM.
ANALYZING
93% COMPLETE
YOU'RE RIGHT. IT'S TIME TO EVEN THINGS UP.
DEEIT
IT'S TIME TO GIVE YOU WHAT YOU WANT.
EEEEEEEEEEEEEEEEE
NAARGH!

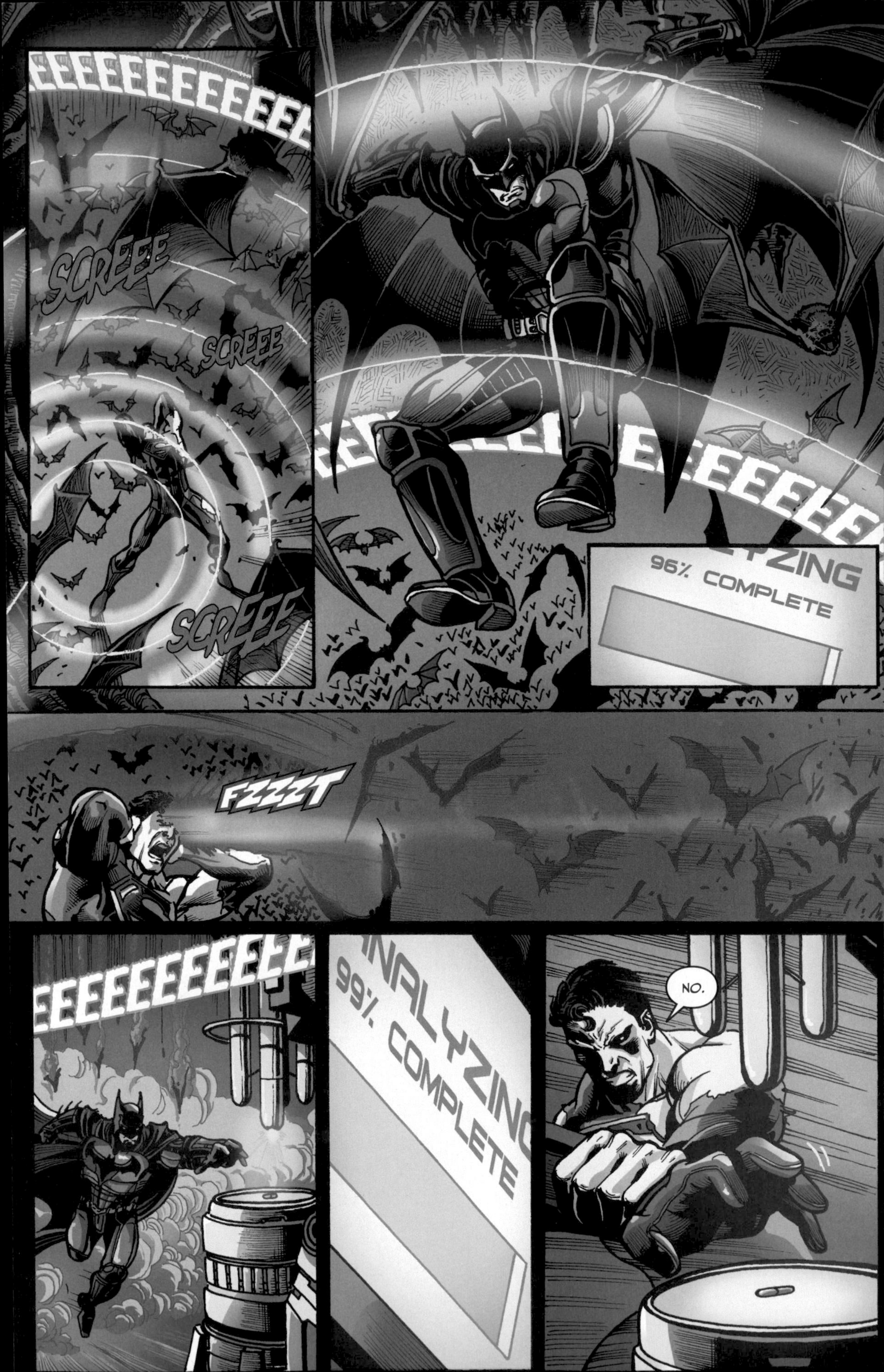
EEEEEEEEEEEEE
SCREEE
SCREEE
SCREEE
EEEEEEEEEEEEE
96% COMPLETE
FZZZT
EEEEEEEEEEEE
ANALYZING
99% COMPLETE
NO.

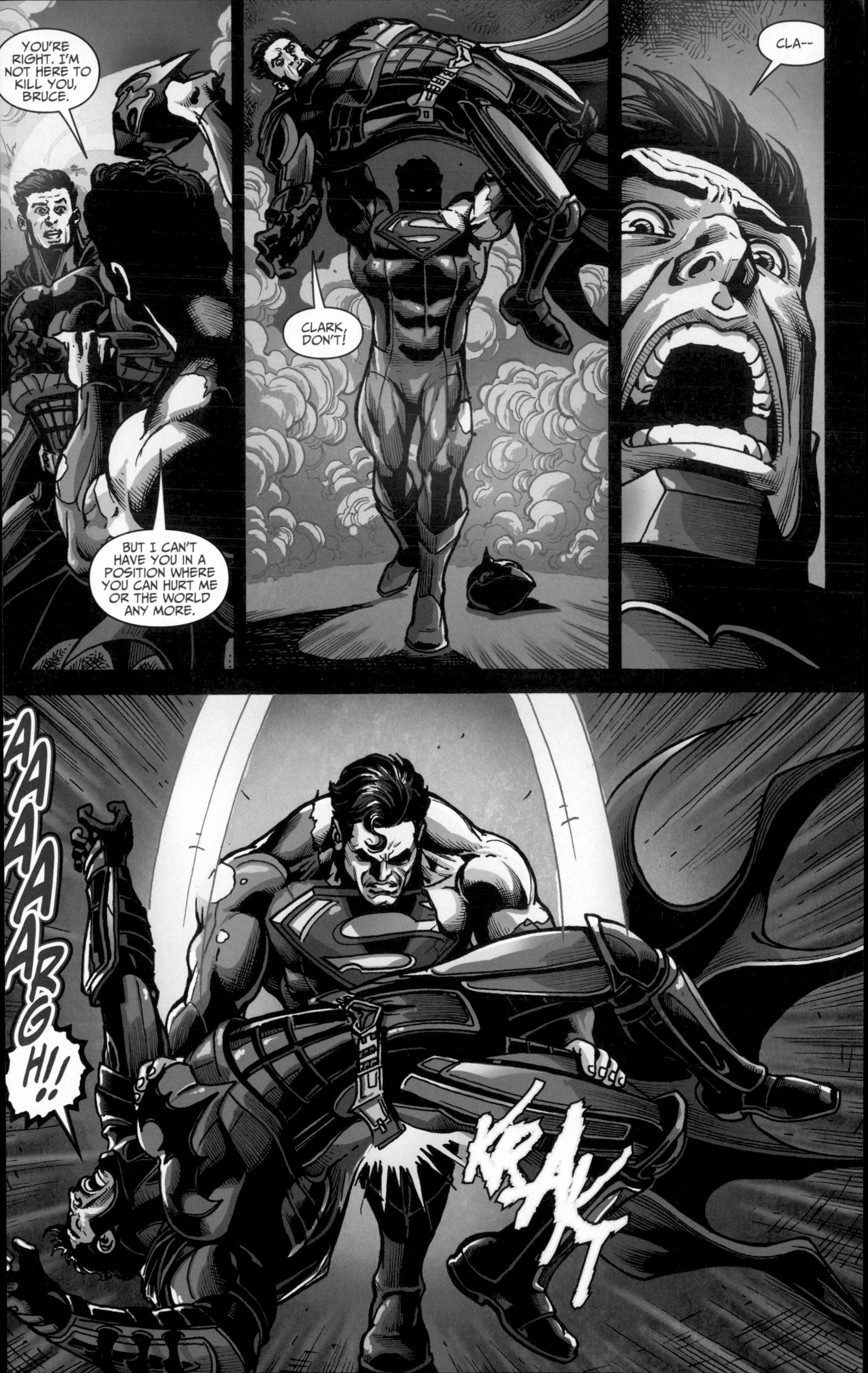
YOU'RE RIGHT. I'M NOT HERE TO KILL YOU, BRUCE.
BUT I CAN'T HAVE YOU IN A POSITION WHERE YOU CAN HURT ME OR THE WORLD ANY MORE.
CLARK, DON'T!
CLA--
AAAAAAARGH!!
KRAK!

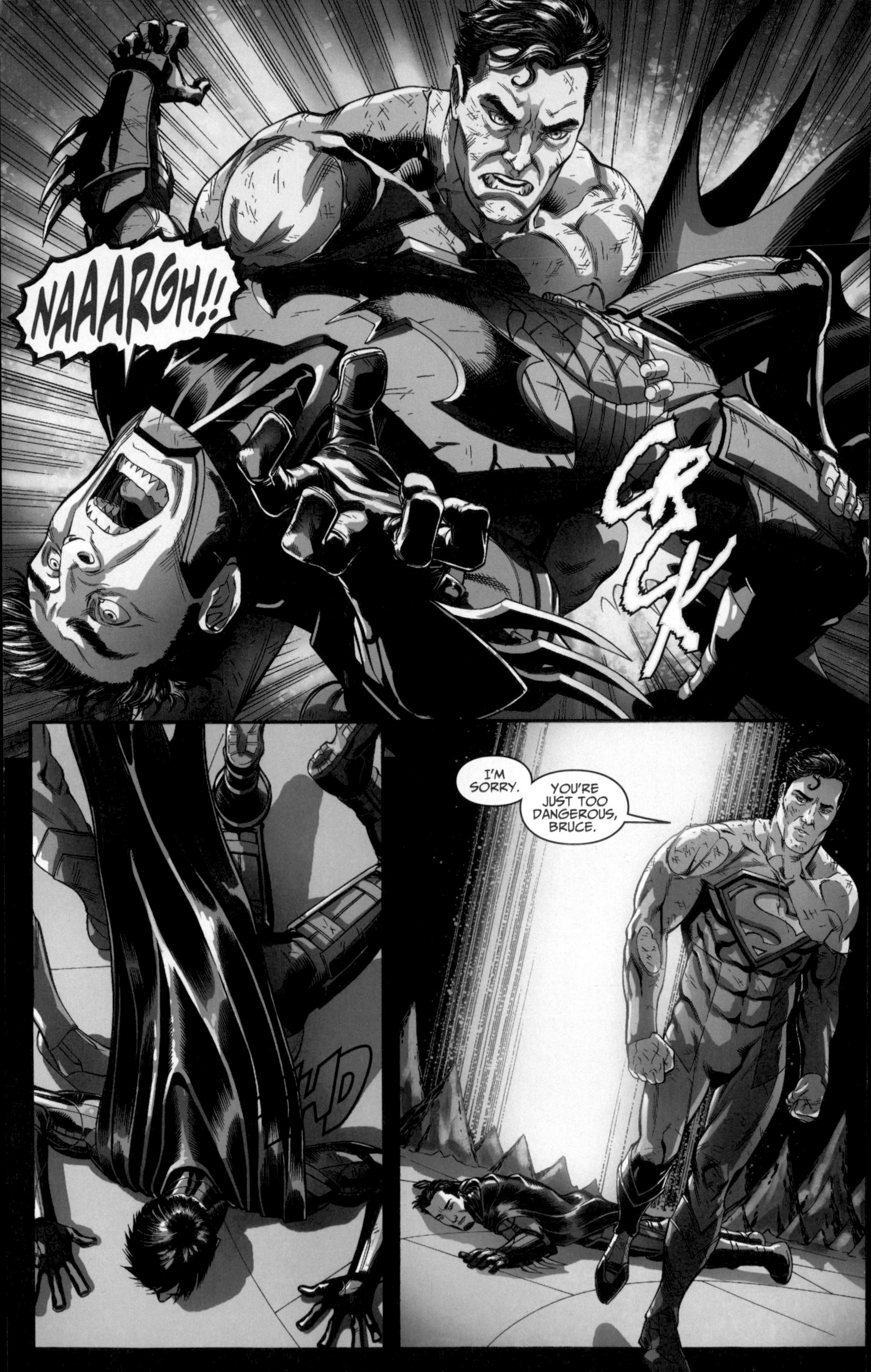
NAAARGH!!
CRCK
I'M SORRY.
YOU'RE JUST TOO DANGEROUS, BRUCE.

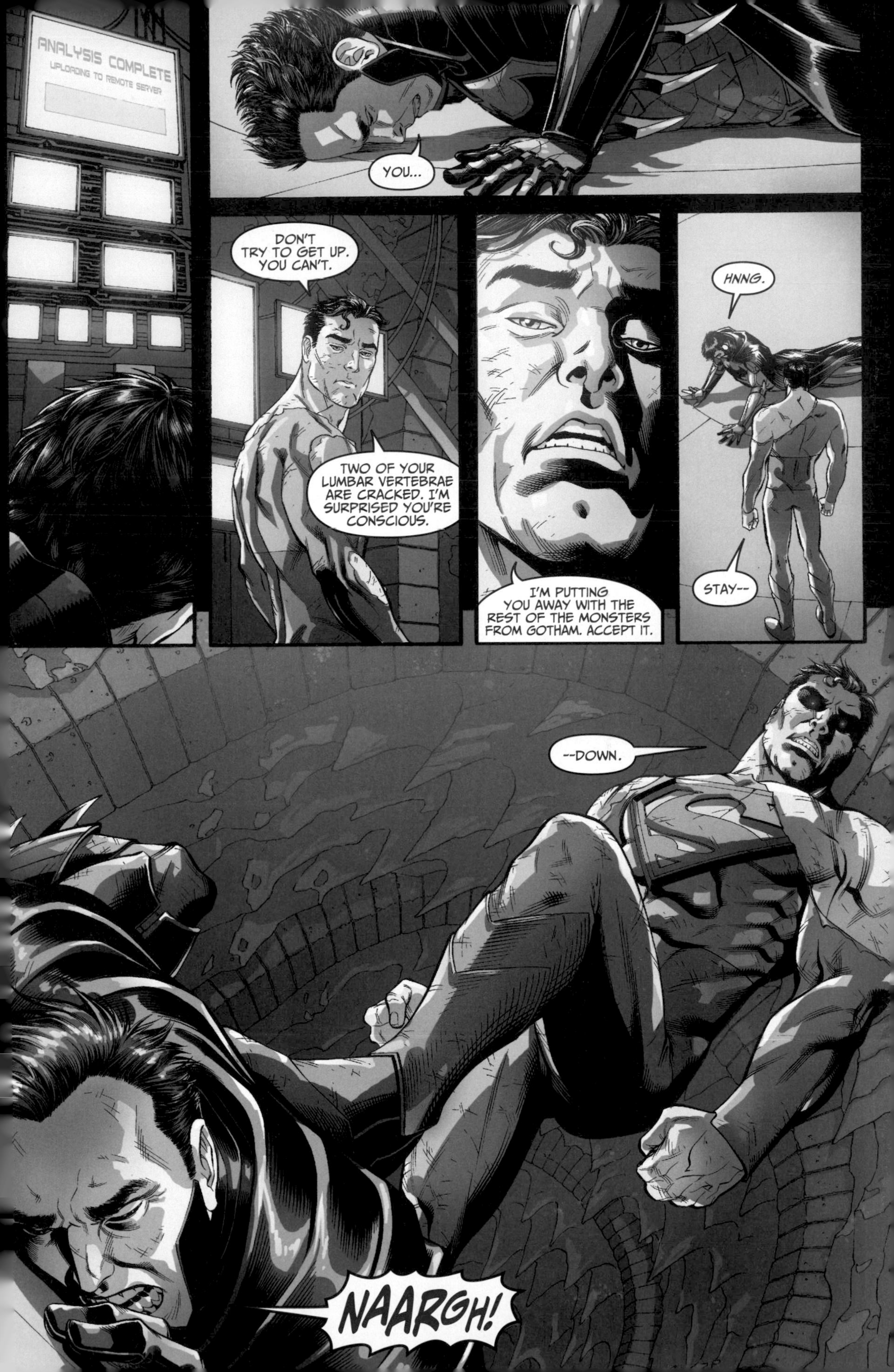
ANALYSIS COMPLETE
UPLOADING TO REMOTE SERVER
YOU...
DON'T TRY TO GET UP. YOU CAN'T.
TWO OF YOUR LUMBAR VERTEBRAE ARE CRACKED. I'M SURPRISED YOU'RE CONSCIOUS.
I'M PUTTING YOU AWAY WITH THE REST OF THE MONSTERS FROM GOTHAM. ACCEPT IT.
HNNG.
STAY--
--DOWN.
NAARGH!

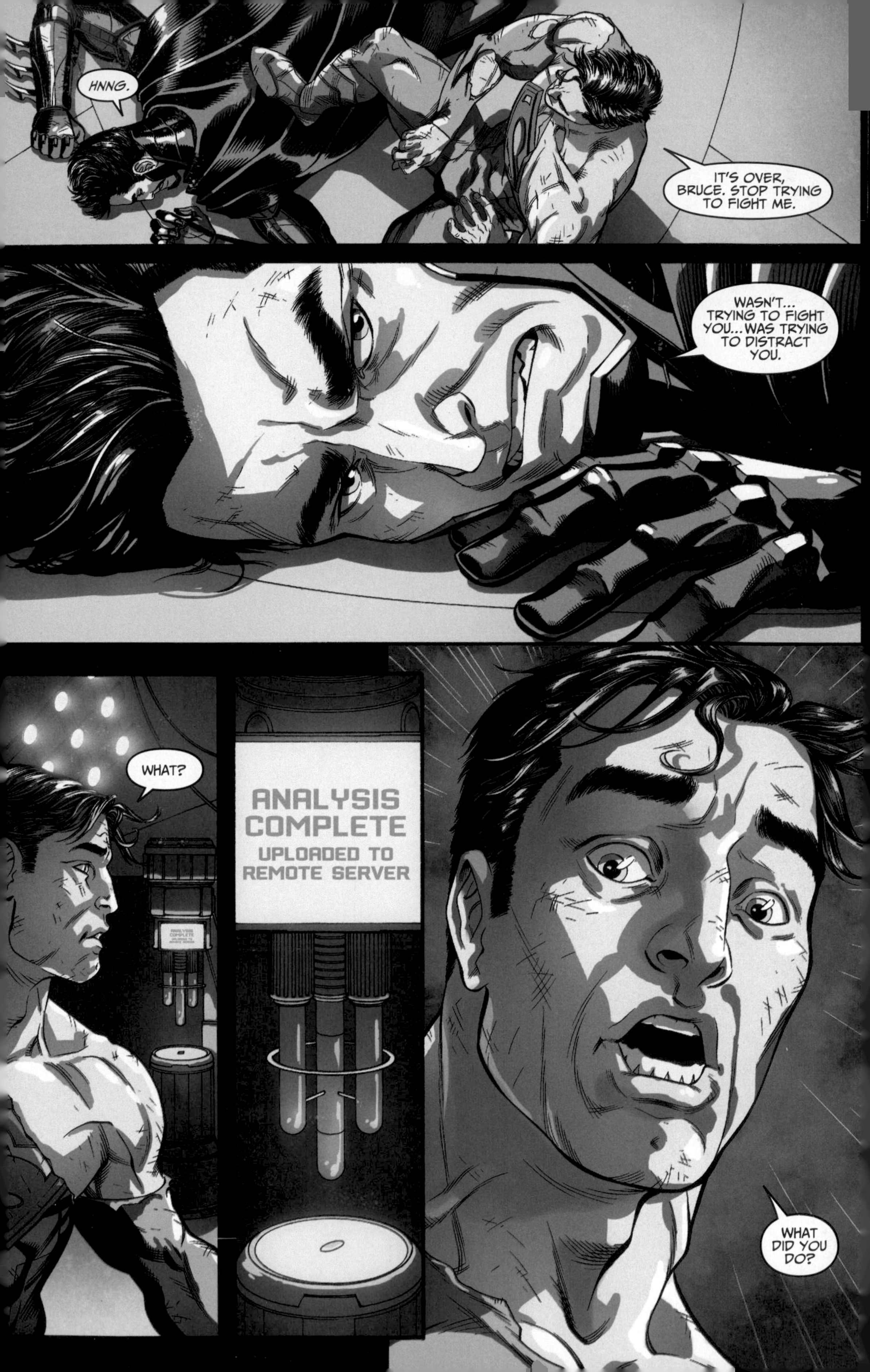
HNNG.
IT'S OVER, BRUCE. STOP TRYING TO FIGHT ME.
WASN'T... TRYING TO FIGHT YOU...WAS TRYING TO DISTRACT YOU.
WHAT?
ANALYSIS COMPLETE
UPLOADED TO REMOTE SERVER
WHAT DID YOU DO?

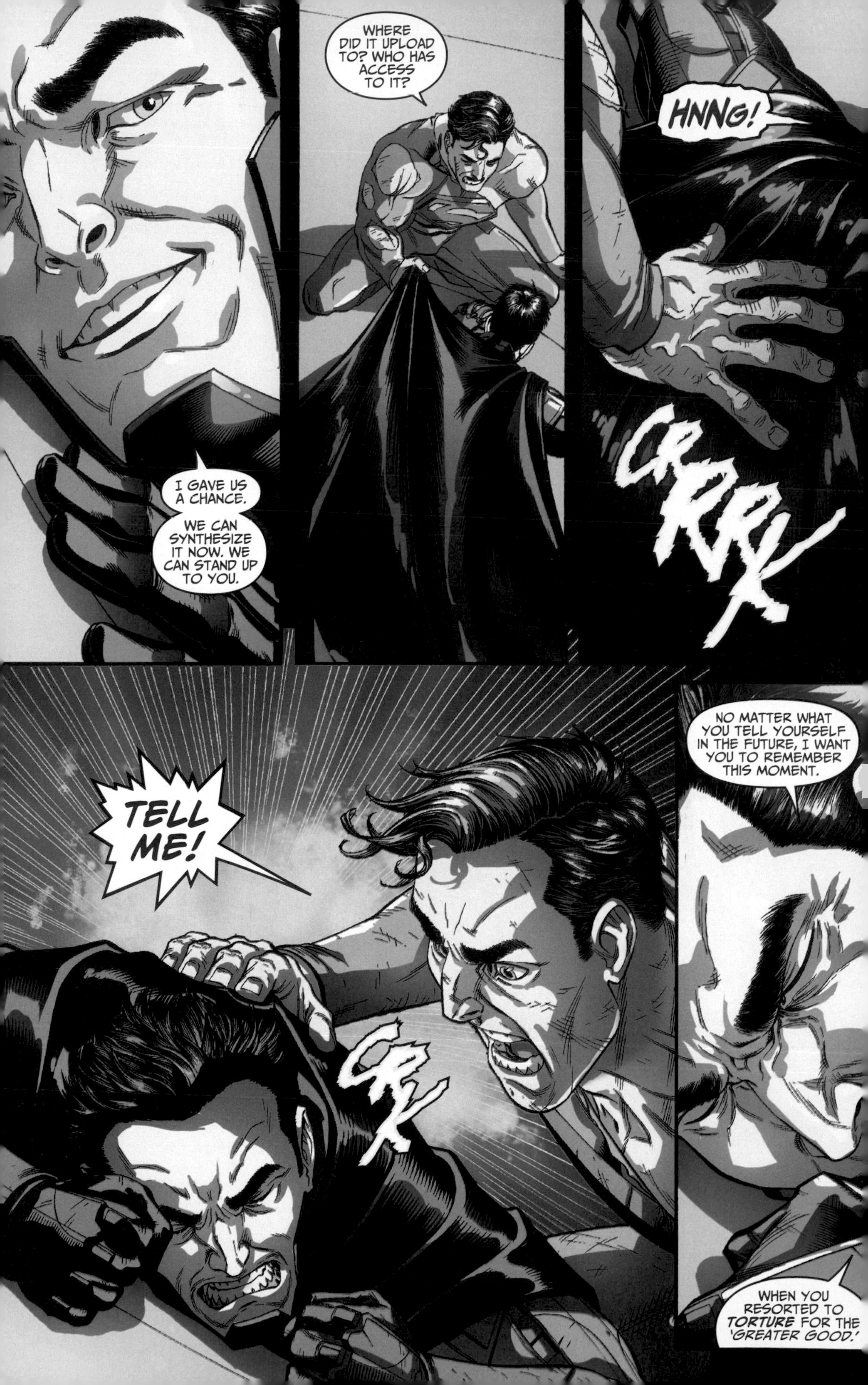
I GAVE US A CHANCE.
WE CAN SYNTHESIZE IT NOW. WE CAN STAND UP TO YOU.
WHERE DID IT UPLOAD TO? WHO HAS ACCESS TO IT?
HNNG!
CRRK
TELL ME!
CRRK
NO MATTER WHAT YOU TELL YOURSELF IN THE FUTURE, I WANT YOU TO REMEMBER THIS MOMENT.
WHEN YOU RESORTED TO *TORTURE* FOR THE 'GREATER GOOD.'

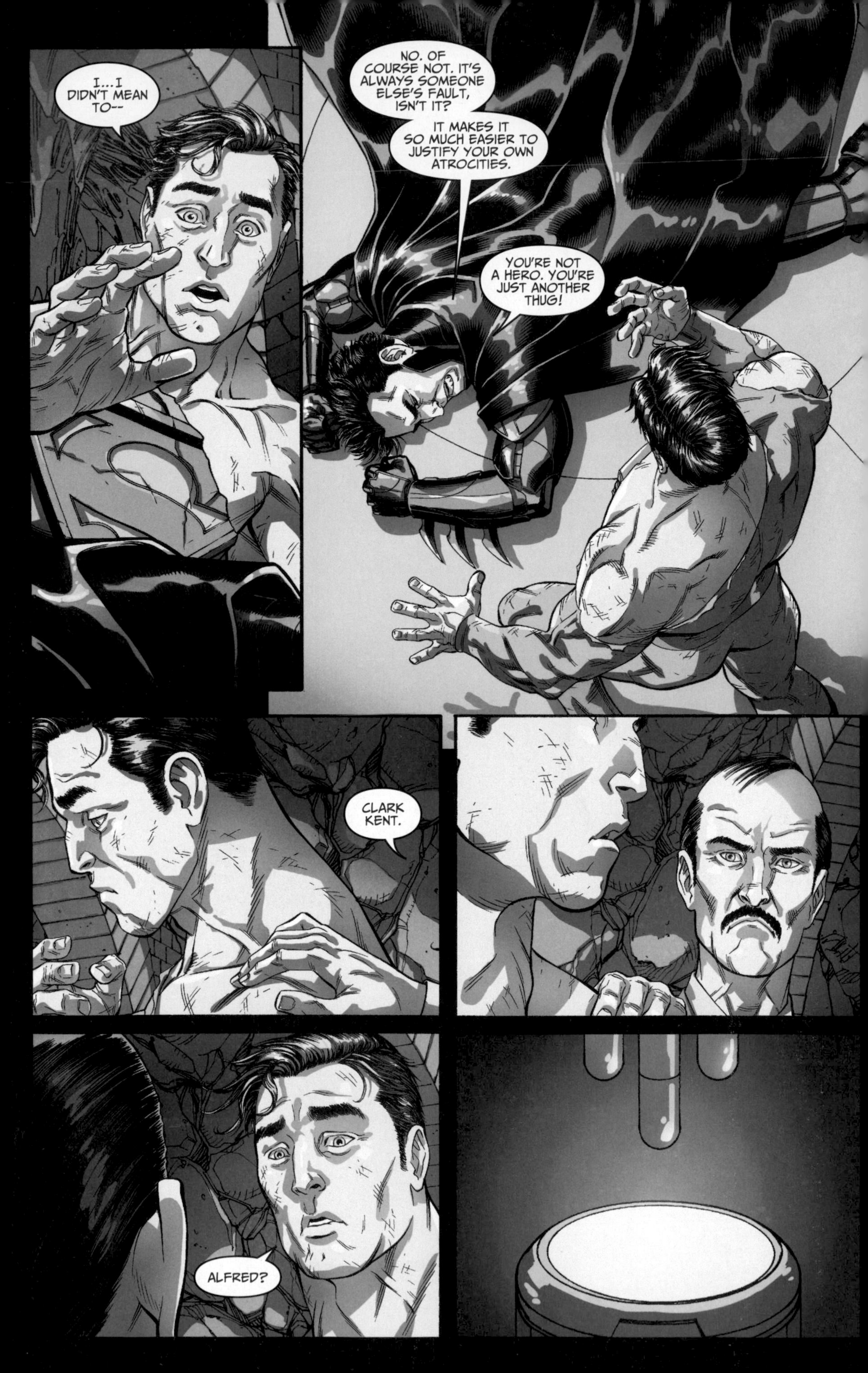
I... I DIDN'T MEAN TO--
NO. OF COURSE NOT. IT'S ALWAYS SOMEONE ELSE'S FAULT, ISN'T IT?
IT MAKES IT SO MUCH EASIER TO JUSTIFY YOUR OWN ATROCITIES.
YOU'RE NOT A HERO. YOU'RE JUST ANOTHER THUG!
CLARK KENT.
ALFRED?

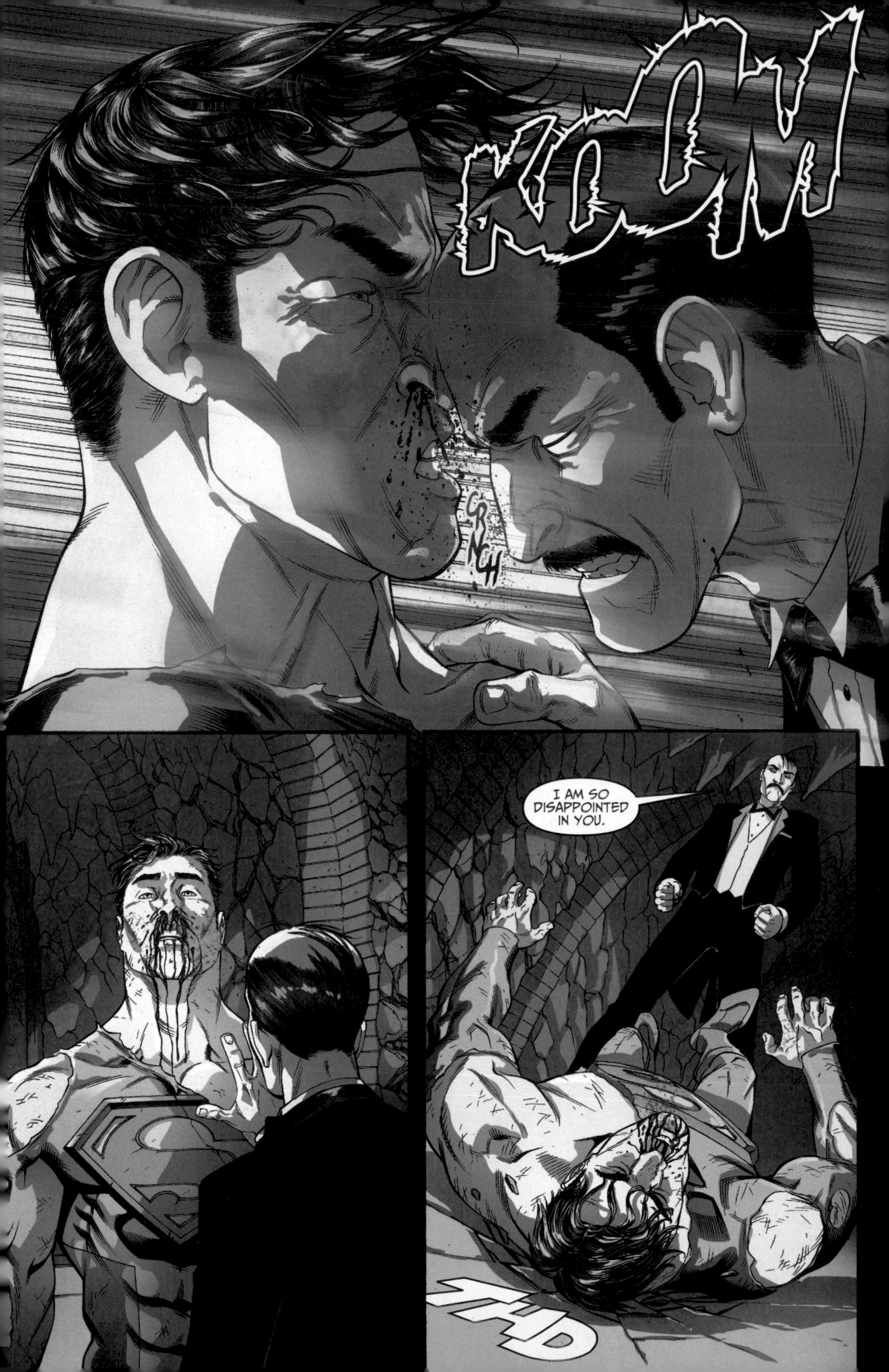
KOOM
CRNCH
I AM SO DISAPPOINTED IN YOU.
THD

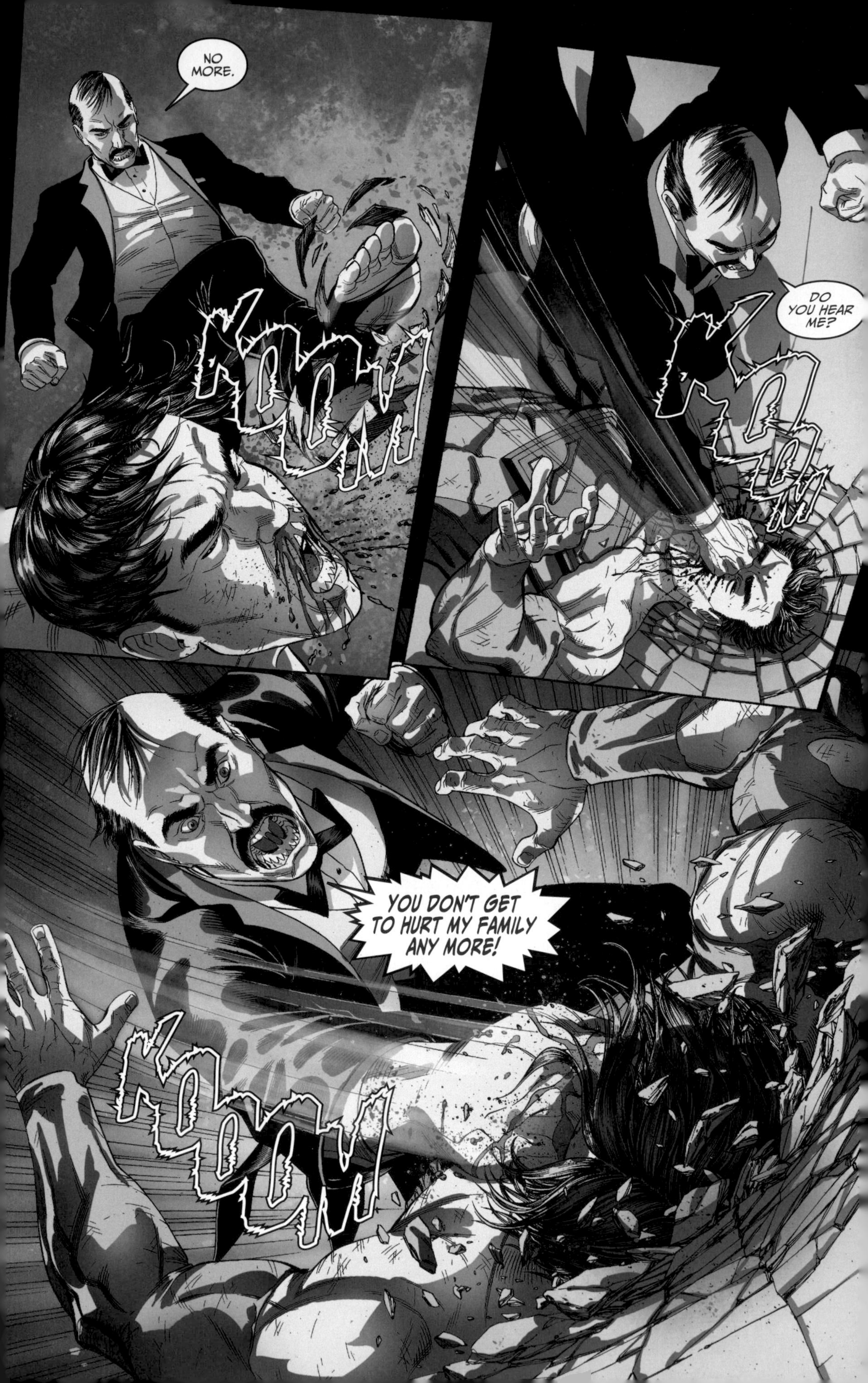
NO MORE.
DO YOU HEAR ME?
YOU DON'T GET TO HURT MY FAMILY ANY MORE!

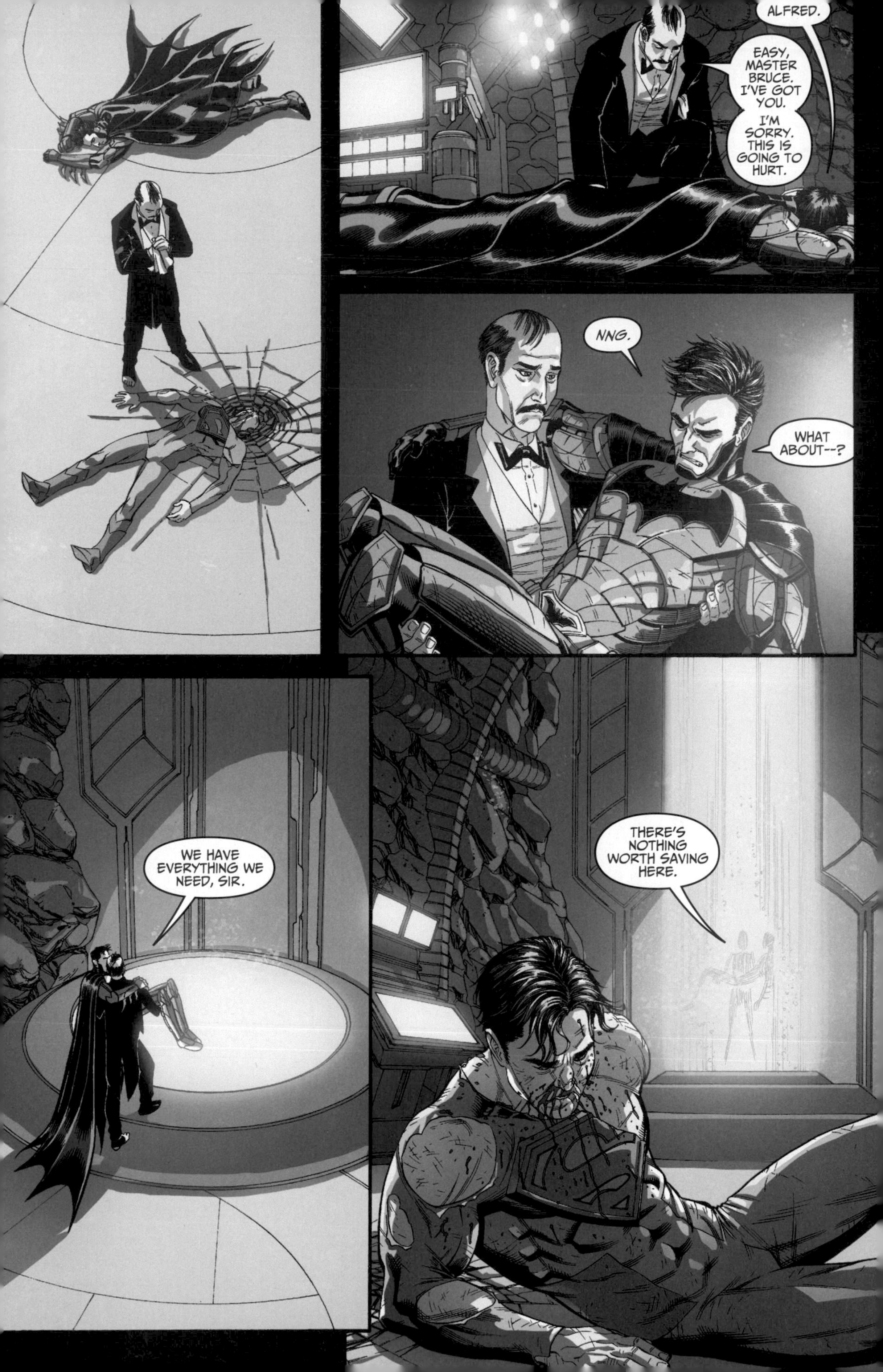
ALFRED.
EASY, MASTER BRUCE. I'VE GOT YOU.
I'M SORRY. THIS IS GOING TO HURT.
NNG.
WHAT ABOUT--?
WE HAVE EVERYTHING WE NEED, SIR.
THERE'S NOTHING WORTH SAVING HERE.

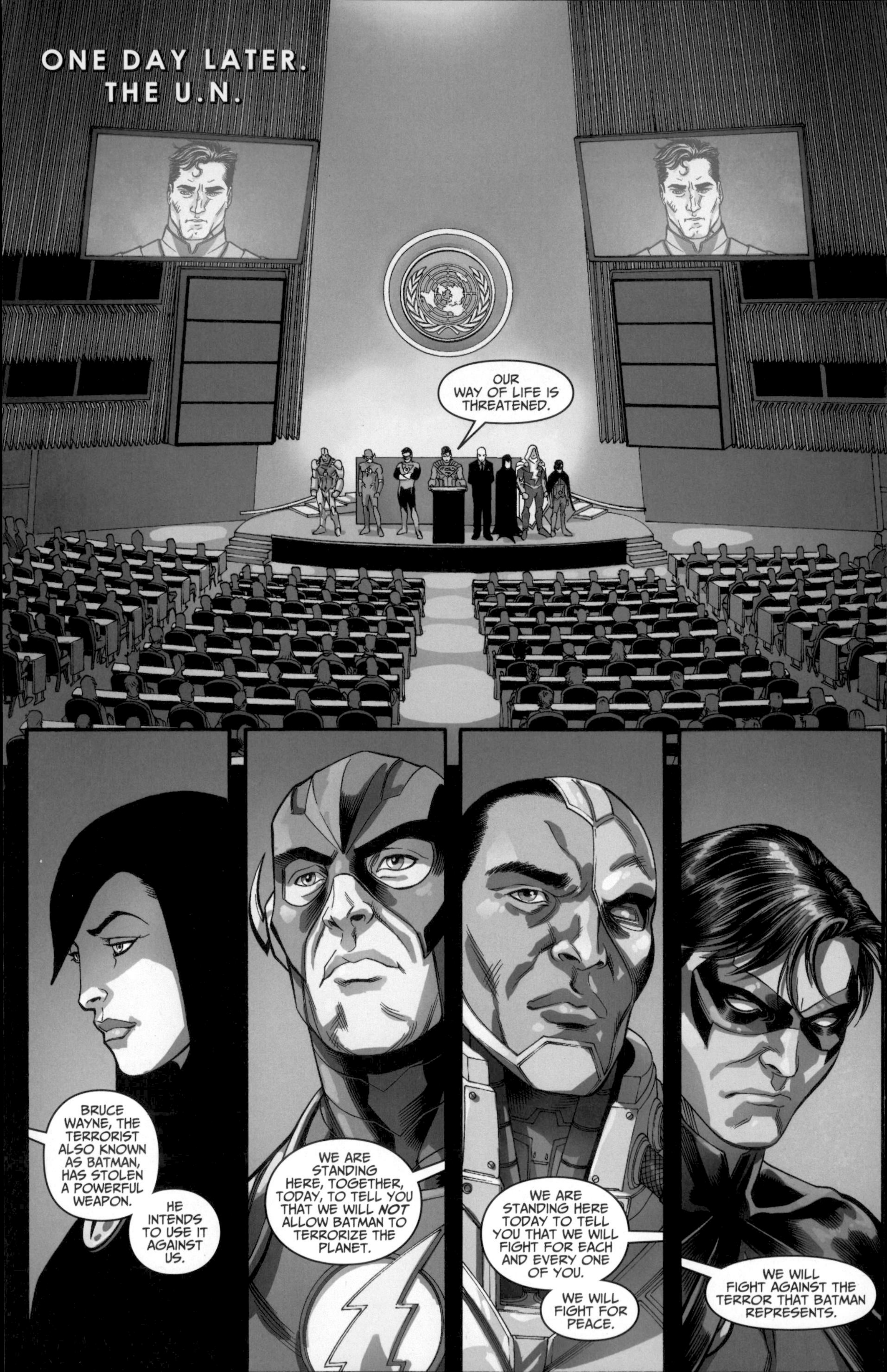
ONE DAY LATER. THE U.N.
OUR WAY OF LIFE IS THREATENED.
BRUCE WAYNE, THE TERRORIST ALSO KNOWN AS BATMAN, HAS STOLEN A POWERFUL WEAPON.
HE INTENDS TO USE IT AGAINST US.
WE ARE STANDING HERE, TOGETHER, TODAY, TO TELL YOU THAT WE WILL NOT ALLOW BATMAN TO TERRORIZE THE PLANET.
WE ARE STANDING HERE TODAY TO TELL YOU THAT WE WILL FIGHT FOR EACH AND EVERY ONE OF YOU.
WE WILL FIGHT FOR PEACE.
WE WILL FIGHT AGAINST THE TERROR THAT BATMAN REPRESENTS.

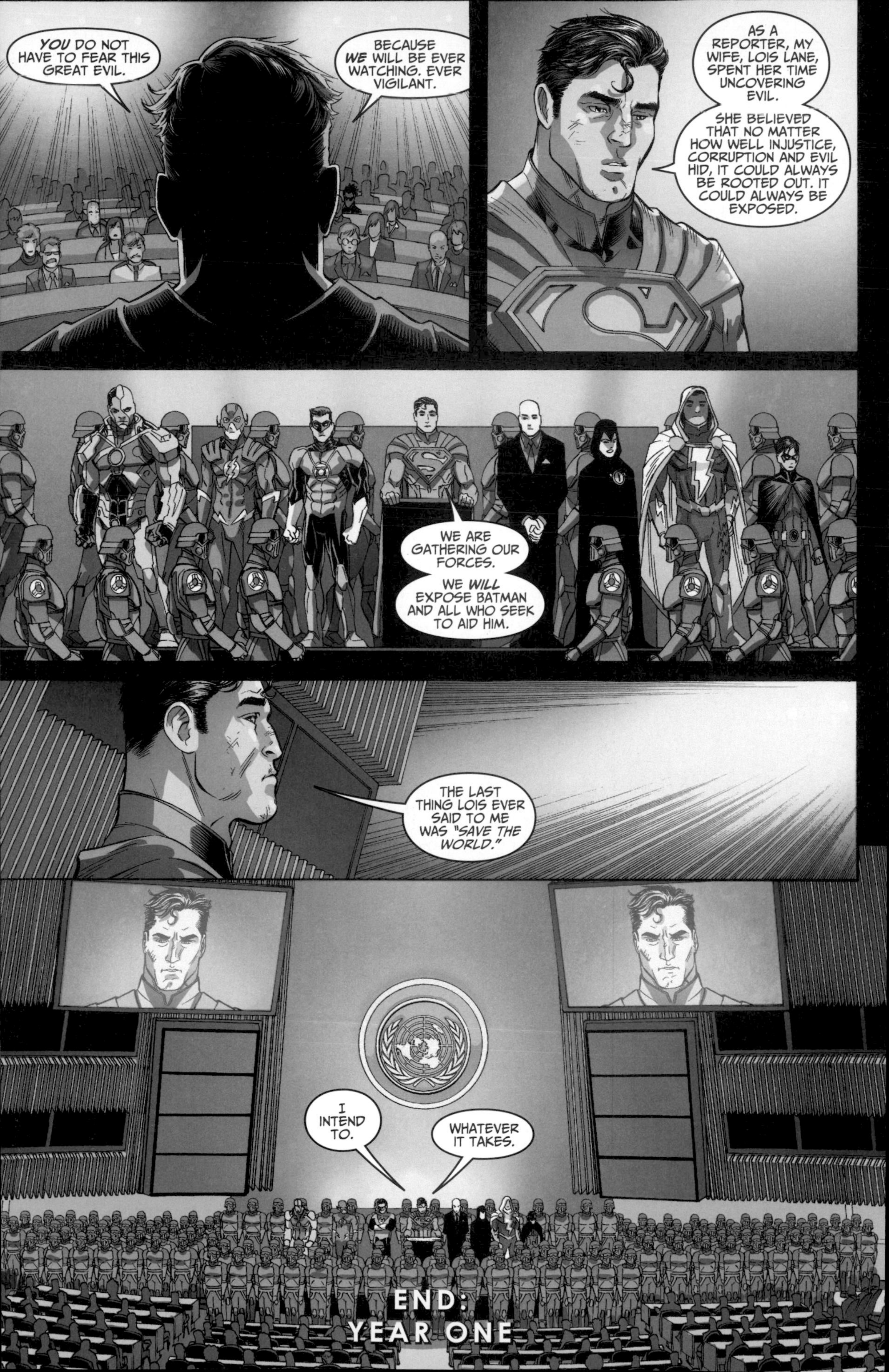
YOU DO NOT HAVE TO FEAR THIS GREAT EVIL.
BECAUSE WE WILL BE EVER WATCHING. EVER VIGILANT.
AS A REPORTER, MY WIFE, LOIS LANE, SPENT HER TIME UNCOVERING EVIL.
SHE BELIEVED THAT NO MATTER HOW WELL INJUSTICE, CORRUPTION AND EVIL HID, IT COULD ALWAYS BE ROOTED OUT. IT COULD ALWAYS BE EXPOSED.
WE ARE GATHERING OUR FORCES.
WE WILL EXPOSE BATMAN AND ALL WHO SEEK TO AID HIM.
THE LAST THING LOIS EVER SAID TO ME WAS "SAVE THE WORLD."
I INTEND TO.
WHATEVER IT TAKES.
END:
YEAR ONE

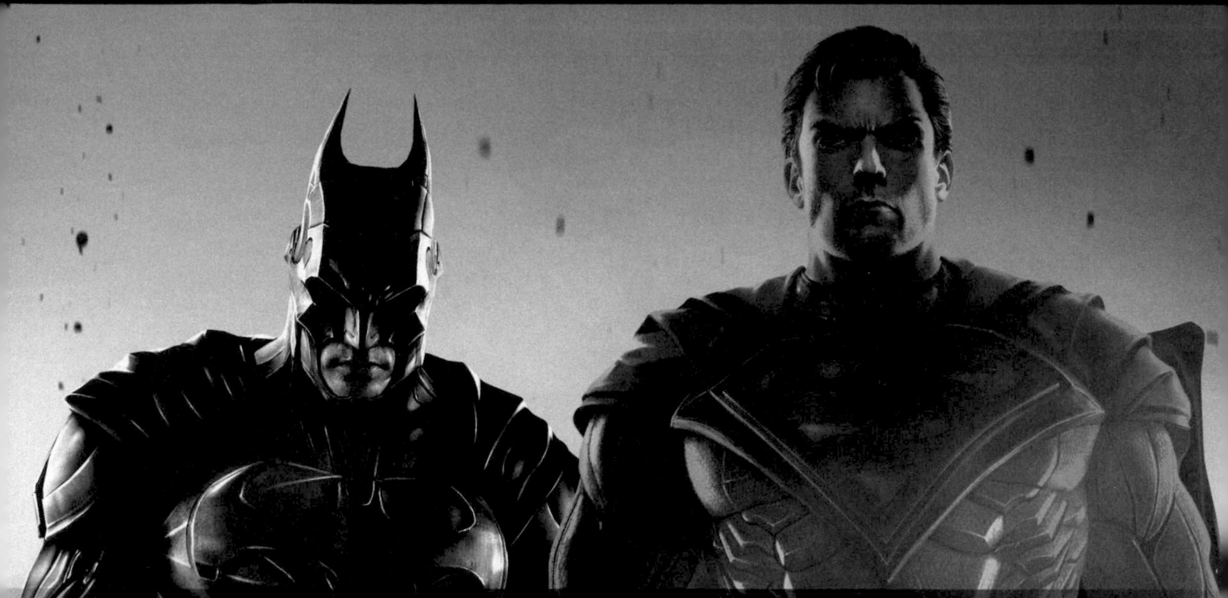

COVER GALLERY

INJUSTICE: GODS AMONG US #1
Game Variant Cover

INJUSTICE: GODS AMONG US #1
3rd Printing Cover

INJUSTICE: GODS AMONG US #2
3rd Printing Cover

INJUSTICE: GODS AMONG US #5
2nd Printing Cover

INJUSTICE: GODS AMONG US #6
Game Variant Cover

INJUSTICE: GODS AMONG US #10
DC Collectibles Variant Cover

INJUSTICE: GODS AMONG US #11
DC Collectibles Variant Cover

INJUSTICE: GODS AMONG US #12
DC Collectibles Variant Cover

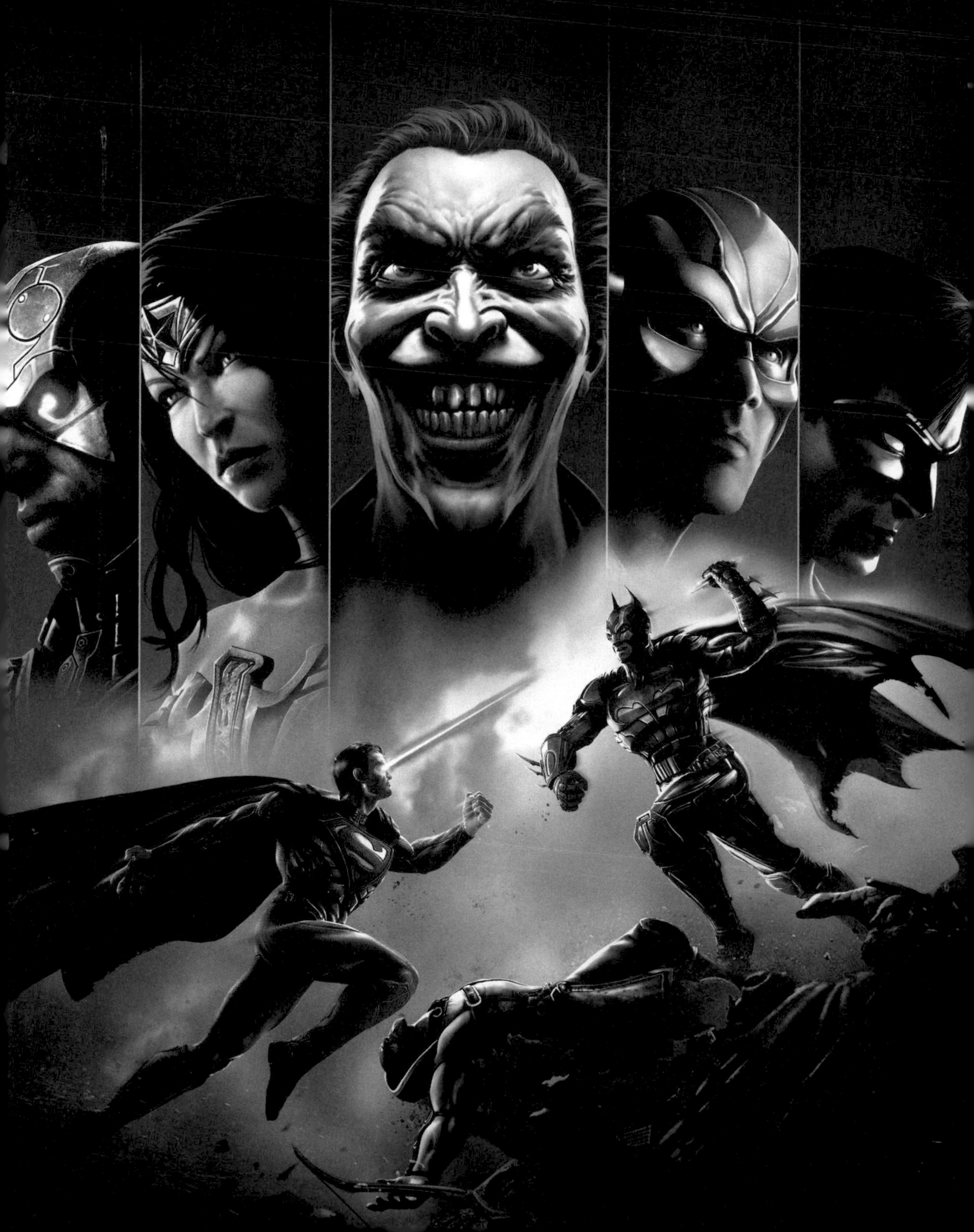

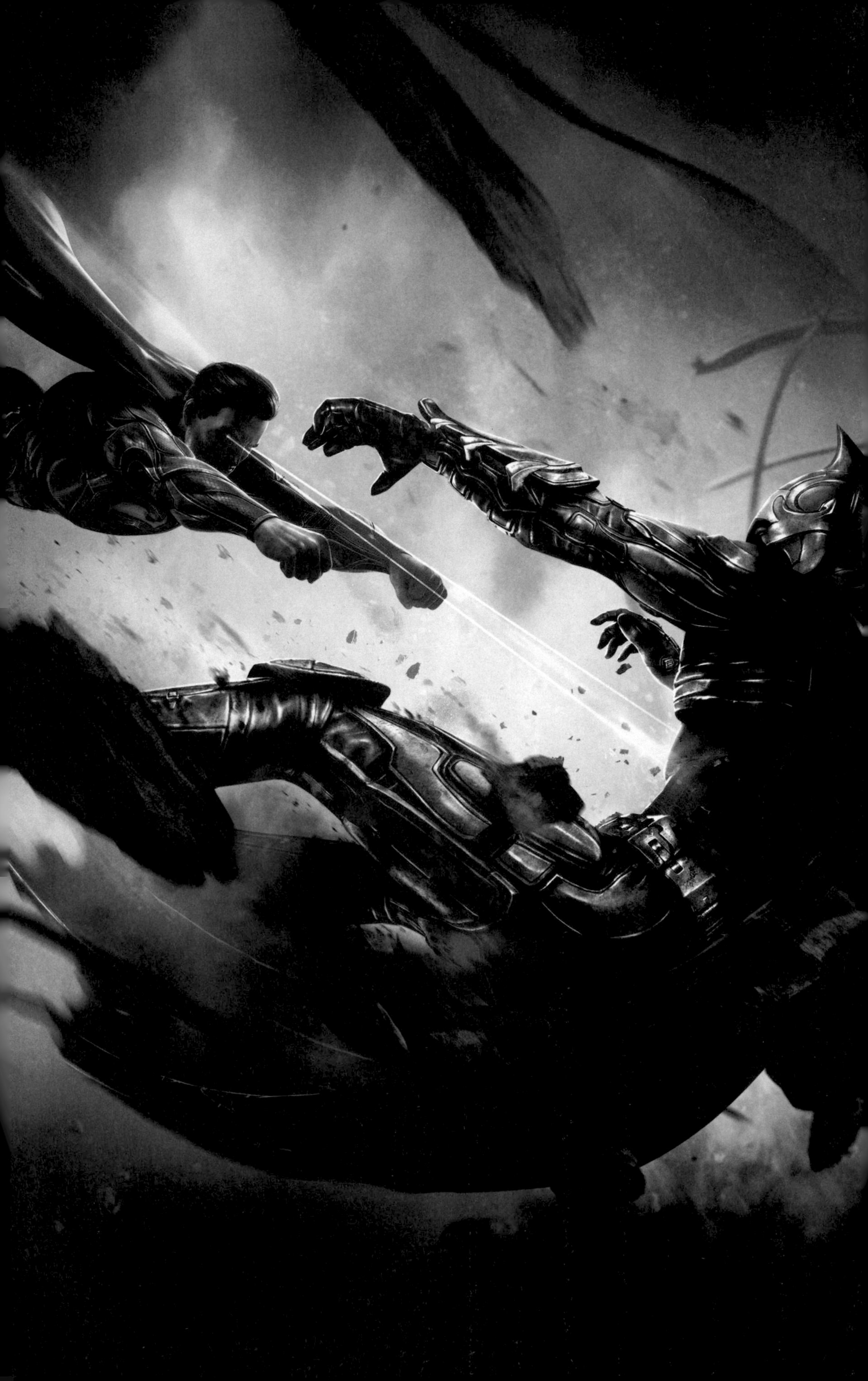

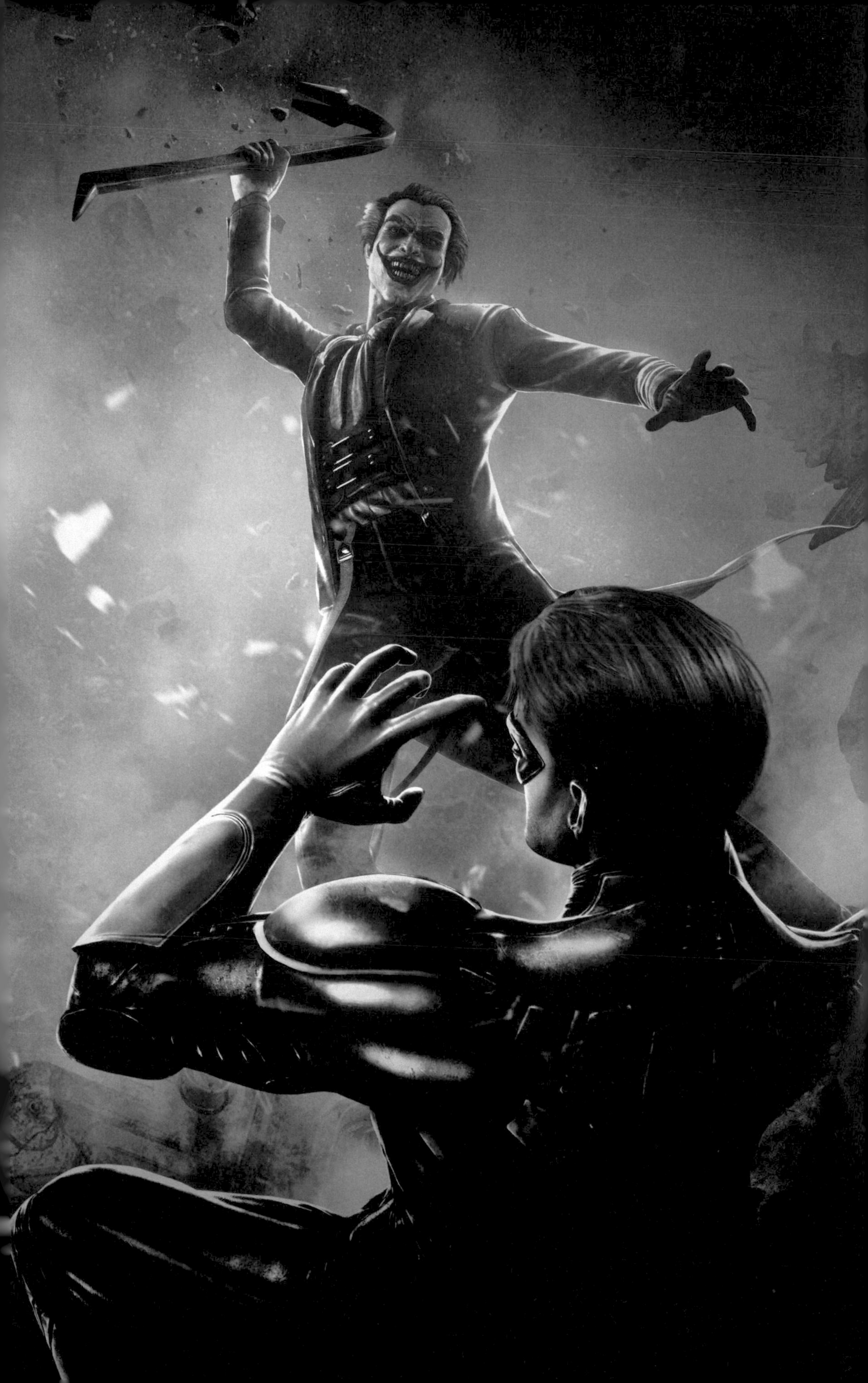

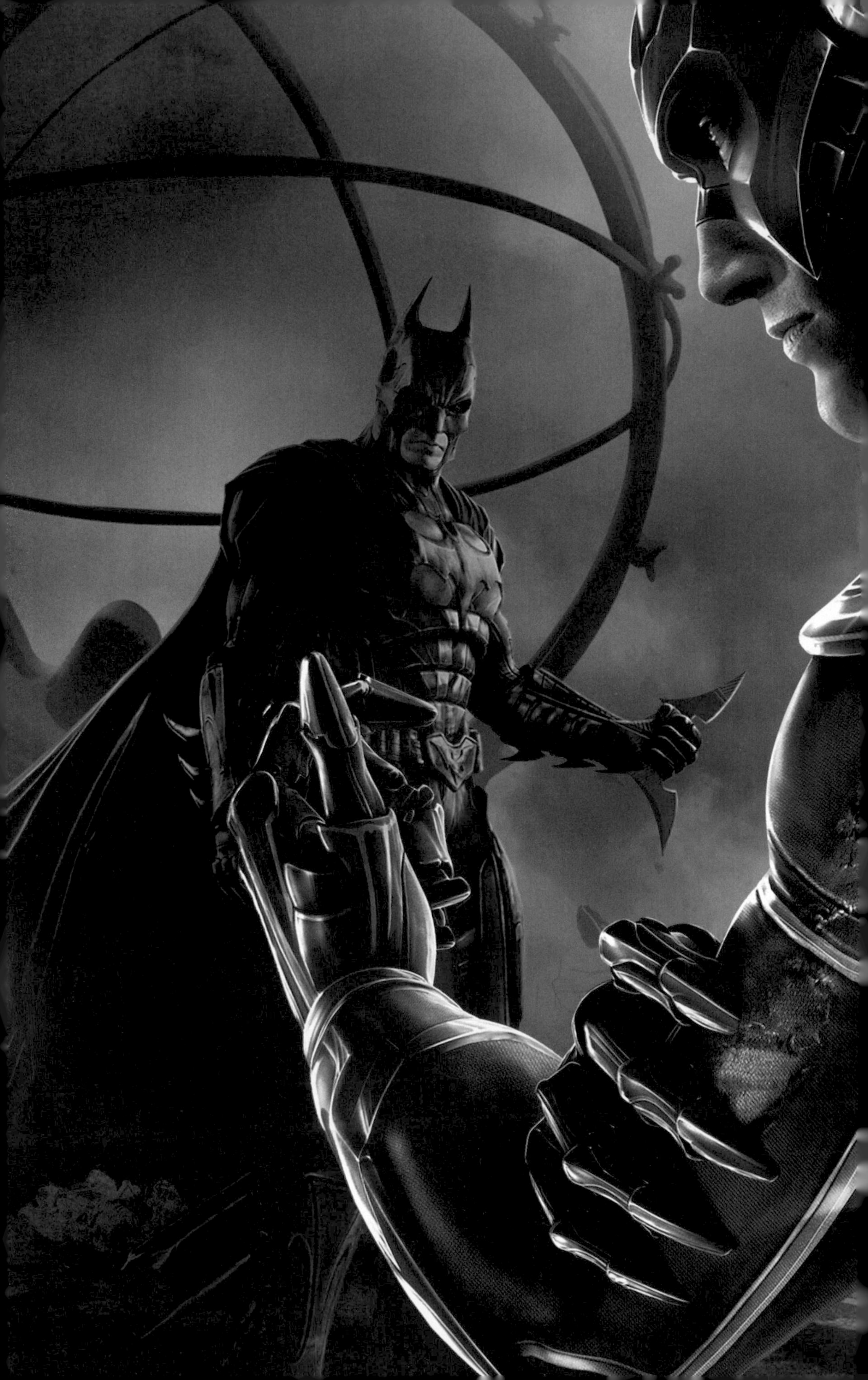

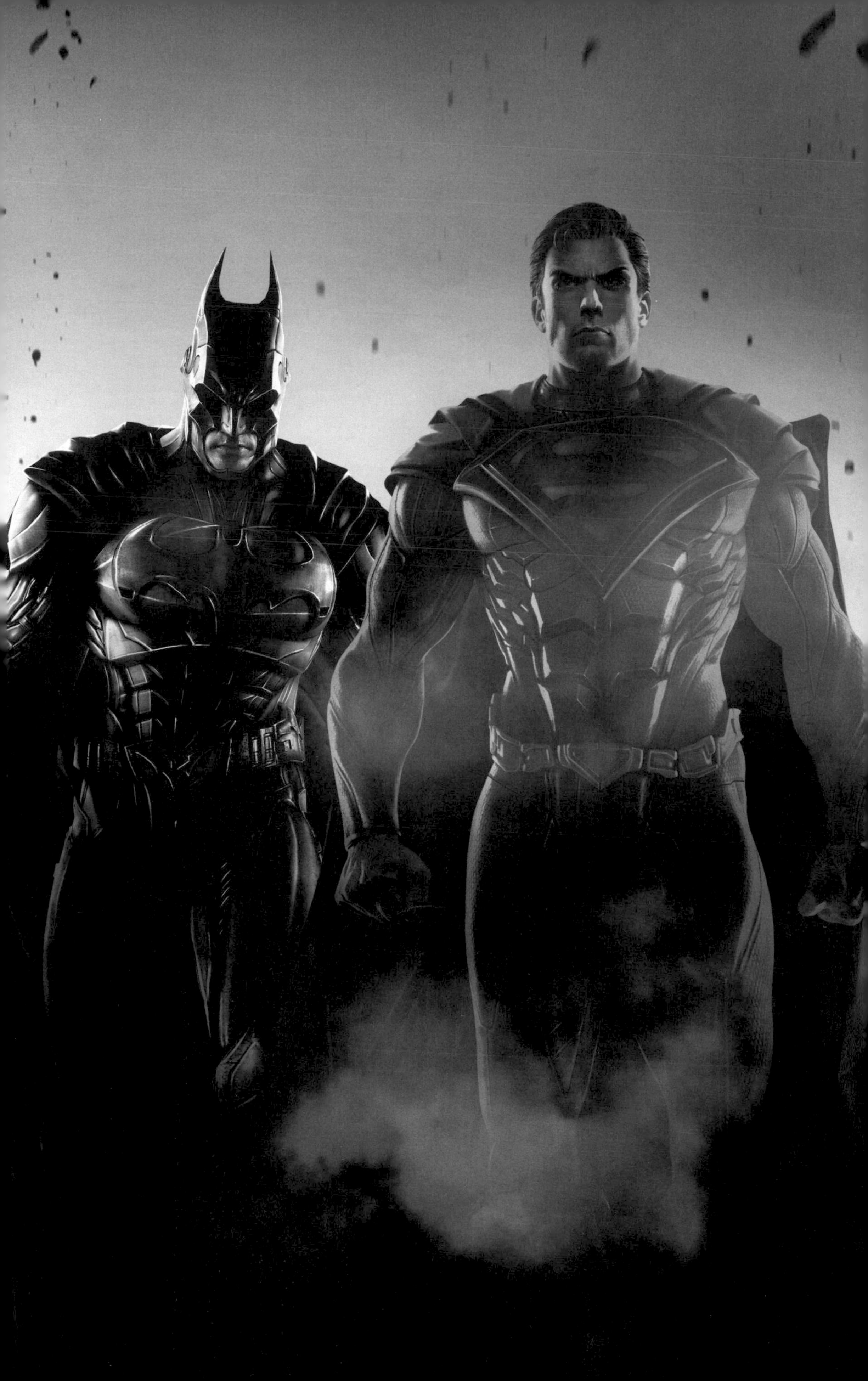

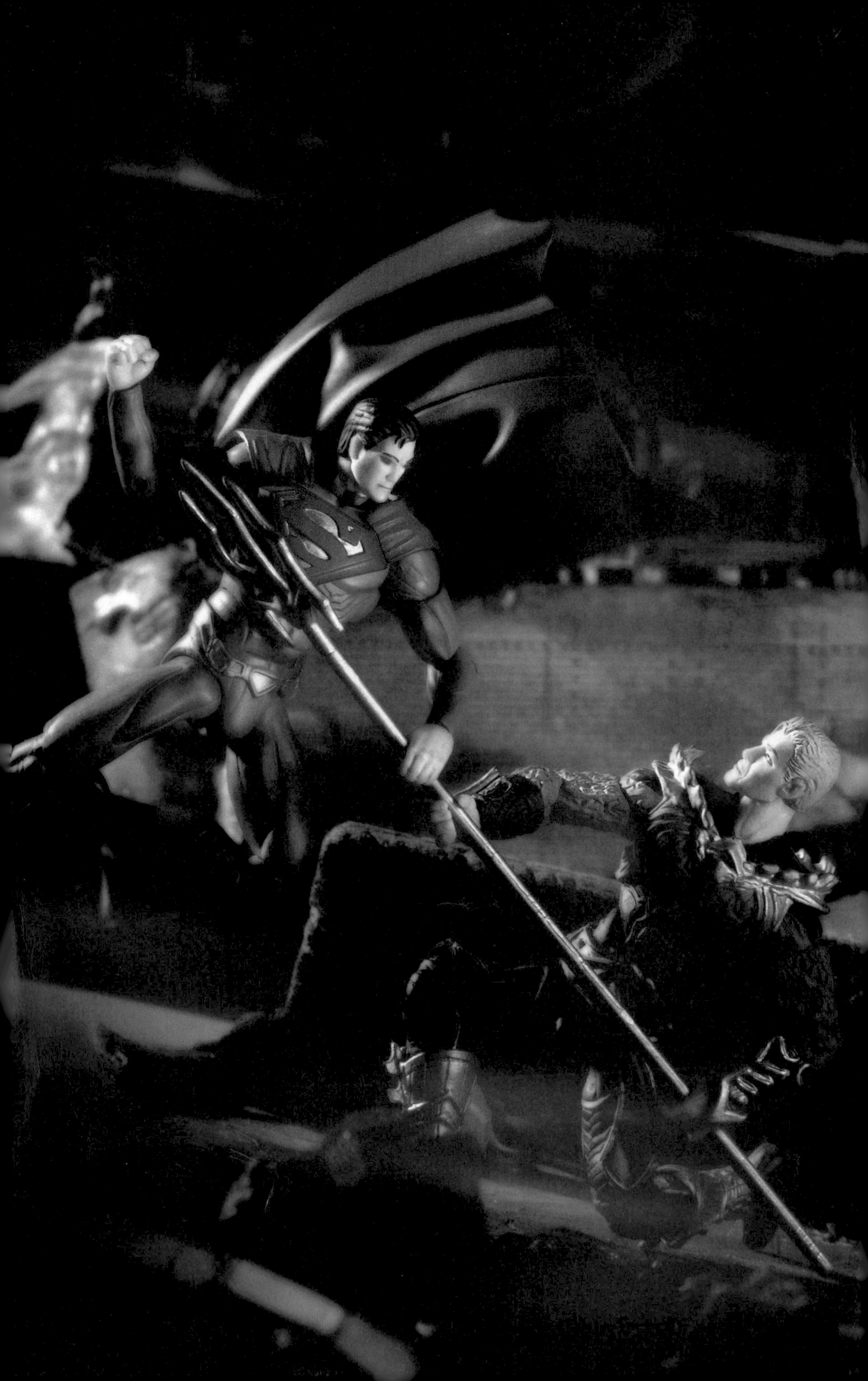

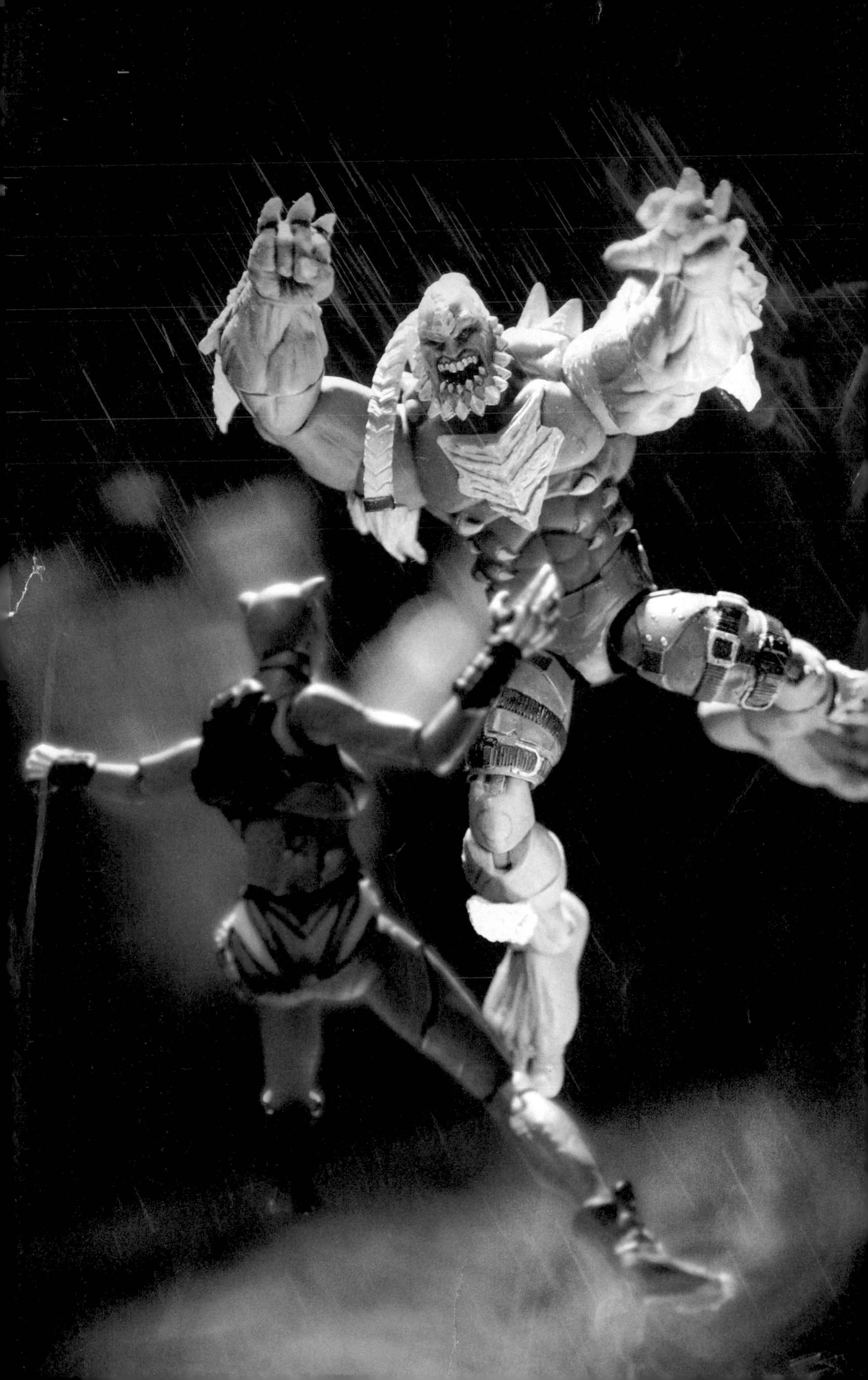

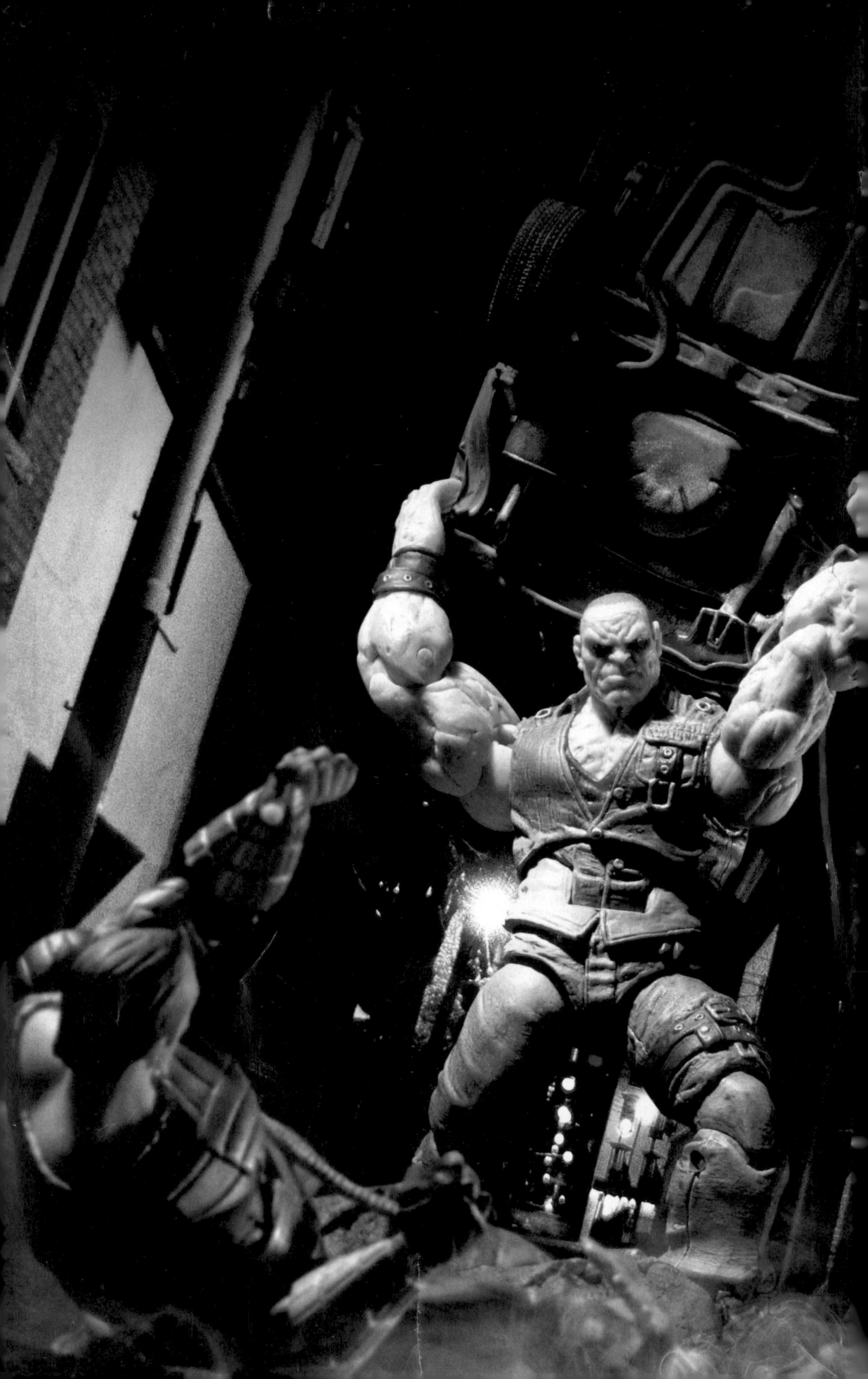